monitoring the future

questionnaire responses from the nation's high school seniors

1986

Jerald G. Bachman, Lloyd D. Johnston, and
Patrick M. O'Malley

Survey Research Center • Institute for Social Research
The University of Michigan
Ann Arbor, Michigan

ISR Code Number 4751
ISSN 0190-9185
ISBN 0-87944-319-7
Library of Congress Catalog Card Number 79-640937

Published in 1987 by:
Institute for Social Research,
The University of Michigan, Ann Arbor, Michigan

6 5 4 3 2 1

Printed in the United States of America

Table of Contents

Preface

This volume is the latest in a series which presents descriptive statistical results from a national survey of young people entitled Monitoring the Future: A continuing Study of the Lifestyles and Values of Youth. Each year the study surveys a large sample of high school seniors, located in approximately 125 schools nationwide, and drawn to be representative of all seniors in the coterminous United States.

The first four volumes in this series, dealing with the high school classes of 1975, 1976, 1977, and 1978 were published simultaneously early in 1980. Additional volumes appear on an annual basis. The most important contribution of this series is likely to be the opportunity it provides for the exploration of trends, a process that obviously involves the use of several different volumes. With that in mind, we have kept the format highly consistent from one volume to another, and we have developed an index (described below) which should facilitate the process of matching data across years. It should be noted that the volume presenting 1975 data is different from the others in several respects.*

Although we designed the volumes to fit together as a series, we also saw distinct advantages in having each volume able to stand alone — to be usable without reference to any of the others. For that reason, the introductory material on research design and questionnaire content, the instructions for accessing the data tables, and the appendices on sampling errors are all included in each volume. Thus, the small price we pay for making each volume self-contained is that much of the text portion is repeated each year.

Purposes of this Series of Publications

Monitoring the Future, which is conducted by the University of Michigan's Institute for Social Research and receives its core funding from the National Institute on Drug Abuse, is an unusually comprehensive research project in several respects: surveys are conducted annually on an ongoing basis; the samples are large and nationally representative; and the subject matter is very broad, encompassing some 1,300 variables per year. Many people — scholars, policy makers, educators, and so on — will have an interest in the results.

The principal investigators are already writing for a number of these audiences and will continue to do so. Because of the limitations in our own time, interests, and expertise, however, there is an enormous amount of valuable information which may never be utilized if the initiative to digest and disseminate all of it must come from us alone. Further, since the project is in part a social indicator series, its value rests to a considerable degree on *timely* dissemination of the results. For these reasons, we wish to share the study's results with others in a number of fields on a rapid and regular basis. We have chosen to provide two major and complementary vehicles for doing this: (a) these annual reference volumes of descriptive results, and (b) machine-readable data archives for direct analysis by others.

We believe that many potential users who would not mount the effort required to conduct computer analyses of archived data will be able to get most of

*The 1975 volume does not include comparison data for black and white subgroups, nor does it include data for the subgroups who did and did not plan to complete four years of college. Also, somewhat fewer questionnaire items appear than in the other volumes. These restrictions are the result primarily of missing data problems that occurred only in the 1975 survey. In most respects, however, those seeking to compare different classes of high school seniors will find the 1975 data useful.

what they want from these volumes of descriptive results. The user of any one of these volumes can estimate – usually with considerable accuracy – a wide variety of characteristics of the high school class described in that volume. To take just one example, the user of the 1984 volume can ascertain that 40.0 percent of seniors in the high school class of 1984 reported using marijuana at least once during the preceding year. Further, by utilizing two or more of these volumes the reader can describe recent trends in any such characteristic. To continue with the same example, the volume describing the high school class of 1975 also indicates that 40.0 percent of these seniors reported marijuana use during the preceding year; and when that is combined with the data from the intervening years the reader is able to discern a steady increase between 1975 and 1979 (50.8 percent of that class reported having used marijuana at least once in the preceding year), and a subsequent steady decrease back down to the 1975 level. The figures for the years 1975 to 1984 are:

1975: 40.0	1980: 48.8
1976: 44.5	1981: 46.1
1977: 47.6	1982: 44.3
1978: 50.2	1983: 42.3
1979: 50.8	1984: 40.0

A similar examination of trends can be carried out for over 1,300 different variables dealing with a wide variety of subject areas (listed in Table 2 of the Introduction). A simple indexing system (described below) has been developed which makes it quite straightforward for the reader wishing to do trend analyses to locate the results for a given question for any year of the study. The index in the present volume lists the location of all items included in the surveys from 1976 onward, as well as most items included in 1975.

Analyses such as those illustrated above need not be limited to the total sample. The data provided in these volumes also permit examination of a variety of subgroups (e.g., males, females, those from different regions, those with different levels of drug use experience).

We recognize that providing ready access to essentially undigested data carries certain risks, particularly the risk of mistaken interpretations based on inadequate controls, lack of awareness of sample limitations, etc. More than offsetting the risks, in our view, are the advantages of prompt and widespread dissemination of these nationally representative survey indicator data. Although we are unable to eliminate the risks, we hope to reduce them by providing the reader with an extensive list of caveats presented at the end of the Introduction section. We ask all who use the data to read these caveats carefully and take them seriously.

A Guide for the Reader

This volume is divided into three main parts: (1) the introductory section, (2) the section giving the descriptive results from the current year's survey, and (3) the cross-time item reference index.

Introductory Section. The introduction contains a description of the study — its purposes, major content areas, design, field procedures, response rates, and methods of publication and data dissemination. Since most of this material remains unchanged from year to year, anyone having read another of the volumes may wish to skim this section. We do, however, suggest reviewing the caveats, located at the end of the introductory section, which deal with interpreting and extrapolating from these data.

Descriptive Results Section. In this section all questions contained in this year's survey are presented along with percentagized frequency distributions of answers for the entire sample and for selected subgroups. The questions in this section are organized according to the number of the questionnaire form in which they were contained (forms one through five) and according to the order in which the questions occurred. There is one important exception, however. A major segment of questions common to all five forms of the questionnaire (dealing with drug use, background characteristics, and some other subjects) is presented only once, at the beginning of the Descriptive Results section, using the data from respondents on all five forms.

The first portion of the descriptive results section contains detailed definitions of all subgroups for whom data are presented. It also describes the statistical conventions used in generating the tables.

Cross-Time Index of Questionnaire Items. Beginning with the 1982 volume, this index is ordered by subject area. (It was ordered by item reference number prior to 1982.) The index is intended to serve two purposes.

First, it should be useful in locating items dealing with a subject area of interest. The subject area key at the beginning of the cross-time item index shows the alphabetical code assigned to various subject areas (e.g., "politics" or "work and leisure"). Having selected a subject area of interest, one can then go to that section of the index to locate all questions in any of the surveys which deal with that subject. (The procedure is slightly different in volumes prior to 1982, as described in those volumes.) To locate the results for any given question in this volume, simply look in column two of the item index for its page location.

The cross-time index can also be used to determine in which other years an item was used and where to locate it. If, in reviewing the Descriptive Results section, one locates an interesting item and would like to know in which of the other annual surveys of seniors it has appeared, it may be found in the cross-time index by the unique "item reference number" within the relevant subject area. The index will indicate all years in which that same item appeared and show the questionnaire form, section, and item number for each year. This information thus can be used to decide which other volumes in this series might be of relevance; and the same item may be readily located by its reference number in the index of any other volume prior to the 1982 volume, and by its subject area and reference number in any volume from 1982 on.

Sampling Appendices. Appendix A is provided for those wishing to determine the confidence limits around a percentage estimate, or to test the statistical significance of an observed difference between two groups, or to test the significance of a change from one year to another. It gives the necessary procedures and tables for such tests and provides the appropriate factors by which to correct for the fact that the study makes use of a multi-stage probability sample clustered in a limited number of schools (usually about 125). Appendix B provides further detail on sample design effects and the procedures which were used to derive the sampling error estimates.

Availability of Archived Data

As was mentioned earlier, this series of volumes is complemented by an archiving of the raw data set for direct analysis by others not associated with the project. The present volumes should be a considerable help to those wishing to access the archived data since they provide a verbatim statement of items and answer categories, and also because they include basic univariate and bivariate frequency distributions for all items, as well as the missing data rates. The cross-time index of items contained in each of these volumes also provides an efficient way to identify the relevant variables in various content areas, as well as to determine when they were measured and their questionnaire locations. In fact, we hope that the availability of this series will not only facilitate the use of the archived data but actually stimulate interest in their use.

The individual level data which are summarized in this and previous volumes are available from:

The Interuniversity Consortium for Political
and Social Research (ICPSR)
Institute for Social Research
P.O. Box 1248
Ann Arbor, Michigan 48106

The ICPSR archive makes individual-level data available to interested investigators for analysis. A few variables have been modified or deleted to ensure that the answers of an individual respondent cannot be located through pattern recognition (i.e., using various descriptor variables in combination to make a unique identification). The changed or deleted variables include month of birth, race, and the sampling weight, which adjusts for selection probability.

Other Publications from the Study

A number of different forms of publications based on Monitoring the Future data have been developed or are being planned. One series of reports, dealing with trends in drug use and drug-related attitudes and beliefs, is being published by the National Institute on Drug Abuse. The first report in that series, *Drug Use Among American High School Students 1975-1977* (Johnston, Bachman, and O'Malley), was published in late 1977. Subsequent reports have been issued annually.

An Occasional Paper series has been launched by the project. It includes papers on design and methodological issues as well as special substantive analyses and early, and sometimes more detailed, drafts of articles planned for journal publication. The first occasional paper, "The Monitoring the Future Project Design and Procedures" (Bachman and Johnston, 1978), provides a detailed description of the study and its underlying rationale.

The present series of reference volumes is being published by the Institute for Social Research. A new volume will be added to this series each year.

To request particular papers, reprints, or periodic notification of publications available from the study, write to Monitoring the Future, Room 2030, Institute for Social Research, The University of Michigan, Box 1248, Ann Arbor, Michigan 48106.

---

*Single copies of these reports may be ordered without cost from the National Clearinghouse for Drug Abuse Information, National Institute on Drug Abuse, 5600 Fishers Lane, Rockville, Maryland 20857. See References for a complete list of reports.

Acknowledgements

A great many people have contributed to the launching and development of this research effort. We are indebted to a number of officials of the National Institute on Drug Abuse and the Special Action Office for Drug Abuse Prevention for their encouragement and advice at the outset — in particular, Richard Bucher, Robert DuPont, William Pollin, and Louise Richards.

Our colleagues at the Institute for Social Research and elsewhere who shared their insights, and often their most cherished instrumentation, are too numerous to mention; but their contributions are greatly appreciated. To the former director of the Survey Research Center's Sampling Section, Irene Hess, and to her colleagues we owe a particular debt for the creativity of the sampling design for the study. The contributions of the SRC Field Section also have been very valuable.

Major contributions to the production of this particular volume were made by staff members Ginger Maggio, Jerome Hiniker, and Dawn Bare. We would also like to thank the staff of the Publishing Division of the Institute for Social Research for their work in arranging publication.

The present and former members of the project staff (listed below) have, of course, contributed greatly to the building of this large and complex research series.

Finally, we would like to acknowledge the tens of thousands of high school seniors, their teachers, and their principals, whose cooperation and generous contributions of time make the Monitoring the Future project possible.

JERALD G. BACHMAN
LLOYD D. JOHNSTON
PATRICK M. O'MALLEY

Present and Former Members of the Project Staff

Donna Ando	Michael Fisher	John Miller
Margaret Bailey	Peter Freedman-Doan	Marion Morse
Dawn Bare	Henry Freeman	Jim Neveaux
Ellen Berger	Walter Gruhn	Dorothy Paulette
Mary Lou Bewley	Lana Harrison	Susan Pauls
Katherine Blatt	James Hersey	Sharon Pietila
Mary Lea Bonucchi	A. Regula Herzog	Joseph Pleck
Katheryn Boris	Jerome Hiniker	Deborah Poinier
Marcy Breslow	Pamela Kittel	Judith Redmond
Susan Burek	Mark Krell	Barbara Renaud
Susan Burling	Zenon Kuzmyn	Don Rubinstein
Mary Danneffel-Mashruwala	Carol Larsen	Maria Sanchez
Mary Lou Davis	Sally Lawson	Tina Smith
Mary Dempsy	Ludmilla Litus	Ann Taylor
William Diedrich	A. Kathryn Loker	Richard Taylor
Robert Doljanac	Regina Lumbard	Lynda Tolen
Karen Donahue	Mary Lutz	Sandra Wronski
Leslie Eveland	Ginger Maggio	Thelma Wurzelbacher
Halford Fairchild	Oksana Malanchuk	Daniel Zahs
Maureen Ferrell	Wayne McCulloch	
Marjorie Fisher	Joan McGraw	

Introduction

The Monitoring the Future project is designed to explore changes in many important values, behaviors, and lifestyle orientations of contemporary American youth. Two general types of tasks may be distinguished. The first is to provide a systematic and accurate *description* of the youth population of interest in a given year, and to quantify the direction and rate of the changes taking place among them over time. The second task, more analytic than descriptive, involves the *explanation* of the relationships and trends observed to exist.

The task of description may be subdivided into three parts: (1) the description of static conditions (which may be accomplished through a single cross-sectional study); (2) the description of cross-cohort or, in longer time-spans, generational changes (usually accomplished using repeated cross sections of the same age groups); and (3) the description of changes with aging (usually accomplished by means of longitudinal studies). The Monitoring the Future project has the capacity to provide each of these three types of description, since it incorporates all three types of research design into a single study. (This complex design, in which multiple cohorts are followed longitudinally, has been referred to as a cohort-sequential design.)

The content of this volume exemplifies the first of these types of description in that it contains cross-sectional data on a single high school class. When the data in this volume are used in combination with data from other such volumes in the series, the nature, direction, and rates of change from one cohort of seniors to another also may be described — the type of reporting which is often labeled as the social indicator approach. The third class of description — dealing with the maturational changes which occur during the years after high school — will not be dealt with in this series of volumes but will be reported in other publications from the study.*

The accurate characterization of American young people and the description of important changes occurring among them is but one class of objectives for the study. The second class of objectives involves the development of a greater understanding of what causes these young people to be as they are, and why the changes being documented are occurring. Explanation will be sought through both the analysis of change at the aggregate level and at the individual level. The results of these explorations will be disseminated via the various publications discussed in the Preface.

The merging of the social indicator approach and the analysis of relationships (particularly longitudinal relations) into a single cohort-sequential design is, in our view, synergistic: the effectiveness of the two approaches combined is greater than if the two were undertaken separately. Because the present series of volumes deals with senior year data only, our remarks here focus primarily on the project's social indicator contributions — the accurate description of high

---

* Panels of students from each graduating class are being randomly selected and followed longitudinally for up to ten years. Thus it soon will be possible to characterize the changes which seem to take place consistently with aging during the early adult years. Not only will longitudinal development in the years after high school be studied, but once enough of these longitudinal panels have accumulated, it will also be possible to characterize cross-sectionally most American young people aged 18 to 28, (at least the major segment of the population who completed high school — roughly 80-85 percent), and to describe the changing characteristics of that age group each year.

school seniors and the documentation of trends over time. It is worth noting, however, that even the limited amount of bivariate data included in the present volumes will suggest promising directions for relational analyses, many of which can be carried out using the archived data tapes from the project.

The Need for Social Indicators

The fundamental argument for developing social indicators is that there are considerable scientific and practical benefits derived from having accurate information about current social realities and the way those realities have been changing. For the scientific community such indicators provide a rich set of information against which existing theory may be tested and from which new theory may be suggested. For the community at large, social indicators permit the "reality testing" of common perceptions and beliefs about the nation and its people. Past experience has demonstrated that widely held conceptions, which themselves may serve to create or exacerbate problems, can be most inaccurate. One example is the exaggerated popular conception of the size and nature of the "gap" between generations (see Adelson, 1970, 1979); another is the mistaken assumption that most young people condone the use of a variety of illegal drugs (Johnston, 1973; Johnston, Bachman, and O'Malley, 1977; 1979 a, b; 1981).

While deflating exaggerated perceptions, a continual monitoring of indicators on youth also can reveal the beginning of new problems and thus give rise to corrective efforts at a relatively early stage. For instance, most would view with concern the emergence of new types of drug use. Monitoring the Future has already documented and reported a sharp increase in regular marijuana use among high school seniors, and as a result more attention has been paid to the issue by policy makers, the media, and the general public. The discovery of such trends may trigger more intense efforts to discover the causes, consequences, and (when appropriate) preventatives of such behaviors.

Although social indicators seldom translate directly into specific policy decisions, the availability of descriptive information can substantially enhance the decision-making capabilities of policy makers. These data provide considerable insight into the size and nature of problems, the rate of change occurring nationally and in subgroups, and in some instances information about related factors and even the likely impacts of major social interventions (such as changed drug laws, or new incentives for recruitment into the military, to name but two). They also provide the possibility of feedback on the consequences of some social interventions as well as major historical events.

The particular topics included in our monitoring system are summarized later in this introduction and, of course, they are presented fully in the complete set of data tables. For present purposes, it is enough to indicate that the range of topics is very broad. This breadth is partly due to the wide interests of the principal investigators; but it also reflects our conviction that the concurrent examination of trends in a variety of areas is not only much more cost efficient but also more scientifically productive.

Research Design and Procedures*

The basic research design involves annual data collections from high school seniors during the spring of each year, beginning with the class of 1975. Each data collection takes place in approximately 125 public and private high schools selected to provide an accurate cross section of high school seniors throughout the coterminous United States. The design also provides for the longitudinal study of a subsample from each class of participating seniors; but since the focus of this series of volumes is exclusively on the data collected annually from seniors, the follow-up procedures will not be discussed here.

Reasons for Focusing on High School Seniors. There are several reasons for choosing the senior year of high school as an optimal point for monitoring the behaviors and attitudes of youth. One is that the completion of high school represents the end of an important developmental stage in this society, since it demarcates both the end of universal public education and, for many, the end of living in the parental home. Therefore, it is a logical point at which to take stock of the accumulated influences of these two environments on American youth.

Further, the completion of high school represents the jumping off point from which young people diverge into widely differing social environments, including college, business firms, military service, and homemaking. But these environmental transitions are not the only important changes which coincide with the end of high school. Most young men and women now reach the formal age of adulthood shortly before or after graduation; more significantly, they begin to assume adult roles, including financial self-support, marriage, and parenthood.

Finally, there are some important practical advantages to building a system of data collections around samples of high school seniors. The last year of high school constitutes the final point at which a reasonably good national sample of an age-specific cohort can be drawn and studied economically. The need for systematically repeated, large-scale samples from which to make reliable estimates of change requires

*A more extensive description of the research design and procedures may be found in Bachman and Johnston (1978).

that considerable stress be laid on efficiency and feasibility; the present design meets those requirements.

One limitation in the design is that it does not include in the target population those young men and women who drop out of high school before graduation (or before the last few months of the senior year, to be more precise). This excludes a relatively small proportion of each age cohort — between 15 and 20 percent (Dearman and Plisko, 1982) — though not an unimportant segment, since we know that certain behaviors such as illicit drug use (Johnston, 1973) and delinquency (Bachman, O'Malley, and Johnston, 1978) tend to be higher than average in this group. However, the addition of a representative sample of dropouts would increase the cost of the present research enormously, because of their dispersion and generally higher level of resistance to being located and interviewed.

For the purposes of estimating characteristics of the entire age group, the omission of high school dropouts does introduce certain biases; however, their small proportion sets outer limits on the bias (Johnston, O'Malley, and Bachman, 1986, Appendix). For the purposes of estimating *changes* from one cohort of high school seniors to another, the omission of dropouts represents a problem only if different cohorts have considerably different proportions who drop out. We have no reason to expect dramatic changes in those rates for the foreseeable future, and recently published government statistics indicate a great deal of stability in dropout rates since 1970 (Dearman and Plisko, 1982, p. 4).

Some may use our high school data to draw conclusions about changes for the entire age group. While we do not encourage such extrapolation, we suspect that the conclusions reached often would be valid, since over 80 percent of the age group is in the surveyed segment of the population *and* we expect that change among those not in school are very likely to parallel the changes among those who are. Nevertheless, for purposes of characterizing the entire age group we would urge the user to check the results emanating from the present monitoring system against those emerging from other data collection systems using different methods, such as household interviews. (It is encouraging to note that when we have compared drug use data for this age group from the present study with those from interview studies, the findings have shown a high degree of similarity.)

Sampling Procedures. The procedure for securing a nationwide sample of high school seniors is a multistage one. Stage 1 is the selection of particular geographic areas, Stage 2 is the selection of one or more high schools in each area, and Stage 3 is the selection of seniors within each high school.

Stage 1: Geographic Areas. The geographic areas used in this study are the primary sampling units (PSUs) developed by the Sampling Section of the Survey Research Center for use in the Center's nationwide interview studies. These consist of 74 primary areas throughout the coterminous United States — including the 12 largest metropolitan areas, which contain about 30 percent of the nation's population. Of the 62 other primary areas, 10 are in the Northeast, 18 in the North Central area, 24 in the South, and 10 in the West. Because these same PSUs are used for personal interview studies by the Survey Research Center (SRC), local field representatives can be assigned to administer the data collections in practically all schools.

Stage 2: Schools. In the major metropolitan areas more than one high school is often included in the sampling design; in most other sampling areas a single high school is sampled. In all cases, the selections of high schools are made such that the probability of drawing a school is proportionate to the size of its senior class (according to recent records), the higher the selection probability assigned to the high school. When a sampled school is unwilling to participate, a replacement school as similar to it as possible is selected from the same geographic area.

Stage 3: Students. Within each selected school, up to about 400 seniors may be included in the data collection. In schools with fewer than 400 seniors, the usual procedure is to include all of them in the data collection. In larger schools, a subset of seniors is selected either by randomly sampling classrooms or by some other random method that is convenient for the school and judged to be unbiased. Sample weights are assigned to each respondent so as to take account of variations in the sizes of samples from one school to another, as well as the (smaller) variations in selection probabilities occurring at the earlier stages of sampling.

The three-stage sampling procedure described above yielded the number of participating schools and students indicated in Table 1.

One other important feature of the base-year sampling procedure should be noted here. All schools (except for half of the initial 1975 sample) are asked to participate in two data collections, thereby permitting replacement of half of the total sample of schools each year. One motivation for requesting that schools participate for two years is administrative efficiency; it is a costly and time-consuming procedure to secure the cooperation of schools, and a two-year period of participation cuts down that effort substantially. Another important advantage is that whenever an appreciable shift in scores from one graduating class to the next is observed, it is possible to check whether the shift might be attributable to some differences in the newly sampled schools. This is done simply by repeating the analysis using only the 60 or so schools which participated both years. Thus far, the half-sample approach

Table 1

Sample Sizes and Student Response Rates

	1975	1976	1977	1978	1979	1980	1981	1982	1983	1984	1985	1986
Number of Public Schools	111	108	108	111	111	107	109	116	112	117	115	113
Number of Private Schools	14	15	16	20	20	20	19	21	22	17	17	16
Number of Schools	125	123	124	131	131	127	128	137	134	134	132	129
Total Number of Students*	15791	16678	18436	18924	16662	16524	18267	18348	16947	16499	16502	15713
Student Response Rate**	78%	77%	79%	83%	82%	82%	81%	83%	84%	83%	84%	83%

* Sample weights are assigned to each respondent to correct for unequal probabilities of selection which arise in the multi-stage sampling procedure.

** The student response rate is derived by dividing the attained sample by the target sample (both based on weighted numbers of cases). The target sample is based upon listings provided by schools. Since such listings may fail to take account of recent student attrition, the actual response rate may be slightly underestimated.

has worked quite well; and examination of drug prevalence data from the "matched half-samples" showed that the half samples of repeat schools yielded drug prevalence trends which were virtually identical to trends based on all schools.

School Recruiting Procedures. Early during the fall semester an initial contact is made with each sampled school. First a letter is sent to the principal describing the study and requesting permission to survey seniors. The letter is followed by a telephone call from a project staff member, who attempts to deal with any questions or problems and (when necessary) makes arrangements to contact and seek permission from other school district officials. Basically the same procedures are followed for schools asked to participate for the second year.

Once the school's agreement to participate is obtained, arrangements are made by phone for administering the questionnaires. A specific date for the survey is mutually agreed upon and a local SRC representative is assigned to carry out the administration.

Advance Contact with Teachers and Students. The local SRC representative is instructed to visit the school two weeks ahead of the actual date of administration. This visit serves as an occasion to meet the teachers whose classes will be affected and to provide them with a brochure describing the study, a brief set of guidelines about the questionnaire administration, and a supply of flyers to be distributed to the students a week to 10 days in advance of the questionnaire administration. The guidelines to the teachers include

a suggested announcement to students at the time the flyers are distributed.

From the students' standpoint, the first information about the study usually consists of the teacher's announcement and the short descriptive flyer. In announcing the study, the teachers are asked to stress that the questionnaires used in the survey are not tests, and that there are no right or wrong answers. The flyer tells students that they will be invited to participate in the study, points out that their participation is strictly voluntary, and stresses confidentiality (including a reference to the fact that the Monitoring the Future project has a special government grant of confidentiality which allows their answers to be protected). The flyer also serves as an informative document which the students can show to their parents.

Questionnaire Administrations. The questionnaire administration in each school is carried out by the local SRC representatives and their assistants, following standardized procedures detailed in a project instruction manual. The questionnaires are administered in classrooms during normal class periods whenever possible, although circumstances in some schools require the use of larger group administrations. Teachers are not asked to do anything more than introduce the SRC staff members and (in most cases) remain in the classroom to help guarantee an orderly atmosphere for the survey. Teachers are urged to avoid walking around the room, so that students may feel free to write their answers without fear of being observed.

The actual process of completing the questionnaires is quite straightforward. Respondents are given sharpened pencils and asked to use them because the questionnaires are designed for automatic scanning. Most respondents can finish within a 45-minute class period; for those who cannot, an effort is made to provide a few minutes of additional time.

Procedures for Protecting Confidentiality. In any study that relies on voluntary reporting of drug use or other illegal acts, it is essential to develop procedures which guarantee the confidentiality of such reports. It is also desirable that these procedures be described adequately to respondents so that they are comfortable about providing honest answers.

We noted that the first information given to students about the survey consists of a descriptive flyer stressing confidentiality and voluntary participation. This theme is repeated at the start of the questionnaire administration. Each participating student is instructed to read the message on the cover of the questionnaire, which stresses the importance and value of the study, notes that answers will be kept strictly confidential, states that the study is completely voluntary, and tells the student "If there is any question you or your parents would find objectionable for any reason, just leave it blank." The instructions then point out that in a few months a summary of nationwide results will be mailed to all participants and also that a follow-up questionnaire will be sent to some students after a year. The cover message explains that these are the reasons for asking that name and address be written on a special form which will be removed from the questionnaire and handed in separately. The message also points out that the two different code numbers (one on the questionnaire and one on the tear-out form) cannot be matched except by a special computer tape at The University of Michigan. (The content of the inside and outside of the standard questionnaire cover, including the tear-out form, may be found in Appendix C.)

Content Areas and Questionnaire Design

Drug use and related attitudes are the topics which receive the most extensive coverage in the Monitoring the Future project; but the questionnaires also deal with a wide range of other subject areas, including attitudes about government, social institutions, race relations, changing roles for women, educational aspirations, occupational aims, and marital and family plans, as well as a variety of background and demographic factors.* (Table 2 provides an outline of the 20

general subject areas into which all items are categorized in the Question Index toward the end of this volume.) Given this breadth of content, the study is not presented to respondents as a "drug use study," nor do they tend to view it as such.

Because many questions are needed to cover all of these topic areas, much of the questionnaire content is divided into five different questionnaire forms which are distributed to participants in an ordered sequence that produces five virtually identical subsamples. About one-third of each questionnaire form consists of key or "core" variables which are common to all forms. All demographic variables and some measures of drug use are included in this "core" set of measures. This use of the full sample for drug and demographic measures provides a more accurate estimation on these dimensions and also makes it possible to link them statistically to all of the other measures which are included in a single form only.**

Representativeness and Validity

The samples for this study are intended to be representative of high school seniors throughout the 48 coterminous states. We have already discussed the fact that this definition of the sample excludes one important portion of the age cohort: those who have dropped out of high school before nearing the end of the senior year. But given the aim of representing high school seniors, it will now be useful to consider the extent to which the obtained samples of schools and students are likely to be representative of all seniors and the degree to which the data obtained are likely to be valid.

We can distinguish at least four ways in which survey data of this sort might fall short of being fully accurate. First, some sampled schools refuse to participate, which could introduce some bias. Second, the failure to obtain questionnaire data from 100 percent of the students sampled in participating schools would also introduce bias. Third, the answers provided by participating students are open to both conscious and unconscious distortions which could reduce validity. Finally, limitations in sample size and/or design could place limits on the accuracy of estimates. Each of these issues is treated extensively elsewhere (Johnston, Bachman, and O'Malley, 1979a, especially Appendices A and B), so in this section we will present only the highlights of each of those discussions.

School Participation. As noted in the description of the sampling design, schools are invited to participate

---

*An example of analyses relating background, demographic, and lifestyle factors to drug use is Bachman, Johnston, and O'Malley (1981); a much broader array of other subject areas included in the study is treated by Bachman and Johnston (1979).

**These core variables are the first ones on which data are presented in the Descriptive Results Section.

Table 2

Measurement Content Areas
(Abbreviated Version*)

A. **Drugs.** Drug use and related attitudes and beliefs, drug availability and exposure, surrounding conditions and social meanings of drug use. Views of significant others regarding drugs.

B. **Education.** Educational lifestyle, values, experiences, and environments.

C. **Work and Leisure.** Vocational values, meaning of work and leisure, work and leisure activities, preferences regarding occupational characteristics and type of work setting.

D. **Sex Roles and Family.** Values, attitudes, and expectations about marriage, family structure, sex roles, and sex discrimination.

E. **Population Concerns.** Values and attitudes about overpopulation and birth control.

F. **Conservation, Materialism, Equity, etc.** Values, attitudes, and expectations related to conservation, pollution, materialism, equity, and the sharing of resources. Preferences regarding type of dwelling and urbanicity.

G. **Religion.** Religious affiliation, practices, and views.

H. **Politics.** Political affiliation, activities, and views.

I. **Social Change.** Values, attitudes, and expectations about social change.

J. **Social Problems.** Concern with various social problems facing the nation and the world.

K. **Major Social Institutions.** Confidence in and commitment to various major social institutions (business, unions, branches of government, press, organized religion, military, etc.).

L. **Military.** Views about the armed services and the use of military force. Personal plans for military service.

M. **Interpersonal Relationships.** Qualitative and quantitative characteristics of cross-age and peer relationships. Interpersonal conflict.

N. **Race Relations.** Attitudes toward and experiences with other racial groups.

O. **Concern for Others.** Concern for others; voluntary and charitable activities.

P. **Happiness.** Happiness and life satisfaction, overall and in specific life domains.

Q. **Other Personality Variables.** Attitudes about self (including self-esteem), locus of control, loneliness, risk-taking, trust in others, importance placed on various life goals, counter-culture orientation, hostility.

R. **Background.** Demographic and family background characteristics, living arrangements.

S. **Deviant Behavior and Victimization.** Delinquent behaviors, driving violations and accidents (including those under the influence of drugs), victimization experiences.

T. **Health Habits and Symptoms.** Health habits, somatic symptoms, medical treatment.

*For more detailed listing of measurement content areas, see Table 3 on page 210.

in the study for a two-year period. With very few exceptions, each school which has participated for one data collection has agreed to participate for a second. Thus far, from 66 percent to 80 percent of the schools initially invited to participate have agreed to do so each year; for each school refusal, a similar school (in terms of size, geographic area, urbanicity, etc.) was recruited as a replacement. The selection of replacement schools almost entirely removes problems of bias in region, urbanicity, and the like that might result from certain schools refusing to participate. Other potential biases are more subtle, however. For example, if it turned out that most schools with "drug problems" refused to participate, that could seriously bias the drug estimates derived from the sample. And if any other single factor were dominant in most refusals, that also might suggest a source of serious bias. In fact, however, the reasons for schools' refusals to participate are varied and largely a function of happenstance events of the particular year. Thus, we feel fairly confident that school refusals have not seriously biased the surveys.

Student Participation. Completed questionnaires are obtained from three-fourths to four-fifths of all students sampled. The single most important reason that students are missed is that they are absent from class at the time of data collection, and in most cases it is not workable to schedule a special follow-up data collection for them. Students with fairly high rates of absenteeism also report above-average rates of drug use; therefore, there is some degree of bias introduced by missing the absentees. That bias could be largely corrected through the use of special weighting; however, this course was not chosen because the bias in estimates (for drug use, where the potential effect was hypothesized to be largest) was determined to be quite small and because the necessary weighting procedures would have introduced undesirable complications (see Johnston et al., 1977).

In addition to absenteeism, student nonparticipation occurs because of schedule conflicts with school trips and other activities which tend to be more frequent than usual during the final months of the senior year. Of course, some students refuse to complete or turn in a questionnaire. However, the SRC representatives in the field estimate this proportion to be only about one percent.

Validity of Self-Report Data. Survey measures of delinquency and of drug use depend upon respondents reporting what are, in many cases, illegal acts. Thus, a critical question is whether such self-reports are likely to be valid. Like most studies dealing with

these areas, we have no direct, objective validation of the present measures; however, the considerable amount of inferential evidence which exists strongly suggests that the self-report questions produce largely valid data. A number of factors have given us reasonable confidence about the validity of the responses to what are presumably among the most sensitive questions in the study: a low nonresponse on the drug questions; a large proportion admitting to some illicit drug use; the consistency of findings across several years of the present study; strong evidence of construct validity (based on relationships observed between variables); a close match between our data and the findings from other studies using other methods; and the findings from several methodological studies which have used objective validation methods.*

As for others of the measures, a few have a long and venerable history — as scholars of the relevant literatures will recognize — though some of these measures have been modified to fit the present questionnaire format. Many (probably most) questions, however, have been developed specifically for this project through a careful process of question writing, pilot testing, pretesting, and question revision or elimination. Some already have been included in other publications from the study, but many have not; therefore, there currently exists little *empirical* evidence of their validity and reliability. On the other hand, the fact that virtually all results presented in this volume are based on individual items, rather than indexes or abstract concepts, should make it easy for the reader to judge the degree to which each item has "face validity" and also the degree to which there is some evidence of construct validity in the bivariate results.

Accuracy of the Sample. A sample survey never can provide the same level of accuracy as would be obtained if the entire target population were to participate in the survey — in the case of the present study, about three million seniors per year. But perfect accuracy of this sort would be extremely expensive and certainly not worthwhile considering the fact that a high level of accuracy can be provided by a carefully designed probability sample. The accuracy of the sample in this study is affected both by the size of the student sample and by the number of schools in which they are clustered. Appendix B presents a discussion of the ways in which this clustering and other aspects of the sampling design are taken into account in computing the precision or accuracy of the samples. For the purposes of this introduction, it is sufficient to note that virtually all estimates based on the total sample have confidence intervals of ±1.5 percentage points or smaller — sometimes considerably smaller.

---

* A more detailed discussion of the evidence for validity of the measures of illicit drug use may be found in Johnston et al. (1977; 1979a), Appendix A. An analysis of inconsistencies in students' reports of monthly versus yearly drug use is provided by Bachman and O'Malley (1981).

This means that, had we been able to invite all schools and all seniors in the 48 coterminous states to participate, the results from such a massive survey would be within an estimated 1.5 percentage points of our present sample findings at least 95 times out of 100. We consider this to be a quite high level of accuracy, and one that permits the detection of fairly small trends from one year to the next.

Consistency and the Measurement of Trends. One other point is worth noting in a discussion of the validity of our findings. The Monitoring the Future project is, by intention, a study designed to be sensitive to changes from one time to another. Accordingly, the measures and procedures have been standardized and applied consistently across each data collection. To the extent that any biases remain because of limits in school and/or student participation, and to the extent that there are distortions (lack of validity) in the responses of some students, it seems very likely that such problems will exist in much the same way from one year to the next. In other words, biases in the survey estimates should tend to be consistent from one year to another, which means that the measurement of *trends* should be affected very little by any such biases.

Caveats to Users of the Data

In attempting to understand and interpret the statistical results contained in this volume, the reader should keep in mind the several considerations discussed below.

Estimation of Sampling Errors. Appendix A provides figures which allow the reader to determine the 95 percent confidence interval around any observed percentage for both the total sample and the several subgroups for which statistics are given. Appendix A also provides tables and guidelines for testing the statistical significance of observed differences between subgroups (e.g., males vs. females) and the significance of year-to-year changes for the entire sample and for the various subgroups on any given variable. Estimates based on subgroups containing relatively few cases (e.g., those who have used heroin) will have substantially larger margins of error than those subgroups with large numbers of cases.

Subgroup Definitions. At the beginning of the Descriptive Results section there is a careful definition of each of the subgroups analyzed in this series of volumes. It is important for the reader to read these definitions so as not to be misled by the necessarily abbreviated descriptions given in the column headings of the data tables. For example, the column labeled "4-year college plans" includes data only for seniors who

expect to be graduated from a four-year college, which is only a subset of all who expect to receive some college training. To take another example, several column headings in the lifetime illicit drug use index use the term "pills"; however, these categories contain people who indicate that they used any of a number of drugs — including some which usually are not taken in pill form (e.g., cocaine and narcotics other than heroin).

Missing Data Notes. Each column of percentages for a given variable adds to 100 percent (with slight variations due to rounding), whether based on the entire sample or any one of the subgroups being described. Missing data were not included in computing these percentages, so it is up to the reader to determine whether an exceptional level of missing data exists on any given question. This can be done by comparing the weighted number of cases on which those percentages were based (given in italics under each percentage distribution) with the total number of weighted cases who took the questionnaire (given at the top of the same column). As would be expected, the missing data rate tends to rise modestly toward the end of each questionnaire. Occasionally there is an exceptional level of nonresponse for some other reason, the most common being that the respondent has been branched around a question or set of questions which are inappropriate for him or her. In this case the percentages are based only on those for whom the question was appropriate *and* who answered. A footnote has been entered to help call attention to the fact that completing a particular question is contingent upon the answer on a prior question. Most such cases are contained in Form 1 of the questionnaire, which has several sets of detailed questions about drug use which are answered only by those respondents who have used a particular class of drug during the past year.

Characterizing Heroin Users. Because this project places a special emphasis on the study of drug use, one set of columns distinguishes respondents according to the extent to which they have been involved with illicit drugs. The five drug use categories are based on an index of seriousness of involvement. The index has Guttman-like properties — that is, anyone classified at a given level is also very likely to have exhibited any drug-using behaviors which are associated with the lower levels in the index.

The most extreme category in the index is defined in terms of the respondent's ever having used heroin during his or her lifetime. However, any interpretations made about heroin users from these data must be tempered with extreme caution, not only because the small number of cases makes estimation in a given year relatively unreliable, but also because heroin users are probably the most selectively represented of all of the subgroups presented here. Heroin users — especially continuing users — are among those most likely to drop out of high school (Johnston, 1973). Therefore, we feel that heroin users are particularly underrepresented in a sample of high school seniors. Furthermore, most of those included in the study report only very occasional heroin use. Frequent users — addicts, if you will — are not well represented in these data.

Given these problems with the representation of heroin users, the readers may wonder why it was decided to present them as a separate category of drug users. There are two reasons for doing so. First, because even occasional heroin use represents such an extreme point on the continuum of drug involvement, it seems preferable that the heroin users not be mixed in with the next highest category of use (the "more pills" category). It remains quite possible, of course, for anyone to *combine* any two or more categories in the drug use continuum (by computing means of percentages weighted by the number of cases in each category); therefore, those wishing to incorporate heroin users with the next category can do so whenever they wish. The second reason for keeping them separate is that we suspect the data based on high school seniors provide some indication of the characteristics which might be found among heavier heroin users who dropped out of school. Some variables in the study are strongly correlated with the drug use continuum, and the present heroin user category provides both an end point for that continuum and an indication of the direction (further out on the continuum) in which heavier heroin users are likely to lie.

In sum, the reporting of separate percentages for heroin users among high school seniors permits greater clarity in analyzing other levels of drug use and provides data which may be suggestive about the larger population of young heroin users. But the particular data are clearly limited and should be interpreted with these cautions in mind.

Interpreting Racial Differences. Data are given for the two largest racial/ethnic subgroups in the population — those who identify themselves as white or Caucasian and those who identify themselves as black or Afro-American. Data are not given for the other ethnic categories (American Indians, Asian Americans, Mexican Americans, Puerto Ricans, or other Latin Americans) since each of these groups comprises less than three percent of the sample in any given year, which means that their small Ns (in combination with their clustered groupings in a limited number of schools) would yield estimates which would be too unreliable. In fact, even blacks — who constitute approximately 12 percent of each year's sample — are represented by only 350 to 425 respondents per year on any single questionnaire form. Further, because our sample is a stratified clustered sam-

ple, it yields less accuracy than would be yielded by a pure random sample of equal size (see Appendix B for details). Therefore, because of the limited number of cases, the margin of sampling error around any statistic describing blacks is larger than for most other subgroups described in this volume.

There exists, however, a quick way to determine the replicability of any finding involving racial comparisons. Since most questions are repeated from year to year, one can readily establish the degree to which a finding is replicated by looking at the results for the same question in prior or subsequent years. Given the relatively small Ns for blacks, the reader is urged to seek such replication before putting much faith in the reliability of any particular racial comparison.

There are factors in addition to unreliability, however, which could be misleading in the interpretation of racial differences. Given the social importance which has been placed on various racial differences reported in the social science literature, we would like to caution the reader to consider the various factors which could account for differences. These factors fall into three categories: differential representation in the sample, differential response tendencies, and the confounding of race with a number of other background and demographic characteristics.

Differential Representation. Census data characterizing American young people in the approximate age range of those in our sample show that somewhat lower proportions of blacks than whites remain in school through the end of twelfth grade (Dearman and Plisko, 1982, p. 23). Therefore, a slightly different segment of the black population than of the white population resides in our target population of high school seniors. Further, our samples appear to underrepresent slightly those black males who, according to census figures, *are* in high school at the twelfth grade level. Identified black males comprise about 6 percent of our sample, whereas census data suggest that they should comprise around 7 percent (U.S. Bureau of the Census, 1978). Therefore, it appears that we are losing more black males from our target population than white males or females of either race. This may be due to generally poorer attendance rates on the part of some black males and/or an unwillingness on the part of some to participate in data collections of this sort.

In sum, a smaller segment of the black population than of the white population of high school age is represented by the data contained here. Insofar as any characteristic is associated with being a school dropout or absentee, it is likely to be somewhat disproportionately underrepresented among blacks in our sample.

Differential Response Tendencies. In examining our full range of variables, we have noted certain racial differences in response tendencies. First, the tendency to state agreement in response to agree-disagree questions is generally somewhat greater among blacks than among whites. For example, blacks tend to agree more with the positively worded items in our index of self-esteem, but they also tend to agree more with the negatively worded items. As it happens, that particular index has an equal number of positively and negatively worded items, so that any overall "agreement bias" should be self-cancelling when the index score is computed. Since all data in this volume are based on single items, however, group differences in agreement bias are likely to affect results on questions employing the agree-disagree format. Fortunately, most of our questions are not of that type.

We have also observed a somewhat greater than average tendency for black respondents to select extreme answer categories on attitudinal scales. For example, even if the same proportion of blacks as whites felt positively (or negatively) about some subject, fewer of the whites are likely to say they feel *very* positively (or *very* negatively). We do not have any ready explanations for these differences in response styles, but what seems important for our present purposes is that, in the process of interpreting racial differences, the reader should be aware that differences in responses to particular questions may be related to these more general tendencies.

A somewhat separate issue in response tendency is a respondent's willingness to answer particular questions. The missing data rate, which can be determined by dividing the number responding to a question by the number taking the questionnaire (given at the top of each page), may reflect willingness to answer particular questions. If a particular question or set of questions has a missing data rate higher than is true for the prior or subsequent questions, then presumably more respondents than usual were unwilling (or perhaps unable) to answer it. We have observed such an exaggerated missing data rate for black males on the set of questions dealing with the respondent's own use of illicit drugs. Clearly a respondent's willingness to be candid on such questions depends on his or her trust of the research process and of the researchers themselves. We interpret the exaggerated missing data rates for black males in these sections as possibly reflecting, at least in part, less trust. The reader is advised to check for exceptional levels of missing data when making comparisons on any variable in which candor is likely to be reduced by lower system trust. One bit of additional evidence related to trust in the research process is that higher proportions of blacks than whites indicated that if they had used marijuana or heroin they would not have been willing to report it in the survey.

Covariance with Other Factors. Some characteristics such as race are highly confounded (correlated) with other variables — variables which may in fact explain some observed racial differences. Put another way, at the aggregate level we might observe a consid-

erable racial difference on some characteristic, but once we control for some background characteristics such as socio-economic level or region of the country — that is, once we compare the black respondents with whites who come from similar backgrounds — there may be no racial difference at all.

Race happens to be correlated with important background and demographic variables much more than some of the other variables dealt with here (like the respondent's sex). When we compare males and females in this sample we know that observed differences between them are not likely to be explained by differences in their family background (such as the socioeconomic level of their families, the region of the country, or the size of the cities in which they grew up) because males and females on the average come from extremely similar backgrounds. A perusal of Section C of Questionnaire Forms 1 through 5, however, will illustrate that on the average the black subgroup in this sample is quite different from the white subgroup in a number of such respects. A higher proportion of blacks live in the South and a higher proportion grew up in families with the father and/or mother absent, and more had mothers who worked while they were growing up. A substantially higher proportion of blacks are Baptists, and blacks tend to attribute more importance to religion in their lives than do whites. Fewer are enrolled in a college-preparatory curriculum (though a higher proportion say they plan to attend some type of college). A slightly higher proportion of black respondents are married and have children, and on the average they are slightly older than the white sample. As was mentioned earlier, black males are more underrepresented in our sample than black females, with the result that each year roughly 58 percent of our black sample is female versus roughly 51 percent of the white sample.

We note these differences in demographic, background, and ascriptive characteristics because, in any attempt to understand *why* a racial difference exists, one would want to be able to examine the role of these covarying characteristics. It is not possible, given the amount of data contained in this volume, to "factor out" the contribution of most of these covarying characteristics when interpreting racial differences. Therefore, while the data here may provide a relatively accurate *description* of racial differences (keeping in mind our earlier cautions about representativeness and response style), they do not by themselves yield a great deal by way of explanation.

However, since the full data sets now reside in an archive, described in the Preface, it is possible for the reader to conduct a more in depth exploration of observed differences—or nondifferences, for that matter. We particularly encourage readers interested in racial comparisons to make further explorations in the data in order to determine the possible role of the other variables discussed here.

Users of the data are also encouraged to contact the principal investigators for information on the most recent analyses of racial differences, some of which are already underway.

Given the long list of caveats about interpreting racial differences, one might ask why we chose to publish the statistics for racial subgroups at all. After considerable deliberation among ourselves as well as with colleagues more knowledgeable in the field of race relations, we concluded that the expected benefits of making these data available (along with this cautionary discussion) outweigh the potential costs of having them misused. Unfortunately, because blacks constitute a relatively small proportion of the American population, they constitute too small a number in most surveys to be characterized separately. Because the sample sizes in the present survey are large in comparison to most, we have at least sufficient numbers of cases to consider publishing data on blacks separately. Further, given the iterative nature of the series, we are also able to provide checks for replication of findings on different samples each year. While there may be some risk that findings will be taken out of context or used carelessly in ways that might tend to increase racial misunderstandings, there is substantially greater risk that valuable information concerning the races (and relative to their well-being) will be lost if it were not included here.

A note on the questions about amphetamine use. Prior to the 1982 survey, we discovered that some respondents' answers to questions on amphetamine use erroneously included use of over-the-counter stay-awake and diet pills, as well as some "look-alike" pills. In the 1982 survey, we introduced some new questions on the use of amphetamines in order to make more clear to the respondents that "look-alike" pills and over-the-counter products should be excluded. We also kept the old version of the questions in two questionnaire forms in the 1982 and 1983 surveys so that it would be possible to "splice" the trend lines resulting from the old and new questions.

As a result of these changes, the reader who uses these volumes to examine trends in amphetamine use must be careful not to make inappropriate comparisons. The response distributions shown in the combined Forms 1 to 5 section (pages 28–29) from 1975 to 1981 contain the responses for Forms 1 through 5. In 1982 and 1983, that section contains two sets of responses. The first set is for Forms 1, 2, and 4 (with Form 1 double-weighted); these provide what we believe to be the best estimates of current amphetamine use and of trends from 1982 on. The second set of responses are based on Forms 3 and 5, the old versions of the questions; thus, these questions provide the best comparisons for looking at trends over time from 1975 to 1983 (although there is reason to be cautious about these trends because of the erroneous inclusion of non-amphetamines, as described above). Beginning with 1984, all forms use the new versions of the questions.

---

* An exended analysis and discussion of black-white differences in response styles may be found in Bachman and O'Malley (1984).

Descriptive Results

Introduction to the Table Format and Conventions

Univariate and selected bivariate percentage distributions are given in this section for all questions asked of this year's senior class. The definitions of column headings and the source of the standard contents for each table are given below under the numbers indicated in Figure 1.

Definitions of Column Headings

① **Questionnaire Form.** The form from which all data on the page were derived is given here. When the designation "Forms 1-5" is used, it indicates that responses from students completing all five questionnaires have been combined; accordingly, the numbers of respondents in each column are five times as large for questions contained in a single form only.

② **Total Sample.** Univariate percentage distributions based on the total sample of respondents are given in this column.

③ **Sex.** Percentage distributions are given separately for males (M) and females (F). Respondents with missing data on the question asking the respondent's sex (Question C03) are omitted from both groupings.

④ **Race.** Percentage distributions are given separately for those describing themselves as "White or Caucasian" (W) and "Black or Afro-American" (B) in answer to Question C04. Comparable columns for the other racial or ethnic groups (Mexican Americans, Asian Americans, American Indians, etc.) are not shown because of the low number of cases in each group. *Note:* See the caveats regarding the interpretation of racial differences in the introduction section of this volume.

⑤ **Region.** Percentage distributions are given separately for respondents living in each of four mutually exclusive regions of the country. The regional classifications are based on Census categories and are defined as follows:

Northeast (NE): Census classifications of New England and Middle Atlantic states; includes Maine, New Hampshire, Vermont, Massachusetts, Rhode Island, Connecticut, New York, New Jersey, and Pennsylvania.

North Central (NC): Census classifications of East North Central and West North Central states; includes Ohio, Indiana, Illinois, Michigan, Wisconsin, Minnesota, Iowa, Missouri, North Dakota, South Dakota, Nebraska, and Kansas.

South (S): Census classifications of South Atlantic, East South Central, and West South Central states; includes Delaware, Maryland, District of Columbia, Virginia, West Virginia, North Carolina, South Carolina, Georgia, Florida, Kentucky, Tennessee, Alabama, Mississippi, Arkansas, Louisiana, Oklahoma, and Texas.

West (W): Census classifications of Mountain and Pacific states; includes Montana, Idaho, Wyoming, Colorado, New Mexico, Arizona, Utah, Nevada, Washington, Oregon, and California.

⑥ **Four-Year College Plans.** Percentage distributions are given separately for (1) respondents who indicate that they "definitely will" or "probably will" graduate from a four-year college program and (2) those who say that they "definitely won't" or "probably won't" graduate from a four-year college program, based on responses to Question C21d. Respondents not answering question C21d are omitted from both columns. (A number of those who do not expect to complete a four-year college program *do* expect to get some post-secondary education, as may be seen in the tables for questions C21a and c.)

⑦ **Illicit Drug Use: Lifetime.** Percentage distributions are given separately for five mutually exclusive subgroups differentiated by their degree of involvement with illicit drugs. Eligibility for each category is defined below.

None. This column contains data from those respondents who indicated that they had not used marijuana at any time and did not report use of any of the following illicit drugs in their lifetime: LSD, other psychedelics, cocaine, amphetamines, tranquilizers, methaqualone, barbiturates, heroin, or other narcotics.*

Marijuana Only. This column contains data from other respondents who indicated that they had used marijuana (or hashish) but had never used any of the other illicit drugs just listed.

Few Pills. This column contains data from those respondents who indicated having used one or more of the above listed drugs (other than marijuana) but who had not used any one class of them on three or more occasions *and* who had not used heroin at all.

More Pills. This column contains data from respondents who had used any of the above listed drugs (other than marijuana) on three or more occasions but who had never used heroin.

Any Heroin. This column contains data from those respondents who indicated having used heroin on one or more occasions in their lifetime.

⑧ **N(Weighted Number of Cases).** This row contains the number of students who turned in questionnaires in each of the categories indicated by the column headings. The number of cases is stated in terms of the weighted number of respondents rather than the actual number, since all percentages in the tables have been calculated using weighted cases. The actual number of respondents generally is about 15 percent higher than the weighted number for data collected in 1975, 1976, and 1977. (A comparison of weighted and unweighted numbers is provided in Tables B-1 and B-2 in Appendix B.) For data collected in 1978 or later, the actual number of respondents is roughly equal to the weighted number. Weighting is used to improve the accuracy of estimates by correcting for unequal probabilities of selection which arise in the multi-stage sampling procedures.

⑨ **Percentage of Weighted Total.** This row indicates the percentage of the total number of respondents who fall into the category indicated by each column heading. Unlike all other percentages on the page, which can be summed vertically, these percentages sum horizontally. To the extent that the subcate-

gories in a column (e.g., Males and Females) fail to sum to 100 percent, cases have been eliminated because of missing data on the variable in question (e.g., Sex), or, in the case of Race, because several subcategories have been omitted intentionally.

Table Contents

⑩ **Questions and Answers.** Each question along with its accompanying answer alternatives is presented verbatim. The alphanumeric prefix to the question indicates the section of the questionnaire in which it is located and its sequence within that section. So, for example, a prefix of B12c indicates that the item was question 12c in the B Section of the questionnaire.

⑪ **Item Reference Number.** This is a unique identification number permanently assigned to each question. Any question may be located in the Question Index of the 1975–1981 volumes by using this number, and in the Question Index of all subsequent volumes by using this number in conjunction with the subject area code.

⑫ **Subject Area Code.** Every question has been classified into one or more subject areas; the alphanumeric code indicates the subject area (or areas) applicable to the question shown. The complete listing of subject areas is presented in Table 3 (at the beginning of the Question Index near the end of this volume). Starting with the 1982 volume, the Question Index is ordered first by subject area, and then (within areas) by item reference number.

⑬ **Percentage Distribution.** Each column of numbers beside a question gives the percentage of each group (defined by the column heading) who chose each answer alternative, rounded to the nearest tenth of a percent. These figures add vertically to 100 percent (with some rounding error). Nonrespondents to the question are excluded from the percentage calculations.

⑭ **Number of Weighted Cases Answering (N).** The number of students in the relevant group (defined by the column heading) who answered the question is given just below the percentage distribution. The number of nonrespondents may be determined by subtracting this weighted number answering from the weighted number taking the questionnaire, shown at the top of the same column. Nonresponse may be due to the subject not answering the question, even though it pertains to him or her, or to the subject skipping inappropriate questions as instructed on a prior item.

---

*Inhalants (including the amyl and butyl nitrites) are not included in this list of illicit drugs because the relevant questions are not contained in all questionnaire forms nor in all years of the study. Similarly, the use of PCP is counted only if it was reported under "other psychedelics" use, because specific questions about PCP are not included in all forms or years. This results in a few apparent inconsistencies in the tables relating the drug use index to specific questions about these drugs.

Figure 1
Guide to Table Format

Column annotations (circled numbers): ① ② ③ ④ ⑤ ⑥ ⑦ across the top; ⑧ ⑨ ⑩ ⑪ ⑫ ⑬ ⑭ along the left side.

QUESTIONNAIRE FORM 1-5 1982	TOTAL	SEX		RACE		REGION				4YR COLLEGE PLANS		ILLICIT DRUG USE: LIFETIME				
		M	F	White	Black	NE	NC	S	W	Yes	No	None	Marijuana Only	Few Pills	More Pills	Any Heroin
N (Weighted No. of Cases):	18348	8828	8788	13887	2080	4741	5383	5551	2672	9360	7507	6328	4040	2439	4839	210
% of Weighted Total:	100.0	48.1	47.9	75.7	11.3	25.8	29.3	30.3	14.6	51.0	40.9	34.5	22.0	13.3	26.4	1.1

These next questions ask for some background information about yourself.

C01: In what year were you born?

	TOTAL	M	F	White	Black	NE	NC	S	W	Yes	No	None	Mari. Only	Few Pills	More Pills	Any Heroin
1. Before '62	.3	.3	.3	.1	.6	.2	.3	.4	.2	.2	.4	.4	.1	.3	.2	1.1
2. 1962	2.0	2.6	1.4	1.3	3.9	1.5	2.0	2.7	1.5	1.0	2.9	2.0	1.9	2.2	1.4	5.3
3. 1963	23.3	26.6	19.6	21.8	26.1	15.2	27.2	25.6	24.4	19.4	27.1	23.4	23.9	23.4	22.0	25.4
4. 1964	72.8	69.3	76.6	75.6	66.3	80.5	69.5	69.9	72.2	77.3	68.6	72.2	72.2	72.7	75.2	67.9
5. 1965	1.6	1.1	2.1	1.2	3.0	2.5	1.0	1.4	1.6	2.1	1.0	1.8	1.9	1.3	1.2	.2
6. 1966	*	*	*	*	*	*	*	*	*	*	-	.1	-	-	-	-
7. 1967	-	-	-	-	-	-	-	-	-	-	-	-	-	-	-	-
8. After 1967	*	*	*	*	-	-	*	*	-	*	*	*	*	*	*	-
Item 10 Subject R01 N	17899	8816	8787	13882	2079	4572	5306	5428	2593	9324	7466	6259	3986	2408	4718	207

C02: In what month were you born?

	TOTAL	M	F	White	Black	NE	NC	S	W	Yes	No	None	Mari. Only	Few Pills	More Pills	Any Heroin
01. January	8.0	8.0	8.3	7.7	10.0	8.4	8.0	8.4	6.9	8.2	7.9	8.2	7.3	9.1	7.5	11.6
02. February	7.3	7.3	7.5	7.2	7.8	7.4	7.2	7.8	6.6	7.4	7.4	7.4	7.6	7.1	7.2	7.0
03. March	7.8	8.2	7.5	7.8	7.7	8.4	7.6	7.0	8.8	8.0	7.6	7.2	8.3	7.2	8.7	4.3
04. April	7.7	7.7	7.7	7.8	7.3	8.1	7.5	7.4	8.1	7.8	7.7	7.5	7.8	7.7	7.6	12.1
05. May	8.2	8.2	8.1	8.4	7.2	8.6	8.5	7.4	8.9	8.4	8.0	8.3	8.2	7.8	8.6	8.4
06. June	8.2	8.7	7.9	8.6	7.4	7.3	8.9	8.2	8.5	7.9	8.8	7.8	8.0	8.1	9.0	6.1
07. July	9.0	9.1	8.9	9.1	9.2	8.6	9.2	8.9	9.3	9.1	8.8	8.9	9.1	9.2	8.7	13.4
08. August	9.1	9.5	8.6	9.1	9.1	9.3	8.9	9.4	8.9	8.9	9.5	9.7	9.4	8.9	8.5	4.9
09. September	9.2	8.7	9.8	9.2	10.0	9.3	9.2	9.5	8.3	8.9	9.5	9.5	8.4	9.8	9.4	4.9
10. October	8.9	8.6	9.0	8.9	8.0	8.6	8.8	9.6	8.5	9.0	8.8	9.2	9.0	9.0	8.5	7.4
11. November	8.1	8.0	7.9	8.2	7.3	7.8	8.0	8.4	8.2	8.0	8.4	8.0	8.2	8.4	8.2	5.4
12. December	8.3	8.0	8.7	8.0	8.8	8.1	8.3	8.0	9.0	8.6	7.8	8.4	8.5	7.8	8.1	11.0
Item 20 Subject R01 N	17871	8802	8779	13863	2079	4566	5294	5420	2591	9312	7455	6253	3986	2398	4706	207

C03: What is your sex?

	TOTAL	M	F	White	Black	NE	NC	S	W	Yes	No	None	Mari. Only	Few Pills	More Pills	Any Heroin
1. Male	50.1	100.0	-	50.9	43.2	49.8	50.6	50.0	49.9	50.0	48.7	47.8	55.3	48.7	48.7	62.6
2. Female	49.9	-	100.0	49.1	56.8	50.2	49.4	50.0	50.1	50.0	51.3	52.2	44.7	51.3	51.3	37.4
Item 30 Subject R01 N	17616	8828	8788	13676	2047	4511	5214	5339	2552	9216	7324	6177	3913	2370	4650	202

C04: How do you describe yourself?

	TOTAL	M	F	White	Black	NE	NC	S	W	Yes	No	None	Mari. Only	Few Pills	More Pills	Any Heroin
1. American Indian	1.4	1.5	1.2	-	-	.8	1.2	1.6	2.4	.6	2.2	.8	1.5	1.4	1.7	3.2
2. Black or Afro-American	11.7	10.1	13.3	-	100.0	10.2	5.1	21.9	6.3	11.3	10.5	13.7	16.1	11.4	4.3	13.1
3. Mexican American or Chicano	2.2	2.3	2.1	-	-	.2	1.0	10.9	1.7	2.4	2.2	2.1	2.4	1.9	2.5	
4. Puerto Rican or other Latin American	1.9	1.8	2.0	-	-	4.1	.5	1.4	1.6	2.1	1.3	2.2	2.0	1.3	1.6	1.5
5. Oriental or Asian American	1.8	1.9	1.7	-	-	2.4	1.3	.3	5.1	3.0	.4	3.4	1.0	.8	.8	1.6
6. White or Caucasian	78.1	79.4	76.9	100.0	-	78.9	87.7	72.4	69.3	78.7	80.0	74.7	74.3	79.8	87.3	68.5
7. Other	2.9	3.1	2.7	-	-	3.4	3.3	1.5	4.4	2.6	3.1	3.0	3.0	2.9	2.4	9.6
Item 40 Subject R01 N	17775	8763	8729	13887	2080	4534	5272	5406	2562	9286	7412	6215	3961	2392	4688	203

C05: Where did you grow up mostly?

	TOTAL	M	F	White	Black	NE	NC	S	W	Yes	No	None	Mari. Only	Few Pills	More Pills	Any Heroin
1. On a farm	7.9	8.3	7.4	8.9	4.0	2.7	9.7	11.7	5.2	5.3	11.3	10.1	6.7	7.2	6.1	4.1
2. In the country, not on a farm	14.6	15.4	13.7	14.8	17.0	12.3	13.1	19.5	11.5	11.1	19.2	16.0	14.2	14.6	12.8	14.0
3. In a small city...					20.8	34.5	31.4	26.4	24.4	29.0	31.0	30.3	28.4	29.4	30.2	30.1
							12.1	11.4	21.8	13.2	13.4	12.0	14.1	13.2	14.5	
							8.8	8.5	7.7	9.6	7.7	7.5	8.5	9.2		
							8.7	12.4		10.0	7.3	8.6	10.2			

QUESTIONNAIRE FORM 1-5 1986	TOTAL	SEX		RACE		REGION				4YR COLLEGE PLANS		ILLICIT DRUG USE: LIFETIME				
		M	F	White	Black	NE	NC	S	W	Yes	No	None	Mari-juana Only	Few Pills	More Pills	Any Her-oin
N (Weighted No. of Cases):	15713	7261	7855	11713	1649	3720	4440	4855	2698	9291	5277	6535	3125	2223	3264	161
% of Weighted Total:	100.0	46.2	50.0	74.5	10.5	23.7	28.3	30.9	17.2	59.1	33.6	41.6	19.9	14.1	20.8	1.0

These next questions ask for some background information about yourself.

C01: In what year were you born?

1. Before '66	0.3	0.4	0.2	0.1	0.4	0.3	0.3	0.4	0.2	0.2	0.4	0.3	0.2	0.4	0.3	1.3
2. 1966	2.1	2.7	1.5	1.3	4.0	1.9	2.3	2.6	1.2	1.0	3.7	1.9	1.8	1.8	2.7	2.1
3. 1967	25.7	30.2	21.3	24.8	27.8	22.7	28.4	26.6	23.6	22.8	30.0	25.3	25.9	26.7	25.4	27.4
4. 1968	70.5	65.8	75.2	72.5	65.5	73.3	68.1	69.1	73.1	74.3	65.1	71.1	70.6	69.9	70.4	68.4
5. 1969	1.3	0.9	1.8	1.2	2.3	1.8	0.9	1.2	1.8	1.6	0.8	1.4	1.5	1.1	1.2	0.8
6. 1970	*	*	*	*	*	*	0.1	*	0.1	0.1	-	*	*	0.1	0.1	-
7. 1971	-	-	-	-	-	-	-	-	-	-	-	-	-	-	-	-
8. After 1971	*	-	-	-	-	-	-	*	-	*	-	-	-	-	-	-
Item 10 Subject R01 N	15346	7254	7849	11702	1647	3609	4379	4722	2635	9250	5240	6471	3072	2196	3212	158

C02: In what month were you born?

01. January	7.8	7.9	7.7	7.6	8.3	7.6	7.9	7.9	7.5	7.7	7.8	7.8	8.4	7.9	7.1	6.0
02. February	7.2	7.5	6.9	7.2	7.6	7.3	7.1	7.5	6.4	7.0	7.3	7.4	6.5	6.8	7.5	10.7
03. March	8.3	8.5	8.1	8.3	7.8	8.9	8.4	7.7	8.2	8.6	7.8	7.7	8.7	9.9	8.1	8.2
04. April	7.8	7.8	7.8	7.8	8.2	8.3	7.8	7.4	8.1	7.8	7.4	7.6	8.0	7.8	8.4	6.3
05. May	8.4	8.3	8.5	8.4	7.9	8.5	8.7	7.8	8.7	8.3	8.2	8.6	8.0	7.8	8.4	10.0
06. June	8.5	8.4	8.7	8.5	8.0	8.8	8.9	7.8	8.7	9.0	7.6	8.8	8.8	7.4	8.5	7.7
07. July	8.7	8.7	8.7	8.8	8.2	8.7	8.6	8.6	9.2	8.5	9.2	8.7	8.7	8.5	8.5	11.4
08. August	8.5	8.3	8.6	8.3	9.5	7.7	7.8	9.6	8.9	8.2	9.4	8.8	8.7	8.3	8.0	11.3
09. September	9.0	8.7	9.5	9.3	8.3	9.1	9.3	8.7	8.8	8.8	9.4	8.9	8.4	9.8	9.6	4.7
10. October	9.2	9.4	8.7	9.5	8.0	8.9	8.9	10.3	7.9	8.9	9.4	9.3	9.0	9.5	8.6	8.1
11. November	8.4	7.8	8.5	8.1	9.3	7.8	8.3	8.5	9.0	8.7	8.2	8.6	8.4	7.7	8.5	8.3
12. December	8.3	8.6	8.3	8.3	9.1	8.4	8.3	8.2	8.6	8.4	8.3	7.9	8.4	8.6	8.9	7.4
Item 20 Subject R01 N	15313	7236	7840	11681	1647	3603	4372	4710	2628	9233	5232	6466	3069	2190	3193	156

C03: What is your sex?

1. Male	48.0	100.0	-	48.2	44.5	49.7	48.0	46.7	48.2	46.7	49.0	46.4	52.5	45.2	47.9	65.3
2. Female	52.0	-	100.0	51.8	55.5	50.3	52.0	53.3	51.8	53.3	51.0	53.6	47.5	54.8	52.1	34.7
Item 30 Subject R01 N	15116	7261	7855	11567	1609	3572	4308	4648	2588	9132	5146	6398	3028	2154	3154	151

C04: How do you describe yourself?

1. American Indian	1.8	1.7	1.7	-	-	1.6	1.4	2.3	1.7	0.9	3.2	1.6	1.5	1.6	2.4	7.8
2. Black or Afro-American	10.8	9.9	11.5	-	100.0	8.3	6.6	21.4	2.3	10.0	10.7	12.9	15.6	7.0	4.1	7.4
3. Mexican American or Chicano	3.4	3.6	3.2	-	-	0.2	1.1	2.7	12.8	2.9	4.0	3.2	3.3	3.5	3.4	3.0
4. Puerto Rican or other Latin American	2.2	2.3	2.1	-	-	5.0	1.2	1.6	1.4	2.2	1.7	2.5	1.7	2.1	2.1	4.9
5. Oriental or Asian American	2.5	2.7	2.2	-	-	2.0	1.9	0.7	7.0	3.3	1.0	3.6	1.6	1.8	1.2	1.4
6. White or Caucasian	77.0	77.4	77.0	100.0	-	79.9	86.2	69.9	70.3	78.8	76.6	73.9	74.4	81.4	84.4	69.7
7. Other	2.4	2.3	2.3	-	-	2.8	1.8	1.3	4.6	1.9	2.8	2.3	1.9	2.6	2.5	5.8
Item 40 Subject R01 N	15221	7203	7785	11713	1649	3560	4355	4698	2608	9186	5202	6425	3054	2172	3181	155

C05: Where did you grow up mostly?

1. On a farm	5.9	6.9	4.9	6.6	2.6	2.7	7.5	7.6	4.6	4.2	9.0	7.5	4.1	5.4	4.7	5.1
2. In the country, not on a farm	13.7	14.6	12.8	14.0	14.0	13.6	11.2	18.9	8.6	10.3	19.4	15.9	11.1	12.6	12.0	14.3
3. In a small city or town (under 50,000 people)	33.2	33.8	33.0	35.2	28.5	40.9	32.5	31.7	26.5	33.0	33.8	33.9	34.6	30.8	32.8	26.5
4. In a medium-sized city (50,000 - 100,000)	13.4	11.1	15.4	12.5	16.8	10.5	11.1	13.5	21.0	13.3	13.6	12.2	13.9	14.2	14.5	17.7
5. In a suburb of a medium-sized city	7.8	7.0	8.6	8.2	6.0	8.9	6.1	7.9	9.0	9.0	5.7	6.4	8.4	10.1	8.6	3.8
6. In a large city (100,000 - 500,000)	8.9	8.7	9.0	7.1	14.8	7.6	9.7	7.8	11.4	9.2	7.7	7.5	9.1	9.6	10.4	14.4
7. In a suburb of a large city	7.9	8.5	7.3	8.8	3.2	6.5	11.2	6.1	7.0	10.0	4.6	7.7	9.1	7.5	7.5	5.6
8. In a very large city (over 500,000)	5.3	5.0	5.5	3.3	11.5	6.3	5.4	3.3	7.1	5.8	4.0	5.0	5.7	5.2	5.4	7.7
9. In a suburb of a very large city	4.0	4.6	3.5	4.2	2.4	3.0	5.3	3.1	4.8	5.2	2.1	3.8	3.9	4.5	4.2	4.9
Item 50 Subject R03 N	14266	6760	7232	10915	1523	3357	4120	4347	2442	8637	4854	6020	2861	2046	2983	141

C06: What is your present marital status?

1. Married	2.2	2.1	2.3	1.7	3.2	1.4	1.7	3.4	1.9	1.6	3.1	2.4	1.7	2.6	1.6	5.6
2. Engaged	6.3	3.6	8.6	6.3	6.5	5.5	6.2	7.8	4.6	3.6	11.1	4.5	5.6	7.3	9.4	15.9
3. Separated/divorced	0.8	0.8	0.7	0.5	2.3	0.7	0.6	1.0	0.7	0.5	1.0	0.5	1.1	1.0	0.8	1.4
4. Single	90.8	93.5	88.4	91.5	88.0	92.3	91.4	87.9	92.7	94.3	84.7	92.6	91.6	89.1	88.1	77.1
Item 60 Subject D01,R01 N	15347	7219	7831	11677	1637	3606	4374	4721	2645	9255	5251	6469	3079	2194	3211	158

*=less than .05 per cent.

QUESTIONNAIRE FORM 1-5 1986	TOTAL	SEX		RACE		REGION				4YR COLLEGE PLANS		ILLICIT DRUG USE: LIFETIME				
		M	F	White	Black	NE	NC	S	W	Yes	No	None	Marijuana Only	Few Pills	More Pills	Any Heroin
N (Weighted No. of Cases):	15713	7261	7855	11713	1649	3720	4440	4855	2698	9291	5277	6535	3125	2223	3264	161
% of Weighted Total:	100.0	46.2	50.0	74.5	10.5	23.7	28.3	30.9	17.2	59.1	33.6	41.6	19.9	14.1	20.8	1.0

C07: How many brothers and sisters do you have? (Include step brothers and sisters and half-brothers and sisters.)

C07A: Older brothers and sisters

0. None	28.5	29.8	27.4	29.8	23.1	26.5	28.0	29.7	30.2	31.8	24.2	31.0	26.2	28.7	26.1	24.4
1. One	27.8	28.0	27.8	29.1	20.9	29.0	27.6	27.6	26.9	28.3	26.9	28.1	29.4	27.3	26.7	24.0
2. Two	17.2	17.1	17.3	17.5	15.6	17.1	17.5	16.6	18.1	16.8	17.6	16.2	18.1	18.3	17.5	20.7
3. Three	10.1	9.9	10.4	10.1	10.0	10.9	10.9	9.2	9.4	9.4	11.0	9.5	10.1	9.5	11.4	14.4
4. Four	6.2	5.7	6.6	5.7	8.3	7.2	6.0	5.6	6.2	5.6	7.2	5.7	6.5	6.5	6.8	1.5
5. Five	3.7	3.5	4.0	3.2	7.1	3.5	4.1	3.9	3.1	3.2	4.6	3.6	3.5	3.5	4.1	7.2
6. Six or more	6.4	6.1	6.6	4.7	15.0	5.7	5.9	7.4	6.3	4.9	8.5	5.9	6.3	6.2	7.4	7.8
Item 75 Subject R02 N	14326	6724	7330	10904	1507	3364	4107	4358	2497	8591	4955	6022	2874	2068	2988	150

C07B: Younger brothers and sisters

0. None	30.3	30.7	30.2	32.4	21.6	32.5	31.7	28.9	27.7	31.0	29.4	28.7	30.5	29.8	34.2	27.0
1. One	35.6	36.6	34.7	36.8	31.2	36.0	34.8	35.9	36.0	36.1	34.7	35.3	36.8	36.8	34.6	34.1
2. Two	19.1	18.4	19.7	18.3	22.3	19.5	19.7	18.8	18.4	18.8	19.7	20.1	17.9	19.5	18.1	20.1
3. Three	7.8	7.4	8.2	6.8	11.2	7.2	7.4	7.8	9.2	7.9	7.5	8.3	8.3	7.0	6.9	6.8
4. Four	3.6	3.5	3.7	2.9	6.0	2.6	3.2	4.5	3.9	3.3	4.0	4.0	3.3	3.6	3.0	3.2
5. Five	1.6	1.7	1.6	1.4	3.1	0.9	1.4	1.9	2.5	1.4	2.0	1.5	1.7	1.7	1.6	2.5
6. Six or more	1.9	1.8	1.9	1.3	4.6	1.3	1.7	2.2	2.4	1.5	2.6	2.1	1.5	1.7	1.6	6.3
Item 76 Subject R02 N	14063	6624	7180	10677	1488	3258	4014	4324	2467	8552	4778	5961	2828	2007	2908	146

C07C: Which of the following people live in the same household with you? (Mark ALL that apply.)

A. I live alone	0.6	0.8	0.4	0.5	0.6	0.7	0.8	0.5	0.6	0.4	0.9	0.3	0.5	0.6	1.1	5.3
B. Father (or male guardian)	76.4	78.1	75.2	81.2	48.8	76.6	78.5	72.6	79.5	79.4	72.9	79.7	74.4	75.8	73.2	68.2
C. Mother (or female guardian)	90.5	89.9	91.3	91.9	84.9	91.6	91.5	88.6	90.8	92.5	87.6	92.3	90.6	90.2	88.1	82.4
D. Brother(s) and/or sister(s)	71.3	70.7	72.0	71.5	66.0	75.6	71.2	67.0	73.4	73.4	68.3	73.9	73.2	69.1	66.8	64.6
E. Grandparent(s)	5.8	5.8	5.9	5.1	9.4	6.6	4.8	6.6	5.3	5.5	6.3	5.3	6.6	6.2	5.9	5.7
F. My husband/wife	1.0	0.6	1.3	0.8	1.2	0.8	0.5	1.7	0.6	0.5	1.8	0.9	0.6	1.1	1.0	5.3
G. My children	1.0	0.3	1.6	0.6	3.6	0.5	0.9	1.7	0.4	0.6	1.6	0.8	1.0	1.3	1.1	0.7
H. Other relative(s)	4.9	4.3	5.5	3.5	10.4	4.8	3.9	6.1	4.6	4.1	6.0	4.8	5.1	4.6	5.0	4.6
I. Non-relative(s)	3.3	2.6	3.9	3.5	2.3	3.8	2.9	3.0	4.0	2.8	4.2	2.4	3.2	3.2	5.3	5.3
Item 80-160 Subject R03 N	15281	7173	7815	11646	1630	3584	4349	4710	2639	9250	5226	6442	3069	2183	3197	157

The next three questions ask about your parents. If you were raised mostly by foster parents, step-parents, or others, answer for them. For example, if you have both a step-father and a natural father, answer for the one that was most important in raising you.

C08: What is the highest level of schooling your father completed?

1. Completed grade school or less	5.5	5.0	5.8	3.5	8.1	4.0	4.1	7.5	6.3	3.8	8.0	6.1	5.0	4.7	4.5	12.6
2. Some high school	13.0	12.8	13.1	11.7	17.0	12.9	11.2	15.7	10.9	8.7	20.1	12.7	12.3	12.6	13.7	18.1
3. Completed high school	29.4	29.3	29.4	29.9	32.4	31.8	33.3	27.4	23.3	24.4	37.8	29.0	29.3	30.1	29.9	26.5
4. Some college	15.4	15.2	15.6	16.6	10.8	12.8	15.4	14.8	20.0	17.8	11.8	15.4	15.1	16.5	15.7	13.5
5. Completed college	18.1	19.2	17.3	19.9	11.4	18.1	18.2	15.8	22.0	22.7	10.5	18.1	18.4	18.7	17.8	14.8
6. Graduate or professional school after college	12.9	13.2	12.7	14.5	5.1	14.2	13.2	11.2	13.6	18.5	3.6	12.9	13.9	12.6	12.7	8.5
7. Don't know, or does not apply	5.7	5.4	6.0	3.9	15.2	6.3	4.6	7.5	3.8	4.1	8.1	5.8	6.1	4.8	5.7	6.0
Item 310 Subject R02 N	15266	7175	7798	11631	1625	3560	4365	4705	2636	9234	5249	6430	3066	2194	3187	159

C09: What is the highest level of schooling your mother completed?

1. Completed grade school or less	3.9	3.4	4.2	2.0	4.7	3.2	2.4	4.5	6.2	2.6	5.8	4.5	3.3	3.0	3.6	5.9
2. Some high school	12.7	11.6	13.7	10.6	19.8	12.0	11.4	16.2	9.5	8.4	20.1	12.4	11.9	13.1	12.9	21.0
3. Completed high school	38.3	40.0	36.9	40.7	33.6	42.1	41.7	36.7	30.5	33.8	45.6	36.9	38.8	38.6	40.5	35.5
4. Some college	18.1	17.3	18.7	19.4	15.6	14.3	17.8	17.4	25.0	21.4	13.2	17.9	18.4	20.3	17.4	14.2
5. Completed college	16.2	16.5	15.9	17.3	13.7	15.3	16.7	15.1	18.2	21.0	7.9	16.7	16.9	15.3	15.5	11.6
6. Graduate or professional school after college	8.0	7.9	8.1	8.3	6.4	9.6	7.7	6.9	8.0	10.7	3.3	8.3	8.0	7.7	7.6	6.5
7. Don't know, or does not apply	2.9	3.2	2.5	1.8	6.1	3.4	2.4	3.2	2.5	2.1	4.2	3.3	2.7	2.0	2.5	5.3
Item 320 Subject R02 N	15269	7169	7805	11632	1627	3560	4368	4705	2636	9243	5252	6437	3065	2191	3188	158

QUESTIONNAIRE FORM 1-5 1986	TOTAL	SEX		RACE		REGION				4YR COLLEGE PLANS		ILLICIT DRUG USE: LIFETIME				
		M	F	White	Black	NE	NC	S	W	Yes	No	None	Marijuana Only	Few Pills	More Pills	Any Heroin
N (Weighted No. of Cases):	15713	7261	7855	11713	1649	3720	4440	4855	2698	9291	5277	6535	3125	2223	3264	161
% of Weighted Total:	100.0	46.2	50.0	74.5	10.5	23.7	28.3	30.9	17.2	59.1	33.6	41.6	19.9	14.1	20.8	1.0

C10: Did your mother have a paid job (half-time or more) during the time you were growing up?

	TOTAL	M	F	White	Black	NE	NC	S	W	Yes	No	None	Marijuana Only	Few Pills	More Pills	Any Heroin
1. No	24.5	25.1	23.8	25.8	11.5	26.1	27.0	20.5	25.1	24.8	24.4	26.8	23.4	22.0	22.1	24.8
2. Yes, some of the time when I was growing up	29.4	29.9	29.2	31.3	18.1	32.0	30.0	25.6	31.7	29.5	29.4	29.2	27.9	30.8	30.9	27.8
3. Yes, most of the time	18.8	18.9	18.3	18.4	20.2	19.0	18.2	19.5	18.0	17.7	20.2	17.3	19.1	19.7	20.1	22.1
4. Yes, all or nearly all of the time	27.4	26.1	28.7	24.5	50.2	22.9	24.8	34.4	25.3	28.0	26.1	26.6	29.7	27.5	26.9	25.3
Item 330 Subject R02 N	15213	7141	7779	11603	1609	3544	4355	4684	2630	9228	5238	6422	3060	2185	3167	157

C11: How would you describe your political preference?

	TOTAL	M	F	White	Black	NE	NC	S	W	Yes	No	None	Marijuana Only	Few Pills	More Pills	Any Heroin
1. Strongly Republican	10.4	13.9	7.0	11.7	4.3	8.9	10.4	12.0	9.5	10.7	9.9	11.0	9.9	9.8	10.4	7.1
2. Mildly Republican	17.3	19.0	15.7	19.8	5.8	12.6	19.3	16.8	21.0	19.9	13.1	17.4	17.7	18.3	16.2	15.0
3. Mildly Democrat	11.1	10.2	12.0	10.1	13.8	8.9	10.4	11.9	13.7	12.1	9.6	11.1	11.3	11.7	10.5	9.4
4. Strongly Democrat	8.9	7.9	9.7	6.1	28.0	8.9	7.1	11.2	7.7	8.8	8.9	9.2	9.5	8.4	7.9	11.2
5. American Independent Party	1.3	1.3	1.2	1.0	2.2	1.5	1.1	1.4	1.1	1.0	1.7	1.0	1.2	2.2	1.3	2.6
6. No preference, independent	22.6	24.5	21.1	24.2	13.9	25.8	25.3	19.6	19.4	22.0	24.1	21.8	21.9	22.1	25.6	27.2
7. Other	1.4	1.9	1.0	1.2	1.5	2.3	1.3	0.8	1.8	1.0	2.1	1.0	1.2	1.1	2.4	3.9
8. Don't know, haven't decided	27.0	21.3	32.3	25.8	30.3	31.1	25.1	26.3	25.7	24.6	30.7	27.6	27.3	26.6	25.7	23.8
Item 340 Subject H01 N	15146	7121	7731	11565	1605	3523	4339	4674	2611	9217	5213	6400	3052	2172	3145	154

C12: How would you describe your political beliefs?

	TOTAL	M	F	White	Black	NE	NC	S	W	Yes	No	None	Marijuana Only	Few Pills	More Pills	Any Heroin
1. Very conservative	3.6	4.7	2.5	3.2	6.1	3.4	3.2	4.4	3.4	3.0	4.4	4.3	3.3	3.0	2.7	3.3
2. Conservative	13.4	15.6	11.4	14.0	12.0	10.9	13.8	14.1	14.9	14.7	11.3	14.9	13.0	13.2	11.1	10.1
3. Moderate	30.9	31.3	30.5	32.2	27.6	27.7	32.4	32.1	30.4	32.8	27.6	30.6	32.2	32.5	29.6	21.7
4. Liberal	15.7	15.1	16.2	15.2	15.5	15.4	15.6	14.5	18.7	17.8	12.3	14.2	16.6	16.1	17.9	18.7
5. Very liberal	3.5	3.4	3.5	3.3	4.3	3.7	3.7	2.9	3.9	3.8	3.1	2.5	3.6	4.2	4.8	5.6
6. Radical	2.8	4.5	1.2	2.7	2.5	3.7	2.3	2.3	3.0	2.4	3.3	1.5	2.4	3.4	4.6	15.2
8. None of the above, or don't know	30.1	25.4	34.8	29.3	32.0	35.3	29.0	29.7	25.8	25.4	38.0	32.0	28.9	27.6	29.2	25.3
Item 350 Subject H01 N	15115	7109	7716	11552	1590	3508	4335	4655	2617	9204	5212	6392	3042	2169	3142	155

C13: The next three questions are about religion.

C13A: What is your religious preference?

	TOTAL	M	F	White	Black	NE	NC	S	W	Yes	No	None	Marijuana Only	Few Pills	More Pills	Any Heroin
01. Baptist	20.9	20.0	21.5	17.3	58.9	7.9	12.8	44.5	9.6	18.3	24.9	23.4	21.9	19.6	16.0	17.4
02. Churches of Christ	6.1	6.5	5.6	5.6	7.5	5.6	5.0	6.9	7.1	4.4	8.7	5.9	6.1	5.7	6.2	5.7
03. Disciples of Christ	0.6	0.6	0.5	0.6	0.6	0.6	0.8	0.6	0.4	0.6	0.5	0.6	0.6	0.6	0.4	0.7
04. Episcopal	1.6	1.6	1.7	1.8	1.4	2.6	1.6	1.2	1.1	1.9	1.0	1.4	1.8	1.6	1.9	3.1
05. Lutheran	5.4	5.3	5.6	6.7	0.8	2.3	12.4	1.3	5.1	5.8	4.9	5.3	6.2	6.3	4.5	5.0
06. Methodist	7.5	7.5	7.5	8.0	7.5	6.1	8.6	9.6	3.5	7.8	6.9	8.2	7.1	7.6	6.6	3.0
07. Presbyterian	3.2	3.0	3.3	3.7	1.0	3.5	3.0	2.6	4.0	3.5	2.7	3.2	3.2	2.9	3.2	2.8
08. United Church of Christ	0.6	0.4	0.7	0.6	0.3	0.7	1.0	0.2	0.1	0.7	0.4	0.6	0.5	0.6	0.5	0.5
09. Other Protestant	4.0	3.9	4.0	4.5	0.9	5.5	4.5	1.8	4.7	3.8	4.3	4.4	3.3	3.9	3.7	4.4
10. Unitarian	0.2	0.1	0.4	0.3	0.1	0.3	0.3	0.2	0.1	0.3	0.1	0.2	0.3	0.1	0.3	-
11. Roman Catholic	28.3	26.9	29.8	29.4	6.3	41.5	30.5	16.1	28.9	31.0	24.0	26.1	29.5	29.7	31.4	26.2
12. Eastern Orthodox	0.4	0.3	0.5	0.4	-	0.5	0.7	0.2	0.2	0.5	0.2	0.4	0.5	0.5	0.3	0.7
13. Jewish	1.6	1.5	1.8	2.0	0.3	4.0	1.2	0.6	1.0	2.3	0.5	1.5	1.7	2.0	1.5	4.5
16. Latter Day Saints	1.7	1.7	1.7	2.1	0.1	0.1	0.9	0.4	7.7	2.0	1.4	2.4	0.9	1.5	1.4	1.2
14. Other religion	6.0	6.1	5.9	4.7	6.8	4.0	5.5	6.2	9.0	5.1	7.3	6.8	4.1	5.8	6.0	9.1
15. None	11.9	14.7	9.5	12.2	7.5	14.7	11.3	7.5	17.4	11.8	12.2	9.6	12.1	11.6	16.1	15.6
Item 360 Subject G N	15055	7041	7722	11497	1590	3481	4328	4658	2589	9182	5178	6361	3028	2164	3119	155

C13B: How often do you attend religious services?

	TOTAL	M	F	White	Black	NE	NC	S	W	Yes	No	None	Marijuana Only	Few Pills	More Pills	Any Heroin
1. Never	12.0	14.1	10.0	12.2	6.3	15.8	12.0	7.5	14.9	10.5	14.3	9.6	11.6	12.2	16.5	21.6
2. Rarely	36.9	39.3	34.4	37.0	33.7	43.6	36.0	31.4	38.9	32.8	43.7	29.4	39.8	40.4	46.5	36.8
3. Once or twice a month	16.8	15.8	17.9	16.1	23.7	14.2	16.8	20.2	14.4	17.9	14.7	15.5	19.0	18.5	16.3	17.1
4. About once a week or more	34.3	30.7	37.7	34.6	36.2	26.5	35.1	40.9	31.9	38.8	27.3	45.4	29.7	28.9	20.7	24.5
Item 370 Subject G N	15225	7135	7789	11614	1604	3547	4360	4680	2637	9261	5259	6421	3055	2189	3173	157

QUESTIONNAIRE FORM 1-5 1986	TOTAL	SEX		RACE		REGION				4YR COLLEGE PLANS		ILLICIT DRUG USE: LIFETIME				
		M	F	White	Black	NE	NC	S	W	Yes	No	None	Marijuana Only	Few Pills	More Pills	Any Heroin
N (Weighted No. of Cases):	15713	7261	7855	11713	1649	3720	4440	4855	2698	9291	5277	6535	3125	2223	3264	161
% of Weighted Total:	100.0	46.2	50.0	74.5	10.5	23.7	28.3	30.9	17.2	59.1	33.6	41.6	19.9	14.1	20.8	1.0
C13C: How important is religion in your life?																
1. Not important	13.3	16.9	9.9	15.0	2.8	19.9	13.4	6.1	17.0	13.4	13.3	10.0	14.0	13.3	19.0	20.9
2. A little important	27.8	29.4	26.4	29.7	15.8	31.9	31.0	20.4	29.8	25.9	30.7	22.3	29.7	32.1	34.3	26.2
3. Pretty important	32.7	31.2	34.1	32.8	30.0	29.8	33.7	35.9	29.4	32.9	32.7	32.6	33.4	34.7	31.4	32.2
4. Very important	26.3	22.5	29.5	22.5	51.3	18.4	21.9	37.6	23.8	27.8	23.3	35.1	22.9	20.0	15.3	20.7
Item 380　Subject G　N	15219	7128	7790	11612	1603	3547	4356	4684	2632	9263	5257	6422	3052	2185	3171	157
C14: When are you most likely to graduate from high school?																
1. By this June	98.5	98.2	99.0	98.9	98.0	98.7	98.5	98.7	98.2	99.3	97.5	99.1	98.8	98.6	97.5	93.6
2. July to January	1.1	1.3	0.8	0.8	1.4	0.8	1.1	1.0	1.5	0.6	1.7	0.6	0.9	1.1	1.8	3.7
3. After next January	-	-	-	-	-	-	-	-	-	-	-	-	-	-	-	-
6. Don't expect to graduate	0.4	0.5	0.3	0.3	0.6	0.5	0.4	0.3	0.4	0.1	0.8	0.3	0.2	0.2	0.7	2.7
Item 390　Subject B01　N	15189	7110	7778	11602	1581	3537	4355	4666	2630	9283	5267	6413	3047	2179	3165	152
C15: Which of the following best describes your present high school program?																
1. Academic or college prep	48.8	47.2	51.0	52.3	38.8	56.2	50.8	42.8	46.3	68.0	17.0	55.1	50.8	45.7	38.7	26.6
2. General	31.6	31.5	31.3	30.5	34.2	23.8	29.4	36.4	37.2	23.6	45.3	26.7	32.8	35.5	36.9	36.2
3. Vocational, technical, or commercial	13.1	15.0	11.0	12.4	16.6	13.8	13.6	13.9	9.7	5.0	26.1	11.3	11.3	13.3	17.3	28.3
4. Other, or don't know	6.5	6.3	6.7	4.7	10.5	6.3	6.1	6.9	6.8	3.4	11.6	6.9	5.1	5.5	7.0	8.9
Item 400　Subject B01　N	15095	7067	7730	11538	1575	3504	4340	4637	2613	9251	5223	6373	3031	2165	3143	155
C16: Compared with others your age throughout the country, how do you rate yourself on school ability?																
1. Far below average	0.7	1.0	0.4	0.5	0.8	0.6	0.7	0.7	0.8	0.3	1.3	0.7	0.6	0.6	0.5	3.3
2. Below average	1.8	2.0	1.5	1.6	1.6	2.1	1.6	1.4	2.4	0.9	3.2	1.4	1.6	1.9	2.6	6.2
3. Slightly below average	4.9	5.4	4.3	4.3	5.4	5.4	5.3	3.8	5.4	3.0	7.9	3.7	4.6	5.9	6.5	5.4
4. Average	37.6	35.5	39.3	34.8	48.2	37.7	35.2	41.4	34.5	28.0	53.2	33.5	37.7	41.4	42.1	39.3
5. Slightly above average	24.6	23.7	25.5	25.5	22.4	23.5	24.4	24.6	26.6	27.2	20.9	24.4	25.1	25.6	24.4	25.1
6. Above average	25.3	25.9	25.1	27.7	17.7	25.6	26.8	23.8	25.1	33.3	12.0	29.4	26.2	20.2	20.8	16.7
7. Far above average	5.1	6.6	3.8	5.5	4.0	5.2	6.0	4.2	5.2	7.3	1.4	6.9	4.3	4.4	3.1	4.0
Item 410　Subject B01　N	14924	7015	7619	11439	1540	3468	4298	4573	2584	9193	5152	6310	2987	2148	3095	152
C17: How intelligent do you think you are compared with others your age?																
1. Far below average	0.6	0.8	0.4	0.4	0.8	0.6	0.7	0.6	0.5	0.2	1.3	0.6	0.4	0.4	0.6	5.8
2. Below average	1.3	1.2	1.3	1.1	0.9	1.0	1.5	1.2	1.5	0.7	2.4	1.3	1.1	1.1	1.4	2.3
3. Slightly below average	4.0	4.0	4.0	3.7	3.3	4.4	4.5	3.2	4.4	2.2	7.3	3.4	4.4	4.5	4.3	8.2
4. Average	35.7	31.1	39.8	34.1	38.8	36.8	34.2	38.3	32.3	26.9	50.4	32.7	34.3	39.6	39.6	37.6
5. Slightly above average	24.2	24.0	24.2	25.1	22.3	23.2	24.1	24.3	25.6	26.4	20.6	23.7	25.1	25.2	24.3	16.5
6. Above average	27.7	30.0	26.0	29.3	25.5	27.7	28.8	26.0	29.3	35.3	15.2	30.7	28.4	24.7	24.4	19.8
7. Far above average	6.4	8.9	4.1	6.3	8.4	6.3	6.3	6.5	6.4	8.3	2.9	7.4	6.3	4.5	5.3	9.7
Item 420　Subject B01　N	14920	6959	7673	11423	1544	3450	4284	4595	2591	9185	5165	6313	2987	2132	3108	153
C18: During the LAST FOUR WEEKS, how many whole days of school have you missed . . .																
C18A: Because of illness																
1. None	57.6	63.7	52.4	58.6	55.9	55.7	58.9	57.8	57.7	60.6	53.1	64.7	57.5	51.2	49.2	43.7
2. 1 day	17.4	15.2	19.3	17.9	15.3	17.6	17.8	17.2	16.6	17.2	17.5	15.7	17.4	21.1	18.2	17.2
3. 2 days	10.5	9.4	11.7	10.5	10.7	10.9	10.0	10.4	11.1	9.8	11.7	8.8	11.1	11.0	12.8	13.3
4. 3 days	6.4	5.5	7.1	5.9	7.7	6.2	5.8	6.9	6.6	5.5	7.7	4.9	6.5	7.7	7.9	10.0
5. 4-5 days	4.8	3.3	6.0	4.3	6.3	5.5	4.4	4.8	4.6	4.0	6.0	3.4	5.0	5.0	7.1	5.9
6. 6-10 days	2.1	1.8	2.3	2.0	2.3	2.7	2.1	1.8	2.0	2.0	2.4	1.6	1.8	2.5	3.2	2.3
7. 11 or more	1.2	1.0	1.3	0.9	1.9	1.5	1.0	1.1	1.4	0.9	1.6	0.9	0.7	1.4	1.6	7.7
Item 430　Subject B06　N	14750	6893	7566	11272	1531	3415	4243	4525	2568	9063	5146	6234	2968	2119	3060	153

QUESTIONNAIRE FORM 1-5 1986	TOTAL	SEX		RACE		REGION				4YR COLLEGE PLANS		ILLICIT DRUG USE: LIFETIME				
		M	F	White	Black	NE	NC	S	W	Yes	No	None	Mari-juana Only	Few Pills	More Pills	Any Her-oin
N (Weighted No. of Cases):	15713	7261	7855	11713	1649	3720	4440	4855	2698	9291	5277	6535	3125	2223	3264	161
% of Weighted Total:	100.0	46.2	50.0	74.5	10.5	23.7	28.3	30.9	17.2	59.1	33.6	41.6	19.9	14.1	20.8	1.0

C18B: Because you skipped or "cut"

1. None	71.7	69.9	73.7	71.4	79.6	71.5	73.2	75.7	62.5	74.9	66.4	83.2	72.1	65.8	53.3	46.0
2. 1 day	13.3	13.6	13.1	14.0	9.8	13.1	13.3	12.1	15.7	12.8	14.2	9.7	14.4	16.7	17.6	9.9
3. 2 days	6.2	6.8	5.5	6.3	5.0	6.4	6.1	5.2	8.0	5.3	7.7	3.5	6.4	7.7	10.3	14.2
4. 3 days	3.8	4.2	3.4	3.9	2.0	4.1	3.7	3.0	5.1	3.2	4.8	1.9	3.2	4.9	7.7	6.4
5. 4-5 days	2.8	3.0	2.6	2.7	1.9	2.8	2.1	2.5	4.7	2.2	3.7	1.2	2.4	2.6	6.3	9.4
6. 6-10 days	1.2	1.4	1.0	1.1	0.6	1.3	1.1	0.7	2.2	0.8	1.8	0.3	0.9	1.5	3.0	3.0
7. 11 or more	0.9	1.2	0.6	0.7	1.1	0.9	0.6	0.7	1.8	0.7	1.3	0.3	0.6	0.8	1.9	11.1
Item 440 Subject B06 N	14327	6705	7352	11000	1453	3287	4152	4374	2514	8842	4994	6045	2885	2061	2997	147

C18C: For other reasons

1. None	58.3	60.7	56.4	58.1	62.0	59.5	55.4	60.3	58.4	57.8	59.3	62.1	57.3	57.1	53.5	47.4
2. 1 day	19.4	17.3	21.3	19.9	18.8	19.1	20.2	19.8	17.9	19.8	18.8	19.4	20.2	18.5	19.2	12.3
3. 2 days	10.6	10.4	10.6	10.8	8.2	9.7	11.0	10.6	11.0	11.2	9.4	9.1	11.9	11.6	11.7	12.4
4. 3 days	5.5	5.1	5.8	5.4	5.5	5.7	6.4	4.6	5.5	5.2	6.1	4.3	5.3	6.7	7.4	6.6
5. 4-5 days	3.8	3.9	3.8	3.8	3.2	3.6	4.5	3.2	4.3	3.7	3.8	3.3	3.6	4.1	4.8	9.0
6. 6-10 days	1.4	1.5	1.4	1.4	1.1	1.2	1.9	1.0	1.7	1.5	1.4	1.4	1.1	1.4	1.9	3.2
7. 11 or more	0.9	1.1	0.6	0.7	1.2	1.2	0.7	0.5	1.2	0.7	1.2	0.4	0.5	0.6	1.5	9.1
Item 450 Subject B06 N	14506	6776	7466	11121	1490	3330	4190	4451	2534	8984	5027	6169	2913	2078	2998	143

C19: During the last four weeks, how often have you gone to school, but skipped a class when you weren't supposed to?

1. Not at all	66.9	63.7	70.0	67.5	70.5	70.3	69.7	74.2	44.6	67.8	65.5	79.2	64.4	60.2	50.2	37.4
2. 1 or 2 times	20.1	21.8	18.5	20.1	18.1	18.2	19.6	16.7	29.9	20.1	20.0	14.8	22.7	24.7	24.9	26.9
3. 3-5 times	7.9	8.4	7.4	7.8	6.9	7.0	6.6	5.6	15.6	7.7	8.3	3.6	8.2	9.1	15.3	15.3
4. 6-10 times	2.9	3.6	2.3	2.8	1.8	2.1	2.3	1.9	6.7	2.7	3.2	1.1	2.5	3.6	5.9	9.4
5. 11-20 times	1.2	1.3	1.0	1.0	0.8	1.2	0.9	0.9	1.9	1.0	1.5	0.7	1.0	1.3	2.0	5.8
6. More than 20 times	1.0	1.1	0.9	0.8	1.9	1.3	0.9	0.8	1.3	0.7	1.6	0.6	1.2	1.0	1.6	5.3
Item 460 Subject B06 N	15105	7062	7744	11556	1565	3502	4338	4647	2618	9279	5266	6377	3025	2170	3150	155

C20: Which of the following best describes your average grade so far in high school?

9. A (93-100)	7.7	6.1	9.3	8.8	3.3	5.3	7.8	9.8	7.3	11.0	2.6	12.2	5.4	5.2	2.7	6.8
8. A- (90-92)	10.6	8.7	12.5	11.5	7.0	9.4	10.4	11.5	10.8	13.8	5.5	13.6	9.4	8.9	7.5	6.0
7. B+ (87-89)	16.3	14.2	18.3	17.2	13.2	16.8	16.1	16.7	15.4	19.3	11.2	18.0	16.2	14.8	14.8	7.5
6. B (83-86)	20.7	19.6	21.9	21.5	17.4	22.0	21.0	19.4	21.0	21.9	19.1	20.7	22.0	21.0	20.1	12.1
5. B- (80-82)	15.8	17.5	14.2	15.3	18.4	17.6	14.4	16.4	14.6	14.7	17.6	13.8	16.6	17.8	17.7	16.8
4. C+ (77-79)	13.3	15.2	11.7	12.0	18.6	13.6	13.7	12.1	14.7	10.0	18.4	10.7	14.0	14.9	16.2	22.6
3. C (73-76)	10.1	12.2	7.9	9.0	13.7	9.9	11.0	9.0	10.7	6.8	15.4	7.6	10.8	11.7	12.4	15.0
2. C- (70-72)	4.1	5.2	3.0	3.5	6.7	3.9	4.4	3.9	4.1	2.1	7.3	2.7	4.3	3.9	6.6	6.0
1. D (69 or below)	1.3	1.5	1.1	1.1	1.7	1.5	1.3	1.2	1.5	0.4	2.9	0.7	1.2	1.9	1.9	7.2
Item 470 Subject B01 N	15017	7027	7693	11509	1542	3473	4314	4624	2606	9232	5241	6344	3008	2157	3129	156

C21: How likely is it that you will do each of the following things after high school?

C21A: Attend a technical or vocational school

1. Definitely won't	47.2	42.2	52.1	49.7	40.0	59.7	47.9	41.6	39.5	60.3	25.9	50.0	48.6	43.3	43.6	34.2
2. Probably won't	27.1	29.2	25.3	27.6	22.9	21.7	27.1	28.8	31.4	26.4	28.8	27.2	26.6	27.7	27.7	21.6
3. Probably will	17.2	19.4	15.2	15.0	26.0	11.4	16.0	20.7	20.6	9.4	29.9	15.6	16.3	19.2	18.9	30.4
4. Definitely will	8.4	9.2	7.5	7.7	11.1	7.2	8.9	8.9	8.5	3.9	15.4	7.2	8.4	9.8	9.8	13.8
Item 480 Subject B09,C03 N	14421	6692	7439	11099	1463	3292	4180	4445	2503	8970	5252	6132	2873	2090	2968	149

C21B: Serve in the armed forces

1. Definitely won't	61.0	43.4	77.2	63.6	45.2	62.6	61.2	57.9	63.9	64.7	55.2	61.4	59.4	61.4	62.5	43.2
2. Probably won't	22.6	30.6	15.5	23.2	17.0	20.9	24.4	22.4	22.3	23.3	21.6	23.7	22.7	21.7	21.4	19.1
3. Probably will	9.0	13.4	4.8	6.9	21.7	8.7	7.3	11.2	8.3	6.4	13.3	7.6	9.9	9.3	9.6	23.4
4. Definitely will	7.4	12.7	2.5	6.3	16.1	7.8	7.1	8.5	5.5	5.6	10.0	7.2	8.0	7.6	6.5	14.3
Item 490 Subject B09,L01 N	13939	6459	7218	10828	1379	3171	4062	4282	2424	8763	5009	5926	2783	2038	2862	135

QUESTIONNAIRE FORM 1-5 1986	TOTAL	SEX		RACE		REGION				4YR COLLEGE PLANS		ILLICIT DRUG USE: LIFETIME				
		M	F	White	Black	NE	NC	S	W	Yes	No	None	Marijuana Only	Few Pills	More Pills	Any Heroin
N (Weighted No. of Cases):	15713	7261	7855	11713	1649	3720	4440	4855	2698	9291	5277	6535	3125	2223	3264	161
% of Weighted Total:	100.0	46.2	50.0	74.5	10.5	23.7	28.3	30.9	17.2	59.1	33.6	41.6	19.9	14.1	20.8	1.0
C21C: Graduate from a two-year college program																
1. Definitely won't	37.2	37.1	37.7	38.5	35.2	47.0	40.4	32.6	27.4	42.7	29.2	39.1	39.7	34.9	32.9	38.4
2. Probably won't	27.1	29.7	24.7	27.9	24.9	22.8	29.1	30.0	24.1	27.3	27.7	28.6	27.2	26.0	24.8	19.6
3. Probably will	22.0	21.8	22.0	20.1	27.8	17.8	19.3	23.4	29.4	17.2	29.3	19.6	20.6	24.1	26.3	24.2
4. Definitely will	13.7	11.4	15.6	13.6	12.1	12.4	11.2	14.0	19.1	12.9	13.9	12.7	12.6	14.9	16.1	17.8
Item 500 Subject B09 N	14399	6672	7446	11075	1467	3301	4149	4426	2522	8936	5251	6123	2883	2080	2957	149
C21D: Graduate from college (four-year program)																
1. Definitely won't	19.4	19.1	19.5	19.0	20.4	22.5	18.9	19.7	15.5	-	53.5	16.4	17.1	22.0	24.6	33.3
2. Probably won't	16.8	18.1	15.5	16.5	17.3	14.9	15.5	19.4	17.2	-	46.5	14.7	16.3	17.4	20.5	22.6
3. Probably will	23.0	24.7	21.4	22.3	25.9	19.1	23.8	23.3	26.6	36.1	-	22.9	24.3	23.9	21.8	20.8
4. Definitely will	40.7	38.1	43.6	42.2	36.4	43.5	41.8	37.6	40.7	63.9	-	45.9	42.4	36.7	33.1	23.3
Item 510 Subject B09 N	14568	6784	7494	11224	1474	3370	4202	4477	2519	9291	5277	6181	2909	2104	3017	153
C21E: Attend graduate or professional school after college																
1. Definitely won't	28.5	28.7	28.0	28.2	30.9	31.8	27.3	29.5	24.3	10.9	58.9	24.4	27.5	31.6	34.4	41.3
2. Probably won't	32.8	33.7	32.0	33.8	28.8	29.0	33.5	33.8	35.1	34.1	31.2	33.0	34.2	33.0	31.5	30.4
3. Probably will	27.2	26.7	27.9	27.3	27.1	28.0	27.4	25.9	27.9	39.1	6.7	29.9	28.4	24.0	23.5	17.6
4. Definitely will	11.5	10.8	12.0	10.8	13.2	11.2	11.8	10.7	12.7	15.9	3.2	12.7	9.9	11.4	10.7	10.7
Item 520 Subject B09 N	14343	6653	7408	11051	1459	3280	4171	4414	2478	8960	5244	6103	2862	2066	2960	146
C22: Suppose you could do just what you'd like and nothing stood in your way. How many of the following things would you WANT to do? (Mark ALL that apply)																
A. Attend a technical or vocational school	22.4	25.6	19.2	20.8	27.8	17.8	21.2	25.0	25.7	10.8	42.7	20.3	21.6	24.5	25.5	31.0
B. Serve in the armed forces	16.3	23.0	10.0	14.1	31.1	16.2	14.7	19.3	13.7	13.2	21.7	15.9	17.5	17.2	14.8	26.5
C. Graduate from a two-year college program	25.4	20.9	29.3	24.5	24.5	21.2	21.9	26.8	34.3	18.1	37.8	23.5	23.0	28.1	29.3	28.5
D. Graduate from college (four-year program)	66.6	64.8	68.7	67.7	64.5	63.3	68.2	65.2	71.0	89.8	27.9	70.0	69.8	66.0	59.2	50.0
E. Attend graduate or professional school after college	43.0	40.7	45.5	43.8	39.8	40.8	45.0	41.5	45.0	57.2	18.6	47.0	43.3	39.8	38.1	33.7
F. None of the above	7.3	8.2	6.4	7.6	4.5	9.7	7.0	6.5	5.9	2.5	15.5	6.1	6.4	7.0	9.8	13.6
Item 530-580 Subject B09,C03 N	14795	6895	7611	11363	1517	3405	4274	4547	2569	9188	5169	6272	2964	2119	3069	150
C23: On the average over the school year, how many hours per week do you work in a paid or unpaid job?																
1. None	23.3	22.3	24.1	20.2	40.9	21.3	21.0	28.0	21.2	23.7	22.6	26.2	22.6	21.5	19.2	14.9
2. 5 or less hours	9.6	9.6	9.7	9.8	7.3	9.2	9.7	9.1	11.0	10.9	7.6	11.6	9.0	7.2	8.1	7.3
3. 6 to 10 hours	9.6	9.6	9.7	9.6	8.9	9.2	9.2	9.6	10.9	10.4	8.3	11.2	9.0	9.5	7.4	7.5
4. 11 to 15 hours	10.8	9.3	12.3	11.7	6.6	11.6	11.5	9.3	11.4	12.2	8.4	11.4	10.9	9.9	10.3	10.9
5. 16 to 20 hours	16.5	15.2	17.6	17.7	10.9	18.4	18.4	13.7	15.7	17.0	15.4	14.5	18.3	17.7	18.2	15.2
6. 21 to 25 hours	12.8	13.0	12.4	13.6	8.8	12.7	13.9	11.7	12.9	12.3	13.4	10.7	13.4	16.1	14.2	13.3
7. 26 to 30 hours	7.8	8.8	6.9	7.9	7.2	8.0	7.7	7.9	7.6	6.8	9.3	6.7	8.0	8.4	9.3	11.0
8. More than 30 hours	9.7	12.2	7.2	9.4	9.4	9.6	8.7	10.8	9.4	6.6	14.9	7.9	8.8	9.8	13.4	19.8
Item 590 Subject C01 N	14868	6930	7648	11421	1517	3423	4299	4564	2581	9219	5202	6284	2986	2136	3089	155
C24: During an average week, how much money do you get from . . .																
C24A: A job or other work																
1. None	26.8	25.3	28.3	24.2	40.7	23.3	24.8	31.3	26.7	27.8	25.3	30.6	26.4	24.9	21.1	14.7
2. $1-5	2.8	2.7	2.9	2.9	2.0	2.4	3.0	2.6	3.2	2.8	2.7	3.4	2.1	2.4	2.2	2.8
3. $6-10	3.4	3.5	3.4	3.7	2.2	2.8	4.0	3.1	3.9	3.5	3.4	4.1	2.6	2.7	3.0	4.5
4. $11-20	5.0	4.7	5.4	5.3	3.9	4.8	5.0	5.5	4.7	5.4	4.4	6.1	4.0	4.3	4.4	5.6
5. $21-35	8.2	7.7	8.9	8.6	5.9	7.9	9.3	7.4	8.5	9.0	7.1	8.7	8.5	8.5	7.1	9.3
6. $36-50	11.8	10.2	13.4	12.9	7.3	13.4	13.6	9.7	10.1	13.2	9.5	11.5	12.7	12.5	11.5	10.6
7. $51-75	17.2	15.7	18.4	18.1	13.8	18.2	18.0	15.7	17.0	17.3	17.0	15.1	18.6	19.0	18.8	18.2
8. $76-125	17.5	20.2	14.8	17.7	15.2	18.8	16.0	17.4	18.2	15.7	20.3	14.4	18.3	19.5	21.7	16.2
9. $126+	7.3	10.2	4.4	6.6	9.0	8.4	6.3	7.3	7.6	5.4	10.2	6.1	6.9	6.1	10.2	18.1
Item 600 Subject C02 N	14245	6667	7308	10995	1416	3285	4146	4350	2464	8857	4979	6042	2886	2048	2932	140

QUESTIONNAIRE FORM 1-5 1986	TOTAL	SEX		RACE		REGION				4YR COLLEGE PLANS		ILLICIT DRUG USE: LIFETIME				
		M	F	White	Black	NE	NC	S	W	Yes	No	None	Mari-juana Only	Few Pills	More Pills	Any Her-oin
N (Weighted No. of Cases):	15713	7261	7855	11713	1649	3720	4440	4855	2698	9291	5277	6535	3125	2223	3264	161
% of Weighted Total:	100.0	46.2	50.0	74.5	10.5	23.7	28.3	30.9	17.2	59.1	33.6	41.6	19.9	14.1	20.8	1.0

C24B: Other sources (allowances, etc.)

	TOTAL	M	F	White	Black	NE	NC	S	W	Yes	No	None	Mari-juana Only	Few Pills	More Pills	Any Her-oin
1. None	32.9	32.4	33.3	34.3	23.0	38.8	33.3	29.0	31.3	30.9	36.4	35.0	32.5	30.9	30.2	27.1
2. $1-5	15.0	13.5	16.4	15.5	12.4	14.5	16.7	12.6	16.7	15.5	14.1	16.8	14.9	13.8	12.7	8.0
3. $6-10	18.8	18.2	19.2	19.3	15.7	18.4	18.8	18.5	19.8	20.0	16.6	19.4	19.1	19.6	17.2	11.0
4. $11-20	16.8	17.9	16.0	16.1	20.2	13.9	17.0	18.6	16.9	17.5	15.6	15.2	17.2	18.5	18.6	13.1
5. $21-35	8.4	8.5	8.3	7.8	13.1	6.6	6.9	11.4	7.9	8.8	7.8	7.0	9.1	9.3	10.0	12.9
6. $36-50	3.4	3.9	2.9	2.9	7.1	3.0	2.9	4.2	3.5	3.3	3.6	2.8	3.3	3.2	4.6	9.7
7. $51-75	1.7	2.0	1.4	1.5	2.9	1.6	1.7	1.8	1.5	1.6	1.7	1.2	1.9	2.0	2.1	3.7
8. $76-125	1.3	1.3	1.3	1.1	2.4	1.3	1.1	1.7	1.0	1.0	1.8	1.2	1.0	1.1	2.0	5.2
9. $126+	1.8	2.3	1.3	1.5	3.2	1.9	1.5	2.1	1.4	1.4	2.5	1.5	1.2	1.6	2.5	9.4
Item 610 Subject C02 N	14070	6518	7288	10849	1416	3182	4081	4334	2473	8823	4883	5966	2831	2035	2899	147

C25: During a typical week, on how many evenings do you go out for fun and recreation?

	TOTAL	M	F	White	Black	NE	NC	S	W	Yes	No	None	Mari-juana Only	Few Pills	More Pills	Any Her-oin
1. Less than one	8.0	6.5	9.4	6.5	13.3	8.1	6.9	8.9	8.5	7.2	9.5	10.9	6.4	7.0	4.6	6.5
2. One	14.1	12.9	15.3	13.0	17.0	13.9	12.3	15.3	15.4	14.7	13.1	18.6	12.3	12.3	8.3	7.3
3. Two	28.8	28.5	29.3	28.7	29.5	28.1	28.6	28.9	30.0	31.2	24.7	32.2	30.2	27.2	22.2	19.2
4. Three	26.5	26.3	26.4	27.7	20.9	26.3	27.9	25.4	26.3	26.7	25.7	24.1	28.9	29.0	28.1	15.7
5. Four or five	15.8	17.2	14.6	17.3	11.8	15.7	17.3	15.2	14.5	15.1	17.2	11.0	16.3	16.6	24.2	26.5
6. Six or seven	6.7	8.6	5.0	6.9	7.5	8.0	7.0	6.4	5.4	5.1	9.7	3.3	5.9	7.8	12.6	24.8
Item 620 Subject C07,M01 N	14831	6912	7629	11415	1509	3402	4296	4564	2570	9197	5182	6271	2974	2132	3086	153

C26: On the average, how often do you go out with a date (or your spouse, if you are married)?

	TOTAL	M	F	White	Black	NE	NC	S	W	Yes	No	None	Mari-juana Only	Few Pills	More Pills	Any Her-oin
1. Never	13.6	14.2	13.0	11.4	20.3	13.8	12.7	12.6	16.5	13.1	14.4	19.7	9.9	10.4	6.8	7.0
2. Once a month or less	18.2	19.4	17.3	18.5	18.0	16.5	19.2	17.8	19.7	19.9	15.6	21.2	18.1	17.1	14.1	7.4
3. 2 or 3 times a month	18.0	18.9	17.3	17.5	22.7	17.2	18.2	17.9	19.0	19.3	15.5	16.9	20.5	18.7	17.6	18.9
4. Once a week	15.8	17.3	14.3	15.7	16.4	15.7	16.0	16.4	14.7	16.3	14.7	14.9	17.8	16.7	14.9	11.0
5. 2 or 3 times a week	22.7	21.4	23.8	24.4	15.3	22.8	22.2	24.9	19.4	22.5	23.3	20.4	22.1	24.1	27.0	25.4
6. Over 3 times a week	11.7	8.8	14.3	12.5	6.2	14.0	11.8	10.4	10.7	9.0	16.6	6.9	11.6	12.9	19.7	30.4
Item 630 Subject C07,M01 N	14705	6829	7590	11331	1478	3358	4270	4528	2549	9098	5133	6210	2947	2116	3056	153

C27: During an average week, how much do you usually drive a car, truck, or motorcycle?

	TOTAL	M	F	White	Black	NE	NC	S	W	Yes	No	None	Mari-juana Only	Few Pills	More Pills	Any Her-oin
1. Not at all	14.6	9.9	18.6	10.2	32.4	23.3	11.6	10.8	14.6	11.9	18.8	15.4	12.9	14.7	13.7	10.2
2. 1 to 10 miles	11.0	7.5	14.2	9.3	18.1	12.4	10.1	11.1	10.3	10.2	12.4	12.6	9.9	9.6	9.3	5.1
3. 11 to 50 miles	29.4	26.4	32.4	30.2	27.6	28.0	31.0	28.3	30.6	31.5	25.9	33.0	30.1	26.9	24.0	21.5
4. 51 to 100 miles	21.4	24.3	18.9	23.5	12.0	19.5	22.8	21.3	21.6	23.0	18.5	19.3	23.9	22.9	22.4	27.1
5. 100 to 200 miles	15.2	20.3	10.6	17.5	4.7	10.8	16.6	17.7	14.3	15.7	14.5	13.3	14.7	16.4	18.9	15.8
6. More than 200 miles	8.5	11.7	5.3	9.3	5.2	6.0	8.0	10.8	8.6	7.7	9.9	6.4	8.5	9.5	11.6	20.3
Item 640 Subject F07 N	14819	6892	7640	11402	1493	3404	4295	4544	2577	9169	5168	6256	2972	2130	3084	152

C28: Within the LAST 12 MONTHS, how many times, if any, have you received a ticket (OR been stopped and warned) for moving violations such as speeding, running a stop light, or improper passing?

	TOTAL	M	F	White	Black	NE	NC	S	W	Yes	No	None	Mari-juana Only	Few Pills	More Pills	Any Her-oin
0. None–GO TO Q.C30	69.6	59.2	79.0	66.5	84.6	77.9	65.8	68.5	66.8	68.6	71.0	77.2	66.9	65.5	59.8	53.0
1. Once	18.9	23.7	14.7	20.6	10.9	13.8	21.1	19.7	20.9	20.2	17.1	15.9	21.6	20.0	21.9	22.4
2. Twice	6.5	9.2	4.0	7.1	3.4	4.6	7.3	6.6	7.1	6.8	5.7	4.2	6.4	8.8	9.5	8.8
3. Three times	2.9	4.4	1.5	3.3	0.7	2.4	3.5	2.9	2.9	2.6	3.6	1.6	3.2	3.3	4.9	7.9
4. Four or more times	2.1	3.4	0.8	2.4	0.5	1.4	2.4	2.3	2.3	1.8	2.7	1.1	1.9	2.4	3.9	8.0
Item 650 Subject S02 N	14588	6773	7547	11289	1442	3341	4249	4461	2538	9082	5035	6195	2925	2096	3029	144

C29: How many of these tickets or warnings occurred after you were . . .

C29A: Drinking alcoholic beverages?

	TOTAL	M	F	White	Black	NE	NC	S	W	Yes	No	None	Mari-juana Only	Few Pills	More Pills	Any Her-oin
0. None	85.9	84.1	88.8	85.2	96.1	87.0	82.9	86.2	89.5	87.9	82.4	93.9	87.6	84.8	76.7	73.6
1. One	11.1	12.1	9.5	11.7	3.0	10.3	12.8	11.0	8.9	9.7	13.2	5.4	9.8	11.9	17.8	15.2
2. Two	2.2	2.8	1.2	2.3	0.6	2.2	3.3	1.9	1.0	1.8	3.0	0.6	2.1	2.6	3.7	6.5
3. Three	0.5	0.6	0.3	0.5	0.3	0.4	0.6	0.5	0.2	0.4	0.7	0.1	0.5	0.7	0.7	1.7
4. Four or more	0.4	0.4	0.2	0.3	-	0.2	0.5	0.3	0.4	0.2	0.8	-	-	-	1.2	3.0
Item 660 Subject A07a,S02 N★	4418	2747	1581	3759	227	734	1448	1396	840	2830	1454	1413	965	721	1209	69

★=excludes respondents for whom question was inappropriate.

QUESTIONNAIRE FORM 1-5 1986	TOTAL	SEX		RACE		REGION				4YR COLLEGE PLANS		ILLICIT DRUG USE: LIFETIME				
		M	F	White	Black	NE	NC	S	W	Yes	No	None	Mari- juana Only	Few Pills	More Pills	Any Her- oin
N (Weighted No. of Cases):	15713	7261	7855	11713	1649	3720	4440	4855	2698	9291	5277	6535	3125	2223	3264	161
% of Weighted Total:	100.0	46.2	50.0	74.5	10.5	23.7	28.3	30.9	17.2	59.1	33.6	41.6	19.9	14.1	20.8	1.0
C29B: Smoking marijuana or hashish?																
0. None	95.1	94.5	96.2	94.9	98.1	96.1	93.6	95.7	95.7	96.4	92.7	100.0	98.7	96.0	86.6	82.8
1. One	3.7	3.9	3.3	4.0	1.3	3.1	4.7	3.5	3.0	3.0	5.1	-	1.1	3.8	10.0	4.6
2. Two	0.6	0.8	0.4	0.6	0.6	0.2	0.9	0.5	0.7	0.4	1.0	-	0.2	-	1.7	8.0
3. Three	0.3	0.4	*	0.2	-	0.3	0.4	0.1	0.3	0.1	0.5	-	-	-	0.9	1.5
4. Four or more	0.3	0.3	0.1	0.3	-	0.3	0.4	0.2	0.3	0.1	0.8	-	-	0.2	0.8	3.1
Item 670 Subject A07a,S02 N★	4375	2715	1575	3731	219	726	1429	1383	836	2816	1433	1400	956	714	1195	67
C29C: Using other illegal drugs?																
0. None	98.7	98.6	99.0	98.8	99.6	99.4	98.1	99.0	98.8	99.1	98.0	100.0	100.0	99.1	97.0	87.3
1. One	0.9	0.8	0.9	0.9	0.4	0.5	1.2	0.6	0.9	0.6	1.2	-	-	0.7	2.0	7.9
2. Two	0.2	0.3	*	0.2	-	-	0.4	0.1	0.1	0.2	0.2	-	-	0.2	0.5	-
3. Three	*	*	-	-	-	0.1	-	-	-	*	-	-	-	-	*	-
4. Four or more	0.2	0.2	0.1	0.1	-	0.1	0.2	0.3	0.2	*	0.5	-	-	-	0.5	4.8
Item 680 Subject A07a,S02 N★	4361	2703	1571	3718	219	724	1426	1377	833	2804	1430	1399	957	713	1182	67
C30: We are interested in any accidents which occurred while you were driving a car, truck, or motorcycle. ("Accidents" means a collision involving property damage or personal injury– not bumps or scratches in parking lots.) During the LAST 12 MONTHS, how many accidents have you had while you were driving (whether or not you were responsible)?																
0. None–GO TO Q.C32	74.9	70.8	78.6	72.1	88.0	76.2	73.0	75.0	75.9	74.1	76.2	80.2	73.4	71.6	68.4	56.4
1. One	18.8	21.3	16.6	21.0	9.9	17.6	20.7	18.2	18.3	19.8	17.0	15.9	20.1	21.3	22.1	20.7
2. Two	4.8	5.8	3.8	5.3	1.7	5.0	4.8	5.1	3.9	4.7	5.0	3.4	5.4	5.0	6.4	10.7
3. Three	1.1	1.5	0.8	1.3	0.5	0.8	1.2	1.1	1.6	1.1	1.1	0.4	0.8	1.4	2.6	4.8
4. Four or more	0.4	0.6	0.2	0.4	-	0.3	0.4	0.6	0.3	0.2	0.7	0.1	0.2	0.8	0.6	7.4
Item 690 Subject S02 N	14450	6712	7467	11209	1402	3294	4210	4428	2519	8989	4995	6146	2897	2081	2982	146
C31: How many of these accidents occurred after you were . . .																
C31A: Drinking alcoholic beverages?																
0. None	91.2	88.6	94.4	91.0	96.9	92.9	89.2	90.4	94.3	93.1	88.0	96.7	92.4	90.7	84.7	72.8
1. One	7.4	9.9	4.5	7.8	2.7	6.4	9.5	7.6	4.6	5.9	10.1	2.8	6.5	8.4	13.0	15.1
2. Two	1.0	1.1	0.8	0.8	0.5	0.3	1.0	1.3	1.0	0.9	0.9	0.5	1.0	0.4	1.6	3.3
3. Three	0.2	0.2	0.2	0.2	-	-	0.3	0.3	0.1	0.1	0.4	*	-	0.5	0.3	1.2
4. Four or more	0.2	0.2	0.1	0.2	-	0.4	-	0.4	0.1	*	0.6	-	-	-	0.3	7.5
Item 700 Subject A07a,S02 N★	3637	1954	1604	3127	176	790	1142	1108	598	2332	1194	1221	775	593	940	65
C31B: Smoking marijuana or hashish?																
0. None	96.5	95.5	97.6	96.5	98.5	97.3	95.4	97.0	96.5	97.6	94.5	100.0	99.4	96.9	89.9	84.6
1. One	2.9	3.6	2.2	3.1	1.2	2.5	3.7	2.4	3.0	2.0	4.5	-	0.6	3.1	8.2	8.5
2. Two	0.4	0.6	0.2	0.4	-	0.1	0.6	0.4	0.4	0.2	0.7	-	-	-	1.5	0.8
3. Three	0.1	0.2	-	0.1	-	-	0.3	0.1	-	0.1	0.1	-	-	-	0.3	1.8
4. Four or more	0.1	0.1	*	*	0.3	0.1	-	0.2	0.1	*	0.2	-	-	-	0.1	4.2
Item 710 Subject A07a,S02 N★	3584	1911	1597	3089	173	777	1123	1089	595	2305	1173	1208	765	584	925	62
C31C: Using other illegal drugs?																
0. None	98.8	98.7	99.1	99.1	99.1	98.3	98.9	99.1	98.8	99.4	97.7	100.0	100.0	99.1	97.6	79.6
1. One	0.8	0.9	0.7	0.7	0.4	1.3	0.7	0.6	0.8	0.5	1.4	-	-	0.7	1.8	13.5
2. Two	*	*	*	*	0.2	-	*	-	0.1	*	*	-	-	-	*	0.8
3. Three	0.2	0.2	0.2	0.1	0.3	0.3	0.3	0.1	-	*	0.6	-	-	0.2	0.5	1.8
4. Four or more	0.1	0.1	-	0.1	-	0.1	-	0.2	0.3	*	0.3	-	-	-	0.1	4.2
Item 720 Subject A07a,S02 N★	3575	1907	1591	3080	173	774	1121	1089	591	2299	1171	1210	765	585	913	62

*=less than .05 per cent.   ★=excludes respondents for whom question was inappropriate.

	TOTAL	SEX		RACE		REGION				4YR COLLEGE PLANS		ILLICIT DRUG USE: LIFETIME				
QUESTIONNAIRE FORM 1-5 1986		M	F	White	Black	NE	NC	S	W	Yes	No	None	Mari- juana Only	Few Pills	More Pills	Any Her- oin
N (Weighted No. of Cases):	15713	7261	7855	11713	1649	3720	4440	4855	2698	9291	5277	6535	3125	2223	3264	161
% of Weighted Total:	100.0	46.2	50.0	74.5	10.5	23.7	28.3	30.9	17.2	59.1	33.6	41.6	19.9	14.1	20.8	1.0

C32: If you have not entered military service, and do not expect to enter, GO TO PART D.

What is, or will be, your branch of service?

	TOTAL	M	F	White	Black	NE	NC	S	W	Yes	No	None	Mari-juana Only	Few Pills	More Pills	Any Heroin
1. Army	27.8	28.4	25.1	26.5	37.3	27.1	27.5	31.8	20.1	25.1	31.0	27.1	31.8	28.4	26.0	15.1
2. Navy	15.3	17.2	9.4	17.7	10.1	16.8	13.7	13.8	19.6	17.2	13.0	18.1	13.2	14.1	12.9	20.4
3. Marine Corps	12.8	15.0	5.7	11.7	12.0	12.5	12.0	13.5	13.0	10.5	15.4	11.4	12.0	13.0	14.2	22.3
4. Air Force	29.7	25.3	44.3	29.1	30.4	27.0	34.3	28.5	28.4	32.2	27.2	30.4	28.6	29.1	30.8	18.6
5. Coast Guard	1.8	1.8	1.9	2.1	1.0	2.6	1.0	1.4	3.2	1.7	1.8	2.2	2.1	1.1	1.5	2.0
6. Uncertain	12.6	12.3	13.7	13.0	9.4	14.1	11.5	11.1	15.8	13.3	11.7	10.9	12.3	14.2	14.6	21.5
Item 730 Subject L01 N★	2583	1891	613	1676	509	581	704	913	386	1231	1223	1000	543	391	527	60

C33: Do you expect to be an officer?

	TOTAL	M	F	White	Black	NE	NC	S	W	Yes	No	None	Mari-juana Only	Few Pills	More Pills	Any Heroin
1. No	14.8	14.5	15.5	14.7	11.6	16.4	16.8	12.0	15.1	9.4	18.6	13.2	15.0	13.6	17.6	10.3
2. Uncertain	42.7	42.2	43.5	44.5	38.6	42.9	45.2	41.5	41.1	33.1	53.0	40.7	44.3	41.7	45.5	42.6
3. Yes	42.5	43.3	41.0	40.8	49.8	40.7	38.0	46.5	43.8	57.5	28.3	46.1	40.7	44.8	36.9	47.2
Item 740 Subject L01 N★	2594	1902	612	1671	512	591	694	913	397	1231	1230	993	550	394	536	59

C34: Do you expect to have a career in the Armed Forces?

	TOTAL	M	F	White	Black	NE	NC	S	W	Yes	No	None	Mari-juana Only	Few Pills	More Pills	Any Heroin
1. No	23.9	25.6	19.8	24.9	19.7	22.0	26.1	22.3	26.6	25.7	20.7	23.9	23.5	24.3	24.3	23.7
2. Uncertain	49.0	49.5	47.7	52.2	38.8	50.0	49.0	45.2	56.6	48.2	50.7	45.8	50.5	50.8	53.4	37.9
3. Yes	27.1	24.9	32.5	22.9	41.5	28.0	25.0	32.5	16.8	26.1	28.6	30.3	26.0	24.9	22.3	38.4
Item 750 Subject L01 N★	2584	1893	610	1659	512	586	694	910	394	1228	1229	988	547	393	534	60

★=excludes respondents for whom question was inappropriate.

QUESTIONNAIRE FORM 1-5 1986	TOTAL	SEX		RACE		REGION				4YR COLLEGE PLANS		ILLICIT DRUG USE: LIFETIME				
		M	F	White	Black	NE	NC	S	W	Yes	No	None	Mari- juana Only	Few Pills	More Pills	Any Her- oin
N (Weighted No. of Cases):	15713	7261	7855	11713	1649	3720	4440	4855	2698	9291	5277	6535	3125	2223	3264	161
% of Weighted Total:	100.0	46.2	50.0	74.5	10.5	23.7	28.3	30.9	17.2	59.1	33.6	41.6	19.9	14.1	20.8	1.0

The following questions are about CIGARETTE SMOKING.

B01: Have you ever smoked cigarettes?

	TOTAL	M	F	White	Black	NE	NC	S	W	Yes	No	None	Mari- juana Only	Few Pills	More Pills	Any Her- oin
1. Never	32.4	34.1	31.1	30.3	43.7	29.1	30.8	34.6	35.9	36.7	25.1	57.3	15.0	18.2	10.1	11.3
2. Once or twice	29.4	30.6	28.4	28.2	38.4	27.6	27.3	31.6	31.3	30.5	27.3	29.3	39.4	30.3	20.6	10.6
3. Occasionally but not regularly	17.3	17.2	17.5	18.5	10.9	16.1	19.2	16.7	17.1	18.0	17.2	8.3	25.3	25.2	21.9	24.0
4. Regularly in the past	6.3	5.6	7.0	6.9	1.9	7.3	7.3	4.7	6.1	5.4	7.8	2.3	7.4	7.8	11.7	13.9
5. Regularly now	14.5	12.6	16.0	16.0	5.1	19.8	15.4	12.4	9.7	9.4	22.6	2.8	12.9	18.5	35.7	40.1
Item 760 Subject A01a N	15336	7118	7736	11573	1574	3625	4354	4715	2642	9155	5176	6400	3091	2196	3225	160

B02: How frequently have you smoked cigarettes during the past 30 days?

	TOTAL	M	F	White	Black	NE	NC	S	W	Yes	No	None	Mari- juana Only	Few Pills	More Pills	Any Her- oin
1. Not at all - incl. (1) in B01	70.4	72.1	69.4	68.0	85.4	64.8	67.5	73.9	76.7	76.0	61.5	90.6	67.5	59.5	42.8	31.3
2. Less than one cigarette per day	10.9	11.0	10.8	11.6	6.8	10.3	12.6	10.3	9.9	11.3	10.3	5.3	14.7	15.9	14.6	17.5
3. One to five cigarettes per day	7.4	6.3	8.3	7.8	4.8	9.3	7.6	5.9	6.9	6.3	9.0	2.0	8.9	11.1	13.6	8.8
4. About one-half pack per day	5.4	4.8	5.8	5.9	2.1	7.8	5.7	4.6	3.4	3.5	8.3	1.1	4.8	7.2	12.5	17.5
5. About one pack per day	4.8	4.8	4.7	5.6	0.5	6.3	5.6	4.3	2.4	2.4	8.6	0.7	3.6	5.4	13.2	17.6
6. About one and one-half packs per day	0.9	0.7	1.0	1.0	0.1	1.2	0.8	0.9	0.5	0.4	1.8	0.1	0.5	0.7	2.8	2.9
7. Two packs or more per day	0.2	0.3	0.1	0.2	0.2	0.3	0.3	0.2	0.2	0.1	0.4	0.1	0.1	0.2	0.4	4.3
Item 780 Subject A01c N	15339	7117	7740	11575	1577	3623	4358	4716	2642	9157	5176	6402	3089	2203	3223	157

B03: Next we want to ask you about drinking alcoholic beverages, including beer, wine, and liquor.

Have you ever had any beer, wine, or liquor to drink?

	TOTAL	M	F	White	Black	NE	NC	S	W	Yes	No	None	Mari- juana Only	Few Pills	More Pills	Any Her- oin
1. No	8.8	7.9	9.4	6.9	16.6	5.7	6.4	12.2	10.8	9.1	7.7	18.8	1.2	1.8	1.0	1.0
2. Yes	91.2	92.1	90.6	93.1	83.4	94.3	93.6	87.8	89.2	90.9	92.3	81.2	98.8	98.2	99.0	99.0
Item 790 Subject A01a N	11980	5570	6091	9100	1236	2817	3403	3680	2080	7245	4092	5029	2382	1745	2554	135

B04: On how many occasions have you had alcoholic beverages to drink . . .

B04A: . . . in your lifetime?

	TOTAL	M	F	White	Black	NE	NC	S	W	Yes	No	None	Mari- juana Only	Few Pills	More Pills	Any Her- oin
1. 0 occasions - incl. (1) in B03	8.7	7.7	9.4	6.7	17.4	5.7	6.5	12.0	10.3	8.9	7.8	18.4	1.1	1.8	1.0	0.9
2. 1-2	7.8	6.9	8.6	5.9	18.4	6.4	5.7	11.1	7.2	7.4	8.0	14.6	3.1	4.1	1.3	3.8
3. 3-5	8.9	7.5	10.2	7.6	15.1	8.7	6.9	10.6	9.1	9.0	8.8	14.6	7.0	6.0	1.4	2.7
4. 6-9	8.5	7.4	9.5	7.7	12.6	8.8	8.0	8.4	8.8	8.8	7.7	12.2	8.7	6.4	2.6	3.8
5. 10-19	12.4	11.2	13.7	12.7	12.6	13.2	12.7	11.6	12.3	13.0	11.6	13.9	14.6	13.8	7.0	3.0
6. 20-39	13.4	11.6	15.3	14.4	8.3	13.8	14.9	11.3	14.4	14.3	12.8	9.9	18.1	19.2	12.4	7.9
7. 40 or more	40.4	47.7	33.4	45.1	15.6	43.4	45.2	35.0	37.8	38.6	43.4	16.3	47.3	48.8	74.3	77.9
Item 810 Subject A01a N	14916	6955	7524	11376	1482	3527	4246	4552	2591	8983	5006	6264	3018	2148	3153	149

B04B: . . . during the last 12 months?

	TOTAL	M	F	White	Black	NE	NC	S	W	Yes	No	None	Mari- juana Only	Few Pills	More Pills	Any Her- oin
1. 0 occasions - incl. (1) in B03	15.5	14.2	16.6	12.2	32.0	11.3	11.6	21.6	17.1	15.4	14.9	29.9	5.6	6.0	3.2	6.2
2. 1-2	14.2	12.2	16.1	12.1	23.8	15.5	11.8	15.9	13.3	13.7	15.2	22.6	11.3	10.8	3.3	4.5
3. 3-5	13.3	11.8	14.6	12.8	17.1	14.2	13.1	13.1	12.5	13.7	12.5	15.2	14.7	14.5	7.8	7.2
4. 6-9	11.2	9.9	12.4	11.4	8.6	12.7	11.3	9.4	12.1	11.5	11.1	10.7	12.9	13.3	9.3	7.6
5. 10-19	15.6	14.7	16.5	17.4	7.3	15.5	17.6	13.5	16.0	16.5	14.7	10.2	21.5	19.9	18.0	9.3
6. 20-39	12.5	13.4	11.7	14.3	4.2	12.9	14.5	10.4	12.1	12.7	11.9	6.1	16.4	15.0	19.6	14.4
7. 40 or more	17.8	23.7	12.1	19.8	7.0	17.8	20.0	16.1	16.9	16.5	19.8	5.4	17.6	20.6	38.8	50.9
Item 820 Subject A01b N	14844	6934	7483	11329	1465	3507	4232	4531	2574	8944	4988	6216	3015	2138	3153	149

B04C: . . . during the last 30 days?

	TOTAL	M	F	White	Black	NE	NC	S	W	Yes	No	None	Mari- juana Only	Few Pills	More Pills	Any Her- oin
1. 0 occasions - incl. (1) in B03	34.7	31.0	38.1	29.8	59.6	32.4	28.7	41.8	35.5	35.2	33.4	57.0	22.8	21.3	12.5	12.0
2. 1-2	22.6	20.3	25.0	22.9	21.6	23.9	23.0	20.9	23.5	23.3	21.8	22.8	26.9	26.6	16.5	15.7
3. 3-5	16.9	17.9	16.1	18.8	8.4	17.7	19.6	13.7	17.1	18.0	15.7	10.6	22.6	20.4	21.5	15.7
4. 6-9	12.0	13.3	10.8	13.5	4.7	12.7	13.3	10.2	11.8	11.6	12.6	5.1	14.5	14.7	21.4	8.1
5. 10-19	8.9	10.8	7.2	9.9	3.8	8.4	10.5	8.5	7.9	8.4	9.6	3.1	9.5	12.6	16.7	24.2
6. 20-39	2.8	3.5	2.1	3.2	1.3	2.8	3.3	2.6	2.6	2.3	3.7	0.8	2.2	2.8	7.1	11.2
7. 40 or more	1.9	3.2	0.6	1.9	0.7	2.1	1.6	2.3	1.6	1.2	3.0	0.7	1.6	1.6	4.2	16.3
Item 830 Subject A01c N	14851	6925	7497	11353	1461	3496	4244	4531	2580	8944	4994	6197	3025	2146	3163	150

QUESTIONNAIRE FORM 1-5 1986	TOTAL	SEX		RACE		REGION				4YR COLLEGE PLANS		ILLICIT DRUG USE: LIFETIME				
		M	F	White	Black	NE	NC	S	W	Yes	No	None	Mari- juana Only	Few Pills	More Pills	Any Her- oin
N (Weighted No. of Cases):	15713	7261	7855	11713	1649	3720	4440	4855	2698	9291	5277	6535	3125	2223	3264	161
% of Weighted Total:	100.0	46.2	50.0	74.5	10.5	23.7	28.3	30.9	17.2	59.1	33.6	41.6	19.9	14.1	20.8	1.0

B05: On the occasions that you drink alcoholic beverages, how often do you drink enough to feel pretty high?

	TOTAL	M	F	White	Black	NE	NC	S	W	Yes	No	None	Mari-juana Only	Few Pills	More Pills	Any Heroin
1. On none of the occasions	25.0	21.4	28.4	20.5	47.9	23.5	21.0	30.5	24.4	26.4	22.6	47.9	14.8	14.8	6.2	5.3
2. On few of the occasions	30.8	27.9	33.4	31.5	27.9	31.3	31.8	30.1	29.8	30.5	31.4	31.2	34.2	34.8	24.9	10.9
3. On about half of the occasions	16.5	17.6	15.6	17.9	9.5	16.9	18.0	15.5	15.2	16.5	16.2	10.2	19.4	19.3	21.8	23.2
4. On most of the occasions	18.4	21.0	16.1	20.6	7.4	18.8	20.5	15.4	19.6	18.8	18.1	7.6	21.5	22.1	30.0	23.8
5. On nearly all of the occasions	9.2	12.1	6.5	9.5	7.4	9.5	8.8	8.5	11.0	7.7	11.6	3.1	10.1	9.0	17.1	36.7
Item 840 Subject A01e N★	11075	5209	5573	8576	1050	2697	3231	3279	1867	6657	3838	4114	2402	1753	2560	132

B06: Think back over the LAST TWO WEEKS. How many times have you had five or more drinks in a row? (A "drink" is a glass of wine, a bottle of beer, a shot glass of liquor, or a mixed drink.)

	TOTAL	M	F	White	Black	NE	NC	S	W	Yes	No	None	Mari-juana Only	Few Pills	More Pills	Any Heroin
1. None - incl. (1) in B03	63.2	53.9	71.9	59.5	83.9	62.9	57.4	68.3	64.1	65.9	58.7	83.7	56.7	53.2	37.4	28.0
2. Once	11.6	12.9	10.5	13.0	5.6	11.2	13.8	9.6	12.3	11.9	11.6	7.3	15.9	15.9	13.6	10.9
3. Twice	9.6	11.9	7.5	10.5	4.2	10.1	10.8	8.2	9.7	9.2	10.4	4.2	12.3	12.5	15.5	10.2
4. Three to five times	10.7	14.2	7.6	11.9	4.1	11.0	12.7	9.1	9.9	9.5	12.6	3.4	11.5	13.8	22.0	23.2
5. Six to nine times	2.9	4.1	1.8	3.2	1.3	2.9	3.6	2.7	2.4	2.3	3.7	0.8	2.3	3.1	7.1	13.8
6. Ten or more times	1.9	3.0	0.7	1.9	1.0	1.8	1.8	2.1	1.6	1.1	3.1	0.6	1.3	1.5	4.5	14.0
Item 850 Subject A01d N	14727	6841	7464	11263	1448	3471	4203	4487	2566	8919	4900	6204	2988	2113	3100	146

The next major section of this questionnaire deals with various other drugs. There is a lot of talk these days about this subject, but very little accurate information. Therefore, we still have a lot to learn about the actual experiences and attitudes of people your age.

We hope that you can answer all questions; but if you find one which you feel you cannot answer honestly, we would prefer that you leave it blank.

Remember that your answers will be kept strictly confidential: they are never connected with your name or your class.

B07: On how many occasions (if any) have you used marijuana (grass, pot) or hashish (hash, hash oil) . . .

B07A: . . . in your lifetime?

	TOTAL	M	F	White	Black	NE	NC	S	W	Yes	No	None	Mari-juana Only	Few Pills	More Pills	Any Heroin
1. 0 occasions	49.1	46.7	51.8	47.7	56.1	43.2	48.0	56.3	46.2	52.5	44.0	100.0	-	27.0	10.2	4.7
2. 1-2	11.6	11.0	12.0	11.3	15.1	11.2	12.1	12.0	10.5	12.2	11.0	-	39.2	16.3	5.5	2.0
3. 3-5	7.2	6.6	7.6	7.3	6.6	7.8	7.8	6.1	7.3	7.4	6.6	-	19.9	11.1	6.7	5.6
4. 6-9	5.6	5.5	5.8	5.9	4.8	5.4	6.2	5.2	5.8	5.5	5.7	-	13.2	9.1	7.5	3.0
5. 10-19	6.7	6.9	6.6	7.1	4.5	7.7	6.7	5.4	7.6	6.7	6.7	-	12.3	12.0	11.0	12.4
6. 20-39	5.4	5.8	5.1	5.7	3.9	6.5	5.4	4.3	5.9	5.0	6.0	-	7.0	9.6	11.7	10.1
7. 40 or more	14.5	17.5	11.2	15.0	9.1	18.2	14.0	10.9	16.7	10.7	20.0	-	8.4	14.8	47.5	62.2
Item 860 Subject A01a N	15186	7093	7679	11490	1585	3565	4331	4676	2613	9135	5115	6535	3116	2178	3189	148

B07B: . . . during the last 12 months?

	TOTAL	M	F	White	Black	NE	NC	S	W	Yes	No	None	Mari-juana Only	Few Pills	More Pills	Any Heroin
1. 0 occasions	61.2	58.8	64.0	59.5	71.5	55.4	59.8	68.3	58.8	63.9	57.3	100.0	34.3	44.8	21.3	11.0
2. 1-2	11.4	10.5	12.1	11.7	10.9	12.0	12.4	9.7	12.0	11.8	10.9	-	31.9	16.9	11.5	8.3
3. 3-5	7.1	7.1	7.0	7.5	4.4	8.2	7.3	6.1	6.8	7.4	6.4	-	14.0	11.7	11.4	11.7
4. 6-9	4.8	4.9	4.7	5.1	3.3	5.4	4.7	4.1	5.5	4.7	5.0	-	8.4	8.4	8.9	6.4
5. 10-19	4.6	4.8	4.4	4.9	2.8	5.5	4.8	3.8	4.6	4.4	4.8	-	6.4	7.9	9.7	11.3
6. 20-39	3.3	3.7	3.0	3.6	2.2	4.5	3.2	2.5	3.5	2.8	4.4	-	2.5	4.5	9.7	11.8
7. 40 or more	7.5	10.3	4.7	7.7	4.9	8.9	7.7	5.5	8.7	4.9	11.2	-	2.6	5.7	27.4	39.6
Item 870 Subject A01b N	15117	7054	7659	11455	1567	3548	4322	4647	2600	9100	5098	6535	3074	2167	3173	147

★=excludes respondents for whom question was inappropriate.

QUESTIONNAIRE FORM 1-5 1986	TOTAL	SEX		RACE		REGION				4YR COLLEGE PLANS		ILLICIT DRUG USE: LIFETIME				
		M	F	White	Black	NE	NC	S	W	Yes	No	None	Mari-juana Only	Few Pills	More Pills	Any Her-oin
N (Weighted No. of Cases):	15713	7261	7855	11713	1649	3720	4440	4855	2698	9291	5277	6535	3125	2223	3264	161
% of Weighted Total:	100.0	46.2	50.0	74.5	10.5	23.7	28.3	30.9	17.2	59.1	33.6	41.6	19.9	14.1	20.8	1.0

B07C: . . . during the last 30 days?

1. 0 occasions	76.6	73.2	80.0	75.4	83.4	71.5	76.0	80.8	76.9	80.0	71.7	100.0	70.4	68.4	42.2	30.2
2. 1-2	9.3	9.7	9.0	10.0	6.9	10.6	9.5	8.3	9.2	9.2	9.4	-	18.7	14.7	15.3	13.8
3. 3-5	4.2	4.5	3.8	4.3	3.6	5.1	4.1	3.7	3.9	4.0	4.4	-	5.5	6.9	9.5	6.7
4. 6-9	2.8	3.1	2.4	2.9	1.8	3.8	2.8	2.2	2.3	2.3	3.6	-	2.7	4.2	7.1	10.1
5. 10-19	3.2	3.8	2.5	3.3	1.8	4.1	3.5	2.2	3.2	2.2	4.6	-	1.6	3.5	10.6	12.2
6. 20-39	1.9	2.5	1.2	2.0	1.2	2.2	2.1	1.4	2.0	1.2	2.8	-	0.4	1.3	7.3	8.2
7. 40 or more	2.1	3.2	1.0	2.0	1.4	2.8	1.9	1.5	2.6	1.1	3.5	-	0.6	1.0	7.9	18.7
Item 880 Subject A01c N	15106	7051	7649	11445	1570	3543	4317	4648	2599	9098	5090	6535	3076	2161	3163	149

B08: On how many occasions (if any) have you used LSD ("acid") . . .

B08A: . . . in your lifetime?

1. 0 occasions	92.8	91.3	94.4	92.2	98.4	92.3	92.0	95.0	90.9	94.6	90.7	100.0	100.0	95.0	72.3	33.8
2. 1-2	3.6	4.0	3.3	4.0	0.9	4.0	3.9	2.6	4.6	3.0	4.5	-	-	5.0	13.0	20.0
3. 3-5	1.5	1.9	1.1	1.6	0.2	1.8	1.8	0.8	1.9	1.1	2.0	-	-	-	6.6	13.3
4. 6-9	0.8	1.0	0.6	0.9	0.1	1.0	0.8	0.5	1.1	0.6	1.1	-	-	-	3.4	8.9
5. 10-19	0.6	0.9	0.3	0.7	0.1	0.6	0.8	0.3	0.8	0.4	0.8	-	-	-	2.5	7.0
6. 20-39	0.3	0.3	0.2	0.3	-	0.2	0.3	0.3	0.4	0.2	0.4	-	-	-	1.2	4.3
7. 40 or more	0.3	0.5	0.2	0.3	0.3	0.1	0.5	0.4	0.3	0.2	0.5	-	-	-	1.0	12.7
Item 890 Subject A01a N	15337	7165	7753	11592	1612	3608	4365	4722	2641	9196	5198	6514	3113	2205	3218	156

B08B: . . . during the last 12 months?

1. 0 occasions	95.5	94.5	96.6	95.2	98.9	94.9	94.7	97.4	94.1	96.7	94.1	100.0	100.0	97.8	82.0	56.8
2. 1-2	2.7	3.2	2.2	2.9	0.7	3.4	3.2	1.4	3.4	2.1	3.6	-	-	2.2	10.8	14.6
3. 3-5	0.9	1.1	0.6	1.0	0.1	1.1	1.0	0.4	1.3	0.7	1.1	-	-	-	4.0	6.7
4. 6-9	0.4	0.5	0.3	0.4	*	0.3	0.4	0.3	0.6	0.2	0.6	-	-	-	1.5	8.9
5. 10-19	0.3	0.4	0.1	0.3	-	0.2	0.3	0.2	0.4	0.2	0.3	-	-	-	1.0	4.5
6. 20-39	0.1	0.2	0.1	0.1	0.1	*	0.2	0.1	0.2	0.1	0.2	-	-	-	0.4	4.5
7. 40 or more	0.1	0.1	*	0.1	0.1	*	0.1	0.1	*	*	0.1	-	-	-	0.2	4.0
Item 900 Subject A01b N	15327	7157	7753	11580	1612	3608	4362	4718	2638	9192	5195	6516	3114	2204	3208	154

B08C: . . . during the last 30 days?

1. 0 occasions	98.3	97.8	99.0	98.3	99.8	98.1	98.2	98.8	97.9	98.9	97.6	100.0	100.0	99.7	93.3	77.4
2. 1-2	1.2	1.6	0.8	1.3	0.1	1.5	1.3	0.8	1.5	0.8	1.7	-	-	0.3	5.2	10.1
3. 3-5	0.2	0.3	0.1	0.3	-	0.2	0.3	0.2	0.4	0.2	0.4	-	-	-	1.1	2.5
4. 6-9	0.1	0.2	0.1	0.1	0.1	0.1	0.1	0.1	0.1	0.1	0.3	-	-	-	0.3	7.2
5. 10-19	*	0.1	-	*	-	0.1	*	*	*	0.1	*	-	-	-	0.1	0.3
6. 20-39	*	*	*	*	-	-	*	*	0.1	*	*	-	-	-	*	1.8
7. 40 or more	*	*	*	*	0.1	*	*	*	-	*	*	-	-	-	0.1	0.7
Item 910 Subject A01c N	15323	7157	7750	11581	1610	3607	4361	4717	2637	9187	5196	6514	3114	2204	3205	155

B09: On how many occasions (if any) have you used psychedelics other than LSD (like mescaline, peyote, psilocybin, PCP) . . .

B09A: . . . in your lifetime?

1. 0 occasions	94.3	93.6	95.1	94.0	98.3	89.9	95.3	97.1	93.7	95.5	92.9	100.0	100.0	94.8	79.1	42.7
2. 1-2	3.1	3.5	2.7	3.3	1.0	4.8	2.6	1.8	4.0	2.4	4.1	-	-	5.2	10.2	23.7
3. 3-5	1.0	1.1	0.7	1.0	0.4	1.9	0.9	0.3	1.1	0.8	1.1	-	-	-	4.3	8.2
4. 6-9	0.5	0.6	0.5	0.5	0.2	1.1	0.4	0.3	0.5	0.5	0.6	-	-	-	2.5	2.8
5. 10-19	0.4	0.5	0.4	0.5	0.1	1.0	0.3	0.3	0.3	0.3	0.5	-	-	-	1.7	6.4
6. 20-39	0.3	0.3	0.4	0.4	-	0.8	0.3	0.2	0.2	0.3	0.4	-	-	-	1.5	3.6
7. 40 or more	0.3	0.4	0.2	0.3	*	0.5	0.2	0.2	0.2	0.2	0.4	-	-	-	0.8	12.7
Item 920 Subject A01a N	15284	7137	7741	11566	1603	3593	4348	4713	2631	9183	5174	6501	3098	2204	3198	154

B09B: . . . during the last 12 months?

1. 0 occasions	97.0	96.6	97.5	96.8	99.0	94.9	97.3	98.6	96.7	97.5	96.7	100.0	100.0	98.3	88.6	64.2
2. 1-2	1.8	1.9	1.6	1.9	0.6	3.1	1.6	0.9	1.9	1.6	2.0	-	-	1.7	6.5	19.1
3. 3-5	0.5	0.6	0.4	0.6	0.2	0.9	0.5	0.2	0.9	0.5	0.6	-	-	-	2.5	1.8
4. 6-9	0.3	0.3	0.2	0.3	0.1	0.5	0.3	0.1	0.3	0.2	0.3	-	-	-	1.1	3.9
5. 10-19	0.2	0.3	0.1	0.2	-	0.4	0.3	0.1	0.1	0.1	0.3	-	-	-	0.7	8.2
6. 20-39	0.1	0.1	0.1	0.1	*	0.2	0.1	0.1	0.1	0.1	0.1	-	-	-	0.4	1.5
7. 40 or more	*	0.1	*	*	*	0.1	*	0.1	*	*	0.1	-	-	-	0.1	1.3
Item 930 Subject A01b N	15265	7126	7737	11551	1603	3589	4344	4707	2624	9177	5165	6501	3098	2201	3184	151

*=less than .05 per cent.

QUESTIONNAIRE FORM 1-5 1986	TOTAL	SEX		RACE		REGION				4YR COLLEGE PLANS		ILLICIT DRUG USE: LIFETIME				
		M	F	White	Black	NE	NC	S	W	Yes	No	None	Marijuana Only	Few Pills	More Pills	Any Heroin
N (Weighted No. of Cases):	15713	7261	7855	11713	1649	3720	4440	4855	2698	9291	5277	6535	3125	2223	3264	161
% of Weighted Total:	100.0	46.2	50.0	74.5	10.5	23.7	28.3	30.9	17.2	59.1	33.6	41.6	19.9	14.1	20.8	1.0

B09C: . . . during the last 30 days?

	TOTAL	M	F	White	Black	NE	NC	S	W	Yes	No	None	Marijuana Only	Few Pills	More Pills	Any Heroin
1. 0 occasions	98.7	98.6	98.9	98.7	99.5	98.2	98.5	99.3	98.9	99.0	98.5	100.0	100.0	99.0	95.6	80.7
2. 1-2	0.9	1.0	0.8	1.0	0.4	1.2	1.1	0.5	0.8	0.8	1.0	-	-	1.0	3.0	10.3
3. 3-5	0.2	0.2	0.2	0.2	0.1	0.4	0.2	0.1	0.1	0.1	0.2	-	-	0.8	4.3
4. 6-9	0.1	0.1	0.1	0.1	-	0.2	0.1	0.1	0.1	0.1	0.2	-	-	-	0.5	2.5
5. 10-19	*	0.1	*	*	-	*	*	*	0.1	*	0.1	-	-	-	0.1	1.9
6. 20-39	*	*	-	-	-	-	*	*	-	-	*	-	-	-	*	-
7. 40 or more	*	*	*	*	*	-	*	*	-	*	*	-	-	-	*	0.3
Item 940 Subject A01c N	15263	7126	7735	11550	1602	3590	4342	4708	2624	9175	5166	6503	3098	2201	3180	152

B10: On how many occasions (if any) have you used cocaine (sometimes called "coke", "crack", "rock") . . .

B10A: . . . in your lifetime?

	TOTAL	M	F	White	Black	NE	NC	S	W	Yes	No	None	Marijuana Only	Few Pills	More Pills	Any Heroin
1. 0 occasions	83.1	80.8	85.7	82.6	91.7	77.0	86.4	89.2	75.2	85.8	79.7	100.0	100.0	72.3	43.2	9.2
2. 1-2	6.9	7.6	6.1	7.0	4.4	8.4	6.4	5.4	8.6	6.4	7.5	-	-	27.7	12.9	21.7
3. 3-5	2.8	3.3	2.2	2.9	1.1	3.8	2.4	1.6	4.0	2.3	3.3	-	-	-	12.7	10.9
4. 6-9	1.8	2.4	1.3	1.8	0.9	2.4	1.4	0.9	3.6	1.6	2.1	-	-	-	8.4	7.7
5. 10-19	2.0	2.1	1.9	2.2	0.5	3.4	1.1	1.2	3.2	1.6	2.8	-	-	-	9.2	8.7
6. 20-39	1.3	1.3	1.2	1.4	0.8	1.9	0.8	0.6	2.4	1.0	1.7	-	-	-	5.7	7.3
7. 40 or more	2.0	2.4	1.6	2.0	0.6	3.2	1.4	1.1	3.1	1.4	3.0	-	-	-	7.9	34.6
Item 950 Subject A01a N	15264	7165	7731	11589	1604	3575	4350	4707	2633	9188	5180	6485	3076	2204	3211	155

B10B: . . . during the last 12 months?

	TOTAL	M	F	White	Black	NE	NC	S	W	Yes	No	None	Marijuana Only	Few Pills	More Pills	Any Heroin
1. 0 occasions	87.3	85.7	89.1	86.7	94.2	82.1	89.9	92.9	80.0	89.6	84.3	100.0	100.0	85.9	52.2	32.6
2. 1-2	5.6	6.1	4.9	5.9	2.9	7.3	5.4	3.5	7.6	5.0	6.2	-	-	14.1	16.4	15.7
3. 3-5	2.4	3.0	1.9	2.6	0.8	3.3	1.9	1.2	4.5	2.0	3.1	-	-	-	11.3	7.0
4. 6-9	1.5	1.7	1.3	1.5	0.6	2.3	0.8	0.8	2.7	1.1	1.9	-	-	-	6.7	9.2
5. 10-19	1.4	1.4	1.3	1.5	0.5	2.3	1.0	0.8	2.1	1.2	1.9	-	-	-	6.1	12.7
6. 20-39	0.9	0.9	0.8	0.9	0.5	1.4	0.3	0.5	1.6	0.6	1.2	-	-	-	3.5	11.3
7. 40 or more	0.9	1.2	0.6	0.9	0.4	1.3	0.7	0.4	1.6	0.6	1.4	-	-	-	3.8	11.4
Item 960 Subject A01b N	15239	7144	7728	11573	1600	3573	4342	4696	2627	9169	5177	6488	3076	2194	3193	154

B10C: . . . during the last 30 days?

	TOTAL	M	F	White	Black	NE	NC	S	W	Yes	No	None	Marijuana Only	Few Pills	More Pills	Any Heroin
1. 0 occasions	93.8	92.8	94.9	93.6	97.3	91.4	95.4	96.6	89.5	95.3	91.5	100.0	100.0	96.4	75.3	49.2
2. 1-2	3.5	4.1	3.0	3.6	1.2	4.8	2.7	2.0	5.8	2.8	4.5	-	-	3.6	13.5	17.6
3. 3-5	1.1	1.4	1.0	1.3	0.4	1.6	0.8	0.6	2.1	0.7	1.8	-	-	-	4.9	11.3
4. 6-9	0.7	0.8	0.5	0.7	0.5	0.9	0.5	0.3	1.1	0.5	0.9	-	-	-	2.8	6.8
5. 10-19	0.4	0.5	0.3	0.4	0.1	0.7	0.2	0.3	0.7	0.3	0.6	-	-	-	1.7	6.9
6. 20-39	0.2	0.2	0.3	0.2	0.3	0.3	0.1	0.1	0.4	0.2	0.2	-	-	-	0.8	5.0
7. 40 or more	0.2	0.3	0.1	0.2	0.2	0.3	0.2	0.1	0.3	0.1	0.4	-	-	-	0.9	3.4
Item 970 Subject A01c N	15232	7141	7725	11569	1599	3568	4341	4697	2626	9163	5178	6488	3076	2193	3188	154

B11: Amphetamines have been prescribed by doctors to help people lose weight or to give people more energy. They are sometimes called uppers, ups, speed, bennies, dexies, pep pills, and diet pills. Drugstores are not supposed to sell them without a prescription from a doctor. Amphetamines do NOT include any non-prescription drugs, such as over-the-counter diet pills (like Dexatrim) or stay-awake pills (like No-Doz), or any mail-order drugs. On how many occasions (if any) have you taken amphetamines on your own–that is, without a doctor telling you to take them...

B11A: . . . in your lifetime?

	TOTAL	M	F	White	Black	NE	NC	S	W	Yes	No	None	Marijuana Only	Few Pills	More Pills	Any Heroin
1. 0 occasions	76.6	78.7	74.8	73.9	91.7	77.0	74.0	79.3	75.3	80.1	70.4	100.0	100.0	49.8	26.7	21.6
2. 1-2	9.2	8.3	10.1	10.2	4.3	8.3	9.8	9.2	9.6	8.6	10.6	-	-	50.2	9.0	14.0
3. 3-5	4.4	3.9	4.9	4.9	1.5	3.9	5.0	3.7	5.3	4.0	5.2	-	-	-	20.6	7.5
4. 6-9	2.5	2.1	2.7	2.8	0.5	2.6	2.9	1.8	2.9	2.0	3.2	-	-	-	11.3	8.4
5. 10-19	2.5	2.5	2.6	2.9	0.9	2.4	2.9	2.3	2.6	2.0	3.3	-	-	-	11.8	5.8
6. 20-39	1.8	1.7	1.9	2.0	0.7	2.2	1.8	1.5	1.7	1.3	2.6	-	-	-	7.9	11.8
7. 40 or more	3.0	2.9	3.1	3.4	0.3	3.4	3.6	2.3	2.8	1.9	4.7	-	-	-	12.8	30.9
Item 980 Subject A01a N	15286	7146	7770	11606	1606	3597	4345	4707	2638	9190	5191	6484	3078	2189	3222	157

*=less than .05 per cent.

QUESTIONNAIRE FORM 1-5 1986	TOTAL	SEX		RACE		REGION				4YR COLLEGE PLANS		ILLICIT DRUG USE: LIFETIME				
		M	F	White	Black	NE	NC	S	W	Yes	No	None	Mari- juana Only	Few Pills	More Pills	Any Her- oin
N (Weighted No. of Cases):	15713	7261	7855	11713	1649	3720	4440	4855	2698	9291	5277	6535	3125	2223	3264	161
% of Weighted Total:	100.0	46.2	50.0	74.5	10.5	23.7	28.3	30.9	17.2	59.1	33.6	41.6	19.9	14.1	20.8	1.0

B11B: . . . during the last 12 months?

1. 0 occasions	86.6	87.3	86.2	85.0	96.4	87.4	84.8	88.5	85.0	89.1	82.3	100.0	100.0	82.6	50.8	40.5
2. 1-2	6.2	5.9	6.4	7.0	1.7	5.2	6.7	6.0	7.2	5.5	7.6	-	-	17.4	17.2	12.5
3. 3-5	2.5	2.3	2.6	2.8	0.6	2.2	3.0	1.9	2.9	2.1	3.1	-	-	-	11.4	7.7
4. 6-9	1.7	1.8	1.6	1.9	0.8	1.8	2.2	1.2	1.6	1.3	2.3	-	-	-	7.5	12.4
5. 10-19	1.5	1.3	1.6	1.6	0.5	1.2	1.8	1.4	1.7	1.1	2.1	-	-	-	6.8	7.5
6. 20-39	0.8	0.7	0.9	1.0	0.1	1.3	0.9	0.5	0.8	0.6	1.3	-	-	-	3.5	9.6
7. 40 or more	0.7	0.7	0.6	0.8	-	0.8	0.8	0.5	0.8	0.3	1.3	-	-	-	2.8	9.9
Item 990 Subject A01b N	15242	7121	7753	11579	1593	3588	4336	4688	2630	9175	5170	6484	3079	2169	3198	156

B11C: . . . during the last 30 days?

1. 0 occasions	94.5	94.9	94.2	93.9	98.7	94.1	93.8	95.6	94.2	96.0	91.8	100.0	100.0	96.2	78.2	57.9
2. 1-2	2.9	2.8	2.9	3.2	0.8	2.5	3.3	2.6	3.2	2.2	3.9	-	-	3.8	10.6	9.5
3. 3-5	1.2	0.9	1.5	1.3	0.5	1.5	1.6	0.8	1.0	0.8	2.0	-	-	-	5.4	11.6
4. 6-9	0.6	0.7	0.5	0.7	*	0.8	0.4	0.5	0.8	0.4	0.9	-	-	-	2.5	6.5
5. 10-19	0.5	0.4	0.5	0.5	-	0.8	0.5	0.3	0.5	0.4	0.7	-	-	-	1.9	10.3
6. 20-39	0.2	0.1	0.3	0.3	-	0.3	0.3	0.1	0.2	0.1	0.4	-	-	-	1.0	2.0
7. 40 or more	0.1	0.2	0.1	0.1	-	0.1	0.1	0.1	0.2	0.1	0.2	-	-	-	0.5	2.2
Item 1000 Subject A01c N	15230	7115	7747	11571	1592	3586	4330	4683	2631	9166	5168	6484	3078	2163	3190	155

B12: On how many occasions (if any) have you used quaaludes (quads, soapers, methaqualone) on your own–that is, without a doctor telling you to take them . . .

B12A: . . . in your lifetime?

1. 0 occasions	94.8	94.1	95.7	94.4	98.6	94.2	95.2	94.5	95.8	96.1	92.9	100.0	100.0	94.6	82.1	37.4
2. 1-2	2.8	2.9	2.6	3.1	0.7	2.9	2.4	3.0	2.6	2.3	3.5	-	-	5.4	8.8	12.8
3. 3-5	0.8	0.9	0.6	0.8	0.4	0.9	0.8	0.9	0.6	0.6	1.1	-	-	-	3.4	10.0
4. 6-9	0.6	0.6	0.4	0.6	0.1	0.8	0.4	0.6	0.4	0.3	0.9	-	-	-	2.3	8.7
5. 10-19	0.4	0.5	0.2	0.4	*	0.5	0.4	0.3	0.4	0.3	0.5	-	-	-	1.5	6.6
6. 20-39	0.4	0.5	0.3	0.4	-	0.4	0.4	0.5	0.1	0.2	0.7	-	-	-	1.1	14.0
7. 40 or more	0.3	0.4	0.2	0.3	0.1	0.4	0.4	0.2	0.2	0.2	0.5	-	-	-	0.9	10.4
Item 1010 Subject A01a N	15284	7162	7764	11609	1608	3590	4351	4712	2631	9187	5198	6479	3083	2203	3208	154

B12B: . . . during the last 12 months?

1. 0 occasions	97.9	97.3	98.6	97.7	99.6	97.1	98.0	98.0	98.6	98.6	96.8	100.0	100.0	98.7	92.6	61.3
2. 1-2	1.2	1.6	0.8	1.4	0.3	1.6	1.2	1.1	0.8	0.9	1.7	-	-	1.3	4.2	12.7
3. 3-5	0.3	0.4	0.3	0.4	*	0.4	0.3	0.5	0.2	0.2	0.6	-	-	-	1.3	8.1
4. 6-9	0.3	0.3	0.2	0.3	*	0.5	0.3	0.2	0.2	0.2	0.4	-	-	-	1.0	7.2
5. 10-19	0.1	0.2	*	0.1	0.1	0.2	0.1	0.1	0.1	0.1	0.2	-	-	-	0.5	1.9
6. 20-39	0.1	0.2	0.1	0.1	-	0.2	0.1	0.1	0.2	*	0.3	-	-	-	0.2	7.0
7. 40 or more	0.1	0.1	*	*	-	0.1	0.1	*	-	*	0.1	-	-	-	0.2	1.9
Item 1020 Subject A01b N	15283	7157	7768	11604	1610	3592	4352	4711	2629	9188	5199	6481	3083	2201	3206	154

B12C: . . . during the last 30 days?

1. 0 occasions	99.2	99.0	99.4	99.1	99.9	98.7	99.3	99.3	99.5	99.6	98.5	100.0	100.0	99.5	97.5	77.7
2. 1-2	0.4	0.4	0.4	0.5	0.1	0.7	0.3	0.4	0.4	0.2	0.8	-	-	0.5	1.4	8.0
3. 3-5	0.2	0.4	0.1	0.2	-	0.4	0.2	0.2	*	0.1	0.4	-	-	-	0.8	5.9
4. 6-9	0.1	0.1	*	0.1	-	0.1	-	0.1	0.1	*	0.1	-	-	-	0.1	4.9
5. 10-19	*	0.1	*	*	-	0.1	0.1	*	-	*	0.1	-	-	-	0.1	2.9
6. 20-39	*	*	-	*	-	*	*	-	-	-	*	-	-	-	*	0.7
7. 40 or more	*	*	*	*	-	*	0.1	-	-	*	*	-	-	-	0.1	-
Item 1030 Subject A01c N	15277	7158	7761	11601	1610	3592	4346	4709	2630	9184	5199	6480	3083	2199	3203	153

B13: Barbiturates are sometimes prescribed by doctors to help people relax or get to sleep. They are sometimes called downs, downers, goofballs, yellows, reds, blues, rainbows. On how many occasions (if any) have you taken barbiturates on your own–that is, without a doctor telling you to take them...

*=less than .05 per cent.

QUESTIONNAIRE FORM 1-5 1986	TOTAL	SEX		RACE		REGION				4YR COLLEGE PLANS		ILLICIT DRUG USE: LIFETIME				
		M	F	White	Black	NE	NC	S	W	Yes	No	None	Marijuana Only	Few Pills	More Pills	Any Heroin
N (Weighted No. of Cases):	15713	7261	7855	11713	1649	3720	4440	4855	2698	9291	5277	6535	3125	2223	3264	161
% of Weighted Total:	100.0	46.2	50.0	74.5	10.5	23.7	28.3	30.9	17.2	59.1	33.6	41.6	19.9	14.1	20.8	1.0

B13A: ... in your lifetime?

	TOTAL	M	F	White	Black	NE	NC	S	W	Yes	No	None	Mar. Only	Few Pills	More Pills	Any Her.
1. 0 occasions	91.6	91.2	92.0	90.9	97.2	90.5	91.7	92.2	91.8	93.8	88.0	100.0	100.0	88.9	71.1	27.6
2. 1-2	4.1	4.0	4.1	4.4	1.9	4.0	3.9	3.9	4.8	3.1	5.8	-	-	11.1	10.7	23.5
3. 3-5	1.5	1.6	1.5	1.7	0.4	1.7	1.6	1.4	1.5	1.4	1.8	-	-	-	6.9	8.6
4. 6-9	0.8	1.0	0.7	0.9	0.2	0.9	1.0	0.7	0.7	0.6	1.3	-	-	-	3.6	7.9
5. 10-19	0.8	0.9	0.8	0.9	0.1	1.3	0.6	0.7	0.6	0.5	1.3	-	-	-	3.4	8.7
6. 20-39	0.5	0.6	0.4	0.5	0.1	0.6	0.5	0.5	0.4	0.3	0.7	-	-	-	1.9	9.2
7. 40 or more	0.7	0.8	0.5	0.7	0.2	1.0	0.7	0.6	0.4	0.4	1.1	-	-	-	2.4	14.4
Item 1040 Subject A01a N	15221	7135	7740	11577	1603	3572	4336	4689	2624	9167	5175	6458	3070	2194	3187	158

B13B: ... during the last 12 months?

	TOTAL	M	F	White	Black	NE	NC	S	W	Yes	No	None	Mar. Only	Few Pills	More Pills	Any Her.
1. 0 occasions	95.8	95.3	96.2	95.5	98.2	94.8	95.8	95.9	96.7	97.0	93.9	100.0	100.0	96.0	85.1	46.9
2. 1-2	2.2	2.4	2.0	2.4	1.3	2.3	2.3	2.2	1.9	1.7	3.1	-	-	4.0	6.7	23.4
3. 3-5	0.8	0.8	0.7	0.8	0.2	1.0	0.7	0.8	0.5	0.6	1.0	-	-	-	3.1	9.3
4. 6-9	0.6	0.7	0.5	0.6	0.1	0.8	0.5	0.6	0.3	0.3	0.9	-	-	-	2.5	4.1
5. 10-19	0.3	0.4	0.2	0.3	-	0.5	0.4	0.2	0.3	0.2	0.5	-	-	-	1.1	8.6
6. 20-39	0.2	0.1	0.3	0.2	-	0.3	0.2	0.3	0.1	0.1	0.4	-	-	-	1.0	1.7
7. 40 or more	0.2	0.2	0.1	0.2	0.2	0.3	0.2	0.1	0.1	0.1	0.2	-	-	-	0.5	5.9
Item 1050 Subject A01b N	15212	7128	7738	11572	1603	3568	4338	4688	2617	9170	5170	6459	3070	2190	3182	157

B13C: ... during the last 30 days?

	TOTAL	M	F	White	Black	NE	NC	S	W	Yes	No	None	Mar. Only	Few Pills	More Pills	Any Her.
1. 0 occasions	98.2	98.1	98.3	98.1	99.2	97.2	98.3	98.4	98.9	98.8	97.3	100.0	100.0	98.5	93.8	70.1
2. 1-2	1.1	1.2	1.0	1.2	0.6	1.5	1.0	1.1	0.8	0.9	1.5	-	-	1.5	3.6	14.3
3. 3-5	0.4	0.3	0.4	0.4	-	0.7	0.3	0.3	0.2	0.2	0.7	-	-	-	1.5	5.7
4. 6-9	0.2	0.2	0.1	0.2	-	0.3	0.2	0.1	0.1	*	0.3	-	-	-	0.6	3.4
5. 10-19	0.1	0.1	0.1	0.1	-	0.3	0.1	0.1	0.1	0.1	0.2	-	-	-	0.4	3.8
6. 20-39	*	*	*	*	0.1	*	0.1	-	*	*	0.1	-	-	-	0.1	0.3
7. 40 or more	*	*	*	*	0.1	0.1	*	*	*	*	*	-	-	-	*	2.4
Item 1060 Subject A01c N	15205	7128	7732	11568	1601	3567	4337	4684	2616	9162	5170	6459	3070	2190	3175	157

B14: Tranquilizers are sometimes prescribed by doctors to calm people down, quiet their nerves, or relax their muscles. Librium, Valium, and Miltown are all tranquilizers. On how many occasions (if any) have you taken tranquilizers on your own–that is, without a doctor telling you to take them...

B14A: ... in your lifetime?

	TOTAL	M	F	White	Black	NE	NC	S	W	Yes	No	None	Mar. Only	Few Pills	More Pills	Any Her.
1. 0 occasions	89.1	89.6	88.7	88.1	96.5	88.1	89.8	88.9	89.6	90.3	87.3	100.0	100.0	78.4	65.8	36.0
2. 1-2	5.9	5.2	6.4	6.4	2.5	5.8	5.5	6.1	6.5	5.6	6.3	-	-	21.6	12.6	15.8
3. 3-5	2.0	2.0	2.0	2.2	0.6	2.2	1.9	2.0	1.9	1.9	2.1	-	-	-	8.9	11.2
4. 6-9	1.0	1.2	0.9	1.1	0.2	1.2	1.0	1.0	0.9	0.8	1.3	-	-	-	4.6	7.9
5. 10-19	0.9	0.8	1.0	1.1	-	0.9	1.0	0.9	0.7	0.8	1.0	-	-	-	4.0	5.4
6. 20-39	0.4	0.4	0.3	0.4	*	0.5	0.2	0.5	0.3	0.3	0.6	-	-	-	1.5	7.0
7. 40 or more	0.7	0.8	0.6	0.7	0.2	1.4	0.6	0.5	0.2	0.4	1.3	-	-	-	2.5	16.7
Item 1070 Subject A01a N	15225	7151	7748	11586	1609	3576	4343	4688	2618	9179	5178	6466	3067	2191	3188	156

B14B: ... during the last 12 months?

	TOTAL	M	F	White	Black	NE	NC	S	W	Yes	No	None	Mar. Only	Few Pills	More Pills	Any Her.
1. 0 occasions	94.2	94.1	94.2	93.5	98.4	93.6	94.5	93.7	95.2	94.9	92.8	100.0	100.0	92.1	79.8	54.5
2. 1-2	3.4	3.3	3.5	3.7	1.3	3.3	3.1	3.9	3.2	3.2	3.9	-	-	7.9	10.1	15.4
3. 3-5	1.0	1.0	1.0	1.1	0.2	0.9	1.2	0.9	0.8	1.0	1.0	-	-	-	4.3	6.3
4. 6-9	0.8	0.8	0.7	0.8	-	0.8	0.7	0.8	0.6	0.5	1.2	-	-	-	3.0	12.1
5. 10-19	0.4	0.5	0.3	0.4	-	0.7	0.3	0.4	0.2	0.2	0.6	-	-	-	1.6	3.6
6. 20-39	0.2	0.1	0.2	0.2	-	0.3	0.1	0.1	0.1	0.1	0.4	-	-	-	0.7	2.4
7. 40 or more	0.2	0.2	0.1	0.2	0.2	0.4	0.1	0.1	*	0.2	0.2	-	-	-	0.5	5.8
Item 1080 Subject A01b N	15206	7143	7739	11576	1610	3574	4338	4684	2609	9170	5176	6467	3067	2182	3176	157

B14C: ... during the last 30 days?

	TOTAL	M	F	White	Black	NE	NC	S	W	Yes	No	None	Mar. Only	Few Pills	More Pills	Any Her.
1. 0 occasions	97.9	97.9	98.0	97.7	99.2	97.2	97.9	98.0	98.7	98.3	97.3	100.0	100.0	98.5	92.4	72.4
2. 1-2	1.3	1.4	1.3	1.4	0.4	1.5	1.5	1.3	0.7	1.2	1.5	-	-	1.5	4.8	9.1
3. 3-5	0.5	0.4	0.5	0.5	0.1	0.6	0.3	0.5	0.5	0.3	0.7	-	-	-	1.7	10.2
4. 6-9	0.2	0.2	0.1	0.2	-	0.3	0.2	0.2	*	0.1	0.3	-	-	-	0.8	2.7
5. 10-19	0.1	*	0.1	0.1	-	0.3	*	*	0.1	0.1	0.2	-	-	-	0.3	3.8
6. 20-39	*	*	*	*	-	0.1	*	-	-	*	*	-	-	-	0.1	0.3
7. 40 or more	*	*	-	-	0.2	0.1	-	*	-	-	-	-	-	-	*	1.5
Item 1090 Subject A01c N	15203	7142	7737	11574	1610	3574	4337	4682	2610	9168	5176	6467	3067	2182	3175	155

*=less than .05 per cent.

QUESTIONNAIRE FORM 1-5 1986	TOTAL	SEX		RACE		REGION				4YR COLLEGE PLANS		ILLICIT DRUG USE: LIFETIME				
		M	F	White	Black	NE	NC	S	W	Yes	No	None	Marijuana Only	Few Pills	More Pills	Any Heroin
N (Weighted No. of Cases):	15713	7261	7855	11713	1649	3720	4440	4855	2698	9291	5277	6535	3125	2223	3264	161
% of Weighted Total:	100.0	46.2	50.0	74.5	10.5	23.7	28.3	30.9	17.2	59.1	33.6	41.6	19.9	14.1	20.8	1.0

B15: On how many occasions (if any) have you used heroin (smack, horse, skag) . . .

B15A: . . . in your lifetime?

	TOTAL	M	F	White	Black	NE	NC	S	W	Yes	No	None	Marijuana Only	Few Pills	More Pills	Any Heroin
1. 0 occasions	98.9	98.6	99.3	99.1	99.3	98.7	99.1	98.8	99.2	99.3	98.4	100.0	100.0	100.0	100.0	-
2. 1-2	0.6	0.7	0.4	0.6	0.3	0.8	0.4	0.8	0.4	0.4	0.9	-	-	-	-	56.2
3. 3-5	0.1	0.1	0.1	0.1	0.1	0.1	0.2	0.1	0.1	0.1	0.2	-	-	-	-	10.8
4. 6-9	0.1	0.2	*	0.1	-	0.1	0.1	0.1	0.1	0.1	0.2	-	-	-	-	10.9
5. 10-19	0.1	0.1	-	*	-	0.1	0.1	0.1	0.1	*	0.2	-	-	-	-	7.3
6. 20-39	*	*	*	*	-	-	*	*	0.1	*	*	-	-	-	-	2.9
7. 40 or more	0.1	0.2	*	0.1	0.3	0.2	0.2	0.1	*	0.1	0.2	-	-	-	-	11.8
Item 1100 Subject A01a N	15216	7155	7740	11594	1607	3565	4346	4691	2614	9179	5183	6460	3061	2186	3194	160

B15B: . . . during the last 12 months?

	TOTAL	M	F	White	Black	NE	NC	S	W	Yes	No	None	Marijuana Only	Few Pills	More Pills	Any Heroin
1. 0 occasions	99.5	99.3	99.8	99.6	99.6	99.3	99.6	99.5	99.5	99.6	99.2	100.0	100.0	100.0	100.0	50.8
2. 1-2	0.2	0.2	0.1	0.2	0.1	0.4	0.1	0.2	0.2	0.2	0.2	-	-	-	-	21.1
3. 3-5	0.1	0.1	0.1	0.1	-	0.1	0.1	*	0.2	0.1	0.2	-	-	-	-	9.6
4. 6-9	0.1	0.1	-	*	-	*	0.1	0.1	*	*	0.1	-	-	-	-	5.0
5. 10-19	*	0.1	*	*	-	0.1	*	0.1	*	*	0.1	-	-	-	-	4.2
6. 20-39	*	*	*	*	0.1	*	*	*	0.1	*	*	-	-	-	-	2.9
7. 40 or more	0.1	0.1	*	*	0.2	0.1	0.1	0.1	-	*	0.1	-	-	-	-	6.5
Item 1110 Subject A01b N	15215	7154	7741	11593	1608	3564	4345	4690	2615	9179	5183	6461	3061	2186	3194	157

B15C: . . . during the last 30 days?

	TOTAL	M	F	White	Black	NE	NC	S	W	Yes	No	None	Marijuana Only	Few Pills	More Pills	Any Heroin
1. 0 occasions	99.8	99.6	99.9	99.9	99.8	99.8	99.8	99.7	99.8	99.9	99.6	100.0	100.0	100.0	100.0	78.2
2. 1-2	0.1	0.2	*	0.1	0.1	0.1	0.1	0.2	*	*	0.3	-	-	-	-	11.4
3. 3-5	*	0.1	*	*	-	0.1	-	0.1	*	*	0.1	-	-	-	-	3.9
4. 6-9	*	*	*	*	0.1	-	-	*	0.1	*	-	-	-	-	-	3.0
5. 10-19	*	*	-	*	0.1	-	*	-	-	*	*	-	-	-	-	0.8
6. 20-39	*	*	-	*	-	-	-	-	-	-	-	-	-	-	-	0.4
7. 40 or more	*	*	*	*	-	*	*	*	*	*	0.1	-	-	-	-	2.2
Item 1120 Subject A01c N	15212	7153	7741	11595	1605	3563	4346	4689	2614	9177	5181	6461	3062	2186	3194	153

B16: There are a number of narcotics other than heroin, such as methadone, opium, morphine, codeine, demerol, paregoric, talwin, and laudanum. These are sometimes prescribed by doctors. On how many occasions (if any) have you taken narcotics other than heroin on your own–that is, without a doctor telling you to take them...

B16A: . . . in your lifetime?

	TOTAL	M	F	White	Black	NE	NC	S	W	Yes	No	None	Marijuana Only	Few Pills	More Pills	Any Heroin
1. 0 occasions	91.0	90.1	91.9	89.9	96.9	90.6	90.4	92.2	90.6	92.1	89.2	100.0	100.0	87.9	69.3	23.7
2. 1-2	4.3	4.5	4.1	4.9	1.8	4.2	4.2	4.2	4.7	4.2	4.7	-	-	12.1	11.0	24.1
3. 3-5	1.7	1.9	1.6	2.0	0.5	1.4	2.2	1.4	1.7	1.5	1.9	-	-	-	7.5	11.4
4. 6-9	1.1	1.1	1.0	1.3	0.3	1.2	1.2	0.7	1.3	0.8	1.6	-	-	-	4.7	9.2
5. 10-19	0.9	1.1	0.7	0.9	0.2	1.2	0.9	0.7	0.7	0.7	1.1	-	-	-	3.6	11.3
6. 20-39	0.4	0.4	0.3	0.4	0.1	0.5	0.6	0.2	0.4	0.3	0.4	-	-	-	1.7	4.8
7. 40 or more	0.6	0.9	0.4	0.7	0.2	0.8	0.6	0.6	0.5	0.3	1.1	-	-	-	2.3	15.5
Item 1130 Subject A01a N	15149	7138	7740	11567	1613	3552	4329	4672	2596	9149	5156	6421	3061	2187	3172	156

B16B: . . . during the last 12 months?

	TOTAL	M	F	White	Black	NE	NC	S	W	Yes	No	None	Marijuana Only	Few Pills	More Pills	Any Heroin
1. 0 occasions	94.8	94.1	95.4	94.1	98.4	94.3	94.2	95.8	94.6	95.7	93.3	100.0	100.0	95.8	80.2	52.4
2. 1-2	2.8	3.0	2.6	3.1	1.1	2.9	3.0	2.5	2.7	2.4	3.4	-	-	4.2	9.6	17.0
3. 3-5	1.1	1.3	0.9	1.3	0.1	1.2	1.4	0.7	1.0	0.9	1.4	-	-	-	4.7	9.3
4. 6-9	0.6	0.6	0.6	0.7	0.2	0.6	0.7	0.5	0.7	0.5	0.9	-	-	-	2.6	8.3
5. 10-19	0.4	0.5	0.3	0.4	0.1	0.4	0.5	0.2	0.5	0.3	0.4	-	-	-	1.6	3.5
6. 20-39	0.2	0.2	0.2	0.2	-	0.3	0.1	0.2	0.3	0.2	0.3	-	-	-	0.8	4.6
7. 40 or more	0.2	0.3	0.1	0.2	0.1	0.4	0.1	0.1	0.2	0.1	0.4	-	-	-	0.5	4.9
Item 1140 Subject A01b N	15130	7129	7732	11557	1611	3549	4323	4665	2593	9141	5153	6424	3061	2177	3162	155

*=less than .05 per cent.

QUESTIONNAIRE FORM 1-5 1986	TOTAL	SEX		RACE		REGION				4YR COLLEGE PLANS		ILLICIT DRUG USE: LIFETIME				
		M	F	White	Black	NE	NC	S	W	Yes	No	None	Mari-juana Only	Few Pills	More Pills	Any Her-oin
N (Weighted No. of Cases):	15713	7261	7855	11713	1649	3720	4440	4855	2698	9291	5277	6535	3125	2223	3264	161
% of Weighted Total:	100.0	46.2	50.0	74.5	10.5	23.7	28.3	30.9	17.2	59.1	33.6	41.6	19.9	14.1	20.8	1.0

B16C: . . . during the last 30 days?

	TOTAL	M	F	White	Black	NE	NC	S	W	Yes	No	None	Mari-juana Only	Few Pills	More Pills	Any Her-oin
1. 0 occasions	98.0	97.6	98.4	97.8	99.1	97.5	97.8	98.6	98.0	98.4	97.3	100.0	100.0	99.0	92.4	73.0
2. 1-2	1.3	1.5	1.1	1.4	0.5	1.5	1.5	1.0	1.0	1.0	1.8	-	-	1.0	4.9	10.0
3. 3-5	0.4	0.4	0.3	0.4	0.2	0.5	0.5	0.1	0.5	0.3	0.3	-	-	-	1.3	7.5
4. 6-9	0.1	0.2	0.1	0.1	0.1	0.1	0.2	0.1	0.1	0.1	0.2	-	-	-	0.5	2.3
5. 10-19	0.1	0.2	0.1	0.1	-	0.2	*	0.1	0.3	0.1	0.2	-	-	-	0.6	2.6
6. 20-39	*	*	*	*	-	*	-	*	0.1	*	0.1	-	-	-	0.1	2.3
7. 40 or more	0.1	0.1	*	0.1	0.1	0.2	*	*	-	*	0.1	-	-	-	0.2	2.3
Item 1150 Subject A01c N	15123	7128	7727	11548	1611	3550	4317	4664	2593	9137	5150	6425	3061	2174	3158	153

B17: On how many occasions (if any) have you sniffed glue, or breathed the contents of aerosol spray cans, or inhaled any other gases or sprays in order to get high . . .

B17A: . . . in your lifetime?

	TOTAL	M	F	White	Black	NE	NC	S	W	Yes	No	None	Mari-juana Only	Few Pills	More Pills	Any Her-oin
1. 0 occasions	84.1	80.4	87.5	82.7	91.9	85.0	83.5	85.2	81.8	85.8	81.0	95.8	85.2	77.7	65.5	52.0
2. 1-2	9.4	11.4	7.6	10.2	5.4	8.8	9.2	9.0	11.5	8.6	11.0	3.2	10.5	14.5	17.5	10.9
3. 3-5	2.8	3.3	2.3	3.1	1.0	2.4	3.3	2.5	3.2	2.5	3.5	0.5	2.2	3.7	6.8	16.5
4. 6-9	1.4	1.8	1.1	1.6	0.4	1.3	2.0	1.0	1.4	1.3	1.8	0.1	0.9	2.2	3.8	5.5
5. 10-19	0.9	1.3	0.5	0.9	0.4	0.9	0.9	0.8	1.0	0.8	1.0	0.1	0.6	1.1	2.4	2.4
6. 20-39	0.6	0.8	0.3	0.7	0.1	0.5	0.5	0.7	0.5	0.4	0.8	0.1	0.2	0.1	2.0	4.4
7. 40 or more	0.8	1.0	0.6	0.8	0.8	1.1	0.6	0.8	0.5	0.6	1.0	0.2	0.3	0.7	2.0	8.4
Item 1160 Subject A01a N	12178	5729	6233	9292	1304	2871	3468	3745	2095	7358	4213	5133	2424	1787	2583	133

B17B: . . . during the last 12 months?

	TOTAL	M	F	White	Black	NE	NC	S	W	Yes	No	None	Mari-juana Only	Few Pills	More Pills	Any Her-oin
1. 0 occasions	93.9	92.2	95.3	93.2	97.3	94.4	93.3	94.3	93.4	94.8	92.3	98.7	94.9	91.7	85.5	73.8
2. 1-2	3.5	4.3	2.7	3.9	1.1	2.9	3.7	3.2	4.4	3.0	4.3	0.8	3.3	4.6	8.0	9.3
3. 3-5	1.1	1.4	0.9	1.3	0.3	0.8	1.7	1.0	0.8	1.1	1.2	0.2	0.9	1.9	2.4	6.1
4. 6-9	0.5	0.7	0.3	0.5	0.6	0.5	0.5	0.5	0.7	0.4	0.8	0.1	0.4	0.7	1.3	1.9
5. 10-19	0.4	0.6	0.3	0.5	0.2	0.5	0.4	0.5	0.3	0.3	0.6	0.1	0.2	0.5	1.4	1.4
6. 20-39	0.2	0.3	0.2	0.3	0.1	0.3	0.2	0.3	0.1	0.2	0.3	*	0.2	0.1	0.7	2.2
7. 40 or more	0.3	0.4	0.2	0.3	0.4	0.6	0.2	0.3	0.2	0.2	0.4	*	0.1	0.5	0.7	5.4
Item 1170 Subject A01b N	12161	5719	6225	9282	1303	2868	3462	3741	2091	7353	4206	5129	2420	1778	2583	132

B17C: . . . during the last 30 days?

	TOTAL	M	F	White	Black	NE	NC	S	W	Yes	No	None	Mari-juana Only	Few Pills	More Pills	Any Her-oin
1. 0 occasions	97.5	96.8	98.1	97.3	98.5	97.3	97.6	97.3	98.1	97.9	96.7	99.5	97.9	96.8	94.3	83.4
2. 1-2	1.6	2.1	1.2	1.8	0.9	1.5	1.7	1.8	1.1	1.3	2.1	0.3	1.7	2.2	3.4	5.8
3. 3-5	0.5	0.6	0.3	0.5	0.2	0.5	0.4	0.5	0.5	0.4	0.5	0.2	0.1	0.4	1.1	5.1
4. 6-9	0.2	0.2	0.1	0.2	0.1	0.2	0.2	0.2	0.1	0.1	0.3	*	*	0.2	0.6	1.1
5. 10-19	0.1	0.1	0.1	0.1	-	0.1	*	0.1	0.1	0.1	0.1	-	0.2	-	0.2	0.4
6. 20-39	0.1	*	0.1	*	-	0.1	*	0.1	-	*	0.2	-	-	0.2	0.1	0.8
7. 40 or more	0.2	0.2	0.1	0.1	0.4	0.3	0.1	0.1	0.1	0.1	0.2	-	0.1	0.3	0.3	3.4
Item 1180 Subject A01c N	12158	5716	6225	9281	1300	2867	3463	3738	2090	7350	4206	5128	2420	1778	2579	133

*=less than .05 per cent.

QUESTIONNAIRE FORM 1 1986	TOTAL	SEX		RACE		REGION				4YR COLLEGE PLANS		ILLICIT DRUG USE: LIFETIME				
		M	F	White	Black	NE	NC	S	W	Yes	No	None	Marijuana Only	Few Pills	More Pills	Any Heroin
N (Weighted No. of Cases):	3179	1469	1562	2351	323	749	897	984	550	1841	999	1333	671	406	643	21
% of Weighted Total:	100.0	46.2	49.1	74.0	10.2	23.5	28.2	30.9	17.3	57.9	31.4	41.9	21.1	12.8	20.2	0.7

A001: Taking all things together, how would you say things are these days–would you say you're very happy, pretty happy, or not too happy these days?

3. Very happy	18.1	18.1	18.2	18.9	11.6	18.3	18.6	16.2	20.4	19.5	15.4	20.8	17.6	19.8	12.9	20.9
2. Pretty happy	69.5	71.4	68.0	70.9	67.9	68.9	70.9	70.5	66.4	69.5	69.9	67.1	72.6	65.7	73.8	63.3
1. Not too happy	12.4	10.5	13.8	10.2	20.5	12.9	10.6	13.3	13.2	11.0	14.7	12.1	9.9	14.6	13.3	15.8
Item 1190 Subject P01,Q01 N	3157	1459	1557	2339	322	740	891	981	545	1833	995	1329	666	403	639	21

A002: How much do you agree or disagree with each of the following statements?

A002A: The nation needs much more long-range planning and coordination to be prepared for the future

1. Disagree	2.4	2.4	1.9	2.1	2.6	2.3	1.9	3.2	2.0	1.6	3.2	2.4	2.5	2.2	2.2	5.7
2. Mostly disagree	5.4	5.7	4.9	5.4	2.6	5.5	5.3	4.9	6.4	4.7	5.7	4.4	6.5	4.9	6.6	9.7
3. Neither	13.3	12.8	13.7	15.0	6.2	14.4	16.0	10.3	13.1	13.2	14.0	13.3	12.1	11.2	16.7	15.8
4. Mostly agree	43.7	41.7	46.4	46.8	36.6	41.6	46.8	42.1	44.4	46.9	41.1	42.4	46.6	46.7	41.5	22.5
5. Agree	35.1	37.4	33.0	30.6	52.0	36.2	30.0	39.5	34.1	33.5	36.0	37.6	32.2	35.0	33.0	46.3
Item 1200 Subject I01 N	3123	1452	1539	2323	319	728	892	970	533	1821	985	1319	659	401	633	20

A002B: I enjoy the fast pace and changes of today's world

1. Disagree	12.0	11.6	11.9	8.9	26.3	11.9	9.8	16.7	7.6	8.9	16.2	13.3	11.1	11.4	9.2	24.7
2. Mostly disagree	13.0	14.3	14.3	13.3	11.6	11.1	15.5	12.3	12.6	11.7	14.4	14.0	13.4	12.4	10.9	12.5
3. Neither	18.7	20.6	16.9	20.2	10.9	20.4	20.2	16.8	17.5	19.1	18.4	19.0	20.3	18.1	16.1	15.4
4. Mostly agree	36.1	34.1	38.8	37.0	31.7	33.1	37.2	35.1	40.0	40.4	31.3	35.5	38.5	34.5	37.1	25.9
5. Agree	20.2	22.2	18.1	20.5	19.5	23.5	17.2	19.1	22.2	19.9	19.7	18.2	16.7	23.5	26.6	21.5
Item 1210 Subject I03,Q02 N	3127	1447	1548	2329	319	732	889	968	538	1822	991	1314	664	403	631	21

A002C: Things change too quickly in today's world

1. Disagree	14.8	15.6	14.2	14.4	18.0	15.5	14.2	14.2	15.8	14.7	15.1	13.0	13.1	16.3	19.1	14.2
2. Mostly disagree	23.5	24.9	22.6	26.4	13.1	20.4	25.8	20.9	28.5	28.7	16.0	22.6	25.2	28.2	22.6	29.9
3. Neither	19.3	20.0	18.6	21.1	11.8	20.8	19.6	18.3	18.3	20.3	18.8	18.7	18.7	16.2	22.5	19.2
4. Mostly agree	21.1	19.8	22.2	21.5	20.6	21.3	21.4	20.3	21.7	19.9	22.8	21.6	22.9	22.9	18.2	16.0
5. Agree	21.4	19.6	22.4	16.6	36.5	22.1	19.0	26.2	15.6	16.4	27.2	24.1	20.1	16.5	17.5	20.7
Item 1220 Subject I03,Q02 N	3132	1450	1548	2331	319	735	891	968	538	1821	992	1321	659	402	636	20

A002D: I think the times ahead for me will be tougher and less fun than things are now

1. Disagree	20.1	20.7	19.4	20.8	16.7	26.5	16.2	18.9	19.8	21.3	18.8	19.0	16.7	19.0	27.9	35.1
2. Mostly disagree	19.6	18.1	21.8	21.8	10.1	17.2	22.0	17.9	22.1	22.2	16.3	20.0	20.0	20.5	19.1	9.2
3. Neither	14.7	15.4	14.5	15.9	8.3	14.2	16.8	13.5	14.4	15.1	14.7	15.8	14.2	14.9	13.3	12.9
4. Mostly agree	21.3	21.6	21.3	21.0	22.3	19.6	21.7	21.2	23.3	21.8	20.1	22.3	20.1	21.8	20.4	26.3
5. Agree	24.2	24.2	23.0	20.4	42.7	22.6	23.3	28.5	20.4	19.6	30.2	22.9	29.0	23.7	19.4	16.5
Item 1230 Subject I01,J N	3130	1449	1545	2330	320	738	883	971	538	1819	994	1314	663	404	634	20

A003: Of all the time you spend with other people, about how much is spent with people over 30?

1. Very little	23.6	25.8	21.3	20.9	36.8	27.3	20.9	22.9	24.2	21.1	27.6	19.8	26.7	25.7	26.1	29.5
2. Some	42.1	44.3	40.0	44.5	30.0	45.2	42.3	38.7	43.4	46.3	33.4	41.4	44.6	46.5	39.6	24.9
3. About half	27.4	24.4	30.8	28.5	26.1	22.2	29.0	30.1	27.1	27.3	29.7	30.9	24.1	22.8	26.6	38.9
4. Most	5.9	4.8	6.7	5.5	5.4	3.9	7.1	7.0	4.7	4.6	7.9	6.9	3.8	4.2	6.7	6.7
5. Nearly all	1.0	0.8	1.2	0.6	1.8	1.3	0.7	1.3	0.7	0.7	1.5	1.0	0.8	0.8	1.0	-
Item 1240 Subject M02 N	3174	1468	1562	2350	323	748	896	983	547	1838	999	1333	671	406	642	21

QUESTIONNAIRE FORM 1 1986	TOTAL	SEX		RACE		REGION				4YR COLLEGE PLANS		ILLICIT DRUG USE: LIFETIME				
		M	F	White	Black	NE	NC	S	W	Yes	No	None	Mari-juana Only	Few Pills	More Pills	Any Her-oin
N (Weighted No. of Cases):	3179	1469	1562	2351	323	749	897	984	550	1841	999	1333	671	406	643	21
% of Weighted Total:	100.0	46.2	49.1	74.0	10.2	23.5	28.2	30.9	17.3	57.9	31.4	41.9	21.1	12.8	20.2	0.7

A004: Would you like to spend more time, or less time, with people over 30 if you could?

1. Much less time	3.6	4.3	2.8	3.1	5.3	3.6	3.3	3.4	4.2	2.7	5.3	2.6	3.6	5.1	4.8	5.2
2. Somewhat less time	6.9	5.7	8.1	6.9	8.1	7.5	8.1	5.8	6.3	5.5	9.1	6.5	7.4	8.5	6.6	15.5
3. About the same as now	68.8	69.4	68.5	71.5	61.8	68.1	69.6	70.0	66.5	70.4	66.8	69.6	68.5	63.3	71.1	49.0
4. Somewhat more time	17.8	17.8	18.3	16.7	18.5	17.7	17.6	16.9	20.3	18.7	16.5	17.9	18.8	21.0	15.3	16.9
5. Much more time	2.8	2.9	2.4	1.7	6.3	3.1	1.4	3.9	2.7	2.7	2.3	3.5	1.8	2.2	2.2	13.5
Item 1250 Subject M02 N	3166	1465	1559	2345	323	741	896	984	546	1834	998	1329	669	406	643	21

A005: Would you like to spend more time, or less time, working with or helping younger children?

1. Much less time	6.6	9.5	3.1	6.8	3.7	7.8	6.2	7.0	5.2	4.8	7.7	5.8	6.2	5.1	9.3	15.8
2. Somewhat less time	7.5	11.1	4.4	7.8	7.5	6.7	8.1	7.0	8.1	7.6	7.8	6.9	7.7	6.3	8.7	18.4
3. About the same as now	35.4	43.3	27.9	37.6	26.1	38.9	36.3	33.3	32.6	36.0	34.2	34.8	34.1	37.9	36.5	43.8
4. Somewhat more time	31.6	25.7	37.6	31.6	28.4	28.3	33.8	29.7	35.8	33.3	29.4	32.6	33.2	31.4	28.4	15.7
5. Much more time	19.0	10.6	27.0	16.3	34.4	18.3	15.5	23.0	18.3	18.3	20.9	19.9	18.7	19.4	17.0	6.4
Item 1260 Subject M02 N	3166	1464	1561	2347	323	744	896	981	546	1836	998	1330	669	405	643	21

A006: The next questions ask how satisfied or dissatisfied you are with several aspects of your life. For each question, mark the circle that shows best how you feel. If you are neutral about something, or are just as satisfied as you are dissatisfied, mark the middle answer.

How satisfied are you with...

A006A: Your job? (If you have no job, leave blank)

7. Completely satisfied	19.1	19.2	18.9	17.6	22.4	22.8	16.9	20.7	15.5	18.0	21.5	21.9	16.9	17.7	16.5	7.2
6.	18.8	19.4	18.9	20.9	7.6	14.8	22.9	17.1	19.9	22.2	14.5	20.4	18.9	17.5	18.0	16.2
5.	15.4	18.5	13.0	16.8	6.6	13.5	15.0	14.7	20.2	16.5	14.3	14.4	14.0	15.8	19.4	32.2
4. Neutral	28.9	26.1	31.1	26.6	46.3	33.1	24.9	32.9	23.6	25.1	33.1	27.3	29.8	29.9	28.8	23.1
3.	7.2	6.9	7.3	8.1	2.4	6.1	8.7	5.0	9.6	8.0	6.2	6.7	8.3	5.9	8.7	-
2.	3.9	3.2	4.6	4.2	2.4	3.3	4.2	3.3	5.1	4.4	3.5	3.4	5.0	4.6	3.1	6.5
1. Completely dissatisfied	6.7	6.7	6.2	5.8	12.3	6.5	7.4	6.4	6.0	5.9	6.9	5.9	7.2	8.6	5.4	14.8
Item 1270 Subject C01,P02 N	2055	975	997	1608	155	500	630	567	358	1214	636	846	430	267	439	15

A006B: The neighborhood where you live?

7. Completely satisfied	30.5	31.3	30.1	29.4	33.8	28.7	32.1	29.9	31.6	29.9	30.8	32.8	32.2	30.0	24.8	21.6
6.	20.2	23.7	17.5	24.1	6.6	17.9	23.8	18.1	21.4	22.8	18.0	20.2	20.4	18.8	21.7	17.2
5.	9.7	11.3	8.6	11.1	3.8	9.9	9.9	8.7	11.0	11.6	7.4	10.7	9.2	10.7	8.6	2.2
4. Neutral	23.3	19.6	26.2	20.7	34.0	24.3	21.0	25.6	21.5	20.4	27.5	22.9	21.1	25.6	23.5	51.9
3.	5.5	4.5	6.2	6.1	3.2	5.4	5.6	5.8	4.8	5.9	5.2	4.0	6.6	3.7	8.4	3.2
2.	3.3	3.4	3.2	3.2	2.6	3.2	3.6	2.8	3.8	3.3	2.8	3.1	2.4	3.3	4.7	-
1. Completely dissatisfied	7.4	6.2	8.1	5.3	16.0	10.6	4.0	9.0	5.8	6.2	8.3	6.2	8.0	7.9	8.3	3.9
Item 1280 Subject P02 N	3168	1467	1562	2350	323	747	895	983	543	1838	998	1332	669	406	643	21

A006C: Your personal safety in your neighborhood, on your job, and in your school–safety from being attacked and injured in some way?

7. Completely satisfied	40.1	46.6	34.8	42.7	33.6	43.4	41.4	36.7	39.4	41.5	39.8	41.7	43.1	39.5	36.5	13.5
6.	21.5	21.8	22.1	24.8	10.2	19.8	23.8	18.1	26.4	24.9	17.3	21.9	20.4	23.8	21.4	25.7
5.	8.9	7.7	9.9	9.0	4.8	7.1	9.0	9.9	9.3	10.1	6.6	8.2	10.0	9.1	9.9	2.2
4. Neutral	18.7	15.4	21.0	14.9	33.5	19.4	17.4	20.9	15.9	14.5	24.9	17.2	18.7	16.8	20.4	46.3
3.	4.2	3.2	5.4	4.2	3.6	2.8	4.2	5.7	3.6	4.0	4.9	4.7	2.6	3.2	4.5	7.2
2.	2.0	1.9	2.1	1.8	2.9	1.8	2.2	1.6	2.9	1.9	1.8	2.2	1.2	1.6	3.1	-
1. Completely dissatisfied	4.5	3.5	4.6	2.5	11.5	5.7	2.0	7.2	2.4	3.2	4.6	4.1	3.9	6.0	4.2	5.2
Item 1290 Subject P02 N	3158	1465	1556	2347	322	746	894	978	540	1835	994	1328	667	404	643	21

QUESTIONNAIRE FORM 1 1986	TOTAL	SEX		RACE		REGION				4YR COLLEGE PLANS		ILLICIT DRUG USE: LIFETIME				
		M	F	White	Black	NE	NC	S	W	Yes	No	None	Mari-juana Only	Few Pills	More Pills	Any Her-oin
N (Weighted No. of Cases):	3179	1469	1562	2351	323	749	897	984	550	1841	999	1333	671	406	643	21
% of Weighted Total:	100.0	46.2	49.1	74.0	10.2	23.5	28.2	30.9	17.3	57.9	31.4	41.9	21.1	12.8	20.2	0.7

A006D: The safety of things you own from being stolen or destroyed in your neighborhood, on your job, and in your school?

7. Completely satisfied	22.3	24.4	20.2	22.6	22.6	24.7	21.9	22.3	19.4	21.0	25.7	23.6	22.1	23.6	18.9	19.5
6.	21.2	21.3	21.9	23.6	11.4	21.7	24.8	17.0	22.2	24.8	16.7	24.1	21.4	18.7	19.3	12.1
5.	13.4	14.6	12.5	15.0	6.4	11.8	15.7	11.0	16.0	14.9	11.8	12.5	14.2	13.8	14.5	26.8
4. Neutral	18.9	17.2	19.6	16.4	28.4	18.8	16.7	21.5	17.7	15.0	23.0	17.0	18.4	17.6	21.7	20.2
3.	8.9	8.8	9.4	9.8	3.2	7.8	9.3	8.9	10.0	9.4	8.3	7.8	9.6	9.8	10.6	-
2.	5.1	4.8	5.5	5.4	4.8	4.7	4.2	5.5	6.1	6.4	3.4	4.7	5.3	5.6	5.2	-
1. Completely dissatisfied	10.3	8.9	10.8	7.2	23.1	10.5	7.4	13.7	8.5	8.5	11.1	10.3	9.0	11.0	9.8	21.3
Item 1300 Subject P02 N	3151	1458	1559	2345	321	740	893	977	541	1833	994	1325	669	404	636	20

A006E: Your educational experiences?

7. Completely satisfied	21.2	20.6	21.5	17.8	40.0	23.0	18.7	24.7	16.4	21.9	20.0	24.6	20.6	21.2	15.1	15.1
6.	24.7	25.7	24.8	27.3	12.9	21.3	30.0	22.3	24.9	28.4	20.3	25.9	26.4	26.7	21.6	18.4
5.	16.7	19.7	14.4	18.7	8.3	16.1	17.3	15.0	19.8	18.8	15.0	15.9	17.9	17.5	18.2	14.3
4. Neutral	22.3	20.1	23.2	20.1	28.1	25.5	19.8	21.9	22.6	17.3	27.4	20.3	24.0	17.3	23.8	26.4
3.	6.9	6.1	8.2	8.2	1.9	5.6	7.7	6.8	7.8	7.1	6.8	6.2	4.7	9.0	10.2	7.3
2.	3.6	3.0	3.8	3.8	2.3	3.9	3.1	3.4	4.7	4.0	3.2	3.2	3.3	3.3	4.7	9.1
1. Completely dissatisfied	4.5	4.8	4.0	4.1	6.4	4.7	3.5	5.9	3.7	2.6	7.4	3.9	3.1	5.0	6.4	9.4
Item 1310 Subject B01,P02 N	3143	1455	1558	2340	319	741	890	973	540	1829	992	1328	665	404	631	21

A006F: Your friends and other people you spend time with?

7. Completely satisfied	45.1	41.8	48.1	44.5	51.9	46.3	41.2	48.9	43.1	43.0	49.4	47.8	48.4	44.6	39.4	23.2
6.	28.1	31.2	25.9	31.4	12.9	26.2	31.4	25.5	29.9	31.5	23.2	28.4	26.3	27.8	30.6	32.3
5.	9.2	11.0	7.8	9.8	6.6	8.9	11.4	7.0	10.1	10.7	7.0	7.7	8.5	10.4	12.1	5.2
4. Neutral	12.2	10.8	12.7	9.0	22.9	12.2	10.6	14.4	10.7	9.7	14.7	11.0	11.4	12.0	12.6	35.3
3.	2.4	1.8	3.0	2.5	2.6	3.4	2.3	1.0	3.9	2.6	2.2	2.1	2.8	2.7	2.4	-
2.	1.4	1.8	1.1	1.5	0.8	1.5	1.7	1.1	1.3	1.3	1.5	1.2	1.6	1.3	1.7	3.9
1. Completely dissatisfied	1.5	1.5	1.3	1.2	2.2	1.4	1.4	2.0	1.0	1.1	2.0	1.7	1.0	1.1	1.2	-
Item 1320 Subject M04,P02 N	3161	1463	1561	2346	321	746	895	979	541	1837	995	1331	669	405	641	21

A006G: The way you get along with your parents?

7. Completely satisfied	33.4	33.9	32.5	30.2	47.0	36.1	28.6	37.3	30.2	30.9	36.3	37.8	34.2	29.6	23.2	17.7
6.	21.2	22.8	20.2	23.5	12.0	18.6	26.5	16.9	23.6	24.3	17.5	22.4	20.8	23.6	19.5	13.2
5.	12.5	14.2	11.2	14.0	6.3	11.6	14.2	10.5	14.6	14.5	10.2	12.1	12.5	13.6	13.1	21.7
4. Neutral	17.6	15.9	18.6	16.2	23.4	17.9	15.8	19.5	16.8	14.9	20.5	16.1	18.3	16.2	20.4	28.8
3.	5.3	5.2	5.6	5.9	3.4	4.5	5.9	5.9	4.5	5.7	5.1	5.0	4.1	5.5	7.6	3.5
2.	3.9	3.7	4.2	4.4	1.0	5.6	3.9	3.5	2.4	4.4	2.7	2.3	3.8	6.0	6.1	10.0
1. Completely dissatisfied	6.1	4.4	7.6	5.7	7.0	5.7	5.1	6.4	7.9	5.3	7.7	4.3	6.2	5.5	9.9	5.2
Item 1330 Subject M03,P02 N	3160	1466	1556	2346	322	744	894	981	541	1831	999	1329	669	406	640	21

A006H: Yourself?

7. Completely satisfied	29.6	33.2	25.5	24.8	56.6	30.7	25.0	34.5	27.0	25.8	34.4	33.3	32.6	25.9	19.9	25.2
6.	27.5	28.5	27.4	30.7	13.8	26.1	31.3	24.0	29.8	31.7	21.8	27.3	27.4	26.8	30.0	20.5
5.	13.3	12.7	13.7	15.3	4.8	13.0	15.4	10.6	15.2	15.2	10.3	13.2	13.3	11.1	15.9	9.0
4. Neutral	19.5	16.2	22.5	18.7	17.1	19.9	18.2	22.0	16.6	17.2	23.3	17.8	17.0	26.4	21.5	19.8
3.	3.9	3.3	4.7	4.5	1.5	3.4	4.8	2.9	5.1	4.5	3.4	3.7	4.5	3.2	4.3	3.5
2.	2.5	2.4	2.7	2.8	1.6	2.9	2.1	2.3	3.2	2.4	2.9	1.8	2.3	3.0	3.8	3.4
1. Completely dissatisfied	3.6	3.5	3.5	3.2	4.6	4.0	3.1	3.8	3.2	3.2	3.9	2.8	2.9	3.6	4.6	18.6
Item 1340 Subject P01,Q01 N	3147	1457	1554	2338	318	740	889	975	543	1827	990	1323	665	402	640	21

A006I: Your standard of living--the things you have like housing, car, furniture, recreation, and the like?

7. Completely satisfied	33.7	33.8	33.1	31.5	44.4	35.6	31.7	34.0	33.9	34.4	31.5	36.4	35.7	34.0	26.1	24.4
6.	26.5	29.2	24.8	29.9	11.6	26.5	29.6	23.8	26.4	30.7	20.7	27.0	28.8	24.7	25.7	20.9
5.	13.4	14.0	13.2	14.8	7.2	11.6	14.5	12.0	16.8	13.9	13.2	12.5	13.2	12.1	17.1	12.6
4. Neutral	15.1	12.5	17.0	13.4	22.6	14.8	14.5	17.9	11.4	10.9	21.3	13.9	13.2	16.5	17.1	14.3
3.	4.8	4.7	5.2	5.0	4.0	3.9	5.6	4.8	5.0	4.8	5.4	4.1	5.0	5.9	5.6	9.1
2.	3.0	2.9	3.2	2.9	2.9	4.1	1.3	3.5	3.6	3.0	3.2	2.8	2.2	3.9	4.0	3.4
1. Completely dissatisfied	3.3	2.8	3.6	2.6	7.4	3.5	2.8	4.0	2.9	2.3	4.6	3.3	1.9	2.9	4.4	15.2
Item 1350 Subject F01,P02 N	3164	1468	1561	2349	323	748	893	981	542	1839	999	1331	670	406	642	21

QUESTIONNAIRE FORM 1 1986	TOTAL	SEX		RACE		REGION				4YR COLLEGE PLANS		ILLICIT DRUG USE: LIFETIME				
		M	F	White	Black	NE	NC	S	W	Yes	No	None	Mari-juana Only	Few Pills	More Pills	Any Her-oin
N (Weighted No. of Cases):	3179	1469	1562	2351	323	749	897	984	550	1841	999	1333	671	406	643	21
% of Weighted Total:	100.0	46.2	49.1	74.0	10.2	23.5	28.2	30.9	17.3	57.9	31.4	41.9	21.1	12.8	20.2	0.7

A006J: The amount of time you have for doing things you want to do?

	TOTAL	M	F	White	Black	NE	NC	S	W	Yes	No	None	Mari-juana Only	Few Pills	More Pills	Any Her-oin
7. Completely satisfied	15.4	15.7	14.9	13.6	23.0	16.8	14.0	16.9	13.3	13.5	18.8	15.7	16.3	16.0	13.6	8.1
6.	16.9	17.8	16.6	18.8	8.9	14.8	19.9	15.2	17.6	18.3	15.7	17.6	15.7	14.9	18.4	13.6
5.	15.0	15.9	13.9	16.4	8.1	14.4	16.7	13.2	16.3	17.7	10.9	14.9	16.4	15.2	14.4	19.7
4. Neutral	19.1	17.1	20.5	16.5	30.4	21.4	18.1	18.9	17.9	15.6	22.8	19.3	19.4	18.4	17.3	32.5
3.	13.6	14.3	13.7	15.8	5.5	15.1	14.5	11.9	13.4	14.7	12.7	14.1	12.2	14.9	14.0	8.2
2.	8.0	7.8	8.3	8.5	4.6	6.4	7.5	9.0	9.1	9.6	6.0	6.9	9.0	10.3	8.4	9.4
1. Completely dissatisfied	12.0	11.4	12.0	10.4	19.6	11.1	9.3	14.8	12.4	10.7	13.0	11.4	11.1	10.2	13.9	8.6
Item 1360 Subject P02 N	3162	1467	1559	2348	323	746	894	981	542	1838	997	1329	669	406	642	21

A006K: The way you spend your leisure time– recreation, relaxation, and so on?

	TOTAL	M	F	White	Black	NE	NC	S	W	Yes	No	None	Mari-juana Only	Few Pills	More Pills	Any Her-oin
7. Completely satisfied	27.1	27.8	25.9	25.7	34.7	28.9	24.1	30.7	23.2	24.7	31.6	26.4	29.6	28.4	25.0	21.7
6.	23.3	24.1	23.5	25.8	14.0	20.3	27.4	21.1	24.8	25.9	19.5	24.8	21.5	20.1	26.4	25.2
5.	15.8	16.7	15.3	17.1	6.6	15.7	17.4	12.0	20.5	18.1	12.4	15.3	16.4	17.8	16.3	-
4. Neutral	17.6	16.8	18.2	16.3	25.6	19.4	16.1	19.4	14.7	16.0	19.1	17.9	19.4	13.8	15.6	40.3
3.	8.0	7.5	8.7	8.6	2.9	9.0	7.6	6.8	9.2	8.3	8.5	6.9	6.3	14.3	8.2	9.4
2.	3.1	3.4	3.0	3.2	2.2	2.6	3.5	2.6	3.8	3.1	3.3	3.3	2.8	2.0	3.3	3.4
1. Completely dissatisfied	5.1	3.7	5.5	3.2	13.9	4.2	3.9	7.4	3.8	3.8	5.6	5.5	4.1	3.5	5.1	-
Item 1370 Subject C08,P02 N	3160	1462	1562	2347	321	745	895	980	541	1836	995	1328	667	405	643	21

A006L: Your life as a whole these days?

	TOTAL	M	F	White	Black	NE	NC	S	W	Yes	No	None	Mari-juana Only	Few Pills	More Pills	Any Her-oin
7. Completely satisfied	18.5	18.8	17.9	17.3	26.4	17.3	16.6	21.4	17.9	16.7	21.7	21.4	18.2	18.0	12.5	2.5
6.	26.6	29.1	25.1	29.3	19.2	25.6	28.1	24.3	29.6	31.4	19.6	28.0	28.3	23.2	25.7	32.6
5.	18.9	19.4	18.9	21.4	5.9	18.7	21.4	16.3	19.9	20.6	17.4	16.4	19.8	25.9	21.0	11.2
4. Neutral	23.7	21.0	25.3	20.2	36.6	25.4	22.4	26.2	18.7	20.2	27.6	24.4	22.5	20.1	23.8	37.3
3.	4.9	5.5	4.5	5.2	2.6	4.5	5.6	4.1	6.0	4.9	5.0	4.7	5.6	4.3	5.9	3.5
2.	3.2	2.8	3.5	3.3	1.7	3.9	3.3	1.9	4.2	2.7	4.2	2.4	2.4	3.7	5.8	-
1. Completely dissatisfied	4.2	3.3	4.7	3.3	7.6	4.7	2.6	5.7	3.7	3.5	4.6	2.8	3.3	4.7	5.3	13.0
Item 1380 Subject P01 N	3149	1458	1554	2340	320	743	893	975	538	1830	993	1327	664	404	639	21

A006M: The way our national government is operating?

	TOTAL	M	F	White	Black	NE	NC	S	W	Yes	No	None	Mari-juana Only	Few Pills	More Pills	Any Her-oin
7. Completely satisfied	5.5	8.2	2.5	4.8	5.8	5.1	3.7	7.6	5.3	4.7	5.4	6.6	4.8	6.1	3.6	-
6.	9.5	13.7	5.8	10.6	3.8	8.9	9.5	9.3	10.8	10.5	8.1	9.1	11.7	8.7	9.6	1.6
5.	15.6	18.9	13.0	17.8	5.4	13.6	19.3	12.7	17.4	19.0	10.7	17.6	13.5	17.8	13.8	8.8
4. Neutral	38.4	32.2	44.4	37.4	45.0	40.8	35.2	40.2	37.1	37.2	42.2	37.3	38.4	36.0	39.8	39.9
3.	11.0	10.0	12.3	11.9	7.4	8.4	14.1	9.5	12.0	12.4	8.9	10.6	11.1	12.5	11.8	10.2
2.	7.3	6.2	8.6	7.6	6.7	9.3	7.9	5.6	6.8	7.3	7.8	6.3	7.8	10.2	7.8	10.6
1. Completely dissatisfied	12.7	10.8	13.4	9.8	25.9	13.9	10.4	15.1	10.5	8.9	16.8	12.6	12.7	8.7	13.6	28.9
Item 1390 Subject H02,K02 N	3149	1459	1557	2341	323	739	890	978	541	1827	996	1322	666	403	642	21

A006N: The amount of fun you are having?

	TOTAL	M	F	White	Black	NE	NC	S	W	Yes	No	None	Mari-juana Only	Few Pills	More Pills	Any Her-oin
7. Completely satisfied	23.8	23.9	23.7	22.0	32.0	24.5	22.3	25.8	22.0	21.7	27.7	22.6	26.6	24.9	22.7	12.6
6.	24.9	27.3	23.6	27.5	15.7	27.0	27.4	21.3	24.7	27.7	20.7	24.8	25.0	24.1	27.2	30.6
5.	18.2	19.1	17.8	20.9	5.5	16.4	19.0	16.8	21.9	20.4	16.5	17.4	20.4	17.8	18.9	26.5
4. Neutral	18.4	15.7	19.8	15.1	32.6	18.4	17.0	20.8	16.4	15.8	20.7	19.6	17.2	16.4	16.7	21.7
3.	6.4	5.8	7.2	7.2	2.6	6.6	7.2	5.1	7.5	6.7	6.1	7.7	4.4	7.3	5.9	-
2.	3.3	3.3	3.4	3.5	2.3	2.1	3.4	4.0	3.4	3.2	3.8	2.9	3.1	3.9	3.6	3.4
1. Completely dissatisfied	4.9	4.9	4.4	3.8	9.3	5.1	3.8	6.2	4.1	4.5	4.6	5.1	3.4	5.6	5.1	5.2
Item 1400 Subject P02,Q01 N	3167	1466	1562	2350	323	746	896	983	542	1838	999	1330	670	406	643	21

A007: How important is each of the following to you in your life?

A007A: Being successful in my line of work

	TOTAL	M	F	White	Black	NE	NC	S	W	Yes	No	None	Mari-juana Only	Few Pills	More Pills	Any Her-oin
1. Not important	1.6	2.2	0.8	1.2	2.2	2.0	0.6	1.3	3.1	0.9	1.9	0.9	2.1	1.2	2.9	-
2. Somewhat important	7.2	6.7	7.2	7.1	5.9	8.9	7.4	5.6	7.2	5.8	9.2	6.7	7.8	7.3	6.4	13.4
3. Quite important	30.8	29.6	32.5	33.4	19.4	28.0	34.7	28.3	32.7	30.8	33.5	31.3	30.6	33.8	28.8	28.7
4. Extremely important	60.5	61.5	59.5	58.3	72.6	61.1	57.2	64.8	57.0	62.4	55.4	61.1	59.6	57.7	61.9	57.9
Item 1410 Subject C06,Q07 N	3140	1455	1552	2339	318	737	891	974	538	1826	991	1322	666	403	633	20

QUESTIONNAIRE FORM 1 1986	TOTAL	SEX		RACE		REGION				4YR COLLEGE PLANS		ILLICIT DRUG USE: LIFETIME				
		M	F	White	Black	NE	NC	S	W	Yes	No	None	Marijuana Only	Few Pills	More Pills	Any Heroin
N (Weighted No. of Cases):	3179	1469	1562	2351	323	749	897	984	550	1841	999	1333	671	406	643	21
% of Weighted Total:	100.0	46.2	49.1	74.0	10.2	23.5	28.2	30.9	17.3	57.9	31.4	41.9	21.1	12.8	20.2	0.7

A007B: Having a good marriage and family life

1. Not important	4.1	5.5	2.2	3.7	5.8	4.5	3.2	4.3	4.8	2.5	6.1	3.2	2.5	3.8	6.5	10.4
2. Somewhat important	6.8	8.3	5.1	6.6	7.8	6.3	7.5	5.8	8.1	7.4	5.3	6.0	5.3	6.9	9.8	14.9
3. Quite important	13.7	16.9	10.6	14.0	10.8	13.4	14.5	13.6	13.1	13.0	13.7	13.4	14.7	13.1	13.5	23.8
4. Extremely important	75.4	69.3	82.1	75.7	75.6	75.9	74.9	76.2	74.0	77.0	74.9	77.4	77.5	76.3	70.2	50.9
Item 1420 Subject D03,Q07 N	3140	1450	1554	2339	314	736	891	973	540	1830	990	1318	667	402	636	21

A007C: Having lots of money

1. Not important	5.2	5.3	5.1	5.6	3.3	5.6	5.1	4.5	6.3	5.8	4.4	6.2	2.7	6.1	5.0	12.2
2. Somewhat important	32.1	26.8	38.2	34.6	26.0	30.3	32.2	34.1	31.0	32.6	34.5	36.9	29.7	29.5	28.2	27.0
3. Quite important	36.2	34.3	38.8	36.3	32.9	36.3	38.1	33.2	38.0	37.6	35.2	34.4	41.5	39.0	34.1	11.0
4. Extremely important	26.5	33.6	18.0	23.5	37.8	27.8	24.5	28.3	24.7	23.9	25.9	22.6	26.2	25.4	32.8	49.8
Item 1430 Subject F01,Q07 N	3148	1456	1555	2339	320	742	892	975	539	1832	992	1323	669	405	634	21

A007D: Having plenty of time for recreation and hobbies

1. Not important	2.2	1.8	2.3	1.1	5.8	2.6	1.8	2.7	1.1	1.1	3.3	2.3	1.5	3.0	2.1	-
2. Somewhat important	28.0	23.4	31.9	26.4	39.3	28.9	27.7	30.4	22.6	23.8	35.3	30.1	25.9	28.6	23.7	34.5
3. Quite important	42.2	41.9	43.6	43.8	30.2	41.7	43.2	39.6	45.9	46.0	37.9	43.4	45.2	42.2	38.7	22.3
4. Extremely important	27.7	32.9	22.2	28.6	24.6	26.7	27.2	27.3	30.4	29.0	23.5	24.1	27.4	26.2	35.5	43.3
Item 1440 Subject C08,Q07 N	3153	1457	1560	2344	319	743	890	979	541	1832	995	1325	669	406	636	21

A007E: Having strong friendships

1. Not important	1.2	1.1	1.2	0.7	4.3	1.5	0.8	1.8	0.6	0.8	1.6	1.2	1.2	1.1	1.1	-
2. Somewhat important	7.4	7.6	6.3	4.7	20.1	7.0	5.0	10.0	7.2	5.6	8.8	7.3	7.2	7.0	7.0	8.7
3. Quite important	28.9	31.9	26.2	28.4	28.9	26.4	33.2	28.5	26.3	26.7	33.0	29.6	29.9	27.9	26.1	49.5
4. Extremely important	62.4	59.5	66.3	66.2	46.7	65.1	61.0	59.8	66.0	66.9	56.6	61.8	61.7	64.0	65.9	41.8
Item 1450 Subject M04,Q07 N	3155	1459	1560	2345	321	745	892	979	539	1833	999	1326	669	406	636	21

A007F: Being able to find steady work

1. Not important	1.0	1.4	0.7	1.1	0.9	1.6	1.1	0.9	0.5	1.1	0.8	0.9	0.9	0.6	1.6	3.9
2. Somewhat important	4.7	4.9	4.4	4.9	3.5	5.5	3.4	5.2	4.5	5.0	4.5	4.6	2.9	6.1	5.7	10.5
3. Quite important	25.4	25.0	26.3	26.9	15.8	25.2	26.6	22.9	28.4	27.2	24.1	27.5	24.4	24.1	22.5	41.9
4. Extremely important	68.9	68.7	68.6	67.2	79.8	67.7	68.9	71.0	66.6	66.7	70.6	66.9	71.7	69.1	70.2	43.7
Item 1460 Subject C04,Q07 N	3147	1453	1561	2340	319	740	891	976	539	1833	994	1323	666	404	635	21

A007G: Making a contribution to society

1. Not important	8.3	9.4	6.9	8.0	8.2	8.7	6.7	8.5	9.9	5.1	12.6	6.3	8.2	8.1	12.1	3.9
2. Somewhat important	39.8	39.2	40.4	40.9	34.9	43.9	39.9	36.6	39.6	36.4	46.2	37.0	41.9	42.9	41.6	56.4
3. Quite important	35.1	33.6	36.8	34.7	36.4	33.4	37.9	35.6	32.0	38.1	29.9	37.0	37.1	30.1	32.7	19.7
4. Extremely important	16.9	17.8	16.0	16.4	20.4	14.0	15.6	19.3	18.6	20.3	11.4	19.7	12.7	18.9	13.6	19.9
Item 1470 Subject O01,Q07 N	3147	1456	1556	2342	318	745	890	976	536	1832	992	1324	665	405	637	21

A007H: Being a leader in my community

1. Not important	34.0	32.6	34.8	34.4	26.6	39.0	33.5	30.1	35.3	28.0	44.3	30.9	32.3	34.3	40.9	42.3
2. Somewhat important	38.2	34.9	41.6	39.0	36.2	36.7	38.9	36.9	41.4	38.8	38.3	37.9	43.3	39.1	33.2	40.0
3. Quite important	19.1	21.4	17.3	18.6	25.0	17.5	19.5	22.1	15.0	22.4	12.8	21.2	17.6	18.3	17.6	-
4. Extremely important	8.7	11.0	6.3	8.0	12.2	6.8	8.1	10.9	8.4	10.8	4.6	10.0	6.7	8.3	8.3	17.7
Item 1480 Subject M05,Q07 N	3153	1456	1560	2341	321	745	894	978	536	1831	998	1325	669	404	637	21

A007I: Being able to give my children better opportunities than I've had

1. Not important	2.2	2.5	2.1	2.4	0.9	1.6	2.6	1.2	4.5	2.4	1.6	2.3	1.1	2.9	2.8	-
2. Somewhat important	9.9	9.7	10.3	11.8	3.4	10.7	11.4	7.5	10.9	9.6	9.6	10.0	9.1	8.6	10.4	33.6
3. Quite important	29.9	31.7	28.9	33.7	12.4	29.1	32.7	26.4	32.6	31.6	28.0	30.7	29.4	31.4	28.9	28.0
4. Extremely important	58.0	56.0	58.7	52.1	83.3	58.6	53.4	65.0	52.1	55.5	60.9	57.0	60.4	57.1	57.9	38.4
Item 1490 Subject Q07 N	3132	1447	1547	2329	316	740	884	969	539	1822	993	1317	660	404	635	21

QUESTIONNAIRE FORM 1 1986	TOTAL	SEX		RACE		REGION				4YR COLLEGE PLANS		ILLICIT DRUG USE: LIFETIME				
		M	F	White	Black	NE	NC	S	W	Yes	No	None	Mari- juana Only	Few Pills	More Pills	Any Her- oin
N (Weighted No. of Cases):	3179	1469	1562	2351	323	749	897	984	550	1841	999	1333	671	406	643	21
% of Weighted Total:	100.0	46.2	49.1	74.0	10.2	23.5	28.2	30.9	17.3	57.9	31.4	41.9	21.1	12.8	20.2	0.7
A007J: Living close to parents and relatives																
1. Not important	24.9	26.7	22.8	24.4	30.9	26.0	23.5	25.8	23.9	25.6	22.5	21.8	26.0	23.9	31.2	20.8
2. Somewhat important	42.3	40.4	44.6	44.4	40.9	40.8	46.9	40.3	40.5	42.0	44.9	41.7	42.6	46.0	40.6	66.1
3. Quite important	22.1	22.1	22.5	21.4	19.1	20.8	19.7	23.8	25.1	22.2	21.5	24.0	22.0	21.4	19.0	7.4
4. Extremely important	10.6	10.8	10.1	9.9	9.1	12.5	9.9	10.0	10.4	10.2	11.0	12.5	9.4	8.7	9.2	5.7
Item 1500 Subject M03,Q07 N	3153	1456	1561	2342	321	744	893	979	538	1832	996	1326	666	406	637	21
A007K: Getting away from this area of the country																
1. Not important	48.4	48.9	48.0	50.7	31.8	46.6	43.5	48.5	58.9	48.6	47.6	50.2	50.1	48.6	44.8	37.1
2. Somewhat important	25.2	24.8	25.6	23.9	29.5	26.5	27.2	24.5	21.5	24.4	26.5	26.7	23.6	23.2	23.2	26.8
3. Quite important	13.2	13.2	13.4	12.8	18.8	12.3	15.2	13.3	10.7	13.9	11.8	11.9	14.1	13.0	15.4	7.6
4. Extremely important	13.2	13.1	13.0	12.5	19.9	14.6	14.0	13.7	8.9	13.1	14.1	11.2	12.3	15.3	16.6	28.4
Item 1510 Subject Q07 N	3157	1458	1561	2343	321	745	894	980	537	1832	999	1328	668	405	638	21
A007L: Working to correct social and economic inequalities																
1. Not important	22.9	26.3	19.9	25.6	12.3	26.4	23.3	18.0	26.2	20.4	27.2	21.1	25.7	21.2	25.9	24.4
2. Somewhat important	45.2	44.0	46.3	46.4	38.0	45.6	47.0	44.1	43.6	46.2	44.7	44.4	44.4	49.5	44.9	37.4
3. Quite important	22.8	22.4	23.2	20.8	30.9	18.8	23.0	26.9	20.6	23.5	21.1	25.3	22.5	21.2	19.6	13.3
4. Extremely important	9.1	7.3	10.6	7.3	18.9	9.2	6.6	11.1	9.6	10.0	7.0	9.2	7.4	8.2	9.6	24.9
Item 1520 Subject N02,O01,Q07 N	3141	1456	1549	2332	320	735	890	978	538	1826	992	1323	664	404	634	21
A007M: Discovering new ways to experience things																
1. Not important	7.9	9.3	6.8	8.2	7.1	8.7	7.6	8.0	7.3	6.4	10.1	9.2	7.5	6.4	7.5	9.4
2. Somewhat important	33.8	34.2	34.0	35.4	30.8	34.2	35.7	33.1	31.6	34.6	34.3	35.4	40.3	31.4	26.1	17.8
3. Quite important	38.6	38.5	39.3	37.9	41.7	34.4	40.0	38.6	42.1	37.7	40.1	37.3	36.2	46.9	37.4	47.8
4. Extremely important	19.6	18.0	19.9	18.5	20.4	22.7	16.6	20.2	19.0	21.3	15.5	18.1	16.1	15.3	29.0	24.9
Item 1530 Subject Q07 N	3152	1452	1562	2339	321	740	894	979	539	1828	998	1328	666	404	638	21
A007N: Finding purpose and meaning in my life																
1. Not important	3.4	5.5	1.2	3.6	1.2	4.8	2.8	1.9	5.1	2.7	4.2	2.7	3.9	1.8	4.9	21.2
2. Somewhat important	11.6	14.1	8.9	12.5	4.6	14.1	11.7	10.0	11.0	11.3	11.7	11.3	13.7	8.0	12.5	9.3
3. Quite important	27.1	30.6	24.4	28.9	22.4	24.3	31.1	24.9	28.4	24.8	31.7	27.7	25.2	32.7	24.2	40.1
4. Extremely important	57.9	49.8	65.5	55.0	71.8	56.9	54.4	63.2	55.5	61.2	52.4	58.2	57.2	57.5	58.3	29.3
Item 1540 Subject Q07 N	3154	1458	1561	2343	321	742	893	980	539	1830	998	1326	669	406	635	21
A008: Generally speaking, would you say that most people can be trusted or that you can't be too careful in dealing with people?																
3. Most people can be trusted	25.1	26.6	24.6	28.1	7.8	22.4	29.7	20.6	29.3	28.5	20.3	27.8	24.4	24.6	21.4	23.9
2. Don't know, undecided	28.1	28.4	27.3	28.2	21.1	32.9	27.2	24.3	29.9	28.3	27.5	29.0	27.3	30.6	24.5	18.4
1. Can't be too careful	46.8	45.0	48.1	43.7	71.2	44.7	43.1	55.1	40.8	43.1	52.2	43.2	48.2	44.8	54.1	57.7
Item 1550 Subject Q05 N	3088	1421	1537	2305	310	725	881	960	522	1800	978	1308	653	397	617	20
A009: Would you say that most of the time people try to be helpful or that they are mostly just looking out for themselves?																
3. Try to be helpful	29.8	27.6	32.6	30.4	27.8	29.0	29.9	28.2	33.8	31.7	28.9	33.0	26.9	28.5	26.8	28.4
2. Don't know, undecided	32.8	34.3	31.4	34.3	25.7	33.9	36.8	29.8	30.0	33.9	31.4	30.5	37.0	31.5	34.2	22.9
1. Just looking out for themselves	37.4	38.1	36.0	35.3	46.5	37.1	33.3	42.0	36.1	34.4	39.7	36.4	36.1	40.0	39.1	48.7
Item 1560 Subject Q05 N	3153	1457	1560	2340	322	744	890	980	539	1834	996	1327	665	406	639	21
A010: Do you think most people would try to take advantage of you if they got a chance or would they try to be fair?																
3. Would try to be fair	27.0	26.8	27.5	28.6	12.3	28.2	29.1	21.8	31.4	29.2	25.2	29.2	25.6	24.7	25.6	21.4
2. Don't know, undecided	32.6	31.2	34.0	35.0	23.6	32.5	31.2	33.9	32.6	33.0	32.4	32.8	31.9	34.8	31.5	22.5
1. Would try to take advantage of you	40.5	42.0	38.5	36.4	64.0	39.3	39.7	44.4	36.0	37.8	42.5	38.0	42.5	40.4	42.9	56.1
Item 1570 Subject Q05 N	3150	1456	1560	2339	322	744	889	979	538	1833	996	1327	665	406	637	21

QUESTIONNAIRE FORM 1 1986	TOTAL	SEX		RACE		REGION				4YR COLLEGE PLANS		ILLICIT DRUG USE: LIFETIME				
		M	F	White	Black	NE	NC	S	W	Yes	No	None	Mari-juana Only	Few Pills	More Pills	Any Her-oin
N (Weighted No. of Cases): % of Weighted Total:	3179 100.0	1469 46.2	1562 49.1	2351 74.0	323 10.2	749 23.5	897 28.2	984 30.9	550 17.3	1841 57.9	999 31.4	1333 41.9	671 21.1	406 12.8	643 20.2	21 0.7

A011: These next questions ask your opinions about a number of different topics. How much do you agree or disagree with each statement below?

A011A: I feel that you can't be a good citizen unless you always obey the law

	TOTAL	M	F	White	Black	NE	NC	S	W	Yes	No	None	Mari-juana Only	Few Pills	More Pills	Any Her-oin
1. Disagree	19.6	20.6	18.2	18.9	20.7	23.6	19.3	17.9	17.6	18.0	20.4	15.6	21.4	20.0	25.6	20.6
2. Mostly disagree	18.3	18.7	18.1	19.8	8.9	18.9	19.9	14.0	22.6	19.1	18.4	15.1	18.7	22.1	22.1	30.4
3. Neither	21.2	20.6	21.9	22.6	14.5	24.0	24.1	17.2	19.6	21.6	22.4	19.4	21.1	22.9	23.8	26.7
4. Mostly agree	30.4	29.9	31.9	31.0	33.8	25.0	29.8	34.2	32.3	31.9	28.0	36.0	27.2	27.6	24.8	22.3
5. Agree	10.5	10.3	10.0	7.7	22.2	8.6	6.9	16.6	8.0	9.4	10.8	14.0	11.5	7.5	3.8	-
Item 1580 Subject H03 N	3150	1457	1558	2339	321	740	891	979	539	1830	996	1327	667	404	636	21

A011B: I feel a good citizen should go along with whatever the government does even if he disagrees with it

	TOTAL	M	F	White	Black	NE	NC	S	W	Yes	No	None	Mari-juana Only	Few Pills	More Pills	Any Her-oin
1. Disagree	39.0	38.5	39.0	37.1	53.2	44.6	36.9	38.4	36.1	38.8	37.6	36.6	39.4	40.2	43.1	20.7
2. Mostly disagree	24.9	23.8	26.9	26.1	17.1	24.6	27.2	22.2	26.1	26.2	24.0	23.6	26.0	28.9	25.4	22.1
3. Neither	18.3	18.2	18.8	19.5	11.7	17.1	18.8	18.1	19.7	17.8	20.5	20.3	16.5	16.7	16.5	36.0
4. Mostly agree	13.5	14.4	12.0	13.7	12.2	9.5	14.2	15.3	14.3	14.0	12.5	14.2	13.6	11.3	11.9	21.2
5. Agree	4.3	5.0	3.4	3.6	5.8	4.2	2.9	6.0	3.8	3.1	5.4	5.3	4.4	2.8	3.0	-
Item 1590 Subject H03 N	3150	1457	1559	2340	321	741	891	980	539	1831	997	1328	668	404	637	21

A011C: I feel a good citizen tries to change the government policies he disagrees with

	TOTAL	M	F	White	Black	NE	NC	S	W	Yes	No	None	Mari-juana Only	Few Pills	More Pills	Any Her-oin
1. Disagree	8.8	8.3	8.7	7.7	12.3	10.9	6.8	9.7	7.6	6.9	11.1	8.1	9.0	9.4	8.8	-
2. Mostly disagree	11.3	9.9	12.9	10.9	11.5	11.3	10.8	10.9	13.0	11.2	12.3	10.1	11.8	12.7	13.0	13.4
3. Neither	27.7	25.0	29.5	27.6	26.2	26.7	31.7	26.1	25.3	27.2	27.7	26.4	27.1	29.2	28.6	49.1
4. Mostly agree	30.1	31.8	29.7	32.3	25.5	28.3	31.9	29.1	31.3	32.0	28.1	31.7	31.6	27.9	27.2	21.0
5. Agree	22.1	25.0	19.3	21.5	24.5	22.8	18.9	24.2	22.8	22.8	20.9	23.7	20.5	20.8	22.4	16.5
Item 1600 Subject H03 N	3133	1449	1550	2332	319	731	888	975	539	1821	990	1318	666	402	635	21

A011D: The way people vote has a major impact on how things are run in this country

	TOTAL	M	F	White	Black	NE	NC	S	W	Yes	No	None	Mari-juana Only	Few Pills	More Pills	Any Her-oin
1. Disagree	5.7	6.2	4.9	5.9	3.2	6.2	4.8	6.3	5.3	5.5	5.9	4.4	4.9	5.0	10.2	-
2. Mostly disagree	9.0	8.9	9.0	10.0	5.4	9.5	9.8	7.5	9.5	8.6	9.5	8.2	8.9	9.4	10.4	16.4
3. Neither	14.8	15.1	14.8	15.6	9.0	14.3	17.7	13.5	13.2	15.3	14.5	15.1	15.6	15.9	12.8	15.1
4. Mostly agree	33.8	33.3	34.8	34.0	30.8	31.4	37.1	31.2	36.4	35.8	31.6	35.6	33.0	33.1	31.2	34.5
5. Agree	36.7	36.6	36.5	34.4	51.5	38.7	30.6	41.4	35.5	34.8	38.5	36.7	37.7	36.7	35.4	34.1
Item 1610 Subject H05,I02 N	3142	1457	1552	2334	321	740	892	972	538	1825	996	1326	667	403	634	21

A011E: People who get together in citizen action groups to influence government policies can have a real effect

	TOTAL	M	F	White	Black	NE	NC	S	W	Yes	No	None	Mari-juana Only	Few Pills	More Pills	Any Her-oin
1. Disagree	3.6	4.0	2.7	3.2	3.2	4.3	2.8	4.7	2.4	2.6	4.4	2.7	2.4	4.4	6.5	-
2. Mostly disagree	9.0	9.3	8.6	9.6	6.2	11.0	8.8	8.3	7.9	9.4	8.7	8.1	8.8	11.4	9.2	8.2
3. Neither	26.3	24.1	28.7	27.8	23.1	27.7	30.1	22.8	24.5	24.4	30.4	26.4	26.1	24.3	28.0	23.6
4. Mostly agree	39.1	41.0	37.5	39.9	32.2	36.5	39.8	38.7	42.2	41.0	36.2	39.5	42.2	39.3	34.8	56.4
5. Agree	22.0	21.6	22.5	19.4	35.3	20.6	18.5	25.6	23.2	22.7	20.3	23.5	20.4	20.6	21.5	11.8
Item 1620 Subject H03,I02 N	3134	1450	1551	2328	321	738	888	970	538	1821	993	1325	665	402	630	21

A011F: Despite its many faults, our system of doing things is still the best in the world

	TOTAL	M	F	White	Black	NE	NC	S	W	Yes	No	None	Mari-juana Only	Few Pills	More Pills	Any Her-oin
1. Disagree	5.9	4.5	6.5	4.7	11.2	6.5	4.1	6.8	6.5	4.4	7.1	5.7	4.7	5.9	6.2	3.4
2. Mostly disagree	6.8	6.1	7.2	5.8	8.6	7.9	7.5	5.7	5.8	5.9	8.4	6.1	8.0	5.8	7.3	8.7
3. Neither	21.6	17.5	25.3	20.4	27.3	25.9	22.8	19.4	17.7	20.7	22.5	22.2	21.2	21.0	20.7	24.2
4. Mostly agree	32.2	32.6	32.4	31.8	33.6	29.6	32.6	32.0	35.1	32.8	32.2	31.1	35.9	34.8	29.8	34.7
5. Agree	33.6	39.2	28.6	37.3	19.3	30.0	33.1	36.0	34.9	36.3	29.9	34.9	30.3	32.5	36.0	29.1
Item 1630 Subject H04 N	3137	1452	1550	2334	316	738	886	975	538	1822	991	1326	664	403	631	21

QUESTIONNAIRE FORM 1 1986	TOTAL	SEX		RACE		REGION				4YR COLLEGE PLANS		ILLICIT DRUG USE: LIFETIME				
		M	F	White	Black	NE	NC	S	W	Yes	No	None	Marijuana Only	Few Pills	More Pills	Any Heroin
N (Weighted No. of Cases):	3179	1469	1562	2351	323	749	897	984	550	1841	999	1333	671	406	643	21
% of Weighted Total:	100.0	46.2	49.1	74.0	10.2	23.5	28.2	30.9	17.3	57.9	31.4	41.9	21.1	12.8	20.2	0.7

A011G: America needs growth to survive, and that is going to require some increase in pollution

1. Disagree	33.0	32.1	34.3	34.0	34.0	34.2	31.5	32.3	35.3	34.1	32.1	32.2	32.1	32.6	37.4	30.2
2. Mostly disagree	21.9	23.1	21.4	23.5	11.9	20.8	23.9	19.9	23.8	23.6	19.6	21.3	21.8	24.6	22.6	15.3
3. Neither	24.5	22.6	25.8	24.7	25.4	24.2	26.8	22.8	23.9	24.6	24.2	24.5	25.7	25.8	22.2	23.4
4. Mostly agree	13.3	14.7	12.2	12.6	16.6	12.5	13.6	15.3	10.2	12.2	15.3	14.0	14.0	11.5	11.8	19.3
5. Agree	7.2	7.4	6.4	5.1	12.2	8.3	4.1	9.5	6.8	5.5	8.8	8.0	6.6	5.4	6.1	11.9
Item 1640 Subject F04 N	3134	1451	1550	2330	320	736	888	975	536	1820	992	1328	664	401	629	21

A011H: If we just leave things to God, they will turn out for the best

1. Disagree	21.4	24.7	18.2	23.3	6.8	32.5	21.0	11.0	25.3	22.8	18.2	17.2	23.8	21.7	28.6	19.7
2. Mostly disagree	13.6	14.7	13.1	14.6	5.7	14.5	15.7	9.6	16.3	14.1	13.4	11.9	13.7	17.6	15.1	11.0
3. Neither	25.2	23.4	27.0	27.4	13.4	27.4	28.9	19.2	26.8	26.4	24.3	24.9	25.7	24.4	26.1	35.1
4. Mostly agree	18.0	16.5	19.2	16.8	22.1	12.2	17.7	24.3	14.8	17.5	18.3	20.2	17.6	16.1	14.0	11.0
5. Agree	21.9	20.6	22.5	17.9	52.1	13.5	16.6	35.9	16.8	19.3	25.9	25.8	19.3	20.2	16.2	23.2
Item 1650 Subject I02 N	3116	1436	1547	2314	319	737	881	964	534	1811	987	1314	663	402	627	19

A011I: Going to school has been an enjoyable experience for me

1. Disagree	6.7	7.2	5.4	6.7	4.2	9.4	6.5	5.0	6.3	4.0	9.8	4.4	5.6	7.6	10.5	30.5
2. Mostly disagree	8.2	8.5	7.7	8.1	7.8	7.5	8.2	8.0	9.2	6.5	10.6	8.0	8.1	6.5	9.4	10.5
3. Neither	16.2	15.7	16.6	17.9	8.8	16.6	16.9	14.3	17.9	15.4	17.7	14.7	15.3	19.1	18.3	17.8
4. Mostly agree	41.7	42.8	41.2	44.1	32.5	41.9	43.3	41.3	39.2	44.3	39.6	41.2	42.8	44.9	40.1	34.2
5. Agree	27.3	25.8	29.0	23.2	46.8	24.5	25.1	31.4	27.3	29.8	22.3	31.8	28.2	22.0	21.7	7.1
Item 1660 Subject B01 N	3137	1451	1553	2334	320	741	888	970	538	1822	996	1321	666	403	634	21

A011J: Doing well in school is important for getting a good job

1. Disagree	2.9	4.0	1.6	2.8	2.8	3.0	2.4	2.6	4.5	1.9	4.5	1.8	2.0	3.4	6.1	-
2. Mostly disagree	3.2	4.9	1.6	3.4	2.0	4.4	2.5	2.6	3.8	2.7	3.2	2.2	4.1	3.6	3.9	9.4
3. Neither	5.9	7.3	4.5	6.6	1.8	7.4	5.9	4.9	5.6	4.4	8.0	4.4	5.6	5.9	8.2	9.6
4. Mostly agree	31.0	31.3	30.5	32.2	24.5	31.3	33.6	27.1	33.1	30.9	30.9	30.2	32.3	34.4	29.5	44.6
5. Agree	57.0	52.5	61.9	54.9	68.9	54.0	55.6	62.8	52.9	60.1	53.4	61.4	56.0	52.7	52.3	36.3
Item 1670 Subject B01 N	3140	1454	1554	2334	321	739	886	976	539	1825	995	1325	667	403	634	21

The following questions are about CIGARETTE SMOKING.

B001: Have you ever smoked cigarettes?

1. Never–GO TO Q.B006	31.7	33.2	30.9	30.1	46.9	25.3	31.2	35.6	34.3	36.3	26.0	55.3	13.3	18.3	11.2	8.1
2. Once or twice	27.6	28.5	27.1	26.4	34.1	28.8	26.2	28.4	26.9	27.1	27.5	29.6	35.6	26.1	17.7	9.2
3. Occasionally but not regularly	18.9	20.1	18.2	20.5	11.5	17.2	20.1	18.4	20.2	20.7	17.0	8.8	27.5	27.7	23.7	41.2
4. Regularly in the past	6.4	5.6	7.1	6.8	0.3	7.8	7.3	5.2	5.4	6.0	6.8	2.3	7.6	9.6	11.8	20.5
5. Regularly now	15.3	12.6	16.8	16.2	7.3	20.9	15.1	12.4	13.1	10.0	22.7	3.9	16.0	18.2	35.6	21.0
Item 760 Subject A01a N	3084	1426	1525	2308	302	726	880	954	524	1792	973	1285	657	397	636	21

B002: When did you smoke your first cigarette?

0. Never smoked a cigarette	31.8	33.2	30.9	30.1	46.9	25.4	31.3	35.6	34.4	36.3	26.0	55.5	13.3	18.3	11.2	8.1
1. Grade 6 or earlier	17.6	20.8	14.3	18.7	12.4	15.0	20.4	18.1	15.6	16.1	19.0	13.9	17.6	17.6	25.2	34.2
2. Grade 7 or 8	21.5	19.0	23.9	22.5	14.3	28.7	19.8	19.7	17.8	19.9	23.9	12.0	30.5	25.8	29.5	33.9
3. Grade 9 (Freshman)	10.4	8.8	11.9	10.5	8.3	12.8	10.8	8.9	9.4	9.1	12.8	6.5	12.2	13.9	14.2	18.2
4. Grade 10 (Sophomore)	8.0	7.4	8.4	7.7	6.7	7.4	6.7	7.3	12.3	7.8	8.4	4.2	11.9	9.5	11.0	-
5. Grade 11 (Junior)	6.9	6.7	7.1	7.2	6.1	6.3	7.1	6.4	8.0	6.7	6.8	4.8	9.1	10.0	7.2	5.6
6. Grade 12 (Senior)	3.8	4.0	3.5	3.4	5.4	4.4	4.0	4.0	2.6	4.2	3.1	3.2	5.4	5.0	1.7	-
Item 1685 Subject A01g N★	3079	1423	1526	2308	302	724	879	953	524	1791	972	1282	655	399	634	21

★=excludes respondents for whom question was inappropriate.

QUESTIONNAIRE FORM 1 1986	TOTAL	SEX		RACE		REGION				4YR COLLEGE PLANS		ILLICIT DRUG USE: LIFETIME				
		M	F	White	Black	NE	NC	S	W	Yes	No	None	Mari- juana Only	Few Pills	More Pills	Any Her- oin
N (Weighted No. of Cases):	3179	1469	1562	2351	323	749	897	984	550	1841	999	1333	671	406	643	21
% of Weighted Total:	100.0	46.2	49.1	74.0	10.2	23.5	28.2	30.9	17.3	57.9	31.4	41.9	21.1	12.8	20.2	0.7
B003: How frequently have you smoked cigarettes during the past 30 days?																
1. Not at all	56.4	58.6	56.2	54.9	72.8	51.5	56.6	58.3	60.4	62.6	49.2	78.3	61.8	48.3	36.7	33.8
2. Less than one cigarette per day	15.1	16.3	14.3	15.8	10.9	12.7	16.3	15.5	15.8	17.1	12.3	11.8	14.8	23.5	14.3	21.6
3. One to five cigarettes per day	10.8	9.5	11.5	11.2	8.8	14.5	9.6	10.0	8.5	9.6	12.3	3.5	11.7	12.4	14.6	10.4
4. About one-half pack per day	8.2	6.1	9.6	8.4	5.2	10.7	7.8	6.9	7.1	5.4	11.7	3.2	4.6	9.9	14.7	16.2
5. About one pack per day	7.8	7.4	7.2	8.1	2.3	9.1	8.2	7.0	6.1	4.9	10.9	2.3	6.6	4.6	16.1	14.3
6. About one and one-half packs per day	1.1	1.2	0.9	1.1	-	0.8	0.8	1.4	1.4	0.4	2.1	-	0.3	1.2	2.7	-
7. Two packs or more per day	0.7	0.8	0.2	0.6	-	0.6	0.6	0.7	0.6	0.1	1.4	0.9	0.2	0.2	0.9	3.7
Item 780 Subject A01c N★	2106	955	1053	1615	160	541	605	616	345	1140	722	574	569	327	564	19
B004: Have you ever tried to stop smoking and found that you could not?																
1. Yes	15.9	12.6	17.1	14.6	14.4	20.6	14.9	14.8	11.9	11.7	18.9	9.4	12.4	11.5	26.8	17.2
2. No	84.1	87.4	82.9	85.4	85.6	79.4	85.1	85.2	88.1	88.3	81.1	90.6	87.6	88.5	73.2	82.8
Item 1690 Subject A01i N★	2027	916	1018	1571	143	526	586	581	334	1101	698	538	545	318	555	19
B005: Do you want to stop smoking now?																
1. Yes	14.5	12.2	15.5	14.0	9.9	17.8	13.1	14.8	10.9	11.5	18.1	5.5	14.4	17.4	20.8	10.0
2. No	20.5	19.4	20.6	21.6	14.5	21.5	20.0	19.3	21.8	16.3	25.6	9.0	14.9	22.2	35.0	44.8
8. Don't smoke now	65.1	68.4	63.9	64.4	75.6	60.7	66.9	65.9	67.3	72.2	56.2	85.5	70.7	60.4	44.3	45.2
Item 1700 Subject A01i N★	2086	951	1040	1607	154	534	599	613	340	1127	719	566	566	327	556	19
B006: Do you think you will be smoking cigarettes five years from now?																
1. I definitely will	0.7	0.7	0.6	0.7	-	0.5	0.9	0.8	0.5	0.4	1.2	0.5	0.6	0.2	1.4	3.4
2. I probably will	12.5	10.7	13.9	12.9	7.3	15.3	11.8	11.5	11.5	8.2	19.0	4.4	13.7	14.3	25.9	36.7
3. I probably will not	26.7	26.5	26.1	26.4	24.1	29.1	27.0	27.7	21.1	24.6	29.8	17.9	31.4	34.8	33.7	24.3
4. I definitely will not	60.1	62.2	59.4	60.0	68.6	55.1	60.3	60.0	66.9	66.9	50.0	77.2	54.3	50.7	39.1	35.7
Item 1710 Subject A04a N	3130	1446	1550	2337	314	735	884	976	536	1822	991	1318	664	402	634	21

The different questionnaire forms used in this study tend to emphasize somewhat different topics. The next major section in this form deals with alcohol and various other drugs. There is a lot of talk these days about these subjects, but very little accurate information. Therefore, we still have a lot to learn about the actual experiences and attitudes of people your age.

We hope that you can answer all questions; but if you find one which you feel you cannot answer honestly, we would prefer that you leave it blank.

Remember that your answers will be strictly confidential. We never connect them with your name or your class.

The next questions are about ALCOHOLIC BEVERAGES, including beer, wine, and liquor.

B007: On how many occasions (if any) have you had alcohol to drink . . .

B007A: . . . in your lifetime?

	TOTAL	M	F	White	Black	NE	NC	S	W	Yes	No	None	Mari- juana Only	Few Pills	More Pills	Any Her- oin
1. 0 occasions	8.0	6.6	8.8	5.5	17.7	5.6	7.1	10.6	8.1	7.8	8.0	16.2	0.6	2.0	1.1	-
2. 1-2	9.3	8.7	9.7	7.3	22.2	6.9	7.7	13.8	7.4	9.6	8.5	17.8	3.1	4.8	1.3	-
3. 3-5	9.2	8.4	10.3	8.1	15.5	8.2	8.0	10.9	9.5	9.0	9.8	14.2	7.2	8.1	1.3	-
4. 6-9	7.5	6.5	8.3	6.7	12.5	6.9	7.4	8.3	7.0	7.5	7.3	11.3	7.6	5.2	1.4	4.8
5. 10-19	12.9	12.1	14.4	13.8	9.1	13.1	13.4	10.9	15.1	13.6	12.9	13.5	17.6	11.9	8.3	-
6. 20-39	14.0	11.3	17.2	15.4	8.3	14.6	15.9	11.5	14.5	13.6	16.6	10.5	16.7	22.3	13.6	9.6
7. 40 or more	39.1	46.4	31.4	43.2	14.6	44.7	40.4	33.9	38.4	38.9	37.0	16.6	47.3	45.7	73.1	85.7
Item 810 Subject A01a N	3033	1420	1493	2296	295	717	859	933	524	1782	957	1287	642	395	620	21

★=excludes respondents for whom question was inappropriate.

QUESTIONNAIRE FORM 1 1986	TOTAL	SEX		RACE		REGION				4YR COLLEGE PLANS		ILLICIT DRUG USE: LIFETIME				
		M	F	White	Black	NE	NC	S	W	Yes	No	None	Mari- juana Only	Few Pills	More Pills	Any Her- oin
N (Weighted No. of Cases):	3179	1469	1562	2351	323	749	897	984	550	1841	999	1333	671	406	643	21
% of Weighted Total:	100.0	46.2	49.1	74.0	10.2	23.5	28.2	30.9	17.3	57.9	31.4	41.9	21.1	12.8	20.2	0.7
B007B: . . . during the last 12 months?																
1. 0 occasions	15.9	15.0	16.3	12.6	33.0	11.1	14.0	21.5	15.7	16.4	14.2	29.9	4.1	8.6	2.9	11.8
2. 1-2	15.1	13.3	17.2	13.1	27.0	15.5	12.3	18.0	13.8	14.1	17.9	24.0	10.8	11.9	3.2	-
3. 3-5	12.7	12.3	13.5	12.6	15.2	11.8	13.0	13.8	11.5	13.0	12.1	14.2	18.8	11.4	5.1	1.6
4. 6-9	11.5	9.6	13.4	11.7	7.5	11.6	12.5	9.9	12.4	11.5	12.6	10.3	14.3	12.3	10.9	14.3
5. 10-19	16.3	14.7	18.0	18.1	7.7	19.1	15.9	13.4	18.3	17.5	15.4	10.0	20.6	24.0	20.0	7.4
6. 20-39	11.9	12.3	11.9	13.6	3.7	12.3	14.4	9.7	11.3	12.7	10.2	6.6	13.0	15.3	19.7	24.9
7. 40 or more	16.6	22.9	9.7	18.3	6.0	18.6	17.8	13.8	17.1	14.8	17.6	5.0	18.5	16.5	38.3	39.9
Item 820 Subject A01b N	3018	1416	1483	2288	286	710	860	929	519	1777	948	1279	641	393	620	21
B007C: . . . during the last 30 days?																
1. 0 occasions	36.0	34.1	38.0	31.3	62.1	31.3	33.5	42.5	34.9	36.8	34.6	59.7	22.5	21.8	11.1	13.5
2. 1-2	21.8	18.1	25.9	21.7	20.9	22.8	20.0	20.8	25.3	21.7	22.6	20.6	27.2	25.1	18.2	3.9
3. 3-5	16.5	17.0	16.3	18.6	7.5	18.5	17.2	14.0	17.2	17.5	16.5	10.0	23.6	21.1	19.2	16.3
4. 6-9	12.5	13.0	11.9	14.2	3.9	14.0	15.6	10.3	9.4	12.6	11.8	5.5	13.6	16.0	23.2	18.8
5. 10-19	8.3	10.7	5.8	9.4	2.8	8.7	8.7	7.5	8.4	7.7	8.4	2.4	9.4	12.0	16.3	22.3
6. 20-39	2.8	3.7	1.7	2.9	1.9	2.9	2.9	2.5	2.9	2.6	2.7	0.8	2.0	1.8	8.0	7.8
7. 40 or more	2.1	3.4	0.5	1.9	0.8	1.9	2.1	2.3	1.9	1.0	3.4	1.1	1.7	2.3	4.1	17.5
Item 830 Subject A01c N	3029	1416	1496	2304	285	712	866	927	524	1780	953	1271	645	398	628	21

IF YOU HAVE NOT HAD ANY BEER, WINE, OR LIQUOR IN THE LAST TWELVE MONTHS, GO TO Q.B016.

B008: When you used alcohol during the last year, how often did you use it in each of the following situations?

B008A: When you were alone	TOTAL	M	F	White	Black	NE	NC	S	W	Yes	No	None	Mari- juana Only	Few Pills	More Pills	Any Her- oin
1. Not at all	70.9	64.1	78.6	71.7	71.4	71.3	73.5	67.8	70.9	73.4	67.4	80.7	74.6	67.6	55.8	57.3
2. A few of the times	22.5	26.3	18.2	22.1	20.1	22.0	21.9	23.6	22.1	22.2	22.5	15.1	19.7	24.8	34.0	21.5
3. Some of the times	5.0	6.9	2.5	5.1	4.6	5.6	3.4	5.6	5.7	3.4	7.1	2.7	4.1	5.3	8.7	14.3
4. Most of the times	1.2	2.0	0.5	0.7	2.6	1.1	0.8	2.1	0.8	0.9	2.0	0.7	1.1	2.2	1.2	6.8
5. Every time	0.5	0.7	0.2	0.4	1.3	-	0.4	0.9	0.6	0.1	1.1	0.8	0.5	-	0.3	-
Item 1720 Subject A05a N★	2540	1197	1247	2007	188	626	746	728	440	1477	813	884	616	362	606	17
B008B: With just 1 or 2 other people																
1. Not at all	13.3	12.3	14.5	12.6	16.2	16.4	13.4	10.6	13.2	16.0	9.5	22.5	11.5	8.4	5.3	-
2. A few of the times	33.8	29.7	37.5	33.1	36.4	34.2	33.0	32.3	36.9	34.4	32.9	35.8	37.1	33.8	27.3	9.5
3. Some of the times	24.8	27.8	21.4	25.5	15.1	28.4	27.5	20.1	23.1	24.3	23.5	14.9	24.4	28.1	35.8	69.7
4. Most of the times	20.5	21.8	19.3	21.4	18.3	15.7	18.6	26.3	20.8	19.2	23.3	15.2	20.7	22.9	27.1	20.8
5. Every time	7.7	8.4	7.3	7.4	13.9	5.3	7.5	10.8	6.0	6.1	10.8	11.5	6.4	6.8	4.5	-
Item 1730 Subject A05b N★	2541	1197	1247	2006	191	625	744	732	440	1476	816	885	617	361	606	17
B008C: At a party																
1. Not at all	13.9	12.3	15.9	13.0	27.1	11.5	13.4	17.5	12.0	13.6	15.3	26.1	9.6	8.1	4.8	-
2. A few of the times	17.9	15.7	20.1	16.4	28.9	14.0	17.7	20.3	20.0	19.0	17.4	24.8	16.2	16.0	11.8	-
3. Some of the times	16.3	15.6	16.1	15.7	15.7	18.3	14.9	15.4	17.1	15.5	16.6	14.6	14.8	17.5	18.4	12.4
4. Most of the times	33.5	34.3	33.3	36.4	16.1	37.9	35.4	29.3	30.9	36.6	28.7	22.7	40.9	37.0	39.3	52.1
5. Every time	18.4	22.0	14.6	18.5	12.2	18.3	18.5	17.6	20.0	15.4	21.9	11.9	18.6	21.4	25.8	35.5
Item 1740 Subject A05c N★	2545	1199	1247	2006	191	629	746	728	441	1485	811	890	614	362	606	18
B008D: When your date or spouse was present																
1. Not at all	36.7	44.3	29.7	33.9	56.5	37.8	32.4	38.1	39.8	37.0	37.1	55.7	32.2	31.3	17.7	4.5
2. A few of the times	26.5	23.9	28.1	26.4	20.6	26.5	26.5	26.2	26.7	27.0	24.1	21.5	29.0	28.2	29.1	19.8
3. Some of the times	18.1	18.1	18.5	19.7	9.1	16.8	20.2	18.1	16.4	18.4	16.9	9.3	20.6	22.6	26.0	30.2
4. Most of the times	12.4	9.8	15.0	13.4	6.8	14.9	11.6	12.0	11.1	12.2	13.3	6.4	13.4	11.9	20.2	39.4
5. Every time	6.4	3.9	8.8	6.6	7.0	4.0	9.2	5.7	6.0	5.3	8.6	7.1	4.9	5.9	7.0	6.1
Item 1750 Subject A05b N★	2524	1190	1238	1993	188	617	741	723	442	1470	811	874	614	361	602	18

★=excludes respondents for whom question was inappropriate.

QUESTIONNAIRE FORM 1 1986	TOTAL	SEX		RACE		REGION				4YR COLLEGE PLANS		ILLICIT DRUG USE: LIFETIME				
		M	F	White	Black	NE	NC	S	W	Yes	No	None	Mari-juana Only	Few Pills	More Pills	Any Her-oin
N (Weighted No. of Cases):	3179	1469	1562	2351	323	749	897	984	550	1841	999	1333	671	406	643	21
% of Weighted Total:	100.0	46.2	49.1	74.0	10.2	23.5	28.2	30.9	17.3	57.9	31.4	41.9	21.1	12.8	20.2	0.7
B008E: When people over age 30 were present																
1. Not at all	37.0	36.9	37.5	35.8	58.7	31.4	35.4	40.8	41.4	37.0	38.3	42.5	42.5	37.0	23.5	10.4
2. A few of the times	37.7	37.7	37.4	37.7	28.2	41.4	38.1	34.6	36.6	39.2	34.0	31.7	37.8	41.9	43.6	56.2
3. Some of the times	14.5	14.3	14.0	14.9	8.2	17.6	14.4	13.7	11.5	14.0	14.3	9.5	12.2	15.1	23.3	17.6
4. Most of the times	5.8	6.1	5.7	6.3	2.4	5.0	6.2	6.4	5.0	4.5	8.5	6.1	4.8	4.5	7.0	15.9
5. Every time	5.1	5.0	5.3	5.3	2.5	4.7	5.9	4.5	5.4	5.3	4.9	10.2	2.7	1.5	2.7	-
Item 1760 Subject A05b N★	2539	1197	1248	2007	190	623	745	731	441	1479	815	887	615	361	605	18
B008F: During the daytime (before 4:00 p.m.)																
1. Not at all	56.4	49.6	63.9	55.0	70.6	54.4	59.0	56.8	54.2	57.0	57.1	71.9	61.2	50.9	34.0	11.1
2. A few of the times	30.4	32.0	28.7	32.1	18.3	32.6	30.4	27.7	31.6	32.7	26.5	20.8	27.8	36.1	41.8	49.2
3. Some of the times	10.3	14.4	5.8	10.3	7.7	9.8	8.4	11.1	12.7	8.8	11.1	4.4	8.7	11.3	20.0	30.7
4. Most of the times	1.9	2.6	0.8	1.7	1.4	2.6	1.2	2.5	1.1	0.7	3.6	1.4	1.6	1.7	2.6	9.0
5. Every time	1.1	1.4	0.8	1.0	2.0	0.7	1.1	1.9	0.4	0.8	1.7	1.5	0.7	-	1.6	-
Item 1770 Subject A05c N★	2541	1195	1249	2006	189	625	744	732	441	1479	816	887	615	360	609	18
B008G: At your home (or apartment or dorm)																
1. Not at all	38.6	38.7	39.2	37.6	40.4	32.6	37.9	43.5	40.5	39.4	38.5	48.3	39.4	37.5	25.6	26.0
2. A few of the times	33.4	30.2	36.5	34.3	30.2	36.0	34.6	31.9	30.4	35.6	29.7	27.8	35.4	38.2	35.0	39.5
3. Some of the times	16.5	19.1	13.5	16.3	17.2	17.8	16.8	13.8	18.5	15.5	16.4	10.9	15.6	14.8	26.6	30.8
4. Most of the times	7.7	7.9	7.4	7.8	8.3	10.9	6.9	6.8	6.0	6.0	11.2	6.2	7.4	8.7	10.1	3.7
5. Every time	3.7	4.2	3.4	3.9	3.9	2.7	3.8	4.0	4.5	3.5	4.2	6.8	2.2	0.8	2.7	-
Item 1780 Subject A05c N★	2540	1195	1247	2005	189	623	745	732	441	1476	816	888	612	361	609	18
B008H: At school																
1. Not at all	85.7	80.4	91.7	86.5	88.2	83.1	89.5	85.4	83.1	89.1	81.2	92.9	88.3	86.1	73.5	58.7
2. A few of the times	10.7	13.9	7.0	9.9	8.9	12.8	8.7	10.7	11.2	8.4	14.4	5.7	8.8	10.4	19.5	19.3
3. Some of the times	2.9	4.5	1.1	2.8	2.2	3.2	1.5	3.0	4.5	1.9	3.3	0.4	2.2	3.3	6.3	22.0
4. Most of the times	0.4	0.7	0.2	0.5	0.6	0.8	*	0.3	0.8	0.5	0.4	0.2	0.7	0.2	0.6	-
5. Every time	0.3	0.6	0.1	0.3	-	-	0.3	0.6	0.3	0.1	0.6	0.8	-	-	0.1	-
Item 1790 Subject A05c N★	2542	1197	1246	2007	189	625	745	732	440	1479	817	887	613	362	609	18
B008I: In a car																
1. Not at all	42.2	38.5	46.2	41.3	50.2	49.2	38.7	37.8	45.5	45.5	38.5	61.3	36.9	32.9	25.6	19.5
2. A few of the times	27.3	26.5	27.9	27.6	28.4	27.1	27.7	25.6	29.8	27.2	26.5	21.9	30.6	31.4	30.4	20.3
3. Some of the times	17.1	19.7	14.7	17.5	10.3	17.2	17.5	17.1	16.5	15.6	18.7	8.4	19.0	20.6	25.5	21.8
4. Most of the times	10.7	12.4	8.9	11.1	7.7	5.3	13.2	14.8	7.5	9.6	12.9	6.3	11.4	12.7	14.9	32.2
5. Every time	2.6	2.8	2.2	2.5	3.3	1.2	2.9	4.7	0.8	2.1	3.4	2.1	2.2	2.5	3.7	6.1
Item 1810 Subject A05c N★	2542	1197	1247	2008	188	625	744	733	441	1479	817	888	613	362	609	18
B009: What have been the most important reasons for your drinking alcoholic beverages? (Mark all that apply.)																
A. To experiment–to see what it's like	42.5	40.7	44.3	39.8	60.7	39.3	37.8	46.8	47.8	44.8	39.1	55.1	39.5	35.7	31.6	34.4
B. To relax or relieve tension	39.9	37.6	41.8	42.9	19.7	41.6	38.7	38.6	41.5	39.1	40.1	31.7	36.1	45.8	52.3	41.1
C. To feel good or get high	49.9	52.0	46.6	52.0	31.7	55.1	47.4	48.0	50.1	49.6	49.0	27.3	55.0	56.9	71.3	73.6
D. To seek deeper insights and understanding	3.7	4.8	2.5	3.0	3.6	2.0	3.5	4.8	4.7	3.7	3.2	2.3	2.4	5.6	5.9	-
E. To have a good time with my friends	75.1	77.1	74.1	78.4	59.7	78.4	77.6	70.6	73.9	76.0	74.1	64.7	81.6	81.2	79.9	72.9
F. To fit in with a group I like	12.1	15.3	9.0	12.0	10.5	9.2	12.0	15.2	11.3	11.8	12.6	12.2	13.3	11.1	11.4	30.1
G. To get away from my problems or troubles	22.9	19.7	26.1	23.7	16.0	22.2	22.8	24.2	22.0	22.4	24.0	10.9	21.9	31.5	35.6	35.1
H. Because of boredom, nothing else to do	22.3	22.6	22.0	22.7	22.0	21.3	24.8	23.9	16.9	22.0	21.1	15.7	20.1	23.8	33.4	11.1
I. Because of anger or frustration	18.8	17.0	20.6	19.8	8.0	16.7	16.9	22.7	18.4	17.6	21.1	10.1	17.2	23.7	29.3	32.2
J. To get through the day	2.2	1.6	2.4	2.0	2.2	2.3	2.0	2.0	2.7	1.5	2.4	0.8	1.7	1.9	4.9	-
K. To increase the effects of some other drug(s)	6.2	8.0	3.2	6.0	3.4	8.3	5.7	4.8	6.2	4.2	7.0	-	2.8	2.7	19.4	43.1
L. To decrease (offset) the effects of some other drug(s)	0.9	1.1	0.5	0.8	-	1.6	0.7	0.3	1.0	0.7	0.6	-	0.3	-	3.1	3.9
M. To get to sleep	7.1	8.5	5.2	6.8	8.9	7.1	5.9	8.6	6.8	6.3	8.0	4.0	8.3	8.5	9.4	15.3
N. Because it tastes good	47.2	47.9	47.1	51.0	25.3	48.8	53.3	43.1	41.6	48.3	45.1	43.2	47.4	48.7	53.8	48.3
O. Because I am "hooked"–I feel I have to drink	0.9	1.0	0.6	0.7	0.4	1.0	0.9	0.7	0.8	0.6	0.9	0.5	0.2	0.3	2.2	-
Item 1820-1960 Subject A06a N★	2487	1177	1219	1966	184	608	730	721	428	1449	797	846	610	362	601	17

*=less than .05 per cent.   ★=excludes respondents for whom question was inappropriate.

QUESTIONNAIRE FORM 1 1986	TOTAL	SEX		RACE		REGION				4YR COLLEGE PLANS		ILLICIT DRUG USE: LIFETIME				
		M	F	White	Black	NE	NC	S	W	Yes	No	None	Mari- juana Only	Few Pills	More Pills	Any Her- oin
N (Weighted No. of Cases):	3179	1469	1562	2351	323	749	897	984	550	1841	999	1333	671	406	643	21
% of Weighted Total:	100.0	46.2	49.1	74.0	10.2	23.5	28.2	30.9	17.3	57.9	31.4	41.9	21.1	12.8	20.2	0.7

B010: When you drink alcoholic beverages, how high do you usually get?

	TOTAL	M	F	White	Black	NE	NC	S	W	Yes	No	None	Mari- juana Only	Few Pills	More Pills	Any Her- oin
1. Not at all high	18.5	16.1	21.3	16.4	35.0	13.3	18.5	23.8	16.6	19.2	19.2	39.0	7.4	9.8	5.2	12.1
2. A little high	34.7	32.6	37.1	35.5	33.2	34.1	35.8	33.6	35.4	37.1	31.3	37.3	39.1	32.1	29.3	31.6
3. Moderately high	39.8	42.8	36.5	41.4	26.6	44.2	38.6	37.1	40.0	37.8	42.6	20.8	48.3	53.5	48.9	26.4
4. Very high	7.1	8.5	5.1	6.7	5.2	8.3	7.1	5.6	8.0	6.0	6.9	2.9	5.2	4.7	16.5	30.0
Item 1970 Subject A01e N★	2531	1194	1243	2003	189	622	742	731	436	1476	811	883	617	360	601	17

B011: When you drink alcoholic beverages, how long do you usually stay high?

	TOTAL	M	F	White	Black	NE	NC	S	W	Yes	No	None	Mari- juana Only	Few Pills	More Pills	Any Her- oin
1. Usually don't get high	20.9	19.2	23.2	18.8	39.3	15.9	21.7	25.7	18.4	22.4	20.0	41.4	12.5	11.4	6.5	12.1
2. One to two hours	40.6	38.3	43.1	42.2	32.5	39.4	39.6	39.8	45.3	43.3	36.8	37.5	44.8	49.0	36.3	15.9
3. Three to six hours	34.9	38.8	30.5	35.7	23.8	40.4	35.3	30.9	33.1	31.8	38.8	18.6	40.0	36.5	51.0	53.7
4. Seven to 24 hours	3.2	3.0	3.1	3.0	3.4	4.2	2.9	3.0	2.7	2.2	3.9	2.2	2.4	3.1	5.2	18.3
5. More than 24 hours	0.4	0.8	0.1	0.4	1.1	0.1	0.4	0.7	0.5	0.2	0.6	0.3	0.3	-	1.0	-
Item 1980 Subject A01f N★	2509	1184	1232	1985	185	614	736	724	436	1464	803	867	612	362	602	17

The following questions ask about how much you have to drink on the occasions when you drink alcoholic beverages. For these questions, a "drink" means any of the following: A 12-ounce can (or bottle) of beer, a 4-ounce glass of wine, a mixed drink or shot glass of liquor.

B012: Think back over the LAST TWO WEEKS. How many times have you had five or more drinks in a row?

	TOTAL	M	F	White	Black	NE	NC	S	W	Yes	No	None	Mari- juana Only	Few Pills	More Pills	Any Her- oin
1. None	60.4	49.5	71.3	57.8	82.9	57.9	57.2	66.4	59.5	63.0	58.0	79.6	58.8	55.2	38.5	30.2
2. Once	13.0	14.8	11.8	14.0	6.6	13.8	13.1	10.1	16.6	13.8	11.8	9.0	16.1	17.8	13.0	20.0
3. Twice	11.0	13.7	8.2	11.8	4.0	13.8	12.1	8.0	10.3	10.4	11.7	5.1	12.5	12.1	16.7	16.3
4. 3 to 5 times	10.9	15.3	6.8	12.0	4.4	10.8	12.1	10.1	10.4	9.5	13.0	3.9	10.0	11.8	21.3	15.6
5. 6 to 9 times	3.0	3.9	1.5	2.8	1.4	2.5	3.8	3.1	2.4	2.5	2.8	0.8	2.0	2.5	7.5	-
6. 10 or more times	1.6	2.9	0.3	1.6	0.6	1.2	1.7	2.3	0.7	0.8	2.6	1.4	0.6	0.6	3.0	17.8
Item 850 Subject A01d N★	2512	1181	1238	1987	188	626	735	717	434	1463	807	880	610	360	594	18

B013: During the last two weeks, how many times have you had 3 or 4 drinks in a row (but no more than that)?

	TOTAL	M	F	White	Black	NE	NC	S	W	Yes	No	None	Mari- juana Only	Few Pills	More Pills	Any Her- oin
1. None	57.0	51.1	63.3	54.4	77.2	54.1	56.0	60.2	57.6	58.4	56.7	75.9	55.1	50.1	37.0	11.1
2. Once	19.4	20.0	18.8	19.9	11.8	21.0	18.2	17.9	21.5	19.0	19.2	14.4	23.7	24.0	18.9	38.3
3. Twice	12.5	14.2	10.9	13.7	5.7	13.0	13.1	10.8	13.2	12.3	12.5	5.3	12.1	15.9	21.2	15.1
4. 3 to 5 times	8.6	11.1	5.9	9.3	5.3	9.4	9.2	8.7	6.3	8.4	8.7	3.1	6.9	9.3	17.5	24.8
5. 6 to 9 times	1.6	1.7	1.1	1.7	-	2.1	2.1	1.0	1.0	1.2	1.7	0.6	1.9	0.7	3.0	4.6
6. 10 or more times	1.0	1.8	*	1.0	-	0.5	1.3	1.5	0.3	0.7	1.2	0.8	0.3	-	2.5	6.1
Item 1990 Subject A01d N★	2521	1189	1240	1999	186	620	745	721	434	1472	808	880	612	358	603	18

B014A: During the last two weeks, how many times have you had two drinks in a row (but no more than that)?

	TOTAL	M	F	White	Black	NE	NC	S	W	Yes	No	None	Mari- juana Only	Few Pills	More Pills	Any Her- oin
1. None	57.7	55.5	60.6	56.1	71.7	53.7	59.8	58.9	57.9	57.8	58.6	72.7	57.7	52.3	39.9	21.2
2. Once	20.2	18.9	21.4	20.5	14.6	22.7	19.0	20.3	18.2	21.0	19.5	15.6	21.6	19.8	25.9	31.4
3. Twice	11.1	12.8	9.6	11.9	7.7	11.5	10.5	10.2	12.9	11.6	9.9	5.7	11.7	14.9	16.2	8.6
4. 3 to 5 times	7.4	8.3	5.8	7.6	5.3	7.9	7.9	5.7	8.6	6.5	7.8	4.1	6.1	10.0	11.7	16.9
5. 6 to 9 times	2.0	1.8	2.1	2.3	-	2.6	1.0	2.7	1.7	1.7	2.5	1.1	2.1	1.3	2.8	17.3
6. 10 to 19 times	0.9	1.4	0.4	1.0	0.7	0.8	1.0	1.2	0.6	1.0	0.9	0.2	0.7	1.7	1.8	4.6
7. 20 or more times	0.7	1.2	0.1	0.6	-	0.8	0.7	0.9	-	0.4	0.8	0.7	0.1	-	1.7	-
Item 2000 Subject A01d N★	2486	1175	1218	1971	187	617	741	706	422	1450	802	873	606	351	593	18

*=less than .05 per cent.　　★=excludes respondents for whom question was inappropriate.

QUESTIONNAIRE FORM 1 1986	TOTAL	SEX		RACE		REGION				4YR COLLEGE PLANS		ILLICIT DRUG USE: LIFETIME				
		M	F	White	Black	NE	NC	S	W	Yes	No	None	Marijuana Only	Few Pills	More Pills	Any Heroin
N (Weighted No. of Cases):	3179	1469	1562	2351	323	749	897	984	550	1841	999	1333	671	406	643	21
% of Weighted Total:	100.0	46.2	49.1	74.0	10.2	23.5	28.2	30.9	17.3	57.9	31.4	41.9	21.1	12.8	20.2	0.7

B014B: During the last two weeks, how many times have you had just one drink?

1. None	57.9	58.4	57.9	57.0	65.6	56.8	60.0	59.3	53.9	57.6	58.5	68.4	54.8	49.5	51.1	58.3
2. Once	24.5	22.6	26.3	25.0	22.3	22.9	25.1	23.3	27.8	24.7	24.1	20.6	24.7	28.1	27.3	25.9
3. Twice	9.9	10.0	9.8	9.9	7.4	12.5	8.1	9.1	10.5	10.2	10.1	5.7	14.6	12.2	10.5	3.7
4. 3 to 5 times	5.1	5.4	4.5	5.3	3.4	4.9	5.2	4.9	5.6	5.0	4.9	3.1	4.4	7.1	7.7	12.0
5. 6 to 9 times	1.5	1.8	1.2	1.4	1.3	1.8	1.0	1.8	1.5	1.5	1.3	1.4	0.8	2.2	2.0	-
6. 10 to 19 times	0.8	1.2	0.3	0.9	-	0.8	0.7	1.0	0.5	0.6	0.7	0.5	0.5	0.6	1.2	-
7. 20 or more times	0.3	0.6	-	0.4	-	0.3	-	0.5	0.3	0.3	0.3	0.4	0.2	0.4	0.2	-
Item 2010 Subject A01d N★	2428	1136	1201	1929	177	606	713	699	411	1422	779	847	582	347	587	18

B015: Have you ever tried to stop using alcoholic beverages and found that you couldn't stop?

1. Yes	3.5	3.4	2.9	2.8	4.1	2.9	4.0	3.9	3.0	2.4	4.7	2.9	2.9	2.7	5.3	-
2. No	96.5	96.6	97.1	97.2	95.9	97.1	96.0	96.1	97.0	97.6	95.3	97.1	97.1	97.3	94.7	100.0
Item 2020 Subject A01i N★	2496	1177	1224	1983	183	619	730	717	430	1455	802	858	609	359	604	18

B016: When (if ever) did you first drink enough to feel drunk or very high?

0. Never got drunk	25.7	23.8	27.7	21.3	52.0	18.6	24.5	33.3	24.0	27.5	24.2	50.5	6.7	11.6	4.5	4.8
1. Grade 6 or earlier	4.1	6.2	1.5	4.3	1.7	5.5	3.5	3.4	4.5	3.4	4.2	1.2	3.4	3.5	11.0	14.3
2. Grade 7 or 8	16.1	17.3	14.4	17.4	4.3	19.8	17.3	13.7	13.4	13.8	17.6	6.2	17.2	19.5	33.8	18.6
3. Grade 9 (Freshman)	18.7	19.1	18.8	20.8	9.1	21.8	19.8	16.1	17.4	18.4	20.0	9.3	28.3	27.0	22.5	38.0
4. Grade 10 (Sophomore)	15.7	15.2	16.5	17.5	10.1	17.5	14.7	14.4	17.2	16.1	15.4	10.5	21.8	20.8	17.4	8.8
5. Grade 11 (Junior)	13.0	12.7	13.6	13.4	8.9	11.8	13.6	11.9	15.3	13.2	13.4	13.6	15.4	13.8	7.6	9.9
6. Grade 12 (Senior)	6.7	5.7	7.5	5.3	13.9	5.1	6.6	7.1	8.2	7.6	5.2	8.7	7.2	3.8	3.3	5.5
Item 2015 Subject A01g N	3058	1435	1505	2319	299	720	877	935	526	1792	965	1285	655	401	629	21

B017: Do you think you will be drinking alcoholic beverages five years from now?

1. I definitely will	16.2	18.5	13.5	18.5	4.4	22.2	20.1	9.5	13.8	17.6	13.6	9.3	17.8	21.5	26.9	19.0
2. I probably will	52.5	50.5	55.0	56.1	38.3	54.4	53.7	49.5	53.2	52.0	54.4	42.9	59.7	56.0	61.3	63.3
3. I probably will not	15.7	16.5	15.2	13.2	25.9	12.6	13.3	20.6	15.1	14.2	17.5	21.7	14.5	13.5	6.5	5.3
4. I definitely will not	15.6	14.4	16.3	12.2	31.4	10.8	12.9	20.4	17.9	16.3	14.5	26.1	8.0	9.0	5.3	12.4
Item 2030 Subject A04a N	3143	1460	1555	2339	322	737	890	974	541	1830	993	1325	670	405	640	20

The next questions are about MARIJUANA and HASHISH.

Marijuana is sometimes called: grass, pot, dope.

Hashish is sometimes called: hash, hash oil.

B018: On how many occasions (if any) have you used hashish . . .

B018A: . . . in your lifetime?

1. 0 occasions	81.2	77.9	85.6	80.3	90.8	71.6	83.4	88.2	78.0	85.3	77.9	100.0	84.7	73.6	44.2	17.3
2. 1-2	8.6	9.1	8.0	9.0	4.0	13.2	7.4	5.9	9.2	7.6	9.5	-	10.1	17.2	19.8	15.0
3. 3-5	2.8	3.7	2.0	3.1	2.3	4.3	2.7	1.7	2.9	2.4	3.4	-	2.1	4.5	8.3	5.9
4. 6-9	2.2	3.0	1.1	2.2	1.9	3.1	2.0	1.2	2.9	1.5	2.2	-	1.2	2.0	7.6	5.3
5. 10-19	2.0	2.2	1.7	2.2	0.2	3.1	1.4	1.1	3.1	1.6	2.1	-	0.7	2.1	7.7	-
6. 20-39	1.1	1.2	0.6	1.0	0.4	1.1	1.3	0.8	1.2	0.5	1.4	-	0.2	0.3	4.3	9.9
7. 40 or more	2.2	2.9	1.0	2.2	0.4	3.8	1.9	1.1	2.7	1.1	3.6	-	1.0	0.3	8.2	46.7
Item 2040 Subject A01a N	3086	1448	1521	2315	312	723	875	959	529	1811	970	1333	671	403	629	20

★=excludes respondents for whom question was inappropriate.

QUESTIONNAIRE FORM 1 1986	TOTAL	SEX		RACE		REGION				4YR COLLEGE PLANS		ILLICIT DRUG USE: LIFETIME				
		M	F	White	Black	NE	NC	S	W	Yes	No	None	Mari-juana Only	Few Pills	More Pills	Any Her-oin
N (Weighted No. of Cases):	3179	1469	1562	2351	323	749	897	984	550	1841	999	1333	671	406	643	21
% of Weighted Total:	100.0	46.2	49.1	74.0	10.2	23.5	28.2	30.9	17.3	57.9	31.4	41.9	21.1	12.8	20.2	0.7
B018B: . . . during the last 12 months?																
1. 0 occasions	88.5	86.2	91.8	88.1	95.3	82.6	89.5	92.6	87.2	91.1	86.3	100.0	91.5	87.7	62.3	42.0
2. 1-2	5.9	6.9	4.8	6.5	1.6	8.2	4.9	4.7	6.4	5.6	6.4	-	5.8	8.2	17.0	4.9
3. 3-5	2.2	2.6	1.4	2.1	1.4	3.4	2.4	0.7	2.6	1.4	2.6	-	1.8	2.7	6.7	8.9
4. 6-9	1.3	1.5	1.0	1.3	1.3	1.9	1.4	0.8	1.3	0.8	1.8	-	0.2	0.5	5.6	4.1
5. 10-19	0.9	1.1	0.7	0.9	0.2	1.7	0.7	0.6	0.9	0.7	0.9	-	-	0.3	3.8	17.4
6. 20-39	0.4	0.5	0.3	0.4	-	0.6	0.6	0.1	0.5	0.2	0.6	-	0.1	0.5	1.6	3.4
7. 40 or more	0.9	1.2	0.1	0.6	0.2	1.6	0.6	0.4	1.2	0.3	1.4	-	0.6	-	3.0	19.2
Item 2050 Subject A01b N	3077	1442	1517	2304	313	719	876	957	525	1808	965	1333	668	402	623	20
B018C: . . . during the last 30 days?																
1. 0 occasions	94.9	93.6	96.9	94.7	98.3	91.1	95.1	97.5	95.0	96.4	93.4	100.0	96.9	95.7	82.3	59.4
2. 1-2	2.9	3.8	2.0	3.4	1.1	4.4	3.3	1.5	3.0	2.4	3.6	-	2.1	2.9	10.0	10.5
3. 3-5	1.0	1.1	0.6	0.8	0.3	2.0	0.7	0.5	0.9	0.6	1.1	-	0.4	1.4	3.5	-
4. 6-9	0.5	0.5	0.4	0.6	0.1	1.1	0.3	0.3	0.2	0.3	0.6	-	0.1	-	1.6	18.7
5. 10-19	0.2	0.5	*	0.3	-	0.5	0.1	0.1	0.3	0.1	0.5	-	-	-	0.8	11.3
6. 20-39	0.2	0.2	-	*	-	0.5	0.2	-	0.1	-	0.3	-	-	-	0.8	-
7. 40 or more	0.3	0.4	*	0.2	0.2	0.4	0.3	0.1	0.5	0.1	0.5	-	0.5	-	1.0	-
Item 2060 Subject A01c N	3076	1443	1516	2302	315	717	874	959	525	1809	964	1333	666	402	621	21

B019: On how many occasions (if any) have you used marijuana . . .

B019A: . . . in your lifetime?

	TOTAL	M	F	White	Black	NE	NC	S	W	Yes	No	None	Mari-juana Only	Few Pills	More Pills	Any Her-oin
1. 0 occasions	48.9	47.2	51.8	47.5	58.1	40.4	49.4	55.7	46.8	52.0	47.5	100.0	-	22.7	10.9	1.7
2. 1-2	10.9	10.6	11.6	11.1	15.9	11.1	10.6	12.4	8.5	12.3	8.9	-	35.2	14.0	6.7	-
3. 3-5	7.1	6.1	7.9	7.2	6.5	7.3	8.2	6.5	6.1	7.2	6.9	-	19.1	14.1	5.1	-
4. 6-9	5.7	6.3	5.1	5.9	5.4	5.5	6.4	4.8	6.2	5.3	5.5	-	12.9	11.0	6.6	-
5. 10-19	6.9	6.9	7.0	7.7	2.1	7.9	6.7	6.0	7.3	6.7	7.4	-	13.7	11.0	11.0	28.5
6. 20-39	5.7	5.7	5.8	6.0	3.2	7.9	5.3	4.1	6.6	5.5	6.5	-	8.3	10.8	11.6	14.9
7. 40 or more	14.8	17.2	10.9	14.7	8.9	19.8	13.4	10.4	18.5	11.0	17.4	-	10.6	16.3	48.1	54.8
Item 2070 Subject A01a N	3065	1442	1508	2304	307	711	873	959	522	1804	956	1333	667	398	628	20

B019B: . . . during the last 12 months?

	TOTAL	M	F	White	Black	NE	NC	S	W	Yes	No	None	Mari-juana Only	Few Pills	More Pills	Any Her-oin
1. 0 occasions	61.3	59.5	64.4	59.8	74.7	52.7	59.8	70.4	59.0	63.9	60.0	100.0	35.0	41.3	21.3	13.5
2. 1-2	10.7	9.5	11.7	11.1	8.2	11.0	13.0	7.8	11.4	11.7	9.0	-	29.4	15.8	10.9	-
3. 3-5	6.9	7.9	5.9	7.3	5.2	7.4	7.7	6.1	6.4	6.9	6.3	-	13.7	14.2	9.5	17.8
4. 6-9	5.3	5.0	5.6	5.5	3.0	7.5	4.2	4.6	5.7	5.2	5.5	-	8.1	9.5	11.2	4.8
5. 10-19	4.7	5.1	4.4	5.4	1.7	6.8	4.4	3.5	4.7	4.3	5.4	-	7.3	8.4	9.2	16.7
6. 20-39	3.9	3.5	4.0	4.3	1.2	4.0	4.0	3.2	4.6	3.5	4.4	-	3.8	6.2	10.2	14.0
7. 40 or more	7.2	9.5	4.0	6.5	6.0	10.5	6.9	4.4	8.1	4.5	9.4	-	2.7	4.6	27.6	33.3
Item 2080 Subject A01b N	3044	1430	1503	2288	305	706	871	946	521	1793	951	1333	655	391	623	21

B019C: . . . during the last 30 days?

	TOTAL	M	F	White	Black	NE	NC	S	W	Yes	No	None	Mari-juana Only	Few Pills	More Pills	Any Her-oin
1. 0 occasions	76.5	73.9	79.8	75.6	83.9	67.6	77.5	81.8	77.1	80.0	73.0	100.0	71.0	63.5	42.1	32.2
2. 1-2	9.1	10.0	8.6	10.0	6.7	11.6	9.5	6.9	9.0	9.0	9.2	-	17.8	14.7	15.4	10.1
3. 3-5	4.0	4.0	3.9	4.3	2.0	5.7	2.9	3.7	3.8	3.8	4.4	-	4.9	8.1	8.6	2.3
4. 6-9	2.7	2.4	2.6	2.7	1.3	4.4	2.1	2.1	2.2	2.0	3.1	-	2.5	6.6	5.6	13.4
5. 10-19	3.3	3.5	3.0	3.5	2.2	4.8	3.6	2.1	2.7	2.7	3.8	-	2.3	3.9	10.6	15.7
6. 20-39	2.1	2.7	1.1	1.7	1.9	3.1	1.8	1.4	2.3	1.1	2.9	-	0.7	1.8	8.2	-
7. 40 or more	2.5	3.6	1.0	2.2	2.0	2.9	2.4	1.9	2.9	1.4	3.5	-	0.8	1.4	9.5	26.3
Item 2090 Subject A01c N	3045	1429	1503	2291	304	709	867	948	521	1792	952	1333	658	390	623	20

IF YOU HAVE NOT USED MARIJUANA OR HASHISH IN THE LAST TWELVE MONTHS, GO TO Q.B028.

B020: When you used marijuana or hashish during the last year, how often did you use it in each of the following situations?

*=less than .05 per cent.

QUESTIONNAIRE FORM 1 1986	TOTAL	SEX		RACE		REGION				4YR COLLEGE PLANS		ILLICIT DRUG USE: LIFETIME				
		M	F	White	Black	NE	NC	S	W	Yes	No	None	Marijuana Only	Few Pills	More Pills	Any Heroin
N (Weighted No. of Cases):	3179	1469	1562	2351	323	749	897	984	550	1841	999	1333	671	406	643	21
% of Weighted Total:	100.0	46.2	49.1	74.0	10.2	23.5	28.2	30.9	17.3	57.9	31.4	41.9	21.1	12.8	20.2	0.7

B020A: When you were alone

	TOTAL	M	F	White	Black	NE	NC	S	W	Yes	No	None	Marijuana Only	Few Pills	More Pills	Any Heroin
1. Not at all	68.4	63.1	78.1	72.0	58.0	65.5	70.7	67.2	70.9	76.8	61.3	-	84.5	79.7	51.2	35.0
2. A few of the times	19.4	22.0	14.8	18.0	22.4	21.8	17.0	19.6	19.4	14.9	22.7	-	12.1	15.4	26.3	38.5
3. Some of the times	9.5	11.1	6.7	8.3	11.8	11.7	8.1	9.9	7.9	7.1	12.6	-	1.6	4.9	18.4	12.1
4. Most of the times	1.5	1.9	0.4	1.0	3.7	1.1	2.1	1.1	1.8	0.9	1.3	-	0.6	-	2.2	14.4
5. Every time	1.2	1.9	-	0.8	4.1	-	2.2	2.3	-	0.3	2.1	-	1.2	-	1.9	-
Item 2100 Subject A05a N★	1177	575	538	918	77	331	345	284	216	637	384	-	422	230	490	18

B020B: With just 1 or 2 other people

	TOTAL	M	F	White	Black	NE	NC	S	W	Yes	No	None	Marijuana Only	Few Pills	More Pills	Any Heroin
1. Not at all	7.5	7.9	7.5	7.6	9.6	6.3	8.7	6.3	9.1	8.7	4.4	-	9.6	9.9	4.7	-
2. A few of the times	33.3	30.2	37.2	33.2	35.9	31.1	34.6	34.8	32.9	33.9	33.8	-	44.0	36.2	23.6	15.1
3. Some of the times	16.5	17.1	14.1	15.3	17.1	17.1	17.4	14.0	17.4	15.2	16.4	-	10.1	13.8	22.3	32.9
4. Most of the times	30.6	32.4	29.0	30.9	27.4	32.6	27.5	31.3	31.9	29.1	34.3	-	23.1	26.8	38.9	34.7
5. Every time	12.0	12.4	12.2	13.0	10.0	12.9	11.9	13.6	8.7	13.0	11.2	-	13.3	13.2	10.5	17.3
Item 2110 Subject A05b N★	1169	572	534	910	77	331	343	280	215	636	379	-	422	224	488	18

B020C: At a party

	TOTAL	M	F	White	Black	NE	NC	S	W	Yes	No	None	Marijuana Only	Few Pills	More Pills	Any Heroin
1. Not at all	23.3	20.2	27.8	22.5	38.5	22.3	22.2	25.7	23.5	27.8	20.2	-	34.9	24.1	14.1	-
2. A few of the times	24.4	26.1	22.9	25.6	19.3	18.9	28.3	27.9	22.0	25.7	22.8	-	30.1	24.5	20.1	4.5
3. Some of the times	19.4	17.3	21.5	20.0	13.4	20.8	19.6	17.1	20.0	18.8	19.0	-	14.6	23.5	21.1	38.6
4. Most of the times	20.6	22.1	18.2	20.8	12.9	23.1	16.9	20.2	23.0	18.4	22.9	-	14.8	17.5	26.3	16.8
5. Every time	12.4	14.2	9.6	11.1	15.9	14.9	13.0	9.2	11.5	9.4	15.1	-	5.6	10.4	18.4	40.1
Item 2120 Subject A05c N★	1169	572	534	910	78	330	344	278	216	637	381	-	420	229	487	18

B020D: When your date or spouse was present

	TOTAL	M	F	White	Black	NE	NC	S	W	Yes	No	None	Marijuana Only	Few Pills	More Pills	Any Heroin
1. Not at all	51.2	59.3	43.7	50.4	54.7	49.4	53.4	51.4	50.1	55.7	45.8	-	67.1	55.7	35.5	41.8
2. A few of the times	24.6	22.4	27.3	25.9	26.0	22.4	27.0	23.3	26.0	23.6	27.2	-	23.3	22.8	26.3	20.7
3. Some of the times	10.8	11.0	9.2	10.1	10.5	12.5	6.5	12.0	13.4	10.3	10.3	-	3.9	11.4	16.6	11.4
4. Most of the times	8.7	4.5	13.5	8.8	3.0	11.3	7.8	7.6	7.9	7.6	9.7	-	3.6	7.1	14.4	3.7
5. Every time	4.6	2.8	6.4	4.8	5.7	4.4	5.2	5.6	2.7	2.8	7.0	-	2.0	3.0	7.1	22.4
Item 2130 Subject A05b N★	1162	565	534	908	77	329	339	277	216	632	378	-	419	226	483	18

B020E: When people over age 30 were present

	TOTAL	M	F	White	Black	NE	NC	S	W	Yes	No	None	Marijuana Only	Few Pills	More Pills	Any Heroin
1. Not at all	69.8	67.1	74.4	72.6	62.8	68.7	73.0	66.3	70.7	76.4	62.6	-	86.2	75.9	54.0	36.3
2. A few of the times	19.1	20.2	17.3	18.1	27.2	21.2	15.5	22.4	17.1	17.0	22.0	-	9.7	17.6	27.2	31.2
3. Some of the times	7.4	8.0	6.6	6.1	9.0	7.3	6.7	7.5	8.7	4.6	10.2	-	2.6	4.3	12.7	21.8
4. Most of the times	2.4	3.6	0.8	2.5	0.7	1.7	3.0	1.4	3.5	0.9	4.1	-	1.0	1.1	4.0	10.7
5. Every time	1.4	1.1	0.9	0.7	0.4	1.1	1.7	2.3	-	1.0	1.0	-	0.5	1.1	2.1	-
Item 2140 Subject A05b N★	1173	572	537	912	77	330	344	282	217	637	381	-	422	230	488	18

B020F: During the daytime (before 4:00 p.m.)

	TOTAL	M	F	White	Black	NE	NC	S	W	Yes	No	None	Marijuana Only	Few Pills	More Pills	Any Heroin
1. Not at all	41.7	37.0	48.1	41.8	54.7	33.2	51.5	42.6	37.6	48.0	33.8	-	59.2	47.3	24.9	10.8
2. A few of the times	26.3	26.6	26.4	26.5	20.3	27.6	22.2	28.6	27.6	25.3	29.0	-	26.1	30.2	24.6	16.5
3. Some of the times	20.3	22.3	17.5	21.1	6.9	26.6	15.0	21.1	18.0	18.3	23.8	-	10.1	15.4	29.8	65.2
4. Most of the times	9.2	10.7	6.8	8.0	15.5	11.1	7.1	5.8	13.9	7.1	10.0	-	3.5	6.6	15.7	7.5
5. Every time	2.6	3.5	1.3	2.6	2.5	1.5	4.1	1.8	2.8	1.3	3.4	-	1.1	0.5	5.1	-
Item 2150 Subject A05c N★	1176	575	537	917	78	332	345	283	216	637	384	-	422	231	489	18

B020G: At your home (or apartment or dorm)

	TOTAL	M	F	White	Black	NE	NC	S	W	Yes	No	None	Marijuana Only	Few Pills	More Pills	Any Heroin
1. Not at all	58.3	55.6	62.3	58.4	53.5	50.3	59.9	63.9	60.7	62.6	53.1	-	73.1	65.8	42.9	38.3
2. A few of the times	18.6	18.7	18.9	19.4	22.8	19.3	19.5	16.7	18.6	17.7	19.1	-	13.9	17.3	22.1	30.3
3. Some of the times	12.2	13.6	9.7	12.2	7.0	16.4	10.0	9.7	12.2	11.4	12.8	-	5.7	10.3	18.6	21.4
4. Most of the times	8.2	9.2	6.9	7.5	13.3	11.0	8.0	6.4	6.7	6.7	10.6	-	5.1	5.4	12.5	6.3
5. Every time	2.8	2.9	2.1	2.4	3.4	3.0	2.7	3.3	1.9	1.7	4.3	-	2.2	1.2	4.0	3.7
Item 2160 Subject A05c N★	1169	573	534	912	78	331	340	282	216	633	384	-	420	229	486	18

★=excludes respondents for whom question was inappropriate.

QUESTIONNAIRE FORM 1 1986	TOTAL	SEX		RACE		REGION				4YR COLLEGE PLANS		ILLICIT DRUG USE: LIFETIME				
		M	F	White	Black	NE	NC	S	W	Yes	No	None	Marijuana Only	Few Pills	More Pills	Any Heroin
N (Weighted No. of Cases):	3179	1469	1562	2351	323	749	897	984	550	1841	999	1333	671	406	643	21
% of Weighted Total:	100.0	46.2	49.1	74.0	10.2	23.5	28.2	30.9	17.3	57.9	31.4	41.9	21.1	12.8	20.2	0.7
B020H: At school																
1. Not at all	67.3	61.6	75.5	68.1	74.0	63.4	71.0	71.1	62.3	74.9	59.1	-	83.1	76.9	50.7	16.3
2. A few of the times	18.5	21.9	14.8	18.4	18.6	20.1	18.1	16.6	19.3	15.3	22.4	-	11.3	14.7	25.5	48.5
3. Some of the times	8.8	9.8	6.4	8.5	-	9.9	6.0	8.4	12.1	6.3	11.6	-	2.5	5.3	15.8	15.3
4. Most of the times	3.5	4.2	2.7	3.5	6.8	4.3	3.2	2.0	4.9	2.8	4.2	-	2.1	3.0	4.8	14.6
5. Every time	1.8	2.5	0.6	1.5	0.6	2.2	1.7	1.9	1.4	0.7	2.7	-	1.0	-	3.3	5.3
Item 2170　Subject A05c　　N★	1179	575	537	917	78	334	345	283	216	640	384	-	422	231	492	18
B020I: In a car																
1. Not at all	27.6	27.0	30.2	29.0	28.3	31.1	24.7	24.6	31.0	33.7	20.7	-	37.3	33.2	16.8	7.4
2. A few of the times	28.7	26.3	30.8	28.4	22.6	26.7	29.7	27.6	31.4	29.9	26.2	-	33.8	27.8	24.2	40.5
3. Some of the times	22.6	23.8	21.3	22.3	23.7	28.5	19.5	21.2	20.1	19.1	28.9	-	15.7	24.3	28.2	23.3
4. Most of the times	15.5	15.7	14.1	15.2	16.4	11.3	16.1	21.3	13.4	13.9	16.7	-	10.4	13.2	21.0	10.8
5. Every time	5.6	7.2	3.6	5.1	8.9	2.4	10.0	5.2	4.0	3.3	7.5	-	2.9	1.4	9.7	18.0
Item 2190　Subject A05c　　N★	1179	577	538	919	78	332	346	284	216	639	384	-	424	231	489	18
B021: How many of the times when you used marijuana or hashish during the last year did you use it along with alcohol–that is, so that their effects overlapped?																
1. Not at all	27.8	24.3	32.3	26.6	39.0	26.6	24.1	30.4	32.4	27.9	28.3	-	43.4	25.5	16.2	6.9
2. A few of the times	32.5	31.3	34.3	33.9	23.2	33.9	35.0	28.3	31.9	33.5	32.5	-	34.5	40.6	27.4	23.0
3. Some of the times	19.7	21.8	16.9	19.8	14.3	24.4	13.8	22.5	18.6	20.4	17.6	-	9.0	16.0	29.7	45.3
4. Most of the times	13.6	15.0	11.5	13.2	15.7	11.8	16.6	12.6	12.6	12.1	15.5	-	9.6	12.9	17.0	22.2
5. Every time	6.3	7.6	5.0	6.5	7.7	3.3	10.5	6.2	4.5	6.0	6.1	-	3.5	5.0	9.6	2.5
Item 2200　Subject A01h　　N★	1157	563	531	910	74	324	344	280	209	624	380	-	410	228	486	18
B022: What have been the most important reasons for your using marijuana or hashish? (Mark all that apply.)																
A. To experiment–to see what it's like	64.8	63.3	66.1	65.1	61.3	63.2	67.4	64.7	62.9	70.4	54.9	-	74.2	69.6	55.0	49.5
B. To relax or relieve tension	40.9	39.3	41.8	39.8	38.6	42.6	34.3	43.4	45.5	36.3	44.2	-	23.9	38.7	55.4	63.6
C. To feel good or get high	75.0	75.6	74.5	76.7	64.0	78.0	73.6	75.9	71.6	75.7	76.0	-	65.6	78.4	81.9	62.4
D. To seek deeper insights and understanding	12.6	15.1	9.8	13.1	2.2	13.7	12.1	11.5	13.2	14.6	9.2	-	4.6	12.5	19.8	13.3
E. To have a good time with my friends	69.1	74.2	64.0	69.9	61.3	73.9	62.7	69.6	71.1	69.0	68.9	-	61.7	73.2	72.8	78.5
F. To fit in with a group I like	12.4	16.2	9.0	12.7	10.7	11.3	11.7	16.4	10.1	11.4	13.1	-	12.9	12.2	11.6	28.4
G. To get away from my problems or troubles	24.9	21.6	28.4	25.0	18.0	25.3	19.2	31.3	25.1	23.5	28.2	-	17.7	25.4	30.8	30.4
H. Because of boredom, nothing else to do	25.9	25.4	25.3	25.6	26.8	27.8	26.2	26.0	22.5	23.7	25.4	-	15.8	22.0	36.1	26.3
I. Because of anger or frustration	16.7	14.2	18.7	15.7	9.8	16.0	14.0	21.4	15.7	14.4	18.2	-	10.2	16.6	21.6	35.9
J. To get through the day	8.3	9.0	7.0	7.5	9.0	7.4	8.4	7.5	10.8	5.4	11.2	-	3.2	5.8	13.8	10.7
K. To increase the effects of some other drug(s)	13.1	15.5	8.8	13.1	12.0	12.5	15.1	14.0	9.4	11.8	12.8	-	5.0	8.4	22.0	21.4
L. To decrease (offset) the effects of some other drug(s)	2.5	2.2	1.7	2.0	0.9	2.9	1.2	1.7	5.2	1.7	1.4	-	0.8	1.0	4.7	3.7
M. Because I am "hooked"–I have to have it	3.0	3.2	2.2	2.4	5.0	3.9	2.1	2.7	3.3	1.3	5.4	-	0.2	0.7	6.0	16.9
Item 2210-2330　Subject A06a　　N★	1178	572	539	916	76	331	345	286	216	642	381	-	420	233	492	18
B023: When you use marijuana or hashish how high do you usually get?																
1. Not at all high	5.1	5.7	4.7	4.8	6.0	2.7	7.8	3.9	5.9	7.1	1.5	-	9.8	4.3	1.6	-
2. A little high	27.6	24.9	31.1	28.3	35.8	25.7	29.3	27.6	27.6	29.7	25.4	-	37.5	33.9	16.3	27.5
3. Moderately high	43.8	42.8	44.8	44.1	33.0	45.3	39.7	47.7	43.2	43.2	45.2	-	38.9	43.8	49.0	28.0
4. Very high	23.5	26.5	19.3	22.8	25.2	26.3	23.3	20.8	23.3	20.0	27.9	-	13.8	18.0	33.1	44.5
Item 2340　Subject A01e　　N★	1177	573	540	919	76	332	345	284	216	642	384	-	420	233	492	18

★=excludes respondents for whom question was inappropriate.

QUESTIONNAIRE FORM 1 1986	TOTAL	SEX		RACE		REGION				4YR COLLEGE PLANS		ILLICIT DRUG USE: LIFETIME				
		M	F	White	Black	NE	NC	S	W	Yes	No	None	Mari- juana Only	Few Pills	More Pills	Any Her- oin
N (Weighted No. of Cases):	3179	1469	1562	2351	323	749	897	984	550	1841	999	1333	671	406	643	21
% of Weighted Total:	100.0	46.2	49.1	74.0	10.2	23.5	28.2	30.9	17.3	57.9	31.4	41.9	21.1	12.8	20.2	0.7
B024: When you use marijuana or hashish, how long do you usually stay high?																
1. Usually don't get high	8.2	8.6	7.9	8.2	10.1	5.1	10.8	6.3	11.1	9.9	4.3	-	15.0	7.5	2.6	-
2. One to two hours	55.0	53.1	58.1	57.0	47.8	56.4	55.1	53.3	55.1	54.6	58.9	-	52.5	62.1	54.2	45.4
3. Three to six hours	32.9	34.3	30.6	31.9	37.0	35.8	29.9	35.5	29.8	32.5	31.5	-	29.5	29.2	37.0	54.6
4. Seven to 24 hours	3.3	3.4	3.1	2.7	4.0	2.4	3.1	4.6	3.2	2.7	4.4	-	2.6	1.3	5.1	-
5. More than 24 hours	0.6	0.6	0.3	0.3	1.1	0.2	1.1	0.3	0.7	0.3	0.9	-	0.4	-	1.1	-
Item 2350 Subject A01f N★	1176	577	537	918	78	331	345	284	216	641	384	-	425	231	490	18
B025: During the LAST MONTH, about how many marijuana cigarettes (joints, reefers), or the equivalent, did you smoke a day, on the average? (If you shared them with other people, count only the amount YOU smoked.)																
1. None	44.3	40.8	49.3	45.6	36.7	36.3	51.1	41.0	50.1	50.3	35.8	-	61.1	44.4	31.7	21.0
2. Less than 1 a day	34.0	35.3	33.6	35.8	26.5	37.7	29.8	35.0	33.6	36.2	33.7	-	29.7	38.4	35.0	37.4
3. 1 a day	7.6	8.1	6.5	7.0	7.2	12.0	4.4	7.0	6.4	4.8	10.9	-	2.4	9.2	10.7	13.8
4. 2 - 3 a day	8.4	9.6	7.0	7.3	21.2	9.3	6.6	12.1	5.0	6.0	10.5	-	4.2	5.6	13.5	-
5. 4 - 6 a day	3.7	4.0	2.4	3.0	2.0	2.8	4.6	3.4	3.9	2.0	6.1	-	1.4	1.5	6.4	9.5
6. 7 - 10 a day	1.2	1.6	0.6	0.7	6.4	1.4	1.8	1.0	0.3	0.6	1.6	-	0.4	-	1.9	18.3
7. 11 or more a day	0.8	0.6	0.5	0.6	-	0.5	1.7	0.4	0.7	-	1.4	-	0.8	0.9	0.9	-
Item 2360 Subject A01d N★	1104	549	503	870	71	314	323	260	206	601	361	-	387	218	474	17
B026: Do you know how much marijuana you have used (in ounces) during the LAST MONTH?																
8. Don't know	21.2	18.2	25.7	22.2	21.4	20.7	19.5	22.9	22.5	20.0	24.5	-	19.9	25.5	20.8	11.7
1. None	40.6	37.7	43.8	40.0	43.9	31.8	45.9	40.1	46.3	44.3	34.7	-	55.8	38.3	29.6	21.0
2. Less than 1/2 ounce	20.3	24.2	16.4	21.5	16.8	26.4	18.1	20.7	13.9	21.1	19.2	-	17.5	25.5	20.6	17.0
3. About 1/2 ounce	7.5	8.6	6.6	7.5	3.1	8.1	5.4	6.3	11.3	7.8	7.4	-	3.6	6.0	11.1	11.5
4. About 1 ounce	4.3	4.5	3.3	4.0	4.3	5.4	4.3	4.0	2.8	3.3	5.4	-	1.2	2.0	7.3	13.6
5. About 2 ounces	2.7	2.1	2.3	1.7	4.5	2.5	3.6	2.3	1.9	1.6	3.5	-	1.4	0.6	4.8	-
6. 3 to 5 ounces	2.7	3.9	1.4	2.6	3.9	4.1	2.3	3.2	0.4	1.9	3.6	-	0.2	1.5	4.9	14.3
7. 6 or more ounces	0.8	0.9	0.5	0.6	2.1	1.1	0.9	0.4	0.8	0.1	1.7	-	0.4	0.7	0.9	10.8
Item 2370 Subject A01d N★	1102	547	502	868	71	315	320	262	205	602	361	-	386	219	473	17
B027: Have you ever tried to stop using marijuana or hashish and found that you couldn't stop?																
1. Yes	6.6	8.6	3.5	5.2	10.2	7.6	6.8	4.6	7.5	4.9	7.5	-	2.7	2.2	11.7	10.7
2. No	93.4	91.4	96.5	94.8	89.8	92.4	93.2	95.4	92.5	95.1	92.5	-	97.3	97.8	88.3	89.3
Item 2380 Subject A01i N★	1161	573	528	910	76	326	342	281	212	639	376	-	419	229	488	18
B028: Thinking back over your whole life, has there ever been a period when you used marijuana or hashish on a daily, or almost daily, basis for at least a month?																
1. No–GO TO Q.B032	85.3	83.5	88.6	85.5	90.2	78.6	89.0	89.1	81.7	89.1	83.2	100.0	89.8	82.2	54.6	31.5
2. Yes	14.7	16.5	11.4	14.5	9.8	21.4	11.0	10.9	18.3	10.9	16.8	-	10.2	17.8	45.4	68.5
Item 21180 Subject A01a N	2998	1410	1482	2273	297	704	859	919	517	1774	940	1257	654	389	624	20
B029: How old were you when you first smoked marijuana or hashish that frequently?																
1. Grade 6 or earlier	6.4	7.6	3.7	6.6	-	4.3	9.3	6.7	6.7	4.7	5.3	-	6.0	4.0	6.4	22.6
2. Grade 7 or 8	24.0	20.9	28.4	25.2	17.3	22.1	25.7	23.4	26.0	18.9	30.0	-	19.2	14.6	29.9	14.5
3. Grade 9(Freshman)	23.0	22.0	22.2	21.1	30.4	23.7	26.1	17.7	25.4	23.0	21.9	-	25.4	25.6	22.2	10.9
4. Grade 10(Sophomore)	21.4	21.2	22.6	22.8	13.2	26.8	16.0	21.7	17.6	25.3	18.3	-	20.2	18.9	22.5	36.9
5. Grade 11(Junior)	16.9	17.8	17.5	16.9	23.8	16.0	13.9	20.2	17.0	17.2	18.6	-	17.2	30.5	12.2	8.4
6. Grade 12(Senior)	8.4	10.5	5.6	7.5	15.3	7.1	8.9	10.4	7.3	10.9	5.9	-	12.0	6.4	6.6	6.7
Item 21190 Subject A01g N★	541	276	212	381	46	177	113	143	107	242	191	-	118	86	301	18

★=excludes respondents for whom question was inappropriate.

QUESTIONNAIRE FORM 1 1986	TOTAL	SEX		RACE		REGION				4YR COLLEGE PLANS		ILLICIT DRUG USE: LIFETIME				
		M	F	White	Black	NE	NC	S	W	Yes	No	None	Mari- juana Only	Few Pills	More Pills	Any Her- oin
N (Weighted No. of Cases):	3179	1469	1562	2351	323	749	897	984	550	1841	999	1333	671	406	643	21
% of Weighted Total:	100.0	46.2	49.1	74.0	10.2	23.5	28.2	30.9	17.3	57.9	31.4	41.9	21.1	12.8	20.2	0.7

B030: How recently did you use marijuana or hashish on a daily, or almost daily, basis for at least a month?

	TOTAL	M	F	White	Black	NE	NC	S	W	Yes	No	None	Mari- juana Only	Few Pills	More Pills	Any Her- oin
1. During the past month	21.6	24.1	16.0	17.6	29.6	25.3	23.0	18.3	18.2	18.2	23.8	-	13.5	17.5	25.2	24.1
2. 2 months ago	10.1	9.3	10.1	10.8	6.7	9.1	7.3	13.6	10.1	7.9	13.0	-	7.7	6.6	10.9	18.1
3. 3 to 9 months ago	22.8	21.7	24.1	21.9	26.6	22.1	18.3	27.6	22.5	25.1	21.3	-	30.8	19.4	21.4	21.1
4. About 1 year ago	14.0	15.6	13.3	15.4	13.1	14.5	13.3	12.4	15.7	15.3	15.8	-	13.9	22.3	12.3	6.8
5. About 2 years ago	14.6	13.8	16.5	15.7	17.2	14.9	17.6	13.7	12.4	14.2	12.6	-	12.4	17.3	14.7	6.9
6. 3 or more years ago	16.9	15.5	19.9	18.5	6.7	14.1	20.5	14.4	21.1	19.2	13.5	-	21.7	16.9	15.5	23.0
Item 21200　Subject A01a　　N★	504	261	196	358	42	169	104	128	103	220	181	-	101	83	294	15

B031: Over your whole lifetime, during how many months have you used marijuana or hashish on a daily or near-daily basis?

	TOTAL	M	F	White	Black	NE	NC	S	W	Yes	No	None	Mari- juana Only	Few Pills	More Pills	Any Her- oin
1. Less than 3 months	38.3	34.6	45.5	38.3	44.1	40.9	38.5	38.0	34.4	40.3	36.7	-	54.3	56.8	28.7	15.5
2. 3 to 9 months	20.7	22.3	19.2	22.2	13.0	16.9	24.2	17.9	26.8	25.8	17.0	-	20.6	20.8	22.0	10.6
3. About 1 year	9.9	11.4	8.0	9.9	14.7	8.1	8.6	13.7	9.4	9.4	9.5	-	11.9	9.3	9.9	6.8
4. About 1 and 1/2 years	7.4	8.8	6.3	7.6	4.6	8.9	4.2	8.8	6.7	8.0	7.1	-	2.5	5.4	9.2	19.5
5. About 2 years	9.4	10.0	8.8	9.7	11.2	11.2	11.0	8.0	6.9	8.9	10.5	-	5.4	5.7	11.6	14.8
6. About 3 to 5 years	9.4	8.0	7.6	7.5	6.7	10.6	7.9	7.2	11.7	4.6	13.0	-	2.0	2.0	13.3	16.5
7. 6 to 9 years	3.4	4.2	2.3	4.2	-	0.4	4.8	5.7	3.8	2.8	3.5	-	2.6	-	4.4	8.9
8. 10 or more years	1.4	0.7	2.3	0.6	5.8	2.9	1.0	0.6	0.4	0.2	2.7	-	0.8	-	0.8	7.5
Item 21210　Subject A01a　　N★	498	261	193	358	40	163	104	127	103	221	180	-	98	79	295	15

B032: Do you think you will be using marijuana or hashish five years from now?

	TOTAL	M	F	White	Black	NE	NC	S	W	Yes	No	None	Mari- juana Only	Few Pills	More Pills	Any Her- oin
1. I definitely will	2.5	2.9	1.6	2.2	1.6	3.8	1.8	2.1	2.3	1.6	3.1	0.5	1.8	0.7	8.4	7.8
2. I probably will	11.7	11.7	10.7	11.8	7.4	17.2	9.2	9.5	11.9	8.7	15.4	0.4	12.1	20.4	28.4	29.8
3. I probably will not	21.0	21.9	20.3	22.8	15.4	24.5	21.7	17.7	20.9	23.0	18.2	7.4	32.4	29.8	31.2	37.6
4. I definitely will not	64.9	63.6	67.4	63.3	75.6	54.4	67.2	70.6	64.9	66.7	63.3	91.7	53.7	49.1	32.0	24.8
Item 2390　Subject A04a　　N	3065	1424	1530	2300	313	718	867	948	532	1800	976	1296	665	399	626	21

The next questions are about LSD, the psychedelic drug which is sometimes called "acid".

B033: On how many occasions (if any) have you taken LSD . . .

B033A: . . . in your lifetime?

	TOTAL	M	F	White	Black	NE	NC	S	W	Yes	No	None	Mari- juana Only	Few Pills	More Pills	Any Her- oin
1. 0 occasions	92.1	91.1	94.1	91.8	98.0	90.0	92.9	94.9	88.6	94.3	91.5	100.0	100.0	93.9	67.5	28.4
2. 1-2	3.8	3.9	3.4	3.9	1.1	4.8	2.9	2.1	6.8	3.1	3.9	-	-	6.1	14.5	3.9
3. 3-5	1.7	2.3	0.9	1.9	0.6	2.0	1.9	1.4	1.7	1.0	1.8	-	-	-	7.4	36.8
4. 6-9	1.0	1.1	0.7	1.2	-	2.4	0.6	0.1	1.2	0.6	1.3	-	-	-	4.9	-
5. 10-19	0.6	0.9	0.3	0.5	0.1	0.7	0.5	0.3	1.1	0.6	0.5	-	-	-	2.6	9.1
6. 20-39	0.4	0.2	0.4	0.4	-	0.1	0.4	0.8	0.2	0.2	0.5	-	-	-	2.0	-
7. 40 or more	0.4	0.5	0.2	0.3	0.2	0.2	0.8	0.2	0.3	0.2	0.7	-	-	-	1.1	21.8
Item 890　Subject A01a　　N	3060	1436	1519	2308	307	719	869	947	525	1806	967	1321	665	400	620	21

B033B: . . . during the last 12 months?

	TOTAL	M	F	White	Black	NE	NC	S	W	Yes	No	None	Mari- juana Only	Few Pills	More Pills	Any Her- oin
1. 0 occasions	94.5	93.9	95.9	94.4	98.4	92.6	94.3	96.9	93.1	96.2	93.7	100.0	100.0	98.5	75.4	51.6
2. 1-2	3.5	3.7	3.1	3.8	1.4	5.1	3.3	1.8	4.9	2.4	4.7	-	-	1.5	16.0	14.6
3. 3-5	1.1	1.5	0.5	1.1	-	1.9	1.3	0.6	0.7	1.0	0.8	-	-	-	5.0	17.2
4. 6-9	0.5	0.4	0.3	0.4	0.2	0.4	0.3	0.4	0.8	0.3	0.2	-	-	-	1.9	9.8
5. 10-19	0.3	0.3	0.2	0.2	-	-	0.4	0.2	0.4	0.1	0.3	-	-	-	1.3	-
6. 20-39	0.1	*	0.1	0.1	-	-	0.3	-	-	-	0.2	-	-	-	0.4	-
7. 40 or more	0.1	0.1	-	0.1	-	-	0.1	0.1	-	*	0.1	-	-	-	0.1	6.8
Item 900　Subject A01b　　N	3060	1436	1520	2304	307	720	871	947	523	1808	965	1323	665	399	620	21

*=less than .05 per cent.　　★=excludes respondents for whom question was inappropriate.

QUESTIONNAIRE FORM 1 1986	TOTAL	SEX		RACE		REGION				4YR COLLEGE PLANS		ILLICIT DRUG USE: LIFETIME				
		M	F	White	Black	NE	NC	S	W	Yes	No	None	Mari-juana Only	Few Pills	More Pills	Any Her-oin
N (Weighted No. of Cases):	3179	1469	1562	2351	323	749	897	984	550	1841	999	1333	671	406	643	21
% of Weighted Total:	100.0	46.2	49.1	74.0	10.2	23.5	28.2	30.9	17.3	57.9	31.4	41.9	21.1	12.8	20.2	0.7

B033C: . . . during the last 30 days?

1. 0 occasions	98.2	97.9	99.2	98.5	100.0	97.3	98.4	98.3	98.6	99.0	98.2	100.0	100.0	100.0	91.6	77.9
2. 1-2	1.5	1.9	0.7	1.3	-	2.7	1.3	1.1	1.2	0.9	1.5	-	-	-	7.2	11.9
3. 3-5	0.2	*	0.1	0.1	-	-	-	0.4	0.2	0.1	*	-	-	-	0.7	3.4
4. 6-9	0.1	0.1	0.1	0.1	-	-	0.1	0.1	-	*	0.3	-	-	-	0.2	4.6
5. 10-19	*	0.1	-	*	-	-	0.1	*	-	*	-	-	-	-	0.2	-
6. 20-39	-	-	-	-	-	-	-	-	-	-	-	-	-	-	-	-
7. 40 or more	*	*	-	*	-	-	0.1	-	-	-	-	-	-	-	-	2.2
Item 910　Subject A01c　N	3055	1433	1517	2303	307	718	869	947	522	1803	965	1321	665	399	617	21

IF YOU HAVE NOT TAKEN LSD IN THE LAST TWELVE MONTHS, GO TO Q.B041.

B034: When you used LSD during the last year, how often did you use it in each of the following situations?

B034A: When you were alone

1. Not at all	79.7	81.9	80.9	79.2	88.1	88.8	71.2	73.4	84.1	81.0	82.8	-	-	87.6	78.2	95.5
2. A few of the times	15.1	15.8	9.6	14.6	11.9	6.8	19.6	21.8	14.8	14.1	12.2	-	-	12.4	16.9	-
3. Some of the times	0.9	-	2.5	1.2	-	-	3.1	-	-	0.7	1.8	-	-	-	1.0	-
4. Most of the times	1.3	1.2	-	0.8	-	-	1.2	4.7	-	0.6	-	-	-	-	0.7	-
5. Every time	3.0	1.0	7.0	4.1	-	4.5	4.9	-	1.1	3.5	3.3	-	-	-	3.2	4.5
Item 2400　Subject A05a　N★	174	89	62	127	7	53	50	33	37	69	59	-	-	7	150	10

B034B: With just 1 or 2 other people

1. Not at all	23.3	23.6	21.1	19.4	58.0	31.7	26.2	17.6	12.0	20.0	20.4	-	-	23.0	22.1	-
2. A few of the times	35.5	37.7	37.1	38.5	21.3	32.9	38.6	31.3	39.1	33.6	48.2	-	-	39.9	35.0	62.4
3. Some of the times	7.1	4.6	11.6	7.8	-	5.7	9.0	5.6	8.0	6.2	5.4	-	-	16.6	7.2	33.1
4. Most of the times	15.8	17.7	11.5	14.7	11.6	16.4	13.7	23.5	10.8	21.4	12.9	-	-	-	16.0	33.1
5. Every time	18.2	16.4	18.8	19.5	9.1	13.3	12.4	21.9	30.2	18.7	13.0	-	-	20.5	19.7	4.5
Item 2410　Subject A05b　N★	173	90	61	127	7	53	50	33	36	67	60	-	-	7	150	10

B034C: At a party

1. Not at all	39.5	44.1	36.7	39.6	51.3	33.4	38.6	46.5	43.0	52.2	24.9	-	-	40.2	40.0	10.5
2. A few of the times	32.7	31.4	30.3	31.7	39.3	38.6	30.9	25.8	33.3	25.6	37.7	-	-	33.5	35.8	6.7
3. Some of the times	11.1	9.1	15.5	10.6	9.4	13.9	13.6	8.3	6.4	10.9	11.6	-	-	-	10.0	42.2
4. Most of the times	7.7	3.7	11.5	8.2	-	9.0	7.0	11.7	3.0	4.0	14.9	-	-	16.6	5.9	16.4
5. Every time	9.0	11.7	6.0	9.9	-	5.1	9.9	7.7	14.4	7.3	10.9	-	-	9.6	8.3	24.3
Item 2420　Subject A05c　N★	171	90	61	127	7	51	50	33	36	68	60	-	-	7	148	10

B034D: When your date or spouse was present

1. Not at all	66.8	81.3	44.1	63.3	100.0	64.9	73.9	69.3	57.1	60.7	60.6	-	-	66.8	67.2	43.2
2. A few of the times	16.7	9.0	24.2	15.8	-	19.6	12.0	10.7	24.8	22.3	15.6	-	-	23.6	18.2	-
3. Some of the times	4.3	4.2	6.0	5.4	-	4.5	4.4	5.6	2.6	3.1	7.9	-	-	-	3.2	25.5
4. Most of the times	3.9	0.5	10.1	5.2	-	4.7	3.1	4.9	3.0	7.5	2.1	-	-	-	4.2	4.5
5. Every time	8.3	5.1	15.6	10.2	-	6.2	6.7	9.4	12.5	6.3	13.7	-	-	9.6	7.3	26.7
Item 2430　Subject A05b　N★	170	87	61	126	7	51	50	32	35	66	59	-	-	7	147	10

B034E: When people over age 30 were present

1. Not at all	77.6	80.5	78.7	78.4	100.0	74.5	83.5	72.3	78.6	81.3	71.1	-	-	76.7	79.7	48.1
2. A few of the times	9.7	7.5	9.6	8.7	-	14.5	9.7	10.0	2.4	10.4	6.9	-	-	-	10.4	10.9
3. Some of the times	8.2	8.8	7.9	8.8	-	7.8	4.1	8.4	14.6	1.4	20.0	-	-	16.6	5.9	41.0
4. Most of the times	2.2	0.7	3.4	2.1	-	2.2	2.1	-	4.5	3.0	2.0	-	-	6.7	2.3	-
5. Every time	2.2	2.6	0.5	2.1	-	0.9	0.6	9.2	-	3.8	-	-	-	-	1.7	-
Item 2440　Subject A05b　N★	171	89	61	126	7	53	50	32	35	68	59	-	-	7	149	10

B034F: During the daytime (before 4:00 p.m.)

1. Not at all	54.2	60.5	51.0	55.5	88.1	56.7	53.2	51.1	54.9	57.6	48.0	-	-	83.2	53.6	34.7
2. A few of the times	24.4	27.7	19.0	24.6	11.9	29.5	17.2	20.8	30.5	28.4	26.9	-	-	16.8	23.9	48.6
3. Some of the times	9.4	4.1	18.3	10.0	-	5.4	17.8	3.5	8.8	5.8	18.3	-	-	-	10.4	5.2
4. Most of the times	6.7	3.5	4.0	4.4	-	5.3	4.8	13.0	5.7	1.0	2.3	-	-	-	6.5	7.0
5. Every time	5.3	4.3	7.7	5.5	-	3.1	7.1	11.6	-	7.1	4.5	-	-	-	5.7	4.5
Item 2450　Subject A05c　N★	172	90	61	127	7	53	50	33	35	68	60	-	-	7	151	10

★=excludes respondents for whom question was inappropriate.　　* = less than .05 per cent.

QUESTIONNAIRE FORM 1 1986	TOTAL	SEX		RACE		REGION				4YR COLLEGE PLANS		ILLICIT DRUG USE: LIFETIME				
		M	F	White	Black	NE	NC	S	W	Yes	No	None	Marijuana Only	Few Pills	More Pills	Any Heroin
N (Weighted No. of Cases):	3179	1469	1562	2351	323	749	897	984	550	1841	999	1333	671	406	643	21
% of Weighted Total:	100.0	46.2	49.1	74.0	10.2	23.5	28.2	30.9	17.3	57.9	31.4	41.9	21.1	12.8	20.2	0.7

B034G: At your home (or apartment or dorm)

1. Not at all	54.6	56.6	54.0	53.7	88.1	57.5	46.8	56.8	59.2	52.1	51.8	-	-	73.1	52.5	63.4
2. A few of the times	24.1	21.7	23.0	23.9	11.9	21.9	29.3	22.8	20.9	23.4	24.2	-	-	20.2	24.8	26.9
3. Some of the times	10.8	8.9	12.2	8.4	-	12.8	13.7	5.5	8.5	9.1	13.6	-	-	-	11.2	5.2
4. Most of the times	3.4	4.9	2.4	4.7	-	3.1	4.5	6.0	-	5.5	2.7	-	-	-	3.9	-
5. Every time	7.2	7.9	8.4	9.3	-	4.6	5.6	8.9	11.4	9.9	7.7	-	-	6.7	7.6	4.5
Item 2460 Subject A05c N★	175	90	64	129	7	53	52	33	37	71	60	-	-	7	154	10

B034H: At school

1. Not at all	75.3	75.1	80.9	77.3	90.6	72.6	72.2	74.9	83.9	79.0	74.4	-	-	95.7	76.6	28.3
2. A few of the times	17.6	17.2	14.3	17.0	9.4	22.9	18.1	15.0	11.4	16.3	20.0	-	-	-	17.4	42.5
3. Some of the times	5.9	5.6	4.3	5.2	-	4.5	9.0	8.0	1.5	4.3	3.7	-	-	-	4.8	29.2
4. Most of the times	0.7	1.3	-	-	-	-	-	-	3.2	-	1.9	-	-	-	0.8	-
5. Every time	0.6	0.8	0.5	0.6	-	-	0.6	2.2	-	0.4	-	-	-	4.3	0.5	-
Item 2470 Subject A05c N★	173	90	61	127	7	54	50	33	35	68	60	-	-	7	151	10

B034I: In a car

1. Not at all	60.3	65.0	60.1	60.2	100.0	58.8	64.2	55.6	61.7	69.6	53.2	-	-	100.0	60.7	17.1
2. A few of the times	25.0	20.0	24.7	23.2	-	31.9	14.8	27.2	27.2	15.0	33.3	-	-	-	27.0	26.4
3. Some of the times	11.5	14.4	9.1	13.2	-	6.8	20.1	12.6	5.6	13.9	9.0	-	-	-	9.8	51.9
4. Most of the times	1.4	-	2.2	1.1	-	-	-	4.7	2.6	-	2.3	-	-	-	0.9	-
5. Every time	1.7	0.5	3.9	2.3	-	2.6	0.9	-	3.0	1.5	2.3	-	-	-	1.6	4.5
Item 2490 Subject A05c N★	173	90	61	127	7	54	50	33	35	68	60	-	-	7	151	10

B035: How many of the times when you used LSD during the last year did you use it along with each of the following drugs–that is, so that their effects overlapped?

B035A: With alcohol

1. Not at all	36.9	36.7	46.2	38.9	88.4	23.9	36.1	35.1	58.0	40.0	35.9	-	-	63.4	34.2	42.1
2. A few of the times	27.0	30.5	18.7	25.4	11.6	37.6	20.5	33.1	15.1	25.0	30.5	-	-	13.4	28.4	26.4
3. Some of the times	9.0	7.1	6.0	7.9	-	6.8	11.7	12.5	5.4	8.0	4.3	-	-	-	10.3	-
4. Most of the times	8.9	3.5	16.6	9.5	-	10.6	7.4	8.2	9.1	9.9	7.9	-	-	6.7	7.9	17.5
5. Every time	18.3	22.2	12.5	18.2	-	21.1	24.4	11.0	12.5	17.1	21.4	-	-	16.6	19.2	14.0
Item 2500 Subject A01h N★	173	90	62	128	7	53	50	33	37	69	60	-	-	7	152	10

B035B: With marijuana

1. Not at all	30.3	29.7	33.8	28.9	69.9	16.9	30.3	34.3	45.9	30.5	26.9	-	-	60.6	26.5	35.4
2. A few of the times	26.1	28.0	24.6	28.0	11.6	31.7	23.1	26.4	21.6	27.2	28.2	-	-	13.4	27.4	26.4
3. Some of the times	5.9	4.1	7.5	6.1	-	-	11.7	7.1	5.4	8.4	4.5	-	-	-	6.7	-
4. Most of the times	15.3	18.1	10.4	13.9	18.5	18.7	15.8	14.4	10.6	18.7	9.5	-	-	26.1	15.4	13.3
5. Every time	22.5	20.1	23.7	23.0	-	32.7	19.1	17.8	16.5	15.3	30.9	-	-	-	24.0	24.8
Item 2510 Subject A01h N★	173	90	63	129	7	53	50	33	37	69	60	-	-	7	152	10

★=excludes respondents for whom question was inappropriate.

QUESTIONNAIRE FORM 1 1986	TOTAL	SEX		RACE		REGION				4YR COLLEGE PLANS		ILLICIT DRUG USE: LIFETIME				
		M	F	White	Black	NE	NC	S	W	Yes	No	None	Mari-juana Only	Few Pills	More Pills	Any Her-oin
N (Weighted No. of Cases):	3179	1469	1562	2351	323	749	897	984	550	1841	999	1333	671	406	643	21
% of Weighted Total:	100.0	46.2	49.1	74.0	10.2	23.5	28.2	30.9	17.3	57.9	31.4	41.9	21.1	12.8	20.2	0.7

B036: What have been the most important reasons for your taking LSD? (Mark all that apply.)

A. To experiment–to see what it's like	88.2	87.5	91.4	89.0	86.5	80.4	93.3	88.8	92.1	91.8	85.7	-	-	100.0	90.3	57.8
B. To relax or relieve tension	7.9	6.6	7.3	5.6	-	8.4	13.1	5.2	2.5	6.6	10.7	-	-	-	8.5	5.2
C. To feel good or get high	63.9	58.6	63.6	61.2	16.7	70.8	64.4	64.5	52.8	56.9	64.4	-	-	31.1	66.9	43.7
D. To seek deeper insights and understanding	29.4	30.2	26.0	27.7	13.1	31.9	28.1	30.4	26.9	39.2	19.3	-	-	17.2	31.6	11.8
E. To have a good time with my friends	45.3	44.6	44.2	44.5	-	50.9	44.6	36.9	45.1	42.4	46.8	-	-	16.6	46.5	56.8
F. To fit in with a group I like	4.6	4.2	1.8	3.7	-	5.5	2.3	5.5	5.4	-	5.0	-	-	-	3.2	29.2
G. To get away from my problems or troubles	11.0	8.6	15.3	10.9	17.2	5.9	16.2	6.0	15.7	13.3	12.8	-	-	20.2	9.4	30.2
H. Because of boredom, nothing else to do	16.6	18.4	14.3	17.3	-	16.3	18.1	14.3	16.8	16.0	23.2	-	-	16.6	16.6	19.4
I. Because of anger or frustration	4.1	2.4	6.9	3.3	-	6.3	6.7	1.4	-	8.4	1.8	-	-	-	4.7	-
J. To get through the day	3.8	3.6	1.5	1.1	-	7.4	1.1	2.9	3.1	3.5	2.7	-	-	-	4.3	-
K. To increase the effects of some other drug(s)	8.0	9.5	3.3	5.7	30.3	10.9	8.7	8.4	2.5	3.9	7.4	-	-	-	7.6	20.6
L. To decrease (offset) the effects of some other drug(s)	2.1	1.7	2.2	1.1	-	4.2	-	1.4	2.5	2.2	2.3	-	-	-	1.9	6.7
M. Because I am "hooked"–I have to have it	0.5	0.5	0.7	0.7	-	-	1.0	1.4	-	-	0.7	-	-	-	0.3	4.5
Item 2520-2640 Subject A06a N★	167	86	61	127	5	52	47	30	37	69	58	-	-	7	148	10

B037: When you take LSD how high do you usually get?

1. Not at all high	3.3	2.6	2.0	0.8	20.1	1.8	-	7.2	6.3	3.3	-	-	-	-	2.3	-
2. A little high	4.1	4.6	4.7	4.4	13.7	-	4.1	4.3	9.9	4.3	5.9	-	-	32.1	1.8	19.8
3. Moderately high	23.3	24.9	25.2	27.5	24.2	21.9	25.2	11.2	34.0	28.5	21.0	-	-	28.7	23.9	6.7
4. Very high	69.3	67.9	68.2	67.3	42.0	76.4	70.8	77.4	49.8	63.9	73.1	-	-	39.1	72.0	73.6
Item 2650 Subject A01e N★	168	86	62	127	6	52	47	33	36	68	58	-	-	7	148	10

B038: When you take LSD how long do you usually stay high?

1. Usually don't get high	3.3	2.6	3.4	0.8	33.8	-	1.8	7.1	6.1	3.2	1.4	-	-	12.4	2.3	-
2. One to two hours	2.0	3.0	1.1	2.6	-	-	1.3	2.1	5.4	1.0	3.4	-	-	-	0.9	19.8
3. Three to six hours	32.8	31.6	39.5	37.9	13.4	35.4	25.6	30.9	39.9	33.0	37.0	-	-	58.1	33.6	53.0
4. Seven to 24 hours	59.8	59.5	56.0	56.5	52.8	62.9	67.1	59.9	46.1	60.9	56.7	-	-	29.5	63.5	27.3
5. More than 24 hours	2.2	3.3	-	2.2	-	1.7	4.2	-	2.5	1.9	1.5	-	-	-	2.5	-
Item 2660 Subject A01f N★	168	86	62	127	6	51	47	33	37	69	59	-	-	7	149	10

B039: Have you ever had a "bad trip" on LSD?

1. No	66.1	64.6	66.5	67.9	89.2	65.7	52.1	79.7	73.5	63.0	67.7	-	-	100.0	65.4	52.2
2. Yes, once	28.4	32.8	27.7	28.7	10.8	29.4	35.7	18.1	26.5	32.2	28.6	-	-	-	29.2	36.6
3. Yes, more than once	5.4	2.5	5.8	3.4	-	4.9	12.3	2.2	-	4.9	3.7	-	-	-	5.4	11.2
Item 2670 Subject A01k N★	172	88	64	128	6	52	50	33	37	71	59	-	-	7	151	10

B040: Have you ever tried to stop using LSD and found that you couldn't stop?

1. Yes	1.7	2.3	1.5	1.1	-	2.9	2.0	1.3	-	2.8	0.7	-	-	-	1.6	4.5
2. No	98.3	97.7	98.5	98.9	100.0	97.1	98.0	98.7	100.0	97.2	99.3	-	-	100.0	98.4	95.5
Item 2680 Subject A01i N★	171	87	64	128	6	52	49	33	36	71	59	-	-	7	151	10

B041: Do you think you will be using LSD five years from now?

1. I definitely will	1.0	0.7	0.9	0.7	0.8	1.1	0.9	0.8	1.2	0.7	1.2	0.5	0.6	0.1	2.7	2.2
2. I probably will	1.0	1.2	0.7	1.1	-	1.5	1.0	0.9	0.7	0.6	1.5	-	0.1	0.9	3.9	14.4
3. I probably will not	7.8	9.0	6.0	8.3	2.6	9.8	6.3	8.0	7.2	6.7	8.1	2.3	4.7	10.4	20.5	24.3
4. I definitely will not	90.2	89.1	92.4	89.8	96.6	87.6	91.7	90.4	90.9	91.9	89.2	97.1	94.5	88.6	72.9	59.1
Item 2690 Subject A04a N	3007	1398	1511	2259	309	699	856	929	523	1772	954	1296	642	385	608	21

The next questions are about PSYCHEDELICS OTHER THAN LSD.

This group would include the following drugs: Mescaline, Peyote, Psilocybin, PCP.

★=excludes respondents for whom question was inappropriate.

QUESTIONNAIRE FORM 1 1986	TOTAL	SEX		RACE		REGION				4YR COLLEGE PLANS		ILLICIT DRUG USE: LIFETIME				
		M	F	White	Black	NE	NC	S	W	Yes	No	None	Mari-juana Only	Few Pills	More Pills	Any Her-oin
N (Weighted No. of Cases):	3179	1469	1562	2351	323	749	897	984	550	1841	999	1333	671	406	643	21
% of Weighted Total:	100.0	46.2	49.1	74.0	10.2	23.5	28.2	30.9	17.3	57.9	31.4	41.9	21.1	12.8	20.2	0.7

B042: On how many occasions (if any) have you taken psychedelics other than LSD . . .

B042A: . . . in your lifetime?

1. 0 occasions	93.3	92.8	94.5	93.3	97.9	87.4	94.9	97.4	91.2	94.2	93.7	100.0	100.0	93.5	72.9	33.2
2. 1-2	3.4	4.2	2.5	3.5	1.3	5.6	2.3	1.3	6.1	3.1	2.8	-	-	6.5	11.6	31.0
3. 3-5	1.3	1.1	1.0	1.2	0.5	2.4	1.1	0.4	1.7	1.2	1.0	-	-	-	6.4	
4. 6-9	0.8	0.5	0.9	0.6	0.3	2.3	0.3	0.2	0.4	0.7	0.9	-	-	-	3.6	8.0
5. 10-19	0.5	0.4	0.5	0.6	-	1.2	0.5	0.1	0.1	0.5	0.4	-	-	-	2.4	
6. 20-39	0.5	0.3	0.5	0.5	-	1.0	0.4	0.2	0.3	0.3	0.6	-	-	-	2.1	5.3
7. 40 or more	0.4	0.7	0.1	0.3	-	0.1	0.6	0.4	0.3	0.1	0.5	-	-	-	1.1	22.5
Item 920 Subject A01a N	3006	1409	1498	2274	299	704	853	931	518	1787	941	1313	647	394	602	21

B042B: . . . during the last 12 months?

1. 0 occasions	96.3	96.1	96.8	96.3	98.3	93.4	96.3	98.6	95.8	96.5	96.9	100.0	100.0	96.9	84.3	66.4
2. 1-2	2.5	2.5	2.3	2.5	1.2	4.4	2.2	0.9	3.2	2.7	1.7	-	-	3.1	9.9	13.4
3. 3-5	0.7	0.7	0.5	0.7	0.5	1.2	0.7	0.3	0.6	0.6	0.5	-	-	-	3.2	3.4
4. 6-9	0.2	0.1	0.2	0.2	-	0.3	0.2	-	0.3	*	0.5	-	-	-	0.9	-
5. 10-19	0.3	0.4	0.2	0.3	-	0.6	0.4	0.1	-	0.2	0.3	-	-	-	1.2	9.7
6. 20-39	0.1	0.1	-	*	-	-	0.2	-	-	-	-	-	-	-	0.3	-
7. 40 or more	0.1	0.1	*	0.1	-	-	0.1	0.1	-	*	0.1	-	-	-	0.1	7.1
Item 930 Subject A01b N	3002	1405	1500	2270	299	700	855	930	517	1788	937	1313	647	394	600	20

B042C: . . . during the last 30 days?

1. 0 occasions	98.3	98.4	98.6	98.3	99.5	97.6	98.0	99.2	98.5	98.8	98.0	100.0	100.0	98.3	93.9	69.8
2. 1-2	1.2	1.2	1.1	1.3	0.5	1.5	1.6	0.6	1.3	1.1	1.3	-	-	1.7	4.2	18.6
3. 3-5	0.4	0.3	0.3	0.3	-	0.8	0.3	0.1	0.3	0.1	0.6	-	-	-	1.7	4.6
4. 6-9	*	*	-	*	-	0.1	-	0.1	-	-	0.1	-	-	-	0.1	4.8
5. 10-19	*	*	*	*	-	-	0.1	*	-	*	-	-	-	-	0.2	-
6. 20-39	-	-	-	-	-	-	-	-	-	-	-	-	-	-	-	-
7. 40 or more	*	*	-	*	-	-	0.1	-	-	-	-	-	-	-	-	2.2
Item 940 Subject A01c N	3002	1405	1498	2268	299	703	852	931	517	1787	938	1315	647	394	596	21

IF YOU HAVE NOT TAKEN ANY PSYCHE-DELICS OTHER THAN LSD IN THE LAST TWELVE MONTHS, GO TO Q.B046.

B043: When you take psychedelics other than LSD how high do you usually get?

1. Not at all high	3.4	-	5.0	2.9	-	2.0	7.7	2.8	-	0.7	6.6	-	-	19.2	0.5	-
2. A little high	13.6	18.7	6.4	13.8	-	11.6	13.5	9.0	22.1	17.7	7.3	-	-	16.8	13.3	13.0
3. Moderately high	36.8	24.7	52.6	40.8	18.6	45.8	30.1	23.8	37.0	39.1	40.3	-	-	34.8	39.2	14.8
4. Very high	46.3	56.6	36.0	42.6	81.4	40.6	48.7	64.4	40.9	42.5	45.9	-	-	29.2	47.0	72.3
Item 2700 Subject A01e N★	114	54	50	85	5	46	32	16	20	63	31	-	-	13	93	8

B044: When you take psychedelics other than LSD how long do you usually stay high?

1. Usually don't get high	5.2	4.2	7.0	6.8	-	2.7	9.7	9.5	-	3.6	11.3	-	-	31.3	1.2	-
2. One to two hours	9.1	8.9	8.8	8.4	16.5	4.1	6.4	19.1	16.3	6.4	15.1	-	-	7.7	9.0	13.0
3. Three to six hours	43.3	40.5	45.6	43.7	44.7	39.6	53.6	20.8	54.6	50.6	34.3	-	-	21.0	48.7	23.5
4. Seven to 24 hours	40.6	42.5	38.6	38.6	38.8	53.6	28.4	50.7	21.4	39.3	34.6	-	-	40.0	38.8	63.5
5. More than 24 hours	1.9	3.9	-	2.5	-	-	1.9	-	7.7	-	4.8	-	-	-	2.3	-
Item 2710 Subject A01f N★	115	56	52	88	5	46	32	17	20	65	32	-	-	16	92	8

B045: What psychedelics other than LSD have you taken during the last year? (Mark all that apply.)

A. Mescaline	54.1	37.8	68.4	53.9	25.6	68.8	54.2	47.3	26.8	52.3	54.5	-	-	35.7	57.7	47.1
B. Peyote	9.1	18.1	0.8	10.5	-	2.1	15.2	22.1	5.5	9.0	7.3	-	-	4.9	8.3	26.7
C. Psilocybin	23.8	41.9	6.7	24.6	32.7	22.3	25.0	16.4	30.4	24.0	19.6	-	-	17.0	25.7	14.8
D. PCP	21.2	20.0	17.2	17.9	26.0	14.1	25.5	38.3	17.8	15.7	22.6	-	-	42.4	14.9	65.5
E. Concentrated THC	20.3	27.6	10.4	21.3	-	14.8	23.6	26.7	22.7	14.2	28.8	-	-	8.9	20.2	43.5
F. Other	24.5	19.9	24.7	23.7	15.7	14.6	28.9	26.9	37.6	16.1	34.3	-	-	26.6	31.3	
G. Don't know the names of some I have used	17.2	15.9	21.5	18.9	26.0	6.4	28.1	25.2	18.5	16.4	19.9	-	-	-	17.7	42.3
Item 2720-2780 Subject A01l N★	115	55	51	87	6	46	32	15	21	63	32	-	-	13	94	8

*=less than .05 per cent.   ★=excludes respondents for whom question was inappropriate.

QUESTIONNAIRE FORM 1 1986	TOTAL	SEX		RACE		REGION				4YR COLLEGE PLANS		ILLICIT DRUG USE: LIFETIME				
		M	F	White	Black	NE	NC	S	W	Yes	No	None	Mari- juana Only	Few Pills	More Pills	Any Her- oin
N (Weighted No. of Cases):	3179	1469	1562	2351	323	749	897	984	550	1841	999	1333	671	406	643	21
% of Weighted Total:	100.0	46.2	49.1	74.0	10.2	23.5	28.2	30.9	17.3	57.9	31.4	41.9	21.1	12.8	20.2	0.7

The next questions are about some non-prescription drugs.

B046: Some types of diet pills (also called appetite suppressants) can be sold legally without a doctor's prescription by drugstores, through the mail, etc. These "over-the-counter" drugs include Dexatrim, Dietac, Prolamine, and others.

On how many occasions (if any) have you taken such non-prescription diet pills ...

B046A: . . . in your lifetime?

	TOTAL	M	F	White	Black	NE	NC	S	W	Yes	No	None	Mari- juana Only	Few Pills	More Pills	Any Her- oin
1. 0 occasions	73.4	86.9	60.3	70.3	85.7	75.7	70.0	76.1	70.8	74.6	70.6	85.6	77.9	66.4	46.7	61.7
2. 1-2	11.0	6.4	15.4	11.7	8.5	10.6	12.5	9.8	11.2	10.2	12.0	7.1	11.6	18.2	13.9	8.3
3. 3-5	4.3	1.7	6.8	4.9	2.1	3.2	4.7	3.8	6.2	4.4	4.6	2.9	3.9	5.2	7.3	9.4
4. 6-9	2.8	1.7	3.8	3.1	2.1	2.2	3.6	2.8	2.4	2.2	3.8	1.0	1.4	4.7	7.2	-
5. 10-19	3.3	1.2	5.4	4.0	0.4	3.3	2.5	3.6	4.1	3.4	3.4	1.6	2.3	2.4	8.8	-
6. 20-39	1.8	0.5	2.9	2.1	0.5	1.5	2.5	1.2	1.8	2.1	1.4	0.7	1.3	1.0	4.8	7.0
7. 40 or more	3.5	1.6	5.3	4.0	0.7	3.5	4.3	2.7	3.4	3.1	4.2	1.1	1.5	2.1	11.4	13.6
Item 21220 Subject A01a N	3043	1438	1515	2308	306	713	858	946	526	1799	969	1315	647	400	617	20

B046B: . . . during the last 12 months?

	TOTAL	M	F	White	Black	NE	NC	S	W	Yes	No	None	Mari- juana Only	Few Pills	More Pills	Any Her- oin
1. 0 occasions	84.7	93.1	76.8	83.0	92.9	85.1	83.4	86.1	83.6	85.0	83.9	92.7	89.0	82.3	64.5	70.6
2. 1-2	6.6	3.4	9.5	6.9	4.9	5.9	7.3	6.1	7.3	6.2	6.6	3.3	5.4	10.8	12.0	5.1
3. 3-5	2.5	0.8	4.2	2.7	1.5	2.5	1.8	3.1	2.4	2.6	2.6	1.2	2.7	1.8	5.6	-
4. 6-9	2.0	1.0	3.0	2.3	0.7	1.6	2.4	1.8	2.1	1.9	2.4	1.1	1.7	2.3	4.0	4.8
5. 10-19	2.0	0.8	3.1	2.3	-	2.5	2.3	1.2	2.4	2.2	1.8	0.9	0.5	0.9	6.8	3.4
6. 20-39	1.3	0.4	2.1	1.6	-	1.5	1.7	0.6	1.5	1.3	1.6	0.7	0.6	0.5	3.5	16.2
7. 40 or more	1.0	0.5	1.3	1.1	-	0.9	1.1	1.1	0.7	0.9	1.1	0.1	0.1	1.4	3.6	-
Item 21230 Subject A01b N	3033	1435	1509	2299	304	710	855	943	525	1797	962	1314	645	397	611	21

B046C: . . . during the last 30 days?

	TOTAL	M	F	White	Black	NE	NC	S	W	Yes	No	None	Mari- juana Only	Few Pills	More Pills	Any Her- oin
1. 0 occasions	93.5	96.8	90.4	92.8	96.8	92.2	94.1	94.2	93.0	93.9	92.7	97.4	97.4	93.2	82.0	75.6
2. 1-2	2.8	1.4	4.2	3.0	2.3	3.6	2.4	2.4	3.3	2.4	3.5	1.2	1.1	3.7	7.6	-
3. 3-5	1.7	0.9	2.6	2.0	0.9	1.3	1.9	1.4	2.4	1.8	1.6	0.4	0.7	1.7	5.8	-
4. 6-9	0.7	0.4	0.9	0.7	-	0.9	0.3	0.8	0.6	0.6	0.8	0.4	0.4	-	1.3	14.8
5. 10-19	0.9	0.4	1.3	0.9	-	1.7	0.7	0.8	0.3	1.0	0.6	0.6	0.4	0.9	2.1	-
6. 20-39	0.3	0.1	0.4	0.4	-	-	0.4	0.3	0.4	0.2	0.6	*	-	0.4	0.7	9.6
7. 40 or more	0.1	0.1	0.2	0.1	-	0.3	0.2	*	-	0.1	0.3	-	0.1	0.1	0.5	-
Item 21240 Subject A01c N	3036	1434	1513	2302	303	710	861	941	525	1801	961	1314	644	397	614	21

B047: Some stay-awake pills can be sold legally without a doctor's prescription by drugstores, through the mail, etc. These non-prescription or "over-the-counter" drugs include No-Doz, Vivarin, Wake, Caffedrine, and others.

On how many occasions (if any) have you taken such non-prescription stay-awake pills...

B047A: . . . in your lifetime?

	TOTAL	M	F	White	Black	NE	NC	S	W	Yes	No	None	Mari- juana Only	Few Pills	More Pills	Any Her- oin
1. 0 occasions	68.5	68.0	68.7	63.6	92.1	72.8	65.5	70.9	63.1	67.2	71.7	86.6	66.6	58.1	38.3	32.3
2. 1-2	12.1	12.6	11.9	13.5	5.1	9.2	12.7	12.1	15.2	12.9	10.0	7.8	15.4	19.0	14.5	4.1
3. 3-5	6.1	6.5	5.9	7.3	1.7	6.0	6.9	5.1	7.1	6.2	6.2	2.1	6.4	7.7	12.9	17.5
4. 6-9	4.1	4.0	4.0	4.7	0.2	3.3	4.5	4.1	4.3	4.1	4.2	1.1	4.4	6.5	8.5	9.8
5. 10-19	4.1	4.0	4.1	4.8	0.5	3.0	5.3	3.1	5.2	4.5	3.2	1.4	4.4	5.1	9.2	-
6. 20-39	2.2	1.9	2.6	2.7	-	2.0	2.1	2.6	2.2	2.4	1.8	0.9	1.4	1.4	6.7	3.5
7. 40 or more	2.9	2.9	2.8	3.4	0.4	3.8	3.1	2.0	2.9	2.6	2.9	0.2	1.4	2.2	9.9	32.8
Item 21250 Subject A01a N	3048	1432	1525	2313	309	718	861	944	525	1807	967	1316	646	399	619	21

*=less than .05 per cent.

QUESTIONNAIRE FORM 1 1986	TOTAL	SEX		RACE		REGION				4YR COLLEGE PLANS		ILLICIT DRUG USE: LIFETIME				
		M	F	White	Black	NE	NC	S	W	Yes	No	None	Mari- juana Only	Few Pills	More Pills	Any Her- oin
N (Weighted No. of Cases):	3179	1469	1562	2351	323	749	897	984	550	1841	999	1333	671	406	643	21
% of Weighted Total:	100.0	46.2	49.1	74.0	10.2	23.5	28.2	30.9	17.3	57.9	31.4	41.9	21.1	12.8	20.2	0.7

B047B: ... during the last 12 months?

	TOTAL	M	F	White	Black	NE	NC	S	W	Yes	No	None	Mari- juana Only	Few Pills	More Pills	Any Her- oin
1. 0 occasions	77.8	77.7	77.8	73.9	95.2	79.6	75.5	80.2	74.5	75.1	81.9	91.4	76.1	68.9	56.2	48.2
2. 1-2	10.1	11.3	9.1	11.7	3.9	10.3	10.6	8.6	11.7	11.9	8.0	4.9	11.9	16.7	15.5	8.1
3. 3-5	4.5	4.5	4.5	5.4	0.5	3.1	5.6	4.2	4.8	4.9	4.0	1.1	5.9	6.0	8.6	14.5
4. 6-9	2.8	2.3	3.1	3.1	-	2.7	2.9	2.5	3.5	2.9	2.3	1.6	2.4	4.0	5.1	8.2
5. 10-19	2.7	2.2	3.1	3.4	-	1.3	3.2	2.9	3.4	3.0	2.0	0.8	2.8	2.3	7.0	3.9
6. 20-39	1.0	0.9	1.2	1.3	-	1.4	1.0	0.8	0.9	1.1	0.6	0.1	0.5	1.1	3.6	
7. 40 or more	1.2	1.0	1.3	1.3	0.3	1.7	1.2	0.8	1.3	1.1	1.2	0.2	0.5	0.9	4.0	17.1
Item 21260 Subject A01b N	3034	1424	1523	2300	309	709	859	942	524	1801	960	1312	643	397	616	21

B047C: ... during the last 30 days?

	TOTAL	M	F	White	Black	NE	NC	S	W	Yes	No	None	Mari- juana Only	Few Pills	More Pills	Any Her- oin
1. 0 occasions	90.4	90.5	90.7	88.9	97.7	91.3	90.1	90.2	90.1	90.0	91.9	96.3	92.8	89.1	76.9	56.8
2. 1-2	5.2	5.4	4.8	6.1	2.0	4.4	4.5	6.5	4.8	5.9	4.0	2.6	4.2	6.1	11.2	8.1
3. 3-5	2.1	2.2	2.1	2.4	0.2	1.3	3.0	1.4	2.9	2.1	1.9	0.9	1.5	3.4	4.2	14.7
4. 6-9	1.2	0.9	1.3	1.4	-	1.2	1.4	0.9	1.1	1.2	0.8	0.1	0.8	0.5	4.0	8.7
5. 10-19	0.7	0.7	0.7	0.9	-	0.8	0.5	0.9	0.6	0.5	0.9	0.1	0.6	0.7	2.2	2.2
6. 20-39	0.3	0.2	0.3	0.3	-	0.7	0.2	-	0.4	0.2	0.4	-	-	0.1	1.1	9.6
7. 40 or more	0.1	0.1	0.1	0.1	-	0.1	0.3	-	-	0.1	0.2	-	0.1	-	0.4	-
Item 21270 Subject A01c N	3025	1420	1518	2294	309	709	853	939	524	1796	958	1310	641	397	611	21

B048: In addition to non-prescription diet and stay-awake pills, there are other stimulants and pep pills which can be sold legally in most states without a prescription–usually by mail. These are sometimes called "fake pep pills," "imitation speed," or "look-alikes," because they look like prescription amphetamines and sometimes have similar names.

Other than diet pills and stay-awake pills you have already told us about, on how many occasions (if any) have you taken other non-prescription stimulants or pep pills ...

B048A: ... in your lifetime?

	TOTAL	M	F	White	Black	NE	NC	S	W	Yes	No	None	Mari- juana Only	Few Pills	More Pills	Any Her- oin
1. 0 occasions	87.3	87.7	87.4	86.3	94.4	86.0	86.2	88.7	88.2	89.8	84.1	99.0	94.6	80.6	59.6	34.7
2. 1-2	4.8	4.8	4.9	5.2	2.0	4.7	5.1	4.7	4.3	4.5	5.5	0.6	3.7	14.2	8.8	10.7
3. 3-5	2.1	1.7	2.4	2.4	0.8	2.1	1.8	1.7	3.3	1.4	2.7	0.1	0.8	2.7	6.9	8.5
4. 6-9	1.3	1.3	1.1	1.2	1.1	1.5	1.9	0.7	0.9	1.2	1.5	0.1	0.3	0.4	5.4	4.9
5. 10-19	1.3	1.1	1.1	1.2	0.7	2.1	1.1	1.2	0.4	1.0	1.6	0.2	0.2	0.8	5.0	3.5
6. 20-39	1.3	1.2	1.4	1.4	0.9	1.0	1.6	1.4	1.1	1.0	1.5	-	0.3	0.9	5.6	4.0
7. 40 or more	2.1	2.2	1.7	2.3	0.1	2.6	2.3	1.7	1.8	1.2	3.0	*	0.1	0.4	8.6	33.8
Item 21280 Subject A01a N	3036	1433	1521	2308	307	708	857	945	526	1807	962	1315	651	394	612	20

B048B: ... during the last 12 months?

	TOTAL	M	F	White	Black	NE	NC	S	W	Yes	No	None	Mari- juana Only	Few Pills	More Pills	Any Her- oin
1. 0 occasions	93.1	93.5	93.3	92.7	97.0	92.6	92.4	94.4	92.3	95.2	90.0	99.6	97.5	93.6	74.6	58.4
2. 1-2	2.6	2.2	2.9	2.8	1.3	2.8	2.3	2.2	3.5	1.6	4.3	0.2	1.5	4.4	7.9	-
3. 3-5	1.4	1.4	1.3	1.6	0.5	1.8	1.9	0.5	1.8	1.3	1.5	-	0.8	0.6	5.5	12.0
4. 6-9	1.0	0.9	1.0	0.9	1.0	0.9	0.9	1.1	1.0	0.6	1.6	0.1	-	0.4	4.2	8.9
5. 10-19	0.6	0.5	0.6	0.7	0.2	0.5	0.8	0.6	0.3	0.4	0.6	0.2	0.1	0.6	2.1	-
6. 20-39	0.5	0.6	0.3	0.4	-	0.2	0.6	0.5	0.5	0.3	0.5	-	0.1	0.2	2.0	-
7. 40 or more	0.9	0.9	0.8	1.0	-	1.1	1.0	0.7	0.6	0.5	1.4	-	-	0.2	3.6	20.8
Item 21290 Subject A01b N	3030	1427	1524	2308	305	707	857	941	526	1805	961	1315	651	394	607	20

B048C: ... during the last 30 days?

	TOTAL	M	F	White	Black	NE	NC	S	W	Yes	No	None	Mari- juana Only	Few Pills	More Pills	Any Her- oin
1. 0 occasions	96.6	96.6	97.0	96.5	98.4	96.4	95.6	97.3	97.2	97.7	95.3	99.8	99.4	98.2	86.4	66.9
2. 1-2	1.5	1.2	1.5	1.6	0.7	1.8	2.0	0.9	1.3	1.0	2.1	0.2	0.6	0.9	5.5	7.5
3. 3-5	0.7	0.9	0.5	0.6	0.9	0.7	0.8	0.6	0.6	0.5	0.8	-	-	0.7	2.9	-
4. 6-9	0.5	0.4	0.4	0.5	-	0.4	0.9	0.4	-	0.3	0.7	-	-	-	2.0	9.6
5. 10-19	0.4	0.5	0.2	0.4	0.1	0.4	0.4	0.4	0.5	0.3	0.4	*	-	0.1	1.7	6.3
6. 20-39	0.1	0.2	0.1	0.2	-	-	-	0.2	0.4	*	0.3	-	-	-	0.4	9.8
7. 40 or more	0.2	0.1	0.3	0.2	-	0.3	0.2	0.2	-	0.1	0.4	-	-	-	1.0	-
Item 21300 Subject A01c N	3028	1427	1521	2308	305	707	855	940	526	1803	961	1314	651	394	605	20

*=less than .05 per cent.

QUESTIONNAIRE FORM 1 1986	TOTAL	SEX		RACE		REGION				4YR COLLEGE PLANS		ILLICIT DRUG USE: LIFETIME				
		M	F	White	Black	NE	NC	S	W	Yes	No	None	Marijuana Only	Few Pills	More Pills	Any Heroin
N (Weighted No. of Cases):	3179	1469	1562	2351	323	749	897	984	550	1841	999	1333	671	406	643	21
% of Weighted Total:	100.0	46.2	49.1	74.0	10.2	23.5	28.2	30.9	17.3	57.9	31.4	41.9	21.1	12.8	20.2	0.7

The next questions are about AMPHETA-MINES, which doctors have prescribed to help people lose weight or to give people more energy. Drugstores are not supposed to sell them without a prescription from a doctor.

Amphetamines are sometimes called: uppers, ups, speed, bennies, dexies, pep pills, diet pills. They include the following drugs: Benzedrine, Dexedrine, Methedrine, Ritalin, Preludin, Dexamyl, Methamphetamine.

IN YOUR ANSWERS ABOUT AMPHETA-MINES, DO NOT INCLUDE ANY NON-PRESCRIPTION OR OVER-THE-COUNTER DRUGS.

B049: Have you ever taken amphetamines because a doctor told you to use them?

	TOTAL	M	F	White	Black	NE	NC	S	W	Yes	No	None	Mari. Only	Few Pills	More Pills	Any Heroin
1. No	92.5	92.9	92.3	92.3	93.8	92.9	93.4	91.5	92.5	93.1	91.7	96.1	96.5	87.7	85.2	56.7
2. Yes, but I had already tried them on my own	1.8	1.7	1.5	1.6	0.4	1.4	1.8	1.8	2.3	1.5	2.1	-	-	2.5	6.0	33.3
3. Yes, and it was the first time I took any	5.7	5.4	6.2	6.1	5.8	5.7	4.8	6.7	5.2	5.4	6.2	3.9	3.5	9.8	8.8	10.0
Item 2790 Subject A01j N	3052	1428	1534	2317	305	704	867	952	530	1811	961	1310	647	397	628	21

B050: On how many occasions (if any) have you taken amphetamines on your own–that is, without a doctor telling you to take them . . .

B050A: . . . in your lifetime?

	TOTAL	M	F	White	Black	NE	NC	S	W	Yes	No	None	Mari. Only	Few Pills	More Pills	Any Heroin
1. 0 occasions	79.8	83.2	77.5	78.4	92.6	79.7	79.0	81.3	78.6	83.2	76.0	100.0	100.0	55.5	32.3	27.0
2. 1-2	7.5	5.9	9.0	8.2	2.8	6.5	7.4	8.9	6.6	6.7	9.4	-	-	44.5	7.8	16.1
3. 3-5	3.7	4.1	3.4	3.7	1.8	2.6	4.4	2.9	5.7	3.7	3.3	-	-	-	17.9	7.2
4. 6-9	2.6	1.5	3.1	2.6	0.8	3.6	2.8	1.7	2.3	2.1	3.0	-	-	-	11.8	19.3
5. 10-19	2.3	2.0	2.6	2.6	0.2	2.7	1.3	2.6	2.9	2.1	2.3	-	-	-	11.1	3.5
6. 20-39	1.5	1.1	1.9	1.5	1.8	2.4	1.3	1.2	1.3	0.9	2.2	-	-	-	7.5	-
7. 40 or more	2.5	2.3	2.5	2.8	-	2.4	3.9	1.3	2.6	1.4	3.8	-	-	-	11.5	26.9
Item 980 Subject A01a N	3044	1431	1526	2312	304	706	863	948	527	1806	966	1314	650	397	624	21

B050B: . . . during the last 12 months?

	TOTAL	M	F	White	Black	NE	NC	S	W	Yes	No	None	Mari. Only	Few Pills	More Pills	Any Heroin
1. 0 occasions	88.7	91.2	87.1	87.9	96.0	89.3	87.6	90.4	86.5	91.4	85.1	100.0	100.0	84.6	56.1	40.4
2. 1-2	5.1	4.0	6.0	5.6	2.5	4.5	5.0	5.0	6.4	3.9	6.9	-	-	15.4	14.8	17.6
3. 3-5	2.3	1.6	2.7	2.5	0.5	2.0	2.1	1.8	3.9	2.0	2.4	-	-	-	11.2	2.5
4. 6-9	1.5	1.2	1.6	1.5	0.7	2.1	1.6	1.1	1.2	1.3	2.2	-	-	-	6.3	28.8
5. 10-19	1.1	0.8	1.3	1.3	-	0.5	1.3	1.2	1.6	0.9	1.3	-	-	-	5.5	-
6. 20-39	0.6	0.4	0.7	0.6	0.3	0.7	1.1	0.2	0.1	0.2	0.9	-	-	-	2.7	-
7. 40 or more	0.8	0.7	0.6	0.8	-	0.9	1.3	0.4	0.3	0.4	1.3	-	-	-	3.4	10.7
Item 990 Subject A01b N	3033	1424	1525	2304	301	702	860	945	526	1806	962	1314	650	392	618	21

B050C: . . . during the last 30 days?

	TOTAL	M	F	White	Black	NE	NC	S	W	Yes	No	None	Mari. Only	Few Pills	More Pills	Any Heroin
1. 0 occasions	95.4	96.4	94.7	95.1	98.6	95.3	94.2	97.1	94.2	96.7	93.7	100.0	100.0	96.8	80.5	60.8
2. 1-2	2.4	1.5	3.2	2.8	0.7	2.0	3.2	1.3	3.9	2.0	3.0	-	-	3.2	9.5	14.3
3. 3-5	1.0	0.9	1.1	0.9	0.8	1.7	1.5	0.4	0.7	0.6	1.6	-	-	-	4.9	9.4
4. 6-9	0.5	0.7	0.2	0.5	-	-	0.2	0.9	0.8	0.3	0.7	-	-	-	1.9	11.5
5. 10-19	0.4	0.3	0.3	0.3	-	0.8	0.5	-	0.4	0.3	0.3	-	-	-	1.9	-
6. 20-39	0.2	0.1	0.3	0.3	-	-	0.4	0.3	-	*	0.6	-	-	-	0.8	3.9
7. 40 or more	0.1	*	0.2	0.2	-	0.3	0.1	*	-	0.1	0.2	-	-	-	0.6	-
Item 1000 Subject A01c N	3030	1425	1521	2303	301	701	855	945	528	1803	961	1314	650	391	614	21

IF YOU HAVE NOT TAKEN AMPHETAMINES IN THE LAST TWELVE MONTHS, GO TO Q.B059.

THE FOLLOWING QUESTIONS REFER ONLY TO TAKING AMPHETAMINES WITHOUT A DOCTOR'S ORDERS. IF YOU HAVE NOT DONE THIS IN THE LAST TWELVE MONTHS, GO TO Q.B059

*=less than .05 per cent.

QUESTIONNAIRE FORM 1 1986	TOTAL	SEX		RACE		REGION				4YR COLLEGE PLANS		ILLICIT DRUG USE: LIFETIME				
		M	F	White	Black	NE	NC	S	W	Yes	No	None	Mari-juana Only	Few Pills	More Pills	Any Her-oin
N (Weighted No. of Cases):	3179	1469	1562	2351	323	749	897	984	550	1841	999	1333	671	406	643	21
% of Weighted Total:	100.0	46.2	49.1	74.0	10.2	23.5	28.2	30.9	17.3	57.9	31.4	41.9	21.1	12.8	20.2	0.7

B051: When you used amphetamines during the last year, how often did you use them in each of the following situations?

B051A: When you were alone

1. Not at all	47.6	49.2	48.4	48.8	50.9	42.4	49.1	46.0	53.1	46.8	47.9	-	-	73.1	41.4	41.3
2. A few of the times	28.1	27.0	28.2	27.1	24.3	34.8	29.0	28.2	19.5	24.8	32.6	-	-	15.9	31.5	24.3
3. Some of the times	8.1	9.8	5.8	7.7	-	7.7	5.4	9.3	11.2	9.4	7.4	-	-	-	9.9	11.7
4. Most of the times	10.6	7.6	11.8	9.5	24.7	11.8	12.3	7.4	10.6	8.9	9.6	-	-	3.9	12.8	-
5. Every time	5.6	6.4	5.8	7.0	-	3.3	4.3	9.2	5.7	10.2	2.5	-	-	7.0	4.4	22.6
Item 2800 Subject A05a N★	316	113	180	253	13	73	99	79	65	141	127	-	-	57	243	12

B051B: With just 1 or 2 other people

1. Not at all	18.6	17.8	20.3	19.6	50.1	18.1	14.0	24.9	18.8	27.0	11.3	-	-	32.8	15.1	6.5
2. A few of the times	42.8	39.3	46.4	42.7	17.2	51.6	48.0	28.9	41.7	38.7	51.4	-	-	44.4	41.1	78.9
3. Some of the times	14.8	16.6	10.5	12.6	19.5	16.6	14.9	14.1	13.4	10.4	15.5	-	-	5.4	17.1	14.6
4. Most of the times	13.7	15.3	13.6	15.3	6.2	7.8	15.1	16.4	14.5	14.0	12.3	-	-	2.7	17.0	-
5. Every time	10.1	11.0	9.2	9.8	7.0	5.9	8.0	15.6	11.6	9.9	9.6	-	-	14.7	9.7	-
Item 2810 Subject A05b N★	317	112	182	252	13	73	100	79	65	142	127	-	-	56	246	12

B051C: At a party

1. Not at all	52.6	44.9	60.7	52.7	78.4	41.1	52.4	58.0	58.9	59.7	51.4	-	-	79.2	47.5	20.1
2. A few of the times	22.5	25.3	18.9	23.0	-	32.4	16.3	20.9	22.8	22.0	19.9	-	-	14.8	25.2	8.5
3. Some of the times	10.6	13.5	8.3	10.6	7.0	9.0	14.9	10.5	5.9	8.6	10.8	-	-	1.9	12.4	18.8
4. Most of the times	8.8	7.9	7.5	8.9	-	13.8	9.6	5.2	6.4	5.1	11.1	-	-	3.5	9.8	15.8
5. Every time	5.5	8.3	4.4	4.8	14.5	3.8	6.7	5.3	6.0	4.6	6.7	-	-	0.6	5.2	36.8
Item 2820 Subject A05c N★	313	113	177	251	13	71	99	79	64	138	127	-	-	57	241	12

B051D: When your date or spouse was present

1. Not at all	67.8	70.0	66.2	67.9	94.6	61.5	69.6	70.2	69.0	70.8	65.1	-	-	80.3	66.3	33.7
2. A few of the times	16.9	17.7	18.6	17.1	5.4	21.8	13.2	17.5	16.6	17.2	17.5	-	-	12.4	18.6	8.5
3. Some of the times	7.1	4.9	7.6	6.8	-	9.9	8.6	5.7	3.4	4.0	8.5	-	-	1.9	7.4	25.9
4. Most of the times	5.1	4.0	4.4	4.7	-	6.2	4.3	3.8	6.9	4.3	5.3	-	-	3.6	4.2	31.9
5. Every time	3.1	3.4	3.2	3.4	-	0.7	4.3	2.9	4.1	3.6	3.6	-	-	1.8	3.6	-
Item 2830 Subject A05b N★	312	112	177	249	13	71	98	79	64	137	127	-	-	56	240	12

B051E: When people over age 30 were present

1. Not at all	71.6	66.7	75.3	72.3	87.4	72.1	68.4	73.4	73.9	79.9	64.8	-	-	87.8	67.9	63.0
2. A few of the times	13.0	19.7	9.8	12.2	12.6	10.3	17.7	12.2	9.9	13.2	13.6	-	-	7.9	15.0	-
3. Some of the times	8.9	8.4	7.8	8.4	-	12.8	6.3	7.4	10.5	3.3	13.3	-	-	1.9	9.5	33.0
4. Most of the times	4.1	2.2	5.0	4.6	-	4.8	7.1	2.9	-	1.9	6.0	-	-	-	5.1	4.0
5. Every time	2.3	3.0	2.2	2.5	-	-	0.5	4.1	5.6	1.7	2.3	-	-	2.4	2.5	-
Item 2840 Subject A05b N★	311	112	177	249	13	70	99	78	64	137	126	-	-	57	240	11

B051F: During the daytime (before 4:00 p.m.)

1. Not at all	27.5	28.5	27.9	28.1	57.9	17.9	26.5	34.4	31.2	26.0	26.2	-	-	48.6	22.5	13.6
2. A few of the times	29.2	35.4	24.6	26.6	15.3	34.4	30.0	23.7	29.0	25.0	35.9	-	-	31.5	28.1	46.4
3. Some of the times	11.3	12.7	8.8	9.9	2.2	15.2	9.6	11.8	8.7	13.7	6.8	-	-	-	12.9	33.5
4. Most of the times	18.2	12.9	23.2	21.4	11.4	25.1	13.3	16.6	20.1	21.0	17.0	-	-	6.8	22.0	-
5. Every time	13.8	10.6	15.5	14.0	13.2	7.3	20.5	13.5	11.0	14.3	14.1	-	-	13.1	14.5	6.5
Item 2850 Subject A05c N★	312	112	177	250	13	71	99	79	64	137	127	-	-	56	240	12

B051G: At your home (or apartment or dorm)

1. Not at all	46.5	56.4	41.1	48.3	57.1	42.8	50.2	44.2	48.0	47.1	46.7	-	-	70.2	41.1	33.1
2. A few of the times	19.8	18.9	20.2	18.0	20.9	24.8	17.5	20.9	16.5	18.4	23.6	-	-	8.7	22.6	20.4
3. Some of the times	14.5	12.0	14.3	13.0	9.9	16.4	16.9	13.5	9.6	14.4	12.7	-	-	3.5	16.1	36.3
4. Most of the times	10.9	7.4	13.5	11.5	12.1	13.7	6.1	10.0	16.5	11.0	9.8	-	-	5.3	12.8	3.7
5. Every time	8.3	5.3	10.4	9.2	-	2.3	9.3	11.4	9.4	9.1	7.3	-	-	12.4	7.5	6.5
Item 2860 Subject A05c N★	316	113	181	253	13	73	100	79	64	141	127	-	-	57	244	12

★=excludes respondents for whom question was inappropriate.

QUESTIONNAIRE FORM 1 1986	TOTAL	SEX		RACE		REGION				4YR COLLEGE PLANS		ILLICIT DRUG USE: LIFETIME				
		M	F	White	Black	NE	NC	S	W	Yes	No	None	Marijuana Only	Few Pills	More Pills	Any Heroin
N (Weighted No. of Cases):	3179	1469	1562	2351	323	749	897	984	550	1841	999	1333	671	406	643	21
% of Weighted Total:	100.0	46.2	49.1	74.0	10.2	23.5	28.2	30.9	17.3	57.9	31.4	41.9	21.1	12.8	20.2	0.7

B051H: At school

	TOTAL	M	F	White	Black	NE	NC	S	W	Yes	No	None	Marijuana Only	Few Pills	More Pills	Any Heroin
1. Not at all	39.8	35.8	45.3	41.6	50.9	35.0	38.0	45.0	41.3	43.6	38.5	-	-	76.5	31.3	23.8
2. A few of the times	23.4	24.6	21.9	20.8	18.8	23.8	22.9	19.5	28.5	21.0	25.5	-	-	15.4	25.9	17.5
3. Some of the times	16.0	17.8	12.3	16.1	11.0	18.2	16.5	15.2	14.0	12.3	18.7	-	-	-	19.0	34.4
4. Most of the times	13.2	12.1	14.7	14.3	4.8	18.4	14.3	10.7	9.0	15.2	12.3	-	-	1.1	15.7	24.3
5. Every time	7.5	9.7	5.8	7.1	14.5	4.6	8.2	9.7	7.1	8.0	5.0	-	-	7.0	8.2	-
Item 2880 Subject A05c N★	312	112	177	250	13	71	99	79	64	137	127			56	241	12

B051I: In a car

	TOTAL	M	F	White	Black	NE	NC	S	W	Yes	No	None	Marijuana Only	Few Pills	More Pills	Any Heroin
1. Not at all	58.5	59.3	60.5	59.3	66.9	59.0	57.6	50.2	69.4	64.2	55.9	-	-	80.0	54.2	32.3
2. A few of the times	16.9	17.2	16.8	15.9	11.5	17.4	17.2	16.6	16.2	12.1	20.2	-	-	15.0	17.1	25.9
3. Some of the times	15.8	14.4	15.6	16.7	7.0	20.6	13.0	20.1	9.4	14.3	18.4	-	-	3.5	18.1	31.4
4. Most of the times	7.0	7.5	5.6	6.3	14.5	3.0	8.6	10.3	4.9	7.0	4.5	-	-	-	8.6	10.3
5. Every time	1.8	1.6	1.5	1.8	-	-	3.6	2.7	-	2.3	0.9	-	-	1.5	2.0	-
Item 2890 Subject A05c N★	310	113	174	248	13	71	96	79	64	136	127			57	238	12

B052: How many of the times when you used amphetamines during the last year did you use them along with each of the following drugs– that is, so that their effects overlapped?

B052A: With alcohol

	TOTAL	M	F	White	Black	NE	NC	S	W	Yes	No	None	Marijuana Only	Few Pills	More Pills	Any Heroin
1. Not at all	45.0	52.8	41.9	45.4	62.2	32.4	45.6	55.4	45.6	47.6	41.4	-	-	79.5	37.7	24.9
2. A few of the times	27.0	23.7	28.0	24.8	31.6	38.8	21.4	19.0	32.3	25.2	26.8	-	-	12.3	29.3	49.1
3. Some of the times	15.3	8.7	19.0	17.1	-	15.9	15.5	14.7	15.2	15.3	18.2	-	-	5.5	18.2	8.0
4. Most of the times	7.1	10.4	5.0	6.7	6.2	6.6	8.5	9.5	2.7	7.6	7.0	-	-	-	8.5	14.3
5. Every time	5.5	4.4	6.1	6.1	-	6.3	9.0	1.4	4.3	4.2	6.5	-	-	2.7	6.3	3.7
Item 2900 Subject A01h N★	314	112	179	252	13	73	99	79	64	139	127			56	243	12

B052B: With marijuana

	TOTAL	M	F	White	Black	NE	NC	S	W	Yes	No	None	Marijuana Only	Few Pills	More Pills	Any Heroin
1. Not at all	59.4	55.0	64.4	60.3	65.6	45.9	59.4	62.0	71.9	64.8	57.8	-	-	91.4	52.9	28.8
2. A few of the times	17.1	22.3	14.7	17.9	15.0	25.5	18.6	13.6	9.2	21.3	14.8	-	-	6.9	18.5	38.7
3. Some of the times	9.8	8.5	10.1	9.5	-	10.4	11.0	8.9	8.4	5.3	12.7	-	-	-	12.0	14.6
4. Most of the times	9.0	10.9	6.2	7.5	19.4	10.7	7.1	9.7	8.8	6.5	9.4	-	-	-	11.2	7.6
5. Every time	4.8	3.3	4.6	4.8	-	7.6	4.0	5.8	1.7	2.1	5.3	-	-	1.8	5.3	10.2
Item 2910 Subject A01h N★	310	112	175	247	13	73	96	79	62	137	127			56	238	12

B052C: With LSD

	TOTAL	M	F	White	Black	NE	NC	S	W	Yes	No	None	Marijuana Only	Few Pills	More Pills	Any Heroin
1. Not at all	96.4	96.2	98.1	97.8	100.0	96.9	96.7	95.3	96.7	97.5	97.1	-	-	100.0	96.0	85.2
2. A few of the times	2.3	2.5	0.4	1.4	-	2.5	0.6	4.2	2.5	0.9	2.1	-	-	-	2.7	6.2
3. Some of the times	0.7	0.5	0.9	-	-	-	1.7	-	0.8	1.2	0.4	-	-	-	0.7	4.6
4. Most of the times	0.5	0.4	0.5	0.6	-	0.7	0.5	0.6	-	0.4	0.3	-	-	-	0.6	-
5. Every time	0.1	0.4	-	0.2	-	-	0.5	-	-	-	-	-	-	-	-	4.0
Item 2920 Subject A01h N★	307	111	176	246	13	71	97	77	62	138	125			56	237	11

B052D: With psychedelics other than LSD

	TOTAL	M	F	White	Black	NE	NC	S	W	Yes	No	None	Marijuana Only	Few Pills	More Pills	Any Heroin
1. Not at all	94.8	94.4	95.0	94.5	94.6	94.9	94.6	94.3	95.6	94.7	94.4	-	-	100.0	94.7	72.5
2. A few of the times	3.1	2.9	3.5	3.5	5.4	3.7	2.8	3.8	1.9	4.2	2.4	-	-	-	3.2	15.8
3. Some of the times	1.3	1.9	0.5	1.0	-	0.8	0.5	1.8	2.5	1.1	2.0	-	-	-	1.3	8.0
4. Most of the times	0.2	0.4	-	0.2	-	0.7	-	-	-	-	-	-	-	-	0.2	-
5. Every time	0.7	0.4	0.9	0.8	-	-	2.1	-	-	-	1.2	-	-	-	0.7	3.7
Item 2930 Subject A01h N★	304	110	174	245	13	70	95	77	62	136	126			56	233	12

★=excludes respondents for whom question was inappropriate.

QUESTIONNAIRE FORM 1 1986	TOTAL	SEX		RACE		REGION				4YR COLLEGE PLANS		ILLICIT DRUG USE: LIFETIME				
		M	F	White	Black	NE	NC	S	W	Yes	No	None	Mari- juana Only	Few Pills	More Pills	Any Her- oin
N (Weighted No. of Cases):	3179	1469	1562	2351	323	749	897	984	550	1841	999	1333	671	406	643	21
% of Weighted Total:	100.0	46.2	49.1	74.0	10.2	23.5	28.2	30.9	17.3	57.9	31.4	41.9	21.1	12.8	20.2	0.7

B053: What have been the most important reasons for your taking amphetamines without a doctor's orders? (Mark all that apply.)

	TOTAL	M	F	White	Black	NE	NC	S	W	Yes	No	None	Mari- juana Only	Few Pills	More Pills	Any Her- oin
A. To experiment–to see what it's like	50.9	59.2	44.5	51.2	35.6	56.0	49.1	43.0	57.6	45.2	51.6	-	-	60.9	48.8	51.1
B. To relax or relieve tension	15.0	14.1	14.8	14.8	8.8	10.8	14.9	17.7	16.5	11.2	17.8	-	-	7.4	14.5	54.4
C. To feel good or get high	49.9	54.7	44.5	50.3	29.4	59.6	51.6	46.5	40.4	44.1	53.9	-	-	22.1	56.7	43.8
D. To seek deeper insights and understanding	3.9	2.8	5.1	3.9	.8	7.3	3.0	3.2	2.2	2.9	5.5	-	-	5.5	3.7	-
E. To have a good time with my friends	29.1	32.3	24.9	30.2	5.8	32.8	23.6	28.2	34.8	25.6	31.2	-	-	6.5	33.9	37.0
F. To fit in with a group I like	3.6	6.3	2.3	4.2	5.8	4.7	1.0	4.5	5.1	4.3	3.5	-	-	1.9	2.9	24.8
G. To get away from my problems or troubles	9.7	6.3	12.2	10.2	5.8	14.7	6.6	7.8	11.4	9.5	12.4	-	-	4.9	10.5	16.8
H. Because of boredom, nothing else to do	14.9	16.6	12.5	14.3	-	22.8	14.8	8.3	14.4	9.9	17.6	-	-	-	17.9	25.0
I. Because of anger or frustration	6.0	4.2	7.8	6.3	-	9.9	3.3	4.8	7.2	6.6	7.1	-	-	1.9	6.4	16.8
J. To get through the day	24.0	27.5	21.7	23.4	15.6	27.0	28.5	14.4	25.1	22.5	26.1	-	-	18.4	24.5	40.8
K. To increase the effects of some other drug(s)	7.5	7.7	7.1	7.4	12.4	6.5	12.7	3.7	4.9	5.9	7.0	-	-	-	9.0	11.8
L. To decrease (offset) the effects of some other drug(s)	1.6	1.6	1.1	1.5	-	3.5	2.0	0.8	-	1.4	0.5	-	-	-	2.1	-
M. To stay awake	56.6	57.3	56.3	54.5	50.8	64.8	56.0	47.6	59.1	58.2	54.7	-	-	35.8	61.4	57.4
N. To get more energy	64.7	62.5	65.2	66.0	52.6	64.5	64.2	60.2	71.4	66.9	61.6	-	-	43.7	69.9	60.2
O. To help me lose weight	35.1	9.0	52.3	36.8	31.3	37.4	37.5	26.9	38.7	42.0	31.3	-	-	19.2	38.4	43.8
P. Because I am "hooked"–I feel I have to have them	1.3	1.8	1.2	1.6	-	-	2.0	-	3.2	0.4	2.8	-	-	-	0.8	16.8
Item 2940-3090 Subject A06a N★	312	112	178	250	12	71	100	77	62	141	124	-	-	55	244	12

B054: When you take amphetamines, how high do you usually get?

	TOTAL	M	F	White	Black	NE	NC	S	W	Yes	No	None	Mari- juana Only	Few Pills	More Pills	Any Her- oin
1. Not at all high	10.8	6.6	13.7	10.0	27.3	8.2	12.9	12.5	8.6	8.3	13.6	-	-	26.9	7.3	-
2. A little high	42.6	44.5	43.7	43.5	34.0	40.9	48.0	30.6	51.4	36.7	49.8	-	-	42.2	43.0	36.3
3. Moderately high	23.3	31.0	15.3	22.2	7.0	24.0	17.3	29.9	23.8	21.8	21.9	-	-	10.8	26.6	20.1
4. Very high	4.6	7.0	3.6	4.7	13.2	8.8	1.7	3.7	5.1	6.7	3.1	-	-	-	4.5	27.1
5. I don't take them to get high	18.7	10.8	23.7	19.6	18.4	18.1	20.1	23.3	11.1	26.5	11.6	-	-	20.0	18.6	16.4
Item 3100 Subject A01e N★	305	109	173	244	13	72	95	77	60	138	121	-	-	55	235	12

B055: When you take amphetamines how long do you usually stay high?

	TOTAL	M	F	White	Black	NE	NC	S	W	Yes	No	None	Mari- juana Only	Few Pills	More Pills	Any Her- oin
1. Usually don't get high	21.3	15.4	26.3	20.8	46.1	16.3	27.1	24.3	13.9	23.1	20.8	-	-	41.1	17.3	-
2. One to two hours	36.8	37.3	35.0	36.1	28.9	32.1	38.0	39.3	37.1	33.8	35.7	-	-	40.8	35.9	41.6
3. Three to six hours	31.0	33.9	29.7	31.9	2.9	32.8	30.1	30.5	31.1	34.1	28.8	-	-	15.3	34.4	37.7
4. Seven to 24 hours	10.1	12.0	8.5	10.4	22.1	18.2	4.4	5.9	15.2	7.5	14.4	-	-	2.8	11.3	20.7
5. More than 24 hours	0.8	1.5	0.5	0.8	-	0.7	0.4	-	2.7	1.6	0.3	-	-	-	1.1	-
Item 3110 Subject A01f N★	309	111	176	248	12	71	100	77	62	139	124	-	-	55	240	12

B056: What amphetamines have you taken during the last year without a doctor's orders? (Mark all that apply.)

	TOTAL	M	F	White	Black	NE	NC	S	W	Yes	No	None	Mari- juana Only	Few Pills	More Pills	Any Her- oin
A. Benzedrine	13.4	17.6	11.8	13.3	21.2	7.1	10.4	20.6	16.6	10.5	13.4	-	-	11.6	12.2	46.6
B. Dexedrine	9.0	5.5	11.7	7.5	5.7	13.3	7.3	8.6	7.5	10.5	8.1	-	-	3.9	10.5	3.7
C. Methedrine	19.3	16.9	19.8	18.3	22.9	13.9	21.8	17.8	23.5	16.2	20.4	-	-	13.3	21.3	8.0
D. Ritalin	2.5	5.3	1.1	3.2	-	2.6	1.8	5.6	-	1.9	3.9	-	-	-	2.8	9.4
E. Preludin	3.2	5.6	1.5	2.3	15.5	-	5.4	6.1	-	2.4	2.4	-	-	-	3.2	18.3
F. Dexamyl	7.6	6.6	9.2	7.4	5.7	4.5	3.8	10.6	13.3	9.8	5.6	-	-	5.6	7.9	9.4
G. Methamphetamine	14.3	15.9	12.0	13.1	27.6	19.0	10.1	12.5	17.9	14.8	13.0	-	-	4.3	15.9	26.8
H. Other	36.4	39.9	34.0	34.1	43.0	47.8	32.4	35.0	31.4	31.7	40.6	-	-	21.1	39.4	39.5
I. Don't know the names of some amphetamines I have used	51.6	45.4	55.0	53.3	43.1	36.2	64.7	54.8	44.7	51.6	49.3	-	-	46.5	53.1	47.9
Item 3120-3200 Subject A01l N★	309	112	174	247	13	71	98	76	62	139	123	-	-	53	242	12

B057: What methods have you used for taking amphetamines? (Mark all that apply.)

	TOTAL	M	F	White	Black	NE	NC	S	W	Yes	No	None	Mari- juana Only	Few Pills	More Pills	Any Her- oin
A. By mouth	92.0	88.5	94.3	92.5	85.5	90.0	91.9	95.7	89.5	92.1	95.6	-	-	82.7	94.0	96.3
B. Injection	1.9	4.4	-	1.2	14.5	2.7	3.0	1.2	-	1.4	0.8	-	-	-	1.1	27.5
C. Other	21.2	27.7	16.1	21.9	4.8	29.7	14.1	18.7	25.9	20.2	19.7	-	-	22.1	20.9	23.1
Item 3210-3230 Subject A05d N★	315	112	182	253	13	71	100	80	63	142	127	-	-	59	243	12

★=excludes respondents for whom question was inappropriate.

QUESTIONNAIRE FORM 1 1986	TOTAL	SEX		RACE		REGION				4YR COLLEGE PLANS		ILLICIT DRUG USE: LIFETIME				
		M	F	White	Black	NE	NC	S	W	Yes	No	None	Mari- juana Only	Few Pills	More Pills	Any Her- oin
N (Weighted No. of Cases):	3179	1469	1562	2351	323	749	897	984	550	1841	999	1333	671	406	643	21
% of Weighted Total:	100.0	46.2	49.1	74.0	10.2	23.5	28.2	30.9	17.3	57.9	31.4	41.9	21.1	12.8	20.2	0.7
B058: Have you ever tried to stop using amphetamines and found that you couldn't stop?																
1. Yes	5.7	6.8	4.2	4.1	12.2	4.7	9.5	3.9	3.2	5.6	3.4	-	-	1.1	5.5	24.1
2. No	94.3	93.2	95.8	95.9	87.8	95.3	90.5	96.1	96.8	94.4	96.6	-	-	98.9	94.5	75.9
Item 3240 Subject A01i N★	308	112	175	248	13	69	98	79	62	138	125	-	-	55	240	12
B059: Do you think you will be using amphetamines without a doctor's orders five years from now?																
1. I definitely will	0.7	0.8	0.6	0.7	0.7	1.2	0.6	0.1	1.2	0.5	1.2	0.2	0.5	0.3	1.6	10.2
2. I probably will	4.3	3.3	4.8	4.0	2.6	4.5	5.6	3.3	3.6	2.9	5.7	0.7	1.2	3.5	15.8	7.2
3. I probably will not	23.1	23.4	22.6	24.5	13.5	25.4	22.0	21.0	25.9	22.8	24.4	12.7	20.9	32.7	41.4	38.9
4. I definitely will not	71.9	72.5	72.0	70.8	83.2	68.9	71.7	75.6	69.3	73.8	68.7	86.3	77.4	63.5	41.2	43.8
Item 3250 Subject A04a N	3037	1421	1533	2301	315	699	869	949	520	1802	973	1305	647	394	612	20

The next questions are about QUAALUDES (Methaqualone).

Quaaludes are sometimes called: soapers, quads, ludes.

B060: On how many occasions (if any) have you taken quaaludes on your own–that is, without a doctor telling you to take them . . .

B060A: . . . in your lifetime?

	TOTAL	M	F	White	Black	NE	NC	S	W	Yes	No	None	Mari- juana Only	Few Pills	More Pills	Any Her- oin
1. 0 occasions	95.0	94.6	96.1	94.8	99.3	94.2	96.0	94.9	94.6	96.4	94.1	100.0	100.0	93.0	82.1	25.9
2. 1-2	2.9	3.5	2.3	3.2	0.5	3.5	2.1	2.9	3.3	2.2	3.6	-	-	7.0	9.4	13.3
3. 3-5	0.7	0.6	0.6	0.7	0.2	1.1	0.7	0.9	0.2	0.5	1.0	-	-	-	3.4	11.1
4. 6-9	0.5	0.2	0.5	0.4	-	0.7	0.1	0.6	0.7	0.3	0.4	-	-	-	2.1	9.4
5. 10-19	0.4	0.5	0.3	0.3	-	-	0.3	0.3	1.0	0.2	0.4	-	-	-	1.3	16.6
6. 20-39	0.2	0.2	0.1	0.2	-	0.2	0.2	0.3	-	0.2	0.1	-	-	-	0.8	4.3
7. 40 or more	0.3	0.5	0.1	0.3	-	0.3	0.6	0.1	0.3	0.2	0.5	-	-	-	1.1	19.4
Item 1010 Subject A01a N	3019	1425	1514	2301	301	698	865	937	519	1795	957	1310	645	399	608	19

B060B: . . . during the last 12 months?

	TOTAL	M	F	White	Black	NE	NC	S	W	Yes	No	None	Mari- juana Only	Few Pills	More Pills	Any Her- oin
1. 0 occasions	97.9	97.7	98.8	98.1	99.8	97.2	98.1	98.2	97.9	98.8	97.4	100.0	100.0	98.3	92.3	51.2
2. 1-2	1.4	1.6	0.8	1.4	0.2	2.4	1.2	0.9	1.2	0.8	1.7	-	-	1.7	5.3	15.2
3. 3-5	0.3	0.3	0.1	0.3	-	0.2	-	0.4	0.6	0.1	0.4	-	-	-	0.8	13.5
4. 6-9	0.3	0.2	0.3	0.2	-	-	0.5	0.4	0.2	0.3	0.2	-	-	-	1.0	13.4
5. 10-19	0.1	0.1	-	-	-	0.2	0.2	-	-	-	0.1	-	-	-	0.4	-
6. 20-39	-	-	-	-	-	-	-	-	-	-	-	-	-	-	-	-
7. 40 or more	0.1	0.1	-	0.1	-	0.1	0.1	0.1	-	-	0.1	-	-	-	0.1	6.8
Item 1020 Subject A01b N	3022	1423	1517	2300	301	701	865	937	519	1797	959	1310	645	398	610	21

B060C: . . . during the last 30 days?

	TOTAL	M	F	White	Black	NE	NC	S	W	Yes	No	None	Mari- juana Only	Few Pills	More Pills	Any Her- oin
1. 0 occasions	99.3	99.0	99.7	99.3	100.0	99.1	99.1	99.5	99.2	99.6	99.1	100.0	100.0	99.6	98.1	56.9
2. 1-2	0.5	0.6	0.2	0.5	-	0.8	0.4	0.1	0.8	0.2	0.6	-	-	0.4	1.3	22.9
3. 3-5	0.2	0.3	*	0.2	-	0.1	0.4	0.1	-	0.2	-	-	-	-	0.5	8.7
4. 6-9	0.1	0.1	0.1	0.1	-	-	-	0.3	-	0.1	0.2	-	-	-	0.1	9.3
5. 10-19	-	-	-	-	-	-	-	-	-	-	-	-	-	-	-	-
6. 20-39	*	*	-	*	-	-	0.1	-	-	-	-	-	-	-	-	2.2
7. 40 or more	-	-	-	-	-	-	-	-	-	-	-	-	-	-	-	-
Item 1030 Subject A01c N	3017	1422	1513	2297	301	701	861	936	519	1795	957	1310	645	395	609	21

IF YOU HAVE NOT TAKEN QUAALUDES IN THE LAST TWELVE MONTHS, GO TO Q.B063.

THE FOLLOWING QUESTIONS REFER ONLY TO TAKING QUAALUDES WITHOUT A DOCTOR'S ORDERS. IF YOU HAVE NOT DONE THIS IN THE LAST TWELVE MONTHS, GO TO Q.B063.

=less than .05 per cent.　　★=excludes respondents for whom question was inappropriate.

QUESTIONNAIRE FORM 1 1986	TOTAL	SEX		RACE		REGION				4YR COLLEGE PLANS		ILLICIT DRUG USE: LIFETIME				
		M	F	White	Black	NE	NC	S	W	Yes	No	None	Marijuana Only	Few Pills	More Pills	Any Heroin
N (Weighted No. of Cases):	3179	1469	1562	2351	323	749	897	984	550	1841	999	1333	671	406	643	21
% of Weighted Total:	100.0	46.2	49.1	74.0	10.2	23.5	28.2	30.9	17.3	57.9	31.4	41.9	21.1	12.8	20.2	0.7

B061: When you take quaaludes how high do you usually get?

1. Not at all high	5.5	6.8	2.5	4.8	-	-	5.1	-	26.5	2.1	9.0	-	-	20.8	-	19.6
2. A little high	23.4	21.2	32.7	25.0	100.0	15.9	20.3	28.9	33.4	20.5	34.3	-	-	57.0	20.1	25.7
3. Moderately high	37.2	38.0	38.6	41.2	-	55.1	28.5	25.5	40.2	40.9	30.8	-	-	-	39.5	43.5
4. Very high	29.6	30.9	17.3	26.7	-	28.9	36.1	40.2	-	24.7	25.9	-	-	-	36.7	11.1
5. I don't take them to get high	4.3	3.1	8.9	2.2	-	-	10.0	5.4	-	11.8	-	-	-	22.1	3.7	-
Item 3260 Subject A01e N★	60	29	19	41	1	17	16	17	9	22	22	-	-	4	45	10

B062: When you take quaaludes how long do you usually stay high?

1. Usually don't get high	7.1	9.6	2.6	6.9	-	-	5.1	-	38.3	2.1	9.0	-	-	35.3	-	19.6
2. One to two hours	29.9	27.4	44.8	34.5	100.0	15.9	32.8	41.8	29.2	34.2	32.0	-	-	64.7	26.5	28.5
3. Three to six hours	53.7	52.4	45.4	48.0	-	59.8	59.3	52.8	32.5	55.9	46.2	-	-	-	61.8	47.3
4. Seven to 24 hours	9.4	10.5	7.2	10.5	-	24.3	2.8	5.4	-	7.8	12.8	-	-	-	11.7	4.5
5. More than 24 hours	-	-	-	-	-	-	-	-	-	-	-	-	-	-	-	-
Item 3270 Subject A01f N★	59	30	17	42	1	17	16	17	9	22	22	-	-	5	44	10

B063: The next questions are about BARBITU-RATES, which doctors sometimes prescribe to help people relax or get to sleep. Drugstores are not supposed to sell them without a pre-scription.

Barbiturates are sometimes called: downs, downers, goofballs, yellows, reds, blues, rain-bows.

They include the following drugs: Phenobarbi-tal, Seconal, Tuinal, Nembutal, Luminal, Des-butal, Amytal.

Have you ever taken barbiturates because a doctor told you to use them?

1. No	95.0	95.2	94.9	94.9	98.8	94.2	96.4	94.1	95.4	95.7	94.3	97.9	97.2	91.5	90.0	64.8
2. Yes, but I had already tried them on my own.	1.5	1.7	1.1	1.3	0.1	1.8	1.2	1.5	1.4	1.1	1.7	0.1	-	0.7	5.5	29.7
3. Yes, and it was the first time I took any	3.5	3.1	4.0	3.8	1.1	4.0	2.4	4.3	3.2	3.2	4.0	2.0	2.8	7.8	4.4	5.5
Item 3280 Subject A01j N	2956	1392	1492	2277	292	676	851	916	513	1778	933	1279	629	387	606	20

B064: On how many occasions (if any) have you taken barbiturates on your own–that is, without a doctor telling you to take them . . .

B064A: . . . in your lifetime?

1. 0 occasions	93.4	93.2	94.0	93.2	98.3	92.8	95.1	93.2	91.8	95.0	91.4	100.0	100.0	92.4	74.7	21.0
2. 1-2	3.2	3.3	3.0	3.3	1.4	2.8	2.1	3.2	5.5	2.4	4.2	-	-	7.6	9.9	32.1
3. 3-5	1.3	1.4	1.1	1.2	0.2	1.7	1.1	1.4	0.6	1.1	1.3	-	-	-	6.0	8.8
4. 6-9	0.8	0.7	0.7	0.8	-	1.0	0.4	1.0	0.6	0.7	1.1	-	-	-	3.3	17.4
5. 10-19	0.5	0.4	0.6	0.6	0.1	0.8	0.3	0.5	0.5	0.4	0.8	-	-	-	2.3	3.4
6. 20-39	0.2	0.1	0.3	0.2	-	0.4	0.2	-	0.4	0.2	0.1	-	-	-	1.0	-
7. 40 or more	0.7	0.9	0.3	0.6	-	0.5	0.9	0.7	0.6	0.2	1.0	-	-	-	2.8	17.4
Item 1040 Subject A01a N	2966	1400	1495	2282	294	679	850	922	514	1779	939	1294	633	394	592	21

B064B: . . . during the last 12 months?

1. 0 occasions	96.7	96.4	97.3	96.7	98.7	96.0	96.8	97.0	97.0	97.8	95.6	100.0	100.0	97.2	86.6	62.5
2. 1-2	1.5	1.8	1.2	1.6	1.3	1.6	1.8	1.3	1.3	0.9	2.4	-	-	2.8	5.3	10.0
3. 3-5	0.8	0.7	1.0	1.0	-	1.4	0.6	0.6	0.9	0.7	0.9	-	-	-	3.8	12.6
4. 6-9	0.3	0.4	0.2	0.3	-	0.4	0.1	0.5	0.2	0.3	0.3	-	-	-	1.3	8.1
5. 10-19	0.2	0.2	0.2	0.2	-	0.2	0.1	0.1	0.5	0.1	0.4	-	-	-	0.8	4.6
6. 20-39	0.3	0.3	0.1	0.1	-	0.5	0.5	0.3	-	-	0.3	-	-	-	1.6	-
7. 40 or more	0.1	0.2	0.1	0.2	-	-	0.1	0.3	0.1	0.1	0.2	-	-	-	0.6	2.2
Item 1050 Subject A01b N	2963	1400	1493	2279	294	678	852	921	512	1780	938	1294	633	393	590	21

★=excludes respondents for whom question was inappropriate.

QUESTIONNAIRE FORM 1 1986	TOTAL	SEX		RACE		REGION				4YR COLLEGE PLANS		ILLICIT DRUG USE: LIFETIME				
		M	F	White	Black	NE	NC	S	W	Yes	No	None	Mari- juana Only	Few Pills	More Pills	Any Her- oin
N (Weighted No. of Cases):	3179	1469	1562	2351	323	749	897	984	550	1841	999	1333	671	406	643	21
% of Weighted Total:	100.0	46.2	49.1	74.0	10.2	23.5	28.2	30.9	17.3	57.9	31.4	41.9	21.1	12.8	20.2	0.7

B064C: . . . during the last 30 days?

	TOTAL	M	F	White	Black	NE	NC	S	W	Yes	No	None	Mari- juana Only	Few Pills	More Pills	Any Her- oin
1. 0 occasions	98.7	98.5	99.2	98.8	100.0	98.1	98.9	98.8	99.0	99.2	98.4	100.0	100.0	99.8	94.4	75.7
2. 1-2	0.6	0.8	0.5	0.7	-	1.0	0.5	0.3	0.7	0.4	0.8	-	-	0.2	2.7	4.6
3. 3-5	0.4	0.3	0.3	0.3	-	0.6	0.2	0.4	0.2	0.3	0.3	-	-	-	1.4	12.8
4. 6-9	0.1	0.2	-	0.1	-	-	0.2	0.3	-	*	0.2	-	-	-	0.5	7.0
5. 10-19	0.2	0.2	-	0.1	-	0.2	0.2	0.2	-	-	0.2	-	-	-	0.8	-
6. 20-39	*	-	*	*	-	-	0.1	-	-	*	-	-	-	-	0.1	-
7. 40 or more	*	-	*	*	-	-	-	-	0.1	*	-	-	-	-	0.1	-
Item 1060 Subject A01c N	2961	1399	1491	2278	294	678	850	920	512	1778	938	1294	633	392	588	21

IF YOU HAVE NOT TAKEN BARBITURATES IN THE LAST TWELVE MONTHS, GO TO Q.B072.

THE FOLLOWING QUESTIONS REFER ONLY TO TAKING BARBITURATES WITHOUT A DOCTOR'S ORDERS. IF YOU HAVE NOT DONE THIS IN THE LAST TWELVE MONTHS, GO TO Q.B072

B065: When you used barbiturates during the last year, how often did you use them in each of the following situations?

B065A: When you were alone

	TOTAL	M	F	White	Black	NE	NC	S	W	Yes	No	None	Mari- juana Only	Few Pills	More Pills	Any Her- oin
1. Not at all	49.9	49.5	54.7	52.2	67.9	59.8	48.0	53.8	25.7	45.8	55.9	-	-	51.5	47.1	47.3
2. A few of the times	24.2	23.9	21.2	20.6	18.2	25.1	29.5	14.1	33.1	25.6	16.0	-	-	18.8	25.0	34.1
3. Some of the times	8.5	10.0	5.5	8.0	-	1.6	6.2	13.0	17.0	7.9	11.0	-	-	-	9.2	18.6
4. Most of the times	7.7	5.5	8.8	7.7	13.9	4.2	8.5	5.9	16.9	5.7	9.5	-	-	18.7	7.4	-
5. Every time	9.8	11.1	9.8	11.5	-	9.3	7.9	13.1	7.3	14.9	7.5	-	-	11.1	11.3	-
Item 3290 Subject A05a N★	98	51	40	74	5	30	24	29	15	38	43	-	-	11	74	8

B065B: With just 1 or 2 other people

	TOTAL	M	F	White	Black	NE	NC	S	W	Yes	No	None	Mari- juana Only	Few Pills	More Pills	Any Her- oin
1. Not at all	29.5	30.5	30.7	25.9	84.5	30.6	20.5	33.6	33.2	33.3	31.3	-	-	55.5	24.5	-
2. A few of the times	37.8	40.5	31.8	40.4	15.5	37.0	34.8	40.4	39.3	39.6	32.9	-	-	35.2	38.2	62.2
3. Some of the times	17.7	19.2	16.3	18.1	-	11.8	27.4	21.5	7.0	5.6	25.3	-	-	5.3	21.3	12.7
4. Most of the times	7.7	6.5	10.7	9.5	-	12.5	8.2	1.5	9.1	12.2	6.6	-	-	-	7.5	25.1
5. Every time	7.3	3.3	10.6	6.2	-	8.0	9.2	2.9	11.4	9.4	4.0	-	-	4.1	8.5	-
Item 3300 Subject A05b N★	97	51	39	73	5	30	23	29	15	38	42	-	-	11	73	8

B065C: At a party

	TOTAL	M	F	White	Black	NE	NC	S	W	Yes	No	None	Mari- juana Only	Few Pills	More Pills	Any Her- oin
1. Not at all	55.4	56.2	61.4	57.4	84.5	40.5	37.9	69.9	83.7	76.5	48.3	-	-	100.0	49.1	21.6
2. A few of the times	13.1	15.4	7.6	13.2	15.5	15.6	15.4	15.5	-	11.6	9.8	-	-	-	15.0	22.6
3. Some of the times	14.7	8.2	20.4	14.2	-	27.6	12.3	5.5	10.6	-	23.5	-	-	-	18.2	12.7
4. Most of the times	7.4	9.6	4.4	4.5	-	8.5	20.2	-	-	8.5	4.0	-	-	-	7.2	25.1
5. Every time	9.4	10.6	6.2	10.7	-	7.9	14.3	9.1	5.6	3.4	14.3	-	-	-	10.6	18.0
Item 3310 Subject A05c N★	97	51	39	73	5	30	23	29	15	38	42	-	-	11	73	8

B065D: When your date or spouse was present

	TOTAL	M	F	White	Black	NE	NC	S	W	Yes	No	None	Mari- juana Only	Few Pills	More Pills	Any Her- oin
1. Not at all	56.0	68.8	44.7	58.2	100.0	56.9	30.7	64.0	81.0	69.0	50.8	-	-	91.7	50.5	33.7
2. A few of the times	22.2	21.0	21.7	19.9	-	19.4	36.4	18.7	10.6	16.0	23.8	-	-	5.3	25.8	26.6
3. Some of the times	8.7	4.1	12.2	6.7	-	11.4	14.7	3.6	2.7	1.0	12.6	-	-	-	9.0	18.6
4. Most of the times	6.4	-	12.6	6.0	-	6.4	14.0	-	5.6	6.9	5.1	-	-	-	8.5	-
5. Every time	6.7	6.1	8.8	9.2	-	5.8	4.2	13.7	-	7.1	7.6	-	-	3.0	6.2	21.1
Item 3320 Subject A05b N★	97	51	39	72	5	30	25	28	15	40	42	-	-	11	73	8

B065E: When people over age 30 were present

	TOTAL	M	F	White	Black	NE	NC	S	W	Yes	No	None	Mari- juana Only	Few Pills	More Pills	Any Her- oin
1. Not at all	60.1	63.9	57.2	59.8	100.0	65.5	62.1	55.4	56.1	65.8	56.8	-	-	59.1	59.6	46.7
2. A few of the times	19.3	24.3	16.5	19.1	-	15.7	20.7	23.0	17.5	16.8	21.9	-	-	22.7	20.0	19.9
3. Some of the times	11.2	5.2	11.9	10.1	-	13.7	14.5	8.7	6.7	4.3	16.3	-	-	-	11.3	33.4
4. Most of the times	2.6	-	6.3	2.0	-	5.1	2.7	-	2.4	1.1	5.1	-	-	-	2.9	-
5. Every time	6.8	6.6	8.1	8.9	-	-	-	12.9	17.3	12.0	-	-	-	18.2	6.2	-
Item 3330 Subject A05b N★	99	51	41	75	5	30	23	29	17	38	42	-	-	11	75	8

*=less than .05 per cent.   ★=excludes respondents for whom question was inappropriate.

QUESTIONNAIRE FORM 1 1986	TOTAL	SEX		RACE		REGION				4YR COLLEGE PLANS		ILLICIT DRUG USE: LIFETIME				
		M	F	White	Black	NE	NC	S	W	Yes	No	None	Marijuana Only	Few Pills	More Pills	Any Heroin
N (Weighted No. of Cases):	3179	1469	1562	2351	323	749	897	984	550	1841	999	1333	671	406	643	21
% of Weighted Total:	100.0	46.2	49.1	74.0	10.2	23.5	28.2	30.9	17.3	57.9	31.4	41.9	21.1	12.8	20.2	0.7

B065F: During the daytime (before 4:00 p.m.)

	TOTAL	M	F	White	Black	NE	NC	S	W	Yes	No	None	Mari. Only	Few Pills	More Pills	Any Heroin
1. Not at all	44.3	50.7	41.0	46.8	29.2	37.4	39.5	50.8	52.5	54.9	38.4	-	-	60.2	40.7	26.6
2. A few of the times	26.7	29.6	22.8	24.2	50.2	22.7	35.6	20.6	31.5	25.4	24.6	-	-	18.2	28.6	33.7
3. Some of the times	13.0	10.9	10.9	11.6	-	23.3	4.5	16.6	-	8.3	16.6	-	-	-	13.3	33.8
4. Most of the times	10.8	1.3	22.2	10.6	20.7	16.5	18.5	2.0	4.4	6.7	15.6	-	-	12.8	12.3	-
5. Every time	5.2	7.5	3.1	6.8	-	-	1.9	9.9	11.6	4.8	4.9	-	-	8.8	5.0	5.9
Item 3340 Subject A05c N★	96	51	38	74	3	28	24	29	15	38	42	-	-	10	74	8

B065G: At your home (or apartment or dorm)

	TOTAL	M	F	White	Black	NE	NC	S	W	Yes	No	None	Mari. Only	Few Pills	More Pills	Any Heroin
1. Not at all	36.9	48.3	24.7	37.6	49.8	50.1	24.8	41.7	24.3	39.0	35.9	-	-	14.5	35.3	46.2
2. A few of the times	21.6	20.0	24.6	23.9	50.2	26.1	20.3	22.6	14.4	26.9	19.9	-	-	40.2	18.7	35.2
3. Some of the times	13.3	10.0	12.9	9.7	-	14.7	26.0	9.2	-	-	18.8	-	-	-	15.3	18.6
4. Most of the times	9.8	12.2	8.4	10.0	-	-	6.7	11.2	27.7	13.9	10.2	-	-	6.1	11.8	-
5. Every time	18.4	9.6	29.4	18.8	-	9.1	22.2	15.3	33.6	20.1	15.2	-	-	39.2	18.8	-
Item 3350 Subject A05c N★	99	51	40	76	3	28	24	29	17	38	42	-	-	10	76	8

B065H: At school

	TOTAL	M	F	White	Black	NE	NC	S	W	Yes	No	None	Mari. Only	Few Pills	More Pills	Any Heroin
1. Not at all	66.4	66.2	71.5	67.4	79.3	53.7	64.3	69.8	87.1	81.5	54.6	-	-	93.3	63.9	35.6
2. A few of the times	9.9	12.0	8.9	11.4	-	13.5	9.9	9.9	3.0	6.9	15.3	-	-	-	11.0	18.0
3. Some of the times	14.8	8.2	18.8	12.2	-	25.9	20.4	7.0	-	4.8	20.6	-	-	-	17.1	21.3
4. Most of the times	6.9	10.5	-	6.4	20.7	6.9	5.4	9.6	4.3	6.8	6.6	-	-	6.7	5.5	25.1
5. Every time	2.0	3.1	0.9	2.6	-	-	-	3.7	5.6	-	2.8	-	-	-	2.6	-
Item 3360 Subject A05c N★	97	51	38	74	3	28	24	29	15	38	42	-	-	10	74	8

B065I: In a car

	TOTAL	M	F	White	Black	NE	NC	S	W	Yes	No	None	Mari. Only	Few Pills	More Pills	Any Heroin
1. Not at all	64.0	67.8	59.7	62.8	100.0	64.6	42.7	67.9	88.2	75.5	55.7	-	-	82.8	64.2	21.1
2. A few of the times	12.8	7.5	22.5	12.6	-	11.7	19.3	9.2	11.8	6.0	20.9	-	-	17.2	12.4	14.1
3. Some of the times	13.6	11.8	15.9	14.6	-	17.2	21.2	10.9	-	6.4	21.0	-	-	-	12.4	49.9
4. Most of the times	6.9	7.7	1.9	6.4	-	6.4	13.3	5.7	-	5.2	2.3	-	-	-	7.4	14.9
5. Every time	2.8	5.1	-	3.6	-	-	3.5	6.3	-	6.8	-	-	-	-	3.6	-
Item 3380 Subject A05c N★	96	51	37	73	3	28	23	29	15	38	41	-	-	10	73	8

B066: How many of the times when you used barbiturates during the last year did you use them along with each of the following drugs– that is, so that their effects overlapped?

B066A: With alcohol

	TOTAL	M	F	White	Black	NE	NC	S	W	Yes	No	None	Mari. Only	Few Pills	More Pills	Any Heroin
1. Not at all	45.8	42.5	50.1	44.0	77.0	20.7	26.8	68.4	76.6	55.1	39.0	-	-	100.0	38.9	17.6
2. A few of the times	18.6	20.0	19.9	17.3	23.0	18.1	35.2	9.1	10.8	14.4	19.1	-	-	-	22.6	12.6
3. Some of the times	13.2	12.8	6.8	10.7	-	15.2	15.9	16.1	-	10.1	14.9	-	-	-	12.9	38.9
4. Most of the times	13.6	13.6	16.0	17.5	-	30.3	11.6	4.3	5.6	16.2	11.0	-	-	-	14.3	31.0
5. Every time	8.8	11.1	7.3	10.5	-	15.6	10.5	2.0	7.0	4.3	16.0	-	-	-	11.3	-
Item 3390 Subject A01h N★	95	50	38	74	3	26	24	29	15	37	42	-	-	10	74	8

B066B: With marijuana

	TOTAL	M	F	White	Black	NE	NC	S	W	Yes	No	None	Mari. Only	Few Pills	More Pills	Any Heroin
1. Not at all	42.7	38.3	52.7	43.1	77.0	26.3	36.2	51.0	65.9	49.3	43.6	-	-	90.6	36.7	12.6
2. A few of the times	19.9	25.0	13.4	18.8	23.0	20.1	29.5	17.3	13.9	18.5	13.2	-	-	9.4	23.4	9.0
3. Some of the times	16.3	20.0	6.9	15.6	-	22.0	12.3	18.9	7.6	11.5	17.9	-	-	-	14.8	58.5
4. Most of the times	9.4	4.3	17.7	10.1	-	7.2	17.8	6.5	5.6	11.6	11.1	-	-	-	10.7	14.1
5. Every time	11.7	12.5	9.3	12.5	-	24.5	7.3	6.3	7.0	9.2	14.1	-	-	-	14.5	5.9
Item 3400 Subject A01h N★	95	50	38	74	3	26	24	29	15	37	42	-	-	10	74	8

B066C: With LSD

	TOTAL	M	F	White	Black	NE	NC	S	W	Yes	No	None	Mari. Only	Few Pills	More Pills	Any Heroin
1. Not at all	92.2	92.3	93.0	93.3	100.0	97.2	82.6	95.9	93.9	86.4	100.0	-	-	90.6	95.3	57.0
2. A few of the times	5.5	6.7	2.9	6.1	-	2.8	9.3	4.1	6.1	9.3	-	-	-	9.4	2.4	36.3
3. Some of the times	2.3	0.9	4.2	0.6	-	-	8.1	-	-	4.3	-	-	-	-	2.3	6.7
4. Most of the times	-	-	-	-	-	-	-	-	-	-	-	-	-	-	-	-
5. Every time	-	-	-	-	-	-	-	-	-	-	-	-	-	-	-	-
Item 3410 Subject A01h N★	93	49	40	73	3	24	26	28	15	38	41	-	-	10	73	7

★=excludes respondents for whom question was inappropriate.

QUESTIONNAIRE FORM 1 1986	TOTAL	SEX		RACE		REGION				4YR COLLEGE PLANS		ILLICIT DRUG USE: LIFETIME				
		M	F	White	Black	NE	NC	S	W	Yes	No	None	Marijuana Only	Few Pills	More Pills	Any Heroin
N (Weighted No. of Cases):	3179	1469	1562	2351	323	749	897	984	550	1841	999	1333	671	406	643	21
% of Weighted Total:	100.0	46.2	49.1	74.0	10.2	23.5	28.2	30.9	17.3	57.9	31.4	41.9	21.1	12.8	20.2	0.7

B066D: With psychedelics other than LSD

1. Not at all	97.3	99.1	97.2	98.8	100.0	100.0	95.5	95.1	100.0	98.8	96.2	-	-	100.0	98.5	81.4
2. A few of the times	1.0	0.9	1.1	1.2	-	-	1.9	1.5	-	1.2	-	-	-	-	0.6	5.9
3. Some of the times	1.1	-	-	-	-	-	-	3.4	-	-	2.4	-	-	-	-	12.7
4. Most of the times	0.7	-	1.6	-	-	-	2.6	-	-	-	1.5	-	-	-	0.9	-
5. Every time	-	-	-	-	-	-	-	-	-	-	-	-	-	-	-	-
Item 3420 Subject A01h N★	93	49	38	74	3	25	24	29	15	37	42	-	-	10	72	8

B066E: With amphetamines

1. Not at all	85.6	90.2	86.4	87.3	100.0	84.7	81.6	89.8	85.2	91.3	85.3	-	-	93.9	84.2	81.4
2. A few of the times	9.5	6.7	11.4	9.5	-	15.3	9.0	5.6	7.8	4.4	11.5	-	-	6.1	11.4	-
3. Some of the times	2.1	0.9	1.3	1.3	-	-	4.0	3.4	-	1.4	2.4	-	-	-	0.7	18.6
4. Most of the times	1.1	2.1	-	1.4	-	-	-	-	7.0	2.9	-	-	-	-	1.4	-
5. Every time	1.8	-	0.9	0.5	-	-	5.4	1.2	-	-	0.8	-	-	-	2.3	-
Item 3430 Subject A01h N★	94	49	38	74	3	26	24	29	15	37	42	-	-	10	73	8

B066F: With quaaludes

1. Not at all	88.6	85.1	95.9	89.0	73.1	86.3	81.2	96.5	89.3	91.7	90.2	-	-	83.9	92.0	58.8
2. A few of the times	4.7	7.5	-	5.0	-	13.7	-	-	6.2	-	3.6	-	-	9.4	3.9	8.6
3. Some of the times	4.0	2.3	4.1	3.6	-	-	11.3	3.5	-	3.0	6.2	-	-	-	2.2	26.7
4. Most of the times	2.7	5.0	-	2.4	26.9	-	7.6	-	4.4	5.4	-	-	-	6.7	1.9	5.9
5. Every time	-	-	-	-	-	-	-	-	-	-	-	-	-	-	-	-
Item 3440 Subject A01h N★	91	48	38	73	2	25	23	28	15	37	41	-	-	10	70	8

B067: What are the most important reasons for your taking barbiturates without a doctor's orders? (Mark all that apply.)

A. To experiment–to see what it's like	50.7	51.5	47.9	48.9	67.5	56.2	55.1	49.1	35.8	36.1	58.2	-	-	31.1	51.6	66.3
B. To relax or relieve tension	61.1	54.2	70.1	64.5	-	61.3	54.3	66.7	63.1	64.6	63.6	-	-	75.1	64.8	8.6
C. To feel good or get high	44.9	43.0	42.2	43.5	-	60.8	58.0	27.4	25.3	28.2	50.2	-	-	-	49.0	62.2
D. To seek deeper insights and understanding	2.3	2.4	-	0.8	-	2.2	-	6.1	-	1.4	4.1	-	-	-	1.5	12.7
E. To have a good time with my friends	30.1	33.2	24.3	30.0	-	38.7	38.4	22.7	13.6	12.5	43.7	-	-	-	32.5	44.6
F. To fit in with a group I like	5.5	6.6	4.9	6.9	-	13.4	-	6.5	-	5.0	6.3	-	-	-	5.5	12.1
G. To get away from my problems or troubles	14.2	2.4	24.9	12.5	-	11.0	20.3	13.2	10.9	9.8	20.8	-	-	9.7	15.0	12.7
H. Because of boredom, nothing else to do	9.6	11.1	3.0	6.6	-	12.1	6.4	3.7	21.6	3.1	4.6	-	-	-	11.9	-
I. Because of anger or frustration	7.0	1.2	14.9	7.6	38.3	6.1	9.3	4.9	8.0	4.6	11.9	-	-	12.3	7.0	-
J. To get through the day	9.4	6.3	8.8	6.4	-	4.9	18.2	8.6	3.1	0.8	14.9	-	-	-	10.3	12.7
K. To increase the effects of some other drug(s)	16.8	19.4	10.9	18.5	-	34.4	16.0	8.3	2.8	9.0	21.5	-	-	-	13.8	65.8
L. To decrease (offset) the effects of some other drug(s)	4.4	7.0	-	4.6	-	7.6	1.8	2.3	7.2	2.7	1.5	-	-	-	3.9	14.5
M. To get to sleep	43.4	40.3	50.7	43.3	32.5	24.5	37.5	59.1	58.8	49.7	37.6	-	-	61.1	42.8	27.6
N. To relieve physical pain	31.4	30.6	32.0	29.1	32.5	28.5	31.6	22.7	51.1	30.9	28.6	-	-	-	35.0	36.0
O. Because I am "hooked"–I have to have them	2.1	-	5.1	2.7	-	-	6.0	-	2.8	1.1	4.0	-	-	-	2.6	-
Item 3450-3580 Subject A06a N★	92	47	39	73	2	25	26	26	15	38	39	-	-	10	74	8

B068: When you take barbiturates how high do you usually get?

1. Not at all high	8.7	12.3	5.7	7.5	-	4.7	10.7	2.8	22.7	12.8	4.5	-	-	9.4	6.7	12.6
2. A little high	33.2	37.4	31.1	35.6	100.0	29.2	27.7	47.2	24.3	32.8	45.6	-	-	31.0	34.7	26.7
3. Moderately high	32.2	29.3	30.1	29.1	-	41.2	46.0	22.9	10.5	23.3	30.2	-	-	-	36.6	35.6
4. Very high	8.0	12.9	3.4	10.2	-	19.1	3.9	2.2	5.5	10.9	4.2	-	-	-	7.4	25.1
5. I don't take them to get high	17.9	8.1	29.8	17.6	-	5.8	11.7	24.9	37.0	20.2	15.5	-	-	59.6	14.7	-
Item 3590 Subject A01e N★	94	48	40	73	2	26	25	27	15	38	38	-	-	10	75	8

★=excludes respondents for whom question was inappropriate.

QUESTIONNAIRE FORM 1 1986	TOTAL	SEX		RACE		REGION				4YR COLLEGE PLANS		ILLICIT DRUG USE: LIFETIME				
		M	F	White	Black	NE	NC	S	W	Yes	No	None	Mari-juana Only	Few Pills	More Pills	Any Her-oin
N (Weighted No. of Cases):	3179	1469	1562	2351	323	749	897	984	550	1841	999	1333	671	406	643	21
% of Weighted Total:	100.0	46.2	49.1	74.0	10.2	23.5	28.2	30.9	17.3	57.9	31.4	41.9	21.1	12.8	20.2	0.7
B069: When you take barbiturates how long do you usually stay high?																
1. Usually don't get high	21.9	20.4	24.6	22.0	-	10.6	17.8	26.4	41.7	26.6	20.4	-	-	65.5	16.0	12.6
2. One to two hours	29.7	25.5	34.0	31.0	61.7	30.1	20.5	37.3	31.3	17.3	40.6	-	-	25.7	31.0	26.7
3. Three to six hours	45.0	49.4	39.2	44.0	-	54.5	54.6	36.3	27.0	56.2	34.2	-	-	-	50.0	60.7
4. Seven to 24 hours	3.3	4.7	2.2	3.1	38.3	4.8	7.1	-	-	-	4.8	-	-	8.8	3.0	-
5. More than 24 hours	-	-	-	-	-	-	-	-	-	-	-	-	-	-	-	-
Item 3600 Subject A01f N★	93	48	39	73	2	26	26	27	14	37	39	-	-	10	74	8
B070: What barbiturates have you taken during the last year without a doctor's orders? (Mark all that apply.)																
A. Phenobarbital	23.9	33.1	13.1	26.9	-	15.9	24.9	27.9	29.2	28.5	19.9	-	-	11.6	26.1	18.6
B. Seconal	14.9	15.5	15.0	12.6	32.5	13.5	29.7	9.9	-	13.8	14.9	-	-	-	16.0	22.6
C. Tuinal	14.7	13.8	18.4	16.4	-	36.7	12.8	2.4	-	1.5	28.8	-	-	-	17.4	5.9
D. Nembutal	11.2	14.6	4.2	10.4	-	4.8	17.9	13.4	7.2	10.2	8.5	-	-	-	10.9	27.1
E. Luminal	7.8	10.0	6.2	5.2	70.8	2.1	10.1	15.7	-	8.1	4.1	-	-	10.8	6.8	14.9
F. Desbutal	3.0	4.2	1.9	2.0	-	-	5.1	5.6	-	1.8	-	-	-	-	2.7	9.0
G. Amytal	12.1	14.2	8.7	11.8	-	2.2	21.7	14.7	8.0	17.9	7.7	-	-	-	12.0	26.7
H. Adrenocal	7.0	9.4	4.9	4.8	-	2.1	6.8	11.8	7.5	12.2	-	-	-	-	7.0	14.9
I. Other	38.8	47.1	31.2	41.1	32.5	38.7	48.1	44.0	13.6	29.7	44.5	-	-	41.0	41.3	18.0
J. Don't know the names of some that I have used	49.2	41.7	55.5	43.2	67.5	51.5	44.1	42.7	65.5	46.4	44.0	-	-	47.4	47.0	64.4
Item 3610-3700 Subject A01l N★	92	49	36	71	2	26	26	25	15	38	39	-	-	8	75	8
B071: Have you ever tried to stop using barbiturates and found that you couldn't stop?																
1. Yes	2.4	1.3	4.1	2.9	-	2.4	6.5	-	-	-	4.1	-	-	-	2.9	-
2. No	97.6	98.7	95.9	97.1	100.0	97.6	93.5	100.0	100.0	100.0	95.9	-	-	100.0	97.1	100.0
Item 3710 Subject A01i N★	90	46	38	72	2	25	24	26	16	36	38	-	-	10	74	7
B072: Do you think you will be using barbiturates without a doctor's prescription five years from now?																
1. I definitely will	0.4	0.3	0.5	0.3	0.8	0.3	0.3	0.2	1.0	0.4	0.4	0.2	0.4	0.2	0.7	-
2. I probably will	1.7	1.9	1.3	1.4	1.1	2.3	1.6	1.4	1.7	0.9	2.4	0.5	0.2	1.9	5.9	8.4
3. I probably will not	17.5	19.5	15.4	17.8	10.1	17.1	15.8	17.6	20.5	16.5	19.0	9.2	15.3	24.3	33.2	31.3
4. I definitely will not	80.4	78.3	82.8	80.4	88.0	80.3	82.3	80.8	76.8	82.2	78.2	90.1	84.1	73.7	60.2	60.3
Item 3720 Subject A04a N	3006	1422	1517	2300	311	691	863	931	521	1800	960	1292	641	398	599	21

The next questions are about TRANQUILIZ-ERS, which doctors sometimes prescribe to calm people down, quiet their nerves, or relax their muscles.

They include the following drugs: Librium, Valium, Miltown, Equanil, Meprobamate, Serax, Atarax, Tranxene, Vistaril.

	TOTAL	M	F	White	Black	NE	NC	S	W	Yes	No	None	Mari-juana Only	Few Pills	More Pills	Any Her-oin
B073: Have you ever taken tranquilizers because a doctor told you to use them?																
1. No	89.3	90.3	88.5	88.4	96.5	89.4	90.6	88.2	88.9	88.9	89.4	94.5	94.5	84.7	76.9	50.9
2. Yes, but I had already tried them on my own.	1.5	1.5	1.4	1.5	0.5	2.0	1.1	1.7	1.2	1.2	1.9	-	0.1	1.0	5.8	26.7
3. Yes, and it was the first time I took any	9.2	8.2	10.1	10.1	2.9	8.6	8.3	10.2	9.9	9.9	8.8	5.5	5.4	14.3	17.3	22.4
Item 3730 Subject A01j N	3004	1421	1522	2304	302	700	858	932	515	1807	951	1304	634	395	608	21

B074: On how many occasions (if any) have you taken tranquilizers on your own–that is, without a doctor telling you to take them . . .

★=excludes respondents for whom question was inappropriate.

QUESTIONNAIRE FORM 1 1986	TOTAL	SEX		RACE		REGION				4YR COLLEGE PLANS		ILLICIT DRUG USE: LIFETIME				
		M	F	White	Black	NE	NC	S	W	Yes	No	None	Mari-juana Only	Few Pills	More Pills	Any Her-oin
N (Weighted No. of Cases):	3179	1469	1562	2351	323	749	897	984	550	1841	999	1333	671	406	643	21
% of Weighted Total:	100.0	46.2	49.1	74.0	10.2	23.5	28.2	30.9	17.3	57.9	31.4	41.9	21.1	12.8	20.2	0.7
B074A: . . . in your lifetime?																
1. 0 occasions	90.8	92.1	90.0	90.1	97.9	89.3	92.1	90.8	90.8	91.4	90.5	100.0	100.0	83.7	67.1	36.7
2. 1-2	4.9	4.2	5.5	5.4	1.5	6.1	3.7	5.2	4.8	4.8	4.8	-	-	16.3	13.1	21.8
3. 3-5	1.6	1.0	2.1	1.7	0.3	1.0	1.4	1.9	2.3	1.9	1.0	-	-	-	7.5	16.7
4. 6-9	0.7	0.7	0.7	0.7	0.3	0.9	0.7	0.6	0.8	0.6	0.9	-	-	-	3.6	3.5
5. 10-19	0.8	0.7	0.9	0.9	-	0.8	1.1	0.7	0.5	0.7	0.7	-	-	-	4.0	-
6. 20-39	0.4	0.5	0.3	0.4	-	0.7	0.2	0.4	0.4	0.2	0.8	-	-	-	1.9	-
7. 40 or more	0.7	0.8	0.6	0.7	-	1.2	0.8	0.3	0.4	0.4	1.2	-	-	-	2.7	21.3
Item 1070 Subject A01a N	2989	1422	1508	2297	300	695	856	926	513	1797	945	1305	634	396	599	20
B074B: . . . during the last 12 months?																
1. 0 occasions	95.3	96.2	94.6	94.8	100.0	95.8	95.7	94.5	95.6	95.6	94.7	100.0	100.0	94.7	81.4	62.9
2. 1-2	2.4	1.5	3.3	2.9	-	1.5	1.8	3.8	2.4	2.6	2.3	-	-	5.3	8.7	3.2
3. 3-5	0.8	0.6	1.1	0.9	-	0.5	0.9	1.1	0.7	1.0	0.7	-	-	-	3.8	12.8
4. 6-9	0.6	0.8	0.3	0.6	-	0.8	0.5	0.4	1.0	0.4	1.2	-	-	-	2.9	4.8
5. 10-19	0.5	0.5	0.5	0.5	-	1.0	0.6	0.1	0.4	0.2	1.0	-	-	-	2.2	9.6
6. 20-39	0.1	0.1	0.1	0.1	-	0.1	0.2	-	-	0.1	-	-	-	-	0.4	-
7. 40 or more	0.2	0.2	0.1	0.2	-	0.3	0.2	0.2	-	0.2	0.1	-	-	-	0.7	6.8
Item 1080 Subject A01b N	2980	1422	1500	2292	300	693	856	925	507	1794	944	1305	634	392	593	21
B074C: . . . during the last 30 days?																
1. 0 occasions	97.8	97.9	97.8	97.6	100.0	97.3	97.3	98.4	98.3	98.1	97.0	100.0	100.0	98.5	91.1	66.1
2. 1-2	1.3	1.1	1.4	1.5	-	1.2	1.7	1.3	0.6	1.3	1.4	-	-	1.5	5.0	12.8
3. 3-5	0.4	0.5	0.4	0.5	-	0.9	0.3	-	0.9	0.1	1.1	-	-	-	1.9	9.6
4. 6-9	0.4	0.5	0.3	0.4	-	0.5	0.6	0.4	0.2	0.4	0.5	-	-	-	1.8	9.3
5. 10-19	*	*	*	*	-	0.1	0.1	-	-	*	-	-	-	-	0.1	2.2
6. 20-39	*	-	*	*	-	-	0.1	-	-	*	-	-	-	-	0.1	-
7. 40 or more	-	-	-	-	-	-	-	-	-	-	-	-	-	-	-	-
Item 1090 Subject A01c N	2979	1422	1500	2291	300	693	855	925	507	1794	944	1305	634	392	593	21

IF YOU HAVE NOT TAKEN TRANQUILIZERS IN THE LAST TWELVE MONTHS, GO TO Q.B082.

THE FOLLOWING QUESTIONS REFER ONLY TO TAKING TRANQUILIZERS WITHOUT A DOCTOR'S ORDERS. IF YOU HAVE NOT DONE THIS IN THE LAST TWELVE MONTHS, GO TO Q.B082.

B075: When you used tranquilizers during the last year, how often did you use them in each of the following situations?

	TOTAL	M	F	White	Black	NE	NC	S	W	Yes	No	None	Mari-juana Only	Few Pills	More Pills	Any Her-oin
B075A: When you were alone																
1. Not at all	40.5	41.7	39.2	40.3	100.0	27.9	45.8	51.0	28.4	39.8	40.6	-	-	74.1	34.3	8.7
2. A few of the times	26.4	28.6	24.9	25.6	-	39.2	15.5	32.0	14.8	23.0	30.0	-	-	7.3	29.5	46.8
3. Some of the times	3.0	1.5	3.0	2.7	-	-	5.6	4.3	-	0.7	6.9	-	-	-	2.9	12.8
4. Most of the times	12.9	17.1	10.9	12.5	-	21.7	9.1	3.9	24.8	18.3	5.6	-	-	8.6	14.7	5.9
5. Every time	17.2	11.1	22.0	18.9	-	11.2	24.0	8.8	32.0	18.1	17.0	-	-	10.0	18.6	25.8
Item 3740 Subject A05a N★	129	53	68	105	1	31	36	42	20	70	48	-	-	19	98	8
B075B: With just 1 or 2 other people																
1. Not at all	38.1	31.6	44.6	39.0	100.0	32.0	26.5	43.0	57.1	45.9	31.0	-	-	45.2	35.3	25.8
2. A few of the times	30.1	34.4	27.6	28.8	-	15.9	30.6	44.4	20.9	28.6	31.5	-	-	37.4	29.9	30.1
3. Some of the times	9.4	13.2	6.1	9.1	-	12.9	11.5	3.4	12.2	9.4	8.9	-	-	-	11.2	12.8
4. Most of the times	14.4	11.1	15.9	15.6	-	37.3	12.6	4.8	4.9	8.8	21.7	-	-	8.1	14.8	31.3
5. Every time	8.0	9.7	5.8	7.5	-	1.9	18.8	4.4	4.9	7.4	6.9	-	-	9.3	8.7	-
Item 3750 Subject A05b N★	129	52	70	102	1	29	37	42	21	70	47	-	-	19	99	8

*=less than .05 per cent.   ★=excludes respondents for whom question was inappropriate.

QUESTIONNAIRE FORM 1 1986	TOTAL	SEX		RACE		REGION				4YR COLLEGE PLANS		ILLICIT DRUG USE: LIFETIME				
		M	F	White	Black	NE	NC	S	W	Yes	No	None	Marijuana Only	Few Pills	More Pills	Any Heroin
N (Weighted No. of Cases):	3179	1469	1562	2351	323	749	897	984	550	1841	999	1333	671	406	643	21
% of Weighted Total:	100.0	46.2	49.1	74.0	10.2	23.5	28.2	30.9	17.3	57.9	31.4	41.9	21.1	12.8	20.2	0.7
B075C: At a party																
1. Not at all	69.6	61.6	79.5	71.4	100.0	48.4	61.1	86.7	80.9	79.8	64.7	-	-	100.0	64.3	50.0
2. A few of the times	11.3	12.7	7.8	8.7	-	25.0	5.9	7.4	8.9	11.0	8.0	-	-	-	12.2	35.9
3. Some of the times	11.4	19.6	6.0	12.7	-	10.8	29.3	2.2	-	7.7	13.9	-	-	-	14.7	-
4. Most of the times	5.3	3.1	6.7	5.6	-	15.7	-	1.5	7.0	1.5	10.0	-	-	-	6.9	-
5. Every time	2.3	3.0	-	1.5	-	-	3.7	2.3	3.1	-	3.4	-	-	-	2.0	14.1
Item 3760 Subject A05c N★	127	53	69	104	1	30	35	41	21	70	47	-	-	19	99	7
B075D: When your date or spouse was present																
1. Not at all	69.4	68.0	70.2	69.7	100.0	60.0	64.1	76.7	75.8	78.4	56.9	-	-	81.5	66.9	59.9
2. A few of the times	7.1	9.5	6.0	5.2	-	10.4	8.3	7.7	-	7.5	7.9	-	-	5.0	8.3	-
3. Some of the times	11.9	11.3	11.1	11.8	-	10.6	22.4	9.8	-	3.8	21.1	-	-	9.7	12.1	18.8
4. Most of the times	7.5	6.3	9.0	9.2	-	14.4	2.9	-	21.1	9.3	6.3	-	-	-	9.8	-
5. Every time	4.1	4.9	3.8	4.2	-	4.6	2.3	5.7	3.1	1.0	7.7	-	-	3.8	2.8	21.4
Item 3770 Subject A05b N★	125	50	70	103	1	27	36	41	21	69	47	-	-	19	96	8
B075E: When people over age 30 were present																
1. Not at all	45.8	46.2	47.3	47.1	100.0	46.1	54.3	42.0	39.0	51.2	42.4	-	-	34.5	44.8	66.2
2. A few of the times	17.2	18.2	15.3	14.7	-	15.1	18.2	16.6	19.4	17.5	14.0	-	-	22.7	17.4	8.7
3. Some of the times	13.5	14.3	12.5	13.3	-	33.8	13.4	7.5	-	10.3	21.0	-	-	-	15.5	25.1
4. Most of the times	8.3	10.5	7.4	8.4	-	3.3	2.9	13.3	14.1	8.6	9.9	-	-	16.7	7.7	-
5. Every time	15.1	10.8	17.6	16.4	-	1.7	11.2	20.5	27.6	12.4	12.7	-	-	26.1	14.7	-
Item 3780 Subject A05b N★	129	52	71	106	1	28	36	41	23	69	48	-	-	19	100	8
B075F: During the daytime (before 4:00 p.m.)																
1. Not at all	48.0	41.7	56.4	49.4	100.0	32.0	51.5	56.2	48.4	53.7	42.7	-	-	67.7	45.4	14.6
2. A few of the times	19.4	23.5	13.6	17.4	-	23.0	14.5	18.1	25.2	17.5	19.7	-	-	7.3	18.8	63.4
3. Some of the times	15.5	15.6	14.7	14.2	-	30.0	14.3	11.5	4.9	9.7	23.6	-	-	9.7	17.3	12.8
4. Most of the times	11.7	9.6	14.4	13.5	-	8.5	11.0	11.1	18.4	13.8	10.0	-	-	3.2	13.8	9.1
5. Every time	5.5	9.5	0.9	5.5	-	6.6	8.7	3.0	3.1	5.4	4.0	-	-	12.1	4.8	-
Item 3790 Subject A05c N★	129	53	69	104	1	30	36	41	21	69	48	-	-	19	99	8
B075G: At your home (or apartment or dorm)																
1. Not at all	27.3	41.7	16.8	27.2	100.0	33.0	28.6	27.4	18.0	31.5	23.9	-	-	27.7	23.5	49.5
2. A few of the times	21.6	11.6	27.5	19.7	-	23.5	13.1	29.8	18.4	17.0	26.5	-	-	22.7	22.5	14.1
3. Some of the times	6.1	5.8	6.7	6.2	-	6.7	15.0	1.1	-	4.6	6.2	-	-	-	7.4	6.8
4. Most of the times	13.0	17.2	10.7	12.4	-	12.7	6.4	13.1	23.4	15.3	11.5	-	-	16.3	13.6	-
5. Every time	32.1	23.6	38.3	34.5	-	24.2	37.0	28.5	40.2	31.6	32.0	-	-	33.3	32.9	29.6
Item 3800 Subject A05c N★	128	52	71	105	1	28	36	39	23	69	47	-	-	19	99	7
B075H: At school																
1. Not at all	65.8	56.7	75.3	67.5	100.0	38.3	63.5	81.0	77.2	71.6	62.5	-	-	79.9	64.1	40.8
2. A few of the times	14.3	19.3	10.5	13.5	-	14.9	17.2	10.6	15.8	14.7	12.4	-	-	9.7	15.1	21.0
3. Some of the times	9.2	10.0	7.2	8.2	-	25.5	8.3	2.4	2.1	7.9	8.0	-	-	-	11.0	12.8
4. Most of the times	8.1	12.1	5.6	9.9	-	18.0	4.4	6.0	4.9	4.3	15.2	-	-	-	8.5	25.4
5. Every time	2.6	2.0	1.4	1.0	-	3.3	6.6	-	-	1.5	2.0	-	-	10.5	1.4	-
Item 3810 Subject A05c N★	126	53	68	103	1	28	35	41	21	69	47	-	-	19	97	8
B075I: In a car																
1. Not at all	71.7	67.1	78.2	72.2	100.0	52.7	60.9	84.9	89.6	76.8	69.2	-	-	100.0	68.4	34.5
2. A few of the times	11.6	18.6	5.5	11.8	-	15.3	18.5	6.4	5.5	8.3	7.1	-	-	-	12.7	31.3
3. Some of the times	13.2	12.6	13.3	13.0	-	32.1	14.0	6.4	-	8.3	21.8	-	-	-	14.5	34.2
4. Most of the times	1.6	1.8	1.5	1.9	-	-	-	2.3	4.9	1.5	2.0	-	-	-	2.1	-
5. Every time	1.9	-	1.5	1.0	-	-	6.6	-	-	1.5	-	-	-	-	2.4	-
Item 3830 Subject A05c N★	126	53	68	103	1	28	35	41	21	69	47	-	-	19	97	8

B076: How many of the times when you used tranquilizers during the last year did you use them along with each of the following drugs– that is, so that their effects overlapped?

★=excludes respondents for whom question was inappropriate.

QUESTIONNAIRE FORM 1 1986	TOTAL	SEX		RACE		REGION				4YR COLLEGE PLANS		ILLICIT DRUG USE: LIFETIME				
		M	F	White	Black	NE	NC	S	W	Yes	No	None	Marijuana Only	Few Pills	More Pills	Any Heroin
N (Weighted No. of Cases):	3179	1469	1562	2351	323	749	897	984	550	1841	999	1333	671	406	643	21
% of Weighted Total:	100.0	46.2	49.1	74.0	10.2	23.5	28.2	30.9	17.3	57.9	31.4	41.9	21.1	12.8	20.2	0.7
B076A: With alcohol																
1. Not at all	61.8	49.2	73.0	64.4	100.0	38.2	57.6	81.1	63.1	67.6	60.0	-	-	94.5	57.2	20.4
2. A few of the times	10.9	15.0	6.0	9.1	-	18.7	5.7	7.7	14.8	12.3	8.7	-	-	-	11.5	36.4
3. Some of the times	11.9	18.0	8.4	11.6	-	18.1	16.5	9.7	-	7.8	14.7	-	-	-	14.4	14.1
4. Most of the times	8.1	7.4	9.2	8.1	-	15.2	8.2	-	14.1	6.6	9.1	-	-	-	8.5	29.1
5. Every time	7.4	10.3	3.3	6.7	-	9.7	12.0	1.5	8.0	5.8	7.4	-	-	5.5	8.5	-
Item 3840 Subject A01h N★	125	50	70	103	1	28	35	41	21	68	47	-	-	19	97	7
B076B: With marijuana																
1. Not at all	67.0	67.0	72.2	72.4	100.0	37.6	67.1	80.2	79.1	72.6	66.8	-	-	100.0	62.9	25.8
2. A few of the times	11.9	11.7	9.3	8.2	-	29.4	7.2	6.6	7.4	14.1	8.3	-	-	-	14.8	8.7
3. Some of the times	8.4	14.1	3.4	7.6	-	7.1	15.0	6.8	2.1	7.2	8.1	-	-	-	6.5	56.4
4. Most of the times	4.8	4.1	5.7	4.5	-	9.1	-	5.4	6.5	3.8	3.2	-	-	-	5.6	9.1
5. Every time	7.9	3.1	9.5	7.3	-	16.8	10.7	1.0	4.9	2.3	13.6	-	-	-	10.2	-
Item 3850 Subject A01h N★	127	52	70	105	1	28	36	42	21	69	48	-	-	19	98	8
B076C: With LSD																
1. Not at all	92.7	90.8	97.1	95.2	100.0	95.5	83.5	95.5	100.0	92.4	95.6	-	-	100.0	92.0	79.1
2. A few of the times	2.3	2.7	0.6	1.7	-	4.5	3.6	1.1	-	2.6	2.4	-	-	-	3.0	-
3. Some of the times	3.5	5.6	2.3	2.7	-	-	9.3	2.3	-	4.4	2.0	-	-	-	3.1	20.9
4. Most of the times	-	-	-	-	-	-	-	-	-	-	-	-	-	-	-	-
5. Every time	1.4	0.9	-	0.4	-	-	3.6	1.1	-	0.7	-	-	-	-	1.8	-
Item 3860 Subject A01h N★	124	48	71	102	1	26	37	41	20	68	47	-	-	19	95	7
B076D: With psychedelics other than LSD																
1. Not at all	94.7	94.9	97.6	95.9	100.0	87.1	94.8	96.6	100.0	96.3	95.3	-	-	100.0	96.7	55.9
2. A few of the times	3.4	5.1	2.4	4.1	-	12.9	1.3	1.0	-	3.7	2.6	-	-	-	1.8	31.3
3. Some of the times	0.8	-	-	-	-	-	-	2.4	-	-	2.1	-	-	-	-	12.8
4. Most of the times	-	-	-	-	-	-	-	-	-	-	-	-	-	-	-	-
5. Every time	1.1	-	-	-	-	-	3.9	-	-	-	-	-	-	-	1.4	-
Item 3870 Subject A01h N★	120	47	70	100	1	25	34	42	20	65	47	-	-	19	91	8
B076E: With amphetamines																
1. Not at all	93.8	93.4	98.6	96.0	100.0	88.0	93.3	96.6	96.7	95.5	94.2	-	-	100.0	95.6	55.9
2. A few of the times	3.3	5.2	0.6	2.8	-	12.0	1.3	1.0	-	3.7	2.4	-	-	-	1.7	31.3
3. Some of the times	1.8	1.4	0.7	1.2	-	-	1.5	2.4	3.3	0.8	3.4	-	-	-	1.3	12.8
4. Most of the times	-	-	-	-	-	-	-	-	-	-	-	-	-	-	-	-
5. Every time	1.1	-	-	-	-	-	3.9	-	-	-	-	-	-	-	1.4	-
Item 3880 Subject A01h N★	121	47	70	100	1	26	34	42	20	65	48	-	-	19	92	8
B076F: With quaaludes																
1. Not at all	93.5	95.3	97.8	96.2	100.0	93.0	86.8	97.6	97.4	97.2	92.4	-	-	100.0	93.7	72.6
2. A few of the times	3.0	3.8	-	1.8	-	7.0	3.7	-	2.6	2.8	2.4	-	-	-	3.2	8.7
3. Some of the times	2.1	-	2.2	1.5	-	-	4.4	2.4	-	-	5.2	-	-	-	1.7	12.8
4. Most of the times	0.4	0.9	-	0.4	-	-	1.3	-	-	-	-	-	-	-	-	5.9
5. Every time	1.1	-	-	-	-	-	3.7	-	-	-	-	-	-	-	1.4	-
Item 3890 Subject A01h N★	123	48	70	102	1	26	35	42	20	66	48	-	-	19	94	8
B076G: With barbiturates																
1. Not at all	89.9	94.9	90.3	90.9	100.0	81.7	85.7	96.4	94.2	90.7	92.2	-	-	100.0	91.3	47.2
2. A few of the times	5.0	4.1	4.9	5.4	-	18.3	2.9	1.1	-	6.7	2.2	-	-	-	3.7	34.1
3. Some of the times	3.6	-	4.8	3.3	-	-	6.1	2.5	5.8	2.6	5.6	-	-	-	3.6	12.8
4. Most of the times	0.4	1.0	-	0.5	-	-	1.3	-	-	-	-	-	-	-	-	5.9
5. Every time	1.1	-	-	-	-	-	3.9	-	-	-	-	-	-	-	1.4	-
Item 3900 Subject A01h N★	118	47	67	98	1	25	34	39	20	64	46	-	-	17	91	8

★=excludes respondents for whom question was inappropriate.

QUESTIONNAIRE FORM 1 1986	TOTAL	SEX		RACE		REGION				4YR COLLEGE PLANS		ILLICIT DRUG USE: LIFETIME				
		M	F	White	Black	NE	NC	S	W	Yes	No	None	Marijuana Only	Few Pills	More Pills	Any Heroin
N (Weighted No. of Cases):	3179	1469	1562	2351	323	749	897	984	550	1841	999	1333	671	406	643	21
% of Weighted Total:	100.0	46.2	49.1	74.0	10.2	23.5	28.2	30.9	17.3	57.9	31.4	41.9	21.1	12.8	20.2	0.7

B077: What have been the most important reasons for taking tranquilizers without a doctor's orders? (Mark all that apply.)

	TOTAL	M	F	White	Black	NE	NC	S	W	Yes	No	None	Marijuana Only	Few Pills	More Pills	Any Heroin
A. To experiment–to see what it's like	28.8	36.2	20.5	28.4	-	40.5	32.4	17.2	28.8	20.7	32.4	-	-	-	32.1	53.7
B. To relax or relieve tension	69.0	63.1	72.8	72.8	-	70.8	70.3	71.4	59.6	67.8	75.5	-	-	55.9	73.1	47.3
C. To feel good or get high	37.6	43.4	29.5	34.8	-	70.1	37.1	20.7	26.7	32.4	39.9	-	-	-	40.2	90.9
D. To seek deeper insights and understanding	3.3	3.2	1.6	1.6	-	5.7	1.4	4.0	2.2	1.5	5.8	-	-	-	3.2	12.8
E. To have a good time with my friends	12.1	13.0	10.2	12.7	-	18.7	14.4	11.6	-	5.3	21.8	-	-	-	12.8	31.0
F. To fit in with a group I like	2.0	3.0	-	0.9	-	2.0	-	4.9	-	0.8	4.3	-	-	-	0.6	25.1
G. To get away from my problems or troubles	19.8	12.5	24.6	21.9	-	27.4	17.7	14.4	23.8	15.0	29.1	-	-	7.2	20.6	38.6
H. Because of boredom, nothing else to do	7.6	14.2	1.2	5.7	-	5.9	4.5	4.9	20.8	3.1	13.8	-	-	-	6.6	38.6
I. Because of anger or frustration	13.5	11.7	14.5	11.7	-	18.4	9.1	10.7	20.1	15.4	13.6	-	-	-	14.0	38.6
J. To get through the day	12.0	8.0	15.9	12.2	-	22.9	18.4	3.6	2.2	12.7	9.2	-	-	3.9	14.4	-
K. To increase the effects of some other drug(s)	9.6	12.7	6.6	10.1	-	11.0	12.1	8.6	5.1	6.3	11.4	-	-	-	9.7	31.0
L. To decrease (offset) the effects of some other drug(s)	2.7	3.7	0.7	1.8	-	2.0	5.1	2.5	-	3.4	2.2	-	-	-	2.4	12.8
M. To get to sleep	47.8	36.9	58.7	50.7	-	67.4	35.0	45.8	47.2	47.4	54.7	-	-	54.8	47.0	40.8
N. To relieve physical pain	38.3	40.6	37.8	38.1	-	35.7	24.1	42.7	58.0	34.8	46.5	-	-	42.0	37.4	40.8
O. Because I am "hooked"–I have to have them	0.4	1.1	-	-	-	2.0	-	-	-	0.8	-	-	-	-	0.6	-
Item 3910-4040 Subject A06a N★	124	50	68	103	-	28	36	40	20	70	45	-	-	18	98	8

B078: When you take tranquilizers how high do you usually get?

	TOTAL	M	F	White	Black	NE	NC	S	W	Yes	No	None	Marijuana Only	Few Pills	More Pills	Any Heroin
1. Not at all high	24.0	17.7	30.0	25.5	-	5.6	20.8	44.7	16.5	26.9	22.8	-	-	36.6	22.1	14.8
2. A little high	19.2	22.9	15.8	21.0	-	28.0	29.7	7.3	11.6	20.8	15.7	-	-	5.7	22.0	14.2
3. Moderately high	17.3	20.1	14.5	14.6	-	27.2	17.5	14.0	9.0	11.8	21.9	-	-	-	20.8	9.7
4. Very high	8.9	14.8	2.8	6.5	-	19.1	6.2	2.5	10.8	8.5	7.6	-	-	-	8.0	61.3
5. I don't take them to get high	30.7	24.6	36.9	32.4	-	20.1	25.8	31.5	52.2	31.9	32.1	-	-	57.7	27.1	-
Item 4050 Subject A01e N★	122	49	69	102	-	29	34	38	20	67	43	-	-	18	99	5

B079: When you take tranquilizers how long do you usually stay high?

	TOTAL	M	F	White	Black	NE	NC	S	W	Yes	No	None	Marijuana Only	Few Pills	More Pills	Any Heroin
1. Usually don't get high	46.0	39.3	54.7	49.2	-	18.7	44.0	66.4	50.2	50.1	47.3	-	-	80.0	40.1	34.9
2. One to two hours	25.3	25.6	22.6	22.1	-	35.7	27.0	14.6	27.1	24.5	18.9	-	-	12.3	28.9	12.8
3. Three to six hours	22.4	28.2	16.3	22.4	-	36.9	21.5	15.2	17.3	20.8	26.5	-	-	7.7	23.9	40.0
4. Seven to 24 hours	4.4	6.9	2.8	3.9	-	2.0	7.5	2.6	5.5	1.8	6.3	-	-	-	4.6	12.3
5. More than 24 hours	1.9	-	3.6	2.3	-	6.8	-	1.2	-	2.9	1.0	-	-	-	2.5	-
Item 4060 Subject A01f N★	121	50	66	101	-	28	35	36	22	66	44	-	-	19	95	8

B080: What tranquilizers have you taken during the last year without a doctor's orders? (Mark all that apply.)

	TOTAL	M	F	White	Black	NE	NC	S	W	Yes	No	None	Marijuana Only	Few Pills	More Pills	Any Heroin
A. Librium	15.8	19.0	13.9	15.3	-	16.4	32.1	5.3	7.6	17.4	11.5	-	-	-	19.0	15.0
B. Valium	69.3	75.6	64.5	70.6	-	81.7	74.3	57.4	67.0	61.2	79.0	-	-	21.6	79.4	61.8
C. Miltown	-	-	-	-	-	-	-	-	-	-	-	-	-	-	-	-
D. Equanil	2.8	3.9	2.3	0.4	-	-	10.0	-	-	2.4	-	-	-	-	3.1	5.9
E. Meprobamate	2.6	2.2	3.0	2.5	-	4.1	5.8	-	-	0.8	5.0	-	-	-	2.8	5.9
F. Serax	3.5	7.0	-	2.7	-	4.3	4.2	3.3	2.0	1.8	6.2	-	-	6.6	2.7	5.9
G. Atarax	5.4	3.1	7.2	6.4	-	-	5.8	11.9	-	7.5	2.2	-	-	3.7	4.6	18.2
H. Tranxene	5.6	3.1	7.6	6.7	-	7.1	5.8	7.6	-	5.7	5.9	-	-	8.6	4.0	18.2
I. Vistaril	4.9	6.6	4.1	5.4	-	-	1.3	10.3	7.0	2.7	8.7	-	-	-	4.0	27.3
J. Don't know the names of some tranquilizers I have used	48.2	37.7	54.5	47.1	-	47.8	48.8	40.4	61.2	42.1	58.4	-	-	64.5	43.8	64.0
Item 4070-4160 Subject A01l N★	121	45	71	101	-	27	34	38	22	68	42	-	-	19	95	8

B081: Have you ever tried to stop using tranquilizers and found that you couldn't stop?

	TOTAL	M	F	White	Black	NE	NC	S	W	Yes	No	None	Marijuana Only	Few Pills	More Pills	Any Heroin
1. Yes	5.5	3.9	7.2	5.2	-	6.6	8.6	-	8.4	5.0	8.0	-	-	-	5.0	29.6
2. No	94.5	96.1	92.8	94.8	-	93.4	91.4	100.0	91.6	95.0	92.0	-	-	100.0	95.0	70.4
Item 4170 Subject A01i N★	128	51	71	105	-	29	37	38	23	71	44	-	-	19	102	7

★=excludes respondents for whom question was inappropriate.

QUESTIONNAIRE FORM 1 1986	TOTAL	SEX		RACE		REGION				4YR COLLEGE PLANS		ILLICIT DRUG USE: LIFETIME				
		M	F	White	Black	NE	NC	S	W	Yes	No	None	Mari- juana Only	Few Pills	More Pills	Any Her- oin
N (Weighted No. of Cases):	3179	1469	1562	2351	323	749	897	984	550	1841	999	1333	671	406	643	21
% of Weighted Total:	100.0	46.2	49.1	74.0	10.2	23.5	28.2	30.9	17.3	57.9	31.4	41.9	21.1	12.8	20.2	0.7

B082: Do you think you will be using tranquilizers without a doctor's orders five years from now?

1. I definitely will	0.6	0.5	0.6	0.5	0.8	0.7	0.4	0.2	1.4	0.6	0.6	0.3	0.5	-	1.0	9.9
2. I probably will	2.5	2.4	2.5	2.3	2.4	2.2	2.6	2.5	2.5	1.8	3.5	1.3	0.7	3.9	6.0	6.4
3. I probably will not	24.8	23.2	26.5	25.8	14.8	27.3	23.9	23.7	25.2	25.3	24.1	16.3	21.3	32.1	42.7	29.3
4. I definitely will not	72.1	73.9	70.5	71.4	82.1	69.8	73.1	73.7	70.9	72.4	71.7	82.1	77.5	63.9	50.3	54.4
Item 4180 Subject A04a N	2982	1407	1514	2280	312	686	849	931	516	1797	951	1287	638	396	590	20

The next questions are about COCAINE, which is sometimes called "coke", "crack", "rock".

B083: On how many occasions (if any) have you taken cocaine . . .

B083A: . . . in your lifetime?

1. 0 occasions	82.8	81.6	84.8	82.2	93.2	74.3	87.7	89.6	73.9	85.8	80.4	100.0	100.0	66.8	40.8	6.7
2. 1-2	6.7	7.3	5.9	7.0	2.1	9.3	4.9	4.7	9.5	6.3	6.5	-	-	33.2	10.3	22.3
3. 3-5	2.7	3.6	1.8	2.9	1.3	3.6	2.0	2.1	3.9	2.1	2.8	-	-	-	13.1	6.7
4. 6-9	1.9	1.6	2.1	2.0	0.7	4.0	1.5	0.8	2.1	1.3	2.7	-	-	-	9.3	5.6
5. 10-19	2.0	2.2	1.8	2.1	0.3	3.5	1.1	0.8	3.8	1.9	2.4	-	-	-	9.3	19.4
6. 20-39	1.4	1.3	1.6	1.6	1.2	1.8	0.7	1.1	2.8	1.1	2.1	-	-	-	6.6	15.5
7. 40 or more	2.3	2.5	2.0	2.3	1.4	3.5	2.1	0.8	3.9	1.5	3.1	-	-	-	10.6	23.9
Item 950 Subject A01a N	3002	1429	1513	2309	299	692	860	931	520	1798	956	1299	635	399	614	21

B083B: . . . during the last 12 months?

1. 0 occasions	86.1	85.5	87.6	85.5	94.6	78.2	89.7	92.7	79.0	88.6	84.0	100.0	100.0	79.4	47.7	35.2
2. 1-2	5.8	6.1	5.0	6.0	1.1	10.0	4.0	3.1	7.8	5.5	5.2	-	-	20.6	14.5	12.0
3. 3-5	2.6	3.1	1.9	2.9	1.0	3.0	2.5	1.8	3.8	1.7	3.9	-	-	-	12.6	3.2
4. 6-9	1.8	1.3	2.1	1.9	0.4	2.7	1.0	0.8	3.4	1.5	2.0	-	-	-	8.4	5.3
5. 10-19	1.4	1.3	1.4	1.4	0.8	2.6	0.7	0.8	1.9	1.2	1.8	-	-	-	6.2	15.4
6. 20-39	1.0	1.0	1.0	1.0	1.2	2.1	0.5	0.4	1.5	0.8	0.9	-	-	-	4.7	8.4
7. 40 or more	1.3	1.6	1.0	1.4	0.8	1.4	1.5	0.4	2.6	0.7	2.2	-	-	-	5.8	20.5
Item 960 Subject A01b N	3001	1431	1510	2307	299	693	858	931	520	1798	956	1301	635	396	614	21

B083C: . . . during the last 30 days?

1. 0 occasions	92.6	92.6	93.0	92.4	96.7	88.4	94.5	96.2	88.9	94.8	89.0	100.0	100.0	92.5	70.2	61.4
2. 1-2	4.2	4.2	4.1	4.4	0.3	6.9	2.9	2.2	6.6	3.2	6.3	-	-	7.5	15.9	-
3. 3-5	1.3	1.4	1.2	1.4	0.7	2.3	0.9	0.6	1.8	0.9	1.9	-	-	-	5.7	14.7
4. 6-9	0.5	0.4	0.6	0.5	0.7	0.5	0.5	0.5	0.6	0.3	0.6	-	-	-	2.3	4.6
5. 10-19	0.7	0.9	0.6	0.7	0.8	1.4	0.4	0.3	1.2	0.5	0.9	-	-	-	3.5	3.4
6. 20-39	0.4	0.2	0.6	0.4	0.5	0.5	0.3	0.1	0.9	0.2	0.8	-	-	-	1.8	3.2
7. 40 or more	0.2	0.4	-	0.2	0.3	0.1	0.5	0.1	0.1	0.1	0.5	-	-	-	0.6	12.7
Item 970 Subject A01c N	3001	1430	1510	2306	299	693	858	931	520	1797	956	1301	635	395	614	21

IF YOU HAVE NOT TAKEN COCAINE IN THE LAST TWELVE MONTHS, GO TO Q.B091.

B084: When you used cocaine during the last year, how often did you use it in each of the following situations?

B084A: When you were alone

1. Not at all	76.8	76.1	79.4	77.9	66.3	81.7	75.5	72.3	74.1	80.4	72.4	-	-	94.0	72.4	58.5
2. A few of the times	14.3	16.1	11.1	13.6	29.0	13.7	10.5	17.0	16.7	11.1	17.7	-	-	2.8	17.8	14.1
3. Some of the times	5.9	4.9	6.1	5.6	4.7	3.7	4.6	9.8	7.4	6.2	6.0	-	-	-	7.2	15.2
4. Most of the times	1.6	1.0	2.4	1.4	-	0.9	5.3	-	0.6	1.4	1.8	-	-	0.8	2.0	-
5. Every time	1.4	1.8	1.0	1.5	-	-	4.1	0.9	1.1	0.9	2.1	-	-	2.4	0.6	12.2
Item 4190 Subject A05a N★	403	198	186	322	18	140	89	68	106	199	154	-	-	83	302	13

★=excludes respondents for whom question was inappropriate.

QUESTIONNAIRE FORM 1 1986	TOTAL	SEX		RACE		REGION				4YR COLLEGE PLANS		ILLICIT DRUG USE: LIFETIME				
		M	F	White	Black	NE	NC	S	W	Yes	No	None	Marijuana Only	Few Pills	More Pills	Any Heroin
N (Weighted No. of Cases):	3179	1469	1562	2351	323	749	897	984	550	1841	999	1333	671	406	643	21
% of Weighted Total:	100.0	46.2	49.1	74.0	10.2	23.5	28.2	30.9	17.3	57.9	31.4	41.9	21.1	12.8	20.2	0.7

B084B: With just 1 or 2 other people

	TOTAL	M	F	White	Black	NE	NC	S	W	Yes	No	None	Mar. Only	Few Pills	More Pills	Any Her.
1. Not at all	11.3	10.4	11.3	12.0	7.5	5.9	16.6	9.5	15.0	10.8	8.5	-	-	30.3	5.3	-
2. A few of the times	29.8	32.1	27.7	30.0	15.1	29.2	28.2	28.5	32.7	33.7	27.5	-	-	38.4	27.9	28.8
3. Some of the times	11.9	10.7	11.9	10.4	18.3	11.6	13.6	10.6	14.9	9.3	14.9	-	-	1.5	14.4	25.4
4. Most of the times	23.2	22.1	24.8	24.7	4.8	26.6	17.6	24.1	22.8	21.8	25.0	-	-	0.5	29.5	27.6
5. Every time	23.8	24.7	24.3	22.8	54.2	26.7	24.0	27.3	17.5	24.4	24.1	-	-	29.2	22.9	18.2
Item 4200 Subject A05b N★	*413*	*203*	*191*	*332*	*18*	*145*	*92*	*68*	*108*	*206*	*154*	*-*	*-*	*84*	*311*	*13*

B084C: At a party

	TOTAL	M	F	White	Black	NE	NC	S	W	Yes	No	None	Mar. Only	Few Pills	More Pills	Any Her.
1. Not at all	29.6	31.5	29.6	28.6	41.3	29.5	29.4	38.4	24.3	35.0	25.1	-	-	46.8	24.9	6.0
2. A few of the times	26.4	25.8	27.1	26.8	24.9	24.3	22.6	30.3	29.8	26.5	23.7	-	-	28.1	26.1	31.9
3. Some of the times	18.0	16.4	18.5	17.6	5.3	19.9	11.0	15.7	22.9	15.5	20.5	-	-	3.0	21.7	29.7
4. Most of the times	13.1	13.1	12.7	12.4	21.8	14.3	16.9	8.4	11.1	12.5	16.5	-	-	1.4	16.4	13.1
5. Every time	13.0	13.2	12.2	14.7	6.7	12.0	20.0	7.2	11.9	10.5	14.3	-	-	20.7	10.9	19.3
Item 4210 Subject A05c N★	*412*	*204*	*187*	*330*	*18*	*144*	*92*	*68*	*108*	*205*	*153*	*-*	*-*	*83*	*311*	*13*

B084D: When your date or spouse was present

	TOTAL	M	F	White	Black	NE	NC	S	W	Yes	No	None	Mar. Only	Few Pills	More Pills	Any Her.
1. Not at all	58.1	73.1	42.9	56.3	78.2	52.7	66.1	63.9	55.3	61.4	53.5	-	-	80.8	52.7	23.9
2. A few of the times	16.0	11.3	19.8	14.9	19.7	18.0	12.9	10.8	18.9	14.2	16.5	-	-	14.1	16.2	28.4
3. Some of the times	8.1	7.5	8.2	8.1	2.1	10.9	4.9	3.5	9.9	8.7	6.9	-	-	-	9.8	23.3
4. Most of the times	7.4	2.8	12.3	7.9	-	7.8	5.5	9.1	7.5	5.3	10.4	-	-	0.9	9.4	7.0
5. Every time	10.4	5.3	16.8	12.8	-	10.6	10.5	12.8	8.4	10.4	12.6	-	-	4.2	11.9	17.5
Item 4220 Subject A05b N★	*404*	*197*	*187*	*324*	*18*	*143*	*86*	*68*	*107*	*200*	*152*	*-*	*-*	*84*	*302*	*13*

B084E: When people over age 30 were present

	TOTAL	M	F	White	Black	NE	NC	S	W	Yes	No	None	Mar. Only	Few Pills	More Pills	Any Her.
1. Not at all	66.9	65.4	69.0	68.8	63.6	65.3	62.2	69.6	71.1	74.2	60.4	-	-	89.6	61.8	28.7
2. A few of the times	14.9	16.3	13.9	13.5	28.9	18.2	13.4	9.0	15.7	14.2	14.5	-	-	4.6	16.7	44.7
3. Some of the times	8.6	9.3	7.1	8.0	-	8.9	4.4	12.0	9.4	6.3	10.9	-	-	1.4	10.4	14.4
4. Most of the times	5.2	4.9	5.5	4.9	-	6.8	9.3	0.6	2.6	3.1	8.7	-	-	0.5	6.8	-
5. Every time	4.4	4.1	4.5	4.7	7.4	0.8	10.7	8.7	1.1	2.2	5.6	-	-	3.8	4.3	12.2
Item 4230 Subject A05b N★	*408*	*200*	*188*	*326*	*18*	*143*	*90*	*68*	*107*	*205*	*152*	*-*	*-*	*84*	*306*	*13*

B084F: During the daytime (before 4:00 p.m.)

	TOTAL	M	F	White	Black	NE	NC	S	W	Yes	No	None	Mar. Only	Few Pills	More Pills	Any Her.
1. Not at all	53.7	51.6	55.1	53.4	57.2	54.2	64.3	48.4	47.7	60.7	43.1	-	-	79.8	46.9	31.6
2. A few of the times	22.9	25.3	21.5	22.6	34.4	27.2	12.4	30.6	21.1	19.7	28.8	-	-	9.2	26.6	30.8
3. Some of the times	13.1	10.0	14.8	12.2	8.4	11.0	10.6	12.8	18.2	10.5	15.0	-	-	0.6	16.2	25.4
4. Most of the times	4.9	6.6	3.7	5.8	-	2.9	5.6	3.0	8.2	4.6	6.5	-	-	-	6.5	-
5. Every time	5.4	6.5	4.8	6.0	-	4.8	7.1	5.3	4.8	4.5	6.6	-	-	10.4	3.8	12.2
Item 4240 Subject A05c N★	*411*	*201*	*188*	*327*	*18*	*145*	*90*	*68*	*108*	*208*	*152*	*-*	*-*	*84*	*309*	*13*

B084G: At your home (or apartment or dorm)

	TOTAL	M	F	White	Black	NE	NC	S	W	Yes	No	None	Mar. Only	Few Pills	More Pills	Any Her.
1. Not at all	54.8	47.9	61.7	54.2	46.2	59.7	55.5	45.4	53.5	56.9	50.3	-	-	79.8	48.4	29.1
2. A few of the times	21.3	25.9	16.1	22.3	8.2	21.8	16.3	24.7	22.9	21.2	23.1	-	-	7.8	24.6	38.5
3. Some of the times	12.4	12.9	11.8	12.0	12.0	9.3	13.6	11.5	16.2	9.2	14.4	-	-	0.5	15.7	15.2
4. Most of the times	6.3	7.7	5.3	5.9	26.3	6.1	6.0	8.3	5.8	6.7	6.7	-	-	0.9	8.0	5.0
5. Every time	5.1	5.6	5.1	5.6	7.3	3.2	8.6	10.0	1.6	6.0	5.4	-	-	11.0	3.3	12.2
Item 4250 Subject A05c N★	*412*	*204*	*188*	*331*	*18*	*145*	*92*	*68*	*107*	*205*	*154*	*-*	*-*	*84*	*310*	*13*

B084H: At school

	TOTAL	M	F	White	Black	NE	NC	S	W	Yes	No	None	Mar. Only	Few Pills	More Pills	Any Her.
1. Not at all	78.4	74.8	84.1	79.5	82.3	75.4	88.8	82.3	71.3	79.0	78.8	-	-	95.7	75.2	36.8
2. A few of the times	11.7	13.2	9.0	11.1	9.3	14.5	5.4	12.5	12.6	11.0	12.9	-	-	3.6	13.5	24.1
3. Some of the times	6.0	6.6	4.6	5.5	3.8	6.0	2.7	3.1	10.8	5.1	6.1	-	-	-	7.5	12.3
4. Most of the times	2.4	3.3	1.7	2.6	4.6	2.6	1.3	1.4	3.7	3.8	1.4	-	-	-	2.6	14.5
5. Every time	1.5	2.1	0.6	1.3	-	1.5	1.8	0.6	1.7	1.2	0.8	-	-	0.7	1.2	12.2
Item 4260 Subject A05c N★	*410*	*202*	*188*	*329*	*18*	*146*	*90*	*68*	*107*	*205*	*152*	*-*	*-*	*84*	*308*	*13*

★=excludes respondents for whom question was inappropriate.

QUESTIONNAIRE FORM 1 1986	TOTAL	SEX		RACE		REGION				4YR COLLEGE PLANS		ILLICIT DRUG USE: LIFETIME				
		M	F	White	Black	NE	NC	S	W	Yes	No	None	Mari-juana Only	Few Pills	More Pills	Any Her-oin
N (Weighted No. of Cases):	3179	1469	1562	2351	323	749	897	984	550	1841	999	1333	671	406	643	21
% of Weighted Total:	100.0	46.2	49.1	74.0	10.2	23.5	28.2	30.9	17.3	57.9	31.4	41.9	21.1	12.8	20.2	0.7
B084I: In a car																
1. Not at all	50.2	45.1	55.4	51.2	42.0	55.7	55.2	42.2	43.4	55.1	45.7	-	-	72.3	44.4	28.4
2. A few of the times	24.7	23.8	25.1	23.3	19.1	24.3	23.4	29.0	23.8	23.2	25.2	-	-	18.6	26.7	25.2
3. Some of the times	16.0	18.0	14.2	15.8	31.6	13.8	14.3	17.4	19.4	14.0	18.7	-	-	3.0	18.9	34.1
4. Most of the times	5.7	7.0	4.4	5.7	7.4	3.9	4.0	7.6	8.4	4.2	7.5	-	-	1.6	7.1	-
5. Every time	3.4	6.1	1.0	4.0	-	2.4	3.1	3.8	5.0	3.5	2.8	-	-	4.5	2.8	12.2
Item 4280 Subject A05c N★	415	204	188	331	18	148	92	68	107	207	154	-	-	84	313	13
B085: How many of the times when you used cocaine during the last year did you use it along with each of the following drugs–that is, so that their effects overlapped?																
B085A: With alcohol																
1. Not at all	26.9	27.1	28.6	27.0	32.9	26.3	22.3	45.9	19.5	28.7	25.2	-	-	37.8	23.8	16.2
2. A few of the times	26.3	26.4	24.2	26.5	22.2	26.4	23.1	19.8	33.0	28.8	23.8	-	-	32.7	24.9	25.7
3. Some of the times	17.1	18.5	15.0	14.3	27.8	16.9	20.7	15.6	15.3	13.9	19.6	-	-	2.0	20.9	24.3
4. Most of the times	11.5	10.8	13.0	12.0	4.8	10.6	10.5	5.6	17.3	11.9	12.5	-	-	3.7	13.5	14.5
5. Every time	18.2	17.3	19.2	20.2	12.2	19.7	23.4	13.1	14.9	16.6	18.9	-	-	23.7	16.9	19.3
Item 4290 Subject A01h N★	411	202	189	329	18	148	90	67	105	205	153	-	-	81	313	13
B085B: With marijuana																
1. Not at all	44.2	44.3	46.3	46.0	24.7	41.1	33.8	52.8	51.8	53.3	36.9	-	-	70.5	38.5	-
2. A few of the times	19.3	17.0	21.5	19.7	11.0	21.0	19.8	15.8	18.7	21.0	17.5	-	-	20.0	19.1	25.0
3. Some of the times	11.7	13.4	8.8	10.6	9.3	12.8	13.3	14.1	7.3	9.5	15.0	-	-	1.5	14.2	17.6
4. Most of the times	12.4	13.2	11.0	11.7	12.2	11.2	17.4	8.5	12.5	10.4	14.0	-	-	2.5	14.5	30.0
5. Every time	12.4	12.0	12.4	12.0	42.8	13.9	15.6	8.8	9.7	5.8	16.6	-	-	5.6	13.7	27.4
Item 4300 Subject A01h N★	409	202	187	329	17	144	92	67	106	198	153	-	-	81	312	12
B085C: With LSD																
1. Not at all	96.1	96.1	97.1	96.7	100.0	97.1	95.5	95.5	95.7	97.6	95.8	-	-	100.0	95.8	74.3
2. A few of the times	2.7	2.6	2.1	2.4	-	2.0	2.7	2.4	3.8	1.9	2.4	-	-	-	3.3	6.9
3. Some of the times	0.6	1.0	0.2	0.4	-	0.4	-	2.1	0.5	0.5	1.0	-	-	-	0.3	14.3
4. Most of the times	-	-	-	-	-	-	-	-	-	-	-	-	-	-	-	-
5. Every time	0.6	0.2	0.6	0.5	-	0.5	1.8	-	-	-	0.8	-	-	-	0.6	4.5
Item 4310 Subject A01h N★	399	195	187	322	18	143	89	66	101	196	150	-	-	81	305	10
B085D: With psychedelics other than LSD																
1. Not at all	96.2	95.8	97.5	97.0	100.0	93.1	97.6	97.9	98.0	96.1	97.5	-	-	99.4	96.2	69.7
2. A few of the times	2.1	2.6	0.9	1.6	-	3.7	1.9	-	1.5	1.3	1.8	-	-	-	2.1	17.4
3. Some of the times	1.4	1.1	1.3	0.9	-	2.9	-	2.1	-	2.3	0.6	-	-	-	1.5	8.8
4. Most of the times	-	-	-	-	-	-	-	-	-	-	-	-	-	-	-	-
5. Every time	0.4	0.5	0.3	0.4	-	0.3	0.5	-	0.5	0.3	-	-	-	0.6	0.2	4.1
Item 4320 Subject A01h N★	398	194	187	321	18	141	88	68	101	193	153	-	-	81	303	11
B085E: With amphetamines																
1. Not at all	94.5	94.1	96.4	94.5	100.0	94.7	93.2	97.9	93.0	96.4	93.0	-	-	100.0	93.9	69.7
2. A few of the times	3.3	3.8	1.5	3.2	-	3.9	4.2	-	3.8	2.2	3.5	-	-	-	3.7	17.4
3. Some of the times	1.3	0.8	1.3	1.1	-	1.1	0.4	2.1	1.6	1.3	1.7	-	-	-	1.3	8.8
4. Most of the times	0.5	0.8	0.2	0.6	-	-	0.3	-	1.5	0.2	1.0	-	-	-	0.6	-
5. Every time	0.5	0.5	0.6	0.7	-	0.3	1.8	-	-	-	0.8	-	-	-	0.5	4.1
Item 4330 Subject A01h N★	398	197	184	321	18	138	89	68	102	195	150	-	-	81	302	11
B085F: With quaaludes																
1. Not at all	97.5	96.9	98.4	97.7	100.0	97.9	96.3	98.6	97.5	98.7	97.6	-	-	100.0	97.2	87.1
2. A few of the times	1.8	2.2	1.6	1.8	-	2.1	3.2	-	1.4	1.3	1.0	-	-	-	2.4	-
3. Some of the times	0.5	0.6	-	0.4	-	-	-	1.4	1.2	-	1.4	-	-	-	0.4	8.8
4. Most of the times	-	-	-	-	-	-	-	-	-	-	-	-	-	-	-	-
5. Every time	0.1	0.2	-	0.1	-	-	0.5	-	-	-	-	-	-	-	-	4.1
Item 4340 Subject A01h N★	401	196	187	323	18	143	89	68	101	197	152	-	-	81	306	11

★=excludes respondents for whom question was inappropriate.

QUESTIONNAIRE FORM 1 1986	TOTAL	SEX		RACE		REGION				4YR COLLEGE PLANS		ILLICIT DRUG USE: LIFETIME				
		M	F	White	Black	NE	NC	S	W	Yes	No	None	Mari- juana Only	Few Pills	More Pills	Any Her- oin
N (Weighted No. of Cases):	3179	1469	1562	2351	323	749	897	984	550	1841	999	1333	671	406	643	21
% of Weighted Total:	100.0	46.2	49.1	74.0	10.2	23.5	28.2	30.9	17.3	57.9	31.4	41.9	21.1	12.8	20.2	0.7
B085G: With barbiturates																
1. Not at all	97.5	97.6	97.7	97.5	100.0	95.7	97.7	97.9	99.6	98.5	96.5	-	-	100.0	97.8	69.7
2. A few of the times	2.0	1.9	2.3	2.3	-	3.9	1.7	0.6	0.4	1.2	2.8	-	-	-	2.0	17.4
3. Some of the times	0.4	0.3	-	-	-	0.4	-	1.4	-	0.3	0.6	-	-	-	0.2	8.8
4. Most of the times	-	-	-	-	-	-	-	-	-	-	-	-	-	-	-	-
5. Every time	0.1	0.2	-	0.1	-	-	0.5	-	-	-	-	-	-	-	-	4.1
Item 4350　Subject A01h　　N★	400	197	186	323	18	141	89	68	101	195	153	-	-	81	304	11
B085H: With tranquilizers																
1. Not at all	98.1	98.7	98.1	98.2	100.0	97.5	98.8	95.5	100.0	98.5	97.9	-	-	100.0	98.5	72.4
2. A few of the times	1.2	0.8	1.6	1.4	-	2.1	0.7	2.0	-	0.9	1.4	-	-	-	1.3	8.4
3. Some of the times	0.6	0.3	0.4	0.2	-	0.4	-	2.5	-	0.6	0.6	-	-	-	0.2	15.1
4. Most of the times	-	-	-	-	-	-	-	-	-	-	-	-	-	-	-	-
5. Every time	0.1	0.2	-	0.1	-	-	0.5	-	-	-	-	-	-	-	-	4.1
Item 4360　Subject A01h　　N★	399	197	187	322	18	142	89	68	100	194	153	-	-	81	304	11
B086: What have been the most important reasons for your taking cocaine? (Mark all that apply.)																
A. To experiment–to see what it's like	77.3	77.7	78.1	79.7	69.3	79.1	81.8	66.5	78.0	79.3	71.8	-	-	88.7	75.8	43.7
B. To relax or relieve tension	17.9	18.3	17.0	15.8	43.8	14.8	21.6	17.8	18.9	16.9	21.9	-	-	9.8	19.8	20.0
C. To feel good or get high	67.4	69.1	65.2	67.8	70.5	66.8	66.2	68.5	68.6	65.6	70.8	-	-	35.4	76.7	45.8
D. To seek deeper insights and understanding	7.3	7.7	6.3	6.4	20.7	7.4	9.8	10.6	2.9	8.0	7.3	-	-	2.5	8.3	12.3
E. To have a good time with my friends	50.1	52.2	48.0	50.6	26.1	50.9	45.6	44.0	56.4	48.7	53.2	-	-	24.8	57.1	40.1
F. To fit in with a group I like	7.5	9.8	5.3	6.2	4.3	3.6	7.9	10.7	10.5	8.0	8.6	-	-	9.6	6.7	14.4
G. To get away from my problems or troubles	7.8	9.0	6.4	8.2	5.6	4.7	11.3	9.3	8.0	4.8	13.2	-	-	1.8	9.0	16.6
H. Because of boredom, nothing else to do	14.4	16.8	9.9	13.5	19.3	13.7	10.7	10.4	20.8	12.1	15.3	-	-	6.7	16.7	7.3
I. Because of anger or frustration	7.3	6.4	7.8	6.6	4.9	7.3	7.9	6.0	7.4	4.8	12.5	-	-	1.8	8.3	16.6
J. To get through the day	7.0	5.7	8.9	7.5	-	4.8	8.6	5.5	9.5	5.1	10.4	-	-	1.1	8.3	11.2
K. To increase the effects of some other drug(s)	11.7	15.0	6.5	11.3	15.2	9.8	13.7	8.4	14.7	10.0	12.9	-	-	3.9	12.9	30.9
L. To decrease (offset) the effects of some other drug(s)	2.6	1.3	3.7	2.5	-	3.0	0.4	2.7	3.7	1.5	3.8	-	-	-	2.7	15.2
M. To stay awake	29.6	27.4	32.4	29.2	11.0	26.1	27.7	22.4	40.2	21.9	40.7	-	-	21.7	31.9	23.5
N. To get more energy	39.1	34.7	43.7	39.9	14.4	35.2	31.9	45.2	46.6	36.9	43.5	-	-	22.7	43.1	46.4
O. Because I am "hooked"–I have to have it	3.6	1.9	5.1	3.2	4.8	3.4	5.5	4.4	1.9	2.0	6.1	-	-	-	3.8	21.4
Item 4370-4510　Subject A06a　　N★	408	204	184	330	17	144	90	67	108	205	150	-	-	82	313	13
B087: When you take cocaine how high do you usually get?																
1. Not at all high	4.6	5.1	4.4	3.9	13.5	4.5	7.6	2.3	3.5	7.1	1.9	-	-	12.7	2.6	-
2. A little high	24.6	21.1	27.8	25.3	9.0	34.4	16.5	21.5	19.6	27.0	22.4	-	-	49.6	18.4	10.0
3. Moderately high	43.4	42.4	44.0	43.1	49.9	39.5	41.5	38.0	53.6	40.2	44.0	-	-	22.4	49.4	33.2
4. Very high	23.5	27.9	19.1	24.0	22.7	18.7	26.9	35.1	19.8	21.5	27.2	-	-	6.5	26.7	56.8
5. I don't take it to get high	4.1	3.5	4.8	3.7	4.9	2.8	7.5	3.1	3.5	4.2	4.5	-	-	8.8	3.0	
Item 4520　Subject A01e　　N★	407	204	185	331	17	146	90	66	106	205	150	-	-	84	311	12
B088: When you take cocaine how long do you usually stay high?																
1. Usually don't get high	8.7	8.5	9.4	7.7	13.5	6.8	11.7	9.2	8.3	13.3	4.0	-	-	27.7	4.1	-
2. One to two hours	55.2	54.1	54.2	57.8	27.7	63.6	48.8	52.2	51.2	53.9	55.1	-	-	60.8	54.0	48.9
3. Three to six hours	27.7	28.6	27.5	26.3	54.0	23.8	28.9	30.6	30.2	26.2	30.3	-	-	10.5	32.5	22.7
4. Seven to 24 hours	7.1	6.1	8.9	7.0	4.8	5.8	6.9	6.6	9.3	6.2	7.5	-	-	1.0	8.3	15.6
5. More than 24 hours	1.3	2.6	-	1.3	-	-	3.6	1.4	1.0	0.3	3.1	-	-	1.1	12.7	
Item 4530　Subject A01f　　N★	408	201	186	330	17	144	90	66	108	202	152	-	-	81	313	13
B089: Have you ever tried to stop using cocaine and found that you couldn't stop?																
1. Yes	6.0	5.1	6.7	5.7	4.0	5.3	6.0	6.2	6.9	5.8	6.8	-	-	0.4	5.6	46.8
2. No	94.0	94.9	93.3	94.3	96.0	94.7	94.0	93.8	93.1	94.2	93.2	-	-	99.6	94.4	53.2
Item 4540　Subject A01i　　N★	404	202	183	328	17	144	88	67	106	202	150	-	-	79	311	13

★=excludes respondents for whom question was inappropriate.

QUESTIONNAIRE FORM 1 1986	TOTAL	SEX		RACE		REGION				4YR COLLEGE PLANS		ILLICIT DRUG USE: LIFETIME				
		M	F	White	Black	NE	NC	S	W	Yes	No	None	Marijuana Only	Few Pills	More Pills	Any Heroin
N (Weighted No. of Cases):	3179	1469	1562	2351	323	749	897	984	550	1841	999	1333	671	406	643	21
% of Weighted Total:	100.0	46.2	49.1	74.0	10.2	23.5	28.2	30.9	17.3	57.9	31.4	41.9	21.1	12.8	20.2	0.7
B090A: What forms of cocaine have you used? (Mark all that apply.)																
A. Cocaine powder	92.7	94.0	90.5	92.4	86.1	90.5	94.3	91.8	95.0	92.9	90.3	-	-	84.8	94.5	100.0
B. "Freebase" or "base"	26.3	23.5	27.4	24.8	50.6	22.3	26.6	26.3	31.6	23.7	27.4	-	-	13.6	28.4	59.5
C. Coca paste	4.2	5.1	3.2	4.8	-	1.5	6.4	6.4	4.8	3.7	5.8	-	-	3.6	3.5	24.8
D. "Rock" or "crack"	29.8	29.6	29.0	28.9	21.4	28.3	30.4	22.1	36.3	24.3	32.9	-	-	9.2	34.9	41.5
Item 4531-4534 Subject A01l N★	408	204	185	332	17	145	88	67	107	205	151	-	-	84	311	13
B090B: What methods have you used for taking cocaine? (Mark all that apply.)																
A. Sniffing or "snorting"	93.6	96.8	90.6	93.1	86.1	91.7	92.8	92.5	97.4	94.7	91.0	-	-	81.7	96.8	92.7
B. Smoking	44.1	40.2	45.5	42.5	61.7	41.4	34.2	46.0	54.8	37.6	49.5	-	-	12.4	51.3	74.0
C. Injection	2.5	3.9	0.3	1.8	11.6	0.8	4.7	7.3	-	1.2	1.9	-	-	-	2.5	19.6
D. Inhaling fumes	8.7	6.6	10.3	8.7	13.8	4.9	8.8	6.7	14.9	8.0	8.3	-	-	3.3	8.6	44.6
E. By mouth	44.7	40.5	49.7	46.3	33.2	45.0	41.8	39.8	50.0	43.9	42.6	-	-	27.2	49.1	53.8
F. Other	5.0	5.5	4.5	5.7	-	4.8	6.6	5.6	3.7	3.7	7.9	-	-	-	5.6	23.5
Item 4550-4590 Subject A05d N★	408	204	186	333	17	144	90	67	107	205	152	-	-	84	311	13
B091: Do you think you will be using cocaine five years from now?																
1. I definitely will	1.1	1.2	0.7	1.0	1.1	1.5	1.4	0.3	1.3	0.5	1.8	0.2	0.7	0.7	2.9	8.1
2. I probably will	4.8	5.1	4.5	5.1	2.2	7.9	2.8	2.9	7.6	3.8	6.6	0.1	0.5	3.2	19.8	36.7
3. I probably will not	15.6	18.2	13.3	17.0	8.2	20.3	15.4	11.6	17.0	16.0	14.7	4.1	16.8	27.6	31.4	20.0
4. I definitely will not	78.5	75.5	81.4	76.9	88.5	70.3	80.4	85.2	74.2	79.7	76.8	95.6	81.9	68.5	45.8	35.1
Item 4600 Subject A04a N	2990	1410	1524	2295	311	691	861	921	518	1798	954	1278	632	397	609	20

The next questions are about HEROIN, which is sometimes called smack, horse, skag.

B092: On how many occasions (if any) have you taken heroin . . .

	TOTAL	M	F	White	Black	NE	NC	S	W	Yes	No	None	Marijuana Only	Few Pills	More Pills	Any Heroin
B092A: . . . in your lifetime?																
1. 0 occasions	99.3	99.0	99.7	99.3	99.8	99.3	99.3	99.5	99.0	99.5	98.9	100.0	100.0	100.0	100.0	-
2. 1-2	0.4	0.5	0.2	0.4	0.2	0.4	0.3	0.2	0.7	0.4	0.4	-	-	-	-	52.0
3. 3-5	*	-	0.1	-	-	0.2	-	-	-	-	0.1	-	-	-	-	5.6
4. 6-9	0.1	0.1	-	0.1	-	-	0.1	0.2	-	-	0.3	-	-	-	-	13.3
5. 10-19	0.1	0.2	-	0.1	-	0.2	-	-	0.3	0.1	0.1	-	-	-	-	12.6
6. 20-39	*	-	*	*	-	-	-	0.1	-	*	-	-	-	-	-	3.4
7. 40 or more	0.1	0.2	-	0.1	-	-	0.3	-	-	-	0.2	-	-	-	-	13.1
Item 1100 Subject A01a N	2967	1419	1497	2290	301	680	857	925	505	1785	948	1297	628	390	597	21
B092B: . . . during the last 12 months?																
1. 0 occasions	99.7	99.5	99.9	99.6	100.0	99.5	99.7	99.6	99.9	99.7	99.5	100.0	100.0	100.0	100.0	52.3
2. 1-2	0.1	0.3	0.1	0.2	-	0.3	0.1	0.1	0.1	0.2	0.1	-	-	-	-	21.1
3. 3-5	*	0.1	-	*	-	-	-	0.1	-	-	0.1	-	-	-	-	4.6
4. 6-9	*	-	-	-	-	-	-	0.1	-	-	0.1	-	-	-	-	4.8
5. 10-19	0.1	0.1	*	0.1	-	0.2	-	0.1	-	*	0.1	-	-	-	-	9.4
6. 20-39	-	-	-	-	-	-	-	-	-	-	-	-	-	-	-	-
7. 40 or more	0.1	0.1	-	0.1	-	-	0.2	-	-	-	0.1	-	-	-	-	7.9
Item 1110 Subject A01b N	2968	1419	1498	2290	301	680	857	925	506	1786	948	1298	628	390	597	21
B092C: . . . during the last 30 days?																
1. 0 occasions	99.9	99.8	100.0	99.9	100.0	100.0	99.8	99.8	100.0	100.0	99.8	100.0	100.0	100.0	100.0	83.3
2. 1-2	*	0.1	-	*	-	-	-	0.1	-	-	0.1	-	-	-	-	4.8
3. 3-5	-	-	-	-	-	-	-	-	-	-	-	-	-	-	-	-
4. 6-9	*	-	*	*	-	-	-	0.1	-	*	-	-	-	-	-	3.5
5. 10-19	*	*	-	*	-	-	0.1	-	-	-	-	-	-	-	-	2.3
6. 20-39	-	-	-	-	-	-	-	-	-	-	-	-	-	-	-	-
7. 40 or more	*	0.1	-	0.1	-	-	0.1	-	-	-	0.1	-	-	-	-	6.0
Item 1120 Subject A01c N	2966	1419	1497	2290	301	680	857	924	505	1785	947	1297	628	390	597	20

*=less than .05 per cent.   ★=excludes respondents for whom question was inappropriate.

QUESTIONNAIRE FORM 1 1986	TOTAL	SEX		RACE		REGION				4YR COLLEGE PLANS		ILLICIT DRUG USE: LIFETIME				
		M	F	White	Black	NE	NC	S	W	Yes	No	None	Mari-juana Only	Few Pills	More Pills	Any Her-oin
N (Weighted No. of Cases):	3179	1469	1562	2351	323	749	897	984	550	1841	999	1333	671	406	643	21
% of Weighted Total:	100.0	46.2	49.1	74.0	10.2	23.5	28.2	30.9	17.3	57.9	31.4	41.9	21.1	12.8	20.2	0.7

The next questions are about NARCOTICS OTHER THAN HEROIN, which are sometimes prescribed by doctors. Drugstores are not supposed to sell them without a prescription. These include:

Methadone, Codeine, Talwin, Morphine, Opium, Demerol, Laudanum, Paregoric.

B093: Have you ever taken any narcotics other than heroin because a doctor told you to use them?

	TOTAL	M	F	White	Black	NE	NC	S	W	Yes	No	None	Mari-juana Only	Few Pills	More Pills	Any Her-oin
1. No	81.8	84.3	79.4	79.2	94.0	78.1	84.5	82.5	80.7	79.3	85.2	87.8	85.7	71.1	72.1	67.9
2. Yes, but I had already tried them on my own.	2.0	2.0	1.7	2.1	-	2.2	2.1	1.7	2.0	1.6	2.4	-	0.2	1.5	7.7	26.5
3. Yes, and it was the first time I took any	16.3	13.7	18.9	18.8	6.0	19.7	13.4	15.9	17.3	19.1	12.4	12.2	14.2	27.4	20.2	5.6
Item 5020 Subject A01j N	2925	1383	1492	2266	287	663	851	908	504	1774	928	1265	620	389	593	21

B094: On how many occasions (if any) have you taken narcotics other than heroin on your own–that is, without a doctor telling you to take them . . .

B094A: . . . in your lifetime?

	TOTAL	M	F	White	Black	NE	NC	S	W	Yes	No	None	Mari-juana Only	Few Pills	More Pills	Any Her-oin
1. 0 occasions	91.7	91.6	92.0	90.4	97.7	90.3	91.7	92.9	91.7	91.9	92.0	100.0	100.0	81.9	72.6	37.0
2. 1-2	4.3	3.9	4.8	5.1	1.8	5.4	3.9	4.1	4.1	4.7	3.9	-	-	18.1	9.2	14.1
3. 3-5	1.5	1.5	1.5	1.8	-	1.4	1.8	1.0	1.8	1.5	1.2	-	-	-	7.3	4.1
4. 6-9	0.9	0.8	1.0	1.0	0.6	0.9	0.6	0.9	1.3	0.7	1.3	-	-	-	4.1	8.9
5. 10-19	0.6	0.7	0.4	0.6	-	1.5	0.4	0.2	0.2	0.5	0.7	-	-	-	2.9	-
6. 20-39	0.4	0.4	0.3	0.4	-	0.5	0.6	0.1	0.4	0.4	-	-	-	-	2.0	3.5
7. 40 or more	0.6	1.1	0.1	0.7	-	0.1	1.0	0.7	0.4	0.4	1.0	-	-	-	1.9	32.3
Item 1130 Subject A01a N	2942	1402	1492	2265	300	674	851	915	502	1773	936	1280	632	392	585	20

B094B: . . . during the last 12 months?

	TOTAL	M	F	White	Black	NE	NC	S	W	Yes	No	None	Mari-juana Only	Few Pills	More Pills	Any Her-oin
1. 0 occasions	95.5	95.4	95.8	95.0	98.6	94.3	94.9	96.5	96.5	96.0	95.2	100.0	100.0	94.9	82.3	57.7
2. 1-2	2.3	1.6	2.9	2.6	0.9	3.1	2.4	2.1	1.3	2.0	2.8	-	-	5.1	7.9	4.2
3. 3-5	0.9	1.5	0.4	1.0	-	1.5	1.2	0.2	1.0	0.9	0.6	-	-	-	4.5	3.5
4. 6-9	0.6	0.7	0.5	0.6	0.6	0.7	0.8	0.6	0.5	0.5	0.8	-	-	-	2.9	10.8
5. 10-19	0.5	0.6	0.3	0.6	-	0.4	0.5	0.5	0.7	0.6	0.3	-	-	-	2.2	7.8
6. 20-39	*	-	*	*	-	-	0.1	-	-	*	-	-	-	-	0.1	-
7. 40 or more	0.1	0.3	-	0.1	-	0.1	0.2	0.1	0.1	*	0.3	-	-	-	0.1	16.1
Item 1140 Subject A01b N	2938	1400	1490	2263	300	672	849	916	501	1770	937	1281	632	391	581	19

B094C: . . . during the last 30 days?

	TOTAL	M	F	White	Black	NE	NC	S	W	Yes	No	None	Mari-juana Only	Few Pills	More Pills	Any Her-oin
1. 0 occasions	98.2	97.6	98.8	97.9	99.7	96.8	98.5	98.6	98.9	98.5	97.5	100.0	100.0	98.5	93.0	63.3
2. 1-2	1.1	1.4	0.9	1.3	-	2.4	1.0	0.6	0.5	0.8	1.8	-	-	1.5	4.4	4.5
3. 3-5	0.4	0.6	0.2	0.4	0.3	0.8	0.4	0.1	0.3	0.5	0.3	-	-	-	1.8	6.0
4. 6-9	0.2	0.3	0.1	0.2	-	-	-	0.5	0.2	0.2	0.2	-	-	-	0.7	10.6
5. 10-19	0.1	0.1	*	0.1	-	-	0.1	0.1	0.1	*	0.1	-	-	-	0.1	9.2
6. 20-39	-	-	-	-	-	-	-	-	-	-	-	-	-	-	-	-
7. 40 or more	*	0.1	-	0.1	-	-	0.1	-	-	-	0.1	-	-	-	-	6.5
Item 1150 Subject A01c N	2935	1400	1488	2258	300	673	845	916	501	1769	935	1282	632	389	580	18

IF YOU HAVE NOT TAKEN NARCOTICS OTHER THAN HEROIN IN THE LAST TWELVE MONTHS, GO TO Q.B103.

THE FOLLOWING QUESTIONS REFER ONLY TO TAKING NARCOTICS OTHER THAN HEROIN WITHOUT A DOCTOR'S ORDERS. IF YOU HAVE NOT DONE THIS IN THE LAST TWELVE MONTHS, GO TO Q.B103.

B095: When you used narcotics other than heroin during the last year, how often did you use them in each of the following situations?

*=less than .05 per cent.

QUESTIONNAIRE FORM 1 1986	TOTAL	SEX		RACE		REGION				4YR COLLEGE PLANS		ILLICIT DRUG USE: LIFETIME				
		M	F	White	Black	NE	NC	S	W	Yes	No	None	Mari-juana Only	Few Pills	More Pills	Any Her-oin
N (Weighted No. of Cases):	3179	1469	1562	2351	323	749	897	984	550	1841	999	1333	671	406	643	21
% of Weighted Total:	100.0	46.2	49.1	74.0	10.2	23.5	28.2	30.9	17.3	57.9	31.4	41.9	21.1	12.8	20.2	0.7
B095A: When you were alone																
1. Not at all	47.8	54.6	42.2	49.5	71.5	50.5	57.9	40.6	30.2	45.8	49.2	-	-	59.6	45.3	50.4
2. A few of the times	25.4	21.9	29.7	24.0	28.5	26.7	11.6	39.7	26.9	23.3	30.2	-	-	18.4	27.4	16.5
3. Some of the times	13.8	11.2	13.1	11.5	-	11.2	16.7	9.3	22.1	15.0	9.9	-	-	-	15.3	21.5
4. Most of the times	6.2	8.9	4.0	7.2	-	6.1	6.9	4.3	9.2	9.8	3.3	-	-	-	7.7	-
5. Every time	6.8	3.4	10.9	7.9	-	5.4	6.9	6.1	11.5	6.0	7.3	-	-	22.0	4.2	11.5
Item 5030 Subject A05a N★	105	52	50	91	3	28	35	30	12	54	39	-	-	13	85	7
B095B: With just 1 or 2 other people																
1. Not at all	24.0	11.1	40.3	26.9	46.8	9.4	25.4	33.7	30.0	28.6	23.5	-	-	32.4	23.0	11.5
2. A few of the times	32.0	34.5	31.6	32.7	7.6	36.4	31.2	33.2	21.8	31.0	31.4	-	-	35.7	33.3	13.5
3. Some of the times	22.5	26.8	13.4	16.9	45.6	20.8	29.8	13.6	26.1	16.2	24.5	-	-	10.5	21.2	63.3
4. Most of the times	12.1	15.8	7.0	12.7	-	25.5	4.5	10.1	8.5	15.0	9.1	-	-	-	14.0	11.7
5. Every time	9.3	11.8	7.8	10.8	-	7.7	9.2	9.3	13.7	9.2	11.6	-	-	21.4	8.4	-
Item 5040 Subject A05b N★	106	52	49	91	2	28	36	29	12	54	38	-	-	13	86	7
B095C: At a party																
1. Not at all	58.9	51.2	70.5	58.6	100.0	54.3	51.0	66.4	73.8	70.5	46.9	-	-	92.1	57.5	11.5
2. A few of the times	16.9	21.4	9.6	17.3	-	23.0	17.4	12.2	12.4	9.8	20.4	-	-	5.6	19.3	9.6
3. Some of the times	13.5	10.7	15.6	13.0	-	16.7	17.6	11.2	-	6.8	24.0	-	-	2.4	13.4	35.8
4. Most of the times	6.2	10.1	1.4	5.9	-	3.6	8.7	2.4	13.8	6.7	4.9	-	-	-	5.2	29.6
5. Every time	4.6	6.5	2.9	5.2	-	2.4	5.2	7.8	-	6.2	3.8	-	-	-	4.5	13.5
Item 5050 Subject A05c N★	105	52	49	91	2	28	35	29	12	54	38	-	-	13	84	7
B095D: When your date or spouse was present																
1. Not at all	60.0	62.8	61.0	61.0	100.0	54.4	49.6	72.8	71.8	62.8	58.5	-	-	89.3	57.6	32.8
2. A few of the times	17.7	17.5	16.3	18.2	-	22.9	25.7	4.7	14.5	15.0	19.9	-	-	10.7	20.4	-
3. Some of the times	12.6	10.4	14.3	11.8	-	16.4	14.5	8.3	9.5	13.5	11.5	-	-	-	12.6	36.3
4. Most of the times	4.1	4.0	2.0	2.7	-	1.9	4.5	5.6	4.2	2.3	4.6	-	-	-	3.4	20.9
5. Every time	5.5	5.3	6.4	6.3	-	4.4	5.8	8.6	-	6.5	5.5	-	-	-	6.0	10.0
Item 5060 Subject A05b N★	103	49	49	91	2	26	36	29	12	51	38	-	-	12	83	7
B095E: When people over age 30 were present																
1. Not at all	47.8	47.6	50.2	49.0	100.0	49.3	47.7	48.0	43.9	58.0	29.0	-	-	55.3	47.8	28.1
2. A few of the times	19.9	25.2	12.1	18.1	-	28.8	22.7	12.2	7.5	12.1	25.5	-	-	14.5	20.4	25.2
3. Some of the times	18.7	21.2	15.8	17.7	-	16.2	16.6	15.9	38.6	13.3	33.5	-	-	10.5	18.7	35.1
4. Most of the times	6.5	2.5	11.3	7.6	-	5.7	5.2	11.3	-	4.3	12.0	-	-	9.2	5.7	11.7
5. Every time	7.2	3.5	10.5	7.7	-	-	7.8	12.6	10.1	12.2	-	-	-	10.5	7.4	-
Item 5070 Subject A05b N★	106	52	49	90	2	29	37	29	11	53	38	-	-	13	86	7
B095F: During the daytime (before 4:00 p.m.)																
1. Not at all	29.0	31.3	26.5	27.3	92.4	26.8	33.9	19.3	44.4	31.5	20.4	-	-	33.2	28.0	25.2
2. A few of the times	34.3	37.7	30.0	36.6	7.6	30.3	29.6	44.8	30.9	35.6	35.5	-	-	25.4	36.3	31.6
3. Some of the times	27.0	21.8	32.1	24.8	-	33.9	28.7	24.6	11.4	16.5	40.8	-	-	34.9	24.6	43.2
4. Most of the times	4.6	2.6	7.4	5.4	-	9.0	5.5	1.5	-	8.9	-	-	-	-	5.8	-
5. Every time	5.1	6.6	4.0	5.9	-	-	2.3	9.8	13.3	7.5	3.3	-	-	6.5	5.3	-
Item 5080 Subject A05c N★	102	51	47	88	2	27	35	29	11	53	36	-	-	13	82	7
B095G: At your home (or apartment or dorm)																
1. Not at all	24.8	34.1	16.5	24.6	71.5	17.5	38.7	14.2	26.8	28.7	16.1	-	-	34.3	24.7	-
2. A few of the times	34.4	38.3	30.1	33.5	28.5	48.4	22.8	39.4	24.9	33.4	39.2	-	-	19.8	33.8	71.9
3. Some of the times	10.2	8.3	10.0	7.9	-	18.0	7.5	8.8	4.2	5.0	12.3	-	-	5.6	10.0	21.5
4. Most of the times	9.0	11.2	7.6	10.2	-	1.8	8.2	10.8	21.9	11.9	6.9	-	-	-	10.6	6.5
5. Every time	21.7	8.1	35.9	23.9	-	14.3	22.7	26.7	22.3	21.0	25.5	-	-	40.3	20.9	-
Item 5090 Subject A05c N★	104	49	50	91	3	27	35	30	12	52	39	-	-	13	84	7

★=excludes respondents for whom question was inappropriate.

QUESTIONNAIRE FORM 1 1986	TOTAL	SEX		RACE		REGION				4YR COLLEGE PLANS		ILLICIT DRUG USE: LIFETIME				
		M	F	White	Black	NE	NC	S	W	Yes	No	None	Marijuana Only	Few Pills	More Pills	Any Heroin
N (Weighted No. of Cases):	3179	1469	1562	2351	323	749	897	984	550	1841	999	1333	671	406	643	21
% of Weighted Total:	100.0	46.2	49.1	74.0	10.2	23.5	28.2	30.9	17.3	57.9	31.4	41.9	21.1	12.8	20.2	0.7
B095H: At school																
1. Not at all	63.5	52.1	78.2	66.0	92.4	41.4	76.3	62.6	84.8	66.3	63.0	-	-	74.0	62.7	47.4
2. A few of the times	14.5	21.3	4.1	13.8	7.6	31.9	4.8	13.4	1.3	12.6	13.0	-	-		16.0	24.9
3. Some of the times	17.7	21.6	13.7	15.3	-	26.7	16.6	16.9	-	16.8	18.4	-	-	19.5	17.9	15.2
4. Most of the times	1.7	1.9	1.6	2.0	-	-	-	6.0	-	1.6	2.5	-	-		1.1	12.5
5. Every time	2.6	3.1	2.4	3.0	-	-	2.4	1.2	13.9	2.9	3.2	-	-	6.5	2.2	-
Item 5100 Subject A05c N★	103	49	49	89	2	29	34	29	11	52	38	-	-	13	83	6
B095I: In a car																
1. Not at all	64.3	48.4	82.4	64.3	54.4	61.2	58.0	68.8	80.9	68.8	64.3	-	-	85.5	64.8	12.5
2. A few of the times	19.0	26.4	11.5	20.0	45.6	36.9	15.6	6.2	19.1	16.2	20.9	-	-	4.1	21.0	24.9
3. Some of the times	10.0	13.5	5.2	8.8	-	-	20.5	10.7	-	9.2	7.5	-	-	10.5	7.5	43.0
4. Most of the times	4.9	8.0	0.9	4.9	-	1.9	3.6	10.9	-	4.2	4.7	-	-	-	4.5	19.7
5. Every time	1.8	3.6	-	2.0	-	-	2.3	3.4	-	1.5	2.6	-	-	-	2.2	-
Item 5120 Subject A05c N★	103	50	49	90	2	28	35	29	11	53	38	-	-	13	83	6
B096: How many of the times when you used narcotics other than heroin during the last year did you use them along with each of the following drugs–that is, so that their effects overlapped?																
B096A: With alcohol																
1. Not at all	50.9	38.6	64.7	53.8	38.9	40.8	48.4	62.4	54.3	59.5	47.2	-	-	92.1	47.0	13.4
2. A few of the times	14.7	20.3	10.0	12.6	61.1	15.6	9.1	19.6	16.7	11.3	19.7	-	-	7.9	16.0	11.7
3. Some of the times	15.3	17.6	10.2	13.5	-	23.3	20.9	3.1	9.5	10.7	14.1	-	-	-	14.6	59.2
4. Most of the times	10.0	8.4	11.4	9.4	-	20.3	4.8	5.4	11.1	7.3	12.4	-	-	-	12.2	-
5. Every time	9.2	15.2	3.7	10.6	-	-	16.8	9.5	8.5	11.3	6.6	-	-	-	10.2	15.7
Item 5130 Subject A01h N★	105	52	50	91	3	29	35	29	12	54	38	-	-	13	86	6
B096B: With marijuana																
1. Not at all	54.0	39.0	69.7	57.3	38.9	47.4	56.1	59.3	50.1	55.8	56.7	-	-	93.6	51.0	11.5
2. A few of the times	12.9	16.6	8.9	13.3	28.5	14.0	12.1	12.5	13.8	17.1	8.3	-	-	2.4	15.0	9.6
3. Some of the times	9.2	16.2	0.9	4.8	-	10.4	6.6	12.9	4.2	8.0	9.9	-	-	-	8.6	33.2
4. Most of the times	13.4	16.5	10.2	12.4	32.6	19.7	12.2	9.8	11.1	13.7	8.6	-	-	-	15.3	16.5
5. Every time	10.6	11.6	10.3	12.2	-	8.5	13.1	5.5	20.9	5.4	16.4	-	-	4.1	10.1	29.1
Item 5140 Subject A01h N★	102	49	50	89	3	28	32	30	12	53	39	-	-	13	82	7
B096C: With LSD																
1. Not at all	95.0	93.4	97.7	95.7	100.0	97.5	95.1	92.4	95.1	95.7	95.8	-	-	100.0	98.0	36.6
2. A few of the times	3.0	3.4	1.4	2.6	-	2.5	4.9	2.6	-	3.5	-	-	-	-	1.4	35.2
3. Some of the times	1.5	3.2	-	1.1	-	-	-	3.5	4.9	-	4.2	-	-	-	-	28.2
4. Most of the times	0.4	-	0.9	0.5	-	-	-	1.6	-	0.8	-	-	-	-	0.6	-
5. Every time	-	-	-	-	-	-	-	-	-	-	-	-	-	-	-	-
Item 5150 Subject A01h N★	97	46	49	85	2	27	32	27	11	52	35	-	-	13	78	5
B096D: With psychedelics other than LSD																
1. Not at all	94.1	92.0	99.1	95.2	100.0	97.5	96.1	91.9	84.9	99.2	88.4	-	-	100.0	97.5	40.2
2. A few of the times	3.1	5.0	-	2.7	-	2.5	2.5	-	15.1	-	6.4	-	-	-	1.9	23.0
3. Some of the times	2.0	2.0	-	1.1	-	-	-	6.6	-	-	5.2	-	-	-	-	29.8
4. Most of the times	0.9	1.0	0.9	1.0	-	-	1.4	1.5	-	0.8	-	-	-	-	0.5	7.0
5. Every time	-	-	-	-	-	-	-	-	-	-	-	-	-	-	-	-
Item 5160 Subject A01h N★	99	47	49	87	2	27	32	29	10	52	37	-	-	13	79	6
B096E: With amphetamines																
1. Not at all	91.2	89.4	94.2	91.9	71.5	100.0	88.9	91.4	74.9	94.7	85.1	-	-	100.0	91.9	58.0
2. A few of the times	4.4	7.2	2.2	4.3	28.5	-	7.9	2.5	11.0	3.4	5.9	-	-	-	3.9	23.7
3. Some of the times	3.1	3.4	1.0	2.4	-	-	1.6	3.4	14.2	-	8.1	-	-	-	2.6	18.3
4. Most of the times	1.3	-	2.6	1.5	-	-	1.6	2.7	-	1.9	0.9	-	-	-	1.6	-
5. Every time	-	-	-	-	-	-	-	-	-	-	-	-	-	-	-	-
Item 5170 Subject A01h N★	98	45	50	86	3	27	31	29	11	51	37	-	-	13	79	5

★=excludes respondents for whom question was inappropriate.

QUESTIONNAIRE FORM 1 1986	TOTAL	SEX		RACE		REGION				4YR COLLEGE PLANS		ILLICIT DRUG USE: LIFETIME				
		M	F	White	Black	NE	NC	S	W	Yes	No	None	Mari-juana Only	Few Pills	More Pills	Any Her-oin
N (Weighted No. of Cases):	3179	1469	1562	2351	323	749	897	984	550	1841	999	1333	671	406	643	21
% of Weighted Total:	100.0	46.2	49.1	74.0	10.2	23.5	28.2	30.9	17.3	57.9	31.4	41.9	21.1	12.8	20.2	0.7

B096F: With quaaludes

	TOTAL	M	F	White	Black	NE	NC	S	W	Yes	No	None	Mari-juana Only	Few Pills	More Pills	Any Her-oin
1. Not at all	97.4	96.6	100.0	98.2	100.0	100.0	95.1	96.6	100.0	97.9	97.3	-	-	100.0	100.0	55.2
2. A few of the times	1.1	2.4	-	1.3	-	-	3.5	-	-	2.1	-	-	-	-	-	19.3
3. Some of the times	1.0	-	-	-	-	-	-	3.4	-	-	2.7	-	-	-	-	17.4
4. Most of the times	0.5	1.0	-	0.5	-	-	1.4	-	-	-	-	-	-	-	-	8.1
5. Every time	-	-	-	-	-	-	-	-	-	-	-	-	-	-	-	-
Item 5180 Subject A01h N★	98	46	49	86	2	27	32	29	10	51	36	-	-	13	79	6

B096G: With barbiturates

	TOTAL	M	F	White	Black	NE	NC	S	W	Yes	No	None	Mari-juana Only	Few Pills	More Pills	Any Her-oin
1. Not at all	94.0	95.4	94.2	94.3	100.0	94.4	93.5	91.8	100.0	95.4	91.5	-	-	100.0	95.7	55.2
2. A few of the times	4.1	3.6	4.9	4.7	-	5.6	5.1	3.2	-	3.8	5.8	-	-	-	3.7	19.3
3. Some of the times	1.5	1.0	-	0.5	-	-	1.4	3.4	-	-	2.7	-	-	-	-	25.5
4. Most of the times	0.4	-	0.9	0.5	-	-	-	1.5	-	0.8	-	-	-	-	0.5	-
5. Every time	-	-	-	-	-	-	-	-	-	-	-	-	-	-	-	-
Item 5190 Subject A01h N★	98	47	49	86	2	27	32	29	11	51	37	-	-	13	79	6

B096H: With tranquilizers

	TOTAL	M	F	White	Black	NE	NC	S	W	Yes	No	None	Mari-juana Only	Few Pills	More Pills	Any Her-oin
1. Not at all	90.2	91.0	90.9	92.7	100.0	84.4	94.5	91.6	88.4	85.3	95.7	-	-	100.0	89.6	77.7
2. A few of the times	4.3	3.0	5.8	4.9	-	7.0	4.1	3.5	-	7.1	1.6	-	-	-	5.4	-
3. Some of the times	5.0	6.0	2.4	1.9	-	8.6	1.4	3.4	11.6	6.8	2.7	-	-	-	4.4	22.3
4. Most of the times	0.4	-	0.9	0.5	-	-	-	1.5	-	0.8	-	-	-	-	0.5	-
5. Every time	-	-	-	-	-	-	-	-	-	-	-	-	-	-	-	-
Item 5200 Subject A01h N★	99	47	49	87	2	27	32	29	10	52	37	-	-	13	79	6

B096I: With cocaine

	TOTAL	M	F	White	Black	NE	NC	S	W	Yes	No	None	Mari-juana Only	Few Pills	More Pills	Any Her-oin
1. Not at all	90.8	85.7	98.2	92.8	54.4	98.1	90.3	90.3	76.1	96.2	85.6	-	-	100.0	92.4	50.5
2. A few of the times	3.0	5.5	0.9	2.5	45.6	-	8.3	1.5	-	3.0	1.8	-	-	-	2.4	17.7
3. Some of the times	2.2	2.5	-	0.8	-	-	-	3.4	10.4	-	5.8	-	-	-	0.8	24.4
4. Most of the times	4.0	6.3	0.9	3.9	-	1.9	1.4	4.9	13.5	0.8	6.8	-	-	-	4.3	7.4
5. Every time	-	-	-	-	-	-	-	-	-	-	-	-	-	-	-	-
Item 5210 Subject A01h N★	100	47	49	87	2	28	32	29	11	52	37	-	-	13	80	6

B096J: With heroin

	TOTAL	M	F	White	Black	NE	NC	S	W	Yes	No	None	Mari-juana Only	Few Pills	More Pills	Any Her-oin
1. Not at all	98.5	99.0	100.0	99.5	100.0	100.0	98.6	96.6	100.0	100.0	97.3	-	-	100.0	100.0	74.5
2. A few of the times	-	-	-	-	-	-	-	-	-	-	-	-	-	-	-	-
3. Some of the times	1.0	-	-	-	-	-	-	3.4	-	-	2.7	-	-	-	-	17.4
4. Most of the times	0.5	1.0	-	0.5	-	-	1.4	-	-	-	-	-	-	-	-	8.1
5. Every time	-	-	-	-	-	-	-	-	-	-	-	-	-	-	-	-
Item 5220 Subject A01h N★	98	47	49	86	2	27	32	29	11	51	37	-	-	13	79	6

★=excludes respondents for whom question was inappropriate.

QUESTIONNAIRE FORM 1 1986	TOTAL	SEX		RACE		REGION				4YR COLLEGE PLANS		ILLICIT DRUG USE: LIFETIME				
		M	F	White	Black	NE	NC	S	W	Yes	No	None	Mari- juana Only	Few Pills	More Pills	Any Her- oin
N (Weighted No. of Cases):	3179	1469	1562	2351	323	749	897	984	550	1841	999	1333	671	406	643	21
% of Weighted Total:	100.0	46.2	49.1	74.0	10.2	23.5	28.2	30.9	17.3	57.9	31.4	41.9	21.1	12.8	20.2	0.7

B097: What have been the most important reasons for your using narcotics other than heroin without a doctor's orders? (Mark all that apply.)

	TOTAL	M	F	White	Black	NE	NC	S	W	Yes	No	None	Mari-juana Only	Few Pills	More Pills	Any Heroin
A. To experiment–to see what it's like	51.0	62.2	34.4	45.0	91.8	69.4	43.9	46.2	41.2	47.1	39.5	-	-	32.6	50.3	88.3
B. To relax or relieve tension	39.2	38.1	38.6	36.8	-	50.3	38.7	28.9	40.6	44.8	27.6	-	-	17.6	43.8	17.0
C. To feel good or get high	49.8	64.6	29.2	44.5	49.1	70.0	48.3	37.1	39.8	42.1	53.0	-	-	-	53.8	78.5
D. To seek deeper insights and understanding	4.5	5.7	2.0	4.3	-	2.5	3.1	9.7	-	5.1	1.7	-	-	4.7	4.0	9.6
E. To have a good time with my friends	23.9	33.6	9.6	22.4	-	30.4	19.4	24.5	20.7	18.6	27.3	-	-	-	24.8	49.8
F. To fit in with a group I like	2.2	4.4	-	2.5	-	-	4.0	3.2	-	2.5	2.7	-	-	-	1.6	13.5
G. To get away from my problems or troubles	16.7	12.5	20.6	16.9	42.8	17.3	10.4	21.5	20.6	16.7	18.0	-	-	7.9	18.0	14.1
H. Because of boredom, nothing else to do	11.1	15.1	7.7	12.5	-	7.1	11.3	9.4	23.2	16.0	4.5	-	-	-	13.4	-
I. Because of anger or frustration	12.7	9.4	15.2	13.2	-	19.4	10.4	14.4	-	9.8	15.0	-	-	7.9	13.1	14.1
J. To get through the day	11.6	13.9	9.0	11.0	-	13.6	17.1	8.5	-	16.5	3.3	-	-	3.2	12.7	11.7
K. To increase the effects of some other drug(s)	13.7	22.4	3.3	11.8	-	8.6	23.1	13.6	-	15.8	7.4	-	-	-	13.6	36.3
L. To decrease (offset) the effects of some other drug(s)	0.5	-	1.1	0.6	-	-	1.5	-	-	1.0	-	-	-	-	0.6	-
M. To get to sleep	27.5	25.2	30.2	27.6	42.8	26.0	23.6	37.0	18.5	23.6	33.7	-	-	20.6	27.9	32.3
N. As a substitute for heroin	2.4	3.5	1.5	1.3	-	-	5.4	2.4	-	1.3	-	-	-	-	1.6	16.5
O. To relieve physical pain	44.7	29.4	63.4	49.1	8.2	38.0	49.6	49.3	35.3	48.6	45.3	-	-	59.3	43.0	42.3
P. To control coughing	14.5	12.5	17.9	16.3	-	4.2	10.5	28.4	14.5	14.1	17.5	-	-	11.0	14.7	16.5
Q. Because I am "hooked"–I have to have it	1.7	-	1.5	0.8	-	-	-	5.8	-	1.3	2.8	-	-	-	-	24.1
Item 5230-5370 Subject A06a N★	102	51	46	90	2	27	33	29	12	54	35	-	-	11	84	7

B098: When you take narcotics other than heroin how high do you usually get?

	TOTAL	M	F	White	Black	NE	NC	S	W	Yes	No	None	Mari-juana Only	Few Pills	More Pills	Any Heroin
1. Not at all high	12.1	0.9	25.7	13.6	-	4.1	9.5	24.0	9.5	14.1	12.0	-	-	27.9	10.8	-
2. A little high	25.2	28.1	20.9	23.7	49.1	20.3	30.4	17.7	39.7	22.3	24.5	-	-	13.3	28.2	9.6
3. Moderately high	24.3	27.5	20.0	22.7	42.8	39.7	19.2	25.8	-	22.6	28.1	-	-	27.5	28.1
4. Very high	18.8	28.3	9.2	19.1	-	20.7	21.2	11.2	25.0	18.5	12.7	-	-	22.3	15.8	48.3
5. I don't take them to get high	19.6	15.2	24.2	20.9	8.2	15.1	19.7	21.3	25.8	22.4	22.7	-	-	36.4	17.7	14.1
Item 5380 Subject A01e N★	104	54	47	92	2	28	34	29	12	54	37	-	-	12	85	7

B099: When you take narcotics other than heroin how long do you usually stay high?

	TOTAL	M	F	White	Black	NE	NC	S	W	Yes	No	None	Mari-juana Only	Few Pills	More Pills	Any Heroin
1. Usually don't get high	24.7	12.3	39.3	27.3	8.2	17.0	25.3	29.7	26.1	28.2	25.4	-	-	62.3	21.6	-
2. One to two hours	30.9	37.1	23.6	29.0	49.1	25.7	35.3	33.3	23.2	29.8	35.5	-	-	11.5	34.1	24.1
3. Three to six hours	35.3	42.8	26.0	33.5	42.8	49.7	31.6	30.0	29.1	35.5	26.6	-	-	21.7	35.9	50.7
4. Seven to 24 hours	9.2	7.8	11.1	10.2	-	7.6	7.7	7.0	21.6	6.5	12.5	-	-	4.5	8.5	25.2
5. More than 24 hours	-	-	-	-	-	-	-	-	-	-	-	-	-	-	-	-
Item 5390 Subject A01f N★	102	52	48	91	2	25	34	30	12	54	37	-	-	11	83	7

B100: What narcotics other than heroin have you taken during the last year without a doctor's orders? (Mark all that apply.)

	TOTAL	M	F	White	Black	NE	NC	S	W	Yes	No	None	Mari-juana Only	Few Pills	More Pills	Any Heroin
A. Methadone	13.4	9.1	15.6	13.1	-	12.0	8.9	12.1	31.5	9.8	17.3	-	-	-	12.2	44.2
B. Opium	44.2	55.2	32.0	42.1	100.0	58.9	39.4	40.2	37.6	42.0	42.1	-	-	36.2	43.1	66.9
C. Morphine	22.1	24.2	19.3	22.2	-	14.8	30.1	21.4	16.5	20.1	17.6	-	-	4.1	18.8	83.0
D. Codeine	87.5	79.1	96.1	86.5	100.0	81.7	90.8	84.9	95.8	86.6	91.0	-	-	67.4	89.1	92.6
E. Demerol	28.6	25.9	30.2	27.1	-	17.6	23.1	31.9	58.2	23.4	37.3	-	-	15.9	28.0	50.8
F. Paregoric	3.2	6.1	-	3.5	-	-	1.4	5.7	8.6	4.0	1.8	-	-	-	3.2	6.5
G. Talwin	3.5	-	7.8	3.9	-	9.8	3.1	-	-	-	10.1	-	-	-	4.1	-
H. Laudanum	3.1	2.8	-	1.6	-	2.8	1.4	7.0	-	-	5.7	-	-	-	-	43.7
I. Other	14.7	18.3	8.0	12.5	-	21.7	6.3	19.2	13.6	19.4	7.2	-	-	-	13.6	44.6
J. Don't know the names of some I have used	12.9	13.3	11.1	9.1	-	16.3	15.3	10.1	5.4	10.9	16.8	-	-	-	13.1	25.8
Item 5400-5490 Subject A01l N★	98	50	44	87	2	24	34	28	12	51	34	-	-	8	83	7

B101: Have you ever tried to stop using narcotics other than heroin and found that you couldn't stop?

	TOTAL	M	F	White	Black	NE	NC	S	W	Yes	No	None	Mari-juana Only	Few Pills	More Pills	Any Heroin
1. Yes	2.9	0.9	3.2	2.2	-	-	2.8	7.0	-	2.2	3.7	-	-	-	1.0	30.7
2. No	97.1	99.1	96.8	97.8	100.0	100.0	97.2	93.0	100.0	97.8	96.3	-	-	100.0	99.0	69.3
Item 5500 Subject A01i N★	103	52	48	91	2	28	34	29	12	54	36	-	-	11	85	7

★=excludes respondents for whom question was inappropriate.

QUESTIONNAIRE FORM 1 1986	TOTAL	SEX		RACE		REGION				4YR COLLEGE PLANS		ILLICIT DRUG USE: LIFETIME				
		M	F	White	Black	NE	NC	S	W	Yes	No	None	Marijuana Only	Few Pills	More Pills	Any Heroin
N (Weighted No. of Cases):	3179	1469	1562	2351	323	749	897	984	550	1841	999	1333	671	406	643	21
% of Weighted Total:	100.0	46.2	49.1	74.0	10.2	23.5	28.2	30.9	17.3	57.9	31.4	41.9	21.1	12.8	20.2	0.7

B102: What methods have you used for taking any of these narcotics other than heroin? (Mark all that apply.)

	TOTAL	M	F	White	Black	NE	NC	S	W	Yes	No	None	Mari juana Only	Few Pills	More Pills	Any Heroin
A. Sniffing or "snorting"	16.1	21.8	8.9	15.1	-	6.5	17.5	19.4	26.1	12.8	15.7	-	-	-	14.4	63.3
B. Smoking	31.9	45.3	15.7	30.4	91.8	33.6	34.0	34.1	16.6	27.3	37.6	-	-	31.6	28.1	78.5
C. Injection	7.3	7.2	5.9	5.7	-	6.9	9.0	8.8	-	5.2	2.7	-	-	-	7.2	20.6
D. By mouth	84.0	74.1	93.8	82.0	100.0	81.3	80.9	83.5	100.0	81.4	93.1	-	-	71.1	85.7	84.4
E. Other	5.8	7.7	1.9	3.4	-	-	5.2	12.5	4.2	5.1	4.1	-	-	-	4.7	28.1
Item 5510-5550 Subject A05d N★	104	53	47	92	2	28	34	30	12	54	37	-	-	11	86	7

B103: Do you think you will be using any narcotics other than heroin without a doctor's orders five years from now?

	TOTAL	M	F	White	Black	NE	NC	S	W	Yes	No	None	Mari juana Only	Few Pills	More Pills	Any Heroin
1. I definitely will	0.6	0.4	0.6	0.4	1.0	0.7	0.8	0.3	0.5	0.5	0.5	0.3	0.5	-	1.6	-
2. I probably will	1.4	1.4	1.3	1.5	0.5	1.8	0.9	1.5	1.2	1.0	2.1	-	0.2	1.1	5.0	21.8
3. I probably will not	15.3	16.5	14.0	16.6	8.8	17.6	13.7	14.7	15.7	15.4	15.5	6.4	15.0	24.8	28.8	23.6
4. I definitely will not	82.8	81.7	84.1	81.5	89.7	79.8	84.6	83.5	82.6	83.1	81.9	93.3	84.3	74.1	64.6	54.7
Item 5560 Subject A04a N	2989	1422	1520	2306	310	686	858	931	513	1803	967	1290	635	398	591	19

B104: When (if ever) did you FIRST do each of the following things? Don't count anything you took because a doctor told you to.

B104A: Smoke cigarettes on a daily basis

	TOTAL	M	F	White	Black	NE	NC	S	W	Yes	No	None	Mari juana Only	Few Pills	More Pills	Any Heroin
8. Never	71.6	75.1	68.7	69.7	88.4	63.8	72.1	76.2	73.0	77.0	62.2	92.0	66.6	62.7	40.4	32.2
1. Grade 6 or below	2.3	2.3	2.0	2.4	0.7	1.8	2.7	2.3	2.0	1.5	3.2	0.8	1.8	3.6	4.5	15.8
2. Grade 7 or 8	6.0	5.7	6.3	6.0	2.6	8.8	5.8	5.5	3.1	4.8	7.6	1.8	7.1	6.5	13.2	14.6
3. Grade 9 (Freshman)	6.8	6.1	7.6	7.2	3.7	9.8	6.2	6.1	5.2	4.9	10.7	2.1	7.1	9.5	13.9	26.6
4. Grade 10 (Sophomore)	5.1	3.8	6.3	5.5	1.4	7.3	4.2	3.8	6.1	4.0	7.3	1.3	7.0	6.5	11.2	-
5. Grade 11 (Junior)	5.1	4.0	6.2	5.8	1.7	4.3	6.4	3.5	7.1	5.3	5.4	1.3	7.1	4.8	11.4	10.9
6. Grade 12 (Senior)	3.1	3.1	2.9	3.3	1.5	4.2	2.6	2.5	3.5	2.4	3.6	0.8	3.2	6.3	5.4	-
Item 5570 Subject A01g N	2857	1356	1463	2221	285	660	822	882	493	1738	906	1235	602	378	578	18

B104B: Try an alcoholic beverage–more than just a few sips

	TOTAL	M	F	White	Black	NE	NC	S	W	Yes	No	None	Mari juana Only	Few Pills	More Pills	Any Heroin
8. Never	8.0	7.1	8.5	5.5	19.8	5.9	6.9	10.7	8.3	8.1	7.7	17.7	0.2	1.8	0.8	-
1. Grade 6 or below	8.2	11.5	5.3	8.6	5.6	8.2	7.7	9.0	7.8	7.6	8.9	5.2	7.8	9.4	13.7	19.8
2. Grade 7 or 8	22.0	24.0	20.2	23.7	9.2	26.0	24.0	17.5	20.9	22.3	20.8	12.6	23.1	26.4	36.7	33.3
3. Grade 9 (Freshman)	24.2	22.9	25.4	26.5	15.5	27.6	25.0	22.3	21.5	23.4	26.6	17.9	30.9	30.1	26.1	31.3
4. Grade 10 (Sophomore)	19.0	17.2	20.8	19.7	14.2	18.3	18.1	19.0	21.3	19.1	18.5	18.0	23.6	19.1	16.0	9.6
5. Grade 11 (Junior)	12.6	11.6	13.5	11.6	17.6	10.1	12.7	13.6	14.0	13.2	12.5	17.7	11.2	9.6	5.5	6.1
6. Grade 12 (Senior)	6.0	5.7	6.3	4.6	18.2	3.9	5.6	8.0	6.2	6.4	4.9	11.0	3.2	3.6	1.3	-
Item 5580 Subject A01g N	2766	1308	1421	2166	273	653	803	834	476	1673	903	1121	609	370	597	19

B104C: Try marijuana or hashish

	TOTAL	M	F	White	Black	NE	NC	S	W	Yes	No	None	Mari juana Only	Few Pills	More Pills	Any Heroin
8. Never	50.2	47.6	52.4	47.9	61.5	41.5	50.7	57.8	47.5	52.7	47.4	100.0	-	22.1	10.5	1.7
1. Grade 6 or below	2.5	3.4	1.6	2.7	2.3	2.8	2.5	1.9	3.4	2.0	2.5	-	2.7	1.7	7.6	28.7
2. Grade 7 or 8	11.4	11.8	11.1	11.6	6.4	16.9	9.3	7.9	13.9	9.6	13.2	-	17.2	15.0	28.8	16.4
3. Grade 9 (Freshman)	11.0	11.8	10.2	11.2	9.3	13.0	10.5	10.0	10.6	9.2	13.8	-	19.5	17.7	21.9	28.3
4. Grade 10 (Sophomore)	10.8	11.4	10.4	12.2	4.9	12.5	10.5	10.3	10.0	11.1	11.2	-	23.0	21.5	15.6	15.7
5. Grade 11 (Junior)	9.3	9.4	9.1	9.2	10.3	8.0	10.7	8.1	10.6	9.7	8.3	-	23.4	14.3	12.1	3.3
6. Grade 12 (Senior)	4.8	4.6	5.1	5.3	5.2	5.3	5.8	3.9	4.1	5.7	3.5	-	14.3	7.7	3.6	5.9
Item 5590 Subject A01g N	2869	1365	1469	2231	278	670	831	874	495	1737	924	1271	578	371	589	20

B104D: Try LSD

	TOTAL	M	F	White	Black	NE	NC	S	W	Yes	No	None	Mari juana Only	Few Pills	More Pills	Any Heroin
8. Never	93.1	92.1	94.1	92.4	98.9	91.8	93.8	95.6	89.5	94.4	92.1	100.0	100.0	95.1	71.1	26.8
1. Grade 6 or below	0.1	0.2	0.1	0.2	-	-	0.2	0.2	0.3	0.2	0.1	-	-	0.3	0.2	7.6
2. Grade 7 or 8	0.4	0.3	0.4	0.4	-	0.1	0.7	0.3	0.4	0.3	0.5	-	-	0.3	1.3	11.2
3. Grade 9 (Freshman)	1.3	1.4	1.2	1.3	0.3	1.3	1.6	1.0	1.1	0.8	2.0	-	-	0.9	5.3	13.6
4. Grade 10 (Sophomore)	1.7	1.6	1.7	1.8	0.2	2.2	0.9	1.0	3.6	1.5	1.7	-	-	1.3	7.0	20.5
5. Grade 11 (Junior)	2.2	3.2	1.4	2.6	0.5	3.2	1.7	1.4	3.2	1.9	2.0	-	-	1.4	9.5	20.3
6. Grade 12 (Senior)	1.2	1.3	1.1	1.3	-	1.5	1.2	0.6	1.8	1.0	1.6	-	-	0.6	5.6	-
Item 5600 Subject A01g N	2927	1383	1508	2262	299	682	839	903	503	1775	940	1283	615	378	583	18

★=excludes respondents for whom question was inappropriate.

QUESTIONNAIRE FORM 1 1986	TOTAL	SEX		RACE		REGION				4YR COLLEGE PLANS		ILLICIT DRUG USE: LIFETIME				
		M	F	White	Black	NE	NC	S	W	Yes	No	None	Mari-juana Only	Few Pills	More Pills	Any Her-oin
N (Weighted No. of Cases):	3179	1469	1562	2351	323	749	897	984	550	1841	999	1333	671	406	643	21
% of Weighted Total:	100.0	46.2	49.1	74.0	10.2	23.5	28.2	30.9	17.3	57.9	31.4	41.9	21.1	12.8	20.2	0.7
B104E: Try a psychedelic other than LSD																
8. Never	95.0	94.2	95.9	94.5	98.9	91.5	96.0	97.8	93.0	95.0	95.6	100.0	100.0	96.3	78.6	22.8
1. Grade 6 or below	0.2	0.3	0.1	0.2	-	0.3	-	-	0.7	0.2	-	-	-	0.3	0.6	8.4
2. Grade 7 or 8	0.4	0.2	0.6	0.5	0.2	0.4	0.4	0.6	0.2	0.2	0.9	-	-	-	2.0	9.3
3. Grade 9 (Freshman)	1.3	1.4	1.1	1.5	-	2.4	0.9	0.7	1.3	1.0	1.5	-	-	0.3	6.0	16.2
4. Grade 10 (Sophomore)	1.1	1.3	1.0	1.3	0.2	1.6	0.7	0.3	2.5	1.2	0.8	-	-	0.5	5.0	15.7
5. Grade 11 (Junior)	1.3	1.7	0.9	1.2	0.7	2.2	1.4	0.5	1.4	1.5	0.8	-	-	1.5	5.4	15.7
6. Grade 12 (Senior)	0.7	0.9	0.4	0.7	-	1.5	0.5	0.2	0.7	0.8	0.3	-	-	1.0	2.5	11.9
Item 5610 Subject A01g N	2897	1373	1487	2235	303	664	832	905	496	1763	927	1286	622	375	548	16
B104F: Try amphetamines																
8. Never	84.7	88.1	81.7	83.1	95.5	84.0	83.1	87.4	83.5	86.7	81.7	100.0	100.0	67.6	37.1	27.7
1. Grade 6 or below	0.2	0.3	0.1	0.2	-	0.4	-	0.2	0.5	0.2	0.3	-	-	-	1.0	8.5
2. Grade 7 or 8	2.2	1.9	2.6	2.3	1.5	2.8	2.8	1.7	1.2	1.6	2.8	-	-	1.7	11.1	5.0
3. Grade 9 (Freshman)	4.1	2.9	5.0	4.6	0.7	3.1	4.7	3.4	5.3	3.6	4.1	-	-	8.7	16.8	13.0
4. Grade 10 (Sophomore)	4.1	3.3	4.9	4.7	-	4.9	3.4	3.7	4.8	3.3	6.0	-	-	8.1	16.9	24.7
5. Grade 11 (Junior)	2.8	2.5	2.9	3.0	1.3	2.9	3.4	2.2	2.5	2.7	2.6	-	-	6.8	10.5	21.2
6. Grade 12 (Senior)	2.0	1.1	2.8	2.1	1.1	1.9	2.6	1.3	2.1	1.9	2.5	-	-	7.1	6.5	-
Item 5620 Subject A01g N	2752	1307	1408	2115	294	647	790	845	469	1676	880	1272	618	304	494	16
B104G: Try quaaludes																
8. Never	96.1	95.8	96.5	95.8	99.3	94.9	97.0	95.9	96.7	96.8	95.4	100.0	100.0	96.0	85.0	30.6
1. Grade 6 or below	0.1	0.2	0.1	0.2	-	0.2	-	0.2	0.3	0.1	0.1	-	-	-	0.5	7.1
2. Grade 7 or 8	0.8	0.5	1.0	0.8	0.2	0.9	0.9	0.8	0.4	0.6	1.1	-	-	1.2	3.4	-
3. Grade 9 (Freshman)	1.2	1.0	1.3	1.4	-	1.1	1.0	1.5	1.0	0.8	1.8	-	-	1.2	4.8	16.4
4. Grade 10 (Sophomore)	1.0	1.6	0.5	1.2	-	1.8	0.4	0.9	1.3	1.0	1.2	-	-	1.2	3.7	24.8
5. Grade 11 (Junior)	0.6	0.7	0.5	0.6	0.2	1.0	0.6	0.6	0.2	0.7	0.4	-	-	0.3	2.4	17.7
6. Grade 12 (Senior)	0.1	0.1	0.1	0.1	0.2	0.1	0.1	0.1	-	0.1	0.1	-	-	0.1	0.2	3.4
Item 5630 Subject A01g N	2918	1376	1506	2254	302	684	842	900	492	1764	939	1286	622	374	567	20
B104H: Try barbiturates																
8. Never	95.1	95.1	95.3	95.0	99.0	94.8	96.0	95.0	94.4	95.8	94.2	100.0	100.0	96.0	79.5	26.6
1. Grade 6 or below	0.2	0.4	-	0.2	-	0.2	-	0.1	0.8	0.3	-	-	-	-	0.8	8.4
2. Grade 7 or 8	0.9	0.7	1.1	1.0	0.4	1.1	1.2	0.6	0.9	0.7	1.6	-	-	-	4.9	-
3. Grade 9 (Freshman)	1.2	1.3	1.1	1.2	0.1	1.3	1.0	1.3	0.9	1.1	1.2	-	-	-	5.7	12.9
4. Grade 10 (Sophomore)	1.1	1.0	1.0	1.0	0.3	0.8	0.8	1.5	1.4	0.9	1.2	-	-	1.8	3.9	24.0
5. Grade 11 (Junior)	1.2	1.2	1.2	1.2	0.2	1.7	0.9	1.0	1.3	1.0	1.3	-	-	1.5	4.3	28.1
6. Grade 12 (Senior)	0.3	0.3	0.2	0.3	-	-	0.1	0.5	0.4	0.2	0.4	-	-	0.7	0.9	-
Item 5640 Subject A01g N	2896	1367	1492	2237	301	673	837	897	490	1761	924	1283	623	368	556	16
B104I: Try tranquilizers																
8. Never	93.4	94.6	92.4	92.8	98.6	91.9	94.6	93.4	93.4	93.8	93.1	100.0	100.0	90.7	73.2	32.8
1. Grade 6 or below	0.3	0.4	0.1	0.3	0.3	0.3	0.1	0.1	0.9	0.1	0.5	-	-	0.2	1.0	10.7
2. Grade 7 or 8	0.8	0.4	1.1	0.9	0.2	0.9	0.6	0.7	1.1	0.6	1.2	-	-	0.6	3.8	-
3. Grade 9 (Freshman)	1.2	1.0	1.3	1.3	0.1	1.3	1.1	1.5	0.8	1.4	0.7	-	-	1.2	4.9	24.6
4. Grade 10 (Sophomore)	2.1	1.5	2.6	2.2	-	3.3	1.7	2.0	1.3	2.0	2.2	-	-	3.9	8.6	3.9
5. Grade 11 (Junior)	1.3	1.2	1.5	1.4	0.2	1.1	1.1	1.2	1.9	1.3	1.2	-	-	1.7	5.2	17.4
6. Grade 12 (Senior)	0.9	0.8	1.0	1.1	0.5	1.1	0.8	1.1	0.6	0.9	1.0	-	-	1.8	3.4	10.5
Item 5650 Subject A01g N	2847	1353	1460	2202	298	661	823	875	488	1716	920	1273	622	353	533	19
B104J: Try cocaine																
8. Never	83.7	82.4	85.2	82.7	93.0	75.5	88.3	90.2	75.3	86.1	81.3	100.0	100.0	69.5	41.4	7.9
1. Grade 6 or below	0.1	0.1	0.2	0.2	-	-	-	-	0.8	0.1	-	-	-	-	0.6	-
2. Grade 7 or 8	0.4	0.4	0.2	0.3	0.7	0.4	0.2	0.1	0.9	0.2	0.5	-	-	0.3	1.2	6.1
3. Grade 9 (Freshman)	2.3	2.0	2.3	2.2	0.7	3.0	2.3	1.1	3.3	1.7	2.7	-	-	3.6	8.5	14.9
4. Grade 10 (Sophomore)	3.1	3.5	2.7	3.4	0.8	5.0	1.9	2.3	4.1	2.3	3.7	-	-	3.5	12.7	16.7
5. Grade 11 (Junior)	5.0	5.4	4.8	5.4	1.7	7.9	3.1	2.8	8.5	4.0	6.6	-	-	6.9	19.3	37.6
6. Grade 12 (Senior)	5.4	6.2	4.6	5.8	3.1	8.1	4.3	3.4	7.2	5.5	5.1	-	-	16.2	16.2	16.9
Item 5660 Subject A01g N	2940	1393	1510	2270	303	682	843	910	506	1779	950	1285	622	374	593	18

QUESTIONNAIRE FORM 1 1986	TOTAL	SEX		RACE		REGION				4YR COLLEGE PLANS		ILLICIT DRUG USE: LIFETIME				
		M	F	White	Black	NE	NC	S	W	Yes	No	None	Mari-juana Only	Few Pills	More Pills	Any Her-oin
N (Weighted No. of Cases):	3179	1469	1562	2351	323	749	897	984	550	1841	999	1333	671	406	643	21
% of Weighted Total:	100.0	46.2	49.1	74.0	10.2	23.5	28.2	30.9	17.3	57.9	31.4	41.9	21.1	12.8	20.2	0.7
B104K: Try heroin																
8. Never	99.5	99.4	99.7	99.5	99.8	99.7	99.3	99.5	99.5	99.4	99.6	100.0	100.0	100.0	100.0	-
1. Grade 6 or below	*	0.1	-	0.1	-	-	-	-	0.3	0.1	-	-	-	-	-	10.9
2. Grade 7 or 8	*	0.1	-	*	-	-	0.1	-	-	-	0.1	-	-	-	-	8.5
3. Grade 9 (Freshman)	*	-	-	-	-	-	-	0.1	-	-	0.1	-	-	-	-	7.8
4. Grade 10 (Sophomore)	0.2	0.1	0.3	0.2	-	-	0.4	0.2	0.2	0.3	0.1	-	-	-	-	41.0
5. Grade 11 (Junior)	0.1	0.1	-	*	0.2	-	0.1	0.1	-	*	0.1	-	-	-	-	12.8
6. Grade 12 (Senior)	0.1	0.2	-	0.1	-	0.3	0.1	-	-	0.1	-	-	-	-	-	19.0
Item 5670 Subject A01g N	2933	1387	1508	2265	302	681	842	906	503	1774	946	1284	617	383	586	13
B104L: Try any narcotic other than heroin																
8. Never	94.7	93.8	95.6	93.8	99.2	95.0	94.2	95.0	94.8	95.0	94.6	100.0	100.0	93.3	78.4	32.2
1. Grade 6 or below	0.2	0.3	-	0.2	-	-	-	0.2	0.6	0.2	0.1	-	-	0.2	0.5	8.3
2. Grade 7 or 8	0.6	0.8	0.5	0.7	0.2	0.3	1.1	0.5	0.5	0.5	0.9	-	-	0.3	2.8	9.6
3. Grade 9 (Freshman)	0.8	0.9	0.7	0.9	-	0.6	1.3	0.6	0.6	0.7	0.8	-	-	0.8	3.3	12.3
4. Grade 10 (Sophomore)	1.5	1.8	1.0	1.7	-	1.7	0.5	1.9	1.9	1.4	1.6	-	-	0.6	6.7	20.9
5. Grade 11 (Junior)	1.3	1.4	1.3	1.6	0.3	1.1	1.9	1.1	0.9	1.3	1.1	-	-	2.7	5.0	9.8
6. Grade 12 (Senior)	0.9	1.0	0.9	1.2	0.3	1.4	0.9	0.7	0.7	1.0	0.9	-	-	2.2	3.3	6.8
Item 5680 Subject A01g N	2805	1345	1423	2154	297	647	816	872	470	1684	910	1274	609	326	530	17
B104M: Smoke your first cigarette																
8. Never	31.8	33.4	30.2	29.7	47.5	25.4	29.7	36.3	36.0	35.7	25.5	57.0	11.0	16.7	10.6	5.0
1. Grade 6 or below	21.2	24.4	18.4	22.9	16.3	19.5	24.3	20.2	19.8	20.3	22.5	14.1	23.3	23.1	31.8	50.0
2. Grade 7 or 8	22.1	21.2	23.3	23.5	12.5	29.5	20.8	19.9	18.4	20.2	26.1	12.4	30.9	26.5	31.4	24.4
3. Grade 9 (Freshman)	9.7	7.8	11.4	9.3	8.8	10.2	9.7	9.5	9.5	8.3	11.3	6.0	13.8	12.7	11.3	14.8
4. Grade 10 (Sophomore)	6.4	5.1	7.4	6.3	3.9	6.1	6.6	5.1	9.3	6.2	6.5	3.9	9.6	8.3	8.1	-
5. Grade 11 (Junior)	5.6	5.4	5.7	5.5	5.4	5.7	5.8	5.5	5.5	6.0	5.1	3.8	7.3	8.7	5.4	5.8
6. Grade 12 (Senior)	3.1	2.8	3.5	2.9	5.6	3.7	3.2	3.5	1.5	3.3	3.1	2.9	4.1	3.9	1.4	-
Item 5575 Subject A01g N	2841	1343	1462	2216	279	667	817	874	482	1732	909	1220	593	369	590	20
B104N: Drink enough to feel drunk or very high																
8. Never	26.3	23.9	28.2	21.4	54.2	19.6	24.5	34.3	24.2	28.1	23.4	52.2	5.9	11.6	3.8	-
1. Grade 6 or below	3.7	5.6	2.0	4.2	2.1	4.7	3.5	2.7	4.6	3.0	4.5	0.9	2.9	3.1	10.2	19.9
2. Grade 7 or 8	14.9	17.1	12.8	16.5	3.3	18.0	16.5	12.3	12.7	13.6	16.0	6.2	17.0	19.0	28.6	17.4
3. Grade 9 (Freshman)	19.6	19.9	19.6	21.5	11.3	22.8	20.2	17.8	17.4	18.6	21.5	8.3	29.3	29.1	27.7	28.1
4. Grade 10 (Sophomore)	16.2	15.2	17.2	17.9	7.8	19.3	15.4	14.4	16.3	16.7	16.3	10.4	23.5	19.4	18.2	18.3
5. Grade 11 (Junior)	12.5	12.4	12.8	12.9	8.9	10.0	12.6	12.5	15.9	12.3	13.0	12.4	15.0	13.1	8.9	16.3
6. Grade 12 (Senior)	6.8	6.0	7.5	5.8	12.3	5.6	7.2	6.0	8.8	7.7	5.3	9.5	6.4	4.7	2.6	-
Item 5585 Subject A01g N	2860	1352	1469	2241	277	666	827	871	496	1740	919	1224	595	381	596	20
The next questions are about your experiences in school.																
D001: Some people like school very much. Others don't. How do you feel about going to school?																
5. I like school very much	10.9	10.2	11.2	8.7	20.9	10.9	10.6	10.9	11.3	12.8	6.4	14.1	7.5	8.8	8.3	2.0
4. I like school quite a lot	29.4	28.9	30.0	29.3	28.6	27.6	27.8	31.6	30.4	34.8	20.3	33.4	32.0	25.3	21.8	17.5
3. I like school some	42.5	44.5	40.7	43.3	39.1	44.0	43.5	41.2	41.4	39.4	48.3	40.0	43.9	44.8	44.9	46.9
2. I don't like school very much	12.8	11.9	13.7	14.0	8.7	14.1	13.4	11.3	12.7	9.9	18.5	9.8	13.1	15.0	17.2	11.7
1. I don't like school at all	4.4	4.4	4.5	4.7	2.7	3.4	4.7	5.0	4.2	3.1	6.5	2.7	3.4	6.1	7.9	21.9
Item 7630 Subject B01,Q08 N	2873	1339	1498	2234	290	643	853	889	488	1795	954	1257	603	374	554	17
D002: How often do you feel that the school work you are assigned is meaningful and important?																
5. Almost always	12.0	10.8	12.6	8.6	26.3	10.9	9.6	14.8	12.4	12.8	9.3	13.9	11.9	9.4	10.1	7.6
4. Often	25.3	26.3	24.2	24.0	31.0	27.4	25.2	24.1	25.2	28.1	20.9	25.9	28.3	23.8	20.5	38.9
3. Sometimes	43.1	41.2	45.4	46.3	32.4	43.0	45.9	43.3	38.1	44.1	41.3	43.9	43.9	46.7	38.6	39.9
2. Seldom	16.9	18.0	16.2	18.5	7.6	15.7	16.6	15.8	21.1	13.4	23.7	14.4	13.1	17.7	26.6	9.7
1. Never	2.6	3.7	1.7	2.6	2.6	3.0	2.7	2.0	3.2	1.6	4.7	1.9	2.8	2.3	4.1	3.9
Item 5700 Subject B01 N	2870	1333	1500	2232	289	643	850	889	487	1792	956	1253	603	373	556	18

*=less than .05 per cent.

QUESTIONNAIRE FORM 1 1986	TOTAL	SEX		RACE		REGION				4YR COLLEGE PLANS		ILLICIT DRUG USE: LIFETIME				
		M	F	White	Black	NE	NC	S	W	Yes	No	None	Mari-juana Only	Few Pills	More Pills	Any Her-oin
N (Weighted No. of Cases):	3179	1469	1562	2351	323	749	897	984	550	1841	999	1333	671	406	643	21
% of Weighted Total:	100.0	46.2	49.1	74.0	10.2	23.5	28.2	30.9	17.3	57.9	31.4	41.9	21.1	12.8	20.2	0.7

D003: How interesting are most of your courses to you?

5. Very exciting and stimulating	4.2	4.4	3.8	2.5	10.6	4.0	3.2	5.3	4.2	4.4	3.6	5.6	3.1	2.9	2.8	15.9
4. Quite interesting	26.8	26.5	27.2	24.1	38.5	27.0	26.3	27.0	27.0	29.3	22.2	30.9	25.2	25.0	19.8	11.0
3. Fairly interesting	46.6	44.7	48.1	48.7	38.2	47.5	46.8	45.6	46.7	46.8	46.1	43.1	52.8	47.6	47.3	46.7
2. Slightly dull	17.6	18.5	17.0	19.7	9.8	17.5	18.4	17.0	17.2	16.4	20.2	16.0	16.4	18.2	22.6	15.9
1. Very dull	4.9	5.9	4.0	4.9	2.9	3.9	5.4	5.0	5.0	3.2	7.9	4.5	2.5	6.3	7.5	10.4
Item 5710 Subject B01 N	2865	1334	1495	2228	288	642	849	886	488	1791	952	1252	601	372	555	18

D004: How important do you think the things you are learning in school are going to be for your later life?

5. Very important	20.6	19.8	21.1	16.2	42.5	19.3	19.0	24.0	19.0	21.4	18.4	23.4	17.8	18.6	17.5	2.0
4. Quite important	26.4	25.5	27.0	26.6	27.1	24.9	27.5	27.8	24.1	28.4	22.7	27.5	27.2	25.6	24.3	31.6
3. Fairly important	31.0	31.6	30.8	33.5	15.2	31.2	32.2	29.2	31.9	31.6	30.8	31.1	30.5	32.3	30.2	47.3
2. Slightly important	18.6	19.1	18.3	20.2	13.8	20.8	17.9	16.3	20.8	16.6	22.5	15.7	21.7	19.9	21.8	8.7
1. Not at all important	3.4	3.9	2.8	3.5	1.4	3.7	3.4	2.7	4.2	2.0	5.6	2.2	2.9	3.6	6.3	10.4
Item 5720 Subject B01 N	2862	1332	1495	2226	289	639	850	886	487	1789	951	1253	601	373	551	17

D005: How much competition for grades is there among students at your school?

1. None	6.4	6.7	6.0	6.0	7.7	8.5	4.9	5.1	8.6	4.1	9.9	6.0	5.5	5.5	8.6	11.4
2. A little	22.1	23.3	20.8	22.2	18.6	22.1	19.5	25.4	20.4	20.1	25.1	20.7	20.6	25.7	23.9	46.0
3. Some	34.0	34.1	34.2	35.9	26.3	32.4	34.6	32.4	38.2	33.4	36.5	33.3	32.7	35.2	36.3	12.4
4. Quite a bit	27.0	26.5	27.5	26.1	32.0	25.5	31.4	26.8	21.9	30.6	20.6	27.4	30.9	26.6	23.3	24.4
5. A great deal	10.5	9.3	11.4	9.8	15.4	11.4	9.6	10.3	11.0	11.9	7.9	12.7	10.3	7.0	7.9	5.7
Item 5730 Subject B04 N	2848	1320	1491	2219	285	635	845	884	483	1781	947	1246	597	370	552	18

D006: How do you think most of the students in your classes would feel if you cheated on a test?

1. They would like it very much	2.6	3.7	1.6	1.9	7.0	2.4	2.5	2.9	2.7	1.9	3.7	2.3	2.5	1.2	3.8	4.5
2. They would like it	2.4	3.1	1.8	1.9	3.8	2.6	1.8	2.9	2.1	1.8	3.1	2.0	1.7	2.7	3.5	15.2
3. They would not care	80.1	78.8	81.2	83.0	73.5	81.7	79.6	78.8	81.0	79.2	82.3	76.4	82.3	84.4	83.1	74.9
4. They would dislike it	11.8	11.8	11.8	11.0	10.3	10.9	13.0	11.1	11.8	13.9	7.6	14.3	11.0	10.5	8.2	5.4
5. They would dislike it very much	3.2	2.6	3.6	2.2	5.5	2.4	3.2	4.2	2.3	3.2	3.3	5.0	2.5	1.2	1.3	-
Item 5740 Subject B04 N	2851	1329	1485	2220	284	637	851	881	482	1782	947	1248	598	372	548	18

D007: How do you think most of the students in your classes would feel if you intentionally did things to make your teachers angry?

1. They would like it very much	4.3	5.9	2.7	3.5	8.3	5.5	3.5	4.5	3.8	3.1	5.5	4.1	3.8	3.8	5.3	5.5
2. They would like it	11.0	15.7	6.9	11.2	11.2	11.5	11.6	11.4	8.6	10.6	11.7	10.3	12.0	12.2	10.9	26.3
3. They would not care	45.0	44.8	45.4	45.1	47.5	44.5	46.4	46.1	41.2	43.6	47.7	42.2	44.8	46.0	49.9	56.9
4. They would dislike it	33.3	28.6	37.3	34.7	24.8	32.3	32.8	30.9	39.6	36.9	27.7	35.5	32.7	33.3	30.2	11.4
5. They would dislike it very much	6.4	5.0	7.7	5.5	8.2	6.2	5.6	7.0	6.7	5.9	7.3	8.1	6.7	4.6	3.7	-
Item 5750 Subject B04 N	2835	1317	1480	2209	282	630	848	877	479	1769	945	1239	597	370	545	18

D008: How often do you find that your friends encourage you to do things which your teachers wouldn't like?

1. Never	34.5	24.7	43.3	32.0	46.7	37.1	32.7	33.5	36.1	34.1	33.6	36.6	37.4	27.7	30.2	3.7
2. Seldom	35.2	35.7	35.0	37.4	28.1	32.5	40.0	33.0	34.5	36.8	33.3	39.2	32.6	36.5	31.4	14.5
3. Sometimes	22.8	28.8	17.1	23.5	15.6	22.4	19.9	25.5	23.8	22.7	23.9	17.8	23.9	28.3	28.5	44.7
4. Often	5.8	8.2	3.9	5.8	6.6	6.0	5.8	6.1	4.9	5.0	6.9	4.8	5.3	6.8	7.2	20.3
5. Almost always	1.6	2.5	0.7	1.3	3.0	1.9	1.6	1.9	0.8	1.3	2.3	1.6	0.8	0.7	2.8	16.8
Item 5760 Subject B04 N	2838	1321	1480	2210	282	630	849	880	480	1774	944	1245	596	369	546	18

QUESTIONNAIRE FORM 1 1986	TOTAL	SEX		RACE		REGION				4YR COLLEGE PLANS		ILLICIT DRUG USE: LIFETIME				
		M	F	White	Black	NE	NC	S	W	Yes	No	None	Mari-juana Only	Few Pills	More Pills	Any Her-oin
N (Weighted No. of Cases):	3179	1469	1562	2351	323	749	897	984	550	1841	999	1333	671	406	643	21
% of Weighted Total:	100.0	46.2	49.1	74.0	10.2	23.5	28.2	30.9	17.3	57.9	31.4	41.9	21.1	12.8	20.2	0.7

D009: Have you ever been in a work-study program–that is, a program where you work on a job as part of your schooling?

	TOTAL	M	F	White	Black	NE	NC	S	W	Yes	No	None	Mari-juana Only	Few Pills	More Pills	Any Her-oin
1. No, not ever	78.1	79.4	77.0	79.4	72.0	83.5	79.0	75.1	75.0	83.3	69.0	81.1	80.7	74.6	72.4	64.7
2. Yes, for a half year or less	8.3	7.6	9.0	7.7	9.3	7.6	7.5	6.7	13.8	6.8	11.0	6.2	9.2	10.2	10.6	-
3. Yes, for about a year	10.1	9.6	10.6	9.5	13.5	6.1	10.7	13.1	9.1	7.7	14.0	9.7	7.5	11.3	12.4	27.7
4. Yes, for about two years	2.5	2.3	2.8	2.5	3.6	1.0	2.4	4.5	1.1	1.3	4.9	2.2	2.2	3.7	2.9	-
5. Yes, for more than two years	0.9	1.2	0.7	0.8	1.5	1.8	0.5	0.6	1.0	0.8	1.2	0.9	0.4	0.2	1.8	7.6
Item 5770 Subject B02,C01 N	2837	1321	1480	2209	281	630	847	876	484	1776	942	1248	594	368	545	18

D010: How many times this school year have you seen a counselor individually?

	TOTAL	M	F	White	Black	NE	NC	S	W	Yes	No	None	Mari-juana Only	Few Pills	More Pills	Any Her-oin
1. No times	19.2	19.4	18.7	20.7	15.6	17.7	15.7	26.8	13.5	14.9	26.1	19.4	17.9	21.2	20.5	12.1
2. 1 time	14.7	12.8	16.5	14.9	13.4	11.4	15.1	16.9	14.3	12.9	18.2	14.6	15.1	17.6	12.3	10.8
3. 2 times	19.5	20.5	18.7	19.4	19.7	20.0	19.3	18.4	21.3	18.8	21.1	19.2	21.9	18.5	19.3	29.0
4. 3 or 4 times	26.5	26.9	26.3	26.3	29.1	26.9	28.0	24.9	26.2	29.6	21.8	25.5	28.1	25.5	26.0	33.1
5. 5 - 7 times	11.5	11.4	11.7	11.5	9.8	12.9	12.5	7.9	14.7	13.9	7.1	12.9	10.4	9.8	10.8	14.9
6. 8 - 10 times	3.6	3.8	3.4	3.1	4.8	3.8	4.8	2.4	3.4	4.2	2.4	4.0	3.1	2.7	4.1	-
7. 11 or more times	4.9	5.3	4.6	4.0	7.6	7.2	4.5	2.7	6.6	5.7	3.2	4.4	3.4	4.8	6.9	-
Item 5780 Subject B05 N	2836	1318	1481	2208	280	626	849	879	482	1770	943	1248	593	366	544	18

D011: How many times this school year have you seen a counselor as a part of a group of other students?

	TOTAL	M	F	White	Black	NE	NC	S	W	Yes	No	None	Mari-juana Only	Few Pills	More Pills	Any Her-oin
1. No times	55.3	53.3	57.1	56.4	46.7	60.5	51.6	54.0	57.7	52.9	59.6	55.1	53.9	57.3	56.5	51.8
2. 1 time	16.1	16.5	15.8	16.3	19.3	13.5	16.2	17.8	16.0	17.3	14.3	16.6	15.6	16.6	15.6	-
3. 2 times	13.8	13.8	13.9	13.3	18.2	13.7	16.4	12.3	11.9	14.4	12.8	12.9	17.3	12.2	12.6	27.7
4. 3 or 4 times	10.3	11.6	8.9	10.1	9.6	7.9	12.0	10.7	9.5	11.1	8.3	10.6	10.6	10.5	8.7	12.8
5. 5 - 7 times	2.3	2.0	2.5	2.4	2.9	2.6	1.7	2.9	2.1	2.3	2.3	2.4	1.6	2.2	3.2	-
6. 8 - 10 times	0.9	1.1	0.8	0.7	2.1	0.7	0.8	1.4	0.7	0.7	1.4	0.5	0.5	0.8	1.7	7.6
7. 11 or more times	1.3	1.7	1.0	0.8	1.2	1.2	1.3	1.0	2.1	1.4	1.2	1.8	0.5	0.4	1.5	-
Item 5790 Subject B05 N	2833	1313	1482	2206	281	624	847	879	482	1768	942	1247	594	366	543	18

D012: Would you have preferred to see a counselor more or less often than you have during the past year?

	TOTAL	M	F	White	Black	NE	NC	S	W	Yes	No	None	Mari-juana Only	Few Pills	More Pills	Any Her-oin
5. Much more often	8.7	9.0	8.3	6.1	20.1	10.5	7.3	8.0	10.4	8.2	8.6	7.8	8.8	8.0	10.6	2.5
4. A little more often	23.7	24.4	23.0	22.6	28.4	21.0	21.7	26.6	25.6	24.8	21.5	21.6	27.8	27.9	22.8	18.4
3. About as often	50.1	47.4	52.9	54.6	32.1	50.1	55.1	46.9	46.7	54.7	43.1	54.8	47.1	48.4	45.1	46.4
2. A little less often	5.4	5.7	5.1	4.5	9.3	5.3	5.2	4.9	6.6	4.6	6.6	4.6	5.7	4.1	7.0	19.2
1. Much less often	12.1	13.4	10.7	12.3	10.2	13.0	10.7	13.6	10.8	7.7	20.2	11.3	10.7	11.5	14.5	13.5
Item 5800 Subject B05 N	2786	1296	1453	2165	279	606	840	865	474	1748	921	1237	585	358	526	18

D013: How helpful have your sessions with a counselor been to you?

	TOTAL	M	F	White	Black	NE	NC	S	W	Yes	No	None	Mari-juana Only	Few Pills	More Pills	Any Her-oin
5. Extremely helpful	10.6	11.5	9.8	8.2	19.8	9.2	10.1	10.9	12.9	11.3	8.8	12.2	10.0	11.8	6.3	17.3
4. Quite helpful	21.2	21.4	20.8	19.4	24.8	19.9	20.6	21.2	24.1	21.3	19.7	22.1	20.8	21.4	19.8	12.6
3. Somewhat helpful	23.8	24.7	23.3	24.2	21.8	21.2	28.3	21.0	24.4	26.6	19.9	23.8	27.3	20.9	22.2	9.6
2. A little helpful	19.5	19.0	20.3	21.3	14.5	22.3	19.4	17.4	20.2	19.7	20.2	18.9	20.5	17.6	20.2	33.0
1. Not at all helpful	11.5	11.6	11.6	12.2	9.5	13.5	11.1	11.7	9.3	10.2	13.6	8.7	10.7	12.9	17.4	21.4
8. Did not see a counselor this year	13.3	11.7	14.2	14.7	9.7	14.0	10.5	17.9	9.1	10.9	17.7	14.3	10.6	15.3	14.0	6.0
Item 5810 Subject B05 N	2809	1300	1471	2189	278	617	834	875	483	1753	923	1239	593	361	540	16

D014: Would you have preferred more or less of each of the following types of counseling in the last year?

D014A: Choosing what courses to take

	TOTAL	M	F	White	Black	NE	NC	S	W	Yes	No	None	Mari-juana Only	Few Pills	More Pills	Any Her-oin
5. Much more	20.3	21.7	18.9	16.4	33.6	19.5	15.0	22.4	27.0	17.4	23.3	19.8	18.3	24.8	21.6	5.1
4. A little more	25.7	23.5	27.6	26.5	22.2	20.8	26.6	27.1	27.5	28.5	22.3	24.6	27.5	25.5	25.6	22.0
3. About right	45.8	45.2	46.7	49.0	32.6	50.1	50.3	41.2	40.7	48.4	41.8	48.1	46.7	43.2	41.5	53.9
2. A little less	2.9	3.1	2.6	2.7	6.4	2.7	4.0	2.6	2.0	2.3	4.2	3.1	1.9	2.2	3.9	4.3
1. Much less	5.3	6.5	4.1	5.4	5.3	6.9	4.1	6.6	2.9	3.4	8.4	4.4	5.6	4.3	7.4	14.7
Item 5811 Subject B05 N	2765	1275	1456	2162	273	601	828	861	475	1726	913	1228	590	353	519	17

QUESTIONNAIRE FORM 1 1986	TOTAL	SEX		RACE		REGION				4YR COLLEGE PLANS		ILLICIT DRUG USE: LIFETIME				
		M	F	White	Black	NE	NC	S	W	Yes	No	None	Mari-juana Only	Few Pills	More Pills	Any Her-oin
N (Weighted No. of Cases):	3179	1469	1562	2351	323	749	897	984	550	1841	999	1333	671	406	643	21
% of Weighted Total:	100.0	46.2	49.1	74.0	10.2	23.5	28.2	30.9	17.3	57.9	31.4	41.9	21.1	12.8	20.2	0.7

D014B: Discussing problems with course work

5. Much more	13.5	13.9	12.8	9.4	27.9	14.9	8.5	14.6	18.4	11.9	15.4	12.9	13.4	13.6	14.6	5.1
4. A little more	21.6	18.9	23.8	20.2	28.2	21.2	19.6	23.6	21.8	22.6	20.2	21.1	23.2	21.4	19.9	10.2
3. About right	51.8	51.7	52.4	57.2	29.6	51.6	57.4	48.6	48.0	55.4	46.5	54.7	49.5	52.0	48.8	70.1
2. A little less	4.2	4.6	3.7	3.9	5.0	5.6	4.1	3.2	4.5	3.5	5.2	2.8	4.0	3.8	8.1	-
1. Much less	8.9	10.9	7.2	9.3	9.3	6.7	10.4	9.9	7.3	6.6	12.7	8.4	9.9	9.2	8.7	14.7
Item 5812 Subject B05 N	2741	1268	1439	2141	272	597	822	852	471	1715	908	1211	587	350	517	17

D014C: Discussing any trouble you've gotten into

5. Much more	9.2	10.7	7.8	6.4	17.3	11.0	4.6	11.5	10.7	7.1	12.5	8.0	7.8	9.7	12.6	7.9
4. A little more	9.6	9.9	8.9	8.4	14.8	8.1	10.9	8.8	10.5	8.6	11.5	7.1	13.0	11.0	9.8	5.8
3. About right	58.6	56.1	61.6	63.4	36.6	57.6	64.1	56.4	54.1	65.0	48.4	64.4	56.1	56.1	50.3	70.4
2. A little less	5.5	6.6	4.7	4.6	9.7	6.6	4.1	5.2	7.3	4.9	6.1	4.5	4.5	5.4	9.7	4.0
1. Much less	17.1	16.8	17.1	17.2	21.6	16.6	16.3	18.1	17.4	14.4	21.5	16.0	18.5	17.9	17.7	11.9
Item 5813 Subject B05 N	2680	1247	1399	2094	261	578	808	832	462	1676	887	1178	574	347	510	17

D014D: Discussing military plans

5. Much more	5.8	8.3	3.4	3.8	15.8	7.8	2.5	6.5	8.0	3.8	8.9	5.6	6.8	6.5	5.0	4.3
4. A little more	8.1	11.6	4.7	6.9	13.2	4.9	9.3	9.8	6.7	7.5	9.4	8.0	11.1	6.0	5.5	2.8
3. About right	44.2	41.7	46.9	47.9	26.4	45.9	49.4	40.1	40.5	50.8	33.9	48.4	43.6	40.7	38.4	60.3
2. A little less	6.0	7.6	4.7	6.1	5.7	6.3	6.8	5.9	4.5	5.7	6.6	5.6	6.6	7.0	4.9	15.5
1. Much less	35.8	30.8	40.4	35.4	39.0	35.1	31.9	37.8	40.3	32.3	41.2	32.4	31.9	39.8	46.2	17.0
Item 5814 Subject B05 N	2645	1243	1370	2067	259	566	803	822	454	1646	887	1170	564	340	497	16

D014E: Discussing education or training plans

5. Much more	24.4	23.0	25.6	20.9	41.2	25.9	19.9	25.8	27.7	26.2	19.8	25.4	23.1	23.0	24.0	14.1
4. A little more	30.0	30.3	29.6	30.9	23.9	24.0	33.9	29.4	31.8	32.8	26.1	31.3	30.2	30.9	26.1	15.4
3. About right	34.0	34.7	33.8	36.4	23.9	38.4	36.3	32.2	28.0	33.9	35.0	34.7	34.3	31.3	35.0	48.2
2. A little less	3.2	3.9	2.6	3.1	2.8	2.5	2.6	3.7	4.2	2.1	5.0	2.1	4.0	4.7	3.4	9.1
1. Much less	8.4	8.2	8.5	8.7	8.1	9.2	7.3	8.9	8.3	5.1	14.1	6.5	8.4	10.0	11.5	13.2
Item 5815 Subject B05 N	2716	1261	1421	2123	269	585	819	846	466	1699	899	1207	577	351	508	17

D014F: Discussing career plans or job choice

5. Much more	28.2	25.6	30.8	24.2	46.8	26.6	24.1	30.6	33.1	29.8	24.3	30.0	27.3	27.0	26.0	16.3
4. A little more	31.6	32.0	31.2	33.5	22.2	28.1	34.6	30.6	32.7	33.3	29.5	31.1	30.7	35.1	31.7	21.3
3. About right	31.7	33.2	30.5	33.6	23.1	35.6	33.4	30.5	26.1	32.1	31.6	32.1	33.4	28.2	31.1	49.9
2. A little less	2.3	2.0	2.4	1.9	4.1	2.0	1.6	2.8	2.7	1.5	3.2	1.9	2.6	2.3	2.5	-
1. Much less	6.2	7.2	5.1	6.8	3.9	7.6	6.3	5.6	5.4	3.4	11.4	4.9	6.0	7.4	8.7	12.5
Item 5816 Subject B05 N	2734	1266	1434	2136	270	595	823	847	468	1712	903	1214	583	350	512	17

D014G: Discussing personal problems

5. Much more	8.3	9.1	7.4	6.6	13.8	9.8	4.5	10.3	9.3	6.6	11.1	6.9	8.2	9.5	9.9	7.9
4. A little more	10.8	10.3	11.0	10.2	10.5	9.5	11.5	10.4	11.7	10.2	11.3	9.5	11.6	12.3	11.9	-
3. About right	51.9	51.9	52.4	56.1	34.5	48.6	57.7	49.8	49.8	58.5	41.2	55.8	52.2	52.2	44.1	50.8
2. A little less	5.1	5.4	4.8	4.7	7.5	7.2	3.8	4.7	5.3	5.1	4.2	4.8	5.9	2.8	6.1	14.1
1. Much less	23.9	23.3	24.3	22.5	33.7	24.9	22.4	24.8	23.9	19.6	32.2	23.0	22.2	23.2	28.0	27.2
Item 5817 Subject B05 N	2687	1247	1406	2098	266	582	810	831	465	1674	893	1181	575	346	511	17

These last questions concern your health.

D015: During the LAST 30 DAYS, on how many days (if any) did you have the following problems or symptoms?

D015A: Headache

1. None	18.8	29.9	8.8	15.5	32.5	21.0	16.6	17.9	21.4	17.6	19.9	21.3	19.8	15.6	14.3	18.3
2. One day	17.4	20.3	15.0	16.3	20.3	15.6	17.5	18.3	18.3	17.4	16.9	20.4	15.6	18.3	11.3	11.1
3. Two days	21.3	21.1	21.8	22.4	23.4	20.6	21.2	21.8	21.6	22.0	20.7	22.5	21.2	20.2	18.8	6.1
4. 3 to 5 days	22.9	17.7	27.5	24.2	14.7	22.8	25.5	23.3	18.0	22.9	23.1	20.2	23.7	25.3	27.6	37.4
5. 6 to 9 days	10.4	6.2	14.2	11.7	5.2	11.0	10.1	9.2	12.3	10.9	10.2	8.6	11.8	10.5	13.4	2.9
6. 10 to 19 days	6.3	3.7	8.7	6.9	2.9	6.7	6.7	6.1	5.4	6.3	6.6	4.8	6.0	7.7	9.6	7.6
7. 20+ days	2.8	1.2	4.0	3.2	1.0	2.3	2.5	3.5	2.9	2.9	2.6	2.3	1.9	2.4	5.1	16.6
Item 21310 Subject T01 N	2778	1278	1465	2173	271	608	831	863	476	1732	919	1225	588	360	526	16

QUESTIONNAIRE FORM 1 1986	TOTAL	SEX		RACE		REGION				4YR COLLEGE PLANS		ILLICIT DRUG USE: LIFETIME				
		M	F	White	Black	NE	NC	S	W	Yes	No	None	Marijuana Only	Few Pills	More Pills	Any Heroin
N (Weighted No. of Cases):	3179	1469	1562	2351	323	749	897	984	550	1841	999	1333	671	406	643	21
% of Weighted Total:	100.0	46.2	49.1	74.0	10.2	23.5	28.2	30.9	17.3	57.9	31.4	41.9	21.1	12.8	20.2	0.7

D015B: Sore throat or hoarse voice

	TOTAL	M	F	White	Black	NE	NC	S	W	Yes	No	None	Marijuana Only	Few Pills	More Pills	Any Heroin
1. None	37.4	44.8	30.8	35.1	51.5	31.7	34.5	42.4	40.8	35.7	39.8	41.7	38.0	33.2	28.7	17.4
2. One day	15.9	16.3	15.9	15.8	16.0	18.0	15.5	15.3	15.1	16.1	15.8	14.9	13.5	22.7	17.1	11.2
3. Two days	17.6	17.7	17.6	17.8	11.7	18.0	19.3	15.5	17.9	17.6	16.6	16.6	19.3	18.8	16.8	21.9
4. 3 to 5 days	18.2	13.7	22.1	19.4	13.5	20.7	17.7	17.7	16.8	18.8	18.0	17.2	17.5	16.2	22.9	35.3
5. 6 to 9 days	7.2	4.9	8.9	7.9	5.8	6.8	8.5	6.6	6.4	7.7	6.4	7.3	7.3	6.6	7.6	-
6. 10 to 19 days	2.7	1.8	3.5	3.0	0.9	3.4	3.4	1.8	2.3	3.1	2.2	1.7	3.5	1.5	5.2	7.4
7. 20+ days	1.0	0.7	1.2	1.0	0.6	1.4	1.1	0.6	0.8	0.9	1.2	0.7	0.9	1.0	1.7	6.8
Item 21320 Subject T01 N	2770	1273	1463	2165	270	611	828	857	473	1731	914	1224	586	359	522	16

D015C: Trouble with sinus congestion, runny nose, or sneezing

	TOTAL	M	F	White	Black	NE	NC	S	W	Yes	No	None	Marijuana Only	Few Pills	More Pills	Any Heroin
1. None	26.4	30.7	22.4	23.5	35.1	25.8	24.6	27.8	27.6	23.6	30.5	28.8	24.9	27.4	21.4	22.8
2. One day	8.9	11.3	6.9	9.0	8.6	7.7	7.4	10.3	10.4	8.3	10.1	8.6	10.1	8.2	8.6	6.9
3. Two days	14.1	14.0	14.3	14.0	14.1	15.0	13.4	14.0	14.1	15.1	11.6	13.6	14.7	13.1	14.0	13.4
4. 3 to 5 days	20.6	18.0	22.9	21.1	18.2	21.4	22.6	18.1	20.4	21.3	19.3	20.1	21.1	20.9	21.2	18.8
5. 6 to 9 days	15.9	14.1	17.6	17.1	13.1	17.3	16.8	15.7	13.1	16.3	15.4	14.9	16.7	16.6	17.2	11.9
6. 10 to 19 days	7.7	6.0	9.3	8.5	5.8	7.4	8.4	7.4	7.5	9.1	6.0	7.5	8.1	6.0	9.8	11.3
7. 20+ days	6.5	6.0	6.6	6.9	5.0	5.4	6.8	6.7	6.7	6.3	7.2	6.5	4.5	7.8	7.8	14.9
Item 21330 Subject T01 N	2778	1279	1468	2177	271	606	829	867	476	1737	917	1226	588	361	525	16

D015D: Coughing spells

	TOTAL	M	F	White	Black	NE	NC	S	W	Yes	No	None	Marijuana Only	Few Pills	More Pills	Any Heroin
1. None	57.5	63.0	52.7	55.9	64.1	58.2	54.0	59.6	59.1	58.4	55.6	62.6	56.5	54.2	50.3	28.4
2. One day	12.8	12.5	13.3	13.1	9.6	10.9	13.3	12.3	15.1	11.5	15.1	11.0	15.2	13.9	12.2	29.0
3. Two days	9.1	7.7	10.5	9.6	7.8	9.2	9.5	9.1	8.3	9.2	9.2	9.1	8.3	10.3	9.4	17.6
4. 3 to 5 days	10.5	9.0	11.5	10.5	9.7	10.3	11.2	10.2	10.0	10.8	10.1	10.5	9.2	11.6	11.4	18.1
5. 6 to 9 days	5.1	4.0	6.1	5.6	4.9	6.1	5.4	4.5	4.6	5.4	4.7	3.7	5.6	5.2	7.9	-
6. 10 to 19 days	3.5	2.5	4.3	3.6	2.3	4.1	4.9	2.3	2.5	3.4	3.3	2.4	3.3	2.3	6.8	-
7. 20+ days	1.5	1.2	1.7	1.6	1.5	1.2	1.8	1.9	0.4	1.2	2.1	0.6	1.9	2.5	2.0	6.9
Item 21340 Subject T01 N	2769	1273	1463	2168	269	603	826	865	475	1729	916	1223	584	360	526	17

D015E: Chest colds

	TOTAL	M	F	White	Black	NE	NC	S	W	Yes	No	None	Marijuana Only	Few Pills	More Pills	Any Heroin
1. None	73.1	75.9	70.8	73.1	70.3	69.8	73.7	70.5	80.8	72.7	74.3	76.8	72.4	68.9	69.7	53.6
2. One day	8.2	8.4	7.9	8.2	7.9	10.0	6.4	9.1	7.3	8.0	8.1	6.9	7.8	12.2	8.4	6.5
3. Two days	6.9	7.0	6.7	6.9	6.7	7.2	7.0	7.8	4.5	7.3	6.4	6.1	8.9	6.1	6.4	11.5
4. 3 to 5 days	6.5	4.9	7.8	6.5	7.5	6.6	6.7	7.5	4.1	6.4	6.3	5.9	5.6	8.6	7.0	16.6
5. 6 to 9 days	3.3	2.2	4.1	3.2	6.3	3.0	3.8	3.3	2.7	3.5	2.6	3.2	3.4	2.7	3.8	2.7
6. 10 to 19 days	1.4	1.2	1.7	1.5	0.9	2.2	1.7	1.3	0.5	1.5	1.6	0.8	1.1	0.9	3.6	4.2
7. 20+ days	0.7	0.5	0.9	0.7	0.4	1.2	0.7	0.6	-	0.6	0.8	0.8	0.8	0.5	1.2	4.8
Item 21350 Subject T01 N	2745	1269	1446	2154	269	596	822	857	471	1718	905	1215	583	356	518	17

D015F: Coughing up phlegm or blood

	TOTAL	M	F	White	Black	NE	NC	S	W	Yes	No	None	Marijuana Only	Few Pills	More Pills	Any Heroin
1. None	82.4	84.7	80.5	80.5	90.1	81.1	79.2	84.1	86.7	82.4	82.5	86.7	82.2	80.6	73.7	66.0
2. One day	4.0	4.1	4.0	4.4	3.2	4.9	4.8	3.1	3.2	4.1	4.0	3.3	3.6	4.1	6.6	-
3. Two days	3.5	3.0	4.1	4.0	2.1	3.2	4.0	3.6	3.0	3.2	3.5	2.6	3.8	5.0	4.4	4.3
4. 3 to 5 days	4.1	3.5	4.5	4.7	1.6	5.1	4.3	3.8	2.9	4.1	4.2	3.5	3.9	4.8	4.6	12.3
5. 6 to 9 days	2.6	2.3	3.0	2.8	1.3	3.1	3.0	2.0	2.5	2.9	2.4	1.5	3.7	1.7	4.9	5.6
6. 10 to 19 days	1.9	1.5	2.1	2.1	0.8	1.2	2.6	2.2	1.2	2.2	1.5	1.1	1.9	2.0	4.2	-
7. 20+ days	1.4	0.9	1.8	1.5	0.9	1.4	2.0	1.3	0.5	1.0	1.9	1.3	0.9	1.8	1.5	11.7
Item 21360 Subject T01 N	2751	1262	1457	2159	267	598	826	855	472	1724	903	1212	582	358	522	17

D015G: Shortness of breath when you were not exercising

	TOTAL	M	F	White	Black	NE	NC	S	W	Yes	No	None	Marijuana Only	Few Pills	More Pills	Any Heroin
1. None	82.8	88.6	77.8	82.7	82.6	83.3	82.1	82.2	84.7	83.9	80.4	86.6	84.2	81.5	75.1	65.5
2. One day	5.9	5.0	6.7	5.8	5.8	6.1	6.5	5.0	6.3	5.3	6.9	5.0	6.4	5.1	7.8	-
3. Two days	3.6	2.2	4.7	3.5	3.9	3.5	3.2	4.5	2.9	3.4	4.7	2.7	3.5	5.6	4.3	10.5
4. 3 to 5 days	3.7	1.9	5.3	3.9	3.5	3.6	4.5	3.1	3.8	3.7	4.0	3.0	3.9	3.0	4.8	12.2
5. 6 to 9 days	1.6	1.2	2.0	1.8	1.7	1.0	1.8	2.2	1.1	1.5	1.8	0.8	1.5	2.9	2.9	-
6. 10 to 19 days	0.9	0.4	1.4	1.0	0.6	0.5	0.7	1.6	0.5	1.0	0.9	0.6	0.3	0.9	2.0	11.7
7. 20+ days	1.3	0.6	2.0	1.4	1.8	2.0	1.1	1.5	0.7	1.1	1.4	1.2	0.2	1.0	3.0	-
Item 21370 Subject T01 N	2766	1270	1463	2169	268	604	826	862	474	1732	910	1222	583	359	523	17

QUESTIONNAIRE FORM 1 1986	TOTAL	SEX		RACE		REGION				4YR COLLEGE PLANS		ILLICIT DRUG USE: LIFETIME				
		M	F	White	Black	NE	NC	S	W	Yes	No	None	Mari-juana Only	Few Pills	More Pills	Any Her-oin
N (Weighted No. of Cases):	3179	1469	1562	2351	323	749	897	984	550	1841	999	1333	671	406	643	21
% of Weighted Total:	100.0	46.2	49.1	74.0	10.2	23.5	28.2	30.9	17.3	57.9	31.4	41.9	21.1	12.8	20.2	0.7

D015H: Wheezing or gasping

	TOTAL	M	F	White	Black	NE	NC	S	W	Yes	No	None	Mari-juana Only	Few Pills	More Pills	Any Her-oin
1. None	87.6	90.1	85.3	87.0	90.4	84.8	86.7	88.9	90.3	88.4	86.8	91.1	89.5	84.3	80.4	68.3
2. One day	4.5	4.7	4.3	4.7	3.1	5.3	4.8	3.7	4.4	3.9	4.8	3.0	4.0	6.8	7.0	6.9
3. Two days	2.2	2.0	2.3	2.3	1.9	2.2	2.8	1.3	2.5	2.2	2.3	1.9	2.6	1.9	2.3	16.1
4. 3 to 5 days	2.4	1.5	3.3	2.5	1.9	3.9	2.3	2.5	0.7	2.2	3.0	1.9	1.6	3.7	2.7	5.9
5. 6 to 9 days	1.1	0.8	1.4	1.1	0.9	0.7	1.3	1.2	0.9	1.2	1.0	0.7	0.7	1.7	2.1	
6. 10 to 19 days	1.2	0.6	1.7	1.3	0.6	0.9	1.3	1.6	0.7	1.3	1.1	0.6	0.8	1.0	3.3	2.7
7. 20+ days	1.0	0.3	1.6	1.1	1.1	2.1	0.8	0.8	0.4	0.9	0.9	0.7	0.6	0.7	2.2	-
Item 21380 Subject T01 N	2763	1268	1463	2166	269	602	826	861	474	1731	909	1220	583	359	523	17

D015I: Trouble remembering things

	TOTAL	M	F	White	Black	NE	NC	S	W	Yes	No	None	Mari-juana Only	Few Pills	More Pills	Any Her-oin
1. None	70.1	73.2	67.2	70.4	70.5	72.6	68.6	69.7	70.0	72.1	66.7	74.6	76.7	67.6	54.2	67.1
2. One day	9.8	9.2	10.2	9.0	12.1	10.7	9.6	9.0	10.2	9.4	10.3	8.9	9.6	12.4	11.1	3.3
3. Two days	7.6	6.5	8.6	7.3	8.5	5.3	8.2	8.8	7.3	7.6	7.5	6.8	4.7	6.7	12.7	6.8
4. 3 to 5 days	5.4	5.0	5.9	5.6	3.2	5.1	6.0	4.9	5.8	5.2	6.5	4.3	4.4	4.1	10.2	-
5. 6 to 9 days	2.9	2.1	3.6	3.2	1.9	3.1	3.3	3.0	1.6	2.3	3.7	2.5	1.9	4.4	3.9	11.2
6. 10 to 19 days	1.8	1.4	2.1	1.8	3.1	1.2	1.5	2.4	1.8	1.4	2.4	1.1	1.7	2.6	2.5	2.9
7. 20+ days	2.5	2.6	2.3	2.7	0.7	2.0	2.8	2.2	3.2	2.1	2.8	1.8	1.0	2.1	5.4	8.7
Item 21390 Subject T01 N	2756	1266	1456	2158	267	607	824	851	475	1726	906	1215	583	356	526	16

D015J: Difficulty thinking or concentrating

	TOTAL	M	F	White	Black	NE	NC	S	W	Yes	No	None	Mari-juana Only	Few Pills	More Pills	Any Her-oin
1. None	52.6	60.5	45.6	50.4	64.2	55.6	49.3	55.5	49.4	51.2	54.2	56.6	57.1	47.2	41.6	49.8
2. One day	13.0	13.3	12.7	12.7	15.6	12.5	13.4	12.5	14.0	13.1	13.1	13.0	12.4	16.0	13.2	-
3. Two days	12.5	9.2	15.5	13.2	10.3	12.6	13.2	11.5	13.1	13.5	11.1	10.2	13.6	12.2	16.4	12.0
4. 3 to 5 days	10.3	8.1	12.4	11.5	5.1	8.5	11.1	9.4	12.9	11.2	9.0	10.3	9.4	10.2	11.8	14.0
5. 6 to 9 days	6.1	4.0	7.9	6.6	2.4	5.3	7.3	6.1	4.7	5.9	6.9	5.8	3.7	8.1	7.9	6.9
6. 10 to 19 days	2.4	2.5	2.4	2.8	0.9	2.2	2.6	2.3	2.4	2.2	2.5	1.6	2.0	3.0	3.6	12.8
7. 20+ days	3.0	2.3	3.5	2.7	1.5	3.3	3.0	2.7	3.5	2.8	3.3	2.4	1.8	3.2	5.5	4.5
Item 21400 Subject T01 N	2755	1266	1454	2164	264	605	823	857	470	1723	907	1214	582	357	526	16

D015K: Trouble learning new things

	TOTAL	M	F	White	Black	NE	NC	S	W	Yes	No	None	Mari-juana Only	Few Pills	More Pills	Any Her-oin
1. None	70.9	74.1	68.2	70.4	75.9	72.7	68.0	71.9	71.9	70.8	71.2	73.2	73.1	68.6	65.7	74.0
2. One day	11.0	9.2	12.6	11.0	12.8	9.5	12.4	10.4	11.5	11.0	10.8	10.1	11.7	13.5	11.4	4.0
3. Two days	7.7	7.3	7.9	8.1	6.1	8.9	7.9	7.0	6.9	7.9	7.0	8.3	5.9	7.2	7.2	4.3
4. 3 to 5 days	5.1	4.5	5.6	5.4	2.3	4.8	5.7	4.7	5.3	5.4	4.9	4.8	4.8	5.2	6.7	5.9
5. 6 to 9 days	2.7	3.0	2.6	2.7	1.5	1.9	3.6	3.1	1.8	2.4	3.5	1.5	2.5	2.4	5.3	7.6
6. 10 to 19 days	1.2	1.1	1.3	1.2	0.5	0.8	1.7	1.1	1.0	1.5	0.8	1.1	0.7	1.6	1.5	
7. 20+ days	1.4	0.8	1.8	1.2	0.9	1.4	0.7	1.8	1.6	1.1	1.7	1.0	1.2	1.6	2.3	4.2
Item 21410 Subject T01 N	2749	1259	1455	2155	266	602	820	857	470	1720	905	1213	583	351	524	17

D015L: Trouble sleeping

	TOTAL	M	F	White	Black	NE	NC	S	W	Yes	No	None	Mari-juana Only	Few Pills	More Pills	Any Her-oin
1. None	45.2	51.3	39.5	43.5	57.5	46.4	39.6	50.9	43.0	42.5	48.0	47.4	44.9	44.8	40.5	35.0
2. One day	12.2	13.1	11.4	12.0	12.7	9.4	13.2	11.7	14.7	12.5	11.3	13.3	12.1	15.4	7.8	-
3. Two days	16.1	13.7	18.5	16.5	9.5	17.3	19.4	10.8	18.4	17.2	15.0	15.5	18.4	15.0	16.0	10.5
4. 3 to 5 days	13.0	11.1	14.6	13.5	9.9	13.4	13.6	12.1	13.3	14.4	11.1	12.4	13.4	9.8	15.5	16.4
5. 6 to 9 days	5.6	4.6	6.7	6.1	4.2	5.1	6.3	6.0	4.4	6.3	4.5	4.1	6.3	6.0	8.1	17.0
6. 10 to 19 days	4.2	3.2	5.1	4.7	3.1	4.3	4.3	4.2	4.1	3.6	5.6	4.0	2.4	5.1	6.3	11.5
7. 20+ days	3.6	3.0	4.3	3.7	3.2	4.0	3.7	4.1	2.2	3.4	4.5	3.2	2.4	3.9	5.7	9.6
Item 21420 Subject T01 N	2747	1261	1451	2152	267	602	818	855	471	1723	902	1213	577	358	523	16

D015M: Trouble getting started in the morning

	TOTAL	M	F	White	Black	NE	NC	S	W	Yes	No	None	Mari-juana Only	Few Pills	More Pills	Any Her-oin
1. None	31.8	36.2	27.9	28.5	47.5	31.1	27.3	37.1	31.0	30.6	32.7	36.0	31.1	27.6	25.1	23.8
2. One day	8.5	7.7	9.3	7.8	10.7	7.8	7.9	9.6	8.7	7.9	9.6	9.4	9.1	6.1	8.2	7.5
3. Two days	12.0	10.2	13.8	12.4	9.3	12.3	13.9	9.6	12.7	12.6	11.4	11.7	12.6	12.6	11.8	-
4. 3 to 5 days	14.1	13.0	14.7	15.2	9.5	13.8	15.6	13.6	13.0	15.2	12.3	15.1	12.2	15.9	12.1	9.6
5. 6 to 9 days	10.2	9.2	11.1	11.0	6.7	11.5	11.2	7.5	11.7	10.9	9.1	8.5	12.7	9.3	11.9	12.8
6. 10 to 19 days	8.6	7.5	9.8	9.4	5.7	10.0	10.1	6.9	7.3	8.5	9.4	7.2	9.2	11.4	9.8	4.3
7. 20+ days	14.7	16.2	13.5	15.8	10.6	13.6	14.0	15.7	15.7	14.4	15.4	12.0	13.1	17.1	21.1	42.0
Item 21430 Subject T01 N	2756	1261	1460	2160	267	605	822	856	472	1726	907	1214	583	357	525	16

QUESTIONNAIRE FORM 1 1986	TOTAL	SEX		RACE		REGION				4YR COLLEGE PLANS		ILLICIT DRUG USE: LIFETIME				
		M	F	White	Black	NE	NC	S	W	Yes	No	None	Mari-juana Only	Few Pills	More Pills	Any Her-oin
N (Weighted No. of Cases):	3179	1469	1562	2351	323	749	897	984	550	1841	999	1333	671	406	643	21
% of Weighted Total:	100.0	46.2	49.1	74.0	10.2	23.5	28.2	30.9	17.3	57.9	31.4	41.9	21.1	12.8	20.2	0.7

D015N: Stayed home most or all of a day because you were not feeling well

1. None	60.7	68.2	54.5	60.7	59.2	57.6	63.6	60.9	59.4	60.8	60.7	68.3	59.6	53.1	50.0	47.5
2. One day	17.3	15.5	18.7	17.6	15.6	16.8	15.6	18.3	18.8	17.7	16.2	13.2	19.3	24.1	19.2	23.8
3. Two days	12.1	9.6	14.2	12.1	12.6	14.3	11.7	11.1	11.8	12.4	11.5	11.1	12.8	12.0	14.4	-
4. 3 to 5 days	7.2	5.8	8.4	6.9	10.0	9.0	6.2	7.5	6.3	6.5	8.5	6.1	5.1	7.8	11.1	28.7
5. 6 to 9 days	1.9	0.5	3.1	2.0	1.7	1.2	2.0	1.5	3.2	1.8	2.1	0.9	2.4	1.7	4.0	-
6. 10 to 19 days	0.5	0.3	0.8	0.5	0.8	0.3	0.9	0.3	0.5	0.7	0.3	0.2	0.8	1.1	0.5	-
7. 20+ days	0.3	0.2	0.4	0.3	0.1	0.7	0.1	0.3	*	0.1	0.7	0.2	0.1	-	0.9	-
Item 21440 Subject T01 N	2761	1264	1463	2165	268	604	826	860	471	1729	907	1218	582	358	524	17

D016: In the LAST 12 MONTHS, how many times (if any) have you seen a doctor or other professional for each of the following?

D016A: For a routine physical check-up

1. None	49.7	49.7	49.5	49.4	44.3	46.6	50.0	50.6	51.5	45.6	58.3	53.0	48.3	48.3	44.8	47.9
2. Once	36.6	36.1	37.2	38.1	33.2	39.7	36.5	35.4	34.9	40.4	29.4	34.6	39.5	35.2	39.0	25.0
3. Twice	9.9	10.8	9.3	9.2	15.2	9.7	10.3	9.6	10.3	10.2	8.9	9.3	9.4	11.5	10.7	27.1
4. 3 to 5 times	2.8	2.7	2.8	2.5	4.4	3.4	2.6	3.0	2.4	2.9	2.5	2.2	2.2	3.4	4.5	-
5. 6 to 9 times	0.5	0.4	0.6	0.4	1.6	0.3	0.5	0.6	0.6	0.4	0.4	0.3	0.5	1.3	0.4	-
6. 10+ times	0.5	0.3	0.6	0.4	1.3	0.3	0.2	0.9	0.3	0.4	0.6	0.6	0.1	0.2	0.7	-
Item 21450 Subject T04 N	2759	1260	1458	2157	265	605	825	863	466	1718	901	1225	574	356	526	16

D016B: For an injury suffered in a fight, assault, or auto accident

1. None	91.2	89.8	92.5	91.0	94.8	91.1	91.2	91.0	91.8	92.4	89.5	94.6	91.0	90.3	84.8	77.6
2. Once	4.7	5.9	3.9	5.1	2.7	5.4	4.7	4.4	4.7	4.1	6.1	2.8	5.5	5.2	7.3	9.1
3. Twice	1.7	2.0	1.5	1.6	1.6	1.8	1.6	2.2	1.1	1.6	1.7	1.1	1.4	2.0	3.2	13.3
4. 3 to 5 times	1.3	1.2	1.2	1.2	0.8	1.0	1.3	1.4	1.4	1.2	1.5	1.1	1.1	1.2	2.1	-
5. 6 to 9 times	0.4	0.6	0.1	0.4	0.1	-	0.4	0.8	-	0.1	0.4	0.3	0.1	1.3	0.1	-
6. 10+ times	0.7	0.6	0.8	0.7	-	0.8	0.8	0.4	1.1	0.6	0.8	0.1	0.8	-	2.6	-
Item 21460 Subject T04 N	2743	1252	1454	2145	264	601	822	855	466	1710	900	1218	569	356	523	16

D016C: For any other accidental injury

1. None	81.3	76.9	85.0	79.4	90.5	77.3	81.2	83.7	82.1	78.3	86.9	84.1	79.6	79.4	76.9	74.8
2. Once	10.7	12.6	9.1	11.7	4.6	12.1	11.6	9.3	9.8	12.7	7.3	8.6	12.5	12.7	12.5	6.7
3. Twice	3.8	5.3	2.4	4.1	2.8	5.3	3.1	3.5	3.6	4.7	2.6	3.5	3.8	3.9	4.8	6.1
4. 3 to 5 times	3.1	3.8	2.5	3.4	1.2	3.4	3.3	2.7	2.7	3.3	2.1	2.9	2.8	2.4	4.4	12.5
5. 6 to 9 times	0.5	0.6	0.3	0.5	0.3	0.4	0.3	0.5	0.8	0.3	0.4	0.1	0.7	1.0	0.6	-
6. 10+ times	0.7	0.8	0.7	0.8	0.5	1.5	0.4	0.3	1.0	0.8	0.7	0.8	0.7	0.7	0.7	-
Item 21470 Subject T04 N	2724	1243	1447	2136	261	598	813	850	464	1700	893	1210	565	354	519	16

D016D: For some physical illness or symptom

1. None	60.0	68.6	52.6	57.3	66.2	56.6	55.8	64.2	64.1	58.1	63.9	63.4	60.3	57.5	53.9	63.5
2. Once	18.9	18.2	19.7	19.4	18.9	20.8	21.3	16.6	16.5	19.0	18.2	18.1	20.8	19.2	18.8	13.1
3. Twice	10.9	7.3	14.1	12.2	8.9	11.9	11.4	9.7	10.8	12.2	8.9	9.8	10.9	9.9	13.2	20.5
4. 3 to 5 times	7.4	4.6	9.5	8.2	3.1	6.6	9.4	6.6	5.9	7.5	7.2	6.4	5.8	9.5	9.8	2.9
5. 6 to 9 times	1.3	0.7	1.7	1.3	1.8	1.7	1.1	1.0	1.6	1.3	1.1	1.0	1.7	1.1	2.0	-
6. 10+ times	1.5	0.6	2.3	1.6	1.2	2.2	0.9	1.8	1.1	1.9	0.7	1.3	0.5	2.8	2.3	-
Item 21480 Subject T04 N	2729	1248	1447	2138	263	596	820	853	460	1704	894	1213	566	354	520	16

D016E: For some emotional or psychological problem or symptom

1. None	94.5	95.3	93.7	94.3	96.5	95.2	94.0	94.7	94.0	94.1	95.4	96.7	95.9	90.9	90.6	70.8
2. Once	2.0	1.8	2.1	2.1	1.7	0.9	2.3	2.2	2.4	2.1	1.8	1.2	2.7	1.8	2.9	13.2
3. Twice	0.8	0.6	0.9	0.7	0.4	0.9	0.3	0.8	1.5	0.8	0.7	0.5	0.4	1.4	1.2	6.3
4. 3 to 5 times	1.1	0.8	1.2	1.1	0.3	0.4	1.9	0.8	1.0	1.0	0.6	0.5	0.2	3.4	1.7	2.9
5. 6 to 9 times	0.6	0.3	0.8	0.6	0.6	1.2	0.3	0.7	-	0.6	0.5	0.5	0.4	0.4	1.2	-
6. 10+ times	1.2	1.1	1.2	1.2	0.6	1.5	1.2	0.9	1.2	1.3	0.9	0.6	0.4	2.1	2.4	6.8
Item 21490 Subject T04 N	2725	1244	1445	2134	261	597	821	850	458	1700	893	1210	567	352	519	16

D017: In the LAST 12 MONTHS, how many times (if any) have you spent one or more nights in the hospital . . .

*=less than .05 per cent.

QUESTIONNAIRE FORM 1 1986	TOTAL	SEX		RACE		REGION				4YR COLLEGE PLANS		ILLICIT DRUG USE: LIFETIME				
		M	F	White	Black	NE	NC	S	W	Yes	No	None	Mari-juana Only	Few Pills	More Pills	Any Her-oin
N (Weighted No. of Cases):	3179	1469	1562	2351	323	749	897	984	550	1841	999	1333	671	406	643	21
% of Weighted Total:	100.0	46.2	49.1	74.0	10.2	23.5	28.2	30.9	17.3	57.9	31.4	41.9	21.1	12.8	20.2	0.7

D017A: Because of an injury

1. None	95.6	94.9	96.3	96.0	97.0	94.4	94.6	96.8	96.7	95.8	95.3	97.1	95.8	96.8	91.3	81.7
2. Once	2.5	3.0	2.1	2.5	1.7	3.1	3.4	1.5	2.0	2.3	2.9	1.8	2.4	2.0	4.7	5.8
3. Twice	1.0	1.3	0.7	0.8	0.3	1.4	1.6	0.4	0.6	1.0	1.0	0.4	1.0	1.2	2.1	12.4
4. 3 to 5 times	0.5	0.7	0.3	0.3	1.1	0.1	0.3	0.9	0.5	0.6	0.1	0.7	0.5	-	0.2	-
5. 6 to 9 times	0.2	0.2	0.3	0.2	-	0.7	0.2	-	0.3	0.3	0.3	-	0.3	-	0.9	-
6. 10+ times	0.2	-	0.3	0.2	-	0.3	-	0.3	-	-	0.5	-	-	-	0.9	-
Item 21500 Subject T04 N	2729	1248	1444	2134	261	593	822	848	466	1700	893	1214	573	349	517	17

D017B: Because of some physical illness

1. None	95.5	95.9	95.2	96.1	92.9	95.5	94.4	95.4	97.7	96.1	95.3	97.4	95.7	93.8	93.3	74.2
2. Once	2.5	2.4	2.6	2.2	3.8	2.3	3.1	2.5	1.7	2.2	3.0	1.8	2.7	3.0	2.7	19.9
3. Twice	0.8	1.2	0.5	0.8	0.8	0.4	0.7	1.5	0.3	0.7	0.6	0.3	0.7	2.3	1.0	5.9
4. 3 to 5 times	0.5	0.3	0.7	0.4	1.6	0.5	1.2	0.2	0.1	0.5	0.5	0.3	0.8	0.1	0.9	-
5. 6 to 9 times	0.3	0.2	0.4	0.1	0.6	0.5	0.3	0.1	0.3	0.3	0.3	*	-	0.3	1.1	-
6. 10+ times	0.3	-	0.6	0.4	0.2	0.7	0.2	0.3	-	0.2	0.3	0.1	0.1	0.5	1.0	-
Item 21510 Subject T04 N	2729	1245	1449	2138	262	591	818	855	465	1702	894	1213	573	353	514	17

D018: Overall, relative to other people your age, do you think your physical health over the past year has been . . .

1. Much poorer than average	2.8	2.3	3.3	2.5	4.6	4.2	2.5	2.6	2.2	2.5	3.5	2.4	2.4	4.2	3.5	-
2. Somewhat poorer	8.4	6.0	10.6	8.6	6.1	8.1	7.7	9.0	9.2	8.4	9.0	6.6	8.1	7.7	13.8	22.6
3. About average	38.5	29.8	45.9	38.6	38.3	37.0	37.8	39.3	40.4	36.8	41.2	36.2	35.6	40.2	43.1	59.3
4. Somewhat better	27.0	29.9	24.4	26.4	27.4	26.5	28.6	26.4	25.7	27.5	26.6	27.3	29.5	27.4	24.8	11.0
5. Much better than average	23.2	32.0	15.7	23.9	23.7	24.3	23.4	22.6	22.5	24.8	19.7	27.5	24.4	20.5	14.8	7.1
Item 21520 Subject T01 N	2739	1250	1450	2148	260	602	822	846	469	1714	889	1209	574	352	528	15

D019: What is your current height (in feet and inches) without shoes?

01. 4'10" or less	0.4	0.3	0.4	0.2	0.4	0.4	0.4	0.2	0.7	0.3	0.4	0.2	0.5	0.3	0.2	5.9
02. 4'11"	0.8	0.1	1.4	0.5	1.9	1.0	0.8	0.7	0.8	0.6	1.2	0.8	0.6	0.7	0.4	5.8
03. 5'0"	1.2	-	2.2	1.2	2.1	1.7	0.8	1.5	0.6	0.9	1.7	1.0	1.0	1.5	1.5	4.8
04. 5'1"	3.4	0.1	6.1	2.7	4.1	3.3	3.3	3.5	3.4	3.3	3.7	3.0	3.0	4.1	3.6	-
05. 5'2"	5.5	-	10.5	5.6	4.3	5.2	3.5	7.3	6.3	4.6	7.2	5.3	4.8	6.9	6.6	-
06. 5'3"	6.1	0.5	10.9	5.9	5.8	6.2	6.2	5.4	7.3	5.5	7.9	5.9	5.1	8.3	6.4	-
07. 5'4"	9.3	0.9	16.6	9.5	7.7	8.8	8.6	9.8	10.1	9.6	8.9	9.6	8.5	9.7	8.9	-
08. 5'5"	8.0	2.7	12.6	7.2	11.3	8.7	8.0	8.0	7.0	8.2	7.4	7.4	7.8	6.0	9.9	14.8
09. 5'6"	9.0	4.0	13.3	8.9	10.0	10.3	9.5	8.0	8.4	8.7	9.7	10.3	6.8	9.0	9.1	-
10. 5'7"	8.3	6.0	10.6	8.1	10.9	7.5	7.8	9.3	8.7	8.6	7.8	9.0	7.8	6.8	9.3	2.0
11. 5'8"	9.7	11.3	8.2	9.6	10.2	9.9	10.3	8.3	10.7	10.3	9.1	10.3	10.9	8.6	6.9	6.4
12. 5'9"	6.4	9.5	3.8	6.2	7.6	5.9	6.3	7.0	6.6	6.8	5.3	6.2	6.6	8.7	5.4	7.4
13. 5'10"	7.2	12.9	2.2	7.9	5.1	6.9	9.0	6.8	5.4	8.2	5.0	7.1	7.7	7.8	6.9	7.1
14. 5'11"	7.6	15.3	0.8	7.3	4.6	6.7	8.0	7.7	7.8	8.1	6.0	6.4	8.4	8.3	8.9	10.9
15. 6'0"	5.3	11.1	0.3	5.8	3.6	6.5	5.6	4.8	3.9	5.2	5.3	4.8	6.6	4.1	5.5	8.0
16. 6'1"	4.9	10.6	-	5.4	4.5	4.6	5.4	4.6	4.9	3.8	6.5	4.3	5.9	6.0	3.9	21.1
17. 6'2"	3.5	7.6	*	4.1	2.6	3.8	3.5	3.2	3.8	4.0	3.0	4.0	3.5	1.7	4.0	-
18. 6'3" or more	3.5	7.1	0.1	4.0	3.2	2.7	3.2	4.1	3.8	3.3	3.8	4.2	4.3	1.3	2.7	5.6
Item 22150 Subject T03 N	2764	1267	1457	2156	269	605	825	860	474	1724	898	1223	575	358	530	17

*=less than .05 per cent.

QUESTIONNAIRE FORM 1 1986	TOTAL	SEX		RACE		REGION				4YR COLLEGE PLANS		ILLICIT DRUG USE: LIFETIME				
		M	F	White	Black	NE	NC	S	W	Yes	No	None	Mari- juana Only	Few Pills	More Pills	Any Her- oin
N (Weighted No. of Cases):	3179	1469	1562	2351	323	749	897	984	550	1841	999	1333	671	406	643	21
% of Weighted Total:	100.0	46.2	49.1	74.0	10.2	23.5	28.2	30.9	17.3	57.9	31.4	41.9	21.1	12.8	20.2	0.7

D020: What is your current weight (in pounds) without shoes or clothing?

		TOTAL	M	F	White	Black	NE	NC	S	W	Yes	No	None	Mari-juana Only	Few Pills	More Pills	Any Heroin
01.	100 lbs. or less	3.1	0.1	5.7	2.9	2.5	4.2	1.5	3.9	3.2	2.4	4.5	3.4	2.2	3.4	3.0	10.7
02.	101-105	3.0	*	5.7	2.8	2.8	2.3	1.8	4.5	3.5	2.6	4.1	3.2	1.7	2.0	4.7	8.5
03.	106-110	5.6	0.5	9.8	5.9	4.3	4.5	4.7	6.8	6.0	6.1	4.9	6.1	5.4	3.9	5.8	-
04.	111-115	6.0	0.9	10.4	6.0	4.7	5.4	5.0	6.7	7.0	5.7	6.9	4.8	7.2	7.9	5.0	5.8
05.	116-120	6.5	1.5	10.9	6.1	5.4	6.6	7.0	6.3	5.9	6.6	6.2	6.9	5.9	7.4	5.6	-
06.	121-125	6.6	2.1	10.7	7.1	3.6	8.0	7.0	4.5	8.0	6.6	7.0	7.2	2.9	7.5	8.8	6.3
07.	126-130	8.1	4.4	11.4	7.6	9.4	9.7	7.1	7.8	8.6	8.2	8.0	7.7	8.2	9.4	8.5	2.0
08.	131-135	7.1	5.0	8.9	7.1	7.5	3.8	9.1	7.0	8.0	7.0	8.1	6.3	7.3	9.3	6.7	6.9
09.	136-140	8.0	7.5	8.5	7.7	11.1	8.5	7.4	8.2	8.4	8.6	6.8	9.1	6.1	10.5	7.2	7.1
10.	141-150	12.4	17.1	8.1	12.4	13.0	11.5	13.9	11.9	11.8	12.9	10.5	12.4	14.1	12.6	11.4	7.4
11.	151-160	10.3	17.0	4.3	10.8	8.5	10.2	12.6	8.7	9.5	10.3	10.4	7.6	12.9	7.7	15.1	16.9
12.	161-170	8.7	16.3	2.0	9.2	8.8	9.7	8.5	9.4	6.2	8.8	7.7	9.7	9.3	7.9	6.3	4.9
13.	171-180	5.4	10.0	1.6	5.2	9.2	5.7	5.4	6.0	4.0	5.3	5.5	6.3	6.6	2.3	4.4	5.6
14.	181-190	3.5	6.8	0.7	3.3	5.0	3.9	3.4	2.8	4.3	3.3	3.5	3.9	3.4	2.9	1.9	14.6
15.	191-200	2.1	3.7	0.7	2.2	1.2	2.2	2.4	2.0	1.5	1.9	2.5	2.2	3.0	0.9	1.8	-
16.	201-210	1.3	2.3	0.3	1.2	1.6	1.2	1.2	1.0	2.0	1.2	1.5	1.2	1.2	1.9	1.1	3.1
17.	211-220	1.1	2.4	0.1	1.3	0.3	1.7	1.1	0.9	1.0	1.4	0.9	1.3	1.3	1.1	0.6	-
18.	221 lbs. or more	1.1	2.3	0.1	1.1	1.0	0.8	0.9	1.5	1.2	1.0	1.1	0.7	1.2	1.3	2.0	-
Item 22160　Subject T03	N	2754	1262	1453	2150	269	599	825	861	469	1715	897	1220	573	356	526	17

* = less than .05 per cent.

QUESTIONNAIRE FORM 2 1986	TOTAL	SEX		RACE		REGION				4YR COLLEGE PLANS		ILLICIT DRUG USE: LIFETIME				
		M	F	White	Black	NE	NC	S	W	Yes	No	None	Mari-juana Only	Few Pills	More Pills	Any Her-oin
N (Weighted No. of Cases):	3179	1481	1591	2367	338	756	902	980	541	1906	1054	1324	625	447	670	37
% of Weighted Total:	100.0	46.6	50.0	74.4	10.6	23.8	28.4	30.8	17.0	59.9	33.2	41.6	19.7	14.1	21.1	1.2

A01: Taking all things together, how would you say things are these days–would you say you're very happy, pretty happy, or not too happy these days?

	TOTAL	M	F	White	Black	NE	NC	S	W	Yes	No	None	Mari-juana Only	Few Pills	More Pills	Any Her-oin
3. Very happy	19.9	19.6	20.4	22.0	12.5	21.5	22.1	16.1	21.1	23.0	15.2	22.0	18.5	16.5	20.2	14.9
2. Pretty happy	68.6	69.9	67.5	69.6	68.8	68.2	67.5	70.6	67.2	66.4	72.2	67.9	70.7	70.8	66.6	59.8
1. Not too happy	11.5	10.5	12.1	8.4	18.7	10.3	10.4	13.2	11.7	10.6	12.6	10.1	10.8	12.7	13.1	25.3
Item 1190 Subject P01,Q01 N	3097	1427	1569	2312	332	732	886	956	524	1868	1025	1289	613	436	652	37

A02: The next questions ask about the kinds of things you might do. How often do you do each of the following?

A02A: Watch TV

	TOTAL	M	F	White	Black	NE	NC	S	W	Yes	No	None	Mari-juana Only	Few Pills	More Pills	Any Her-oin
5. Almost everyday	73.7	76.7	70.5	72.2	81.6	72.2	73.7	77.8	68.1	70.9	78.8	77.2	75.8	68.3	69.5	68.6
4. At least once a week	21.8	19.2	24.6	22.8	15.4	22.6	21.9	18.3	27.0	24.1	17.9	19.7	20.3	26.1	24.4	23.6
3. Once or twice a month	3.3	2.7	3.9	3.8	1.5	3.7	3.6	2.6	3.8	4.2	1.9	2.3	3.1	4.6	4.3	7.8
2. A few times a year	0.8	1.0	0.7	0.8	1.3	0.5	0.8	1.0	0.8	0.5	0.9	0.5	0.8	0.5	1.2	-
1. Never	0.4	0.4	0.3	0.4	0.2	1.0	-	0.3	0.4	0.3	0.5	0.3	-	0.5	0.6	-
Item 5820 Subject C07 N	3162	1475	1584	2359	336	748	900	977	537	1901	1051	1318	624	444	667	37

A02B: Go to movies

	TOTAL	M	F	White	Black	NE	NC	S	W	Yes	No	None	Mari-juana Only	Few Pills	More Pills	Any Her-oin
5. Almost everyday	0.1	*	0.1	0.1	-	0.2	-	0.2	0.3	0.1	*	0.1	-	-	-	-
4. At least once a week	10.8	11.0	10.4	9.9	12.9	9.6	11.5	12.1	9.3	10.1	11.6	10.6	9.7	11.6	12.5	5.1
3. Once or twice a month	55.2	54.6	56.1	58.8	43.5	55.1	57.3	50.7	59.8	58.0	50.9	54.1	56.8	59.3	54.7	46.9
2. A few times a year	31.3	32.3	30.3	29.3	37.5	32.7	29.9	32.7	29.1	29.9	34.1	31.7	31.9	27.4	31.0	46.7
1. Never	2.6	2.1	3.1	1.9	6.1	2.5	1.3	4.4	1.5	1.9	3.3	3.5	1.5	1.8	1.8	1.3
Item 5830 Subject C07 N	3159	1473	1583	2358	335	750	899	976	535	1896	1050	1314	624	446	667	37

A02C: Go to rock concerts

	TOTAL	M	F	White	Black	NE	NC	S	W	Yes	No	None	Mari-juana Only	Few Pills	More Pills	Any Her-oin
5. Almost everyday	0.1	0.2	-	0.1	-	0.1	-	0.2	-	*	0.2	0.2	-	-	-	-
4. At least once a week	0.3	0.4	0.1	0.2	0.5	0.2	0.2	0.2	0.6	0.1	0.4	0.1	0.3	0.4	0.4	-
3. Once or twice a month	4.2	5.1	3.5	4.6	3.5	4.1	5.5	2.9	4.8	3.3	6.0	2.2	3.5	2.6	8.2	24.3
2. A few times a year	52.0	54.2	50.5	56.7	33.2	50.8	55.5	49.6	52.3	56.2	46.4	40.7	55.6	61.8	66.7	62.6
1. Never	43.4	40.2	45.9	38.4	62.7	44.9	38.8	47.2	42.4	40.4	47.0	56.9	40.7	35.2	24.7	13.2
Item 5845 Subject C07 N	3164	1475	1585	2359	336	751	898	977	538	1898	1051	1316	625	444	669	37

A02D: Ride around in a car (or motorcycle) just for fun

	TOTAL	M	F	White	Black	NE	NC	S	W	Yes	No	None	Mari-juana Only	Few Pills	More Pills	Any Her-oin
5. Almost everyday	36.1	40.5	31.3	35.6	40.6	30.2	36.3	41.6	34.1	30.3	47.0	27.3	35.4	37.7	50.2	67.4
4. At least once a week	35.0	35.0	35.4	36.1	31.0	34.5	35.0	36.9	32.1	36.6	32.3	33.9	37.9	38.5	33.7	20.2
3. Once or twice a month	13.8	11.4	16.2	14.2	11.2	15.1	14.1	11.3	16.0	16.1	10.1	16.5	14.4	13.7	8.9	-
2. A few times a year	9.0	7.6	10.5	9.2	8.3	12.1	9.3	5.6	10.5	10.4	5.7	13.2	7.5	7.0	3.7	8.0
1. Never	6.1	5.4	6.6	5.0	8.9	8.1	5.4	4.5	7.3	6.6	5.0	9.1	4.7	3.1	3.4	4.4
Item 5850 Subject C07 N	3159	1473	1582	2356	335	750	895	976	537	1895	1050	1312	624	444	669	37

A02E: Participate in community affairs or volunteer work

	TOTAL	M	F	White	Black	NE	NC	S	W	Yes	No	None	Mari-juana Only	Few Pills	More Pills	Any Her-oin
5. Almost everyday	1.7	1.5	1.8	1.2	2.9	2.3	1.8	1.6	1.2	1.7	1.7	2.0	1.0	0.7	1.7	1.8
4. At least once a week	8.4	6.7	10.1	7.7	12.3	10.8	7.6	7.7	7.9	9.8	6.1	11.5	6.5	6.9	5.3	11.0
3. Once or twice a month	14.0	11.6	16.1	14.4	14.0	12.2	14.8	14.9	13.3	16.5	10.4	16.7	13.3	13.1	10.4	7.1
2. A few times a year	44.9	43.2	46.9	46.5	40.4	38.6	48.3	47.4	43.4	47.2	41.0	45.1	45.7	49.8	41.8	45.9
1. Never	31.0	37.1	25.1	30.3	30.4	36.1	27.5	28.3	34.3	24.9	40.7	24.7	33.6	29.6	40.8	34.2
Item 5860 Subject C07,O02 N	3160	1474	1583	2358	334	752	899	973	536	1895	1053	1314	623	445	668	37

A02F: Play a musical instrument or sing

	TOTAL	M	F	White	Black	NE	NC	S	W	Yes	No	None	Mari-juana Only	Few Pills	More Pills	Any Her-oin
5. Almost everyday	27.1	21.5	32.1	26.4	37.3	28.0	26.8	30.1	20.9	31.1	21.0	31.3	24.6	23.1	24.2	20.7
4. At least once a week	9.4	7.9	11.2	9.5	9.7	9.2	9.6	8.6	11.0	10.5	8.1	12.0	6.5	8.7	8.5	2.8
3. Once or twice a month	6.4	6.0	6.7	6.2	7.1	5.7	5.9	7.2	6.6	6.9	5.5	6.1	7.2	7.1	5.5	8.2
2. A few times a year	11.7	11.0	12.4	11.7	13.7	9.9	11.7	10.2	16.8	12.7	9.0	11.6	12.5	12.4	10.4	1.9
1. Never	45.4	53.6	37.6	46.2	32.2	47.2	45.9	44.0	44.7	38.9	56.3	38.9	49.3	48.7	51.5	66.4
Item 5870 Subject C07 N	3160	1475	1584	2361	335	753	895	978	534	1897	1049	1319	621	444	666	37

*=less than .05 per cent.

QUESTIONNAIRE FORM 2 1986	TOTAL	SEX		RACE		REGION				4YR COLLEGE PLANS		ILLICIT DRUG USE: LIFETIME				
		M	F	White	Black	NE	NC	S	W	Yes	No	None	Mari- juana Only	Few Pills	More Pills	Any Her- oin
N (Weighted No. of Cases):	3179	1481	1591	2367	338	756	902	980	541	1906	1054	1324	625	447	670	37
% of Weighted Total:	100.0	46.6	50.0	74.4	10.6	23.8	28.4	30.8	17.0	59.9	33.2	41.6	19.7	14.1	21.1	1.2
A02G: Do creative writing																
5. Almost everyday	6.7	5.9	7.4	6.5	7.9	7.5	6.6	5.2	8.3	7.9	4.4	6.0	6.6	5.9	9.0	6.9
4. At least once a week	11.5	10.3	12.8	10.6	15.0	11.6	11.3	10.9	12.8	14.1	6.7	13.4	9.1	11.7	10.2	11.0
3. Once or twice a month	19.3	15.8	22.7	19.2	21.0	17.6	17.7	18.7	25.2	23.4	12.4	22.2	17.9	20.6	14.9	10.5
2. A few times a year	28.0	25.6	30.1	28.4	26.3	27.8	28.8	28.6	25.6	27.8	28.0	27.3	29.0	26.6	29.5	30.3
1. Never	34.6	42.5	27.0	35.2	29.8	35.5	35.5	36.5	28.1	26.8	48.5	31.1	37.4	35.3	36.5	41.2
Item 5880 Subject C07 N	3150	1466	1581	2349	335	750	895	968	537	1895	1046	1315	620	440	666	37
A02H: Actively participate in sports, athletics or exercising																
5. Almost everyday	44.4	54.2	35.6	45.7	43.3	47.4	47.4	38.5	45.9	49.6	34.8	44.7	46.5	47.0	40.9	43.4
4. At least once a week	23.8	21.6	25.8	24.0	20.3	24.6	23.8	22.7	24.7	24.7	23.6	23.4	23.9	25.2	24.2	25.6
3. Once or twice a month	13.5	9.9	17.4	14.2	10.7	11.8	13.9	15.0	12.6	13.1	15.1	13.7	11.3	14.1	15.2	14.2
2. A few times a year	11.4	8.7	13.3	10.3	15.6	9.9	8.5	15.6	11.0	8.5	15.8	11.2	11.8	10.1	12.2	6.2
1. Never	6.8	5.5	7.9	5.8	10.1	6.2	6.3	8.3	5.9	4.1	10.7	7.0	6.5	3.6	7.5	10.6
Item 5890 Subject C07 N	3166	1474	1587	2361	336	754	897	976	538	1902	1052	1315	625	446	669	37
A02I: Do art or craft work																
5. Almost everyday	13.8	13.9	13.2	13.5	12.2	14.0	13.6	13.6	13.9	13.4	14.5	12.1	13.0	18.1	15.1	17.0
4. At least once a week	9.4	9.9	8.7	9.3	8.9	9.2	8.3	8.6	12.7	8.9	9.7	9.6	8.2	11.7	8.2	13.7
3. Once or twice a month	15.3	14.1	16.7	15.7	12.0	16.1	17.1	11.7	17.8	16.8	12.9	17.1	14.4	15.0	13.1	10.7
2. A few times a year	30.1	27.4	32.9	31.7	23.4	28.9	32.2	29.1	30.0	32.7	25.9	31.1	30.7	28.2	29.6	27.0
1. Never	31.5	34.6	28.5	29.8	43.5	31.7	28.8	37.0	25.6	28.1	36.9	30.2	33.7	27.0	34.0	31.7
Item 5900 Subject C07 N	3149	1470	1575	2348	336	748	892	970	538	1889	1047	1318	622	440	660	36
A02J: Work around the house, yard, garden, car, etc.																
5. Almost everyday	34.2	26.6	40.7	32.2	46.0	31.0	35.0	36.9	32.5	31.1	39.8	34.4	33.0	33.0	35.8	29.9
4. At least once a week	40.5	47.2	34.9	42.6	30.1	37.7	40.6	40.5	44.3	42.8	36.1	41.4	40.6	40.4	39.2	43.8
3. Once or twice a month	17.0	18.4	16.0	18.0	11.2	18.7	16.7	14.9	18.7	17.7	16.3	16.7	18.0	16.0	17.8	9.5
2. A few times a year	6.0	5.4	6.3	5.8	6.3	10.2	5.2	5.1	2.9	6.1	5.4	5.1	6.5	7.7	5.3	12.0
1. Never	2.4	2.5	2.1	1.4	6.5	2.4	2.5	2.6	1.6	2.3	2.4	2.4	2.0	3.0	1.9	4.9
Item 5910 Subject C07 N	3165	1473	1588	2361	337	751	900	978	537	1901	1051	1319	624	444	670	37
A02K: Get together with friends, informally																
5. Almost everyday	48.8	52.2	45.6	50.6	47.1	47.2	48.7	49.9	49.5	47.7	50.6	37.7	51.3	53.9	62.6	67.4
4. At least once a week	39.4	37.3	42.1	39.8	39.0	40.1	41.9	36.1	40.5	41.5	37.3	45.8	39.6	38.8	30.3	19.7
3. Once or twice a month	8.5	7.2	9.4	7.6	8.7	8.8	7.5	9.4	8.2	8.5	8.0	11.0	7.7	6.4	5.3	2.9
2. A few times a year	2.5	2.3	2.4	1.5	3.5	2.6	1.6	3.8	1.8	2.0	2.9	4.2	1.1	0.9	1.5	3.1
1. Never	0.7	1.0	0.4	0.5	1.7	1.4	0.4	0.9	0.1	0.3	1.2	1.3	0.2	-	0.2	6.9
Item 5920 Subject C07,M04 N	3162	1472	1589	2358	334	751	900	974	536	1902	1045	1317	625	443	669	37
A02L: Go shopping or window-shopping																
5. Almost everyday	4.0	1.8	5.8	3.3	6.2	5.3	3.3	3.6	4.0	3.2	5.1	2.9	3.6	4.1	6.3	4.8
4. At least once a week	37.7	24.6	49.8	37.1	42.6	39.5	38.8	36.3	35.7	37.6	38.1	36.5	32.6	43.7	40.0	49.5
3. Once or twice a month	43.7	48.3	40.0	44.7	39.9	41.3	43.6	45.3	44.3	46.9	38.7	46.1	46.7	41.4	40.1	25.4
2. A few times a year	11.0	18.2	4.2	11.2	8.4	10.7	10.9	10.4	12.6	9.6	12.9	11.3	12.9	8.6	9.8	6.3
1. Never	3.6	7.1	0.2	3.8	2.9	3.1	3.4	4.4	3.3	2.7	5.2	3.1	4.2	2.2	3.7	14.0
Item 5930 Subject C07,F01 N	3158	1470	1584	2353	337	750	893	976	539	1892	1052	1312	621	446	669	37
A02M: Spend at least an hour of leisure time alone																
5. Almost everyday	41.8	40.4	43.1	40.5	50.8	41.3	41.7	41.6	42.9	43.2	40.0	41.1	41.4	42.7	44.2	36.4
4. At least once a week	34.8	34.4	35.3	36.5	24.5	36.0	35.4	32.9	35.8	35.8	32.9	34.6	34.8	35.0	35.6	21.9
3. Once or twice a month	12.7	12.4	12.8	12.7	13.2	12.0	11.8	13.5	13.8	12.8	12.3	13.4	12.8	11.5	11.8	13.9
2. A few times a year	5.6	6.7	4.6	5.5	5.3	5.9	5.9	5.7	4.7	4.5	7.2	5.2	6.7	6.2	4.5	13.2
1. Never	5.1	6.1	4.2	4.8	6.2	4.7	5.2	6.4	2.8	3.8	7.6	5.8	4.3	4.5	3.9	14.7
Item 5940 Subject C07 N	3164	1473	1587	2363	334	752	898	975	539	1902	1050	1318	625	444	670	36

QUESTIONNAIRE FORM 2 1986	TOTAL	SEX		RACE		REGION				4YR COLLEGE PLANS		ILLICIT DRUG USE: LIFETIME				
		M	F	White	Black	NE	NC	S	W	Yes	No	None	Mari- juana Only	Few Pills	More Pills	Any Her- oin
N (Weighted No. of Cases):	3179	1481	1591	2367	338	756	902	980	541	1906	1054	1324	625	447	670	37
% of Weighted Total:	100.0	46.6	50.0	74.4	10.6	23.8	28.4	30.8	17.0	59.9	33.2	41.6	19.7	14.1	21.1	1.2

A02N: Read books, magazines, or newspapers

5. Almost everyday	50.2	49.5	50.9	51.9	46.8	52.4	51.1	48.1	49.2	55.2	42.5	51.3	48.4	54.3	49.3	29.4
4. At least once a week	30.5	29.0	31.6	29.2	33.4	26.2	30.3	32.8	32.6	29.5	31.9	31.1	29.8	29.3	30.2	30.2
3. Once or twice a month	12.8	13.3	12.5	12.6	12.6	14.0	12.9	11.2	13.5	10.4	16.2	11.6	15.6	10.8	13.1	20.3
2. A few times a year	4.3	5.1	3.4	4.0	5.5	3.7	4.1	5.6	3.1	3.9	4.7	4.5	4.1	3.8	4.2	10.0
1. Never	2.3	3.1	1.6	2.3	1.6	3.6	1.6	2.3	1.5	0.9	4.7	1.6	2.1	1.7	3.2	10.1
Item 5950 Subject C07 N	3166	1473	1589	2361	338	752	899	977	538	1901	1053	1322	623	445	668	37

A02O: Go to taverns, bars or nightclubs

5. Almost everyday	1.3	2.0	0.4	1.2	1.3	1.1	1.5	1.2	1.5	1.0	1.6	0.7	2.0	0.7	1.8	9.0
4. At least once a week	11.1	12.4	9.6	10.4	13.0	12.6	9.8	11.9	9.5	9.6	12.8	4.6	12.0	13.2	18.1	43.0
3. Once or twice a month	18.0	18.2	18.0	19.0	15.5	18.4	18.8	17.4	17.2	18.2	17.6	11.9	20.9	23.5	24.3	17.2
2. A few times a year	22.7	24.8	21.3	24.2	17.0	22.5	24.1	22.3	21.5	24.3	21.2	19.7	23.2	27.0	27.3	10.5
1. Never	46.9	42.5	50.7	45.1	53.1	45.4	45.7	47.2	50.2	46.9	46.7	63.1	42.0	35.6	28.5	20.2
Item 5960 Subject C07 N	3166	1475	1587	2361	335	752	899	975	539	1903	1048	1318	624	446	668	37

A02P: Go to parties or other social affairs

5. Almost everyday	3.0	4.0	1.5	2.9	3.9	4.0	3.1	2.0	3.2	2.0	4.2	1.6	1.8	3.1	5.8	15.8
4. At least once a week	35.5	39.4	32.3	36.7	28.7	34.9	41.9	28.3	38.9	35.7	35.2	21.7	41.0	43.0	51.5	55.9
3. Once or twice a month	36.3	32.6	40.2	36.9	36.5	35.1	34.4	39.4	35.5	39.2	31.9	39.8	37.1	33.9	31.8	15.3
2. A few times a year	21.2	19.8	22.3	20.2	23.2	22.0	17.6	24.9	19.2	20.6	22.3	30.7	17.4	17.1	9.0	10.8
1. Never	4.0	4.3	3.7	3.3	7.8	4.0	3.0	5.4	3.3	2.4	6.5	6.2	2.7	2.9	1.9	2.2
Item 5970 Subject C07 N	3173	1478	1591	2365	337	754	901	979	539	1905	1052	1322	625	446	669	37

A03: How much do you agree or disagree with each of the following statements?

A03A: In the United States, we put too much emphasis on making profits and not enough on human well-being

1. Disagree	6.1	8.8	3.4	6.1	4.6	6.1	6.6	5.8	5.6	6.3	5.0	6.0	6.6	5.4	4.6	15.6
2. Mostly disagree	12.7	15.4	10.5	13.8	6.4	8.8	13.1	15.1	13.2	13.3	10.5	13.6	11.6	11.9	13.1	6.4
3. Neither	19.5	21.2	18.2	21.0	11.4	20.8	21.3	17.3	18.5	19.2	20.5	20.2	18.8	18.7	19.4	28.3
4. Mostly agree	41.1	34.3	47.4	41.5	41.5	38.7	41.2	40.2	46.2	42.4	40.2	41.1	43.4	39.1	42.4	21.0
5. Agree	20.6	20.2	20.4	17.6	36.1	25.6	17.7	21.7	16.6	18.8	23.9	19.1	19.7	24.8	20.5	28.7
Item 5990 Subject F03,O03 N	3154	1474	1577	2353	336	747	896	976	536	1895	1048	1312	621	444	670	37

A03B: People are too much concerned with material things these days

1. Disagree	3.8	5.8	2.0	3.8	3.9	4.3	3.7	4.3	2.4	3.1	4.9	3.5	2.5	4.8	4.4	5.8
2. Mostly disagree	6.4	7.9	5.0	6.9	4.0	5.9	6.6	6.8	6.1	6.5	5.9	5.0	7.7	5.9	7.2	8.5
3. Neither	10.7	13.7	7.9	11.3	8.6	10.9	13.5	8.2	10.5	9.6	12.1	10.3	12.3	11.1	9.1	20.2
4. Mostly agree	39.9	38.0	42.4	41.9	32.1	41.7	39.8	35.7	45.4	42.2	37.5	40.0	42.4	39.1	40.0	27.0
5. Agree	39.1	34.6	42.7	36.2	51.4	37.2	36.4	45.0	35.7	38.6	39.6	41.1	35.0	39.0	39.4	38.5
Item 6000 Subject F02 N	3158	1473	1581	2356	337	743	896	979	539	1898	1045	1314	623	445	667	37

A03C: Since it helps the economy to grow, people should be encouraged to buy more

1. Disagree	15.4	14.1	16.6	14.1	22.5	17.9	14.2	16.4	12.3	13.2	18.6	15.5	13.8	14.2	17.6	19.0
2. Mostly disagree	19.9	17.5	22.2	20.5	21.0	18.9	21.2	19.8	19.1	20.5	19.3	18.8	23.8	17.8	20.9	17.3
3. Neither	34.7	30.1	39.4	36.3	27.7	33.9	35.3	32.8	38.4	37.5	31.0	35.7	35.0	35.6	32.8	29.3
4. Mostly agree	19.8	23.4	15.9	19.5	19.1	18.2	19.3	19.9	22.5	19.3	19.8	19.4	18.3	21.6	20.1	15.4
5. Agree	10.2	14.8	5.8	9.5	9.7	11.1	10.0	11.1	7.7	9.5	11.3	10.5	9.1	10.7	8.6	18.9
Item 6010 Subject F02 N	3149	1471	1575	2354	332	743	895	972	538	1891	1044	1309	623	443	666	37

QUESTIONNAIRE FORM 2 1986	TOTAL	SEX		RACE		REGION				4YR COLLEGE PLANS		ILLICIT DRUG USE: LIFETIME				
		M	F	White	Black	NE	NC	S	W	Yes	No	None	Marijuana Only	Few Pills	More Pills	Any Heroin
N (Weighted No. of Cases):	3179	1481	1591	2367	338	756	902	980	541	1906	1054	1324	625	447	670	37
% of Weighted Total:	100.0	46.6	50.0	74.4	10.6	23.8	28.4	30.8	17.0	59.9	33.2	41.6	19.7	14.1	21.1	1.2

A03D: There is nothing wrong with advertising that gets people to buy things they don't really need

1. Disagree	27.3	26.0	28.0	27.0	28.7	28.7	26.6	29.8	21.9	27.6	26.8	29.1	25.5	26.7	25.4	28.9
2. Mostly disagree	24.3	21.9	27.1	25.3	21.6	25.3	23.9	23.4	25.4	26.6	21.4	24.0	23.9	26.1	25.7	12.8
3. Neither	16.2	15.7	17.3	17.2	11.5	15.8	18.2	13.4	18.7	16.6	15.5	18.0	15.8	15.0	14.5	15.1
4. Mostly agree	17.0	18.1	16.1	17.7	14.7	15.1	17.5	16.5	19.9	16.5	18.0	15.4	17.6	17.9	18.9	21.6
5. Agree	15.1	18.3	11.6	12.8	23.4	15.2	13.7	16.9	14.2	12.7	18.3	13.6	17.1	14.3	15.5	21.6
Item 6020 Subject F02 N	3149	1468	1579	2349	333	743	895	972	539	1892	1043	1312	624	440	666	37

A03E: There will probably be more shortages in the future, so Americans will have to learn how to be happy with fewer "things"

1. Disagree	11.4	13.0	9.3	11.4	10.0	13.6	12.7	9.6	9.7	11.1	11.8	9.9	10.1	13.0	13.2	23.7
2. Mostly disagree	14.5	16.5	13.0	15.9	10.5	15.3	16.5	12.7	13.5	15.9	12.5	13.3	14.9	16.1	15.7	15.1
3. Neither	19.1	16.9	21.0	19.7	11.8	21.9	20.0	15.4	20.3	19.9	16.8	19.9	19.4	18.9	17.1	24.8
4. Mostly agree	27.2	27.3	27.6	27.8	27.9	23.4	26.5	30.1	28.2	29.1	23.5	29.2	27.0	25.6	25.9	9.1
5. Agree	27.8	26.3	29.0	25.1	39.9	25.8	24.3	32.2	28.3	24.0	35.4	27.7	28.6	26.5	28.0	27.3
Item 6030 Subject F02 N	3153	1473	1576	2352	335	744	895	977	537	1894	1045	1314	620	439	670	37

A04: Below are several ways that people have used to protest about serious social issues. How much do you approve or disapprove of these actions?

A04A: Signing petitions

4. Strongly approve	21.7	22.7	21.3	23.1	20.1	24.7	24.0	18.5	19.3	24.7	15.7	23.1	20.4	19.3	22.5	27.0
3. Approve	45.8	44.6	47.0	47.7	37.2	38.3	48.1	44.8	53.9	50.3	40.0	45.8	47.1	50.3	43.5	29.8
2. Disapprove	3.4	5.3	1.5	3.2	4.7	3.4	3.4	3.7	2.5	2.6	4.7	2.6	3.9	2.5	3.6	4.9
1. Strongly disapprove	1.2	1.7	0.6	1.0	2.4	1.2	0.8	1.6	1.0	1.0	1.5	1.0	1.3	0.3	1.9	-
8. Don't know, or it depends	28.1	25.6	29.6	25.0	35.6	32.4	23.6	31.5	23.3	21.4	38.1	27.6	27.3	27.7	28.5	38.4
Item 6040 Subject I02 N	3151	1467	1582	2352	336	745	895	974	537	1898	1043	1314	624	442	667	37

A04B: Boycotting certain products or stores

4. Strongly approve	11.8	13.5	10.3	12.1	12.2	13.7	11.8	10.2	12.1	13.7	8.2	11.3	9.6	15.3	12.8	15.3
3. Approve	32.8	36.5	29.3	33.1	32.0	34.1	32.6	31.9	32.8	34.9	30.3	33.9	34.1	31.5	33.3	7.5
2. Disapprove	15.9	17.3	14.5	15.8	14.3	13.3	18.8	15.4	15.3	14.8	17.5	15.8	16.9	16.6	13.2	17.5
1. Strongly disapprove	3.6	3.1	3.9	3.3	6.0	4.7	3.1	3.0	4.0	3.5	4.0	3.4	2.9	3.2	4.4	5.8
8. Don't know, or it depends	36.0	29.6	41.9	35.8	35.6	34.1	33.8	39.4	35.9	33.2	40.0	35.6	36.4	33.4	36.3	53.9
Item 6050 Subject I02 N	3142	1465	1577	2346	334	746	895	963	539	1889	1042	1310	623	442	665	37

A04C: Lawful demonstrations

4. Strongly approve	14.9	17.4	12.5	14.9	13.3	17.2	16.0	12.0	15.3	17.5	10.6	13.9	15.1	16.9	15.7	21.0
3. Approve	45.6	44.8	46.9	47.3	45.4	43.6	47.7	45.1	45.7	49.6	40.0	46.7	48.6	44.4	44.0	29.7
2. Disapprove	9.9	12.3	7.4	9.8	9.1	9.9	8.9	11.7	8.4	8.0	13.2	7.8	9.1	12.1	12.2	21.3
1. Strongly disapprove	3.6	4.5	2.4	3.4	3.7	3.2	3.2	3.9	4.5	2.6	4.9	4.1	3.4	1.8	3.6	2.2
8. Don't know, or it depends	26.0	21.0	30.8	24.7	28.5	26.1	24.3	27.3	26.2	22.3	31.4	27.5	23.8	24.8	24.6	25.9
Item 6060 Subject I02 N	3126	1455	1569	2339	331	739	893	959	536	1890	1031	1304	617	441	664	37

A04D: Occupying buildings or factories

4. Strongly approve	4.6	5.7	3.4	4.0	8.3	4.7	4.5	5.3	3.5	3.6	6.5	2.9	6.3	5.5	5.6	8.6
3. Approve	21.3	22.1	20.2	20.3	26.3	20.7	22.0	22.5	18.9	18.0	27.0	17.7	24.0	19.2	26.2	34.0
2. Disapprove	25.2	26.6	24.3	26.1	19.5	24.2	24.8	25.4	26.7	28.5	19.7	29.0	20.7	22.0	24.7	18.4
1. Strongly disapprove	9.7	12.0	7.4	10.4	6.8	8.2	11.2	9.6	9.6	11.3	6.9	9.5	11.5	10.2	8.4	5.4
8. Don't know, or it depends	39.1	33.6	44.7	39.1	39.1	42.1	37.6	37.2	41.2	38.6	39.9	40.9	37.5	43.1	35.0	33.6
Item 6070 Subject I02 N	3116	1458	1559	2337	329	735	888	958	535	1880	1031	1304	617	438	654	37

A04E: Wildcat strikes

4. Strongly approve	1.9	2.5	1.1	1.6	2.9	1.4	1.9	2.3	2.0	1.4	2.9	1.5	1.7	1.9	2.8	4.1
3. Approve	10.5	13.9	7.2	10.4	10.9	11.4	11.3	8.7	11.0	9.4	12.7	7.1	8.8	10.5	18.5	17.2
2. Disapprove	28.0	28.4	27.7	28.9	25.6	28.6	28.6	28.3	25.4	28.3	27.9	29.2	28.7	29.0	25.3	20.1
1. Strongly disapprove	15.8	17.2	14.4	15.8	17.1	14.8	17.4	15.8	14.3	16.0	14.9	17.3	15.1	16.5	11.8	17.7
8. Don't know, or it depends	43.9	38.1	49.6	43.4	43.5	43.8	40.8	44.9	47.4	45.0	41.5	44.9	45.7	42.1	41.6	40.9
Item 6080 Subject I02 N	3100	1448	1550	2319	326	728	887	954	530	1865	1026	1293	616	433	653	37

QUESTIONNAIRE FORM 2 1986	TOTAL	SEX		RACE		REGION				4YR COLLEGE PLANS		ILLICIT DRUG USE: LIFETIME				
		M	F	White	Black	NE	NC	S	W	Yes	No	None	Mari-juana Only	Few Pills	More Pills	Any Her-oin
N (Weighted No. of Cases):	3179	1481	1591	2367	338	756	902	980	541	1906	1054	1324	625	447	670	37
% of Weighted Total:	100.0	46.6	50.0	74.4	10.6	23.8	28.4	30.8	17.0	59.9	33.2	41.6	19.7	14.1	21.1	1.2
A04F: Blocking traffic																
4. Strongly approve	2.0	2.7	1.3	1.5	3.6	1.6	1.5	2.9	2.0	1.6	3.0	2.2	1.3	2.1	1.6	2.3
3. Approve	3.4	3.5	3.0	2.6	4.9	3.4	3.3	3.0	4.0	3.2	3.2	2.8	4.2	2.9	3.9	4.0
2. Disapprove	39.8	36.3	43.0	39.9	38.0	39.3	41.2	38.2	41.2	38.9	41.3	39.1	39.3	38.4	43.2	35.3
1. Strongly disapprove	41.4	44.9	38.4	43.2	38.1	40.0	42.4	41.9	40.6	44.2	37.4	43.4	41.1	43.8	37.4	29.9
8. Don't know, or it depends	13.4	12.6	14.3	12.9	15.4	15.8	11.6	14.0	12.2	12.2	15.0	12.4	14.2	12.9	13.9	28.5
Item 6090 Subject I02 N	3143	1465	1577	2350	333	745	893	971	534	1897	1039	1313	622	442	664	37
A04G: Damaging things																
4. Strongly approve	2.7	3.8	1.6	2.2	3.9	4.0	1.9	3.0	2.0	2.2	3.8	2.7	2.5	1.9	2.7	15.9
3. Approve	2.2	2.9	1.3	1.6	4.9	3.3	1.8	2.4	1.0	1.7	2.3	1.1	1.7	1.7	4.7	3.4
2. Disapprove	22.4	23.1	21.1	21.1	24.3	23.8	21.1	23.2	21.1	20.1	26.2	20.6	22.8	24.7	23.4	29.8
1. Strongly disapprove	66.2	61.9	71.3	69.4	57.0	62.5	69.3	64.7	68.7	71.1	58.8	70.1	67.7	64.2	61.4	41.4
8. Don't know, or it depends	6.5	8.3	4.8	5.6	9.8	6.4	6.0	6.8	7.1	5.0	9.0	5.5	5.5	7.5	7.8	9.5
Item 6100 Subject I02 N	3152	1469	1581	2353	336	746	895	973	537	1897	1048	1315	624	443	666	37
A04H: Personal violence																
4. Strongly approve	3.6	4.9	2.1	2.7	5.7	4.3	3.7	3.4	2.9	2.7	5.3	2.9	3.0	2.5	5.1	24.4
3. Approve	2.7	3.8	1.4	2.1	4.3	3.9	2.6	2.9	1.1	1.9	3.3	1.9	1.5	3.8	3.6	9.6
2. Disapprove	18.2	20.8	15.4	18.3	19.3	19.5	16.7	18.1	19.3	16.9	20.4	16.6	19.4	17.9	20.5	20.3
1. Strongly disapprove	65.7	57.8	74.1	68.9	55.9	62.6	68.3	64.2	68.2	71.8	57.4	70.1	68.2	64.5	59.7	27.0
8. Don't know, or it depends	9.7	12.6	6.9	7.9	14.8	9.7	8.6	11.5	8.5	6.8	13.6	8.4	7.9	11.3	11.2	18.6
Item 6110 Subject I02 N	3149	1468	1581	2351	336	745	897	972	535	1895	1046	1316	622	443	665	37
A05: Do you think that you would prefer having a mate for most of your life, or would you prefer not having a mate?																
5. Definitely prefer to have a mate	57.5	52.6	61.8	59.4	49.5	59.2	55.1	58.1	58.1	57.5	58.7	57.4	57.7	57.9	57.4	57.6
4. Probably prefer to have a mate	27.7	28.8	27.2	28.0	25.3	28.6	28.5	26.6	27.1	29.2	24.7	28.6	29.7	27.0	25.4	23.4
3. Not sure	10.5	13.0	8.0	8.5	20.0	8.1	11.3	12.0	10.0	8.9	12.7	9.8	9.0	12.5	10.7	18.9
2. Probably prefer not to have a mate	3.3	4.1	2.5	3.1	4.0	3.1	4.3	2.6	3.4	3.5	3.0	2.9	3.2	2.3	5.2	-
1. Definitely prefer not to have a mate	0.9	1.4	0.5	0.9	1.1	1.0	0.8	0.8	1.3	0.9	0.9	1.3	0.3	0.2	1.3	-
Item 6120 Subject D01 N	3159	1470	1586	2358	336	751	897	976	534	1896	1048	1319	624	445	664	37
A06: Which do you think you are most likely to choose in the long run?																
3. Getting married	77.7	74.7	80.8	80.6	67.9	77.5	78.9	76.0	78.8	80.5	74.1	80.0	78.1	79.0	72.8	67.9
2. I have no idea	16.6	19.2	13.9	14.1	24.2	17.3	15.2	17.8	15.9	14.0	19.8	14.4	17.9	15.7	19.2	16.1
1. Not getting married	5.2	5.9	4.6	4.8	7.9	5.2	5.6	5.1	4.8	5.0	5.5	4.8	3.6	5.0	7.6	16.0
8. Am already married	0.5	0.3	0.7	0.5	-	-	0.3	1.1	0.5	0.5	0.6	0.7	0.5	0.3	0.4	-
Item 6130 Subject D01 N	3104	1444	1559	2320	326	746	886	942	530	1861	1034	1296	617	432	654	36
A07: If you did get married (or are married) . . .																
A07A: How likely do you think it is that you would stay married to the same person for life?																
5. Very likely	59.3	53.8	64.5	60.7	50.4	58.4	59.2	59.3	60.4	59.1	60.4	65.4	54.8	53.7	56.3	57.9
4. Fairly likely	24.3	26.8	22.5	25.8	19.6	25.4	24.6	21.9	26.9	26.7	20.6	21.4	27.4	29.2	24.7	22.4
3. Uncertain	13.3	15.8	10.5	11.1	23.4	12.9	13.9	15.1	9.9	11.4	15.2	10.8	15.5	13.3	15.1	8.2
2. Fairly unlikely	1.8	2.0	1.6	1.6	3.1	1.9	1.3	2.0	2.3	1.7	2.1	1.2	2.2	2.4	1.8	8.4
1. Very unlikely	1.2	1.7	0.9	0.8	3.6	1.4	1.0	1.7	0.5	1.1	1.6	1.2	0.2	1.3	2.1	3.1
Item 6140 Subject D01 N	3052	1420	1529	2269	329	710	866	961	515	1823	1019	1272	607	428	643	31
A07B: How likely is it that you would want to have children?																
5. Very likely	62.5	60.1	64.5	63.7	55.4	63.4	60.2	63.7	62.9	63.2	61.4	64.7	61.3	61.3	60.7	52.6
4. Fairly likely	19.0	22.5	15.7	18.4	22.4	20.0	20.2	17.6	17.9	19.5	18.1	18.3	22.6	18.8	16.3	22.7
3. Uncertain	11.9	11.6	12.2	12.0	11.6	12.3	12.0	11.1	12.9	11.4	12.8	10.8	11.7	13.8	12.8	20.7
2. Fairly unlikely	2.7	2.3	3.1	2.6	3.6	0.9	3.7	2.6	3.5	2.6	3.1	2.4	1.7	3.0	4.4	-
1. Very unlikely	2.7	2.1	3.2	2.4	3.5	2.7	2.4	2.8	2.7	2.6	2.2	2.5	1.8	2.1	4.1	2.9
8. Already have child(ren)	1.3	1.4	1.2	0.8	3.5	0.8	1.5	2.2	0.1	0.7	2.4	1.3	0.9	1.0	1.7	-
Item 6150 Subject D02 N	3071	1434	1534	2286	326	719	872	959	521	1836	1026	1278	610	433	645	33

QUESTIONNAIRE FORM 2 1986	TOTAL	SEX		RACE		REGION				4YR COLLEGE PLANS		ILLICIT DRUG USE: LIFETIME				
		M	F	White	Black	NE	NC	S	W	Yes	No	None	Marijuana Only	Few Pills	More Pills	Any Heroin
N (Weighted No. of Cases):	3179	1481	1591	2367	338	756	902	980	541	1906	1054	1324	625	447	670	37
% of Weighted Total:	100.0	46.6	50.0	74.4	10.6	23.8	28.4	30.8	17.0	59.9	33.2	41.6	19.7	14.1	21.1	1.2

The questions in the next column ask you to imagine different kinds of married life that you might have. We want you to think about different ways you might share responsibilities for working, taking care of the home, and taking care of children. Please indicate how acceptable for you each of the different arrangements would be.

A08: Imagine you are married and have no children–how would you feel about each of the following working arrangements?

A08A: Husband works full-time, wife doesn't work

	TOTAL	M	F	White	Black	NE	NC	S	W	Yes	No	None	Marijuana Only	Few Pills	More Pills	Any Heroin
1. Not at all acceptable	27.2	15.0	38.5	24.8	36.9	29.5	27.9	24.5	27.9	30.0	22.5	27.2	29.5	27.3	24.0	25.3
2. Somewhat acceptable	34.5	33.1	36.2	35.4	32.5	35.1	34.1	32.3	38.5	34.7	34.2	33.5	35.7	35.2	35.4	38.5
3. Acceptable	30.9	41.8	20.6	32.6	21.2	29.1	31.3	33.8	27.5	29.6	33.9	32.4	28.9	30.8	31.6	24.6
4. Desirable	7.3	10.1	4.7	7.1	9.4	6.3	6.7	9.3	6.1	5.7	9.4	6.9	5.8	6.7	8.9	11.7
Item 6160 Subject C05,D04 N	3144	1463	1580	2351	334	745	891	974	534	1892	1041	1312	621	446	659	37

A08B: Husband works full-time, wife works about half-time

	TOTAL	M	F	White	Black	NE	NC	S	W	Yes	No	None	Marijuana Only	Few Pills	More Pills	Any Heroin
1. Not at all acceptable	4.9	2.7	6.7	3.7	9.0	6.5	4.5	4.8	3.5	4.6	5.0	4.5	4.3	5.7	5.3	5.4
2. Somewhat acceptable	23.0	16.5	28.9	21.4	29.7	24.0	20.8	24.3	23.2	23.9	20.7	24.1	22.3	21.4	22.2	14.9
3. Acceptable	57.4	63.0	52.3	58.8	52.2	56.9	59.0	55.7	58.5	55.3	61.8	58.6	57.4	58.5	54.6	69.4
4. Desirable	14.7	17.8	12.1	16.2	9.1	12.7	15.7	15.2	14.8	16.2	12.5	12.7	16.0	14.4	18.0	10.4
Item 6170 Subject C05,D04 N	3145	1467	1577	2349	333	748	891	973	533	1892	1042	1311	620	445	662	37

A08C: Both work full-time

	TOTAL	M	F	White	Black	NE	NC	S	W	Yes	No	None	Marijuana Only	Few Pills	More Pills	Any Heroin
1. Not at all acceptable	10.5	13.5	7.5	9.4	11.7	10.6	9.1	11.6	10.9	7.9	14.2	9.9	11.8	8.3	11.0	12.0
2. Somewhat acceptable	16.3	19.6	13.4	16.4	14.9	14.0	16.0	17.9	17.1	14.6	18.7	16.6	12.7	17.0	18.2	19.4
3. Acceptable	48.9	47.8	49.6	49.3	46.6	49.6	48.6	48.6	49.0	50.3	46.6	49.4	51.0	45.2	47.9	49.6
4. Desirable	24.3	19.1	29.5	24.9	26.8	25.8	26.4	21.9	23.0	27.2	20.4	24.0	24.5	29.4	22.9	19.0
Item 6180 Subject C05,D04 N	3138	1459	1580	2346	332	749	889	970	530	1892	1040	1309	623	443	660	37

A08D: Both work about half-time

	TOTAL	M	F	White	Black	NE	NC	S	W	Yes	No	None	Marijuana Only	Few Pills	More Pills	Any Heroin
1. Not at all acceptable	39.9	41.8	37.3	38.2	48.3	37.8	39.6	45.2	33.4	37.3	42.3	39.0	37.9	39.3	41.9	22.3
2. Somewhat acceptable	29.6	29.4	30.3	31.0	23.4	29.3	29.8	28.3	31.9	30.4	28.6	30.0	30.3	31.9	28.1	39.1
3. Acceptable	22.6	20.6	25.0	22.9	20.7	23.1	23.2	20.1	25.6	24.0	21.8	23.5	23.4	20.6	22.6	15.0
4. Desirable	7.9	8.2	7.5	7.9	7.6	9.8	7.3	6.3	9.2	8.2	7.3	7.5	8.3	8.2	7.4	23.6
Item 6190 Subject C05,D04 N	3113	1453	1561	2329	326	739	886	961	526	1876	1034	1300	618	439	652	37

A08E: Husband works about half-time, wife works full-time

	TOTAL	M	F	White	Black	NE	NC	S	W	Yes	No	None	Marijuana Only	Few Pills	More Pills	Any Heroin
1. Not at all acceptable	46.6	52.3	40.8	44.4	55.1	44.7	38.5	54.9	47.7	42.5	53.3	46.4	44.2	48.8	47.0	40.4
2. Somewhat acceptable	29.4	25.8	33.4	31.7	22.5	30.0	33.7	26.0	27.6	32.3	25.6	31.0	29.4	26.2	29.6	31.4
3. Acceptable	20.5	17.4	23.6	20.9	17.9	21.9	24.3	15.5	21.0	22.8	16.4	19.2	23.7	21.4	19.8	23.7
4. Desirable	3.5	4.5	2.2	3.0	4.5	3.4	3.5	3.5	3.7	2.5	4.7	3.4	2.8	3.6	3.7	4.5
Item 6200 Subject C05,D04 N	3137	1463	1575	2349	331	747	887	970	533	1889	1039	1308	621	445	659	37

A08F: Husband doesn't work, wife works full-time

	TOTAL	M	F	White	Black	NE	NC	S	W	Yes	No	None	Marijuana Only	Few Pills	More Pills	Any Heroin
1. Not at all acceptable	76.0	74.5	77.1	74.9	84.3	74.0	73.0	81.1	74.3	73.6	80.2	76.6	74.7	77.2	75.3	62.7
2. Somewhat acceptable	13.2	11.6	15.1	14.9	4.7	13.7	15.8	9.3	15.4	16.1	8.8	13.1	14.6	12.8	13.1	15.4
3. Acceptable	7.0	8.6	5.8	7.4	4.7	8.3	7.6	5.4	7.2	7.8	5.9	6.4	8.4	7.6	6.9	8.9
4. Desirable	3.8	5.4	1.9	2.8	6.2	3.9	3.6	4.3	3.1	2.5	5.1	3.9	2.3	2.4	4.7	13.0
Item 6210 Subject C05,D04 N	3141	1460	1580	2349	334	746	888	973	534	1888	1044	1312	621	443	659	37

A09: Imagine you are married and have one or more pre-school children. How would you feel about each of the following working arrangements?

QUESTIONNAIRE FORM 2 1986	TOTAL	SEX		RACE		REGION				4YR COLLEGE PLANS		ILLICIT DRUG USE: LIFETIME				
		M	F	White	Black	NE	NC	S	W	Yes	No	None	Mari-juana Only	Few Pills	More Pills	Any Her-oin
N (Weighted No. of Cases):	3179	1481	1591	2367	338	756	902	980	541	1906	1054	1324	625	447	670	37
% of Weighted Total:	100.0	46.6	50.0	74.4	10.6	23.8	28.4	30.8	17.0	59.9	33.2	41.6	19.7	14.1	21.1	1.2

A09A: Husband works full-time, wife doesn't work

	TOTAL	M	F	White	Black	NE	NC	S	W	Yes	No	None	Mari Only	Few Pills	More Pills	Any Heroin
1. Not at all acceptable	9.9	6.1	12.8	7.0	20.6	10.1	9.7	10.6	8.6	9.9	9.2	9.4	10.7	11.4	8.0	12.4
2. Somewhat acceptable	20.2	16.4	24.0	18.9	26.6	20.8	18.6	19.5	23.6	19.8	21.0	20.0	19.2	22.1	21.2	10.2
3. Acceptable	41.3	41.8	40.7	42.3	38.5	41.2	42.9	40.3	40.9	39.6	44.8	41.7	41.9	39.0	41.4	39.2
4. Desirable	28.6	35.6	22.6	31.7	14.3	27.9	28.8	29.6	27.0	30.7	25.1	28.9	28.2	27.5	29.4	38.2
Item 6220 Subject C05,D04 N	3147	1463	1583	2352	334	747	892	974	534	1896	1044	1312	623	444	662	37

A09B: Husband works full-time, wife works about half-time

	TOTAL	M	F	White	Black	NE	NC	S	W	Yes	No	None	Mari Only	Few Pills	More Pills	Any Heroin
1. Not at all acceptable	7.3	9.4	5.2	7.1	5.8	9.9	5.2	7.9	6.0	5.9	8.6	6.9	6.2	8.0	7.5	9.7
2. Somewhat acceptable	25.4	26.4	24.2	24.5	29.9	25.7	25.9	25.6	23.6	23.9	28.8	26.2	25.3	24.7	23.1	26.9
3. Acceptable	53.2	51.9	54.6	53.7	54.0	50.9	55.9	51.5	54.9	54.7	50.8	54.1	53.2	53.4	53.4	42.5
4. Desirable	14.1	12.3	16.0	14.7	10.3	13.5	12.9	15.1	15.4	15.5	11.8	12.9	15.4	14.0	16.0	20.9
Item 6230 Subject C05,D04 N	3150	1465	1584	2354	334	747	893	976	534	1894	1047	1313	623	445	663	37

A09C: Both work full-time

	TOTAL	M	F	White	Black	NE	NC	S	W	Yes	No	None	Mari Only	Few Pills	More Pills	Any Heroin
1. Not at all acceptable	50.9	56.4	46.2	53.2	38.9	57.9	51.1	43.1	55.2	50.6	51.2	49.4	50.3	51.3	54.5	61.3
2. Somewhat acceptable	24.4	21.8	27.5	25.2	18.2	19.7	24.6	28.3	23.7	26.0	22.5	25.6	24.5	23.5	23.5	27.5
3. Acceptable	17.8	15.0	19.9	15.7	28.8	15.8	17.7	20.4	15.7	17.5	18.2	18.0	18.7	15.7	17.3	7.5
4. Desirable	6.9	6.8	6.5	5.9	14.1	6.6	6.6	8.2	5.3	5.8	8.2	7.1	6.5	9.6	4.8	3.7
Item 6240 Subject C05,D04 N	3135	1459	1576	2341	333	744	891	970	530	1888	1041	1310	618	445	657	37

A09D: Both work about half-time

	TOTAL	M	F	White	Black	NE	NC	S	W	Yes	No	None	Mari Only	Few Pills	More Pills	Any Heroin
1. Not at all acceptable	37.3	40.4	34.1	36.0	44.0	38.6	34.4	42.2	31.4	34.0	42.2	38.6	36.2	34.2	38.1	17.5
2. Somewhat acceptable	33.6	32.3	35.3	34.8	30.3	32.5	33.0	32.8	37.4	34.2	32.1	31.1	35.2	34.0	35.3	61.2
3. Acceptable	22.2	20.6	23.7	22.7	16.3	21.3	25.7	19.1	23.6	24.2	19.7	22.7	22.2	24.5	21.1	14.4
4. Desirable	6.9	6.8	6.9	6.4	9.4	7.6	6.9	5.9	7.6	7.6	5.9	7.6	6.4	7.4	5.4	6.8
Item 6250 Subject C05,D04 N	3125	1457	1571	2341	327	743	890	964	528	1885	1035	1305	619	440	657	37

A09E: Husband works about half-time, wife works full-time

	TOTAL	M	F	White	Black	NE	NC	S	W	Yes	No	None	Mari Only	Few Pills	More Pills	Any Heroin
1. Not at all acceptable	53.0	56.3	49.2	52.4	52.0	52.7	47.0	59.5	51.5	49.4	59.5	50.7	50.8	55.5	56.4	58.2
2. Somewhat acceptable	27.0	24.9	29.6	27.9	28.1	25.4	30.1	24.6	28.6	28.4	24.3	28.7	27.6	23.1	26.9	26.4
3. Acceptable	17.2	15.7	18.9	17.4	15.8	19.1	20.0	13.0	17.4	19.9	13.0	17.7	19.2	17.9	15.0	9.3
4. Desirable	2.8	3.1	2.3	2.3	4.1	2.8	2.9	2.9	2.6	2.4	3.2	2.9	2.4	3.5	1.8	6.1
Item 6260 Subject C05,D04 N	3145	1463	1582	2351	334	748	892	972	534	1893	1044	1311	622	445	662	36

A09F: Husband doesn't work, wife works full-time

	TOTAL	M	F	White	Black	NE	NC	S	W	Yes	No	None	Mari Only	Few Pills	More Pills	Any Heroin
1. Not at all acceptable	68.1	68.8	67.1	66.3	77.6	64.4	64.6	75.6	65.6	63.9	75.8	67.9	67.2	68.6	68.7	60.4
2. Somewhat acceptable	15.5	14.2	17.0	16.8	8.4	17.8	17.6	10.8	17.1	17.3	12.2	15.4	15.5	13.0	17.5	21.7
3. Acceptable	12.1	11.2	13.0	13.0	8.0	13.8	13.7	8.9	12.8	14.9	7.0	12.7	13.2	13.4	9.6	12.9
4. Desirable	4.4	5.8	2.9	3.8	6.0	4.0	4.2	4.7	4.5	3.9	5.0	4.0	4.1	5.0	4.3	5.0
Item 6270 Subject C05,D04 N	3137	1459	1580	2349	331	744	890	971	533	1892	1039	1307	620	444	662	37

A10: Imagine you are married and have one or more pre-school children. Imagine also that the husband is working full-time and the wife does not have a job outside the home. How would you feel about each of these arrangements for the day-to-day care of the child(ren)?

A10A: Wife does all child care

	TOTAL	M	F	White	Black	NE	NC	S	W	Yes	No	None	Mari Only	Few Pills	More Pills	Any Heroin
1. Not at all acceptable	34.1	27.7	40.2	33.7	35.3	34.2	35.8	32.5	33.9	37.2	29.7	34.6	34.5	36.4	31.4	30.0
2. Somewhat acceptable	27.7	27.3	28.4	28.7	24.0	30.2	27.4	26.6	26.6	26.1	29.3	27.7	25.2	30.8	27.8	35.1
3. Acceptable	28.3	30.8	25.9	27.2	32.0	25.6	28.3	29.2	30.6	26.9	30.8	28.7	30.1	23.6	29.1	29.3
4. Desirable	9.9	14.2	5.6	10.3	8.7	9.9	8.5	11.8	9.0	9.8	10.1	9.0	10.2	9.2	11.7	5.7
Item 6280 Subject D04 N	3135	1456	1579	2346	334	742	890	971	531	1885	1044	1308	619	444	658	37

QUESTIONNAIRE FORM 2 1986	TOTAL	SEX		RACE		REGION				4YR COLLEGE PLANS		ILLICIT DRUG USE: LIFETIME				
		M	F	White	Black	NE	NC	S	W	Yes	No	None	Mari-juana Only	Few Pills	More Pills	Any Her-oin
N (Weighted No. of Cases):	3179	1481	1591	2367	338	756	902	980	541	1906	1054	1324	625	447	670	37
% of Weighted Total:	100.0	46.6	50.0	74.4	10.6	23.8	28.4	30.8	17.0	59.9	33.2	41.6	19.7	14.1	21.1	1.2

A10B: Wife does most of it

1. Not at all acceptable	10.5	10.3	10.7	8.5	19.3	11.3	9.7	11.3	9.5	10.9	9.9	9.9	11.5	10.6	10.0	10.1
2. Somewhat acceptable	31.2	28.6	33.7	31.4	29.5	31.0	32.9	28.8	33.0	29.2	35.5	30.6	31.0	32.2	31.8	36.2
3. Acceptable	44.7	45.4	44.1	45.3	42.1	44.3	44.9	45.1	44.0	45.5	41.9	45.8	42.7	42.6	46.3	34.9
4. Desirable	13.6	15.7	11.5	14.8	9.1	13.4	12.6	14.8	13.6	14.4	12.6	13.7	14.8	14.6	11.8	18.8
Item 6290 Subject D04 N	3141	1459	1584	2350	335	742	892	974	533	1890	1045	1310	620	445	662	37

A10C: Both do it equally

1. Not at all acceptable	4.2	5.8	2.6	3.9	4.3	3.0	4.2	5.5	3.3	3.9	4.7	3.9	3.6	4.7	4.6	5.5
2. Somewhat acceptable	16.4	19.9	12.8	16.4	18.4	13.9	15.8	19.0	16.3	15.5	17.6	15.8	16.3	14.0	18.8	16.8
3. Acceptable	40.5	41.1	39.7	39.0	49.5	41.5	38.2	43.0	38.6	38.4	43.0	39.9	41.9	39.9	40.5	24.3
4. Desirable	38.8	33.3	44.9	40.7	27.8	41.7	41.7	32.5	41.7	42.2	34.6	40.4	38.2	41.4	36.2	53.4
Item 6300 Subject D04 N	3131	1454	1580	2343	332	742	888	970	530	1882	1043	1307	618	442	660	37

A10D: Husband does most of it

1. Not at all acceptable	45.6	45.4	45.7	44.2	48.8	45.0	44.8	48.3	42.7	45.3	45.7	44.2	45.1	47.2	47.2	39.9
2. Somewhat acceptable	39.2	38.5	40.1	41.7	32.3	38.1	40.0	36.7	43.8	40.4	37.3	39.4	39.3	36.9	41.1	42.3
3. Acceptable	12.4	13.9	11.2	12.3	11.3	14.4	13.1	10.7	11.8	12.4	13.0	13.7	12.7	12.3	9.4	17.8
4. Desirable	2.8	2.2	3.0	1.8	7.6	2.5	2.1	4.3	1.8	2.0	4.0	2.7	2.9	3.6	2.2	-
Item 6310 Subject D04 N	3129	1453	1580	2345	331	740	892	967	530	1883	1044	1306	617	444	659	37

A10E: Husband does all of it

1. Not at all acceptable	81.5	79.4	83.9	82.4	77.2	80.3	82.4	81.4	82.2	82.4	80.4	80.8	82.5	80.6	83.1	82.1
2. Somewhat acceptable	11.7	13.4	10.3	12.1	10.5	13.3	12.1	9.7	12.4	11.6	12.0	12.3	10.7	12.5	11.3	15.7
3. Acceptable	3.8	4.5	3.1	3.6	4.4	3.9	3.3	4.4	3.7	4.0	3.4	3.6	4.4	4.3	3.7	-
4. Desirable	2.9	2.7	2.7	1.9	7.9	2.6	2.3	4.6	1.7	2.0	4.2	3.3	2.4	2.7	1.9	2.2
Item 6320 Subject D04 N	3134	1457	1581	2347	333	743	892	969	530	1884	1046	1308	618	444	660	37

The next section of this questionnaire is about government and public affairs.

A11: Some people think about what's going on in government very often, and others are not that interested. How much of an interest do you take in government and current events?

1. No interest at all	3.7	3.8	3.3	3.0	6.1	4.5	2.9	3.6	4.1	2.0	6.2	3.5	4.0	2.3	3.8	15.6
2. Very little interest	14.4	10.8	17.8	13.0	20.2	17.3	15.9	12.2	12.0	11.5	20.2	12.8	14.7	16.1	15.6	21.0
3. Some interest	47.3	41.1	53.3	48.2	43.7	46.4	48.3	47.1	47.0	45.3	50.2	48.7	46.5	44.8	47.6	39.1
4. A lot of interest	24.9	31.5	19.2	26.0	21.5	23.9	23.9	25.1	27.4	29.4	17.7	25.9	25.3	24.4	23.6	17.4
5. A very great interest	9.7	12.9	6.4	9.8	8.4	7.9	9.0	12.0	9.5	11.8	5.7	9.1	9.5	12.5	9.4	6.9
Item 6330 Subject H01,Q08 N	3143	1467	1581	2353	335	750	890	968	535	1896	1042	1318	623	444	659	36

A12: Do you think some of the people running the government are crooked or dishonest?

1. Most of them are crooked or dishonest	7.1	7.8	6.3	5.9	16.1	7.6	5.8	9.5	4.3	5.4	10.4	5.9	6.6	6.0	9.6	24.9
2. Quite a few are	26.5	27.4	25.4	25.3	32.8	28.4	26.3	27.0	23.2	26.8	26.2	25.0	24.8	31.3	28.5	25.2
3. Some are	57.2	55.0	59.7	59.1	45.6	55.1	58.8	55.6	60.4	58.9	53.5	60.1	58.5	53.7	53.3	41.4
4. Hardly any are	8.6	9.2	8.0	9.3	4.6	8.2	8.3	7.3	11.7	8.3	9.1	8.2	9.3	9.0	8.1	8.5
5. None at all are crooked or dishonest	0.6	0.6	0.6	0.4	0.8	0.7	0.7	0.6	0.3	0.5	0.7	0.8	0.8	-	0.5	-
Item 6340 Subject H04,K01 N	3132	1468	1569	2344	335	741	889	968	533	1887	1042	1314	622	442	655	35

A13: Do you think the government wastes much of the money we pay in taxes?

1. Nearly all tax money is wasted	6.0	6.6	5.2	4.7	12.3	7.8	3.9	7.2	4.8	4.2	9.3	5.0	6.8	6.1	6.8	7.6
2. A lot of tax money is wasted	45.8	47.9	43.9	46.3	43.8	48.0	47.4	43.5	44.1	45.9	47.2	47.1	41.6	43.4	48.9	55.4
3. Some tax money is wasted	39.4	36.3	42.8	40.7	33.6	36.6	40.5	39.7	40.8	41.9	33.8	39.4	40.8	41.7	36.8	28.1
4. A little tax money wasted	7.8	8.2	7.3	7.6	8.1	6.4	7.3	8.1	9.8	7.6	8.0	7.6	10.2	6.7	6.9	6.9
5. No tax money is wasted	1.1	1.0	0.8	0.7	2.2	1.3	0.8	1.5	0.5	0.4	1.7	0.9	0.6	2.0	0.7	1.9
Item 6350 Subject H04,K01 N	3137	1465	1577	2348	334	748	890	967	533	1891	1043	1317	622	440	659	35

QUESTIONNAIRE FORM 2 1986	TOTAL	SEX		RACE		REGION				4YR COLLEGE PLANS		ILLICIT DRUG USE: LIFETIME				
		M	F	White	Black	NE	NC	S	W	Yes	No	None	Mari- juana Only	Few Pills	More Pills	Any Her- oin
N (Weighted No. of Cases):	3179	1481	1591	2367	338	756	902	980	541	1906	1054	1324	625	447	670	37
% of Weighted Total:	100.0	46.6	50.0	74.4	10.6	23.8	28.4	30.8	17.0	59.9	33.2	41.6	19.7	14.1	21.1	1.2

A14: How much of the time do you think you can trust the government in Washington to do what is right?

1. Almost always	11.2	12.7	9.5	11.9	7.0	9.4	10.5	12.7	12.0	11.9	10.4	10.1	12.5	11.2	12.1	3.7
2. Often	44.9	47.3	43.3	48.8	25.9	41.6	48.2	41.8	50.0	48.8	37.8	46.8	43.2	45.7	43.8	49.6
3. Sometimes	35.1	30.9	38.7	32.6	44.6	37.4	33.1	36.8	32.2	32.8	39.5	34.7	35.5	34.5	35.3	21.5
4. Seldom	7.5	7.5	7.6	5.9	18.8	10.2	7.1	7.2	5.2	5.8	10.6	7.2	7.6	8.0	7.2	23.7
5. Never	1.2	1.5	0.9	0.8	3.7	1.5	1.1	1.6	0.5	0.7	1.7	1.2	1.3	0.6	1.6	1.5
Item 6360　Subject H04,K01　N	3137	1466	1577	2349	334	748	888	969	533	1891	1043	1317	622	441	660	35

A15: Do you feel that the people running the government are smart people who usually know what they are doing?

1. They almost always know what they are doing	15.5	19.7	11.4	15.9	15.1	14.1	14.5	17.2	15.9	14.4	17.4	16.1	14.1	15.3	16.1	15.4
2. They usually know what they are doing	57.4	54.8	59.9	59.9	41.6	55.8	58.8	54.4	62.5	62.6	47.8	58.6	58.5	57.7	55.0	38.9
3. They sometimes know what they are doing	22.8	21.3	24.4	20.4	35.8	25.2	21.3	24.4	19.0	19.2	29.8	21.6	21.7	22.2	25.4	33.7
4. They seldom know what they are doing	3.5	3.3	3.7	3.4	5.4	3.8	4.3	3.2	2.3	3.3	3.9	3.0	4.6	4.3	2.8	8.5
5. They never know what they are doing	0.8	1.0	0.6	0.5	2.1	1.0	1.0	0.7	0.4	0.5	1.1	0.7	1.1	0.5	0.5	3.5
Item 6370　Subject H04,K01　N	3137	1467	1577	2350	333	748	888	967	534	1892	1042	1315	622	443	659	35

A16: Would you say the government is pretty much run for a few big interests looking out for themselves, or is it run for the benefit of all the people?

1. Nearly always run for a few big interests	6.4	7.1	5.4	5.3	12.8	5.9	6.8	6.9	5.4	4.7	8.8	5.9	6.8	7.6	5.3	1.3
2. Usually run for a few big interests	18.3	20.7	16.2	17.2	20.0	17.0	18.6	17.9	20.2	17.1	20.5	19.3	16.7	16.5	17.3	39.6
3. Run some for the big interests, some for the people	49.0	43.8	53.8	48.5	48.8	51.4	47.8	49.7	46.6	48.6	50.0	48.1	48.2	52.0	51.3	50.2
4. Usually run for the benefit of all the people	21.4	22.1	21.0	23.8	13.5	19.5	21.9	21.6	22.6	24.6	15.9	21.8	23.8	19.4	20.1	6.5
5. Nearly always run for the benefit of all the people	4.9	6.3	3.7	5.2	4.8	6.2	4.8	3.9	5.1	5.0	4.7	4.9	4.5	4.5	5.9	2.5
Item 6380　Subject H04,K01　N	3129	1463	1575	2343	335	746	887	965	531	1887	1040	1312	621	443	656	35

A17: Have you ever done, or do you plan to do, the following things?

A17A: Vote in a public election

1. I probably won't do this	3.9	5.1	2.8	2.9	7.1	4.7	2.8	4.3	4.0	2.6	6.0	3.8	3.2	4.4	4.0	9.8
2. Don't know	8.3	6.5	9.8	6.4	12.9	9.7	6.7	8.3	8.9	5.3	13.2	8.5	7.2	7.5	7.6	23.5
3. I probably will do this	83.5	83.0	84.7	86.3	77.2	80.1	85.9	83.1	85.1	88.2	76.4	84.5	85.3	84.3	83.2	57.6
4. I have already done this	4.3	5.4	2.7	4.3	2.8	5.4	4.6	4.3	2.1	3.9	4.4	3.2	4.3	3.8	5.1	9.1
Item 6390　Subject H05,I02　N	3141	1468	1579	2353	333	749	889	968	534	1894	1044	1319	621	444	660	36

A17B: Write to public officials

1. I probably won't do this	22.9	21.3	24.6	21.2	25.8	23.1	23.4	23.9	20.5	18.3	31.8	21.2	22.4	20.5	27.6	43.7
2. Don't know	47.1	47.5	46.8	48.2	45.2	46.4	47.2	47.5	47.2	45.7	49.1	47.5	46.2	49.0	45.1	31.8
3. I probably will do this	19.1	20.2	17.7	18.9	19.8	19.8	18.6	17.9	21.2	23.1	11.7	19.3	20.8	21.6	16.4	13.3
4. I have already done this	10.9	11.0	10.9	11.7	9.2	10.8	10.9	10.8	11.1	13.0	7.4	12.0	10.6	8.8	10.9	11.3
Item 6400　Subject H05,I02　N	3136	1466	1578	2350	333	748	887	968	534	1893	1044	1316	620	444	660	36

A17C: Give money to a political candidate or cause

1. I probably won't do this	34.8	38.6	31.4	33.9	34.3	34.4	35.5	32.5	38.5	31.1	42.2	32.4	34.8	38.0	36.4	41.3
2. Don't know	42.3	39.7	44.7	42.8	40.1	43.3	39.7	44.2	41.5	42.8	40.3	46.0	40.8	37.1	39.7	38.3
3. I probably will do this	19.3	18.1	20.3	19.7	21.0	19.4	21.3	19.2	16.2	22.1	14.4	18.6	20.2	22.1	19.1	16.8
4. I have already done this	3.6	3.6	3.5	3.6	4.5	2.9	3.5	4.1	3.8	4.0	3.0	3.0	4.1	2.7	4.8	3.7
Item 6410　Subject H05,I02　N	3132	1465	1576	2349	332	746	888	964	534	1892	1043	1314	620	443	660	36

QUESTIONNAIRE FORM 2 1986	TOTAL	SEX		RACE		REGION				4YR COLLEGE PLANS		ILLICIT DRUG USE: LIFETIME				
		M	F	White	Black	NE	NC	S	W	Yes	No	None	Mari-juana Only	Few Pills	More Pills	Any Her-oin
N (Weighted No. of Cases):	3179	1481	1591	2367	338	756	902	980	541	1906	1054	1324	625	447	670	37
% of Weighted Total:	100.0	46.6	50.0	74.4	10.6	23.8	28.4	30.8	17.0	59.9	33.2	41.6	19.7	14.1	21.1	1.2
A17D: Work in a political campaign																
1. I probably won't do this	49.4	50.6	48.8	49.8	40.6	50.1	49.7	45.9	54.1	43.7	60.4	50.0	48.4	46.3	51.5	43.1
2. Don't know	36.7	38.2	35.1	36.5	42.0	37.8	34.0	40.2	33.3	39.2	30.9	35.5	38.6	38.6	35.6	43.6
3. I probably will do this	9.2	6.8	11.0	8.5	13.2	8.6	9.3	9.2	9.8	11.4	5.3	9.3	9.2	10.8	8.0	5.2
4. I have already done this	4.7	4.4	5.2	5.1	4.2	3.5	7.1	4.7	2.8	5.7	3.4	5.2	3.8	4.3	5.0	8.1
Item 6420 Subject H05,I02 N	3127	1462	1574	2346	331	746	884	963	533	1889	1041	1311	620	442	659	36
A17E: Participate in a lawful demonstration																
1. I probably won't do this	37.7	36.7	39.0	38.5	30.3	34.8	37.1	39.4	39.9	34.5	44.2	40.3	38.3	29.4	38.4	21.6
2. Don't know	45.4	45.0	45.5	44.7	51.9	45.5	45.4	47.8	41.2	45.6	44.4	44.5	44.8	52.9	42.8	39.6
3. I probably will do this	14.4	15.3	13.4	14.0	16.7	16.2	15.2	11.0	16.5	17.1	9.9	12.7	15.1	16.0	15.5	28.6
4. I have already done this	2.5	3.0	2.1	2.8	1.1	3.6	2.3	1.9	2.3	2.8	1.5	2.6	1.8	1.7	3.3	10.3
Item 6430 Subject H05,I02 N	3130	1463	1575	2348	332	747	885	964	534	1892	1042	1312	620	443	660	36
A17F: Boycott certain products or stores																
1. I probably won't do this	41.6	38.5	44.2	42.6	38.4	39.1	40.7	45.1	40.0	37.3	49.5	42.0	41.8	39.3	42.2	32.8
2. Don't know	41.9	43.7	40.2	41.3	44.3	41.3	41.7	42.0	42.6	44.1	38.0	41.9	42.7	43.7	39.4	42.4
3. I probably will do this	12.8	14.0	11.6	12.0	14.1	14.6	12.5	10.5	14.8	13.7	10.7	12.1	12.8	12.7	14.6	15.0
4. I have already done this	3.8	3.7	4.1	4.1	3.2	4.9	5.1	2.4	2.6	4.9	1.8	4.0	2.7	4.2	3.9	9.8
Item 6440 Subject H05,I02 N	3130	1464	1574	2348	332	746	885	966	534	1891	1041	1313	620	443	660	36
A18: How much do you agree or disagree with each of the following statements?																
A18A: The U.S. should begin a gradual program of disarming whether other countries do or not																
1. Disagree	39.8	53.7	26.6	42.6	31.2	35.3	39.0	47.6	33.0	39.7	39.4	39.3	38.1	38.5	42.7	39.9
2. Mostly disagree	18.0	16.7	19.4	18.1	15.5	17.1	19.4	16.6	19.4	19.0	16.9	18.5	17.8	19.0	16.7	9.9
3. Neither	18.6	12.9	23.9	17.2	21.8	20.5	18.8	15.6	21.0	17.3	20.5	18.8	19.2	19.2	16.4	28.6
4. Mostly agree	15.1	10.8	19.5	14.8	18.5	16.6	14.6	13.8	16.3	15.0	15.8	14.5	15.5	17.5	15.1	11.6
5. Agree	8.5	6.0	10.6	7.3	13.0	10.4	8.3	6.4	10.3	8.9	7.4	8.8	9.3	5.8	9.2	10.0
Item 6450 Subject H02,L03 N	3104	1461	1554	2331	329	733	886	957	529	1882	1030	1302	620	438	652	35
A18B: There may be times when the U.S. should go to war to protect the rights of other countries																
1. Disagree	19.2	16.6	21.4	17.7	27.9	22.2	18.6	20.1	14.1	17.3	23.0	19.3	18.3	18.0	20.0	32.1
2. Mostly disagree	21.8	18.1	25.1	20.9	21.9	21.0	21.9	20.5	24.9	20.7	22.9	22.1	23.6	21.3	20.7	11.9
3. Neither	18.7	17.1	19.9	19.3	16.0	19.3	19.3	16.4	21.1	19.2	17.9	18.3	18.0	20.5	19.4	15.9
4. Mostly agree	25.5	27.2	24.4	26.3	21.1	21.9	26.0	26.4	27.8	28.4	20.3	25.7	26.1	27.2	23.4	12.7
5. Agree	14.9	21.0	9.2	15.8	13.0	15.8	14.1	16.6	12.0	14.4	16.0	14.6	14.1	13.0	16.5	27.3
Item 5690 Subject H02,L03 N	3123	1466	1566	2341	335	744	885	963	531	1890	1037	1308	621	443	658	35
A18C: The U.S. should be willing to go to war to protect its own economic interests																
1. Disagree	9.6	8.0	10.9	8.9	9.8	12.5	8.6	8.4	9.4	9.5	9.3	9.0	8.8	9.3	11.4	15.9
2. Mostly disagree	15.3	12.3	18.0	15.8	13.0	16.3	16.3	12.7	16.8	16.6	12.9	17.0	16.3	13.1	13.3	12.0
3. Neither	20.5	18.1	23.3	20.8	15.8	20.9	22.4	16.9	23.6	20.3	21.5	21.7	20.4	21.9	18.4	12.8
4. Mostly agree	31.0	32.1	30.1	32.1	28.7	25.0	31.3	34.2	33.2	31.1	31.9	30.9	31.6	33.0	30.1	32.0
5. Agree	23.6	29.5	17.6	22.5	32.6	25.3	21.4	27.8	17.0	22.4	24.5	21.4	22.8	22.6	26.8	27.3
Item 6460 Subject H02,L03 N	3115	1464	1561	2337	331	738	883	963	531	1884	1035	1305	621	439	657	35
A18D: The only good reason for the U.S. to go to war is to defend against an attack on our own country																
1. Disagree	8.5	11.6	5.6	8.8	6.8	9.0	7.7	9.3	7.9	8.5	7.9	9.2	7.8	8.2	6.9	8.8
2. Mostly disagree	12.0	15.1	9.3	12.1	10.8	9.9	13.1	12.7	11.9	13.8	8.8	12.2	13.0	13.3	11.1	6.7
3. Neither	9.1	8.8	9.7	9.8	4.3	10.7	9.9	7.8	7.7	8.9	9.5	9.5	10.1	8.4	8.6	-
4. Mostly agree	32.5	29.4	35.6	32.9	35.8	32.9	31.1	33.2	32.9	34.0	30.5	30.6	36.8	32.4	33.9	16.5
5. Agree	37.9	35.1	39.9	36.3	42.3	37.4	38.2	37.0	39.6	34.8	43.3	38.4	32.2	37.7	39.4	68.0
Item 6470 Subject H02,L03 N	3117	1464	1562	2334	334	740	886	960	531	1889	1034	1308	622	441	656	33

QUESTIONNAIRE FORM 2 1986	TOTAL	SEX		RACE		REGION				4YR COLLEGE PLANS		ILLICIT DRUG USE: LIFETIME				
		M	F	White	Black	NE	NC	S	W	Yes	No	None	Mari-juana Only	Few Pills	More Pills	Any Her-oin
N (Weighted No. of Cases):	3179	1481	1591	2367	338	756	902	980	541	1906	1054	1324	625	447	670	37
% of Weighted Total:	100.0	46.6	50.0	74.4	10.6	23.8	28.4	30.8	17.0	59.9	33.2	41.6	19.7	14.1	21.1	1.2
A18E: The U.S. does not need to have greater military power than the Soviet Union																
1. Disagree	34.8	39.4	30.1	33.7	44.5	31.4	33.8	44.0	24.8	31.5	39.0	32.8	38.3	32.6	36.2	36.4
2. Mostly disagree	21.0	20.0	22.3	21.2	21.0	20.0	19.2	22.1	23.5	21.1	21.4	19.9	20.0	22.5	23.8	15.8
3. Neither	17.9	14.9	21.1	18.2	16.0	18.5	17.0	15.4	23.5	18.5	17.5	19.2	16.8	17.4	17.1	16.4
4. Mostly agree	14.5	14.4	14.7	14.9	12.8	15.2	17.0	11.1	15.4	16.3	12.2	16.9	13.4	13.7	11.3	19.4
5. Agree	11.7	11.3	11.9	12.0	5.7	15.0	13.0	7.4	12.9	12.6	9.8	11.2	11.5	13.8	11.6	12.0
Item 6480 Subject H02,L03 N	3108	1461	1557	2334	329	738	882	960	527	1880	1036	1304	618	441	653	35
A18F: The U.S. ought to have much more military power than any other nation in the world																
1. Disagree	17.2	15.6	18.9	17.5	13.2	22.4	17.5	14.3	14.8	18.8	14.5	17.1	15.6	19.5	17.0	16.1
2. Mostly disagree	18.7	17.7	19.7	20.3	13.3	19.0	19.5	15.4	22.9	21.5	14.2	22.6	17.4	16.4	14.8	9.2
3. Neither	25.9	22.8	29.0	25.9	23.4	26.3	25.9	23.7	29.5	25.3	27.8	26.0	27.2	25.8	25.5	31.6
4. Mostly agree	18.6	19.6	17.6	18.3	21.1	16.1	18.5	20.5	18.7	17.5	20.5	15.9	20.6	17.1	22.6	16.4
5. Agree	19.6	24.3	14.7	18.1	29.0	16.2	18.6	26.1	14.1	16.9	22.9	18.3	19.2	21.2	20.1	26.6
Item 6490 Subject H02,L03 N	3114	1464	1560	2335	333	739	885	960	530	1886	1035	1306	621	440	655	35
A18G: Our present foreign policy is based on our own narrow economic and power interests																
1. Disagree	6.2	8.3	4.4	6.3	7.4	6.0	6.3	7.8	3.7	6.5	5.9	5.7	5.1	7.4	7.3	17.2
2. Mostly disagree	11.1	13.8	8.9	11.9	8.7	9.7	11.4	13.0	9.2	11.7	10.5	11.4	11.1	11.1	9.6	24.2
3. Neither	45.1	37.5	52.2	46.1	35.9	45.2	46.9	40.9	49.4	44.8	45.9	44.3	46.3	47.6	44.9	33.3
4. Mostly agree	24.8	26.5	23.1	25.1	24.4	25.0	24.4	25.4	23.8	24.9	24.3	25.9	23.7	24.1	24.3	18.4
5. Agree	12.8	14.0	11.4	10.7	23.6	14.1	11.0	12.9	13.8	12.0	13.4	12.7	13.8	9.9	13.9	6.8
Item 6500 Subject H02,L03 N	3072	1454	1532	2311	324	720	877	949	526	1856	1026	1289	612	434	651	33
A18H: Servicemen should obey orders without question																
1. Disagree	13.5	12.3	14.1	11.3	21.8	14.2	13.8	13.6	11.6	12.7	14.5	12.5	12.4	13.2	15.1	20.1
2. Mostly disagree	18.9	14.3	23.5	18.4	20.3	19.6	19.3	17.5	19.5	20.5	16.4	19.0	18.5	21.5	18.3	11.8
3. Neither	22.2	18.8	25.4	22.3	16.8	26.5	21.0	17.5	26.6	23.1	20.2	22.4	24.4	20.0	21.2	20.8
4. Mostly agree	28.6	31.5	26.5	30.6	25.5	23.8	28.5	33.3	27.3	28.8	29.1	30.4	28.1	29.3	27.2	16.8
5. Agree	16.8	23.1	10.5	17.4	15.6	15.9	17.4	18.0	15.0	14.9	19.8	15.7	16.5	16.0	18.3	30.5
Item 6510 Subject L03 N	3109	1465	1556	2334	333	737	884	960	528	1883	1033	1306	621	438	655	35
A19: This section deals with activities which may be against the rules or against the law. We hope you will answer all of these questions. However, if you find a question which you cannot answer honestly, we would prefer that you leave it blank. Remember, your answers will never be connected with your name. During the LAST 12 MONTHS, how often have you...																
A19A: Argued or had a fight with either of your parents																
1. Not at all	11.1	13.0	8.9	7.1	30.4	9.1	9.8	15.7	7.9	9.4	13.1	15.7	10.4	8.7	4.3	5.3
2. Once	8.7	10.4	7.1	7.1	17.1	8.5	6.9	10.5	9.2	8.4	8.6	10.5	7.9	6.7	5.7	3.4
3. Twice	11.6	12.8	10.4	10.9	15.3	14.9	10.7	9.2	12.7	11.1	12.4	13.1	9.5	10.8	11.3	1.8
4. 3 or 4 times	24.2	24.5	24.0	25.6	17.2	24.7	25.6	22.4	24.9	25.5	23.1	23.8	27.1	27.3	21.5	22.8
5. 5 or more times	44.3	39.2	49.6	49.3	19.9	42.9	47.1	42.3	45.4	45.6	42.8	36.9	45.1	46.5	57.2	66.7
Item 6520 Subject M03,S01 N	3134	1467	1577	2345	336	737	894	967	536	1895	1040	1318	622	443	664	36
A19B: Hit an instructor or supervisor																
1. Not at all	96.9	95.5	98.3	97.3	97.1	95.6	97.6	97.2	96.9	97.6	95.9	98.3	97.6	96.8	95.0	74.4
2. Once	1.9	2.7	1.3	1.7	2.4	3.1	1.2	1.8	1.8	1.5	2.7	0.9	1.4	2.9	3.2	13.7
3. Twice	0.6	1.0	*	0.6	-	0.8	0.9	0.3	0.3	0.6	0.6	0.5	0.4	-	1.0	5.0
4. 3 or 4 times	0.4	0.4	0.3	0.2	0.3	0.3	0.2	0.5	0.5	0.1	0.8	0.3	0.1	0.3	0.5	4.1
5. 5 or more times	0.2	0.4	0.1	0.2	0.2	0.2	0.1	0.2	0.5	0.2	-	0.1	0.5	-	0.2	2.9
Item 6530 Subject M02,S01 N	3140	1471	1580	2351	336	743	894	967	536	1902	1041	1318	624	445	665	36

*=less than .05 per cent.

QUESTIONNAIRE FORM 2 1986	TOTAL	SEX		RACE		REGION				4YR COLLEGE PLANS		ILLICIT DRUG USE: LIFETIME				
		M	F	White	Black	NE	NC	S	W	Yes	No	None	Mari-juana Only	Few Pills	More Pills	Any Her-oin
N (Weighted No. of Cases):	3179	1481	1591	2367	338	756	902	980	541	1906	1054	1324	625	447	670	37
% of Weighted Total:	100.0	46.6	50.0	74.4	10.6	23.8	28.4	30.8	17.0	59.9	33.2	41.6	19.7	14.1	21.1	1.2

A19C: Gotten into a serious fight in school or at work

1. Not at all	82.8	79.5	86.6	83.3	83.1	81.4	84.0	84.0	80.8	86.2	77.9	89.1	82.1	79.1	76.4	41.2
2. Once	11.3	12.6	9.4	10.9	10.3	12.7	9.6	10.9	13.0	9.8	13.3	7.1	11.6	15.2	14.5	42.8
3. Twice	3.4	4.6	2.2	3.7	2.9	4.3	3.5	3.0	2.6	2.1	5.2	2.0	4.0	3.6	5.1	5.4
4. 3 or 4 times	1.7	2.1	1.4	1.5	2.2	1.2	2.2	1.5	1.8	1.4	2.3	1.3	1.2	1.7	2.7	7.8
5. 5 or more times	0.9	1.2	0.4	0.6	1.5	0.4	0.8	0.7	1.9	0.5	1.4	0.5	1.1	0.5	1.4	2.8
Item 6540 Subject B07,C01,S01 N	3138	1470	1581	2350	337	742	891	968	537	1901	1039	1318	624	447	663	36

A19D: Taken part in a fight where a group of your friends were against another group

1. Not at all	80.5	76.5	84.6	81.3	82.1	79.3	82.4	80.8	78.7	84.4	73.8	87.7	81.9	78.5	70.0	37.1
2. Once	11.3	12.4	10.2	11.3	10.4	10.0	11.1	12.6	11.3	9.4	15.0	7.7	11.7	13.1	16.2	21.5
3. Twice	4.4	6.1	2.7	3.8	4.3	5.2	4.1	3.7	5.2	3.6	5.9	2.5	4.1	4.7	7.3	19.5
4. 3 or 4 times	2.4	3.2	1.7	2.4	2.3	3.6	1.6	2.0	2.9	1.9	3.0	1.8	1.4	2.8	3.9	1.3
5. 5 or more times	1.3	1.7	0.8	1.1	0.9	1.9	0.9	0.8	1.9	0.7	2.3	0.3	0.9	0.9	2.5	20.6
Item 6550 Subject S01 N	3141	1475	1579	2352	337	745	891	968	537	1900	1044	1323	622	447	665	36

A19E: Hurt someone badly enough to need bandages or a doctor

1. Not at all	88.9	81.0	97.0	89.8	88.8	88.5	88.3	90.0	88.7	92.2	84.0	93.5	91.0	87.9	82.5	52.9
2. Once	7.0	11.7	2.2	6.4	8.4	7.0	6.3	7.0	8.0	5.0	10.2	4.1	5.5	9.0	10.9	27.7
3. Twice	2.3	4.3	0.4	2.2	1.5	2.0	4.0	1.7	1.1	1.6	3.7	1.5	1.7	1.8	4.1	3.6
4. 3 or 4 times	0.9	1.5	0.4	0.9	0.9	1.3	0.8	0.7	1.1	0.7	1.2	0.8	0.6	0.6	1.3	12.0
5. 5 or more times	0.8	1.5	0.1	0.7	0.4	1.2	0.5	0.7	1.1	0.6	0.9	0.1	1.2	0.8	1.3	3.7
Item 6560 Subject S01 N	3140	1473	1580	2353	337	744	891	968	537	1900	1044	1323	622	446	665	36

A19F: Used a knife or gun or some other thing (like a club) to get something from a person

1. Not at all	96.6	95.1	98.5	96.9	96.5	96.1	96.6	97.3	96.0	97.8	95.2	98.8	97.7	96.1	93.4	72.4
2. Once	1.8	2.8	0.8	1.8	2.2	1.1	2.2	1.8	2.1	1.3	2.8	0.4	1.2	3.1	3.5	16.4
3. Twice	0.6	0.8	0.3	0.5	0.3	0.8	0.8	0.3	0.6	0.5	0.7	0.3	0.6	-	1.6	2.5
4. 3 or 4 times	0.6	0.9	0.2	0.5	0.8	1.6	0.3	0.3	0.4	0.4	0.6	0.2	0.3	0.4	1.0	7.4
5. 5 or more times	0.4	0.5	0.1	0.3	0.2	0.4	0.1	0.4	0.9	-	0.7	0.2	0.2	0.5	0.5	1.3
Item 6570 Subject S01 N	3142	1474	1581	2352	337	745	892	968	537	1901	1044	1323	622	447	665	36

A19G: Taken something not belonging to you worth under $50

1. Not at all	68.0	62.3	72.8	65.2	83.6	69.2	65.5	72.1	62.9	68.2	66.9	79.8	65.7	62.7	50.0	58.7
2. Once	16.2	18.5	14.4	17.5	8.0	15.5	15.6	15.9	18.7	16.3	16.8	11.6	17.3	19.1	22.8	13.2
3. Twice	6.9	7.2	6.7	7.7	4.3	7.0	9.0	4.0	8.4	7.2	6.1	3.8	8.1	8.7	10.9	7.8
4. 3 or 4 times	4.5	5.0	4.0	5.0	1.3	3.8	5.4	3.9	5.1	4.5	4.7	2.8	4.2	4.7	8.1	9.1
5. 5 or more times	4.4	6.9	2.2	4.6	2.8	4.6	4.5	4.0	4.9	3.9	5.4	1.9	4.7	4.8	8.2	11.2
Item 6580 Subject S01 N	3126	1464	1576	2341	335	741	888	962	535	1891	1038	1319	617	444	661	36

A19H: Taken something not belonging to you worth over $50

1. Not at all	93.4	90.6	96.0	93.7	95.0	92.8	93.6	94.5	91.7	94.6	91.6	98.1	92.6	92.0	86.6	79.8
2. Once	3.5	4.6	2.5	3.2	2.7	3.9	3.2	2.6	4.7	3.4	3.5	1.2	4.5	3.3	7.1	4.8
3. Twice	1.2	1.9	0.7	1.2	1.2	1.2	1.3	1.1	1.5	0.8	1.9	0.4	0.9	2.1	2.8	1.5
4. 3 or 4 times	1.0	1.7	0.2	0.8	0.9	1.2	0.9	1.0	0.8	0.7	1.3	0.1	1.0	1.0	1.8	9.9
5. 5 or more times	0.9	1.3	0.6	1.1	0.2	0.8	0.9	0.8	1.3	0.5	1.6	0.2	0.9	1.6	1.6	4.1
Item 6590 Subject S01 N	3131	1467	1578	2347	334	743	891	962	534	1893	1042	1321	621	444	661	36

A19I: Taken something from a store without paying for it

1. Not at all	72.1	67.2	76.8	71.2	80.8	70.6	71.7	76.9	66.1	74.2	67.6	85.7	67.6	67.3	55.0	39.8
2. Once	12.8	13.5	12.0	12.7	10.6	14.6	11.5	11.0	15.9	12.4	14.1	6.9	16.2	17.0	18.4	14.9
3. Twice	6.1	7.5	4.6	6.6	3.6	7.2	7.6	3.9	6.1	5.7	6.6	3.6	7.5	5.7	8.5	21.8
4. 3 or 4 times	4.4	4.9	4.0	4.7	2.9	4.1	5.1	3.2	6.0	4.4	4.5	2.3	4.1	5.0	8.4	6.7
5. 5 or more times	4.5	6.9	2.6	4.7	2.2	3.5	4.2	5.0	5.9	3.3	7.1	1.5	4.7	5.0	9.6	16.8
Item 6600 Subject S01 N	3130	1470	1574	2343	336	741	890	965	534	1893	1041	1315	622	446	662	36

MONITORING THE FUTURE

QUESTIONNAIRE FORM 2 1986	TOTAL	SEX		RACE		REGION				4YR COLLEGE PLANS		ILLICIT DRUG USE: LIFETIME				
		M	F	White	Black	NE	NC	S	W	Yes	No	None	Mari-juana Only	Few Pills	More Pills	Any Her-oin
N (Weighted No. of Cases):	3179	1481	1591	2367	338	756	902	980	541	1906	1054	1324	625	447	670	37
% of Weighted Total:	100.0	46.6	50.0	74.4	10.6	23.8	28.4	30.8	17.0	59.9	33.2	41.6	19.7	14.1	21.1	1.2

A19J: Taken a car that didn't belong to someone in your family without permission of the owner

	TOTAL	M	F	White	Black	NE	NC	S	W	Yes	No	None	Mari-juana Only	Few Pills	More Pills	Any Her-oin
1. Not at all	94.9	93.3	96.6	95.0	96.1	94.5	95.2	95.6	93.7	96.3	92.8	97.0	94.4	94.8	92.5	78.1
2. Once	3.1	4.1	2.1	3.2	2.3	3.5	3.1	2.6	3.6	2.3	4.7	2.1	3.8	2.6	4.3	11.4
3. Twice	1.1	1.2	1.0	1.0	1.2	1.1	1.2	0.7	1.6	0.9	1.2	0.7	0.9	1.8	1.3	6.5
4. 3 or 4 times	0.4	0.7	0.2	0.4	-	0.1	0.4	0.8	0.2	0.4	0.6	-	0.7	0.8	0.6	2.4
5. 5 or more times	0.4	0.7	0.1	0.4	0.4	0.8	*	0.3	0.9	0.1	0.7	0.2	0.2	-	1.3	1.6
Item 6610 Subject S01 N	3134	1469	1579	2348	336	743	891	964	536	1900	1041	1320	624	446	664	36

A19K: Taken part of a car without permission of the owner

	TOTAL	M	F	White	Black	NE	NC	S	W	Yes	No	None	Mari-juana Only	Few Pills	More Pills	Any Her-oin
1. Not at all	94.4	90.6	98.0	94.2	98.0	93.7	95.1	95.7	91.9	95.9	91.6	97.5	94.4	93.5	90.6	60.1
2. Once	3.2	5.2	1.3	3.3	0.8	3.2	2.9	2.2	5.1	2.6	4.7	1.7	3.2	4.2	4.5	18.2
3. Twice	1.2	2.2	0.3	1.3	0.7	1.1	1.3	1.5	0.9	1.0	1.8	0.4	1.5	1.3	2.4	3.2
4. 3 or 4 times	0.6	0.9	0.4	0.5	0.1	0.8	0.7	0.2	0.9	0.3	1.1	0.1	0.4	0.8	1.1	9.3
5. 5 or more times	0.6	1.1	0.1	0.6	0.4	1.3	-	0.4	1.2	0.2	0.9	0.3	0.4	0.1	1.3	9.2
Item 6620 Subject S01 N	3128	1464	1578	2344	335	742	889	962	534	1897	1042	1322	621	446	660	36

A19L: Gone into some house or building when you weren't supposed to be there

	TOTAL	M	F	White	Black	NE	NC	S	W	Yes	No	None	Mari-juana Only	Few Pills	More Pills	Any Her-oin
1. Not at all	75.5	70.6	80.1	74.2	82.6	75.0	72.9	79.1	74.0	76.2	74.6	84.2	72.7	67.6	67.0	53.4
2. Once	12.1	12.2	11.8	13.0	7.3	10.0	13.1	11.5	14.0	12.1	12.1	8.8	13.9	16.9	14.4	9.8
3. Twice	6.3	8.4	4.4	6.5	5.5	8.3	7.5	3.8	6.3	6.2	6.3	4.1	6.3	7.5	9.6	12.2
4. 3 or 4 times	3.1	4.3	1.9	3.3	1.7	2.7	4.3	2.3	3.2	2.7	3.6	1.5	3.4	4.8	4.2	11.9
5. 5 or more times	3.0	4.4	1.8	3.0	2.9	4.1	2.2	3.2	2.5	2.8	3.4	1.4	3.7	3.3	4.9	12.8
Item 6630 Subject S01 N	3123	1463	1576	2339	337	740	890	958	535	1891	1042	1315	622	443	664	36

A19M: Set fire to someone's property on purpose

	TOTAL	M	F	White	Black	NE	NC	S	W	Yes	No	None	Mari-juana Only	Few Pills	More Pills	Any Her-oin
1. Not at all	98.0	96.7	99.4	98.4	96.2	96.3	99.0	98.8	97.3	98.6	97.6	99.2	97.9	99.2	96.2	84.4
2. Once	1.1	1.9	0.2	0.9	2.4	2.4	0.7	0.6	0.7	0.8	1.2	0.5	1.0	0.5	2.1	6.5
3. Twice	0.3	0.3	0.2	0.1	1.1	0.2	0.2	0.4	0.5	0.2	0.4	0.2	0.5	0.1	0.3	0.9
4. 3 or 4 times	0.3	0.4	0.1	0.2	0.1	0.1	-	*	1.3	*	0.4	-	0.2	0.3	0.8	-
5. 5 or more times	0.4	0.7	0.1	0.3	0.1	1.0	0.1	0.2	0.3	0.3	0.4	0.1	0.3	-	0.6	8.3
Item 6640 Subject S01 N	3130	1465	1580	2344	335	742	892	960	536	1895	1043	1322	618	447	664	36

A19N: Damaged school property on purpose

	TOTAL	M	F	White	Black	NE	NC	S	W	Yes	No	None	Mari-juana Only	Few Pills	More Pills	Any Her-oin
1. Not at all	86.8	81.3	92.4	86.7	90.2	83.9	87.9	87.7	87.4	88.3	84.0	93.4	85.7	82.9	78.6	73.5
2. Once	6.8	9.0	4.8	6.8	5.4	7.7	6.4	6.4	7.2	6.8	7.4	3.5	7.9	9.8	10.7	6.0
3. Twice	3.0	4.6	1.6	3.2	3.0	3.8	2.6	3.3	2.2	2.4	4.3	1.7	3.2	5.6	4.0	1.0
4. 3 or 4 times	1.9	3.2	0.7	2.0	0.6	2.1	2.0	1.8	1.8	1.8	2.0	0.9	1.9	0.9	3.7	13.7
5. 5 or more times	1.4	1.9	0.6	1.2	0.7	2.4	1.0	0.9	1.4	0.7	2.3	0.5	1.3	0.9	2.9	5.7
Item 6650 Subject B07,S01 N	3121	1462	1575	2337	336	739	889	959	533	1892	1040	1316	621	442	661	36

A19O: Damaged property at work on purpose

	TOTAL	M	F	White	Black	NE	NC	S	W	Yes	No	None	Mari-juana Only	Few Pills	More Pills	Any Her-oin
1. Not at all	94.8	91.0	98.3	94.7	95.9	93.1	95.1	95.8	94.6	95.0	94.4	97.4	94.9	93.1	91.2	85.4
2. Once	2.7	4.2	1.2	2.6	1.9	4.4	2.3	1.4	3.1	2.2	3.6	1.6	2.2	3.7	4.4	3.4
3. Twice	1.2	2.2	0.3	1.4	0.6	0.8	1.6	1.3	0.9	1.1	1.4	0.4	1.2	1.7	2.2	5.6
4. 3 or 4 times	0.8	1.5	0.1	0.8	0.8	1.0	0.8	0.6	0.9	1.0	0.4	0.4	1.3	0.5	1.1	3.3
5. 5 or more times	0.6	1.1	*	0.5	0.7	0.7	0.2	0.8	0.5	0.7	0.3	0.2	0.3	1.0	1.0	2.3
Item 6660 Subject C01,S01 N	3130	1466	1579	2346	336	743	891	961	535	1897	1042	1323	623	444	661	36

A19P: Gotten into trouble with police because of something you did

	TOTAL	M	F	White	Black	NE	NC	S	W	Yes	No	None	Mari-juana Only	Few Pills	More Pills	Any Her-oin
1. Not at all	78.6	69.5	86.9	77.4	89.9	79.4	73.1	85.1	74.8	80.6	76.0	89.8	75.6	76.2	62.0	55.5
2. Once	13.2	16.8	10.1	13.9	7.0	12.4	16.3	9.0	16.6	13.0	13.4	7.2	15.9	15.6	21.1	17.4
3. Twice	5.1	8.0	2.2	5.3	1.6	4.6	6.3	3.9	5.5	4.4	5.4	2.3	5.9	6.0	8.8	7.3
4. 3 or 4 times	2.1	3.7	0.6	2.1	1.1	2.0	3.3	1.3	1.6	1.7	2.7	0.5	1.5	2.0	5.2	7.4
5. 5 or more times	1.2	2.1	0.2	1.2	0.3	1.7	1.0	0.7	1.5	0.3	2.5	0.2	1.0	0.1	2.9	12.3
Item 6670 Subject S01 N	3131	1467	1580	2346	336	740	892	962	536	1899	1042	1321	623	446	662	36

*=less than .05 per cent.

QUESTIONNAIRE FORM 2 1986	TOTAL	SEX		RACE		REGION				4YR COLLEGE PLANS		ILLICIT DRUG USE: LIFETIME				
		M	F	White	Black	NE	NC	S	W	Yes	No	None	Mari- juana Only	Few Pills	More Pills	Any Her- oin
N (Weighted No. of Cases):	3179	1481	1591	2367	338	756	902	980	541	1906	1054	1324	625	447	670	37
% of Weighted Total:	100.0	46.6	50.0	74.4	10.6	23.8	28.4	30.8	17.0	59.9	33.2	41.6	19.7	14.1	21.1	1.2

A20: The next questions are about some things which may have happened TO YOU. During the LAST 12 MONTHS, how often...

A20A: Has something of yours (worth under $50) been stolen?

	TOTAL	M	F	White	Black	NE	NC	S	W	Yes	No	None	Mar.J	Few	More	Her
1. Not at all	52.7	47.7	57.4	53.0	53.8	53.4	53.7	53.2	49.3	50.3	58.4	57.9	50.8	49.7	45.8	61.9
2. Once	28.6	29.8	27.7	28.2	27.8	28.0	29.3	27.3	30.7	29.6	26.4	28.1	30.3	27.8	29.1	17.3
3. Twice	11.2	12.3	9.8	11.1	10.7	12.6	10.3	10.5	12.0	12.5	8.4	7.5	11.8	14.5	15.4	11.9
4. 3 or 4 times	5.4	7.1	3.8	5.5	5.2	3.7	5.1	6.8	5.6	5.7	4.7	4.5	5.7	5.8	6.6	7.4
5. 5 or more times	2.1	3.1	1.3	2.1	2.5	2.4	1.7	2.3	2.4	2.0	2.1	2.0	1.3	2.3	3.2	1.4
Item 6680 Subject S03 N	3124	1464	1574	2342	335	741	890	961	532	1896	1036	1316	623	440	664	36

A20B: Has something of yours (worth over $50) been stolen?

	TOTAL	M	F	White	Black	NE	NC	S	W	Yes	No	None	Mar.J	Few	More	Her
1. Not at all	82.5	77.9	86.9	84.2	79.8	82.8	82.6	82.5	82.0	82.4	83.6	86.1	82.4	80.2	78.2	80.8
2. Once	13.5	16.8	10.5	12.6	15.2	13.4	13.6	13.3	13.7	14.1	12.4	11.4	13.7	17.1	14.3	17.9
3. Twice	2.6	3.5	1.8	2.3	2.3	2.8	2.3	3.0	2.4	2.4	2.7	1.9	2.3	1.0	5.7	-
4. 3 or 4 times	1.0	1.3	0.7	0.7	1.7	0.4	1.2	1.1	1.6	0.9	1.2	0.4	1.3	1.5	1.5	-
5. 5 or more times	0.3	0.5	0.1	0.2	0.9	0.6	0.2	0.1	0.3	0.3	0.1	0.2	0.3	0.2	0.3	1.3
Item 6690 Subject S03 N	3123	1462	1577	2342	335	741	888	961	534	1897	1036	1316	622	443	664	36

A20C: Has someone deliberately damaged your property (your car, clothing, etc.)?

	TOTAL	M	F	White	Black	NE	NC	S	W	Yes	No	None	Mar.J	Few	More	Her
1. Not at all	67.9	61.1	74.0	67.8	72.6	70.8	67.1	69.0	63.2	69.6	65.3	72.4	70.8	64.4	60.5	59.9
2. Once	21.7	25.2	18.5	22.1	18.5	18.9	23.3	20.1	25.5	19.9	24.5	19.9	19.6	24.1	24.4	20.5
3. Twice	7.0	8.8	5.5	7.3	5.5	6.6	7.0	6.8	8.0	7.5	6.4	5.4	5.8	8.4	10.2	7.0
4. 3 or 4 times	2.5	3.8	1.3	2.3	2.2	2.6	1.8	2.9	2.7	2.2	2.9	1.6	2.7	2.3	3.9	9.9
5. 5 or more times	0.9	1.0	0.7	0.6	1.2	1.0	0.8	1.1	0.7	0.7	0.9	0.7	1.1	0.8	0.9	2.7
Item 6700 Subject S03 N	3122	1463	1575	2340	335	740	890	959	533	1896	1036	1316	623	442	663	36

A20D: Has someone injured you with a weapon (like a knife, gun, or club)?

	TOTAL	M	F	White	Black	NE	NC	S	W	Yes	No	None	Mar.J	Few	More	Her
1. Not at all	95.3	93.3	97.4	96.1	94.8	94.1	95.5	97.0	93.4	96.4	94.5	97.1	95.6	95.6	93.1	71.2
2. Once	3.3	4.6	1.9	2.6	4.1	3.8	3.3	2.0	5.0	2.4	4.0	2.1	3.6	3.3	4.5	14.2
3. Twice	0.9	1.2	0.6	0.9	0.8	1.4	0.9	0.5	0.8	0.8	0.7	0.5	0.7	0.4	1.6	10.1
4. 3 or 4 times	0.3	0.5	0.1	0.2	0.4	0.3	0.2	0.3	0.6	0.2	0.4	0.3	-	0.1	0.6	2.7
5. 5 or more times	0.2	0.4	*	0.2	-	0.4	0.1	0.2	0.3	0.1	0.4	-	0.1	0.5	0.2	1.8
Item 6710 Subject S03 N	3126	1465	1577	2342	336	741	891	959	535	1898	1038	1318	623	444	663	36

A20E: Has someone threatened you with a weapon, but not actually injured you?

	TOTAL	M	F	White	Black	NE	NC	S	W	Yes	No	None	Mar.J	Few	More	Her
1. Not at all	84.2	79.4	89.2	85.8	78.4	83.2	86.2	83.7	83.1	87.6	79.6	90.1	82.8	81.2	78.2	56.6
2. Once	10.4	12.6	8.1	9.8	12.9	10.4	9.5	10.6	11.9	8.5	13.0	6.9	11.7	13.1	14.3	11.0
3. Twice	3.3	4.9	1.6	2.8	4.8	3.7	2.9	3.9	2.3	2.5	4.0	2.1	3.3	3.7	4.4	13.7
4. 3 or 4 times	1.1	1.7	0.4	0.7	2.1	1.0	0.8	1.0	1.8	0.9	1.3	0.5	1.5	1.2	1.5	2.5
5. 5 or more times	1.0	1.4	0.7	0.9	1.7	1.8	0.6	0.9	0.9	0.5	2.1	0.4	0.7	0.8	1.6	16.1
Item 6720 Subject S03 N	3124	1462	1578	2342	335	738	891	960	535	1899	1036	1316	623	443	664	36

A20F: Has someone injured you on purpose without using a weapon?

	TOTAL	M	F	White	Black	NE	NC	S	W	Yes	No	None	Mar.J	Few	More	Her
1. Not at all	84.4	83.8	85.4	83.9	88.7	82.9	82.3	87.7	84.3	86.4	81.9	89.6	87.0	82.8	74.3	62.4
2. Once	10.1	10.4	9.5	10.7	8.3	10.6	11.9	8.3	9.4	9.4	11.2	7.5	9.6	11.3	14.8	11.0
3. Twice	2.9	3.2	2.5	3.1	1.5	3.0	3.1	2.3	3.2	2.7	2.8	1.8	1.9	3.7	5.2	6.0
4. 3 or 4 times	1.6	1.3	1.6	1.3	1.3	2.7	1.5	1.0	1.1	0.9	2.4	0.8	0.7	0.8	3.3	11.5
5. 5 or more times	1.1	1.3	0.9	1.0	0.3	0.7	1.2	0.7	2.0	0.7	1.8	0.3	0.6	1.4	2.4	9.1
Item 6730 Subject S03 N	3125	1464	1577	2343	334	740	891	959	535	1899	1036	1319	622	442	664	36

*=less than .05 per cent.

QUESTIONNAIRE FORM 2 1986	TOTAL	SEX		RACE		REGION				4YR COLLEGE PLANS		ILLICIT DRUG USE: LIFETIME				
		M	F	White	Black	NE	NC	S	W	Yes	No	None	Marijuana Only	Few Pills	More Pills	Any Heroin
N (Weighted No. of Cases):	3179	1481	1591	2367	338	756	902	980	541	1906	1054	1324	625	447	670	37
% of Weighted Total:	100.0	46.6	50.0	74.4	10.6	23.8	28.4	30.8	17.0	59.9	33.2	41.6	19.7	14.1	21.1	1.2

A20G: Has an unarmed person threatened you with injury, but not actually injured you?

	TOTAL	M	F	White	Black	NE	NC	S	W	Yes	No	None	Mari. Only	Few Pills	More Pills	Any Heroin
1. Not at all	71.7	65.6	77.8	71.3	72.4	73.0	71.4	71.7	70.5	73.6	68.8	80.1	70.3	64.3	62.5	48.3
2. Once	15.2	16.9	13.3	15.4	15.2	15.5	15.1	14.1	17.0	14.3	16.8	11.6	16.3	19.2	18.9	14.6
3. Twice	5.8	7.4	4.4	5.9	5.1	5.5	5.0	7.2	5.3	6.0	5.8	3.4	6.1	9.4	7.9	13.1
4. 3 or 4 times	4.0	5.3	2.6	4.1	3.7	2.1	4.7	4.9	3.7	3.5	4.7	3.0	4.8	4.3	5.0	7.6
5. 5 or more times	3.3	4.8	1.8	3.3	3.7	3.9	3.8	2.2	3.5	2.6	3.9	2.0	2.5	2.7	5.7	16.4
Item 6740 Subject S03 N	3126	1464	1579	2343	336	741	890	960	534	1899	1038	1318	623	444	663	36

A21: The following questions concern cigarettes, alcohol, and a number of other drugs. How difficult do you think it would be for you to get each of the following types of drugs, if you wanted some?

A21A: Marijuana (pot, grass)

	TOTAL	M	F	White	Black	NE	NC	S	W	Yes	No	None	Mari. Only	Few Pills	More Pills	Any Heroin
1. Probably impossible	5.8	4.5	6.7	3.5	14.7	5.7	5.0	7.3	4.5	4.9	6.8	11.3	0.8	2.6	0.7	4.1
2. Very difficult	3.2	3.2	3.0	2.3	5.7	2.2	3.7	3.7	2.5	2.9	3.3	5.8	2.1	1.7	0.2	-
3. Fairly difficult	5.8	5.4	6.2	5.7	3.6	5.7	6.3	5.4	6.2	6.0	5.7	9.5	4.6	2.8	2.3	-
4. Fairly easy	30.4	30.3	30.9	31.8	22.8	28.1	31.2	32.4	28.5	32.3	26.6	36.1	30.8	29.7	19.8	12.8
5. Very easy	54.8	56.7	53.3	56.8	53.3	58.2	53.9	51.2	58.3	53.8	57.6	37.3	61.7	63.2	77.0	83.1
Item 6750 Subject A03a N	3115	1461	1571	2334	336	741	891	954	529	1892	1037	1306	622	444	665	36

A21B: LSD

	TOTAL	M	F	White	Black	NE	NC	S	W	Yes	No	None	Mari. Only	Few Pills	More Pills	Any Heroin
1. Probably impossible	22.7	20.2	24.3	18.1	41.7	23.9	21.3	24.8	19.6	20.2	26.5	27.2	25.3	19.3	13.3	6.1
2. Very difficult	20.5	20.4	20.4	20.9	17.4	21.9	19.2	20.6	20.5	21.7	17.5	19.4	22.4	23.8	18.9	8.3
3. Fairly difficult	28.3	28.9	28.3	30.9	19.7	26.1	30.5	29.0	26.4	28.3	29.2	27.9	28.3	29.9	29.3	21.7
4. Fairly easy	21.2	21.3	22.0	23.2	15.4	19.9	22.7	18.6	25.5	22.8	19.4	20.6	18.7	21.5	25.1	33.9
5. Very easy	7.3	9.2	5.1	6.9	5.7	8.2	6.3	7.0	8.0	7.0	7.5	4.8	5.4	5.5	13.3	30.0
Item 6760 Subject A03a N	3091	1454	1557	2317	333	737	883	948	523	1877	1029	1298	614	442	661	36

A21C: Some other psychedelic (mescaline, peyote, psilocybin, PCP, etc.)

	TOTAL	M	F	White	Black	NE	NC	S	W	Yes	No	None	Mari. Only	Few Pills	More Pills	Any Heroin
1. Probably impossible	26.8	24.8	28.1	22.3	46.2	25.3	25.5	31.1	23.2	23.8	31.2	30.1	33.2	23.1	16.9	8.0
2. Very difficult	24.8	24.9	24.8	26.5	15.6	24.8	24.8	23.5	27.5	25.3	24.0	25.0	22.7	26.5	24.9	30.9
3. Fairly difficult	23.5	24.7	22.8	25.4	18.4	21.4	22.3	25.6	24.7	25.1	21.4	22.2	23.3	24.2	27.3	8.0
4. Fairly easy	18.1	18.2	18.6	19.9	12.0	18.2	22.2	14.8	17.4	19.5	16.3	18.6	14.3	20.8	19.8	19.0
5. Very easy	6.8	7.4	5.6	5.9	7.9	10.4	5.2	5.2	7.2	6.3	7.0	4.2	6.5	5.4	11.1	34.1
Item 6770 Subject A03a N	3080	1450	1549	2311	330	734	877	945	525	1867	1028	1293	616	437	658	36

A21D: Amphetamines (uppers, pep pills, bennies, speed)

	TOTAL	M	F	White	Black	NE	NC	S	W	Yes	No	None	Mari. Only	Few Pills	More Pills	Any Heroin
1. Probably impossible	12.1	10.9	12.6	7.8	31.5	11.7	9.6	15.5	10.7	10.2	14.4	18.0	12.1	6.7	3.5	
2. Very difficult	9.2	9.5	8.5	7.9	10.0	9.9	8.6	7.9	11.4	10.2	7.1	11.9	9.9	9.1	3.2	1.0
3. Fairly difficult	14.4	15.2	13.9	14.6	13.0	16.1	13.1	14.3	14.5	16.1	11.4	15.5	17.2	14.2	10.3	10.9
4. Fairly easy	33.8	34.4	34.0	37.0	24.3	33.7	34.0	32.7	35.9	34.7	33.0	32.8	38.6	36.1	31.2	23.4
5. Very easy	30.5	30.0	31.0	32.7	21.1	28.6	34.8	29.7	27.5	28.9	34.1	21.9	22.3	33.9	51.7	64.6
Item 6780 Subject A03a N	3097	1454	1561	2322	335	736	883	951	527	1878	1033	1295	620	443	663	36

A21E: Barbiturates (downers, goofballs, reds, yellows, etc.)

	TOTAL	M	F	White	Black	NE	NC	S	W	Yes	No	None	Mari. Only	Few Pills	More Pills	Any Heroin
1. Probably impossible	15.9	14.6	16.5	10.9	37.6	16.3	13.6	19.1	13.5	13.7	18.9	21.1	18.0	9.9	7.4	
2. Very difficult	14.3	15.2	13.5	14.2	11.8	13.7	11.7	11.3	16.0	15.1	12.2	15.5	17.1	12.4	10.6	1.0
3. Fairly difficult	21.4	22.4	20.8	23.3	13.2	22.7	21.4	20.0	22.3	22.6	19.7	19.7	23.1	25.3	22.1	12.2
4. Fairly easy	27.9	26.3	30.2	30.2	21.8	26.7	25.3	29.3	31.8	29.0	26.9	28.4	26.9	28.8	28.5	22.7
5. Very easy	20.4	21.6	19.1	21.4	15.6	20.5	22.7	20.3	16.4	19.6	22.3	15.4	14.8	23.5	31.4	64.1
Item 6790 Subject A03a N	3083	1448	1553	2313	330	734	881	946	521	1870	1028	1291	615	441	660	36

A21F: Tranquilizers

	TOTAL	M	F	White	Black	NE	NC	S	W	Yes	No	None	Mari. Only	Few Pills	More Pills	Any Heroin
1. Probably impossible	16.0	16.6	15.0	11.4	37.0	15.4	14.7	18.8	14.3	13.2	20.4	18.2	20.5	11.2	9.9	3.8
2. Very difficult	12.9	14.2	11.8	11.9	15.7	13.9	13.2	11.0	14.1	12.3	12.9	12.4	14.7	11.5	13.1	9.0
3. Fairly difficult	19.9	20.8	19.5	21.4	12.2	19.2	21.5	18.3	21.3	20.4	19.4	19.2	20.4	18.6	22.5	16.6
4. Fairly easy	29.1	26.6	31.6	30.9	20.9	28.3	29.3	29.5	28.7	30.9	26.4	30.7	28.9	32.5	24.8	18.4
5. Very easy	22.1	21.7	22.2	24.5	14.2	23.2	21.2	22.4	21.6	23.2	20.9	19.5	15.4	26.2	29.8	52.1
Item 6800 Subject A03a N	3084	1445	1558	2312	333	736	884	942	523	1873	1026	1292	615	440	661	36

QUESTIONNAIRE FORM 2 1986	TOTAL	SEX		RACE		REGION				4YR COLLEGE PLANS		ILLICIT DRUG USE: LIFETIME				
		M	F	White	Black	NE	NC	S	W	Yes	No	None	Marijuana Only	Few Pills	More Pills	Any Heroin
N (Weighted No. of Cases):	3179	1481	1591	2367	338	756	902	980	541	1906	1054	1324	625	447	670	37
% of Weighted Total:	100.0	46.6	50.0	74.4	10.6	23.8	28.4	30.8	17.0	59.9	33.2	41.6	19.7	14.1	21.1	1.2
A21G: Cocaine																
1. Probably impossible	17.4	17.2	17.5	14.8	28.6	15.2	18.1	21.0	12.9	15.4	20.8	24.9	16.7	11.8	6.8	3.8
2. Very difficult	13.6	14.0	13.3	13.9	10.2	11.3	15.0	15.4	11.1	13.5	14.0	18.4	14.1	12.0	5.4	6.0
3. Fairly difficult	17.5	17.6	17.5	18.5	14.3	15.1	19.4	18.9	14.3	18.2	16.8	20.8	15.9	18.5	13.3	5.0
4. Fairly easy	27.9	25.9	30.1	30.1	21.2	28.1	29.4	25.8	29.0	30.4	23.4	23.4	33.5	31.1	30.4	16.0
5. Very easy	23.6	25.3	21.7	22.7	25.7	30.3	17.6	18.9	32.7	22.5	25.0	12.5	19.9	26.6	44.1	69.2
Item 6810 Subject A03a N	3093	1452	1559	2322	332	737	884	946	526	1876	1033	1291	620	444	662	36
A21H: Heroin (smack, horse)																
1. Probably impossible	30.1	29.4	30.0	26.7	44.5	29.3	30.5	32.7	26.0	27.6	34.4	33.3	30.6	30.5	23.7	4.8
2. Very difficult	24.0	25.7	22.8	25.4	18.0	23.9	25.9	22.6	23.3	24.7	23.2	22.3	25.1	25.0	26.5	5.0
3. Fairly difficult	23.9	23.0	25.2	26.8	11.0	22.9	22.7	24.1	27.1	25.0	22.3	22.5	23.4	23.5	28.5	31.0
4. Fairly easy	14.7	13.5	16.1	15.4	13.6	15.3	16.7	12.4	14.8	15.6	12.9	15.7	14.1	14.2	14.0	15.6
5. Very easy	7.3	8.3	5.8	5.8	12.8	8.6	4.2	8.3	8.8	7.0	7.2	6.3	6.7	6.9	7.2	43.5
Item 6820 Subject A03a N	3077	1449	1546	2311	329	733	875	944	524	1867	1025	1286	614	442	658	36
A21I: Some other narcotic (methadone, opium, codeine, paregoric, etc.)																
1. Probably impossible	25.5	24.4	25.7	20.6	43.7	25.3	24.7	29.1	20.4	23.0	29.2	30.5	29.6	22.9	13.6	5.6
2. Very difficult	20.8	22.0	20.0	22.0	17.5	18.6	23.5	19.7	21.4	21.4	19.6	21.1	23.0	23.1	16.7	12.4
3. Fairly difficult	21.5	21.9	21.7	23.3	14.3	22.5	19.1	21.1	25.0	22.6	19.6	20.4	21.1	26.1	22.3	17.7
4. Fairly easy	21.3	19.3	23.1	22.9	14.5	23.3	22.0	19.6	20.3	21.7	21.2	19.9	17.9	19.2	28.6	24.6
5. Very easy	11.0	12.3	9.5	11.3	10.0	10.4	10.8	10.5	13.0	11.2	10.3	8.1	8.4	8.7	18.8	39.6
Item 6830 Subject A03a N	3087	1453	1552	2316	332	733	880	948	526	1872	1031	1291	615	443	662	36

This section asks for your views and feelings about a number of different things.

D01: How satisfied are you with your life as a whole these days?	TOTAL	M	F	White	Black	NE	NC	S	W	Yes	No	None	Marijuana Only	Few Pills	More Pills	Any Heroin
1. Completely dissatisfied	2.5	2.7	2.2	1.7	5.3	2.3	2.9	2.4	2.1	1.9	3.6	2.0	1.7	3.2	2.6	15.5
2. Quite dissatisfied	8.9	9.1	8.8	8.5	9.8	9.7	8.2	8.7	9.4	9.1	8.3	8.1	8.8	10.3	9.9	9.3
3. Somewhat dissatisfied	11.9	10.8	13.1	11.6	11.7	13.5	10.8	12.4	10.9	11.5	12.6	9.8	10.0	14.5	16.1	5.5
4. Neither, or mixed feelings	13.2	14.0	12.4	12.5	11.1	11.5	12.3	14.9	14.1	11.6	16.1	12.2	13.3	13.3	14.1	15.2
5. Somewhat satisfied	23.3	23.6	23.0	23.7	24.6	21.0	22.4	25.7	23.7	23.6	22.7	21.9	25.1	22.5	24.7	40.6
6. Quite satisfied	33.8	33.4	34.6	36.2	27.5	33.3	37.3	29.9	35.2	36.2	29.5	38.2	36.4	29.4	27.4	11.3
7. Completely satisfied	6.4	6.5	6.0	5.7	9.9	8.7	6.1	6.0	4.6	6.0	7.3	7.8	4.8	6.7	5.2	2.6
Item 6840 Subject P01,Q01 N	2966	1378	1535	2274	297	686	861	903	516	1867	1023	1240	598	427	637	36

D02: These next questions ask you to guess how well you might do in several different situations. How good do you think you would be...

D02A: As a husband or wife?	TOTAL	M	F	White	Black	NE	NC	S	W	Yes	No	None	Marijuana Only	Few Pills	More Pills	Any Heroin
1. Poor	1.0	1.8	0.4	1.0	1.4	0.4	1.0	1.5	1.1	1.0	1.1	0.5	1.3	1.0	1.7	6.0
2. Not so good	2.0	2.3	1.8	1.9	3.3	1.6	2.0	2.3	2.1	1.5	3.2	1.5	1.6	2.6	2.8	-
3. Fairly good	9.4	9.9	9.0	8.5	10.8	7.2	9.9	10.1	9.9	9.8	8.3	8.4	8.3	10.0	11.5	13.9
4. Good	34.7	38.6	31.7	35.9	29.4	32.8	34.3	36.6	35.0	35.9	32.5	36.1	36.7	36.9	30.6	24.1
5. Very good	49.9	43.9	54.7	50.4	50.9	54.8	48.9	46.7	50.4	49.9	50.1	50.8	49.1	46.6	50.2	52.5
8. Don't know	3.0	3.5	2.5	2.3	4.3	3.2	3.8	2.8	1.5	3.0	2.9	2.8	2.9	2.9	3.1	3.5
Item 6850 Subject D01,Q01 N	2963	1376	1533	2272	297	687	859	903	514	1866	1018	1243	596	422	638	35

D02B: As a parent?	TOTAL	M	F	White	Black	NE	NC	S	W	Yes	No	None	Marijuana Only	Few Pills	More Pills	Any Heroin
1. Poor	1.2	1.9	0.6	1.1	1.8	1.3	0.9	1.5	0.8	0.9	1.7	0.7	0.7	1.8	2.0	4.2
2. Not so good	2.0	1.6	2.4	2.3	1.1	1.7	2.3	1.8	2.0	1.9	2.3	1.1	2.5	3.9	1.9	-
3. Fairly good	10.0	10.9	9.4	10.0	10.6	7.8	9.5	12.1	10.1	9.9	10.2	9.8	9.7	9.9	11.0	9.8
4. Good	32.0	34.0	30.5	33.6	23.0	29.0	33.8	31.1	34.5	32.6	30.6	32.8	33.2	34.2	29.0	28.0
5. Very good	49.7	46.2	52.3	48.4	58.7	55.1	47.6	47.3	50.0	49.1	50.9	49.5	49.3	45.4	51.9	54.4
8. Don't know	5.1	5.4	4.9	4.7	4.7	5.0	5.9	6.0	2.6	5.6	4.4	6.0	4.5	4.8	4.2	3.6
Item 6860 Subject D02,Q01 N	2960	1374	1532	2270	297	688	857	903	513	1867	1018	1242	595	422	637	34

QUESTIONNAIRE FORM 2 1986	TOTAL	SEX		RACE		REGION				4YR COLLEGE PLANS		ILLICIT DRUG USE: LIFETIME				
		M	F	White	Black	NE	NC	S	W	Yes	No	None	Mari-juana Only	Few Pills	More Pills	Any Her-oin
N (Weighted No. of Cases):	3179	1481	1591	2367	338	756	902	980	541	1906	1054	1324	625	447	670	37
% of Weighted Total:	100.0	46.6	50.0	74.4	10.6	23.8	28.4	30.8	17.0	59.9	33.2	41.6	19.7	14.1	21.1	1.2

D02C: As a worker on a job?

	TOTAL	M	F	White	Black	NE	NC	S	W	Yes	No	None	Mari-juana Only	Few Pills	More Pills	Any Her-oin
1. Poor	0.3	0.6	0.1	0.4	0.1	0.1	0.3	0.6	0.3	0.2	0.6	0.1	-	0.6	1.0	1.4
2. Not so good	0.4	0.6	0.3	0.5	0.5	0.1	0.3	0.8	0.4	0.2	0.9	0.4	0.3	0.1	0.4	-
3. Fairly good	3.6	4.3	2.9	3.4	3.5	4.3	3.3	3.9	2.6	3.2	3.9	3.1	3.6	3.6	4.2	4.1
4. Good	31.0	28.7	33.5	32.0	21.3	27.1	32.0	33.6	30.1	30.2	32.4	29.8	30.6	36.8	30.7	33.8
5. Very good	63.6	64.5	62.5	63.0	72.7	68.0	62.5	60.2	65.5	65.2	61.3	65.8	63.4	58.4	63.0	57.1
8. Don't know	1.1	1.3	0.6	0.6	1.8	0.5	1.6	0.9	1.0	1.0	1.0	0.7	2.1	0.6	0.8	3.6
Item 6870　Subject C03,Q01　N	2959	1374	1531	2269	297	687	857	902	512	1865	1016	1243	594	421	637	34

D03: Some people think a lot about the social problems of the nation and the world, and about how they might be solved. Others spend little time thinking about these issues. How much do you think about such things?

	TOTAL	M	F	White	Black	NE	NC	S	W	Yes	No	None	Mari-juana Only	Few Pills	More Pills	Any Her-oin
1. Never	4.9	6.6	3.1	4.2	6.8	6.8	5.5	4.2	2.8	2.7	9.2	4.7	4.6	4.9	4.3	23.0
2. Seldom	19.1	17.8	20.6	19.0	17.3	20.5	19.4	18.5	17.5	16.9	23.0	17.4	22.3	17.8	21.0	10.7
3. Sometimes	51.2	50.1	52.5	52.6	50.1	51.4	49.1	51.8	53.3	51.9	50.0	52.3	51.0	51.6	49.0	46.4
4. Quite often	19.4	20.0	18.6	19.2	19.4	16.2	20.3	19.3	22.5	21.7	14.9	21.0	16.4	19.9	19.4	15.4
5. A great deal	5.4	5.6	5.2	5.0	6.4	5.2	5.6	6.2	4.0	6.8	2.9	4.6	5.6	5.8	6.3	4.5
Item 6880　Subject J,Q08　N	2936	1356	1527	2256	293	673	856	897	510	1851	1010	1235	592	416	629	35

D04: Now we'd like you to make some ratings of how honest and moral the people are who run the following organizations. To what extent are there problems of dishonesty and immorality in the leadership of...

D04A: Large corporations?

	TOTAL	M	F	White	Black	NE	NC	S	W	Yes	No	None	Mari-juana Only	Few Pills	More Pills	Any Her-oin
1. Not at all	3.5	4.7	2.4	2.5	6.9	4.6	3.6	3.0	2.6	2.2	5.7	2.8	3.7	3.3	3.8	14.8
2. Slight	17.8	20.8	15.1	18.4	16.8	16.9	18.4	17.4	18.6	17.1	18.5	17.4	17.4	21.8	15.8	23.8
3. Moderate	35.7	34.4	37.1	37.0	29.4	36.8	35.7	33.4	38.1	38.9	30.9	35.8	36.9	35.2	36.6	20.2
4. Considerable	21.1	21.8	20.4	21.9	18.3	19.8	20.9	22.6	20.2	22.7	17.6	20.8	24.7	21.4	17.7	16.3
5. Great	4.6	4.7	4.4	4.1	7.8	3.9	5.4	4.7	4.2	4.6	4.6	4.0	5.0	5.0	5.5	1.4
8. No opinion	17.3	13.6	20.7	16.2	20.8	18.0	15.9	18.8	16.2	14.5	22.6	19.2	12.2	13.4	20.7	23.6
Item 6890　Subject K01　N	2892	1341	1501	2227	285	655	848	893	496	1809	984	1235	574	400	614	36

D04B: Major labor unions?

	TOTAL	M	F	White	Black	NE	NC	S	W	Yes	No	None	Mari-juana Only	Few Pills	More Pills	Any Her-oin
1. Not at all	3.9	5.5	2.3	3.0	7.5	5.2	4.1	3.1	3.1	2.5	5.9	3.6	3.2	5.5	3.5	7.2
2. Slight	18.1	17.8	18.3	18.5	17.6	20.1	16.9	17.3	19.3	16.9	20.3	17.4	20.2	18.3	17.7	18.6
3. Moderate	33.1	32.9	33.4	35.1	26.1	33.8	35.0	30.4	34.0	35.8	28.2	34.1	34.2	33.2	30.6	30.8
4. Considerable	18.3	21.5	15.6	17.6	19.2	14.6	20.8	18.8	18.0	19.4	16.3	17.7	20.5	18.0	17.2	19.2
5. Great	5.8	7.0	4.5	5.9	6.0	5.2	5.9	5.9	6.3	6.0	5.6	5.5	5.0	7.7	6.0	7.5
8. No opinion	20.8	15.3	25.8	19.9	23.7	21.3	17.3	24.5	19.2	19.3	23.6	21.6	17.0	17.2	25.1	16.6
Item 6900　Subject K01　N	2879	1336	1494	2219	285	651	845	892	492	1803	979	1231	572	398	611	36

D04C: The nation's colleges and universities?

	TOTAL	M	F	White	Black	NE	NC	S	W	Yes	No	None	Mari-juana Only	Few Pills	More Pills	Any Her-oin
1. Not at all	8.3	9.5	7.0	8.1	8.4	11.9	7.5	6.3	8.2	7.1	10.5	8.8	8.1	5.9	8.3	7.8
2. Slight	27.2	29.4	25.4	29.3	19.4	28.1	31.0	24.5	24.0	31.5	18.8	28.7	29.1	28.2	22.4	20.5
3. Moderate	25.4	23.3	27.3	25.7	23.2	23.5	25.1	25.8	27.7	26.2	23.9	25.9	24.7	21.7	27.8	32.3
4. Considerable	18.5	18.6	18.5	18.8	19.0	17.3	18.0	20.6	17.0	18.4	18.6	18.5	18.9	21.8	15.3	16.3
5. Great	6.9	6.7	6.7	5.5	13.6	5.9	5.8	7.2	9.4	6.9	7.0	5.5	8.0	10.0	6.4	12.4
8. No opinion	13.9	12.6	15.1	12.7	16.4	13.4	12.5	15.6	13.7	9.9	21.3	12.6	11.2	12.3	19.7	10.7
Item 6910　Subject B10,K01　N	2870	1338	1482	2209	285	647	841	889	493	1799	973	1230	573	394	604	36

D04D: The nation's public schools?

	TOTAL	M	F	White	Black	NE	NC	S	W	Yes	No	None	Mari-juana Only	Few Pills	More Pills	Any Her-oin
1. Not at all	8.2	9.4	6.9	8.4	7.5	11.0	7.4	7.2	7.6	6.8	10.4	8.7	7.1	6.7	8.5	10.6
2. Slight	28.6	30.1	27.5	29.6	23.5	28.8	29.2	29.6	25.5	30.8	24.7	29.5	30.0	34.1	22.6	39.0
3. Moderate	26.4	24.7	28.0	27.1	23.6	25.1	27.1	26.0	27.6	27.4	23.8	26.1	23.4	26.8	29.3	8.3
4. Considerable	18.9	19.1	18.8	18.8	22.5	16.7	18.7	19.7	20.6	20.3	17.1	18.9	21.8	18.1	17.1	17.2
5. Great	6.9	6.9	6.5	5.9	9.8	8.4	6.5	5.5	8.2	6.3	8.5	6.6	6.9	5.7	7.8	16.0
8. No opinion	11.0	9.7	12.3	10.1	13.1	10.0	11.1	11.9	10.6	8.4	15.5	10.2	10.8	8.6	14.6	9.0
Item 6920　Subject B10,K01　N	2873	1334	1489	2215	281	645	846	890	492	1803	974	1228	571	398	608	36

QUESTIONNAIRE FORM 2 1986	TOTAL	SEX		RACE		REGION				4YR COLLEGE PLANS		ILLICIT DRUG USE: LIFETIME				
		M	F	White	Black	NE	NC	S	W	Yes	No	None	Marijuana Only	Few Pills	More Pills	Any Heroin
N (Weighted No. of Cases):	3179	1481	1591	2367	338	756	902	980	541	1906	1054	1324	625	447	670	37
% of Weighted Total:	100.0	46.6	50.0	74.4	10.6	23.8	28.4	30.8	17.0	59.9	33.2	41.6	19.7	14.1	21.1	1.2

D04E: Churches and religious organizations?

1. Not at all	14.7	15.6	13.9	15.2	10.4	19.9	13.8	12.4	13.5	14.0	16.1	15.2	16.7	12.9	12.4	34.2
2. Slight	29.1	28.2	29.9	30.8	21.9	23.6	32.2	31.3	27.0	32.7	22.0	30.8	27.0	31.7	27.9	12.4
3. Moderate	15.3	15.7	15.1	15.1	15.4	12.7	16.9	13.5	19.1	16.2	14.4	14.7	14.1	15.2	17.3	16.9
4. Considerable	14.8	14.2	15.4	15.2	15.2	15.3	14.0	16.3	13.1	14.3	15.5	14.2	15.3	15.2	14.9	13.5
5. Great	13.6	13.9	13.0	12.0	24.7	14.9	11.8	14.3	13.7	13.1	14.5	12.8	17.4	12.9	11.6	11.7
8. No opinion	12.5	12.4	12.7	11.7	12.4	13.7	11.3	12.2	13.6	9.7	17.5	12.3	9.5	12.1	15.9	11.4
Item 6930 Subject G,K01 N	2882	1337	1495	2219	285	653	847	890	492	1806	977	1232	571	400	610	36

D04F: The national news media (TV, magazines, news services)?

1. Not at all	4.3	6.3	2.4	3.6	6.2	4.6	4.1	4.2	4.7	3.0	6.6	3.6	4.0	5.1	5.1	12.4
2. Slight	20.8	22.3	19.2	21.3	15.5	23.1	18.6	20.6	21.8	20.6	21.2	22.2	20.8	21.6	17.5	33.6
3. Moderate	29.8	28.5	31.6	31.4	22.1	29.2	32.4	27.6	29.9	32.4	24.9	29.7	30.1	28.9	31.4	13.5
4. Considerable	22.9	21.6	24.0	23.1	25.4	21.1	23.6	23.6	23.0	25.2	19.1	24.3	23.9	20.1	23.1	13.1
5. Great	11.5	11.2	11.5	10.9	16.9	10.5	11.2	12.7	11.3	10.6	13.2	10.4	10.2	13.6	11.9	22.6
8. No opinion	10.7	10.2	11.3	9.6	13.9	11.5	10.1	11.3	9.3	8.1	14.9	9.9	10.9	10.6	12.1	4.8
Item 6940 Subject K01 N	2873	1332	1491	2213	284	649	845	887	492	1800	975	1230	569	396	610	36

D04G: The Presidency and the administration?

1. Not at all	7.0	8.7	5.2	6.6	6.8	7.0	7.2	7.1	6.4	6.3	8.3	7.0	7.4	6.5	6.3	17.3
2. Slight	23.3	24.9	22.0	24.8	20.3	20.9	24.2	24.5	23.1	24.4	20.9	23.7	23.6	24.6	21.5	27.0
3. Moderate	29.2	28.5	30.1	29.4	26.7	29.5	30.2	26.5	32.0	31.9	24.6	29.7	29.9	27.5	29.0	28.3
4. Considerable	18.7	19.0	18.4	19.1	20.2	20.7	17.3	19.3	17.7	19.9	16.6	19.7	18.6	20.0	17.2	10.6
5. Great	6.7	6.4	6.9	6.1	10.3	6.3	8.0	6.4	5.3	5.5	8.8	5.8	5.6	6.5	9.6	4.3
8. No opinion	15.0	12.5	17.5	14.0	15.7	15.5	13.1	16.3	15.4	12.0	20.9	14.2	14.9	15.0	16.4	12.5
Item 6950 Subject H04,K01 N	2872	1332	1492	2215	283	649	843	886	493	1800	974	1230	568	396	610	36

D04H: Congress–that is, the U.S. Senate and House of Representatives?

1. Not at all	5.9	7.5	4.1	5.1	7.2	6.5	4.8	5.8	7.0	4.8	7.6	5.5	6.2	5.0	6.1	18.0
2. Slight	21.2	21.4	20.8	22.5	18.0	18.6	23.7	21.1	20.8	22.2	19.7	21.9	21.9	21.3	19.3	23.6
3. Moderate	30.4	30.0	31.1	30.8	27.9	30.0	33.2	27.0	32.0	33.6	25.0	31.6	28.1	33.1	28.2	19.3
4. Considerable	19.0	20.5	17.8	19.1	22.1	20.9	16.2	20.4	19.0	20.2	16.5	19.4	21.5	18.1	17.2	11.9
5. Great	6.0	6.6	5.2	5.8	7.4	3.9	7.0	7.2	4.8	4.8	8.0	5.4	5.2	7.4	6.8	11.9
8. No opinion	17.5	14.1	20.9	16.7	17.4	20.2	15.1	18.5	16.4	14.4	23.2	16.1	17.1	15.0	21.9	15.3
Item 6960 Subject H04,K01 N	2872	1331	1491	2212	284	650	842	888	492	1798	976	1229	569	398	609	36

D04I: The U.S. Supreme Court?

1. Not at all	13.4	17.5	9.5	13.6	10.4	14.4	13.0	11.8	15.4	13.8	12.9	15.4	10.7	12.1	12.7	14.8
2. Slight	25.2	26.0	24.6	27.0	20.2	23.8	26.0	25.9	24.4	28.2	18.9	25.6	25.6	27.6	22.9	26.8
3. Moderate	20.2	17.9	22.4	20.1	20.1	19.6	21.7	18.5	21.6	20.9	19.6	19.6	21.6	21.0	19.4	22.5
4. Considerable	15.4	15.2	15.4	15.0	21.5	14.3	14.7	17.1	14.8	15.7	14.6	15.7	16.8	14.8	14.3	13.9
5. Great	7.8	9.0	6.5	7.5	8.2	7.9	7.6	8.5	6.9	6.2	10.7	7.1	8.0	7.2	9.3	4.6
8. No opinion	18.0	14.4	21.6	16.7	19.6	20.0	17.0	18.2	16.9	15.2	23.4	16.6	17.2	17.3	21.4	17.4
Item 6970 Subject H04,K01 N	2858	1325	1484	2204	281	649	835	883	491	1794	970	1223	567	397	605	36

D04J: All the courts and the justice system in general?

1. Not at all	7.1	8.9	5.2	6.6	7.8	8.7	5.7	6.8	8.0	5.4	10.5	7.6	6.3	7.3	6.2	7.8
2. Slight	25.8	26.9	24.7	27.8	19.5	25.2	27.7	24.2	26.2	26.4	24.1	26.7	24.6	30.0	23.0	31.8
3. Moderate	28.5	27.7	29.4	28.7	25.4	27.7	28.4	27.9	30.8	33.0	20.9	29.5	28.7	28.0	27.6	20.5
4. Considerable	17.5	18.3	16.9	17.6	21.3	15.9	18.7	19.2	14.5	17.7	17.2	17.4	18.2	15.7	18.0	19.5
5. Great	5.3	6.0	4.7	4.9	7.6	5.0	4.9	5.7	6.0	4.6	6.5	4.6	6.8	4.5	5.8	6.7
8. No opinion	15.7	12.2	19.1	14.4	18.4	17.5	14.5	16.2	14.4	12.8	20.9	14.2	15.4	14.5	19.3	13.6
Item 6980 Subject H04,K01 N	2868	1331	1487	2214	281	647	843	885	493	1802	971	1229	569	394	608	36

QUESTIONNAIRE FORM 2 1986	TOTAL	SEX		RACE		REGION				4YR COLLEGE PLANS		ILLICIT DRUG USE: LIFETIME				
		M	F	White	Black	NE	NC	S	W	Yes	No	None	Mari- juana Only	Few Pills	More Pills	Any Her- oin
N (Weighted No. of Cases):	3179	1481	1591	2367	338	756	902	980	541	1906	1054	1324	625	447	670	37
% of Weighted Total:	100.0	46.6	50.0	74.4	10.6	23.8	28.4	30.8	17.0	59.9	33.2	41.6	19.7	14.1	21.1	1.2

D04K: The police and other law enforcement agencies?

1. Not at all	5.2	6.5	3.6	4.5	7.3	5.7	5.1	5.3	4.4	3.7	8.0	5.4	4.6	5.1	5.2	4.7
2. Slight	23.7	24.2	23.2	25.4	16.7	25.1	23.8	23.6	21.9	23.8	23.3	25.1	22.8	28.3	19.3	29.0
3. Moderate	31.2	30.0	32.6	32.3	28.9	31.0	33.3	29.1	31.6	34.6	25.3	32.8	33.4	29.2	27.9	25.1
4. Considerable	20.3	20.2	20.5	19.8	17.4	18.5	18.9	21.0	24.0	21.5	17.9	18.3	21.0	20.3	23.6	15.2
5. Great	8.1	9.1	7.3	7.3	15.2	6.8	9.1	8.2	8.0	7.3	9.5	6.9	8.5	6.8	10.1	16.6
8. No opinion	11.5	10.0	12.9	10.6	14.6	12.9	9.9	12.8	10.0	9.1	16.0	11.4	9.6	10.3	13.9	9.4
Item 6990　Subject K01　N	2868	1330	1489	2213	281	650	841	885	492	1799	973	1226	568	397	609	36

D04L: The U.S. military?

1. Not at all	8.6	9.3	7.7	7.8	10.4	8.0	8.0	10.2	7.5	7.8	9.9	8.9	9.9	7.7	7.1	12.3
2. Slight	24.6	25.2	24.3	26.8	17.4	24.0	24.5	25.3	24.5	26.4	21.6	26.4	21.8	24.9	24.2	29.9
3. Moderate	25.8	27.2	24.5	26.4	21.6	24.7	28.3	21.5	30.7	28.5	20.9	26.4	26.8	26.1	24.0	17.7
4. Considerable	15.2	16.0	14.4	15.0	19.4	16.6	14.1	15.6	14.4	15.5	14.8	14.9	15.2	18.2	14.4	6.9
5. Great	8.6	9.6	7.7	8.2	11.1	7.1	9.9	8.8	8.4	6.9	11.7	7.6	9.7	7.5	9.3	22.4
8. No opinion	17.1	12.7	21.4	15.8	20.2	19.6	15.2	18.6	14.5	15.0	21.1	15.8	16.5	15.6	21.0	10.8
Item 7000　Subject K01,L04　N	2865	1325	1490	2211	282	648	843	883	491	1800	967	1227	569	396	607	36

D05: How much do you agree or disagree with each of the following statements?

D05A: There is too much competition in this society

1. Disagree	9.8	15.1	5.0	10.4	11.4	10.3	9.4	11.3	6.9	9.8	9.2	10.1	8.7	10.1	9.4	9.8
2. Mostly disagree	13.2	16.1	10.7	14.5	8.2	9.5	14.0	14.9	13.9	15.4	9.5	14.6	11.7	14.8	10.9	2.4
3. Neither	24.2	26.1	23.0	24.7	22.8	22.6	24.0	25.2	25.2	24.0	25.5	23.5	26.6	25.7	22.2	29.2
4. Mostly agree	33.3	27.5	38.4	33.1	31.1	36.0	34.2	29.1	35.9	33.7	31.9	33.4	36.6	28.2	34.6	35.3
5. Agree	19.5	15.2	22.8	17.2	26.5	21.7	18.5	19.6	18.2	17.1	24.0	18.4	16.3	21.2	22.9	23.3
Item 7010　Subject Q08　N	2897	1336	1511	2235	283	660	846	890	500	1827	971	1233	571	413	614	36

D05B: Too many young people are sloppy about their grooming and clothing, and just don't care how they look

1. Disagree	18.6	21.3	16.6	19.3	16.6	21.0	18.6	17.2	18.0	18.8	17.7	16.7	18.9	20.6	20.7	33.4
2. Mostly disagree	29.5	28.2	31.0	31.6	21.2	26.9	30.7	30.4	29.2	32.8	23.8	29.7	29.6	29.2	30.3	23.4
3. Neither	19.4	20.2	18.7	19.6	12.4	21.9	19.6	16.6	20.6	19.1	20.5	19.4	18.3	18.2	20.2	20.9
4. Mostly agree	21.5	20.6	22.2	20.6	27.9	19.5	20.7	22.3	23.8	19.9	23.5	21.6	23.6	20.7	20.5	3.0
5. Agree	11.0	9.7	11.5	9.0	21.8	10.7	10.3	13.5	8.4	9.4	14.5	12.5	9.7	11.3	8.3	19.3
Item 7020　Subject Q08　N	2899	1336	1512	2235	283	663	848	886	502	1826	972	1236	572	411	614	36

D05C: There is too much hard rock music on the radio these days

1. Disagree	38.4	42.4	35.3	42.3	25.7	39.0	40.0	39.8	32.7	36.9	41.0	30.2	42.3	40.2	49.6	46.4
2. Mostly disagree	22.8	20.9	24.2	23.9	16.6	19.9	25.4	22.1	23.1	25.1	18.3	22.6	21.1	25.0	24.1	18.9
3. Neither	18.4	18.9	18.3	16.9	21.2	20.9	17.4	16.3	20.7	19.4	17.2	20.5	16.9	18.5	14.4	23.5
4. Mostly agree	11.3	9.3	13.0	9.6	21.2	11.1	9.7	11.5	13.9	10.6	12.8	14.9	10.3	9.6	6.4	4.6
5. Agree	9.1	8.6	9.3	7.4	15.4	9.1	7.5	10.3	9.6	8.1	10.7	11.8	9.5	6.8	5.5	6.7
Item 7030　Subject Q08　N	2895	1331	1515	2229	284	660	849	888	499	1823	974	1232	571	414	614	36

D05D: People should do their own thing, even if other people think it's strange

1. Disagree	3.2	4.5	1.7	2.8	6.1	3.2	3.0	4.3	1.9	3.0	3.6	3.2	3.0	3.9	3.2	4.5
2. Mostly disagree	4.8	5.3	4.5	4.7	5.8	4.5	3.5	5.3	6.5	4.1	6.0	6.2	2.9	3.2	5.1	1.9
3. Neither	12.0	14.8	9.7	11.5	15.3	8.5	13.4	13.0	12.5	11.2	13.8	14.5	9.9	10.4	9.9	8.2
4. Mostly agree	33.9	32.5	35.5	34.3	29.4	33.7	34.6	33.5	33.7	36.0	29.6	34.9	38.1	34.4	28.2	21.6
5. Agree	46.1	43.0	48.6	46.7	43.5	50.1	45.5	43.9	45.5	45.8	46.9	41.2	46.0	48.1	53.6	63.9
Item 7040　Subject Q08　N	2894	1333	1511	2231	281	661	849	886	499	1822	973	1234	570	411	614	36

QUESTIONNAIRE FORM 2 1986	TOTAL	SEX		RACE		REGION				4YR COLLEGE PLANS		ILLICIT DRUG USE: LIFETIME				
		M	F	White	Black	NE	NC	S	W	Yes	No	None	Mari-juana Only	Few Pills	More Pills	Any Her-oin
N (Weighted No. of Cases):	3179	1481	1591	2367	338	756	902	980	541	1906	1054	1324	625	447	670	37
% of Weighted Total:	100.0	46.6	50.0	74.4	10.6	23.8	28.4	30.8	17.0	59.9	33.2	41.6	19.7	14.1	21.1	1.2

D05E: I get a real kick out of doing things that are a little dangerous

	TOTAL	M	F	White	Black	NE	NC	S	W	Yes	No	None	Mari-juana Only	Few Pills	More Pills	Any Her-oin
1. Disagree	19.9	13.3	25.4	16.9	40.8	20.4	17.2	25.3	14.7	18.7	22.4	24.7	18.2	17.2	14.2	6.9
2. Mostly disagree	17.2	14.7	19.5	17.4	18.1	18.0	15.5	18.9	15.7	17.8	16.5	19.0	18.9	18.0	12.0	8.7
3. Neither	28.0	27.5	28.6	28.9	18.5	27.6	30.6	23.6	31.7	28.9	26.1	29.6	29.5	22.5	26.5	24.8
4. Mostly agree	22.3	27.0	18.1	23.6	14.4	18.2	26.0	20.5	24.3	22.5	21.1	18.4	22.9	27.0	26.4	27.1
5. Agree	12.7	17.5	8.4	13.2	8.2	15.8	10.7	11.7	13.6	12.1	13.9	8.3	10.5	15.4	20.8	32.4
Item 7050 Subject Q04 N	2890	1326	1514	2227	284	661	849	882	498	1826	969	1232	572	410	614	36

D05F: I like to test myself every now and then by doing something a little risky

	TOTAL	M	F	White	Black	NE	NC	S	W	Yes	No	None	Mari-juana Only	Few Pills	More Pills	Any Her-oin
1. Disagree	16.5	11.3	21.0	14.3	31.0	16.9	14.2	20.6	12.7	15.0	19.4	21.6	14.5	15.1	9.3	13.9
2. Mostly disagree	14.5	12.0	17.0	14.9	14.4	15.9	13.4	15.7	12.6	15.2	13.1	15.2	19.5	14.1	10.5	5.3
3. Neither	23.3	21.8	24.7	23.3	17.1	25.5	24.8	19.7	24.5	24.3	22.1	27.6	19.5	15.1	23.3	24.7
4. Mostly agree	30.9	35.3	27.1	32.5	22.6	26.2	33.6	28.9	36.1	32.4	27.2	26.5	31.9	38.1	35.1	17.2
5. Agree	14.7	19.5	10.2	15.0	14.9	15.6	14.0	15.1	14.1	13.2	17.6	9.4	14.6	17.7	21.8	38.9
Item 7060 Subject Q04 N	2863	1320	1492	2206	279	650	845	875	493	1813	957	1222	565	402	611	33

D05G: I take a positive attitude toward myself

	TOTAL	M	F	White	Black	NE	NC	S	W	Yes	No	None	Mari-juana Only	Few Pills	More Pills	Any Her-oin
1. Disagree	3.3	2.8	3.7	3.3	3.1	3.9	2.5	3.4	3.5	2.7	4.2	3.4	1.9	3.8	3.4	9.3
2. Mostly disagree	6.6	5.2	8.0	7.1	5.3	6.2	7.0	7.7	4.6	5.9	7.6	6.5	4.8	8.6	6.8	5.7
3. Neither	13.7	12.3	15.1	14.0	8.1	10.2	13.5	13.8	18.8	12.0	16.6	12.5	15.5	15.0	14.3	11.3
4. Mostly agree	43.2	43.5	43.2	44.7	33.1	41.8	43.4	43.7	43.7	45.2	40.5	43.1	46.8	40.7	42.9	39.1
5. Agree	33.2	36.2	30.1	31.0	50.5	37.8	33.7	31.4	29.4	34.2	31.0	34.5	30.9	32.0	32.6	34.6
Item 12550 Subject Q01 N	2878	1325	1502	2221	278	657	846	880	495	1811	967	1230	566	403	610	36

D05H: I feel I am a person of worth, on an equal plane with others

	TOTAL	M	F	White	Black	NE	NC	S	W	Yes	No	None	Mari-juana Only	Few Pills	More Pills	Any Her-oin
1. Disagree	2.5	2.8	2.2	2.2	3.0	2.9	2.8	2.3	1.9	1.7	3.8	2.0	2.1	3.1	2.4	14.7
2. Mostly disagree	4.1	3.4	4.6	3.6	6.4	3.7	4.3	4.8	3.1	3.7	4.3	4.1	3.4	4.5	4.7	3.4
3. Neither	10.9	11.1	11.0	10.7	7.2	11.3	9.8	10.6	12.7	9.8	13.4	9.8	10.9	11.7	12.3	14.7
4. Mostly agree	37.4	36.3	38.7	39.5	28.2	32.7	39.5	37.0	40.9	37.5	37.6	39.6	36.4	35.7	36.3	23.9
5. Agree	45.0	46.4	43.5	44.1	55.3	49.3	43.5	45.4	41.5	47.2	40.9	44.6	47.2	45.1	44.4	43.4
Item 12570 Subject Q01 N	2863	1316	1496	2212	277	650	842	880	492	1805	959	1221	563	403	608	36

D05I: I am able to do things as well as most other people

	TOTAL	M	F	White	Black	NE	NC	S	W	Yes	No	None	Mari-juana Only	Few Pills	More Pills	Any Her-oin
1. Disagree	1.6	2.0	1.0	1.1	3.4	1.2	1.4	2.5	0.7	1.2	2.2	1.9	1.0	1.3	1.2	8.0
2. Mostly disagree	2.3	2.2	2.5	2.3	3.2	2.2	2.4	2.8	1.7	2.0	2.8	1.8	2.1	4.4	1.7	2.9
3. Neither	7.4	7.5	7.4	7.1	5.7	8.4	7.7	6.0	8.2	5.7	11.2	5.9	6.0	8.9	10.4	10.8
4. Mostly agree	43.5	38.9	47.9	44.9	32.7	41.3	44.6	42.8	45.6	43.7	43.3	44.4	44.2	42.1	43.2	35.8
5. Agree	45.2	49.3	41.2	44.5	55.0	46.9	43.9	45.9	43.7	47.5	40.5	46.1	46.8	43.3	43.4	42.5
Item 12580 Subject Q01 N	2869	1325	1493	2215	280	655	843	876	495	1812	960	1222	565	405	608	36

D05J: On the whole, I'm satisfied with myself

	TOTAL	M	F	White	Black	NE	NC	S	W	Yes	No	None	Mari-juana Only	Few Pills	More Pills	Any Her-oin
1. Disagree	2.8	2.5	2.9	2.6	2.9	2.2	2.9	3.1	3.1	2.4	3.5	3.1	2.5	2.6	2.3	15.0
2. Mostly disagree	5.6	4.6	6.6	5.8	5.4	6.9	5.3	4.9	6.0	4.9	7.0	4.2	4.6	7.9	7.4	10.1
3. Neither	11.0	11.3	10.8	10.2	8.8	9.5	10.2	11.8	13.1	10.4	12.1	8.4	13.4	13.1	12.2	13.5
4. Mostly agree	41.4	41.0	41.6	42.9	30.9	39.4	40.5	43.3	42.0	42.1	40.2	43.5	40.0	41.8	38.7	39.9
5. Agree	39.1	40.5	38.0	38.5	52.0	42.0	41.2	36.9	35.8	40.2	37.2	40.7	39.5	34.6	39.4	21.5
Item 12620 Subject P01,Q01 N	2865	1320	1496	2220	277	655	843	874	494	1808	960	1225	564	408	602	36

D05K: I feel I do not have much to be proud of

	TOTAL	M	F	White	Black	NE	NC	S	W	Yes	No	None	Mari-juana Only	Few Pills	More Pills	Any Her-oin
1. Disagree	41.6	40.9	42.0	42.0	46.5	44.6	41.3	42.5	36.8	44.8	36.2	45.2	37.6	40.7	38.8	41.0
2. Mostly disagree	32.0	31.1	33.4	33.7	26.4	29.2	32.2	33.3	33.0	34.2	29.1	34.2	36.4	35.0	30.5	14.6
3. Neither	11.8	12.8	11.1	11.4	6.6	11.5	12.9	9.1	14.9	10.2	13.6	10.8	12.5	11.6	13.0	17.6
4. Mostly agree	8.5	8.6	8.3	7.7	10.6	8.5	8.3	8.1	9.8	6.3	12.8	7.9	6.9	7.2	11.1	15.7
5. Agree	6.0	6.7	5.2	5.2	9.9	6.2	5.3	7.0	5.6	4.5	8.3	5.5	6.6	5.6	6.6	11.0
Item 12660 Subject Q01 N	2863	1311	1501	2211	279	654	841	876	492	1806	958	1223	557	408	607	36

QUESTIONNAIRE FORM 2 1986	TOTAL	SEX		RACE		REGION				4YR COLLEGE PLANS		ILLICIT DRUG USE: LIFETIME				
		M	F	White	Black	NE	NC	S	W	Yes	No	None	Marijuana Only	Few Pills	More Pills	Any Heroin
N (Weighted No. of Cases):	3179	1481	1591	2367	338	756	902	980	541	1906	1054	1324	625	447	670	37
% of Weighted Total:	100.0	46.6	50.0	74.4	10.6	23.8	28.4	30.8	17.0	59.9	33.2	41.6	19.7	14.1	21.1	1.2

D05L: Sometimes I think that I am no good at all

1. Disagree	35.2	38.6	31.9	33.9	49.5	37.9	32.6	36.3	33.9	37.3	31.2	37.9	34.6	32.5	32.1	30.6
2. Mostly disagree	23.4	24.3	22.7	24.4	20.5	22.9	25.1	22.4	23.3	24.3	22.3	23.9	24.3	24.1	21.6	29.2
3. Neither	17.9	18.3	17.8	17.9	12.1	17.4	19.4	16.0	19.4	17.1	19.3	15.7	19.3	18.0	21.2	11.5
4. Mostly agree	14.3	11.3	16.7	14.5	10.7	13.7	14.9	14.4	13.7	13.3	16.2	14.6	14.5	14.6	13.2	8.8
5. Agree	9.2	7.5	10.8	9.2	7.3	8.1	8.0	10.9	9.7	8.0	11.0	7.9	7.4	10.8	11.8	20.0
Item 12680 Subject Q01 N	2856	1314	1491	2212	276	645	841	878	492	1805	952	1222	559	406	603	36

D05M: I feel that I can't do anything right

1. Disagree	44.5	47.6	41.4	44.5	55.6	50.4	43.4	43.3	40.6	46.7	40.3	46.4	46.1	42.4	41.5	38.6
2. Mostly disagree	27.9	28.0	28.2	28.5	20.1	24.8	27.7	29.7	29.4	29.8	25.7	28.8	29.0	29.8	25.6	16.6
3. Neither	15.9	14.5	17.1	15.7	13.9	13.9	17.8	13.8	19.3	15.1	17.1	14.5	14.9	15.3	19.0	13.2
4. Mostly agree	7.5	6.1	8.8	7.2	6.9	7.5	7.4	7.8	7.2	5.5	10.9	6.7	7.6	7.5	8.6	15.7
5. Agree	4.1	3.7	4.5	4.1	3.5	3.3	3.6	5.4	3.6	2.9	6.1	3.5	2.4	4.9	5.3	15.8
Item 12720 Subject Q01 N	2867	1319	1498	2218	279	654	841	880	492	1808	961	1223	562	408	607	36

D05N: I feel that my life is not very useful

1. Disagree	55.4	58.3	52.9	56.2	59.3	60.8	54.6	53.7	52.7	59.7	47.6	58.0	55.7	52.6	52.4	49.1
2. Mostly disagree	22.0	19.8	24.0	22.6	19.7	19.1	20.6	25.3	22.7	21.2	24.2	22.5	22.1	24.9	20.3	11.8
3. Neither	13.1	12.8	13.4	12.7	10.2	11.1	15.7	11.6	14.0	12.1	14.8	11.5	14.0	12.3	15.4	15.9
4. Mostly agree	5.4	5.1	5.5	4.9	5.8	4.6	5.6	4.9	6.8	4.4	7.1	4.2	6.1	4.9	6.8	16.5
5. Agree	4.0	4.0	4.1	3.5	5.0	4.5	3.4	4.4	3.8	2.6	6.3	3.8	2.1	5.3	5.1	6.7
Item 12750 Subject Q01 N	2861	1316	1495	2214	278	651	839	879	492	1806	956	1222	560	409	604	36

D06: How many of your friends would you estimate . . .

D06A: Smoke cigarettes?

1. None	12.2	11.6	12.3	10.4	23.4	9.2	10.1	12.5	19.1	13.5	9.3	19.0	7.6	10.6	4.0	1.9
2. A few	37.6	37.9	37.8	38.0	39.0	32.8	39.7	36.9	41.4	41.6	30.1	45.3	41.6	32.3	24.1	10.7
3. Some	28.7	32.3	25.7	29.6	20.7	29.9	28.0	30.8	24.6	28.7	29.3	26.9	31.3	30.7	29.0	22.4
4. Most	19.4	16.7	21.5	20.1	13.7	24.9	19.9	18.8	12.2	14.9	27.7	8.3	18.2	22.9	38.1	57.3
5. All	2.2	1.6	2.7	1.9	3.2	3.2	2.3	1.0	2.6	1.4	3.6	0.6	1.2	3.4	4.9	7.7
Item 7070 Subject A02a N	2873	1316	1506	2225	276	653	849	873	498	1813	963	1225	564	408	612	36

D06B: Smoke marijuana (pot, grass) or hashish?

1. None	20.8	17.5	23.5	20.2	21.5	16.8	20.1	24.0	21.7	21.8	19.2	38.1	7.1	11.8	5.7	5.1
2. A few	35.2	35.3	35.5	36.6	33.9	32.2	36.0	35.9	36.5	37.6	30.6	42.0	39.2	35.2	19.3	10.9
3. Some	25.8	27.9	23.7	25.8	22.5	26.2	28.7	24.0	23.7	25.6	26.5	16.3	34.3	30.4	34.1	29.8
4. Most	15.3	15.8	15.1	14.9	17.7	20.8	13.2	13.5	14.7	12.9	19.6	3.1	17.2	19.6	33.3	43.5
5. All	2.9	3.5	2.3	2.5	4.4	4.0	2.0	2.6	3.4	2.1	4.2	0.5	2.3	3.0	7.7	10.7
Item 7080 Subject A02a N	2870	1316	1503	2223	278	651	849	874	495	1809	964	1223	563	408	613	36

D06C: Take LSD?

1. None	75.5	72.5	77.9	74.9	79.8	74.7	76.2	78.2	70.5	78.5	69.9	83.0	79.0	78.5	58.1	28.6
2. A few	17.3	19.0	16.0	18.0	13.7	17.0	16.6	15.8	21.8	17.1	18.0	13.6	16.3	17.1	25.7	30.6
3. Some	5.4	5.9	4.9	5.4	4.8	4.8	5.4	5.2	6.4	3.2	9.4	3.1	3.3	3.9	11.9	15.2
4. Most	1.2	1.4	1.0	1.1	0.4	2.7	1.5	0.3	0.4	0.6	2.1	0.2	0.7	0.3	3.0	24.2
5. All	0.6	1.1	0.1	0.6	1.2	0.9	0.3	0.5	1.0	0.6	0.6	0.2	0.8	0.3	1.3	1.4
Item 7090 Subject A02a N	2855	1309	1495	2214	275	649	844	870	492	1807	954	1216	563	402	610	36

D06D: Take other psychedelics (mescaline, peyote, PCP, etc.)?

1. None	77.7	75.5	79.6	77.5	81.4	72.6	79.1	81.5	75.4	80.5	73.0	84.5	83.0	78.9	61.1	29.6
2. A few	16.7	18.5	15.3	17.8	11.1	18.9	15.6	15.0	19.1	15.8	18.9	12.8	14.1	16.8	26.2	40.8
3. Some	4.2	4.1	4.3	3.5	4.6	6.1	4.2	2.7	4.3	2.9	6.3	2.2	2.4	2.6	10.2	12.5
4. Most	0.8	1.4	0.3	0.8	1.3	1.3	0.9	0.5	0.4	0.5	1.1	0.2	0.2	1.2	1.8	9.2
5. All	0.5	0.6	0.4	0.4	1.6	1.0	0.3	0.3	0.9	0.4	0.7	0.3	0.2	0.6	0.7	8.0
Item 7100 Subject A02a N	2861	1314	1496	2218	275	648	848	872	493	1805	959	1220	560	407	610	36

QUESTIONNAIRE FORM 2 1986	TOTAL	SEX		RACE		REGION				4YR COLLEGE PLANS		ILLICIT DRUG USE: LIFETIME				
		M	F	White	Black	NE	NC	S	W	Yes	No	None	Mari-juana Only	Few Pills	More Pills	Any Her-oin
N (Weighted No. of Cases):	3179	1481	1591	2367	338	756	902	980	541	1906	1054	1324	625	447	670	37
% of Weighted Total:	100.0	46.6	50.0	74.4	10.6	23.8	28.4	30.8	17.0	59.9	33.2	41.6	19.7	14.1	21.1	1.2

D06E: Take amphetamines (uppers, pep pills, bennies, speed)?

	TOTAL	M	F	White	Black	NE	NC	S	W	Yes	No	None	Mari.	Few	More	Any
1. None	58.2	57.0	59.2	56.1	69.1	59.0	55.9	59.8	58.4	62.0	51.2	72.9	64.5	53.1	28.3	20.7
2. A few	29.2	29.5	29.0	31.5	19.9	27.3	31.6	28.6	28.5	28.2	31.4	22.9	28.3	32.7	40.0	37.3
3. Some	9.2	9.4	9.1	9.1	7.5	9.4	9.3	9.1	8.8	8.1	11.4	3.2	5.6	12.5	21.8	14.6
4. Most	2.6	2.7	2.6	2.6	1.6	3.1	2.7	2.2	2.7	1.5	4.5	0.5	1.1	1.2	8.0	24.3
5. All	0.8	1.4	0.2	0.6	1.9	1.2	0.4	0.3	1.6	0.3	1.5	0.4	0.5	0.4	1.9	3.0
Item 7110 Subject A02a N	2847	1310	1486	2209	272	643	845	868	491	1801	953	1217	557	403	608	36

D06F: Take quaaludes (quads, methaqualone)?

	TOTAL	M	F	White	Black	NE	NC	S	W	Yes	No	None	Mari.	Few	More	Any
1. None	76.5	73.1	79.5	75.7	82.6	73.9	78.1	76.6	77.0	78.8	72.7	84.2	81.2	74.5	61.2	27.2
2. A few	17.4	19.3	15.9	18.6	10.6	18.3	17.0	17.2	17.6	17.2	17.5	13.1	14.9	19.2	26.6	40.4
3. Some	4.5	5.6	3.5	4.3	3.6	4.7	4.1	5.0	3.8	3.0	7.5	2.1	2.6	5.7	9.2	7.0
4. Most	1.1	1.3	0.9	1.0	1.3	2.1	0.5	1.0	0.9	0.7	1.4	0.2	1.1	0.4	2.2	22.4
5. All	0.5	0.7	0.2	0.3	1.9	1.0	0.3	0.2	0.7	0.2	0.9	0.4	0.2	0.3	0.8	3.0
Item 7120 Subject A02a N	2842	1307	1485	2209	271	642	844	863	493	1795	953	1212	558	404	605	36

D06G: Take barbiturates (downers, goofballs, reds, yellows, etc.)?

	TOTAL	M	F	White	Black	NE	NC	S	W	Yes	No	None	Mari.	Few	More	Any
1. None	74.4	71.8	76.6	73.8	78.9	72.1	74.9	74.8	75.9	76.9	69.9	82.6	78.9	71.8	58.1	33.4
2. A few	19.4	20.9	18.1	20.6	14.3	20.5	19.8	18.9	18.0	18.4	21.1	14.4	16.6	22.4	29.2	30.8
3. Some	4.8	5.5	4.3	4.4	4.2	5.1	4.3	5.4	4.3	3.6	7.3	2.3	3.9	5.5	9.4	17.1
4. Most	1.0	1.2	0.9	1.0	1.6	1.5	0.9	0.7	1.2	0.8	1.3	0.4	0.2	-	2.9	15.7
5. All	0.4	0.6	0.1	0.2	1.0	0.8	0.1	0.2	0.7	0.3	0.5	0.3	0.4	0.3	0.4	3.0
Item 7130 Subject A02a N	2855	1313	1491	2215	273	646	847	868	493	1802	957	1216	560	406	609	36

D06H: Take tranquilizers?

	TOTAL	M	F	White	Black	NE	NC	S	W	Yes	No	None	Mari.	Few	More	Any
1. None	75.8	73.1	78.2	75.0	81.5	76.2	76.9	74.2	76.4	76.8	74.1	82.6	81.1	72.6	62.1	31.7
2. A few	18.4	19.9	17.3	19.7	12.2	17.7	17.5	20.2	17.8	18.4	18.7	14.8	15.0	21.0	26.6	30.4
3. Some	4.4	5.2	3.7	4.1	3.8	4.5	4.8	4.3	4.0	3.7	6.0	1.9	2.8	5.7	8.6	26.9
4. Most	0.9	1.1	0.7	0.8	1.5	1.0	0.8	0.7	1.1	0.7	0.8	0.4	0.2	0.4	2.3	8.0
5. All	0.4	0.7	0.1	0.4	1.1	0.7	-	0.6	0.7	0.4	0.4	0.2	0.8	0.3	0.4	3.0
Item 7140 Subject A02a N	2847	1310	1486	2210	272	645	845	866	491	1798	955	1212	560	406	607	36

D06I: Take cocaine?

	TOTAL	M	F	White	Black	NE	NC	S	W	Yes	No	None	Mari.	Few	More	Any
1. None	54.4	53.0	55.2	53.7	60.6	45.8	59.1	62.2	43.6	56.1	51.6	74.0	52.7	47.8	23.2	22.4
2. A few	27.3	27.4	27.3	28.2	25.7	30.1	26.9	23.8	30.5	28.1	25.8	20.8	34.7	32.0	30.7	20.5
3. Some	12.2	13.4	11.3	12.3	6.5	13.6	9.9	10.6	17.1	11.8	12.9	4.1	10.3	15.6	27.2	15.8
4. Most	4.4	3.8	5.1	4.3	5.2	6.2	3.5	2.6	6.9	3.0	6.8	0.7	1.2	3.9	13.6	28.0
5. All	1.7	2.4	1.0	1.5	2.0	4.3	0.6	0.9	1.9	1.0	2.9	0.3	1.1	0.6	5.3	13.3
Item 7150 Subject A02a N	2848	1309	1488	2209	273	642	844	869	492	1798	956	1213	560	404	608	36

D06J: Take heroin (smack, horse)?

	TOTAL	M	F	White	Black	NE	NC	S	W	Yes	No	None	Mari.	Few	More	Any
1. None	84.7	84.0	85.1	85.3	82.0	82.6	87.9	83.7	83.3	86.4	81.1	86.7	86.6	82.2	83.4	38.7
2. A few	11.7	11.3	12.2	11.7	11.3	13.4	9.4	11.7	13.4	11.0	13.5	11.5	10.2	13.1	12.6	21.3
3. Some	2.6	3.1	2.2	2.1	4.4	2.8	2.0	3.4	1.8	2.1	3.6	1.3	2.4	3.5	3.3	15.7
4. Most	0.5	0.7	0.5	0.5	1.3	0.7	0.4	0.6	0.5	*	1.2	0.3	-	0.9	0.3	17.6
5. All	0.5	0.9	0.1	0.5	1.1	0.4	0.2	0.6	1.1	0.5	0.6	0.3	0.8	0.3	0.4	6.7
Item 7160 Subject A02a N	2835	1302	1482	2205	268	641	840	863	490	1794	948	1208	556	402	606	36

D06K: Take other narcotics (methadone, opium, codeine, paregoric, etc.)?

	TOTAL	M	F	White	Black	NE	NC	S	W	Yes	No	None	Mari.	Few	More	Any
1. None	78.2	75.3	80.7	77.6	80.7	78.4	78.1	78.6	77.2	81.1	72.9	85.5	84.0	76.4	62.0	34.3
2. A few	15.8	16.7	15.2	16.8	10.1	15.8	16.0	15.4	16.4	14.8	17.9	12.1	12.3	19.0	24.1	24.1
3. Some	4.2	5.4	3.2	4.1	5.1	3.1	4.3	4.5	5.1	3.1	6.4	1.6	2.5	3.9	10.5	16.3
4. Most	1.2	1.7	0.7	1.1	2.8	2.1	1.4	0.9	0.4	0.5	2.3	0.5	0.2	0.4	2.7	22.4
5. All	0.6	0.8	0.2	0.5	1.3	0.6	0.3	0.6	1.0	0.6	0.6	0.3	1.0	0.3	0.6	3.0
Item 7170 Subject A02a N	2845	1306	1488	2207	273	642	843	868	492	1799	953	1212	558	404	608	36

*=less than .05 per cent.

QUESTIONNAIRE FORM 2 1986	TOTAL	SEX		RACE		REGION				4YR COLLEGE PLANS		ILLICIT DRUG USE: LIFETIME				
		M	F	White	Black	NE	NC	S	W	Yes	No	None	Marijuana Only	Few Pills	More Pills	Any Heroin
N (Weighted No. of Cases):	3179	1481	1591	2367	338	756	902	980	541	1906	1054	1324	625	447	670	37
% of Weighted Total:	100.0	46.6	50.0	74.4	10.6	23.8	28.4	30.8	17.0	59.9	33.2	41.6	19.7	14.1	21.1	1.2
D06L: Use inhalants (sniffing glue, aerosols, laughing gas, etc.)?																
1. None	77.6	74.3	80.3	77.5	78.5	80.2	79.2	73.3	79.1	78.4	75.9	82.0	78.4	74.6	72.3	44.9
2. A few	15.8	17.4	14.4	16.1	12.9	13.8	15.2	17.8	15.7	16.0	15.8	13.2	15.3	18.3	19.7	21.0
3. Some	4.6	4.9	4.4	4.5	5.1	4.1	4.0	6.3	3.3	3.9	6.1	3.8	4.3	5.2	5.0	22.5
4. Most	1.4	2.2	0.8	1.5	2.1	0.8	1.6	2.1	0.8	1.2	1.3	0.9	0.8	1.6	2.0	10.2
5. All	0.6	1.2	0.1	0.4	1.5	1.1	-	0.5	1.1	0.4	1.0	0.1	1.2	0.3	1.0	1.4
Item 7180 Subject A02a N	2835	1304	1481	2203	270	640	840	863	492	1794	950	1205	558	402	608	36
D06M: Drink alcoholic beverages (liquor, beer, wine)?																
1. None	4.4	3.8	4.7	2.9	11.1	2.6	3.4	6.2	5.7	3.6	5.6	7.8	2.0	2.1	1.0	3.7
2. A few	10.9	9.7	12.2	8.9	22.8	11.8	7.5	12.3	13.4	10.8	11.8	18.4	6.6	7.6	2.5	3.5
3. Some	16.6	15.0	17.8	15.4	20.1	15.4	13.9	18.9	18.8	17.0	15.9	23.4	15.6	11.0	8.0	5.8
4. Most	41.7	43.9	40.3	44.8	29.7	36.4	47.2	42.4	38.2	44.3	37.3	37.5	51.0	45.6	40.4	44.8
5. All	26.3	27.6	25.0	28.0	16.3	33.8	28.1	20.2	23.9	24.3	29.3	12.8	24.9	33.7	48.0	42.2
Item 7190 Subject A02a N	2847	1308	1489	2213	273	646	845	866	491	1801	954	1214	560	405	604	36
D06N: Get drunk at least once a week?																
1. None	15.3	12.7	17.4	12.8	27.3	17.6	12.2	14.5	19.1	15.2	15.7	26.3	9.0	8.4	4.4	3.7
2. A few	26.0	22.6	28.9	25.7	26.9	25.1	24.9	27.8	25.6	25.2	25.8	29.6	28.8	23.7	18.1	15.9
3. Some	26.9	28.3	25.9	28.5	19.3	23.7	28.0	28.8	25.7	29.3	22.1	26.1	29.4	28.0	25.9	16.8
4. Most	22.9	25.6	20.7	23.8	18.9	20.7	26.5	21.6	21.6	22.0	24.5	14.5	26.0	30.4	31.6	29.1
5. All	9.0	10.8	7.1	9.2	7.5	12.9	8.4	7.3	7.9	7.3	11.9	3.4	6.8	9.6	20.0	34.5
Item 7200 Subject A02a N	2850	1309	1491	2212	274	645	845	870	490	1801	956	1216	558	404	609	36

Lately there has been increased attention paid to two types of drugs: PCP and amyl or butyl nitrite.

E01: How many of your friends would you estimate . . .

E01A: Take PCP (angel dust, crystal, peace pill, killer weed, supergrass, crystal cyclone)?

	TOTAL	M	F	White	Black	NE	NC	S	W	Yes	No	None	Marijuana Only	Few Pills	More Pills	Any Heroin
1. None	83.9	83.7	84.0	85.2	83.2	84.6	86.2	84.4	78.3	86.9	78.8	88.5	87.0	84.6	74.0	43.8
2. A few	11.6	11.9	11.4	11.0	9.4	10.4	10.7	11.7	14.3	10.5	13.5	9.3	8.5	10.2	18.6	35.9
3. Some	3.3	3.2	3.4	2.9	5.3	3.4	2.4	3.4	4.6	2.0	5.6	1.7	3.9	3.6	5.2	7.8
4. Most	0.9	0.7	1.2	0.8	1.0	1.1	0.7	0.4	2.1	0.6	1.5	0.4	0.3	1.4	1.8	10.1
5. All	0.3	0.5	0.1	0.2	1.1	0.4	0.1	0.1	0.7	*	0.6	0.1	0.3	0.3	0.5	2.5
Item 7201 Subject A02a N	2816	1294	1473	2184	273	631	837	862	485	1776	945	1199	552	401	600	36

E01B: Take amyl or butyl nitrites (poppers, snappers, Locker Room, Vaporole, Rush, Kick, Bullet)?

	TOTAL	M	F	White	Black	NE	NC	S	W	Yes	No	None	Marijuana Only	Few Pills	More Pills	Any Heroin
1. None	82.0	80.9	82.8	81.9	84.5	86.1	78.8	81.9	82.3	83.0	80.1	89.6	82.5	81.4	69.0	40.3
2. A few	13.3	13.0	13.8	13.3	11.0	9.5	15.6	13.4	14.1	13.2	13.6	8.5	13.2	11.9	22.5	32.0
3. Some	3.5	4.2	2.9	3.5	3.0	3.1	4.3	3.7	2.4	2.8	4.8	1.4	2.9	5.2	6.5	14.5
4. Most	0.8	1.2	0.4	0.9	0.3	0.9	1.0	0.6	0.5	0.7	1.0	0.3	0.5	1.2	1.1	11.9
5. All	0.5	0.7	0.2	0.4	1.1	0.5	0.4	0.5	0.6	0.4	0.5	0.1	0.9	0.3	0.9	1.4
Item 7202 Subject A02a N	2798	1282	1466	2170	271	628	838	850	482	1766	941	1191	548	402	596	34

E02: On how many occasions (if any) have you used PCP (angel dust, crystal, peace pill, killer weed, supergrass, crystal cyclone)?

E02A: . . . in your lifetime?

	TOTAL	M	F	White	Black	NE	NC	S	W	Yes	No	None	Marijuana Only	Few Pills	More Pills	Any Heroin
1. 0 occasions	95.2	94.5	95.9	95.6	96.1	95.1	97.5	95.8	90.5	96.8	92.3	99.8	97.0	96.1	87.3	43.9
2. 1-2	3.1	3.4	2.7	2.7	2.8	3.5	1.3	2.8	6.0	1.8	5.4	0.1	1.8	3.4	8.3	28.9
3. 3-5	0.5	0.5	0.5	0.5	0.6	0.8	0.3	0.4	0.6	0.3	0.9	-	0.2	0.2	1.1	8.1
4. 6-9	0.4	0.3	0.4	0.4	-	0.4	0.1	0.1	1.2	0.4	0.3	-	0.4	-	0.9	6.3
5. 10-19	0.2	0.2	0.2	0.2	-	0.1	0.2	0.1	0.6	0.2	0.2	-	-	0.1	1.0	-
6. 20-39	0.2	0.4	*	0.1	0.3	-	0.3	0.1	0.5	0.2	0.2	-	-	0.2	0.4	7.3
7. 40 or more	0.4	0.6	0.2	0.4	0.3	0.1	0.3	0.7	0.7	0.3	0.6	0.1	0.6	-	1.0	5.5
Item 1181 Subject A01a N	2797	1286	1461	2174	266	623	838	855	481	1767	937	1199	552	392	595	36

*=less than .05 per cent.

QUESTIONNAIRE FORM 2 1986	TOTAL	SEX		RACE		REGION				4YR COLLEGE PLANS		ILLICIT DRUG USE: LIFETIME				
		M	F	White	Black	NE	NC	S	W	Yes	No	None	Marijuana Only	Few Pills	More Pills	Any Heroin
N (Weighted No. of Cases):	3179	1481	1591	2367	338	756	902	980	541	1906	1054	1324	625	447	670	37
% of Weighted Total:	100.0	46.6	50.0	74.4	10.6	23.8	28.4	30.8	17.0	59.9	33.2	41.6	19.7	14.1	21.1	1.2
E02B: ... during the last 12 months?																
1. 0 occasions	97.6	97.2	98.0	97.9	96.3	98.4	98.8	98.0	93.7	97.9	96.9	99.8	97.4	98.6	93.8	75.3
2. 1-2	1.4	1.4	1.4	1.1	2.8	1.0	0.6	1.0	4.0	1.1	1.9	0.1	1.7	0.9	3.2	16.8
3. 3-5	0.2	0.3	0.2	0.3	-	0.5	0.2	0.2	0.1	0.3	0.2	-	0.3	-	0.5	5.6
4. 6-9	0.3	0.4	0.3	0.3	0.3	0.1	0.2	0.2	1.0	0.3	0.5	-	-	0.3	1.3	-
5. 10-19	0.1	0.1	0.2	0.1	0.3	-	0.3	0.1	0.2	0.1	0.3	-	-	0.2	0.6	-
6. 20-39	0.1	0.2	-	*	-	-	-	-	0.5	0.1	*	-	-	-	0.3	1.2
7. 40 or more	0.2	0.3	0.1	0.2	0.3	-	-	0.5	0.4	0.2	0.2	0.1	0.6	-	0.3	1.2
Item 1182 Subject A01b　N	2798	1286	1462	2174	267	623	838	854	482	1766	938	1199	552	392	595	36
E02C: ... during the last 30 days?																
1. 0 occasions	98.7	98.2	99.2	98.8	98.8	98.9	99.5	98.9	96.9	98.7	98.8	99.8	98.9	99.1	96.8	87.5
2. 1-2	0.7	1.0	0.6	0.8	0.6	1.1	0.3	0.4	1.8	0.8	0.8	0.1	0.4	0.6	1.9	8.7
3. 3-5	0.3	0.3	0.2	0.2	0.3	0.1	0.2	0.2	0.7	0.2	0.4	-	-	0.3	0.9	2.6
4. 6-9	0.1	0.2	-	*	-	-	-	-	0.4	0.1	*	-	-	-	0.3	1.2
5. 10-19	*	*	-	*	-	-	-	-	0.1	*	-	-	-	-	0.1	-
6. 20-39	-	-	-	-	-	-	-	-	-	-	-	-	-	-	-	-
7. 40 or more	0.2	0.3	-	0.2	0.3	-	-	0.5	0.1	0.2	-	0.1	0.6	-	0.1	-
Item 1183 Subject A01c　N	2797	1285	1462	2175	266	623	838	854	481	1766	938	1199	552	392	595	36
E03: On how many occasions (if any) have you used amyl or butyl nitrites (poppers, snappers, Locker Room, Vaporole, Rush, Kick, Bullet)?																
E03A: ... in your lifetime?																
1. 0 occasions	91.4	88.8	93.8	90.8	95.1	95.3	87.8	90.9	93.9	91.7	91.1	98.4	92.6	91.2	78.6	48.6
2. 1-2	5.0	5.9	4.0	5.2	3.1	2.8	7.0	4.8	4.4	5.2	4.6	1.3	4.6	4.5	12.7	13.5
3. 3-5	1.1	1.7	0.6	1.4	-	0.4	2.0	1.0	0.8	1.0	1.5	0.1	0.8	1.8	2.8	6.6
4. 6-9	0.8	1.1	0.5	0.8	-	1.0	1.5	0.1	0.4	0.6	0.9	-	0.5	0.3	2.5	7.7
5. 10-19	0.6	0.9	0.3	0.5	1.4	0.3	0.3	1.3	0.1	0.5	0.7	-	0.3	0.9	1.6	2.8
6. 20-39	0.3	0.1	0.4	0.4	-	-	0.7	0.2	-	0.1	0.7	0.1	0.1	0.2	0.5	3.7
7. 40 or more	0.9	1.5	0.4	1.0	0.3	0.3	0.8	1.6	0.4	1.0	0.6	0.1	1.1	1.0	1.2	17.1
Item 1184 Subject A01a　N	2791	1279	1464	2167	267	623	836	854	478	1765	933	1193	552	396	588	36
E03B: ... during the last 12 months?																
1. 0 occasions	95.3	93.1	97.1	94.8	96.8	97.8	93.4	94.2	97.2	95.6	94.7	99.3	94.9	94.1	90.2	60.0
2. 1-2	2.9	4.0	2.1	3.2	1.6	1.7	4.8	2.4	2.1	2.7	3.3	0.5	3.5	2.6	6.4	21.7
3. 3-5	0.5	0.8	0.3	0.6	-	0.1	1.0	0.4	0.4	0.4	0.7	0.1	-	1.2	1.3	-
4. 6-9	0.2	0.3	0.1	0.2	-	0.1	0.4	0.2	0.1	0.2	0.2	-	0.1	0.2	0.5	4.8
5. 10-19	0.5	0.7	0.3	0.4	1.3	0.3	0.2	1.2	-	0.4	0.7	-	0.3	0.9	1.0	4.8
6. 20-39	0.1	0.2	*	0.1	-	-	-	0.2	0.2	0.1	0.2	-	0.1	-	0.2	3.2
7. 40 or more	0.5	1.0	0.1	0.6	0.3	-	0.2	1.5	-	0.7	0.2	0.1	1.1	1.0	0.3	5.4
Item 1185 Subject A01b　N	2791	1280	1463	2166	267	625	834	854	478	1765	935	1195	552	396	586	36
E03C: ... during the last 30 days?																
1. 0 occasions	98.7	97.9	99.3	98.5	99.4	99.5	99.1	97.3	99.3	98.7	98.5	99.9	98.4	97.9	97.8	83.1
2. 1-2	0.5	0.6	0.3	0.5	0.3	0.2	0.7	0.4	0.4	0.5	0.5	0.1	0.3	-	1.3	6.6
3. 3-5	0.1	0.1	0.1	0.1	-	0.2	0.1	0.1	0.1	0.1	0.1	-	-	0.2	0.3	1.4
4. 6-9	0.2	0.3	0.1	0.2	-	-	-	0.6	-	-	0.5	-	-	0.9	0.3	-
5. 10-19	0.1	0.1	0.2	0.1	-	0.2	0.1	0.1	0.2	0.1	0.1	-	0.2	-	0.2	4.4
6. 20-39	0.1	0.2	-	0.1	-	-	-	0.3	-	0.1	-	-	0.5	-	-	-
7. 40 or more	0.4	0.8	*	0.4	0.3	-	0.1	1.2	-	0.4	0.2	0.1	0.6	1.0	0.1	4.5
Item 1186 Subject A01c　N	2792	1280	1463	2166	267	625	834	854	478	1765	935	1195	552	396	587	36
E04: When (if ever) did you FIRST do each of the following things?																
E04A: Try PCP																
8. Never	96.9	96.4	97.4	97.1	98.1	96.9	98.3	97.4	93.6	98.0	94.8	99.9	98.8	97.4	91.2	44.9
1. Grade 6 or below	0.4	0.8	-	0.3	1.3	0.1	0.2	0.8	0.3	0.2	0.7	-	0.6	1.2	0.4	-
2. Grade 7 or 8	0.5	0.7	0.4	0.5	0.1	0.6	0.7	0.2	0.7	0.2	1.2	0.1	-	0.5	0.5	21.7
3. Grade 9 (Freshman)	0.4	0.6	0.3	0.3	-	0.3	0.4	0.5	0.4	0.3	0.6	-	0.1	-	1.2	12.2
4. Grade 10 (Sophomore)	0.7	0.8	0.7	0.6	-	1.4	0.1	0.3	1.7	0.5	1.0	-	-	0.5	2.7	8.3
5. Grade 11 (Junior)	0.8	0.5	0.9	0.7	-	0.6	0.3	0.6	1.9	0.5	1.3	-	0.5	0.1	2.4	13.0
6. Grade 12 (Senior)	0.4	0.3	0.4	0.4	0.4	0.1	0.1	0.3	1.3	0.3	0.4	-	-	0.3	1.5	-
Item 5686 Subject A01g　N	2720	1239	1432	2115	257	607	820	829	464	1735	895	1186	536	384	559	32

*=less than .05 per cent.

QUESTIONNAIRE FORM 2 1986	TOTAL	SEX		RACE		REGION				4YR COLLEGE PLANS		ILLICIT DRUG USE: LIFETIME				
		M	F	White	Black	NE	NC	S	W	Yes	No	None	Marijuana Only	Few Pills	More Pills	Any Heroin
N (Weighted No. of Cases):	3179	1481	1591	2367	338	756	902	980	541	1906	1054	1324	625	447	670	37
% of Weighted Total:	100.0	46.6	50.0	74.4	10.6	23.8	28.4	30.8	17.0	59.9	33.2	41.6	19.7	14.1	21.1	1.2

E04B: Try amyl or butyl nitrites

8. Never	93.4	91.0	95.4	92.7	97.3	96.3	91.4	92.4	94.8	93.5	93.0	99.3	94.2	92.6	82.8	48.4
1. Grade 6 or below	0.3	0.4	0.2	0.2	0.9	0.5	0.5	0.1	0.1	0.2	0.5	0.1	-	-	1.1	1.6
2. Grade 7 or 8	1.0	1.4	0.7	1.1	0.1	1.3	1.5	0.7	0.4	0.7	1.6	-	-	0.2	3.6	22.0
3. Grade 9 (Freshman)	0.7	1.1	0.5	1.0	-	0.3	1.1	0.7	0.7	0.8	0.7	0.1	0.2	0.2	2.6	9.4
4. Grade 10 (Sophomore)	1.1	1.4	0.7	1.1	0.3	0.5	0.7	1.5	1.7	1.1	1.1	0.1	1.3	0.7	2.9	7.8
5. Grade 11 (Junior)	2.1	2.9	1.4	2.3	1.3	1.0	3.5	1.8	1.6	2.3	1.8	0.1	2.5	3.0	4.9	9.3
6. Grade 12 (Senior)	1.4	1.7	1.2	1.7	-	0.2	1.4	2.7	0.8	1.4	1.3	0.3	1.9	3.1	2.1	1.4
Item 5687 Subject A01g N	2704	1227	1431	2100	256	610	792	830	473	1719	901	1177	537	382	553	30

E05: What is your best guess about whether your parents think you drink alcoholic beverages (beer, wine, liquor)?

1. They feel sure I don't drink	28.8	23.8	32.6	25.2	49.8	25.9	21.5	37.1	30.6	30.3	26.9	47.7	15.9	19.8	8.9	24.4
2. They think I probably don't drink	13.7	12.8	14.5	12.9	15.4	15.2	11.6	14.0	14.6	13.8	12.7	14.2	15.2	15.4	10.7	0.9
3. I don't know, or they differ in whether they think I do	9.0	8.5	9.6	9.5	7.1	10.3	10.6	7.4	7.5	8.9	9.3	8.6	10.7	9.6	7.6	11.8
4. They think I probably drink	19.7	21.9	17.8	21.0	13.6	22.4	18.9	19.0	18.7	20.2	18.2	12.6	25.1	25.2	25.3	14.8
5. They feel sure (or know) that I drink	28.8	32.9	25.6	31.4	14.0	26.3	37.3	22.5	28.7	26.7	32.9	16.9	33.1	29.9	47.5	48.2
Item 7510 Subject A09a N	2794	1280	1466	2165	273	622	838	857	477	1761	939	1192	551	399	591	35

E06: What's your best guess about whether your parents think you smoke marijuana?

1. They feel sure I don't	74.3	70.1	78.4	74.9	73.7	75.3	72.8	77.1	70.8	77.7	68.4	94.1	68.5	67.0	47.6	43.2
2. They think I probably don't	11.4	11.9	11.1	11.8	10.6	11.7	13.1	10.1	10.1	11.1	12.1	3.9	17.9	17.2	16.4	11.4
3. I don't know, or they differ in whether they think I do	4.9	6.2	3.4	4.9	3.7	3.8	4.2	5.2	7.0	3.9	6.3	1.1	7.6	4.3	9.3	13.1
4. They think I probably do	4.8	5.9	3.8	4.3	6.7	6.2	4.7	3.6	5.4	4.0	6.3	0.3	4.4	6.6	12.0	18.2
5. They feel sure (or know) that I do	4.6	6.0	3.3	4.0	5.3	2.9	5.2	3.9	6.8	3.3	6.9	0.6	1.5	4.9	14.7	14.2
Item 7520 Subject A09a N	2775	1267	1459	2149	269	616	834	850	474	1751	931	1184	547	395	587	36

E07: To what extent have you participated in the following school activities during this school year?

E07A: School newspaper or yearbook

1. Not at all	71.7	74.9	69.0	71.2	70.9	65.7	71.7	71.4	79.9	66.7	81.3	69.6	73.9	68.0	76.7	75.3
2. Slight	10.6	10.0	11.0	11.1	10.3	12.3	9.6	11.2	8.9	11.5	8.8	11.1	8.5	14.3	8.5	6.5
3. Moderate	6.4	5.9	6.9	6.6	5.2	9.5	8.2	4.5	2.7	7.5	4.3	6.5	7.6	5.5	6.2	1.9
4. Considerable	4.1	3.5	4.6	4.2	4.4	6.8	2.4	3.8	4.0	4.9	2.6	4.5	3.1	6.1	2.5	6.8
5. Great	7.3	5.7	8.4	7.0	9.1	5.8	8.1	9.1	4.5	9.4	2.9	8.4	6.9	6.0	6.1	9.5
Item 22170 Subject B01,C07 N	2757	1261	1451	2135	267	612	832	839	475	1736	930	1182	545	388	582	34

E07B: Music or other performing arts

1. Not at all	63.1	71.3	56.8	63.8	52.1	58.8	65.0	62.8	65.5	58.5	71.1	57.2	67.3	63.1	71.0	71.4
2. Slight	9.5	8.7	10.2	9.7	10.1	11.1	9.6	7.7	10.0	8.4	10.8	9.9	7.7	9.4	8.5	20.8
3. Moderate	5.6	3.9	7.0	5.2	6.0	6.0	4.8	5.5	6.9	6.3	4.5	6.2	6.4	5.0	4.5	5.4
4. Considerable	6.6	4.9	7.9	5.9	10.2	7.2	6.4	6.7	5.7	7.9	4.5	7.7	4.4	8.2	5.5	1.1
5. Great	15.3	11.2	18.2	15.4	21.6	16.9	14.1	17.2	12.0	18.9	9.0	19.1	14.2	14.3	10.5	1.2
Item 22180 Subject B01,C07 N	2757	1254	1457	2137	266	611	831	839	476	1739	928	1186	545	389	577	35

E07C: Athletic teams

1. Not at all	46.4	36.7	55.0	45.5	44.1	40.9	43.2	52.5	48.3	40.1	58.8	47.5	42.5	40.2	52.8	42.6
2. Slight	10.2	10.4	10.1	10.0	12.0	11.0	10.4	9.8	9.6	9.7	11.3	9.7	9.0	13.5	10.0	9.9
3. Moderate	9.4	10.8	8.2	9.9	8.2	10.4	10.6	8.5	8.0	9.8	8.7	8.9	11.9	10.7	6.5	16.5
4. Considerable	10.6	13.3	8.3	11.5	5.7	11.6	12.4	7.4	11.9	11.7	8.7	10.7	10.8	9.0	11.4	10.9
5. Great	23.4	28.8	18.4	23.1	30.1	26.2	23.5	21.8	22.2	28.8	12.5	23.2	25.9	26.6	19.4	20.2
Item 22190 Subject B01,C07 N	2764	1265	1450	2140	267	615	831	843	475	1743	927	1186	549	389	578	35

QUESTIONNAIRE FORM 2 1986	TOTAL	SEX		RACE		REGION				4YR COLLEGE PLANS		ILLICIT DRUG USE: LIFETIME				
		M	F	White	Black	NE	NC	S	W	Yes	No	None	Mari- juana Only	Few Pills	More Pills	Any Her- oin
N (Weighted No. of Cases):	3179	1481	1591	2367	338	756	902	980	541	1906	1054	1324	625	447	670	37
% of Weighted Total:	100.0	46.6	50.0	74.4	10.6	23.8	28.4	30.8	17.0	59.9	33.2	41.6	19.7	14.1	21.1	1.2

E07D: Other school clubs or activities

1. Not at all	30.0	37.0	23.5	29.3	27.9	34.7	30.6	22.7	35.7	21.2	45.6	24.9	27.9	23.1	46.1	43.2
2. Slight	15.6	16.4	15.2	16.3	13.9	13.2	17.4	16.1	14.9	15.8	15.4	16.1	18.1	15.1	12.5	19.8
3. Moderate	16.7	16.9	16.8	17.1	14.7	14.0	17.9	18.9	14.5	19.5	11.9	16.2	17.8	21.0	13.8	19.0
4. Considerable	17.0	15.5	18.4	17.7	15.2	16.1	16.4	19.8	14.1	18.8	13.4	19.8	17.6	17.5	10.9	9.1
5. Great	20.7	14.2	26.1	19.8	28.3	22.0	17.8	22.6	20.8	24.8	13.7	22.9	18.6	23.3	16.7	8.9
Item 22200 Subject B01,C07 N	2782	1266	1468	2154	268	620	834	847	482	1755	935	1193	552	395	582	35

The next questions are about military service.

E08: Do you favor or oppose a military draft at the present time?

1. Strongly oppose	23.8	29.1	19.1	23.7	24.8	26.4	24.1	21.3	24.4	24.1	23.1	22.0	24.2	23.9	27.0	26.8
2. Mostly oppose	18.8	18.6	19.0	20.1	14.9	18.0	20.1	18.9	17.3	19.4	18.3	19.6	20.0	20.8	15.0	24.3
3. No opinion, or mixed	40.2	31.3	48.2	39.9	40.3	37.5	39.6	39.8	45.4	40.8	39.3	40.9	41.5	38.6	40.1	21.7
4. Mostly favor	11.5	11.8	11.5	11.3	11.7	12.6	10.6	13.9	7.5	10.9	12.4	11.3	10.3	10.4	13.0	18.9
5. Strongly favor	5.6	9.1	2.3	5.1	8.3	5.3	5.6	6.1	5.3	4.8	6.9	6.2	3.9	6.3	4.8	8.3
Item 21060 Subject L02 N	2760	1265	1449	2141	266	614	827	845	474	1736	929	1185	548	393	575	33

E09: Do you think any military draft in the U.S. should include women as well as men?

1. No	27.9	18.4	35.9	28.7	27.2	24.9	27.2	32.3	25.1	27.4	29.1	30.8	26.2	29.4	24.0	18.0
2. Uncertain	34.7	27.5	41.9	33.5	42.0	31.7	32.5	37.3	38.0	36.0	32.2	34.9	37.3	33.8	33.2	16.6
3. Yes	37.4	54.1	22.2	37.8	30.8	43.5	40.3	30.4	36.9	36.6	38.8	34.4	36.5	36.7	42.8	65.4
Item 21070 Subject L02 N	2778	1277	1453	2152	269	616	834	851	476	1748	933	1190	552	395	580	33

One idea for getting more high school grad- uates to serve in the military is to offer them a paid college education after three years of service in the armed forces. During the three years of military duty their pay would be fairly low, but afterward the government would pay their tuition plus $300 a month living expenses for up to four academic years.

E10: Do you think it would be a good idea for the U.S. to have such a program of paid college in return for military service?

1. Definitely not	1.9	1.9	1.6	1.5	2.3	1.6	2.4	1.8	1.6	1.6	2.4	2.2	2.0	0.9	1.8	3.7
2. Probably not	2.4	2.6	2.3	2.1	5.1	2.4	2.1	2.8	2.4	2.0	3.4	2.4	3.6	2.9	1.1	3.5
3. No opinion or uncertain	16.4	16.5	16.2	15.6	17.7	16.3	15.7	15.3	19.4	13.5	21.9	17.4	14.4	16.0	15.7	15.4
4. Yes, probably	32.2	29.8	34.5	33.7	26.7	35.0	33.0	30.5	30.1	34.0	29.2	30.5	36.0	30.8	33.3	31.3
5. Yes, definitely	47.1	49.2	45.4	47.1	48.2	44.7	46.8	49.6	46.5	49.0	43.1	47.5	43.9	49.4	48.2	46.1
Item 21080 Subject L02 N	2747	1256	1443	2130	262	605	827	841	474	1727	927	1183	542	385	576	33

E11: If paid college in return for military service were available NOW, how likely is it that you would sign up for such a plan?

1. Definitely would not	32.7	27.6	37.7	34.4	23.2	33.3	30.9	35.3	30.7	33.1	32.9	34.5	31.1	31.7	32.1	28.8
2. Probably would not	37.4	37.0	37.5	40.3	27.0	37.6	40.4	33.4	38.8	39.7	32.4	41.1	34.6	39.4	32.7	15.9
3. Probably would	23.5	26.5	20.8	19.7	36.4	24.7	19.6	25.2	25.5	21.4	27.2	18.4	27.7	21.9	28.6	45.0
4. Definitely would	6.5	8.8	4.1	5.6	13.5	4.4	9.2	6.1	5.0	5.8	7.5	6.0	6.6	7.0	6.7	10.2
Item 21090 Subject L02 N	2726	1249	1430	2114	262	603	817	837	469	1715	922	1177	536	387	569	33

E12: Some people like school very much. Oth- ers don't. How do you feel about going to school?

5. I like school very much	11.9	10.9	12.7	10.2	22.1	10.6	11.4	13.3	12.3	12.7	10.9	16.3	8.1	10.7	7.1	10.2
4. I like school quite a lot	29.6	29.6	29.5	29.6	28.7	27.4	30.2	28.2	33.7	34.4	20.9	34.3	29.4	28.3	21.9	18.9
3. I like school some	40.3	41.7	38.9	40.9	40.7	43.9	42.0	38.6	35.9	38.4	43.6	37.2	43.9	43.5	42.2	33.3
2. I don't like school very much	12.1	10.8	13.6	13.1	6.0	11.8	10.8	13.0	12.9	10.7	14.5	8.4	12.8	12.5	17.7	26.8
1. I don't like school at all	6.1	7.0	5.3	6.2	2.5	6.3	5.6	6.8	5.2	3.8	10.2	3.9	5.8	5.0	11.1	10.8
Item 7630 Subject B01,Q08 N	2787	1276	1462	2160	270	617	836	853	481	1760	929	1192	560	392	581	33

QUESTIONNAIRE FORM 2 1986	TOTAL	SEX		RACE		REGION				4YR COLLEGE PLANS		ILLICIT DRUG USE: LIFETIME				
		M	F	White	Black	NE	NC	S	W	Yes	No	None	Mari-juana Only	Few Pills	More Pills	Any Her-oin
N (Weighted No. of Cases):	3179	1481	1591	2367	338	756	902	980	541	1906	1054	1324	625	447	670	37
% of Weighted Total:	100.0	46.6	50.0	74.4	10.6	23.8	28.4	30.8	17.0	59.9	33.2	41.6	19.7	14.1	21.1	1.2

E13: About how many hours do you spend in an average week on all your homework including both in school and out of school?

	TOTAL	M	F	White	Black	NE	NC	S	W	Yes	No	None	Mari-juana Only	Few Pills	More Pills	Any Her-oin
1. 0 hours	7.1	11.0	3.5	7.3	4.5	6.6	6.5	8.2	6.6	4.7	11.0	5.7	5.7	7.2	9.8	19.8
2. 1-4 hours	44.5	46.0	43.8	44.3	47.8	44.6	44.0	46.9	41.2	39.6	54.5	40.7	46.1	46.1	49.0	59.6
3. 5-9 hours	22.4	20.9	23.3	22.5	24.3	24.3	24.3	19.8	21.2	23.9	19.9	20.8	23.2	26.4	22.4	10.8
4. 10-14 hours	13.4	11.7	14.8	13.5	13.1	12.2	13.0	12.5	17.2	15.8	8.6	16.7	12.4	8.9	11.7	4.5
5. 15-19 hours	5.2	3.8	6.3	5.5	3.4	6.1	4.7	4.9	5.4	6.9	2.2	6.2	6.5	3.4	3.4	3.7
6. 20-24 hours	3.7	3.5	4.0	3.7	5.1	4.2	3.5	3.2	4.3	4.3	2.3	4.8	2.8	4.1	2.5	1.6
7. 25 or more hours	3.7	3.1	4.3	3.2	1.9	2.0	3.9	4.5	4.0	4.9	1.6	5.2	3.3	3.9	1.3	-
Item 7640 Subject B01 N	2770	1269	1452	2145	267	614	831	848	477	1751	922	1184	557	386	582	33

E14: In general, how much say or influence do you feel each of the following has on HOW YOUR SCHOOL IS RUN?

E14A: The principal

	TOTAL	M	F	White	Black	NE	NC	S	W	Yes	No	None	Mari-juana Only	Few Pills	More Pills	Any Her-oin
1. Little or no influence	12.8	14.0	11.9	11.5	17.8	12.6	11.1	13.0	15.7	10.7	16.3	9.9	12.7	15.4	15.5	10.9
2. Some influence	13.5	14.1	12.8	12.2	19.8	13.2	12.0	14.3	15.0	11.1	18.0	13.1	12.3	12.0	15.8	31.5
3. Moderate influence	14.3	14.9	13.8	14.2	10.7	11.9	15.5	12.9	17.6	13.7	15.3	12.6	17.7	13.1	15.4	11.6
4. Considerable influence	24.5	24.0	25.4	26.1	18.2	26.9	26.6	22.4	21.5	27.4	18.6	26.7	22.8	25.8	21.8	21.9
5. A great deal of influence	34.9	33.0	36.1	35.9	33.6	35.4	34.9	37.4	30.1	37.1	31.8	37.8	34.5	33.6	31.6	24.1
Item 7650 Subject B10 N	2745	1251	1447	2125	266	600	828	843	475	1733	915	1177	546	386	574	33

E14B: The teachers

	TOTAL	M	F	White	Black	NE	NC	S	W	Yes	No	None	Mari-juana Only	Few Pills	More Pills	Any Her-oin
1. Little or no influence	8.4	10.3	6.8	7.7	10.9	9.4	7.7	7.8	9.7	6.8	11.7	7.6	7.7	8.9	9.4	11.0
2. Some influence	18.6	19.2	18.0	18.5	18.8	18.7	18.1	19.1	18.1	16.0	23.3	16.1	20.4	19.7	21.5	20.3
3. Moderate influence	30.2	29.1	31.7	31.3	26.7	29.9	31.7	28.4	31.1	31.6	28.0	28.9	30.7	34.5	29.9	26.4
4. Considerable influence	31.4	30.7	32.0	32.0	28.0	26.5	34.5	32.0	31.3	34.1	25.2	34.4	30.2	28.8	29.5	29.0
5. A great deal of influence	11.4	10.7	11.4	10.5	15.6	15.4	8.0	12.7	9.8	11.5	11.8	13.0	10.9	8.1	9.7	13.3
Item 7660 Subject B10 N	2735	1246	1444	2122	262	601	826	835	472	1730	908	1176	544	386	570	33

E14C: The students

	TOTAL	M	F	White	Black	NE	NC	S	W	Yes	No	None	Mari-juana Only	Few Pills	More Pills	Any Her-oin
1. Little or no influence	27.7	29.7	25.9	28.4	25.5	25.4	26.2	32.6	24.6	25.7	31.4	25.6	26.8	31.9	30.0	30.3
2. Some influence	25.0	25.0	25.4	26.0	20.6	28.8	26.1	22.8	22.2	26.0	23.8	24.9	27.0	24.3	24.7	16.4
3. Moderate influence	21.4	20.4	22.3	20.7	22.1	18.5	23.7	19.9	23.7	22.9	18.0	22.7	24.2	18.0	18.5	16.7
4. Considerable influence	15.0	15.4	14.6	14.7	17.2	15.4	14.8	12.2	19.5	15.6	14.3	16.1	12.8	14.9	14.7	15.3
5. A great deal of influence	10.9	9.5	11.8	10.2	14.6	11.9	9.1	12.4	10.0	9.8	12.5	10.7	9.2	10.9	12.0	21.3
Item 7670 Subject B10 N	2728	1242	1440	2114	263	598	824	836	470	1724	907	1172	545	381	571	32

E14D: Parents of students

	TOTAL	M	F	White	Black	NE	NC	S	W	Yes	No	None	Mari-juana Only	Few Pills	More Pills	Any Her-oin
1. Little or no influence	21.2	23.7	19.4	21.4	18.5	22.8	19.4	20.7	23.3	16.8	29.6	17.3	19.2	23.7	27.6	37.5
2. Some influence	28.5	29.0	28.0	30.0	26.0	29.9	29.1	29.8	23.8	29.8	27.4	27.8	30.2	27.4	30.7	20.7
3. Moderate influence	24.4	21.3	26.9	24.5	21.0	20.4	27.9	22.0	27.2	26.7	19.7	26.4	24.4	22.7	21.7	25.2
4. Considerable influence	15.6	16.0	15.2	15.7	15.4	14.6	15.4	16.1	16.3	17.6	11.3	16.8	17.7	15.0	12.0	6.2
5. A great deal of influence	10.3	10.1	10.4	8.4	19.2	12.3	8.2	11.4	9.4	9.0	12.0	11.6	8.5	11.2	8.0	10.3
Item 7680 Subject B10 N	2724	1237	1441	2111	263	596	824	833	472	1722	907	1170	540	384	571	33

E15: Have you had any drug education courses or lectures in school?

	TOTAL	M	F	White	Black	NE	NC	S	W	Yes	No	None	Mari-juana Only	Few Pills	More Pills	Any Her-oin
1. No–GO TO Q.E19	23.8	25.7	22.6	23.0	31.2	17.5	24.5	27.7	23.8	20.7	29.7	26.2	24.9	19.8	20.8	14.4
2. No, and I wish I had– GO TO Q.E19	3.9	2.4	5.0	3.9	3.8	3.2	3.8	4.1	4.6	3.4	4.8	3.5	4.3	3.9	4.5	4.1
3. Yes	72.3	71.9	72.4	73.0	65.0	79.3	71.7	68.2	71.6	76.0	65.5	70.3	70.8	76.3	74.7	81.4
Item 7690 Subject A10a N	2568	1156	1374	2012	225	558	793	770	447	1661	821	1109	503	360	544	33

QUESTIONNAIRE FORM 2 1986	TOTAL	SEX		RACE		REGION				4YR COLLEGE PLANS		ILLICIT DRUG USE: LIFETIME				
		M	F	White	Black	NE	NC	S	W	Yes	No	None	Mari-juana Only	Few Pills	More Pills	Any Her-oin
N (Weighted No. of Cases):	3179	1481	1591	2367	338	756	902	980	541	1906	1054	1324	625	447	670	37
% of Weighted Total:	100.0	46.6	50.0	74.4	10.6	23.8	28.4	30.8	17.0	59.9	33.2	41.6	19.7	14.1	21.1	1.2

E16: Would you say that the information about drugs that you received in school classes or programs has . . .

	TOTAL	M	F	White	Black	NE	NC	S	W	Yes	No	None	Mari-juana Only	Few Pills	More Pills	Any Her-oin
1. Made you less interested in trying drugs	57.2	54.1	59.3	54.5	73.1	58.3	49.2	64.2	58.4	57.7	56.0	72.5	59.1	51.9	33.2	8.9
2. Not changed your interest in trying drugs	40.0	41.7	39.1	42.4	23.7	38.8	47.7	32.6	39.6	39.9	39.8	26.6	39.6	45.7	59.8	67.8
3. Made you more interested in trying drugs	2.9	4.3	1.6	3.1	3.2	2.8	3.1	3.2	1.9	2.3	4.2	0.9	1.4	2.4	7.0	23.2
Item 7840 Subject A10a N★	1868	836	999	1474	149	443	575	522	328	1268	547	784	361	277	409	27

E17: How many of the following drug education experiences have you had in high school? (Mark all that apply.)

	TOTAL	M	F	White	Black	NE	NC	S	W	Yes	No	None	Mari-juana Only	Few Pills	More Pills	Any Her-oin
A. A special course about drugs	24.1	24.8	22.5	23.8	27.4	34.7	22.6	18.3	21.8	26.3	19.6	25.4	24.2	19.6	22.9	39.5
B. Films, lectures, or discussions in one of my regular courses	77.4	75.3	79.5	78.3	70.1	75.4	75.9	79.4	79.8	79.6	73.6	80.9	75.6	75.3	75.4	67.8
C. Films or lectures, outside of my regular courses	30.4	29.2	30.5	31.3	32.9	31.3	31.3	30.3	27.6	31.0	28.8	31.9	27.8	30.3	29.6	33.8
D. Special discussions ("rap" groups) about drugs	22.5	19.6	24.4	22.9	25.5	23.3	22.0	19.4	27.2	23.6	20.4	20.9	19.0	19.3	29.8	35.1
Item 7850-7880 Subject A10a N★	1840	827	980	1455	146	434	571	514	322	1247	538	776	353	273	401	27

E18: Overall, how valuable were the experiences to you?

	TOTAL	M	F	White	Black	NE	NC	S	W	Yes	No	None	Mari-juana Only	Few Pills	More Pills	Any Her-oin
1. Little or no value	17.1	20.5	14.3	16.8	13.5	17.2	17.8	15.5	18.3	17.3	16.2	15.4	11.7	19.2	22.3	32.0
2. Some value	43.8	46.1	43.1	46.0	30.9	41.0	47.6	42.7	42.9	46.0	39.6	40.8	45.5	40.1	50.9	46.0
3. Considerable value	25.5	22.6	27.6	26.0	25.6	29.4	22.7	25.1	25.8	24.7	26.8	26.0	29.7	28.2	20.0	18.9
4. Great value	13.5	10.8	15.0	11.1	29.9	12.3	11.8	16.7	13.0	12.0	17.4	17.8	13.1	12.4	6.7	3.1
Item 7890 Subject A10a N★	1854	830	991	1467	145	438	573	517	325	1258	541	781	356	273	409	27

E19: During the LAST TWO WEEKS, how many times (if any) have you driven a car, truck, or motorcycle after . . .

E19A: Drinking alcohol?

	TOTAL	M	F	White	Black	NE	NC	S	W	Yes	No	None	Mari-juana Only	Few Pills	More Pills	Any Her-oin
1. None	73.2	66.1	79.1	70.3	86.8	80.1	66.5	70.8	80.8	73.8	72.3	87.9	66.7	66.0	56.6	49.0
2. Once	12.1	13.5	11.0	13.4	6.5	11.3	14.6	13.1	7.0	12.5	10.8	6.4	15.3	17.7	16.7	21.0
3. Twice	7.7	9.7	6.0	8.3	3.6	4.8	10.2	7.6	6.9	7.2	8.5	2.9	10.5	7.3	13.7	16.2
4. 3-5 times	5.3	7.6	3.5	6.1	1.5	2.3	6.9	6.6	4.0	4.8	6.4	2.2	5.5	7.2	9.6	11.1
5. 6-9 times	0.9	1.4	0.4	0.9	1.1	0.4	1.3	1.0	0.4	0.9	0.9	0.4	0.7	0.9	1.8	-
6. 10 or more	0.9	1.7	0.1	0.9	0.5	1.1	0.6	1.0	0.9	0.7	1.2	0.2	1.3	0.9	1.7	2.7
Item 1811 Subject A07a N	2728	1251	1429	2115	260	591	825	832	479	1732	900	1173	544	384	570	31

E19B: Having 5 or more drinks in a row?

	TOTAL	M	F	White	Black	NE	NC	S	W	Yes	No	None	Mari-juana Only	Few Pills	More Pills	Any Her-oin
1. None	84.2	77.4	90.0	82.5	95.0	89.9	77.7	84.0	88.7	85.3	81.8	94.7	80.2	82.1	70.5	60.8
2. Once	7.3	10.4	4.7	8.0	3.4	4.4	10.8	6.6	6.0	7.5	7.0	2.7	9.9	8.8	12.0	14.5
3. Twice	4.2	5.5	3.0	4.4	0.4	2.5	5.8	4.1	3.6	3.9	4.7	1.3	5.5	2.9	9.2	10.3
4. 3-5 times	3.0	4.6	1.6	3.5	1.2	2.0	3.9	4.4	0.4	2.4	4.2	1.2	3.7	4.5	5.1	1.0
5. 6-9 times	0.9	1.4	0.5	1.1	-	0.7	1.2	0.7	1.0	0.6	1.5	0.1	0.5	0.9	1.9	11.8
6. 10 or more	0.5	0.9	0.1	0.5	-	0.6	0.7	0.2	0.3	0.3	0.8	-	0.3	0.8	1.3	1.5
Item 1812 Subject A07a N	2701	1233	1421	2101	253	586	814	827	474	1722	890	1162	537	377	565	33

E20: During the LAST TWO WEEKS, how many times (if any) have you been a passenger in a car . . .

E20A: When the driver had been drinking?

	TOTAL	M	F	White	Black	NE	NC	S	W	Yes	No	None	Mari-juana Only	Few Pills	More Pills	Any Her-oin
1. None	61.8	62.8	60.7	59.7	70.1	69.5	56.5	59.0	66.6	63.7	58.3	78.0	53.9	50.6	45.0	30.1
2. Once	18.6	16.3	20.8	20.0	12.8	15.4	20.6	18.8	18.6	18.5	18.5	14.3	22.7	24.3	20.1	18.3
3. Twice	10.4	11.5	9.8	11.0	8.1	8.2	12.6	11.1	8.1	10.0	10.9	4.8	11.9	13.1	18.6	11.9
4. 3-5 times	6.5	6.6	6.0	6.9	6.0	4.1	7.8	8.2	4.0	6.2	7.1	1.9	9.6	8.4	11.3	15.3
5. 6-9 times	1.3	1.4	1.3	1.2	2.5	0.6	1.5	1.7	1.2	0.7	2.5	0.4	1.7	0.7	2.5	13.4
6. 10 or more	1.4	1.4	1.5	1.2	0.5	2.1	1.0	1.2	1.6	0.9	2.7	0.5	0.1	2.9	2.5	11.1
Item 1815 Subject A07a N	2712	1243	1421	2108	258	591	825	824	473	1723	899	1166	536	381	570	33

★=excludes respondents for whom question was inappropriate.

QUESTIONNAIRE FORM 2 1986	TOTAL	SEX		RACE		REGION				4YR COLLEGE PLANS		ILLICIT DRUG USE: LIFETIME				
		M	F	White	Black	NE	NC	S	W	Yes	No	None	Marijuana Only	Few Pills	More Pills	Any Heroin
N (Weighted No. of Cases):	3179	1481	1591	2367	338	756	902	980	541	1906	1054	1324	625	447	670	37
% of Weighted Total:	100.0	46.6	50.0	74.4	10.6	23.8	28.4	30.8	17.0	59.9	33.2	41.6	19.7	14.1	21.1	1.2

E20B: When you think the driver had 5 or more drinks?

1. None	78.8	75.2	81.8	76.8	86.5	83.8	73.3	77.9	83.9	81.5	73.7	91.2	74.6	75.6	62.8	35.7
2. Once	10.2	11.3	9.2	11.5	4.3	9.0	12.8	9.4	8.8	10.1	10.4	5.1	12.6	13.2	16.4	11.5
3. Twice	5.7	7.6	4.2	5.9	4.3	3.5	7.6	5.3	5.9	4.0	8.4	2.1	5.6	4.3	12.2	23.2
4. 3-5 times	3.5	3.9	3.1	3.8	4.1	1.7	4.7	4.9	1.0	3.2	4.4	1.1	6.0	3.5	5.2	13.7
5. 6-9 times	0.8	1.1	0.7	0.9	0.5	0.9	0.7	1.3	0.2	0.7	1.3	0.2	0.9	1.2	1.4	9.0
6. 10 or more	1.0	0.9	1.1	1.0	0.4	1.1	1.0	1.3	0.2	0.5	1.9	0.3	0.2	2.1	2.0	6.9
Item 1816 Subject A07a N	2693	1225	1421	2097	253	585	820	820	469	1709	897	1156	530	379	570	33

E21: How often do you . . .

E21A: Eat breakfast?

1. Never	10.3	10.0	10.2	9.8	8.0	10.0	12.2	9.4	8.7	9.6	11.7	7.9	7.8	10.5	15.0	24.9
2. Seldom	29.8	25.3	34.0	29.3	35.4	31.4	29.4	28.9	30.4	27.4	34.0	26.6	29.5	35.4	33.6	24.6
3. Sometimes	16.0	14.7	16.9	14.8	26.5	14.3	15.8	19.2	12.8	15.2	17.6	14.7	18.5	15.2	16.0	26.6
4. Most days	9.7	9.6	10.0	9.6	11.3	9.7	8.7	8.9	13.1	10.2	8.9	9.9	10.4	8.8	9.6	8.0
5. Nearly every day	10.8	10.8	10.6	11.3	7.3	9.8	11.2	10.6	11.5	12.0	8.1	10.3	11.6	13.1	10.2	2.5
6. Every day	23.4	29.6	18.4	25.3	11.5	24.9	22.7	23.0	23.5	25.6	19.7	30.5	22.2	17.0	15.5	13.3
Item 20740 Subject T02 N	2731	1245	1437	2119	257	595	829	830	477	1736	902	1170	543	382	576	33

E21B: Eat at least some green vegetables?

1. Never	4.0	4.4	3.5	3.0	5.6	3.9	3.5	4.2	4.5	3.0	5.6	3.9	3.9	2.1	4.4	13.1
2. Seldom	12.2	12.4	12.0	11.8	14.2	9.9	12.5	13.8	11.8	10.3	16.2	10.9	11.5	12.7	14.1	22.9
3. Sometimes	22.9	22.3	23.7	22.4	29.1	22.8	23.3	24.0	20.3	19.8	28.2	21.7	22.7	25.3	24.1	22.7
4. Most days	24.5	23.6	25.1	25.2	22.8	23.9	23.7	23.9	27.7	25.6	23.1	21.6	27.9	25.9	26.7	25.2
5. Nearly every day	17.9	17.7	18.3	18.1	17.6	15.9	19.6	18.2	16.7	20.4	12.9	18.4	19.7	19.8	14.4	4.8
6. Every day	18.6	19.6	17.4	19.4	10.7	23.7	17.4	15.9	19.0	20.9	14.0	23.5	14.3	14.1	16.4	11.3
Item 20750 Subject T02 N	2719	1239	1433	2109	258	591	826	827	476	1728	899	1164	539	380	577	33

E21C: Eat at least some fruit?

1. Never	1.8	2.0	1.4	1.7	2.4	1.7	1.5	1.8	2.5	1.0	2.8	1.1	1.6	0.9	3.3	6.6
2. Seldom	10.1	10.8	9.5	10.0	12.1	7.8	10.4	12.7	8.0	7.4	15.3	8.0	12.2	11.4	11.4	11.8
3. Sometimes	28.4	26.7	30.4	28.1	29.9	26.6	28.0	32.3	24.6	26.3	33.4	26.2	27.9	33.0	29.9	32.4
4. Most days	23.2	22.5	23.7	22.7	27.6	20.6	22.3	24.5	25.9	24.4	20.4	22.4	23.8	22.8	25.2	19.6
5. Nearly every day	18.5	18.2	18.7	18.6	14.5	20.1	19.2	15.0	21.0	20.3	14.7	20.1	18.3	18.1	16.0	10.3
6. Every day	18.0	19.9	16.3	19.0	13.5	23.2	18.7	13.7	18.1	20.7	13.3	22.2	16.2	13.4	14.1	19.3
Item 20760 Subject T02 N	2722	1239	1435	2111	258	590	828	828	477	1729	902	1167	543	377	575	33

E21D: Exercise vigorously (jogging, swimming, calisthenics, or any other active sports)?

1. Never	5.3	4.5	5.7	4.4	8.9	5.2	3.6	7.0	5.3	3.5	8.6	4.4	5.5	3.8	6.9	14.9
2. Seldom	18.4	14.1	22.3	18.1	21.5	17.4	19.2	20.6	14.4	15.1	24.6	16.6	18.7	18.4	22.1	11.6
3. Sometimes	24.4	18.7	29.8	24.5	23.7	22.3	23.1	27.8	23.7	24.4	24.5	26.6	21.8	25.5	22.5	20.1
4. Most days	16.1	17.2	15.2	16.3	16.0	13.3	16.8	16.4	17.9	16.9	14.7	16.1	15.6	14.7	18.2	18.3
5. Nearly every day	16.3	20.1	12.6	16.8	15.0	17.5	17.1	14.5	16.4	18.4	12.4	17.2	15.8	22.0	11.3	16.1
6. Every day	19.5	25.5	14.3	20.0	14.9	24.1	20.2	13.6	22.4	21.6	15.2	19.2	22.7	15.7	19.0	19.0
Item 20770 Subject T02 N	2708	1231	1430	2103	255	589	827	821	472	1718	898	1164	532	380	572	33

E21E: Get at least seven hours of sleep?

1. Never	2.4	3.0	1.7	2.2	3.6	2.6	1.9	3.1	1.7	1.9	3.2	2.1	2.0	0.9	3.0	14.2
2. Seldom	12.3	10.9	13.6	12.3	11.9	10.6	13.8	12.4	11.7	11.2	14.0	10.4	12.2	14.8	14.4	21.5
3. Sometimes	20.6	18.9	22.2	20.1	19.8	16.6	22.8	24.0	16.2	21.2	19.2	18.1	21.2	22.9	22.8	36.0
4. Most days	22.4	23.3	21.5	23.0	18.9	19.9	24.5	21.2	24.2	22.5	22.3	21.6	19.7	23.6	27.2	7.4
5. Nearly every day	22.6	21.0	24.3	23.4	23.0	26.2	20.1	21.5	24.3	24.0	20.3	25.4	25.0	22.3	16.1	13.1
6. Every day	19.6	23.0	16.7	19.0	22.8	24.1	16.9	17.8	22.1	19.1	21.0	22.5	19.9	15.5	16.5	7.8
Item 20780 Subject T02 N	2709	1232	1429	2104	256	589	824	822	475	1721	898	1163	533	379	574	33

QUESTIONNAIRE FORM 2 1986	TOTAL	SEX		RACE		REGION				4YR COLLEGE PLANS		ILLICIT DRUG USE: LIFETIME				
		M	F	White	Black	NE	NC	S	W	Yes	No	None	Mari-juana Only	Few Pills	More Pills	Any Her-oin
N (Weighted No. of Cases):	3179	1481	1591	2367	338	756	902	980	541	1906	1054	1324	625	447	670	37
% of Weighted Total:	100.0	46.6	50.0	74.4	10.6	23.8	28.4	30.8	17.0	59.9	33.2	41.6	19.7	14.1	21.1	1.2

E21F: Get less sleep than you think you should?

	TOTAL	M	F	White	Black	NE	NC	S	W	Yes	No	None	Mari-juana Only	Few Pills	More Pills	Any Her-oin
1. Never	8.0	8.8	7.0	6.7	14.2	9.2	6.7	8.5	8.2	5.6	12.4	8.6	6.8	6.7	7.9	10.9
2. Seldom	17.4	17.6	17.3	16.9	21.7	21.4	14.2	17.1	18.8	16.2	19.6	18.8	18.1	15.5	15.7	7.9
3. Sometimes	29.5	28.3	30.5	29.7	27.0	28.3	29.8	29.7	29.8	30.5	27.9	30.8	31.8	27.2	26.5	38.5
4. Most days	18.0	17.5	18.8	18.3	15.6	16.2	20.1	17.9	16.6	19.6	14.4	18.1	19.1	17.3	17.2	17.0
5. Nearly every day	14.5	14.6	14.6	15.5	9.2	11.3	16.4	14.6	15.3	15.7	13.0	12.7	13.6	18.0	17.5	10.2
6. Every day	12.6	13.2	11.8	12.8	12.3	13.6	12.8	12.3	11.3	12.3	12.8	11.0	10.6	15.3	15.1	15.5
Item 20790 Subject T02　N	2707	1230	1429	2103	255	588	822	822	475	1719	898	1165	531	377	574	32

E22: When you drive a car, how often do you wear a seatbelt?

	TOTAL	M	F	White	Black	NE	NC	S	W	Yes	No	None	Mari-juana Only	Few Pills	More Pills	Any Her-oin
1. Never	26.7	33.7	20.6	26.9	27.4	27.1	30.2	27.9	18.0	20.5	38.2	20.5	25.5	30.5	36.7	54.1
2. Seldom	16.5	17.2	16.1	16.8	17.8	11.3	18.8	20.4	12.0	16.0	17.2	14.8	15.4	16.2	15.7	18.8
3. Sometimes	15.1	12.3	17.5	15.5	14.8	10.2	16.9	15.3	17.6	14.2	15.7	15.1	13.8	15.9	16.6	3.6
4. Often	13.7	12.5	14.6	13.4	13.1	12.1	13.8	14.5	14.0	15.2	11.3	15.0	13.4	11.4	13.1	3.2
5. Always	25.0	22.7	26.8	25.2	21.3	33.4	18.7	19.8	34.6	31.4	13.6	31.0	24.3	23.4	15.2	15.4
8. Does not apply	3.1	1.6	4.4	2.3	5.6	6.0	1.6	2.1	3.8	2.7	4.0	3.7	2.6	2.5	2.8	4.8
Item 22210 Subject F07,S02,T02　N	2713	1240	1427	2109	254	590	821	828	474	1723	895	1166	537	379	571	33

E23: When you are riding in the front passenger seat of a car, how often do you wear a seatbelt?

	TOTAL	M	F	White	Black	NE	NC	S	W	Yes	No	None	Mari-juana Only	Few Pills	More Pills	Any Her-oin
1. Never	27.2	34.4	21.2	27.2	31.0	27.4	32.5	28.6	15.7	21.3	38.2	22.2	26.2	28.5	35.9	54.1
2. Seldom	19.4	18.7	20.3	20.4	18.2	15.2	21.3	22.4	16.0	18.4	21.3	16.4	21.3	21.2	21.8	24.8
3. Sometimes	16.4	13.9	18.4	16.9	15.0	13.9	15.7	16.7	20.3	17.2	15.1	16.8	16.5	16.8	16.2	1.5
4. Often	14.5	12.2	16.1	14.3	12.5	13.4	16.3	12.9	15.9	16.6	10.5	15.8	16.3	14.1	11.2	10.0
5. Always	22.0	20.1	23.8	21.1	20.9	29.9	14.1	18.7	31.8	26.3	14.3	28.6	19.4	18.5	14.3	9.5
8. Does not apply	0.4	0.6	0.2	0.1	2.4	0.3	0.1	0.8	0.3	0.2	0.6	0.1	0.4	0.9	0.6	-
Item 22220 Subject F07,S02,T02　N	2711	1234	1430	2108	251	590	819	827	474	1720	897	1167	534	378	572	33

QUESTIONNAIRE FORM 3 1986	TOTAL	SEX		RACE		REGION				4YR COLLEGE PLANS		ILLICIT DRUG USE: LIFETIME				
		M	F	White	Black	NE	NC	S	W	Yes	No	None	Mari-juana Only	Few Pills	More Pills	Any Her-oin
N (Weighted No. of Cases):	3159	1456	1581	2348	342	746	901	978	534	1801	1138	1328	641	437	648	29
% of Weighted Total:	100.0	46.1	50.1	74.3	10.8	23.6	28.5	31.0	16.9	57.0	36.0	42.0	20.3	13.8	20.5	0.9
A01: Taking all things together, how would you say things are these days-would you say you're very happy, pretty happy, or not too happy these days?																
3. Very happy	17.0	17.3	16.8	18.7	11.0	15.7	18.1	15.0	20.3	19.1	13.6	19.2	18.4	13.1	13.7	15.3
2. Pretty happy	70.6	71.3	70.5	71.3	68.8	69.8	70.8	72.2	68.1	70.3	72.8	69.2	71.1	74.6	72.0	68.0
1. Not too happy	12.5	11.5	12.7	10.0	20.2	14.5	11.1	12.8	11.6	10.5	13.6	11.6	10.4	12.3	14.2	16.7
Item 1190 Subject P01,Q01 N	3138	1443	1575	2333	339	737	896	975	529	1794	1128	1317	638	437	644	29
A02: Some people think a lot about the social problems of the nation and the world, and about how they might be solved. Others spend little time thinking about these issues. How much do you think about such things?																
1. Never	2.4	2.5	2.2	2.5	1.7	5.1	2.3	1.1	1.3	1.0	4.3	1.9	3.1	3.0	2.1	9.4
2. Seldom	13.5	13.0	13.6	12.8	15.6	14.7	13.1	12.8	13.8	12.1	14.8	12.3	15.8	12.6	14.3	3.2
3. Sometimes	50.5	50.1	51.0	51.2	45.2	51.1	50.8	47.8	54.0	49.3	52.2	51.9	48.4	50.0	49.5	56.0
4. Quite often	28.1	28.6	28.0	28.5	30.4	23.5	28.9	31.8	26.1	31.2	24.7	29.0	27.8	27.7	27.5	26.0
5. A great deal	5.5	5.8	5.2	5.0	7.1	5.6	4.9	6.4	4.7	6.4	4.0	4.9	4.9	6.7	6.5	5.3
Item 6880 Subject J,Q08 N	3141	1446	1577	2337	339	737	897	976	531	1797	1130	1321	638	437	643	29
A03: The next questions ask your opinions about a number of different topics. How much do you agree or disagree with each statement below?																
A03A: Men and women should be paid the same money if they do the same work																
1. Disagree	2.5	3.7	1.1	2.1	2.7	3.2	1.9	3.0	1.6	1.4	3.3	2.6	2.3	0.5	3.2	10.1
2. Mostly disagree	1.7	2.8	0.6	1.7	1.3	2.0	1.3	1.2	3.0	1.4	1.9	1.5	1.8	2.2	1.6	3.1
3. Neither	1.7	3.3	0.3	1.7	1.2	1.9	1.9	2.0	0.8	1.5	2.0	1.6	2.7	1.0	0.7	4.0
4. Mostly agree	14.6	19.8	9.2	14.9	13.3	13.7	14.8	14.7	15.2	14.4	14.7	14.1	13.5	14.0	15.2	30.2
5. Agree	79.5	70.4	88.8	79.5	81.4	79.3	80.1	79.1	79.4	81.3	78.1	80.2	79.7	82.2	79.3	52.5
Item 7930 Subject D06 N	3147	1449	1577	2339	339	739	898	978	531	1796	1131	1323	636	436	646	29
A03B: Women should be considered as seriously as men for jobs as executives or politicians																
1. Disagree	3.6	6.9	0.4	3.7	2.8	4.0	3.2	3.9	2.8	2.3	5.4	3.6	3.6	2.1	4.0	11.5
2. Mostly disagree	4.7	8.7	0.9	4.9	1.5	4.5	4.1	5.1	5.4	4.3	5.1	4.4	4.7	4.7	4.5	8.3
3. Neither	3.3	5.9	0.9	3.0	2.9	3.4	3.7	3.6	2.0	2.5	4.1	3.5	2.4	1.5	4.0	10.0
4. Mostly agree	21.5	29.3	13.6	21.8	18.7	19.4	19.9	22.8	24.5	21.2	21.6	20.7	21.5	23.8	21.1	32.4
5. Agree	66.9	49.2	84.2	66.6	74.1	68.7	69.1	64.6	65.2	69.5	63.8	67.7	67.8	67.8	66.4	37.9
Item 7940 Subject D06,H02 N	3145	1450	1576	2341	337	738	899	978	530	1796	1133	1319	639	437	645	29
A03C: A woman should have exactly the same job opportunities as a man																
1. Disagree	5.8	10.2	1.5	5.1	6.1	7.2	4.3	6.8	4.4	3.7	8.4	6.5	4.4	4.7	5.2	17.3
2. Mostly disagree	5.8	11.0	1.2	6.5	4.9	6.8	6.4	4.6	5.9	5.1	7.1	4.4	7.4	5.8	7.3	12.5
3. Neither	4.9	6.9	3.0	5.0	3.1	4.4	5.0	5.1	5.1	4.6	5.7	5.2	4.9	5.8	3.4	5.3
4. Mostly agree	29.2	29.7	28.4	30.9	20.8	25.6	31.3	29.2	30.8	28.5	30.2	29.0	29.0	29.1	31.3	16.9
5. Agree	54.2	42.2	66.0	52.6	65.2	55.9	53.0	54.3	53.7	58.1	48.6	54.9	54.4	54.5	52.8	47.9
Item 7950 Subject D06 N	3130	1444	1568	2332	335	733	894	975	528	1789	1126	1316	633	437	641	29
A03D: A woman should have exactly the same educational opportunities as a man																
1. Disagree	1.1	1.6	0.6	0.7	2.5	1.2	0.7	1.8	0.6	0.7	1.7	1.3	0.7	0.8	1.0	4.0
2. Mostly disagree	0.8	1.3	0.2	0.7	1.0	1.0	0.9	0.7	0.4	0.3	0.9	0.6	0.7	0.3	1.1	4.9
3. Neither	1.1	2.1	0.1	1.2	0.4	1.0	1.3	0.9	1.0	1.0	1.2	1.6	1.2	0.5	0.2	1.7
4. Mostly agree	8.4	10.5	5.6	7.6	7.0	9.4	6.0	9.4	9.0	6.7	10.0	7.9	9.4	7.1	7.8	10.9
5. Agree	88.7	84.4	93.5	89.9	89.0	87.4	91.1	87.2	89.1	91.2	86.2	88.7	88.1	91.3	89.9	78.5
Item 7960 Subject D06 N	3134	1443	1572	2329	336	736	895	972	530	1790	1126	1320	633	434	643	28

QUESTIONNAIRE FORM 3 1986	TOTAL	SEX		RACE		REGION				4YR COLLEGE PLANS		ILLICIT DRUG USE: LIFETIME				
		M	F	White	Black	NE	NC	S	W	Yes	No	None	Marijuana Only	Few Pills	More Pills	Any Heroin
N (Weighted No. of Cases):	3159	1456	1581	2348	342	746	901	978	534	1801	1138	1328	641	437	648	29
% of Weighted Total:	100.0	46.1	50.1	74.3	10.8	23.6	28.5	31.0	16.9	57.0	36.0	42.0	20.3	13.8	20.5	0.9

A03E: It is usually better for everyone involved if the man is the achiever outside the home and the woman takes care of the home and family

1. Disagree	31.3	17.6	44.2	30.2	40.8	35.6	29.5	30.6	29.6	33.6	28.5	30.2	34.2	29.5	32.1	31.0
2. Mostly disagree	18.3	14.8	21.9	18.9	13.7	16.0	18.6	17.4	22.3	20.0	16.8	20.4	16.9	17.8	15.4	14.4
3. Neither	17.1	21.5	12.9	18.6	10.1	17.0	19.4	14.4	18.6	17.3	16.8	16.6	15.1	20.0	19.1	10.2
4. Mostly agree	19.4	24.2	14.8	19.1	18.9	17.4	19.5	21.5	17.9	18.0	20.4	20.3	18.1	20.3	18.4	27.7
5. Agree	14.0	21.9	6.2	13.1	16.5	14.0	13.0	16.1	11.6	11.1	17.5	12.6	15.7	12.4	15.0	16.7
Item 7970 Subject D05 N	3147	1452	1576	2341	338	739	899	977	533	1795	1134	1324	639	436	645	29

A03F: A preschool child is likely to suffer if the mother works

1. Disagree	18.2	12.4	23.4	16.1	37.8	18.2	16.8	21.4	14.9	17.3	19.7	18.5	18.2	15.9	18.8	7.4
2. Mostly disagree	19.1	13.0	24.1	18.9	18.6	19.6	20.2	18.6	17.5	20.3	16.5	19.3	21.5	19.8	16.2	33.3
3. Neither	16.8	16.3	17.4	18.2	10.6	16.9	17.4	14.4	20.0	18.3	15.1	14.2	16.1	21.5	19.7	4.9
4. Mostly agree	24.2	26.6	22.8	25.4	15.7	23.4	26.5	21.5	26.6	25.3	23.3	25.7	25.0	23.1	22.5	28.5
5. Agree	21.7	31.6	12.3	21.5	17.4	21.9	19.2	24.1	21.1	18.8	25.4	22.3	19.1	19.6	22.9	25.9
Item 7980 Subject D05 N	3128	1448	1564	2329	337	731	894	974	530	1788	1126	1315	635	434	641	29

A03G: A working mother can establish just as warm and secure a relationship with her children as a mother who does not work

1. Disagree	11.3	16.9	6.0	10.9	8.4	12.5	11.9	10.1	11.0	9.4	13.3	11.3	11.3	9.2	11.4	14.1
2. Mostly disagree	17.9	24.7	11.9	19.5	10.8	16.4	19.1	17.4	19.2	18.4	17.8	17.5	16.5	20.3	18.7	28.3
3. Neither	8.8	11.2	6.4	9.7	2.2	9.7	9.3	6.6	10.6	9.7	7.5	8.6	7.2	9.3	10.5	4.9
4. Mostly agree	28.1	25.2	31.3	28.9	24.4	27.1	27.7	27.6	31.2	28.8	27.9	28.6	27.7	28.8	28.1	33.8
5. Agree	33.9	22.0	44.5	31.0	54.3	34.3	32.1	38.4	28.1	33.6	33.5	33.9	37.2	32.4	31.4	18.8
Item 7990 Subject D05 N	3141	1450	1572	2336	339	736	897	976	532	1791	1133	1321	639	437	640	29

A04: The next questions are about pollution and the environment. How much do you agree or disagree with each statement below?

A04A: Pollution of most types has increased in the U.S. in the last ten years

1. Disagree	2.3	3.5	1.1	1.9	3.8	3.2	1.4	3.3	0.8	2.0	2.3	2.6	2.0	1.1	2.4	3.9
2. Mostly disagree	4.8	6.5	3.2	5.2	3.5	5.0	5.3	5.4	2.7	4.7	4.6	4.4	5.2	4.5	5.3	10.8
3. Neither	10.1	9.6	10.8	10.9	8.6	11.1	12.0	8.3	9.0	10.7	9.8	11.0	8.7	9.2	10.4	5.8
4. Mostly agree	32.9	28.2	37.1	34.8	26.5	28.4	38.3	30.8	33.8	33.3	32.7	31.5	35.0	34.6	32.6	34.1
5. Agree	49.9	52.2	47.8	47.1	57.6	52.3	43.1	52.2	53.8	49.3	50.6	50.5	49.2	50.5	49.4	45.4
Item 8000 Subject F04 N	3138	1445	1577	2335	338	736	897	975	531	1788	1135	1319	636	436	643	29

A04B: Government should take steps to deal with our environmental problems, even if it means that most of us pay higher prices or taxes

1. Disagree	8.5	11.3	6.0	6.6	18.0	8.9	5.8	12.1	5.7	5.6	12.8	7.9	8.8	7.4	7.8	12.7
2. Mostly disagree	9.5	10.7	8.5	9.0	11.8	8.8	9.2	9.6	10.8	9.3	9.4	8.8	10.8	8.4	10.7	5.8
3. Neither	19.6	15.3	23.8	20.0	15.9	19.0	20.8	18.3	20.6	18.2	21.8	17.0	19.2	20.5	24.0	30.5
4. Mostly agree	38.4	34.8	41.8	40.8	30.3	37.0	39.4	37.9	39.9	41.3	35.6	42.3	37.4	38.7	34.3	28.9
5. Agree	24.0	27.9	19.9	23.6	24.0	26.4	24.8	22.1	23.0	25.6	20.5	23.9	23.9	25.0	23.3	22.1
Item 8010 Subject F04,H02 N	3137	1448	1573	2336	337	732	897	976	533	1790	1132	1321	635	434	643	29

A04C: I would prefer to pay more money for things that will last a long time, rather than have them cost less and break sooner

1. Disagree	1.1	1.7	0.5	0.9	1.1	1.3	0.9	1.4	0.7	0.5	2.0	1.1	0.6	0.8	1.4	3.7
2. Mostly disagree	1.6	1.5	1.5	1.3	3.0	1.7	1.6	1.5	1.3	1.6	1.4	1.2	1.9	2.1	1.2	3.1
3. Neither	3.5	3.2	3.4	3.5	1.1	4.4	3.3	2.9	3.4	3.3	3.6	3.0	2.5	2.8	5.0	3.9
4. Mostly agree	24.5	24.9	24.2	25.5	17.5	24.0	27.0	21.0	27.7	24.3	24.6	25.2	23.1	25.0	23.7	30.4
5. Agree	69.3	68.7	70.3	68.8	77.4	68.6	67.2	73.2	67.0	70.3	68.5	69.5	71.9	69.3	68.7	58.9
Item 8020 Subject F01 N	3136	1442	1577	2333	337	736	898	969	533	1788	1133	1320	636	436	642	29

QUESTIONNAIRE FORM 3 1986	TOTAL	SEX		RACE		REGION				4YR COLLEGE PLANS		ILLICIT DRUG USE: LIFETIME				
		M	F	White	Black	NE	NC	S	W	Yes	No	None	Mari- juana Only	Few Pills	More Pills	Any Her- oin
N (Weighted No. of Cases):	3159	1456	1581	2348	342	746	901	978	534	1801	1138	1328	641	437	648	29
% of Weighted Total:	100.0	46.1	50.1	74.3	10.8	23.6	28.5	31.0	16.9	57.0	36.0	42.0	20.3	13.8	20.5	0.9

A04D: I would probably be willing to use a bicycle or mass transit (if available) rather than a car to get to work

	TOTAL	M	F	White	Black	NE	NC	S	W	Yes	No	None	Mari.	Few	More	Heroin
1. Disagree	38.5	40.5	36.2	36.1	49.5	39.7	32.9	44.0	36.3	33.1	45.8	34.9	40.6	38.0	43.8	55.4
2. Mostly disagree	21.8	21.4	22.0	22.6	18.2	19.3	24.0	21.4	22.1	22.4	21.6	22.3	20.6	22.3	21.6	16.6
3. Neither	10.3	10.4	10.5	10.7	7.9	9.1	12.1	9.6	10.1	11.5	8.9	10.6	10.2	11.8	8.3	4.5
4. Mostly agree	16.7	15.7	18.0	17.8	15.3	16.0	18.4	14.9	18.1	19.5	12.5	19.2	15.3	16.6	14.0	11.8
5. Agree	12.7	12.0	13.3	12.7	9.1	15.8	12.6	10.0	13.4	13.5	11.2	13.0	13.3	11.4	12.3	11.7
Item 8030　Subject F07　N	3135	1446	1576	2336	337	733	899	971	532	1789	1131	1323	637	430	643	29

A04E: I would be willing to eat less meat and more grains and vegetables, if it would help provide food for starving people

	TOTAL	M	F	White	Black	NE	NC	S	W	Yes	No	None	Mari.	Few	More	Heroin
1. Disagree	10.8	18.1	3.8	11.0	10.4	12.8	10.1	10.4	9.8	8.8	13.3	9.2	10.8	10.5	13.3	23.7
2. Mostly disagree	9.5	13.3	6.1	10.2	7.0	11.8	10.2	7.7	8.3	9.2	9.8	8.4	9.3	11.5	11.2	5.7
3. Neither	16.7	20.4	13.1	17.5	13.8	16.7	19.5	13.7	17.2	16.8	16.5	16.9	18.2	16.2	15.4	7.2
4. Mostly agree	29.2	27.5	31.2	29.2	26.3	26.4	29.4	30.2	30.5	29.5	28.6	30.1	24.9	31.1	28.7	53.4
5. Agree	33.9	20.8	45.8	32.1	42.6	32.2	30.7	38.0	34.2	35.8	31.8	35.3	36.8	30.7	31.3	10.0
Item 8040　Subject F03,O03　N	3131	1445	1574	2332	337	731	897	972	531	1789	1132	1319	635	431	642	29

A05: In the following list you will find some statements about leisure time and work. Please show whether you agree or disagree with each statement.

A05A: I like the kind of work you can forget about after the work day is over

	TOTAL	M	F	White	Black	NE	NC	S	W	Yes	No	None	Mari.	Few	More	Heroin
1. Disagree	12.2	13.8	10.8	10.7	21.3	14.2	12.4	12.5	8.4	12.7	11.2	13.7	10.1	10.5	11.2	17.1
2. Mostly disagree	15.0	14.2	15.3	15.1	13.1	13.2	17.0	13.7	16.3	18.1	9.9	14.7	17.4	14.7	13.2	30.6
3. Neither	13.6	13.2	14.4	13.9	13.4	13.3	15.2	11.7	14.9	16.4	9.6	15.3	13.5	12.9	11.7	3.3
4. Mostly agree	25.7	23.3	28.5	27.1	17.4	24.2	26.4	23.2	31.2	24.7	27.3	26.8	23.9	27.3	24.6	11.6
5. Agree	33.6	35.4	31.1	33.2	34.8	35.1	29.0	38.9	29.2	28.0	42.0	29.5	35.1	34.5	39.3	37.3
Item 8050　Subject C04　N	3133	1446	1569	2335	339	730	898	975	530	1789	1130	1317	636	437	643	29

A05B: To me, work is nothing more than making a living

	TOTAL	M	F	White	Black	NE	NC	S	W	Yes	No	None	Mari.	Few	More	Heroin
1. Disagree	38.5	33.3	43.1	38.1	40.4	41.3	35.9	40.3	36.0	42.8	32.6	40.7	39.8	37.8	33.3	35.9
2. Mostly disagree	29.4	29.6	29.7	32.3	16.5	22.6	34.9	27.4	32.9	31.0	27.9	30.0	28.2	33.7	28.4	16.5
3. Neither	8.8	10.0	8.1	10.0	3.2	8.6	10.7	6.6	10.1	8.1	10.1	8.2	8.5	9.4	9.5	11.0
4. Mostly agree	12.4	13.8	10.9	11.9	14.8	13.0	10.8	13.1	13.0	10.8	14.8	11.9	12.2	11.8	14.7	7.2
5. Agree	10.9	13.3	8.2	7.7	25.1	14.6	7.6	12.7	8.1	7.3	14.7	9.2	11.3	7.3	14.1	29.4
Item 8060　Subject C06　N	3137	1446	1573	2339	338	731	899	975	532	1791	1132	1323	636	436	640	29

A05C: I expect my work to be a very central part of my life

	TOTAL	M	F	White	Black	NE	NC	S	W	Yes	No	None	Mari.	Few	More	Heroin
1. Disagree	5.2	6.0	4.5	4.9	6.8	6.3	3.9	5.2	5.9	3.2	8.4	5.9	4.8	3.9	4.6	12.6
2. Mostly disagree	8.7	8.3	9.0	9.0	6.5	9.3	9.6	7.1	9.1	9.2	8.2	8.5	8.6	10.1	8.1	10.6
3. Neither	14.2	14.6	14.2	16.9	5.4	14.3	17.1	11.3	14.4	15.0	13.4	12.9	13.3	14.5	18.0	12.6
4. Mostly agree	37.0	35.9	38.1	38.7	24.7	32.7	38.2	36.8	41.1	38.8	35.1	37.9	34.0	37.8	38.6	48.0
5. Agree	35.0	35.2	34.2	30.4	56.7	37.4	31.2	39.5	29.6	33.8	34.9	34.8	39.3	33.7	30.7	16.1
Item 8070　Subject C06　N	3132	1444	1571	2339	334	731	897	973	532	1787	1133	1319	634	437	643	27

A05D: I want to do my best in my job, even if this sometimes means working overtime

	TOTAL	M	F	White	Black	NE	NC	S	W	Yes	No	None	Mari.	Few	More	Heroin
1. Disagree	1.2	2.2	0.5	0.8	2.1	2.4	0.6	1.1	1.1	0.8	1.9	1.3	0.8	1.5	1.4	-
2. Mostly disagree	3.0	3.2	2.6	3.0	3.3	3.7	2.6	2.8	3.2	3.1	2.6	3.4	2.4	2.7	3.0	3.1
3. Neither	5.0	5.6	4.2	5.7	1.4	5.9	4.9	3.8	5.9	5.2	5.1	4.8	3.9	5.0	6.5	1.7
4. Mostly agree	33.1	32.4	33.5	34.4	24.7	32.0	38.0	28.4	34.9	33.8	32.7	33.0	35.1	32.0	32.7	30.3
5. Agree	57.7	56.6	59.2	56.0	68.4	56.0	53.9	63.8	55.0	57.1	57.8	57.5	57.7	58.7	56.4	64.9
Item 8080　Subject C06　N	3136	1446	1573	2337	338	730	898	976	533	1792	1131	1321	638	434	642	29

QUESTIONNAIRE FORM 3 1986	TOTAL	SEX		RACE		REGION				4YR COLLEGE PLANS		ILLICIT DRUG USE: LIFETIME				
		M	F	White	Black	NE	NC	S	W	Yes	No	None	Mari-juana Only	Few Pills	More Pills	Any Her-oin
N (Weighted No. of Cases):	3159	1456	1581	2348	342	746	901	978	534	1801	1138	1328	641	437	648	29
% of Weighted Total:	100.0	46.1	50.1	74.3	10.8	23.6	28.5	31.0	16.9	57.0	36.0	42.0	20.3	13.8	20.5	0.9

A05E: I would like to stay in the same job for most of my adult life

1. Disagree	14.4	14.7	14.0	13.1	19.9	17.2	13.5	13.7	13.7	12.1	17.5	13.1	15.3	13.9	16.8	12.3
2. Mostly disagree	13.3	12.3	14.4	13.2	14.4	13.2	13.8	10.9	17.0	13.4	13.2	12.7	12.1	12.1	16.8	3.1
3. Neither	16.8	17.1	16.9	18.0	9.9	18.1	17.4	14.3	18.7	18.9	12.9	16.9	17.8	15.0	17.6	15.0
4. Mostly agree	25.7	23.0	27.9	26.2	23.3	23.1	27.1	24.9	28.0	26.9	23.8	28.5	24.2	27.7	19.6	32.3
5. Agree	29.8	33.0	26.8	29.5	32.4	28.4	28.2	36.2	22.6	28.6	32.6	28.8	30.6	31.2	29.2	37.3
Item 8090 Subject C03 N	3135	1446	1573	2338	337	731	897	975	532	1791	1132	1319	635	437	644	29

A06: If you were to get enough money to live as comfortably as you'd like for the rest of your life, would you want to work?

1. I would want to work	74.1	70.0	77.8	72.9	80.7	70.9	74.6	74.8	76.2	76.3	71.3	80.2	72.6	73.2	63.1	76.4
2. I would not want to work	25.9	30.0	22.2	27.1	19.3	29.1	25.4	25.2	23.8	23.7	28.7	19.8	27.4	26.8	36.9	23.6
Item 8100 Subject C06 N	3078	1406	1561	2305	325	722	889	948	519	1761	1108	1296	621	429	635	28

The next questions are about living or work-ing with people of different races. Please rate each of the statements below using the follow-ing terms:

Not at all acceptable: I'd avoid this if I possibly could.

Somewhat acceptable: I could live with this, but not be happy about it.

Acceptable: This would be O.K., or I'd be neu-tral about this.

Desirable: I'd really like this.

A07: How would you feel about . . .

A07A: Having close personal friends of another race?

1. Not at all acceptable	2.1	3.1	0.7	2.0	0.6	1.1	2.1	3.2	1.2	1.3	3.2	2.0	1.9	0.3	2.9	12.6
2. Somewhat acceptable	5.5	7.9	3.4	6.3	2.3	5.5	5.7	5.8	4.3	3.9	8.0	5.1	4.9	5.3	6.8	11.6
3. Acceptable	55.1	58.9	51.6	59.2	41.9	60.3	57.0	54.9	45.3	51.8	59.8	55.4	53.5	53.4	56.7	50.3
4. Desirable	37.3	30.0	44.3	32.5	55.2	33.1	35.1	36.1	49.1	43.1	29.1	37.4	39.7	40.9	33.7	25.5
Item 8110 Subject N01 N	3146	1453	1574	2339	342	737	899	977	533	1796	1134	1322	641	436	644	29

A07B: Having a job with a supervisor of a dif-ferent race?

1. Not at all acceptable	3.2	5.4	1.0	3.3	1.2	1.9	3.9	3.9	2.2	1.9	5.1	2.7	3.0	1.9	4.6	14.2
2. Somewhat acceptable	7.2	9.6	4.8	7.7	5.8	7.8	6.3	9.1	4.3	5.9	8.8	7.2	7.0	6.1	7.7	11.3
3. Acceptable	68.2	68.9	67.6	70.8	61.9	70.9	69.6	67.2	63.7	68.7	68.0	68.3	67.7	67.2	68.9	63.2
4. Desirable	21.5	16.1	26.7	18.1	31.0	19.4	20.1	19.8	29.8	23.5	18.1	21.8	22.3	24.9	18.8	11.3
Item 8120 Subject C05,N01 N	3146	1455	1573	2339	342	739	899	977	531	1794	1134	1323	641	436	644	29

A07C: Having a family of a different race (but same level of education and income) move next door to you?

1. Not at all acceptable	5.7	7.8	3.7	5.8	1.8	7.0	3.8	8.1	2.4	3.7	8.4	5.1	4.6	4.5	7.6	19.2
2. Somewhat acceptable	8.6	9.8	7.1	9.5	6.0	9.5	8.5	11.9	1.5	6.2	12.0	8.3	8.0	5.9	10.2	13.6
3. Acceptable	58.1	63.1	53.5	60.2	55.1	60.7	60.1	55.3	55.9	58.6	57.3	57.4	59.8	59.3	57.4	53.2
4. Desirable	27.7	19.3	35.7	24.5	37.1	22.8	27.6	24.7	40.2	31.5	22.3	29.2	27.5	30.2	24.9	13.9
Item 8130 Subject N01 N	3145	1454	1574	2339	342	738	899	975	533	1794	1135	1322	641	436	644	29

A07D: Having your (future) children's friends be all of your race?

1. Not at all acceptable	17.3	15.2	19.6	15.2	25.1	17.7	14.1	18.6	19.7	19.3	14.7	18.0	16.0	17.7	16.3	11.8
2. Somewhat acceptable	19.1	19.2	18.8	18.7	19.1	18.6	19.6	17.7	21.3	20.6	16.3	19.7	19.5	20.1	17.2	10.3
3. Acceptable	43.8	43.9	43.4	45.5	36.1	44.4	46.8	41.2	42.7	42.7	45.5	43.4	45.3	43.7	43.1	50.7
4. Desirable	19.8	21.7	18.1	20.6	19.7	19.3	19.5	22.4	16.3	17.5	23.5	18.9	19.1	18.5	23.4	27.1
Item 8140 Subject N01 N	3123	1445	1560	2329	334	734	892	967	530	1779	1130	1316	634	435	636	29

QUESTIONNAIRE FORM 3 1986	TOTAL	SEX		RACE		REGION				4YR COLLEGE PLANS		ILLICIT DRUG USE: LIFETIME				
		M	F	White	Black	NE	NC	S	W	Yes	No	None	Mari- juana Only	Few Pills	More Pills	Any Her- oin
N (Weighted No. of Cases):	3159	1456	1581	2348	342	746	901	978	534	1801	1138	1328	641	437	648	29
% of Weighted Total:	100.0	46.1	50.1	74.3	10.8	23.6	28.5	31.0	16.9	57.0	36.0	42.0	20.3	13.8	20.5	0.9

A07E: Having some of your (future) children's friends be of other races?

1. Not at all acceptable	3.1	4.3	1.7	2.7	3.2	2.5	2.3	4.4	2.8	1.8	5.0	2.7	2.7	2.8	3.8	15.1
2. Somewhat acceptable	8.1	10.2	5.6	9.1	2.7	10.5	7.3	9.5	3.7	5.8	11.7	8.3	6.6	5.5	9.2	20.8
3. Acceptable	52.1	56.9	48.0	53.5	49.3	55.5	53.6	51.5	46.1	49.2	56.9	50.8	56.0	49.3	52.8	45.7
4. Desirable	36.7	28.6	44.7	34.7	44.7	31.5	36.8	34.6	47.4	43.1	26.4	38.3	34.6	42.4	34.1	18.4
Item 8150 Subject N01 N	3141	1449	1574	2337	339	738	894	976	532	1793	1131	1321	638	436	643	29

A08: How would you feel about having a job where . . .

A08A: . . . all the employees are of your race?

1. Not at all acceptable	7.1	5.9	7.9	4.2	17.2	6.2	5.8	8.5	8.0	7.4	6.6	8.3	7.8	5.5	4.9	5.1
2. Somewhat acceptable	14.2	11.8	16.2	10.9	25.3	13.9	12.3	13.9	18.1	14.7	12.7	14.8	12.6	12.6	15.1	10.0
3. Acceptable	55.0	56.3	53.9	58.4	41.7	56.5	56.4	52.2	55.4	57.5	51.8	55.2	57.3	58.9	48.3	58.1
4. Desirable	23.8	26.0	22.1	26.5	15.8	23.5	25.4	25.4	18.5	20.4	28.9	21.7	22.3	23.0	31.7	26.8
Item 8160 Subject C05,N01 N	3141	1454	1574	2339	341	738	899	972	532	1791	1135	1326	639	436	643	26

A08B: . . . some employees are of a different race?

1. Not at all acceptable	1.2	1.9	0.3	1.0	1.0	0.8	1.6	1.5	0.6	0.5	2.2	1.3	0.6	0.8	1.4	4.7
2. Somewhat acceptable	3.9	5.6	2.0	3.9	3.6	3.7	3.6	5.4	2.0	2.9	4.9	3.7	4.9	1.8	4.6	3.7
3. Acceptable	67.2	72.6	62.5	70.3	55.3	73.0	67.7	65.6	61.2	66.0	69.2	65.3	66.5	70.6	68.3	80.9
4. Desirable	27.7	19.9	35.2	24.8	40.1	22.5	27.1	27.5	36.3	30.5	23.7	29.7	28.0	26.7	25.8	10.7
Item 8170 Subject C05,N01 N	3145	1454	1574	2342	340	739	898	975	532	1793	1135	1324	639	436	643	29

A08C: . . . most employees are of a different race?

1. Not at all acceptable	10.8	13.5	8.1	12.9	4.1	11.2	10.5	12.8	6.9	10.5	11.5	10.4	9.5	5.5	15.8	20.8
2. Somewhat acceptable	30.0	32.5	28.2	34.1	15.1	29.2	32.2	32.1	23.8	29.5	31.0	29.3	29.5	33.9	29.9	20.0
3. Acceptable	49.8	46.6	52.5	46.7	60.7	51.3	49.3	45.4	56.7	50.9	48.1	50.4	52.2	51.8	45.1	51.2
4. Desirable	9.4	7.4	11.2	6.3	20.1	8.2	8.0	9.8	12.7	9.1	9.3	9.9	8.8	8.8	9.2	8.0
Item 8180 Subject C05,N01 N	3135	1452	1570	2333	339	734	898	971	532	1789	1132	1319	637	436	643	26

A09: How would you feel about living in an area where . . .

A09A: . . . all the neighbors are of your race?

1. Not at all acceptable	4.5	3.1	5.7	2.1	11.7	5.2	4.1	4.0	4.9	4.1	5.1	5.1	4.9	3.8	3.3	1.6
2. Somewhat acceptable	10.7	10.3	10.7	6.9	20.0	12.8	7.5	9.8	14.7	11.6	8.9	10.5	11.4	9.2	10.3	8.7
3. Acceptable	51.1	51.6	50.3	52.5	48.8	48.0	52.0	51.1	54.0	54.3	46.1	53.2	52.5	55.1	42.8	37.5
4. Desirable	33.7	35.0	33.3	38.5	19.6	34.0	36.4	35.1	26.4	30.0	39.9	31.2	31.2	31.9	43.7	52.2
Item 8190 Subject N01 N	3148	1455	1576	2344	340	742	899	975	533	1796	1136	1325	639	436	646	29

A09B: . . . some of the neighbors are of other races?

1. Not at all acceptable	2.0	2.8	1.1	2.0	1.4	2.2	1.8	2.8	1.0	0.9	3.6	1.8	2.1	0.8	2.9	8.5
2. Somewhat acceptable	7.6	9.5	5.4	7.7	3.7	9.3	7.2	9.5	2.6	5.8	9.9	7.9	5.4	7.3	8.5	13.3
3. Acceptable	68.1	71.2	65.7	70.1	63.2	71.4	69.0	67.1	63.7	68.4	67.7	67.0	71.8	69.9	65.4	67.2
4. Desirable	22.3	16.6	27.7	20.2	31.8	17.1	22.1	20.7	32.8	24.9	18.8	23.3	20.7	22.0	23.2	11.0
Item 8200 Subject N01 N	3145	1453	1574	2339	342	739	899	975	532	1793	1135	1324	639	436	643	29

A09C: . . . most of the neighbors are of other races?

1. Not at all acceptable	18.2	21.3	15.6	21.8	6.8	18.2	20.0	21.8	8.5	18.5	18.2	17.1	19.0	14.0	22.8	28.0
2. Somewhat acceptable	34.6	36.2	33.3	38.6	21.6	32.5	33.2	38.1	33.3	33.4	37.2	34.3	34.3	35.7	35.2	15.2
3. Acceptable	40.1	37.3	42.4	35.1	56.0	42.8	41.2	33.6	46.6	40.7	38.3	40.4	39.5	43.6	36.6	53.2
4. Desirable	7.1	5.1	8.7	4.5	15.7	6.5	5.5	6.5	11.7	7.4	6.3	8.3	7.2	6.7	5.5	3.6
Item 8210 Subject N01 N	3135	1450	1570	2331	340	737	896	971	531	1787	1132	1317	639	434	646	26

A10: How would you feel about having your (future) children go to schools where . . .

QUESTIONNAIRE FORM 3 1986	TOTAL	SEX		RACE		REGION				4YR COLLEGE PLANS		ILLICIT DRUG USE: LIFETIME				
		M	F	White	Black	NE	NC	S	W	Yes	No	None	Marijuana Only	Few Pills	More Pills	Any Heroin
N (Weighted No. of Cases):	3159	1456	1581	2348	342	746	901	978	534	1801	1138	1328	641	437	648	29
% of Weighted Total:	100.0	46.1	50.1	74.3	10.8	23.6	28.5	31.0	16.9	57.0	36.0	42.0	20.3	13.8	20.5	0.9
A10A: . . . all the children are of your race?																
1. Not at all acceptable	8.5	6.3	10.5	5.3	21.7	8.2	6.7	9.8	9.6	9.2	7.1	9.7	9.0	6.8	7.5	6.2
2. Somewhat acceptable	12.6	11.8	13.1	9.4	19.9	10.8	12.0	12.4	16.4	14.5	9.3	12.2	13.3	13.8	10.9	12.3
3. Acceptable	48.3	48.9	47.1	49.8	43.2	49.5	48.4	46.0	50.5	50.0	45.2	49.0	51.9	48.3	41.9	48.1
4. Desirable	30.6	33.1	29.4	35.6	15.1	31.4	33.0	31.7	23.5	26.4	38.3	29.0	25.8	31.1	39.8	33.4
Item 8220 Subject B03,N01 N	3132	1451	1568	2332	340	734	897	970	531	1783	1134	1320	635	435	643	26
A10B: . . . some of the children are of other races?																
1. Not at all acceptable	1.3	1.9	0.7	1.1	0.9	1.2	0.5	2.6	0.5	0.7	2.2	1.3	1.3	0.4	1.4	8.5
2. Somewhat acceptable	5.6	7.6	3.1	5.4	2.6	6.5	4.8	7.0	3.0	3.6	8.0	6.0	3.9	2.1	7.5	12.4
3. Acceptable	63.9	67.9	60.3	65.6	58.3	67.2	64.6	63.0	59.6	61.4	67.4	63.2	66.2	65.0	62.0	56.7
4. Desirable	29.3	22.6	35.9	27.8	38.2	25.1	30.0	27.5	37.0	34.3	22.4	29.4	28.6	32.4	29.1	22.4
Item 8230 Subject B03,N01 N	3133	1450	1567	2335	339	732	898	973	531	1786	1133	1320	634	435	643	29
A10C: . . . most of the children are of other races?																
1. Not at all acceptable	21.1	23.8	18.8	25.1	7.9	21.9	22.3	24.6	11.4	21.3	21.3	19.3	21.5	19.1	25.9	33.2
2. Somewhat acceptable	34.4	35.7	33.2	37.7	24.0	32.9	34.6	36.3	32.5	33.9	36.2	33.6	36.0	34.8	35.4	19.9
3. Acceptable	37.4	34.1	40.0	33.0	49.9	37.6	38.2	31.9	45.9	37.9	35.6	39.5	33.8	39.3	33.2	43.4
4. Desirable	7.1	6.4	8.0	4.1	18.2	7.6	4.9	7.1	10.2	7.0	6.9	7.6	8.7	6.9	5.4	3.6
Item 8240 Subject B03,N01 N	3130	1450	1567	2331	339	733	897	969	532	1783	1133	1317	634	435	646	26
A11: What race are your close friends?																
1. All my race	30.9	32.7	29.7	34.7	25.8	28.4	37.0	34.7	17.0	29.0	33.4	34.0	32.0	24.8	27.8	27.5
2. Almost all my race	29.6	27.6	31.4	34.0	17.0	30.4	30.1	27.3	32.0	31.5	27.7	28.2	30.3	29.2	31.9	15.3
3. Mostly my race	21.8	21.8	21.6	21.8	24.5	22.9	19.6	22.9	21.7	22.2	21.5	19.3	22.7	27.3	22.6	26.7
4. About half my race	10.9	10.6	10.8	7.4	23.0	10.6	8.4	10.5	16.3	10.2	11.5	11.0	10.0	12.3	10.2	18.1
5. Mostly other race(s)	4.0	4.5	3.7	1.3	5.3	5.3	3.0	1.9	8.0	3.8	4.0	4.0	2.7	4.6	4.9	7.3
6. Almost all other race(s)	2.8	2.8	2.7	0.7	4.3	2.4	1.9	2.7	5.0	3.3	1.9	3.5	2.2	1.9	2.6	5.1
Item 8250 Subject N03 N	3130	1442	1575	2337	336	733	894	973	531	1788	1133	1318	635	434	642	29
A12: What race are the people in your neighborhood?																
1. All my race	43.4	42.5	44.8	49.8	32.8	41.4	50.5	49.2	23.6	42.4	45.8	45.8	41.1	39.6	43.8	42.3
2. Almost all my race	26.0	26.5	25.4	29.9	13.5	28.4	27.6	22.1	27.4	27.1	24.8	24.6	26.8	29.3	26.9	23.4
3. Mostly my race	12.8	13.6	12.2	13.2	13.9	12.8	10.7	11.4	18.9	13.3	11.7	12.5	12.5	12.4	14.3	12.8
4. About half my race	7.9	6.9	8.5	5.2	14.5	7.5	4.9	8.6	12.6	7.4	8.7	7.3	7.9	10.3	7.1	1.9
5. Mostly other race(s)	6.1	6.3	5.8	0.9	17.7	5.3	3.8	6.1	11.0	5.8	5.9	5.7	7.6	5.4	4.5	19.6
6. Almost all other race(s)	3.7	4.2	3.3	0.9	7.6	4.5	2.5	2.7	6.5	4.0	3.2	4.0	4.1	3.0	3.5	-
Item 8260 Subject N03 N	3125	1441	1570	2333	337	729	892	974	529	1781	1133	1315	634	434	641	29
A13: What race were the students in the elementary school where you spent the most time?																
1. All my race	32.4	32.3	32.7	36.7	25.2	33.2	41.7	30.7	18.5	29.8	37.0	34.3	29.8	31.7	32.9	20.1
2. Almost all my race	29.6	31.1	28.6	34.5	13.1	30.4	32.2	24.3	33.9	32.4	26.1	28.5	32.2	27.2	29.6	32.6
3. Mostly my race	14.5	15.1	14.2	15.9	8.6	14.8	11.7	16.5	15.2	15.3	14.0	13.9	12.0	17.7	17.6	12.2
4. About half my race	12.8	11.0	13.8	9.7	27.1	11.7	6.3	17.9	16.1	10.9	15.3	11.9	14.1	15.9	10.8	9.0
5. Mostly other race(s)	6.9	7.2	6.7	2.3	17.7	5.3	5.1	7.9	10.5	7.7	5.4	7.8	7.3	4.8	5.2	24.1
6. Almost all other race(s)	3.7	3.3	4.0	0.9	8.3	4.5	2.9	2.6	5.8	4.0	2.3	3.5	4.7	2.7	3.9	2.1
Item 8270 Subject B03,N03 N	3128	1441	1573	2335	337	732	892	974	530	1785	1134	1316	636	434	642	29
A14: What race are the students in your present school (if you are in school)?																
1. All my race	14.6	14.9	14.2	17.2	6.9	10.1	18.1	21.7	1.8	12.1	18.2	19.2	9.0	11.9	12.4	8.7
2. Almost all my race	28.1	30.3	26.1	32.9	8.8	34.9	34.9	15.6	30.1	29.8	25.5	25.8	29.3	28.5	30.8	26.1
3. Mostly my race	23.6	24.4	23.2	27.6	11.1	26.1	23.8	18.6	29.1	25.2	22.3	23.3	23.3	25.5	24.2	28.7
4. About half my race	19.7	17.0	22.1	17.6	36.3	16.2	13.5	29.0	18.0	18.4	22.2	16.9	23.9	23.6	20.0	7.1
5. Mostly other race(s)	9.4	8.9	9.9	3.7	24.5	8.6	6.8	10.4	13.1	9.4	8.6	9.5	8.5	8.6	9.1	22.4
6. Almost all other race(s)	4.6	4.4	4.6	1.2	12.5	4.2	2.9	4.6	7.9	5.2	3.2	5.3	6.0	1.9	3.6	7.0
Item 8280 Subject B03,N03 N	3123	1441	1572	2333	337	729	892	972	530	1782	1132	1316	635	434	640	29

QUESTIONNAIRE FORM 3 1986	TOTAL	SEX		RACE		REGION				4YR COLLEGE PLANS		ILLICIT DRUG USE: LIFETIME				
		M	F	White	Black	NE	NC	S	W	Yes	No	None	Mari-juana Only	Few Pills	More Pills	Any Her-oin
N (Weighted No. of Cases):	3159	1456	1581	2348	342	746	901	978	534	1801	1138	1328	641	437	648	29
% of Weighted Total:	100.0	46.1	50.1	74.3	10.8	23.6	28.5	31.0	16.9	57.0	36.0	42.0	20.3	13.8	20.5	0.9

A15: What race are the people that you work with on your job (if you have a job)?

	TOTAL	M	F	White	Black	NE	NC	S	W	Yes	No	None	Mari-juana Only	Few Pills	More Pills	Any Her-oin
1. All my race	36.8	34.0	40.1	44.2	8.6	43.1	42.7	31.3	27.7	35.0	41.0	37.8	33.5	36.0	40.2	41.2
2. Almost all my race	23.4	24.7	22.1	27.3	8.9	23.8	25.6	20.1	24.6	25.1	20.9	22.9	23.7	20.5	24.9	23.2
3. Mostly my race	13.7	14.9	12.4	15.0	9.1	13.0	13.2	14.9	13.5	14.3	13.1	13.1	14.6	17.6	12.2	13.2
4. About half my race	12.3	12.1	12.3	9.5	28.5	10.6	8.9	17.1	11.8	12.2	12.0	12.3	14.0	13.1	9.7	3.6
5. Mostly other race(s)	8.3	9.1	7.4	2.8	26.4	5.0	6.1	10.1	13.7	7.9	8.7	8.2	7.7	8.3	7.6	15.2
6. Almost all other race(s)	5.6	5.2	5.7	1.2	18.6	4.5	3.5	6.6	8.7	5.6	4.4	5.8	6.5	4.5	5.4	3.7
Item 8290 Subject N03 N	2645	1243	1303	2002	263	640	758	790	458	1487	980	1070	553	379	560	28

A16: How often do you do things (like having a conversation, eating together, playing sports) with people of other races?

	TOTAL	M	F	White	Black	NE	NC	S	W	Yes	No	None	Mari-juana Only	Few Pills	More Pills	Any Her-oin
1. Not at all	9.4	9.6	9.3	10.2	7.1	9.5	11.1	10.0	5.5	6.2	14.2	10.6	8.8	7.2	9.2	18.7
2. A little	27.8	27.3	28.4	31.5	16.8	31.3	30.7	25.4	22.5	25.4	31.1	26.5	27.6	28.0	31.2	13.6
3. Some	37.3	37.5	37.0	38.6	35.2	35.1	38.9	38.4	35.6	38.5	35.4	36.8	38.2	36.1	37.5	39.0
4. A lot	25.5	25.6	25.3	19.7	40.9	24.1	19.3	26.3	36.4	29.9	19.3	26.0	25.4	28.7	22.1	28.8
Item 8300 Subject N03 N	3127	1441	1572	2333	338	727	895	973	532	1787	1130	1315	638	434	642	29

A17: Generally, how do you feel about the experiences you have had with people of other races?

	TOTAL	M	F	White	Black	NE	NC	S	W	Yes	No	None	Mari-juana Only	Few Pills	More Pills	Any Her-oin
5. Very good	25.3	21.3	29.2	22.7	34.7	24.9	23.9	23.4	31.8	30.1	17.8	28.8	23.4	26.9	18.8	27.9
4. Mostly good	43.9	41.2	46.7	44.7	39.1	42.8	45.6	39.9	49.9	45.1	43.1	44.1	48.8	42.1	42.1	28.5
3. Mixed	27.4	32.6	22.6	28.8	23.8	28.6	27.3	33.1	15.7	22.2	34.5	24.2	24.4	29.4	33.9	32.5
2. Mostly bad	2.2	3.2	1.2	2.6	1.4	2.6	1.9	2.6	1.5	1.7	3.3	1.9	2.1	1.5	3.5	2.6
1. Very bad	1.1	1.8	0.3	1.1	1.0	1.2	1.3	1.0	1.1	0.9	1.2	1.0	1.2	0.1	1.7	8.5
Item 8310 Subject N03 N	3123	1440	1569	2331	338	728	895	970	530	1784	1130	1314	636	434	640	29

A18: The next questions are about some of your own plans. Are you married or engaged?

	TOTAL	M	F	White	Black	NE	NC	S	W	Yes	No	None	Mari-juana Only	Few Pills	More Pills	Any Her-oin
1. Married–SKIP TO Q.A20	0.6	0.5	0.7	0.6	1.4	0.1	0.1	1.7	0.4	0.3	1.2	0.1	0.9	1.2	1.1	2.1
2. Engaged	8.3	4.1	11.6	8.1	8.0	5.6	7.9	11.1	7.3	4.4	14.6	6.0	7.3	8.6	12.7	22.9
3. Neither	91.1	95.4	87.7	91.4	90.6	94.3	92.0	87.2	92.3	95.2	84.2	93.9	91.9	90.2	86.2	75.0
Item 8320 Subject D01,R01 N	2975	1370	1508	2258	313	699	858	911	507	1732	1063	1254	611	414	612	25

A19: If it were just up to you, what would be the ideal time for you to get married?

	TOTAL	M	F	White	Black	NE	NC	S	W	Yes	No	None	Mari-juana Only	Few Pills	More Pills	Any Her-oin
1. Within the next year or so	6.9	3.4	9.8	7.0	5.4	4.5	6.4	10.8	4.3	3.0	13.3	5.9	5.4	7.0	9.5	12.5
2. Two or three years from now	17.1	13.6	20.3	17.4	16.0	13.6	18.3	19.8	15.3	11.3	26.6	17.7	14.8	18.0	18.4	21.0
3. Four or five years from now	33.3	31.3	35.3	34.7	27.5	34.8	31.5	34.5	32.1	35.1	30.2	34.4	33.6	32.5	31.3	26.2
4. Over five years from now	37.4	45.2	30.5	36.7	41.8	42.8	39.4	29.4	41.0	46.0	24.2	36.9	41.0	38.2	35.5	27.1
5. I don't want to marry	5.2	6.4	4.1	4.2	9.4	4.3	4.4	5.5	7.3	4.6	5.8	5.2	5.2	4.3	5.3	13.2
Item 8330 Subject D01 N★	3006	1380	1521	2275	316	706	861	919	520	1742	1075	1268	615	422	616	26

A20: Have you thought at all about whether you'd like to have children or how many you'd like to have?

	TOTAL	M	F	White	Black	NE	NC	S	W	Yes	No	None	Mari-juana Only	Few Pills	More Pills	Any Her-oin
3. I've thought about it a lot	37.9	24.9	50.2	37.4	49.3	35.1	36.2	43.1	35.4	36.9	41.0	36.7	40.3	37.7	39.2	25.0
2. I've thought about it a little	52.4	60.7	44.3	54.2	42.9	55.0	54.6	47.1	54.7	54.5	48.4	53.0	51.6	54.6	50.5	60.3
1. I haven't thought about it at all	9.7	14.4	5.5	8.3	7.8	10.0	9.2	9.9	9.8	8.6	10.6	10.3	8.1	7.6	10.3	14.8
Item 8340 Subject D02 N	3063	1413	1538	2292	328	715	883	946	519	1764	1099	1283	627	424	634	29

A21: All things considered, if you could have exactly the number of children you want, what number would you choose to have?

	TOTAL	M	F	White	Black	NE	NC	S	W	Yes	No	None	Mari-juana Only	Few Pills	More Pills	Any Her-oin
1. None	4.5	4.5	4.5	4.4	4.7	4.3	5.3	3.9	4.4	4.3	4.6	5.3	3.4	3.3	4.7	8.3
2. One	7.2	7.0	7.3	6.9	10.0	7.1	7.0	8.0	6.2	5.9	9.4	6.3	7.1	6.5	9.8	8.4
3. Two	47.8	49.3	46.2	47.9	49.2	43.8	47.3	50.2	49.5	45.1	50.9	47.1	49.3	49.3	46.1	53.4
4. Three	20.8	19.9	21.5	21.1	21.0	21.7	19.9	19.7	22.8	23.4	17.1	20.7	22.7	22.7	17.9	17.7
5. Four	9.6	7.7	11.8	9.3	9.2	10.5	11.4	8.5	7.5	10.5	8.4	9.9	7.8	9.7	11.3	-
6. Five	1.7	1.9	1.7	1.9	0.7	2.0	1.7	1.4	1.9	1.9	1.6	1.9	1.8	2.1	1.4	-
7. Six or more	1.4	1.1	1.5	1.4	1.0	1.4	1.0	1.1	2.7	1.3	1.5	1.6	0.4	1.2	1.7	7.7
8. Don't know	7.0	8.6	5.5	7.0	4.1	9.2	6.3	7.1	5.0	7.6	6.5	7.2	7.5	5.2	7.0	4.5
Item 8350 Subject D02 N	3112	1442	1557	2316	337	732	893	964	523	1782	1122	1311	632	433	640	29

★=excludes respondents for whom question was inappropriate.

QUESTIONNAIRE FORM 3 1986	TOTAL	SEX		RACE		REGION				4YR COLLEGE PLANS		ILLICIT DRUG USE: LIFETIME				
		M	F	White	Black	NE	NC	S	W	Yes	No	None	Marijuana Only	Few Pills	More Pills	Any Heroin
N (Weighted No. of Cases):	3159	1456	1581	2348	342	746	901	978	534	1801	1138	1328	641	437	648	29
% of Weighted Total:	100.0	46.1	50.1	74.3	10.8	23.6	28.5	31.0	16.9	57.0	36.0	42.0	20.3	13.8	20.5	0.9

A22: If the "population explosion" were NOT a problem, would you choose to have a larger number of children?

4. Yes, I'm sure I would want more	3.8	4.2	3.6	3.9	3.1	5.4	3.1	3.6	3.0	3.1	5.3	3.8	3.4	2.0	4.8	10.9
3. I probably would want more	9.8	8.8	10.0	8.4	10.6	11.4	7.7	10.4	10.2	9.6	9.8	9.9	8.0	10.5	10.0	18.8
2. I probably would not want more	36.4	36.1	36.7	38.8	26.1	34.5	38.6	35.7	36.3	38.2	33.7	37.4	35.1	38.8	33.9	18.6
1. I'm sure I would not want more	33.2	33.4	33.1	32.7	41.6	28.9	32.1	35.8	36.5	32.0	34.6	31.5	36.6	32.1	36.1	30.6
8. Don't know, no idea	16.8	17.5	16.6	16.2	18.6	19.7	18.5	14.6	13.9	17.2	16.7	17.4	16.9	16.6	15.2	21.1
Item 8360 Subject D02,E01 N	3137	1449	1576	2341	341	737	897	973	531	1797	1133	1320	638	436	645	29

A23: If it were just up to you, how soon after getting married would you want to have your first child?

1. I don't want to have children (or get married)	4.7	4.6	5.0	4.6	5.2	4.6	5.1	4.4	4.8	4.5	5.0	5.6	3.7	3.3	4.9	8.3
2. I wouldn't wait at all	4.6	7.2	1.6	3.6	8.3	5.5	3.8	4.0	5.7	4.0	5.5	4.2	4.5	5.7	4.3	7.7
3. I would wait one year	26.9	30.7	23.9	26.5	32.0	29.1	23.3	28.7	26.5	25.4	29.1	27.2	26.1	27.2	25.3	35.6
4. I would wait two years	30.5	27.6	32.7	30.9	27.2	30.2	31.8	29.8	29.7	30.4	30.2	30.0	33.1	30.6	29.3	34.6
5. I would wait three years	14.3	10.6	17.7	14.5	12.2	12.0	16.1	14.0	15.0	16.5	11.1	14.4	13.8	13.9	15.5	10.4
6. I would wait four or five years	8.1	5.4	10.6	8.9	4.7	6.1	8.0	9.3	9.0	7.6	8.9	8.2	7.2	7.5	9.8	1.4
7. I would wait more than five years	1.8	2.0	1.6	1.9	1.6	1.1	2.1	2.1	1.6	2.1	1.4	1.4	2.1	2.9	1.5	2.1
8. Don't know, or already have a child	9.1	11.8	6.9	9.1	8.9	11.4	9.7	7.6	7.8	9.6	8.7	8.9	9.4	9.0	9.4	-
Item 8370 Subject D02 N	3106	1440	1553	2317	336	729	890	964	523	1783	1119	1310	631	432	640	29

A24: Now we'd like you to make some ratings of how good or bad a job you feel each of the following organizations is doing for the country as a whole. For each one, mark the circle that best describes how you feel.

How good or bad a job is being done for the country as a whole by...

A24A: Large corporations?

1. Very poor	1.9	2.4	1.4	1.4	2.5	3.0	1.1	2.1	1.4	1.6	2.1	2.1	1.3	0.6	2.7	-
2. Poor	5.8	8.1	3.8	6.4	4.6	6.7	5.8	5.0	6.0	5.9	5.5	6.2	3.5	8.0	5.9	5.9
3. Fair	26.7	27.9	25.6	26.7	26.1	23.2	27.9	27.4	28.3	25.7	29.1	27.8	25.8	27.4	24.7	40.0
4. Good	37.2	38.3	36.5	38.6	33.0	36.4	38.7	37.0	36.0	39.3	34.6	34.9	39.1	42.6	37.6	17.8
5. Very good	10.4	10.4	10.0	9.7	13.8	9.5	9.1	13.0	9.4	10.7	9.5	11.0	10.9	9.0	9.4	21.9
8. No opinion	17.9	12.9	22.7	17.1	20.1	21.2	17.4	15.4	18.9	16.7	19.1	17.9	19.5	12.4	19.7	14.4
Item 8380 Subject K02 N	3136	1452	1570	2340	339	739	898	969	530	1793	1133	1322	637	436	643	29

A24B: Major labor unions?

1. Very poor	3.6	5.8	1.7	3.7	3.9	4.0	4.1	4.0	1.8	3.8	3.4	4.5	2.7	2.6	4.0	-
2. Poor	10.6	13.9	7.4	10.7	7.2	8.7	11.1	10.0	13.5	11.1	9.3	11.6	8.7	12.4	8.7	9.4
3. Fair	30.6	32.3	29.4	31.2	30.3	27.8	31.6	33.1	27.9	30.7	30.8	31.5	30.1	34.3	28.0	23.1
4. Good	26.1	26.5	25.7	26.1	29.2	24.8	27.2	24.5	29.1	25.4	27.7	23.8	27.5	28.8	27.4	30.9
5. Very good	6.5	6.0	6.7	6.0	6.5	10.2	5.0	5.4	5.9	5.9	7.0	5.5	7.8	4.3	8.2	16.6
8. No opinion	22.6	15.5	29.1	22.3	22.8	24.5	21.1	23.0	21.7	23.0	21.9	23.1	23.2	17.5	23.6	20.0
Item 8390 Subject K02 N	3129	1451	1564	2333	340	733	897	970	529	1790	1130	1317	636	435	642	29

A24C: The nation's colleges and universities?

1. Very poor	1.0	1.4	0.6	0.6	1.6	0.9	0.8	1.4	0.7	0.6	1.5	1.1	0.1	0.9	1.3	2.9
2. Poor	2.8	3.1	2.6	2.3	4.2	4.5	1.5	2.4	3.5	2.4	3.2	1.4	4.2	3.6	4.0	7.0
3. Fair	12.3	12.5	11.9	10.6	16.9	13.7	11.4	12.7	11.3	9.5	15.8	9.7	12.5	11.4	12.4	8.3
4. Good	44.4	46.1	43.0	46.2	39.3	41.8	46.1	44.4	45.0	45.7	43.3	45.3	42.7	51.2	39.7	61.4
5. Very good	34.2	31.3	36.9	35.1	32.5	31.9	33.7	35.7	35.2	38.1	29.2	34.7	35.4	29.4	36.8	14.4
8. No opinion	5.3	5.7	5.0	5.2	5.5	7.2	6.4	3.4	4.3	3.6	7.0	4.9	6.2	3.5	5.7	6.1
Item 8400 Subject B10,K02 N	3115	1447	1557	2323	339	724	896	965	529	1784	1125	1315	635	433	635	29

	TOTAL	SEX		RACE		REGION				4YR COLLEGE PLANS		ILLICIT DRUG USE: LIFETIME				
QUESTIONNAIRE FORM 3 **1986**		M	F	White	Black	NE	NC	S	W	Yes	No	None	Mari-juana Only	Few Pills	More Pills	Any Her-oin
N (Weighted No. of Cases):	3159	1456	1581	2348	342	746	901	978	534	1801	1138	1328	641	437	648	29
% of Weighted Total:	100.0	46.1	50.1	74.3	10.8	23.6	28.5	31.0	16.9	57.0	36.0	42.0	20.3	13.8	20.5	0.9
A24D: The nation's public schools?																
1. Very poor	3.8	3.6	4.0	3.5	2.1	4.9	3.2	3.5	3.7	3.0	4.9	3.1	2.2	2.3	7.7	13.0
2. Poor	12.2	12.5	12.3	12.0	14.2	13.0	12.1	11.8	12.2	13.5	10.8	11.9	12.4	11.8	13.5	15.4
3. Fair	33.7	32.1	35.3	33.8	36.8	37.6	32.5	32.1	33.5	34.3	32.7	32.9	29.0	40.3	37.1	19.6
4. Good	35.3	37.1	33.2	37.2	28.9	29.0	36.6	37.9	37.1	35.9	34.9	36.7	40.1	31.6	29.2	40.3
5. Very good	11.5	10.9	12.2	10.5	14.0	11.3	12.5	11.4	10.4	11.0	12.3	12.4	12.9	11.6	8.9	9.7
8. No opinion	3.4	3.8	2.9	2.9	3.9	4.1	3.2	3.3	3.1	2.3	4.4	2.9	3.4	2.4	3.6	2.1
Item 8410 Subject B10,K02 N	3119	1445	1562	2325	339	728	894	966	530	1785	1126	1314	635	434	638	29
A24E: Churches and religious organizations?																
1. Very poor	3.1	4.2	2.0	3.0	2.6	3.4	3.5	2.4	3.2	2.9	3.6	2.7	1.7	3.9	4.9	6.6
2. Poor	4.7	6.3	3.4	5.2	3.2	6.8	4.9	2.6	5.4	4.6	4.8	3.3	5.7	6.0	6.4	3.8
3. Fair	23.5	24.0	23.1	24.0	20.2	27.7	24.5	19.1	23.8	23.8	22.8	23.2	22.7	24.6	23.6	33.1
4. Good	36.9	36.2	37.4	37.9	35.4	28.7	38.7	41.0	37.9	37.1	37.4	36.7	39.0	37.4	35.6	22.1
5. Very good	17.9	15.1	19.8	16.3	28.1	12.7	14.5	25.9	16.2	18.0	17.3	20.5	17.4	15.4	14.0	23.4
8. No opinion	13.9	14.3	13.8	13.6	10.5	20.7	13.9	9.0	13.5	13.5	14.1	13.6	13.5	12.6	15.4	11.1
Item 8420 Subject G,K02 N	3123	1448	1563	2331	335	732	897	964	530	1787	1132	1315	634	435	640	29
A24F: The national news media (TV, maga-zines, news services)?																
1. Very poor	2.5	3.0	2.2	2.4	2.9	3.8	1.9	2.0	2.8	2.3	2.6	2.7	1.8	2.2	2.9	6.2
2. Poor	5.9	7.1	4.9	6.3	4.9	6.1	6.7	5.5	5.2	6.6	5.2	5.9	5.2	4.3	8.1	6.1
3. Fair	21.6	21.5	22.2	22.6	16.8	22.6	20.1	22.2	21.8	22.1	21.4	20.6	20.0	24.3	24.1	9.4
4. Good	39.2	38.3	39.0	39.0	38.1	34.7	41.4	39.1	41.9	40.1	37.5	41.9	39.9	39.5	32.8	49.4
5. Very good	26.3	25.6	27.2	25.9	31.8	27.0	24.9	27.7	24.9	25.8	27.5	24.2	28.0	26.8	28.3	22.8
8. No opinion	4.5	4.5	4.4	3.9	5.5	5.9	4.9	3.5	3.3	3.1	5.8	4.7	5.2	3.0	3.7	6.1
Item 8430 Subject K02 N	3125	1447	1567	2336	337	733	896	966	530	1790	1130	1318	636	433	641	29
A24G: The President and his administration?																
1. Very poor	5.8	4.7	7.0	4.1	14.8	7.9	5.6	5.4	3.9	4.9	7.0	4.4	5.1	6.5	8.7	3.3
2. Poor	7.8	6.8	8.8	6.6	15.0	9.0	8.5	6.5	7.1	7.7	8.0	7.1	8.9	6.8	8.4	9.8
3. Fair	23.1	19.8	26.1	22.0	30.2	23.6	24.3	21.2	24.2	23.3	22.9	23.5	20.9	24.5	23.4	29.5
4. Good	32.6	34.2	31.3	35.6	18.1	31.0	31.4	33.8	35.0	33.8	31.8	32.3	30.5	38.9	32.2	33.7
5. Very good	21.8	28.1	16.2	23.9	9.7	19.1	20.5	24.6	22.9	23.6	19.2	23.7	25.7	18.0	17.5	11.8
8. No opinion	8.8	6.5	10.7	7.7	12.2	9.4	9.7	8.5	7.0	6.7	11.2	9.0	9.0	5.3	9.7	12.0
Item 8440 Subject H04,K02 N	3128	1448	1567	2333	340	733	896	967	531	1791	1129	1316	637	435	642	29
A24H: Congress–that is, the U.S. Senate and House of Representatives?																
1. Very poor	2.7	3.3	2.1	1.8	5.8	3.9	3.0	2.2	1.4	2.2	3.3	2.1	1.6	2.8	4.2	10.0
2. Poor	6.7	7.7	5.5	6.5	8.1	9.1	6.6	5.3	5.8	5.8	8.2	6.5	5.0	7.1	8.0	8.0
3. Fair	29.5	29.1	29.7	28.8	35.3	27.4	31.9	29.1	29.1	30.0	28.7	28.6	28.1	33.4	30.3	29.7
4. Good	33.6	37.4	30.2	35.9	28.3	30.9	32.3	34.7	37.8	37.0	29.2	35.7	35.3	35.2	27.6	33.3
5. Very good	8.7	9.2	8.4	9.2	6.6	7.5	7.0	11.6	8.0	8.1	9.3	9.4	9.7	6.3	8.7	7.0
8. No opinion	18.8	13.3	24.2	17.8	20.7	21.2	19.2	17.1	17.9	16.9	21.3	17.7	20.2	15.3	21.2	12.0
Item 8450 Subject H04,K02 N	3124	1449	1563	2331	340	730	896	968	530	1787	1130	1314	637	435	641	29
A24I: The U.S. Supreme Court?																
1. Very poor	2.2	2.8	1.6	1.9	3.7	3.5	2.2	1.9	1.0	1.8	2.4	2.4	1.4	1.9	2.5	-
2. Poor	4.2	4.4	4.1	3.9	4.6	5.6	4.2	3.4	4.1	4.4	3.6	4.0	4.8	3.2	4.9	8.1
3. Fair	24.0	25.1	22.8	23.5	26.9	25.4	22.5	24.0	24.7	24.2	25.5	22.7	22.8	30.7	23.3	30.0
4. Good	35.2	37.5	33.1	36.9	30.6	30.8	36.7	35.7	37.9	36.4	33.2	35.5	37.7	33.8	32.8	31.6
5. Very good	11.1	11.3	10.9	11.2	11.7	10.3	10.4	12.8	10.4	11.4	10.8	11.9	11.0	9.7	10.8	19.4
8. No opinion	23.2	18.8	27.5	22.6	22.4	24.5	24.1	22.2	21.8	21.7	24.5	23.4	22.3	20.7	25.6	10.9
Item 8460 Subject H04,K02 N	3106	1446	1550	2320	337	722	892	965	528	1783	1122	1308	631	435	638	28
A24J: All the courts and the justice system in general?																
1. Very poor	5.1	6.3	3.9	4.6	7.1	6.7	4.4	4.8	4.7	4.8	5.3	5.1	4.7	3.7	6.1	-
2. Poor	11.5	12.6	10.9	12.5	6.2	12.6	12.3	9.5	12.5	12.4	10.0	12.1	11.9	10.9	10.3	23.2
3. Fair	33.3	34.4	32.5	33.9	33.3	32.9	32.7	33.3	34.8	35.7	31.5	32.8	30.5	37.1	34.9	27.7
4. Good	28.6	27.3	29.3	29.6	27.7	22.0	30.0	30.8	30.9	29.5	27.8	28.2	30.3	30.3	26.9	26.8
5. Very good	5.8	5.7	5.9	5.1	7.7	7.2	4.8	6.0	5.4	4.7	6.8	5.7	6.1	5.8	6.2	13.4
8. No opinion	15.7	13.7	17.4	14.3	18.0	18.5	15.8	15.6	11.7	13.0	18.5	16.1	16.4	12.3	15.6	9.0
Item 8470 Subject H04,K02 N	3118	1449	1557	2326	338	728	895	964	530	1785	1125	1311	635	432	641	29

QUESTIONNAIRE FORM 3 1986	TOTAL	SEX		RACE		REGION				4YR COLLEGE PLANS		ILLICIT DRUG USE: LIFETIME				
		M	F	White	Black	NE	NC	S	W	Yes	No	None	Mari- juana Only	Few Pills	More Pills	Any Her- oin
N (Weighted No. of Cases):	3159	1456	1581	2348	342	746	901	978	534	1801	1138	1328	641	437	648	29
% of Weighted Total:	100.0	46.1	50.1	74.3	10.8	23.6	28.5	31.0	16.9	57.0	36.0	42.0	20.3	13.8	20.5	0.9

A24K: The police and other law enforcement agencies?

1. Very poor	5.4	5.8	4.9	4.5	7.9	7.5	4.9	5.5	3.1	3.8	6.6	4.1	4.2	4.8	8.2	18.0
2. Poor	11.4	12.8	10.2	10.4	15.9	12.7	11.4	10.2	11.5	11.5	11.1	10.2	11.9	11.9	12.6	17.1
3. Fair	36.6	35.9	37.6	36.9	39.6	39.6	35.2	36.6	35.1	39.9	33.0	35.8	38.5	39.0	36.4	13.3
4. Good	32.9	32.3	33.2	35.4	21.8	25.2	34.4	33.9	39.1	33.6	33.3	34.8	32.7	34.5	29.8	34.6
5. Very good	7.6	7.6	7.7	7.0	8.5	7.3	7.0	8.8	7.1	6.3	9.3	8.6	6.9	5.8	7.1	7.7
8. No opinion	6.1	5.6	6.5	5.8	6.3	7.7	7.2	5.0	4.0	4.9	6.7	6.5	5.8	4.1	5.9	9.3
Item 8480 Subject K02 N	3125	1449	1564	2332	340	731	896	968	531	1786	1132	1318	637	434	639	29

A24L: The U.S. military?

1. Very poor	2.2	2.2	2.0	1.7	3.3	2.7	2.1	1.7	2.5	1.8	2.4	2.0	1.3	1.9	2.7	12.7
2. Poor	2.1	2.7	1.6	2.2	1.8	2.9	2.4	1.0	2.5	2.3	1.9	2.1	2.0	1.1	3.0	3.2
3. Fair	15.8	15.1	16.6	15.3	15.5	17.8	15.9	12.5	19.2	17.0	14.5	16.8	13.3	16.1	16.5	18.6
4. Good	37.2	35.3	39.1	39.2	31.8	33.9	40.1	37.2	37.1	38.6	35.8	35.5	39.7	38.2	38.2	32.5
5. Very good	29.2	35.9	23.1	28.4	37.4	27.0	25.0	36.1	26.8	27.2	32.5	30.0	30.3	31.2	24.9	24.9
8. No opinion	13.4	8.8	17.6	13.2	10.3	15.7	14.5	11.5	11.9	13.1	13.0	13.5	13.5	11.5	14.7	8.1
Item 8490 Subject K02,L04 N	3115	1447	1556	2323	339	730	891	964	531	1782	1127	1315	633	434	637	29

A25: All things considered, do you think the armed services presently have too much or too little influence on the way this country is run?

1. Far too little	2.9	3.5	2.3	2.5	3.7	2.6	2.6	4.2	1.4	2.4	3.7	2.9	2.2	3.7	3.4	-
2. Too little	12.6	10.4	14.6	12.0	16.2	14.3	9.3	14.5	12.2	10.1	16.0	11.7	13.4	12.7	13.1	12.2
3. About right	66.7	69.2	64.2	68.3	61.8	65.8	69.3	67.1	63.1	68.6	64.2	68.8	67.9	66.6	62.5	67.1
4. Too much	14.2	13.3	15.5	14.5	11.2	13.5	15.8	11.6	17.4	15.5	13.0	14.0	13.1	13.5	16.2	12.9
5. Far too much	3.6	3.6	3.3	2.8	7.0	3.8	3.0	2.6	5.9	3.4	3.2	2.6	3.4	3.4	4.8	7.7
Item 8500 Subject K03,L04 N	3092	1442	1537	2306	338	722	888	959	523	1770	1122	1309	627	423	637	29

A26: Do you think the U.S. spends too much or too little on the armed services?

1. Far too little	3.2	5.3	1.4	2.9	2.4	3.9	2.6	3.9	2.0	2.6	3.8	2.9	3.1	5.0	2.2	6.9
2. Too little	13.3	16.8	9.9	14.0	14.5	11.7	13.0	16.0	10.8	11.5	16.1	12.6	14.4	13.4	14.1	5.7
3. About right	43.0	40.4	45.1	43.9	39.7	40.3	44.8	45.6	39.0	42.3	44.0	45.4	43.9	38.1	40.3	57.4
4. Too much	29.0	27.4	30.6	28.7	26.6	30.5	29.1	26.0	32.0	31.4	25.6	28.1	28.1	34.0	28.5	22.9
5. Far too much	11.6	10.0	13.1	10.5	16.9	13.5	10.6	8.5	16.2	12.2	10.5	11.1	10.6	9.4	15.0	7.1
Item 8510 Subject K03,L04 N	3095	1443	1541	2311	337	725	888	962	521	1771	1122	1306	627	429	638	29

A27: Next are some questions which ask about your experiences and attitudes concerning particular drugs. First we want your answers about some drugs that can be bought at a drugstore without a doctor's prescription– sometimes called over-the-counter or non-prescription drugs.

DURING THE LAST 12 MONTHS, on how many occasions have you...

A27A: . . . used non-prescription drugs which are supposed to relieve pain (such as aspirin, Anacin, Bufferin, Excedrin, Tylenol, Nuprin, Advil)?

1. 0 occasions	7.0	9.1	4.1	4.6	14.0	7.3	6.0	8.3	5.7	5.3	7.8	9.5	6.9	2.8	3.1	10.6
2. 1-2	16.8	18.2	15.1	13.4	26.0	15.4	14.7	19.1	18.5	14.1	19.1	20.2	16.1	14.8	11.8	13.1
3. 3-5	16.9	19.9	14.4	15.8	22.0	16.8	18.0	16.9	15.3	17.6	16.3	19.2	18.3	16.5	11.4	9.4
4. 6-9	14.9	15.7	14.5	15.3	14.0	16.5	14.0	13.7	16.2	15.5	14.2	15.4	14.5	13.1	15.7	6.1
5. 10-19	18.5	18.3	19.5	20.7	13.7	16.4	19.4	18.5	20.0	19.7	17.9	16.5	19.8	23.9	19.6	8.9
6. 20-39	12.8	9.3	15.9	15.2	4.6	12.4	13.5	11.9	14.0	14.1	11.5	10.4	11.7	16.5	16.3	26.0
7. 40 or more	13.0	9.5	16.4	14.9	5.8	15.2	14.4	11.5	10.4	13.6	13.1	8.7	12.7	12.4	22.1	25.8
Item 8520 Subject A01b N	3126	1450	1566	2336	339	735	895	964	531	1793	1128	1324	637	437	639	29

QUESTIONNAIRE FORM 3 1986	TOTAL	SEX		RACE		REGION				4YR COLLEGE PLANS		ILLICIT DRUG USE: LIFETIME				
		M	F	White	Black	NE	NC	S	W	Yes	No	None	Mari-juana Only	Few Pills	More Pills	Any Her-oin
N (Weighted No. of Cases):	3159	1456	1581	2348	342	746	901	978	534	1801	1138	1328	641	437	648	29
% of Weighted Total:	100.0	46.1	50.1	74.3	10.8	23.6	28.5	31.0	16.9	57.0	36.0	42.0	20.3	13.8	20.5	0.9
A27B: . . . used non-prescription drugs that are supposed to help people get to sleep (such as Sleep-Eze, Sominex, or Nytol)?																
1. 0 occasions	88.6	88.9	88.6	88.3	91.1	89.5	89.0	88.6	86.5	90.0	86.5	94.6	89.3	84.9	79.3	61.4
2. 1-2	6.5	6.2	6.9	6.9	4.7	5.1	6.1	6.9	8.7	6.4	7.0	3.1	6.6	11.6	9.8	17.6
3. 3-5	2.3	2.4	2.1	2.2	2.3	2.5	2.6	1.9	2.1	1.7	3.0	1.3	1.9	1.9	4.9	2.1
4. 6-9	1.4	1.0	1.7	1.5	0.5	1.9	1.4	1.1	1.4	0.9	2.0	0.3	1.4	1.0	3.8	4.8
5. 10-19	0.6	0.9	0.4	0.6	1.2	0.2	0.5	1.0	0.6	0.7	0.6	0.3	0.7	0.2	1.3	8.5
6. 20-39	0.3	0.2	0.2	0.2	-	0.5	0.2	0.1	0.4	0.1	0.6	0.1	-	0.4	0.7	5.7
7. 40 or more	0.3	0.4	0.1	0.3	0.2	0.3	0.1	0.3	0.3	0.2	0.3	0.3	0.2	-	0.2	-
Item 8530 Subject A01b N	3125	1450	1566	2333	338	736	894	965	530	1791	1131	1322	640	437	638	29
A27C: . . . used non-prescription drugs that are supposed to help people stay awake (such as No-Doz, Wake, or Vivarin)?																
1. 0 occasions	77.5	75.9	79.3	74.3	90.2	78.3	75.6	79.7	75.3	76.9	77.3	89.7	78.0	74.2	55.2	34.7
2. 1-2	9.8	10.1	9.9	11.2	4.3	9.1	11.1	8.0	12.2	10.3	10.1	5.5	8.8	16.5	16.2	5.8
3. 3-5	5.5	6.3	4.7	6.1	2.9	4.6	5.5	5.7	6.3	5.4	5.1	2.3	6.6	4.6	11.0	18.4
4. 6-9	2.5	2.6	2.3	3.0	1.2	1.8	3.0	2.8	2.0	2.7	2.3	0.9	2.9	1.8	6.0	-
5. 10-19	2.5	2.5	2.4	2.9	0.9	2.3	3.3	2.1	2.2	2.8	2.3	1.3	1.8	1.7	6.1	12.0
6. 20-39	1.2	1.2	0.8	1.3	0.1	1.6	1.1	0.7	1.6	1.3	1.2	0.4	1.1	0.4	2.6	20.3
7. 40 or more	1.0	1.4	0.6	1.3	0.4	2.3	0.4	1.0	0.3	0.6	1.6	0.1	0.8	0.7	2.9	8.8
Item 8540 Subject A01b N	3121	1448	1562	2332	337	734	893	963	530	1790	1127	1320	639	436	640	28
A27D: . . . used non-prescription drugs that are supposed to calm people down–keep them from being nervous or in a bad mood (such as Cope, Compoz, Devarex, or Miles Nervine)?																
1. 0 occasions	95.4	95.4	95.7	95.9	95.8	96.3	96.8	93.9	94.6	96.5	94.2	97.7	97.0	95.5	91.6	62.7
2. 1-2	2.3	2.3	2.3	2.1	1.8	1.5	1.6	3.0	3.4	2.5	2.0	1.4	1.6	3.1	3.7	10.8
3. 3-5	0.6	0.6	0.6	0.6	0.3	0.6	0.5	0.8	0.5	0.3	0.9	0.3	0.5	0.2	1.3	7.3
4. 6-9	0.4	0.4	0.3	0.3	0.6	0.1	0.4	0.5	0.4	0.2	0.6	0.2	0.1	0.6	1.0	-
5. 10-19	0.6	0.6	0.3	0.4	1.3	0.4	0.3	1.0	0.2	0.2	0.8	0.3	0.5	0.3	0.7	7.0
6. 20-39	0.3	*	0.5	0.3	-	0.2	0.3	0.3	0.4	0.2	0.5	0.1	-	0.1	0.8	5.7
7. 40 or more	0.5	0.6	0.3	0.4	0.2	0.9	0.1	0.5	0.4	0.1	0.9	0.2	0.3	0.3	1.0	6.5
Item 8550 Subject A01b N	3121	1451	1561	2334	338	732	895	964	531	1792	1128	1320	639	437	640	29
A28: Individuals differ in whether or not they disapprove of people doing certain things. Do YOU disapprove of people (who are 18 or older) doing each of the following?																
A28A: Smoking one or more packs of cigarettes per day																
1. Don't disapprove	24.6	26.2	23.4	26.7	14.6	28.0	26.6	23.1	19.4	19.7	33.2	13.4	22.7	25.8	47.6	55.2
2. Disapprove	37.1	35.3	38.3	36.7	39.6	34.2	35.5	39.8	39.0	36.8	36.8	38.2	39.5	44.9	28.1	16.5
3. Strongly disapprove	38.3	38.5	38.3	36.6	45.8	37.9	37.9	37.1	41.6	43.5	29.9	48.4	37.7	29.3	24.3	28.3
Item 8560 Subject A11a N	3131	1450	1573	2338	339	737	898	966	530	1798	1131	1327	640	437	641	29
A28B: Trying marijuana (pot, grass) once or twice																
1. Don't disapprove	45.4	46.0	44.2	48.2	34.5	55.5	47.3	34.8	47.1	45.6	45.0	15.6	59.9	59.8	81.6	79.2
2. Disapprove	25.0	26.0	24.5	25.2	25.6	23.0	26.7	26.0	23.3	24.9	24.9	32.0	25.5	21.7	13.2	14.3
3. Strongly disapprove	29.6	28.0	31.3	26.5	39.8	21.4	25.9	39.2	29.6	29.5	30.1	52.4	14.6	18.5	5.3	6.5
Item 8570 Subject A11a N	3129	1449	1572	2336	339	736	898	965	529	1794	1130	1324	639	436	641	29
A28C: Smoking marijuana occasionally																
1. Don't disapprove	31.0	32.8	29.1	32.8	23.9	39.8	30.6	23.6	32.7	28.2	34.4	6.7	36.7	37.8	69.3	67.5
2. Disapprove	25.6	25.8	24.9	25.7	25.0	26.0	28.6	23.3	24.0	27.0	23.3	23.6	32.1	31.9	19.4	20.5
3. Strongly disapprove	43.5	41.4	46.0	41.5	51.1	34.1	40.9	53.1	43.2	44.8	42.3	69.7	31.2	30.3	11.3	12.0
Item 8580 Subject A11a N	3126	1445	1574	2335	338	740	893	964	530	1795	1126	1326	637	435	642	29

*=less than .05 per cent.

QUESTIONNAIRE FORM 3 1986	TOTAL	SEX		RACE		REGION				4YR COLLEGE PLANS		ILLICIT DRUG USE: LIFETIME				
		M	F	White	Black	NE	NC	S	W	Yes	No	None	Mari-juana Only	Few Pills	More Pills	Any Her-oin
N (Weighted No. of Cases):	3159	1456	1581	2348	342	746	901	978	534	1801	1138	1328	641	437	648	29
% of Weighted Total:	100.0	46.1	50.1	74.3	10.8	23.6	28.5	31.0	16.9	57.0	36.0	42.0	20.3	13.8	20.5	0.9
A28D: Smoking marijuana regularly																
1. Don't disapprove	13.4	17.1	9.6	13.3	10.6	18.3	13.9	8.6	14.4	9.7	18.2	2.7	9.7	11.1	38.4	55.5
2. Disapprove	22.5	22.2	22.0	22.8	24.1	26.5	22.8	20.0	21.2	21.4	23.6	12.7	30.6	29.3	30.2	16.3
3. Strongly disapprove	64.1	60.8	68.5	63.9	65.3	55.2	63.3	71.4	64.4	68.9	58.2	84.6	59.7	59.6	31.5	28.2
Item 8590 Subject A11a N	3130	1448	1574	2337	339	740	896	965	530	1795	1129	1327	639	436	642	28
A28E: Trying LSD once or twice																
1. Don't disapprove	10.8	12.5	9.1	11.0	7.0	12.7	12.3	8.0	10.9	10.1	12.3	3.4	7.0	11.9	27.5	53.0
2. Disapprove	17.7	15.8	18.6	17.9	15.6	18.6	18.8	16.2	17.1	17.8	16.8	14.1	17.4	17.8	25.4	22.8
3. Strongly disapprove	71.5	71.7	72.3	71.1	77.5	68.7	68.9	75.8	72.1	72.2	70.9	82.5	75.6	70.3	47.1	24.2
Item 8600 Subject A11a N	3132	1452	1572	2340	338	740	898	964	530	1798	1130	1325	640	437	643	29
A28F: Taking LSD regularly																
1. Don't disapprove	3.4	4.7	1.7	2.7	3.1	5.3	2.9	2.6	3.2	2.5	4.5	1.8	2.5	2.0	6.7	26.6
2. Disapprove	10.5	11.5	9.3	10.5	10.6	10.3	12.2	10.1	8.8	9.0	12.3	7.3	8.1	8.2	20.9	23.4
3. Strongly disapprove	86.1	83.8	89.0	86.9	86.4	84.4	84.9	87.4	88.1	88.5	83.2	90.9	89.4	89.9	72.3	50.0
Item 8610 Subject A11a N	3126	1448	1572	2337	339	738	895	964	529	1795	1129	1325	638	437	640	29
A28G: Trying heroin (smack, horse) once or twice																
1. Don't disapprove	6.7	6.8	6.1	6.1	4.9	8.5	7.1	5.3	5.8	6.4	7.2	3.2	4.2	6.5	13.3	63.7
2. Disapprove	16.5	15.1	17.3	16.9	14.0	17.2	17.7	15.8	14.8	15.9	16.3	13.5	18.0	14.3	23.2	11.7
3. Strongly disapprove	76.8	78.2	76.6	77.0	81.1	74.3	75.2	78.9	79.3	77.7	76.5	83.3	77.8	79.2	63.5	24.6
Item 8620 Subject A11a N	3127	1446	1573	2336	338	741	895	961	530	1796	1127	1325	638	436	640	29
A28H: Taking heroin occasionally																
1. Don't disapprove	3.4	4.4	2.3	2.7	3.3	5.5	3.0	2.4	2.8	2.7	4.2	2.2	2.5	1.4	6.1	33.1
2. Disapprove	11.2	10.4	10.9	10.7	11.9	11.3	12.7	11.3	8.1	10.1	11.9	8.3	11.2	9.3	17.1	37.9
3. Strongly disapprove	85.4	85.3	86.8	86.7	84.8	83.2	84.3	86.3	89.1	87.2	84.0	89.5	86.3	89.3	76.8	29.0
Item 8630 Subject A11a N	3131	1449	1575	2339	339	741	896	963	530	1797	1130	1326	640	437	641	29
A28I: Taking heroin regularly																
1. Don't disapprove	2.4	3.3	1.2	1.5	3.2	3.7	1.9	2.2	1.7	1.7	3.2	1.6	2.1	1.4	3.3	22.0
2. Disapprove	8.0	7.8	7.5	7.3	9.4	8.3	9.0	8.2	5.6	6.1	9.6	7.1	6.7	4.7	13.0	23.7
3. Strongly disapprove	89.6	88.9	91.3	91.2	87.4	87.9	89.0	89.5	92.7	92.2	87.2	91.3	91.2	93.9	83.7	54.4
Item 8640 Subject A11a N	3118	1442	1570	2331	336	735	895	959	529	1795	1122	1323	638	434	638	29
A28J: Trying a barbiturate (downer, goofball, red, yellow, etc.) once or twice																
1. Don't disapprove	13.2	14.1	12.5	13.8	8.1	14.8	15.0	10.6	12.4	11.9	15.6	4.1	7.6	12.6	36.4	49.3
2. Disapprove	22.6	22.7	22.0	23.3	18.3	23.6	24.2	20.1	23.0	22.8	22.6	17.5	22.4	28.1	30.0	25.6
3. Strongly disapprove	64.2	63.2	65.5	62.9	73.6	61.5	60.8	69.2	64.6	65.3	61.8	78.4	70.0	59.3	33.6	25.1
Item 8650 Subject A11a N	3129	1448	1574	2338	338	739	896	965	529	1795	1130	1326	639	437	642	29
A28K: Taking barbiturates regularly																
1. Don't disapprove	5.1	6.1	3.8	4.1	4.5	6.9	4.2	5.2	4.0	3.5	7.3	2.0	3.5	2.7	12.2	28.9
2. Disapprove	19.4	21.7	17.2	19.5	18.4	21.6	20.1	18.1	17.3	15.7	24.0	12.5	18.2	20.7	33.5	40.8
3. Strongly disapprove	75.5	72.2	79.0	76.4	77.1	71.5	75.7	76.7	78.8	80.8	68.7	85.5	78.3	76.6	54.4	30.3
Item 8660 Subject A11a N	3115	1445	1565	2329	338	734	894	960	526	1786	1127	1320	638	431	641	29
A28L: Trying an amphetamine (upper, pep pill, bennie, speed) once or twice																
1. Don't disapprove	23.5	22.7	23.6	25.7	12.5	26.9	26.0	19.0	22.9	21.9	27.0	6.6	15.3	28.4	61.3	69.6
2. Disapprove	25.2	26.2	24.0	25.9	20.3	26.4	26.9	23.1	24.5	24.7	26.1	23.2	28.2	34.3	21.6	15.0
3. Strongly disapprove	51.3	51.1	52.5	48.4	67.2	46.7	47.2	57.9	52.6	53.4	47.0	70.2	56.5	37.3	17.1	15.4
Item 8670 Subject A11a N	3122	1446	1571	2332	339	738	893	961	529	1794	1126	1321	639	436	642	29

QUESTIONNAIRE FORM 3 1986	TOTAL	SEX		RACE		REGION				4YR COLLEGE PLANS		ILLICIT DRUG USE: LIFETIME				
		M	F	White	Black	NE	NC	S	W	Yes	No	None	Mari- juana Only	Few Pills	More Pills	Any Her- oin
N (Weighted No. of Cases):	3159	1456	1581	2348	342	746	901	978	534	1801	1138	1328	641	437	648	29
% of Weighted Total:	100.0	46.1	50.1	74.3	10.8	23.6	28.5	31.0	16.9	57.0	36.0	42.0	20.3	13.8	20.5	0.9
A28M: Taking amphetamines regularly																
1. Don't disapprove	6.5	7.4	5.2	6.4	4.5	8.5	6.2	6.2	4.8	4.2	10.0	2.0	2.6	4.7	18.8	39.6
2. Disapprove	20.2	20.7	19.1	20.5	18.7	21.2	22.5	17.1	20.8	17.6	23.7	11.1	19.7	22.0	37.3	47.2
3. Strongly disapprove	73.3	71.9	75.6	73.2	76.8	70.3	71.4	76.7	74.4	78.2	66.3	86.8	77.7	73.3	43.8	13.2
Item 8680 Subject A11a N	3118	1448	1565	2328	339	736	894	961	526	1790	1126	1320	639	434	640	29
A28N: Trying cocaine once or twice																
1. Don't disapprove	19.8	21.7	17.3	20.7	10.7	26.4	18.4	14.3	22.7	18.4	21.8	4.2	11.9	23.5	55.2	66.5
2. Disapprove	17.9	17.5	18.2	17.8	18.8	21.1	17.4	15.3	19.4	17.5	18.5	15.0	20.6	23.2	17.2	20.7
3. Strongly disapprove	62.3	60.8	64.5	61.6	70.5	52.6	64.2	70.5	57.9	64.2	59.8	80.8	67.5	53.3	27.6	12.7
Item 8690 Subject A11a N	3118	1446	1567	2334	335	738	895	957	528	1791	1126	1323	638	434	641	29
A28O: Taking cocaine regularly																
1. Don't disapprove	5.7	7.7	3.4	5.3	4.0	9.4	4.6	3.3	6.6	3.7	8.5	1.7	2.9	1.9	16.7	45.0
2. Disapprove	14.5	14.9	13.1	14.9	11.2	15.8	15.0	13.7	13.5	12.5	17.0	7.7	10.8	13.8	32.3	33.3
3. Strongly disapprove	79.7	77.4	83.5	79.7	84.7	74.8	80.4	82.9	79.8	83.9	74.5	90.6	86.2	84.3	51.0	21.6
Item 8700 Subject A11a N	3113	1443	1567	2328	334	736	890	957	529	1788	1126	1316	636	436	641	29
A28P: Trying one or two drinks of an alcoholic beverage (beer, wine, liquor)																
1. Don't disapprove	79.1	82.0	76.8	83.8	62.9	83.5	84.5	70.8	78.7	80.2	78.8	66.2	87.6	86.4	93.0	91.6
2. Disapprove	12.9	11.3	14.1	10.0	22.4	11.3	9.6	16.8	13.5	12.9	12.1	20.1	8.6	9.8	4.2	3.9
3. Strongly disapprove	8.1	6.7	9.1	6.2	14.7	5.2	5.9	12.4	7.8	6.9	9.1	13.7	3.7	3.8	2.8	4.5
Item 8710 Subject A11a N	3126	1448	1574	2337	339	738	896	963	528	1795	1130	1325	638	436	642	29
A28Q: Taking one or two drinks nearly every day																
1. Don't disapprove	27.2	35.4	19.7	29.5	18.4	31.3	29.7	24.7	21.9	23.5	32.5	17.6	29.2	26.9	44.0	66.9
2. Disapprove	42.1	39.3	44.7	43.0	37.0	42.7	43.3	40.1	42.7	44.3	40.0	41.9	43.3	46.8	39.4	14.6
3. Strongly disapprove	30.7	25.4	35.6	27.5	44.7	26.0	27.0	35.2	35.4	32.3	27.4	40.5	27.4	26.3	16.6	18.5
Item 8720 Subject A11a N	3117	1447	1569	2328	339	739	894	957	527	1787	1128	1321	638	435	642	26
A28R: Taking four or five drinks nearly every day																
1. Don't disapprove	8.6	12.4	4.5	9.3	4.1	11.6	8.1	8.4	5.6	5.7	13.0	4.5	8.5	7.2	16.7	37.2
2. Disapprove	25.0	29.5	20.8	25.7	23.2	26.0	28.2	23.2	21.3	21.7	28.9	19.7	26.4	26.8	32.3	34.1
3. Strongly disapprove	66.5	58.1	74.7	65.0	72.8	62.5	63.8	68.4	73.1	72.6	58.1	75.8	65.1	66.0	51.0	28.7
Item 8730 Subject A11a N	3125	1447	1573	2336	339	737	896	962	529	1793	1130	1325	638	436	640	29
A28S: Having five or more drinks once or twice each weekend																
1. Don't disapprove	37.6	46.5	29.1	41.1	19.7	43.5	41.4	32.4	32.2	33.5	43.2	20.2	41.8	43.4	64.2	60.4
2. Disapprove	27.6	24.9	30.0	28.8	22.3	26.3	28.5	25.6	31.3	29.6	25.5	30.9	28.0	30.3	20.1	8.6
3. Strongly disapprove	34.9	28.5	40.9	30.1	58.0	30.2	30.1	42.0	36.6	36.9	31.3	48.9	30.3	26.3	15.7	31.0
Item 8740 Subject A11a N	3124	1446	1573	2334	338	738	896	963	527	1792	1130	1325	636	436	642	29
A29: During the LAST 12 MONTHS, how often have you been around people who were taking each of the following to get high or for "kicks"?																
A29A: Marijuana (pot, grass) or hashish																
1. Not at all	28.0	23.8	32.1	26.4	29.8	23.2	28.1	32.8	26.2	28.4	26.5	52.1	11.7	13.5	6.1	3.1
2. Once or twice	24.5	26.1	23.1	24.0	28.2	19.5	26.3	27.5	22.9	25.6	23.3	29.1	28.9	22.4	11.9	9.4
3. Occasionally	23.4	25.8	21.4	24.6	20.6	25.6	24.2	19.6	26.1	25.2	21.8	13.0	36.3	36.7	23.7	14.9
4. Often	24.0	24.2	23.4	25.0	21.4	31.7	21.4	20.2	24.7	20.8	28.3	5.8	23.2	27.4	58.4	72.6
Item 20590 Subject A02b N	3119	1444	1570	2327	340	739	894	957	529	1789	1128	1321	637	437	642	29

QUESTIONNAIRE FORM 3 1986	TOTAL	SEX		RACE		REGION				4YR COLLEGE PLANS		ILLICIT DRUG USE: LIFETIME				
		M	F	White	Black	NE	NC	S	W	Yes	No	None	Marijuana Only	Few Pills	More Pills	Any Heroin
N (Weighted No. of Cases):	3159	1456	1581	2348	342	746	901	978	534	1801	1138	1328	641	437	648	29
% of Weighted Total:	100.0	46.1	50.1	74.3	10.8	23.6	28.5	31.0	16.9	57.0	36.0	42.0	20.3	13.8	20.5	0.9

A29B: LSD

	TOTAL	M	F	White	Black	NE	NC	S	W	Yes	No	None	Mar. Only	Few Pills	More Pills	Any Heroin
1. Not at all	86.9	86.2	88.3	85.6	95.6	86.3	85.8	89.4	85.0	87.6	85.5	95.0	92.7	85.2	68.0	26.5
2. Once or twice	8.0	8.5	7.1	8.9	2.5	9.0	8.6	6.2	8.5	8.2	8.5	3.7	5.3	11.7	16.8	14.7
3. Occasionally	3.5	3.5	3.5	4.0	0.8	2.8	3.9	2.9	5.1	3.2	4.0	0.8	1.4	2.2	10.6	33.9
4. Often	1.6	1.8	1.2	1.5	1.0	1.9	1.6	1.5	1.4	1.0	2.0	0.4	0.5	0.9	4.7	24.8
Item 20600 Subject A02b N	3078	1426	1547	2300	334	731	884	944	519	1761	1117	1303	625	431	638	29

A29C: Other psychedelics (mescaline, peyote, PCP, etc.)

	TOTAL	M	F	White	Black	NE	NC	S	W	Yes	No	None	Mar. Only	Few Pills	More Pills	Any Heroin
1. Not at all	88.2	87.2	89.4	87.6	94.0	83.4	88.3	92.3	87.6	88.7	88.3	95.7	93.3	88.8	69.7	38.0
2. Once or twice	7.5	8.0	6.9	8.2	2.8	8.8	8.1	5.3	8.6	7.6	7.1	3.1	5.3	8.5	18.2	12.2
3. Occasionally	2.8	3.2	2.3	2.8	2.1	5.1	2.1	1.5	3.1	2.8	3.1	0.9	1.2	2.3	7.6	27.3
4. Often	1.5	1.6	1.3	1.4	1.1	2.7	1.5	1.0	0.7	0.9	1.5	0.4	0.2	0.5	4.5	22.5
Item 20610 Subject A02b N	3110	1440	1565	2324	338	734	893	955	528	1783	1126	1316	633	437	642	29

A29D: Amphetamines (uppers, pep pills, bennies, speed)

	TOTAL	M	F	White	Black	NE	NC	S	W	Yes	No	None	Mar. Only	Few Pills	More Pills	Any Heroin
1. Not at all	63.5	64.3	63.1	59.1	81.9	64.6	58.2	66.0	66.5	65.9	58.1	82.1	69.4	53.6	27.5	12.1
2. Once or twice	19.9	19.9	20.0	22.1	12.2	17.4	22.5	20.2	18.4	20.6	20.2	13.4	21.9	29.6	26.3	10.3
3. Occasionally	10.8	10.8	10.8	12.1	4.7	11.6	12.1	9.5	9.6	9.2	13.7	3.4	7.1	14.6	26.4	24.6
4. Often	5.8	5.0	6.1	6.8	1.1	6.4	7.2	4.3	5.5	4.2	8.0	1.1	1.6	2.1	19.8	52.9
Item 20620 Subject A02b N	3111	1440	1568	2322	340	736	892	955	529	1784	1127	1314	634	437	643	29

A29E: Barbiturates (downers, goofballs, reds, yellows, etc.)

	TOTAL	M	F	White	Black	NE	NC	S	W	Yes	No	None	Mar. Only	Few Pills	More Pills	Any Heroin
1. Not at all	84.2	83.5	85.1	82.7	92.7	82.1	82.4	85.3	88.2	86.2	80.8	93.7	91.8	80.4	62.0	21.5
2. Once or twice	9.8	10.2	9.2	10.8	5.9	10.4	10.8	9.6	8.0	9.6	10.9	4.5	6.5	15.1	20.3	24.1
3. Occasionally	3.9	4.3	3.5	4.5	0.3	4.8	4.3	3.9	2.1	3.0	5.1	1.4	1.4	4.0	10.8	15.2
4. Often	2.1	2.0	2.1	2.1	1.0	2.7	2.6	1.3	1.7	1.2	3.2	0.4	0.3	0.5	6.9	39.3
Item 20630 Subject A02b N	3109	1440	1565	2321	340	736	891	954	528	1782	1127	1315	634	437	641	29

A29F: Tranquilizers (Librium, Valium, Miltown)

	TOTAL	M	F	White	Black	NE	NC	S	W	Yes	No	None	Mar. Only	Few Pills	More Pills	Any Heroin
1. Not at all	80.4	80.9	80.3	78.1	92.8	78.5	80.9	81.7	79.9	81.2	78.7	89.5	88.1	76.3	59.1	30.0
2. Once or twice	12.6	12.7	12.4	14.6	4.3	12.5	11.7	12.3	15.1	13.3	12.5	8.0	9.6	19.1	21.0	28.1
3. Occasionally	4.4	4.0	4.7	4.5	2.0	5.3	4.0	4.5	3.8	3.7	5.3	2.0	2.2	2.8	11.5	14.7
4. Often	2.5	2.4	2.6	2.9	0.9	3.6	3.4	1.6	1.3	1.8	3.6	0.5	0.2	1.8	8.4	27.2
Item 20640 Subject A02b N	3108	1437	1565	2319	338	734	894	953	528	1781	1126	1314	635	435	643	29

A29G: Cocaine ("coke")

	TOTAL	M	F	White	Black	NE	NC	S	W	Yes	No	None	Mar. Only	Few Pills	More Pills	Any Heroin
1. Not at all	62.6	62.2	63.8	61.7	69.4	51.6	66.1	72.0	55.1	63.2	61.8	83.6	61.9	49.6	30.3	17.0
2. Once or twice	17.7	18.1	17.3	17.9	19.0	21.7	16.8	15.8	17.2	19.3	15.6	11.3	23.4	28.7	19.0	3.2
3. Occasionally	11.9	11.9	12.0	12.4	7.7	15.9	11.4	7.5	15.1	11.1	13.0	3.6	12.5	16.5	25.3	16.6
4. Often	7.8	7.9	6.9	8.1	3.9	10.8	5.7	4.7	12.7	6.4	9.5	1.6	2.2	5.2	25.4	63.2
Item 20650 Subject A02b N	3109	1439	1567	2322	338	732	892	956	529	1781	1128	1318	634	437	639	29

A29H: Heroin (smack, horse)

	TOTAL	M	F	White	Black	NE	NC	S	W	Yes	No	None	Mar. Only	Few Pills	More Pills	Any Heroin
1. Not at all	94.0	94.1	94.4	94.5	95.2	93.8	93.6	95.2	93.0	94.8	93.3	96.7	95.4	94.4	90.4	18.6
2. Once or twice	3.9	3.8	4.1	3.8	2.9	4.3	3.8	2.9	5.1	3.7	4.1	2.3	3.7	3.8	6.9	19.3
3. Occasionally	1.1	0.9	0.9	0.9	0.5	0.8	1.4	1.0	1.2	1.0	1.0	0.6	0.5	0.9	0.9	30.0
4. Often	1.0	1.3	0.5	0.8	1.4	1.2	1.3	0.9	0.7	0.5	1.6	0.4	0.4	0.9	1.7	32.1
Item 20660 Subject A02b N	3099	1432	1562	2311	340	733	889	954	524	1774	1125	1308	635	436	638	29

A29I: Other narcotics (methadone, opium, codeine, paregoric, etc.)

	TOTAL	M	F	White	Black	NE	NC	S	W	Yes	No	None	Mar. Only	Few Pills	More Pills	Any Heroin
1. Not at all	84.4	85.3	83.8	82.8	93.1	81.6	83.3	87.9	83.8	85.6	82.2	93.0	91.4	86.6	61.4	16.9
2. Once or twice	9.8	9.3	10.2	10.6	4.0	11.2	10.0	7.8	11.2	9.5	11.0	5.2	7.1	9.7	21.9	18.3
3. Occasionally	3.6	3.4	3.9	4.3	1.5	4.8	4.0	2.9	2.7	3.6	3.8	1.2	1.3	2.9	9.2	42.7
4. Often	2.1	2.0	2.1	2.2	1.3	2.4	2.7	1.3	2.3	1.3	3.1	0.5	0.2	0.9	7.5	22.1
Item 20670 Subject A02b N	3108	1435	1567	2320	340	735	892	956	526	1780	1125	1315	634	436	642	29

QUESTIONNAIRE FORM 3 1986	TOTAL	SEX		RACE		REGION				4YR COLLEGE PLANS		ILLICIT DRUG USE: LIFETIME				
		M	F	White	Black	NE	NC	S	W	Yes	No	None	Mari- juana Only	Few Pills	More Pills	Any Her- oin
N (Weighted No. of Cases):	3159	1456	1581	2348	342	746	901	978	534	1801	1138	1328	641	437	648	29
% of Weighted Total:	100.0	46.1	50.1	74.3	10.8	23.6	28.5	31.0	16.9	57.0	36.0	42.0	20.3	13.8	20.5	0.9

A29J: Alcoholic beverages (beer, wine, liquor)

	TOTAL	M	F	White	Black	NE	NC	S	W	Yes	No	None	Mari- juana Only	Few Pills	More Pills	Any Her- oin
1. Not at all	5.9	4.6	6.5	4.5	7.3	5.8	4.1	6.5	7.8	4.9	6.2	10.8	2.4	1.8	1.4	3.1
2. Once or twice	10.9	8.5	12.8	8.6	19.6	10.3	8.9	13.2	10.8	11.2	9.6	19.0	6.6	4.3	2.4	2.1
3. Occasionally	25.2	24.9	26.3	22.7	38.4	24.3	22.5	26.2	29.5	25.9	24.3	32.6	26.3	21.5	12.8	12.5
4. Often	58.0	62.0	54.4	64.2	34.8	59.6	64.4	54.1	52.0	58.0	59.8	37.6	64.7	72.3	83.4	82.4
Item 20680 Subject A02b N	3119	1444	1570	2329	340	739	894	956	530	1789	1129	1322	636	437	643	29

This section asks for your views and feelings about a number of different things.

D01: How satisfied are you with your life as a whole these days?

	TOTAL	M	F	White	Black	NE	NC	S	W	Yes	No	None	Mari- juana Only	Few Pills	More Pills	Any Her- oin
1. Completely dissatisfied	2.5	3.4	1.6	2.0	4.8	4.4	1.4	3.1	0.7	1.6	3.7	2.2	2.8	2.0	2.4	8.3
2. Quite dissatisfied	9.5	8.5	10.4	8.9	6.5	10.9	8.5	8.9	10.3	10.6	7.8	10.3	9.2	9.9	7.5	0.5
3. Somewhat dissatisfied	10.5	8.8	11.6	10.0	12.2	10.5	10.5	9.1	12.7	9.9	11.4	8.6	10.0	12.6	6.2	6.2
4. Neither, or mixed feelings	13.0	12.8	12.9	12.7	13.6	13.3	12.0	12.3	15.7	12.0	14.5	11.2	14.9	12.2	15.1	17.3
5. Somewhat satisfied	26.8	28.7	25.6	27.6	26.8	22.5	28.6	29.4	24.8	27.8	25.4	25.0	27.7	32.2	26.5	22.1
6. Quite satisfied	32.4	33.0	32.0	33.8	27.9	34.1	34.0	30.3	30.9	33.1	31.5	36.2	30.0	27.4	30.5	39.0
7. Completely satisfied	5.4	4.9	5.9	5.0	8.1	4.3	4.9	6.9	5.0	5.0	5.7	6.5	5.4	3.7	4.3	6.6
Item 6840 Subject P01,Q01 N	2972	1370	1531	2283	300	672	874	916	510	1771	1100	1268	603	418	613	28

D02: These questions are about your health during the last MONTH.

D02A: Have you been bothered by shortness of breath when you were not exercising or working hard?

	TOTAL	M	F	White	Black	NE	NC	S	W	Yes	No	None	Mari- juana Only	Few Pills	More Pills	Any Her- oin
1. Never	71.5	76.8	67.0	72.1	71.6	69.9	70.7	72.5	73.3	73.1	68.3	77.0	74.1	67.3	62.0	51.5
2. Seldom	18.2	15.5	20.5	18.3	14.8	18.3	20.1	16.5	18.0	17.2	20.1	14.5	18.6	23.1	21.5	19.5
3. Sometimes	8.6	6.8	10.2	8.0	12.1	8.7	7.5	10.1	8.0	8.2	9.6	7.4	6.4	9.4	11.9	29.0
4. Often	1.6	0.9	2.3	1.6	1.5	3.2	1.7	1.0	0.7	1.5	2.0	1.0	0.8	0.2	4.6	-
Item 8850 Subject T01 N	2972	1368	1533	2283	299	671	873	915	513	1771	1099	1267	603	418	613	28

D02B: Have you been bothered by your heart beating hard?

	TOTAL	M	F	White	Black	NE	NC	S	W	Yes	No	None	Mari- juana Only	Few Pills	More Pills	Any Her- oin
1. Never	73.0	77.4	69.2	72.8	73.0	72.4	73.4	72.5	73.8	73.6	72.3	79.7	75.0	66.8	60.4	72.3
2. Seldom	17.9	16.4	19.0	18.0	16.0	17.8	18.4	17.1	18.4	18.0	17.9	14.0	17.3	22.3	23.7	22.5
3. Sometimes	8.0	5.5	10.3	8.1	8.9	8.6	7.0	9.3	6.6	7.4	8.5	5.3	6.8	9.8	13.8	5.2
4. Often	1.2	0.7	1.6	1.1	2.1	1.2	1.2	1.1	1.2	1.0	1.4	1.0	0.8	1.2	2.1	-
Item 8860 Subject T01 N	2965	1366	1528	2278	299	668	873	912	511	1768	1095	1264	601	418	611	28

D02C: Have you had spells of dizziness?

	TOTAL	M	F	White	Black	NE	NC	S	W	Yes	No	None	Mari- juana Only	Few Pills	More Pills	Any Her- oin
1. Never	58.9	68.1	50.6	57.9	66.0	62.4	58.9	57.3	57.2	59.7	57.4	63.9	62.9	52.7	49.4	31.7
2. Seldom	24.9	21.2	28.3	25.8	17.2	22.5	23.3	26.5	27.5	25.6	24.1	23.2	22.0	28.6	28.2	37.9
3. Sometimes	13.6	8.5	17.9	13.9	13.8	12.7	14.4	13.6	13.2	12.6	14.9	10.9	12.1	17.4	18.0	22.9
4. Often	2.7	2.1	3.2	2.5	3.0	2.3	3.4	2.6	2.1	2.2	3.6	1.9	3.0	1.3	4.4	7.4
Item 8870 Subject T01 N	2954	1359	1524	2271	298	664	869	909	512	1761	1093	1259	601	418	608	28

D02D: Have your hands trembled enough to bother you?

	TOTAL	M	F	White	Black	NE	NC	S	W	Yes	No	None	Mari- juana Only	Few Pills	More Pills	Any Her- oin
1. Never	79.2	84.5	74.2	78.5	82.5	83.8	76.2	77.9	80.3	80.7	77.1	83.5	82.6	80.2	66.6	60.4
2. Seldom	13.1	10.1	15.9	14.0	9.2	9.4	15.2	14.8	11.3	12.6	14.3	10.6	10.9	12.3	20.4	22.9
3. Sometimes	6.2	4.1	8.0	6.1	6.9	5.2	6.9	5.9	6.8	5.6	6.5	4.9	4.9	5.2	10.7	12.7
4. Often	1.6	1.2	1.9	1.4	1.4	1.6	1.7	1.4	1.6	1.2	2.1	1.0	1.5	2.3	2.3	4.1
Item 8880 Subject T01 N	2957	1361	1525	2275	296	663	872	909	512	1763	1093	1262	599	416	610	28

D02E: Have you been troubled by your hands sweating so that they felt damp and clammy?

	TOTAL	M	F	White	Black	NE	NC	S	W	Yes	No	None	Mari- juana Only	Few Pills	More Pills	Any Her- oin
1. Never	66.5	70.9	62.9	65.4	78.3	70.0	67.3	66.4	60.7	69.0	62.4	69.7	70.0	62.8	59.9	55.7
2. Seldom	20.3	17.8	22.3	21.1	12.0	17.3	19.2	20.3	26.2	19.1	22.2	18.6	18.6	25.6	21.7	24.5
3. Sometimes	9.7	7.9	11.3	10.2	7.0	9.0	9.8	10.1	9.9	8.3	12.2	9.1	8.6	8.4	12.7	14.2
4. Often	3.5	3.4	3.4	3.3	2.7	3.6	3.8	3.2	3.2	3.6	3.3	2.7	2.8	3.1	5.7	5.6
Item 8890 Subject T01 N	2959	1361	1526	2276	296	660	873	913	512	1766	1095	1266	598	418	608	28

QUESTIONNAIRE FORM 3 1986	TOTAL	SEX		RACE		REGION				4YR COLLEGE PLANS		ILLICIT DRUG USE: LIFETIME				
		M	F	White	Black	NE	NC	S	W	Yes	No	None	Marijuana Only	Few Pills	More Pills	Any Heroin
N (Weighted No. of Cases):	3159	1456	1581	2348	342	746	901	978	534	1801	1138	1328	641	437	648	29
% of Weighted Total:	100.0	46.1	50.1	74.3	10.8	23.6	28.5	31.0	16.9	57.0	36.0	42.0	20.3	13.8	20.5	0.9

D02F: Have there been times when you couldn't take care of things because you just couldn't get going?

	TOTAL	M	F	White	Black	NE	NC	S	W	Yes	No	None	Marijuana Only	Few Pills	More Pills	Any Heroin
1. Never	51.9	60.9	43.7	51.3	56.2	50.0	52.6	50.5	55.5	51.6	51.6	55.9	55.6	47.0	43.2	46.7
2. Seldom	28.8	25.7	31.6	30.1	20.2	31.5	29.5	27.3	26.6	29.9	27.3	25.9	29.5	32.2	31.1	38.3
3. Sometimes	15.5	11.4	19.1	14.8	19.4	13.2	14.6	18.3	14.8	14.9	16.6	14.8	12.0	17.9	19.1	7.8
4. Often	3.9	2.0	5.6	3.8	4.2	5.3	3.3	3.8	3.1	3.5	4.4	3.4	2.9	2.8	6.6	7.3
Item 8900 Subject T01 N	2963	1364	1528	2279	297	666	873	912	513	1770	1093	1265	600	419	611	27

D03: At any time during the LAST 12 MONTHS, have you felt in your own mind that you should REDUCE or STOP your use of . . .

D03A: Alcohol?

	TOTAL	M	F	White	Black	NE	NC	S	W	Yes	No	None	Marijuana Only	Few Pills	More Pills	Any Heroin
1. Yes	34.0	37.4	30.5	34.1	34.7	26.0	35.8	37.5	35.3	32.8	36.2	23.4	40.4	45.7	38.3	44.8
2. No	51.3	49.7	53.1	53.9	34.4	63.8	53.7	42.2	46.8	51.4	51.3	47.0	53.7	50.0	59.1	47.1
8. Haven't used in last 12 months	14.6	12.9	16.4	11.9	30.9	10.2	10.5	20.3	17.9	15.8	12.6	29.6	5.9	4.3	2.6	8.1
Item 8910 Subject A01i N	2558	1209	1292	2038	222	573	780	767	439	1554	916	1014	530	372	582	26

D03B: Cigarettes?

	TOTAL	M	F	White	Black	NE	NC	S	W	Yes	No	None	Marijuana Only	Few Pills	More Pills	Any Heroin
1. Yes	25.4	23.3	26.6	25.9	18.2	28.2	27.6	23.9	20.3	20.3	33.6	9.2	29.0	36.9	46.2	45.4
2. No	15.2	15.0	15.3	15.4	10.0	17.5	14.4	13.9	16.1	14.0	16.9	9.3	17.2	17.4	23.4	41.1
8. Haven't used in last 12 months	59.4	61.7	58.1	58.7	71.8	54.2	58.0	62.2	63.6	65.7	49.6	81.5	53.8	45.6	30.4	13.6
Item 8920 Subject A01i N	2883	1322	1495	2232	283	644	864	879	496	1727	1052	1233	575	411	603	28

D03C: Marijuana?

	TOTAL	M	F	White	Black	NE	NC	S	W	Yes	No	None	Marijuana Only	Few Pills	More Pills	Any Heroin
1. Yes	21.2	23.1	18.9	22.2	18.1	22.8	22.7	18.6	21.2	17.9	26.9	-	33.8	34.3	44.7	30.0
2. No	16.5	16.6	16.3	16.6	13.2	24.5	14.4	12.2	17.3	15.6	17.3	-	28.5	20.9	35.6	60.2
8. Haven't used in last 12 months	62.3	60.3	64.8	61.2	68.7	52.6	62.9	69.2	61.5	66.4	55.8	100.0	37.7	44.8	19.7	9.9
Item 8930 Subject A01i N	2583	1192	1335	2024	244	580	768	781	453	1577	917	1139	472	364	562	26

D03D: Psychedelics (LSD, etc.)?

	TOTAL	M	F	White	Black	NE	NC	S	W	Yes	No	None	Marijuana Only	Few Pills	More Pills	Any Heroin
1. Yes	2.5	3.5	1.6	2.7	0.6	3.6	2.6	1.4	2.8	1.7	3.9	-	-	1.6	10.5	32.6
2. No	1.9	2.6	1.2	2.0	0.2	2.5	2.7	0.8	1.7	1.0	2.9	-	-	0.6	7.9	31.3
8. Haven't used in last 12 months	95.6	93.9	97.2	95.2	99.2	93.9	94.7	97.8	95.5	97.3	93.2	100.0	100.0	97.8	81.6	36.1
Item 8940 Subject A01i N	2578	1187	1337	2015	248	561	776	780	461	1592	901	1137	534	363	494	23

D03E: Amphetamines (uppers)?

	TOTAL	M	F	White	Black	NE	NC	S	W	Yes	No	None	Marijuana Only	Few Pills	More Pills	Any Heroin
1. Yes	3.8	3.7	3.5	4.2	1.2	3.9	4.6	3.6	2.6	2.9	5.5	-	-	2.6	16.6	54.4
2. No	4.9	4.9	4.9	5.8	0.2	6.0	6.2	3.1	4.6	3.7	6.8	-	-	1.3	25.7	24.8
8. Haven't used in last 12 months	91.3	91.4	91.6	90.1	98.6	90.1	89.2	93.3	92.8	93.4	87.6	100.0	100.0	96.0	57.7	20.8
Item 8950 Subject A01i N	2471	1146	1276	1930	243	553	736	749	433	1537	853	1136	534	315	437	22

D03F: Tranquilizers?

	TOTAL	M	F	White	Black	NE	NC	S	W	Yes	No	None	Marijuana Only	Few Pills	More Pills	Any Heroin
1. Yes	1.4	1.3	1.7	1.5	0.3	2.5	1.5	0.9	0.9	0.5	3.2	-	-	0.9	5.9	27.0
2. No	2.0	1.9	2.1	2.0	0.1	2.6	2.3	1.4	1.7	1.2	2.9	-	-	1.0	8.7	30.1
8. Haven't used in last 12 months	96.6	96.9	96.3	96.5	99.5	95.0	96.2	97.6	97.4	98.2	93.9	100.0	100.0	98.1	85.3	43.0
Item 9005 Subject A01i N	2531	1170	1308	1984	240	555	778	748	449	1556	892	1131	531	350	473	19

D03G: Barbiturates/Quaaludes (downers)?

	TOTAL	M	F	White	Black	NE	NC	S	W	Yes	No	None	Marijuana Only	Few Pills	More Pills	Any Heroin
1. Yes	1.3	1.7	0.8	1.2	1.3	1.5	1.7	1.0	0.7	0.9	1.9	-	-	0.5	4.5	36.4
2. No	1.8	1.7	1.9	1.9	0.5	2.8	1.3	1.7	1.5	1.1	2.9	-	-	1.5	6.9	34.9
8. Haven't used in last 12 months	96.9	96.6	97.3	96.9	98.2	95.7	96.9	97.3	97.8	98.0	95.3	100.0	100.0	98.1	88.6	28.6
Item 8970 Subject A01i N	2571	1187	1332	2015	246	557	780	773	462	1600	887	1138	532	370	483	21

D03H: Cocaine?

	TOTAL	M	F	White	Black	NE	NC	S	W	Yes	No	None	Marijuana Only	Few Pills	More Pills	Any Heroin
1. Yes	5.1	5.9	3.8	4.5	5.5	7.6	4.0	3.9	5.8	3.7	7.7	-	-	7.2	18.7	30.9
2. No	6.6	7.4	5.8	7.2	1.5	11.7	5.0	2.9	9.2	5.3	8.1	-	-	3.4	27.3	48.2
8. Haven't used in last 12 months	88.4	86.7	90.4	88.2	93.1	80.7	91.0	93.2	85.0	91.1	84.1	100.0	100.0	89.3	53.9	20.8
Item 8980 Subject A01i N	2608	1195	1353	2046	246	568	789	789	463	1610	911	1136	532	361	527	25

QUESTIONNAIRE FORM 3 1986	TOTAL	SEX		RACE		REGION				4YR COLLEGE PLANS		ILLICIT DRUG USE: LIFETIME				
		M	F	White	Black	NE	NC	S	W	Yes	No	None	Mari- juana Only	Few Pills	More Pills	Any Her- oin
N (Weighted No. of Cases):	3159	1456	1581	2348	342	746	901	978	534	1801	1138	1328	641	437	648	29
% of Weighted Total:	100.0	46.1	50.1	74.3	10.8	23.6	28.5	31.0	16.9	57.0	36.0	42.0	20.3	13.8	20.5	0.9
D03I: Heroin?																
1. Yes	0.2	0.4	-	0.1	-	0.2	0.4	0.2	-	0.2	0.3	-	-	-	-	22.1
2. No	0.5	0.5	0.1	0.4	-	0.3	0.4	0.5	0.7	0.3	0.9	-	-	-	-	54.4
8. Haven't used in last 12 months	99.3	99.1	99.9	99.5	100.0	99.5	99.2	99.3	99.3	99.6	98.8	100.0	100.0	100.0	100.0	23.5
Item 8990 Subject A01i N	2625	1207	1358	2063	246	574	798	791	462	1622	919	1138	532	376	529	23
D03J: Other narcotics?																
1. Yes	1.2	1.2	1.0	1.2	0.8	0.7	1.9	1.2	0.7	0.9	1.7	-	-	-	5.2	34.5
2. No	1.9	1.8	1.9	2.1	-	3.4	2.3	0.8	1.1	1.5	2.5	-	-	0.5	8.6	37.2
8. Haven't used in last 12 months	96.9	97.0	97.1	96.7	99.2	95.9	95.8	98.0	98.2	97.6	95.8	100.0	100.0	99.5	86.2	28.3
Item 9000 Subject A01i N	2529	1167	1309	1974	245	554	778	759	439	1584	864	1137	528	359	460	18
D04: How likely is it that you will use marijuana in the next 12 months?																
1. Definitely will-GO TO Q.D05	9.7	11.3	8.5	10.3	6.0	14.1	9.4	7.0	9.4	7.9	12.3	1.6	6.1	9.9	31.6	32.8
2. Probably will-GO TO Q.D05	12.8	13.5	12.2	13.5	9.6	17.1	13.1	10.0	12.0	11.8	14.3	1.4	21.7	19.7	25.0	23.9
3. Probably will not	18.8	19.1	18.0	19.9	15.2	20.5	21.0	16.1	17.7	20.4	17.2	9.5	32.5	23.5	22.4	20.3
4. Definitely will not	58.7	56.0	61.3	56.4	69.2	48.4	56.6	66.9	60.8	59.9	56.2	87.5	39.7	46.9	21.0	23.0
Item 9010 Subject A04a N	2697	1228	1408	2103	263	586	816	817	477	1631	973	1214	540	368	522	22

Here are some reasons people give for not using marijuana, or for stopping use. Please tell us which reasons are true for you. (Mark all that apply.)

	TOTAL	M	F	White	Black	NE	NC	S	W	Yes	No	None	Mari- juana Only	Few Pills	More Pills	Any Her- oin
A. Concerned about possible psychological damage	67.1	65.1	69.3	67.2	64.5	65.9	68.4	67.3	65.9	70.6	62.0	71.9	60.0	65.9	58.1	55.0
B. Concerned about possible physical damage	68.1	65.4	70.3	69.0	62.4	65.6	68.3	69.6	67.5	72.1	61.7	73.4	61.4	64.1	58.9	55.0
C. Concerned about getting arrested	43.8	47.5	40.6	44.8	38.9	39.7	46.7	48.2	35.2	45.1	42.1	46.7	38.8	42.0	39.1	49.6
D. Concerned about becoming addicted to marijuana	51.6	49.7	53.4	51.2	53.2	47.8	52.5	54.3	49.2	52.2	51.7	56.3	48.1	49.3	38.8	55.0
E. It's against my beliefs	52.3	50.1	54.7	53.6	48.1	46.1	52.7	54.5	54.1	55.4	45.6	64.8	39.5	37.1	27.9	44.7
F. Concerned about loss of energy or ambition	35.3	35.9	34.7	34.1	38.0	29.1	34.7	37.1	39.6	36.4	34.4	38.0	32.2	31.8	31.7	53.0
G. Concerned about possible loss of control of myself	51.0	47.2	55.2	51.0	55.8	48.3	51.9	52.5	50.0	54.1	46.0	58.4	40.7	46.1	40.4	24.4
H. It might lead to stronger drugs	54.0	53.0	55.1	54.1	52.6	50.6	54.4	58.1	49.6	54.7	53.6	58.1	47.5	52.9	47.2	23.9
I. Not enjoyable, I didn't like it	32.6	31.7	32.7	31.5	38.0	32.2	34.5	30.0	34.4	30.8	36.0	23.4	49.9	45.5	36.1	44.7
J. My parents would disapprove	58.4	56.8	60.6	58.0	58.7	50.0	59.5	60.8	61.0	60.3	56.4	62.5	56.1	56.0	48.3	42.8
K. My husband/wife (or boyfriend/ girlfriend) would disapprove	33.9	34.4	33.5	34.0	32.1	27.7	35.7	36.0	33.9	32.5	36.7	33.6	36.5	30.9	36.2	32.5
L. I don't like being with the people who use it	47.0	44.8	49.5	46.5	45.9	42.4	46.6	48.9	48.8	47.7	44.5	58.5	29.6	36.8	30.4	13.5
M. My friends don't use it	37.1	36.1	38.5	39.0	28.9	31.2	40.0	37.8	37.3	39.0	33.3	46.2	27.2	28.5	19.7	5.4
N. I might have a bad trip	25.5	25.9	25.2	24.6	28.2	24.2	26.0	27.2	22.8	25.8	24.7	27.3	25.1	21.4	23.7	24.4
O. Too expensive	24.7	28.6	21.2	26.0	21.5	21.1	27.3	25.0	23.7	24.0	26.8	24.8	25.9	22.5	27.0	5.3
P. Not available	7.6	6.4	8.6	7.2	8.0	5.4	8.0	9.3	6.1	6.4	10.1	7.9	7.2	6.9	7.7	-
Q. Don't feel like getting high	62.3	59.6	65.2	63.3	56.7	62.5	62.9	59.5	65.9	62.9	61.3	65.2	57.6	64.3	58.4	32.5
Item 9020-9180 Subject A06a N★	2022	886	1086	1550	215	387	612	659	363	1268	689	1131	380	250	220	11

D05A: Has your use of alcohol ever caused any of the following problems for you?

Responses to this set of questions are not included because of complexities in the presentation and interpretation of the data.

Item 9190-9350 Subject A07b   N

★=excludes respondents for whom question was inappropriate.

QUESTIONNAIRE FORM 3 1986	TOTAL	SEX		RACE		REGION				4YR COLLEGE PLANS		ILLICIT DRUG USE: LIFETIME				
		M	F	White	Black	NE	NC	S	W	Yes	No	None	Mari-juana Only	Few Pills	More Pills	Any Her-oin
N (Weighted No. of Cases):	3159	1456	1581	2348	342	746	901	978	534	1801	1138	1328	641	437	648	29
% of Weighted Total:	100.0	46.1	50.1	74.3	10.8	23.6	28.5	31.0	16.9	57.0	36.0	42.0	20.3	13.8	20.5	0.9

D05M: Has your use of marijuana ever caused any of the following problems for you? (Mark all that apply.)

Responses to this set of questions are not included because of complexities in the presentation and interpretation of the data.

Item 9360-9520   Subject A07b   N

D05O: Has your use of other drugs ever caused any of the following problems for you? (Mark all that apply.)

Responses to this set of questions are not included because of complexities in the presentation and interpretation of the data.

Item 9530-9690   Subject A07b   N

E01A: Have you ever taken or used smokeless tobacco (snuff, plug, dipping tobacco, chewing tobacco)?

	TOTAL	M	F	White	Black	NE	NC	S	W	Yes	No	None	Mari-juana Only	Few Pills	More Pills	Any Her-oin
1. Never–GO TO Q.E02	68.6	44.6	90.2	64.8	87.8	72.6	65.7	67.4	70.9	69.3	67.5	78.9	63.9	60.6	58.9	34.5
2. Once or twice	16.7	25.8	8.5	17.8	10.6	16.3	16.4	17.1	17.4	17.3	16.0	10.9	20.2	18.9	23.3	34.6
3. Occasionally but not regularly	7.2	14.0	1.1	8.3	1.5	4.5	10.0	7.0	6.1	7.4	6.8	6.2	7.0	9.6	7.3	17.3
4. Regularly in the past	3.0	6.3	0.2	3.7	-	2.7	3.4	3.2	2.5	2.6	3.3	1.0	3.6	5.5	4.9	7.3
5. Regularly now	4.4	9.4	0.1	5.3	-	4.0	4.5	5.4	3.1	3.3	6.4	2.9	5.3	5.4	5.6	6.3

Item 22230   Subject A01a   N | 2789 | 1274 | 1446 | 2174 | 265 | 606 | 847 | 855 | 481 | 1693 | 993 | 1197 | 552 | 403 | 580 | 26 |

E01B: How frequently have you taken smokeless tobacco during the past 30 days?

	TOTAL	M	F	White	Black	NE	NC	S	W	Yes	No	None	Mari-juana Only	Few Pills	More Pills	Any Her-oin
1. Not at all	88.5	77.7	98.4	87.0	98.6	90.5	86.5	87.8	90.7	90.2	85.5	91.5	88.3	87.5	84.9	66.3
2. Once or twice	4.6	8.1	1.1	4.7	0.9	3.4	6.1	3.9	4.6	4.4	5.0	3.3	4.3	4.6	6.5	27.4
3. Once or twice per week	1.3	2.3	0.3	1.5	0.4	0.8	1.6	1.5	0.9	1.3	1.3	1.4	1.0	0.7	1.4	-
4. Three to five times per week	0.9	1.9	0.1	1.2	-	0.8	1.3	0.7	0.8	0.8	1.2	0.5	0.8	1.3	1.6	-
5. About once a day	0.9	1.9	-	1.2	-	0.7	0.9	1.3	0.5	1.0	0.6	0.6	1.1	1.8	0.7	-
6. More than once a day	3.8	8.0	0.1	4.5	-	3.8	3.6	4.8	2.4	2.3	6.5	2.7	4.6	4.1	4.9	6.3

Item 22240   Subject A01c   N★ | 2795 | 1279 | 1449 | 2179 | 268 | 605 | 850 | 857 | 483 | 1694 | 998 | 1202 | 554 | 402 | 580 | 26 |

E02: There has been talk about shortages of energy, food, and raw materials in this country. Do you think that in the coming years we will have plenty to meet our needs, a sufficient amount, or will we have to consume less?

	TOTAL	M	F	White	Black	NE	NC	S	W	Yes	No	None	Mari-juana Only	Few Pills	More Pills	Any Her-oin
1. Plenty to meet our needs	17.9	24.3	12.3	17.4	16.8	15.8	18.9	17.7	19.1	18.2	17.4	19.2	18.5	14.1	17.4	18.3
2. A sufficient amount	56.4	55.9	56.8	57.8	53.8	58.8	58.5	55.9	50.8	55.3	58.2	56.6	52.6	57.2	58.4	57.5
3. Will have to consume less	25.7	19.8	30.8	24.8	29.4	25.4	22.6	26.4	30.1	26.5	24.5	24.3	28.9	28.7	24.2	24.2

Item 9750   Subject F05   N | 2788 | 1271 | 1450 | 2162 | 272 | 596 | 846 | 865 | 481 | 1685 | 1006 | 1200 | 557 | 393 | 580 | 27 |

E03: The questions in this section deal with population problems. How much do you agree or disagree with each statement?

E03A: Our government should help other countries to control their population

	TOTAL	M	F	White	Black	NE	NC	S	W	Yes	No	None	Mari-juana Only	Few Pills	More Pills	Any Her-oin
1. Disagree	20.2	24.9	15.9	19.6	28.3	22.8	18.3	22.2	16.5	16.7	25.4	18.2	22.3	18.5	22.8	35.4
2. Mostly disagree	17.1	18.4	16.1	17.2	15.6	17.5	17.7	15.7	18.2	18.2	16.0	16.6	17.8	19.8	15.1	30.0
3. Neither	29.3	25.6	32.3	30.1	26.2	25.6	31.2	29.3	30.7	30.2	27.5	29.2	29.0	26.7	32.3	16.1
4. Mostly agree	22.5	19.9	25.3	23.0	17.8	21.6	22.4	21.8	25.1	25.2	18.2	25.3	21.6	21.2	18.5	11.3
5. Agree	10.9	11.2	10.4	10.1	12.1	12.5	10.4	11.1	9.5	9.9	12.9	10.7	9.3	13.8	11.3	7.3

Item 9760   Subject E01,H02   N | 2809 | 1277 | 1463 | 2176 | 275 | 605 | 851 | 865 | 488 | 1697 | 1017 | 1212 | 556 | 401 | 581 | 27 |

★=excludes respondents for whom question was inappropriate.

QUESTIONNAIRE FORM 3 1986	TOTAL	SEX M	F	RACE White	Black	REGION NE	NC	S	W	4YR COLLEGE PLANS Yes	No	ILLICIT DRUG USE: LIFETIME None	Marijuana Only	Few Pills	More Pills	Any Heroin
N (Weighted No. of Cases):	3159	1456	1581	2348	342	746	901	978	534	1801	1138	1328	641	437	648	29
% of Weighted Total:	100.0	46.1	50.1	74.3	10.8	23.6	28.5	31.0	16.9	57.0	36.0	42.0	20.3	13.8	20.5	0.9

E03B: Governments should avoid making policy about population and let the individual decide

	TOTAL	M	F	White	Black	NE	NC	S	W	Yes	No	None	Mar. Only	Few Pills	More Pills	Any Heroin
1. Disagree	12.9	15.0	11.0	12.0	18.5	15.5	10.8	14.0	11.6	10.7	16.6	12.9	15.6	9.9	13.1	10.3
2. Mostly disagree	21.4	22.1	20.7	22.6	16.1	19.4	22.1	21.5	22.8	23.6	18.2	22.0	20.6	24.5	18.8	14.8
3. Neither	30.5	29.3	31.7	31.8	24.7	30.5	31.2	30.2	29.7	32.0	28.3	28.1	30.7	35.4	30.6	39.1
4. Mostly agree	23.3	21.1	25.6	23.5	20.4	22.0	24.5	22.1	24.7	23.6	21.8	24.9	22.9	19.9	23.7	17.0
5. Agree	11.9	12.5	11.1	10.1	20.3	12.7	11.3	12.2	11.2	10.0	15.0	12.1	10.3	10.3	13.8	18.8
Item 9770 Subject E01,H02 N	2793	1275	1449	2166	273	598	847	864	484	1686	1010	1207	551	400	575	27

E03C: I feel strongly enough about preventing overpopulation that I'd be willing to limit my family to two children

	TOTAL	M	F	White	Black	NE	NC	S	W	Yes	No	None	Mar. Only	Few Pills	More Pills	Any Heroin
1. Disagree	17.4	17.1	17.5	16.9	21.9	21.5	15.9	17.0	15.7	16.1	19.7	17.1	19.0	17.5	16.7	17.8
2. Mostly disagree	14.4	15.5	13.1	14.3	13.3	13.9	17.1	13.3	12.0	14.4	13.8	15.1	13.0	16.4	11.1	32.1
3. Neither	25.9	25.2	26.7	26.2	24.4	27.7	26.8	24.8	24.2	28.2	22.4	26.7	23.9	22.7	28.0	23.8
4. Mostly agree	21.6	20.5	22.7	22.2	14.4	18.2	21.4	21.1	27.2	22.9	19.8	21.9	20.5	22.1	22.4	13.8
5. Agree	20.7	21.6	20.0	20.3	25.9	18.8	18.8	23.7	21.0	18.4	24.4	19.1	23.6	21.3	21.7	12.6
Item 9780 Subject E01 N	2789	1270	1451	2165	275	598	849	858	485	1681	1010	1206	549	396	578	27

E03D: To help prevent overpopulation, I might decide not to have any children of my own

	TOTAL	M	F	White	Black	NE	NC	S	W	Yes	No	None	Mar. Only	Few Pills	More Pills	Any Heroin
1. Disagree	55.7	53.3	58.4	57.0	55.9	58.0	56.4	55.4	51.9	56.7	54.7	55.4	62.0	56.1	51.4	39.3
2. Mostly disagree	17.4	18.8	15.9	17.5	15.1	15.9	18.2	17.7	17.4	18.0	15.8	18.5	14.4	17.6	17.7	21.4
3. Neither	18.0	19.4	16.5	17.9	16.7	17.4	19.1	16.7	19.0	17.6	18.7	17.2	15.0	17.9	21.1	33.1
4. Mostly agree	4.3	4.2	4.4	3.8	5.6	4.1	3.3	4.5	5.6	3.7	4.9	3.8	3.9	4.3	5.5	4.2
5. Agree	4.7	4.4	4.9	3.9	6.8	4.6	3.0	5.6	6.1	3.9	5.8	5.1	4.7	4.1	4.3	2.0
Item 9790 Subject E01 N	2789	1269	1452	2163	273	598	848	860	483	1683	1007	1205	551	395	578	27

E03E: High schools should offer instruction in birth control methods

	TOTAL	M	F	White	Black	NE	NC	S	W	Yes	No	None	Mar. Only	Few Pills	More Pills	Any Heroin
1. Disagree	5.7	6.0	5.5	4.9	9.2	6.0	4.7	6.5	5.9	3.3	9.9	6.8	4.1	6.0	4.3	11.2
2. Mostly disagree	3.5	3.6	3.1	3.1	2.7	2.7	4.0	3.9	3.0	3.0	4.3	4.4	2.1	2.5	3.3	1.7
3. Neither	12.6	15.0	10.5	12.6	6.1	12.6	14.3	10.7	13.1	12.2	13.1	14.6	10.0	9.9	12.3	16.5
4. Mostly agree	24.5	25.8	23.5	24.8	22.7	21.7	26.7	22.6	27.5	25.7	22.3	25.6	23.2	25.3	23.8	12.6
5. Agree	53.6	49.6	57.3	54.6	59.3	57.1	50.3	56.3	50.5	55.8	50.3	48.7	60.6	56.4	56.4	58.0
Item 9800 Subject E02 N	2789	1268	1452	2166	270	600	849	856	483	1684	1006	1204	551	396	579	27

E03F: I personally consider most methods of birth control to be immoral

	TOTAL	M	F	White	Black	NE	NC	S	W	Yes	No	None	Mar. Only	Few Pills	More Pills	Any Heroin
1. Disagree	47.1	44.1	49.6	49.8	41.6	53.7	45.4	44.7	46.5	51.2	39.9	40.9	53.7	51.4	52.0	55.5
2. Mostly disagree	17.4	18.5	16.6	18.1	13.1	15.4	17.6	18.6	17.2	17.6	17.8	18.8	15.9	17.3	16.0	11.3
3. Neither	23.3	24.9	22.2	22.9	20.7	19.4	26.3	21.6	25.9	22.0	26.4	25.4	20.9	21.5	22.0	21.8
4. Mostly agree	6.5	7.0	5.8	5.1	12.4	7.2	4.7	7.9	6.4	5.0	8.3	6.9	5.8	5.3	6.6	4.0
5. Agree	5.7	5.6	5.8	4.1	12.4	4.3	6.0	7.2	4.1	4.2	7.7	8.0	3.6	4.5	3.4	7.7
Item 9810 Subject E02 N	2778	1264	1445	2156	270	593	846	854	483	1681	999	1200	545	396	576	27

E03G: The government should make birth control information and services available without cost to anyone who wants them

	TOTAL	M	F	White	Black	NE	NC	S	W	Yes	No	None	Mar. Only	Few Pills	More Pills	Any Heroin
1. Disagree	6.7	7.6	5.4	6.0	7.0	7.1	5.5	7.4	6.8	5.4	8.7	7.0	4.8	7.0	7.2	9.5
2. Mostly disagree	5.9	5.3	6.3	6.4	2.6	4.4	7.0	5.5	6.3	5.8	6.2	5.1	7.0	5.1	6.6	5.4
3. Neither	16.3	18.0	14.9	16.3	11.0	15.2	17.6	15.1	17.2	16.5	15.9	18.1	13.8	16.1	13.8	26.9
4. Mostly agree	25.8	23.2	28.6	27.1	18.9	25.3	26.6	23.9	28.1	27.0	23.8	27.3	26.8	26.1	22.8	14.2
5. Agree	45.4	45.9	44.8	44.4	60.5	47.9	43.3	48.1	41.6	45.2	45.5	42.5	47.6	45.7	49.6	44.0
Item 9820 Subject E02,H02 N	2780	1264	1448	2156	271	592	849	856	484	1680	1002	1202	548	397	575	27

E04: Did you have a unit on sex education when you were in high school?

	TOTAL	M	F	White	Black	NE	NC	S	W	Yes	No	None	Mar. Only	Few Pills	More Pills	Any Heroin
1. No, and I'm glad I didn't	8.2	9.6	7.2	8.3	6.2	7.0	7.3	8.9	9.9	6.6	10.8	9.4	6.7	5.7	8.2	
2. No, and I wish I had	19.6	17.3	21.5	20.1	24.0	17.2	17.3	25.7	15.6	17.9	21.4	17.7	20.2	22.0	20.8	21.6
3. Yes, and it was very worthwhile	26.3	24.5	27.7	23.3	37.6	28.3	24.9	25.2	28.2	25.7	27.5	27.8	27.1	27.1	22.8	14.3
4. Yes, and it was somewhat worthwhile	34.6	35.4	33.8	36.3	24.0	35.5	37.5	30.0	36.7	38.9	28.1	36.8	32.9	33.3	33.2	25.1
5. Yes, but it was not worthwhile at all	11.4	13.2	9.9	12.1	8.1	12.0	13.1	10.2	9.6	10.8	12.3	8.3	13.1	12.0	15.0	39.0
Item 9860 Subject B01,E02 N	2761	1251	1441	2140	268	598	837	848	478	1674	985	1195	547	388	573	27

QUESTIONNAIRE FORM 3 1986	TOTAL	SEX		RACE		REGION				4YR COLLEGE PLANS		ILLICIT DRUG USE: LIFETIME				
		M	F	White	Black	NE	NC	S	W	Yes	No	None	Mari-juana Only	Few Pills	More Pills	Any Her-oin
N (Weighted No. of Cases):	3159	1456	1581	2348	342	746	901	978	534	1801	1138	1328	641	437	648	29
% of Weighted Total:	100.0	46.1	50.1	74.3	10.8	23.6	28.5	31.0	16.9	57.0	36.0	42.0	20.3	13.8	20.5	0.9

E05: Did you ever study about birth control methods in high school?

	TOTAL	M	F	White	Black	NE	NC	S	W	Yes	No	None	Mari-juana Only	Few Pills	More Pills	Any Her-oin
1. No, and I'm glad I didn't	10.8	13.4	8.4	10.1	9.2	9.3	9.3	13.0	11.3	8.3	14.4	11.9	9.0	9.6	10.5	14.9
2. No, and I wish I had	26.0	23.8	28.2	26.6	28.0	24.7	23.9	28.7	26.3	25.0	26.9	23.8	29.1	26.9	26.4	28.8
3. Yes, and it was very worthwhile	26.7	23.8	28.9	25.1	37.0	29.4	25.4	26.1	26.6	27.5	25.3	27.3	26.0	29.5	24.3	29.8
4. Yes, and it was somewhat worthwhile	30.1	31.3	28.8	31.5	19.9	29.7	34.2	25.6	31.1	33.1	26.0	31.2	29.2	27.5	31.3	17.5
5. Yes, but it was not worthwhile at all	6.5	7.7	5.6	6.6	5.9	6.9	7.2	6.5	4.6	6.1	7.4	5.8	6.6	6.5	7.6	8.9
Item 9870 Subject B01,E02 N	2738	1234	1436	2124	267	594	833	840	470	1663	975	1184	541	389	568	27

E06: How important is each of the following for being looked up to or having high status in your school?

E06A: Coming from the right family

	TOTAL	M	F	White	Black	NE	NC	S	W	Yes	No	None	Mari-juana Only	Few Pills	More Pills	Any Her-oin
1. No importance	13.8	15.7	12.1	12.5	19.2	18.2	10.5	12.3	16.5	12.3	16.0	11.5	14.9	15.7	16.0	9.8
2. Little importance	22.1	23.8	20.5	23.0	17.1	22.2	21.1	20.6	26.3	25.0	17.0	24.3	23.4	20.1	17.2	36.5
3. Moderate importance	31.2	29.6	32.4	33.6	18.3	30.5	33.5	31.0	28.2	33.3	28.1	31.0	29.4	34.4	31.0	21.0
4. Great importance	16.3	16.1	16.6	16.0	20.2	14.1	18.0	16.5	15.6	15.9	17.2	16.0	18.3	14.9	16.6	5.7
5. Very great importance	16.7	14.8	18.4	14.9	25.3	15.1	16.7	19.6	13.4	13.4	21.6	17.3	14.0	15.0	19.2	26.9
Item 13580 Subject B04 N	2755	1247	1439	2141	269	588	845	847	475	1674	981	1204	542	389	561	27

E06B: Being a leader in student activities

	TOTAL	M	F	White	Black	NE	NC	S	W	Yes	No	None	Mari-juana Only	Few Pills	More Pills	Any Her-oin
1. No importance	10.2	11.7	8.9	9.9	9.6	12.3	9.7	8.9	10.6	6.9	16.1	7.7	11.2	9.5	14.4	11.9
2. Little importance	15.2	15.7	14.5	15.3	15.3	19.7	11.2	15.8	15.6	13.2	18.6	14.2	14.3	18.2	16.2	13.5
3. Moderate importance	33.9	34.0	34.3	35.9	27.9	31.8	36.1	34.0	32.5	36.2	29.6	31.6	34.9	36.6	36.3	26.1
4. Great importance	25.8	23.9	27.3	25.4	27.3	22.4	29.0	24.9	26.1	29.0	20.8	29.2	24.7	24.8	20.0	34.1
5. Very great importance	14.9	14.7	15.0	13.5	19.9	13.8	14.0	16.4	15.3	14.7	14.9	17.3	14.9	10.8	13.1	14.4
Item 13590 Subject B04,M05 N	2750	1246	1436	2137	267	589	842	844	475	1672	977	1203	541	387	561	27

E06C: Having a nice car

	TOTAL	M	F	White	Black	NE	NC	S	W	Yes	No	None	Mari-juana Only	Few Pills	More Pills	Any Her-oin
1. No importance	14.1	13.2	14.7	12.1	22.8	18.4	11.8	14.7	11.6	13.5	15.7	13.7	16.9	13.5	12.6	9.5
2. Little importance	21.5	18.7	24.3	22.2	21.0	24.4	23.8	18.0	20.3	23.6	19.2	24.1	19.5	19.0	20.5	14.1
3. Moderate importance	32.3	33.1	32.2	34.7	23.4	33.1	31.8	30.8	35.0	34.3	28.9	32.5	32.3	33.7	31.4	19.4
4. Great importance	18.7	20.8	16.5	18.4	17.5	13.8	19.4	20.8	19.6	18.1	19.1	18.4	19.6	19.2	17.8	23.5
5. Very great importance	13.4	14.2	12.3	12.6	15.3	10.4	13.1	15.6	13.6	10.6	17.2	11.2	11.6	14.6	17.7	33.5
Item 13600 Subject B04,F01 N	2746	1245	1433	2133	266	586	843	842	475	1668	977	1200	540	388	562	26

E06D: Getting good grades

	TOTAL	M	F	White	Black	NE	NC	S	W	Yes	No	None	Mari-juana Only	Few Pills	More Pills	Any Her-oin
1. No importance	5.6	7.2	4.2	5.4	4.3	8.1	4.9	4.8	5.1	3.9	8.4	3.5	6.5	4.6	8.9	17.5
2. Little importance	13.0	13.5	12.5	14.8	4.8	11.5	12.7	13.8	13.8	12.5	13.0	12.3	13.4	12.9	13.7	15.6
3. Moderate importance	34.9	36.6	33.6	38.8	16.8	34.1	38.5	30.3	37.5	35.9	34.3	32.7	34.3	37.9	38.2	26.1
4. Great importance	27.8	25.8	29.7	26.0	34.3	27.1	27.3	29.4	26.6	28.2	27.7	29.5	27.0	30.0	24.4	15.0
5. Very great importance	18.8	16.8	20.1	15.0	39.9	19.2	16.7	21.8	16.9	19.6	16.7	21.9	18.6	14.6	14.8	25.7
Item 13610 Subject B04 N	2743	1242	1434	2133	267	586	840	843	474	1667	976	1201	539	387	558	27

E06E: Being a good athlete

	TOTAL	M	F	White	Black	NE	NC	S	W	Yes	No	None	Mari-juana Only	Few Pills	More Pills	Any Her-oin
1. No importance	10.3	9.2	11.1	9.7	10.7	13.1	8.3	10.5	9.9	7.3	15.4	8.1	11.1	11.8	13.3	6.0
2. Little importance	11.4	9.7	12.9	10.9	14.6	10.6	10.7	13.5	10.0	10.0	13.8	12.0	11.1	11.6	10.4	12.6
3. Moderate importance	28.5	26.4	30.4	29.2	28.2	32.4	25.4	29.2	28.1	28.8	28.8	26.6	28.2	29.0	32.1	31.9
4. Great importance	28.8	31.1	27.0	29.3	23.4	25.8	33.8	23.8	32.5	32.1	23.0	32.2	27.0	28.6	23.9	20.9
5. Very great importance	21.0	23.6	18.6	21.0	23.2	18.1	21.8	23.0	19.5	21.8	19.0	21.2	22.7	18.9	20.3	28.5
Item 13620 Subject B04 N	2735	1239	1429	2125	269	583	841	838	474	1666	971	1196	541	382	558	27

E06F: Knowing a lot about intellectual matters

	TOTAL	M	F	White	Black	NE	NC	S	W	Yes	No	None	Mari-juana Only	Few Pills	More Pills	Any Her-oin
1. No importance	11.5	12.1	11.1	12.5	7.7	14.2	11.1	10.0	11.7	9.0	15.9	10.0	10.9	12.0	14.6	8.6
2. Little importance	26.2	24.2	28.3	28.1	15.7	21.1	28.5	26.1	28.5	38.5	21.7	28.9	24.5	23.6	24.4	26.0
3. Moderate importance	38.5	38.6	38.3	40.4	27.1	41.3	39.8	35.2	38.9	38.5	38.7	35.6	40.8	45.0	38.7	28.5
4. Great importance	15.3	16.0	14.5	12.9	28.4	15.3	14.3	16.1	15.6	16.1	14.5	17.3	14.1	13.6	13.7	10.7
5. Very great importance	8.5	9.1	7.8	6.2	21.2	8.2	6.3	12.5	5.3	7.5	9.1	8.3	9.6	5.8	8.6	26.3
Item 13630 Subject B04 N	2735	1237	1430	2127	265	581	841	838	475	1666	971	1201	538	383	556	27

	TOTAL	SEX		RACE		REGION				4YR COLLEGE PLANS		ILLICIT DRUG USE: LIFETIME				
QUESTIONNAIRE FORM 3 **1986**		M	F	White	Black	NE	NC	S	W	Yes	No	None	Mari-juana Only	Few Pills	More Pills	Any Her-oin
N (Weighted No. of Cases):	3159	1456	1581	2348	342	746	901	978	534	1801	1138	1328	641	437	648	29
% of Weighted Total:	100.0	46.1	50.1	74.3	10.8	23.6	28.5	31.0	16.9	57.0	36.0	42.0	20.3	13.8	20.5	0.9
E06G: Planning to go to college																
1. No importance	10.9	11.8	10.3	10.7	10.2	13.4	8.6	11.8	10.1	5.3	20.1	8.3	8.9	12.7	16.1	18.8
2. Little importance	16.1	17.9	14.6	17.4	9.9	15.1	15.8	17.0	16.3	13.9	19.6	17.8	14.9	15.1	14.0	15.9
3. Moderate importance	31.2	32.1	30.5	32.9	22.8	29.6	33.0	29.3	33.4	31.8	30.8	30.9	32.8	32.7	30.2	15.9
4. Great importance	21.3	21.2	21.7	21.4	22.6	20.3	22.9	20.2	21.7	23.2	18.4	21.6	22.2	19.1	21.3	30.4
5. Very great importance	20.5	17.1	23.0	17.7	34.6	21.6	19.7	21.6	18.5	25.8	11.1	21.3	21.3	20.4	18.4	19.0
Item 13640 Subject B04 N	2743	1244	1430	2132	264	586	841	842	475	1670	973	1203	538	387	557	27
E07: How about using drugs (other than marijuana or alcohol)–does that cause a student to be looked up to or looked down on?																
E07A: Among the majority of students in my school, such drug use is . . .																
1. Looked down on a lot	23.9	26.9	21.5	24.5	24.4	19.3	23.8	31.0	16.8	23.0	25.7	30.4	21.5	21.8	14.6	6.7
2. Looked down on some	22.6	22.5	23.0	24.3	13.0	19.1	22.0	23.5	26.5	23.1	21.5	25.4	19.5	22.4	19.6	12.5
3. Neither, or mixed	43.4	40.5	45.6	42.5	47.6	49.5	44.6	36.4	46.2	44.9	41.4	35.6	49.6	45.8	52.9	45.3
4. Looked up to some	8.1	8.1	8.0	7.3	10.3	9.7	7.4	7.0	9.2	7.3	9.0	6.6	7.2	9.4	11.0	16.7
5. Looked up to a lot	2.0	2.1	2.0	1.4	4.7	2.4	2.1	2.0	1.3	1.7	2.4	2.1	2.1	0.5	1.8	18.8
Item 13650 Subject A12b N	2731	1235	1430	2126	265	582	837	838	474	1669	967	1194	537	383	563	27
E07B: Among my own group of friends, such drug use is . . .																
1. Looked down on a lot	40.2	38.1	42.5	41.2	37.8	32.2	39.1	45.2	43.2	43.0	35.5	60.1	32.2	28.6	15.5	-
2. Looked down on some	18.1	17.2	19.1	18.0	17.6	17.5	19.1	18.6	16.3	19.1	16.2	16.6	21.2	22.9	15.7	14.9
3. Neither, or mixed	33.0	34.1	31.8	32.6	34.5	39.5	33.5	29.1	31.4	31.8	35.5	19.9	40.0	39.1	49.5	44.9
4. Looked up to some	6.1	7.5	4.7	5.9	5.7	6.8	5.8	5.0	7.7	4.6	8.3	2.7	5.3	6.9	12.4	22.4
5. Looked up to a lot	2.5	3.1	1.9	2.2	4.4	4.1	2.5	2.1	1.4	1.4	4.4	0.7	1.4	2.4	6.9	17.8
Item 13660 Subject A12b N	2727	1235	1426	2123	265	580	835	838	474	1667	965	1193	535	383	560	27
E07C: My own feelings about such drug use is that . . .																
1. I look down on it a lot	54.8	54.3	56.0	54.0	61.5	48.8	52.0	61.2	56.0	57.9	49.7	77.8	50.3	42.5	20.7	8.5
2. I look down on it some	17.1	16.0	17.4	17.5	16.2	17.6	19.6	15.4	15.2	17.8	16.0	11.6	21.6	24.9	19.4	9.9
3. Neither, or mixed	24.4	25.7	23.5	25.2	18.1	29.1	25.1	20.8	24.0	21.5	29.6	9.8	25.5	30.5	49.1	54.9
4. I look up to it some	2.7	2.7	2.6	2.4	2.3	3.4	2.1	2.1	3.9	2.2	3.3	0.6	2.0	2.2	7.8	13.0
5. I look up to it a lot	0.9	1.4	0.4	0.8	1.9	1.1	1.2	0.5	1.0	0.6	1.3	0.2	0.6	-	3.0	13.7
Item 13670 Subject A11c N	2717	1230	1421	2118	265	578	835	836	468	1660	962	1187	535	383	557	27
E08: The next questions are about some things which may have happened TO YOU while you were at school (inside or outside or in a schoolbus).																
During the LAST 12 MONTHS, how often ...																
E08A: Has something of yours (worth under $50) been stolen?																
1. Not at all	63.0	59.9	65.8	61.8	68.3	61.8	64.3	64.5	59.4	60.7	65.6	68.4	62.7	57.2	57.0	41.3
2. Once	24.3	25.7	23.4	25.1	21.4	25.7	24.4	22.0	26.7	25.9	22.2	23.3	24.5	28.0	24.9	21.1
3. Twice	8.6	8.4	8.3	8.7	6.7	7.6	8.1	8.2	11.4	9.0	8.4	5.8	8.2	9.8	12.7	15.1
4. 3 or 4 times	3.0	4.4	1.9	3.2	3.0	3.8	2.2	3.8	2.3	3.4	2.7	1.7	3.5	3.9	4.4	10.2
5. 5 or more times	1.1	1.6	0.6	1.2	0.7	1.2	1.1	1.5	0.2	1.1	1.1	0.8	1.1	1.1	1.1	12.3
Item 9871 Subject B07,S03 N	2759	1255	1434	2140	267	589	837	853	479	1672	983	1199	544	381	571	27
E08B: Has something of yours (worth over $50) been stolen?																
1. Not at all	85.9	82.1	89.5	86.8	84.3	84.9	87.2	85.0	86.2	85.7	85.7	89.7	86.3	83.5	80.8	55.4
2. Once	11.2	13.1	9.4	10.9	11.0	13.2	10.3	10.8	10.9	11.8	10.7	8.7	10.9	12.9	15.6	20.7
3. Twice	1.8	2.9	0.9	1.3	3.0	1.0	1.6	2.4	2.2	1.6	2.0	1.4	1.6	1.3	2.8	5.8
4. 3 or 4 times	1.0	1.5	0.3	1.1	0.3	0.8	0.8	1.3	0.7	0.9	1.2	0.2	0.3	2.3	0.6	18.1
5. 5 or more times	0.2	0.4	-	*	1.3	-	0.2	0.4	-	*	0.4	-	0.8	-	0.1	
Item 9872 Subject B07,S03 N	2748	1244	1434	2132	265	584	835	852	477	1665	981	1197	543	379	566	27

*=less than .05 per cent.

QUESTIONNAIRE FORM 3 1986	TOTAL	SEX		RACE		REGION				4YR COLLEGE PLANS		ILLICIT DRUG USE: LIFETIME				
		M	F	White	Black	NE	NC	S	W	Yes	No	None	Mari- juana Only	Few Pills	More Pills	Any Her- oin
N (Weighted No. of Cases):	3159	1456	1581	2348	342	746	901	978	534	1801	1138	1328	641	437	648	29
% of Weighted Total:	100.0	46.1	50.1	74.3	10.8	23.6	28.5	31.0	16.9	57.0	36.0	42.0	20.3	13.8	20.5	0.9

E08C: Has someone deliberately damaged your property (your car, clothing, etc.)?

1. Not at all	74.1	68.5	78.9	74.3	75.5	75.2	76.0	72.0	73.1	76.4	69.9	78.3	79.8	70.0	64.4	40.6
2. Once	18.5	20.6	17.1	18.6	16.5	18.1	17.1	19.2	20.4	17.1	21.0	16.8	13.4	22.7	24.3	29.6
3. Twice	4.5	6.7	2.7	4.5	6.2	3.6	4.5	6.0	3.1	3.9	5.7	3.4	4.6	4.8	6.5	7.6
4. 3 or 4 times	1.9	2.9	1.0	1.8	0.6	1.5	1.9	1.6	2.9	1.8	2.2	0.9	1.9	1.5	4.0	5.2
5. 5 or more times	1.0	1.3	0.4	0.9	1.2	1.6	0.6	1.2	0.5	0.9	1.2	0.6	0.3	1.1	0.8	17.0
Item 9873 Subject B07,S03　N	2748	1249	1429	2129	268	588	837	850	473	1665	980	1196	545	379	565	27

E08D: Has someone injured you with a weapon (like a knife, gun, or club)?

1. Not at all	94.6	91.4	97.6	95.1	93.1	93.8	94.1	94.1	97.5	96.2	91.9	96.7	96.1	95.4	91.0	60.1
2. Once	2.9	4.4	1.7	2.6	4.8	3.9	2.8	3.2	1.5	2.2	4.2	2.0	2.4	2.7	5.2	7.6
3. Twice	1.5	2.8	0.3	1.4	1.0	1.4	2.2	1.5	0.2	0.8	2.8	0.9	1.2	1.3	2.1	15.0
4. 3 or 4 times	0.5	0.9	0.2	0.4	0.7	0.7	0.4	0.3	0.8	0.3	0.9	0.2	0.2	0.6	1.0	2.1
5. 5 or more times	0.5	0.6	0.1	0.4	0.3	0.2	0.5	0.8	0.1	0.5	0.2	0.3	0.1	-	0.6	15.2
Item 9874 Subject B07,S03　N	2748	1248	1431	2132	265	585	835	853	476	1665	980	1199	542	380	566	27

E08E: Has someone threatened you with a weapon, but not actually injured you?

1. Not at all	86.8	79.8	93.3	87.4	84.3	84.9	87.0	85.8	90.9	90.3	80.6	91.1	90.1	84.4	79.2	50.2
2. Once	8.3	12.1	4.8	7.9	9.6	10.4	7.3	8.7	6.5	5.9	12.4	5.8	6.7	10.3	12.2	16.9
3. Twice	2.4	4.0	1.1	2.5	2.8	2.6	2.7	2.6	0.9	2.2	2.9	2.2	2.2	1.6	3.0	13.2
4. 3 or 4 times	1.2	1.7	0.6	0.9	2.7	0.7	1.5	1.6	0.6	0.9	1.8	0.5	0.7	1.1	2.7	14.3
5. 5 or more times	1.3	2.5	0.3	1.3	0.7	1.5	1.4	1.3	1.1	0.7	2.4	0.5	0.3	2.5	2.8	5.3
Item 9875 Subject B07,S03　N	2740	1250	1424	2127	266	584	835	850	471	1660	979	1197	539	379	562	27

E08F: Has someone injured you on purpose without using a weapon?

1. Not at all	86.2	82.8	89.2	85.5	87.2	83.5	85.8	87.1	88.7	87.9	82.9	89.8	87.3	85.8	79.4	56.6
2. Once	8.5	10.3	7.2	8.8	9.1	10.7	8.0	8.7	6.5	8.1	9.7	7.1	9.1	7.0	12.5	9.3
3. Twice	2.4	3.3	1.7	2.6	2.0	2.6	3.0	1.7	2.5	1.8	3.6	1.5	1.4	3.3	4.8	-
4. 3 or 4 times	1.6	1.7	1.2	1.7	0.9	1.8	2.0	1.1	1.6	1.4	2.0	1.0	1.2	2.3	1.1	32.1
5. 5 or more times	1.2	1.9	0.7	1.4	0.9	1.4	1.2	1.4	0.7	0.8	1.8	0.6	1.0	1.6	2.2	2.0
Item 9876 Subject B07,S03　N	2743	1246	1429	2128	267	582	835	852	473	1663	979	1198	539	380	564	27

E08G: Has an unarmed person threatened you with injury, but not actually injured you?

1. Not at all	75.2	67.0	82.3	74.3	77.3	71.4	74.0	76.6	79.3	77.5	71.2	81.7	75.5	69.3	67.4	40.9
2. Once	13.4	15.7	11.5	13.5	11.8	14.1	14.2	12.2	13.2	12.7	14.6	10.6	13.7	17.7	15.7	10.3
3. Twice	5.2	8.0	2.6	5.7	3.1	6.9	5.6	4.0	4.4	4.9	5.7	3.6	4.6	6.8	7.2	21.2
4. 3 or 4 times	2.9	3.9	2.0	2.9	3.0	3.2	3.6	2.7	1.2	2.3	3.9	2.1	3.2	1.0	5.3	3.5
5. 5 or more times	3.4	5.4	1.5	3.6	4.8	4.3	2.6	4.5	1.9	2.7	4.7	2.1	3.0	5.2	4.3	24.1
Item 9877 Subject B07,S03　N	2736	1243	1425	2122	267	585	831	850	469	1658	978	1192	541	378	561	27

E09: Looking toward the future, how important would it be for you to have each of the following things?

E09A: At least one car

1. Not important	2.4	2.7	2.0	1.9	2.0	3.7	1.9	2.6	1.4	1.5	3.7	2.6	2.0	0.7	2.7	3.8
2. Somewhat important	13.8	12.3	15.1	12.7	18.5	14.1	12.6	15.2	13.1	12.8	15.9	13.9	13.0	14.9	12.6	28.7
3. Quite important	34.5	34.1	35.3	34.4	31.9	35.4	35.3	32.8	35.1	36.2	30.9	37.3	30.7	36.2	31.1	27.5
4. Extremely important	49.2	50.8	47.6	51.0	47.5	46.8	50.2	49.4	50.4	49.5	49.5	46.3	54.3	48.2	53.6	40.0
Item 13835 Subject F01　N	2720	1225	1426	2107	261	576	833	842	469	1652	968	1191	530	378	560	27

E09B: At least two cars

1. Not important	37.2	28.8	44.9	36.0	45.6	37.4	38.2	37.7	34.1	36.4	37.9	40.8	34.6	33.0	35.2	21.6
2. Somewhat important	34.2	36.2	32.6	35.1	29.5	37.6	34.3	31.2	34.9	34.5	34.1	33.4	32.8	36.8	35.0	30.0
3. Quite important	19.4	22.5	16.4	19.5	16.4	16.2	19.2	20.6	21.4	19.8	18.9	18.2	23.4	18.8	18.2	32.8
4. Extremely important	9.3	12.6	6.1	9.4	8.4	8.7	8.3	10.5	9.5	9.3	9.0	7.5	9.2	11.4	11.6	15.6
Item 13840 Subject F01　N	2718	1226	1424	2107	260	576	831	842	469	1652	965	1192	528	375	561	27

QUESTIONNAIRE FORM 3 1986	TOTAL	SEX		RACE		REGION				4YR COLLEGE PLANS		ILLICIT DRUG USE: LIFETIME				
		M	F	White	Black	NE	NC	S	W	Yes	No	None	Marijuana Only	Few Pills	More Pills	Any Heroin
N (Weighted No. of Cases):	3159	1456	1581	2348	342	746	901	978	534	1801	1138	1328	641	437	648	29
% of Weighted Total:	100.0	46.1	50.1	74.3	10.8	23.6	28.5	31.0	16.9	57.0	36.0	42.0	20.3	13.8	20.5	0.9
E09C: A large (full-sized) car																
1. Not important	60.6	51.4	68.7	60.8	61.2	60.6	57.1	62.3	63.9	60.3	61.1	62.0	60.2	59.3	60.9	34.4
2. Somewhat important	24.2	27.5	21.7	24.4	22.8	20.7	25.5	24.5	25.6	25.0	23.3	24.8	23.2	23.8	24.0	31.8
3. Quite important	9.7	12.3	7.1	9.4	11.7	12.1	11.0	8.1	7.2	10.4	8.2	9.0	10.3	12.4	7.8	18.2
4. Extremely important	5.5	8.7	2.6	5.4	4.4	6.6	6.3	5.1	3.3	4.3	7.4	4.3	6.4	4.5	7.3	15.6
Item 13850 Subject F01 N	2698	1216	1417	2094	256	572	825	838	464	1639	962	1189	527	370	551	27
E09D: A new car every two or three years																
1. Not important	56.9	48.3	64.6	56.5	61.5	58.2	52.6	58.6	59.5	56.9	58.4	62.0	55.3	53.7	51.3	23.5
2. Somewhat important	25.9	27.6	24.5	27.1	19.5	26.3	28.7	24.1	23.3	26.3	24.5	24.5	28.2	25.6	27.3	22.7
3. Quite important	9.8	12.9	7.2	9.6	10.7	8.4	10.9	9.0	11.3	9.9	9.1	8.2	9.3	13.4	11.7	14.4
4. Extremely important	7.4	11.1	3.8	6.8	8.2	7.0	7.7	8.3	5.9	6.8	8.1	5.4	7.2	7.3	9.7	39.5
Item 13860 Subject F01 N	2712	1227	1417	2107	257	574	829	841	468	1646	965	1191	525	372	562	27
E09E: Clothes in the latest style																
1. Not important	10.9	15.3	7.3	11.7	4.1	13.1	10.6	9.4	11.7	9.1	14.8	12.9	6.6	10.8	10.6	6.5
2. Somewhat important	33.1	35.4	31.6	34.3	27.3	33.1	30.7	34.7	34.2	32.7	34.5	37.0	34.0	30.5	26.5	29.5
3. Quite important	33.9	30.9	36.0	33.8	31.6	28.9	38.1	32.6	35.2	37.3	27.0	33.4	35.6	33.3	33.4	34.3
4. Extremely important	22.0	18.4	25.1	20.2	37.0	24.9	20.7	23.2	18.9	20.8	23.8	16.7	23.8	25.5	29.4	29.7
Item 13870 Subject F01 N	2707	1225	1416	2102	259	573	827	840	466	1644	962	1184	527	375	559	27
E09F: A house of my own (instead of an apartment or condominium)																
1. Not important	15.5	14.0	17.0	15.9	13.1	15.6	15.7	15.2	15.7	15.0	16.0	14.5	12.5	18.3	18.3	17.6
2. Somewhat important	23.5	21.6	25.3	24.6	16.5	22.5	26.3	21.6	23.1	24.7	21.9	23.9	22.5	24.9	23.1	16.0
3. Quite important	28.8	30.7	27.7	29.3	23.3	26.8	30.2	28.2	29.7	29.6	27.9	30.8	27.9	28.5	25.5	21.4
4. Extremely important	32.2	33.8	30.0	30.2	47.1	35.1	27.8	35.0	31.5	30.7	34.1	30.7	37.1	28.3	33.2	45.0
Item 13880 Subject F01 N	2714	1224	1421	2109	259	579	828	839	468	1647	964	1187	529	376	562	27
E09G: Lots of space around my house, a big yard																
1. Not important	15.3	13.6	17.0	15.3	14.1	14.1	15.5	14.6	17.8	14.4	17.6	13.4	14.5	18.0	18.4	12.8
2. Somewhat important	26.2	25.3	26.9	26.5	25.0	24.3	25.9	26.7	28.3	26.8	24.2	25.3	26.6	29.8	26.1	18.2
3. Quite important	31.6	32.4	31.3	32.1	27.5	32.9	34.1	28.5	31.1	33.6	28.9	34.6	30.3	28.6	28.8	20.5
4. Extremely important	26.9	28.8	24.9	26.1	33.3	28.7	24.5	30.2	22.8	25.2	29.3	26.7	28.6	23.6	26.6	48.4
Item 13890 Subject F01 N	2710	1225	1417	2107	258	579	828	836	467	1647	962	1183	529	376	561	27
E09H: A well-kept garden and lawn																
1. Not important	14.6	14.2	14.6	14.8	12.4	15.3	15.6	14.7	11.7	13.6	16.6	12.1	14.2	16.4	19.0	13.5
2. Somewhat important	29.8	30.6	29.7	31.3	23.0	34.8	29.5	26.6	29.8	30.1	28.7	29.3	29.6	32.8	29.7	16.5
3. Quite important	34.0	33.2	34.4	33.7	34.3	30.1	37.2	33.1	34.7	35.5	31.9	36.8	32.0	34.5	29.7	30.2
4. Extremely important	21.6	22.0	21.3	20.2	30.3	19.8	17.7	25.6	23.8	20.8	22.8	21.8	24.2	16.4	21.7	39.8
Item 13900 Subject F01 N	2700	1220	1412	2102	257	576	825	833	466	1642	956	1179	525	377	558	27
E09I: Major labor-saving appliances (washer, drier, dishwasher, etc.)																
1. Not important	6.6	7.6	5.9	5.7	6.8	7.1	6.3	6.5	6.8	5.4	8.6	6.3	5.8	5.9	7.6	4.7
2. Somewhat important	23.1	23.3	23.2	23.8	21.1	23.2	24.1	23.3	20.6	22.7	23.6	24.2	19.9	24.8	22.5	21.2
3. Quite important	38.0	39.2	36.9	38.5	29.9	38.5	41.0	32.9	41.1	39.0	36.6	39.4	38.2	41.1	33.4	23.1
4. Extremely important	32.4	30.0	34.0	32.0	42.1	31.2	28.6	37.3	31.5	32.9	31.1	30.1	36.2	28.2	36.5	51.0
Item 13910 Subject F01 N	2708	1222	1417	2107	258	578	827	836	467	1647	959	1182	527	376	562	27
E09J: A high-quality stereo																
1. Not important	11.6	8.2	14.8	10.9	14.1	13.4	8.8	14.4	9.4	10.4	13.9	14.8	8.8	11.1	7.7	
2. Somewhat important	31.9	27.1	36.1	32.2	30.6	29.7	33.8	32.3	30.5	33.5	29.5	37.3	31.8	31.9	21.6	13.6
3. Quite important	28.3	29.6	27.0	28.7	25.4	25.8	30.0	26.4	31.6	29.3	27.3	26.7	31.5	28.3	28.1	32.4
4. Extremely important	28.2	35.2	22.2	28.2	29.9	31.0	27.5	26.8	28.6	26.8	29.3	21.2	27.9	28.7	42.5	54.0
Item 13920 Subject F01 N	2708	1223	1417	2106	258	578	828	835	467	1648	958	1183	527	375	562	27

QUESTIONNAIRE FORM 3 1986	TOTAL	SEX		RACE		REGION				4YR COLLEGE PLANS		ILLICIT DRUG USE: LIFETIME				
		M	F	White	Black	NE	NC	S	W	Yes	No	None	Mari- juana Only	Few Pills	More Pills	Any Her- oin
N (Weighted No. of Cases):	3159	1456	1581	2348	342	746	901	978	534	1801	1138	1328	641	437	648	29
% of Weighted Total:	100.0	46.1	50.1	74.3	10.8	23.6	28.5	31.0	16.9	57.0	36.0	42.0	20.3	13.8	20.5	0.9
E09K: A vacation house																
1. Not important	50.5	47.4	53.6	50.8	53.2	48.4	48.8	55.7	46.7	48.3	54.1	56.1	50.8	42.4	45.1	28.9
2. Somewhat important	27.1	25.8	28.2	27.8	23.3	27.3	29.4	22.9	30.4	29.1	24.3	25.9	27.8	33.3	26.0	14.4
3. Quite important	12.2	14.8	9.8	12.1	10.7	13.4	12.8	10.6	12.5	13.0	11.2	10.9	10.5	12.8	14.8	22.1
4. Extremely important	10.2	12.0	8.4	9.3	12.8	10.9	9.1	10.7	10.3	9.7	10.4	7.1	10.8	11.5	14.1	34.6
Item 13930 Subject F01 N	2700	1218	1414	2098	258	578	824	832	466	1640	957	1177	524	376	561	27
E09L: A motor-powered, recreational vehicle (powerboat, snowmobile)																
1. Not important	47.4	34.7	58.6	44.5	68.4	47.8	42.5	53.5	44.8	48.6	45.6	53.3	48.3	44.4	36.4	33.7
2. Somewhat important	27.0	28.8	25.5	28.3	17.4	26.2	29.1	24.6	28.7	27.1	26.7	26.2	28.1	29.9	27.1	11.2
3. Quite important	13.8	18.9	9.1	15.0	7.0	14.7	16.3	11.1	13.2	13.8	13.9	12.1	12.6	13.5	18.2	34.9
4. Extremely important	11.7	17.5	6.8	12.3	7.1	11.3	12.1	10.7	13.3	10.5	13.8	8.5	11.0	12.1	18.3	20.2
Item 13940 Subject F01 N	2702	1220	1414	2101	257	578	823	834	467	1646	954	1182	526	375	557	27
E10: When (if ever) did you FIRST do each of the following things? Don't count anything you took because a doctor told you to.																
E10A: Smoke cigarettes on a daily basis																
8. Never	71.0	74.5	68.8	69.0	88.3	61.0	69.3	76.5	76.5	77.7	59.1	92.6	69.2	59.2	36.6	20.1
1. Grade 6 or below	2.8	3.2	2.4	3.1	0.5	5.0	3.2	1.4	2.0	2.5	3.5	0.7	2.7	4.6	5.3	24.9
2. Grade 7 or 8	7.0	6.0	7.7	7.5	2.1	11.7	6.7	5.3	4.3	4.4	11.5	1.5	7.6	8.2	17.5	5.0
3. Grade 9 (Freshman)	5.5	4.5	6.3	5.9	1.8	5.6	4.9	6.3	4.9	3.2	9.6	1.7	5.6	7.3	11.6	24.3
4. Grade 10 (Sophomore)	5.6	4.6	6.4	6.2	2.7	8.8	6.6	3.4	3.8	5.1	6.5	1.6	5.5	7.7	12.7	3.7
5. Grade 11 (Junior)	4.9	4.4	5.0	4.5	3.2	4.5	5.3	4.0	6.0	4.1	6.3	0.7	5.4	8.6	10.4	8.4
6. Grade 12 (Senior)	3.3	2.8	3.4	3.8	1.3	3.3	3.9	3.2	2.5	3.0	3.5	1.2	4.0	4.4	5.9	13.6
Item 5570 Subject A01g N	2527	1125	1336	1967	239	544	773	776	433	1549	887	1121	480	341	530	25
E10B: Try an alcoholic beverage - more than just a few sips																
8. Never	8.8	7.2	10.2	7.0	16.6	5.4	6.2	12.9	10.8	9.2	8.0	19.5	1.0	2.0	0.5	-
1. Grade 6 or below	8.6	11.9	5.7	8.3	7.8	6.3	11.5	8.2	7.0	8.6	8.4	7.5	5.6	8.7	12.1	25.8
2. Grade 7 or 8	21.9	23.8	20.5	23.3	13.3	26.5	22.4	17.8	22.5	19.0	26.3	11.3	24.0	24.1	37.4	39.9
3. Grade 9 (Freshman)	25.3	24.4	26.0	27.4	15.8	28.5	27.0	23.6	21.4	25.3	25.7	17.6	28.8	32.0	33.0	14.4
4. Grade 10 (Sophomore)	16.8	16.0	17.5	17.9	12.4	16.5	17.0	16.4	17.6	18.9	14.6	17.0	21.8	18.4	11.7	17.7
5. Grade 11 (Junior)	12.3	10.7	13.6	11.5	17.7	11.2	11.0	13.1	14.6	12.1	12.1	16.5	15.0	11.8	3.0	2.2
6. Grade 12 (Senior)	6.2	6.0	6.6	4.6	16.5	5.6	5.0	8.1	6.0	7.0	4.9	10.7	3.8	3.1	2.3	-
Item 5580 Subject A01g N	2446	1105	1279	1944	205	530	769	730	418	1480	872	1000	498	353	542	26
E10C: Try marijuana or hashish																
8. Never	50.4	49.2	52.5	48.6	56.9	42.1	49.8	58.3	47.5	54.9	42.6	100.0	-	26.0	7.7	3.4
1. Grade 6 or below	3.0	4.2	1.7	2.9	3.1	3.5	3.5	1.7	3.7	2.1	3.7	-	2.8	2.9	7.8	22.7
2. Grade 7 or 8	10.3	10.9	9.7	11.1	7.5	13.0	9.9	8.1	11.3	8.6	13.5	-	12.6	14.6	26.6	26.3
3. Grade 9 (Freshman)	11.6	10.7	11.8	12.4	8.3	15.0	13.0	9.0	9.4	9.6	15.4	-	18.2	17.1	26.6	12.9
4. Grade 10 (Sophomore)	10.9	11.9	10.1	11.2	6.9	11.4	9.9	11.2	11.4	10.1	12.4	-	21.8	16.8	20.7	11.2
5. Grade 11 (Junior)	8.2	8.3	7.7	8.1	9.4	8.7	8.7	6.6	9.5	8.1	8.5	-	24.4	13.7	7.5	23.5
6. Grade 12 (Senior)	5.8	4.9	6.4	5.6	7.9	6.3	5.2	5.1	7.3	6.7	4.0	-	20.2	9.0	3.1	-
Item 5590 Subject A01g N	2557	1153	1343	1996	233	545	784	786	441	1569	893	1140	470	353	544	27
E10D: Try LSD																
8. Never	94.1	93.0	95.5	93.3	99.4	93.9	91.5	96.3	94.9	95.9	91.6	100.0	100.0	95.3	77.4	19.9
1. Grade 6 or below	0.1	0.2	-	0.1	-	-	0.2	-	-	0.1	-	-	-	-	0.1	6.2
2. Grade 7 or 8	0.4	0.5	0.3	0.5	-	0.1	0.3	0.3	1.1	0.3	0.5	-	-	1.5	10.4
3. Grade 9 (Freshman)	1.1	1.4	0.8	1.2	-	1.2	1.7	0.5	1.1	0.6	1.9	-	-	0.4	3.9	29.9
4. Grade 10 (Sophomore)	1.1	1.5	0.6	1.2	-	0.8	1.7	0.4	1.5	0.7	1.5	-	-	0.5	4.2	15.8
5. Grade 11 (Junior)	2.0	2.0	1.5	2.3	-	2.0	3.0	1.5	0.9	1.7	2.4	-	-	2.4	7.6	9.7
6. Grade 12 (Senior)	1.3	1.4	1.3	1.5	0.6	2.0	1.7	1.0	0.5	0.7	2.0	-	-	1.3	5.3	8.0
Item 5600 Subject A01g N	2627	1184	1381	2035	256	557	800	813	457	1602	926	1158	522	366	532	21

QUESTIONNAIRE FORM 3 1986	TOTAL	SEX		RACE		REGION				4YR COLLEGE PLANS		ILLICIT DRUG USE: LIFETIME				
		M	F	White	Black	NE	NC	S	W	Yes	No	None	Marijuana Only	Few Pills	More Pills	Any Heroin
N (Weighted No. of Cases):	3159	1456	1581	2348	342	746	901	978	534	1801	1138	1328	641	437	648	29
% of Weighted Total:	100.0	46.1	50.1	74.3	10.8	23.6	28.5	31.0	16.9	57.0	36.0	42.0	20.3	13.8	20.5	0.9

E10E: Try any psychedelic other than LSD

	TOTAL	M	F	White	Black	NE	NC	S	W	Yes	No	None	Mari-juana Only	Few Pills	More Pills	Any Heroin
8. Never	97.2	96.5	98.1	96.9	99.6	96.7	96.5	98.2	97.3	97.5	96.7	100.0	100.0	98.8	89.2	33.9
1. Grade 6 or below	*	0.1	-	*	-	0.1	0.1	-	-	-	0.1	-	-	-	0.1	2.4
2. Grade 7 or 8	0.4	0.6	0.1	0.4	-	-	0.6	0.3	0.5	0.4	0.4	-	-	-	1.2	18.6
3. Grade 9 (Freshman)	0.7	0.7	0.7	0.8	-	1.6	0.7	0.3	0.2	0.4	1.1	-	-	0.1	2.4	28.0
4. Grade 10 (Sophomore)	1.0	1.2	0.6	1.0	0.2	1.0	1.2	0.9	0.7	1.0	1.0	-	-	-	4.3	17.0
5. Grade 11 (Junior)	0.4	0.4	0.4	0.5	0.2	0.5	0.4	0.1	0.9	0.5	0.3	-	-	0.1	2.1	-
6. Grade 12 (Senior)	0.3	0.5	*	0.3	-	0.1	0.5	0.1	0.3	0.2	0.4	-	-	1.0	0.6	-
Item 5610 Subject A01g N	2582	1160	1364	1996	255	540	790	806	445	1584	904	1158	522	359	498	19

E10F: Try amphetamines

	TOTAL	M	F	White	Black	NE	NC	S	W	Yes	No	None	Mari-juana Only	Few Pills	More Pills	Any Heroin
8. Never	87.0	88.6	86.4	84.6	96.8	87.1	83.7	88.8	89.0	89.0	83.4	100.0	100.0	78.3	36.6	17.6
1. Grade 6 or below	0.2	0.2	0.2	0.2	-	-	0.4	-	0.4	0.2	-	-	-	-	1.1	-
2. Grade 7 or 8	2.3	1.8	2.8	2.8	-	4.2	1.2	2.1	2.3	1.3	4.1	-	-	1.0	13.3	11.8
3. Grade 9 (Freshman)	4.4	3.5	4.9	5.3	1.5	3.5	6.0	4.0	3.9	3.6	5.8	-	-	7.0	22.7	15.5
4. Grade 10 (Sophomore)	3.1	3.0	3.1	3.7	0.7	3.4	4.4	2.5	1.3	2.8	3.7	-	-	5.7	14.1	23.4
5. Grade 11 (Junior)	1.7	2.1	1.0	1.7	0.4	1.0	2.2	1.3	2.4	1.5	1.8	-	-	2.8	7.0	28.4
6. Grade 12 (Senior)	1.4	0.8	1.6	1.6	0.5	0.8	2.1	1.4	0.7	1.5	1.2	-	-	5.2	5.1	3.3
Item 5620 Subject A01g N	2331	1060	1215	1781	248	515	689	738	389	1450	794	1157	520	235	368	23

E10G: Try quaaludes

	TOTAL	M	F	White	Black	NE	NC	S	W	Yes	No	None	Mari-juana Only	Few Pills	More Pills	Any Heroin
8. Never	95.9	96.1	95.6	95.6	98.6	95.0	96.2	95.3	97.3	96.8	94.2	100.0	100.0	96.6	84.8	19.9
1. Grade 6 or below	0.2	0.3	0.1	0.3	-	-	0.4	0.1	0.3	0.3	0.1	-	-	-	0.8	7.4
2. Grade 7 or 8	1.1	0.9	1.3	1.2	-	1.4	0.9	1.3	0.7	0.8	1.7	-	-	1.1	4.0	18.0
3. Grade 9 (Freshman)	1.1	0.7	1.3	1.1	0.2	1.4	0.4	1.6	0.8	0.7	1.6	-	-	0.5	4.4	7.1
4. Grade 10 (Sophomore)	0.9	1.0	0.9	1.0	-	1.0	1.4	0.8	0.1	0.8	1.0	-	-	0.7	3.0	30.0
5. Grade 11 (Junior)	0.6	0.6	0.6	0.5	0.9	0.6	0.6	0.5	0.7	0.5	0.7	-	-	1.1	2.0	5.3
6. Grade 12 (Senior)	0.3	0.4	0.2	0.3	0.3	0.7	0.1	0.4	-	0.1	0.7	-	-	-	1.0	12.2
Item 5630 Subject A01g N	2621	1181	1382	2032	257	557	799	812	451	1609	917	1159	524	359	534	18

E10H: Try barbiturates

	TOTAL	M	F	White	Black	NE	NC	S	W	Yes	No	None	Mari-juana Only	Few Pills	More Pills	Any Heroin
8. Never	96.1	95.9	96.5	95.6	99.2	95.2	95.8	96.2	97.3	97.3	94.7	100.0	100.0	98.0	83.5	23.7
1. Grade 6 or below	0.2	0.2	0.1	0.2	-	0.2	0.4	-	-	0.3	-	-	-	-	0.6	7.4
2. Grade 7 or 8	0.9	0.9	1.0	1.1	-	1.5	1.1	0.8	0.4	0.6	1.7	-	-	0.2	4.2	16.9
3. Grade 9 (Freshman)	1.4	1.2	1.2	1.5	0.2	2.3	0.6	1.9	0.6	1.0	1.3	-	-	1.0	5.7	17.6
4. Grade 10 (Sophomore)	1.0	1.3	0.8	1.1	0.3	0.3	1.3	1.0	1.1	0.7	1.4	-	-	0.2	4.3	23.8
5. Grade 11 (Junior)	0.3	0.5	0.1	0.4	-	0.5	0.5	-	0.5	0.2	0.6	-	-	0.6	1.0	6.4
6. Grade 12 (Senior)	0.1	-	0.3	0.2	0.3	-	0.3	0.1	0.2	0.1	0.2	-	-	-	0.6	4.2
Item 5640 Subject A01g N	2538	1145	1335	1955	254	537	775	789	437	1566	876	1157	524	331	479	18

E10I: Try tranquilizers

	TOTAL	M	F	White	Black	NE	NC	S	W	Yes	No	None	Mari-juana Only	Few Pills	More Pills	Any Heroin
8. Never	95.1	95.7	94.8	94.4	99.7	93.7	95.0	95.5	96.5	96.3	93.3	100.0	100.0	95.4	78.8	36.1
1. Grade 6 or below	0.2	0.3	0.1	0.2	-	0.1	0.1	0.4	0.2	0.2	0.1	-	-	0.5	0.6	2.7
2. Grade 7 or 8	0.9	0.3	1.3	1.1	-	1.5	1.0	0.4	0.8	0.7	1.3	-	-	0.8	3.8	15.2
3. Grade 9 (Freshman)	1.4	1.0	1.7	1.5	-	2.5	0.6	1.4	1.2	0.9	2.1	-	-	0.2	6.8	18.3
4. Grade 10 (Sophomore)	0.9	1.0	0.8	1.1	-	0.1	1.4	1.2	0.6	1.0	0.9	-	-	1.3	3.8	14.9
5. Grade 11 (Junior)	0.7	1.2	0.4	0.8	-	1.1	0.9	0.4	0.5	0.5	1.1	-	-	0.7	3.0	8.5
6. Grade 12 (Senior)	0.8	0.6	0.9	0.9	0.3	1.0	0.9	0.7	0.2	0.4	1.2	-	-	1.2	3.2	4.3
Item 5650 Subject A01g N	2447	1117	1278	1888	251	524	759	745	420	1509	852	1157	520	286	439	17

E10J: Try cocaine

	TOTAL	M	F	White	Black	NE	NC	S	W	Yes	No	None	Mari-juana Only	Few Pills	More Pills	Any Heroin
8. Never	85.2	83.4	87.3	85.0	90.8	76.7	88.4	90.3	80.5	87.8	81.3	100.0	100.0	74.6	49.2	1.8
1. Grade 6 or below	0.2	0.3	-	0.1	0.7	-	0.4	0.2	-	0.2	0.1	-	-	0.5	0.6	-
2. Grade 7 or 8	1.0	1.2	0.8	1.0	0.2	1.4	0.7	0.5	1.7	0.8	1.2	-	-	0.2	3.5	22.7
3. Grade 9 (Freshman)	1.5	2.1	0.9	1.4	1.4	2.1	1.8	0.6	1.9	0.9	2.5	-	-	3.3	4.3	17.5
4. Grade 10 (Sophomore)	4.1	3.1	4.7	4.7	0.8	6.6	1.9	3.4	6.2	3.7	4.8	-	-	6.7	14.5	17.6
5. Grade 11 (Junior)	4.1	5.0	3.0	4.0	1.2	6.3	2.8	2.7	5.8	3.6	4.7	-	-	5.8	14.8	22.9
6. Grade 12 (Senior)	4.0	4.8	3.3	3.8	4.9	6.9	3.9	2.2	3.9	3.0	5.3	-	-	8.8	13.1	17.5
Item 5660 Subject A01g N	2613	1169	1382	2028	254	552	795	815	450	1605	913	1156	519	355	529	26

*=less than .05 per cent.

QUESTIONNAIRE FORM 3 1986	TOTAL	SEX		RACE		REGION				4YR COLLEGE PLANS		ILLICIT DRUG USE: LIFETIME				
		M	F	White	Black	NE	NC	S	W	Yes	No	None	Marijuana Only	Few Pills	More Pills	Any Heroin
N (Weighted No. of Cases):	3159	1456	1581	2348	342	746	901	978	534	1801	1138	1328	641	437	648	29
% of Weighted Total:	100.0	46.1	50.1	74.3	10.8	23.6	28.5	31.0	16.9	57.0	36.0	42.0	20.3	13.8	20.5	0.9
E10K: Try heroin																
8. Never	99.1	98.8	99.7	99.3	99.7	99.3	98.9	99.0	99.3	99.3	98.7	100.0	100.0	100.0	100.0	-
1. Grade 6 or below	0.1	0.2	-	0.1	-	0.1	0.2	-	-	0.1	0.1	-	-	-	-	7.7
2. Grade 7 or 8	0.1	0.1	0.1	*	-	-	0.2	0.1	-	*	0.2	-	-	-	-	9.8
3. Grade 9 (Freshman)	0.1	0.1	*	*	-	-	0.2	0.1	-	0.1	0.1	-	-	-	-	7.1
4. Grade 10 (Sophomore)	0.2	0.3	0.1	0.1	-	0.5	-	0.1	0.5	0.1	0.5	-	-	-	-	25.6
5. Grade 11 (Junior)	0.2	0.3	0.1	0.2	-	-	0.4	0.1	0.3	0.2	0.2	-	-	-	-	22.7
6. Grade 12 (Senior)	0.2	0.2	0.1	0.2	0.3	0.2	0.1	0.5	-	0.2	0.3	-	-	-	-	27.0
Item 5670 Subject A01g N	2628	1180	1384	2044	254	558	802	811	457	1616	916	1152	523	359	543	23
E10L: Try any narcotic other than heroin																
8. Never	96.7	96.7	97.2	96.5	99.4	95.3	96.0	97.6	97.9	96.9	96.5	100.0	100.0	98.4	87.0	13.5
1. Grade 6 or below	0.1	0.2	-	0.1	-	-	0.3	-	-	0.1	-	-	-	-	0.2	5.6
2. Grade 7 or 8	0.4	0.3	0.4	0.4	-	0.5	0.7	0.4	-	0.3	0.5	-	-	-	1.4	11.6
3. Grade 9 (Freshman)	1.0	0.8	0.9	1.1	-	1.1	0.7	1.4	0.6	0.9	1.1	-	-	-	4.5	25.0
4. Grade 10 (Sophomore)	0.6	0.8	0.4	0.6	-	0.3	1.0	0.3	0.7	0.5	0.7	-	-	0.6	2.5	7.5
5. Grade 11 (Junior)	0.8	1.1	0.4	0.9	-	1.7	0.8	0.1	0.8	0.9	0.6	-	-	0.2	2.7	31.3
6. Grade 12 (Senior)	0.5	0.2	0.6	0.4	0.6	1.1	0.5	0.2	-	0.4	0.6	-	-	0.7	1.8	5.3
Item 5680 Subject A01g N	2488	1112	1314	1913	252	529	764	774	421	1542	857	1153	522	330	430	23
E10M: Try inhalants																
8. Never	90.9	88.7	93.3	90.1	96.4	92.0	91.5	90.5	89.2	92.0	88.9	98.6	94.7	88.4	73.0	38.1
1. Grade 6 or below	1.1	1.8	0.6	1.3	-	1.2	1.0	1.1	1.2	1.3	0.8	0.4	0.6	1.5	2.7	10.6
2. Grade 7 or 8	2.1	2.3	1.9	2.2	0.8	1.5	2.1	2.2	2.6	1.6	3.2	0.2	0.6	2.8	7.2	10.1
3. Grade 9 (Freshman)	1.6	1.9	1.1	1.8	0.4	0.2	1.3	2.0	3.0	1.1	2.4	*	0.9	2.6	5.0	4.8
4. Grade 10 (Sophomore)	1.6	1.9	1.2	1.8	0.3	1.8	1.2	1.8	1.9	2.0	1.1	0.3	0.7	2.4	4.6	16.6
5. Grade 11 (Junior)	1.5	1.8	1.2	1.5	1.6	1.8	2.3	0.8	1.1	1.1	2.2	0.3	1.8	1.5	4.4	-
6. Grade 12 (Senior)	1.2	1.6	0.7	1.4	0.5	1.5	0.6	1.6	1.1	1.0	1.4	0.3	0.6	0.9	3.2	19.8
Item 5685 Subject A01g N	2409	1063	1286	1860	237	506	726	767	409	1496	824	1107	462	324	467	22
E10N: Smoke your first cigarette																
8. Never	33.7	35.8	32.2	30.5	49.3	30.8	32.1	36.4	35.4	37.3	25.7	59.6	15.6	19.0	7.5	10.5
1. Grade 6 or below	24.3	27.0	22.1	26.6	13.4	29.0	24.8	22.1	21.7	21.0	30.9	12.9	26.4	25.9	44.1	42.4
2. Grade 7 or 8	18.0	17.4	18.5	18.9	13.7	21.4	17.6	17.8	14.9	17.2	19.8	9.1	24.3	25.4	26.1	15.7
3. Grade 9 (Freshman)	10.3	8.9	11.4	10.7	7.9	10.5	9.9	10.2	11.3	9.6	12.3	6.2	16.7	14.3	10.6	9.7
4. Grade 10 (Sophomore)	7.0	6.4	7.8	7.0	9.2	5.1	8.9	6.1	7.7	7.5	6.2	4.4	11.3	7.4	8.2	-
5. Grade 11 (Junior)	3.8	2.9	4.5	3.6	2.3	2.5	4.7	3.1	5.3	4.3	2.8	4.4	3.4	4.4	2.4	8.3
6. Grade 12 (Senior)	2.8	1.6	3.6	2.6	4.3	0.8	2.0	4.4	3.7	3.0	2.4	3.3	2.2	3.6	1.0	13.4
Item 5575 Subject A01g N	2442	1089	1294	1922	216	537	748	733	425	1513	840	1050	482	335	523	26
E10O: Try smokeless tobacco (snuff, plug or chewing tobacco)																
8. Never	70.3	45.9	90.8	66.2	90.9	74.2	66.2	69.6	74.0	70.5	70.0	80.9	65.6	61.5	59.8	23.6
1. Grade 6 or below	5.8	11.0	1.4	6.5	1.4	4.2	6.2	7.7	3.7	5.3	6.2	4.2	6.5	7.1	7.5	13.5
2. Grade 7 or 8	7.8	14.6	2.1	9.0	2.6	6.8	7.4	9.2	7.2	7.8	8.4	4.0	9.8	12.0	10.1	26.2
3. Grade 9 (Freshman)	7.4	13.7	2.1	8.5	2.5	8.4	7.4	7.2	6.6	7.1	7.9	4.7	8.9	6.5	11.8	21.3
4. Grade 10 (Sophomore)	4.1	7.7	1.2	4.7	2.1	2.7	5.0	3.8	5.0	4.3	4.1	2.4	4.8	6.7	5.8	4.6
5. Grade 11 (Junior)	3.0	5.1	1.2	3.7	0.4	2.4	6.0	1.4	1.4	3.3	2.0	2.7	3.3	3.9	2.7	-
6. Grade 12 (Senior)	1.5	2.0	1.2	1.4	-	1.3	1.8	1.0	2.1	1.7	1.3	1.0	1.1	2.2	2.2	10.9
Item 5576 Subject A01g N	2549	1124	1368	1988	240	548	779	779	444	1564	894	1131	493	347	525	24
E10P: Drink enough to feel drunk or very high																
8. Never	31.2	28.8	33.4	25.3	56.6	27.8	25.5	38.9	31.5	32.3	28.0	55.6	14.7	14.5	6.2	5.1
1. Grade 6 or below	3.1	4.5	1.7	3.3	1.2	3.2	3.8	2.6	2.5	2.6	3.6	1.2	0.9	4.2	7.5	24.5
2. Grade 7 or 8	13.3	16.4	10.9	15.1	4.6	15.7	15.3	10.1	12.9	10.9	17.8	4.6	15.0	16.1	27.8	31.6
3. Grade 9 (Freshman)	18.5	17.1	19.9	21.4	8.1	20.4	21.2	14.9	18.0	18.0	19.6	7.9	22.5	23.5	35.2	6.3
4. Grade 10 (Sophomore)	15.1	16.6	13.5	16.7	9.3	14.9	16.1	14.2	15.0	17.2	12.3	10.8	22.7	21.2	12.9	13.7
5. Grade 11 (Junior)	13.1	11.4	14.2	13.3	9.1	13.5	13.2	12.1	14.3	13.0	13.3	13.4	19.2	13.0	6.7	16.0
6. Grade 12 (Senior)	5.7	5.2	6.4	5.0	11.0	4.5	5.0	7.2	5.9	6.0	5.3	6.5	4.9	7.4	3.7	2.8
Item 5585 Subject A01g N	2656	1200	1391	2066	256	565	813	825	453	1621	936	1158	528	363	549	27

*=less than .05 per cent.

QUESTIONNAIRE FORM 4 1986	TOTAL	SEX		RACE		REGION				4YR COLLEGE PLANS		ILLICIT DRUG USE: LIFETIME				
		M	F	White	Black	NE	NC	S	W	Yes	No	None	Mari- juana Only	Few Pills	More Pills	Any Her- oin
N (Weighted No. of Cases):	3123	1441	1571	2352	333	744	873	961	545	1904	1002	1314	604	446	654	26
% of Weighted Total:	100.0	46.1	50.3	75.3	10.7	23.8	27.9	30.8	17.4	61.0	32.1	42.1	19.3	14.3	20.9	0.8

A01: Taking all things together, how would you say things are these days-would you say you're very happy, pretty happy, or not too happy these days?

	TOTAL	M	F	White	Black	NE	NC	S	W	Yes	No	None	Mari- juana Only	Few Pills	More Pills	Any Her- oin
3. Very happy	17.9	17.7	18.4	19.9	12.9	17.8	17.5	17.3	20.1	20.2	14.6	19.9	18.3	16.8	14.9	16.6
2. Pretty happy	68.8	69.4	68.6	69.5	63.1	68.2	71.0	69.6	64.9	68.7	69.3	67.4	69.8	69.4	70.6	73.4
1. Not too happy	13.3	12.9	13.1	10.6	24.0	14.0	11.6	13.1	15.0	11.0	16.1	12.7	11.9	13.8	14.5	10.0
Item 1190 Subject P01,Q01 N	3116	1438	1569	2349	333	741	871	960	544	1900	1001	1312	604	445	652	26

A02: Looking ahead to the next five years, do you think that things in this country will get better or worse?

	TOTAL	M	F	White	Black	NE	NC	S	W	Yes	No	None	Mari- juana Only	Few Pills	More Pills	Any Her- oin
1. Get much better	3.4	4.0	2.6	2.9	4.7	3.2	2.7	4.1	3.8	3.2	3.7	3.8	2.6	2.7	3.8	-
2. Get somewhat better	31.2	35.9	27.0	31.2	30.9	32.5	34.7	29.2	27.4	32.4	29.7	32.0	32.1	32.8	29.1	11.8
3. Stay about the same	30.5	30.3	31.3	32.9	20.8	29.7	32.8	28.5	31.3	32.3	27.5	30.5	32.4	31.2	28.9	23.8
4. Get somewhat worse	29.7	25.6	33.2	28.9	34.7	28.8	26.7	31.4	32.5	27.7	32.8	28.4	27.4	28.9	33.2	47.0
5. Get much worse	5.2	4.2	6.0	4.0	9.0	5.8	3.1	6.9	4.9	4.4	6.3	5.2	5.5	4.3	4.9	17.4
Item 9940 Subject I01 N	3115	1440	1567	2348	333	739	872	960	544	1901	1001	1311	604	446	652	26

A03: Looking ahead to the next five years, do you think that things in the rest of the world will get better or worse?

	TOTAL	M	F	White	Black	NE	NC	S	W	Yes	No	None	Mari- juana Only	Few Pills	More Pills	Any Her- oin
1. Get much better	1.3	1.2	1.2	0.7	2.7	1.1	1.1	1.8	1.1	1.2	1.5	1.2	1.1	2.6	1.0	-
2. Get somewhat better	17.3	17.9	16.3	16.9	22.1	17.9	18.5	16.6	16.0	18.0	15.6	18.8	17.8	17.4	13.9	-
3. Stay about the same	26.3	27.4	25.6	27.7	20.1	26.0	27.8	25.3	25.8	25.9	26.2	25.9	27.3	27.3	25.3	28.6
4. Get somewhat worse	44.7	43.1	47.0	45.9	42.1	45.0	44.8	44.8	44.2	45.7	45.2	43.9	43.8	45.5	47.4	59.9
5. Get much worse	10.3	10.4	9.9	8.9	13.0	10.1	7.7	11.5	12.9	9.3	11.4	10.2	10.0	7.2	12.4	11.4
Item 9950 Subject I01 N	3110	1438	1564	2343	333	735	871	960	543	1898	997	1307	604	446	650	26

A04: How do you think your own life will go in the next five years–do you think it will get better or worse?

	TOTAL	M	F	White	Black	NE	NC	S	W	Yes	No	None	Mari- juana Only	Few Pills	More Pills	Any Her- oin
1. Get much better	41.6	40.9	41.6	39.6	54.0	41.5	38.6	43.7	42.7	41.8	42.2	41.0	38.0	44.6	43.7	26.8
2. Get somewhat better	47.5	48.3	47.4	49.1	40.0	47.3	50.1	45.5	47.1	48.2	45.9	47.4	51.8	48.1	44.3	49.5
3. Stay about the same	7.9	7.9	8.1	8.5	2.9	8.3	7.9	8.3	6.8	7.1	9.0	8.8	6.7	4.6	9.2	16.1
4. Get somewhat worse	2.3	2.5	2.1	2.2	2.7	2.2	2.9	1.6	2.9	2.6	2.0	2.1	2.7	2.5	2.3	5.2
5. Get much worse	0.7	0.4	0.8	0.5	0.3	0.7	0.5	0.9	0.4	0.4	0.8	0.7	1.0	0.3	0.4	2.4
Item 9960 Subject I01 N	3119	1441	1570	2352	332	742	873	960	545	1904	1001	1314	604	446	653	26

A05: Some people think a lot about the social problems of the nation and the world, and about how they might be solved. Others spend little time thinking about these issues. How much do you think about such things?

	TOTAL	M	F	White	Black	NE	NC	S	W	Yes	No	None	Mari- juana Only	Few Pills	More Pills	Any Her- oin
1. Never	2.0	2.6	1.2	1.8	3.7	2.8	1.4	1.7	2.0	1.2	2.9	1.7	1.9	1.6	2.8	2.0
2. Seldom	16.5	16.9	16.0	17.2	14.9	20.2	19.2	12.2	14.8	14.6	20.9	16.3	17.2	12.3	17.6	35.0
3. Sometimes	49.8	48.0	51.4	51.4	39.8	47.5	49.8	51.7	49.5	49.6	49.5	49.1	51.4	51.9	49.3	31.6
4. Quite often	26.1	25.7	26.9	24.3	34.3	22.9	24.7	28.0	29.2	28.0	22.6	27.9	22.1	30.2	24.1	31.4
5. A great deal	5.7	6.8	4.5	5.3	7.4	6.5	4.9	6.4	4.5	6.6	4.1	5.1	7.3	4.0	6.3	-
Item 6880 Subject J,Q08 N	3116	1439	1568	2351	332	742	873	958	543	1901	1000	1309	604	446	653	26

A06: These questions are about pollution and the environment. Please mark the circle that shows how much you agree or disagree with each statement below.

A06A: In general, pollution has increased in the U.S. in the last ten years

	TOTAL	M	F	White	Black	NE	NC	S	W	Yes	No	None	Mari- juana Only	Few Pills	More Pills	Any Her- oin
1. Disagree	3.7	5.5	2.1	3.4	6.5	5.8	3.1	3.5	2.4	3.1	4.5	4.3	2.9	3.1	4.2	-
2. Mostly disagree	8.0	9.1	6.9	8.7	6.3	6.7	11.1	8.0	5.0	7.6	8.2	7.8	8.9	8.2	7.7	7.7
3. Neither	8.4	8.5	8.2	8.6	5.4	7.8	12.0	6.5	6.9	8.3	7.8	7.6	8.8	9.9	8.7	2.5
4. Mostly agree	35.5	32.9	38.1	36.8	31.3	33.3	39.0	34.8	34.0	37.1	34.4	35.5	36.6	32.7	35.5	51.1
5. Agree	44.3	44.1	44.6	42.5	50.5	46.4	34.8	47.2	51.7	44.0	45.1	44.8	42.8	46.2	43.9	38.6
Item 9970 Subject F04 N	3111	1437	1568	2348	331	740	873	955	543	1899	1000	1310	604	445	651	26

QUESTIONNAIRE FORM 4 1986	TOTAL	SEX		RACE		REGION				4YR COLLEGE PLANS		ILLICIT DRUG USE: LIFETIME				
		M	F	White	Black	NE	NC	S	W	Yes	No	None	Marijuana Only	Few Pills	More Pills	Any Heroin
N (Weighted No. of Cases):	3123	1441	1571	2352	333	744	873	961	545	1904	1002	1314	604	446	654	26
% of Weighted Total:	100.0	46.1	50.3	75.3	10.7	23.8	27.9	30.8	17.4	61.0	32.1	42.1	19.3	14.3	20.9	0.8

A06B: The dangers of pollution are not really as great as government, the media, and environmental groups would like us to believe

	TOTAL	M	F	White	Black	NE	NC	S	W	Yes	No	None	Mari	Few	More	Heroin
1. Disagree	36.9	36.7	37.3	36.2	40.8	40.8	34.0	36.7	36.5	38.3	33.7	35.9	36.1	36.5	39.7	35.4
2. Mostly disagree	27.0	26.2	27.9	29.5	16.4	24.2	29.2	27.0	27.1	29.6	23.9	29.2	27.4	27.2	23.2	34.0
3. Neither	12.3	11.9	12.5	12.7	7.4	13.5	12.5	10.6	13.3	11.7	12.5	10.5	13.8	13.8	13.0	21.2
4. Mostly agree	15.5	16.3	14.9	14.9	20.8	13.2	16.4	15.7	16.6	13.8	19.6	16.3	15.2	13.9	15.4	3.4
5. Agree	8.4	8.9	7.4	6.7	14.6	8.3	7.9	10.0	6.5	6.7	10.3	8.2	7.5	8.6	8.6	6.0
Item 9980 Subject F04 N	3096	1430	1560	2341	327	734	871	951	540	1893	991	1301	604	444	647	26

A06C: America needs growth to survive, and that is going to require some increase in pollution

	TOTAL	M	F	White	Black	NE	NC	S	W	Yes	No	None	Mari	Few	More	Heroin
1. Disagree	33.8	33.0	34.4	34.0	30.6	36.7	31.6	33.8	33.1	34.0	33.4	32.8	35.6	32.4	36.2	35.6
2. Mostly disagree	21.4	20.8	22.0	22.9	14.5	19.4	25.3	18.0	24.1	23.1	18.6	20.4	22.5	23.9	20.7	14.3
3. Neither	13.5	13.1	14.1	14.1	12.6	12.8	15.1	11.8	14.7	14.4	12.5	13.3	13.2	14.9	13.4	16.9
4. Mostly agree	19.1	19.6	18.9	18.7	22.5	18.5	18.3	21.0	18.0	18.9	20.0	20.1	18.1	19.6	18.4	6.1
5. Agree	12.2	13.4	10.6	10.4	19.8	12.6	9.7	15.3	10.1	9.5	15.5	13.4	10.6	9.2	11.3	27.0
Item 9990 Subject F04 N	3086	1431	1550	2335	328	733	865	951	537	1887	994	1298	600	442	644	26

A06D: People will have to change their buying habits and way of life to correct our environmental problems

	TOTAL	M	F	White	Black	NE	NC	S	W	Yes	No	None	Mari	Few	More	Heroin
1. Disagree	14.6	15.9	12.9	13.7	21.0	13.9	15.1	18.1	8.6	12.4	17.9	14.5	13.6	11.9	16.3	12.9
2. Mostly disagree	16.1	17.1	15.1	17.4	10.7	17.6	16.1	15.7	14.8	16.4	16.3	16.2	16.5	15.5	15.5	34.3
3. Neither	17.8	17.5	18.1	19.0	11.0	17.3	20.3	15.0	19.5	18.3	18.0	16.1	19.4	18.7	19.6	23.0
4. Mostly agree	30.3	28.7	32.4	30.9	26.5	31.4	30.7	27.1	33.9	31.8	27.1	34.1	28.6	27.3	28.2	7.9
5. Agree	21.2	20.8	21.5	19.1	30.8	19.8	17.9	24.2	23.2	21.2	20.6	19.1	22.0	26.6	20.4	21.9
Item 10000 Subject F04 N	3101	1436	1558	2343	330	734	868	955	543	1897	996	1303	603	446	648	26

A06E: Government should take action to solve our environmental problems even if it means that some of the products we now use would have to be changed or banned

	TOTAL	M	F	White	Black	NE	NC	S	W	Yes	No	None	Mari	Few	More	Heroin
1. Disagree	7.0	8.5	5.2	6.2	10.2	7.7	6.7	7.2	6.2	4.8	10.1	6.3	6.7	6.5	8.9	3.8
2. Mostly disagree	9.4	10.0	8.8	9.7	8.0	9.7	9.2	9.2	9.6	9.4	9.5	9.2	7.6	9.8	9.8	21.4
3. Neither	14.5	13.7	15.2	14.5	11.1	13.6	14.5	14.8	15.3	12.7	17.9	13.3	14.1	12.6	18.7	27.4
4. Mostly agree	35.5	35.0	36.2	36.8	31.1	32.1	38.8	34.3	37.2	38.2	30.7	37.1	36.0	39.2	30.0	24.3
5. Agree	33.5	32.7	34.5	31.9	39.6	36.8	30.8	34.5	31.7	34.9	31.8	34.2	35.6	31.8	32.6	23.2
Item 10010 Subject F04,H02 N	3097	1433	1557	2340	329	736	867	954	539	1894	996	1300	604	445	646	26

A06F: Government should place higher taxes on products which cause pollution in their manufacture or disposal, so that companies will be encouraged to find better ways to produce them

	TOTAL	M	F	White	Black	NE	NC	S	W	Yes	No	None	Mari	Few	More	Heroin
1. Disagree	14.1	13.8	13.6	11.8	22.7	15.3	11.4	15.6	14.2	12.5	16.0	14.5	11.7	12.3	15.8	17.2
2. Mostly disagree	11.8	13.0	11.0	12.5	10.4	12.9	11.3	12.7	9.3	11.3	12.0	11.9	9.8	11.4	12.3	11.3
3. Neither	13.9	12.0	15.5	13.9	15.8	14.0	14.7	13.1	13.7	14.0	13.8	14.0	15.5	14.1	13.0	9.4
4. Mostly agree	27.5	27.4	28.1	29.0	22.9	24.5	29.9	26.6	29.5	28.5	26.6	28.0	26.5	30.2	25.9	41.0
5. Agree	32.7	33.8	31.8	32.8	28.2	33.3	32.8	31.9	33.3	33.7	31.5	31.7	36.4	31.9	33.0	21.1
Item 10020 Subject F04,H02 N	3096	1433	1556	2336	332	736	866	955	539	1893	994	1302	603	444	646	25

A06G: I wish that government would ban throw-away bottles and beverage cans

	TOTAL	M	F	White	Black	NE	NC	S	W	Yes	No	None	Mari	Few	More	Heroin
1. Disagree	32.5	35.5	29.9	32.9	31.0	30.7	29.9	36.1	33.1	30.7	36.0	31.6	33.1	30.9	35.6	21.9
2. Mostly disagree	15.6	13.9	17.2	16.3	13.3	13.7	14.6	18.5	14.8	15.6	15.7	15.9	15.8	14.4	14.9	15.8
3. Neither	25.0	19.6	29.8	24.7	24.5	25.5	27.6	20.9	27.4	27.2	21.7	26.1	23.9	28.1	22.3	27.6
4. Mostly agree	13.6	14.4	12.9	13.3	15.2	15.2	14.2	11.6	14.0	14.0	12.6	13.2	15.2	12.3	13.5	28.2
5. Agree	13.3	16.6	10.2	12.8	16.1	14.9	13.7	12.9	10.7	12.6	14.0	13.1	12.1	14.3	13.8	6.3
Item 10030 Subject F04,H02 N	3075	1421	1548	2322	329	727	864	948	535	1879	988	1294	597	440	643	26

QUESTIONNAIRE FORM 4 1986	TOTAL	SEX		RACE		REGION				4YR COLLEGE PLANS		ILLICIT DRUG USE: LIFETIME				
		M	F	White	Black	NE	NC	S	W	Yes	No	None	Mari-juana Only	Few Pills	More Pills	Any Her-oin
N (Weighted No. of Cases):	3123	1441	1571	2352	333	744	873	961	545	1904	1002	1314	604	446	654	26
% of Weighted Total:	100.0	46.1	50.3	75.3	10.7	23.8	27.9	30.8	17.4	61.0	32.1	42.1	19.3	14.3	20.9	0.8

A06H: T.V. commercials stimulate people to buy a lot of things they don't really need

1. Disagree	6.2	7.4	5.2	5.8	9.5	6.8	6.9	6.3	4.2	5.5	6.9	5.9	5.5	6.8	5.9	10.2
2. Mostly disagree	8.5	10.0	7.0	8.7	7.9	7.5	9.6	8.0	8.8	8.7	7.8	8.0	9.3	9.2	8.0	12.2
3. Neither	9.4	11.6	7.2	10.2	3.7	10.2	9.9	9.0	8.1	9.5	8.7	7.8	10.1	12.1	8.3	28.4
4. Mostly agree	26.9	27.6	26.9	28.3	22.6	25.7	28.1	25.5	29.3	27.7	26.3	27.5	28.9	22.4	28.3	14.0
5. Agree	49.0	43.5	53.8	47.0	56.3	49.8	45.6	51.2	49.5	48.6	50.3	50.9	46.2	49.5	49.4	35.2
Item 10040 Subject F02 N	3099	1435	1557	2339	331	735	868	956	542	1896	995	1306	598	444	648	26

A06I: T.V. commercials do a lot of good by showing new products that we might not know about otherwise

1. Disagree	5.3	6.8	3.8	5.3	5.0	8.0	4.4	3.9	5.8	4.8	6.3	5.6	2.9	5.3	7.0	7.4
2. Mostly disagree	10.0	10.2	9.7	10.4	6.0	11.8	8.7	7.2	14.8	11.0	8.2	8.4	10.0	10.5	11.6	33.1
3. Neither	14.5	15.1	13.9	15.4	6.4	17.1	16.1	9.6	17.0	16.3	10.8	15.0	13.6	15.2	15.0	14.6
4. Mostly agree	35.9	36.0	36.1	38.1	29.1	32.0	38.5	36.8	35.2	37.0	35.3	36.8	37.8	37.4	32.2	22.2
5. Agree	34.3	31.9	36.4	30.7	53.5	31.2	32.4	42.5	27.2	31.0	39.3	34.3	35.7	31.7	34.2	22.7
Item 10050 Subject F02 N	3103	1434	1564	2342	331	736	868	957	541	1894	997	1302	604	444	650	26

A06J: My family and I often buy things we don't really need; we could get along with much less

1. Disagree	14.1	15.1	12.8	11.8	25.6	15.8	10.9	14.5	16.4	12.8	15.3	13.4	14.3	12.2	14.7	24.3
2. Mostly disagree	16.5	16.1	17.4	16.6	16.5	18.0	17.5	14.1	17.4	16.3	16.2	16.5	17.8	13.9	17.1	16.8
3. Neither	12.8	15.6	9.8	13.6	6.4	13.4	15.3	10.5	12.0	12.9	12.3	12.3	13.1	12.6	13.5	13.1
4. Mostly agree	27.1	26.0	28.4	28.7	22.6	24.6	28.4	26.4	29.8	28.8	25.4	27.6	25.2	28.5	27.4	38.2
5. Agree	29.4	27.2	31.6	29.3	28.9	28.2	27.9	34.6	24.4	29.3	30.9	30.3	29.6	32.9	27.3	7.6
Item 10060 Subject F01 N	3095	1435	1551	2337	331	728	868	955	543	1896	991	1301	601	446	646	25

A06K: By the year 2000, engineers and scientists will probably have invented devices that will solve our pollution problems

1. Disagree	11.7	12.4	11.0	11.4	11.3	15.6	9.8	12.3	8.6	10.8	13.0	11.8	10.7	9.8	12.9	21.2
2. Mostly disagree	17.8	18.8	17.4	19.6	10.8	21.3	17.3	13.3	21.9	18.8	16.9	17.9	16.3	21.8	17.0	7.7
3. Neither	23.7	23.2	24.2	24.8	16.5	20.7	24.2	23.5	27.1	23.4	24.5	22.3	23.4	23.2	27.0	36.8
4. Mostly agree	31.3	28.7	33.1	31.8	29.8	26.8	33.4	32.7	31.3	32.9	27.6	31.8	34.6	27.9	29.7	23.3
5. Agree	15.5	16.8	14.2	12.4	31.5	15.6	15.2	18.1	11.3	14.0	18.1	16.1	15.0	17.3	13.3	11.0
Item 10070 Subject F04 N	3102	1437	1558	2343	329	736	869	956	541	1898	993	1303	603	446	652	26

A07: In your own actions–the things you buy and the things you do–how much of an effort do you make to conserve energy and protect the environment?

1. None	8.9	8.9	8.6	9.1	9.6	10.6	8.6	8.5	7.6	7.8	11.3	7.3	6.1	7.5	14.3	42.2
2. A little	27.4	27.2	27.7	27.2	31.7	26.3	28.7	25.9	29.6	28.4	26.6	23.4	35.0	30.2	27.0	15.6
3. Some	51.2	51.2	51.4	51.9	43.8	52.2	50.4	53.2	47.6	50.7	50.5	55.1	46.8	51.6	48.5	20.7
4. Quite a bit	12.5	12.7	12.2	11.8	14.9	10.9	12.3	12.4	15.1	13.2	11.6	14.2	12.1	10.7	10.3	21.6
Item 10080 Subject F04 N	2998	1382	1525	2288	303	714	839	917	527	1854	946	1258	585	428	636	25

The next questions are about work.

A08: Different people may look for different things in their work. Below is a list of some of these things. Please read each one, then indicate how important this thing is for you.

A08A: A job where you can see the results of what you do

1. Not important	1.2	2.2	0.4	1.1	1.5	1.1	1.6	1.1	1.0	1.1	1.4	1.0	0.4	0.8	2.1	11.4
2. A little important	5.8	7.1	4.4	6.0	4.1	6.1	6.3	5.5	5.0	5.0	6.6	4.9	5.7	5.4	7.0	16.7
3. Pretty important	35.5	35.8	34.8	37.2	22.8	37.6	38.4	29.1	39.4	35.7	36.0	34.2	34.2	42.7	33.9	49.2
4. Very important	57.5	54.9	60.4	55.7	71.6	55.1	53.7	64.3	54.6	58.1	55.9	59.8	59.7	51.0	57.0	22.8
Item 10090 Subject C04 N	3107	1441	1561	2344	332	738	868	958	543	1897	1000	1313	602	445	648	26

QUESTIONNAIRE FORM 4 1986	TOTAL	SEX		RACE		REGION				4YR COLLEGE PLANS		ILLICIT DRUG USE: LIFETIME				
		M	F	White	Black	NE	NC	S	W	Yes	No	None	Marijuana Only	Few Pills	More Pills	Any Heroin
N (Weighted No. of Cases):	3123	1441	1571	2352	333	744	873	961	545	1904	1002	1314	604	446	654	26
% of Weighted Total:	100.0	46.1	50.3	75.3	10.7	23.8	27.9	30.8	17.4	61.0	32.1	42.1	19.3	14.3	20.9	0.8

A08B: A job that has high status and prestige

1. Not important	7.1	8.4	6.2	8.2	4.1	8.8	7.7	6.5	5.0	6.7	8.6	7.2	6.9	4.7	7.7	27.9
2. A little important	22.8	21.1	24.7	25.3	13.7	23.5	23.0	20.1	26.4	22.7	23.6	24.3	21.4	23.4	21.5	22.6
3. Pretty important	38.6	38.7	38.3	39.4	32.3	35.5	41.6	37.5	39.9	37.5	39.6	38.3	38.7	40.3	39.1	24.3
4. Very important	31.5	31.7	30.9	27.1	49.8	32.1	27.7	35.9	28.7	33.1	28.2	30.2	33.0	31.6	31.7	25.1
Item 10100 Subject C04 N	3098	1434	1560	2338	330	737	865	953	543	1896	994	1308	600	442	648	26

A08C: A job which is interesting to do

1. Not important	0.6	0.8	0.4	0.3	2.4	0.8	0.6	0.5	0.5	0.6	0.6	0.7	0.4	-	0.4	11.6
2. A little important	1.4	1.7	0.9	0.9	3.3	1.6	1.2	1.6	1.1	0.8	1.9	1.3	0.8	1.6	1.2	5.6
3. Pretty important	11.5	12.7	9.9	10.5	14.5	10.9	12.0	10.4	13.6	9.4	15.1	11.9	10.7	10.6	11.0	15.4
4. Very important	86.5	84.8	88.8	88.3	79.9	86.6	86.2	87.5	84.8	89.2	82.3	86.0	88.1	87.8	87.4	67.4
Item 10110 Subject C04 N	3082	1433	1545	2330	326	736	856	951	540	1885	991	1305	597	439	641	26

A08D: A job where the chances for advancement and promotion are good

1. Not important	1.5	1.7	1.3	1.6	1.6	2.5	1.4	0.8	1.4	1.6	1.3	2.2	0.9	0.7	0.4	11.6
2. A little important	6.1	5.1	7.2	6.7	4.0	5.7	5.7	6.0	7.5	6.6	5.9	6.7	4.5	5.5	6.2	14.2
3. Pretty important	25.4	26.2	24.8	27.2	16.9	23.4	29.8	21.7	27.7	27.4	22.8	27.3	26.4	24.5	22.2	2.7
4. Very important	67.0	67.0	66.7	64.5	77.5	68.4	63.1	71.6	63.4	64.4	70.1	63.7	68.3	69.4	71.2	71.5
Item 10120 Subject C04 N	3101	1440	1556	2342	332	736	867	956	542	1894	999	1310	601	445	646	26

A08E: A job that gives you an opportunity to be directly helpful to others

1. Not important	2.8	4.8	1.0	3.0	3.8	3.4	3.1	2.2	2.7	2.2	4.0	2.0	2.3	2.8	3.7	31.2
2. A little important	14.5	21.2	8.5	15.7	11.6	14.4	16.7	12.3	15.2	13.7	15.5	12.6	16.1	14.7	17.1	13.0
3. Pretty important	37.3	42.0	33.0	38.8	27.1	36.0	36.0	38.1	39.9	36.6	39.7	36.8	38.7	39.7	35.2	39.1
4. Very important	45.3	32.0	57.4	42.5	57.5	46.1	44.3	47.5	42.2	47.5	40.9	48.6	42.9	42.8	44.0	16.8
Item 10130 Subject C04,O01 N	3103	1440	1558	2342	331	737	867	956	543	1895	998	1311	602	443	647	26

A08F: A job which provides you with a chance to earn a good deal of money

1. Not important	1.7	1.7	1.7	2.0	2.0	1.9	2.1	1.1	1.8	2.0	1.5	2.1	1.2	1.0	1.4	12.1
2. A little important	7.7	6.1	9.4	8.8	4.2	7.5	8.8	7.9	5.9	9.3	5.5	9.1	7.0	6.7	6.3	10.3
3. Pretty important	32.2	30.3	34.0	34.8	16.7	29.1	34.8	28.1	39.5	34.6	28.6	33.4	31.2	35.1	30.2	29.5
4. Very important	58.4	61.9	54.9	54.4	77.1	61.5	54.3	62.9	52.9	54.1	64.4	55.4	60.6	57.2	62.1	48.2
Item 10140 Subject C04,F01 N	3102	1438	1560	2341	330	733	869	957	542	1894	996	1310	604	443	644	26

A08G: A job where you have the chance to be creative

1. Not important	4.5	6.3	2.9	4.6	5.8	5.5	4.1	4.3	4.1	4.3	5.1	4.3	4.7	4.2	4.1	13.0
2. A little important	22.0	22.3	21.7	22.2	22.1	24.3	20.9	22.2	20.2	20.3	26.0	21.5	24.0	21.1	22.6	13.1
3. Pretty important	35.7	37.1	34.6	35.9	35.3	31.4	37.3	37.7	35.4	36.2	34.4	35.4	34.4	36.4	37.7	30.6
4. Very important	37.8	34.3	40.8	37.4	36.7	38.8	37.6	35.8	40.3	39.3	34.6	38.8	36.9	38.3	35.6	43.3
Item 10150 Subject C04 N	3100	1438	1558	2340	330	739	863	955	543	1890	1000	1308	603	444	646	26

A08H: A job where the skills you learn will not go out of date

1. Not important	4.3	4.5	4.0	3.9	7.0	4.9	4.9	3.3	4.3	4.4	4.2	4.8	3.0	2.8	4.9	9.0
2. A little important	10.4	10.6	10.1	11.3	8.3	11.6	11.3	8.1	11.5	11.7	8.2	11.6	7.7	9.0	11.6	17.7
3. Pretty important	29.8	28.9	30.8	31.8	20.0	30.9	30.3	28.7	29.5	30.4	30.1	28.0	30.6	32.9	30.8	18.5
4. Very important	55.5	55.9	55.0	53.0	64.7	52.7	53.5	59.9	54.7	53.6	57.6	55.6	58.7	55.4	52.7	54.8
Item 10160 Subject C04 N	3104	1437	1562	2342	331	739	867	957	542	1895	998	1311	604	445	645	26

A08I: A job that gives you a chance to make friends

1. Not important	2.3	2.8	1.5	1.4	7.0	3.4	1.7	2.1	2.0	1.9	2.4	2.0	1.9	1.7	2.3	18.1
2. A little important	9.8	11.9	7.7	8.9	15.7	9.0	10.5	9.8	9.5	8.5	11.5	9.7	9.4	8.1	10.2	27.4
3. Pretty important	35.2	39.2	31.4	35.2	31.7	34.4	34.7	35.4	36.6	34.6	36.3	34.9	36.6	33.9	35.9	34.6
4. Very important	52.8	46.2	59.3	54.5	45.6	53.2	53.1	52.6	51.9	55.0	49.8	53.4	52.1	56.3	51.7	19.9
Item 10170 Subject C04,M04 N	3101	1439	1557	2341	330	739	864	957	541	1893	998	1308	604	445	645	26

QUESTIONNAIRE FORM 4 1986	TOTAL	SEX		RACE		REGION				4YR COLLEGE PLANS		ILLICIT DRUG USE: LIFETIME				
		M	F	White	Black	NE	NC	S	W	Yes	No	None	Mari- juana Only	Few Pills	More Pills	Any Her- oin
N (Weighted No. of Cases):	3123	1441	1571	2352	333	744	873	961	545	1904	1002	1314	604	446	654	26
% of Weighted Total:	100.0	46.1	50.3	75.3	10.7	23.8	27.9	30.8	17.4	61.0	32.1	42.1	19.3	14.3	20.9	0.8

A08J: A job which uses your skills and abilities– lets you do the things you can do best

1. Not important	0.6	1.0	0.3	0.4	1.7	1.2	0.4	0.3	1.0	0.6	0.6	0.6	0.2	0.2	1.0	9.0
2. A little important	3.7	4.5	2.8	3.7	3.4	3.8	4.6	3.0	3.3	3.2	4.4	3.3	4.5	3.4	3.3	12.8
3. Pretty important	23.3	25.4	21.5	23.5	24.1	22.3	26.4	21.7	22.3	22.8	23.6	20.8	27.4	24.2	24.5	21.8
4. Very important	72.4	69.1	75.4	72.3	70.8	72.8	68.6	75.0	73.5	73.4	71.5	75.3	67.9	72.3	71.3	56.3
Item 10180 Subject C04 N	3109	1441	1562	2345	332	739	869	958	543	1898	1000	1312	604	445	648	26

A08K: A job that is worthwhile to society

1. Not important	3.9	5.9	2.0	3.5	4.4	6.8	2.5	2.4	4.7	3.1	4.6	3.3	3.2	2.2	5.7	17.4
2. A little important	14.6	17.9	11.5	15.2	14.6	16.8	14.7	14.2	12.3	13.3	17.1	12.7	13.0	17.9	17.2	41.6
3. Pretty important	40.3	41.7	39.3	41.5	32.8	38.4	42.3	39.0	42.0	40.0	40.4	39.7	44.6	39.5	38.3	29.1
4. Very important	41.2	34.5	47.2	39.8	48.2	38.0	40.5	44.4	41.0	43.6	37.9	44.4	39.3	40.3	38.7	11.9
Item 10190 Subject C04,O01 N	3076	1428	1546	2324	325	731	859	944	542	1880	989	1297	599	442	639	26

A08L: A job where you have more than two weeks vacation

1. Not important	17.1	14.8	19.4	16.6	24.7	16.3	17.4	19.6	13.5	17.2	17.8	17.9	15.6	15.3	17.6	32.3
2. A little important	34.7	30.6	38.4	35.4	31.1	35.0	34.0	35.9	33.1	34.9	34.5	34.6	35.8	34.4	34.2	23.0
3. Pretty important	27.6	29.5	26.0	28.5	22.3	25.2	29.5	26.7	29.8	28.3	26.6	28.8	28.1	29.0	24.7	23.8
4. Very important	20.5	25.1	16.1	19.5	21.9	23.5	19.2	17.8	23.5	19.6	21.1	18.7	20.5	21.3	23.6	20.9
Item 10200 Subject C04 N	3102	1438	1559	2341	332	736	866	957	543	1897	996	1310	603	443	648	26

A08M: A job where you get a chance to partic- ipate in decision making

1. Not important	3.0	3.8	2.5	2.8	5.2	3.6	3.7	2.6	1.8	2.1	4.8	3.0	3.6	1.9	2.1	11.3
2. A little important	19.4	18.9	19.6	20.2	14.4	19.0	20.0	19.5	18.8	16.5	25.6	20.0	16.2	18.9	19.9	38.0
3. Pretty important	44.7	46.3	43.2	45.1	39.4	41.6	46.6	43.6	47.6	44.5	43.8	43.5	47.1	48.8	42.6	41.4
4. Very important	32.9	31.0	34.8	32.0	40.9	35.8	29.7	34.3	31.7	36.9	25.8	33.4	33.1	30.4	35.4	9.3
Item 10210 Subject C04 N	3095	1434	1555	2336	330	736	862	956	540	1890	997	1305	602	445	644	26

A08N: A job which leaves a lot of time for other things in your life

1. Not important	2.6	2.5	2.5	1.9	7.4	1.9	2.8	3.2	2.0	2.2	3.1	3.1	1.5	2.6	1.7	9.0
2. A little important	15.5	13.2	17.2	15.6	14.8	16.5	16.7	14.3	14.3	15.6	14.6	15.6	16.3	14.4	15.7	8.6
3. Pretty important	41.1	38.1	43.9	41.9	38.8	41.2	41.0	40.2	42.8	41.8	40.4	43.1	39.2	40.3	39.6	63.0
4. Very important	40.8	46.2	36.4	40.6	39.0	40.3	39.5	42.3	41.0	40.4	41.9	38.2	43.0	42.8	42.9	19.4
Item 10220 Subject C04 N	3100	1438	1557	2338	331	735	869	957	539	1894	996	1310	599	444	647	26

A08O: A job which allows you to establish roots in a community and not have to move from place to place

1. Not important	10.2	11.2	9.5	10.3	11.1	13.5	9.5	8.3	10.0	11.1	8.4	7.9	10.1	10.1	13.6	21.9
2. A little important	19.3	17.7	19.9	19.0	20.5	19.6	22.8	14.8	21.0	21.0	16.4	18.8	20.9	17.6	20.4	8.7
3. Pretty important	32.8	33.4	31.9	33.1	29.9	33.3	34.1	30.2	34.7	32.9	31.6	32.8	32.0	35.5	31.3	48.1
4. Very important	37.8	37.8	38.6	37.6	38.5	33.6	33.6	46.7	34.2	35.0	43.5	40.5	36.9	36.8	34.7	21.2
Item 10230 Subject C04 N	3105	1438	1562	2343	331	737	869	956	543	1895	1000	1312	602	445	646	26

A08P: A job which leaves you mostly free of supervision by others

1. Not important	8.2	7.7	8.4	7.8	14.3	7.6	8.3	9.6	6.5	6.8	10.5	9.5	8.5	4.3	6.7	19.5
2. A little important	25.7	23.9	27.1	26.5	23.6	24.5	25.4	27.2	25.3	25.7	26.1	25.6	25.1	26.1	26.4	37.9
3. Pretty important	39.5	39.2	40.2	39.7	36.4	38.4	41.9	36.8	42.1	40.9	37.0	39.6	40.3	41.8	37.8	22.9
4. Very important	26.6	29.2	24.2	26.0	25.7	29.5	24.3	26.5	26.1	26.6	26.3	25.2	26.1	27.8	29.0	19.8
Item 10240 Subject C04 N	3106	1439	1562	2343	332	737	868	958	543	1895	1000	1312	602	445	647	26

QUESTIONNAIRE FORM 4 1986	TOTAL	SEX		RACE		REGION				4YR COLLEGE PLANS		ILLICIT DRUG USE: LIFETIME				
		M	F	White	Black	NE	NC	S	W	Yes	No	None	Mari-juana Only	Few Pills	More Pills	Any Her-oin
N (Weighted No. of Cases):	3123	1441	1571	2352	333	744	873	961	545	1904	1002	1314	604	446	654	26
% of Weighted Total:	100.0	46.1	50.3	75.3	10.7	23.8	27.9	30.8	17.4	61.0	32.1	42.1	19.3	14.3	20.9	0.8

A08Q: A job that offers a reasonably predictable, secure future

1. Not important	1.3	1.7	0.8	1.2	1.1	1.8	1.9	0.4	1.1	1.4	1.0	1.4	0.7	1.1	1.3	7.2
2. A little important	5.7	6.4	4.7	5.5	6.9	7.2	6.7	3.8	5.6	5.7	5.1	5.1	5.2	4.4	6.9	18.5
3. Pretty important	28.9	29.4	28.7	30.5	18.8	28.9	29.5	25.8	33.2	31.1	25.1	29.5	29.3	27.2	27.5	39.9
4. Very important	64.1	62.5	65.8	62.8	73.2	62.1	61.9	70.1	60.0	61.8	68.8	64.0	64.8	67.3	64.3	34.4
Item 10250 Subject C04 N	3100	1433	1562	2341	332	737	866	955	542	1893	997	1309	602	443	645	26

A08R: A job where you can learn new things, learn new skills

1. Not important	1.5	2.2	0.9	1.6	1.2	2.8	1.6	0.9	0.7	1.4	1.3	1.4	0.7	1.0	1.7	6.9
2. A little important	10.9	14.1	8.1	11.8	7.3	10.2	11.9	10.1	11.9	12.1	8.5	10.8	11.8	10.2	10.7	39.6
3. Pretty important	40.7	40.9	40.9	43.7	28.7	38.4	43.3	39.9	41.0	40.3	42.9	41.5	38.4	40.2	43.5	37.9
4. Very important	46.9	42.7	50.1	42.9	62.7	48.6	43.1	49.2	46.4	46.2	47.3	46.4	49.1	48.6	44.2	15.6
Item 10260 Subject B02,C04 N	3097	1431	1562	2341	330	736	863	955	542	1891	996	1308	602	443	644	26

A08S: A job where you do not have to pretend to be a type of person that you are not

1. Not important	4.8	6.6	3.0	4.3	6.3	5.4	4.8	4.9	3.6	4.0	5.6	4.3	4.9	3.3	5.0	13.3
2. A little important	5.8	8.1	3.5	5.1	6.3	7.1	5.9	3.6	7.7	5.0	6.6	5.1	5.8	4.5	7.0	24.8
3. Pretty important	18.5	24.4	13.2	18.8	17.2	16.6	20.9	18.3	18.0	17.2	20.4	17.3	19.8	19.8	19.4	18.1
4. Very important	70.9	60.9	80.4	71.8	70.2	70.9	68.4	73.2	70.8	73.9	67.4	73.3	69.5	72.3	68.6	43.8
Item 10270 Subject C04 N	3092	1429	1557	2337	329	735	865	952	540	1886	995	1306	601	443	644	26

A08T: A job that most people look up to and respect

1. Not important	4.9	6.4	3.5	5.1	5.8	6.9	4.8	4.1	3.6	4.2	6.1	4.6	3.8	2.8	6.9	24.4
2. A little important	15.5	16.3	15.1	17.0	9.2	17.5	15.1	12.9	18.1	14.8	17.2	15.9	14.5	14.6	16.5	23.4
3. Pretty important	38.0	40.5	35.3	39.3	31.5	31.8	41.6	38.2	40.1	37.8	38.7	38.0	40.3	37.7	37.4	9.9
4. Very important	41.6	36.7	46.2	38.5	53.5	43.8	38.5	44.7	38.2	43.3	38.0	41.5	41.4	44.9	39.2	42.3
Item 10280 Subject C04 N	3090	1428	1557	2333	330	732	863	955	539	1888	993	1307	599	442	642	26

A08U: A job that permits contact with a lot of people

1. Not important	7.1	9.9	4.6	7.4	9.7	7.4	8.5	6.1	6.2	5.9	8.9	6.9	6.7	5.6	7.7	21.0
2. A little important	23.0	27.5	18.8	22.3	25.5	19.0	22.4	25.5	25.0	19.4	29.4	23.9	24.7	19.2	21.9	24.4
3. Pretty important	38.0	40.6	35.8	39.2	32.4	36.4	38.4	39.4	37.0	38.1	37.2	36.7	36.5	43.5	39.2	33.2
4. Very important	31.9	22.0	40.7	31.1	32.4	37.2	30.8	29.0	31.8	36.5	24.5	32.4	32.1	31.7	31.2	21.5
Item 10290 Subject C04,M05 N	3099	1432	1561	2340	332	737	865	955	542	1893	996	1309	601	443	646	25

A08V: A job with an easy pace that lets you work slowly

1. Not important	25.0	25.2	24.7	25.9	24.3	23.7	26.5	23.6	26.9	26.1	23.7	26.1	23.4	22.0	25.6	21.3
2. A little important	38.5	39.3	37.9	38.9	36.6	38.5	38.7	39.0	37.5	39.8	36.9	36.9	39.6	38.0	42.8	27.6
3. Pretty important	26.0	25.5	26.7	26.0	25.2	26.6	26.1	25.8	25.3	24.9	27.3	26.8	27.0	28.9	21.4	40.4
4. Very important	10.5	10.0	10.6	9.2	13.9	11.2	8.7	11.6	10.4	9.3	12.1	10.3	10.1	11.2	10.2	10.7
Item 10300 Subject C04 N	3095	1430	1559	2340	327	737	866	951	541	1892	994	1306	601	441	646	26

A08W: A job where most problems are quite difficult and challenging

1. Not important	16.2	16.6	16.1	16.1	16.9	18.4	14.7	16.6	14.9	13.6	19.7	14.8	16.7	14.1	19.5	24.3
2. A little important	36.4	32.9	40.0	37.6	31.4	35.4	35.5	37.1	38.1	34.1	41.2	35.6	36.9	37.3	38.8	15.8
3. Pretty important	34.2	36.6	31.4	34.3	34.3	31.7	37.5	32.6	34.9	38.2	28.2	35.0	35.4	34.8	30.1	43.2
4. Very important	13.2	13.9	12.5	12.0	17.4	14.5	12.2	13.7	12.1	14.1	10.9	14.5	11.0	13.8	11.7	16.7
Item 10310 Subject C04 N	3095	1429	1561	2337	332	733	866	955	542	1889	996	1305	602	443	645	26

QUESTIONNAIRE FORM 4 1986	TOTAL	SEX		RACE		REGION				4YR COLLEGE PLANS		ILLICIT DRUG USE: LIFETIME				
		M	F	White	Black	NE	NC	S	W	Yes	No	None	Mari-juana Only	Few Pills	More Pills	Any Her-oin
N (Weighted No. of Cases):	3123	1441	1571	2352	333	744	873	961	545	1904	1002	1314	604	446	654	26
% of Weighted Total:	100.0	46.1	50.3	75.3	10.7	23.8	27.9	30.8	17.4	61.0	32.1	42.1	19.3	14.3	20.9	0.8

A09: What kind of work do you think you will be doing when you are 30 years old? Mark the one that comes closest to what you expect to be doing.

	TOTAL	M	F	White	Black	NE	NC	S	W	Yes	No	None	Mari-juana Only	Few Pills	More Pills	Any Her-oin
01. Laborer (car washer, sanitary worker, farm laborer)	0.4	0.7	0.1	0.3	0.6	0.4	0.6	0.1	0.6	0.1	0.8	0.1	-	0.8	0.7	3.4
02. Service worker (cook, waiter, barber, janitor, gas station attendant, practical nurse, beautician)	2.0	0.9	3.0	1.7	4.9	2.7	1.1	3.1	0.3	0.4	5.1	1.8	1.2	2.9	2.3	-
03. Operative or semi-skilled worker (garage worker, taxicab, bus or truck driver, assembly line worker, welder)	1.8	3.6	0.2	2.0	0.6	1.1	2.7	2.1	0.9	0.3	4.3	1.1	1.4	1.3	3.0	11.0
04. Sales clerk in a retail store (shoe salesperson, department store clerk, drug store clerk)	1.1	0.4	1.9	1.1	1.8	0.9	0.6	1.6	1.4	0.4	2.5	1.5	0.8	0.8	0.9	-
05. Clerical or office worker (bank teller, bookkeeper, secretary, typist, postal clerk or carrier, ticket agent)	10.3	1.6	18.0	9.3	13.4	10.5	9.4	12.4	7.6	5.0	20.5	10.7	9.1	10.1	10.6	10.0
06. Protective service (police officer, fireman, detective)	2.3	3.5	1.2	2.3	2.1	2.9	1.7	2.1	2.8	1.9	2.9	1.9	4.2	2.0	1.6	-
07. Military service	4.0	7.0	1.3	3.3	10.1	3.2	3.8	5.8	2.3	2.5	6.4	3.6	4.0	5.4	3.7	-
08. Craftsman or skilled worker (carpenter, electrician, brick layer, mechanic, machinist, tool and die maker, telephone installer)	8.2	16.5	0.4	8.6	6.3	9.0	7.8	8.8	6.5	2.0	19.3	7.5	8.4	6.0	10.8	2.3
09. Farm owner, farm manager	0.7	1.1	0.4	0.8	-	0.8	0.7	0.6	1.0	0.4	1.1	0.8	0.7	0.6	0.7	-
10. Owner of small business (restaurant owner, shop owner)	6.7	8.2	5.3	7.1	5.3	7.1	7.5	5.6	6.6	6.4	7.5	5.0	6.3	8.7	8.6	24.6
11. Sales representative (insurance agent, real estate broker, bond salesman)	1.9	2.7	1.1	1.8	1.2	0.8	2.0	2.1	3.1	2.1	1.6	1.3	1.8	3.5	2.4	3.6
12. Manager or administrator (office manager, sales manager, school administrator, government official)	9.5	9.3	9.7	9.5	11.0	9.8	9.2	9.1	10.1	12.1	4.9	7.5	13.5	11.0	8.7	-
13. Professional without doctoral degree (registered nurse, librarian, engineer, architect, social worker, technician, accountant, actor, artist, musician)	29.6	27.2	31.9	30.2	21.3	28.1	33.2	25.9	32.2	39.1	12.3	31.9	30.4	27.7	25.6	26.2
14. Professional with doctoral degree or equivalent (lawyer, physician, dentist, scientist, college professor)	13.3	11.2	15.4	13.1	14.8	13.4	11.8	12.9	16.2	19.7	1.7	16.6	10.5	11.7	11.2	14.6
15. Full-time homemaker or housewife	1.9	0.1	3.4	1.9	1.8	2.6	1.8	1.7	1.4	0.9	3.0	2.1	0.8	3.2	1.5	2.7
16. Don't know-GO TO Q.A13	6.4	6.2	6.7	7.0	4.8	6.6	6.1	6.0	7.1	6.7	5.8	6.3	6.8	4.2	7.8	1.6
Item 10320 Subject C03 N	2937	1358	1488	2255	298	699	811	910	517	1824	925	1238	589	411	614	24

A10: How likely do you think it is that you will actually get to do this kind of work?

	TOTAL	M	F	White	Black	NE	NC	S	W	Yes	No	None	Mari-juana Only	Few Pills	More Pills	Any Her-oin
1. Not very likely	1.1	1.4	0.8	1.1	1.5	0.7	1.8	0.9	1.2	0.8	1.8	1.4	0.8	1.1	1.1	4.2
2. Somewhat likely	6.6	6.5	6.2	6.0	7.1	9.2	6.4	4.2	7.6	6.4	5.9	5.0	7.4	8.0	7.3	4.9
3. Fairly likely	22.1	25.3	19.7	22.5	19.7	21.9	22.4	22.8	20.6	23.2	20.7	22.5	25.0	18.3	21.6	20.7
4. Very likely	46.4	43.7	48.5	47.0	46.9	38.3	49.2	48.3	49.2	50.1	40.0	45.5	48.4	49.7	44.5	41.0
5. Certain	17.2	14.9	19.7	16.7	19.9	20.3	15.4	16.7	16.9	17.0	17.7	19.0	13.7	16.6	18.0	6.3
6. I already do this kind of work	6.6	8.1	5.1	6.7	4.9	9.6	4.8	7.2	4.4	2.5	13.9	6.6	4.7	6.3	7.5	22.8
Item 10330 Subject C03 N★	2844	1315	1433	2141	306	671	790	890	493	1741	918	1209	557	411	576	26

A11: How certain are you that this kind of work is a good choice for you?

	TOTAL	M	F	White	Black	NE	NC	S	W	Yes	No	None	Mari-juana Only	Few Pills	More Pills	Any Her-oin
1. Not at all certain	2.5	3.0	1.8	2.2	3.8	3.3	1.9	2.0	3.3	2.5	2.0	2.0	3.1	3.1	2.2	9.1
2. Somewhat certain	7.7	7.6	7.5	7.0	9.0	9.0	7.7	6.0	8.9	7.9	7.0	5.9	10.7	8.9	6.7	2.6
3. Fairly certain	30.6	28.8	32.9	32.9	20.7	30.7	34.7	26.7	31.0	33.2	27.3	30.2	33.7	27.6	32.1	18.9
4. Very certain	40.6	42.7	38.6	40.2	45.5	34.9	39.9	46.0	39.9	39.7	42.5	40.8	40.0	44.1	39.6	30.2
5. Completely certain	18.6	17.9	19.2	17.7	21.0	22.1	15.8	19.4	16.8	16.7	21.1	21.0	12.5	16.2	19.4	39.2
Item 10340 Subject C03 N★	2858	1322	1439	2153	307	676	795	891	496	1742	927	1212	558	416	581	26

★=excludes respondents for whom question was inappropriate.

QUESTIONNAIRE FORM 4 1986	TOTAL	SEX		RACE		REGION				4YR COLLEGE PLANS		ILLICIT DRUG USE: LIFETIME				
		M	F	White	Black	NE	NC	S	W	Yes	No	None	Marijuana Only	Few Pills	More Pills	Any Heroin
N (Weighted No. of Cases):	3123	1441	1571	2352	333	744	873	961	545	1904	1002	1314	604	446	654	26
% of Weighted Total:	100.0	46.1	50.3	75.3	10.7	23.8	27.9	30.8	17.4	61.0	32.1	42.1	19.3	14.3	20.9	0.8

A12: How satisfying do you think this kind of work will be for you?

1. Not very satisfying	0.7	0.4	1.0	0.5	0.5	0.3	0.9	0.6	0.8	0.4	1.1	0.8	0.2	1.5	0.3	-
2. Somewhat satisfying	6.7	6.7	6.4	5.7	10.7	8.4	5.4	6.5	6.6	5.7	7.3	7.1	7.3	3.9	6.2	13.9
3. Quite satisfying	23.5	25.7	21.6	24.2	18.8	25.3	26.6	21.7	19.5	21.8	27.0	22.2	24.9	23.8	25.5	14.9
4. Very satisfying	41.6	40.8	42.2	43.0	37.7	37.7	42.9	42.0	44.4	43.2	39.0	42.1	43.5	42.9	38.3	38.7
5. Extremely satisfying	27.5	26.4	28.9	26.5	32.3	28.3	24.1	29.2	28.6	28.9	25.6	27.8	24.1	27.8	29.7	32.6
Item 10350 Subject C03,P02 N★	2859	1323	1438	2152	307	677	794	892	497	1744	925	1212	558	416	584	26

A13: To what extent do you think the things listed below will prevent you from getting the kind of work you would like to have?

A13A: Your religion

1. Not at all	91.1	91.6	91.6	93.0	86.4	90.1	92.0	91.2	91.0	93.0	90.7	91.0	92.4	92.9	91.0	82.4
2. Somewhat	3.8	4.0	3.6	3.4	5.7	4.4	3.4	3.8	3.8	3.3	3.9	3.5	3.8	2.3	5.2	4.5
3. A lot	1.4	1.4	0.7	0.7	3.0	1.5	0.8	2.0	1.1	0.8	1.6	1.4	0.7	1.5	0.5	7.5
8. Don't know	3.7	3.0	4.1	2.9	5.0	4.0	3.8	3.0	4.1	2.9	3.9	4.1	3.1	3.3	3.3	5.6
Item 10360 Subject C03,G N	2998	1389	1510	2277	317	720	840	914	524	1835	966	1266	586	430	620	26

A13B: Your sex

1. Not at all	77.7	89.9	66.8	79.4	68.6	78.0	76.2	76.7	81.5	76.4	82.2	76.8	80.8	75.9	78.3	83.1
2. Somewhat	16.4	6.0	26.3	16.0	19.3	15.5	17.2	17.5	14.6	18.7	10.9	17.1	15.2	18.9	15.5	5.3
3. A lot	3.3	2.4	3.8	2.6	8.1	3.7	4.2	2.9	1.8	2.2	4.9	2.7	2.8	3.7	3.6	11.6
8. Don't know	2.6	1.6	3.1	2.1	4.0	2.8	2.4	2.8	2.2	2.6	2.0	3.3	1.3	1.5	2.7	-
Item 10370 Subject C03,D06 N	3000	1388	1513	2277	318	723	841	912	524	1837	966	1267	587	429	620	26

A13C: Your race

1. Not at all	84.4	85.2	84.9	94.2	42.7	83.3	86.5	82.7	85.7	85.8	85.3	83.0	85.1	86.3	88.6	75.6
2. Somewhat	9.4	8.8	9.1	3.4	33.5	9.5	8.1	10.2	9.8	8.7	8.9	9.5	10.0	9.4	7.0	12.7
3. A lot	3.1	2.4	3.4	1.1	14.3	3.9	2.9	3.9	1.2	2.8	2.7	2.9	2.8	3.0	3.2	3.8
8. Don't know	3.1	3.6	2.5	1.3	9.6	3.4	2.6	3.2	3.3	2.7	3.1	4.6	2.1	1.3	1.3	7.9
Item 10380 Subject C03,N02 N	2993	1388	1508	2274	316	719	841	909	524	1835	964	1264	587	428	620	26

A13D: Your family background

1. Not at all	88.0	88.0	88.8	90.7	81.8	88.3	88.1	88.0	87.3	89.9	86.9	88.3	90.7	83.4	89.5	82.2
2. Somewhat	7.3	7.7	7.0	6.5	9.1	5.9	7.3	7.5	8.7	6.7	7.3	7.1	5.4	11.1	6.8	13.0
3. A lot	1.8	1.5	1.5	0.9	4.4	2.8	1.6	1.4	1.2	1.2	2.4	1.8	1.1	1.9	1.7	4.8
8. Don't know	2.9	2.8	2.8	1.9	4.7	2.9	2.9	3.1	2.8	2.3	3.3	2.8	2.8	3.5	2.0	-
Item 10390 Subject C03 N	2998	1389	1511	2276	317	721	841	911	525	1837	965	1266	587	428	620	26

A13E: Your political views

1. Not at all	83.7	85.1	83.5	87.2	71.9	82.4	86.3	83.3	81.7	83.7	85.0	83.9	85.0	81.1	86.2	91.9
2. Somewhat	8.5	7.7	8.8	7.3	12.4	9.9	7.3	8.6	8.6	9.5	6.3	7.4	9.7	10.4	7.8	8.1
3. A lot	1.5	2.0	0.8	1.1	2.6	2.3	0.9	1.1	2.1	1.3	1.6	1.5	0.9	1.0	1.8	-
8. Don't know	6.3	5.3	6.8	4.4	13.0	5.5	5.5	7.0	7.6	5.5	7.0	7.2	4.4	7.6	4.1	-
Item 10400 Subject C03,H01 N	2992	1388	1506	2271	318	716	842	910	524	1836	962	1262	586	429	618	26

A13F: Your education

1. Not at all	46.5	44.8	48.6	46.7	48.9	48.9	41.7	50.1	44.7	50.5	40.1	47.4	49.7	45.1	43.7	57.0
2. Somewhat	26.8	28.5	24.7	26.9	24.0	26.0	31.8	21.9	28.4	23.8	33.0	24.2	26.8	29.3	31.0	22.1
3. A lot	23.1	23.4	22.8	23.2	23.1	22.4	23.2	23.6	22.7	22.3	23.3	24.5	19.3	23.6	22.4	20.9
8. Don't know	3.7	3.3	3.8	3.1	4.0	2.7	3.4	4.4	4.3	3.4	3.6	3.9	4.2	1.9	2.9	-
Item 10410 Subject B09,C03 N	3008	1395	1515	2282	319	722	845	915	526	1839	973	1267	590	433	623	26

A13G: Lack of vocational training

1. Not at all	55.0	56.7	54.2	56.5	51.4	58.0	50.9	59.1	50.5	59.1	48.9	55.9	56.7	52.5	54.1	64.5
2. Somewhat	24.7	26.3	23.0	24.5	24.5	23.8	30.4	19.7	25.6	23.0	27.3	23.2	25.0	29.3	25.7	20.4
3. A lot	12.4	10.3	14.1	11.5	14.3	11.2	10.8	13.8	14.0	9.5	17.3	12.5	11.4	10.8	13.6	10.9
8. Don't know	7.9	6.7	8.7	7.4	9.8	7.0	7.9	7.4	9.9	8.4	6.6	8.4	6.9	7.8	6.7	4.3
Item 10420 Subject C03 N	2986	1386	1501	2266	314	716	839	909	522	1826	963	1261	585	427	616	26

★=excludes respondents for whom question was inappropriate.

QUESTIONNAIRE FORM 4 1986	TOTAL	SEX		RACE		REGION				4YR COLLEGE PLANS		ILLICIT DRUG USE: LIFETIME				
		M	F	White	Black	NE	NC	S	W	Yes	No	None	Mari-juana Only	Few Pills	More Pills	Any Her-oin
N (Weighted No. of Cases):	3123	1441	1571	2352	333	744	873	961	545	1904	1002	1314	604	446	654	26
% of Weighted Total:	100.0	46.1	50.3	75.3	10.7	23.8	27.9	30.8	17.4	61.0	32.1	42.1	19.3	14.3	20.9	0.8

A13H: Lack of ability

	TOTAL	M	F	White	Black	NE	NC	S	W	Yes	No	None	Mari-juana Only	Few Pills	More Pills	Any Her-oin
1. Not at all	58.7	61.0	56.9	58.7	63.3	58.8	55.6	62.1	57.8	60.3	57.5	57.4	61.6	61.2	58.0	72.2
2. Somewhat	16.4	16.1	16.8	16.6	14.0	18.7	18.0	14.0	15.2	15.4	17.2	15.4	15.8	16.4	19.4	8.5
3. A lot	20.9	19.6	21.9	21.3	19.7	19.0	22.5	20.4	22.1	20.5	22.0	22.8	18.7	19.0	19.8	15.0
8. Don't know	3.9	3.3	4.3	3.4	3.0	3.5	3.9	3.5	4.9	3.8	3.3	4.3	3.9	3.4	2.8	4.3
Item 10430　Subject C03　N	2990	1389	1505	2271	316	718	838	911	523	1830	965	1262	587	429	617	26

A13I: Not knowing the right people

	TOTAL	M	F	White	Black	NE	NC	S	W	Yes	No	None	Mari-juana Only	Few Pills	More Pills	Any Her-oin
1. Not at all	44.7	43.5	45.9	45.4	48.7	44.8	41.0	49.0	43.0	40.6	52.9	44.3	45.0	44.2	46.6	47.1
2. Somewhat	38.9	39.4	38.8	39.7	31.5	37.1	44.1	34.8	40.4	43.0	32.1	40.1	40.0	40.9	34.5	36.0
3. A lot	10.1	11.3	8.8	9.4	12.4	12.7	8.6	9.5	9.8	10.1	9.6	8.7	10.2	8.7	13.8	9.5
8. Don't know	6.3	5.8	6.6	5.5	7.3	5.4	6.3	6.7	6.8	6.3	5.4	6.9	4.7	6.2	5.0	7.4
Item 10440　Subject C03　N	2998	1390	1509	2274	319	723	840	912	523	1834	966	1271	586	429	618	26

A13J: Not wanting to work hard

	TOTAL	M	F	White	Black	NE	NC	S	W	Yes	No	None	Mari-juana Only	Few Pills	More Pills	Any Her-oin
1. Not at all	61.0	61.7	60.3	60.9	63.3	58.7	59.0	64.0	61.9	61.4	60.4	61.1	62.9	59.3	61.8	63.5
2. Somewhat	10.7	10.1	11.3	11.1	8.4	11.4	12.3	9.6	9.0	11.0	9.5	9.6	10.8	12.9	9.7	11.2
3. A lot	25.9	25.7	26.2	26.0	25.6	26.2	27.0	24.7	25.9	25.4	27.3	26.7	24.1	25.4	26.3	25.4
8. Don't know	2.4	2.6	2.2	1.9	2.7	3.7	1.8	1.6	3.2	2.2	2.9	2.6	2.2	2.4	2.2	-
Item 10450　Subject C03　N	2994	1387	1508	2274	317	720	840	912	523	1833	965	1262	586	429	621	26

A13K: Not wanting to conform

	TOTAL	M	F	White	Black	NE	NC	S	W	Yes	No	None	Mari-juana Only	Few Pills	More Pills	Any Her-oin
1. Not at all	52.1	50.3	53.7	51.5	54.7	52.4	47.6	55.1	53.7	50.6	55.3	53.3	53.3	50.6	50.1	72.8
2. Somewhat	22.3	24.4	20.4	23.4	17.1	21.6	24.0	21.0	22.8	24.2	18.7	21.6	21.5	22.5	24.5	21.7
3. A lot	14.9	14.5	15.3	15.4	13.7	14.1	16.6	14.8	13.5	16.0	13.5	14.6	13.3	16.2	16.6	-
8. Don't know	10.7	10.7	10.6	9.8	14.5	11.9	11.8	9.0	10.1	9.2	12.5	10.5	11.9	10.8	8.8	5.5
Item 10460　Subject C03,Q08　N	2978	1383	1497	2263	313	713	838	908	519	1826	960	1257	584	427	613	26

A14: If you were to get enough money to live as comfortably as you'd like for the rest of your life, would you want to work?

	TOTAL	M	F	White	Black	NE	NC	S	W	Yes	No	None	Mari-juana Only	Few Pills	More Pills	Any Her-oin
1. I would want to work	79.6	75.9	83.0	78.6	84.1	78.5	79.2	80.5	80.0	81.8	75.7	83.3	80.7	80.3	72.1	40.4
2. I would not want to work	20.4	24.1	17.0	21.4	15.9	21.5	20.8	19.5	20.0	18.2	24.3	16.7	19.3	19.7	27.9	59.6
Item 8100　Subject C06　N	3082	1429	1552	2332	327	724	866	952	540	1888	988	1305	601	439	641	26

A15: How much do you agree or disagree with each statement below?

A15A: One sees so few good or happy marriages that one questions it as a way of life

	TOTAL	M	F	White	Black	NE	NC	S	W	Yes	No	None	Mari-juana Only	Few Pills	More Pills	Any Her-oin
1. Disagree	26.7	27.6	26.2	29.2	19.6	24.1	26.0	28.8	27.6	29.0	23.7	30.8	26.7	20.8	23.2	38.2
2. Mostly disagree	19.0	17.6	20.5	20.2	13.0	18.0	20.7	16.5	21.8	21.5	15.5	19.2	16.2	22.7	19.0	15.6
3. Neither	20.7	24.2	17.2	20.5	15.8	20.9	21.4	17.8	24.5	19.6	22.5	19.1	22.1	22.6	20.7	28.1
4. Mostly agree	20.8	19.5	22.4	20.1	26.8	23.3	19.7	21.9	17.5	19.6	21.6	18.7	24.0	21.8	22.1	-
5. Agree	12.8	11.0	13.8	10.0	24.9	13.7	12.1	15.1	8.7	10.3	16.6	12.2	10.9	12.2	15.0	18.1
Item 10470　Subject D03　N	3080	1429	1550	2332	327	730	864	949	537	1887	992	1304	600	444	640	26

A15B: It is usually a good idea for a couple to live together before getting married in order to find out whether they really get along

	TOTAL	M	F	White	Black	NE	NC	S	W	Yes	No	None	Mari-juana Only	Few Pills	More Pills	Any Her-oin
1. Disagree	24.6	18.1	31.0	24.4	26.1	18.3	22.1	30.9	26.0	26.9	21.4	35.0	17.8	19.7	12.9	39.0
2. Mostly disagree	13.7	12.0	15.6	14.2	12.7	11.7	15.8	14.6	11.4	15.3	12.1	15.6	12.9	13.7	10.7	5.3
3. Neither	14.7	14.6	14.9	15.2	11.1	15.3	16.6	12.1	15.3	15.3	13.2	14.0	14.1	17.7	14.7	5.8
4. Mostly agree	22.6	26.3	18.2	22.8	17.2	25.1	20.7	21.8	23.6	20.5	26.2	17.7	25.8	24.6	27.2	37.8
5. Agree	24.4	29.0	20.3	23.4	32.8	29.5	24.7	20.5	23.7	22.1	27.1	17.6	29.4	24.4	34.5	12.1
Item 10480　Subject D03　N	3101	1438	1561	2343	332	738	869	953	541	1897	999	1312	603	444	647	26

QUESTIONNAIRE FORM 4 1986	TOTAL	SEX		RACE		REGION				4YR COLLEGE PLANS		ILLICIT DRUG USE: LIFETIME				
		M	F	White	Black	NE	NC	S	W	Yes	No	None	Mari-juana Only	Few Pills	More Pills	Any Her-oin
N (Weighted No. of Cases):	3123	1441	1571	2352	333	744	873	961	545	1904	1002	1314	604	446	654	26
% of Weighted Total:	100.0	46.1	50.3	75.3	10.7	23.8	27.9	30.8	17.4	61.0	32.1	42.1	19.3	14.3	20.9	0.8

A15C: Having a close intimate relationship with only one partner is too restrictive for the average person

1. Disagree	41.2	35.0	47.2	42.3	42.0	40.6	39.9	43.5	39.9	41.2	42.8	45.9	41.1	35.5	37.0	22.3
2. Mostly disagree	23.1	23.8	22.6	24.7	16.8	23.7	26.3	20.6	21.6	25.2	20.2	21.4	24.6	27.8	22.0	35.5
3. Neither	14.2	15.9	12.2	13.8	9.7	14.7	14.1	13.2	15.6	13.7	14.3	13.3	14.0	13.8	15.8	25.5
4. Mostly agree	13.9	16.1	12.3	13.3	16.2	12.3	13.0	14.6	16.4	13.1	14.4	12.5	13.6	17.2	15.2	8.8
5. Agree	7.5	9.2	5.7	5.9	15.3	8.6	6.6	8.0	6.6	6.8	8.3	6.9	6.6	5.7	9.9	7.9
Item 10490 Subject D03 N	3090	1437	1556	2336	331	733	867	950	541	1892	996	1307	603	441	646	26

A15D: Having a job takes away from a woman's relationship with her husband

1. Disagree	47.7	36.1	58.3	47.3	61.0	47.5	46.8	50.3	44.8	50.2	43.9	48.4	50.4	43.9	46.7	42.5
2. Mostly disagree	27.3	28.5	26.4	28.5	20.8	28.2	28.1	24.4	29.7	27.5	26.6	25.3	30.6	26.7	28.5	28.3
3. Neither	13.4	19.1	7.9	13.5	7.2	12.2	14.7	12.1	15.2	12.5	14.2	14.8	7.9	16.9	12.1	26.6
4. Mostly agree	7.7	10.4	5.1	7.4	6.2	7.9	7.7	7.7	7.4	6.7	10.3	7.4	7.8	7.6	8.8	-
5. Agree	4.0	5.9	2.3	3.3	4.8	4.2	2.8	5.4	2.9	3.0	5.0	4.1	3.3	4.8	3.8	2.5
Item 10500 Subject D05 N	3094	1435	1559	2341	332	736	864	953	541	1896	996	1310	602	444	645	26

A15E: Having a job gives a wife more of a chance to develop herself as a person

1. Disagree	3.5	4.7	2.2	3.0	7.1	4.1	3.2	3.8	2.7	2.5	5.0	4.2	2.3	1.8	3.6	15.1
2. Mostly disagree	2.4	2.9	1.7	2.2	3.0	2.8	2.7	1.7	2.9	2.0	2.5	2.1	1.4	2.5	3.6	-
3. Neither	9.4	14.1	5.1	9.6	5.5	8.2	10.0	10.0	9.0	7.4	13.3	8.7	9.0	11.8	8.4	25.3
4. Mostly agree	30.2	37.8	23.2	30.9	20.9	28.4	31.1	27.5	35.8	31.1	28.6	30.2	30.9	30.4	29.0	34.0
5. Agree	54.5	40.5	67.8	54.3	63.5	56.5	53.0	57.1	49.7	57.0	50.5	54.8	56.4	53.5	55.4	25.7
Item 10510 Subject D05 N	3097	1437	1561	2343	330	736	866	953	541	1896	999	1311	602	444	647	26

A15F: Being a father and raising children is one of the most fulfilling experiences a man can have

1. Disagree	4.5	6.4	2.7	4.3	4.6	6.2	3.7	3.9	4.7	3.3	6.4	3.2	4.9	3.9	6.5	20.1
2. Mostly disagree	4.5	5.0	4.0	4.3	4.3	6.7	3.2	3.0	6.0	3.8	5.4	4.6	4.5	3.5	4.7	6.5
3. Neither	18.9	17.4	20.6	20.3	11.5	20.1	21.9	14.3	20.6	19.0	18.6	16.9	19.6	18.8	22.5	10.7
4. Mostly agree	32.7	32.8	32.5	34.5	26.4	30.1	34.7	32.7	33.1	33.3	32.6	33.7	33.3	36.1	28.5	27.1
5. Agree	39.4	38.4	40.1	36.6	53.3	36.9	36.4	46.1	35.7	40.6	37.1	41.7	37.7	37.7	37.8	35.7
Item 10520 Subject D05 N	3083	1433	1552	2333	329	733	862	949	538	1888	997	1303	601	441	645	26

A15G: Most mothers should spend more time with their children than they do now

1. Disagree	5.5	5.1	5.8	5.3	7.8	7.2	6.0	4.6	4.0	5.6	5.5	4.7	6.0	4.3	6.3	17.2
2. Mostly disagree	10.5	11.0	10.3	11.5	6.3	12.0	11.8	8.0	10.8	11.6	9.5	9.8	11.1	10.3	12.4	7.5
3. Neither	28.9	33.6	24.9	31.5	16.4	31.5	31.9	22.8	31.3	30.8	26.4	26.2	29.4	29.4	34.1	35.1
4. Mostly agree	30.7	28.2	33.0	30.8	28.6	27.9	29.6	32.7	32.7	30.3	31.1	31.2	31.0	32.6	27.1	31.0
5. Agree	24.4	22.2	26.1	20.9	40.8	21.5	20.7	31.9	21.2	21.7	27.5	28.1	22.5	23.4	20.1	9.2
Item 10530 Subject D05 N	3091	1435	1559	2339	330	734	867	951	540	1893	998	1309	603	444	644	26

A15H: If a wife works, her husband should take a greater part in housework and child-care

1. Disagree	5.4	7.3	3.4	4.6	7.6	7.4	5.6	3.8	5.5	3.9	7.8	5.8	3.0	3.4	7.3	27.8
2. Mostly disagree	5.9	7.1	4.6	5.5	6.1	6.3	5.8	4.8	7.4	4.6	8.1	5.4	6.7	5.1	6.6	6.8
3. Neither	14.6	15.3	13.7	15.1	8.3	15.9	14.0	12.7	17.1	15.7	15.7	13.4	14.7	15.9	15.5	19.9
4. Mostly agree	34.4	36.9	32.3	35.4	30.1	31.5	37.9	33.7	34.2	34.8	35.0	34.8	32.9	37.4	33.6	31.1
5. Agree	39.6	33.4	46.0	39.4	47.8	38.8	36.8	45.0	35.9	41.0	36.6	40.6	42.7	38.3	37.1	14.3
Item 10540 Subject D05 N	3088	1432	1558	2337	329	734	866	948	540	1893	995	1308	602	441	646	26

QUESTIONNAIRE FORM 4 1986	TOTAL	SEX		RACE		REGION				4YR COLLEGE PLANS		ILLICIT DRUG USE: LIFETIME				
		M	F	White	Black	NE	NC	S	W	Yes	No	None	Marijuana Only	Few Pills	More Pills	Any Heroin
N (Weighted No. of Cases):	3123	1441	1571	2352	333	744	873	961	545	1904	1002	1314	604	446	654	26
% of Weighted Total:	100.0	46.1	50.3	75.3	10.7	23.8	27.9	30.8	17.4	61.0	32.1	42.1	19.3	14.3	20.9	0.8

A16: How much TV do you estimate you watch on an average weekday?

1. None	3.5	4.0	3.0	3.9	1.4	4.5	4.5	2.2	2.7	4.2	2.3	3.5	3.3	2.8	4.2	9.2
2. Half-hour or less	12.2	10.9	13.5	13.5	6.6	13.8	12.4	9.0	15.5	13.2	10.5	11.3	12.4	13.9	12.5	23.8
3. About one hour	20.3	21.4	19.4	22.6	8.8	19.9	22.5	17.3	22.4	22.4	16.1	19.3	20.7	24.1	20.4	3.6
4. About two hours	22.2	22.8	22.0	23.7	14.5	19.3	24.3	21.5	24.2	23.8	19.8	21.7	20.4	21.4	26.5	7.5
5. About three hours	17.8	17.3	18.3	17.3	16.9	19.3	13.9	19.8	18.5	17.2	19.3	18.0	20.4	13.8	16.8	29.9
6. About four hours	11.9	12.3	11.3	10.8	17.0	11.6	11.6	13.8	9.5	9.7	16.3	11.7	11.6	13.7	10.7	17.3
7. Five hours or more	12.1	11.3	12.4	8.1	34.8	11.6	10.8	16.5	7.2	9.6	15.6	14.4	11.1	10.3	8.9	8.6
Item 10550 Subject C07 N	3083	1427	1560	2338	329	737	863	946	538	1891	993	1306	600	443	646	26

A17: In the past year, how many books have you read just because you wanted to–that is, without their being assigned?

1. None	20.6	26.8	15.2	20.3	20.4	20.3	19.8	22.7	18.7	17.1	27.4	18.1	22.6	20.6	23.1	35.0
2. One	14.7	15.3	13.7	14.2	14.4	14.9	16.3	12.6	15.5	13.5	15.8	14.2	15.0	16.0	14.5	6.8
3. Two to five	37.0	35.8	38.3	36.6	42.4	38.9	34.6	38.4	35.9	38.6	34.0	38.2	36.1	36.5	36.5	15.3
4. Six to ten	11.4	10.3	12.5	11.5	9.2	11.3	12.6	9.8	12.2	12.8	9.3	10.8	12.6	13.6	10.5	7.0
5. Ten or more	16.3	11.8	20.3	17.4	13.6	14.6	16.7	16.4	17.7	18.0	13.5	18.7	13.6	13.3	15.5	35.8
Item 10560 Subject C07 N	3094	1433	1564	2342	331	733	867	949	544	1897	996	1313	601	444	650	23

A18: Some people think about what's going on in government very often, and others are not that interested. How much of an interest do you take in government and current events?

1. No interest at all	3.9	4.1	3.5	3.6	4.0	5.5	3.1	3.3	4.0	2.7	6.2	3.3	4.2	2.7	5.0	13.1
2. Very little interest	16.7	11.9	21.2	16.0	21.1	19.9	19.0	14.5	12.8	13.5	22.2	18.5	16.1	16.2	13.6	19.9
3. Some interest	44.9	42.2	47.3	45.3	42.5	41.3	46.1	44.9	47.9	44.9	45.1	44.2	44.4	45.8	47.1	29.7
4. A lot of interest	24.3	27.7	21.3	24.6	22.9	22.5	22.8	25.8	26.3	27.1	19.5	25.5	23.8	23.5	22.9	29.2
5. A very great interest	10.2	14.1	6.7	10.5	9.5	10.9	9.0	11.5	9.0	11.9	7.0	8.6	11.5	11.8	11.4	8.1
Item 6330 Subject H01,Q08 N	3090	1432	1563	2340	331	732	867	948	542	1896	995	1311	603	443	648	23

A19: Some people think that there ought to be changes in the amount of influence and power that certain organizations have in our society. Do you think the following organizations should have more influence, less influence, or about the same amount of influence as they have now?

How much influence should there be for...

A19A: Large corporations?

1. Much less	4.5	6.2	2.9	4.3	5.7	5.6	4.8	3.7	3.7	4.9	3.7	4.2	5.7	2.7	4.1	19.3
2. Less	25.9	28.0	24.2	28.4	15.4	24.6	26.9	24.2	28.9	28.5	21.4	27.2	24.9	26.8	24.2	31.8
3. Same as now	39.5	37.7	40.9	40.8	28.8	39.9	39.6	37.9	41.5	41.6	36.3	37.2	41.5	42.0	41.3	30.8
4. More	11.0	11.8	10.3	9.5	20.4	8.8	13.0	12.7	7.8	8.2	16.1	11.0	9.8	12.4	11.1	9.3
5. Much more	3.7	4.8	2.6	2.4	11.9	3.6	3.1	5.7	1.4	2.6	5.3	4.2	3.0	3.7	3.1	2.4
8. No opinion	15.5	11.4	19.1	14.7	17.8	17.5	12.7	15.8	16.7	14.2	17.2	16.2	15.2	12.4	16.3	6.3
Item 10570 Subject K03 N	3071	1430	1548	2327	329	724	864	945	539	1882	993	1299	601	442	643	26

A19B: Major labor unions?

1. Much less	7.5	12.4	3.2	8.5	2.9	5.4	9.1	7.9	6.8	8.6	6.1	7.9	8.1	7.0	5.7	20.2
2. Less	18.2	21.6	15.4	20.9	6.9	12.6	20.2	19.3	20.5	20.1	15.4	19.0	15.9	19.8	18.7	8.5
3. Same as now	31.0	30.5	31.4	33.1	19.4	33.1	31.3	29.5	30.1	30.5	33.0	30.0	31.8	31.4	31.5	48.9
4. More	20.4	17.7	22.6	17.7	31.3	24.6	18.7	18.7	20.4	19.6	20.3	19.2	21.2	19.6	22.1	18.3
5. Much more	7.2	7.2	7.0	4.4	22.9	7.8	6.5	8.4	5.3	5.5	10.6	8.2	6.6	7.1	5.3	2.4
8. No opinion	15.8	10.6	20.4	15.4	16.5	16.5	14.1	16.2	16.9	15.9	14.6	15.5	16.4	15.1	16.8	1.7
Item 10580 Subject K03 N	3066	1428	1545	2329	327	721	863	946	535	1881	989	1296	600	440	642	26

QUESTIONNAIRE FORM 4 1986	TOTAL	SEX		RACE		REGION				4YR COLLEGE PLANS		ILLICIT DRUG USE: LIFETIME				
		M	F	White	Black	NE	NC	S	W	Yes	No	None	Mari-juana Only	Few Pills	More Pills	Any Her-oin
N (Weighted No. of Cases):	3123	1441	1571	2352	333	744	873	961	545	1904	1002	1314	604	446	654	26
% of Weighted Total:	100.0	46.1	50.3	75.3	10.7	23.8	27.9	30.8	17.4	61.0	32.1	42.1	19.3	14.3	20.9	0.8

A19C: Churches and religious organizations?

1. Much less	8.5	11.9	5.7	9.9	2.4	11.2	9.6	4.7	9.8	9.0	8.6	6.8	7.8	9.5	12.1	16.3
2. Less	10.5	11.5	9.7	11.4	4.6	12.1	9.6	8.4	13.7	11.6	8.7	9.8	10.5	9.7	12.9	16.9
3. Same as now	33.2	30.7	35.5	35.4	20.0	37.8	36.5	26.9	32.5	32.9	33.9	31.2	36.0	34.4	34.3	28.6
4. More	22.2	22.5	21.9	21.7	26.1	16.4	24.0	26.9	18.9	22.8	21.4	23.5	21.0	23.7	19.1	32.1
5. Much more	15.8	12.8	18.3	12.4	38.4	10.9	11.1	25.8	12.4	14.0	17.7	19.2	14.4	14.9	10.6	2.0
8. No opinion	9.8	10.6	9.0	9.1	8.6	11.6	9.3	7.2	12.7	9.7	9.7	9.4	10.3	7.9	11.0	4.1
Item 10590 Subject G,K03 N	3075	1431	1553	2331	329	727	864	947	538	1887	993	1301	603	443	643	26

A19D: The national news media (TV, magazines, news services)?

1. Much less	8.0	9.5	6.6	8.5	7.3	6.6	10.0	8.2	6.7	8.5	7.4	7.4	7.2	9.3	9.3	18.7
2. Less	22.8	23.5	22.7	25.6	11.2	23.5	22.3	21.8	24.2	26.3	18.3	23.4	25.6	21.9	20.4	13.7
3. Same as now	43.2	42.4	43.9	43.4	41.2	41.6	44.4	42.8	44.3	43.7	42.0	44.8	44.7	39.0	42.4	37.1
4. More	12.6	11.7	13.2	11.2	16.5	13.1	11.8	12.7	12.8	10.7	15.5	11.1	11.6	15.0	13.9	9.2
5. Much more	5.4	5.5	5.3	4.1	12.3	5.2	4.5	7.5	3.3	4.1	7.4	5.9	4.5	7.9	3.6	13.1
8. No opinion	8.0	7.5	8.4	7.2	11.4	10.0	7.0	7.0	8.7	6.6	9.3	7.5	6.3	7.0	10.4	8.2
Item 10600 Subject K03 N	3069	1428	1547	2325	329	722	862	946	538	1882	990	1295	602	443	641	26

A19E: The Presidency and the administration?

1. Much less	3.1	3.8	2.4	2.5	6.7	3.5	3.9	2.7	1.9	2.1	4.6	3.0	2.6	2.8	3.0	11.4
2. Less	9.8	8.0	11.3	9.6	14.4	10.5	10.8	8.5	9.7	10.0	9.2	9.2	10.5	8.4	11.0	19.4
3. Same as now	42.9	45.0	41.6	44.6	35.5	43.8	44.1	40.4	44.2	45.9	38.4	43.5	43.9	43.8	42.1	34.7
4. More	22.4	24.0	21.0	24.2	13.4	18.9	22.6	24.1	24.1	23.6	21.5	22.0	24.3	23.1	21.4	5.4
5. Much more	11.0	11.5	10.6	9.9	15.8	8.2	9.5	15.9	8.5	8.7	14.5	11.2	8.9	12.6	11.7	8.8
8. No opinion	10.8	7.8	13.1	9.2	14.0	15.1	9.2	8.5	11.7	9.6	11.8	11.2	9.9	9.3	11.0	20.3
Item 10610 Subject H04,K03 N	3077	1430	1554	2331	330	727	864	947	538	1887	993	1302	602	443	643	26

A19F: The Congress–that is, the U.S. Senate and House of Representatives?

1. Much less	2.3	3.1	1.6	2.0	4.8	2.1	2.8	2.6	1.4	1.6	3.8	2.1	1.4	2.0	2.7	13.7
2. Less	8.5	9.7	7.3	8.4	9.1	8.1	8.0	9.6	7.9	8.1	8.9	8.9	8.0	8.4	8.2	7.8
3. Same as now	44.2	46.5	42.8	46.9	32.3	42.9	46.7	41.8	46.4	46.7	40.8	44.9	44.9	45.8	42.1	39.1
4. More	23.2	22.2	24.1	23.8	19.5	24.2	23.1	23.5	21.5	24.8	21.0	23.4	24.7	21.6	23.4	14.3
5. Much more	8.7	9.1	8.4	7.4	16.9	6.1	7.3	12.1	8.5	7.2	11.0	8.1	7.7	9.8	10.0	20.2
8. No opinion	13.0	9.5	15.8	11.6	17.4	16.6	12.1	10.4	14.3	11.6	14.5	12.7	13.3	12.5	13.7	4.9
Item 10620 Subject H04,K03 N	3077	1430	1554	2332	330	726	863	949	539	1889	993	1302	602	443	643	26

A19G: The U.S. Supreme Court?

1. Much less	1.8	2.6	1.2	1.5	3.1	2.0	2.2	1.6	1.5	1.5	2.5	2.0	1.1	1.4	1.9	11.4
2. Less	5.3	5.0	5.3	5.0	5.5	5.0	4.7	6.2	5.1	4.4	6.9	4.7	4.4	6.9	5.7	16.9
3. Same as now	45.1	47.1	43.7	46.9	36.0	43.0	49.6	42.8	44.5	47.4	40.9	45.4	46.7	43.1	44.4	36.9
4. More	25.0	25.4	24.9	25.9	20.0	24.3	23.8	26.3	25.5	26.8	23.0	25.6	25.6	26.7	23.1	23.9
5. Much more	10.3	11.2	9.2	8.8	20.1	9.8	7.8	13.3	9.4	8.5	12.9	9.8	9.7	10.1	12.1	-
8. No opinion	12.5	8.7	15.7	11.8	15.3	15.9	11.9	9.7	14.0	11.3	13.7	12.5	12.5	11.8	12.9	10.9
Item 10630 Subject H04,K03 N	3068	1424	1553	2330	327	725	862	943	538	1885	990	1299	601	442	639	26

A19H: All the courts and the justice system in general?

1. Much less	1.7	1.7	1.4	1.1	3.3	1.7	2.1	1.8	0.9	1.3	2.2	1.6	0.7	0.7	1.8	15.4
2. Less	6.1	7.7	4.7	6.3	4.5	6.7	5.9	5.6	6.6	4.9	7.6	4.9	5.8	7.5	7.6	8.2
3. Same as now	43.4	44.4	42.9	44.7	39.5	39.2	47.8	43.1	42.7	45.3	41.8	43.7	44.7	43.2	41.6	60.1
4. More	27.1	26.4	27.8	27.7	22.1	26.9	24.4	28.8	28.8	29.0	24.6	28.4	27.0	28.1	24.8	9.5
5. Much more	10.1	11.3	9.1	9.1	17.1	10.1	8.0	12.6	9.1	9.4	10.8	9.7	10.8	9.2	11.4	-
8. No opinion	11.6	8.5	14.2	11.1	13.5	15.5	11.8	8.2	12.0	10.2	13.1	11.5	11.0	11.3	12.8	6.9
Item 10640 Subject H04,K03 N	3073	1429	1551	2330	329	726	864	945	538	1885	992	1301	601	443	641	26

QUESTIONNAIRE FORM 4 1986	TOTAL	SEX		RACE		REGION				4YR COLLEGE PLANS		ILLICIT DRUG USE: LIFETIME				
		M	F	White	Black	NE	NC	S	W	Yes	No	None	Mari-juana Only	Few Pills	More Pills	Any Her-oin
N (Weighted No. of Cases):	3123	1441	1571	2352	333	744	873	961	545	1904	1002	1314	604	446	654	26
% of Weighted Total:	100.0	46.1	50.3	75.3	10.7	23.8	27.9	30.8	17.4	61.0	32.1	42.1	19.3	14.3	20.9	0.8

A19I: The police and other law enforcement agencies?

1. Much less	3.3	5.2	1.6	2.9	5.3	4.2	4.8	2.2	1.9	2.4	4.5	2.6	2.3	1.9	5.4	20.1
2. Less	7.1	9.0	5.4	7.0	7.5	7.5	7.2	6.2	8.3	6.7	7.6	4.3	8.4	9.6	33.6
3. Same as now	32.1	34.7	30.1	33.7	24.9	31.2	36.1	28.6	33.2	33.3	30.7	30.1	34.4	32.1	34.8	30.9
4. More	31.6	28.0	34.6	33.2	21.3	28.4	31.5	32.7	34.0	34.0	28.6	37.0	27.3	29.5	27.4	10.5
5. Much more	18.8	17.2	20.7	16.9	33.1	20.3	13.6	25.3	13.9	17.0	21.6	19.4	21.5	19.7	14.9	-
8. No opinion	7.0	5.9	7.6	6.3	8.0	8.3	6.9	5.1	8.7	6.6	7.0	6.5	6.0	8.0	7.9	4.9
Item 10650 Subject K03 N	3074	1429	1553	2329	330	725	864	947	538	1887	991	1301	603	442	642	26

A19J: The U.S. military?

1. Much less	4.2	5.0	3.2	4.0	4.9	6.0	4.4	2.5	4.5	4.0	4.2	3.1	4.5	2.9	6.0	33.7
2. Less	8.1	8.6	7.7	8.9	4.6	7.8	8.1	6.6	11.2	8.8	7.3	10.1	6.1	8.6	6.1	9.7
3. Same as now	39.5	39.5	40.1	40.9	30.9	37.3	42.5	36.8	42.4	43.4	34.0	41.8	39.8	37.7	38.1	14.3
4. More	21.6	21.8	21.3	22.0	17.1	23.6	20.0	22.3	20.1	20.6	24.0	18.8	24.4	22.9	23.5	27.0
5. Much more	15.7	18.0	13.5	14.0	29.8	13.8	14.4	21.9	9.4	12.7	19.9	15.1	14.2	17.0	16.3	10.3
8. No opinion	10.9	7.1	14.1	10.2	12.7	11.5	10.5	9.9	12.4	10.4	10.6	11.1	11.1	10.9	9.9	4.9
Item 10660 Subject K03,L04 N	3072	1430	1549	2327	330	724	864	947	536	1883	992	1302	599	442	642	26

The next questions ask your views about drugs.

A20: Do you think that people (who are 18 or older) should be prohibited by law from doing each of the following?

A20A: Smoking marijuana (pot, grass) in private

1. No	39.8	40.5	39.1	39.3	41.5	46.3	39.8	35.1	39.2	37.5	43.6	21.2	47.6	43.4	66.8	73.4
2. Not sure	16.4	14.7	17.8	16.0	16.4	16.3	16.1	16.2	17.4	16.7	15.6	16.2	19.4	19.0	12.4	6.6
3. Yes	43.8	44.7	43.1	44.7	42.0	37.4	44.1	48.7	43.4	45.9	40.7	62.6	32.9	37.6	20.9	19.9
Item 10780 Subject A13a N	3084	1433	1555	2338	327	731	867	945	541	1889	998	1305	602	443	645	26

A20B: Smoking marijuana in public places

1. No	13.6	17.3	9.8	11.4	20.2	14.3	13.5	13.6	13.0	10.3	18.7	9.6	14.4	11.8	18.9	51.7
2. Not sure	7.5	8.4	6.5	7.9	5.7	7.4	9.5	6.3	6.6	6.6	8.3	3.5	7.5	8.8	14.5	17.4
3. Yes	78.9	74.4	83.7	80.7	74.1	78.3	77.1	80.1	80.4	83.1	73.1	86.9	78.1	79.4	66.6	30.9
Item 10790 Subject A13a N	3084	1434	1555	2339	326	731	868	944	541	1887	998	1306	601	443	645	26

A20C: Taking LSD in private

1. No	21.0	23.0	18.3	18.2	32.1	23.7	20.9	19.8	19.3	17.7	25.3	17.2	17.8	18.4	30.8	53.9
2. Not sure	10.0	9.3	10.6	8.3	13.4	9.7	8.8	10.8	11.1	8.7	11.8	8.3	8.8	12.3	12.9	3.2
3. Yes	69.0	67.8	71.1	73.5	54.5	66.6	70.3	69.4	69.6	73.6	62.9	74.6	73.4	69.3	56.4	42.9
Item 10800 Subject A13a N	3084	1433	1555	2339	326	731	868	944	541	1889	996	1305	603	443	644	26

A20D: Taking LSD in public places

1. No	12.1	14.9	8.7	9.6	20.1	12.5	11.9	11.8	12.3	9.1	15.8	10.2	12.0	10.5	14.3	46.0
2. Not sure	3.1	3.4	2.8	2.8	2.4	2.5	4.4	3.0	1.9	1.9	4.8	2.3	2.3	2.2	4.8	19.4
3. Yes	84.9	81.8	88.5	87.7	77.6	85.1	83.7	85.2	85.9	89.0	79.4	87.5	85.7	87.3	80.9	34.6
Item 10810 Subject A13a N	3078	1433	1550	2332	325	728	868	940	541	1884	995	1303	603	442	642	26

A20E: Taking amphetamines (uppers) or barbiturates (downers) in private

1. No	27.4	28.5	26.1	26.6	31.5	30.4	27.1	26.5	25.7	24.3	33.0	19.1	22.9	26.3	47.1	64.4
2. Not sure	15.8	14.4	16.8	14.5	18.2	15.7	15.2	15.1	18.0	15.4	15.9	13.7	16.5	20.1	16.7	9.2
3. Yes	56.8	57.1	57.2	58.9	50.2	53.9	57.7	58.4	56.3	60.3	51.0	67.3	60.5	53.6	36.2	26.4
Item 10820 Subject A13a N	3081	1431	1556	2335	328	731	868	944	538	1885	998	1305	603	443	643	26

QUESTIONNAIRE FORM 4 1986	TOTAL	SEX		RACE		REGION				4YR COLLEGE PLANS		ILLICIT DRUG USE: LIFETIME				
		M	F	White	Black	NE	NC	S	W	Yes	No	None	Mari-juana Only	Few Pills	More Pills	Any Her-oin
N (Weighted No. of Cases):	3123	1441	1571	2352	333	744	873	961	545	1904	1002	1314	604	446	654	26
% of Weighted Total:	100.0	46.1	50.3	75.3	10.7	23.8	27.9	30.8	17.4	61.0	32.1	42.1	19.3	14.3	20.9	0.8
A20F: Taking amphetamines or barbiturates in public places																
1. No	13.9	17.0	10.5	12.1	19.7	14.4	14.1	13.9	13.0	11.0	17.8	10.6	13.1	13.6	19.1	42.1
2. Not sure	7.0	7.9	6.2	6.9	6.0	7.7	7.7	6.1	6.4	5.6	8.7	4.1	6.6	7.8	11.9	22.2
3. Yes	79.1	75.1	83.3	81.1	74.3	77.9	78.1	80.0	80.6	83.4	73.5	85.3	80.3	78.5	69.0	35.7
Item 10830 Subject A13a N	*3078*	*1431*	*1554*	*2337*	*325*	*730*	*866*	*941*	*540*	*1885*	*996*	*1305*	*602*	*442*	*644*	*26*
A20G: Taking heroin (smack, horse) in private																
1. No	19.5	21.3	17.1	17.0	29.9	21.7	19.2	18.9	17.8	16.3	23.4	16.6	18.2	17.9	24.6	55.0
2. Not sure	8.8	7.1	10.1	7.3	10.4	9.4	8.4	8.0	10.2	7.3	11.1	7.6	8.8	10.1	10.4	3.2
3. Yes	71.7	71.5	72.8	75.6	59.7	68.9	72.3	73.1	72.1	76.4	65.5	75.8	73.0	72.0	65.0	41.8
Item 10840 Subject A13a N	*3081*	*1434*	*1553*	*2337*	*327*	*730*	*867*	*944*	*540*	*1886*	*997*	*1304*	*602*	*443*	*645*	*26*
A20H: Taking heroin in public places																
1. No	11.9	14.8	8.5	9.5	18.9	11.9	12.0	11.5	12.3	8.5	16.1	10.3	11.3	10.4	13.7	45.5
2. Not sure	3.1	3.5	2.9	2.7	3.4	3.1	3.9	3.1	1.8	1.9	5.0	2.0	3.4	2.2	4.7	20.5
3. Yes	85.0	81.7	88.6	87.8	77.7	85.0	84.1	85.4	85.9	89.6	78.9	87.7	85.3	87.4	81.5	34.1
Item 10850 Subject A13a N	*3078*	*1430*	*1554*	*2333*	*327*	*731*	*865*	*944*	*538*	*1884*	*997*	*1305*	*602*	*441*	*643*	*26*
A20I: Getting drunk in private																
1. No	67.4	70.2	65.6	70.3	57.3	69.3	70.2	65.8	62.9	67.2	68.3	55.5	73.9	75.0	81.3	74.3
2. Not sure	14.1	11.5	16.1	12.8	16.6	14.1	13.8	13.7	15.3	15.7	10.8	20.2	11.6	9.6	8.0	2.1
3. Yes	18.5	18.3	18.3	16.9	26.1	16.6	16.1	20.4	21.8	17.1	20.8	24.3	14.4	15.4	10.6	23.6
Item 10860 Subject A13a N	*3074*	*1434*	*1546*	*2328*	*326*	*728*	*861*	*945*	*540*	*1882*	*993*	*1301*	*599*	*442*	*645*	*26*
A20J: Getting drunk in public places																
1. No	26.1	29.9	22.3	27.1	23.5	29.7	29.6	21.9	22.9	23.8	30.2	17.4	29.3	28.9	36.1	58.2
2. Not sure	21.7	23.0	21.0	23.4	11.8	17.8	27.8	19.9	·20.8	21.8	21.4	18.0	26.2	21.8	25.5	20.0
3. Yes	52.2	47.1	56.7	49.5	64.7	52.5	42.6	58.3	56.4	54.4	48.4	64.6	44.4	49.2	38.5	21.8
Item 10870 Subject A13a N	*3087*	*1436*	*1556*	*2338*	*328*	*731*	*868*	*947*	*540*	*1888*	*999*	*1309*	*603*	*442*	*645*	*26*
A20K: Smoking tobacco in certain specified public places																
1. No	38.5	38.8	38.2	40.4	35.6	38.9	41.0	39.6	32.4	35.8	43.8	28.4	43.2	44.0	49.5	60.7
2. Not sure	16.3	15.5	17.0	15.7	19.9	15.5	16.0	17.5	16.2	15.8	16.7	18.6	14.8	16.4	12.9	2.3
3. Yes	45.1	45.7	44.8	43.9	44.5	45.6	43.0	43.0	51.5	48.4	39.5	52.9	42.0	39.6	37.6	37.0
Item 10760 Subject A13a N	*3085*	*1432*	*1558*	*2338*	*328*	*730*	*867*	*947*	*541*	*1889*	*998*	*1308*	*602*	*442*	*645*	*26*
A21: In particular, there has been a great deal of public debate about whether marijuana use should be legal. Which of the following policies would you favor?																
1. Using marijuana should be entirely legal	14.9	18.0	12.0	15.3	13.9	16.4	15.0	14.2	13.7	12.7	18.3	5.3	18.0	16.5	29.2	31.9
2. It should be a minor violation –like a parking ticket– but not a crime	25.9	23.6	27.8	25.7	25.2	29.5	27.1	19.7	29.9	26.7	24.2	14.5	32.5	30.0	38.6	43.9
3. It should be a crime	42.5	42.7	42.6	42.9	40.0	34.8	41.7	49.3	42.5	44.8	40.4	64.8	29.2	34.1	18.7	7.0
4. Don't know	16.7	15.7	17.6	16.1	20.9	19.4	16.2	16.7	13.9	15.8	17.0	15.4	20.3	19.4	13.5	17.2
Item 10880 Subject A13b N	*3081*	*1432*	*1556*	*2338*	*328*	*728*	*864*	*947*	*541*	*1892*	*993*	*1309*	*601*	*442*	*644*	*26*
A22: If it were legal for people to USE marijuana, should it also be legal to SELL marijuana?																
1. No	33.0	31.8	34.0	33.3	31.8	33.1	33.3	33.0	32.3	34.2	31.9	44.5	24.6	32.3	19.5	19.1
2. Yes, but only to adults	42.2	45.1	39.8	43.5	40.0	44.6	43.5	39.3	42.2	42.9	41.9	31.1	50.7	44.9	55.7	64.1
3. Yes, to anyone	10.4	10.1	10.7	9.0	13.8	8.0	10.4	11.8	10.8	8.7	12.2	9.7	9.4	6.6	13.3	16.8
4. Don't know	14.4	12.9	15.6	14.2	14.5	14.3	12.8	15.9	14.6	14.3	14.0	14.7	15.2	16.2	11.6	-
Item 10890 Subject A13b N	*3074*	*1430*	*1554*	*2333*	*328*	*725*	*863*	*945*	*541*	*1887*	*995*	*1305*	*599*	*442*	*645*	*26*

QUESTIONNAIRE FORM 4 1986	TOTAL	SEX M	SEX F	RACE White	RACE Black	REGION NE	REGION NC	REGION S	REGION W	4YR COLLEGE PLANS Yes	4YR COLLEGE PLANS No	None	Mari-juana Only	Few Pills	More Pills	Any Her-oin
N (Weighted No. of Cases):	3123	1441	1571	2352	333	744	873	961	545	1904	1002	1314	604	446	654	26
% of Weighted Total:	100.0	46.1	50.3	75.3	10.7	23.8	27.9	30.8	17.4	61.0	32.1	42.1	19.3	14.3	20.9	0.8

A23: If marijuana were legal to use and legally available, which of the following would you be most likely to do?

	TOTAL	M	F	White	Black	NE	NC	S	W	Yes	No	None	Mari-juana Only	Few Pills	More Pills	Any Her-oin
1. Not use it, even if it were legal and available	62.4	59.0	65.6	61.8	68.9	58.5	57.8	69.4	62.8	63.9	61.3	90.2	49.9	51.0	28.6	14.6
2. Try it	7.6	7.1	8.0	7.6	8.1	7.7	10.1	6.6	5.4	8.1	7.5	5.5	11.3	9.5	6.1	24.1
3. Use it about as often as I do now	16.8	19.7	14.3	18.7	7.1	18.7	20.5	11.6	17.7	16.8	16.5	0.4	22.1	22.5	41.9	23.8
4. Use it more often than I do now	5.0	5.8	4.4	5.2	4.4	6.6	5.2	3.8	4.7	4.2	6.2	0.2	5.4	6.2	12.5	28.5
5. Use it less than I do now	2.0	2.1	1.7	1.2	2.4	2.3	1.3	1.9	2.8	1.7	2.0	0.1	1.0	2.8	6.0	-
6. Don't know	6.1	6.2	6.0	5.4	9.2	6.3	5.2	6.7	6.4	5.4	6.5	3.6	10.2	8.0	5.0	9.0
Item 10900 Subject A13b N	3079	1434	1558	2341	328	728	863	946	542	1893	994	1309	603	440	646	26

This section asks for your views and feelings about a number of different things.

D01: How satisfied are you with your life as a whole these days?

	TOTAL	M	F	White	Black	NE	NC	S	W	Yes	No	None	Mari-juana Only	Few Pills	More Pills	Any Her-oin
1. Completely dissatisfied	2.9	2.5	3.0	2.4	5.6	4.2	2.6	3.2	1.3	1.6	5.8	3.0	2.6	2.1	2.9	6.4
2. Quite dissatisfied	9.3	8.9	9.8	9.3	9.2	8.4	9.1	10.3	9.1	10.0	7.7	10.7	7.5	7.1	10.0	7.1
3. Somewhat dissatisfied	9.9	9.4	10.3	10.0	7.3	10.3	8.8	9.3	11.9	9.1	11.4	7.4	10.2	14.0	11.4	2.6
4. Neither, or mixed feelings	15.2	15.6	14.8	14.5	14.1	15.4	13.9	15.3	16.7	12.9	19.5	13.1	14.5	16.1	19.6	20.4
5. Somewhat satisfied	24.7	25.2	24.2	25.2	27.0	22.2	28.9	24.9	21.1	25.6	22.3	23.3	28.0	25.1	26.0	10.5
6. Quite satisfied	32.8	32.4	33.3	33.5	30.3	33.8	32.7	30.4	35.7	36.4	26.6	36.4	31.8	33.9	25.9	20.7
7. Completely satisfied	5.3	6.0	4.7	5.0	6.4	5.7	4.2	6.6	4.2	4.5	6.7	6.1	5.4	1.8	4.2	32.3
Item 6840 Subject P01,Q01 N	2947	1358	1528	2286	290	673	844	903	527	1873	965	1254	582	421	623	23

D02: FOR THOSE WHO HAVE A JOB: All things considered, how satisfied are you with your present job?

	TOTAL	M	F	White	Black	NE	NC	S	W	Yes	No	None	Mari-juana Only	Few Pills	More Pills	Any Her-oin
1. Completely dissatisfied	4.0	4.2	3.5	3.3	9.8	4.8	3.4	3.8	4.3	3.5	5.0	4.0	3.5	3.8	3.4	14.2
2. Quite dissatisfied	9.2	9.1	9.5	9.4	7.2	9.0	9.3	9.5	9.0	8.9	9.5	8.8	9.0	8.5	11.2	4.0
3. Somewhat dissatisfied	13.3	13.4	13.0	13.7	14.2	12.7	12.6	14.0	13.9	13.3	13.0	11.1	17.2	14.2	13.7	6.9
4. Neither, or mixed feelings	15.4	15.5	15.3	14.6	9.8	16.1	17.0	13.3	15.2	16.0	13.7	14.0	16.1	14.6	17.5	17.6
5. Somewhat satisfied	29.3	26.7	32.0	30.2	29.0	31.8	26.4	29.3	30.9	29.5	29.8	30.1	28.3	28.8	29.7	20.9
6. Quite satisfied	22.8	24.7	21.4	22.6	23.7	21.3	25.0	21.8	22.6	23.4	21.7	25.6	20.7	24.6	18.6	29.5
7. Completely satisfied	6.0	6.4	5.3	6.2	6.4	4.2	6.3	8.3	4.1	5.4	7.4	6.4	5.3	5.5	5.9	7.0
Item 10910 Subject C01,P02 N★	1936	928	963	1560	136	452	585	540	359	1195	661	765	390	279	455	21

D03A: Which best describes your recent employment experience?

	TOTAL	M	F	White	Black	NE	NC	S	W	Yes	No	None	Mari-juana Only	Few Pills	More Pills	Any Her-oin
1. I have a paid job now.	63.7	64.9	62.7	65.6	49.7	66.6	65.3	60.4	62.7	61.4	66.9	59.2	67.8	65.8	67.5	62.7
2. No paid job now, but I had one during the past 3 months.	10.7	11.8	9.5	10.2	12.9	9.0	11.1	10.0	13.6	11.1	9.6	10.0	10.7	12.8	10.2	19.8
3. No paid job in the past 3 months –GO TO Q.D10	18.2	18.5	17.9	18.2	20.4	18.2	17.8	19.0	17.2	19.4	16.8	20.4	16.1	14.3	18.0	15.5
4. Never had a paid job–GO TO Q.D10	7.4	4.8	9.9	6.0	17.0	6.2	5.7	10.6	6.5	8.0	6.6	10.3	5.4	7.0	4.2	2.0
Item 21530 Subject C01 N	2671	1234	1379	2101	242	615	776	790	490	1700	871	1141	520	384	568	22

The next questions are about your present or most recent paid job. (If you presently hold more than one paid job, answer for the more important one.)

D03B: On the average, how many hours per week do (did) you work on this particular job?

	TOTAL	M	F	White	Black	NE	NC	S	W	Yes	No	None	Mari-juana Only	Few Pills	More Pills	Any Her-oin
1. 5 or less hours	8.5	8.5	8.0	8.1	13.0	7.9	8.8	8.7	8.5	8.6	8.5	11.3	6.4	4.7	6.6	30.4
2. 6 to 10 hours	10.4	8.6	12.4	9.4	15.9	9.4	9.6	10.9	11.9	11.9	8.4	13.5	9.9	8.4	6.4	25.0
3. 11 to 15 hours	15.1	12.7	17.9	16.0	10.9	12.9	16.1	14.6	17.0	16.9	12.6	15.6	16.7	13.6	15.0	-
4. 16 to 20 hours	22.2	20.5	24.5	23.3	22.0	26.0	21.7	18.2	24.3	23.1	20.7	20.0	25.7	25.5	21.7	3.3
5. 21 to 25 hours	19.9	20.8	18.7	20.9	13.1	18.1	21.0	21.8	17.7	19.2	19.8	17.5	18.7	20.7	25.2	8.1
6. 26 to 30 hours	10.9	11.4	10.4	10.0	11.6	9.0	11.1	12.6	10.6	10.1	12.6	10.4	10.0	11.6	11.4	31.3
7. 31 to 35 hours	5.2	6.8	3.6	5.3	5.7	6.7	5.3	4.3	4.3	4.0	6.6	4.7	4.7	6.6	5.2	2.0
8. 36 or more hours	7.8	10.7	4.6	7.1	7.8	9.5	6.5	8.9	5.6	6.1	10.9	7.1	7.7	8.9	8.5	-
Item 21540 Subject C01 N★	2123	1021	1054	1694	164	508	626	602	387	1326	710	843	442	316	472	21

★=excludes respondents for whom question was inappropriate.

QUESTIONNAIRE FORM 4 1986	TOTAL	SEX		RACE		REGION				4YR COLLEGE PLANS		ILLICIT DRUG USE: LIFETIME				
		M	F	White	Black	NE	NC	S	W	Yes	No	None	Mari-juana Only	Few Pills	More Pills	Any Her-oin
N (Weighted No. of Cases):	3123	1441	1571	2352	333	744	873	961	545	1904	1002	1314	604	446	654	26
% of Weighted Total:	100.0	46.1	50.3	75.3	10.7	23.8	27.9	30.8	17.4	61.0	32.1	42.1	19.3	14.3	20.9	0.8

D04: About how old is (was) your supervisor?

	TOTAL	M	F	White	Black	NE	NC	S	W	Yes	No	None	Mari-juana Only	Few Pills	More Pills	Any Her-oin
1. Age 20 or younger	1.9	2.2	1.5	1.7	4.0	1.5	2.5	1.6	2.0	1.5	2.6	1.5	1.4	2.6	2.0	12.2
2. 21 to 25	17.0	16.0	18.2	16.8	16.1	17.2	19.5	12.8	19.5	18.6	14.8	14.2	16.7	17.9	21.8	12.0
3. 26 to 30	24.2	23.2	24.9	24.0	26.3	21.4	26.7	24.2	24.2	24.6	24.1	24.2	24.4	24.4	23.0	47.8
4. 31 or older	56.8	58.6	55.4	57.5	53.6	60.0	51.3	61.3	54.4	55.3	58.5	60.1	57.5	55.0	53.2	27.9
Item 21550 Subject C01,M02 N★	2123	1016	1059	1691	161	512	622	609	381	1319	714	848	436	315	473	23

D05: How many of the other workers are within 2 or 3 years of your own age?

	TOTAL	M	F	White	Black	NE	NC	S	W	Yes	No	None	Mari-juana Only	Few Pills	More Pills	Any Her-oin
1. None	19.7	20.7	18.7	19.4	16.0	17.0	18.2	22.1	22.0	18.2	22.5	23.6	14.8	18.3	17.6	25.5
2. A few	27.8	26.8	28.8	26.6	30.6	30.7	25.4	27.6	28.0	26.2	31.2	25.7	31.7	28.8	27.9	14.5
3. About half	17.1	18.0	15.9	17.4	18.1	17.2	18.2	16.3	16.2	17.5	15.1	16.9	17.0	14.9	19.1	15.4
4. Most	14.6	14.5	14.6	14.7	15.9	16.6	13.2	14.9	13.5	15.0	14.0	14.0	13.0	14.7	16.4	25.7
5. Nearly all	15.3	14.3	16.6	15.8	13.4	14.7	18.3	12.5	15.4	17.5	12.1	14.5	16.4	18.4	14.0	4.9
6. All	5.6	5.8	5.3	6.1	6.1	3.7	6.6	6.5	5.0	5.6	5.2	5.3	7.1	4.9	5.0	14.0
Item 21560 Subject C01 N★	2114	1013	1054	1686	159	505	625	605	379	1310	716	843	437	312	472	22

D06: To what extent does (did) this job . . .

D06A: Use your skills and abilities–let you do the things you do best?

	TOTAL	M	F	White	Black	NE	NC	S	W	Yes	No	None	Mari-juana Only	Few Pills	More Pills	Any Her-oin
1. Not at all	20.8	24.6	16.9	20.1	24.8	21.2	20.1	21.9	19.9	21.3	18.7	19.4	22.3	22.4	19.9	51.4
2. A little	32.9	32.3	34.1	33.7	30.1	30.7	36.7	31.8	31.4	35.8	28.5	33.9	35.4	28.4	33.9	2.5
3. Some extent	24.4	21.7	26.6	25.0	18.7	25.1	23.2	23.0	27.6	24.5	23.9	22.3	24.9	27.4	25.7	7.9
4. Considerable extent	13.3	14.3	12.7	13.4	13.6	12.3	13.6	13.6	13.6	12.1	16.2	14.3	11.1	14.5	12.1	29.5
5. A great extent	8.6	7.2	9.8	7.7	12.8	10.7	6.5	9.8	7.5	6.3	12.7	10.2	6.3	7.4	8.3	8.7
Item 21570 Subject C01 N★	2118	1010	1059	1686	161	502	627	608	382	1319	711	850	432	316	471	22

D06B: Teach you new skills that will be useful in your future work?

	TOTAL	M	F	White	Black	NE	NC	S	W	Yes	No	None	Mari-juana Only	Few Pills	More Pills	Any Her-oin
1. Not at all	25.0	30.1	20.1	25.0	23.2	27.3	25.4	25.1	21.3	26.3	21.8	23.9	22.5	26.2	27.4	48.6
2. A little	25.7	24.7	26.9	25.6	27.4	23.2	26.6	25.4	27.7	27.5	23.1	25.9	28.9	22.7	25.0	23.6
3. Some extent	22.3	18.5	25.8	23.5	14.6	20.6	23.1	21.2	25.1	22.3	23.1	22.5	22.4	21.0	22.9	13.0
4. Considerable extent	15.2	14.9	15.4	15.2	15.7	16.8	15.9	13.9	13.7	14.1	17.0	13.5	17.0	18.8	14.8	5.2
5. A great extent	11.8	11.8	11.8	10.8	19.1	12.1	9.0	14.4	12.2	9.8	15.0	14.2	9.2	11.5	9.8	9.6
Item 21580 Subject C01 N★	2111	1005	1058	1684	156	498	626	605	381	1316	707	846	430	316	471	22

D06C: Make good use of special skills you learned in technical, vocational, business, or professional studies?

	TOTAL	M	F	White	Black	NE	NC	S	W	Yes	No	None	Mari-juana Only	Few Pills	More Pills	Any Her-oin
1. Not at all	55.3	57.3	53.9	58.2	42.2	56.0	57.8	53.9	52.9	60.4	46.8	53.1	61.4	49.6	57.8	71.5
2. A little	16.3	14.4	18.1	15.3	16.3	12.7	16.9	16.6	19.2	16.4	16.6	17.8	15.8	17.7	13.2	20.2
3. Some extent	13.5	14.3	12.4	12.6	15.7	13.4	14.6	12.9	13.0	11.9	16.1	13.6	12.5	14.8	13.8	1.6
4. Considerable extent	8.4	8.2	8.6	7.8	16.8	9.5	6.7	8.7	9.0	7.3	10.3	7.2	6.2	11.0	10.8	-
5. A great extent	6.5	5.8	7.0	6.1	9.1	8.4	4.0	7.9	5.8	3.9	10.2	8.3	4.1	6.9	4.4	6.8
Item 21590 Subject C01 N★	2104	1003	1053	1679	158	496	623	605	380	1311	706	840	429	316	471	22

D06D: Let you get to know people with social backgrounds very different from yours?

	TOTAL	M	F	White	Black	NE	NC	S	W	Yes	No	None	Mari-juana Only	Few Pills	More Pills	Any Her-oin
1. Not at all	18.1	20.8	15.6	17.8	19.8	17.3	21.0	16.3	17.2	18.1	17.2	19.9	19.8	10.6	18.0	30.7
2. A little	22.8	22.3	23.2	23.9	16.0	21.6	20.2	25.4	24.3	22.2	22.8	23.1	21.4	24.3	22.9	19.1
3. Some extent	22.2	22.1	22.6	21.3	26.4	23.8	22.4	20.3	22.7	22.9	21.4	20.2	23.5	23.2	24.0	20.0
4. Considerable extent	20.5	20.5	20.5	20.6	22.8	20.2	19.5	22.5	19.2	20.7	21.0	19.6	19.7	28.1	17.7	17.7
5. A great extent	16.5	14.3	18.1	16.5	14.9	17.1	16.9	15.5	16.7	16.0	17.6	17.2	15.5	13.8	17.4	12.6
Item 21600 Subject C01,M05 N★	2098	1000	1051	1675	156	493	623	601	381	1313	699	839	427	315	469	22

D06E: Let you get to know people over age 30?

	TOTAL	M	F	White	Black	NE	NC	S	W	Yes	No	None	Mari-juana Only	Few Pills	More Pills	Any Her-oin
1. Not at all	11.3	12.2	10.2	10.1	19.0	9.3	12.6	10.3	13.3	11.4	11.1	12.0	10.2	6.4	12.7	40.5
2. A little	17.9	18.6	16.9	18.6	17.2	17.7	18.1	18.3	17.0	17.7	18.3	20.1	16.5	14.7	18.2	-
3. Some extent	21.8	24.5	19.5	21.5	18.2	21.6	22.3	20.6	22.8	22.0	21.7	20.2	22.4	25.2	21.1	33.9
4. Considerable extent	23.1	23.3	23.1	23.4	21.4	22.5	22.1	24.3	23.4	23.2	21.7	22.0	26.3	24.7	21.4	13.0
5. A great extent	26.0	21.5	30.3	26.4	24.1	28.9	24.9	26.5	23.5	25.8	27.1	25.7	24.6	29.0	26.5	12.6
Item 21610 Subject C01,M02 N★	2093	999	1046	1674	156	493	623	596	381	1309	699	838	427	310	470	22

★=excludes respondents for whom question was inappropriate.

QUESTIONNAIRE FORM 4 1986	TOTAL	SEX		RACE		REGION				4YR COLLEGE PLANS		ILLICIT DRUG USE: LIFETIME				
		M	F	White	Black	NE	NC	S	W	Yes	No	None	Marijuana Only	Few Pills	More Pills	Any Heroin
N (Weighted No. of Cases):	3123	1441	1571	2352	333	744	873	961	545	1904	1002	1314	604	446	654	26
% of Weighted Total:	100.0	46.1	50.3	75.3	10.7	23.8	27.9	30.8	17.4	61.0	32.1	42.1	19.3	14.3	20.9	0.8

D06F: Cause you stress and tension?

1. Not at all	26.8	30.2	23.7	26.9	27.8	30.8	25.9	26.4	23.7	27.1	26.4	30.8	26.3	18.9	25.1	26.2
2. A little	29.8	29.0	29.9	30.4	23.9	25.6	29.1	28.9	37.6	30.7	28.1	30.2	28.5	30.6	29.8	34.7
3. Some extent	21.2	20.3	22.6	21.1	22.4	19.8	23.7	21.5	18.3	21.4	20.7	19.3	21.6	25.0	21.4	18.3
4. Considerable extent	12.2	11.5	12.5	11.9	13.2	12.4	13.3	11.7	10.6	12.0	12.9	11.3	13.0	16.3	10.7	9.6
5. A great extent	10.1	9.0	11.4	9.8	12.8	11.4	8.1	11.4	9.9	8.8	11.8	8.4	10.6	9.3	12.9	11.1
Item 21620　Subject C01　N★	2096	999	1049	1674	155	493	622	600	381	1310	700	837	427	314	470	22

D06G: Interfere with your education?

1. Not at all	48.8	47.2	50.1	50.2	44.1	54.8	45.5	48.5	47.0	48.6	50.3	53.6	49.7	38.7	46.3	43.2
2. A little	24.9	26.7	23.5	24.9	22.2	23.3	28.4	23.1	24.3	25.7	22.8	22.6	24.3	27.6	28.3	27.7
3. Some extent	15.2	15.3	15.4	15.2	19.7	12.0	16.5	15.4	16.9	15.3	15.2	14.6	14.0	21.3	12.8	23.4
4. Considerable extent	6.6	6.7	6.1	5.6	9.1	5.7	6.0	8.7	5.6	6.4	6.9	5.1	6.6	10.3	7.1	5.7
5. A great extent	4.5	4.1	4.9	4.0	4.9	4.2	3.7	4.3	6.2	3.9	4.9	4.2	5.4	2.2	5.5	-
Item 21630　Subject C01　N★	2092	997	1047	1670	153	489	622	601	380	1307	698	834	427	314	469	22

D06H: Interfere with your social life?

1. Not at all	24.8	24.4	24.8	23.2	35.4	25.4	21.1	28.9	23.5	22.6	29.2	28.6	23.4	18.5	22.5	39.5
2. A little	30.6	29.4	31.7	31.9	19.3	32.3	30.7	27.9	32.4	32.0	28.1	29.5	30.0	34.3	30.9	27.6
3. Some extent	21.3	21.9	20.8	21.7	22.4	20.0	23.8	19.9	21.0	22.6	19.0	19.7	23.7	25.5	20.0	4.1
4. Considerable extent	13.3	14.9	11.8	13.7	12.0	13.3	14.7	12.3	12.2	13.4	13.1	12.1	13.7	13.2	14.7	28.8
5. A great extent	10.1	9.3	10.8	9.5	10.9	9.0	9.7	10.9	10.9	9.4	10.6	10.1	9.1	8.6	11.9	-
Item 21640　Subject C01　N★	2089	996	1046	1669	153	490	620	599	381	1307	697	835	427	311	469	22

D06I: Interfere with your family life?

1. Not at all	46.8	45.5	47.6	46.4	56.0	50.4	44.9	48.2	42.9	46.7	47.7	46.2	50.4	35.7	52.1	48.1
2. A little	26.0	26.9	25.4	27.0	17.2	23.7	27.8	25.7	26.8	26.5	25.1	26.9	23.1	32.5	23.2	28.1
3. Some extent	15.8	17.2	14.8	15.6	14.1	13.6	17.8	14.7	17.5	16.5	14.7	16.3	14.1	20.1	13.3	13.1
4. Considerable extent	6.6	6.2	6.8	6.5	7.5	7.5	5.4	6.3	7.8	6.8	5.5	5.5	8.5	7.5	6.0	10.7
5. A great extent	4.8	4.2	5.4	4.5	5.2	4.7	4.2	5.2	5.0	3.4	7.1	5.0	3.8	4.2	5.4	-
Item 21650　Subject C01　N★	2085	992	1045	1668	152	489	619	600	377	1306	696	832	425	317	465	22

D07: To what extent is (was) this job . . .

D07A: An interesting job to do?

1. Not at all	18.3	21.8	15.3	17.6	22.4	18.8	18.2	19.9	15.2	18.2	18.3	15.5	19.9	18.6	20.0	52.6
2. A little	24.5	25.6	23.8	25.2	18.3	23.0	24.6	23.9	27.4	26.4	21.5	24.9	24.1	25.7	24.9	6.6
3. Some extent	29.0	25.8	31.4	29.4	26.2	28.3	30.9	28.4	27.8	29.4	27.4	28.5	31.4	26.9	29.6	13.0
4. Considerable extent	17.6	15.9	19.4	17.9	16.8	18.7	18.2	14.7	19.6	17.4	18.6	18.4	17.1	21.1	14.5	17.9
5. A great extent	10.6	11.0	10.1	9.9	16.2	11.2	8.2	13.1	10.0	8.6	14.3	12.7	7.4	7.7	11.0	9.9
Item 21660　Subject C01　N★	2088	995	1046	1669	153	491	617	600	380	1303	698	836	427	314	465	22

D07B: A job you COULD be happy doing for most of your life?

1. Not at all	68.7	68.4	69.7	69.3	61.6	70.4	70.6	64.3	70.1	77.1	54.6	66.1	73.8	68.0	70.3	63.9
2. A little	10.3	8.3	12.1	10.6	9.5	9.0	11.2	9.7	11.3	8.7	13.0	11.2	9.4	10.9	10.0	2.5
3. Some extent	9.8	9.9	9.4	9.5	10.4	8.4	9.8	11.0	9.8	7.8	12.8	10.1	7.0	8.2	12.6	13.6
4. Considerable extent	6.6	7.9	5.2	6.0	12.4	6.8	5.2	8.7	5.4	4.3	10.9	6.8	6.8	8.1	4.3	13.2
5. A great extent	4.6	5.5	3.6	4.6	6.1	5.4	3.3	6.2	3.4	2.1	8.7	5.8	3.0	4.8	2.8	6.8
Item 21670　Subject C01　N★	2083	991	1043	1665	152	491	616	597	378	1301	694	832	426	314	463	22

D07C: The type of work you EXPECT to be doing for most of your life?

1. Not at all	75.4	73.6	77.7	76.6	66.5	71.6	79.5	72.8	77.5	84.2	60.4	75.1	80.2	74.6	74.1	52.0
2. A little	8.1	7.8	8.0	7.6	10.5	9.8	6.6	7.4	9.2	6.5	10.5	7.9	5.7	7.4	10.8	19.1
3. Some extent	7.2	7.9	6.2	6.5	11.6	7.9	6.0	9.0	5.5	4.8	11.8	5.9	6.2	8.6	8.4	14.2
4. Considerable extent	5.1	5.8	4.7	5.1	6.0	5.7	4.9	5.0	5.0	2.8	8.8	5.3	5.2	6.2	3.8	14.8
5. A great extent	4.2	4.9	3.5	4.2	5.4	5.0	3.0	5.7	2.7	1.7	8.5	5.8	2.7	3.2	2.9	-
Item 21680　Subject C01　N★	2078	987	1044	1661	152	488	617	596	377	1298	693	832	424	313	461	22

★=excludes respondents for whom question was inappropriate.

QUESTIONNAIRE FORM 4 1986	TOTAL	SEX		RACE		REGION				4YR COLLEGE PLANS		ILLICIT DRUG USE: LIFETIME				
		M	F	White	Black	NE	NC	S	W	Yes	No	None	Mari-juana Only	Few Pills	More Pills	Any Her-oin
N (Weighted No. of Cases):	3123	1441	1571	2352	333	744	873	961	545	1904	1002	1314	604	446	654	26
% of Weighted Total:	100.0	46.1	50.3	75.3	10.7	23.8	27.9	30.8	17.4	61.0	32.1	42.1	19.3	14.3	20.9	0.8

D07D: A good stepping-stone toward the kind of work you want in the long run?

1. Not at all	55.7	57.2	54.7	55.8	50.4	54.6	58.4	54.9	54.1	61.8	45.8	55.6	57.6	54.8	55.6	52.0
2. A little	16.2	14.7	17.7	16.7	11.5	14.8	15.6	15.1	20.9	16.6	15.0	17.0	15.8	16.2	15.1	31.3
3. Some extent	10.9	10.9	10.7	10.7	14.0	12.6	10.3	11.9	7.9	9.8	12.4	9.7	11.8	13.3	10.6	-
4. Considerable extent	8.1	8.5	7.4	8.1	8.0	9.6	7.3	7.2	8.9	5.6	13.0	8.3	8.6	5.3	8.9	9.9
5. A great extent	9.1	8.7	9.5	8.7	16.1	8.3	8.4	10.9	8.2	6.2	13.7	9.4	6.2	10.4	9.7	6.8
Item 21690 Subject C01 N★	2074	985	1042	1657	152	485	616	594	378	1298	693	830	424	313	459	22

D07E: The kind of work people do just for the money?

1. Not at all	20.4	17.0	23.9	20.4	23.6	21.1	17.5	23.7	19.4	19.5	22.6	21.9	16.9	20.9	20.7	16.0
2. A little	19.0	17.6	19.6	19.4	10.3	18.6	19.5	17.4	21.3	17.6	21.7	20.8	18.3	20.0	16.6	9.8
3. Some extent	18.6	18.4	18.7	17.7	24.1	20.0	18.8	17.7	18.0	18.0	20.2	20.0	18.0	16.8	17.1	29.5
4. Considerable extent	16.3	17.1	15.5	16.8	12.5	14.7	16.0	15.5	20.0	17.6	14.3	14.6	20.3	15.5	16.5	26.3
5. A great extent	25.6	29.8	22.3	25.7	29.5	25.7	28.1	25.8	21.3	27.4	21.2	22.7	26.5	26.8	29.1	18.4
Item 21700 Subject C01 N★	2062	987	1029	1649	151	482	614	587	379	1290	688	823	421	308	462	22

D08: To what extent did any high school teacher or counselor help you get this job?

1. Not at all	81.2	81.4	81.7	83.5	68.3	81.0	81.5	78.8	84.7	86.1	72.7	82.6	83.4	77.0	80.6	74.9
2. A little	4.2	4.8	3.3	4.1	3.1	3.9	5.3	3.9	3.4	3.9	4.8	4.1	4.5	5.5	3.7	-
3. Some extent	3.9	4.1	3.6	3.1	7.9	3.8	3.7	4.0	4.1	2.3	6.7	3.0	3.4	5.8	4.7	-
4. Considerable extent	4.3	4.0	4.2	3.6	7.4	4.4	3.5	6.4	1.9	3.3	5.5	4.3	4.4	3.6	3.5	18.3
5. A great extent	6.4	5.8	7.1	5.7	13.2	6.9	5.9	6.9	5.9	4.4	10.3	6.0	4.3	8.1	7.5	6.8
Item 21710 Subject C01,M02 N★	2049	972	1031	1635	150	484	610	584	371	1280	684	818	420	308	457	22

D09: Is (was) this job part of a work-study program?

1. Yes	13.9	12.0	15.6	12.7	24.3	9.0	12.1	21.8	10.6	9.7	21.3	12.0	11.5	18.1	16.9	6.5
2. No	86.1	88.0	84.4	87.3	75.7	91.0	87.9	78.2	89.4	90.3	78.7	88.0	88.5	81.9	83.1	93.5
Item 21720 Subject C01 N★	2018	947	1029	1629	132	475	594	577	372	1270	664	809	410	304	454	19

D10: People have different opinions about world problems. How much do you agree or disagree with each of the following statements?

D10A: I feel that I can do very little to change the way the world is today

1. Disagree	9.5	8.7	10.2	7.9	19.4	12.9	7.4	9.4	9.0	9.6	9.1	11.3	6.3	7.5	9.4	28.2
2. Mostly disagree	20.2	19.6	20.8	20.7	17.6	17.8	19.3	22.1	21.4	23.6	13.6	22.3	21.0	18.8	15.4	18.2
3. Neither	25.2	25.9	24.2	25.7	25.2	25.2	27.5	23.3	24.5	24.2	25.1	24.9	27.0	24.6	25.0	17.4
4. Mostly agree	27.8	25.8	30.2	29.2	24.3	26.1	28.5	27.7	29.3	29.5	25.8	26.4	30.7	32.7	25.6	13.4
5. Agree	17.3	20.1	14.7	16.5	19.6	18.0	17.3	17.6	15.8	13.1	25.1	15.1	15.0	16.3	24.6	22.7
Item 10920 Subject I02,J N	2816	1289	1471	2198	269	630	820	870	496	1797	914	1209	554	410	578	23

D10B: It does little good to clean up air and water pollution because this society will not last long enough for it to matter

1. Disagree	39.8	39.3	40.2	40.9	37.4	36.7	39.5	40.2	43.4	44.3	31.3	42.9	40.2	37.1	35.6	33.5
2. Mostly disagree	30.1	29.3	30.5	31.7	23.5	27.0	30.8	31.3	30.8	30.6	29.9	30.6	29.4	31.9	28.1	34.5
3. Neither	16.1	18.1	14.4	16.1	12.3	18.4	17.4	13.5	15.3	14.1	19.1	12.9	17.7	18.2	19.8	20.4
4. Mostly agree	9.2	8.6	9.8	7.9	14.7	10.1	9.3	10.0	6.3	7.4	12.6	8.8	9.7	9.3	9.3	3.2
5. Agree	4.9	4.8	5.0	3.4	12.0	7.9	3.0	5.0	4.3	3.6	7.0	4.9	3.0	3.5	7.2	8.4
Item 10930 Subject F05,J N	2804	1282	1465	2192	264	626	816	868	493	1793	907	1205	552	404	577	23

D10C: When things get tough enough, we'll put our minds to it and find a technological solution

1. Disagree	6.1	5.3	6.7	6.1	5.8	7.7	5.3	6.6	4.6	5.8	6.5	6.2	4.7	8.2	5.6	15.3
2. Mostly disagree	10.3	10.9	9.8	10.7	7.4	12.3	9.1	10.5	9.6	10.2	10.5	9.0	11.3	10.9	12.0	8.5
3. Neither	23.3	21.5	24.8	23.6	18.2	24.8	26.3	20.7	20.9	23.1	23.2	23.3	22.0	21.1	25.7	17.7
4. Mostly agree	39.2	40.1	38.5	40.8	31.9	34.1	42.3	38.0	42.5	39.8	38.6	38.5	41.7	38.8	38.5	43.1
5. Agree	21.1	22.2	20.2	18.8	36.7	21.2	17.0	24.1	22.5	21.0	21.3	23.0	20.3	21.1	18.2	15.4
Item 10940 Subject I01,J N	2793	1278	1460	2185	263	624	813	863	493	1786	902	1202	549	404	573	23

★=excludes respondents for whom question was inappropriate.

QUESTIONNAIRE FORM 4 1986	TOTAL	SEX		RACE		REGION				4YR COLLEGE PLANS		ILLICIT DRUG USE: LIFETIME				
		M	F	White	Black	NE	NC	S	W	Yes	No	None	Marijuana Only	Few Pills	More Pills	Any Heroin
N (Weighted No. of Cases):	3123	1441	1571	2352	333	744	873	961	545	1904	1002	1314	604	446	654	26
% of Weighted Total:	100.0	46.1	50.3	75.3	10.7	23.8	27.9	30.8	17.4	61.0	32.1	42.1	19.3	14.3	20.9	0.8

D10D: When I think about all the terrible things that have been happening, it is hard for me to hold out much hope for the world

1. Disagree	17.7	20.4	15.5	18.3	18.0	18.7	16.1	18.9	16.9	19.5	14.6	19.6	19.6	13.3	14.5	16.9
2. Mostly disagree	29.0	28.9	29.2	31.5	18.2	28.0	30.8	27.4	30.3	32.4	22.6	29.6	30.6	33.0	24.6	7.2
3. Neither	26.0	27.6	24.3	26.6	19.6	28.0	27.2	21.6	29.3	23.6	30.8	24.9	25.6	24.2	30.7	20.5
4. Mostly agree	18.5	15.5	21.3	16.6	25.1	14.9	18.7	21.9	16.4	17.1	20.9	17.1	17.3	20.9	19.3	53.4
5. Agree	8.8	7.6	9.7	7.1	19.1	10.4	7.2	10.1	7.1	7.4	11.1	8.8	6.9	8.6	10.9	1.9
Item 10950　Subject J　　N	2785	1272	1458	2180	263	623	810	860	492	1790	895	1202	547	402	570	23

D10E: I often wonder if there is any real purpose to my life in light of the world situation

1. Disagree	27.0	28.6	25.5	27.7	28.2	27.6	24.1	25.8	33.2	29.9	22.5	30.6	27.5	25.4	20.8	21.4
2. Mostly disagree	20.9	20.6	21.3	22.3	13.7	21.4	23.2	19.9	18.0	22.7	17.1	21.6	22.4	18.3	20.2	-
3. Neither	27.2	28.4	25.8	27.2	20.8	25.5	30.6	24.6	28.1	24.3	32.0	26.3	25.6	28.9	29.5	38.9
4. Mostly agree	16.8	14.8	18.8	16.0	19.4	14.2	15.3	20.7	15.7	16.4	17.7	13.9	17.6	19.9	19.5	25.1
5. Agree	8.2	7.6	8.6	6.8	17.8	11.4	6.8	9.0	5.0	6.8	10.7	7.6	7.0	7.5	10.0	14.6
Item 10960　Subject J　　N	2766	1258	1452	2165	258	620	808	849	488	1777	887	1192	548	402	561	23

D10F: My guess is that this country will be caught up in a major world upheaval in the next 10 years

1. Disagree	12.1	14.3	10.2	12.3	16.4	12.4	13.2	11.3	11.5	12.2	11.9	13.1	15.2	9.1	8.9	12.0
2. Mostly disagree	16.2	19.2	13.6	17.0	12.3	16.3	14.0	17.7	17.1	19.0	11.3	16.0	18.3	20.7	12.8	2.4
3. Neither	31.7	29.2	33.8	32.3	27.5	34.7	35.4	27.0	29.9	31.1	33.0	33.9	28.9	29.9	31.0	28.9
4. Mostly agree	25.8	24.9	26.7	25.8	23.2	22.3	25.8	28.3	26.0	25.2	26.7	24.3	23.8	27.3	29.3	44.2
5. Agree	14.2	12.4	15.6	12.6	20.6	14.4	11.6	15.7	15.6	12.5	17.1	12.7	13.8	13.0	18.1	12.4
Item 10970　Subject J　　N	2763	1261	1449	2167	255	618	809	848	489	1774	888	1192	544	396	567	23

D10G: Nuclear or biological annihilation will probably be the fate of all mankind, within my lifetime

1. Disagree	20.6	27.1	15.0	22.3	19.3	20.8	21.0	19.7	21.0	23.1	15.9	23.3	19.3	18.1	17.9	21.7
2. Mostly disagree	18.7	22.0	15.7	20.1	10.9	18.1	19.5	18.0	19.0	19.9	15.2	18.1	23.9	20.7	13.9	22.7
3. Neither	29.8	25.9	33.3	29.6	24.8	28.0	33.5	28.1	28.7	29.7	30.5	31.3	27.7	28.7	30.7	19.0
4. Mostly agree	18.3	14.3	21.7	17.5	21.5	19.7	16.0	20.0	17.6	17.2	21.5	17.5	15.9	18.9	21.0	17.5
5. Agree	12.7	10.6	14.2	10.5	23.4	13.4	9.9	14.2	13.7	10.1	16.9	9.8	13.2	13.6	16.6	19.1
Item 10980　Subject J　　N	2758	1266	1438	2164	257	616	808	847	487	1774	882	1190	544	395	565	23

D10H: The human race has come through tough times before, and will do so again

1. Disagree	4.3	5.0	3.9	4.0	6.2	4.7	3.3	4.5	5.5	3.3	5.9	4.4	3.0	4.8	4.3	13.1
2. Mostly disagree	6.6	7.3	5.9	5.5	13.3	7.3	5.9	6.7	6.7	6.3	6.3	5.8	6.0	5.5	6.8	50.3
3. Neither	23.2	22.2	23.9	22.9	19.0	24.7	23.0	21.4	24.5	21.2	26.6	22.5	23.8	21.2	25.8	20.0
4. Mostly agree	37.1	35.1	38.9	39.2	26.6	35.9	39.7	35.5	37.0	38.3	35.9	37.5	37.9	39.4	36.0	8.1
5. Agree	28.8	30.4	27.4	28.3	35.0	27.4	28.2	32.0	26.3	30.9	25.3	29.8	29.3	29.1	27.2	8.5
Item 10990　Subject J　　N	2765	1265	1446	2170	258	620	807	851	487	1773	891	1191	544	397	570	23

The next questions are about alcohol use–this time asking separately about beer, wine, and hard liquor.

D11: On how many occasions (if any) have you had beer to drink . . .

D11A: . . . in your lifetime?

1. 0 occasions	13.4	10.0	16.3	11.0	29.0	12.5	9.3	16.4	15.9	13.9	12.0	26.3	4.4	6.6	1.6	-
2. 1-2	10.9	7.6	13.5	10.1	18.2	8.6	10.1	13.4	10.8	11.2	10.9	19.5	6.5	6.3	1.9	-
3. 3-5	9.1	6.9	11.0	8.4	12.3	9.6	7.5	8.8	11.4	9.8	7.7	13.5	7.0	6.4	4.1	-
4. 6-9	8.4	7.4	9.4	8.3	9.1	9.3	8.0	8.0	8.5	8.2	9.2	9.8	10.9	7.1	4.3	-
5. 10-19	10.7	10.4	11.0	10.8	11.8	12.0	10.4	11.1	9.1	11.6	9.1	10.6	13.7	14.2	6.6	-
6. 20-39	11.2	10.3	12.0	11.8	7.5	12.8	11.1	9.2	12.6	11.3	11.3	7.8	13.2	15.4	13.3	-
7. 40 or more	36.4	47.4	26.7	39.5	12.2	35.2	43.6	33.1	31.7	34.0	39.9	12.5	44.3	44.0	68.2	100.0
Item 11000　Subject A01a　　N	2663	1221	1392	2122	222	596	776	817	474	1715	857	1111	537	396	570	21

QUESTIONNAIRE FORM 4 1986	TOTAL	SEX		RACE		REGION				4YR COLLEGE PLANS		ILLICIT DRUG USE: LIFETIME				
		M	F	White	Black	NE	NC	S	W	Yes	No	None	Mari-juana Only	Few Pills	More Pills	Any Her-oin
N (Weighted No. of Cases):	3123	1441	1571	2352	333	744	873	961	545	1904	1002	1314	604	446	654	26
% of Weighted Total:	100.0	46.1	50.3	75.3	10.7	23.8	27.9	30.8	17.4	61.0	32.1	42.1	19.3	14.3	20.9	0.8

D11B: . . . during the last 12 months?

1. 0 occasions	26.0	19.9	31.4	22.4	49.2	27.2	19.1	31.3	26.8	26.1	26.1	44.1	15.6	16.6	7.8	3.1
2. 1-2	13.8	10.7	16.2	13.4	16.3	15.0	12.2	13.1	16.3	14.3	13.2	19.2	11.8	11.8	6.9	-
3. 3-5	11.5	10.7	12.3	11.5	13.6	11.4	12.4	11.6	10.1	11.3	12.1	12.3	14.1	11.5	7.8	-
4. 6-9	9.5	10.0	8.9	10.0	4.5	9.6	8.8	7.9	12.9	10.6	7.4	8.5	10.3	13.6	8.3	4.6
5. 10-19	12.0	11.7	12.4	12.7	8.7	11.8	14.7	11.5	8.6	12.0	12.1	7.5	16.9	12.4	15.5	5.1
6. 20-39	10.9	13.2	8.9	12.5	1.8	12.3	12.6	9.3	9.2	11.5	9.1	4.0	13.3	16.6	18.3	11.5
7. 40 or more	16.3	23.8	9.9	17.6	5.9	12.7	20.3	15.3	16.2	14.1	20.0	4.4	17.9	17.4	35.4	75.7
Item 11010 Subject A01b N	2633	1203	1381	2107	216	587	770	808	468	1695	849	1103	531	383	566	21

D11C: . . . during the last 30 days?

1. 0 occasions	44.5	35.7	52.1	40.9	69.4	48.5	33.7	51.4	45.6	44.3	45.8	65.4	33.1	38.0	20.2	5.2
2. 1-2	18.1	16.9	19.1	18.5	15.0	14.7	21.1	15.5	22.0	19.7	15.3	18.6	22.9	18.7	13.6	-
3. 3-5	13.6	15.8	11.8	14.9	7.9	15.2	16.6	11.2	10.8	13.7	13.3	8.6	17.6	15.2	18.5	8.7
4. 6-9	11.1	14.3	8.5	12.0	3.7	10.1	12.5	10.5	11.1	11.6	10.5	4.0	14.3	13.4	20.6	-
5. 10-19	7.8	9.4	6.4	8.8	1.3	7.1	10.7	5.6	7.5	6.6	8.9	1.5	9.0	9.4	17.4	16.4
6. 20-39	3.5	5.3	1.8	3.7	0.8	3.1	3.9	4.1	2.1	3.2	4.4	1.5	2.2	4.8	6.9	27.4
7. 40 or more	1.4	2.6	0.3	1.2	1.9	1.3	1.4	1.6	1.0	0.9	1.7	0.3	0.9	0.5	2.8	42.3
Item 11020 Subject A01c N	2629	1201	1379	2106	215	586	769	807	466	1693	848	1101	531	384	565	21

D12: Think back over the LAST TWO WEEKS. How many times have you had five or more 12-ounce cans of beer (or the equivalent) in a row?

1. None	66.9	54.6	77.6	64.6	86.5	67.4	59.2	70.6	72.5	69.2	64.0	85.6	61.9	59.2	42.7	11.8
2. Once	9.8	12.2	7.7	10.4	4.0	10.6	11.8	7.1	10.0	9.3	10.3	6.1	13.6	12.9	12.0	-
3. Twice	8.6	11.1	6.6	9.5	3.5	7.6	11.4	8.9	4.6	8.3	9.0	4.6	10.5	11.2	12.8	3.7
4. Three to five times	9.3	13.7	5.2	10.2	2.4	9.6	11.4	7.8	8.1	9.0	10.1	2.0	11.2	10.0	19.8	25.6
5. Six to nine times	3.1	4.5	1.9	3.3	1.4	2.6	4.1	2.8	2.4	2.7	2.7	1.1	1.4	5.6	6.8	-
6. Ten or more times	2.4	4.0	1.0	1.9	2.2	2.2	2.1	2.8	2.5	1.5	4.0	0.5	1.3	1.1	5.8	58.9
Item 11030 Subject A01d N	2620	1195	1377	2097	214	586	764	801	469	1695	837	1101	524	380	566	21

D13: On how many occasions (if any) have you had wine to drink . . .

D13A: . . . in your lifetime?

1. 0 occasions	16.0	16.5	14.9	13.9	30.9	12.0	11.2	23.6	15.7	14.2	19.0	27.7	9.5	6.6	5.8	3.3
2. 1-2	17.3	17.6	17.2	16.5	24.6	15.2	13.7	20.8	19.9	16.2	19.7	25.3	13.6	14.6	7.7	-
3. 3-5	16.4	16.5	16.6	16.2	16.6	19.7	16.5	14.4	15.6	17.3	14.7	17.3	17.5	18.8	12.5	-
4. 6-9	14.3	14.4	14.4	14.7	11.1	17.7	16.1	11.2	12.2	14.6	13.7	12.4	17.0	17.0	13.4	8.5
5. 10-19	14.6	14.1	15.2	15.8	6.0	14.3	16.8	12.5	14.7	15.4	12.2	9.4	17.6	15.0	21.3	33.3
6. 20-39	10.7	9.9	11.1	11.3	5.2	10.9	13.7	8.9	8.5	12.3	7.8	4.2	15.1	13.9	17.3	11.0
7. 40 or more	10.8	11.0	10.7	11.5	5.6	10.3	11.9	8.6	13.4	10.0	12.8	3.8	9.8	13.9	22.0	43.9
Item 11040 Subject A01a N	2670	1233	1384	2126	229	590	787	818	475	1723	857	1118	533	398	571	20

D13B: . . . during the last 12 months?

1. 0 occasions	34.8	36.2	33.3	31.8	54.4	32.5	25.8	44.1	36.7	31.7	40.5	50.7	26.1	27.5	18.3	8.7
2. 1-2	24.3	26.1	22.9	24.6	22.7	27.7	26.6	21.6	20.8	25.0	23.2	24.9	25.0	27.0	21.1	2.0
3. 3-5	15.6	14.4	16.7	16.6	10.6	17.4	17.3	14.0	13.4	17.1	12.3	12.7	20.1	14.8	17.7	10.1
4. 6-9	11.1	10.2	11.9	11.9	6.5	9.4	14.0	8.4	12.8	11.6	10.2	6.7	13.9	12.5	16.0	11.0
5. 10-19	8.1	7.3	9.1	8.5	2.6	8.0	10.0	7.3	6.4	9.2	6.3	3.9	8.4	10.2	13.9	29.7
6. 20-39	3.1	2.3	3.6	3.4	1.7	1.8	3.5	2.3	5.8	2.8	3.9	0.6	4.5	4.2	6.2	6.3
7. 40 or more	2.9	3.5	2.5	3.2	1.5	3.2	2.7	2.2	4.1	2.6	3.7	0.5	1.9	3.8	6.8	32.1
Item 11050 Subject A01b N	2642	1222	1369	2111	225	586	781	809	466	1701	856	1102	530	392	569	20

D13C: . . . during the last 30 days?

1. 0 occasions	65.5	69.2	61.9	63.5	79.3	68.0	59.0	72.0	61.9	63.8	68.5	79.1	59.6	61.5	48.9	20.5
2. 1-2	20.3	19.0	22.0	21.6	11.9	20.5	24.1	16.1	21.1	22.2	16.8	14.8	26.6	22.6	24.1	4.5
3. 3-5	7.9	6.7	9.1	8.7	4.9	5.8	9.4	7.7	8.6	8.0	7.7	4.0	9.2	6.5	15.2	23.8
4. 6-9	4.0	3.0	4.6	4.1	2.3	4.3	4.1	2.4	5.8	4.0	4.0	1.5	2.5	6.0	7.6	23.7
5. 10-19	1.7	1.3	2.0	1.5	0.2	0.5	2.9	1.3	1.6	1.4	2.2	0.6	1.3	3.2	2.6	13.9
6. 20-39	0.4	0.4	0.2	0.3	-	0.2	0.3	0.2	0.9	0.3	0.5	-	0.5	-	1.1	-
7. 40 or more	0.3	0.5	0.1	0.1	1.5	0.7	0.2	0.2	-	0.3	0.1	-	0.2	0.2	0.5	13.6
Item 11060 Subject A01c N	2637	1223	1363	2107	225	583	780	809	465	1702	852	1102	529	393	566	21

QUESTIONNAIRE FORM 4 1986	TOTAL	SEX		RACE		REGION				4YR COLLEGE PLANS		ILLICIT DRUG USE: LIFETIME				
		M	F	White	Black	NE	NC	S	W	Yes	No	None	Mari- juana Only	Few Pills	More Pills	Any Her- oin
N (Weighted No. of Cases):	3123	1441	1571	2352	333	744	873	961	545	1904	1002	1314	604	446	654	26
% of Weighted Total:	100.0	46.1	50.3	75.3	10.7	23.8	27.9	30.8	17.4	61.0	32.1	42.1	19.3	14.3	20.9	0.8

D14: Think back over the LAST TWO WEEKS. How many times have you had five or more 4-ounce glasses of wine in a row (or the equivalent, which is about three-fourths of a bottle)?

1. None	86.3	87.6	85.4	85.9	91.7	88.5	82.8	87.1	87.8	86.7	85.4	93.8	83.9	85.0	76.5	19.0
2. Once	6.7	5.9	7.2	7.3	2.7	5.1	9.1	7.0	4.1	7.0	6.0	3.8	8.6	7.5	10.5	2.0
3. Twice	3.9	3.6	4.2	4.1	1.2	3.2	4.7	3.5	3.9	3.6	4.5	1.6	4.7	3.3	7.0	41.5
4. Three to five times	1.8	1.4	2.1	1.9	1.6	2.0	1.7	1.4	2.7	1.6	2.2	0.6	1.7	3.2	3.5	4.2
5. Six to nine times	0.7	0.6	0.8	0.4	1.1	0.5	0.9	0.5	1.0	0.6	0.9	0.2	0.9	0.2	1.1	16.8
6. Ten or more times	0.7	0.9	0.4	0.4	1.7	0.6	0.9	0.6	0.4	0.4	1.0	0.1	0.2	0.9	1.5	16.5
Item 11070 Subject A01d N	*2590*	*1183*	*1356*	*2072*	*222*	*568*	*767*	*797*	*458*	*1686*	*819*	*1088*	*510*	*389*	*556*	*17*

The next questions are about hard liquor. (Hard liquor includes whiskey, Scotch, bourbon, gin, vodka, rum, etc., or mixed drinks made with liquor.)

D15: On how many occasions (if any) have you had liquor to drink . . .

D15A: . . . in your lifetime?

1. 0 occasions	19.7	17.9	21.0	15.5	47.0	17.7	13.7	24.1	24.8	20.5	18.8	38.1	8.1	7.4	3.4	3.1
2. 1-2	13.8	12.9	14.7	13.2	22.7	12.9	12.4	15.1	15.3	14.0	13.7	21.4	13.2	10.5	2.7	-
3. 3-5	12.5	11.6	13.7	13.0	10.8	14.2	12.8	12.3	10.5	12.6	12.1	12.6	14.9	16.2	8.2	-
4. 6-9	11.0	10.2	11.7	11.4	6.4	11.5	11.0	10.5	11.6	11.5	10.4	8.7	15.5	14.2	9.5	6.9
5. 10-19	14.3	15.6	13.1	15.8	5.4	14.7	16.5	13.4	11.7	15.1	12.7	9.5	19.3	16.3	18.1	9.9
6. 20-39	12.5	13.3	12.0	13.9	1.6	13.6	14.2	10.8	11.5	12.2	12.9	5.0	16.7	15.1	21.3	16.0
7. 40 or more	16.1	18.5	13.7	17.2	6.1	15.4	19.6	13.9	14.7	14.2	19.5	4.7	12.3	20.3	36.8	64.1
Item 11080 Subject A01a N	*2643*	*1220*	*1370*	*2109*	*219*	*581*	*779*	*812*	*471*	*1702*	*856*	*1102*	*532*	*392*	*570*	*21*

D15B: . . . during the last 12 months?

1. 0 occasions	34.0	31.7	36.0	29.3	67.7	35.9	24.8	40.5	36.0	33.1	36.4	55.6	24.0	22.0	11.0	7.8
2. 1-2	18.9	18.4	19.3	18.9	17.4	17.7	20.5	17.3	20.3	19.0	18.4	20.2	23.7	19.2	12.0	-
3. 3-5	13.3	12.8	13.9	14.6	6.1	13.1	13.9	14.0	11.4	14.6	10.7	9.0	18.5	19.6	12.9	1.9
4. 6-9	11.4	12.5	10.5	12.2	4.1	13.4	12.5	9.3	10.8	12.7	9.3	7.9	12.2	13.1	16.3	17.9
5. 10-19	12.2	13.3	11.2	13.5	2.8	12.3	14.7	9.3	12.6	11.7	12.6	4.5	13.3	15.3	22.9	28.0
6. 20-39	6.2	6.1	6.4	7.3	0.8	5.2	9.3	5.1	4.3	5.7	6.8	2.1	5.8	6.1	14.6	18.8
7. 40 or more	4.0	5.2	2.8	4.2	1.1	2.4	4.3	4.4	4.6	3.3	5.7	0.8	2.5	4.3	10.3	25.6
Item 11090 Subject A01b N	*2615*	*1206*	*1356*	*2087*	*218*	*573*	*776*	*801*	*464*	*1682*	*851*	*1091*	*525*	*387*	*563*	*21*

D15C: . . . during the last 30 days?

1. 0 occasions	59.0	56.3	61.4	55.8	84.5	62.8	50.2	64.1	60.4	58.2	61.1	78.1	52.1	52.0	35.2	14.5
2. 1-2	20.9	23.2	19.0	22.4	10.5	20.0	25.1	17.9	20.0	23.0	16.6	13.2	29.4	24.5	26.0	10.8
3. 3-5	10.2	11.2	9.2	11.1	3.9	8.3	11.5	9.6	11.4	10.4	9.3	5.3	10.9	12.9	16.6	6.5
4. 6-9	6.3	5.5	6.9	6.9	0.7	6.5	7.9	4.7	6.5	5.5	8.0	2.1	4.2	8.1	14.5	27.4
5. 10-19	2.9	2.6	3.2	3.4	-	1.8	4.6	3.0	1.3	2.1	4.2	1.2	2.5	2.5	6.1	23.8
6. 20-39	0.5	0.8	0.2	0.4	0.5	0.4	0.6	0.5	0.2	0.4	0.6	-	0.7	-	1.0	13.1
7. 40 or more	0.2	0.4	-	0.2	-	0.3	0.2	0.3	0.2	0.3	0.1	0.1	0.2	-	0.5	3.9
Item 11100 Subject A01c N	*2612*	*1205*	*1355*	*2086*	*217*	*574*	*771*	*802*	*465*	*1680*	*850*	*1090*	*525*	*385*	*565*	*22*

D16: Think back over the LAST TWO WEEKS. How many times have you had five or more mixed drinks or shot-glasses of hard liquor in a row?

1. None	78.6	75.3	81.4	77.1	92.4	79.9	74.1	80.9	80.4	80.1	76.0	89.7	77.2	79.1	59.8	20.3
2. Once	9.6	11.8	7.9	10.4	3.2	7.8	12.2	8.0	10.4	10.1	8.8	5.4	12.4	9.4	15.6	2.2
3. Twice	5.7	6.1	5.4	6.0	0.8	5.5	7.0	4.9	5.2	4.7	7.7	3.1	5.7	5.6	11.2	6.6
4. Three to five times	4.3	4.8	3.7	4.8	1.7	4.8	4.7	4.1	3.3	3.9	4.4	1.4	3.7	3.7	10.4	10.0
5. Six to nine times	1.4	1.2	1.4	1.2	1.9	1.6	1.6	1.4	0.5	0.8	2.4	0.1	0.8	1.6	2.5	53.7
6. Ten or more times	0.5	0.7	0.2	0.5	-	0.4	0.4	0.6	0.2	0.3	0.7	0.3	0.2	0.5	0.6	7.2
Item 11110 Subject A01d N	*2552*	*1177*	*1328*	*2040*	*212*	*548*	*760*	*785*	*459*	*1664*	*805*	*1079*	*517*	*374*	*542*	*16*

These next questions ask for your opinions about the military services in the United States.

E01: To what extent do you think the following opportunities are available to people who work in the military services?

QUESTIONNAIRE FORM 4 1986	TOTAL	SEX		RACE		REGION				4YR COLLEGE PLANS		ILLICIT DRUG USE: LIFETIME				
		M	F	White	Black	NE	NC	S	W	Yes	No	None	Marijuana Only	Few Pills	More Pills	Any Heroin
N (Weighted No. of Cases):	3123	1441	1571	2352	333	744	873	961	545	1904	1002	1314	604	446	654	26
% of Weighted Total:	100.0	46.1	50.3	75.3	10.7	23.8	27.9	30.8	17.4	61.0	32.1	42.1	19.3	14.3	20.9	0.8

E01A: A chance to get ahead

1. To a very little extent	6.2	8.4	4.1	5.4	9.8	7.4	6.3	4.1	8.0	5.7	6.6	5.9	5.9	5.6	6.7	24.7
2. To a little extent	11.3	12.7	10.0	12.0	6.5	11.1	12.3	8.2	15.5	11.5	10.9	11.3	12.1	12.4	10.2	11.7
3. To some extent	42.6	41.6	44.2	44.0	28.8	38.0	44.7	43.1	44.1	44.3	39.4	42.8	42.6	43.3	42.7	47.4
4. To a great extent	25.3	23.4	26.8	25.4	25.1	24.9	25.8	26.2	23.4	26.2	24.0	24.8	26.4	24.6	26.3	7.0
5. To a very great extent	14.5	13.9	14.9	13.3	29.7	18.6	11.0	18.3	9.0	12.2	19.0	15.2	12.9	14.1	14.1	9.2
Item 11120 Subject L04 N	2695	1242	1399	2120	250	593	792	830	480	1740	862	1158	534	387	556	22

E01B: A chance to get more education

1. To a very little extent	4.9	6.8	3.2	4.2	8.9	5.7	5.7	3.2	5.6	4.6	5.8	5.1	4.3	3.0	5.8	20.8
2. To a little extent	8.5	9.7	7.1	8.9	5.3	8.4	7.5	7.2	12.2	8.6	8.4	8.1	9.3	9.0	7.4	23.3
3. To some extent	29.8	31.2	28.8	31.6	19.5	27.7	31.4	28.5	32.3	31.0	27.0	29.8	31.5	28.3	30.6	12.6
4. To a great extent	34.9	32.4	37.2	34.9	34.0	34.7	37.6	35.6	29.8	35.8	33.5	34.7	34.5	37.9	33.7	29.9
5. To a very great extent	21.8	19.9	23.7	20.5	32.3	23.5	17.9	25.5	20.1	19.9	25.4	22.3	20.4	21.7	22.5	13.4
Item 11130 Subject B10,L04 N	2694	1244	1401	2123	249	592	791	831	480	1738	865	1158	532	387	554	23

E01C: A chance to advance to a more responsible position

1. To a very little extent	4.8	6.7	3.3	4.1	9.2	5.5	6.0	2.5	6.1	3.8	6.6	5.2	3.9	3.1	4.9	27.8
2. To a little extent	7.3	9.0	5.6	7.4	5.7	4.9	8.2	6.5	10.3	7.3	7.5	7.9	8.1	6.8	6.0	2.6
3. To some extent	30.1	29.8	30.6	31.3	19.6	29.1	31.7	27.6	32.8	31.9	25.8	30.1	30.8	27.2	32.3	7.9
4. To a great extent	35.4	34.9	35.6	36.3	30.1	35.8	36.7	36.1	31.5	36.5	34.3	34.6	36.6	38.2	33.8	48.3
5. To a very great extent	22.4	19.5	24.9	21.0	35.4	24.8	17.4	27.2	19.3	20.5	25.8	22.2	20.6	24.7	23.0	13.4
Item 11140 Subject L04 N	2692	1243	1398	2122	247	592	792	829	479	1738	863	1158	534	386	554	23

E01D: A chance to have a personally more fulfilling job

1. To a very little extent	6.7	8.8	4.8	6.2	9.3	5.9	8.0	5.1	8.3	6.1	8.0	7.7	5.3	5.0	6.4	29.9
2. To a little extent	12.3	14.5	10.1	13.2	6.2	9.5	13.3	10.7	16.7	13.8	9.5	12.3	14.1	12.7	10.6	7.7
3. To some extent	34.5	33.4	36.1	36.8	24.4	32.4	37.9	32.2	35.5	35.8	31.6	34.2	36.7	29.8	36.9	28.1
4. To a great extent	28.4	27.7	28.8	27.7	25.1	31.4	25.8	29.6	27.1	29.3	26.8	27.3	27.3	31.4	30.8	18.6
5. To a very great extent	18.1	15.7	20.3	16.1	35.0	20.8	15.0	22.4	12.5	15.1	24.1	18.5	16.7	21.1	15.3	15.7
Item 11150 Subject C05,L04 N	2684	1238	1396	2114	247	588	792	825	479	1735	859	1157	533	386	551	20

E01E: A chance to get their ideas heard

1. To a very little extent	15.4	20.3	11.2	15.7	13.2	16.2	17.1	12.0	17.6	16.5	13.5	16.3	14.8	12.3	15.9	31.3
2. To a little extent	22.6	24.8	20.6	24.0	13.5	18.5	25.1	19.3	29.1	24.5	18.3	22.0	25.4	22.2	23.3	6.4
3. To some extent	33.5	30.2	36.7	34.3	28.1	35.0	32.9	33.3	32.8	34.1	32.9	34.1	36.3	32.0	30.4	28.3
4. To a great extent	17.9	15.4	19.9	16.7	22.6	17.0	17.4	20.7	15.0	17.5	18.8	17.1	15.3	23.0	19.0	12.5
5. To a very great extent	10.6	9.3	11.7	9.4	22.7	13.2	7.5	14.7	5.5	7.4	16.5	10.5	8.2	10.4	11.5	21.4
Item 11160 Subject L04 N	2680	1236	1393	2112	247	587	791	827	476	1732	860	1155	532	387	547	23

E02: To what extent is it likely that a person in the military can get things changed and set right if he is being treated unjustly by a superior?

1. To a very little extent	19.2	22.8	15.9	19.7	14.5	19.7	18.6	17.0	23.7	20.1	16.5	18.7	20.4	18.8	17.9	71.9
2. To a little extent	27.8	27.2	28.4	28.1	24.4	25.8	26.8	29.2	29.4	30.7	22.9	27.1	30.1	28.1	29.1	4.9
3. To some extent	38.1	34.0	41.9	38.6	31.9	39.1	42.0	34.9	36.0	37.5	39.9	38.6	38.0	38.4	36.9	21.3
4. To a great extent	10.9	11.5	10.4	10.4	17.8	10.7	9.6	13.8	8.3	9.3	13.4	11.2	8.5	11.3	12.8	-
5. To a very great extent	4.0	4.5	3.4	3.2	11.3	4.7	3.0	5.1	2.7	2.3	7.3	4.4	3.0	3.5	3.3	1.9
Item 11170 Subject L04 N	2652	1219	1381	2088	248	577	786	822	467	1708	849	1136	524	381	549	24

E03: To what extent do you think there is any discrimination against women who are in the armed services?

1. To a very little extent	16.4	19.4	13.8	15.4	23.2	18.9	12.7	18.4	16.3	13.7	21.9	16.9	17.2	13.7	15.6	27.6
2. To a little extent	30.0	32.4	27.7	31.1	23.4	27.5	29.3	30.7	33.0	29.7	30.9	29.5	35.2	30.9	26.7	34.4
3. To some extent	38.1	35.2	41.0	38.2	38.9	36.3	41.4	37.4	36.2	40.8	32.6	35.5	35.5	39.6	44.8	33.4
4. To a great extent	11.3	9.4	12.8	11.5	9.4	12.1	12.7	9.8	10.3	12.1	9.6	13.2	8.2	12.1	10.5	-
5. To a very great extent	4.1	3.6	4.6	3.8	5.2	5.2	3.9	3.6	4.1	3.7	5.0	5.0	4.0	3.7	2.5	4.6
Item 11180 Subject D06,L04 N	2651	1225	1375	2085	248	575	788	821	468	1714	847	1140	526	379	544	23

QUESTIONNAIRE FORM 4 1986	TOTAL	SEX		RACE		REGION				4YR COLLEGE PLANS		ILLICIT DRUG USE: LIFETIME				
		M	F	White	Black	NE	NC	S	W	Yes	No	None	Mari-juana Only	Few Pills	More Pills	Any Her-oin
N (Weighted No. of Cases):	3123	1441	1571	2352	333	744	873	961	545	1904	1002	1314	604	446	654	26
% of Weighted Total:	100.0	46.1	50.3	75.3	10.7	23.8	27.9	30.8	17.4	61.0	32.1	42.1	19.3	14.3	20.9	0.8

E04: To what extent do you think there is any discrimination against black people who are in the armed services?

1. To a very little extent	33.4	37.7	29.1	34.2	34.2	34.1	29.3	37.5	32.4	31.5	36.5	32.6	38.9	31.0	29.8	55.4
2. To a little extent	29.4	28.6	29.9	30.5	21.4	28.6	29.7	28.8	31.1	31.3	26.1	30.6	28.1	31.3	29.1	21.4
3. To some extent	28.5	25.5	31.7	28.3	26.5	28.1	33.0	24.7	28.0	29.6	26.4	28.6	24.6	29.5	31.9	21.3
4. To a great extent	6.1	6.0	6.4	5.4	9.6	6.4	5.7	6.1	6.5	5.4	7.4	4.9	6.4	7.2	7.4	-
5. To a very great extent	2.5	2.2	2.9	1.6	8.3	2.8	2.3	2.9	2.0	2.1	3.5	3.4	2.0	0.9	1.8	1.9
Item 11190 Subject L04,N02 N	2629	1215	1362	2069	242	569	787	810	462	1700	841	1128	525	375	540	23

E05: Do you personally feel that you would receive more just and fair treatment as a civilian or as a member of the military service?

1. Much more fair in the military service	6.5	8.8	4.5	5.7	8.6	8.4	4.5	7.7	5.7	4.5	9.8	7.1	6.2	6.8	5.7	6.3
2. More fair in the military service	12.3	12.4	12.1	12.5	13.4	12.6	15.1	11.2	9.0	11.6	13.6	9.2	15.8	14.3	13.0	35.2
3. About the same	44.2	39.5	48.1	44.3	44.9	42.4	45.7	45.5	41.8	45.4	42.1	45.4	44.3	46.5	40.8	23.8
4. More fair as a civilian	15.1	17.4	13.2	15.8	10.3	14.7	14.3	15.0	17.2	15.9	13.8	15.2	14.2	10.9	18.7	14.5
5. Much more fair as a civilian	9.4	13.7	5.6	9.7	8.0	10.0	9.1	7.8	11.9	10.7	7.1	9.2	8.6	9.4	10.5	10.7
6. Question not appropriate for me	12.4	8.1	16.4	12.0	14.8	12.0	11.3	12.9	14.2	11.9	13.6	13.9	10.8	12.1	11.4	9.5
Item 11200 Subject L04 N	2645	1214	1380	2081	245	578	784	814	469	1711	840	1136	519	382	546	23

E06: If YOU felt that it was necessary for the U.S. to fight in some future war, how likely is it that you would volunteer for military service in that war?

1. I'm sure that I would volunteer	13.9	21.9	6.7	14.0	14.6	15.9	12.6	15.4	11.2	11.8	17.9	12.7	14.4	14.6	15.0	20.6
2. I would very likely volunteer	6.1	8.6	3.6	6.5	4.3	5.6	6.2	6.6	5.5	5.8	6.8	6.2	8.2	4.4	5.2	2.5
3. I would probably volunteer	16.6	24.0	10.2	17.1	9.3	14.3	17.9	15.1	19.6	17.3	14.6	15.1	17.5	17.7	17.5	32.3
4. I would probably NOT volunteer	19.5	17.1	21.4	18.8	17.3	16.5	19.9	18.2	24.8	21.3	16.6	19.7	20.4	21.2	16.6	21.6
5. I would very likely NOT volunteer	8.4	5.6	10.9	9.4	4.8	6.8	10.0	8.7	7.1	9.4	5.7	8.3	8.0	8.3	9.6	4.7
6. I would definitely NOT volunteer	16.6	9.4	23.4	15.3	30.3	18.0	14.8	19.4	13.1	15.8	18.5	18.8	15.3	15.6	14.2	10.4
7. In my opinion, there is no such thing as a "necessary" war	18.9	13.4	23.7	18.9	19.2	22.9	18.7	16.5	18.8	18.6	20.0	19.1	16.2	18.2	22.0	7.9
Item 11220 Subject L03 N	2655	1224	1382	2095	243	580	782	820	473	1712	849	1139	526	380	548	24

E07: How closely do your ideas agree with your PARENTS' ideas about . . .

Our ideas are . . .

E07A: What you should do with your life.

1. Very similar	27.2	26.2	28.5	27.0	28.7	29.0	25.9	28.2	25.4	29.2	24.1	31.8	25.3	24.5	21.5	21.8
2. Mostly similar	44.4	44.3	44.5	47.4	30.6	43.5	48.0	39.8	47.5	48.0	37.4	43.4	48.6	48.4	42.2	23.1
3. Mostly different	13.4	13.0	13.7	12.2	18.8	12.4	13.3	14.2	13.1	10.8	18.3	11.8	12.4	13.3	16.4	38.5
4. Very different	8.0	7.6	8.1	6.7	14.6	8.7	7.0	9.3	6.4	5.8	11.3	5.2	8.8	6.9	13.1	10.7
8. Don't know	7.1	8.8	5.3	6.7	7.3	6.5	5.8	8.5	7.6	6.3	9.0	7.7	5.0	6.9	6.9	6.0
Item 11230 Subject M03 N	2693	1234	1409	2125	244	587	789	835	482	1740	860	1154	529	387	559	24

E07B: What you do in your leisure time

1. Very similar	9.0	7.2	10.6	8.4	13.0	11.0	8.5	9.2	7.4	8.5	10.5	10.9	9.1	7.9	5.7	10.7
2. Mostly similar	33.1	30.7	35.5	34.7	24.4	32.7	34.9	32.1	32.3	35.7	28.6	38.3	33.0	33.5	23.3	13.4
3. Mostly different	27.3	29.9	24.9	27.7	26.2	25.6	27.9	25.6	31.5	27.3	27.1	25.4	28.5	27.7	31.0	19.5
4. Very different	24.9	25.1	24.6	23.8	26.9	24.5	23.6	27.1	23.8	23.6	26.8	19.0	24.0	27.7	34.9	31.5
8. Don't know	5.7	7.1	4.4	5.3	9.4	6.3	5.1	6.0	5.1	4.9	6.9	6.5	5.4	3.1	5.2	24.8
Item 11240 Subject C08,M03 N	2688	1231	1407	2123	245	584	789	833	481	1736	860	1152	528	387	559	23

E07C: How you dress–what clothes you wear

1. Very similar	23.8	19.7	27.4	23.8	25.8	25.5	20.6	26.4	22.2	23.5	24.4	25.4	20.4	27.4	21.6	7.6
2. Mostly similar	41.4	41.4	41.8	44.1	26.6	37.5	45.6	39.2	42.9	44.0	36.0	43.8	43.7	38.3	38.4	10.1
3. Mostly different	16.8	18.2	15.3	16.8	17.0	17.1	16.7	15.5	18.9	16.5	17.7	14.7	17.1	18.6	19.5	29.9
4. Very different	13.4	14.5	12.1	11.5	21.3	13.7	12.8	14.9	11.3	11.9	16.1	11.4	15.2	11.6	15.6	34.9
8. Don't know	4.7	6.2	3.4	3.9	9.3	6.2	4.3	4.1	4.7	4.1	5.7	4.8	3.6	4.1	4.9	17.6
Item 11250 Subject M03 N	2681	1228	1403	2116	243	585	785	830	481	1735	855	1151	527	386	558	20

QUESTIONNAIRE FORM 4 1986	TOTAL	SEX		RACE		REGION				4YR COLLEGE PLANS		ILLICIT DRUG USE: LIFETIME				
		M	F	White	Black	NE	NC	S	W	Yes	No	None	Mari- juana Only	Few Pills	More Pills	Any Her- oin
N (Weighted No. of Cases):	3123	1441	1571	2352	333	744	873	961	545	1904	1002	1314	604	446	654	26
% of Weighted Total:	100.0	46.1	50.3	75.3	10.7	23.8	27.9	30.8	17.4	61.0	32.1	42.1	19.3	14.3	20.9	0.8

E07D: How you spend your money

1. Very similar	11.5	9.3	13.6	10.6	16.1	15.1	9.1	13.7	7.3	11.2	12.8	14.9	6.3	12.8	8.9	1.8
2. Mostly similar	31.8	29.6	33.8	34.3	21.7	29.0	35.8	27.6	36.0	35.5	24.1	35.1	35.5	28.3	25.7	4.7
3. Mostly different	27.0	28.9	25.6	27.4	21.8	25.3	26.0	27.5	29.6	27.0	27.1	25.3	26.8	32.3	27.1	36.3
4. Very different	24.9	26.9	22.9	23.3	35.4	25.0	25.3	27.6	19.6	21.9	30.5	20.2	27.0	22.3	33.1	45.5
8. Don't know	4.8	5.3	4.1	4.4	5.0	5.5	3.8	3.7	7.5	4.4	5.6	4.6	4.4	4.3	5.2	11.7
Item 11260 Subject M03 N	2678	1227	1402	2118	241	584	783	831	480	1732	855	1149	528	385	555	23

E07E: What things are O.K. to do when you are on a date

1. Very similar	16.6	14.4	18.3	16.0	21.2	18.4	12.8	17.9	18.1	15.6	18.7	18.7	11.9	19.1	14.2	14.7
2. Mostly similar	29.1	27.3	30.5	30.4	22.4	27.1	32.3	28.3	27.6	31.2	25.5	33.5	26.8	30.3	22.7	10.9
3. Mostly different	20.6	21.6	20.2	21.4	16.0	20.3	21.3	20.4	20.4	21.1	20.2	16.7	27.8	20.8	22.7	23.9
4. Very different	21.4	21.9	20.7	20.3	24.7	21.4	20.4	22.4	21.1	19.4	24.5	16.4	21.2	21.6	30.2	30.1
8. Don't know	12.4	14.8	10.3	11.9	15.7	12.8	13.2	11.0	12.8	12.8	11.0	14.6	12.2	8.3	10.2	20.4
Item 11270 Subject M03 N	2682	1231	1402	2119	242	584	785	831	482	1734	856	1151	528	386	557	23

E07F: Whether it is O.K. to drink

1. Very similar	24.6	22.1	26.6	22.5	35.3	25.1	21.4	27.1	24.9	25.8	23.0	36.0	14.6	20.7	13.5	18.9
2. Mostly similar	29.6	28.1	30.9	31.5	19.2	28.7	30.3	27.8	32.6	31.1	27.4	27.7	32.0	30.9	33.0	2.5
3. Mostly different	19.4	21.1	18.0	21.0	9.9	19.2	23.9	16.1	18.2	18.9	19.9	14.7	24.3	21.6	23.1	15.6
4. Very different	21.5	22.5	20.6	21.1	24.4	22.2	20.0	23.7	19.2	19.7	24.3	15.6	25.5	23.5	26.7	37.1
8. Don't know	4.9	6.3	3.8	4.0	11.3	4.7	4.5	5.3	5.1	4.5	5.5	6.1	3.5	3.3	3.7	25.8
Item 11280 Subject M03 N	2699	1243	1403	2129	247	590	793	833	483	1730	873	1150	526	392	567	25

E07G: Whether it is O.K. to use marijuana

1. Very similar	50.5	47.3	53.5	51.2	49.3	45.3	47.3	57.0	51.1	54.7	43.6	76.8	31.4	42.3	23.4	11.3
2. Mostly similar	11.6	10.7	12.6	12.4	8.8	10.3	14.7	9.4	12.1	12.0	11.4	8.6	15.8	16.2	11.7	2.6
3. Mostly different	7.5	7.4	7.4	7.9	5.5	8.1	8.4	6.0	7.6	7.2	8.0	2.6	11.7	7.7	12.8	9.3
4. Very different	23.2	25.7	20.9	21.9	24.5	26.9	21.7	22.0	23.0	19.9	28.3	5.6	31.3	28.1	45.0	64.6
8. Don't know	7.2	8.9	5.6	6.7	11.9	9.4	7.9	5.5	6.2	6.3	8.6	6.4	9.8	5.7	7.1	12.2
Item 11290 Subject M03 N	2697	1240	1405	2130	246	588	794	832	483	1730	871	1151	525	391	567	24

E07H: Whether it is O.K. to use other drugs

1. Very similar	59.2	56.2	62.1	60.9	51.8	53.8	57.0	64.6	60.1	65.0	48.6	79.4	53.3	56.7	29.1	5.1
2. Mostly similar	11.9	10.0	13.5	12.8	8.0	11.2	14.2	9.4	13.1	11.9	12.0	6.9	15.4	18.6	14.8	6.2
3. Mostly different	4.9	5.6	4.2	4.8	5.4	5.3	6.1	4.0	3.8	3.9	7.0	2.3	5.1	3.5	9.1	27.6
4. Very different	17.5	20.5	14.8	15.5	23.2	22.1	15.3	16.2	17.5	13.4	24.6	4.6	19.2	15.4	41.1	48.8
8. Don't know	6.6	7.8	5.4	6.0	11.5	7.5	7.4	5.7	5.5	5.7	7.7	6.8	7.0	5.8	6.0	12.2
Item 11300 Subject M03 N	2681	1230	1397	2117	241	584	790	830	477	1724	865	1144	521	389	564	24

E07I: What values are important in life

1. Very similar	36.2	34.1	38.2	34.9	42.0	34.3	34.1	41.7	32.5	38.1	33.0	42.1	32.9	37.6	27.4	5.9
2. Mostly similar	40.8	41.7	39.9	43.4	29.6	38.4	42.8	37.6	45.7	42.0	38.9	39.5	45.1	37.8	42.4	26.8
3. Mostly different	12.4	13.1	11.9	12.3	11.4	13.8	13.7	10.7	11.1	11.1	14.5	9.3	12.0	15.9	15.3	35.7
4. Very different	6.5	6.4	6.4	6.0	9.4	8.1	6.1	6.0	6.0	5.3	7.9	4.8	7.7	4.2	10.3	15.8
8. Don't know	4.1	4.7	3.6	3.5	7.7	5.4	3.2	3.9	4.7	3.5	5.7	4.3	2.4	4.5	4.6	15.9
Item 11310 Subject M03 N	2686	1231	1402	2121	243	582	792	832	479	1727	863	1146	522	390	565	24

E07J: The value of education

1. Very similar	57.0	54.3	59.6	56.0	62.6	56.0	52.1	62.5	56.7	63.9	43.3	62.7	55.0	56.2	49.8	32.1
2. Mostly similar	30.1	30.9	29.5	32.0	19.8	29.0	32.9	26.6	32.9	28.6	33.8	27.2	32.4	30.9	32.6	32.1
3. Mostly different	6.6	7.4	5.8	6.8	6.5	7.8	8.2	4.7	5.5	4.0	11.0	5.0	6.6	7.6	9.0	10.7
4. Very different	4.2	4.4	3.9	3.5	7.9	4.7	4.1	4.2	3.8	2.1	8.2	2.9	4.4	4.0	6.6	13.7
8. Don't know	2.1	3.0	1.2	1.7	3.2	2.4	2.7	1.9	1.1	1.3	3.7	2.3	1.5	1.3	2.0	11.4
Item 11320 Subject B09,M03 N	2679	1231	1397	2114	245	580	791	829	478	1726	857	1146	524	387	562	24

QUESTIONNAIRE FORM 4 1986	TOTAL	SEX		RACE		REGION				4YR COLLEGE PLANS		ILLICIT DRUG USE: LIFETIME				
		M	F	White	Black	NE	NC	S	W	Yes	No	None	Marijuana Only	Few Pills	More Pills	Any Heroin
N (Weighted No. of Cases):	3123	1441	1571	2352	333	744	873	961	545	1904	1002	1314	604	446	654	26
% of Weighted Total:	100.0	46.1	50.3	75.3	10.7	23.8	27.9	30.8	17.4	61.0	32.1	42.1	19.3	14.3	20.9	0.8
E07K: What are appropriate roles for women																
1. Very similar	31.3	25.0	36.9	31.7	34.6	32.6	28.5	34.3	29.4	33.4	27.8	34.7	30.6	26.2	29.2	8.9
2. Mostly similar	39.4	40.5	38.8	41.8	27.0	33.2	42.0	40.3	40.8	40.1	38.6	37.6	41.2	43.7	39.1	22.3
3. Mostly different	9.8	11.1	8.6	9.7	8.0	11.6	10.6	7.9	9.3	9.3	10.8	8.0	11.1	10.4	11.5	19.9
4. Very different	6.4	5.6	6.8	4.7	13.9	7.6	6.3	5.9	5.9	4.9	9.3	5.3	5.7	7.2	8.0	24.1
8. Don't know	13.1	17.7	9.0	12.1	16.6	15.0	12.5	11.6	14.6	12.3	13.4	14.4	11.3	12.4	12.2	24.9
Item 11330 Subject D05,M03 N	2674	1229	1395	2113	243	580	790	825	479	1721	858	1140	523	386	563	24
E07L: Conservation and pollution issues																
1. Very similar	20.4	20.6	20.0	20.6	21.4	22.8	16.8	23.2	18.7	20.8	19.9	23.1	20.3	14.3	19.2	1.9
2. Mostly similar	30.0	33.4	27.1	32.1	18.2	26.0	33.4	28.4	32.1	31.7	27.5	31.5	32.0	28.3	27.5	14.8
3. Mostly different	7.9	10.2	5.9	7.3	11.5	10.3	8.2	7.8	4.8	6.3	11.4	6.7	6.1	13.1	7.4	33.2
4. Very different	3.5	3.7	2.8	2.6	7.0	4.8	3.0	2.8	3.7	2.5	4.7	2.7	3.1	4.7	3.9	13.5
8. Don't know	38.2	32.1	44.1	37.4	42.0	36.1	38.6	37.8	40.7	38.6	36.5	36.0	38.2	39.6	42.1	36.6
Item 11340 Subject F04,M03 N	2674	1233	1391	2114	242	579	789	828	477	1722	857	1140	524	385	563	24
E07M: Racial issues																
1. Very similar	32.2	33.2	31.7	31.5	40.7	31.2	25.4	38.7	33.6	33.7	30.1	33.3	33.3	29.3	31.7	16.6
2. Mostly similar	30.2	31.6	28.7	31.4	20.6	29.2	32.1	29.0	30.1	31.4	27.7	29.7	33.2	33.7	26.1	21.2
3. Mostly different	10.4	9.4	11.3	10.9	7.5	12.7	12.9	8.0	7.6	10.3	10.7	10.0	8.1	12.4	12.0	19.7
4. Very different	7.1	6.4	7.6	7.1	9.0	9.6	6.1	7.0	5.8	5.6	9.5	6.3	8.6	5.5	7.7	26.0
8. Don't know	20.1	19.5	20.7	19.0	22.3	17.2	23.4	17.3	22.9	19.0	21.9	20.7	16.8	19.2	22.6	16.5
Item 11350 Subject M03,N02 N	2666	1224	1391	2108	239	576	787	825	478	1720	853	1137	524	383	559	24
E07N: Religion																
1. Very similar	38.8	35.2	42.1	38.1	47.0	33.6	35.2	47.3	36.1	40.4	36.6	45.8	35.3	34.7	31.4	16.9
2. Mostly similar	31.3	32.3	30.2	32.7	21.0	32.2	35.8	27.6	29.4	32.0	30.0	28.5	37.3	34.0	30.2	26.3
3. Mostly different	10.4	11.6	9.4	10.9	7.7	11.1	11.7	7.4	12.7	10.4	9.9	10.2	9.8	12.3	10.1	7.6
4. Very different	8.0	8.8	7.4	7.7	11.1	10.4	7.5	7.0	8.0	7.2	9.4	6.1	7.5	8.6	12.0	13.5
8. Don't know	11.4	12.1	10.9	10.7	13.2	12.8	9.8	10.8	13.7	10.0	14.2	9.4	10.1	10.3	16.3	35.7
Item 11360 Subject G,M03 N	2673	1232	1391	2112	243	578	789	827	479	1723	855	1141	523	384	562	24
E07O: Politics																
1. Very similar	20.2	20.5	19.7	20.4	23.7	20.9	15.6	24.8	18.7	19.0	23.3	21.7	19.6	17.7	19.6	10.1
2. Mostly similar	28.3	30.6	26.2	30.5	15.9	26.0	31.3	27.3	27.5	31.1	23.2	28.3	30.9	28.2	26.9	11.5
3. Mostly different	9.6	11.0	8.4	8.7	12.0	9.6	9.8	9.5	9.4	9.8	9.2	8.5	7.9	15.3	8.7	23.3
4. Very different	5.4	6.6	3.9	4.8	9.5	7.9	4.0	4.5	5.9	4.6	6.4	4.2	6.0	6.3	5.8	10.9
8. Don't know	36.6	31.2	41.7	35.7	39.0	35.6	39.2	33.8	38.4	35.5	37.9	37.3	35.6	32.3	39.0	44.2
Item 11370 Subject H01,M03 N	2669	1232	1387	2108	243	579	789	823	478	1721	852	1137	523	383	562	24
E08: How do you think your CLOSE FRIENDS feel (or would feel) about YOU doing each of the following things?																
E08A: Smoking one or more packs of cigarettes per day																
1. Not disapprove	23.8	25.0	22.8	24.9	18.9	30.3	25.5	21.7	16.6	19.0	32.3	12.7	23.2	24.2	44.3	61.5
2. Disapprove	36.8	38.0	35.7	37.1	36.4	31.9	36.6	41.2	35.5	37.1	36.0	39.0	38.7	37.9	31.3	18.1
3. Strongly disapprove	39.4	37.0	41.5	38.1	44.8	37.8	37.8	37.1	47.9	43.9	31.7	48.3	38.1	37.9	24.4	20.4
Item 11470 Subject A12b N	2657	1211	1393	2095	245	580	782	822	473	1713	851	1137	517	383	556	24
E08B: Trying marijuana (pot, grass) once or twice																
1. Not disapprove	43.3	46.2	41.2	45.6	34.0	49.3	46.5	36.6	42.4	42.3	43.9	17.4	62.5	50.7	73.4	57.5
2. Disapprove	23.2	25.0	21.7	22.6	26.4	21.9	23.7	24.4	21.8	23.8	21.9	28.3	21.1	23.1	14.4	40.0
3. Strongly disapprove	33.5	28.8	37.1	31.9	39.7	28.8	29.8	39.0	35.9	33.8	34.3	54.3	16.4	26.2	12.2	2.5
Item 11480 Subject A12b N	2653	1209	1394	2092	243	573	785	824	471	1714	846	1136	520	379	555	24

QUESTIONNAIRE FORM 4 1986	TOTAL	SEX		RACE		REGION				4YR COLLEGE PLANS		ILLICIT DRUG USE: LIFETIME				
		M	F	White	Black	NE	NC	S	W	Yes	No	None	Mari-juana Only	Few Pills	More Pills	Any Her-oin
N (Weighted No. of Cases):	3123	1441	1571	2352	333	744	873	961	545	1904	1002	1314	604	446	654	26
% of Weighted Total:	100.0	46.1	50.3	75.3	10.7	23.8	27.9	30.8	17.4	61.0	32.1	42.1	19.3	14.3	20.9	0.8
E08C: Smoking marijuana occasionally																
1. Not disapprove	35.6	40.2	31.8	37.4	27.6	41.5	38.3	30.3	33.3	33.4	39.7	12.6	45.1	41.4	68.8	66.7
2. Disapprove	23.0	23.3	23.0	23.1	22.4	22.6	25.1	21.8	22.3	23.4	21.3	25.0	27.0	24.1	14.5	23.7
3. Strongly disapprove	41.3	36.5	45.2	39.4	50.0	35.8	36.6	47.9	44.4	43.3	39.1	62.4	27.9	34.4	16.8	9.6
Item 11490　Subject A12b 　N	2654	1209	1394	2096	242	577	781	822	474	1712	846	1133	518	381	560	24
E08D: Smoking marijuana regularly																
1. Not disapprove	17.7	22.3	13.8	17.7	17.2	20.9	17.4	16.5	16.4	13.5	25.3	5.9	16.2	17.8	41.6	61.3
2. Disapprove	28.4	30.9	26.0	29.1	25.5	29.2	31.1	25.8	27.3	28.5	27.8	22.3	37.3	32.1	29.8	28.6
3. Strongly disapprove	54.0	46.8	60.2	53.2	57.2	49.9	51.6	57.7	56.4	58.0	46.9	71.8	46.5	50.1	28.6	10.1
Item 11500　Subject A12b 　N	2644	1202	1392	2086	241	571	781	821	471	1712	838	1133	518	376	554	24
E08E: Trying LSD once or twice																
1. Not disapprove	11.0	13.7	8.7	11.3	12.1	13.9	11.2	10.5	7.9	9.4	13.9	5.8	9.7	9.7	21.2	52.4
2. Disapprove	24.4	26.3	22.7	24.5	22.7	21.0	27.6	24.0	24.1	22.1	27.8	21.7	21.3	28.9	29.1	46.1
3. Strongly disapprove	64.6	60.0	68.6	64.2	65.2	65.2	61.3	65.5	68.0	68.5	58.3	72.5	69.0	61.4	49.8	1.5
Item 11510　Subject A12b 　N	2652	1208	1392	2094	241	578	781	821	472	1714	843	1131	519	382	558	23
E08F: Trying an amphetamine (upper, pep pill, bennie, speed) once or twice																
1. Not disapprove	20.6	22.6	19.0	21.8	14.2	21.4	23.5	18.8	17.8	19.5	23.0	8.9	17.5	22.4	44.9	50.7
2. Disapprove	26.3	27.9	24.8	26.9	23.2	25.1	27.1	26.7	25.6	25.3	26.4	24.8	24.9	30.1	27.9	27.1
3. Strongly disapprove	53.2	49.4	56.3	51.3	62.6	53.5	49.4	54.5	56.5	55.1	50.7	66.3	57.6	47.5	27.1	22.3
Item 11520　Subject A12b 　N	2648	1203	1393	2089	243	578	776	823	471	1711	845	1132	519	380	554	24
E08G: Trying cocaine once or twice																
1. Not disapprove	20.4	23.5	17.8	20.7	15.4	25.6	19.6	15.6	24.0	18.7	23.4	6.4	16.7	20.7	50.8	53.5
2. Disapprove	22.8	24.6	21.0	23.1	20.4	20.7	24.0	24.4	20.6	21.5	24.6	21.5	23.5	27.1	22.6	18.5
3. Strongly disapprove	56.8	51.8	61.2	56.1	64.2	53.7	56.5	60.1	55.4	59.9	52.0	72.0	59.9	52.2	26.6	28.0
Item 11525　Subject A12b 　N	2649	1204	1393	2089	243	576	777	824	472	1714	841	1133	519	380	554	24
E08H: Taking cocaine occasionally																
1. Not disapprove	12.7	15.6	10.1	12.5	11.2	17.8	10.3	10.4	14.2	9.9	17.7	4.6	7.3	6.8	36.0	43.3
2. Disapprove	24.0	26.6	21.9	24.8	21.8	20.8	26.9	24.8	22.1	22.9	25.5	19.8	25.7	27.8	28.6	45.5
3. Strongly disapprove	63.3	57.8	68.1	62.7	67.0	61.3	62.9	64.8	63.7	67.2	56.8	75.6	67.0	65.4	35.4	11.3
Item 11526　Subject A12b 　N	2648	1204	1393	2090	242	578	777	820	473	1712	843	1132	519	378	556	24
E08I: Taking one or two drinks nearly every day																
1. Not disapprove	24.1	32.5	16.3	25.2	18.1	23.6	27.0	26.3	16.0	20.7	29.7	14.2	24.6	25.2	41.1	74.8
2. Disapprove	36.0	35.5	36.9	36.5	30.8	35.0	40.5	33.2	34.6	36.5	35.5	34.0	39.0	38.8	36.4	20.9
3. Strongly disapprove	39.9	32.0	46.8	38.2	51.1	41.5	32.5	40.4	49.5	42.8	34.8	51.8	36.4	36.0	22.5	4.3
Item 11530　Subject A12b 　N	2648	1204	1392	2088	243	576	777	823	472	1712	843	1132	519	380	554	24
E08J: Taking four or five drinks nearly every day																
1. Not disapprove	12.6	18.0	7.8	12.5	12.3	11.4	13.9	15.0	7.8	8.8	20.4	7.5	10.9	11.4	22.9	62.1
2. Disapprove	27.2	31.0	23.6	27.6	21.4	27.5	31.4	25.0	23.6	25.6	29.1	23.2	28.3	29.6	33.0	26.8
3. Strongly disapprove	60.2	51.0	68.6	59.9	66.2	61.2	54.7	59.9	68.6	65.6	50.5	69.4	60.8	59.0	44.1	11.1
Item 11540　Subject A12b 　N	2639	1196	1392	2083	241	573	777	819	471	1708	837	1131	517	377	550	24
E08K: Having five or more drinks once or twice each weekend																
1. Not disapprove	45.1	53.7	37.8	49.0	24.0	46.1	53.7	40.7	37.6	44.5	46.6	27.2	53.3	53.5	68.9	60.1
2. Disapprove	23.4	20.8	25.7	23.4	24.4	22.3	21.6	25.3	24.4	23.6	22.2	25.8	23.2	25.2	16.6	24.7
3. Strongly disapprove	31.5	25.4	36.5	27.6	51.6	31.6	24.7	34.0	38.1	31.9	31.2	46.9	23.5	21.3	14.5	15.2
Item 11550　Subject A12b 　N	2647	1206	1389	2088	242	574	778	823	473	1712	842	1132	518	379	555	25

QUESTIONNAIRE FORM 4 1986	TOTAL	SEX		RACE		REGION				4YR COLLEGE PLANS		ILLICIT DRUG USE: LIFETIME				
		M	F	White	Black	NE	NC	S	W	Yes	No	None	Mari-juana Only	Few Pills	More Pills	Any Her-oin
N (Weighted No. of Cases):	3123	1441	1571	2352	333	744	873	961	545	1904	1002	1314	604	446	654	26
% of Weighted Total:	100.0	46.1	50.3	75.3	10.7	23.8	27.9	30.8	17.4	61.0	32.1	42.1	19.3	14.3	20.9	0.8

E08L: Driving a car after having 1-2 drinks

1. Not disapprove	33.0	42.6	24.5	36.2	15.3	28.4	44.2	29.8	25.8	32.8	33.8	18.3	37.3	40.9	52.9	57.5
2. Disapprove	31.0	29.2	33.0	31.2	29.9	31.6	29.9	31.9	30.6	31.5	29.3	32.1	34.2	31.3	26.0	25.8
3. Strongly disapprove	36.0	28.2	42.5	32.6	54.8	40.0	25.9	38.3	43.5	35.7	36.9	49.6	28.4	27.8	21.1	16.7
Item 11551 Subject A12b N	2644	1206	1387	2088	240	575	776	821	472	1711	840	1130	517	379	555	24

E08M: Driving a car after having 5 or more drinks

1. Not disapprove	8.1	12.4	4.1	8.1	10.9	5.7	11.9	7.8	5.2	6.1	12.6	5.1	6.7	8.0	13.5	36.3
2. Disapprove	22.2	25.5	19.2	22.6	19.4	18.1	26.7	24.1	16.5	21.6	22.3	18.0	25.5	24.8	26.0	20.8
3. Strongly disapprove	69.7	62.0	76.7	69.3	69.7	76.3	61.4	68.1	78.4	72.4	65.2	76.9	67.9	67.2	60.5	42.8
Item 11552 Subject A12b N	2643	1204	1388	2086	242	573	777	822	472	1709	841	1131	517	378	554	24

E09: In some communities parents who are particularly concerned with drug or alcohol abuse among young people have formed groups of concerned parents to deal with these problems. In these groups parents try to become more informed and sometimes to set some common guidelines for young peoples' behavior. In general, what do you think of the idea of having parents get together in groups such as these?

1. A bad idea	5.1	7.1	3.2	4.3	9.0	7.6	4.7	3.8	4.9	4.0	7.1	4.9	3.6	5.0	6.5	14.7
2. More bad than good	8.1	10.9	5.5	8.3	3.9	8.3	10.4	7.1	5.8	7.7	8.4	4.8	8.5	9.2	12.1	29.5
3. Don't know or can't say	27.5	31.3	24.2	29.3	15.2	23.0	31.6	25.7	29.1	25.3	31.5	22.6	28.3	30.5	34.6	20.1
4. More good than bad	23.8	22.3	25.2	24.8	22.2	23.4	24.0	23.0	25.4	26.0	19.5	21.4	27.2	25.9	25.2	21.0
5. A good idea	35.5	28.4	41.8	33.3	49.7	37.7	29.2	40.3	34.8	37.0	33.6	46.2	32.4	29.5	21.6	14.7
Item 21730 Subject A16a N	2600	1189	1360	2052	233	566	771	802	461	1683	825	1114	509	377	538	24

E10: To the best of your knowledge, how many of your close friends have parents who are involved in such parent groups?

1. None	69.1	63.7	74.4	69.9	62.2	67.1	69.9	69.0	70.4	68.4	69.7	69.5	67.4	66.3	73.0	48.3
2. A few	22.1	26.0	18.3	22.5	19.8	23.5	22.2	21.1	21.9	23.3	20.7	21.3	24.5	25.0	19.1	38.5
3. Some	8.0	9.5	6.5	7.0	15.1	8.6	7.1	9.0	7.0	8.0	7.8	8.2	7.1	8.0	7.6	8.3
4. Most or all	0.8	0.7	0.8	0.6	2.9	0.9	0.8	0.9	0.7	0.4	1.7	1.0	1.0	0.7	0.2	4.9
Item 21740 Subject A16a N	2599	1185	1363	2051	233	568	769	802	459	1680	824	1113	510	375	538	23

E11: Has either (or both) of your own parents been involved in such a group?

1. No–GO TO Q.E14	92.2	91.5	93.2	92.7	87.2	90.0	92.2	92.1	95.1	92.9	91.3	93.0	93.6	92.9	90.5	65.4
2. Yes, in the past, but not now	5.1	5.8	4.4	4.7	8.7	5.9	5.5	5.6	2.8	4.4	6.2	4.1	4.3	4.1	7.2	28.9
3. Yes, now	2.6	2.7	2.4	2.7	4.1	4.2	2.3	2.2	2.1	2.7	2.6	2.9	2.1	3.0	2.3	5.7
Item 21750 Subject A16a N	2553	1161	1344	2024	220	560	752	785	456	1656	805	1103	503	357	528	24

E12: Has the involvement of your parent(s) in such a group had any impact on your own feelings about drug or alcohol use?

1. Made me much less likely to use drugs or alcohol	27.9	24.5	31.2	20.0	54.5	36.3	21.8	26.0	27.0	24.7	32.3	42.7	16.7	21.0	16.8	29.8
2. Made me somewhat less likely to use drugs or alcohol	16.9	17.4	15.6	19.0	8.7	12.7	20.3	16.1	20.6	15.5	17.0	13.4	25.0	24.1	14.0	5.7
3. No impact either way	49.3	49.8	50.1	55.5	32.5	46.5	50.5	52.7	44.9	52.5	46.3	43.1	54.9	44.3	58.0	47.5
4. Made me somewhat more likely to use drugs or alcohol	3.5	3.7	3.0	4.0	4.4	4.5	4.4	2.4	2.2	3.1	4.1	-	3.4	6.7	5.0	17.0
5. Made me much more likely to use drugs or alcohol	2.4	4.5	-	1.5	-	-	3.0	2.8	5.3	4.2	0.3	0.8	-	3.8	6.2	-
Item 21760 Subject A16a N★	313	167	129	214	49	87	81	103	42	170	120	118	51	45	77	12

★=excludes respondents for whom question was inappropriate.

	TOTAL	SEX		RACE		REGION				4YR COLLEGE PLANS		ILLICIT DRUG USE: LIFETIME				
QUESTIONNAIRE FORM 4 **1986**		M	F	White	Black	NE	NC	S	W	Yes	No	None	Mari-juana Only	Few Pills	More Pills	Any Her-oin
N (Weighted No. of Cases):	3123	1441	1571	2352	333	744	873	961	545	1904	1002	1314	604	446	654	26
% of Weighted Total:	100.0	46.1	50.3	75.3	10.7	23.8	27.9	30.8	17.4	61.0	32.1	42.1	19.3	14.3	20.9	0.8

E13: What about your relationship with your parents? Has their involvement in the parent group made your relationship better or worse?

	TOTAL	M	F	White	Black	NE	NC	S	W	Yes	No	None	Mari-juana Only	Few Pills	More Pills	Any Her-oin
1. Much worse	6.9	9.4	2.5	5.1	11.8	5.5	7.6	9.0	3.2	4.5	10.5	7.8	3.8	4.9	8.8	10.7
2. Somewhat worse	12.2	14.6	9.0	10.8	12.7	14.9	7.9	12.7	13.3	9.0	16.2	8.1	11.6	7.9	15.4	47.9
3. No effect, don't know	45.5	40.0	56.9	51.2	17.7	45.6	44.5	43.7	50.9	53.5	35.4	41.3	59.0	52.7	48.0	10.5
4. Somewhat better	20.7	21.9	16.2	20.5	25.8	21.7	22.1	17.5	23.9	18.8	22.1	21.9	19.8	19.2	17.5	20.8
5. Much better	14.8	14.1	15.4	12.4	31.9	12.2	18.0	17.1	8.7	14.2	15.9	20.9	5.7	15.3	10.2	10.1
Item 21770 Subject A16a **N★**	306	171	119	205	50	80	78	102	47	173	113	115	45	47	78	11

E14: In some communities young people them-selves have formed groups aimed at avoiding drug use, such as Youth for Drug-Free Alter-natives. How many of your close friends have been members of such a group?

	TOTAL	M	F	White	Black	NE	NC	S	W	Yes	No	None	Mari-juana Only	Few Pills	More Pills	Any Her-oin
1. None	69.6	68.7	70.8	68.8	73.8	62.7	68.6	73.9	72.2	69.3	69.5	69.3	70.1	67.9	71.7	45.1
2. A few	19.8	20.4	19.1	20.7	14.7	23.7	20.4	16.3	20.0	19.8	20.3	20.2	18.9	20.2	19.6	13.1
3. Some	9.3	9.8	8.5	9.2	9.6	11.4	9.8	8.4	7.4	9.5	8.8	8.6	9.8	10.8	8.4	32.5
4. Most or all	1.3	1.1	1.6	1.4	1.9	2.2	1.2	1.4	0.4	1.3	1.4	1.9	1.2	1.2	0.3	9.3
Item 21780 Subject A16a **N**	2597	1181	1366	2050	233	567	770	800	460	1681	821	1111	507	375	540	24

E15: Have you ever participated in such a group?

	TOTAL	M	F	White	Black	NE	NC	S	W	Yes	No	None	Mari-juana Only	Few Pills	More Pills	Any Her-oin
3. Yes, now	5.2	4.4	5.6	5.1	6.8	8.1	4.5	5.0	3.0	5.5	4.8	5.8	5.0	4.5	3.8	23.6
2. Yes, in the past, but not now	6.9	5.4	8.2	6.9	7.1	6.7	6.3	7.2	7.4	6.8	6.6	5.3	6.1	9.0	8.7	16.2
1. No	88.0	90.2	86.2	88.0	86.1	85.2	89.1	87.8	89.6	87.7	88.5	88.9	88.9	86.6	87.5	60.2
Item 21790 Subject A16a **N**	2540	1146	1346	2014	223	552	761	780	447	1663	787	1091	501	364	523	21

★=excludes respondents for whom question was inappropriate.

QUESTIONNAIRE FORM 5 1986	TOTAL	SEX		RACE		REGION				4YR COLLEGE PLANS		ILLICIT DRUG USE: LIFETIME				
		M	F	White	Black	NE	NC	S	W	Yes	No	None	Mari-juana Only	Few Pills	More Pills	Any Her-oin
N (Weighted No. of Cases):	3073	1413	1550	2295	312	725	867	952	529	1839	1084	1237	583	487	648	47
% of Weighted Total:	100.0	46.0	50.4	74.7	10.2	23.6	28.2	31.0	17.2	59.9	35.3	40.3	19.0	15.8	21.1	1.5

A01: Taking all things together, how would you say things are these days–would you say you're very happy, pretty happy, or not too happy these days?

	TOTAL	M	F	White	Black	NE	NC	S	W	Yes	No	None	Mari-juana Only	Few Pills	More Pills	Any Her-oin
3. Very happy	17.3	17.0	17.6	18.7	10.5	17.1	17.5	17.1	17.7	18.0	16.2	17.1	18.6	15.3	18.3	7.3
2. Pretty happy	68.6	69.0	68.3	70.9	62.1	66.9	72.2	67.4	67.1	69.3	68.2	69.6	68.9	70.3	65.7	71.2
1. Not too happy	14.1	13.9	14.1	10.3	27.4	15.9	10.3	15.5	15.2	12.7	15.7	13.4	12.6	14.3	16.0	21.5
Item 1190 Subject P01,Q01 N	3060	1407	1546	2286	311	724	861	952	523	1832	1083	1234	580	485	645	47

A02: Some people think a lot about the social problems of the nation and the world, and about how they might be solved. Others spend little time thinking about these issues. How much do you think about such things?

	TOTAL	M	F	White	Black	NE	NC	S	W	Yes	No	None	Mari-juana Only	Few Pills	More Pills	Any Her-oin
1. Never	1.4	1.6	1.1	1.4	0.6	3.3	1.3	0.4	0.7	1.0	1.9	0.8	0.5	1.6	3.2	2.1
2. Seldom	12.9	13.6	12.4	13.2	10.0	15.8	12.9	11.1	12.1	11.7	14.6	10.9	12.6	10.7	17.2	21.5
3. Sometimes	50.6	49.1	52.0	51.7	44.3	52.7	50.8	47.3	53.1	50.1	51.7	50.6	55.0	53.2	46.9	36.3
4. Quite often	30.1	29.6	30.5	29.1	35.8	25.6	28.1	34.8	31.1	31.5	27.9	31.8	27.8	30.2	28.6	29.5
5. A great deal	5.1	6.1	4.0	4.6	9.3	2.7	7.0	6.3	3.0	5.7	3.9	6.0	4.1	4.3	4.2	10.6
Item 6880 Subject J,Q08 N	3062	1407	1548	2289	311	724	860	952	526	1833	1083	1235	580	485	647	47

A03: Of all the problems facing the nation today, how often do you worry about each of the following?

A03A: Chance of nuclear war

	TOTAL	M	F	White	Black	NE	NC	S	W	Yes	No	None	Mari-juana Only	Few Pills	More Pills	Any Her-oin
1. Never	7.6	8.6	6.3	7.2	9.4	7.7	8.0	6.5	8.7	7.7	7.3	8.5	7.3	5.3	7.3	7.5
2. Seldom	23.3	27.0	20.1	25.1	15.5	23.7	23.1	22.5	24.5	23.7	23.4	25.0	21.3	21.5	22.9	26.8
3. Sometimes	41.6	40.4	42.9	43.0	31.8	41.7	44.3	38.8	42.2	42.3	40.1	38.9	42.3	44.2	45.4	34.5
4. Often	27.5	24.0	30.7	24.7	43.4	26.8	24.6	32.1	24.6	26.3	29.2	27.6	29.0	29.0	24.4	31.2
Item 11660 Subject J N	3063	1408	1549	2293	310	723	864	951	524	1836	1083	1235	581	486	647	47

A03B: Population growth

	TOTAL	M	F	White	Black	NE	NC	S	W	Yes	No	None	Mari-juana Only	Few Pills	More Pills	Any Her-oin
1. Never	34.4	34.4	33.8	36.4	29.4	41.9	35.5	32.5	25.8	32.9	37.3	33.4	34.0	34.9	36.1	34.3
2. Seldom	41.6	42.0	41.9	42.7	36.3	38.8	41.7	41.7	44.9	43.7	38.4	40.9	44.7	41.7	41.1	40.9
3. Sometimes	18.6	18.0	19.0	16.7	25.3	12.5	18.4	20.6	23.5	17.8	18.9	20.4	17.1	18.1	16.7	15.5
4. Often	5.5	5.6	5.2	4.2	9.1	6.9	4.4	5.2	5.8	5.6	5.4	5.3	4.2	5.4	6.1	9.3
Item 11670 Subject E01,J N	3059	1407	1548	2292	310	722	864	949	524	1835	1082	1235	580	485	647	47

A03C: Crime and violence

	TOTAL	M	F	White	Black	NE	NC	S	W	Yes	No	None	Mari-juana Only	Few Pills	More Pills	Any Her-oin
1. Never	2.5	3.6	1.3	2.2	1.9	3.4	2.9	1.8	2.0	1.7	3.8	2.0	2.3	2.6	3.4	1.2
2. Seldom	18.1	25.6	11.3	19.4	16.1	19.7	18.2	16.0	19.6	17.4	19.1	17.7	18.5	17.3	18.8	31.5
3. Sometimes	42.5	44.2	41.4	46.4	25.8	40.7	45.3	38.6	47.7	44.1	41.0	42.2	42.2	43.1	44.2	31.0
4. Often	36.9	26.6	46.0	32.0	56.1	36.3	33.6	43.7	30.7	36.8	36.2	38.1	37.0	36.9	33.6	36.3
Item 11680 Subject J N	3057	1406	1545	2290	310	720	863	950	524	1835	1079	1236	578	484	647	46

A03D: Pollution

	TOTAL	M	F	White	Black	NE	NC	S	W	Yes	No	None	Mari-juana Only	Few Pills	More Pills	Any Her-oin
1. Never	15.2	15.8	14.8	15.0	20.8	18.0	15.8	15.6	9.7	13.6	18.4	12.1	18.9	14.6	18.3	19.8
2. Seldom	40.6	38.2	43.4	42.7	36.7	37.2	40.4	42.7	41.5	42.4	38.6	41.7	42.1	41.5	37.5	34.4
3. Sometimes	32.0	30.6	33.3	31.6	29.2	33.1	31.5	30.3	34.7	32.6	30.5	33.0	28.1	33.2	32.2	36.1
4. Often	12.2	15.5	8.5	10.8	13.3	11.7	12.4	11.4	14.2	11.4	12.5	13.2	10.9	10.7	12.0	9.7
Item 11690 Subject F04,J N	3039	1400	1536	2279	308	716	859	944	521	1825	1074	1229	577	481	640	47

A03E: Energy shortages

	TOTAL	M	F	White	Black	NE	NC	S	W	Yes	No	None	Mari-juana Only	Few Pills	More Pills	Any Her-oin
1. Never	27.4	25.4	29.2	28.7	22.7	28.8	27.4	25.8	28.5	25.2	30.8	22.6	29.8	30.8	32.0	23.5
2. Seldom	44.0	41.4	46.4	46.3	36.7	43.0	43.7	45.0	43.8	46.2	41.9	48.2	41.9	38.8	42.6	39.9
3. Sometimes	22.4	25.1	19.9	20.8	28.7	22.3	23.8	21.0	22.4	22.8	21.0	23.0	21.8	24.1	19.6	28.1
4. Often	6.3	8.2	4.5	4.2	11.9	5.9	5.1	8.1	5.3	5.8	6.4	6.2	6.5	6.3	5.7	8.5
Item 11700 Subject F05,J N	3047	1403	1539	2285	309	715	861	947	523	1827	1077	1229	578	483	645	47

QUESTIONNAIRE FORM 5 1986	TOTAL	SEX		RACE		REGION				4YR COLLEGE PLANS		ILLICIT DRUG USE: LIFETIME				
		M	F	White	Black	NE	NC	S	W	Yes	No	None	Mari- juana Only	Few Pills	More Pills	Any Her- oin
N (Weighted No. of Cases):	3073	1413	1550	2295	312	725	867	952	529	1839	1084	1237	583	487	648	47
% of Weighted Total:	100.0	46.0	50.4	74.7	10.2	23.6	28.2	31.0	17.2	59.9	35.3	40.3	19.0	15.8	21.1	1.5

A03F: Race relations

1. Never	23.0	26.9	19.7	24.6	13.4	23.2	23.5	20.3	27.1	19.7	28.8	20.4	20.5	23.0	29.0	37.7
2. Seldom	33.6	34.3	33.1	37.5	14.1	32.7	35.3	32.7	33.6	34.4	32.9	33.4	37.6	31.5	32.6	30.3
3. Sometimes	27.4	24.8	29.5	26.3	31.0	27.8	26.6	29.2	25.0	28.3	25.4	29.4	24.7	32.1	23.5	18.6
4. Often	16.0	14.0	17.7	11.7	41.4	16.3	14.6	17.9	14.3	17.6	12.9	16.8	17.2	13.4	14.9	13.5
Item 11710 Subject J,N02 N	3044	1404	1537	2279	310	719	860	946	519	1830	1075	1234	574	481	644	47

A03G: Hunger and poverty

1. Never	7.6	12.1	3.2	8.1	4.2	10.1	7.8	6.3	5.9	5.8	10.0	6.1	8.1	6.9	9.7	12.2
2. Seldom	26.6	35.2	19.2	29.7	14.2	24.3	27.6	26.3	28.5	25.9	28.6	24.9	27.6	25.8	28.9	36.6
3. Sometimes	41.9	38.4	45.2	42.7	37.5	43.4	41.8	40.3	42.8	45.1	37.3	44.3	41.2	41.4	40.4	21.6
4. Often	24.0	14.3	32.4	19.6	44.0	22.2	22.7	27.1	22.9	23.1	24.1	24.7	23.1	25.9	21.1	29.6
Item 11720 Subject F03,J N	3050	1406	1538	2285	309	721	859	944	524	1826	1081	1227	580	484	645	47

A03H: Using open land for housing or industry

1. Never	41.3	38.8	43.9	42.3	39.2	44.3	42.6	42.4	33.3	41.1	41.4	39.0	44.5	42.6	42.3	46.4
2. Seldom	31.9	30.9	32.8	31.9	35.8	33.2	30.4	32.0	32.2	33.2	30.1	33.4	34.1	31.2	27.8	25.8
3. Sometimes	17.9	18.9	17.1	17.3	16.1	14.2	18.7	16.3	24.7	17.5	18.5	19.7	13.9	17.8	18.3	16.3
4. Often	8.9	11.4	6.1	8.4	8.9	8.2	8.4	9.2	9.8	8.2	10.0	7.9	7.6	8.4	11.5	11.5
Item 11730 Subject F05,J N	3056	1404	1546	2290	308	720	864	947	524	1832	1081	1230	580	486	647	47

A03I: Urban decay

1. Never	49.3	46.2	52.5	50.4	48.7	48.3	49.4	51.6	46.1	46.9	53.7	48.9	52.1	48.2	48.8	49.2
2. Seldom	33.8	33.7	33.9	33.9	35.0	33.9	31.8	34.3	36.0	35.6	31.1	34.7	32.9	33.6	32.7	34.4
3. Sometimes	14.0	16.8	11.2	13.2	14.3	14.2	16.0	11.2	15.3	14.3	13.1	14.1	13.1	14.9	13.7	11.7
4. Often	3.0	3.4	2.5	2.5	2.1	3.6	2.9	2.8	2.6	3.3	2.1	2.3	1.9	3.3	4.8	4.7
Item 11740 Subject J N	3028	1394	1531	2276	303	712	858	943	515	1818	1073	1217	574	484	642	45

A03J: Economic problems

1. Never	10.2	9.9	10.3	10.0	10.9	14.9	9.8	9.2	6.4	7.9	14.3	8.0	12.1	10.9	11.6	11.7
2. Seldom	29.2	26.9	31.3	30.3	24.4	32.5	25.6	28.4	31.7	27.4	32.1	27.5	27.5	34.6	29.6	30.0
3. Sometimes	42.0	42.4	42.0	43.3	38.6	37.2	43.6	42.0	46.0	45.0	38.3	44.7	41.8	37.4	41.9	34.2
4. Often	18.6	20.8	16.3	16.4	26.2	15.4	21.0	20.4	15.8	19.7	15.3	19.8	18.6	17.1	17.0	24.1
Item 11750 Subject J N	3051	1405	1541	2285	308	721	858	946	525	1829	1079	1230	580	481	647	47

A03K: Drug abuse

1. Never	9.0	13.8	4.4	9.1	8.8	12.4	9.4	6.9	7.2	7.4	11.2	7.9	8.8	6.1	12.6	23.5
2. Seldom	21.8	27.3	16.8	23.9	14.3	20.9	22.2	21.9	22.4	23.3	20.2	20.2	25.4	22.1	22.3	14.0
3. Sometimes	37.3	36.1	39.1	39.1	27.1	37.9	38.6	34.8	38.8	39.6	34.2	39.3	35.9	38.4	34.1	27.5
4. Often	31.9	22.7	39.6	27.9	49.7	28.8	29.7	36.4	31.6	29.7	34.4	32.6	29.8	33.5	30.9	35.0
Item 11760 Subject J N	3063	1408	1550	2293	311	723	864	951	524	1837	1083	1235	581	486	647	47

A04: How well do you think your experiences and training (at home, school, work, etc.) have prepared you to be a good...

A04A: Husband or wife

1. Poorly	2.0	2.8	1.3	1.7	2.4	1.6	2.4	1.3	2.9	1.7	2.6	1.2	1.9	1.8	3.0	7.9
2. Not so well	4.3	4.9	3.5	4.4	2.0	4.2	4.0	3.6	6.1	4.3	4.0	3.6	3.8	4.9	5.3	6.4
3. Fairly well	22.2	26.5	18.5	23.4	15.4	24.1	22.8	19.9	22.9	21.6	24.0	21.1	20.1	19.2	27.4	23.3
4. Well	41.4	42.8	40.1	41.1	43.8	40.9	40.6	43.3	39.6	42.0	41.0	41.1	46.3	45.6	37.1	29.0
5. Very well	30.1	23.1	36.4	29.4	36.4	29.1	30.1	31.9	28.5	30.5	28.4	33.0	27.9	28.5	27.1	33.4
Item 11770 Subject D01 N	2997	1376	1518	2252	301	711	847	928	511	1802	1058	1218	565	467	638	47

A04B: Parent

1. Poorly	2.2	3.1	1.3	2.2	1.4	1.5	2.4	1.7	3.5	1.8	2.8	1.6	2.0	1.8	3.5	2.7
2. Not so well	5.5	7.0	4.3	5.6	3.6	5.2	5.6	5.1	6.0	5.1	6.3	4.8	4.8	4.8	7.5	11.4
3. Fairly well	20.7	24.6	17.2	22.1	14.1	23.5	18.1	20.4	21.9	20.2	22.4	20.5	19.6	18.7	23.9	16.3
4. Well	36.8	37.4	36.4	37.9	33.8	34.5	39.1	38.1	33.8	37.3	36.8	35.5	41.3	39.8	34.7	26.5
5. Very well	34.8	27.9	40.7	32.3	47.2	35.2	34.8	34.7	34.7	35.8	31.7	37.6	32.3	35.0	30.3	43.1
Item 11780 Subject D02 N	3017	1383	1529	2266	304	714	854	935	513	1816	1063	1219	573	475	642	45

QUESTIONNAIRE FORM 5 1986	TOTAL	SEX M	F	RACE White	Black	REGION NE	NC	S	W	4YR COLLEGE PLANS Yes	No	None	Mari- juana Only	Few Pills	More Pills	Any Her- oin
N (Weighted No. of Cases):	3073	1413	1550	2295	312	725	867	952	529	1839	1084	1237	583	487	648	47
% of Weighted Total:	100.0	46.0	50.4	74.7	10.2	23.6	28.2	31.0	17.2	59.9	35.3	40.3	19.0	15.8	21.1	1.5

A04C: Worker on a job

	TOTAL	M	F	White	Black	NE	NC	S	W	Yes	No	None	Mari Only	Few	More	Heroin
1. Poorly	0.9	1.4	0.4	0.7	0.6	1.0	1.2	0.5	0.8	0.8	1.0	0.7	0.3	0.7	1.7	1.2
2. Not so well	2.3	2.4	2.1	2.2	2.1	3.0	2.4	1.3	2.9	2.3	2.6	2.3	1.7	3.3	2.6	-
3. Fairly well	12.7	13.7	12.0	13.0	11.5	12.4	12.9	11.5	14.8	12.2	13.4	12.0	12.0	14.9	12.6	8.5
4. Well	40.5	40.1	40.6	41.2	34.3	40.4	40.6	39.7	41.9	41.0	39.9	40.3	42.1	39.0	40.3	46.9
5. Very well	43.7	42.4	44.9	42.9	51.5	43.2	42.9	47.0	39.5	43.8	43.1	44.7	43.9	42.2	42.7	43.3
Item 11790 Subject C01 N	3038	1393	1542	2276	308	717	860	943	519	1825	1071	1231	579	478	641	45

A05: Apart from the particular kind of work you want to do, how would you rate each of the following settings as a place to work?

A05A: Working in a large corporation

	TOTAL	M	F	White	Black	NE	NC	S	W	Yes	No	None	Mari Only	Few	More	Heroin
1. Not at all acceptable	4.4	4.3	4.2	4.6	2.3	5.8	4.1	3.3	4.8	3.4	5.6	3.4	4.6	5.1	4.7	4.0
2. Somewhat acceptable	21.7	19.5	23.5	22.6	18.3	22.2	20.1	22.9	21.2	19.8	25.0	21.4	20.4	23.5	21.8	25.3
3. Acceptable	46.9	48.1	46.1	47.3	45.3	48.4	48.0	46.1	44.5	47.6	46.6	50.0	42.9	45.6	46.4	39.4
4. Desirable	27.1	28.1	26.2	25.5	34.1	23.6	27.8	27.7	29.5	29.3	22.8	25.2	32.2	25.7	27.1	31.4
Item 11800 Subject C05 N	3057	1407	1546	2289	310	724	863	947	524	1834	1082	1232	581	486	646	47

A05B: Working in a small business

	TOTAL	M	F	White	Black	NE	NC	S	W	Yes	No	None	Mari Only	Few	More	Heroin
1. Not at all acceptable	4.6	5.0	4.1	3.6	9.3	7.0	3.9	3.9	3.6	4.0	5.5	3.6	4.5	4.3	5.9	2.9
2. Somewhat acceptable	23.8	24.3	22.9	21.5	38.6	24.7	20.2	26.7	23.4	22.5	24.8	22.9	24.6	24.2	23.8	26.0
3. Acceptable	53.2	52.8	53.7	54.5	43.7	51.8	56.9	52.6	49.9	53.9	51.9	54.7	50.7	54.5	52.6	46.9
4. Desirable	18.5	17.9	19.3	20.4	8.3	16.5	19.1	16.8	23.2	19.6	17.8	18.8	20.2	16.9	17.7	24.2
Item 11810 Subject C05 N	3054	1405	1545	2287	309	723	861	947	522	1834	1080	1231	580	485	644	47

A05C: Working in a government agency

	TOTAL	M	F	White	Black	NE	NC	S	W	Yes	No	None	Mari Only	Few	More	Heroin
1. Not at all acceptable	16.4	16.1	16.3	17.5	9.7	18.4	17.1	13.1	18.8	13.5	21.4	13.0	16.2	19.7	20.5	18.5
2. Somewhat acceptable	29.8	30.0	30.6	31.7	23.3	27.1	32.6	30.1	28.6	31.7	27.6	32.0	31.5	27.0	26.4	26.7
3. Acceptable	34.3	34.1	34.5	34.3	31.3	34.9	31.1	34.2	38.8	36.1	31.0	37.5	30.4	34.9	32.5	29.7
4. Desirable	19.5	19.7	18.6	16.6	35.8	19.7	19.2	22.7	13.8	18.8	20.0	17.5	21.9	18.4	20.7	25.1
Item 11820 Subject C05,H05 N	3048	1400	1544	2284	308	721	860	947	521	1831	1077	1227	579	486	644	47

A05D: Working in the military service

	TOTAL	M	F	White	Black	NE	NC	S	W	Yes	No	None	Mari Only	Few	More	Heroin
1. Not at all acceptable	44.8	38.7	51.0	46.4	33.9	42.7	47.0	41.4	50.2	47.8	40.3	43.2	47.1	46.0	45.3	47.2
2. Somewhat acceptable	28.2	27.5	28.8	28.9	25.2	26.6	29.1	28.3	28.7	29.5	26.2	28.8	28.2	27.1	28.5	27.2
3. Acceptable	16.6	18.0	14.8	15.7	18.1	19.6	16.2	15.1	15.6	15.0	18.0	17.7	14.3	17.2	16.1	9.3
4. Desirable	10.5	15.8	5.4	9.0	22.8	11.2	7.8	15.2	5.5	7.6	15.5	10.4	10.5	9.8	10.1	16.4
Item 11830 Subject C05,L04 N	3048	1406	1538	2284	306	722	860	947	520	1831	1078	1232	577	484	643	47

A05E: Working in a school or university

	TOTAL	M	F	White	Black	NE	NC	S	W	Yes	No	None	Mari Only	Few	More	Heroin
1. Not at all acceptable	23.2	28.3	17.8	23.7	19.9	27.0	20.4	23.3	22.4	17.1	33.6	18.3	23.3	23.8	31.0	34.8
2. Somewhat acceptable	36.6	38.4	35.9	37.4	32.2	34.0	37.5	37.1	38.0	34.9	39.6	36.7	36.9	39.2	35.5	29.3
3. Acceptable	27.4	23.2	31.0	26.5	31.9	26.5	29.1	26.0	28.4	30.8	21.0	30.5	27.9	26.3	22.5	20.2
4. Desirable	12.8	10.1	15.4	12.5	16.0	12.6	13.1	13.5	11.2	17.2	5.9	14.5	12.0	10.7	11.0	15.7
Item 11840 Subject B10,C05 N	3048	1405	1539	2284	307	719	863	945	521	1828	1080	1229	580	483	643	47

A05F: Working in a police department or police agency

	TOTAL	M	F	White	Black	NE	NC	S	W	Yes	No	None	Mari Only	Few	More	Heroin
1. Not at all acceptable	27.9	28.6	27.2	27.3	34.2	28.8	25.8	29.4	27.1	27.9	28.5	26.3	29.9	26.4	30.9	23.8
2. Somewhat acceptable	33.3	32.8	33.9	33.3	29.6	30.8	36.9	31.0	34.9	34.9	30.6	36.4	36.4	29.8	28.5	25.9
3. Acceptable	28.5	27.4	29.4	28.9	26.2	28.4	27.6	30.2	26.8	27.3	29.9	29.6	24.6	30.2	26.9	32.9
4. Desirable	10.4	11.2	9.5	10.6	10.0	12.0	9.7	9.3	11.2	9.9	11.0	7.8	9.0	13.7	13.6	17.4
Item 11850 Subject C05 N	3054	1407	1543	2287	309	723	863	946	522	1832	1081	1233	580	484	644	47

A05G: Working in a social service organization

	TOTAL	M	F	White	Black	NE	NC	S	W	Yes	No	None	Mari Only	Few	More	Heroin
1. Not at all acceptable	22.1	34.3	10.4	23.3	17.6	22.6	21.3	23.1	20.8	20.1	25.5	21.7	21.0	21.1	24.5	13.8
2. Somewhat acceptable	36.8	43.7	30.8	37.0	31.9	36.7	35.0	37.2	39.3	37.0	36.4	36.8	40.0	35.2	35.4	46.8
3. Acceptable	28.2	17.9	37.4	26.7	33.6	28.1	28.4	28.8	26.7	28.4	27.4	29.8	27.0	29.4	24.3	27.1
4. Desirable	13.0	4.2	21.4	13.0	16.9	12.7	15.3	10.9	13.2	14.5	10.7	11.6	12.0	14.4	15.8	12.3
Item 11860 Subject C05,O01 N	3040	1402	1535	2277	307	718	861	942	520	1829	1073	1229	576	482	644	47

QUESTIONNAIRE FORM 5 1986	TOTAL	SEX		RACE		REGION				4YR COLLEGE PLANS		ILLICIT DRUG USE: LIFETIME				
		M	F	White	Black	NE	NC	S	W	Yes	No	None	Mari- juana Only	Few Pills	More Pills	Any Her- oin
N (Weighted No. of Cases):	3073	1413	1550	2295	312	725	867	952	529	1839	1084	1237	583	487	648	47
% of Weighted Total:	100.0	46.0	50.4	74.7	10.2	23.6	28.2	31.0	17.2	59.9	35.3	40.3	19.0	15.8	21.1	1.5
A05H: Working with a small group of partners																
1. Not at all acceptable	10.4	10.8	9.7	8.8	18.0	12.4	7.2	12.1	9.7	7.9	14.0	8.8	11.0	10.6	11.7	23.2
2. Somewhat acceptable	27.2	26.7	27.2	24.6	39.0	25.8	27.0	31.5	21.7	26.4	28.0	28.3	29.0	25.2	23.6	27.6
3. Acceptable	44.4	43.4	45.3	46.9	32.9	44.7	46.6	40.4	47.6	44.9	44.1	45.1	42.6	46.3	44.6	30.2
4. Desirable	18.1	19.1	17.7	19.6	10.1	17.1	19.3	16.1	21.0	20.7	13.8	17.8	17.4	17.9	20.1	19.0
Item 11870 Subject C05 N	3050	1405	1540	2282	310	723	860	946	522	1831	1078	1231	580	484	641	47
A05I: Working on your own (self-employed)																
1. Not at all acceptable	7.8	6.2	9.1	6.4	11.1	7.4	5.9	9.6	8.3	7.4	8.0	8.6	5.8	7.7	8.1	1.8
2. Somewhat acceptable	14.8	13.6	16.4	15.2	13.9	15.6	15.6	14.3	13.5	15.0	14.4	13.3	17.1	16.9	14.3	10.6
3. Acceptable	31.7	29.9	33.3	31.9	29.3	32.6	33.5	29.2	32.1	31.8	31.7	34.4	32.6	33.0	26.3	22.6
4. Desirable	45.6	50.3	41.3	46.4	45.6	44.5	45.0	46.9	46.1	45.8	45.9	43.7	44.5	42.4	51.2	64.9
Item 11880 Subject C05 N	3052	1405	1542	2285	309	723	862	945	523	1833	1078	1232	579	484	645	47
A06: If you were to get enough money to live as comfortably as you'd like for the rest of your life, would you want to work?																
1. I would want to work	81.4	79.5	83.2	81.0	84.9	78.7	83.2	82.0	81.0	83.9	77.4	84.9	82.3	79.7	76.5	68.4
2. I would not want to work	18.6	20.5	16.8	19.0	15.1	21.3	16.8	18.0	19.0	16.1	22.6	15.1	17.7	20.3	23.5	31.6
Item 8100 Subject C06 N	3034	1391	1539	2276	304	716	853	945	521	1825	1069	1224	575	485	639	46
A07: The next questions are about race re- lations. How much have you gotten to know people of other races...																
A07A: In school?																
1. Not at all	7.8	9.2	6.9	9.4	2.0	6.7	10.5	8.7	3.6	7.0	9.4	8.0	6.7	7.2	9.2	10.9
2. A little	20.1	19.3	21.3	23.2	13.2	20.5	25.3	16.4	17.4	21.5	17.9	20.3	20.3	21.6	19.3	14.0
3. Some	28.9	29.9	27.8	30.4	21.6	31.5	29.6	24.2	32.6	28.4	29.4	29.2	27.6	27.0	29.1	38.9
4. A lot	40.6	38.4	42.0	34.0	62.7	40.2	30.2	47.3	45.8	40.8	39.7	39.8	42.7	42.0	39.5	36.2
8. Does not apply to me	2.6	3.3	2.0	3.0	0.6	1.0	4.5	3.4	0.6	2.2	3.7	2.7	2.8	2.3	2.9	-
Item 11890 Subject B03,N03 N	3055	1408	1542	2283	310	725	860	944	526	1835	1076	1232	582	482	645	47
A07B: In your neighborhood?																
1. Not at all	32.5	31.1	34.6	38.4	13.8	33.0	38.5	30.9	25.1	34.5	30.6	31.4	33.6	31.3	35.8	33.4
2. A little	23.2	23.6	22.9	23.6	22.0	23.5	22.1	21.9	27.2	22.8	22.8	24.7	23.4	24.6	21.0	10.7
3. Some	19.6	19.3	19.5	16.5	24.2	20.7	16.4	19.4	23.7	19.6	19.9	18.7	19.2	19.6	19.7	29.5
4. A lot	15.1	15.4	14.5	10.6	35.1	16.4	10.3	17.3	17.3	13.5	17.0	14.6	15.5	14.9	14.7	21.9
8. Does not apply to me	9.5	10.5	8.5	10.9	5.0	6.4	12.8	10.5	6.7	9.6	9.6	10.6	8.3	9.6	8.9	4.5
Item 11900 Subject N03 N	3051	1407	1539	2281	311	724	857	945	525	1834	1076	1232	581	481	644	47
A07C: In church?																
1. Not at all	36.3	37.8	35.0	39.5	26.0	43.2	37.1	34.5	28.6	36.0	37.1	34.0	39.0	38.5	37.3	27.7
2. A little	22.1	22.1	22.1	22.6	19.6	21.0	23.0	20.8	24.4	22.8	21.8	23.7	21.0	22.0	20.6	28.2
3. Some	13.9	12.2	15.1	12.4	16.0	11.1	9.9	17.5	17.8	13.3	15.1	15.5	11.4	15.1	11.0	15.6
4. A lot	9.0	7.2	10.7	5.6	26.0	5.7	7.5	11.7	10.9	8.7	8.3	10.4	9.0	7.3	6.7	13.8
8. Does not apply to me	18.8	20.7	17.0	19.8	12.3	19.0	22.4	15.5	18.3	19.2	17.8	16.5	19.6	17.1	24.4	14.7
Item 11910 Subject G,N03 N	3039	1400	1534	2273	308	716	858	940	525	1825	1072	1221	580	480	645	47
A07D: On sports teams?																
1. Not at all	18.1	15.4	20.9	20.0	9.9	20.6	22.4	13.9	14.8	16.2	21.1	17.7	14.7	19.1	20.8	20.4
2. A little	16.8	18.2	15.6	18.0	12.2	18.3	19.9	14.1	14.9	18.6	14.1	18.0	18.2	14.7	15.9	14.0
3. Some	21.1	22.2	20.3	21.2	17.8	20.7	19.7	22.7	21.4	21.0	21.4	21.4	19.2	22.6	21.0	21.7
4. A lot	25.0	30.2	19.3	21.2	43.4	22.8	16.4	31.9	29.7	25.9	22.5	25.0	30.8	21.9	21.6	16.9
8. Does not apply to me	19.0	13.9	23.8	19.7	16.7	17.7	21.7	17.4	19.3	18.3	21.0	17.8	17.0	21.7	20.7	26.9
Item 11920 Subject N03 N	3045	1407	1536	2278	310	724	857	941	523	1829	1076	1226	582	478	645	47

QUESTIONNAIRE FORM 5 1986	TOTAL	SEX		RACE		REGION				4YR COLLEGE PLANS		ILLICIT DRUG USE: LIFETIME				
		M	F	White	Black	NE	NC	S	W	Yes	No	None	Mari-juana Only	Few Pills	More Pills	Any Her-oin
N (Weighted No. of Cases):	3073	1413	1550	2295	312	725	867	952	529	1839	1084	1237	583	487	648	47
% of Weighted Total:	100.0	46.0	50.4	74.7	10.2	23.6	28.2	31.0	17.2	59.9	35.3	40.3	19.0	15.8	21.1	1.5
A07E: In clubs?																
1. Not at all	25.4	27.0	24.0	27.9	13.8	29.3	28.4	21.2	22.4	23.8	27.5	22.3	26.7	27.8	28.0	18.7
2. A little	19.8	20.4	19.1	20.4	16.7	20.9	17.6	22.5	17.4	21.6	17.9	22.9	18.6	17.6	16.0	20.7
3. Some	19.7	18.4	21.4	19.7	20.7	18.3	19.1	21.1	20.2	21.1	17.7	21.2	19.0	19.6	17.2	32.3
4. A lot	16.3	12.9	19.1	13.2	29.9	13.2	12.4	20.0	20.1	16.7	15.0	16.3	16.6	17.3	15.7	12.5
8. Does not apply to me	18.8	21.3	16.5	18.9	19.0	18.3	22.5	15.2	19.9	16.8	21.9	17.2	19.0	17.7	23.1	15.9
Item 11930 Subject N03 N	3049	1408	1537	2282	310	724	858	944	524	1830	1078	1228	582	481	645	47
A07F: On a job?																
1. Not at all	14.0	14.3	14.2	16.0	5.5	14.6	17.7	11.3	11.9	13.8	14.6	14.5	15.1	12.6	14.3	7.5
2. A little	16.0	17.9	14.5	17.1	11.3	16.7	18.7	13.6	14.8	16.6	15.0	17.1	16.6	16.4	13.1	16.3
3. Some	23.4	24.8	22.0	23.6	20.0	25.8	20.8	22.3	26.2	24.6	21.7	22.7	20.0	29.1	22.8	30.1
4. A lot	34.2	31.9	35.5	31.4	48.2	32.7	28.6	39.9	35.1	32.4	35.8	30.6	36.8	32.9	38.8	33.8
8. Does not apply to me	12.4	11.1	13.7	11.9	15.0	10.1	14.2	12.8	11.9	12.7	12.8	15.1	11.5	9.1	11.0	12.3
Item 11940 Subject C01,N03 N	3056	1408	1541	2286	310	724	859	947	524	1835	1079	1231	582	482	646	47
A08: Thinking about the country as a whole, would you say relations between white people and black people have been getting better, getting worse, or staying pretty much the same?																
1. Better	27.7	28.5	26.8	29.4	19.2	24.8	27.5	26.3	34.4	30.0	24.0	27.9	25.3	29.0	28.3	27.3
2. A little better	44.7	42.5	47.3	42.9	57.2	44.2	47.7	43.9	41.9	45.1	44.5	47.2	46.8	40.5	42.5	38.3
3. Same	21.0	21.7	20.2	20.7	17.9	23.5	18.7	21.2	21.1	19.7	22.8	19.1	21.9	22.9	21.0	27.7
4. A little worse	4.7	4.5	4.5	4.8	4.7	6.3	5.1	4.9	1.4	3.6	6.0	4.0	4.7	5.6	5.4	5.3
5. Worse	1.9	2.8	1.2	2.1	1.0	1.1	1.0	3.7	1.2	1.6	2.7	1.8	1.3	2.1	2.8	1.4
Item 11950 Subject N02 N	3052	1409	1536	2282	310	724	853	948	527	1828	1078	1226	582	482	646	47
The next questions are about driving.																
A09: Do you have a driver's license?																
1. Yes	85.3	89.7	81.9	90.0	62.4	75.4	90.5	88.0	85.3	87.7	81.9	84.7	87.1	84.2	86.6	85.4
2. No, but I soon will– GO TO Q.A13	12.1	8.4	15.4	8.8	29.4	20.9	8.3	9.8	10.6	10.2	15.3	11.9	10.8	13.8	11.7	12.7
3. No–GO TO Q.A13	2.6	1.9	2.8	1.2	8.2	3.7	1.2	2.1	4.1	2.1	2.8	3.4	2.1	1.9	1.7	1.9
Item 11960 Subject F07 N	2924	1352	1479	2250	267	685	839	903	498	1792	1010	1172	562	467	618	45
A10: Do you own a car?																
1. Yes	56.5	65.2	47.1	59.1	34.2	43.5	55.3	62.6	62.7	52.7	63.5	52.6	54.4	61.5	61.3	79.1
2. No, but I expect to own one in another year or two	27.8	21.7	34.1	25.2	46.6	35.8	25.0	26.6	25.3	27.7	27.9	28.9	26.4	26.7	28.1	20.9
3. No	15.7	13.1	18.7	15.7	19.2	20.7	19.7	10.7	12.0	19.5	8.6	18.5	19.2	11.8	10.6	-
Item 11970 Subject F07 N★	2502	1214	1214	2029	170	517	760	798	427	1575	831	999	490	393	535	39
A11: Are you able to use someone else's car when you want to?																
1. Yes, whenever I wish	32.0	29.2	35.4	34.0	23.3	28.6	31.3	35.6	30.6	34.4	28.7	31.2	31.0	28.1	37.1	44.5
2. Yes, most of the time	43.9	44.1	43.5	43.6	49.0	47.8	44.2	41.8	42.5	44.0	43.9	47.3	43.8	47.4	35.3	38.8
3. Sometimes	17.1	19.0	15.0	15.9	18.0	16.0	16.8	17.5	18.4	14.9	20.7	14.9	17.5	18.5	19.3	13.5
4. Rarely	4.8	5.4	4.1	4.6	7.1	4.6	5.8	3.7	5.5	5.0	4.2	4.2	5.6	3.9	6.3	3.1
5. Never	2.2	2.4	2.0	1.9	2.6	3.0	1.9	1.4	3.1	1.8	2.5	2.4	2.0	2.1	1.9	-
Item 11980 Subject F07 N★	2492	1210	1208	2020	169	517	756	796	423	1567	829	995	489	390	534	39
A12: Do you make an effort to cut down on driving, in order to save gasoline?																
1. Not at all	26.7	26.2	26.9	27.7	23.2	33.3	25.7	22.5	28.2	27.3	25.5	21.9	31.3	23.8	33.6	21.9
2. Not very much	33.5	33.7	32.9	34.2	26.6	32.9	34.4	34.6	30.6	35.4	30.1	33.4	33.6	37.6	29.6	42.9
3. Yes, to some extent	32.0	33.0	31.5	31.2	36.0	25.7	32.3	34.7	34.0	30.5	35.3	34.9	29.5	31.4	29.9	32.3
4. Yes, quite a bit	4.8	4.4	5.2	4.3	8.9	4.2	5.2	5.4	3.9	4.2	5.4	5.7	3.1	4.9	4.8	-
8. Don't know	3.0	2.7	3.4	2.6	5.3	4.0	2.5	2.7	3.3	2.6	3.7	4.1	2.6	2.3	2.1	2.9
Item 11990 Subject F07 N★	2495	1212	1210	2025	168	514	760	796	426	1571	829	995	490	391	535	39

★=excludes respondents for whom question was inappropriate.

QUESTIONNAIRE FORM 5 1986	TOTAL	SEX		RACE		REGION				4YR COLLEGE PLANS		ILLICIT DRUG USE: LIFETIME				
		M	F	White	Black	NE	NC	S	W	Yes	No	None	Mari-juana Only	Few Pills	More Pills	Any Her-oin
N (Weighted No. of Cases):	3073	1413	1550	2295	312	725	867	952	529	1839	1084	1237	583	487	648	47
% of Weighted Total:	100.0	46.0	50.4	74.7	10.2	23.6	28.2	31.0	17.2	59.9	35.3	40.3	19.0	15.8	21.1	1.5

A13: Do you make an effort to cut down on the amount of electricity you use in order to save energy?

1. Not at all	10.6	12.2	9.0	12.2	4.9	13.7	12.2	8.0	8.6	10.5	11.1	8.8	10.7	10.7	13.4	12.1
2. Not very much	29.6	29.4	30.0	31.2	21.8	30.5	29.8	28.6	29.8	30.6	28.6	29.1	30.1	29.3	30.2	34.9
3. Yes, to some extent	43.4	43.0	44.4	43.6	45.1	41.7	41.6	45.3	45.4	44.6	42.0	45.7	43.2	43.2	42.0	32.6
4. Yes, quite a bit	14.0	12.4	15.0	11.3	24.3	12.7	12.9	15.7	14.4	12.9	15.1	14.2	14.2	14.1	12.5	14.0
8. Don't know	2.3	3.0	1.6	1.8	3.9	1.4	3.5	2.4	1.7	1.5	3.3	2.3	1.7	2.7	1.9	6.6
Item 12000 Subject F05 N	3048	1406	1536	2279	309	718	857	948	525	1828	1077	1231	583	482	639	47

A14: In the house or apartment where you live, is an effort made to reduce heat during the winter, in order to save energy?

1. Not at all	7.3	7.8	6.6	6.3	13.0	9.7	6.9	6.8	5.7	5.4	9.7	7.0	6.8	7.6	7.7	7.6
2. Not very much	17.7	18.1	17.8	16.9	23.5	18.3	16.0	19.2	17.4	18.0	17.4	16.7	18.9	18.7	18.0	18.0
3. Yes, to some extent	40.4	38.5	42.3	42.0	31.0	39.6	39.7	40.2	42.7	40.7	39.9	40.5	42.6	41.1	38.3	34.7
4. Yes, quite a bit	31.6	32.4	30.6	32.7	27.5	29.5	35.0	30.5	30.9	33.4	29.7	33.6	28.9	30.5	31.8	32.6
8. Don't know	3.0	3.2	2.7	2.1	5.0	2.9	2.4	3.3	3.3	2.5	3.3	2.3	2.8	2.1	4.1	7.2
Item 12010 Subject F05 N	3046	1404	1537	2277	309	718	855	948	526	1829	1077	1230	580	482	641	47

A15: How do you feel about each of the following?

A15A: How much do you enjoy shopping for things like clothes, records, sporting goods, and books?

1. Not at all	1.4	2.7	0.1	1.3	1.2	1.2	2.0	1.3	0.8	1.1	1.9	1.7	1.0	1.2	1.0	2.5
2. Not very much	9.1	15.7	2.9	9.7	4.3	6.6	9.3	9.7	10.9	7.6	11.2	10.1	5.0	9.3	10.0	18.6
3. Pretty much	31.4	42.8	20.6	33.3	19.1	30.3	33.2	30.0	32.3	30.6	33.1	32.7	34.8	26.8	30.1	30.6
4. Very much	58.2	38.8	76.4	55.7	75.4	61.9	55.5	59.0	56.0	60.8	53.8	55.6	59.2	62.7	58.9	48.3
Item 12020 Subject F01 N	3055	1408	1542	2284	311	723	856	949	526	1832	1080	1231	583	482	646	47

A15B: How much do you care about having the latest fashion in your clothes, records, leisure activities, and so on?

1. Not at all	5.5	8.7	2.7	5.9	2.6	6.2	5.9	4.8	4.9	5.0	6.3	6.0	4.3	6.6	4.7	6.6
2. Not very much	27.7	32.8	23.1	28.0	18.3	23.5	26.1	28.0	35.3	27.5	28.0	30.2	25.2	23.4	29.4	29.9
3. Pretty much	37.3	35.3	39.2	38.8	31.8	39.1	39.4	34.2	37.1	38.8	35.7	38.3	37.0	37.4	36.4	30.9
4. Very much	29.5	23.1	35.1	27.3	47.4	31.2	28.5	33.0	22.7	28.8	30.0	25.5	33.5	32.6	29.4	32.6
Item 12030 Subject F01 N	3052	1406	1542	2284	311	723	856	948	526	1832	1080	1230	583	482	645	47

A15C: How much do you care about whether your family has most of the things your friends and neighbors have?

1. Not at all	24.5	25.3	23.8	23.6	25.0	25.4	23.7	22.2	28.5	25.0	23.3	23.4	22.7	24.2	29.8	18.5
2. Not very much	47.0	45.9	47.8	47.3	44.0	46.8	49.1	45.0	47.5	45.4	50.6	49.1	45.6	49.5	43.4	37.4
3. Pretty much	21.6	22.0	21.1	22.5	20.3	20.8	20.3	25.3	17.9	22.9	19.1	20.8	25.2	19.5	19.2	29.8
4. Very much	7.0	6.7	7.3	6.6	10.8	7.0	6.8	7.5	6.1	6.7	6.9	6.7	6.5	6.8	7.6	14.3
Item 12040 Subject F01 N	3044	1401	1542	2282	307	723	854	943	523	1829	1075	1224	582	482	645	47

A16: When you are older, do you expect to own more possessions than your parents do now, or about the same, or less?

I expect to own . . .

1. Much less than my parents	1.7	2.0	1.0	1.6	1.4	1.5	1.5	1.4	2.6	1.2	2.2	1.4	0.5	1.9	2.5	6.7
2. Somewhat less than my parents	5.4	5.5	5.1	5.7	4.0	6.1	5.2	4.9	5.5	4.9	6.2	5.9	5.0	5.5	4.9	0.9
3. About as much as my parents	34.9	31.1	38.9	38.0	22.6	34.3	36.5	33.2	36.1	32.6	39.0	36.3	34.7	38.8	31.1	25.5
4. Somewhat more than my parents	38.6	39.3	38.0	37.3	42.5	39.1	38.0	41.5	33.6	40.3	36.1	41.0	37.7	32.3	39.1	37.5
5. Much more than my parents	19.5	22.0	16.9	17.4	29.6	18.9	18.8	19.1	22.2	21.0	16.5	15.5	22.1	21.5	22.4	29.4
Item 12050 Subject F01 N	3042	1403	1535	2277	310	722	853	946	522	1823	1078	1223	583	482	643	47

QUESTIONNAIRE FORM 5 1986	TOTAL	SEX		RACE		REGION				4YR COLLEGE PLANS		ILLICIT DRUG USE: LIFETIME				
		M	F	White	Black	NE	NC	S	W	Yes	No	None	Mari-juana Only	Few Pills	More Pills	Any Her-oin
N (Weighted No. of Cases):	3073	1413	1550	2295	312	725	867	952	529	1839	1084	1237	583	487	648	47
% of Weighted Total:	100.0	46.0	50.4	74.7	10.2	23.6	28.2	31.0	17.2	59.9	35.3	40.3	19.0	15.8	21.1	1.5

A17: Compared with your parents, what is the smallest amount that you could be content or satisfied to own?

The least I could be content to own is . . .

1. Much less than my parents	8.4	8.5	8.2	8.9	3.7	8.6	8.9	7.4	9.4	9.1	7.5	10.0	7.3	10.1	5.7	5.5
2. Somewhat less than my parents	29.4	29.0	30.2	32.8	17.7	28.7	32.3	26.7	30.6	31.0	27.6	29.8	29.3	27.1	32.6	21.7
3. About as much as my parents	43.4	44.0	43.3	42.9	46.0	43.1	43.3	45.6	40.0	42.3	45.2	42.7	46.4	42.0	42.2	55.4
4. Somewhat more than my parents	14.3	13.6	14.3	12.5	20.9	14.9	11.4	15.7	15.7	13.1	15.3	13.3	13.6	16.0	14.6	15.0
5. Much more than my parents	4.4	4.8	4.0	2.9	11.7	4.7	4.0	4.7	4.3	4.6	4.4	4.2	3.4	4.8	4.9	2.4
Item 12060 Subject F01 N	3020	1396	1523	2265	302	711	850	938	522	1816	1068	1216	578	479	639	47

A18: These next questions ask your opinions about a number of different topics. How much do you agree or disagree with each statement below?

A18A: We ought to worry about our own country and let the rest of the world take care of itself

1. Disagree	22.5	25.3	19.6	20.2	31.3	21.8	21.6	23.2	23.7	23.8	20.7	25.8	22.2	20.7	18.0	16.9
2. Mostly disagree	25.6	22.2	28.9	27.5	18.7	25.3	26.2	23.4	28.8	29.7	19.1	26.7	25.6	26.8	23.1	19.9
3. Neither	14.6	14.2	14.9	14.5	12.8	14.0	15.3	12.3	18.2	14.0	14.9	14.0	13.1	15.5	15.7	18.3
4. Mostly agree	23.5	22.5	24.7	25.0	18.5	24.8	24.3	24.3	18.6	22.0	25.8	22.7	25.6	23.3	24.8	25.7
5. Agree	13.9	15.9	11.9	12.7	18.9	14.0	12.5	16.7	10.7	10.5	19.6	10.8	13.6	13.8	18.3	19.2
Item 12070 Subject O03 N	3055	1410	1541	2285	312	725	859	945	526	1833	1080	1231	583	482	647	47

A18B: It would be better if we all felt more like citizens of the world than of any particular country

1. Disagree	9.9	12.0	7.9	10.7	7.4	13.0	9.3	8.8	8.6	9.1	11.3	10.1	8.3	9.7	10.7	15.6
2. Mostly disagree	11.4	13.0	9.5	11.6	8.4	9.7	12.2	12.0	11.1	12.4	10.2	11.6	11.4	10.5	11.3	13.0
3. Neither	19.2	19.3	19.1	19.7	14.1	22.0	17.4	17.1	22.3	18.0	20.6	17.4	19.9	23.4	19.0	21.9
4. Mostly agree	30.7	28.6	33.3	31.8	27.3	28.8	32.0	30.4	31.3	31.2	30.5	31.2	31.8	31.0	29.1	30.5
5. Agree	28.8	27.1	30.2	26.2	42.8	26.4	29.0	31.7	26.7	29.2	27.3	29.7	28.6	25.4	29.9	19.0
Item 12080 Subject O03 N	3045	1411	1532	2278	312	723	855	945	523	1827	1077	1232	582	477	643	47

A18C: I find it hard to be sympathetic toward starving people in foreign lands, when there is so much trouble in our own country

1. Disagree	31.1	21.6	39.7	27.4	48.5	32.9	27.9	32.5	31.4	30.9	30.4	34.0	33.4	31.0	24.0	21.2
2. Mostly disagree	24.0	21.6	26.8	25.5	18.6	22.7	24.9	24.3	23.7	26.1	21.5	25.0	22.5	28.6	21.6	14.7
3. Neither	14.3	18.6	10.3	15.0	11.6	12.3	16.4	13.6	15.2	14.2	14.7	13.9	13.7	12.2	15.9	28.6
4. Mostly agree	17.9	21.3	14.6	19.1	13.0	19.7	17.5	16.6	18.1	17.5	18.3	16.1	18.9	15.7	22.8	15.1
5. Agree	12.7	17.0	8.6	13.0	8.3	12.3	13.3	13.0	11.7	11.3	15.2	11.1	11.5	12.5	15.7	20.4
Item 12090 Subject F03,O03 N	3051	1407	1540	2285	310	725	859	943	524	1833	1078	1229	583	482	646	47

A18D: Maybe some minority groups do get unfair treatment, but that's no business of mine

1. Disagree	40.5	33.9	47.0	37.3	55.4	44.2	38.4	37.8	43.6	46.0	30.7	44.6	39.7	38.8	36.4	33.2
2. Mostly disagree	27.6	26.2	29.0	30.4	16.5	26.0	31.4	24.3	29.6	28.0	27.6	26.5	26.4	31.2	28.5	14.8
3. Neither	18.6	22.0	15.6	19.7	14.9	16.8	18.9	20.6	17.2	15.9	23.6	17.5	21.0	17.8	19.1	25.9
4. Mostly agree	8.1	10.5	5.5	8.2	5.9	6.8	7.5	10.5	6.6	6.3	10.9	7.4	7.2	6.7	10.0	17.4
5. Agree	5.2	7.4	3.0	4.5	7.3	6.2	3.7	6.9	3.0	3.9	7.3	4.0	5.7	5.5	5.9	8.7
Item 12100 Subject N02,O03 N	3042	1406	1533	2282	309	723	852	943	525	1829	1076	1227	580	482	643	47

A18E: I get very upset when I see other people treated unfairly

1. Disagree	3.1	3.7	2.5	3.0	4.3	4.1	3.0	3.1	2.1	3.0	3.5	2.7	3.1	3.8	3.3	6.5
2. Mostly disagree	4.7	6.7	2.6	4.9	4.6	3.8	6.3	4.3	4.3	3.7	6.4	4.4	6.4	5.5	2.8	9.1
3. Neither	8.8	12.9	4.9	9.9	4.0	8.7	10.5	7.5	8.8	7.7	11.1	6.1	8.6	11.1	11.8	23.9
4. Mostly agree	32.3	37.7	27.5	33.9	24.2	30.7	36.2	30.8	30.7	31.5	34.4	31.8	32.1	29.3	35.5	28.0
5. Agree	51.0	39.0	62.5	48.2	62.8	52.6	44.1	54.4	54.1	54.1	44.6	54.9	49.9	50.3	46.6	32.5
Item 12110 Subject O03 N	3042	1403	1537	2278	310	720	856	941	525	1828	1074	1229	580	482	642	46

QUESTIONNAIRE FORM 5 1986	TOTAL	SEX		RACE		REGION				4YR COLLEGE PLANS		ILLICIT DRUG USE: LIFETIME				
		M	F	White	Black	NE	NC	S	W	Yes	No	None	Mari- juana Only	Few Pills	More Pills	Any Her- oin
N (Weighted No. of Cases):	3073	1413	1550	2295	312	725	867	952	529	1839	1084	1237	583	487	648	47
% of Weighted Total:	100 0	46.0	50.4	74.7	10.2	23.6	28.2	31.0	17.2	59.9	35.3	40.3	19.0	15.8	21.1	1.5

A18F: I would agree to a good plan to make a better life for the poor, even if it cost me money

	TOTAL	M	F	White	Black	NE	NC	S	W	Yes	No	None	Mari- juana Only	Few Pills	More Pills	Any Her- oin
1. Disagree	6.5	9.7	3.6	7.3	2.9	9.3	6.4	4.8	6.2	5.1	8.9	4.7	8.0	5.9	9.2	8.9
2. Mostly disagree	10.0	12.0	7.9	10.6	6.2	7.5	11.6	10.6	9.6	9.7	11.1	9.1	9.9	8.0	13.0	18.6
3. Neither	23.2	26.3	20.5	25.3	7.2	23.3	25.8	20.6	23.7	23.4	23.6	21.7	24.4	27.0	22.6	18.7
4. Mostly agree	36.3	31.6	40.9	36.6	38.2	36.3	36.4	34.8	38.7	37.4	34.6	38.7	34.2	36.0	35.1	21.1
5. Agree	23.9	20.4	27.1	20.2	45.5	23.7	19.7	29.1	21.8	24.4	21.9	25.8	23.4	23.1	20.0	32.7
Item 12120 Subject O03 N	3041	1404	1534	2276	311	725	851	943	522	1827	1075	1226	579	481	644	47

A18G: It's not really my problem if others are in trouble and need help

	TOTAL	M	F	White	Black	NE	NC	S	W	Yes	No	None	Mari- juana Only	Few Pills	More Pills	Any Her- oin
1. Disagree	39.5	31.2	47.1	37.3	56.3	42.9	35.9	41.9	36.2	41.6	35.8	43.9	39.9	38.4	33.0	16.0
2. Mostly disagree	36.5	39.1	34.5	39.1	23.2	35.0	39.4	34.5	37.4	38.3	34.4	35.4	37.8	36.2	38.1	39.7
3. Neither	13.8	16.0	11.6	14.2	9.8	12.9	14.7	12.0	16.5	11.7	17.6	11.9	12.1	14.5	17.5	22.0
4. Mostly agree	7.0	8.7	5.2	6.7	5.2	5.5	7.1	8.0	7.4	6.1	7.9	6.4	6.2	7.5	8.4	11.4
5. Agree	3.3	5.0	1.7	2.7	5.7	3.7	2.9	3.6	2.5	2.3	4.3	2.4	4.1	3.5	3.1	10.8
Item 12130 Subject O03 N	3044	1407	1534	2278	311	723	854	945	523	1830	1074	1230	581	480	643	47

A18H: Americans could change their eating habits to provide more food for the hungry people in other parts of the world, and at the same time be healthier themselves

	TOTAL	M	F	White	Black	NE	NC	S	W	Yes	No	None	Mari- juana Only	Few Pills	More Pills	Any Her- oin
1. Disagree	12.1	17.4	7.4	12.8	10.8	13.4	11.8	13.1	9.2	12.1	12.7	9.8	11.9	13.6	15.6	15.0
2. Mostly disagree	11.8	13.9	9.8	12.3	11.8	11.1	12.7	11.6	11.6	12.5	10.6	12.6	9.9	10.3	12.4	18.1
3. Neither	19.9	21.9	17.6	18.8	16.8	19.1	23.6	17.0	20.1	19.6	20.5	19.1	22.7	20.3	18.2	26.2
4. Mostly agree	29.2	27.3	30.9	29.9	24.2	26.7	29.3	29.9	30.9	28.8	30.1	29.0	29.7	30.6	27.5	35.6
5. Agree	27.1	19.5	34.2	25.3	36.4	29.7	22.6	28.4	28.3	27.0	26.1	29.5	25.8	25.2	26.2	5.1
Item 12140 Subject F03,O03 N	3045	1405	1538	2281	311	723	857	944	522	1830	1078	1231	580	480	644	47

A18I: My family and I often buy things we really don't need; we could get along with much less

	TOTAL	M	F	White	Black	NE	NC	S	W	Yes	No	None	Mari- juana Only	Few Pills	More Pills	Any Her- oin
1. Disagree	12.6	13.5	11.6	11.2	21.4	17.3	10.8	11.1	11.9	11.1	14.7	11.5	12.9	11.7	15.1	14.8
2. Mostly disagree	17.4	20.9	13.4	16.5	15.9	18.8	16.1	16.6	19.0	17.5	16.3	16.3	18.1	16.9	17.8	16.3
3. Neither	17.3	20.0	14.6	18.0	12.0	18.8	19.2	13.2	19.6	18.1	16.5	18.5	17.1	20.0	13.2	18.6
4. Mostly agree	29.1	27.0	31.8	31.0	25.5	23.7	31.8	32.8	25.3	29.4	29.1	29.8	31.0	29.3	27.7	25.1
5. Agree	23.6	18.6	28.6	23.3	25.2	21.4	22.1	26.4	24.1	23.9	23.3	24.1	20.8	22.1	26.2	25.2
Item 10060 Subject F01 N	3041	1404	1536	2276	311	721	854	943	523	1830	1072	1227	583	482	640	47

A18J: Most people will have fuller and happier lives if they choose legal marriage rather than staying single, or just living with someone

	TOTAL	M	F	White	Black	NE	NC	S	W	Yes	No	None	Mari- juana Only	Few Pills	More Pills	Any Her- oin
1. Disagree	23.3	19.7	26.6	22.8	29.2	32.7	21.0	18.6	22.2	24.5	21.8	16.6	25.9	25.2	30.3	33.2
2. Mostly disagree	14.5	14.3	14.7	15.0	10.8	11.6	18.3	13.4	14.3	14.8	14.6	13.8	12.6	15.2	16.9	15.4
3. Neither	29.9	33.0	27.3	29.8	27.9	31.5	29.9	26.9	33.2	29.4	30.0	29.1	32.4	31.5	28.9	32.0
4. Mostly agree	15.3	17.9	13.0	16.2	11.6	12.9	15.1	17.1	15.4	15.2	15.3	18.2	15.8	14.3	10.9	6.1
5. Agree	17.1	15.2	18.4	16.3	20.5	11.3	15.7	24.0	14.8	16.1	18.2	22.3	13.2	13.9	12.9	13.4
Item 12150 Subject D03 N	3048	1408	1539	2285	309	724	858	942	524	1832	1078	1232	581	482	644	47

A18K: Parents should encourage just as much independence in their daughters as in their sons

	TOTAL	M	F	White	Black	NE	NC	S	W	Yes	No	None	Mari- juana Only	Few Pills	More Pills	Any Her- oin
1. Disagree	4.1	7.0	1.3	3.7	6.3	5.1	3.4	4.6	3.0	3.5	5.4	3.5	4.3	4.2	4.6	2.4
2. Mostly disagree	5.9	9.8	2.5	5.4	7.2	5.1	5.2	7.1	6.3	5.5	6.6	5.9	5.5	6.9	5.2	5.1
3. Neither	8.9	15.4	2.7	8.5	6.9	7.7	9.4	8.6	10.0	9.1	8.1	8.9	8.0	7.8	9.5	15.4
4. Mostly agree	22.4	29.7	16.2	22.6	17.5	23.2	22.1	21.5	23.5	21.2	25.0	23.0	25.7	20.6	19.8	22.0
5. Agree	58.7	38.1	77.4	59.8	62.0	58.9	59.9	58.2	57.2	60.7	54.9	58.6	56.4	60.4	60.9	55.0
Item 12160 Subject D05 N	3041	1402	1538	2277	311	723	852	944	523	1831	1072	1227	581	480	643	47

QUESTIONNAIRE FORM 5 1986	TOTAL	SEX		RACE		REGION				4YR COLLEGE PLANS		ILLICIT DRUG USE: LIFETIME				
		M	F	White	Black	NE	NC	S	W	Yes	No	None	Mari- juana Only	Few Pills	More Pills	Any Her- oin
N (Weighted No. of Cases):	3073	1413	1550	2295	312	725	867	952	529	1839	1084	1237	583	487	648	47
% of Weighted Total:	100.0	46.0	50.4	74.7	10.2	23.6	28.2	31.0	17.2	59.9	35.3	40.3	19.0	15.8	21.1	1.5

A18L: Being a mother and raising children is one of the most fulfilling experiences a woman can have

1. Disagree	4.8	3.2	6.2	4.7	5.5	4.7	5.1	3.8	6.2	5.0	4.3	3.5	5.8	3.2	7.7	7.2
2. Mostly disagree	6.0	3.9	7.9	6.1	5.9	5.5	7.4	5.0	6.2	6.7	5.1	4.4	5.3	6.0	9.6	8.8
3. Neither	30.8	45.8	17.8	33.9	20.9	30.2	32.2	28.9	32.6	33.7	26.9	31.7	32.3	30.4	29.8	20.5
4. Mostly agree	26.8	23.9	29.6	26.8	22.8	27.0	26.1	27.1	27.1	25.9	28.2	26.6	27.5	27.3	25.8	27.9
5. Agree	31.6	23.3	38.6	28.4	44.8	32.5	29.2	35.1	27.9	28.8	35.5	33.8	29.2	33.0	27.1	35.6
Item 12170 Subject D05 N	3005	1373	1532	2252	308	711	843	935	516	1809	1061	1213	568	477	640	47

A18M: Most fathers should spend more time with their children than they do now

1. Disagree	1.6	2.1	1.3	1.4	2.1	2.0	1.4	1.5	1.9	1.9	1.3	1.9	1.2	0.3	2.3	-
2. Mostly disagree	3.0	3.8	2.2	3.1	2.6	3.2	2.8	2.7	3.7	3.1	2.4	3.0	2.1	2.7	3.6	6.0
3. Neither	16.1	16.6	15.9	17.5	9.8	19.6	16.6	12.8	16.5	16.7	15.3	13.8	16.0	17.7	19.8	24.0
4. Mostly agree	36.1	38.8	33.7	38.0	26.2	33.4	39.5	33.4	39.0	37.0	35.8	36.5	40.4	32.2	35.1	29.1
5. Agree	43.1	38.6	47.0	39.9	59.3	41.8	39.8	49.6	38.9	41.3	45.1	44.9	40.2	47.1	39.1	40.9
Item 12180 Subject D05 N	3040	1401	1538	2278	310	721	854	940	525	1830	1072	1224	580	481	645	47

A18N: The husband should make all the important decisions in the family

1. Disagree	44.0	25.4	61.8	45.1	49.5	48.4	46.2	39.4	42.3	49.1	36.3	42.7	43.7	47.5	44.5	45.2
2. Mostly disagree	20.3	21.0	19.5	20.0	19.3	21.0	18.6	20.4	22.0	20.5	19.8	22.0	20.4	18.7	18.9	20.7
3. Neither	17.8	26.2	9.9	18.5	11.6	15.8	20.8	16.4	18.3	15.9	21.3	16.2	18.7	20.6	18.8	5.2
4. Mostly agree	10.7	16.0	5.8	10.1	11.9	8.8	8.0	14.1	11.5	9.0	13.0	11.6	10.3	8.5	10.7	14.1
5. Agree	7.2	11.4	3.1	6.3	7.7	6.1	6.3	9.6	5.8	5.4	9.7	7.5	6.9	4.7	7.1	14.8
Item 12190 Subject D05 N	3048	1405	1541	2282	312	724	853	946	525	1832	1078	1229	582	482	645	47

A19: Some people think about what's going on in government very often, and others are not that interested. How much of an interest do you take in government and current events?

1. No interest at all	3.6	3.9	3.3	3.7	3.2	6.5	2.8	2.3	3.0	1.9	6.2	2.2	3.4	3.6	5.9	5.9
2. Very little interest	13.9	10.2	17.6	14.1	15.3	17.1	14.6	12.2	11.6	12.3	16.3	12.2	11.9	18.6	15.5	16.6
3. Some interest	47.5	42.8	52.1	45.7	50.5	48.9	44.9	46.1	52.6	44.8	51.9	48.4	49.5	47.7	43.6	47.9
4. A lot of interest	26.0	30.3	21.6	27.1	21.8	19.5	28.3	28.8	26.1	30.2	20.3	27.4	26.1	22.8	26.6	16.7
5. A very great interest	9.0	12.7	5.4	9.4	9.1	8.0	9.4	10.6	6.8	10.8	5.3	9.8	9.1	7.2	8.4	12.9
Item 6330 Subject H01,Q08 N	3038	1406	1532	2280	305	718	857	940	524	1829	1071	1226	581	481	642	47

A20: If you have at least an average income in the future, how likely is it that you will contribute money to the following organizations? If you have already contributed, mark the last circle only. Are you likely to contribute to...

A20A: The United Fund or other community charities?

1. Definitely not	5.3	7.4	3.2	4.8	4.5	6.1	4.2	4.2	8.3	3.8	7.9	3.6	4.1	6.9	7.8	7.3
2. Probably not	17.6	20.8	14.4	19.3	9.6	19.8	19.0	14.3	18.2	16.3	20.2	16.9	18.0	15.7	21.1	16.8
3. Don't know	44.8	45.7	44.9	45.8	37.3	40.6	44.3	46.1	49.2	44.8	45.4	43.1	45.1	50.5	44.0	36.3
4. Probably will	23.5	20.0	26.4	22.0	34.8	25.2	23.5	25.4	17.5	25.3	19.5	26.5	26.6	18.8	17.7	29.3
5. Definitely will	2.5	1.7	3.0	1.8	7.9	2.3	1.5	3.6	2.6	2.8	2.0	3.2	1.7	2.1	2.2	1.7
6. Already have	6.3	4.4	8.1	6.3	5.9	6.1	7.5	6.4	4.2	7.0	4.9	6.6	4.5	6.0	7.1	8.6
Item 12200 Subject O02 N	3031	1400	1534	2274	310	719	852	938	522	1823	1073	1220	579	482	645	47

A20B: International relief organizations (CARE, UNICEF, etc.)?

1. Definitely not	5.5	8.3	2.9	5.7	3.6	5.5	5.5	4.9	6.9	4.4	7.9	3.9	4.7	5.9	8.0	13.3
2. Probably not	15.9	21.1	10.9	17.8	10.1	13.9	16.3	17.3	15.5	14.4	18.8	16.5	12.9	12.8	20.1	12.1
3. Don't know	31.9	34.9	29.5	32.0	24.9	28.5	30.9	32.7	36.6	30.1	35.1	31.0	35.1	31.6	30.2	42.0
4. Probably will	32.6	25.7	39.0	30.9	41.9	34.8	32.5	32.8	29.5	35.0	27.9	34.4	35.1	34.5	26.7	12.1
5. Definitely will	6.0	3.8	7.8	4.4	13.4	6.6	4.8	6.7	5.9	6.6	4.2	6.4	5.5	6.2	5.4	4.9
6. Already have	8.1	6.3	9.9	9.1	6.1	10.6	10.1	5.6	5.6	9.4	6.1	7.7	6.6	8.9	9.5	15.5
Item 12210 Subject O02 N	3028	1399	1533	2274	306	721	850	937	520	1824	1070	1221	577	482	643	47

QUESTIONNAIRE FORM 5 1986	TOTAL	SEX		RACE		REGION				4YR COLLEGE PLANS		ILLICIT DRUG USE: LIFETIME				
		M	F	White	Black	NE	NC	S	W	Yes	No	None	Marijuana Only	Few Pills	More Pills	Any Heroin
N (Weighted No. of Cases):	3073	1413	1550	2295	312	725	867	952	529	1839	1084	1237	583	487	648	47
% of Weighted Total:	100.0	46.0	50.4	74.7	10.2	23.6	28.2	31.0	17.2	59.9	35.3	40.3	19.0	15.8	21.1	1.5

A20C: Minority group organizations (NAACP, SCLC, etc.)?

	TOTAL	M	F	White	Black	NE	NC	S	W	Yes	No	None	Marij. Only	Few Pills	More Pills	Any Heroin
1. Definitely not	10.8	14.9	7.1	12.3	4.5	9.4	11.2	12.1	9.7	9.7	13.0	9.5	9.0	13.3	13.0	13.3
2. Probably not	26.2	27.6	24.6	30.4	6.6	25.1	29.4	24.0	26.2	27.0	26.0	26.6	23.5	23.6	30.6	27.4
3. Don't know	40.3	38.9	42.4	42.8	20.7	42.1	40.2	37.3	43.5	39.8	41.1	39.0	42.9	41.4	39.8	37.2
4. Probably will	17.0	13.7	19.6	13.0	34.6	18.1	14.1	18.5	17.4	17.3	15.6	18.2	18.0	16.2	13.3	19.2
5. Definitely will	4.4	3.6	5.0	1.0	26.0	3.3	4.0	6.4	2.9	4.9	3.2	5.2	5.6	4.3	2.0	-
6. Already have	1.4	1.4	1.3	0.6	7.6	2.0	1.1	1.7	0.3	1.2	1.2	1.5	1.0	1.2	1.3	2.9
Item 12220 Subject N02,O02 N	3024	1400	1528	2270	308	716	851	937	519	1817	1072	1219	577	482	642	47

A20D: Church or religious organizations?

	TOTAL	M	F	White	Black	NE	NC	S	W	Yes	No	None	Marij. Only	Few Pills	More Pills	Any Heroin
1. Definitely not	5.9	7.1	4.8	7.0	1.4	8.0	6.1	2.6	8.9	5.6	6.3	4.0	5.0	6.7	9.7	7.3
2. Probably not	9.8	11.3	8.4	10.5	3.0	10.0	12.3	6.9	10.7	10.3	8.8	7.7	10.3	10.1	13.1	16.1
3. Don't know	13.7	15.5	12.2	13.5	13.3	15.4	11.3	12.2	18.1	12.1	16.4	11.2	13.7	16.0	16.4	15.7
4. Probably will	26.4	26.9	25.1	25.9	24.7	29.2	24.0	27.5	24.3	24.4	29.8	27.2	27.3	25.9	23.8	26.0
5. Definitely will	15.3	12.8	17.4	13.5	26.4	12.2	16.3	18.8	11.8	16.1	13.5	17.1	18.6	14.7	10.2	3.9
6. Already have	28.8	26.5	32.0	29.6	31.3	25.2	30.0	32.0	26.2	31.5	25.3	32.8	25.0	26.5	26.8	30.9
Item 12230 Subject G,O02 N	3020	1396	1530	2271	305	715	850	936	520	1815	1072	1217	577	482	640	47

A20E: Political parties or organizations?

	TOTAL	M	F	White	Black	NE	NC	S	W	Yes	No	None	Marij. Only	Few Pills	More Pills	Any Heroin
1. Definitely not	17.4	18.3	16.8	17.9	12.7	17.8	18.6	15.3	18.5	14.7	22.1	14.7	16.0	20.8	20.7	28.7
2. Probably not	28.0	28.5	27.1	29.0	23.9	30.4	28.8	24.9	28.6	27.9	28.9	27.7	27.5	26.1	30.5	33.3
3. Don't know	35.7	33.5	38.1	34.7	39.1	35.0	34.1	37.0	37.0	35.1	36.5	37.4	36.9	37.1	30.6	25.3
4. Probably will	14.2	13.9	14.3	13.7	18.6	12.2	13.1	18.3	11.4	16.8	9.3	14.9	16.5	11.6	12.9	11.5
5. Definitely will	2.2	2.8	1.7	2.2	3.6	1.9	2.0	2.4	2.9	3.0	0.9	2.4	1.9	2.1	2.5	-
6. Already have	2.5	3.0	2.0	2.5	2.1	2.7	3.4	2.1	1.6	2.6	2.3	2.9	1.2	2.3	3.0	1.2
Item 12240 Subject H05,O02 N	3024	1399	1529	2272	306	719	850	935	520	1821	1071	1221	577	480	642	47

A20F: Citizen lobbies (Common Cause, Public Citizen, etc.)?

	TOTAL	M	F	White	Black	NE	NC	S	W	Yes	No	None	Marij. Only	Few Pills	More Pills	Any Heroin
1. Definitely not	10.2	11.1	8.8	9.8	11.3	9.9	9.3	10.6	11.3	8.8	13.2	8.6	10.3	9.3	12.9	19.9
2. Probably not	26.3	27.2	25.1	28.6	15.8	26.3	30.7	23.2	24.4	27.0	25.5	26.5	21.7	27.9	29.8	23.0
3. Don't know	44.7	42.8	47.6	45.8	37.7	45.0	41.9	44.6	48.9	46.1	42.4	44.7	47.8	45.5	42.2	40.6
4. Probably will	15.5	15.4	15.2	13.5	27.1	15.4	14.3	17.9	13.3	14.7	16.3	17.8	16.3	13.1	10.9	9.5
5. Definitely will	2.4	2.4	2.3	1.6	6.0	2.8	2.4	2.6	1.3	2.7	1.4	1.7	3.0	3.3	2.4	5.9
6. Already have	1.0	1.0	1.0	0.7	2.2	0.6	1.3	1.2	0.8	0.7	1.2	0.7	0.9	0.8	1.9	1.2
Item 12250 Subject H05,I02,O02 N	3019	1395	1527	2268	306	716	850	933	521	1817	1069	1217	575	481	640	47

A20G: Charities to help fight diseases (Cancer, Heart Disease, etc.)?

	TOTAL	M	F	White	Black	NE	NC	S	W	Yes	No	None	Marij. Only	Few Pills	More Pills	Any Heroin
1. Definitely not	2.1	3.0	1.3	1.8	2.9	2.3	1.5	1.6	3.8	1.1	4.0	1.4	1.1	2.2	3.4	11.3
2. Probably not	4.0	6.3	1.7	4.2	3.3	3.7	4.4	4.4	5.5	3.7	4.4	4.4	2.9	3.0	5.3	5.2
3. Don't know	13.8	18.4	9.2	14.1	10.6	12.2	16.1	12.1	15.2	13.4	14.4	13.6	14.7	12.4	14.5	10.3
4. Probably will	38.6	41.9	35.6	39.8	30.6	36.7	40.9	36.2	41.5	38.5	38.5	39.5	39.1	40.5	36.2	33.2
5. Definitely will	27.2	20.1	33.7	24.6	43.4	29.1	23.7	30.6	24.0	28.9	24.5	27.6	30.4	26.3	23.4	24.9
6. Already have	14.3	10.2	18.5	15.5	9.2	16.0	14.9	15.0	10.0	14.4	14.3	13.5	11.8	15.5	17.2	15.0
Item 12260 Subject O02 N	3027	1394	1535	2271	308	718	850	938	521	1820	1072	1221	577	481	642	47

A20H: Organizations concerned with population problems (Planned Parenthood, ZPG, etc.)?

	TOTAL	M	F	White	Black	NE	NC	S	W	Yes	No	None	Marij. Only	Few Pills	More Pills	Any Heroin
1. Definitely not	9.2	12.4	6.3	10.1	6.3	10.2	8.4	8.2	11.1	8.2	11.0	8.9	8.6	8.6	10.3	14.4
2. Probably not	20.3	22.5	18.2	21.4	14.3	17.7	21.6	21.6	19.5	21.2	18.7	23.4	17.8	17.3	19.1	20.0
3. Don't know	40.1	43.0	37.6	40.7	30.8	41.7	39.4	39.9	39.0	40.5	40.6	41.2	43.3	39.7	36.6	28.4
4. Probably will	22.5	17.2	27.3	21.0	33.7	22.5	22.8	22.3	22.4	22.8	21.0	20.5	21.5	27.9	22.4	32.3
5. Definitely will	6.6	4.1	8.9	5.6	13.1	6.7	6.2	6.8	6.9	6.3	7.0	5.0	7.6	5.4	9.7	2.3
6. Already have	1.2	0.8	1.7	1.1	1.8	1.0	1.6	1.2	1.1	0.9	1.8	1.0	1.2	0.9	2.0	2.6
Item 12270 Subject E01,O02 N	3029	1399	1534	2275	306	719	852	938	520	1822	1073	1224	577	481	642	47

QUESTIONNAIRE FORM 5 1986	TOTAL	SEX		RACE		REGION				4YR COLLEGE PLANS		ILLICIT DRUG USE: LIFETIME				
		M	F	White	Black	NE	NC	S	W	Yes	No	None	Mari-juana Only	Few Pills	More Pills	Any Her-oin
N (Weighted No. of Cases):	3073	1413	1550	2295	312	725	867	952	529	1839	1084	1237	583	487	648	47
% of Weighted Total:	100.0	46.0	50.4	74.7	10.2	23.6	28.2	31.0	17.2	59.9	35.3	40.3	19.0	15.8	21.1	1.5

A20I: Organizations concerned with environmental problems (Sierra Club, Friends of Earth, etc.)?

	TOTAL	M	F	White	Black	NE	NC	S	W	Yes	No	None	Mari-juana Only	Few Pills	More Pills	Any Her-oin
1. Definitely not	9.7	11.1	8.8	9.5	10.2	10.6	9.6	8.2	11.5	8.5	12.5	8.1	10.2	8.7	12.2	19.9
2. Probably not	21.9	20.3	23.4	23.3	19.5	20.3	21.1	24.0	21.8	21.8	22.2	22.3	18.6	21.2	25.0	25.2
3. Don't know	40.4	36.4	43.9	40.0	37.5	39.8	40.8	40.8	39.6	40.0	41.7	41.5	42.4	44.9	34.7	31.2
4. Probably will	19.1	21.1	17.1	18.4	24.5	20.3	18.6	18.8	18.9	20.0	17.1	20.1	19.2	15.0	19.2	15.2
5. Definitely will	7.0	8.2	5.8	6.9	7.3	6.2	8.1	6.4	7.2	8.0	4.4	6.4	6.9	8.4	7.1	5.8
6. Already have	1.9	2.8	1.1	1.9	0.9	2.8	1.8	1.8	1.0	1.7	2.2	1.6	2.6	1.8	1.9	2.7
Item 12280 Subject F04,O02 N	3030	1401	1532	2276	306	720	852	938	520	1824	1072	1223	579	482	642	47

Now we have a different kind of question.

A21: How satisfied are you with your life as a whole these days?

	TOTAL	M	F	White	Black	NE	NC	S	W	Yes	No	None	Mari-juana Only	Few Pills	More Pills	Any Her-oin
1. Completely dissatisfied	2.1	2.5	1.7	1.8	2.5	3.1	1.5	2.1	2.1	1.8	2.6	2.1	2.0	1.2	3.2	1.1
2. Quite dissatisfied	6.9	5.7	7.5	6.8	6.1	6.9	5.6	7.1	8.5	7.2	6.5	6.1	7.5	7.2	8.0	6.3
3. Somewhat dissatisfied	9.7	10.3	9.5	9.3	10.8	8.6	10.0	9.3	11.7	9.3	10.3	8.6	8.6	11.9	10.6	13.4
4. Neither, or mixed feelings	15.0	13.6	16.7	14.8	19.3	14.8	14.4	16.4	13.9	13.7	17.3	13.2	12.2	18.3	18.5	20.3
5. Somewhat satisfied	26.5	27.7	25.2	26.2	27.6	29.3	26.3	25.2	25.5	26.4	26.5	23.9	27.9	31.1	25.4	38.8
6. Quite satisfied	34.5	35.1	34.3	36.8	25.3	32.4	38.5	33.2	33.0	36.9	31.4	39.1	38.2	25.6	31.0	15.5
7. Completely satisfied	5.2	5.1	5.1	4.3	8.3	4.9	3.8	6.6	5.3	4.8	5.4	7.0	3.6	4.6	3.3	4.5
Item 6840 Subject P01,Q01 N	3040	1403	1541	2285	309	719	858	942	521	1829	1077	1232	582	484	642	46

A22: These questions are about whether you think women are discriminated against in each of the following areas. To what extent are women discriminated against...

A22A: In getting a college education?

	TOTAL	M	F	White	Black	NE	NC	S	W	Yes	No	None	Mari-juana Only	Few Pills	More Pills	Any Her-oin
1. Not at all	44.4	49.8	39.2	45.7	42.1	44.7	46.4	45.7	38.1	46.4	42.1	43.0	47.0	42.2	46.0	47.6
2. Very little	31.4	28.0	35.1	33.2	25.2	32.5	32.4	28.2	34.1	32.6	30.1	31.5	32.4	30.3	32.3	25.8
3. Some	11.9	8.7	14.9	11.7	12.0	12.6	10.3	11.6	14.1	10.6	14.0	11.9	8.5	15.7	12.1	7.2
4. A good deal	3.0	2.7	3.3	2.2	5.3	1.9	3.1	3.6	3.3	2.4	3.4	2.3	2.2	4.0	3.7	10.6
5. A great deal	1.8	1.8	1.3	0.7	6.5	1.5	0.8	3.4	1.0	1.1	2.6	3.0	0.9	0.4	1.0	4.8
8. Don't know	7.5	8.9	6.2	6.5	8.9	6.7	7.0	7.5	9.4	7.0	7.9	8.2	9.0	7.3	4.9	3.9
Item 12290 Subject D06 N	3037	1397	1543	2284	310	717	857	943	520	1827	1075	1230	580	485	642	47

A22B: In gaining positions of leadership over men and women?

	TOTAL	M	F	White	Black	NE	NC	S	W	Yes	No	None	Mari-juana Only	Few Pills	More Pills	Any Her-oin
1. Not at all	7.1	9.6	4.4	6.9	7.3	6.3	6.7	8.3	6.5	6.2	8.3	4.5	8.3	6.5	10.2	20.3
2. Very little	13.9	17.2	11.1	14.7	10.9	12.7	13.8	14.9	13.7	15.3	11.9	15.0	13.4	14.3	12.4	9.8
3. Some	36.6	40.6	33.5	39.3	26.1	33.5	38.3	35.1	40.6	38.0	35.1	40.4	32.4	36.2	34.4	31.1
4. A good deal	24.5	18.3	30.1	24.2	27.1	27.9	24.1	22.8	23.5	25.1	23.3	23.4	27.4	24.0	24.2	21.5
5. A great deal	12.9	7.8	17.3	10.8	21.9	15.7	11.1	13.7	10.4	11.3	15.2	11.4	12.8	14.5	14.8	13.8
8. Don't know	5.1	6.5	3.6	4.0	6.8	3.8	6.0	5.2	5.3	4.2	6.2	5.3	5.7	4.4	4.0	3.5
Item 12300 Subject D06 N	3031	1396	1542	2283	310	715	856	941	518	1825	1075	1229	580	485	639	47

A22C: In obtaining executive positions in business?

	TOTAL	M	F	White	Black	NE	NC	S	W	Yes	No	None	Mari-juana Only	Few Pills	More Pills	Any Her-oin
1. Not at all	7.9	11.0	5.0	7.9	8.0	7.5	6.5	8.8	9.5	7.0	9.5	6.9	8.3	7.8	8.9	17.7
2. Very little	16.8	18.5	15.0	16.9	14.6	15.7	18.0	16.0	17.7	16.9	15.5	15.1	17.4	17.6	19.3	13.5
3. Some	32.8	33.5	33.1	35.2	25.7	33.1	34.5	31.4	32.1	34.3	31.9	35.0	32.3	32.9	30.3	28.7
4. A good deal	23.3	20.4	25.6	24.3	20.7	26.4	23.9	22.8	19.3	24.4	21.3	24.0	25.5	23.8	20.0	17.3
5. A great deal	11.2	7.3	15.0	8.9	20.7	10.0	9.7	12.7	12.6	10.6	12.1	10.8	9.2	11.7	14.0	10.0
8. Don't know	7.9	9.3	6.3	6.9	10.3	7.3	7.4	8.4	8.8	6.8	9.6	8.3	7.3	6.3	7.4	12.8
Item 12310 Subject D06 N	3029	1396	1540	2282	310	713	856	942	517	1824	1074	1228	580	484	640	47

A22D: In obtaining top jobs in the professions?

	TOTAL	M	F	White	Black	NE	NC	S	W	Yes	No	None	Mari-juana Only	Few Pills	More Pills	Any Her-oin
1. Not at all	10.6	13.2	7.9	10.2	11.3	10.3	9.5	11.7	10.9	9.9	12.1	9.2	11.1	9.8	12.9	18.0
2. Very little	18.6	21.1	16.8	19.7	15.9	16.2	20.2	19.2	18.3	19.3	17.7	17.9	17.6	19.8	20.3	20.7
3. Some	30.4	29.5	31.5	31.9	24.6	33.2	30.6	29.3	28.3	31.5	28.6	33.0	29.3	32.0	26.3	18.2
4. A good deal	21.3	19.6	23.0	22.0	21.1	21.2	22.8	19.6	22.2	22.0	20.5	21.0	24.8	21.1	19.7	17.5
5. A great deal	11.8	7.2	15.7	9.5	20.5	12.9	10.5	12.4	11.2	11.2	12.0	11.6	9.8	11.3	13.3	20.8
8. Don't know	7.3	9.4	5.1	6.6	6.5	6.2	6.4	7.8	9.0	6.1	9.0	7.3	7.5	6.0	7.5	4.7
Item 12320 Subject D06 N	3026	1393	1539	2284	308	713	856	939	518	1824	1072	1225	580	485	640	47

QUESTIONNAIRE FORM 5 1986	TOTAL	SEX		RACE		REGION				4YR COLLEGE PLANS		ILLICIT DRUG USE: LIFETIME				
		M	F	White	Black	NE	NC	S	W	Yes	No	None	Mari-juana Only	Few Pills	More Pills	Any Her-oin
N (Weighted No. of Cases):	3073	1413	1550	2295	312	725	867	952	529	1839	1084	1237	583	487	648	47
% of Weighted Total:	100.0	46.0	50.4	74.7	10.2	23.6	28.2	31.0	17.2	59.9	35.3	40.3	19.0	15.8	21.1	1.5

A22E: In getting skilled labor jobs?

1. Not at all	11.7	14.4	9.2	12.0	9.8	12.3	12.4	11.2	10.6	11.8	11.5	10.4	11.3	9.5	15.5	17.1
2. Very little	21.4	20.9	22.2	22.8	18.2	18.4	24.6	20.4	22.0	21.9	20.8	22.3	23.3	24.5	16.7	12.5
3. Some	30.2	31.8	29.3	30.9	26.8	29.7	29.0	31.3	31.0	30.5	30.1	30.5	29.6	28.1	31.2	36.2
4. A good deal	17.6	15.8	19.4	17.6	19.1	19.8	17.4	17.2	15.7	17.6	18.0	18.6	15.9	19.1	17.1	9.0
5. A great deal	8.1	6.5	9.1	6.7	13.5	8.6	6.7	8.2	9.7	7.8	8.4	7.0	6.9	7.9	10.2	18.3
8. Don't know	11.0	10.6	10.9	10.0	12.5	11.2	9.9	11.6	11.1	10.5	11.2	11.3	13.0	11.0	9.3	6.9
Item 12330 Subject D06 N	3020	1389	1538	2273	309	714	854	937	516	1821	1070	1224	580	484	639	44

A22F: In getting elected to political office?

1. Not at all	6.1	9.2	3.1	5.7	5.8	5.3	4.8	7.8	6.2	5.9	6.3	4.8	7.0	7.0	6.2	13.8
2. Very little	11.7	15.3	8.3	11.9	11.2	10.4	12.8	12.1	10.9	12.7	10.1	11.4	12.7	9.5	12.7	15.5
3. Some	25.6	28.0	23.7	26.9	21.3	21.7	28.9	24.6	27.2	25.8	25.4	27.8	24.4	26.2	23.0	16.8
4. A good deal	24.9	23.7	26.5	26.0	22.6	26.5	25.7	23.3	24.4	26.8	21.3	26.4	26.7	22.5	22.5	20.2
5. A great deal	25.8	16.8	34.1	24.6	33.1	29.8	23.4	25.4	24.7	24.5	28.7	23.3	23.7	29.9	30.1	24.2
8. Don't know	6.0	7.1	4.3	5.0	6.0	6.3	4.3	6.8	6.6	4.4	8.1	6.2	5.5	4.8	5.6	9.5
Item 12340 Subject D06,H02 N	3031	1396	1542	2284	308	715	856	940	519	1826	1073	1229	579	485	640	47

A22G: In getting equal pay for equal work?

1. Not at all	15.6	21.1	10.1	15.1	19.9	14.5	13.5	19.1	14.3	15.5	15.8	14.7	15.9	15.4	16.6	23.8
2. Very little	18.8	23.2	14.9	20.4	11.6	17.8	20.6	17.2	20.1	19.9	17.5	20.0	20.7	15.7	17.2	22.4
3. Some	24.1	21.9	26.5	25.6	21.8	26.0	23.0	24.0	23.6	25.6	22.4	24.7	22.8	27.0	23.8	8.8
4. A good deal	17.5	15.4	19.7	17.1	18.8	17.9	19.5	14.8	18.9	17.8	16.6	18.6	17.5	20.6	13.3	12.9
5. A great deal	17.7	10.6	24.3	16.2	21.7	17.4	18.3	17.7	17.0	16.4	19.4	15.6	17.8	16.2	21.7	28.6
8. Don't know	6.2	7.8	4.5	5.6	6.1	6.4	5.1	7.1	6.2	4.8	8.3	6.5	5.3	5.2	7.4	3.5
Item 12350 Subject D06 N	3030	1395	1541	2283	308	715	856	940	518	1825	1074	1228	580	485	639	47

A23: The next questions ask for your opinions on the effects of using certain drugs and other substances. First, how much do you think people risk harming themselves (physically or in other ways), if they...

A23A: Smoke one or more packs of cigarettes per day

1. No risk	1.4	1.7	1.1	0.6	2.7	1.4	1.1	1.9	1.1	0.8	1.9	0.9	0.9	0.7	2.5	7.6
2. Slight risk	4.9	4.8	5.0	5.1	5.7	6.3	5.0	4.8	3.1	3.4	7.5	3.8	4.0	5.3	7.0	12.9
3. Moderate risk	26.4	26.7	26.1	28.2	17.2	22.9	29.0	26.5	26.8	23.2	32.0	23.1	25.5	30.5	30.6	34.4
4. Great risk	66.0	64.8	67.3	65.5	69.8	68.4	64.1	65.0	67.7	71.7	57.0	70.8	68.4	62.2	59.3	40.6
5. Can't say, drug unfamiliar	1.3	1.9	0.6	0.5	4.6	1.1	0.9	1.8	1.2	0.9	1.6	1.5	1.2	1.3	0.6	4.5
Item 12360 Subject A14a N	3038	1402	1541	2286	310	718	857	942	521	1831	1074	1232	580	483	644	47

A23B: Try marijuana (pot, grass) once or twice

1. No risk	30.3	36.6	25.3	33.3	19.5	39.3	32.1	20.7	32.6	31.3	28.7	12.1	40.7	34.6	51.6	50.2
2. Slight risk	36.3	30.7	41.2	37.5	31.3	36.3	37.6	35.7	35.1	36.9	36.0	36.6	38.5	38.9	32.1	38.5
3. Moderate risk	15.5	13.8	17.1	15.2	16.2	12.7	15.0	18.1	15.2	15.9	15.1	21.7	9.5	16.3	9.4	4.1
4. Great risk	15.1	15.7	14.1	12.1	27.2	9.9	12.1	21.6	15.2	13.8	16.7	24.6	9.7	9.1	6.3	5.4
5. Can't say, drug unfamiliar	2.8	3.2	2.3	1.9	5.9	1.8	3.1	3.9	1.9	2.1	3.5	5.0	1.6	1.1	0.6	1.7
Item 12370 Subject A14a N	3039	1400	1543	2286	310	720	857	943	519	1830	1076	1232	582	485	642	47

A23C: Smoke marijuana occasionally

1. No risk	7.1	9.9	4.7	6.9	7.5	9.4	5.8	6.7	6.7	5.6	8.8	2.3	6.7	6.7	14.8	28.7
2. Slight risk	25.7	28.2	23.6	29.1	14.2	30.7	28.3	18.6	27.7	26.7	24.7	12.3	34.4	29.7	40.1	34.9
3. Moderate risk	39.5	33.5	45.0	40.8	34.7	39.2	41.4	39.0	37.5	40.9	37.6	42.2	42.3	40.4	33.0	22.9
4. Great risk	25.0	24.8	24.9	21.2	38.5	19.0	21.5	32.0	26.4	24.7	25.4	38.3	15.2	21.9	11.6	11.8
5. Can't say, drug unfamiliar	2.7	3.6	1.8	2.0	5.1	1.7	3.1	3.7	1.7	2.1	3.5	4.9	1.4	1.3	0.6	1.7
Item 12380 Subject A14a N	3035	1399	1540	2284	308	717	856	940	521	1829	1073	1230	580	484	643	47

QUESTIONNAIRE FORM 5 1986	TOTAL	SEX		RACE		REGION				4YR COLLEGE PLANS		ILLICIT DRUG USE: LIFETIME				
		M	F	White	Black	NE	NC	S	W	Yes	No	None	Mari-juana Only	Few Pills	More Pills	Any Her-oin
N (Weighted No. of Cases):	3073	1413	1550	2295	312	725	867	952	529	1839	1084	1237	583	487	648	47
% of Weighted Total:	100.0	46.0	50.4	74.7	10.2	23.6	28.2	31.0	17.2	59.9	35.3	40.3	19.0	15.8	21.1	1.5

A23D: Smoke marijuana regularly

1. No risk	2.2	2.8	1.4	1.5	3.4	3.2	1.6	2.3	1.7	1.2	2.9	1.2	1.0	2.0	4.0	10.6
2. Slight risk	5.4	8.1	3.2	5.6	6.5	5.3	5.6	5.3	5.7	3.9	7.7	1.4	5.1	5.2	12.7	15.0
3. Moderate risk	18.6	20.6	16.3	20.0	13.7	23.9	18.4	13.5	20.9	19.2	17.5	9.6	23.5	20.0	29.3	35.8
4. Great risk	71.3	65.3	77.5	71.2	71.4	66.0	71.6	75.6	70.5	73.9	68.7	83.7	69.0	71.5	53.4	36.9
5. Can't say, drug unfamiliar	2.4	3.1	1.6	1.7	5.1	1.7	2.8	3.3	1.2	1.8	3.1	4.2	1.4	1.3	0.6	1.7
Item 12390 Subject A14a N	3035	1398	1542	2285	309	718	857	941	519	1828	1074	1232	578	484	643	47

A23E: Try LSD once or twice

1. No risk	4.1	5.0	3.3	3.9	3.8	5.0	3.6	3.7	4.3	3.4	4.5	1.5	1.7	5.5	7.3	25.8
2. Slight risk	17.0	16.6	17.6	18.1	11.1	18.5	19.1	14.2	16.4	17.0	17.4	13.9	16.6	15.1	25.1	28.5
3. Moderate risk	25.5	22.8	28.4	27.3	20.7	27.9	23.5	25.1	26.2	26.6	24.2	24.4	29.0	24.7	26.6	17.0
4. Great risk	42.0	42.9	40.3	40.9	44.2	37.3	42.6	43.2	45.0	43.5	39.6	48.2	38.1	43.8	33.6	20.2
5. Can't say, drug unfamiliar	11.5	12.7	10.4	9.7	20.2	11.3	11.3	13.7	8.0	9.5	14.3	12.1	14.5	10.9	7.5	8.4
Item 12400 Subject A14a N	3037	1401	1539	2284	310	717	859	942	520	1828	1078	1231	580	485	642	47

A23F: Take LSD regularly

1. No risk	1.2	1.6	0.7	0.7	2.6	1.2	0.8	1.7	0.9	0.5	1.8	0.8	0.8	0.9	1.7	6.2
2. Slight risk	1.1	1.3	1.0	0.9	1.2	1.5	1.4	1.0	0.5	0.8	1.3	0.4	0.3	1.4	2.4	6.4
3. Moderate risk	4.5	5.5	3.5	4.3	3.5	5.4	3.7	4.4	4.8	3.7	5.8	2.7	4.5	4.5	7.5	13.0
4. Great risk	82.6	79.6	85.5	85.4	72.1	81.7	84.0	79.7	86.7	86.4	77.3	84.9	81.3	83.4	81.3	66.0
5. Can't say, drug unfamiliar	10.6	11.9	9.3	8.7	20.5	10.2	10.0	13.2	7.1	8.5	13.8	11.2	13.1	9.8	7.1	8.4
Item 12410 Subject A14a N	3030	1398	1538	2282	310	716	856	941	518	1825	1076	1228	579	484	641	47

A23G: Try heroin (smack, horse) once or twice

1. No risk	2.9	3.9	1.9	2.4	3.6	2.7	3.2	3.2	1.9	2.2	3.2	1.6	1.4	3.7	4.6	19.5
2. Slight risk	14.7	13.5	16.2	15.9	11.7	18.0	15.7	12.6	12.6	14.9	15.0	15.0	12.2	11.8	18.0	26.0
3. Moderate risk	25.7	23.6	28.1	27.4	18.4	25.2	27.5	22.9	28.3	26.6	24.3	23.7	30.2	26.4	25.7	26.9
4. Great risk	45.8	47.4	43.5	44.5	49.4	43.7	43.4	47.3	50.3	47.0	44.5	48.3	42.8	47.5	44.1	25.8
5. Can't say, drug unfamiliar	10.9	11.6	10.4	9.9	17.0	10.4	10.3	14.1	7.0	9.4	13.0	11.4	13.4	10.6	7.5	1.7
Item 12420 Subject A14a N	3026	1400	1532	2279	309	714	854	941	517	1820	1078	1229	580	481	638	47

A23H: Take heroin occasionally

1. No risk	1.3	1.8	0.7	0.7	3.1	1.1	0.9	2.1	0.7	0.8	1.4	1.2	0.5	0.9	2.0	1.9
2. Slight risk	2.2	2.9	1.7	1.9	3.6	2.3	2.1	2.2	2.6	1.9	2.6	1.1	1.8	2.2	3.0	24.2
3. Moderate risk	18.1	15.2	21.2	19.7	14.6	21.2	19.8	16.2	14.4	16.8	20.8	19.8	14.6	16.2	19.7	28.7
4. Great risk	68.2	69.3	66.8	68.5	62.9	66.0	67.5	66.1	76.3	71.8	62.9	67.1	71.0	70.7	67.9	45.2
5. Can't say, drug unfamiliar	10.2	10.8	9.6	9.3	15.9	9.4	9.6	13.5	6.0	8.7	12.3	10.8	12.1	10.0	7.4	-
Item 12430 Subject A14a N	3030	1399	1536	2281	308	715	857	939	519	1823	1076	1226	582	484	640	47

A23I: Take heroin regularly

1. No risk	1.2	1.7	0.6	0.5	2.3	1.0	1.0	1.7	0.7	0.5	1.3	1.0	0.4	1.3	1.7	4.3
2. Slight risk	0.2	0.2	0.3	0.2	0.3	0.4	0.2	0.2	0.2	0.1	0.5	0.3	-	-	-	3.5
3. Moderate risk	1.6	2.2	1.0	1.5	2.4	1.3	1.9	1.5	1.7	1.3	1.9	1.0	2.2	0.6	2.7	5.6
4. Great risk	87.1	85.0	89.0	88.9	78.3	87.7	87.9	83.2	91.8	90.0	83.8	87.7	85.6	88.2	87.9	82.6
5. Can't say, drug unfamiliar	9.9	10.8	9.1	8.9	16.8	9.5	9.0	13.5	5.6	8.1	12.5	10.0	11.8	9.9	7.7	4.1
Item 12440 Subject A14a N	3020	1393	1534	2276	306	715	854	933	517	1818	1075	1221	581	482	639	47

A23J: Try barbiturates (downers, goofballs, reds, yellows, etc.) once or twice

1. No risk	9.0	10.5	7.6	9.7	4.8	10.9	9.5	6.7	9.7	7.9	10.3	3.7	5.0	8.8	20.2	38.3
2. Slight risk	26.3	25.1	28.0	28.7	14.0	27.8	28.9	22.8	26.4	28.4	24.0	21.2	26.2	30.8	33.6	36.7
3. Moderate risk	27.4	25.9	28.6	28.5	21.3	27.5	24.9	27.7	30.8	28.2	26.0	29.3	27.9	26.1	25.8	8.5
4. Great risk	25.4	26.0	24.1	23.4	35.3	23.3	24.7	27.6	25.4	24.5	26.3	33.1	24.1	22.2	14.6	11.4
5. Can't say, drug unfamiliar	12.0	12.5	11.6	9.8	24.7	10.5	12.0	15.3	7.8	11.1	13.4	12.7	16.8	12.2	5.9	5.2
Item 12450 Subject A14a N	3031	1401	1536	2285	309	715	856	940	520	1827	1074	1226	581	485	641	47

QUESTIONNAIRE FORM 5 1986	TOTAL	SEX		RACE		REGION				4YR COLLEGE PLANS		ILLICIT DRUG USE: LIFETIME				
		M	F	White	Black	NE	NC	S	W	Yes	No	None	Marijuana Only	Few Pills	More Pills	Any Heroin
N (Weighted No. of Cases):	3073	1413	1550	2295	312	725	867	952	529	1839	1084	1237	583	487	648	47
% of Weighted Total:	100.0	46.0	50.4	74.7	10.2	23.6	28.2	31.0	17.2	59.9	35.3	40.3	19.0	15.8	21.1	1.5

A23K: Take barbiturates regularly

1. No risk	1.4	1.6	1.0	0.9	2.9	1.6	1.2	1.8	0.7	0.6	1.8	0.9	0.4	1.6	1.9	12.1
2. Slight risk	3.1	3.6	2.7	3.6	1.3	4.6	3.4	1.9	3.0	2.3	4.5	0.8	1.9	2.4	8.5	11.9
3. Moderate risk	16.0	17.2	15.3	17.6	8.2	16.6	16.8	13.9	17.8	14.5	19.1	8.4	16.3	19.3	27.4	29.0
4. Great risk	67.2	64.7	69.3	68.1	62.5	66.4	66.8	66.4	70.3	71.6	60.3	77.5	63.8	63.0	56.3	40.0
5. Can't say, drug unfamiliar	12.2	12.9	11.7	9.9	25.1	10.8	11.8	15.9	8.3	10.9	14.3	12.4	17.6	13.7	5.8	6.9
Item 12460 Subject A14a N	3022	1398	1530	2282	307	716	849	939	518	1818	1073	1222	578	485	640	47

A23L: Try amphetamines (uppers, pep pills, bennies, speed) once or twice

1. No risk	12.1	13.1	11.3	13.6	6.6	13.3	13.7	9.7	11.9	11.4	12.7	4.7	8.4	13.8	26.0	37.4
2. Slight risk	27.2	25.4	29.1	29.9	10.9	28.0	31.0	21.4	30.1	28.9	25.9	20.1	27.1	32.6	37.4	22.3
3. Moderate risk	27.4	25.7	28.5	27.6	25.0	28.0	23.9	29.4	28.4	28.5	25.0	31.3	28.3	24.7	22.2	18.0
4. Great risk	25.1	26.4	23.7	22.3	41.0	23.6	22.7	29.1	24.1	24.3	25.8	34.3	25.8	21.0	11.1	13.0
5. Can't say, drug unfamiliar	8.3	9.4	7.4	6.6	16.6	7.1	8.8	10.4	5.4	6.8	10.6	9.6	10.4	7.9	3.3	9.4
Item 12470 Subject A14a N	3035	1402	1539	2285	310	717	857	943	518	1829	1075	1230	582	485	642	47

A23M: Take amphetamines regularly

1. No risk	1.6	2.2	0.9	0.8	2.9	1.6	1.0	2.2	1.4	0.7	2.2	0.9	0.5	1.5	2.8	7.5
2. Slight risk	5.2	6.2	4.3	5.7	3.1	5.3	6.2	4.8	3.8	4.1	6.8	1.4	3.3	5.7	13.1	12.9
3. Moderate risk	17.4	17.6	17.3	19.5	7.7	19.1	18.2	13.7	20.4	16.6	19.5	9.2	18.8	20.5	29.3	26.6
4. Great risk	67.3	64.7	69.6	67.2	68.6	65.8	66.1	68.9	68.3	71.3	61.2	78.7	66.6	64.7	50.6	46.0
5. Can't say, drug unfamiliar	8.6	9.3	7.9	6.8	17.8	8.2	8.4	10.3	6.1	7.4	10.3	9.8	10.7	7.7	4.1	7.0
Item 12480 Subject A14a N	3033	1400	1539	2284	308	716	858	941	518	1826	1076	1230	582	483	640	47

A23N: Try cocaine once or twice

1. No risk	9.5	11.3	8.0	10.0	6.2	13.9	8.2	6.5	11.3	8.5	11.0	2.3	7.2	9.4	21.9	50.7
2. Slight risk	22.5	21.3	23.7	24.1	15.3	25.9	23.3	17.0	26.1	22.8	22.2	15.9	22.3	23.2	36.5	10.8
3. Moderate risk	28.8	26.2	31.3	29.1	26.7	26.9	28.0	30.8	29.0	29.5	27.9	30.4	30.1	31.6	23.4	21.8
4. Great risk	33.5	34.6	32.1	32.0	42.5	28.6	33.7	38.6	30.5	34.3	31.9	43.9	34.3	30.5	16.0	15.0
5. Can't say, drug unfamiliar	5.8	6.6	5.0	4.9	9.3	4.7	6.8	7.2	3.0	4.8	7.1	7.4	6.2	5.2	2.1	1.7
Item 12490 Subject A14a N	3033	1402	1537	2286	308	717	858	940	518	1830	1073	1228	581	484	642	47

A23O: Take cocaine regularly

1. No risk	1.6	2.2	0.9	0.8	3.9	1.3	0.9	2.5	1.4	0.7	2.2	0.9	0.8	1.7	3.2	3.5
2. Slight risk	2.2	3.1	1.4	1.9	1.1	3.0	1.6	1.9	2.7	1.8	2.8	0.3	0.8	1.1	6.6	22.1
3. Moderate risk	8.6	10.7	6.6	8.9	7.6	12.4	7.5	5.3	11.2	7.7	9.7	3.0	9.5	8.6	18.0	16.3
4. Great risk	82.2	77.6	86.8	83.8	79.0	78.9	83.6	83.9	81.4	85.7	78.3	89.1	82.9	83.5	70.3	56.4
5. Can't say, drug unfamiliar	5.4	6.4	4.3	4.5	8.4	4.4	6.4	6.4	3.2	4.1	7.0	6.6	6.1	5.2	2.0	1.7
Item 12500 Subject A14a N	3027	1398	1535	2283	305	714	856	938	519	1825	1074	1228	579	482	642	47

A23P: Try one or two drinks of an alcoholic beverage (beer, wine, liquor)

1. No risk	50.0	55.5	45.4	54.6	29.6	57.7	54.3	40.6	49.2	52.9	46.7	35.3	59.2	54.8	64.9	73.7
2. Slight risk	34.2	30.2	38.1	33.4	37.4	31.7	32.4	37.3	35.1	33.5	35.1	42.6	28.7	33.4	25.8	16.2
3. Moderate risk	9.9	8.3	11.5	8.1	18.1	7.1	7.9	13.6	10.2	8.5	11.6	13.1	9.1	7.7	6.3	-
4. Great risk	4.6	4.3	4.3	3.1	12.5	2.2	4.2	7.1	4.1	4.0	5.2	7.3	2.3	2.9	2.5	5.6
5. Can't say, drug unfamiliar	1.3	1.7	0.7	0.7	2.5	1.3	1.2	1.3	1.4	1.1	1.3	1.6	0.8	1.3	0.5	4.6
Item 12510 Subject A14a N	3036	1399	1543	2287	309	718	856	942	519	1829	1076	1233	581	485	642	46

A23Q: Take one or two drinks nearly every day

1. No risk	8.4	12.6	4.6	8.4	10.0	11.4	7.4	8.4	5.8	6.7	11.2	5.1	10.7	7.4	11.9	20.6
2. Slight risk	26.1	31.5	21.5	28.0	18.0	27.5	26.7	24.9	25.2	25.7	27.5	23.0	25.6	29.5	31.4	22.4
3. Moderate risk	39.1	35.1	42.9	40.4	33.4	36.7	38.9	39.4	42.1	40.7	37.1	39.6	39.2	42.9	35.5	38.1
4. Great risk	25.1	19.2	30.1	22.6	36.0	23.5	25.4	25.9	25.5	25.8	22.9	30.4	23.7	19.6	20.8	13.6
5. Can't say, drug unfamiliar	1.4	1.6	0.9	0.7	2.5	1.0	1.6	1.5	1.3	1.1	1.3	1.9	0.8	0.7	0.6	5.3
Item 12520 Subject A14a N	3031	1396	1541	2281	308	717	857	939	517	1826	1076	1232	579	481	642	47

QUESTIONNAIRE FORM 5 1986	TOTAL	SEX		RACE		REGION				4YR COLLEGE PLANS		ILLICIT DRUG USE: LIFETIME				
		M	F	White	Black	NE	NC	S	W	Yes	No	None	Mari- juana Only	Few Pills	More Pills	Any Her- oin
N (Weighted No. of Cases):	3073	1413	1550	2295	312	725	867	952	529	1839	1084	1237	583	487	648	47
% of Weighted Total:	100.0	46.0	50.4	74.7	10.2	23.6	28.2	31.0	17.2	59.9	35.3	40.3	19.0	15.8	21.1	1.5

A23R: Take four or five drinks nearly every day

1. No risk	2.9	4.4	1.4	2.3	4.2	3.3	2.6	3.4	1.6	1.6	4.5	1.9	2.2	1.8	5.1	13.6
2. Slight risk	6.3	9.6	3.4	6.6	2.7	6.0	4.9	7.6	6.4	4.9	8.5	4.2	9.1	3.9	8.8	13.0
3. Moderate risk	22.9	27.8	18.8	24.7	17.1	22.0	25.7	23.1	19.1	21.3	26.1	20.3	20.8	28.2	25.8	21.2
4. Great risk	66.5	56.4	75.4	65.6	73.5	67.6	65.0	64.2	71.7	71.0	59.4	71.6	67.1	65.5	59.6	46.9
5. Can't say, drug unfamiliar	1.4	1.7	1.0	0.8	2.5	1.1	1.7	1.7	1.2	1.2	1.5	2.0	0.8	0.7	0.7	5.3
Item 12530 Subject A14a N	*3027*	*1396*	*1541*	*2279*	*308*	*717*	*854*	*936*	*520*	*1825*	*1074*	*1228*	*579*	*482*	*643*	*47*

A23S: Have five or more drinks once or twice each weekend

1. No risk	8.2	11.2	5.7	8.3	6.2	11.3	8.7	6.7	5.8	6.4	11.0	4.5	9.3	8.4	13.1	20.5
2. Slight risk	19.5	22.8	16.4	21.5	11.3	20.3	21.5	17.2	19.3	19.2	20.5	13.1	22.9	21.8	26.6	24.4
3. Moderate risk	31.9	32.4	31.5	33.0	25.8	31.0	32.8	29.9	35.3	33.2	29.9	28.9	32.8	34.6	35.2	23.0
4. Great risk	39.1	31.9	45.7	36.4	54.4	36.3	35.8	44.7	38.3	40.1	37.2	51.6	34.2	34.8	24.7	26.0
5. Can't say, drug unfamiliar	1.4	1.8	0.7	0.8	2.3	1.2	1.3	1.6	1.3	1.1	1.4	1.9	0.8	0.5	0.5	6.1
Item 12540 Subject A14a N	*3035*	*1400*	*1542*	*2285*	*310*	*720*	*856*	*941*	*517*	*1829*	*1078*	*1233*	*582*	*485*	*639*	*47*

A23T: Take cocaine occasionally

1. No risk	3.5	4.5	2.4	3.0	3.9	4.2	2.4	4.3	2.7	2.4	4.2	1.1	1.4	3.7	8.2	17.3
2. Slight risk	9.0	10.4	8.0	10.1	4.7	11.8	8.2	6.8	10.1	8.4	10.0	3.4	7.3	7.9	19.1	44.7
3. Moderate risk	27.7	25.4	30.0	30.0	21.6	29.4	26.7	25.3	31.3	28.2	27.5	24.3	28.4	30.7	34.4	7.1
4. Great risk	54.2	53.3	54.9	52.2	61.8	50.1	56.3	56.7	52.0	56.4	51.6	63.8	56.4	53.3	36.5	28.2
5. Can't say, drug unfamiliar	5.6	6.4	4.8	4.7	8.0	4.4	6.5	7.0	3.3	4.7	6.7	7.4	6.5	4.3	1.7	2.7
Item 12495 Subject A14a N	*3020*	*1393*	*1536*	*2278*	*305*	*714*	*855*	*933*	*518*	*1824*	*1069*	*1229*	*579*	*480*	*638*	*47*

A23U: Use smokeless tobacco regularly (chewing tobacco, plug, dipping tobacco, snuff)

1. No risk	7.8	9.4	6.1	6.8	14.5	8.6	6.2	9.6	5.9	6.0	10.1	5.1	7.4	10.8	10.3	6.6
2. Slight risk	27.8	29.9	26.5	29.7	24.0	26.8	30.1	29.8	21.9	27.6	29.0	27.6	31.2	28.5	24.8	30.5
3. Moderate risk	32.8	33.9	31.9	34.1	25.9	29.6	35.7	31.5	34.7	34.9	29.6	32.7	34.7	31.3	33.7	25.9
4. Great risk	25.8	21.2	29.7	25.3	25.8	27.4	23.6	23.5	31.4	26.1	25.6	29.2	21.7	23.9	25.0	25.0
5. Can't say, drug unfamiliar	5.8	5.6	5.8	4.1	9.8	7.6	4.4	5.6	6.2	5.5	5.7	5.4	4.9	5.5	6.3	12.1
Item 12365 Subject A14a N	*3038*	*1403*	*1542*	*2289*	*309*	*720*	*857*	*941*	*520*	*1830*	*1078*	*1233*	*582*	*485*	*642*	*47*

This section asks for your views and feelings about a number of different things.

D01: Do you agree or disagree with each of the following?

D01A: I take a positive attitude toward myself

1. Disagree	2.3	2.1	2.6	1.9	5.1	2.0	2.6	1.9	3.1	2.1	2.6	2.6	2.3	1.8	2.1	4.3
2. Mostly disagree	6.4	5.1	7.6	7.0	2.5	7.0	5.5	7.3	5.5	6.3	6.6	4.3	7.5	6.7	8.7	17.2
3. Neither	9.1	10.0	8.0	9.4	4.0	10.0	9.0	7.9	10.0	8.5	10.1	9.5	7.8	9.0	9.3	11.1
4. Mostly agree	49.0	44.7	53.3	51.6	35.1	49.8	50.9	46.3	49.9	48.2	50.3	47.5	47.5	51.7	52.3	39.8
5. Agree	33.2	38.1	28.5	30.1	53.2	31.1	32.1	36.7	31.5	34.9	30.4	36.0	34.8	30.8	27.6	27.6
Item 12550 Subject Q01 N	*2920*	*1348*	*1506*	*2243*	*283*	*674*	*842*	*903*	*501*	*1806*	*1041*	*1188*	*557*	*469*	*622*	*46*

D01B: Good luck is more important than hard work for success

1. Disagree	37.3	35.0	39.4	36.9	46.1	41.3	33.0	38.2	37.4	37.6	37.1	38.5	37.2	37.5	34.8	34.0
2. Mostly disagree	37.4	36.7	38.5	39.2	28.9	31.1	43.0	35.5	39.6	39.8	33.0	38.9	38.5	34.8	37.2	18.8
3. Neither	15.7	17.2	14.3	16.4	9.1	17.3	14.8	16.1	14.6	14.7	17.3	14.8	14.5	16.4	17.4	29.4
4. Mostly agree	7.1	7.8	6.0	6.0	9.1	7.6	7.4	6.5	7.0	6.3	8.5	5.5	8.0	7.7	8.1	12.0
5. Agree	2.5	3.2	1.8	1.5	6.8	2.6	1.7	3.8	1.3	1.5	4.2	2.2	1.8	3.5	2.5	5.9
Item 12560 Subject Q02 N	*2917*	*1346*	*1504*	*2242*	*280*	*673*	*839*	*902*	*503*	*1806*	*1040*	*1189*	*554*	*466*	*624*	*46*

QUESTIONNAIRE FORM 5 1986	TOTAL	SEX		RACE		REGION				4YR COLLEGE PLANS		ILLICIT DRUG USE: LIFETIME				
		M	F	White	Black	NE	NC	S	W	Yes	No	None	Mari-juana Only	Few Pills	More Pills	Any Her-oin
N (Weighted No. of Cases):	3073	1413	1550	2295	312	725	867	952	529	1839	1084	1237	583	487	648	47
% of Weighted Total:	100.0	46.0	50.4	74.7	10.2	23.6	28.2	31.0	17.2	59.9	35.3	40.3	19.0	15.8	21.1	1.5
D01C: I feel I am a person of worth, on an equal plane with others																
1. Disagree	1.6	2.2	1.2	1.5	3.1	1.8	1.6	1.3	1.9	1.3	2.1	1.6	1.2	1.7	1.7	5.5
2. Mostly disagree	3.7	3.9	3.6	3.6	2.4	3.0	4.0	4.0	3.7	3.8	3.6	3.5	2.8	3.0	5.7	4.5
3. Neither	10.2	11.1	9.4	10.1	7.2	10.8	12.5	8.1	9.2	8.8	12.1	10.5	9.7	11.6	9.4	9.2
4. Mostly agree	42.4	40.7	43.8	44.3	31.8	44.0	42.7	41.6	41.1	40.8	45.2	40.9	43.6	42.1	43.9	47.2
5. Agree	42.1	42.2	42.0	40.6	55.5	40.4	39.1	45.1	44.1	45.3	37.0	43.6	42.7	41.7	39.3	33.7
Item 12570 Subject Q01 N	2908	1343	1500	2241	278	668	839	899	502	1802	1034	1185	549	466	624	46
D01D: I am able to do things as well as most other people																
1. Disagree	1.2	1.3	1.1	0.8	2.5	1.0	0.7	1.8	1.4	1.0	1.8	1.4	2.2	0.2	1.0	-
2. Mostly disagree	2.0	1.7	2.3	2.2	1.5	1.9	2.4	1.9	1.7	2.2	1.8	2.7	1.4	0.9	2.0	1.8
3. Neither	5.7	5.3	6.1	5.6	3.0	6.2	7.6	3.3	6.3	4.7	6.9	6.1	5.6	6.1	5.4	5.2
4. Mostly agree	45.0	42.2	47.6	46.7	34.3	45.2	45.7	42.9	47.1	43.7	47.3	44.0	44.6	44.8	47.6	48.4
5. Agree	46.1	49.5	43.0	44.7	58.6	45.7	43.6	50.1	43.6	48.4	42.3	45.8	46.2	48.1	44.0	44.7
Item 12580 Subject Q01 N	2899	1340	1493	2230	277	665	835	898	501	1801	1027	1185	550	463	617	46
D01E: Every time I try to get ahead, something or somebody stops me																
1. Disagree	17.0	16.9	17.4	15.6	25.0	20.1	14.2	16.1	19.0	18.7	13.8	17.3	20.0	15.6	14.7	21.5
2. Mostly disagree	32.0	29.7	34.0	34.7	20.9	31.1	34.4	28.4	35.4	35.6	26.3	32.1	35.7	30.8	28.6	33.1
3. Neither	25.1	25.0	25.0	25.4	19.4	22.2	28.3	24.0	25.2	24.7	25.3	24.9	25.1	25.9	25.8	18.0
4. Mostly agree	20.2	21.8	18.7	19.1	24.9	20.8	16.7	25.4	16.0	16.5	26.4	20.0	15.5	23.3	23.0	15.4
5. Agree	5.8	6.6	4.8	5.2	9.8	5.7	6.4	6.1	4.4	4.5	8.2	5.7	3.7	4.4	7.9	12.1
Item 12590 Subject Q02 N	2907	1340	1500	2240	275	668	839	899	501	1803	1033	1185	550	464	623	46
D01F: Planning only makes a person unhappy since plans hardly ever work out anyway																
1. Disagree	28.9	26.8	30.9	28.7	35.5	25.9	27.9	30.1	32.5	32.6	23.0	33.2	25.8	26.7	25.7	16.7
2. Mostly disagree	33.6	33.1	34.0	35.6	22.2	31.9	38.4	30.5	33.6	36.3	28.9	34.0	34.7	33.5	30.6	28.6
3. Neither	17.7	19.7	16.5	18.7	14.1	18.4	18.2	17.2	16.8	15.6	21.2	14.7	18.1	20.4	21.0	28.8
4. Mostly agree	13.3	13.5	12.4	11.4	16.2	16.1	10.8	14.2	11.9	10.9	17.1	12.9	12.3	11.8	15.4	16.1
5. Agree	6.5	6.8	6.2	5.6	12.0	7.7	4.7	8.0	5.3	4.6	9.7	5.1	6.4	7.6	7.4	9.8
Item 12600 Subject Q02 N	2902	1335	1502	2239	274	668	836	898	500	1799	1031	1182	550	463	622	45
D01G: People who accept their condition in life are happier than those who try to change things																
1. Disagree	17.9	18.0	18.0	18.1	23.5	18.8	17.9	16.5	19.4	20.6	13.6	18.6	18.8	15.5	17.8	14.3
2. Mostly disagree	24.2	25.0	23.5	26.4	16.4	23.9	26.2	23.2	23.2	26.6	20.6	24.4	27.3	22.3	24.0	14.9
3. Neither	21.7	21.5	21.7	21.3	19.6	23.8	21.3	19.2	23.9	20.9	22.7	23.1	17.8	24.0	19.2	39.6
4. Mostly agree	22.1	21.6	22.2	21.8	17.3	19.6	22.0	24.6	21.2	19.0	27.2	20.8	21.1	24.4	23.9	20.9
5. Agree	14.0	13.9	14.6	12.4	23.2	13.9	12.6	16.5	12.3	12.9	15.9	13.0	15.1	13.9	15.1	10.3
Item 12610 Subject Q02 N	2899	1335	1497	2237	273	666	835	898	500	1795	1034	1183	547	463	622	46
D01H: On the whole, I'm satisfied with myself																
1. Disagree	3.4	3.6	3.4	3.1	8.0	3.1	2.8	4.1	3.6	3.5	3.3	3.1	2.5	3.7	3.8	19.4
2. Mostly disagree	7.5	8.1	6.9	7.2	6.4	7.4	8.6	6.5	7.8	6.7	9.0	7.2	7.4	6.5	8.7	14.8
3. Neither	9.6	10.5	8.9	9.6	6.0	10.6	9.2	8.5	10.6	9.7	9.2	8.5	7.1	10.3	13.5	10.8
4. Mostly agree	41.0	37.9	43.5	42.1	34.8	40.6	44.6	38.0	40.7	41.0	40.9	39.5	42.5	43.3	41.7	26.9
5. Agree	38.5	39.9	37.3	38.0	44.9	38.3	34.7	43.0	37.3	39.0	37.7	41.8	40.5	36.1	32.3	28.1
Item 12620 Subject P01,Q01 N	2894	1334	1494	2232	274	667	835	894	499	1796	1027	1176	548	462	622	46
D01I: People like me don't have much of a chance to be successful in life																
1. Disagree	59.8	58.0	61.4	59.5	69.6	61.0	56.7	60.8	61.3	65.4	51.2	62.1	62.5	56.2	55.4	50.8
2. Mostly disagree	25.0	24.1	25.8	26.7	15.9	24.5	27.8	23.5	24.0	23.2	27.7	24.5	24.8	26.2	26.0	19.0
3. Neither	9.1	10.0	8.5	8.9	5.1	9.2	9.6	8.1	10.0	7.2	12.6	7.7	7.3	10.7	12.6	11.9
4. Mostly agree	4.5	5.5	3.7	3.8	5.4	4.1	4.7	5.5	3.2	3.2	6.3	3.9	4.1	5.6	5.0	13.6
5. Agree	1.5	2.4	0.7	1.2	4.0	1.1	1.3	2.1	1.4	1.1	2.2	1.9	1.2	1.3	1.0	4.6
Item 12630 Subject Q02 N	2892	1333	1494	2232	274	666	836	893	498	1797	1024	1180	550	462	617	46

QUESTIONNAIRE FORM 5 1986	TOTAL	SEX		RACE		REGION				4YR COLLEGE PLANS		ILLICIT DRUG USE: LIFETIME				
		M	F	White	Black	NE	NC	S	W	Yes	No	None	Marijuana Only	Few Pills	More Pills	Any Heroin
N (Weighted No. of Cases):	3073	1413	1550	2295	312	725	867	952	529	1839	1084	1237	583	487	648	47
% of Weighted Total:	100.0	46.0	50.4	74.7	10.2	23.6	28.2	31.0	17.2	59.9	35.3	40.3	19.0	15.8	21.1	1.5

D01J: When I make plans, I am almost certain that I can make them work

	TOTAL	M	F	White	Black	NE	NC	S	W	Yes	No	None	Mari Only	Few	More	Any Her
1. Disagree	2.0	2.4	1.8	1.5	5.3	2.1	2.0	1.8	2.5	1.6	2.9	2.5	0.7	1.2	2.7	2.7
2. Mostly disagree	6.5	6.0	6.9	6.4	8.1	8.0	7.4	6.5	2.8	6.5	6.5	5.3	7.0	5.5	9.0	7.9
3. Neither	15.5	16.6	14.6	16.0	8.9	14.8	17.8	13.0	16.8	15.3	16.0	13.6	17.0	18.1	15.7	19.5
4. Mostly agree	49.1	45.9	51.8	50.1	38.8	47.4	48.9	50.2	50.0	49.5	48.2	50.8	50.4	49.2	46.8	25.7
5. Agree	26.8	29.0	25.0	26.0	38.8	27.7	23.9	28.4	27.9	27.2	26.4	27.8	24.8	26.0	25.8	44.2
Item 12640 Subject Q02 N	2897	1333	1497	2236	275	669	836	897	496	1795	1030	1181	550	460	623	44

D01K: A lot of times I feel lonely

	TOTAL	M	F	White	Black	NE	NC	S	W	Yes	No	None	Mari Only	Few	More	Any Her
1. Disagree	16.8	18.1	15.5	15.4	21.2	21.6	13.7	16.3	16.4	15.2	19.7	15.7	19.4	13.8	17.1	24.5
2. Mostly disagree	28.3	28.2	28.4	30.2	19.7	28.7	28.8	26.2	30.5	30.0	25.7	28.3	31.8	27.0	26.4	31.2
3. Neither	18.4	20.0	16.7	19.7	9.3	19.0	21.2	14.3	20.0	18.9	17.5	17.3	18.8	18.4	20.3	12.7
4. Mostly agree	24.2	23.3	25.0	23.7	25.1	21.1	23.2	28.5	22.3	24.5	23.3	26.3	20.0	25.6	23.6	22.4
5. Agree	12.4	10.4	14.4	11.0	24.8	9.6	13.0	14.7	10.7	11.5	13.7	12.4	10.0	15.3	12.6	9.2
Item 12650 Subject Q03 N	2878	1316	1494	2224	271	661	834	891	491	1782	1025	1176	543	457	617	46

D01L: I feel I do not have much to be proud of

	TOTAL	M	F	White	Black	NE	NC	S	W	Yes	No	None	Mari Only	Few	More	Any Her
1. Disagree	41.3	42.0	40.6	39.6	52.8	43.1	36.1	43.9	43.0	44.6	36.0	44.5	44.2	36.9	35.1	42.7
2. Mostly disagree	32.6	31.2	34.1	34.9	20.9	33.4	35.7	30.4	30.4	32.8	32.4	32.1	32.1	34.2	33.7	25.9
3. Neither	11.1	12.8	9.3	11.2	10.1	10.8	12.5	10.4	10.6	10.0	13.0	10.7	9.7	10.9	13.7	6.5
4. Mostly agree	10.7	9.7	11.8	10.3	10.0	9.5	10.7	10.9	11.7	9.2	13.0	9.1	9.8	14.5	11.6	19.2
5. Agree	4.3	4.3	4.2	3.8	6.1	3.2	4.9	4.4	4.3	3.4	5.6	3.7	4.2	3.5	5.9	5.7
Item 12660 Subject Q01 N	2881	1319	1494	2227	271	662	834	891	493	1784	1026	1177	543	458	619	46

D01M: There is always someone I can turn to if I need help

	TOTAL	M	F	White	Black	NE	NC	S	W	Yes	No	None	Mari Only	Few	More	Any Her
1. Disagree	3.6	4.4	2.7	2.7	8.3	2.7	3.4	3.4	5.1	3.1	4.5	3.5	3.3	3.0	4.2	7.9
2. Mostly disagree	6.7	8.6	5.1	7.1	4.6	5.6	7.6	6.0	8.1	6.1	7.6	6.9	6.1	8.1	5.8	10.6
3. Neither	5.9	8.1	4.0	6.3	3.7	8.0	6.7	4.6	4.2	6.1	5.9	5.5	5.4	6.1	7.5	4.9
4. Mostly agree	27.7	30.9	24.6	28.1	20.5	28.9	27.5	26.4	29.0	27.8	28.0	25.2	32.4	28.5	27.3	41.1
5. Agree	56.1	47.9	63.6	55.8	62.8	54.7	54.8	59.6	53.6	56.9	54.0	58.9	52.8	54.4	55.2	35.4
Item 12670 Subject Q03 N	2868	1311	1489	2218	268	659	830	888	490	1779	1019	1170	541	458	614	46

D01N: Sometimes I think that I am no good at all

	TOTAL	M	F	White	Black	NE	NC	S	W	Yes	No	None	Mari Only	Few	More	Any Her
1. Disagree	31.3	36.8	26.4	28.8	50.7	35.1	27.1	33.1	29.9	31.9	29.9	33.0	34.3	25.2	28.6	31.1
2. Mostly disagree	25.2	24.9	25.8	26.6	18.3	24.3	25.5	24.5	27.1	26.6	23.2	26.2	25.8	23.8	24.1	23.9
3. Neither	16.9	16.8	16.4	17.9	6.9	15.9	17.5	16.9	16.9	15.4	19.1	16.2	16.4	20.4	17.1	15.9
4. Mostly agree	15.9	13.8	17.6	16.1	12.3	12.9	18.2	16.4	15.1	15.6	16.4	13.7	14.3	19.6	18.8	23.6
5. Agree	10.8	7.6	13.8	10.6	11.9	11.8	11.8	9.1	11.0	10.5	11.3	11.0	9.6	11.1	11.4	5.4
Item 12680 Subject Q01 N	2862	1307	1489	2213	267	657	829	889	488	1777	1016	1172	537	455	613	46

D01O: I often feel left out of things

	TOTAL	M	F	White	Black	NE	NC	S	W	Yes	No	None	Mari Only	Few	More	Any Her
1. Disagree	20.2	21.4	19.3	18.8	29.9	19.4	17.6	22.8	20.7	20.5	20.5	19.1	24.7	17.9	18.8	33.8
2. Mostly disagree	26.5	26.1	26.8	28.1	18.0	29.2	24.6	23.1	31.9	28.5	23.3	25.3	28.3	25.7	28.2	21.9
3. Neither	20.4	22.5	18.1	21.0	11.6	20.9	23.1	17.3	20.5	20.2	20.0	20.5	20.6	22.2	19.0	12.0
4. Mostly agree	22.1	20.6	23.6	22.2	22.6	19.4	22.4	26.3	17.7	20.9	23.4	23.6	18.0	23.0	22.9	23.6
5. Agree	10.9	9.3	12.2	9.9	17.9	11.1	12.2	10.5	9.2	9.9	12.8	11.5	8.4	11.3	11.1	8.7
Item 12690 Subject Q03 N	2858	1306	1485	2210	267	653	829	888	488	1771	1016	1169	539	456	610	46

D01P: I believe a person is master of his/her own fate

	TOTAL	M	F	White	Black	NE	NC	S	W	Yes	No	None	Mari Only	Few	More	Any Her
1. Disagree	4.7	3.7	5.7	4.1	8.5	5.5	3.4	5.3	4.8	3.9	6.3	5.9	2.2	2.8	5.9	10.7
2. Mostly disagree	6.2	4.7	7.6	6.7	3.9	5.2	8.4	5.6	5.3	7.0	5.0	6.6	7.1	6.4	5.0	6.1
3. Neither	20.0	16.6	23.0	20.8	14.0	22.2	20.6	18.4	18.8	18.5	22.6	18.5	19.2	24.6	20.8	16.6
4. Mostly agree	33.8	34.9	32.7	35.2	24.2	34.4	35.1	32.8	32.6	35.0	31.4	36.5	35.0	28.0	32.1	33.5
5. Agree	35.3	40.1	31.0	33.2	49.3	32.7	32.5	37.9	38.6	35.5	34.7	32.5	36.4	38.2	36.2	33.1
Item 12700 Subject Q02 N	2847	1308	1473	2205	263	651	826	882	488	1765	1012	1164	538	456	607	46

QUESTIONNAIRE FORM 5 1986	TOTAL	SEX		RACE		REGION				4YR COLLEGE PLANS		ILLICIT DRUG USE: LIFETIME				
		M	F	White	Black	NE	NC	S	W	Yes	No	None	Marijuana Only	Few Pills	More Pills	Any Heroin
N (Weighted No. of Cases):	3073	1413	1550	2295	312	725	867	952	529	1839	1084	1237	583	487	648	47
% of Weighted Total:	100.0	46.0	50.4	74.7	10.2	23.6	28.2	31.0	17.2	59.9	35.3	40.3	19.0	15.8	21.1	1.5

D01Q: There is usually someone I can talk to, if I need to

1. Disagree	3.4	4.1	2.9	2.8	7.9	2.5	4.0	2.8	4.7	2.8	4.6	3.6	2.2	2.6	4.5	8.2
2. Mostly disagree	5.1	6.4	4.0	4.9	3.8	4.7	6.0	4.5	5.0	5.0	5.2	5.4	4.1	6.3	3.9	13.2
3. Neither	4.9	7.1	2.8	4.8	4.4	6.4	5.5	3.3	4.5	4.6	5.5	4.6	5.7	4.3	5.7	1.9
4. Mostly agree	27.8	31.8	24.2	28.7	18.1	27.4	28.1	26.3	30.4	27.3	29.1	26.4	27.3	31.2	29.3	25.5
5. Agree	58.8	50.5	66.1	58.9	65.8	58.9	56.3	63.0	55.4	60.4	55.7	60.0	60.6	55.6	56.6	51.2
Item 12710 Subject Q03 N	2857	1305	1486	2210	266	654	828	887	488	1772	1015	1168	539	457	609	46

D01R: I feel that I can't do anything right

1. Disagree	39.8	42.1	37.8	38.7	53.2	44.1	35.5	40.0	41.1	42.8	34.8	40.8	44.3	38.0	35.0	34.9
2. Mostly disagree	31.4	29.9	32.6	32.9	20.6	28.8	33.4	30.8	32.3	32.8	29.0	31.9	30.3	31.3	31.9	35.0
3. Neither	15.4	15.1	15.6	15.9	10.2	14.5	17.6	14.6	14.2	13.8	18.1	14.3	15.2	17.3	16.8	7.0
4. Mostly agree	9.5	8.5	10.4	9.1	10.7	9.5	9.9	10.0	8.2	7.7	12.4	9.6	6.4	10.3	11.2	13.4
5. Agree	3.9	4.3	3.5	3.4	5.3	3.1	3.5	4.6	4.3	2.9	5.8	3.4	3.8	3.1	5.2	9.7
Item 12720 Subject Q01 N	2846	1304	1475	2204	264	652	827	881	486	1767	1009	1165	538	454	605	46

D01S: I often wish I had more good friends

1. Disagree	16.9	15.4	17.8	15.9	18.4	21.9	14.1	15.1	18.3	16.9	17.1	15.8	20.6	16.6	16.9	11.1
2. Mostly disagree	17.0	15.6	18.3	18.2	10.8	19.1	17.0	14.4	19.0	18.1	15.4	17.6	16.7	16.1	16.7	18.7
3. Neither	16.0	18.4	14.0	16.7	12.9	17.2	17.1	13.3	13.7	16.7	14.5	15.4	17.5	15.9	15.1	27.7
4. Mostly agree	26.3	27.4	25.6	27.6	19.2	21.5	28.9	26.9	27.3	24.9	28.7	25.8	26.3	28.6	26.0	29.0
5. Agree	23.8	23.1	24.3	21.6	38.7	20.3	22.9	28.2	21.7	23.4	24.3	25.4	18.9	22.8	25.4	13.5
Item 12730 Subject Q03 N	2852	1300	1486	2209	265	654	828	883	487	1772	1011	1169	537	456	605	46

D01T: Planning ahead makes things turn out better

1. Disagree	3.7	4.1	3.4	3.0	6.7	4.3	3.6	3.4	3.5	3.1	4.9	3.1	2.3	3.2	5.4	16.8
2. Mostly disagree	6.8	6.2	7.1	6.9	6.4	8.3	7.2	6.3	4.8	5.9	8.2	5.0	6.6	8.0	9.3	13.5
3. Neither	21.6	19.8	22.9	22.4	16.5	27.9	21.1	20.0	16.7	20.6	23.1	17.5	23.8	27.9	22.4	18.9
4. Mostly agree	40.0	40.3	40.0	41.4	29.1	33.8	43.4	38.9	44.4	41.2	38.0	43.1	39.9	37.4	36.8	33.3
5. Agree	28.0	29.6	26.5	26.4	41.2	25.6	24.7	31.4	30.6	29.3	25.8	31.3	27.4	23.4	26.2	17.5
Item 12740 Subject Q02 N	2854	1300	1486	2207	266	653	828	883	489	1770	1013	1165	538	457	609	46

D01U: I feel that my life is not very useful

1. Disagree	47.7	47.4	48.1	45.8	67.6	48.5	43.3	50.0	49.8	50.3	43.2	51.9	48.1	45.1	40.3	38.8
2. Mostly disagree	28.6	27.7	29.4	30.4	16.0	28.0	30.2	28.1	27.8	29.5	27.4	26.0	32.2	31.1	28.9	32.0
3. Neither	14.5	14.6	14.1	15.0	7.3	15.9	16.5	11.9	13.8	12.0	18.7	13.3	12.3	17.4	17.5	7.8
4. Mostly agree	6.7	7.1	6.4	6.8	4.6	5.4	7.4	7.0	6.3	5.9	8.0	6.0	4.8	5.2	10.5	14.7
5. Agree	2.5	3.2	2.0	2.0	4.5	2.1	2.5	2.9	2.3	2.3	2.7	2.8	2.6	1.1	2.8	6.7
Item 12750 Subject Q01 N	2839	1296	1475	2200	262	649	829	876	485	1766	1002	1162	535	450	608	45

D01V: I usually have a few friends around that I can get together with

1. Disagree	5.1	5.6	4.6	4.1	10.3	5.2	4.1	6.1	4.7	4.5	6.0	5.1	3.5	5.3	5.7	7.3
2. Mostly disagree	6.3	6.1	6.5	6.1	6.4	4.7	6.2	6.2	8.7	5.4	8.1	6.3	2.8	7.6	8.2	2.9
3. Neither	8.1	9.4	6.6	8.2	6.0	8.3	10.4	6.8	6.3	7.2	9.0	9.0	7.2	7.3	8.0	11.1
4. Mostly agree	36.6	36.7	36.6	37.6	30.7	34.7	38.4	35.5	37.7	35.8	38.1	38.1	37.6	36.2	33.2	43.8
5. Agree	44.0	42.3	45.7	44.0	46.6	47.1	40.8	45.4	42.6	47.1	38.8	41.5	48.9	43.5	44.9	34.9
Item 12760 Subject Q03 N	2846	1295	1483	2203	264	648	829	883	485	1769	1006	1166	536	452	609	45

D01W: I am eager to leave home and live on my own—independent from my parents

1. Disagree	8.2	8.0	8.5	6.8	14.5	7.5	7.1	10.1	7.4	7.3	9.7	8.8	8.7	8.3	6.1	3.6
2. Mostly disagree	11.1	12.5	9.7	10.6	10.9	10.7	10.7	10.5	13.4	10.9	11.5	13.5	8.0	12.1	9.5	1.4
3. Neither	20.7	24.0	17.9	20.4	15.7	20.8	21.2	19.9	21.3	21.8	19.2	24.0	20.8	19.1	15.7	22.4
4. Mostly agree	28.2	28.6	27.7	29.6	22.7	24.5	27.5	32.0	27.3	30.2	24.8	29.6	32.0	27.0	23.1	21.9
5. Agree	31.8	26.9	36.3	32.6	36.2	36.5	33.5	27.5	30.6	29.7	34.7	24.1	30.5	33.5	45.7	50.6
Item 13950 Subject I03,Q01 N	2841	1292	1482	2204	262	647	828	881	486	1765	1006	1160	536	453	609	46

QUESTIONNAIRE FORM 5 1986	TOTAL	SEX		RACE		REGION				4YR COLLEGE PLANS		ILLICIT DRUG USE: LIFETIME				
		M	F	White	Black	NE	NC	S	W	Yes	No	None	Mari-juana Only	Few Pills	More Pills	Any Her-oin
N (Weighted No. of Cases):	3073	1413	1550	2295	312	725	867	952	529	1839	1084	1237	583	487	648	47
% of Weighted Total:	100.0	46.0	50.4	74.7	10.2	23.6	28.2	31.0	17.2	59.9	35.3	40.3	19.0	15.8	21.1	1.5

D01X: I feel hesitant about taking a full-time job and becoming part of the "adult world"

1. Disagree	31.7	32.4	31.2	30.4	45.1	30.9	29.4	32.7	34.8	29.1	35.9	29.6	32.1	31.2	34.6	39.6
2. Mostly disagree	21.8	21.6	22.2	22.9	14.2	24.5	21.4	21.1	20.1	23.7	19.4	21.9	21.2	25.8	19.4	20.6
3. Neither	14.4	16.8	12.1	14.9	10.6	15.4	15.3	12.3	15.3	14.0	15.1	16.1	14.5	12.4	13.0	14.7
4. Mostly agree	21.5	20.5	22.4	22.0	15.6	19.2	23.6	21.5	21.1	22.9	18.7	22.5	20.8	21.7	20.7	14.3
5. Agree	10.6	8.6	12.0	9.7	14.5	9.9	10.2	12.4	8.6	10.3	10.8	9.8	11.3	8.9	12.2	10.9
Item 13960 Subject I03,Q01 N	2838	1287	1484	2198	263	648	825	879	486	1768	999	1158	537	453	607	46

The next two questions ask your views about different lifestyles that have been in the news lately.

D02: A man and a woman who live together without being married are ... (Mark ONE circle.)

1. Experimenting with a worthwhile alternative lifestyle	24.8	24.4	24.9	25.8	23.8	25.9	26.9	21.3	26.0	24.2	25.3	17.4	26.8	31.3	31.4	35.6
2. Doing their own thing and not affecting anyone else	50.8	51.4	50.7	52.1	40.6	59.4	49.8	46.1	49.8	50.7	51.3	48.1	54.8	47.7	55.0	44.2
3. Living in a way that could be destructive to society	4.9	5.6	4.4	4.6	9.2	2.9	4.1	7.5	4.5	5.0	4.8	6.8	4.2	4.4	2.0	7.6
4. Violating a basic principle of human morality	12.4	10.8	14.0	11.8	13.1	3.8	11.8	18.7	13.6	13.2	11.5	19.2	9.3	8.0	6.0	7.9
8. None of the above	7.1	7.9	6.1	5.7	13.3	8.1	7.4	6.5	6.1	6.8	7.2	8.5	4.9	8.6	5.6	4.8
Item 12770 Subject D03 N	2796	1259	1470	2172	254	641	813	861	482	1752	976	1146	529	446	594	43

D03: A man and a woman who decide to have and raise a child out of wedlock are ...

1. Experimenting with a worthwhile alternative lifestyle	8.7	9.4	8.1	8.3	13.2	10.5	8.5	8.1	7.9	8.3	9.6	7.0	8.9	10.9	10.3	12.7
2. Doing their own thing and not affecting anyone else	38.2	38.4	37.8	37.5	41.4	44.5	38.3	30.4	43.3	36.3	41.1	34.1	42.3	40.5	40.5	31.6
3. Living in a way that could be destructive to society	17.2	16.4	18.1	18.0	13.1	14.9	18.8	18.6	15.2	18.5	15.4	17.4	17.5	14.1	18.6	19.6
4. Violating a basic principle of human morality	22.8	23.3	22.6	24.1	16.4	12.0	21.8	32.3	21.8	24.5	20.1	28.8	17.9	20.9	16.7	26.2
8. None of the above	13.0	12.4	13.4	12.1	15.8	18.1	12.6	10.5	11.7	12.4	13.7	12.8	13.4	13.5	13.9	9.8
Item 12775 Subject D03 N	2778	1246	1466	2163	253	633	811	855	479	1738	972	1137	526	445	589	43

D04: These next questions ask how you feel about your present financial situation and your future financial security.

D04A: I feel that I have enough money to get along pretty well

1. Never	11.6	12.7	10.7	9.3	23.9	12.5	10.3	12.4	11.3	9.2	15.3	11.7	11.1	9.9	12.9	11.0
2. Seldom	20.3	19.0	21.1	19.4	23.7	19.9	20.5	20.6	20.2	18.8	23.5	19.7	17.9	25.7	20.5	10.7
3. Sometimes	33.7	31.7	35.4	34.2	30.5	33.0	35.7	32.0	34.1	32.3	36.5	34.2	34.4	33.0	33.8	33.8
4. Often	25.1	26.5	24.2	26.9	15.8	26.2	23.5	25.3	25.9	28.7	18.7	25.7	25.6	25.1	22.2	38.0
5. Always	9.3	10.0	8.6	10.2	6.1	8.4	10.0	9.6	8.6	11.1	6.1	8.7	10.8	6.9	11.4	6.5
Item 12990 Subject C02 N	2796	1271	1461	2167	255	629	817	867	483	1742	983	1144	527	447	595	46

D04B: I get very concerned about how I am going to be able to pay my next bills

1. Never	25.3	22.9	27.5	24.8	37.2	28.5	23.7	25.3	23.7	27.0	22.0	25.7	28.3	20.7	25.0	15.0
2. Seldom	27.8	28.6	27.5	29.4	21.3	27.7	28.8	26.3	28.9	29.7	24.5	29.1	28.8	28.0	25.4	28.3
3. Sometimes	27.6	27.9	27.0	27.5	22.8	26.2	28.2	28.2	27.1	25.5	31.4	26.1	22.5	30.6	31.9	31.2
4. Often	13.4	14.7	11.9	13.1	10.7	10.7	13.3	14.0	15.9	13.0	14.1	12.9	14.1	15.8	12.3	13.2
5. Always	6.0	5.9	6.1	5.1	8.1	6.8	6.0	6.2	4.5	4.9	8.1	6.3	6.3	5.0	5.4	12.3
Item 13000 Subject C02 N	2756	1265	1429	2140	252	618	809	854	475	1716	971	1126	512	444	590	46

QUESTIONNAIRE FORM 5 1986	TOTAL	SEX		RACE		REGION				4YR COLLEGE PLANS		ILLICIT DRUG USE: LIFETIME				
		M	F	White	Black	NE	NC	S	W	Yes	No	None	Mari- juana Only	Few Pills	More Pills	Any Her- oin
N (Weighted No. of Cases):	3073	1413	1550	2295	312	725	867	952	529	1839	1084	1237	583	487	648	47
% of Weighted Total:	100.0	46.0	50.4	74.7	10.2	23.6	28.2	31.0	17.2	59.9	35.3	40.3	19.0	15.8	21.1	1.5

D04C: I worry whether I will have any job at all in a few months

	TOTAL	M	F	White	Black	NE	NC	S	W	Yes	No	None	Mari- juana Only	Few Pills	More Pills	Any Her- oin
1. Never	38.0	37.3	38.9	40.3	37.1	40.5	37.1	38.4	35.8	42.2	30.7	38.8	40.4	34.1	37.0	34.5
2. Seldom	26.0	28.0	24.5	27.4	17.9	28.5	25.1	23.8	28.1	26.4	25.2	25.2	27.6	27.2	26.2	17.7
3. Sometimes	18.9	18.3	18.6	17.3	21.6	18.1	18.6	20.3	17.9	17.5	21.1	19.1	17.6	19.4	19.5	15.7
4. Often	11.4	10.2	12.7	10.5	13.0	8.7	12.7	11.8	12.4	9.2	15.8	11.5	9.3	14.7	10.2	18.4
5. Always	5.7	6.2	5.3	4.5	10.4	4.3	6.5	5.8	5.8	4.7	7.2	5.4	5.1	4.6	7.1	13.7
Item 13010 Subject C02 N	2760	1262	1435	2141	254	617	809	857	478	1717	974	1130	516	443	590	45

D04D: I feel sure that I could go out and get a new job (with decent pay) whenever I want one

	TOTAL	M	F	White	Black	NE	NC	S	W	Yes	No	None	Mari- juana Only	Few Pills	More Pills	Any Her- oin
1. Never	9.0	8.3	9.7	7.0	19.9	9.3	7.4	10.1	9.5	7.1	12.3	9.5	8.8	8.2	8.9	4.3
2. Seldom	22.8	20.6	24.8	22.9	21.5	23.2	23.6	22.4	21.7	21.1	25.9	23.5	22.6	23.5	21.8	10.6
3. Sometimes	32.8	30.9	34.1	33.8	25.4	32.5	34.7	30.9	33.4	33.3	31.4	32.3	32.3	34.7	32.4	42.3
4. Often	22.3	24.4	20.8	23.7	17.3	23.3	22.5	22.5	20.5	24.6	18.5	23.5	21.7	22.4	21.2	17.7
5. Always	13.0	15.8	10.5	12.5	15.8	11.6	11.8	14.0	14.9	13.8	11.8	11.2	14.6	11.1	15.7	25.0
Item 13020 Subject C02 N	2755	1263	1428	2138	252	620	805	856	474	1712	975	1126	516	442	589	46

FOR THOSE WHO HAVE A JOB:

D04E: I feel sure I that can keep working steadily with my present employer as long as I want to

	TOTAL	M	F	White	Black	NE	NC	S	W	Yes	No	None	Mari- juana Only	Few Pills	More Pills	Any Her- oin
1. Never	4.6	5.6	3.6	3.1	9.4	5.0	4.2	4.5	4.8	2.4	7.7	4.3	4.1	3.1	5.4	10.7
2. Seldom	5.3	6.3	4.4	4.5	10.6	5.8	4.5	5.4	5.8	5.0	5.7	5.0	5.3	5.0	5.3	18.3
3. Sometimes	16.1	13.5	18.0	15.0	20.0	15.0	16.3	17.8	14.5	13.6	20.1	15.8	15.7	18.7	15.3	11.1
4. Often	29.2	28.3	29.8	30.3	20.0	24.8	30.0	30.6	31.2	29.7	28.4	30.6	31.7	31.0	24.8	23.5
5. Always	44.8	46.3	44.2	47.1	39.9	49.4	45.0	41.7	43.6	49.3	38.2	44.2	43.2	42.1	49.1	36.5
Item 13030 Subject C02 N★	1871	864	956	1491	145	436	570	551	314	1150	674	728	347	325	416	32

D04F: I worry about getting fired or laid-off from my job

	TOTAL	M	F	White	Black	NE	NC	S	W	Yes	No	None	Mari- juana Only	Few Pills	More Pills	Any Her- oin
1. Never	53.5	52.2	54.7	55.0	54.3	57.2	54.0	50.1	53.2	55.3	50.6	53.5	56.1	50.6	53.5	45.1
2. Seldom	29.3	30.7	28.7	30.9	20.4	26.5	30.4	30.3	29.5	29.9	28.5	29.5	28.3	32.7	28.4	26.1
3. Sometimes	12.1	11.9	11.6	10.3	15.0	11.5	11.0	13.4	12.6	10.8	13.7	11.7	12.0	11.7	13.6	5.8
4. Often	3.1	3.2	3.0	2.3	6.3	2.8	2.3	4.5	2.4	2.5	4.0	2.5	2.3	3.7	3.5	13.0
5. Always	2.0	2.0	2.0	1.5	3.9	2.0	2.4	1.7	2.2	1.5	3.2	2.8	1.3	1.4	1.1	9.9
Item 13040 Subject C02 N★	1863	860	953	1487	145	435	571	544	312	1144	671	723	346	320	418	32

D05: Please think about all the money you earned during the past year, including last summer.

About how much of your past year's earnings have gone into:

D05A: Savings for your future education

	TOTAL	M	F	White	Black	NE	NC	S	W	Yes	No	None	Mari- juana Only	Few Pills	More Pills	Any Her- oin
1. None	52.5	52.8	51.7	51.2	60.8	49.4	45.6	58.0	58.6	45.1	66.2	46.2	50.2	57.7	62.0	59.2
2. A little (1-20%)	22.7	24.2	21.8	24.0	14.9	22.1	26.5	20.6	20.5	24.8	18.3	25.4	22.3	22.5	18.0	22.9
3. Some (21-40%)	11.4	10.7	12.0	11.5	7.6	13.1	11.6	9.8	11.4	13.1	8.2	11.2	12.3	11.0	10.8	11.9
4. About half (41-60%)	5.5	5.0	5.9	5.4	7.0	5.6	7.0	5.5	2.8	6.8	3.1	7.0	6.3	5.1	2.8	0.3
5. Most (61-80%)	4.3	4.2	4.2	4.4	6.0	6.0	5.0	3.1	2.9	4.9	3.2	5.2	4.2	2.7	3.9	2.1
6. Almost all (81-99%)	2.9	2.1	3.7	3.0	1.0	3.0	3.7	1.9	3.2	4.4	0.5	3.9	3.4	0.9	1.8	3.6
7. All	0.8	1.0	0.6	0.5	2.7	0.8	0.5	1.1	0.6	0.9	0.4	1.0	1.1	0.1	0.6	-
Item 20830 Subject C02 N	2655	1220	1373	2085	219	606	784	806	459	1665	925	1087	499	429	563	46

D05B: Savings or payments for a car or car expenses

	TOTAL	M	F	White	Black	NE	NC	S	W	Yes	No	None	Mari- juana Only	Few Pills	More Pills	Any Her- oin
1. None	45.8	36.7	54.0	43.0	63.5	53.8	45.0	41.6	43.9	49.0	40.4	49.2	48.7	42.3	40.3	36.3
2. A little (1-20%)	16.5	17.2	16.0	17.3	10.1	14.7	18.4	14.5	19.4	16.6	16.4	16.4	17.5	14.9	17.4	11.6
3. Some (21-40%)	13.9	16.5	11.9	14.9	7.1	11.3	14.2	16.7	11.8	13.1	15.7	14.0	12.2	15.0	13.8	18.9
4. About half (41-60%)	11.3	14.1	8.7	12.1	11.6	8.6	10.4	14.5	10.9	10.1	13.3	10.7	10.0	13.5	12.3	14.8
5. Most (61-80%)	7.2	9.2	5.1	7.5	3.3	5.8	8.4	6.5	8.2	6.6	7.9	5.8	6.3	9.2	9.1	6.6
6. Almost all (81-99%)	3.8	4.5	3.0	3.9	2.1	3.6	2.9	4.2	4.9	3.4	4.4	2.6	3.8	4.2	5.5	4.5
7. All	1.5	1.7	1.3	1.2	2.3	2.2	0.7	2.0	1.0	1.2	1.9	1.4	1.3	0.8	1.7	7.4
Item 20840 Subject C02 N	2650	1221	1368	2083	217	604	781	807	458	1661	924	1087	497	428	561	46

★=excludes respondents for whom question was inappropriate.

QUESTIONNAIRE FORM 5 1986	TOTAL	SEX		RACE		REGION				4YR COLLEGE PLANS		ILLICIT DRUG USE: LIFETIME				
		M	F	White	Black	NE	NC	S	W	Yes	No	None	Mari- juana Only	Few Pills	More Pills	Any Her- oin
N (Weighted No. of Cases):	3073	1413	1550	2295	312	725	867	952	529	1839	1084	1237	583	487	648	47
% of Weighted Total:	100.0	46.0	50.4	74.7	10.2	23.6	28.2	31.0	17.2	59.9	35.3	40.3	19.0	15.8	21.1	1.5

D05C: Other savings for long-range purposes

1. None	49.0	48.1	49.6	48.0	58.2	52.9	48.4	48.9	44.9	48.6	50.3	45.0	51.9	50.1	53.1	54.0
2. A little (1-20%)	21.1	22.0	20.5	22.1	17.1	16.1	22.4	22.3	23.4	22.4	19.3	22.7	20.3	22.0	18.1	22.7
3. Some (21-40%)	13.8	14.6	12.9	14.3	8.4	14.6	14.0	12.8	14.0	13.7	13.4	15.7	12.4	11.5	14.0	3.1
4. About half (41-60%)	7.2	7.0	7.4	7.2	6.6	5.9	7.7	7.2	7.8	6.9	7.6	7.2	6.3	8.3	6.2	9.2
5. Most (61-80%)	5.3	5.4	5.2	5.2	6.1	5.9	5.2	5.0	5.4	4.8	6.1	5.7	5.3	4.5	5.2	3.7
6. Almost all (81-99%)	2.7	1.9	3.3	2.4	2.0	3.5	1.7	2.7	3.6	2.8	2.5	2.7	2.6	3.2	2.3	5.8
7. All	1.0	1.0	1.0	0.8	1.6	1.1	0.6	1.1	1.0	0.9	0.8	0.9	1.2	0.4	1.2	1.5
Item 20850 Subject C02 N	2639	1215	1363	2075	215	601	779	804	456	1657	918	1081	497	426	559	45

D05D: Spending on your own needs and activities – things such as clothing, stereo, TV, records, other possessions, movies, eating out, other recreation, hobbies, gifts for others, and other personal expenses

1. None	4.7	5.7	3.6	3.0	10.2	4.0	4.4	4.9	5.7	3.5	6.4	5.4	3.7	4.3	4.7	4.1
2. A little (1-20%)	15.2	15.8	14.0	15.3	12.9	16.9	13.3	15.2	16.3	16.2	13.9	19.4	13.2	10.3	12.3	21.7
3. Some (21-40%)	19.5	19.8	19.3	19.5	18.3	18.6	21.7	19.2	17.4	20.3	18.1	20.9	18.2	19.1	17.7	21.4
4. About half (41-60%)	17.7	18.5	17.0	18.7	14.7	16.6	15.8	19.2	19.6	16.9	19.2	17.6	18.0	20.6	16.1	3.3
5. Most (61-80%)	18.9	19.9	18.4	19.9	14.7	16.7	21.9	17.1	19.9	19.2	18.6	16.7	20.8	21.5	19.5	20.4
6. Almost all (81-99%)	15.4	12.0	18.8	15.8	16.2	16.3	15.6	15.8	13.3	16.5	13.4	13.8	17.8	15.6	16.6	14.0
7. All	8.6	8.2	8.9	7.9	13.1	10.8	7.3	8.5	7.9	7.4	10.2	6.2	8.2	8.6	13.0	15.0
Item 20860 Subject C02 N	2645	1218	1366	2083	214	604	781	804	457	1663	919	1083	497	427	561	46

D05E: Helping to pay family living expenses (groceries, housing, etc.)

1. None	55.6	55.7	55.5	61.2	29.2	56.2	63.0	47.8	56.0	61.2	45.9	56.1	59.6	52.4	54.5	50.2
2. A little (1-20%)	25.6	26.0	25.4	25.3	27.1	23.7	25.1	27.1	26.4	24.5	27.6	24.6	24.6	26.8	26.9	30.4
3. Some (21-40%)	9.3	9.0	9.8	7.6	19.2	10.0	5.8	11.7	10.1	7.3	12.6	10.7	7.1	9.7	8.1	6.3
4. About half (41-60%)	4.1	4.9	3.4	2.7	10.5	4.8	2.2	6.2	3.0	2.9	6.4	2.8	4.1	5.1	5.8	8.0
5. Most (61-80%)	2.7	2.4	3.1	1.8	9.4	3.2	2.3	3.4	1.6	1.7	4.3	2.6	2.6	4.4	2.0	1.2
6. Almost all (81-99%)	1.6	1.0	2.1	0.8	3.1	1.4	0.9	2.4	1.9	1.7	1.6	1.8	1.8	1.3	1.6	-
7. All	1.0	0.9	0.8	0.5	1.4	0.8	0.7	1.4	1.0	0.6	1.5	1.5	0.1	0.4	1.0	3.9
Item 20870 Subject C02 N	2640	1215	1363	2078	214	601	781	805	454	1657	920	1081	498	428	557	45

The next questions ask about characteristics which some people associate with the use of particular drugs. We want to know what you think.

E01: Do YOU think that people who smoke marijuana several times a week tend to be . . .

E01A: More creative than average

1. No	62.5	59.7	64.7	63.6	58.4	60.9	61.6	61.7	67.7	65.2	57.9	66.9	68.6	60.6	53.0	32.0
2. Yes	14.8	17.3	12.3	14.5	14.5	15.0	15.6	14.8	13.4	12.1	19.4	7.8	10.5	15.5	29.3	45.2
3. Not sure, no opinion	22.7	22.9	23.0	21.9	27.1	24.2	22.8	23.6	19.0	22.7	22.7	25.3	20.9	23.9	17.7	22.9
Item 13060 Subject A11c N	2755	1246	1448	2147	240	622	808	857	469	1726	963	1132	511	444	585	46

E01B: Less sensible than average

1. No	23.6	26.0	20.8	22.8	25.5	27.6	21.4	22.6	23.8	21.5	26.5	14.7	24.0	23.4	39.3	28.1
2. Yes	59.6	56.6	62.5	61.5	52.5	55.2	61.4	59.9	61.9	62.0	56.5	67.1	59.9	58.4	47.4	52.8
3. Not sure, no opinion	16.8	17.4	16.7	15.7	22.0	17.2	17.2	17.5	14.3	16.6	17.0	18.2	16.1	18.2	13.3	19.2
Item 13070 Subject A11c N	2753	1247	1444	2146	239	621	807	856	469	1722	965	1131	511	442	585	46

E01C: More interesting people than average

1. No	65.7	62.3	68.8	67.2	56.0	65.1	64.6	65.1	69.7	67.7	62.9	71.6	68.4	63.3	56.9	40.0
2. Yes	16.0	18.9	13.2	15.3	19.5	16.1	16.1	16.7	14.3	14.0	19.1	7.6	15.2	16.3	30.3	41.5
3. Not sure, no opinion	18.3	18.8	18.0	17.5	24.6	18.8	19.4	18.2	16.0	18.3	18.0	20.8	16.4	20.4	12.8	18.5
Item 13080 Subject A11c N	2747	1240	1445	2140	241	620	805	854	468	1718	964	1132	510	437	585	46

QUESTIONNAIRE FORM 5 1986	TOTAL	SEX		RACE		REGION				4YR COLLEGE PLANS		ILLICIT DRUG USE: LIFETIME				
		M	F	White	Black	NE	NC	S	W	Yes	No	None	Mari-juana Only	Few Pills	More Pills	Any Her-oin
N (Weighted No. of Cases):	3073	1413	1550	2295	312	725	867	952	529	1839	1084	1237	583	487	648	47
% of Weighted Total:	100.0	46.0	50.4	74.7	10.2	23.6	28.2	31.0	17.2	59.9	35.3	40.3	19.0	15.8	21.1	1.5
E01D: Less hard-working than average																
1. No	25.5	27.1	24.1	25.1	29.1	29.1	25.2	23.4	25.1	23.1	29.6	16.5	28.5	25.2	38.5	40.8
2. Yes	56.9	55.6	58.2	58.4	46.6	53.2	58.4	57.3	58.6	58.3	54.6	63.5	55.2	55.7	48.5	42.7
3. Not sure, no opinion	17.6	17.3	17.6	16.5	24.2	17.6	16.4	19.3	16.4	18.6	15.8	20.0	16.2	19.1	13.0	16.5
Item 13090 Subject A11c N	2748	1242	1445	2142	240	619	807	855	468	1717	965	1130	510	441	585	46
E01E: More independent than average																
1. No	53.6	47.5	58.7	53.4	55.4	51.6	54.9	53.7	53.6	53.2	54.3	55.1	57.4	50.9	50.2	40.0
2. Yes	25.9	31.8	20.9	27.2	19.9	27.7	24.3	25.0	28.0	25.1	27.2	21.1	21.9	29.7	34.5	44.3
3. Not sure, no opinion	20.5	20.7	20.4	19.4	24.7	20.7	20.8	21.3	18.4	21.7	18.5	23.8	20.7	19.4	15.4	15.7
Item 13100 Subject A11c N	2739	1240	1438	2134	241	612	807	853	466	1713	960	1129	510	436	580	46
E01F: More emotionally unstable than average																
1. No	20.5	22.8	18.2	21.0	15.7	25.8	19.2	17.9	20.7	19.1	23.2	10.6	22.9	22.2	35.3	38.3
2. Yes	62.2	59.2	65.2	62.1	65.0	57.1	62.4	64.7	64.1	64.3	58.4	71.9	58.2	59.1	51.0	43.4
3. Not sure, no opinion	17.3	18.0	16.6	16.9	19.4	17.1	18.4	17.4	15.2	16.6	18.4	17.5	18.9	18.6	13.8	18.4
Item 13110 Subject A11c N	2741	1241	1439	2141	239	617	807	851	466	1715	958	1126	512	441	582	46
E01G: More concerned about other people than average																
1. No	70.6	68.6	72.5	72.0	69.2	67.3	71.7	70.8	72.8	72.2	67.7	73.6	73.7	70.3	64.4	46.9
2. Yes	8.8	10.4	7.4	8.0	9.9	10.1	8.0	9.1	8.0	6.7	12.4	5.3	6.6	8.2	17.3	25.7
3. Not sure, no opinion	20.6	21.0	20.1	20.0	20.9	22.6	20.4	20.1	19.2	21.2	19.9	21.1	19.7	21.5	18.3	27.3
Item 13120 Subject A11c N	2746	1240	1445	2140	241	619	805	854	467	1715	965	1129	510	442	582	46
E01H: More weak-willed than average																
1. No	24.8	25.7	24.1	25.5	19.0	30.2	22.7	22.5	25.6	21.8	29.7	14.6	24.9	27.0	41.6	42.1
2. Yes	54.9	54.3	55.5	54.3	59.3	47.8	56.9	56.7	57.3	56.4	52.4	62.6	53.0	54.8	43.1	43.3
3. Not sure, no opinion	20.3	20.0	20.5	20.2	21.7	21.9	20.4	20.7	17.1	21.7	17.9	22.8	22.1	18.3	15.3	14.6
Item 13130 Subject A11c N	2741	1237	1443	2138	240	617	805	852	466	1715	962	1129	508	437	584	46
E01I: More criminal than average																
1. No	24.6	25.0	23.9	25.7	16.6	28.7	25.5	19.1	27.4	24.1	25.7	13.2	30.2	26.9	39.6	31.8
2. Yes	54.9	56.2	53.9	53.9	63.2	46.9	54.5	60.6	55.7	54.5	55.5	65.2	47.9	51.2	44.4	51.6
3. Not sure, no opinion	20.5	18.7	22.2	20.4	20.1	24.4	20.0	20.3	16.9	21.4	18.9	21.6	21.9	21.9	16.0	16.6
Item 13140 Subject A11c N	2743	1238	1444	2139	239	619	807	851	466	1717	961	1130	506	442	582	46

The next questions are similar, but ask about illegal drugs other than marijuana–like psychedelics, barbiturates, narcotics, and amphetamines.

E02: Do YOU think that people who use illegal drugs (other than marijuana) several times a week tend to be . . .

	TOTAL	M	F	White	Black	NE	NC	S	W	Yes	No	None	Mari-juana Only	Few Pills	More Pills	Any Her-oin
E02A: More creative than average																
1. No	62.9	58.9	66.1	63.8	60.6	62.0	62.6	63.4	63.7	64.2	60.6	68.1	62.2	63.7	55.5	38.9
2. Yes	11.4	13.1	9.8	10.5	14.6	11.2	11.8	11.7	10.4	9.1	15.3	7.3	9.4	10.0	19.5	38.1
3. Not sure, no opinion	25.7	28.0	24.1	25.7	24.8	26.8	25.7	24.9	25.9	26.7	24.2	24.6	28.4	26.3	25.0	23.0
Item 13330 Subject A11c N	2708	1216	1433	2113	237	610	797	840	461	1692	951	1111	507	434	576	46
E02B: Less sensible than average																
1. No	13.9	15.0	12.8	11.7	19.5	15.7	12.2	13.4	15.5	11.9	17.1	9.8	13.1	14.5	20.8	29.2
2. Yes	65.2	62.0	68.1	67.5	60.1	64.3	66.9	64.9	63.9	67.2	62.0	70.8	62.7	63.9	59.2	44.0
3. Not sure, no opinion	20.9	23.1	19.1	20.8	20.4	20.0	20.9	21.7	20.6	20.9	20.9	19.4	24.2	21.6	19.9	26.8
Item 13340 Subject A11c N	2705	1217	1428	2110	235	607	797	839	462	1693	948	1111	506	433	576	46

QUESTIONNAIRE FORM 5 1986	TOTAL	SEX		RACE		REGION				4YR COLLEGE PLANS		ILLICIT DRUG USE: LIFETIME				
		M	F	White	Black	NE	NC	S	W	Yes	No	None	Marijuana Only	Few Pills	More Pills	Any Heroin
N (Weighted No. of Cases):	3073	1413	1550	2295	312	725	867	952	529	1839	1084	1237	583	487	648	47
% of Weighted Total:	100.0	46.0	50.4	74.7	10.2	23.6	28.2	31.0	17.2	59.9	35.3	40.3	19.0	15.8	21.1	1.5

E02C: More interesting people than average

	TOTAL	M	F	White	Black	NE	NC	S	W	Yes	No	None	Mar. Only	Few Pills	More Pills	Any Her.
1. No	65.6	62.4	68.5	67.1	61.6	64.6	64.9	67.4	65.0	66.0	65.1	71.0	66.2	64.2	57.2	57.1
2. Yes	10.3	11.7	8.9	9.3	13.6	11.0	10.9	9.8	9.4	8.8	12.9	6.7	7.6	9.0	19.5	21.6
3. Not sure, no opinion	24.0	26.0	22.5	23.5	24.8	24.4	24.2	22.7	25.6	25.2	22.0	22.3	26.2	26.8	23.3	21.3
Item 13350 Subject A11c N	2701	1217	1425	2107	234	606	795	838	462	1691	945	1110	503	433	576	46

E02D: Less hard-working than average

	TOTAL	M	F	White	Black	NE	NC	S	W	Yes	No	None	Mar. Only	Few Pills	More Pills	Any Her.
1. No	15.6	16.3	14.9	14.4	21.1	20.1	13.2	15.8	13.4	13.6	18.8	13.3	15.5	11.8	22.0	27.1
2. Yes	61.0	58.6	63.0	62.1	55.9	57.9	62.4	60.5	63.7	62.3	59.2	66.3	58.5	60.4	53.8	56.9
3. Not sure, no opinion	23.4	25.1	22.1	23.4	23.0	22.1	24.4	23.7	22.9	24.2	22.1	20.4	25.9	27.8	24.2	16.0
Item 13360 Subject A11c N	2700	1217	1423	2105	234	606	793	839	462	1692	944	1109	502	433	577	46

E02E: More independent than average

	TOTAL	M	F	White	Black	NE	NC	S	W	Yes	No	None	Mar. Only	Few Pills	More Pills	Any Her.
1. No	54.3	48.5	59.0	53.7	58.2	55.2	52.4	55.4	54.5	53.8	54.9	57.9	56.3	50.9	49.9	33.0
2. Yes	20.0	23.9	16.7	20.5	17.3	18.9	21.0	20.3	19.1	19.2	21.7	18.3	16.6	20.9	24.0	43.1
3. Not sure, no opinion	25.7	27.6	24.4	25.7	24.4	25.9	26.6	24.3	26.4	27.0	23.4	23.7	27.1	28.2	26.1	23.9
Item 13370 Subject A11c N	2694	1215	1420	2102	233	605	794	836	459	1687	942	1106	501	431	576	46

E02F: More emotionally unstable than average

	TOTAL	M	F	White	Black	NE	NC	S	W	Yes	No	None	Mar. Only	Few Pills	More Pills	Any Her.
1. No	11.5	12.7	10.4	10.2	13.3	15.0	9.2	10.6	12.5	8.8	16.0	7.7	12.3	9.9	17.5	34.2
2. Yes	66.6	63.1	69.7	68.0	63.0	64.6	67.1	67.3	67.1	69.7	61.2	73.2	61.1	66.6	59.9	55.0
3. Not sure, no opinion	21.9	24.2	20.0	21.8	23.8	20.4	23.7	22.1	20.4	21.4	22.8	19.1	26.6	23.5	22.6	10.8
Item 13380 Subject A11c N	2699	1216	1424	2105	234	606	794	837	462	1689	945	1107	503	432	577	46

E02G: More concerned about other people than average

	TOTAL	M	F	White	Black	NE	NC	S	W	Yes	No	None	Mar. Only	Few Pills	More Pills	Any Her.
1. No	69.1	66.6	71.2	69.9	67.1	67.8	70.7	69.5	67.5	69.7	68.1	72.7	68.5	68.1	65.2	60.0
2. Yes	6.9	6.9	6.8	6.0	9.4	7.6	5.3	7.5	7.6	5.6	9.1	5.9	4.6	6.6	9.7	22.5
3. Not sure, no opinion	24.0	26.5	22.0	24.1	23.5	24.6	24.1	23.0	24.9	24.8	22.9	21.4	26.8	25.3	25.1	17.5
Item 13390 Subject A11c N	2700	1216	1424	2105	234	606	794	838	462	1690	945	1108	502	433	577	46

E02H: More weak-willed than average

	TOTAL	M	F	White	Black	NE	NC	S	W	Yes	No	None	Mar. Only	Few Pills	More Pills	Any Her.
1. No	13.0	13.2	13.0	12.6	10.3	18.5	11.5	10.4	13.1	10.9	16.9	9.0	13.0	10.8	21.4	25.7
2. Yes	62.3	60.3	63.7	62.0	67.2	57.2	63.4	64.2	63.8	63.9	59.3	68.2	58.7	62.4	54.7	63.7
3. Not sure, no opinion	24.7	26.5	23.3	25.4	22.5	24.3	25.1	25.4	23.1	25.2	23.8	22.8	28.2	26.9	23.8	10.6
Item 13400 Subject A11c N	2697	1216	1421	2104	234	604	794	838	462	1691	941	1105	503	433	576	46

E02I: More criminal than average

	TOTAL	M	F	White	Black	NE	NC	S	W	Yes	No	None	Mar. Only	Few Pills	More Pills	Any Her.
1. No	12.4	11.5	13.1	12.0	11.0	15.0	12.0	9.6	14.9	11.3	14.2	9.2	13.5	11.2	17.1	30.8
2. Yes	63.6	63.4	63.9	64.0	66.2	60.8	62.4	67.2	62.5	64.1	62.7	70.3	58.7	63.0	57.8	44.7
3. Not sure, no opinion	24.0	25.1	23.0	24.1	22.8	24.3	25.5	23.2	22.6	24.6	23.1	20.5	27.8	25.8	25.1	24.4
Item 13410 Subject A11c N	2691	1213	1419	2101	233	601	793	838	459	1685	941	1107	502	431	572	46

The next few questions ask how YOU view cigarette smoking.

E03: In my opinion, when a guy my age is smoking a cigarette, it makes him look . . .

E03A: Cool, calm, in-control

	TOTAL	M	F	White	Black	NE	NC	S	W	Yes	No	None	Mar. Only	Few Pills	More Pills	Any Her.
1. Disagree	61.6	60.4	63.0	60.0	70.1	59.4	59.8	63.3	64.9	65.7	54.1	76.7	56.6	53.6	45.2	31.9
2. Mostly disagree	13.1	12.7	13.5	13.7	9.1	10.7	14.8	12.8	13.7	12.9	13.8	9.9	16.1	16.4	14.1	19.8
3. Neither	19.8	20.7	18.7	21.1	13.0	23.5	20.5	17.4	17.9	17.0	24.6	10.0	20.9	24.5	32.9	36.1
4. Mostly agree	3.6	3.4	3.5	3.5	3.5	3.1	3.4	4.7	2.5	3.1	4.4	2.4	4.0	3.5	5.4	5.5
5. Agree	1.9	2.8	1.2	1.6	4.4	3.3	1.5	1.7	1.0	1.3	3.1	1.0	2.4	2.0	2.5	6.7
Item 20880 Subject A11c N	2687	1223	1405	2105	226	607	798	821	461	1684	938	1105	495	430	577	45

QUESTIONNAIRE FORM 5 1986	TOTAL	SEX		RACE		REGION				4YR COLLEGE PLANS		ILLICIT DRUG USE: LIFETIME				
		M	F	White	Black	NE	NC	S	W	Yes	No	None	Mari- juana Only	Few Pills	More Pills	Any Her- oin
N (Weighted No. of Cases):	3073	1413	1550	2295	312	725	867	952	529	1839	1084	1237	583	487	648	47
% of Weighted Total:	100.0	46.0	50.4	74.7	10.2	23.6	28.2	31.0	17.2	59.9	35.3	40.3	19.0	15.8	21.1	1.5
E03B: Insecure																
1. Disagree	14.2	14.3	14.3	13.3	20.6	17.5	14.6	14.3	9.2	12.3	17.6	10.5	14.4	14.2	21.7	13.4
2. Mostly disagree	8.3	7.4	9.3	8.8	5.9	8.9	8.0	8.8	7.1	7.8	9.3	7.0	7.8	11.8	7.5	20.0
3. Neither	33.9	34.6	32.8	35.0	26.2	37.5	33.7	34.5	28.5	32.1	37.4	28.3	35.8	35.3	41.2	40.4
4. Mostly agree	20.1	20.2	19.9	21.0	15.4	16.5	22.2	17.7	25.3	22.0	17.1	23.1	19.9	19.3	15.3	16.6
5. Agree	23.5	23.5	23.7	21.9	31.9	19.6	21.5	24.7	29.9	25.8	18.5	31.2	22.1	19.4	14.2	9.6
Item 20890 Subject A11c N	2682	1218	1404	2104	224	605	795	820	461	1683	935	1102	493	429	577	45
E03C: Rugged, tough, independent																
1. Disagree	50.6	50.9	50.7	49.5	57.5	48.9	46.8	51.5	57.9	53.0	46.0	60.9	48.7	44.6	40.2	22.6
2. Mostly disagree	15.7	14.6	16.6	16.0	11.1	13.8	16.6	15.5	17.1	15.9	15.9	15.5	14.9	17.4	15.7	15.3
3. Neither	23.7	26.0	21.7	24.8	17.9	24.7	26.7	23.0	18.6	22.0	26.8	15.9	24.8	30.6	30.8	44.5
4. Mostly agree	7.2	5.7	8.7	7.7	5.5	8.6	8.8	6.1	4.8	6.7	8.2	5.0	8.7	5.3	11.4	13.0
5. Agree	2.7	2.8	2.4	2.0	8.1	3.9	1.1	4.0	1.5	2.5	3.2	2.7	3.0	2.1	2.0	4.6
Item 20900 Subject A11c N	2681	1221	1400	2103	224	604	797	821	460	1678	937	1103	493	429	576	45
E03D: Conforming																
1. Disagree	27.1	25.1	29.1	24.1	42.1	27.9	22.2	31.5	27.0	25.6	29.1	30.2	25.1	24.8	25.9	10.7
2. Mostly disagree	9.8	11.9	8.0	9.7	9.3	9.9	10.3	9.4	9.4	9.4	10.9	8.8	11.5	8.6	11.2	8.9
3. Neither	41.8	42.0	41.4	43.4	32.7	40.6	46.7	39.7	38.9	38.9	46.7	35.8	42.2	50.9	45.5	55.2
4. Mostly agree	10.9	10.8	10.7	11.4	9.0	11.4	11.5	9.2	12.2	13.1	6.8	11.5	13.0	8.4	9.2	12.0
5. Agree	10.4	10.3	10.8	11.4	6.9	10.2	9.3	10.3	12.5	13.0	6.4	13.7	8.2	7.3	8.2	13.2
Item 20910 Subject A11c N	2659	1210	1390	2091	222	601	790	815	453	1668	926	1090	491	428	571	45
E03E: Mature, sophisticated																
1. Disagree	61.2	59.5	63.0	60.4	67.4	61.7	58.1	60.8	66.4	65.6	52.9	75.1	56.4	53.8	47.0	23.8
2. Mostly disagree	12.5	12.2	13.0	12.5	10.2	11.1	13.0	13.2	12.6	12.5	12.8	10.1	14.2	15.2	14.2	14.0
3. Neither	21.7	23.0	20.3	23.2	13.0	22.0	24.8	20.7	17.8	18.8	26.9	11.7	23.4	27.7	31.6	58.2
4. Mostly agree	2.9	2.8	2.9	2.7	2.5	2.8	3.4	2.9	2.6	2.2	4.4	1.6	3.5	1.8	6.0	1.5
5. Agree	1.7	2.5	0.9	1.2	7.0	2.4	0.8	2.5	0.7	1.0	2.9	1.4	2.6	1.5	1.1	2.5
Item 20920 Subject A11c N	2674	1216	1400	2101	223	603	790	822	458	1675	932	1103	487	427	577	45
E03F: Like he's TRYING to appear mature and sophisticated																
1. Disagree	12.5	12.0	12.6	11.1	15.4	16.5	11.3	12.5	9.1	9.6	16.8	9.2	11.6	11.9	20.0	10.8
2. Mostly disagree	4.9	4.4	5.4	4.6	5.9	5.2	4.8	4.3	6.0	4.9	5.0	2.8	6.5	7.1	6.3	3.4
3. Neither	19.9	22.5	17.5	21.2	11.2	20.9	23.5	17.7	16.2	18.0	23.4	12.6	21.2	23.5	26.8	44.6
4. Mostly agree	21.5	21.2	21.6	22.8	12.2	19.8	22.3	21.2	23.0	22.3	20.2	22.4	21.6	23.1	19.3	20.0
5. Agree	41.2	39.8	42.9	40.3	55.2	37.6	38.1	44.3	45.7	45.2	34.5	53.0	39.0	34.4	27.6	21.2
Item 20930 Subject A11c N	2688	1224	1404	2108	227	606	795	828	459	1683	939	1110	494	429	575	45
E04: In my opinion, when a girl my age is smoking a cigarette, it makes her look . . .																
E04A: Cool, calm, in-control																
1. Disagree	67.2	67.1	67.8	65.5	76.4	61.8	64.8	70.2	73.3	71.8	59.1	78.4	65.2	63.1	52.5	42.8
2. Mostly disagree	11.5	11.8	11.3	11.9	8.1	12.4	13.5	9.3	10.5	10.8	12.7	9.8	13.3	14.0	11.6	10.8
3. Neither	16.8	16.8	16.4	18.4	9.3	19.6	17.8	15.7	13.4	13.7	22.1	8.9	17.7	18.8	27.6	36.8
4. Mostly agree	2.8	2.4	3.3	3.2	1.1	3.4	2.9	2.7	2.2	2.6	3.4	1.6	2.4	2.4	5.9	5.6
5. Agree	1.7	2.0	1.3	1.1	5.1	2.9	0.9	2.1	0.6	1.1	2.8	1.3	1.4	1.7	2.4	4.0
Item 20940 Subject A11c N	2649	1180	1409	2082	220	597	787	810	454	1666	917	1089	487	425	569	44
E04B: Insecure																
1. Disagree	15.5	16.0	15.1	13.4	22.2	19.2	13.3	16.6	12.3	13.3	19.6	12.7	12.7	15.3	22.9	18.5
2. Mostly disagree	7.1	6.8	7.7	7.4	8.1	9.7	6.3	7.1	5.2	7.4	6.6	5.8	7.4	6.9	9.3	13.7
3. Neither	27.9	28.3	26.7	29.1	19.1	29.4	30.1	25.7	26.3	25.6	32.2	19.7	31.1	31.4	36.1	41.8
4. Mostly agree	18.4	17.3	19.4	19.3	14.9	17.5	20.0	18.7	16.1	19.6	16.2	22.0	16.0	19.1	14.0	8.9
5. Agree	31.1	31.6	31.1	30.7	35.6	24.2	30.3	31.9	40.1	34.2	25.5	39.8	32.8	27.3	17.8	17.1
Item 20950 Subject A11c N	2645	1180	1405	2079	219	597	787	807	454	1665	914	1085	488	425	569	44

QUESTIONNAIRE FORM 5 1986	TOTAL	SEX		RACE		REGION				4YR COLLEGE PLANS		ILLICIT DRUG USE: LIFETIME				
		M	F	White	Black	NE	NC	S	W	Yes	No	None	Mari- juana Only	Few Pills	More Pills	Any Her- oin
N (Weighted No. of Cases):	3073	1413	1550	2295	312	725	867	952	529	1839	1084	1237	583	487	648	47
% of Weighted Total:	100.0	46.0	50.4	74.7	10.2	23.6	28.2	31.0	17.2	59.9	35.3	40.3	19.0	15.8	21.1	1.5

E04C: Independent and liberated

	TOTAL	M	F	White	Black	NE	NC	S	W	Yes	No	None	Mari-juana Only	Few Pills	More Pills	Any Heroin
1. Disagree	55.0	54.5	56.0	53.8	64.0	51.3	52.5	57.8	59.1	57.7	50.0	64.2	52.8	54.7	42.9	27.2
2. Mostly disagree	13.5	13.8	13.0	14.3	12.0	12.6	12.9	13.2	15.9	13.7	13.1	13.0	15.7	11.3	13.8	13.7
3. Neither	22.0	23.2	20.7	23.0	14.3	26.0	24.4	19.0	18.1	19.2	26.6	13.3	24.3	27.4	30.1	35.5
4. Mostly agree	6.5	5.5	7.4	6.8	4.2	6.7	7.8	6.0	4.9	6.2	7.1	5.6	4.6	5.6	10.2	14.3
5. Agree	3.0	3.0	2.9	2.1	5.5	3.3	2.4	4.0	2.0	3.1	3.1	3.9	2.5	0.9	3.0	9.3
Item 20960 Subject A11c N	2638	1177	1401	2077	218	593	784	807	454	1659	915	1080	487	423	569	44

E04D: Conforming

	TOTAL	M	F	White	Black	NE	NC	S	W	Yes	No	None	Mari-juana Only	Few Pills	More Pills	Any Heroin
1. Disagree	31.6	29.8	33.0	27.6	49.7	28.5	26.3	37.8	33.5	29.6	35.2	33.9	29.1	29.2	32.0	21.2
2. Mostly disagree	8.4	10.6	6.6	8.1	7.6	8.7	7.6	8.4	9.0	7.6	9.7	6.4	9.3	10.4	10.3	3.0
3. Neither	38.4	38.1	38.3	39.9	29.5	40.3	41.7	36.0	34.6	35.5	43.2	33.6	38.4	42.1	43.1	59.3
4. Mostly agree	9.5	9.2	9.6	10.6	5.8	10.3	11.5	7.2	8.9	12.2	4.7	9.9	12.4	8.4	7.1	7.3
5. Agree	12.2	12.3	12.5	13.8	7.4	12.2	12.8	10.6	14.0	15.2	7.2	16.2	10.8	10.0	7.5	9.2
Item 20970 Subject A11c N	2614	1168	1387	2059	219	590	775	801	448	1650	899	1067	482	422	566	44

E04E: Mature, sophisticated

	TOTAL	M	F	White	Black	NE	NC	S	W	Yes	No	None	Mari-juana Only	Few Pills	More Pills	Any Heroin
1. Disagree	64.3	64.4	64.7	63.7	69.2	60.8	62.6	64.4	71.6	69.2	55.4	75.9	62.3	57.7	51.2	36.2
2. Mostly disagree	11.5	11.7	11.5	11.8	10.1	11.3	11.7	11.7	11.2	10.8	13.1	9.6	13.5	13.0	13.3	4.6
3. Neither	18.8	18.4	18.8	19.9	9.8	21.4	20.8	17.6	14.2	15.6	24.2	10.5	18.4	25.2	27.0	52.1
4. Mostly agree	2.7	2.7	2.7	2.7	2.5	2.8	3.2	2.5	1.7	2.2	3.5	1.7	3.3	2.0	4.3	5.6
5. Agree	2.7	2.8	2.3	1.8	8.3	3.7	1.6	3.8	1.3	2.2	3.7	2.4	2.5	2.0	4.1	1.5
Item 20980 Subject A11c N	2636	1175	1402	2070	220	592	782	808	454	1659	911	1084	486	424	565	44

E04F: Like she's TRYING to appear mature and sophisticated

	TOTAL	M	F	White	Black	NE	NC	S	W	Yes	No	None	Mari-juana Only	Few Pills	More Pills	Any Heroin
1. Disagree	12.6	11.8	13.0	10.9	16.1	16.5	11.2	12.5	10.1	9.8	17.1	9.3	10.6	13.8	19.6	13.6
2. Mostly disagree	4.9	4.5	5.3	4.6	6.0	6.7	4.2	4.8	4.3	4.9	5.2	4.0	6.3	5.2	5.2	3.7
3. Neither	17.4	19.4	15.6	18.6	9.9	18.4	20.7	15.5	14.1	15.5	21.0	9.9	17.4	21.5	25.7	46.2
4. Mostly agree	17.6	17.1	18.0	19.0	9.8	15.7	20.2	16.0	18.3	19.0	15.1	19.2	17.0	16.7	16.3	16.6
5. Agree	47.4	47.2	48.1	47.0	58.3	42.6	43.7	51.2	53.3	50.8	41.7	57.7	49.0	41.7	33.2	19.8
Item 20990 Subject A11c N	2631	1175	1397	2070	217	588	781	809	453	1657	909	1084	483	422	564	44

E05: Do you agree or disagree..

E05A: Smokers know how to enjoy life more than nonsmokers

	TOTAL	M	F	White	Black	NE	NC	S	W	Yes	No	None	Mari-juana Only	Few Pills	More Pills	Any Heroin
1. Disagree	75.3	71.3	79.0	75.4	76.8	74.7	74.2	75.1	78.1	80.9	65.2	83.3	76.9	68.7	65.0	53.6
2. Mostly disagree	8.7	9.4	8.0	9.0	5.1	8.3	9.3	8.0	9.3	7.1	11.8	6.7	9.0	11.0	10.9	5.8
3. Neither	13.7	16.1	11.4	13.8	12.6	15.1	14.3	13.5	11.2	10.7	18.7	7.7	12.9	18.7	20.2	37.7
4. Mostly agree	1.2	1.6	0.7	1.0	1.7	0.8	1.4	1.5	0.6	0.7	2.0	1.1	0.5	0.4	2.4	1.8
5. Agree	1.2	1.6	0.9	0.8	3.8	1.1	0.7	1.9	0.8	0.6	2.3	1.2	0.7	1.1	1.6	1.0
Item 21000 Subject A11c N	2678	1212	1406	2103	223	600	788	831	459	1682	930	1106	488	429	576	45

E05B: I prefer to date people who don't smoke

	TOTAL	M	F	White	Black	NE	NC	S	W	Yes	No	None	Mari-juana Only	Few Pills	More Pills	Any Heroin
1. Disagree	7.1	6.3	7.8	7.0	7.3	9.9	6.6	6.7	5.1	5.5	9.8	3.5	6.1	7.3	14.1	13.7
2. Mostly disagree	3.6	3.3	4.0	3.6	1.6	3.8	4.7	2.6	3.5	3.0	4.6	1.6	3.3	3.4	6.9	19.3
3. Neither	18.3	17.4	18.8	19.7	9.7	23.0	20.7	15.2	13.4	15.8	23.0	10.6	18.7	22.5	28.0	38.1
4. Mostly agree	10.2	11.1	9.6	10.1	7.0	9.8	10.5	10.0	10.3	9.9	10.5	9.7	12.7	8.0	11.3	1.2
5. Agree	60.8	62.0	59.8	59.5	74.5	53.4	57.6	65.4	67.7	65.8	52.2	74.6	59.2	58.9	39.7	27.7
Item 21010 Subject A11c N	2677	1212	1406	2101	223	600	786	830	461	1681	930	1103	490	429	575	45

E05C: The harmful effects of cigarettes have been exaggerated

	TOTAL	M	F	White	Black	NE	NC	S	W	Yes	No	None	Mari-juana Only	Few Pills	More Pills	Any Heroin
1. Disagree	51.0	49.1	52.8	51.9	49.2	54.5	47.9	49.4	54.7	56.5	40.1	59.4	50.1	45.5	41.8	33.5
2. Mostly disagree	18.8	18.6	19.1	20.0	18.4	16.0	20.6	19.3	18.4	19.5	18.2	17.3	21.7	21.5	17.6	14.9
3. Neither	14.0	16.2	12.1	14.1	8.0	12.8	15.6	14.1	12.6	12.0	18.0	10.4	13.8	16.6	19.5	10.3
4. Mostly agree	8.5	8.6	8.3	8.2	6.6	9.1	10.2	7.5	6.6	6.5	12.0	5.9	6.8	7.9	13.2	32.7
5. Agree	7.7	7.5	7.8	5.7	22.6	7.6	5.7	9.6	7.6	5.5	11.8	7.0	7.6	8.5	7.8	8.6
Item 21020 Subject A11c N	2673	1213	1400	2099	222	599	788	829	457	1680	927	1101	488	429	575	45

QUESTIONNAIRE FORM 5 1986	TOTAL	SEX		RACE		REGION				4YR COLLEGE PLANS		ILLICIT DRUG USE: LIFETIME				
		M	F	White	Black	NE	NC	S	W	Yes	No	None	Mari- juana Only	Few Pills	More Pills	Any Her- oin
N (Weighted No. of Cases):	3073	1413	1550	2295	312	725	867	952	529	1839	1084	1237	583	487	648	47
% of Weighted Total:	100.0	46.0	50.4	74.7	10.2	23.6	28.2	31.0	17.2	59.9	35.3	40.3	19.0	15.8	21.1	1.5
E05D: I think that becoming a smoker reflects poor judgment																
1. Disagree	10.2	9.4	10.8	9.2	14.7	13.1	9.1	9.0	10.4	8.5	13.1	6.9	10.1	11.3	14.9	18.1
2. Mostly disagree	7.4	7.6	7.2	7.6	4.2	8.5	7.7	6.9	6.7	7.3	7.8	4.8	8.1	6.4	12.5	13.7
3. Neither	23.0	21.1	24.4	23.6	14.2	26.1	24.6	20.6	20.7	19.7	29.1	17.0	24.8	27.4	26.8	52.0
4. Mostly agree	18.0	19.1	17.3	19.0	14.5	15.9	20.8	16.7	18.5	19.6	15.5	16.9	20.5	21.0	17.4	1.5
5. Agree	41.3	42.8	40.2	40.5	52.3	36.4	37.8	46.8	43.7	44.8	34.5	54.4	36.5	33.9	28.3	14.6
Item 21030 Subject A11c N	2662	1206	1398	2090	221	598	782	827	456	1675	922	1099	486	425	573	45
E05E: I personally don't mind being around people who are smoking																
1. Disagree	34.0	33.5	34.5	31.5	49.9	34.1	30.6	34.8	38.4	37.9	26.9	47.6	26.1	28.7	19.7	19.8
2. Mostly disagree	15.7	16.6	15.0	16.2	12.1	15.5	14.2	16.3	17.3	17.0	13.4	16.0	20.0	14.8	12.7	12.5
3. Neither	13.4	14.9	11.7	13.7	6.8	13.8	15.6	10.6	14.2	11.9	16.2	11.4	14.5	17.4	13.8	9.7
4. Mostly agree	18.8	19.5	18.3	19.2	14.2	16.0	20.2	20.0	17.7	18.8	18.6	15.4	22.9	20.3	20.3	17.7
5. Agree	18.1	15.5	20.6	19.4	17.0	20.5	19.4	18.2	12.4	14.4	24.9	9.5	16.5	18.8	33.5	40.3
Item 21040 Subject A11c N	2670	1210	1400	2099	220	601	787	825	457	1677	927	1101	486	429	576	45
E05F: Smoking is a dirty habit																
1. Disagree	9.3	9.2	9.5	8.8	11.7	11.4	9.6	8.2	7.8	8.1	11.5	6.0	7.6	7.6	16.5	30.4
2. Mostly disagree	5.5	6.1	4.9	5.5	3.9	5.3	4.8	6.5	5.2	5.7	5.2	3.7	6.0	6.0	7.7	24.3
3. Neither	16.7	17.5	15.9	17.2	13.4	18.3	19.5	14.5	13.5	14.7	20.4	11.7	20.8	21.7	17.8	14.5
4. Mostly agree	18.4	18.7	18.2	19.4	9.9	16.2	20.1	17.9	19.0	19.7	16.2	16.8	17.4	21.8	20.0	14.5
5. Agree	50.2	48.4	51.5	49.1	61.1	48.7	46.0	52.8	54.5	51.8	46.7	61.8	48.3	42.8	37.9	16.7
Item 21050 Subject A11c N	2661	1206	1398	2094	220	597	783	824	458	1675	920	1100	484	429	571	45
E05G: I strongly dislike being near people who are smoking																
1. Disagree	21.4	18.9	23.6	22.6	20.1	25.4	23.8	20.4	14.1	17.3	28.9	12.6	21.6	23.1	36.1	34.7
2. Mostly disagree	13.5	14.2	12.9	13.9	10.4	12.1	12.7	14.2	15.2	13.4	13.7	10.1	15.3	13.7	16.4	35.9
3. Neither	19.8	22.9	16.8	20.3	12.6	20.0	22.2	17.6	19.1	19.0	21.4	16.5	24.5	23.5	19.6	15.3
4. Mostly agree	14.9	14.7	15.2	15.1	11.7	14.5	14.6	15.9	13.7	15.9	13.1	17.4	15.3	13.9	10.9	1.8
5. Agree	30.5	29.4	31.5	28.1	45.3	27.9	26.6	31.9	38.0	34.4	23.0	43.4	23.2	25.8	17.0	12.3
Item 21055 Subject A11c N	2667	1208	1398	2094	220	601	783	824	458	1676	925	1102	486	428	573	45
E06: The next questions ask how you feel about the amount of supervision that you received from your parents (or guardians) during your high school years. For each of the following areas, do you feel that you received about the right amount of supervision, too little, or too much?																
E06A: What kinds of parties, dances or other events you could go to																
1. Far too little supervision	9.1	11.9	6.7	8.7	9.0	8.9	8.2	10.4	8.6	7.2	12.6	5.5	8.9	8.7	15.8	12.1
2. Too little	9.9	10.8	8.9	9.5	9.6	8.3	10.8	9.7	10.8	9.6	10.0	7.5	8.7	11.5	12.7	21.4
3. About right	64.1	61.8	66.1	65.4	62.4	63.7	63.6	64.5	64.8	67.4	58.8	71.3	62.6	64.2	54.3	49.0
4. Too much supervision	11.1	10.6	11.8	11.1	12.8	11.3	12.5	10.4	10.1	10.9	11.7	10.6	14.6	10.0	9.6	7.7
5. Far too much	5.8	5.0	6.4	5.3	6.1	7.8	5.0	5.0	5.8	5.0	6.9	5.1	5.2	5.5	7.6	9.8
Item 21800 Subject M03 N	2635	1195	1379	2069	213	588	785	810	452	1654	914	1080	487	431	557	45
E06B: How late you stayed out on dates																
1. Far too little supervision	4.8	6.7	3.1	4.3	7.1	3.3	5.3	6.2	3.4	3.2	7.6	4.1	3.3	3.7	7.9	3.3
2. Too little	7.3	8.2	6.4	6.7	7.7	4.9	8.5	6.8	9.2	5.9	9.9	5.4	5.8	9.4	9.3	20.3
3. About right	58.8	60.0	58.1	59.7	58.1	63.1	56.2	57.9	59.7	61.7	53.8	65.3	61.1	59.3	45.9	41.4
4. Too much supervision	19.2	17.1	20.8	20.0	14.9	18.3	21.3	19.5	16.2	20.2	17.4	17.1	21.0	18.8	23.1	12.0
5. Far too much	9.9	8.0	11.6	9.3	12.2	10.4	8.8	9.7	11.5	9.0	11.3	8.1	8.8	8.8	13.7	23.0
Item 21810 Subject M03 N	2616	1182	1373	2062	211	583	781	805	447	1639	913	1063	481	429	563	44

QUESTIONNAIRE FORM 5 1986	TOTAL	SEX		RACE		REGION				4YR COLLEGE PLANS		ILLICIT DRUG USE: LIFETIME				
		M	F	White	Black	NE	NC	S	W	Yes	No	None	Mari-juana Only	Few Pills	More Pills	Any Her-oin
N (Weighted No. of Cases):	3073	1413	1550	2295	312	725	867	952	529	1839	1084	1237	583	487	648	47
% of Weighted Total:	100.0	46.0	50.4	74.7	10.2	23.6	28.2	31.0	17.2	59.9	35.3	40.3	19.0	15.8	21.1	1.5

E06C: The way you dressed

	TOTAL	M	F	White	Black	NE	NC	S	W	Yes	No	None	Mari-juana Only	Few Pills	More Pills	Any Her-oin
1. Far too little supervision	5.2	6.1	4.3	4.9	3.5	4.9	4.7	5.8	5.1	3.4	8.4	2.7	4.4	6.5	8.9	7.9
2. Too little	5.0	6.4	4.0	4.5	7.1	6.1	4.7	4.7	4.8	4.3	6.3	3.7	5.5	5.8	5.7	9.7
3. About right	76.5	72.9	79.4	78.1	73.2	76.3	78.3	75.0	76.3	79.7	70.9	80.5	80.8	74.4	68.9	60.2
4. Too much supervision	9.1	9.9	8.5	8.8	10.1	9.1	8.3	10.0	9.0	9.2	9.4	9.2	6.1	9.9	10.8	10.1
5. Far too much	4.2	4.7	3.9	3.7	6.1	3.5	4.0	4.5	4.8	3.6	4.9	3.9	3.3	3.4	5.6	12.0
Item 21820 Subject M03 N	2615	1180	1376	2057	209	583	775	807	450	1641	908	1075	478	428	558	43

E06D: What you did with your money

	TOTAL	M	F	White	Black	NE	NC	S	W	Yes	No	None	Mari-juana Only	Few Pills	More Pills	Any Her-oin
1. Far too little supervision	4.4	5.5	3.4	4.4	4.7	5.2	4.2	4.5	3.6	3.3	6.5	2.6	3.8	4.5	7.3	15.2
2. Too little	12.3	13.3	11.3	11.8	10.7	10.8	12.6	12.8	12.8	12.2	12.5	9.6	12.3	15.4	13.6	20.7
3. About right	60.3	55.5	64.5	61.8	52.1	59.3	62.4	56.9	63.7	63.0	55.6	66.6	62.0	55.8	52.5	36.5
4. Too much supervision	16.2	18.6	14.0	15.7	21.4	17.0	15.3	17.9	13.5	16.1	16.5	15.4	16.4	16.4	17.6	11.8
5. Far too much	6.9	7.2	6.8	6.3	11.1	7.7	5.4	7.9	6.4	5.5	8.8	5.7	5.5	7.9	9.0	15.8
Item 21830 Subject M03 N	2620	1186	1374	2057	211	581	780	809	450	1648	905	1076	480	426	557	44

E06E: How often you went out in the evening

	TOTAL	M	F	White	Black	NE	NC	S	W	Yes	No	None	Mari-juana Only	Few Pills	More Pills	Any Her-oin
1. Far too little supervision	4.3	5.3	3.3	4.0	5.0	4.0	4.2	4.9	3.5	2.8	6.8	3.0	4.6	3.2	6.9	2.3
2. Too little	6.9	8.2	5.6	6.4	7.0	6.2	7.0	6.8	7.6	5.4	9.2	4.6	6.3	9.6	8.5	14.6
3. About right	59.8	59.9	60.2	60.6	62.2	60.8	60.5	58.7	59.6	64.3	52.4	66.4	57.6	58.9	50.6	57.8
4. Too much supervision	19.9	19.2	20.3	20.5	16.8	20.4	19.8	20.3	18.6	20.0	19.8	19.0	22.7	19.7	20.5	6.0
5. Far too much	9.1	7.4	10.6	8.6	9.0	8.6	8.5	9.3	10.7	7.5	11.8	6.9	8.9	8.7	13.5	19.4
Item 21840 Subject M03 N	2608	1182	1366	2055	207	577	780	800	450	1638	904	1067	477	428	556	44

E06F: How much time you spent on homework

	TOTAL	M	F	White	Black	NE	NC	S	W	Yes	No	None	Mari-juana Only	Few Pills	More Pills	Any Her-oin
1. Far too little supervision	7.9	9.5	6.6	8.1	4.7	7.3	7.5	8.3	9.0	6.3	11.0	6.3	6.5	8.4	11.0	17.9
2. Too little	20.5	22.7	18.1	20.8	13.1	18.6	23.1	19.2	21.0	20.7	20.3	17.1	21.3	21.6	26.3	22.4
3. About right	52.4	47.3	57.5	53.1	61.7	52.6	52.3	52.7	52.0	55.0	47.6	59.8	52.6	48.8	40.9	42.2
4. Too much supervision	12.5	13.4	11.6	12.3	11.6	14.2	11.6	13.4	10.2	12.8	12.2	11.6	13.0	14.0	13.5	4.3
5. Far too much	6.6	7.2	6.1	5.5	8.9	7.4	5.5	6.4	7.9	5.2	8.8	5.2	6.6	7.2	8.2	13.1
Item 21850 Subject M03 N	2616	1181	1375	2059	210	581	783	803	449	1647	905	1076	475	429	557	44

E06G: What courses you took in school

	TOTAL	M	F	White	Black	NE	NC	S	W	Yes	No	None	Mari-juana Only	Few Pills	More Pills	Any Her-oin
1. Far too little supervision	6.2	7.2	5.3	5.7	7.0	6.0	6.6	6.2	5.6	4.1	9.9	4.4	4.5	8.1	9.1	10.9
2. Too little	11.5	12.8	10.6	11.2	11.4	10.3	12.8	10.3	13.2	10.9	13.1	10.2	12.4	10.7	14.1	19.0
3. About right	70.1	67.1	73.0	72.6	65.1	71.6	68.5	72.9	66.4	74.1	63.1	75.5	68.8	66.4	65.7	48.8
4. Too much supervision	8.0	7.8	7.8	7.2	7.4	9.4	8.3	5.8	9.6	7.7	8.1	6.5	11.5	10.1	5.7	7.1
5. Far too much	4.1	5.1	3.3	3.3	9.0	2.7	3.8	4.8	5.3	3.2	5.8	3.5	2.8	4.8	5.4	14.2
Item 21860 Subject M03 N	2608	1181	1367	2052	207	576	781	801	450	1643	901	1074	475	428	553	44

E06H: The hours you could work during the school year

	TOTAL	M	F	White	Black	NE	NC	S	W	Yes	No	None	Mari-juana Only	Few Pills	More Pills	Any Her-oin
1. Far too little supervision	5.9	6.5	5.2	5.3	7.8	5.8	6.1	6.8	4.0	4.3	8.6	5.1	4.7	6.9	6.5	14.2
2. Too little	9.3	11.8	7.1	8.4	11.1	7.5	8.4	10.6	10.7	7.4	12.6	6.7	12.2	9.3	11.8	9.7
3. About right	71.3	66.8	75.1	73.4	62.5	72.5	73.7	68.7	70.3	75.5	64.0	74.7	70.4	70.4	67.5	59.7
4. Too much supervision	8.4	8.4	8.4	8.3	9.4	8.6	7.9	8.3	9.4	8.3	8.4	8.4	8.5	9.6	7.7	4.7
5. Far too much	5.1	6.4	4.1	4.5	9.1	5.5	4.0	5.7	5.6	4.4	6.4	5.1	4.2	3.8	6.5	11.7
Item 21870 Subject M03 N	2577	1170	1347	2035	198	570	769	789	449	1614	898	1049	468	429	555	44

E06I: How much TV you watched

	TOTAL	M	F	White	Black	NE	NC	S	W	Yes	No	None	Mari-juana Only	Few Pills	More Pills	Any Her-oin
1. Far too little supervision	8.6	9.4	7.7	7.9	9.5	9.8	7.6	8.7	8.3	5.7	14.0	6.6	6.9	9.6	13.0	3.3
2. Too little	11.3	12.6	10.3	10.1	12.1	11.2	10.3	11.2	12.9	10.6	12.9	9.4	13.7	13.8	10.7	18.8
3. About right	67.4	65.3	69.7	70.6	60.2	65.9	71.3	66.0	65.2	72.1	59.2	71.2	68.0	63.5	63.7	62.7
4. Too much supervision	7.6	7.5	7.4	7.1	10.8	8.8	6.3	8.0	7.6	7.7	6.4	8.1	7.5	7.0	6.9	4.4
5. Far too much	5.1	5.2	5.0	4.3	7.4	4.3	4.5	6.1	5.8	3.8	7.5	4.8	4.0	6.2	5.7	10.8
Item 21880 Subject M03 N	2613	1183	1370	2054	207	577	780	804	452	1646	904	1073	475	428	558	44

QUESTIONNAIRE FORM 5 1986	TOTAL	SEX		RACE		REGION				4YR COLLEGE PLANS		ILLICIT DRUG USE: LIFETIME				
		M	F	White	Black	NE	NC	S	W	Yes	No	None	Mari-juana Only	Few Pills	More Pills	Any Her-oin
N (Weighted No. of Cases):	3073	1413	1550	2295	312	725	867	952	529	1839	1084	1237	583	487	648	47
% of Weighted Total:	100.0	46.0	50.4	74.7	10.2	23.6	28.2	31.0	17.2	59.9	35.3	40.3	19.0	15.8	21.1	1.5
E06J: What kinds of TV programs you watched																
1. Far too little supervision	9.1	10.3	8.0	7.9	11.7	9.8	8.0	8.8	10.4	6.6	13.7	6.5	6.9	11.3	13.5	10.3
2. Too little	8.0	9.0	7.2	6.8	11.9	8.1	6.2	9.1	8.8	7.2	9.2	5.6	8.7	9.2	9.2	26.6
3. About right	71.8	69.0	74.5	75.0	59.4	71.6	75.2	69.8	69.5	76.7	62.8	76.0	72.4	67.4	69.5	49.5
4. Too much supervision	7.2	7.7	6.3	7.1	6.7	7.1	7.6	7.4	6.1	6.6	8.2	7.0	8.2	9.9	4.6	1.5
5. Far too much	4.1	4.0	4.0	3.2	10.3	3.4	3.0	5.0	5.2	2.9	6.0	4.9	3.9	2.2	3.2	12.1
Item 21890 Subject M03 N	2607	1177	1369	2049	207	575	780	803	449	1642	902	1071	474	428	556	43
E07: Over the LAST 12 MONTHS, about how often have you gone to parties?																
1. Not at all–GO TO Q.9	15.7	15.0	16.3	14.0	27.4	11.2	11.7	21.2	18.7	13.3	20.1	26.4	9.3	10.0	5.1	11.2
2. Once a month or less	32.1	31.0	33.4	32.3	28.4	31.7	32.3	31.8	32.9	34.9	27.2	41.3	27.9	29.3	20.6	23.4
3. 2 or 3 times a month	25.5	24.6	26.4	26.3	23.8	28.0	26.7	25.6	20.1	26.4	24.6	20.0	30.8	31.2	27.2	19.0
4. About once a week	14.6	14.9	13.9	15.3	8.8	16.7	15.1	12.7	14.2	15.6	11.9	8.9	16.1	18.5	21.9	10.6
5. 2 or 3 times a week	9.2	10.4	8.1	9.1	7.9	8.9	11.1	5.7	12.3	7.6	11.9	2.3	12.8	9.6	18.8	18.6
6. Over 3 times a week	2.9	4.1	1.9	3.0	3.7	3.5	3.1	2.9	1.9	2.1	4.3	1.0	3.1	1.4	6.3	17.2
Item 21900 Subject C07 N	2574	1150	1366	2028	207	574	762	790	448	1620	886	1071	471	418	537	45
E08: Now think about the parties you went to in the last 12 months. How often...																
E08A: Were people over age 30 present at least some of the time?																
1. Never	40.9	39.7	42.0	41.5	44.2	40.8	44.7	37.2	40.4	42.8	37.5	40.2	46.7	40.4	38.1	27.2
2. Seldom	31.7	34.6	28.8	32.1	23.0	31.4	30.8	32.7	32.1	31.0	32.3	28.6	35.1	35.4	30.3	43.5
3. Sometimes	18.4	18.4	18.4	18.2	17.5	18.2	17.7	18.9	18.9	17.6	20.2	19.5	13.9	16.7	21.8	18.3
4. Most times	6.0	4.6	7.4	5.7	7.4	5.4	5.2	7.5	5.9	5.8	6.5	8.1	2.8	5.5	6.5	1.7
5. Always	3.0	2.6	3.4	2.5	8.0	4.3	1.6	3.6	2.6	2.8	3.5	3.7	1.4	2.0	3.4	9.2
Item 21910 Subject C07,M02 N★	2247	1027	1169	1793	163	528	689	651	379	1439	752	820	438	384	533	41
E08B: Did someone get high on alcohol?																
1. Never	10.1	7.9	12.3	8.6	15.6	8.5	7.8	12.7	12.3	9.7	11.1	21.2	2.6	6.4	2.1	5.8
2. Seldom	5.4	5.2	5.2	4.4	10.0	7.0	3.0	5.9	6.4	5.1	5.8	9.1	3.5	3.7	2.4	2.0
3. Sometimes	14.7	15.7	13.9	13.8	23.3	17.5	12.9	17.0	10.1	14.1	15.8	15.6	15.7	13.5	13.5	11.4
4. Most times	27.8	27.2	28.0	28.3	18.8	29.5	30.3	25.0	25.9	27.5	28.0	26.6	30.3	32.2	25.7	22.6
5. Always	42.0	43.9	40.7	44.9	32.3	37.5	46.0	39.4	45.3	43.6	39.3	27.5	47.9	44.3	56.3	58.2
Item 21920 Subject A02b,C07 N★	2243	1028	1164	1786	163	529	687	647	379	1436	752	819	434	383	535	41
E08C: Did most people get high on alcohol?																
1. Never	12.4	10.0	14.7	10.7	16.0	10.7	9.7	15.3	14.9	12.9	11.6	24.0	4.7	8.6	3.6	8.6
2. Seldom	10.6	10.8	10.3	9.4	23.3	9.8	9.1	13.3	9.5	11.3	9.1	18.3	8.8	5.8	4.3	3.7
3. Sometimes	18.2	18.9	17.4	18.0	21.3	21.2	18.3	19.0	14.2	17.7	19.6	19.0	23.2	16.0	15.6	10.3
4. Most times	31.3	31.6	31.1	32.8	18.8	30.6	33.6	29.0	31.9	31.7	30.1	25.2	32.2	39.4	34.0	37.8
5. Always	27.5	28.7	26.5	29.1	20.6	28.7	29.3	23.4	29.5	26.4	29.7	13.5	31.1	30.1	42.5	39.6
Item 21930 Subject A02b,C07 N★	2230	1020	1159	1779	163	527	687	643	373	1430	746	817	432	377	533	41
E08D: Did you get high on alcohol?																
1. Never	27.2	22.5	31.7	22.8	54.6	21.7	22.6	33.2	32.9	30.0	22.3	51.8	14.9	16.2	8.5	11.6
2. Seldom	15.1	13.7	16.1	14.8	19.5	17.9	15.3	15.6	10.2	14.1	17.4	15.8	18.9	16.1	9.6	23.8
3. Sometimes	25.4	24.9	26.0	26.9	14.3	23.9	27.8	23.7	25.9	26.4	22.8	19.3	30.0	34.1	26.3	11.1
4. Most times	20.3	23.7	17.4	22.3	6.4	23.0	22.4	17.1	18.3	19.5	21.8	10.7	25.2	22.3	28.2	33.2
5. Always	12.0	15.2	8.8	13.2	5.2	13.5	11.9	10.4	12.7	10.0	15.7	2.4	11.1	11.3	27.5	20.3
Item 21940 Subject A05c,C07 N★	2228	1020	1156	1778	162	521	686	642	378	1426	746	815	430	377	533	41
E08E: Did you feel pressure to drink alcohol?																
1. Never	63.7	59.3	68.0	61.5	72.8	66.4	58.8	63.3	69.5	63.0	64.7	63.8	65.1	60.7	65.8	53.4
2. Seldom	20.4	22.2	18.5	22.2	9.3	18.4	25.3	18.4	17.4	21.5	18.4	19.5	19.8	24.8	19.2	24.7
3. Sometimes	10.7	11.7	9.7	11.0	12.5	9.7	10.9	13.0	7.5	10.9	10.1	10.7	12.2	8.3	10.1	11.9
4. Most times	2.8	3.6	2.2	3.0	2.3	3.3	2.5	2.6	3.0	2.3	3.8	3.7	1.3	2.6	2.5	5.5
5. Always	2.5	3.3	1.7	2.2	3.1	2.1	2.5	2.7	2.6	2.3	3.0	2.4	1.6	3.6	2.5	4.5
Item 21950 Subject A02b,C07 N★	2233	1021	1163	1781	162	526	686	642	379	1427	750	815	430	382	534	41

★=excludes respondents for whom question was inappropriate.

QUESTIONNAIRE FORM 5 1986	TOTAL	SEX		RACE		REGION				4YR COLLEGE PLANS		ILLICIT DRUG USE: LIFETIME				
		M	F	White	Black	NE	NC	S	W	Yes	No	None	Marijuana Only	Few Pills	More Pills	Any Heroin
N (Weighted No. of Cases):	3073	1413	1550	2295	312	725	867	952	529	1839	1084	1237	583	487	648	47
% of Weighted Total:	100.0	46.0	50.4	74.7	10.2	23.6	28.2	31.0	17.2	59.9	35.3	40.3	19.0	15.8	21.1	1.5
E08F: Did you feel pressure to drink enough to get high?																
1. Never	73.4	67.0	79.1	72.3	80.8	73.0	71.1	73.9	77.3	74.0	72.2	77.4	73.3	68.4	71.6	57.7
2. Seldom	14.7	18.2	11.6	15.7	8.5	12.5	18.2	14.5	12.1	14.6	15.1	11.4	15.1	20.6	14.6	28.7
3. Sometimes	7.7	9.7	5.9	8.0	5.8	9.1	8.3	7.1	5.8	8.3	6.4	7.2	8.2	7.1	9.0	3.6
4. Most times	2.5	2.8	2.2	2.5	2.6	3.2	1.6	2.7	2.6	2.0	3.4	3.1	1.1	1.3	3.0	5.5
5. Always	1.7	2.3	1.2	1.6	2.2	2.2	0.8	1.9	2.2	1.1	3.0	0.9	2.2	2.5	1.7	4.5
Item 21960 Subject A02b,C07 N★	2234	1024	1162	1781	162	527	684	645	378	1430	749	815	435	382	531	41
E08G: Did someone get high on marijuana?																
1. Never	31.6	28.4	34.3	30.9	27.3	24.1	33.4	35.7	31.6	32.7	30.3	56.0	17.4	27.6	11.3	7.9
2. Seldom	14.1	15.3	13.1	13.6	14.3	14.8	12.8	16.9	10.8	15.5	11.4	16.1	17.0	13.0	11.2	1.6
3. Sometimes	21.6	23.7	19.9	22.3	22.1	26.0	20.9	19.2	20.6	23.0	18.6	14.4	32.7	24.4	20.6	26.2
4. Most times	16.9	16.6	16.8	17.6	12.2	17.5	17.9	15.8	15.9	15.1	19.8	7.6	16.7	20.8	27.4	21.0
5. Always	15.8	16.0	15.8	15.5	24.1	17.4	14.9	12.4	21.1	13.7	19.9	5.9	16.2	14.3	29.5	43.4
Item 21970 Subject A02b,C07 N★	2231	1018	1162	1779	162	522	688	644	377	1428	748	813	433	382	530	41
E08H: Did most people get high on marijuana?																
1. Never	39.6	38.4	41.2	39.9	34.2	34.0	40.5	46.2	34.8	43.2	34.0	66.6	27.4	32.8	16.2	9.6
2. Seldom	22.7	23.3	21.8	23.7	18.5	22.4	25.9	21.5	19.2	23.5	20.6	17.7	33.0	24.1	22.1	14.0
3. Sometimes	17.0	18.7	15.3	16.4	21.0	17.7	15.2	14.8	22.3	17.7	15.0	9.4	19.9	21.7	20.7	34.6
4. Most times	11.6	10.6	12.3	11.8	8.0	14.7	11.2	9.7	11.2	8.9	16.7	3.6	11.1	14.1	22.7	5.1
5. Always	9.1	8.9	9.3	8.1	18.3	11.1	7.2	7.7	12.1	6.8	13.6	2.8	8.6	7.2	18.3	36.7
Item 21980 Subject A02b,C07 N★	2231	1019	1161	1780	162	522	688	643	378	1428	748	811	433	382	532	41
E08I: Did you get high on marijuana?																
1. Never	65.8	62.8	68.7	64.4	75.5	60.1	66.9	70.3	63.9	69.4	59.6	97.5	58.9	59.5	31.3	27.2
2. Seldom	13.5	13.8	13.1	14.3	9.3	15.3	14.9	11.1	12.3	13.8	12.9	1.3	25.4	19.6	18.0	16.3
3. Sometimes	9.8	9.6	9.9	10.4	6.0	11.8	8.6	7.3	13.6	9.5	9.9	0.3	11.2	13.0	19.2	20.3
4. Most times	6.1	7.8	4.6	6.3	4.5	7.4	5.1	6.8	5.2	4.3	9.4	0.4	3.1	5.3	17.1	13.9
5. Always	4.8	6.1	3.7	4.6	4.7	5.4	4.5	4.4	5.0	3.0	8.2	0.4	1.5	2.6	14.4	22.3
Item 21990 Subject A05c,C07 N★	2239	1022	1166	1784	164	527	688	646	378	1436	749	821	433	381	533	41
E08J: Did you feel pressure to use marijuana?																
1. Never	84.1	79.4	87.8	84.3	82.7	84.4	85.1	83.4	82.9	86.1	80.0	89.4	83.1	82.6	78.1	78.6
2. Seldom	8.8	11.8	6.2	8.9	7.5	7.5	9.4	8.0	10.8	8.9	8.7	6.0	10.6	11.1	9.8	12.6
3. Sometimes	4.7	4.9	4.7	4.8	4.6	4.8	4.4	5.0	4.6	3.5	7.0	2.2	4.7	5.6	8.5	-
4. Most times	0.9	1.5	0.4	0.9	-	0.9	0.5	1.7	0.4	0.6	1.5	0.9	0.3	-	1.8	3.6
5. Always	1.5	2.3	0.9	1.1	5.2	2.3	0.6	2.0	1.3	1.0	2.8	1.6	1.3	0.8	1.8	5.2
Item 22000 Subject A02b,C07 N★	2238	1022	1165	1784	163	524	689	645	379	1435	750	818	433	383	533	41
E08K: Did someone get high on other drugs?																
1. Never	53.2	51.7	54.2	51.8	64.0	45.0	55.4	64.3	41.8	55.2	49.6	72.7	55.9	50.6	26.8	15.3
2. Seldom	18.0	19.5	16.9	19.6	8.8	20.8	18.8	15.3	17.1	17.8	18.3	13.1	20.6	22.4	20.1	11.5
3. Sometimes	17.3	17.2	17.3	17.3	14.5	20.3	17.4	12.0	22.1	16.7	18.2	9.7	14.8	17.7	29.3	30.7
4. Most times	5.9	6.4	5.6	6.2	4.7	6.8	5.0	4.1	9.4	5.5	6.7	2.8	4.3	4.4	13.1	11.1
5. Always	5.6	5.2	6.0	5.1	7.9	7.2	3.4	4.3	9.6	4.8	7.1	1.8	4.4	4.9	10.8	31.4
Item 22010 Subject A02b,C07 N★	2213	1008	1154	1767	160	518	685	635	374	1412	748	807	427	381	526	41
E08L: Did most people get high on other drugs?																
1. Never	59.3	58.7	59.7	60.0	58.1	54.3	60.9	68.8	46.9	62.9	52.7	77.9	64.3	56.3	33.7	11.0
2. Seldom	20.3	20.7	19.9	21.7	13.1	21.5	23.1	14.8	22.8	20.6	19.7	12.8	20.5	23.3	28.5	23.8
3. Sometimes	12.6	12.5	12.6	11.2	17.1	13.5	11.2	9.6	19.2	10.3	16.2	6.2	9.0	13.1	22.3	36.7
4. Most times	4.0	4.7	3.5	3.9	2.2	4.9	2.9	3.2	6.0	3.3	5.6	1.4	2.9	4.0	8.7	8.4
5. Always	3.8	3.3	4.3	3.1	9.4	5.8	1.9	3.6	5.0	2.9	5.8	1.6	3.3	3.2	6.9	20.1
Item 22020 Subject A02b,C07 N★	2218	1010	1157	1772	160	517	689	637	376	1416	748	808	428	383	529	41

★=excludes respondents for whom question was inappropriate.

QUESTIONNAIRE FORM 5 1986	TOTAL	SEX		RACE		REGION				4YR COLLEGE PLANS		ILLICIT DRUG USE: LIFETIME				
		M	F	White	Black	NE	NC	S	W	Yes	No	None	Marijuana Only	Few Pills	More Pills	Any Heroin
N (Weighted No. of Cases):	3073	1413	1550	2295	312	725	867	952	529	1839	1084	1237	583	487	648	47
% of Weighted Total:	100.0	46.0	50.4	74.7	10.2	23.6	28.2	31.0	17.2	59.9	35.3	40.3	19.0	15.8	21.1	1.5

E08M: Did you get high on other drugs?

	TOTAL	M	F	White	Black	NE	NC	S	W	Yes	No	None	Marijuana Only	Few Pills	More Pills	Any Heroin
1. Never	85.3	82.5	87.7	84.9	91.4	79.0	88.6	89.0	81.6	88.7	79.2	97.2	96.6	88.7	58.7	38.9
2. Seldom	6.4	7.7	5.6	6.7	3.6	8.4	5.4	4.4	9.2	5.6	8.1	1.0	1.4	7.3	17.3	19.7
3. Sometimes	5.2	5.8	4.6	5.3	2.9	8.6	3.7	3.8	5.9	3.9	7.5	1.0	1.3	3.2	16.1	12.4
4. Most times	2.0	2.6	1.4	2.0	1.3	2.2	1.5	2.1	2.4	1.2	3.5	0.8	0.5	-	5.2	17.7
5. Always	1.0	1.4	0.7	1.0	0.8	1.9	0.8	0.7	0.9	0.7	1.8	-	0.3	0.8	2.7	11.3
Item 22030 Subject A05c,C07 N★	2221	1011	1160	1773	163	516	688	640	377	1422	745	814	430	383	523	41

E08N: Did you feel pressure to use other drugs?

	TOTAL	M	F	White	Black	NE	NC	S	W	Yes	No	None	Marijuana Only	Few Pills	More Pills	Any Heroin
1. Never	89.1	85.3	92.5	89.5	87.0	88.2	89.1	90.0	88.6	92.0	83.2	93.2	93.1	88.7	80.3	81.9
2. Seldom	5.2	7.0	3.8	5.4	4.0	4.8	6.2	4.3	5.7	3.8	8.2	3.0	3.1	6.2	9.8	6.9
3. Sometimes	3.1	3.7	2.4	3.1	2.2	4.3	3.0	2.2	3.3	2.2	4.8	1.5	1.8	3.5	6.6	4.4
4. Most times	0.9	1.2	0.5	0.9	1.1	0.3	0.6	1.4	1.3	1.0	0.8	0.7	0.5	1.1	1.4	-
5. Always	1.7	2.7	0.8	1.2	5.7	2.4	1.1	2.1	1.1	1.0	3.1	1.6	1.4	0.6	1.9	6.8
Item 22040 Subject A02b,C07 N★	2224	1013	1161	1773	162	517	688	642	377	1427	745	815	429	383	526	41

E09: Now think about how you would LIKE parties to be. At the parties you go to, how often...

E09A: Would you like people over age 30 to be present at least some of the time?

	TOTAL	M	F	White	Black	NE	NC	S	W	Yes	No	None	Marijuana Only	Few Pills	More Pills	Any Heroin
1. Never	42.6	44.2	40.7	42.3	46.0	45.6	43.7	39.2	43.1	42.0	43.9	37.8	51.9	43.5	43.7	32.7
2. Seldom	27.4	27.2	27.8	28.3	23.8	27.4	30.0	27.4	22.7	29.2	24.1	27.2	29.6	27.8	26.0	20.1
3. Sometimes	23.3	22.3	24.2	22.9	21.3	20.9	21.7	25.1	25.7	22.9	23.9	25.8	15.7	24.9	24.0	26.6
4. Most times	3.6	2.6	4.4	3.5	3.9	2.8	2.6	4.3	5.0	3.5	3.9	5.2	1.5	1.5	3.9	4.3
5. Always	3.1	3.7	2.8	3.0	5.0	3.3	1.9	4.0	3.4	2.5	4.3	4.0	1.4	2.4	2.5	16.3
Item 22050 Subject C08,M02 N	2579	1164	1355	2033	203	567	769	793	451	1619	894	1054	472	423	554	44

E09B: Would you like to get high on alcohol?

	TOTAL	M	F	White	Black	NE	NC	S	W	Yes	No	None	Marijuana Only	Few Pills	More Pills	Any Heroin
1. Never	34.7	30.6	38.3	29.5	64.0	28.5	27.4	43.5	39.7	34.8	34.3	59.9	17.1	19.6	15.0	22.4
2. Seldom	17.3	14.7	19.7	17.4	14.0	17.4	18.2	16.2	17.5	17.3	17.2	15.2	22.5	22.6	13.9	10.5
3. Sometimes	27.5	29.6	25.7	30.3	12.9	32.0	31.8	22.7	23.1	29.0	25.1	18.2	36.5	35.2	30.6	35.1
4. Most times	12.3	14.2	10.6	13.8	3.6	13.0	14.7	10.5	10.7	12.1	12.7	4.8	14.4	14.5	22.5	15.2
5. Always	8.2	10.9	5.7	9.0	5.5	9.1	7.9	7.2	9.0	6.7	10.7	2.0	9.4	8.2	18.0	16.9
Item 22060 Subject A05c,C08 N	2561	1156	1348	2019	202	563	764	781	452	1609	889	1044	468	418	554	44

E09C: Would you like other people to get high on alcohol?

	TOTAL	M	F	White	Black	NE	NC	S	W	Yes	No	None	Marijuana Only	Few Pills	More Pills	Any Heroin
1. Never	34.7	30.4	38.4	29.6	64.4	28.2	27.6	44.2	38.2	34.2	35.2	57.0	19.2	23.4	15.7	17.4
2. Seldom	17.1	13.7	20.2	17.4	13.2	18.3	16.8	16.5	17.2	17.2	16.7	15.3	21.7	20.8	14.3	12.9
3. Sometimes	28.6	30.3	27.2	31.3	14.1	33.0	33.4	23.1	24.8	30.2	26.6	21.4	36.5	32.7	31.3	38.5
4. Most times	12.0	15.0	9.2	13.3	3.5	12.5	14.2	9.8	11.4	12.2	11.9	4.3	13.6	15.1	23.0	13.9
5. Always	7.6	10.6	5.1	8.4	4.9	8.0	8.1	6.3	8.4	6.3	9.7	2.0	9.0	8.0	15.8	17.3
Item 22070 Subject A11d,C08 N	2560	1153	1346	2014	203	562	763	785	449	1601	892	1049	465	423	547	43

E09D: Would you like to use marijuana?

	TOTAL	M	F	White	Black	NE	NC	S	W	Yes	No	None	Marijuana Only	Few Pills	More Pills	Any Heroin
1. Never	69.6	66.6	72.5	68.3	76.0	61.5	69.2	74.6	71.3	71.7	65.9	96.2	59.9	63.1	36.5	32.1
2. Seldom	12.0	11.7	12.4	12.5	7.3	15.5	12.4	9.3	11.8	12.3	12.2	2.5	21.3	16.9	18.5	15.5
3. Sometimes	9.6	11.2	7.9	9.8	8.4	11.4	9.3	8.0	10.7	9.3	9.6	0.7	13.0	12.2	18.6	30.1
4. Most times	4.9	5.4	4.4	5.4	2.6	5.9	5.1	5.0	3.1	4.2	6.2	0.6	2.8	4.7	14.3	13.6
5. Always	3.9	5.1	2.8	4.0	5.7	5.6	4.0	3.1	3.1	2.5	6.0	0.1	3.0	3.1	12.1	8.6
Item 22080 Subject A05c,C08 N	2565	1158	1346	2023	201	563	765	788	448	1608	894	1051	464	422	551	42

E09E: Would you like other people to use marijuana?

	TOTAL	M	F	White	Black	NE	NC	S	W	Yes	No	None	Marijuana Only	Few Pills	More Pills	Any Heroin
1. Never	66.9	64.5	69.2	65.3	76.4	59.1	65.8	74.6	65.3	68.7	64.0	92.8	57.1	60.9	35.2	22.8
2. Seldom	13.4	13.2	13.6	14.1	9.8	15.5	14.4	10.0	15.0	13.6	13.3	4.1	21.6	18.7	19.0	18.8
3. Sometimes	12.1	13.4	10.8	12.5	6.9	14.6	12.1	8.7	14.9	12.0	12.3	2.1	15.9	13.8	23.9	39.0
4. Most times	4.6	5.6	3.7	5.0	2.6	6.7	4.1	4.5	2.9	3.6	6.3	0.7	2.6	4.6	13.1	12.6
5. Always	3.0	3.3	2.7	3.1	4.3	4.1	3.6	2.2	1.9	2.2	4.1	0.2	2.7	2.1	8.8	6.7
Item 22090 Subject A11d,C08 N	2555	1151	1344	2012	201	561	760	786	448	1601	889	1050	462	422	544	43

★=excludes respondents for whom question was inappropriate.

QUESTIONNAIRE FORM 5 1986	TOTAL	SEX		RACE		REGION				4YR COLLEGE PLANS		ILLICIT DRUG USE: LIFETIME				
		M	F	White	Black	NE	NC	S	W	Yes	No	None	Mari- juana Only	Few Pills	More Pills	Any Her- oin
N (Weighted No. of Cases):	3073	1413	1550	2295	312	725	867	952	529	1839	1084	1237	583	487	648	47
% of Weighted Total:	100.0	46.0	50.4	74.7	10.2	23.6	28.2	31.0	17.2	59.9	35.3	40.3	19.0	15.8	21.1	1.5
E09F: Would you like to use other drugs?																
1. Never	85.4	82.5	88.0	85.1	89.9	79.7	87.0	89.4	82.9	88.3	80.5	96.8	92.8	87.1	58.6	50.6
2. Seldom	6.5	7.3	5.8	6.2	6.9	9.2	5.3	5.0	7.9	5.4	8.6	1.5	3.3	7.9	17.2	13.2
3. Sometimes	5.6	7.2	4.4	6.1	2.1	7.6	5.8	3.7	6.1	4.4	7.5	1.1	2.7	4.7	16.6	18.1
4. Most times	1.5	1.5	1.4	1.6	1.0	2.0	1.3	1.1	1.9	1.4	1.6	0.6	0.5	0.3	4.4	9.0
5. Always	1.0	1.5	0.4	1.0	-	1.6	0.6	0.8	1.3	0.5	1.8	-	0.7	-	3.1	9.1
Item 22100 Subject A05c,C08 N	2566	1161	1344	2021	201	562	765	788	450	1607	893	1052	465	424	549	43
E09G: Would you like other people to use other drugs?																
1. Never	83.5	80.1	86.1	83.3	87.3	78.2	84.3	88.3	80.1	85.4	79.9	95.3	89.9	83.5	57.6	44.1
2. Seldom	6.9	6.7	7.2	6.8	6.2	8.4	7.4	4.6	8.4	6.8	7.5	1.9	3.8	9.1	17.0	17.7
3. Sometimes	7.3	9.7	5.5	7.4	5.5	10.5	6.2	5.4	8.6	6.2	9.0	1.8	5.2	6.2	19.9	24.5
4. Most times	1.3	2.0	0.8	1.4	0.4	1.3	1.2	1.1	2.0	1.0	1.9	0.9	0.3	0.2	3.7	5.4
5. Always	1.0	1.5	0.4	1.0	0.5	1.6	1.0	0.6	0.9	0.6	1.6	0.2	0.8	1.0	1.8	8.3
Item 22110 Subject A11d,C08 N	2547	1148	1339	2003	202	559	757	786	445	1599	884	1050	460	422	539	43
E10: If you had ever used marijuana or hashish, do you think that you would have said so in this questionnaire?																
1. No	6.5	8.2	4.8	4.5	17.2	6.5	7.1	7.2	4.6	4.9	9.2	8.8	5.9	5.4	3.1	9.8
2. Not sure	6.5	6.3	6.5	6.0	9.4	6.4	5.4	6.9	7.8	6.8	6.2	10.7	3.3	4.9	3.0	3.7
3. Yes	55.1	54.9	55.4	55.3	56.8	49.1	53.8	60.9	54.6	57.6	51.3	77.0	43.4	46.6	32.5	33.4
4. I did say so	31.9	30.6	33.3	34.3	16.6	38.0	33.7	25.0	32.9	30.7	33.4	3.5	47.4	43.1	61.4	53.0
Item 20800 Subject A15a N	2552	1149	1344	2010	201	564	758	786	444	1598	891	1036	470	419	549	45
E11: If you had ever used amphetamines (without a doctor's orders), do you think that you would have said so in this questionnaire?																
1. No	8.7	11.1	6.4	6.8	20.8	9.8	8.6	8.9	7.3	6.3	12.8	8.8	10.5	8.5	5.3	17.8
2. Not sure	7.1	7.1	7.1	6.9	9.8	6.0	7.4	7.8	6.9	7.7	6.4	10.8	4.1	4.9	4.9	6.7
3. Yes	67.7	66.6	68.5	68.2	62.4	67.3	65.7	69.2	69.1	70.6	63.1	76.9	75.6	66.5	48.2	29.3
4. I did say so	16.4	15.2	18.0	18.1	6.9	16.9	18.3	14.1	16.7	15.5	17.7	3.5	9.9	20.1	41.5	46.2
Item 20810 Subject A15a N	2541	1141	1340	2004	198	563	754	780	443	1592	885	1030	469	419	548	43
E12: If you had ever used heroin, do you think that you would have said so in this questionnaire?																
1. No	10.0	11.9	7.8	8.0	21.7	11.6	9.5	10.2	8.6	7.5	14.1	9.1	11.4	9.4	9.2	3.8
2. Not sure	8.9	8.7	9.2	8.7	10.4	8.4	9.4	8.2	9.8	10.2	6.6	11.9	5.5	8.8	5.8	16.2
3. Yes	71.9	70.2	73.5	73.7	62.6	68.4	70.3	75.4	73.2	74.0	69.0	75.7	74.5	72.3	68.4	18.6
4. I did say so	9.2	9.2	9.5	9.6	5.4	11.6	10.9	6.3	8.5	8.3	10.2	3.3	8.6	9.5	16.5	61.4
Item 20820 Subject A15a N	2546	1146	1341	2008	199	563	759	780	444	1594	888	1031	469	420	550	43

Cross-Time Index of Questionnaire Items, 1975-1986

Introduction to the Indexing Conventions

Beginning with the 1982 volume, the cross-time index of question locations is organized first by subject area (see Table 3 for complete listing). Within each subject area, questions are listed in numerical sequence according to item reference number, which is the unique numerical identifier assigned to each question in the study.

The Question Index may be used in two major ways:

1. **Locating a Question Across Years.** Having located a question of interest in the Descriptive Results section, the reader may determine in what other years that same question has appeared by simply looking it up by subject area and item reference number. The Index will show all years in which that item has appeared and also show its location each year (by questionnaire form, section, and item number). All items will retain their unique reference numbers in future years as well, and thus may be located in exactly the same way in subsequent volumes in this series.

EXAMPLE: A reader interested in a particular item about the nation needing more long-range planning would note that it has been classified under subject area I01 ("Expectations concerning social change") and that it has been assigned item reference number 1200. The index entry for item 1200 shows that this item has appeared in Section A of questionnaire Form 1 in all annual surveys in the series. Its question number was 4A in 1975 and 2A thereafter.

2. **Locating Questions by Subject Area.** Given an interest in some particular subject area, one can quickly scan the Index to locate all questions dealing with that area. Table 3 lists all the subject areas into which items are classified, along with the alphanumeric code assigned to each area.

EXAMPLE: A reader interested in items dealing with religion should first locate the relevant code in Table 3: Code G, "Religion." The second step is to scan that section of the item index, noting for every item its item reference number and page location in this volume. The reader may or may not find the abbreviated description of the item (given in the third column of the index and further described below) helpful in deciding whether to look up a particular item in the Descriptive Results section. Some of these descriptions are rather clear as to their meaning, but others are less so.

Definition of the Column Headings

The definitions of column headings, and the conventions used for the entries in each column, are given below under the numbers indicated in the following key.

①**Item Reference Number.** A unique identification number is assigned to each question for the duration of this research and reporting series. It appears below that question in the Descriptive Results section, as well as in this index and the indices of all other volumes in this series.

②**Page Location.** The second column of the Question Index gives the page number of the present volume on which a verbatim statement of the question may be found along with this year's descriptive results.

③**Item Description (Abbreviated).** This is a brief mnemonic description — up to 16 characters in length — that attempts to characterize the content of the question. Originally developed for question identification on OSIRIS computer files, it may in many cases allow one to determine the relevance of the question to one's own interest and thus reduce the number of irrelevant questions that must be looked up in the Descriptive Results section.

④ **Questionnaire Location by Year.** An entry is provided for every year in which an item appeared in one of the study's questionnaire forms. The six (or fewer) characters comprising the entry indicate the form in which the question appeared, the section of that form, and the question number. Take as an example the questionnaire location 1A004A. This location code indicates that the question appeared in Form 1, Section A, and was labeled as Question 4a.

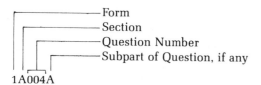

Occasionally an entry will be enclosed in parentheses. This indicates that there was a change (usually minor) in the wording of the question and/or the answer alternatives in subsequent years.

A form number (ranging from 1 to 5) is usually shown in the first character location. However, two substitute characters will replace the form number at times:

+ A plus sign indicates that the item appeared in all five forms that year and that it appeared in the same location on all forms.
* An asterisk indicates that the item appeared in four forms (Forms 2 through 5) and in the same location on all forms.

⑤ **Subject Area.** Table 3 shows the subject content areas that have been distinguished here and gives the alphanumeric code assigned to each of them. Every question item in the index has been classified into (and listed under) one or more of the subject areas, and the index (beginning with the 1982 volume) has been organized by subject area.

Figure 2

Guide to Cross-Time Index

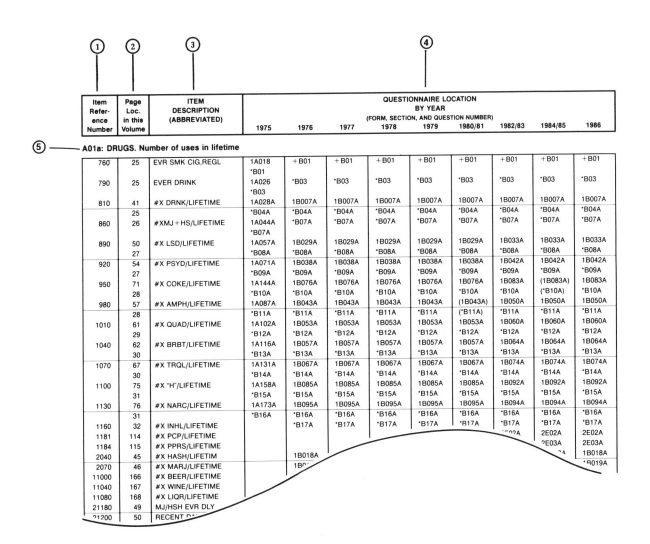

① Item Refer- ence Number	② Page Loc. in this Volume	③ ITEM DESCRIPTION (ABBREVIATED)	④ QUESTIONNAIRE LOCATION BY YEAR (FORM, SECTION, AND QUESTION NUMBER)								
			1975	1976	1977	1978	1979	1980/81	1982/83	1984/85	1986
⑤ A01a: DRUGS. Number of uses in lifetime											
760	25	EVR SMK CIG,REGL	1A018 *B01	+B01	+B01	+B01	+B01	+B01	+B01	+B01	+B01
790	25	EVER DRINK	1A026 *B03	*B03	*B03	*B03	*B03	*B03	*B03	*B03	*B03
810	41	#X DRNK/LIFETIME	1A028A	1B007A	1B007A	1B007A	1B007A	1B007A	1B007A	1B007A	1B007A
	25		*B04A	*B04A	*B04A	*B04A	*B04A	*B04A	*B04A	*B04A	*B04A
860	26	#XMJ+HS/LIFETIME	1A044A *B07A	*B07A	*B07A	*B07A	*B07A	*B07A	*B07A	*B07A	*B07A
890	50	#X LSD/LIFETIME	1A057A	1B029A	1B029A	1B029A	1B029A	1B029A	1B033A	1B033A	1B033A
	27		*B08A	*B08A	*B08A	*B08A	*B08A	*B08A	*B08A	*B08A	*B08A
920	54	#X PSYD/LIFETIME	1A071A	1B038A	1B038A	1B038A	1B038A	1B038A	1B042A	1B042A	1B042A
	27		*B09A	*B09A	*B09A	*B09A	*B09A	*B09A	*B09A	*B09A	*B09A
950	71	#X COKE/LIFETIME	1A144A	1B076A	1B076A	1B076A	1B076A	1B076A	1B083A	(1B083A)	1B083A
	28		*B10A	*B10A	*B10A	*B10A	*B10A	*B10A	*B10A	(*B10A)	*B10A
980	57	#X AMPH/LIFETIME	1A087A	1B043A	1B043A	1B043A	1B043A	(1B043A)	1B050A	1B050A	1B050A
	28		*B11A	*B11A	*B11A	*B11A	*B11A	(*B11A)	*B11A	*B11A	*B11A
1010	61	#X QUAD/LIFETIME	1A102A	1B053A	1B053A	1B053A	1B053A	1B053A	1B060A	1B060A	1B060A
	29		*B12A	*B12A	*B12A	*B12A	*B12A	*B12A	*B12A	*B12A	*B12A
1040	62	#X BRBT/LIFETIME	1A116A	1B057A	1B057A	1B057A	1B057A	1B057A	1B064A	1B064A	1B064A
	30		*B13A	*B13A	*B13A	*B13A	*B13A	*B13A	*B13A	*B13A	*B13A
1070	67	#X TRQL/LIFETIME	1A131A	1B067A	1B067A	1B067A	1B067A	1B067A	1B074A	1B074A	1B074A
	30		*B14A	*B14A	*B14A	*B14A	*B14A	*B14A	*B14A	*B14A	*B14A
1100	75	#X "H"/LIFETIME	1A158A	1B085A	1B085A	1B085A	1B085A	1B085A	1B092A	1B092A	1B092A
	31		*B15A	*B15A	*B15A	*B15A	*B15A	*B15A	*B15A	*B15A	*B15A
1130	76	#X NARC/LIFETIME	1A173A	1B095A	1B095A	1B095A	1B095A	1B095A	1B094A	1B094A	1B094A
	31		*B16A	*B16A	*B16A	*B16A	*B16A	*B16A	*B16A	*B16A	*B16A
1160	32	#X INHL/LIFETIME		*B17A	*B17A	*B17A	*B17A	*B17A	*B17A	*B17A	*B17A
1181	114	#X PCP/LIFETIME							?E02A	2E02A	2E02A
1184	115	#X PPRS/LIFETIME							?E03A	2E03A	2E03A
2040	45	#X HASH/LIFETIM		1B018A							1B018A
2070	46	#X MARJ/LIFETIME		1B0...							*B019A
11000	166	#X BEER/LIFETIME									
11040	167	#X WINE/LIFETIME									
11080	168	#X LIQR/LIFETIME									
21180	49	MJ/HSH EVR DLY									
21200	50	RECENT D...									

Table 3

Subject Area Key
(Referenced by letter in the Question Index)

A. **Drugs.** Drug use and related attitudes and beliefs, drug availabilty and exposure, surrounding conditions and social meaning of drug use. Views of significant others regarding drugs.

A01   Use of Various Licit and Illicit Drugs
    A01a — . . . in lifetime
    A01b — . . . in the last 12 months
    A01c — . . . in the last 30 days
    A01d —Quantity used
    A01e —How high? (How often?)
    A01f —How long high?
    A01g —Incidence of first use
    A01h —Use with other drugs
    A01i —Try to stop?
    A01j —Use on doctor's orders?
    A01k —Bad trip?
    A01l —Kinds of drugs

A02   Exposure to Drug Use
    A02a —Friends' use of drugs
    A02b —Exposure to users

A03   Availability of Drugs

A04   Expected Future Use

A05   Conditions of Use
    A05a —Alone
    A05b —With others
    A05c —Settings
    A05d —Mode of drug administration

A06   Reasons for Use, Abstention, and Stopping

A07   Drug Problems
    A07a —Driving, tickets, and accidents after use
    A07b —Other problems

A08   Sources of Help regarding Drugs

A09   Parental Awareness of Use

A10   Drug Education and Communication
    A10a —In school

A11   Own Attitudes regarding Drugs and Drug Users
    A11a —For adults
    A11b —For own children
    A11c —Perception of drug users
    A11d —Use by high school age people

A12   Others' Attitudes regarding Drugs and Drug Users
    A12a —Parents
    A12b —Friends and students
    A12c —Perception of drug users

A13   Legal Issues regarding Drugs
    A13a —Preferred legality for adults
    A13b —Own response to legalization
    A13c —Knowledge of marijuana laws

A14   Risk of Drug Harm
    A14a —To self
    A14b —To others

A15   Admitting Use in Questionnaire

A16   Parent Groups

B. **Education.**

B01   High school: scholastic status, objectives, experiences

B02   Combining work and school: attitudes, experiences

B03   Interracial contact at school

B04   Student norms

B05   Counseling

B06   Absenteeism and truancy

B07   Delinquency and victimization at school

B08   Opinions regarding competency testing

B09   Post high school: status, plans, characteristics

B10   Attitudes regarding educational institutions

Table 3 (continued)

C. Work and Leisure.

C01   Present or recent work experience

C02   Income sources; financial security

C03   Vocational plans, aspirations, expectations

C04   Preferences regarding job characteristics

C05   Desirability of different working arrangements and settings

C06   Work ethic/success orientation

C07   Leisure time: extent, activities

C08   Attitudes toward leisure time

D. Sex Roles and Family.

D01   Dating and marriage: status, attitudes, expectations

D02   Parenthood: status, attitudes, expectations

D03   Values surrounding marriage and family

D04   Preferences regarding marital/familial arrangements

D05   Sex role attitudes

D06   Opinions regarding sex discrimination

E. Population Concerns.

E01   Overpopulation

E02   Birth control

F. Conservation, Materialism, Equity, etc.

F01   Personal materialism

F02   Societal materialism and advertising

F03   Concern with world hunger and poverty

F04   Ecological concerns

F05   Concern with conservation of resources

F06   Preferences regarding dwelling type and urbanicity

F07   Driving and use of mass transit

G. Religion.   **Religious preferences, activities, views.**

H. Politics.

H01   Political interest and preferences

H02   Attitudes toward governmental policies and practices

H03   Views about the role of citizens in government. (See also I02: Attitudes regarding activism)

H04   Confidence in government

H05   Voting, political activism

I. Social Change.

I01   Expectations concerning societal change

I02   Attitudes regarding activism

I03   Reactions to personal and social change

J. Social Problems. Interest and concerns.

K. Major Social Institutions.

K01   Trust (See also C05: Institutions as work settings)

K02   Satisfaction with performance

K03   Preferred influence

L. Military.

L01   Plans for military service

L02   Attitudes toward a draft

Table 3 (continued)

L03 Views about the use of military force

L04 Attitudes toward the military as an institution and occupation

M. Interpersonal Relationships.

M01 Dating

M02 Cross-age relationships with adults outside the family (See also B05)

M03 Agreement/disagreement with parents

M04 Friendships (See also Q03: Loneliness)

M05 Community at large

N. Race Relations.

N01 Preferred interracial contact

N02 Attitudes about discrimination

N03 Actual interracial contacts

O. Concern for Others.

O01 Attitudes regarding social service, charitable activism

O02 Involvement in community, altruistic activities

O03 Concern with the problems of others

P. Happiness.

P01 Happiness; satisfaction with life and self

P02 Satisfaction with specific life domains

Q. Other Personality Variables.

Q01 Attitudes about self, self-esteem

Q02 Locus of control

Q03 Loneliness

Q04 Risk taking

Q05 Trust in others

Q06 (Changed to Subject Areas T01-T04.)

Q07 Importance placed on various life goals

Q08 Social, political, cultural orientation

Q09 Hostility

R. Background.

R01 Age, sex, race, and marital status

R02 Family characteristics

R03 Living arrangements and household characteristics

S. Deviance and Victimization.

S01 Delinquent behaviors

S02 Driving violations and accidents

S03 Victimization experiences

T. Health.

T01 Symptoms

T02 Habits

T03 Height and weight

T04 Medical treatment

Item Reference Number	Page Loc. in this Volume	Item Description (Abbreviated)	1975	1976	1977	1978	1979	1980/81	1982/83	1984/85	1986

A01a: DRUGS. Number of uses in lifetime

Item Ref. No.	Page Loc.	Item Description	1975	1976	1977	1978	1979	1980/81	1982/83	1984/85	1986
760	25	EVR SMK CIG,REGL	1A018 *B01	+B01	+B01	+B01	+B01	+B01	+B01	+B01	+B01
790	25	EVER DRINK	1A026 *B03	*B03	*B03	*B03	*B03	*B03	*B03	*B03	*B03
810	41	#X DRNK/LIFETIME	1A028A	1B007A	1B007A	1B007A	1B007A	1B007A	1B007A	1B007A	1B007A
	25			*B04A	*B04A	*B04A	*B04A	*B04A	*B04A	*B04A	*B04A
860	26	#XMJ+HS/LIFETIME	1A044A *B07A	*B07A	*B07A	*B07A	*B07A	*B07A	*B07A	*B07A	*B07A
890	50	#X LSD/LIFETIME	1A057A	1B029A	1B029A	1B029A	1B029A	1B029A	1B033A	1B033A	1B033A
	27			*B08A	*B08A	*B08A	*B08A	*B08A	*B08A	*B08A	*B08A
920	54	#X PSYD/LIFETIME	1A071A	1B038A	1B038A	1B038A	1B038A	1B038A	1B042A	1B042A	1B042A
	27			*B09A	*B09A	*B09A	*B09A	*B09A	*B09A	*B09A	*B09A
950	71	#X COKE/LIFETIME	1A144A	1B076A	1B076A	1B076A	1B076A	1B076A	1B083A	(1B083A)	1B083A
	28			*B10A	*B10A	*B10A	*B10A	*B10A	*B10A	(*B10A)	*B10A
980	57	#X AMPH/LIFETIME	1A087A	1B043A	1B043A	1B043A	1B043A	(1B043A)	1B050A	1B050A	1B050A
	28			*B11A	*B11A	*B11A	*B11A	(*B11A)	*B11A	*B11A	*B11A
1010	61	#X QUAD/LIFETIME	1A102A	1B053A	1B053A	1B053A	1B053A	1B053A	1B060A	1B060A	1B060A
	29			*B12A	*B12A	*B12A	*B12A	*B12A	*B12A	*B12A	*B12A
1040	62	#X BRBT/LIFETIME	1A116A	1B057A	1B057A	1B057A	1B057A	1B057A	1B064A	1B064A	1B064A
	30			*B13A	*B13A	*B13A	*B13A	*B13A	*B13A	*B13A	*B13A
1070	67	#X TRQL/LIFETIME	1A131A	1B067A	1B067A	1B067A	1B067A	1B067A	1B074A	1B074A	1B074A
	30			*B14A	*B14A	*B14A	*B14A	*B14A	*B14A	*B14A	*B14A
1100	75	#X "H"/LIFETIME	1A158A	1B085A	1B085A	1B085A	1B085A	1B085A	1B092A	1B092A	1B092A
	31			*B15A	*B15A	*B15A	*B15A	*B15A	*B15A	*B15A	*B15A
1130	76	#X NARC/LIFETIME	1A173A	1B095A	1B095A	1B095A	1B095A	1B095A	1B094A	1B094A	1B094A
	31			*B16A	*B16A	*B16A	*B16A	*B16A	*B16A	*B16A	*B16A
1160	32	#X INHL/LIFETIME		*B17A	*B17A	*B17A	*B17A	*B17A	*B17A	*B17A	*B17A
1181	114	#X PCP/LIFETIME					2E02A	2E02A	2E02A	2E02A	2E02A
1184	115	#X PPRS/LIFETIME					2E03A	2E03A	2E03A	2E03A	2E03A
2040	45	#X HASH/LIFETIM		1B018A	1B018A	1B018A	1B018A	1B018A	1B018A	1B018A	1B018A
2070	46	#X MARJ/LIFETIME		1B019A	1B019A	1B019A	1B019A	1B019A	1B019A	1B019A	1B019A
11000	166	#X BEER/LIFETIME		4D04A	4D04A	4D04A	4D04A	4D04A	4D11A	4D11A	4D11A
11040	167	#X WINE/LIFETIME		4D06A	4D06A	4D06A	4D06A	4D06A	4D13A	4D13A	4D13A
11080	168	#X LIQR/LIFETIME		4D08A	4D08A	4D08A	4D08A	4D08A	4D15A	4D15A	4D15A
21180	49	MJ/HSH EVR DLY							1B028	1B028	1B028
21200	50	RECENT DAILY MJ							1B030	1B030	1B030
21210	50	#X DAILY MJ/LFT							1B031	1B031	1B031
21220	55	#X DIETPILL/LFT							1B046A	1B046A	1B046A
21250	55	#X STA-AWAK/LFT							1B047A	1B047A	1B047A
21280	56	#X LOOKALIK/LFT							1B048A	1B048A	1B048A
22230	139	EVR USE SMOKELESS									3E01A

A01b: DRUGS. Number of uses in last 12 months

Item Ref. No.	Page Loc.	Item Description	1975	1976	1977	1978	1979	1980/81	1982/83	1984/85	1986
820	42	#X DRNK/LAST12MO	1A028B	1B007B	1B007B	1B007B	1B007B	1B007B	1B007B	1B007B	1B007B
	25			*B04B	*B04B	*B04B	*B04B	*B04B	*B04B	*B04B	*B04B
870	26	#XMJ+HS/LAST12MO	1A044B *B07B	*B07B	*B07B	*B07B	*B07B	*B07B	*B07B	*B07B	*B07B
900	50	#X LSD/LAST 12MO	1A057B	1B029B	1B029B	1B029B	1B029B	1B029B	1B033B	1B033B	1B033B
	27			*B08B	*B08B	*B08B	*B08B	*B08B	*B08B	*B08B	*B08B
930	54	#X PSYD/LAST12MO	1A071B	1B038B	1B038B	1B038B	1B038B	1B038B	1B042B	1B042B	1B042B
	27			*B09B	*B09B	*B09B	*B09B	*B09B	*B09B	*B09B	*B09B
960	71	#X COKE/LAST12MO	1A144B	1B076B	1B076B	1B076B	1B076B	1B076B	1B083B	(1B083B)	1B083B
	28			*B10B	*B10B	*B10B	*B10B	*B10B	*B10B	(*B10B)	*B10B
990	57	#X AMPH/LAST12MO	1A087B	1B043B	1B043B	1B043B	1B043B	(1B043B)	1B050B	1B050B	1B050B
	29			*B11B	*B11B	*B11B	*B11B	(*B11B)	*B11B	*B11B	*B11B
1020	61	#X QUAD/LAST12MO	1A102B	1B053B	1B053B	1B053B	1B053B	1B053B	1B060B	1B060B	1B060B
	29			*B12B	*B12B	*B12B	*B12B	*B12B	*B12B	*B12B	*B12B
1050	62	#X BRBT/LAST12MO	1A116B	1B057B	1B057B	1B057B	1B057B	1B057B	1B064B	1B064B	1B064B
	30			*B13B	*B13B	*B13B	*B13B	*B13B	*B13B	*B13B	*B13B
1080	67	#X TRQL/LAST12MO	1A131B	1B067B	1B067B	1B067B	1B067B	1B067B	1B074B	1B074B	1B074B
	30			*B14B	*B14B	*B14B	*B14B	*B14B	*B14B	*B14B	*B14B
1110	75	#X "H"/LAST 12MO	1A158B	1B085B	1B085B	1B085B	1B085B	1B085B	1B092B	1B092B	1B092B

(continued)

Item Reference Number	Page Loc. in this Volume	ITEM DESCRIPTION (ABBREVIATED)	QUESTIONNAIRE LOCATION BY YEAR (FORM, SECTION, AND QUESTION NUMBER)								
			1975	1976	1977	1978	1979	1980/81	1982/83	1984/85	1986

A01b: DRUGS. Number of uses in last 12 months *(continued)*

Item Ref	Page	Item Description	1975	1976	1977	1978	1979	1980/81	1982/83	1984/85	1986
	31		*B15B	*B15B	*B15B	*B15B	*B15B	*B15B	*B15B	*B15B	*B15B
1140	76	#X NARC/LAST12MO	1A173B	1B095B	1B095B	1B095B	1B095B	1B095B	1B094B	1B094B	1B094B
	31		*B16B	*B16B	*B16B	*B16B	*B16B	*B16B	*B16B	*B16B	*B16B
1170	32	#X INHL/LAST12MO		*B17B	*B17B	*B17B	*B17B	*B17B	*B17B	*B17B	*B17B
1182	115	#X PCP/LAST12MO					2E02B	2E02B	2E02B	2E02B	2E02B
1185	115	#X PPRS/LAST12MO					2E03B	2E03B	2E03B	2E03B	2E03B
2050	46	#X HASH/LAST12M		1B018B	1B018B	1B018B	1B018B	1B018B	1B018B	1B018B	1B018B
2080	46	#X MARJ/LAST12MO		1B019B	1B019B	1B019B	1B019B	1B019B	1B019B	1B019B	1B019B
8520	131	12MO,#OCC PAINRF	3A48A	3A27A	3A27A	3A27A	3A27A	3A27A	3A27A	(3A27A)	3A27A
8530	132	12MO,#OCC SLP PL	3A48B	3A27B	3A27B	3A27B	3A27B	3A27B	3A27B	3A27B	3A27B
8540	132	12MO,#OCC AWK PL	3A48C	3A27C	3A27C	3A27C	3A27C	3A27C	3A27C	3A27C	3A27C
8550	132	12MO,#OCC CALM P	3A48D	3A27D	3A27D	3A27D	3A27D	3A27D	3A27D	3A27D	3A27D
11010	167	#X BEER/LAST12MO		4D04B	4D04B	4D04B	4D04B	4D04B	4D11B	4D11B	4D11B
11050	167	#X WINE/LAST12MO		4D06B	4D06B	4D06B	4D06B	4D06B	4D13B	4D13B	4D13B
11090	168	#X LIQR/LAST12MO		4D08B	4D08B	4D08B	4D08B	4D08B	4D15B	4D15B	4D15B
21230	55	#X DIETPILL/12M							1B046B	1B046B	1B046B
21260	56	#X STA-AWAK/12M							1B047B	1B047B	1B047B
21290	56	#X LOOKALIK/12M							1B048B	1B048B	1B048B

A01c: DRUGS. Number of uses in last 30 days

Item Ref	Page	Item Description	1975	1976	1977	1978	1979	1980/81	1982/83	1984/85	1986
780	41	#CIGS SMKD/30DAY	1A020	1B003	1B003	1B003	1B003	1B003	1B003	1B003	1B003
	25		*B02	*B02	*B02	*B02	*B02	*B02	*B02	*B02	*B02
830	42	#X DRNK/LAST30DA	1A028C	1B007C	1B007C	1B007C	1B007C	1B007C	1B007C	1B007C	1B007C
	25		*B04C	*B04C	*B04C	*B04C	*B04C	*B04C	*B04C	*B04C	*B04C
880	27	#XMJ+HS/LAST30DA	1A044C	*B07C	*B07C	*B07C	*B07C	*B07C	*B07C	*B07C	*B07C
			*B07C								
910	51	#X LSD/LAST 30DA	1A057C	1B029C	1B029C	1B029C	1B029C	1B029C	1B033C	1B033C	1B033C
	27		*B08C	*B08C	*B08C	*B08C	*B08C	*B08C	*B08C	*B08C	*B08C
940	54	#X PSYD/LAST30DA	1A071C	1B038C	1B038C	1B038C	1B038C	1B038C	1B042C	1B042C	1B042C
	28		*B09C	*B09C	*B09C	*B09C	*B09C	*B09C	*B09C	*B09C	*B09C
970	71	#X COKE/LAST30DA	1A144C	1B076C	1B076C	1B076C	1B076C	1B076C	1B083C	(1B083C)	1B083C
	28		*B10C	*B10C	*B10C	*B10C	*B10C	*B10C	*B10C	(*B10C)	*B10C
1000	57	#X AMPH/LAST30DA	1A087C	1B043C	1B043C	1B043C	1B043C	(1B043C)	1B050C	1B050C	1B050C
	29		*B11C	*B11C	*B11C	*B11C	*B11C	(*B11C)	*B11C	*B11C	*B11C
1030	61	#X QUAD/LAST30DA	1A102C	1B053C	1B053C	1B053C	1B053C	1B053C	1B060C	1B060C	1B060C
	29		*B12C	*B12C	*B12C	*B12C	*B12C	*B12C	*B12C	*B12C	*B12C
1060	63	#X BRBT/LAST30DA	1A116C	1B057C	1B057C	1B057C	1B057C	1B057C	1B064C	1B064C	1B064C
	30		*B13C	*B13C	*B13C	*B13C	*B13C	*B13C	*B13C	*B13C	*B13C
1090	67	#X TRQL/LAST30DA	1A131C	1B067C	1B067C	1B067C	1B067C	1B067C	1B074C	1B074C	1B074C
	30		*B14C	*B14C	*B14C	*B14C	*B14C	*B14C	*B14C	*B14C	*B14C
1120	75	#X "H"/LAST 30DA	1A158C	1B085C	1B085C	1B085C	1B085C	1B085C	1B092C	1B092C	1B092C
	31		*B15C	*B15C	*B15C	*B15C	*B15C	*B15C	*B15C	*B15C	*B15C
1150	76	#X NARC/LAST30DA	1A173C	1B095C	1B095C	1B095C	1B095C	1B095C	1B094C	1B094C	1B094C
	32		*B16C	*B16C	*B16C	*B16C	*B16C	*B16C	*B16C	*B16C	*B16C
1180	32	#X INHL/LAST30DA		*B17C	*B17C	*B17C	*B17C	*B17C	*B17C	*B17C	*B17C
1183	115	#X PCP/LAST30DA					2E02C	2E02C	2E02C	2E02C	2E02C
1186	115	#X PPRS/LAST30DA					2E03C	2E03C	2E03C	2E03C	2E03C
2060	46	#X HASH/LAST30D		1B018C	1B018C	1B018C	1B018C	1B018C	1B018C	1B018C	1B018C
2090	46	#X MARJ/LAST30DA		1B019C	1B019C	1B019C	1B019C	1B019C	1B019C	1B019C	1B019C
11020	167	#X BEER/LAST30DA		4D04C	4D04C	4D04C	4D04C	4D04C	4D11C	4D11C	4D11C
11060	167	#X WINE/LAST30DA		4D06C	4D06C	4D06C	4D06C	4D06C	4D13C	4D13C	4D13C
11100	168	#X LIQR/LAST30DA		4D08C	4D08C	4D08C	4D08C	4D08C	4D15C	4D15C	4D15C
21240	55	#X DIETPILL/30D							1B046C	1B046C	1B046C
21270	56	#X STA-AWAK/30D							1B047C	1B047C	1B047C
21300	56	#X LOOKALIK/30D							1B048C	1B048C	1B048C
22240	139	#X SMKLESS/30 DA									3E01B

A01d: DRUGS. Quantity used

Item Ref	Page	Item Description	1975	1976	1977	1978	1979	1980/81	1982/83	1984/85	1986
850	44	5+DRK ROW/LST 2W	1A035	1B012	1B012	1B012	1B012	1B012	1B012	1B012	1B012
	26		*B06	*B06	*B06	*B06	*B06	*B06	*B06	*B06	*B06
1990	44	#X/2W,3-4 DR RW	1A036	1B013	1B013	1B013	1B013	1B013	1B013	1B013	1B013
		(continued)									

Item Reference Number	Page Loc. in this Volume	ITEM DESCRIPTION (ABBREVIATED)	QUESTIONNAIRE LOCATION BY YEAR (FORM, SECTION, AND QUESTION NUMBER)								
			1975	1976	1977	1978	1979	1980/81	1982/83	1984/85	1986

A01d: DRUGS. Quantity used *(continued)*

Item Reference Number	Page Loc. in this Volume	ITEM DESCRIPTION (ABBREVIATED)	1975	1976	1977	1978	1979	1980/81	1982/83	1984/85	1986
2000	44	#X/2WK,2 DRK RW	1A037	1B014	1B014	1B014	1B014	1B014	1B014	1B014	1B014A
2010	45	#X/2WK,JST 1DRK	1A038	1B015	1B015	1B015	1B015	1B015	1B015	1B015	1B014B
2360	49	JOINT/DA LST MO		1B025	1B025	1B025	1B025	1B025	1B025	1B025	1B025
2370	49	OZS.MJ LST MO/6		1B026	1B026	1B026	1B026	1B026	1B026	1B026	1B026
11030	167	5+BR/LST2WK,10+X		4D05	4D05	4D05	4D05	4D05	4D12	4D12	4D12
11070	168	#X 20OZ+ WN/2 WK		4D07	4D07	4D07	4D07	4D07	4D14	4D14	4D14
11110	168	#X 5+LIQ/LST 2WK		4D09	4D09	4D09	4D09	4D09	4D16	4D16	4D16
21100		#CANS COLA/DAY						5E10‡			
21110		#CUPS COFFEE/DAY						5E11‡			
21120		#CUPS TEA/DAY						5E12‡			
21130		#12OZ CAF DRK/DA							5E08		
21140		#12OZ OTH DRK/DA							5E09		
21150		#CUPS COFFEE/DA							5E10		
21160		#CUPS OF TEA/DAY							5E11		
21170		#CUPS DECAFF/DAY							5E12		

A01e: DRUGS. How high, how often high

Item Reference Number	Page Loc. in this Volume	ITEM DESCRIPTION (ABBREVIATED)	1975	1976	1977	1978	1979	1980/81	1982/83	1984/85	1986
840	26	#X DRK ENF FL HI	*B05	*B05	*B05	*B05	*B05	*B05	*B05	*B05	*B05
1970	44	#X DRK ENF FL 4	1A033	1B010	1B010	1B010	1B010	1B010	1B010	1B010	1B010
2340	48	MJ/HSH,VRY HIGH	1A050	1B023	1B023	1B023	1B023	1B023	1B023	1B023	1B023
2650	53	LSD,GET VERY HI	1A063	1B033	1B033	1B033	1B033	1B033	1B037	1B037	1B037
2700	54	PSYD,GT VERY HI	1A077	1B039	1B039	1B039	1B039	1B039	1B043	1B043	1B043
3100	60	AMPH,GT VERY HI	1A093	1B047	1B047	1B047	1B047	1B047	1B054	1B054	1B054
3260	62	QUAD,GT VERY HI	1A108	1B054	1B054	1B054	1B054	1B054	1B061	1B061	1B061
3590	65	BARB,GT VERY HI	1A122	1B061	1B061	1B061	1B061	1B061	1B068	1B068	1B068
4050	70	TRNQ,GT VERY HI	1A137	1B071	1B071	1B071	1B071	1B071	1B078	1B078	1B078
4520	74	COK,GET VERY HI	1A150	1B080	1B080	1B080	1B080	1B080	1B087	1B087	1B087
4930		HER,GT VERY HI	1A164	1B089	1B089	1B089	1B089	1B089			
5380	80	NARC,GT VERY HI	1A179	1B099	1B099	1B099	1B099	1B099	1B098	1B098	1B098

A01f: DRUGS. How long high

Item Reference Number	Page Loc. in this Volume	ITEM DESCRIPTION (ABBREVIATED)	1975	1976	1977	1978	1979	1980/81	1982/83	1984/85	1986
1980	44	DRK AL,HI24+HR	1A034	1B011	1B011	1B011	1B011	1B011	1B011	1B011	1B011
2350	49	MJ/HSH,HI 24+HR	1A051	1B024	1B024	1B024	1B024	1B024	1B024	1B024	1B024
2660	53	LSD,HIGH 24+ HR	1A064	1B034	1B034	1B034	1B034	1B034	1B038	1B038	1B038
2710	54	PSYD,HI 24+ HRS	1A078	1B040	1B040	1B040	1B040	1B040	1B044	1B044	1B044
3110	60	AMPH,HI 24+ HRS	1A094	1B048	1B048	1B048	1B048	1B048	1B055	1B055	1B055
3270	62	QUAD,HI 24+ HRS	1A109	1B055	1B055	1B055	1B055	1B055	1B062	1B062	1B062
3600	66	BARB,HI 24+ HRS	1A123	1B062	1B062	1B062	1B062	1B062	1B069	1B069	1B069
4060	70	TRNQ,HI 24+ HRS	1A138	1B072	1B072	1B072	1B072	1B072	1B079	1B079	1B079
4530	74	COK,HIGH 24+ HR	1A151	1B081	1B081	1B081	1B081	1B081	1B088	1B088	1B088
4940		HER,HI 24+ HRS	1A165	1B090	1B090	1B090	1B090	1B090			
5390	80	NARC,HI 24+ HRS	1A180	1B100	1B100	1B100	1B100	1B100	1B099	1B099	1B099

A01g: DRUGS. Incidence of first use

Item Reference Number	Page Loc. in this Volume	ITEM DESCRIPTION (ABBREVIATED)	1975	1976	1977	1978	1979	1980/81	1982/83	1984/85	1986
1680		SMK CIG DLY/12G	1A019	1B002	(1B002)	1B002	1B002	1B002	1B002	1B002	
1685	40	GR 1ST SMOK 0=N									1B002
2015	45	GR 1ST DRUNK0=N									1B016
5570	81	GR 1ST SMOK DLY	1A019	1B105A	1B105A	1B105A	1B105A	1B105A	1B104A	1B104A	1B104A
	145				3E12A	3E12A	3E12A	3E12A	3E10A	3E10A	3E10A
5575	83	GR 1ST SMOKE EVR									1B104M
	147										3E10N
5576	147	GR 1ST SMOKELESS									3E10O
5580	81	GR 1ST TRY ALC	1A027	1B105B	1B105B	1B105B	1B105B	1B105B	1B104B	1B104B	1B104B
	145				3E12B	3E12B	3E12B	3E12B	3E10B	3E10B	3E10B
5585	83	GR 1ST DRUNK									1B104N
	147										3E10P
5590	81	GR 1ST TRY MJ	1A043	1B105C	1B105C	1B105C	1B105C	1B105C	1B104C	1B104C	1B104C
	145				3E12C	3E12C	3E12C	3E12C	3E10C	3E10C	3E10C
5600	81	GR 1ST TRY LSD	1A056	1B105D	1B105D	1B105D	1B105D	1B105D	1B104D	1B104D	1B104D
	145	*(continued)*			3E12D	3E12D	3E12D	3E12D	3E10D	3E10D	3E10D

‡ This question appears in 1981 but does not appear in 1980.

Item Reference Number	Page Loc. in this Volume	ITEM DESCRIPTION (ABBREVIATED)	QUESTIONNAIRE LOCATION BY YEAR (FORM, SECTION, AND QUESTION NUMBER)								
			1975	1976	1977	1978	1979	1980/81	1982/83	1984/85	1986

A01g: DRUGS. Incidence of first use *(continued)*

Item Reference Number	Page Loc. in this Volume	ITEM DESCRIPTION (ABBREVIATED)	1975	1976	1977	1978	1979	1980/81	1982/83	1984/85	1986
5610	82	GR 1ST TRY PSY	1A070	1B105E	1B105E	1B105E	1B105E	1B105E	1B104E	(1B104E)	1B104E
	146				3E12E	3E12E	3E12E	3E12E	3E10E	3E10E	3E10E
5620	82	GR 1ST TRY AMP	1A086	1B105F	1B105F	1B105F	1B105F	1B105F	1B104F	1B104F	1B104F
	146				3E12F	3E12F	3E12F	3E12F	3E10F	3E10F	3E10F
5630	82	GR 1ST TRY QUA	1A101	1B105G	1B105G	1B105G	1B105G	1B105G	1B104G	1B104G	1B104G
	146				3E12G	3E12G	3E12G	3E12G	3E10G	3E10G	3E10G
5640	82	GR 1ST TRY BRB	1A115	1B105H	1B105H	1B105H	1B105H	1B105H	1B104H	1B104H	1B104H
	146				3E12H	3E12H	3E12H	3E12H	3E10H	3E10H	3E10H
5650	82	GR 1ST TRY TRN	1A130	1B105I	1B105I	1B105I	1B105I	1B105I	1B104I	1B104I	1B104I
	146				3E12I	3E12I	3E12I	3E12I	3E10I	3E10I	3E10I
5660	82	GR 1ST TRY COK	1A143	1B105J	1B105J	1B105J	1B105J	1B105J	1B104J	1B104J	1B104J
	146				3E12J	3E12J	3E12J	3E12J	3E10J	3E10J	3E10J
5670	83	GR 1ST TRY HER	1A157	1B105K	1B105K	1B105K	1B105K	1B105K	1B104K	1B104K	1B104K
	147				3E12K	3E12K	3E12K	3E12K	3E10K	3E10K	3E10K
5680	83	GR 1ST TRY NRC	1A172	1B105L	1B105L	1B105L	1B105L	1B105L	1B104L	1B104L	1B104L
	147				3E12L	3E12L	3E12L	3E12L	3E10L	3E10L	3E10L
5685	147	GR 1ST TRY INHAL				3E12M	3E12M	3E12M	3E10M	3E10M	3E10M
5686	115	GR 1ST TRY PCP						2E04A	2E04A	2E04A	2E04A
5687	116	GR 1ST TRY PPRS						2E04B	2E04B	2E04B	2E04B
21190	49	GR 1ST DAILY MJ							1B029	1B029	1B029

A01h: DRUGS. Use with other drugs

Item Reference Number	Page Loc. in this Volume	ITEM DESCRIPTION (ABBREVIATED)	1975	1976	1977	1978	1979	1980/81	1982/83	1984/85	1986
2200	48	#X OVL MJ+ ALC		1B021	1B021	1B021	1B021	1B021	1B021	1B021	1B021
2500	52	#X OVL LSD+ ALC		1B031A	1B031A	1B031A	1B031A	1B031A	1B035A	1B035A	1B035A
2510	52	#X OVL LSD+ MJ		1B031B	1B031B	1B031B	1B031B	1B031B	1B035B	1B035B	1B035B
2900	59	#X OVL AMPH+ALC		1B045A	1B045A	1B045A	1B045A	1B045A	1B052A	1B052A	1B052A
2910	59	#X OVL AMPH+MJ		1B045B	1B045B	1B045B	1B045B	1B045B	1B052B	1B052B	1B052B
2920	59	#X OVL AMPH+LSD		1B045C	1B045C	1B045C	1B045C	1B045C	1B052C	1B052C	1B052C
2930	59	#X OVL AMPH+PSY		1B045D	1B045D	1B045D	1B045D	1B045D	1B052D	1B052D	1B052D
3390	64	#X OVL BARB+ALC		1B059A	1B059A	1B059A	1B059A	1B059A	1B066A	1B066A	1B066A
3400	64	#X OVL BARB+MJ		1B059B	1B059B	1B059B	1B059B	1B059B	1B066B	1B066B	1B066B
3410	64	#X OVL BARB+LSD		1B059C	1B059C	1B059C	1B059C	1B059C	1B066C	1B066C	1B066C
3420	65	#X OVL BARB+PSY		1B059D	1B059D	1B059D	1B059D	1B059D	1B066D	1B066D	1B066D
3430	65	#X OVL BARB+AMP		1B059E	1B059E	1B059E	1B059E	1B059E	1B066E	1B066E	1B066E
3440	65	#X OVL BARB+QUA		1B059F	1B059F	1B059F	1B059F	1B059F	1B066F	1B066F	1B066F
3840	69	#X OVL TRQL+ALC		1B069A	1B069A	1B069A	1B069A	1B069A	1B076A	1B076A	1B076A
3850	69	#X OVL TRQL+MJ		1B069B	1B069B	1B069B	1B069B	1B069B	1B076B	1B076B	1B076B
3860	69	#X OVL TRQL+LSD		1B069C	1B069C	1B069C	1B069C	1B069C	1B076C	1B076C	1B076C
3870	69	#X OVL TRQL+PSY		1B069D	1B069D	1B069D	1B069D	1B069D	1B076D	1B076D	1B076D
3880	69	#X OVL TRQL+AMP		1B069E	1B069E	1B069E	1B069E	1B069E	1B076E	1B076E	1B076E
3890	69	#X OVL TRQL+QUA		1B069F	1B069F	1B069F	1B069F	1B069F	1B076F	1B076F	1B076F
3900	69	#X OVL TRQL+BRB		1B069G	1B069G	1B069G	1B069G	1B069G	1B076G	1B076G	1B076G
4290	73	#X OVL COKE+ALC		1B078A	1B078A	1B078A	1B078A	1B078A	1B085A	1B085A	1B085A
4300	73	#X OVL COKE+MJ		1B078B	1B078B	1B078B	1B078B	1B078B	1B085B	1B085B	1B085B
4310	73	#X OVL COKE+LSD		1B078C	1B078C	1B078C	1B078C	1B078C	1B085C	1B085C	1B085C
4320	73	#X OVL COKE+PSY		1B078D	1B078D	1B078D	1B078D	1B078D	1B085D	1B085D	1B085D
4330	73	#X OVL COKE+AMP		1B078E	1B078E	1B078E	1B078E	1B078E	1B085E	1B085E	1B085E
4340	73	#X OVL COKE+QUA		1B078F	1B078F	1B078F	1B078F	1B078F	1B085F	1B085F	1B085F
4350	74	#X OVL COKE+BRB		1B078G	1B078G	1B078G	1B078G	1B078G	1B085G	1B085G	1B085G
4360	74	#X OVL COKE+TRN		1B078H	1B078H	1B078H	1B078H	1B078H	1B085H	1B085H	1B085H
4710		#X OVL HER +ALC		1B087A	1B087A	1B087A	1B087A	1B087A			
4720		#X OVL HER +MJ		1B087B	1B087B	1B087B	1B087B	1B087B			
4730		#X OVL HER +LSD		1B087C	1B087C	1B087C	1B087C	1B087C			
4740		#X OVL HER +PSY		1B087D	1B087D	1B087D	1B087D	1B087D			
4750		#X OVL HER +AMP		1B087E	1B087E	1B087E	1B087E	1B087E			
4760		#X OVL HER +QUA		1B087F	1B087F	1B087F	1B087F	1B087F			
4770		#X OVL HER +BRB		1B087G	1B087G	1B087G	1B087G	1B087G			
4780		#X OVL HER +TRN		1B087H	1B087H	1B087H	1B087H	1B087H			
4790		#X OVL HER +COK		1B087I	1B087I	1B087I	1B087I	1B087I			
5130	78	#X OVL NARC+ALC		1B097A	1B097A	1B097A	1B097A	1B097A	1B096A	1B096A	1B096A
5140	78	#X OVL NARC+MJ		1B097B	1B097B	1B097B	1B097B	1B097B	1B096B	1B096B	1B096B
5150	78	#X OVL NARC+LSD		1B097C	1B097C	1B097C	1B097C	1B097C	1B096C	1B096C	1B096C

(continued)

Item Reference Number	Page Loc. in this Volume	ITEM DESCRIPTION (ABBREVIATED)	QUESTIONNAIRE LOCATION BY YEAR (FORM, SECTION, AND QUESTION NUMBER)								
			1975	1976	1977	1978	1979	1980/81	1982/83	1984/85	1986

A01h: DRUGS. Use with other drugs *(continued)*

Item Reference Number	Page Loc. in this Volume	ITEM DESCRIPTION (ABBREVIATED)	1975	1976	1977	1978	1979	1980/81	1982/83	1984/85	1986
5160	78	#X OVL NARC+PSY		1B097D	1B097D	1B097D	1B097D	1B097D	1B096D	1B096D	1B096D
5170	78	#X OVL NARC+AMP		1B097E	1B097E	1B097E	1B097E	1B097E	1B096E	1B096E	1B096E
5180	79	#X OVL NARC+QUA		1B097F	1B097F	1B097F	1B097F	1B097F	1B096F	1B096F	1B096F
5190	79	#X OVL NARC+BRB		1B097G	1B097G	1B097G	1B097G	1B097G	1B096G	1B096G	1B096G
5200	79	#X OVL NARC+TRN		1B097H	1B097H	1B097H	1B097H	1B097H	1B096H	1B096H	1B096H
5210	79	#X OVL NARC+COK		1B097I	1B097I	1B097I	1B097I	1B097I	1B096I	1B096I	1B096I
5220	79	#X OVL NARC+HER		1B097J	1B097J	1B097J	1B097J	1B097J	1B096J	1B096J	1B096J

A01i: DRUGS. Tried to stop

Item Reference Number	Page Loc. in this Volume	ITEM DESCRIPTION (ABBREVIATED)	1975	1976	1977	1978	1979	1980/81	1982/83	1984/85	1986
1690	41	*TRY STP SMK&FL	1A021	1B004	1B004	1B004	1B004	1B004	1B004	1B004	1B004
1700	41	*WNT STP SMK NW	1A022	1B005	1B005	1B005	1B005	1B005	1B005	1B005	1B005
2020	45	*TRY STP ALC&FL	1A039	1B016	1B016	1B016	1B016	1B016	1B016	1B016	1B015
2380	49	*TRY STP MJ &FL	1A052	1B027	1B027	1B027	1B027	1B027	1B027	1B027	1B027
2680	53	*TRY STP LSD&FL	1A066	1B036	1B036	1B036	1B036	1B036	1B040	1B040	1B040
3240	61	*TRY STP AMP&FL	1A096	1B051	1B051	1B051	1B051	1B051	1B058	1B058	1B058
3710	66	TRY STP BARB&FL	1A125	1B064	1B064	1B064	1B064	1B064	1B071	1B071	1B071
4170	70	*TRY STP TRQ&FL	1A139	1B074	1B074	1B074	1B074	1B074	1B081	1B081	1B081
4540	74	*TRY STP COK&FL	1A152	1B082	1B082	1B082	1B082	1B082	1B089	1B089	1B089
4950		TRY STP HER& FL	1A166	1B091	1B091	1B091	1B091	1B091			
5500	80	TRY STP NARC&FL	1A182	1B102	1B102	1B102	1B102	1B102	1B101	1B101	1B101
8910	137	12MO REDUCE ALCL		3D03A	3D03A	3D03A	3D03A	3D03A	3D03A	3D03A	3D03A
8920	137	12MO REDUCE CIG		3D03B	3D03B	3D03B	3D03B	3D03B	3D03B	3D03B	3D03B
8930	137	12MO REDUCE MARJ		3D03C	3D03C	3D03C	3D03C	3D03C	3D03C	3D03C	3D03C
8940	137	12MO REDUCE PSYC		3D03D	3D03D	3D03D	3D03D	3D03D	3D03D	3D03D	3D03D
8950	137	12MO REDUCE AMPH		3D03E	3D03E	3D03E	3D03E	3D03E	3D03E	3D03E	3D03E
8960		12MO REDUCE QUAL		3D03F	3D03F	3D03F					
8970	137	12MO REDUCE BARB		3D03G	3D03G	(3D03G)	3D03G	3D03G	3D03G	3D03G	3D03G
8980	137	12MO REDUCE COKE		3D03H	3D03H	3D03H	3D03H	3D03H	3D03H	3D03H	3D03H
8990	138	12MO REDUCE HRN		3D03I	3D03I	3D03I	3D03I	3D03I	3D03I	3D03I	3D03I
9000	138	12MO REDUCE NARC		3D03J	3D03J	3D03J	3D03J	3D03J	3D03J	3D03J	3D03J
9005	137	12MO REDUCE TRQL					3D03F	3D03F	3D03F	3D03F	3D03F

A01j: DRUGS. Use on doctor's orders

Item Reference Number	Page Loc. in this Volume	ITEM DESCRIPTION (ABBREVIATED)	1975	1976	1977	1978	1979	1980/81	1982/83	1984/85	1986
2790	57	DR TOLD TK AMPH	1A085	1B042	1B042	1B042	1B042	1B042	1B049	1B049	1B049
3280	62	DR TOLD TK BARB	1A114	1B056	1B056	1B056	1B056	1B056	1B063	1B063	1B063
3730	66	DR TOLD TK TRNQ	1A129	1B066	1B066	1B066	1B066	1B066	1B073	1B073	1B073
5020	76	DR TOLD TK NARC	1A171	1B094	1B094	1B094	1B094	1B094	1B093	1B093	1B093

A01k: DRUGS. Bad trip

Item Reference Number	Page Loc. in this Volume	ITEM DESCRIPTION (ABBREVIATED)	1975	1976	1977	1978	1979	1980/81	1982/83	1984/85	1986
2670	53	1+ BAD TRIP LSD	1A065	1B035	1B035	1B035	1B035	1B035	1B039	1B039	1B039

A01l: DRUGS. Specific kinds of drugs

Item Reference Number	Page Loc. in this Volume	ITEM DESCRIPTION (ABBREVIATED)	1975	1976	1977	1978	1979	1980/81	1982/83	1984/85	1986
2720	54	TKN YR,MESCALIN	1A079A	1B041A	1B041A	1B041A	1B041A	1B041A	1B045A	1B045A	1B045A
2730	54	TKN YR,PEYOTE	1A079B	1B041B	1B041B	1B041B	1B041B	1B041B	1B045B	1B045B	1B045B
2740	54	TKN YR,PSILOCYB	1A079C	1B041C	1B041C	1B041C	1B041C	1B041C	1B045C	1B045C	1B045C
2750	54	TKN YR,PCP		1B041D	1B041D	1B041D	1B041D	1B041D	1B045D	1B045D	1B045D
2760	54	TKN YR,CNCT THC	1A079D	1B041E	1B041E	1B041E	1B041E	1B041E	1B045E	1B045E	1B045E
2770	54	TKN YR,OTH PSYD	1A079E	1B041F	1B041F	1B041F	1B041F	1B041F	1B045F	1B045F	1B045F
2780	54	TKN YR,DK NAME	1A079F	1B041G	1B041G	1B041G	1B041G	1B041G	1B045G	1B045G	1B045G
3120	60	TKN YR,BENZDRIN	1A095A	1B049A	1B049A	1B049A	1B049A	1B049A	1B056A	1B056A	1B056A
3130	60	TKN YR,DEXEDRIN	1A095B	1B049B	1B049B	1B049B	1B049B	1B049B	1B056B	1B056B	1B056B
3140	60	TKN YR,METHDRIN	1A095C	1B049C	1B049C	1B049C	1B049C	1B049C	1B056C	1B056C	1B056C
3150	60	TKN YR,RITALIN	1A095D	1B049D	1B049D	1B049D	1B049D	1B049D	1B056D	1B056D	1B056D
3160	60	TKN YR,PRELUDIN	1A095E	1B049E	1B049E	1B049E	1B049E	1B049E	1B056E	1B056E	1B056E
3170	60	TKN YR,DEXAMYL	1A095F	1B049F	1B049F	1B049F	1B049F	1B049F	1B056F	1B056F	1B056F
3180	60	TKN YR,METHAMPH	1A095G	1B049G	1B049G	1B049G	1B049G	1B049G	1B056G	1B056G	1B056G
3190	60	TKN YR,OTH AMPH	1A095H	1B049H	1B049H	1B049H	1B049H	1B049H	1B056H	1B056H	1B056H
3200	60	TKN YR,DNT KN N	1A095I	1B049I	1B049I	1B049I	1B049I	1B049I	1B056I	1B056I	1B056I
3610	66	TKN YR,PHNOBARB	1A124A	1B063A	1B063A	1B063A	1B063A	1B063A	1B070A	1B070A	1B070A
		(continued)									

Item Reference Number	Page Loc. in this Volume	ITEM DESCRIPTION (ABBREVIATED)	QUESTIONNAIRE LOCATION BY YEAR (FORM, SECTION, AND QUESTION NUMBER)								
			1975	1976	1977	1978	1979	1980/81	1982/83	1984/85	1986

A01I: DRUGS. Specific kinds of drugs *(continued)*

3620	66	TKN YR,SECONAL	1A124B	1B063B	1B063B	1B063B	1B063B	1B063B	1B070B	1B070B	1B070B
3630	66	TKN YR,TUINAL	1A124C	1B063C	1B063C	1B063C	1B063C	1B063C	1B070C	1B070C	1B070C
3640	66	TKN YR,NEMBUTAL	1A124D	1B063D	1B063D	1B063D	1B063D	1B063D	1B070D	1B070D	1B070D
3650	66	TKN YR,LUMINAL	1A124E	1B063E	1B063E	1B063E	1B063E	1B063E	1B070E	1B070E	1B070E
3660	66	TKN YR,DESBUTAL	1A124F	1B063F	1B063F	1B063F	1B063F	1B063F	1B070F	1B070F	1B070F
3670	66	TKN YR,AMYTAL	1A124G	1B063G	1B063G	1B063G	1B063G	1B063G	1B070G	1B070G	1B070G
3680	66	TKN YR,ADRNOCAL	1A124H	1B063H	1B063H	1B063H	1B063H	1B063H	1B070H	1B070H	1B070H
3690	66	TKN YR,OTH BRBT	1A124I	1B063I	1B063I	1B063I	1B063I	1B063I	1B070I	1B070I	1B070I
3700	66	TKN YR,DNT KNOW	1A124J	1B063J	1B063J	1B063J	1B063J	1B063J	1B070J	1B070J	1B070J
4070	70	TKN YR,LIBRIUM		1B073A	1B073A	1B073A	1B073A	1B073A	1B080A	1B080A	1B080A
4080	70	TKN YR,VALIUM		1B073B	1B073B	1B073B	1B073B	1B073B	1B080B	1B080B	1B080B
4090	70	TKN YR,MILTOWN		1B073C	1B073C	1B073C	1B073C	1B073C	1B080C	1B080C	1B080C
4100	70	TKN YR,EQUANIL		1B073D	1B073D	1B073D	1B073D	1B073D	1B080D	1B080D	1B080D
4110	70	TKN YR,MEPRBMTE		1B073E	1B073E	1B073E	1B073E	1B073E	1B080E	1B080E	1B080E
4120	70	TKN YR,SERAX		1B073F	1B073F	1B073F	1B073F	1B073F	1B080F	1B080F	1B080F
4130	70	TKN YR,ATARAX		1B073G	1B073G	1B073G	1B073G	1B073G	1B080G	1B080G	1B080G
4140	70	TKN YR,TRANXENE		1B073H	1B073H	1B073H	1B073H	1B073H	1B080H	1B080H	1B080H
4150	70	TKN YR,VISTARIL		1B073I	1B073I	1B073I	1B073I	1B073I	1B080I	1B080I	1B080I
4160	70	TKN YR,DNT KNW		1B073J	1B073J	1B073J	1B073J	1B073J	1B080J	1B080J	1B080J
4531	75	FRM COKE-POWDER									1B090Aa
4532	75	FRM COKE-FRBASE									1B090Ab
4533	75	FRM COKE-PASTE									1B090Ac
4534	75	FRM COKE-CRACK									1B090Ad
5400	80	NARC TKN MTHDNE	1A181A	1B101A	1B101A	1B101A	1B101A	1B101A	1B100A	1B100A	1B100A
5410	80	NARC TKN OPIUM	1A181B	1B101B	1B101B	1B101B	1B101B	1B101B	1B100B	1B100B	1B100B
5420	80	NARC TKN MRPHNE	1A181C	1B101C	1B101C	1B101C	1B101C	1B101C	1B100C	1B100C	1B100C
5430	80	NARC TKN CODEIN	1A181D	1B101D	1B101D	1B101D	1B101D	1B101D	1B100D	1B100D	1B100D
5440	80	NARC TKN DEMROL	1A181E	1B101E	1B101E	1B101E	1B101E	1B101E	1B100E	1B100E	1B100E
5450	80	NARC TKN PARGRC	1A181F	1B101F	1B101F	1B101F	1B101F	1B101F	1B100F	1B100F	1B100F
5460	80	NARC TKN TALWIN	1A181G	1B101G	1B101G	1B101G	1B101G	1B101G	1B100G	1B100G	1B100G
5470	80	NARC TKN LDANUM	1A181H	1B101H	1B101H	1B101H	1B101H	1B101H	1B100H	1B100H	1B100H
5480	80	NARC TKN OTHER	1A181I	1B101I	1B101I	1B101I	1B101I	1B101I	1B100I	1B100I	1B100I
5490	80	NARC TKN DNT KN	1A181J	1B101J	1B101J	1B101J	1B101J	1B101J	1B100J	1B100J	1B100J

A02a: DRUGS. Friends' use

7070	112	ALL FRD SMK CIGS	2A41A	2D06A	2D06A	2D06A	2D06A	2D06A	2D06A	2D06A	2D06A
7080	112	ALL FRD SMK MARJ	2A41B	2D06B	2D06B	2D06B	2D06B	2D06B	2D06B	2D06B	2D06B
7090	112	ALL FRD TAKE LSD	2A41C	2D06C	2D06C	2D06C	2D06C	2D06C	2D06C	2D06C	2D06C
7100	112	ALL FRD TK PSYDL	2A41D	2D06D	2D06D	2D06D	2D06D	2D06D	2D06D	2D06D	2D06D
7110	113	ALL FRD TK AMPH	2A41E	2D06E	2D06E	2D06E	2D06E	2D06E	2D06E	2D06E	2D06E
7120	113	ALL FRD TK QUALD	2A41F	2D06F	2D06F	2D06F	2D06F	2D06F	2D06F	2D06F	2D06F
7130	113	ALL FRD TK BARBT	2A41G	2D06G	2D06G	2D06G	2D06G	2D06G	2D06G	2D06G	2D06G
7140	113	ALL FRD TK TRNQL	2A41H	2D06H	2D06H	2D06H	2D06H	2D06H	2D06H	2D06H	2D06H
7150	113	ALL FRD TK COKE	2A41I	2D06I	2D06I	2D06I	2D06I	2D06I	2D06I	2D06I	2D06I
7160	113	ALL FRD TK HERON	2A41J	2D06J	2D06J	2D06J	2D06J	2D06J	2D06J	2D06J	2D06J
7170	113	ALL FRD TK NARC	2A41K	2D06K	2D06K	2D06K	2D06K	2D06K	2D06K	2D06K	2D06K
7180	114	ALL FRD TK INHL	2A41L	2D06L	2D06L	2D06L	2D06L	2D06L	2D06L	2D06L	2D06L
7190	114	ALL FRD DRK ALCL	2A41M	2D06M	2D06M	2D06M	2D06M	2D06M	2D06M	2D06M	2D06M
7200	114	ALL FRD GT DRUNK	2A41N	2D06N	2D06N	2D06N	2D06N	2D06N	2D06N	2D06N	2D06N
7201	114	# FRNDS TAKE PCP					2E01A	2E01A	2E01A	2E01A	2E01A
7202	114	# FRNDS TK PPRS					2E01B	2E01B	2E01B	2E01B	2E01B

A02b: DRUGS. Exposure to users

8750		OFT W PL TK MARJ	3A55A	5E07A	5E08A	5E08A					
8760		OFT W PL TK LSD	3A55B	5E07B	5E08B	5E08B					
8770		OFT W PL TK PSYC	3A55C	5E07C	5E08C	5E08C					
8780		OFT W PL TK QUAL		5E07D	5E08D	5E08D					
8790		OFT W PL TK BARB	3A55E	5E07E	5E08E	5E08E					
8800		OFT W PL TK TRQL	3A55F	5E07F	5E08F	5E08F					
8810		OFT W PL TK COKE	3A55G	5E07G	5E08G	5E08G					
8820		OFT W PL TK HRN	3A55H	5E07H	5E08H	5E08H					
		(continued)									

Item Reference Number	Page Loc. in this Volume	ITEM DESCRIPTION (ABBREVIATED)	QUESTIONNAIRE LOCATION BY YEAR (FORM, SECTION, AND QUESTION NUMBER)								
			1975	1976	1977	1978	1979	1980/81	1982/83	1984/85	1986

A02b: DRUGS. Exposure to users (continued)

Item Reference Number	Page Loc. in this Volume	ITEM DESCRIPTION (ABBREVIATED)	1975	1976	1977	1978	1979	1980/81	1982/83	1984/85	1986
8830		OFT W PL TK NARC	3A55I	5E07I	5E08I	5E08I					
8835		OFT W PL TK INHL		5E07J	5E08J	5E08J					
8840		OFT W PL TK ALCL	3A55K	5E07K	5E08K	5E08K					
20590	134	12MO NR OTH MARJ		3A29A	3A29A	3A29A	3A29A	3A29A	3A29A	3A29A	3A29A
20600	135	12MO NR OTH LSD		3A29B	3A29B	3A29B	3A29B	3A29B	3A29B	3A29B	3A29B
20610	135	12MO NR OTH PSYC		3A29C	3A29C	3A29C	3A29C	3A29C	3A29C	3A29C	3A29C
20620	135	12MO NR OTH AMPH		3A29D	3A29D	3A29D	3A29D	3A29D	3A29D	3A29D	3A29D
20630	135	12MO NR OTH BARB		3A29E	3A29E	3A29E	3A29E	3A29E	3A29E	3A29E	3A29E
20640	135	12MO NR OTH TRQL		3A29F	3A29F	3A29F	3A29F	3A29F	3A29F	3A29F	3A29F
20650	135	12MO NR OTH COKE		3A29G	3A29G	3A29G	3A29G	3A29G	3A29G	3A29G	3A29G
20660	135	12MO NR OTH HRN		3A29H	3A29H	3A29H	3A29H	3A29H	3A29H	3A29H	3A29H
20670	135	12MO NR OTH NARC		3A29I	3A29I	3A29I	3A29I	3A29I	3A29I	3A29I	3A29I
20680	136	12MO NR OTH ALCL		3A29J	3A29J	3A29J	3A29J	3A29J	3A29J	3A29J	3A29J
21920	203	PARTY-ONE HI ALC								5E08B	5E08B
21930	203	PARTY-OTH HI ALC								5E08C	5E08C
21950	203	PARTY-PRESS ALCL								5E08E	5E08E
21960	204	PARTY-PRS HI ALC								5E08F	5E08F
21970	204	PARTY-ONE HI MJ								5E08G	5E08G
21980	204	PARTY-OTH HI MJ								5E08H	5E08H
22000	204	PARTY-PRESS MJ								5E08J	5E08J
22010	204	PARTY-ONE HI OTD								5E08K	5E08K
22020	204	PARTY-OTH HI OTD								5E08L	5E08L
22040	205	PARTY-PRESS OTDG								5E08N	5E08N

A03a: DRUGS. Availability

Item Reference Number	Page Loc. in this Volume	ITEM DESCRIPTION (ABBREVIATED)	1975	1976	1977	1978	1979	1980/81	1982/83	1984/85	1986
6750	106	EASY GT MARIJUAN	2A40A	2A21A	2A21A	2A21A	2A21A	2A21A	2A21A	2A21A	2A21A
6760	106	EASY GT LSD	2A40B	2A21B	2A21B	2A21B	2A21B	2A21B	2A21B	2A21B	2A21B
6770	106	EASY GT PSYDELIC	2A40C	2A21C	2A21C	2A21C	2A21C	2A21C	2A21C	2A21C	2A21C
6780	106	EASY GT AMPHTMNS	2A40D	2A21D	2A21D	2A21D	2A21D	2A21D	2A21D	2A21D	2A21D
6790	106	EASY GT BBTUATES	2A40F	2A21E	2A21E	2A21E	2A21E	2A21E	2A21E	2A21E	2A21E
6800	106	EASY GT TRANQLIZ	2A40G	2A21F	2A21F	2A21F	2A21F	2A21F	2A21F	2A21F	2A21F
6810	107	EASY GT COCAINE	2A40H	2A21G	2A21G	2A21G	2A21G	2A21G	2A21G	2A21G	2A21G
6820	107	EASY GT HEROIN	2A40I	2A21H	2A21H	2A21H	2A21H	2A21H	2A21H	2A21H	2A21H
6830	107	EASY GT NARCOTIC	2A40J	2A21I	2A21I	2A21I	2A21I	2A21I	2A21I	2A21I	2A21I

A04a: DRUGS. Expected future use

Item Reference Number	Page Loc. in this Volume	ITEM DESCRIPTION (ABBREVIATED)	1975	1976	1977	1978	1979	1980/81	1982/83	1984/85	1986
1710	41	NO SMK IN 5 YR	1A023	1B006	1B006	1B006	1B006	1B006	1B006	1B006	1B006
2030	45	NO ALC IN 5 YR	1A040	1B017	1B017	1B017	1B017	1B017	1B017	1B017	1B017
2390	50	NO MJ/HSH IN5YR	1A053	1B028	1B028	1B028	1B028	1B028	1B032	1B032	1B032
2690	53	NO LSD IN 5 YRS	1A067	1B037	1B037	1B037	1B037	1B037	1B041	1B041	1B041
3250	61	NO AMPH IN 5YR	1A097	1B052	1B052	1B052	1B052	1B052	1B059	1B059	1B059
3720	66	NO BARB IN 5YR	1A126	1B065	1B065	1B065	1B065	1B065	1B072	1B072	1B072
4180	71	NO TRNQ IN 5YR	1A140	1B075	1B075	1B075	1B075	1B075	1B082	1B082	1B082
4600	75	NO COKE IN 5YR	1A154	1B084	1B084	1B084	1B084	1B084	1B091	1B091	1B091
5010		NO HER IN 5 YR	1A168	1B093	1B093	1B093	1B093	1B093			
5560	81	NO NARC IN 5YR	1A184	1B104	1B104	1B104	1B104	1B104	1B103	1B103	1B103
9010	138	NXT 12MOS USE MJ		3D04	3D04	3D04	3D04	3D04	3D04	3D04	3D04

A05a: DRUGS. Use alone

Item Reference Number	Page Loc. in this Volume	ITEM DESCRIPTION (ABBREVIATED)	1975	1976	1977	1978	1979	1980/81	1982/83	1984/85	1986
1720	42	#X/YR ALC ALONE		1B008A	1B008A	1B008A	1B008A	1B008A	1B008A	1B008A	1B008A
2100	47	#X/YR MJ ALONE	1A045	1B020A	1B020A	1B020A	1B020A	1B020A	1B020A	1B020A	1B020A
2400	51	#X/YR LSD ALONE		1B030A	1B030A	1B030A	1B030A	1B030A	1B034A	1B034A	1B034A
2800	58	#X/YR AMPH ALNE		1B044A	1B044A	1B044A	1B044A	1B044A	1B051A	1B051A	1B051A
3290	63	#X/YR BRBT ALNE		1B058A	1B058A	1B058A	1B058A	1B058A	1B065A	1B065A	1B065A
3740	67	#X/YR TRQL ALNE		1B068A	1B068A	1B068A	1B068A	1B068A	1B075A	1B075A	1B075A
4190	71	#X/YR COKE ALNE		1B077A	1B077A	1B077A	1B077A	1B077A	1B084A	1B084A	1B084A
4610		#X/YR HER ALONE		1B086A	1B086A	1B086A	1B086A	1B086A			
5030	77	#X/YR NARC ALNE		1B096A	1B096A	1B096A	1B096A	1B096A	1B095A	1B095A	1B095A

Item Reference Number	Page Loc. in this Volume	ITEM DESCRIPTION (ABBREVIATED)	QUESTIONNAIRE LOCATION BY YEAR (FORM, SECTION, AND QUESTION NUMBER)								
			1975	1976	1977	1978	1979	1980/81	1982/83	1984/85	1986
A05b: DRUGS. Use with others											
1730	42	#X/YR ALC-2 PPL		1B008B	1B008B	1B008B	1B008B	1B008B	1B008B	1B008B	1B008B
1750	42	#X/YR ALC-DT/SP		1B008D	1B008D	1B008D	1B008D	1B008D	1B008D	1B008D	1B008D
1760	43	#X/YR ALC-ADLTS		1B008E	1B008E	1B008E	1B008E	1B008E	1B008E	1B008E	1B008E
2110	47	#X/YR MJ-2 PPL		1B020B	1B020B	1B020B	1B020B	1B020B	1B020B	1B020B	1B020B
2130	47	#X/YR MJ-DT/SP		1B020D	1B020D	1B020D	1B020D	1B020D	1B020D	1B020D	1B020D
2140	47	#X/YR MJ-ADLTS		1B020E	1B020E	1B020E	1B020E	1B020E	1B020E	1B020E	1B020E
2410	51	#X/YR LSD-2 PPL		1B030B	1B030B	1B030B	1B030B	1B030B	1B034B	1B034B	1B034B
2430	51	#X/YR LSD-DT/SP		1B030D	1B030D	1B030D	1B030D	1B030D	1B034D	1B034D	1B034D
2440	51	#X/YR LSD-ADLTS		1B030E	1B030E	1B030E	1B030E	1B030E	1B034E	1B034E	1B034E
2810	58	#X/YR AMPH-2PPL		1B044B	1B044B	1B044B	1B044B	1B044B	1B051B	1B051B	1B051B
2830	58	#X/YR AMPH-DT/S		1B044D	1B044D	1B044D	1B044D	1B044D	1B051D	1B051D	1B051D
2840	58	#X/YR AMPH-ADLT		1B044E	1B044E	1B044E	1B044E	1B044E	1B051E	1B051E	1B051E
3300	63	#X/YR BRBT-2PPL		1B058B	1B058B	1B058B	1B058B	1B058B	1B065B	1B065B	1B065B
3320	63	#X/YR BRBT-DT/S		1B058D	1B058D	1B058D	1B058D	1B058D	1B065D	1B065D	1B065D
3330	63	#X/YR BRBT-ADLT		1B058E	1B058E	1B058E	1B058E	1B058E	1B065E	1B065E	1B065E
3750	67	#X/YR TRQL-2PPL		1B068B	1B068B	1B068B	1B068B	1B068B	1B075B	1B075B	1B075B
3770	68	#X/YR TRQL-DT/S		1B068D	1B068D	1B068D	1B068D	1B068D	1B075D	1B075D	1B075D
3780	68	#X/YR TRQL-ADLT		1B068E	1B068E	1B068E	1B068E	1B068E	1B075E	1B075E	1B075E
4200	72	#X/YR COKE-2PPL		1B077B	1B077B	1B077B	1B077B	1B077B	1B084B	1B084B	1B084B
4220	72	#X/YR COKE-DT/S		1B077D	1B077D	1B077D	1B077D	1B077D	1B084D	1B084D	1B084D
4230	72	#X/YR COKE-ADLT		1B077E	1B077E	1B077E	1B077E	1B077E	1B084E	1B084E	1B084E
4620		#X/YR HER-2 PPL		1B086B	1B086B	1B086B	1B086B	1B086B			
4640		#X/YR HER-DA/SP		1B086D	1B086D	1B086D	1B086D	1B086D			
4650		#X/YR HER-ADULT		1B086E	1B086E	1B086E	1B086E	1B086E			
5040	77	#X/YR NARC-2PPL		1B096B	1B096B	1B096B	1B096B	1B096B	1B095B	1B095B	1B095B
5060	77	#X/YR NARC-DT/S		1B096D	1B096D	1B096D	1B096D	1B096D	1B095D	1B095D	1B095D
5070	77	#X/YR NARC-ADLT		1B096E	1B096E	1B096E	1B096E	1B096E	1B095E	1B095E	1B095E
A05c: DRUGS. Settings of use											
1740	42	#X/YR ALC@PARTY		1B008C	1B008C	1B008C	1B008C	1B008C	1B008C	1B008C	1B008C
1770	43	#X/YR ALC-DATIM		1B008F	1B008F	1B008F	1B008F	1B008F	1B008F	1B008F	1B008F
1780	43	#X/YR ALC@HOME		1B008G	1B008G	1B008G	1B008G	1B008G	1B008G	1B008G	1B008G
1790	43	#X/YR ALC@SCHL		1B008H	1B008H	1B008H	1B008H	1B008H	1B008H	1B008H	1B008H
1810	43	#X/YR ALCIN CAR		1B008I	1B008I	1B008I	1B008I	1B008I	1B008I	1B008I	1B008I
2120	47	#X/YR MJ@PARTY		1B020C	1B020C	1B020C	1B020C	1B020C	1B020C	1B020C	1B020C
2150	47	#X/YR MJ-DATIME		1B020F	1B020F	1B020F	1B020F	1B020F	1B020F	1B020F	1B020F
2160	47	#X/YR MJ@HOME		1B020G	1B020G	1B020G	1B020G	1B020G	1B020G	1B020G	1B020G
2170	48	#X/YR MJ@SCHL		1B020H	1B020H	1B020H	1B020H	1B020H	1B020H	1B020H	1B020H
2190	48	#X/YR MJIN CAR		1B020I	1B020I	1B020I	1B020I	1B020I	1B020I	1B020I	1B020I
2420	51	#X/YR LSD@PARTY		1B030C	1B030C	1B030C	1B030C	1B030C	1B034C	1B034C	1B034C
2450	51	#X/YR LSD-DATIM		1B030F	1B030F	1B030F	1B030F	1B030F	1B034F	1B034F	1B034F
2460	52	#X/YR LSD@HOME		1B030G	1B030G	1B030G	1B030G	1B030G	1B034G	1B034G	1B034G
2470	52	#X/YR LSD@SCHL		1B030H	1B030H	1B030H	1B030H	1B030H	1B034H	1B034H	1B034H
2490	52	#X/YR LSDIN CAR		1B030I	1B030I	1B030I	1B030I	1B030I	1B034I	1B034I	1B034I
2820	58	#X/YR AMPH@PRTY		1B044C	1B044C	1B044C	1B044C	1B044C	1B051C	1B051C	1B051C
2850	58	#X/YR AMPH-DATM		1B044F	1B044F	1B044F	1B044F	1B044F	1B051F	1B051F	1B051F
2860	58	#X/YR AMPH@HOME		1B044G	1B044G	1B044G	1B044G	1B044G	1B051G	1B051G	1B051G
2880	59	#X/YR AMPH@SCHL		1B044H	1B044H	1B044H	1B044H	1B044H	1B051H	1B051H	1B051H
2890	59	#X/YR AMPH@CAR		1B044I	1B044I	1B044I	1B044I	1B044I	1B051I	1B051I	1B051I
3310	63	#X/YR BRBT@PRTY		1B058C	1B058C	1B058C	1B058C	1B058C	1B065C	1B065C	1B065C
3340	64	#X/YR BRBT-DATM		1B058F	1B058F	1B058F	1B058F	1B058F	1B065F	1B065F	1B065F
3350	64	#X/YR BRBT@HOME		1B058G	1B058G	1B058G	1B058G	1B058G	1B065G	1B065G	1B065G
3360	64	#X/YR BRBT@SCHL		1B058H	1B058H	1B058H	1B058H	1B058H	1B065H	1B065H	1B065H
3380	64	#X/YR BRBT@CAR		1B058I	1B058I	1B058I	1B058I	1B058I	1B065I	1B065I	1B065I
3760	68	#X/YR TRQL@PRTY		1B068C	1B068C	1B068C	1B068C	1B068C	1B075C	1B075C	1B075C
3790	68	#X/YR TRQL-DATM		1B068F	1B068F	1B068F	1B068F	1B068F	1B075F	1B075F	1B075F
3800	68	#X/YR TRQL@HOME		1B068G	1B068G	1B068G	1B068G	1B068G	1B075G	1B075G	1B075G
3810	68	#X/YR TRQL@SCHL		1B068H	1B068H	1B068H	1B068H	1B068H	1B075H	1B075H	1B075H
3830	68	#X/YR TRQL@CAR		1B068I	1B068I	1B068I	1B068I	1B068I	1B075I	1B075I	1B075I
4210	72	#X/YR COKE@PRTY		1B077C	1B077C	1B077C	1B077C	1B077C	1B084C	1B084C	1B084C
4240	72	#X/YR COKE-DATM		1B077F	1B077F	1B077F	1B077F	1B077F	1B084F	1B084F	1B084F
4250	72	#X/YR COKE@HOME		1B077G	1B077G	1B077G	1B077G	1B077G	1B084G	1B084G	1B084G
		(continued)									

Item Reference Number	Page Loc. in this Volume	ITEM DESCRIPTION (ABBREVIATED)	QUESTIONNAIRE LOCATION BY YEAR (FORM, SECTION, AND QUESTION NUMBER)								
			1975	1976	1977	1978	1979	1980/81	1982/83	1984/85	1986

A05c: DRUGS. Settings of use *(continued)*

4260	72	#X/YR COKE@SCHL		1B077H	1B077H	1B077H	1B077H	1B077H	1B084H	1B084H	1B084H
4280	73	#X/YR COKE@CAR		1B077I	1B077I	1B077I	1B077I	1B077I	1B084I	1B084I	1B084I
4630		#X/YR HER@PARTY		1B086C	1B086C	1B086C	1B086C	1B086C			
4660		#X/YR HER-DATIM		1B086F	1B086F	1B086F	1B086F	1B086F			
4670		#X/YR HER@HOME		1B086G	1B086G	1B086G	1B086G	1B086G			
4680		#X/YR HER@SCHL		1B086H	1B086H	1B086H	1B086H	1B086H			
4700		#X/YR HER@CAR		1B086I	1B086I	1B086I	1B086I	1B086I			
5050	77	#X/YR NARC@PRTY		1B096C	1B096C	1B096C	1B096C	1B096C	1B095C	1B095C	1B095C
5080	77	#X/YR NARC-DATM		1B096F	1B096F	1B096F	1B096F	1B096F	1B095F	1B095F	1B095F
5090	77	#X/YR NARC@HOME		1B096G	1B096G	1B096G	1B096G	1B096G	1B095G	1B095G	1B095G
5100	78	#X/YR NARC@SCHL		1B096H	1B096H	1B096H	1B096H	1B096H	1B095H	1B095H	1B095H
5120	78	#X/YR NARC @CAR		1B096I	1B096I	1B096I	1B096I	1B096I	1B095I	1B095I	1B095I
21940	203	PARTY-YOU HI ALC								5E08D	5E08D
21990	204	PARTY-YOU HI MJ								5E08I	5E08I
22030	205	PARTY-YOU HI OTD								5E08M	5E08M
22060	205	PRF PTY-U HI ALC								5E09B	5E09B
22080	205	PRF PTY-U USE MJ								5E09D	5E09D
22100	206	PR PTY-U USE OTD								5E09F	5E09F

A05d: DRUGS. Mode of administration

3210	60	MTHD AMPH-MOUTH		1B050A	1B050A	1B050A	1B050A	1B050A	1B057A	1B057A	1B057A
3220	60	MTHD AMPH-INJCT		1B050B	1B050B	1B050B	1B050B	1B050B	1B057B	1B057B	1B057B
3230	60	MTHD AMPH-OTHER		1B050C	1B050C	1B050C	1B050C	1B050C	1B057C	1B057C	1B057C
4550	75	MTHD COKE SNORT	1A153A	1B083A	1B083A	1B083A	1B083A	1B083A	1B090A	1B090A	1B090Ba
4560	75	MTHD COKE-SMOKE	1A153B	1B083B	1B083B	1B083B	1B083B	1B083B	1B090B	1B090B	1B090Bb
4570	75	MTHD COKE-INJCT	1A153C	1B083C	1B083C	1B083C	1B083C	1B083C	1B090C	1B090C	1B090Bc
4575	75	MTHD COKE-INHAL									1B090Bd
4580	75	MTHD COKE-MOUTH	1A153D	1B083D	1B083D	1B083D	1B083D	1B083D	1B090D	1B090D	1B090Be
4590	75	MTHD COKE-OTHER	1A153E	1B083E	1B083E	1B083E	1B083E	1B083E	1B090E	1B090E	1B090Bf
4960		METHD HRN SNORT	1A167A	1B092A	1B092A	1B092A	1B092A	1B092A			
4970		METHD HRN-SMOKE	1A167B	1B092B	1B092B	1B092B	1B092B	1B092B			
4980		METHD HRN-INJCT	1A167C	1B092C	1B092C	1B092C	1B092C	1B092C			
4990		METHD HRN-MOUTH	1A167D	1B092D	1B092D	1B092D	1B092D	1B092D			
5000		METHD HRN-OTHER	1A167E	1B092E	1B092E	1B092E	1B092E	1B092E			
5510	81	METH NARC SNORT	1A183A	1B103A	1B103A	1B103A	1B103A	1B103A	1B102A	1B102A	1B102A
5520	81	METH NARC SMOKE	1A183B	1B103B	1B103B	1B103B	1B103B	1B103B	1B102B	1B102B	1B102B
5530	81	METH NARC INJCT	1A183C	1B103C	1B103C	1B103C	1B103C	1B103C	1B102C	1B102C	1B102C
5540	81	METH NARC MOUTH	1A183D	1B103D	1B103D	1B103D	1B103D	1B103D	1B102D	1B102D	1B102D
5550	81	METH NARC OTHER	1A183E	1B103E	1B103E	1B103E	1B103E	1B103E	1B102E	1B102E	1B102E

A06a: DRUGS. Reasons for use, abstention, and stopping

1820	43	ALC EXPERIMENT		1B009A	1B009A	1B009A	1B009A	1B009A	1B009A	1B009A	1B009A
1830	43	ALC RELAX	1A032A	1B009B	1B009B	1B009B	1B009B	1B009B	1B009B	1B009B	1B009B
1840	43	ALC GET HIGH	1A032B	1B009C	1B009C	1B009C	1B009C	1B009C	1B009C	1B009C	1B009C
1850	43	ALC SEEK INSGHT	1A032C	1B009D	1B009D	1B009D	1B009D	1B009D	1B009D	1B009D	1B009D
1860	43	ALC GD TM FRNDS	1A032D	1B009E	1B009E	1B009E	1B009E	1B009E	1B009E	1B009E	1B009E
1870	43	ALC FIT IN GRP	1A032E	1B009F	1B009F	1B009F	1B009F	1B009F	1B009F	1B009F	1B009F
1880	43	ALC GET AWY PRB	1A032F	1B009G	1B009G	1B009G	1B009G	1B009G	1B009G	1B009G	1B009G
1890	43	ALC BOREDOM	1A032G	1B009H	1B009H	1B009H	1B009H	1B009H	1B009H	1B009H	1B009H
1900	43	ALC ANGR&FRSTRN	1A032H	1B009I	1B009I	1B009I	1B009I	1B009I	1B009I	1B009I	1B009I
1910	43	ALC GT THRU DAY	1A032J	1B009J	1B009J	1B009J	1B009J	1B009J	1B009J	1B009J	1B009J
1920	43	ALC INCRS EF DR	1A032K	1B009K	1B009K	1B009K	1B009K	1B009K	1B009K	1B009K	1B009K
1930	43	ALC DECRS EF DR	1A032L	1B009L	1B009L	1B009L	1B009L	1B009L	1B009L	1B009L	1B009L
1940	43	ALC GET SLEEP		1B009M	1B009M	1B009M	1B009M	1B009M	1B009M	1B009M	1B009M
1950	43	ALC TASTES GOOD	1A032N	1B009N	1B009N	1B009N	1B009N	1B009N	1B009N	1B009N	1B009N
1960	43	ALC I AM HOOKED	1A032M	1B009O	1B009O	1B009O	1B009O	1B009O	1B009O	1B009O	1B009O
2210	48	MJ EXPERIMENT	1A049A	1B022A	1B022A	1B022A	1B022A	1B022A	1B022A	1B022A	1B022A
2220	48	MJ RELAX	1A049B	1B022B	1B022B	1B022B	1B022B	1B022B	1B022B	1B022B	1B022B
2230	48	MJ GET HIGH	1A049C	1B022C	1B022C	1B022C	1B022C	1B022C	1B022C	1B022C	1B022C
2240	48	MJ SEEK INSIGHT	1A049D	1B022D	1B022D	1B022D	1B022D	1B022D	1B022D	1B022D	1B022D
2250	48	MJ GD TM FRNDS	1A049E	1B022E	1B022E	1B022E	1B022E	1B022E	1B022E	1B022E	1B022E
		(continued)									

Item Refer- ence Number	Page Loc. in this Volume	ITEM DESCRIPTION (ABBREVIATED)	QUESTIONNAIRE LOCATION BY YEAR (FORM, SECTION, AND QUESTION NUMBER)								
			1975	1976	1977	1978	1979	1980/81	1982/83	1984/85	1986

A06a: DRUGS. Reasons for use, abstention, and stopping (continued)

Item Refer- ence Number	Page Loc. in this Volume	ITEM DESCRIPTION (ABBREVIATED)	1975	1976	1977	1978	1979	1980/81	1982/83	1984/85	1986
2260	48	MJ FIT IN GRP	1A049F	1B022F	1B022F	1B022F	1B022F	1B022F	1B022F	1B022F	1B022F
2270	48	MJ GET AWY PRB	1A049G	1B022G	1B022G	1B022G	1B022G	1B022G	1B022G	1B022G	1B022G
2280	48	MJ BOREDOM	1A049H	1B022H	1B022H	1B022H	1B022H	1B022H	1B022H	1B022H	1B022H
2290	48	MJ ANGR&FRUSTRN	1A049I	1B022I	1B022I	1B022I	1B022I	1B022I	1B022I	1B022I	1B022I
2300	48	MJ GET THRU DAY	1A049K	1B022J	1B022J	1B022J	1B022J	1B022J	1B022J	1B022J	1B022J
2310	48	MJ INCRS EF DRG	1A049L	1B022K	1B022K	1B022K	1B022K	1B022K	1B022K	1B022K	1B022K
2320	48	MJ DECRS EF DRG	1A049M	1B022L	1B022L	1B022L	1B022L	1B022L	1B022L	1B022L	1B022L
2330	48	MJ I AM HOOKED		1B022M	1B022M	1B022M	1B022M	1B022M	1B022M	1B022M	1B022M
2520	53	LSD EXPERIMENT	1A062A	1B032A	1B032A	1B032A	1B032A	1B032A	1B036A	1B036A	1B036A
2530	53	LSD RELAX	1A062B	1B032B	1B032B	1B032B	1B032B	1B032B	1B036B	1B036B	1B036B
2540	53	LSD GET HIGH	1A062C	1B032C	1B032C	1B032C	1B032C	1B032C	1B036C	1B036C	1B036C
2550	53	LSD SEEK INSGHT	1A062D	1B032D	1B032D	1B032D	1B032D	1B032D	1B036D	1B036D	1B036D
2560	53	LSD GD TM FRNDS	1A062E	1B032E	1B032E	1B032E	1B032E	1B032E	1B036E	1B036E	1B036E
2570	53	LSD FIT IN GRP	1A062F	1B032F	1B032F	1B032F	1B032F	1B032F	1B036F	1B036F	1B036F
2580	53	LSD GT AWY PRB	1A062G	1B032G	1B032G	1B032G	1B032G	1B032G	1B036G	1B036G	1B036G
2590	53	LSD BOREDOM	1A062H	1B032H	1B032H	1B032H	1B032H	1B032H	1B036H	1B036H	1B036H
2600	53	LSD ANGR&FRSTRN	1A062I	1B032I	1B032I	1B032I	1B032I	1B032I	1B036I	1B036I	1B036I
2610	53	LSD GT THRU DAY	1A062K	1B032J	1B032J	1B032J	1B032J	1B032J	1B036J	1B036J	1B036J
2620	53	LSD INCRS EF DR	1A062L	1B032K	1B032K	1B032K	1B032K	1B032K	1B036K	1B036K	1B036K
2630	53	LSD DCRS EF DRG	1A062M	1B032L	1B032L	1B032L	1B032L	1B032L	1B036L	1B036L	1B036L
2640	53	LSD I AM HOOKED		1B032M	1B032M	1B032M	1B032M	1B032M	1B036M	1B036M	1B036M
2940	60	AMPH EXPERIMENT	1A092A	1B046A	1B046A	1B046A	1B046A	1B046A	1B053A	1B053A	1B053A
2950	60	AMPH RELAX	1A092B	1B046B	1B046B	1B046B	1B046B	1B046B	1B053B	1B053B	1B053B
2960	60	AMPH GET HIGH	1A092C	1B046C	1B046C	1B046C	1B046C	1B046C	1B053C	1B053C	1B053C
2970	60	AMPH SK INSIGHT	1A092D	1B046D	1B046D	1B046D	1B046D	1B046D	1B053D	1B053D	1B053D
2980	60	AMPH GD TM FRND	1A092E	1B046E	1B046E	1B046E	1B046E	1B046E	1B053E	1B053E	1B053E
2990	60	AMPH FIT IN GRP	1A092F	1B046F	1B046F	1B046F	1B046F	1B046F	1B053F	1B053F	1B053F
3000	60	AMPH GT AWY PRB	1A092G	1B046G	1B046G	1B046G	1B046G	1B046G	1B053G	1B053G	1B053G
3010	60	AMPH BOREDOM	1A092H	1B046H	1B046H	1B046H	1B046H	1B046H	1B053H	1B053H	1B053H
3020	60	AMPH ANGR&FRSTN	1A092I	1B046I	1B046I	1B046I	1B046I	1B046I	1B053I	1B053I	1B053I
3030	60	AMPH GT THRU DA	1A092K	1B046J	1B046J	1B046J	1B046J	1B046J	1B053J	1B053J	1B053J
3040	60	AMPH INCR EF DR	1A092L	1B046K	1B046K	1B046K	1B046K	1B046K	1B053K	1B053K	1B053K
3050	60	AMPH DCRS EF DR	1A092M	1B046L	1B046L	1B046L	1B046L	1B046L	1B053L	1B053L	1B053L
3060	60	AMPH STAY AWAKE	1A092N	1B046M	1B046M	1B046M	1B046M	1B046M	1B053M	1B053M	1B053M
3070	60	AMPH GET>ENERGY	1A092O	1B046N	1B046N	1B046N	1B046N	1B046N	1B053N	1B053N	1B053N
3080	60	AMPH LOSE WGHT	1A092P	1B046O	1B046O	1B046O	1B046O	1B046O	1B053O	1B053O	1B053O
3090	60	AMPH I AM HOOKD	1A092Q	1B046P	1B046P	1B046P	1B046P	1B046P	1B053P	1B053P	1B053P
3450	65	BARB EXPERIMENT	1A121A	1B060A	1B060A	1B060A	1B060A	1B060A	1B067A	1B067A	1B067A
3460	65	BARB RELAX	1A121B	1B060B	1B060B	1B060B	1B060B	1B060B	1B067B	1B067B	1B067B
3470	65	BARB GET HIGH	1A121C	1B060C	1B060C	1B060C	1B060C	1B060C	1B067C	1B067C	1B067C
3480	65	BARB SK INSIGHT	1A121D	1B060D	1B060D	1B060D	1B060D	1B060D	1B067D	1B067D	1B067D
3490	65	BARB GD TM FRND	1A121E	1B060E	1B060E	1B060E	1B060E	1B060E	1B067E	1B067E	1B067E
3500	65	BARB FIT IN GRP	1A121F	1B060F	1B060F	1B060F	1B060F	1B060F	1B067F	1B067F	1B067F
3510	65	BARB GT AWY PRB	1A121G	1B060G	1B060G	1B060G	1B060G	1B060G	1B067G	1B067G	1B067G
3520	65	BARB BOREDOM	1A121H	1B060H	1B060H	1B060H	1B060H	1B060H	1B067H	1B067H	1B067H
3530	65	BARB ANGR&FRSTN	1A121I	1B060I	1B060I	1B060I	1B060I	1B060I	1B067I	1B067I	1B067I
3540	65	BARB GT THRU DA	1A121K	1B060J	1B060J	1B060J	1B060J	1B060J	1B067J	1B067J	1B067J
3550	65	BARB INCR EF DR	1A121L	1B060K	1B060K	1B060K	1B060K	1B060K	1B067K	1B067K	1B067K
3560	65	BARB DCRS EF DR	1A121M	1B060L	1B060L	1B060L	1B060L	1B060L	1B067L	1B067L	1B067L
3570	65	BARB GET SLEEP	1A121N	1B060M	1B060M	1B060M	1B060M	1B060M	1B067M	1B067M	1B067M
3575	65	BARB RLV PHYS PN				1B060N	1B060N	1B060N	1B067N	1B067N	1B067N
3580	65	BARB I AM HOOKD	1A121O	1B060N	1B060N	1B060O	1B060O	1B060O	1B067O	1B067O	1B067O
3910	70	TRNQ EXPERIMENT	1A136A	1B070A	1B070A	1B070A	1B070A	1B070A	1B077A	1B077A	1B077A
3920	70	TRNQ RELAX	1A136B	1B070B	1B070B	1B070B	1B070B	1B070B	1B077B	1B077B	1B077B
3930	70	TRNQ GET HIGH	1A136C	1B070C	1B070C	1B070C	1B070C	1B070C	1B077C	1B077C	1B077C
3940	70	TRNQ SK INSIGHT	1A136D	1B070D	1B070D	1B070D	1B070D	1B070D	1B077D	1B077D	1B077D
3950	70	TRNQ GD TM FRND	1A136E	1B070E	1B070E	1B070E	1B070E	1B070E	1B077E	1B077E	1B077E
3960	70	TRNQ FIT IN GRP	1A136F	1B070F	1B070F	1B070F	1B070F	1B070F	1B077F	1B077F	1B077F
3970	70	TRNQ GT AWY PRB	1A136G	1B070G	1B070G	1B070G	1B070G	1B070G	1B077G	1B077G	1B077G
3980	70	TRNQ BOREDOM	1A136H	1B070H	1B070H	1B070H	1B070H	1B070H	1B077H	1B077H	1B077H
3990	70	TRNQ ANGR&FRSTN	1A136I	1B070I	1B070I	1B070I	1B070I	1B070I	1B077I	1B077I	1B077I
4000	70	TRNQ GT THRU DA	1A136K	1B070J	1B070J	1B070J	1B070J	1B070J	1B077J	1B077J	1B077J
4010	70	TRNQ INCR EF DR	1A136L	1B070K	1B070K	1B070K	1B070K	1B070K	1B077K	1B077K	1B077K

(continued)

Item Reference Number	Page Loc. in this Volume	ITEM DESCRIPTION (ABBREVIATED)	QUESTIONNAIRE LOCATION BY YEAR (FORM, SECTION, AND QUESTION NUMBER)								
			1975	1976	1977	1978	1979	1980/81	1982/83	1984/85	1986

A06a: DRUGS. Reasons for use, abstention, and stopping (continued)

Item Reference Number	Page Loc. in this Volume	ITEM DESCRIPTION (ABBREVIATED)	1975	1976	1977	1978	1979	1980/81	1982/83	1984/85	1986
4020	70	TRNQ DCRS EF DR	1A136M	1B070L	1B070L	1B070L	1B070L	1B070L	1B077L	1B077L	1B077L
4030	70	TRNQ GET SLEEP	1A136N	1B070M	1B070M	1B070M	1B070M	1B070M	1B077M	1B077M	1B077M
4035	70	TRNQ RLV PHYS PN				1B070N	1B070N	1B070N	1B077N	1B077N	1B077N
4040	70	TRNQ I AM HOOKD	1A136O	1B070N	1B070N	1B070O	1B070O	1B070O	1B077O	1B077O	1B077O
4370	74	COKE EXPERIMENT	1A149A	1B079A	1B079A	1B079A	1B079A	1B079A	1B086B	1B086A	1B086A
4380	74	COKE RELAX	1A149B	1B079B	1B079B	1B079B	1B079B	1B079B	1B086B	1B086B	1B086B
4390	74	COKE GET HIGH	1A149C	1B079C	1B079C	1B079C	1B079C	1B079C	1B086C	1B086C	1B086C
4400	74	COKE SK INSIGHT	1A149D	1B079D	1B079D	1B079D	1B079D	1B079D	1B086D	1B086D	1B086D
4410	74	COKE GD TM FRND	1A149E	1B079E	1B079E	1B079E	1B079E	1B079E	1B086E	1B086E	1B086E
4420	74	COKE FIT IN GRP	1A149F	1B079F	1B079F	1B079F	1B079F	1B079F	1B086F	1B086F	1B086F
4430	74	COKE GT AWY PRB	1A149G	1B079G	1B079G	1B079G	1B079G	1B079G	1B086G	1B086G	1B086G
4440	74	COKE BOREDOM	1A149H	1B079H	1B079H	1B079H	1B079H	1B079H	1B086H	1B086H	1B086H
4450	74	COKE ANGR&FRSTN	1A149I	1B079I	1B079I	1B079I	1B079I	1B079I	1B086I	1B086I	1B086I
4460	74	COKE GT THRU DA	1A149K	1B079J	1B079J	1B079J	1B079J	1B079J	1B086J	1B086J	1B086J
4470	74	COKE INCR EF DR	1A149L	1B079K	1B079K	1B079K	1B079K	1B079K	1B086K	1B086K	1B086K
4480	74	COKE DCRS EF DR	1A149M	1B079L	1B079L	1B079L	1B079L	1B079L	1B086L	1B086L	1B086L
4490	74	COKE STAY AWAKE		1B079M	1B079M	1B079M	1B079M	1B079M	1B086M	1B086M	1B086M
4500	74	COKE GET>ENERGY	1A149N	1B079N	1B079N	1B079N	1B079N	1B079N	1B086N	1B086N	1B086N
4510	74	COKE I AM HOOKD	1A149O	1B079O	1B079O	1B079O	1B079O	1B079O	1B086O	1B086O	1B086O
4800		HERIN EXPERMENT	1A163A	1B088A	1B088A	1B088A	1B088A	1B088A			
4810		HERIN RELAX	1A163B	1B088B	1B088B	1B088B	1B088B	1B088B			
4820		HERIN GET HIGH	1A163C	1B088C	1B088C	1B088C	1B088C	1B088C			
4830		HERIN SK INSIGT	1A163D	1B088D	1B088D	1B088D	1B088D	1B088D			
4840		HERIN GD TM FRN	1A163E	1B088E	1B088E	1B088E	1B088E	1B088E			
4850		HERIN FT IN GRP	1A163F	1B088F	1B088F	1B088F	1B088F	1B088F			
4860		HERIN GT AWY PB	1A163G	1B088G	1B088G	1B088G	1B088G	1B088G			
4870		HERIN BOREDOM	1A163H	1B088H	1B088H	1B088H	1B088H	1B088H			
4880		HERIN ANGR&FRST	1A163I	1B088I	1B088I	1B088I	1B088I	1B088I			
4890		HERIN GT THR DA	1A163K	1B088J	1B088J	1B088J	1B088J	1B088J			
4900		HERIN INC EF DG	1A163L	1B088K	1B088K	1B088K	1B088K	1B088K			
4910		HERIN DEC EF DG	1A163M	1B088L	1B088L	1B088L	1B088L	1B088L			
4920		HERIN I AM HOOK	1A163N	1B088M	1B088M	1B088M	1B088M	1B088M			
5230	80	NARC EXPERIMENT	1A178A	1B098A	1B098A	1B098A	1B098A	1B098A	1B097A	1B097A	1B097A
5240	80	NARC RELAX	1A178B	1B098B	1B098B	1B098B	1B098B	1B098B	1B097B	1B097B	1B097B
5250	80	NARC GET HIGH	1A178C	1B098C	1B098C	1B098C	1B098C	1B098C	1B097C	1B097C	1B097C
5260	80	NARC SK INSIGTS	1A178D	1B098D	1B098D	1B098D	1B098D	1B098D	1B097D	1B097D	1B097D
5270	80	NARC GD TM FRND	1A178E	1B098E	1B098E	1B098E	1B098E	1B098E	1B097E	1B097E	1B097E
5280	80	NARC FIT IN GRP	1A178F	1B098F	1B098F	1B098F	1B098F	1B098F	1B097F	1B097F	1B097F
5290	80	NARC GT AWY PBM	1A178G	1B098G	1B098G	1B098G	1B098G	1B098G	1B097G	1B097G	1B097G
5300	80	NARC BOREDOM	1A178H	1B098H	1B098H	1B098H	1B098H	1B098H	1B097H	1B097H	1B097H
5310	80	NARC ANGR&FRSTN	1A178I	1B098I	1B098I	1B098I	1B098I	1B098I	1B097I	1B097I	1B097I
5320	80	NARC GT THRU DA	1A178K	1B098J	1B098J	1B098J	1B098J	1B098J	1B097J	1B097J	1B097J
5330	80	NARC INC EF DG	1A178L	1B098K	1B098K	1B098K	1B098K	1B098K	1B097K	1B097K	1B097K
5340	80	NARC DEC EF DG	1A178M	1B098L	1B098L	1B098L	1B098L	1B098L	1B097L	1B097L	1B097L
5350	80	NARC GET SLEEP		1B098M	1B098M	1B098M	1B098M	1B098M	1B097M	1B097M	1B097M
5360	80	NARC SBST HERIN	1A178O	1B098N	1B098N	1B098N	1B098N	1B098N	1B097N	1B097N	1B097N
5363	80	NARC RLV PHYS PN				1B098O	1B098O	1B098O	1B097O	1B097O	1B097O
5366	80	NARC RLV COUGHNG				1B098P	1B098P	1B098P	1B097P	1B097P	1B097P
5370	80	NARC I AM HOOKD	1A178N	1B098O	1B098O	1B098Q	1B098Q	1B098Q	1B097Q	1B097Q	1B097Q
9020	138	CNCRN PSYCH DAMG		(3D04A)	(3D04A)	3D04A	3D04A	3D04A	3D04A	3D04A	3D04A
9030	138	CNCRN PHYSCL DMG		(3D04B)	(3D04B)	3D04B	3D04B	3D04B	3D04B	3D04B	3D04B
9040	138	CNCRN GT ARRESTD		(3D04C)	(3D04C)	3D04C	3D04C	3D04C	3D04C	3D04C	3D04C
9050	138	CNCRN BECOM ADCT		(3D04D)	(3D04D)	3D04D	3D04D	3D04D	3D04D	3D04D	3D04D
9060	138	AGST MY BELIEFS		(3D04E)	(3D04E)	3D04E	3D04E	3D04E	3D04E	3D04E	3D04E
9070	138	CNCRN LEGY&AMBTN		(3D04F)	(3D04F)	3D04F	3D04F	3D04F	3D04F	3D04F	3D04F
9080	138	CNCRN LOSS CNTRL		(3D04G)	(3D04G)	3D04G	3D04G	3D04G	3D04G	3D04G	3D04G
9090	138	MJ ->STRNGR DRGS		(3D04H)	(3D04H)	3D04H	3D04H	3D04H	3D04H	3D04H	3D04H
9100	138	MJ NOT ENJOYABLE		(3D04I)	(3D04I)	3D04I	3D04I	3D04I	3D04I	3D04I	3D04I
9110	138	PRNTS DISAPPROVE		(3D04J)	(3D04J)	3D04J	3D04J	3D04J	3D04J	3D04J	3D04J
9120	138	HS/WF DISAPPROVE		(3D04K)	(3D04K)	3D04K	3D04K	3D04K	3D04K	3D04K	3D04K
9130	138	DONT LIKE USERS		(3D04L)	(3D04L)	3D04L	3D04L	3D04L	3D04L	3D04L	3D04L
9140	138	FRNDS DNT USE IT		(3D04M)	(3D04M)	3D04M	3D04M	3D04M	3D04M	3D04M	3D04M
9150	138	PSSBLY BAD TRIP		(3D04N)	(3D04N)	3D04N	3D04N	3D04N	3D04N	3D04N	3D04N

(continued)

Item Reference Number	Page Loc. in this Volume	ITEM DESCRIPTION (ABBREVIATED)	QUESTIONNAIRE LOCATION BY YEAR (FORM, SECTION, AND QUESTION NUMBER)								
			1975	1976	1977	1978	1979	1980/81	1982/83	1984/85	1986

A06a: DRUGS. Reasons for use, abstention, and stopping *(continued)*

Item Ref.	Page	Description	1975	1976	1977	1978	1979	1980/81	1982/83	1984/85	1986
9160	138	TOO EXPENSIVE			3D04O	3D04O	3D04O	3D04O	3D04O	3D04O	3D04O
9170	138	NOT AVAILABLE			3D04P	3D04P	3D04P	3D04P	3D04P	3D04P	3D04P
9180	138	NOT WNT GET HIGH			3D04Q	3D04Q	3D04Q	3D04Q	3D04Q	3D04Q	3D04Q

A07a: DRUGS. Driving, tickets, and accidents after use

Item Ref.	Page	Description	1975	1976	1977	1978	1979	1980/81	1982/83	1984/85	1986
660	22	#TCKTS AFT DRNK		+C29A	+C29A	+C29A	+C29A	+C29A	+C29A	+C29A	+C29A
670	23	#TCKTS AFT MARJ		+C29B	+C29B	+C29B	+C29B	+C29B	+C29B	+C29B	+C29B
680	23	#TCKTS AFT OTDG		+C29C	+C29C	+C29C	+C29C	+C29C	+C29C	+C29C	+C29C
700	23	#ACDTS AFT DRNK		+C31A	+C31A	+C31A	+C31A	+C31A	+C31A	+C31A	+C31A
710	23	#ACDTS AFT MARJ		+C31B	+C31B	+C31B	+C31B	+C31B	+C31B	+C31B	+C31B
720	23	#ACDTS AFT OTDG		+C31C	+C31C	+C31C	+C31C	+C31C	+C31C	+C31C	+C31C
1811	119	#X/2W DRIVE+ALCL								2E19A	2E19A
1812	119	#X/2W DRIVE+5DRK								2E19B	2E19B
1815	119	#X/2W RIDE+ALCL								2E20A	2E20A
1816	120	#X/2W RIDE+5DRK								2E20B	2E20B

A07b: DRUGS. Other problems

Item Ref.	Page	Description	1975	1976	1977	1978	1979	1980/81	1982/83	1984/85	1986
9190	138	AL CS BEHV REGRT		3D05A	3D05A	3D05A	3D05A	3D05A	3D05A	3D05A	3D05A
9200	138	AL HURT REL PRNT		3D05A	3D05A	3D05A	3D05A	3D05A	3D05A	3D05A	3D05A
9210	138	AL HURT REL SPSE		3D05A	3D05A	3D05A	3D05A	3D05A	3D05A	3D05A	3D05A
9220	138	AL HURT REL FRND		3D05A	3D05A	3D05A	3D05A	3D05A	3D05A	3D05A	3D05A
9230	138	AL HURT REL TCHR		3D05A	3D05A	3D05A	3D05A	3D05A	3D05A	3D05A	3D05A
9240	138	AL INV PL BD INF		3D05A	3D05A	3D05A	3D05A	3D05A	3D05A	3D05A	3D05A
9250	138	AL HURT PERF JOB		3D05A	3D05A	3D05A	3D05A	3D05A	3D05A	3D05A	3D05A
9260	138	AL CAUS<INTERSTD		3D05A	3D05A	3D05A	3D05A	3D05A	3D05A	3D05A	3D05A
9270	138	AL CS<STABL EMTN		3D05A	3D05A	3D05A	3D05A	3D05A	3D05A	3D05A	3D05A
9280	138	AL CS HAV<ENERGY		3D05A	3D05A	3D05A	3D05A	3D05A	3D05A	3D05A	3D05A
9290	138	AL INTF THNK CLR		3D05A	3D05A	3D05A	3D05A	3D05A	3D05A	3D05A	3D05A
9300	138	AL BD PSYCH EFCT		3D05A	3D05A	3D05A	3D05A	3D05A	3D05A	3D05A	3D05A
9310	138	AL CS HEALTH BAD		3D05A	3D05A	3D05A	3D05A	3D05A	3D05A	3D05A	3D05A
9320	138	AL CS DRIV UNSAF		3D05A	3D05A	3D05A	3D05A	3D05A	3D05A	3D05A	3D05A
9330	138	AL GT TRBL W POL		3D05A	3D05A	3D05A	3D05A	3D05A	3D05A	3D05A	3D05A
9340	138	AL CS NO PROBLEM			3D05A	3D05A	3D05A	3D05A	3D05A	3D05A	3D05A
9350	138	AL NEVER USED DG			3D05A	3D05A	3D05A	3D05A	3D05A	3D05A	3D05A
9360	139	MJ CS BEHV REGRT		3D05M	3D05M	3D05M	3D05M	3D05M	3D05M	3D05M	3D05M
9370	139	MJ HURT REL PRNT		3D05M	3D05M	3D05M	3D05M	3D05M	3D05M	3D05M	3D05M
9380	139	MJ HURT REL SPSE		3D05M	3D05M	3D05M	3D05M	3D05M	3D05M	3D05M	3D05M
9390	139	MJ HURT REL FRND		3D05M	3D05M	3D05M	3D05M	3D05M	3D05M	3D05M	3D05M
9400	139	MJ HURT REL TCHR		3D05M	3D05M	3D05M	3D05M	3D05M	3D05M	3D05M	3D05M
9410	139	MJ INV PL BD INF		3D05M	3D05M	3D05M	3D05M	3D05M	3D05M	3D05M	3D05M
9420	139	MJ HURT PERF JOB		3D05M	3D05M	3D05M	3D05M	3D05M	3D05M	3D05M	3D05M
9430	139	MJ CAUS<INTERSTD		3D05M	3D05M	3D05M	3D05M	3D05M	3D05M	3D05M	3D05M
9440	139	MJ CS<STABL EMTN		3D05M	3D05M	3D05M	3D05M	3D05M	3D05M	3D05M	3D05M
9450	139	MJ CS HAV<ENERGY		3D05M	3D05M	3D05M	3D05M	3D05M	3D05M	3D05M	3D05M
9460	139	MJ INTF THNK CLR		3D05M	3D05M	3D05M	3D05M	3D05M	3D05M	3D05M	3D05M
9470	139	MJ BD PSYCH EFCT		3D05M	3D05M	3D05M	3D05M	3D05M	3D05M	3D05M	3D05M
9480	139	MJ CS HEALTH BAD		3D05M	3D05M	3D05M	3D05M	3D05M	3D05M	3D05M	3D05M
9490	139	MJ CS DRIV UNSAF		3D05M	3D05M	3D05M	3D05M	3D05M	3D05M	3D05M	3D05M
9500	139	MJ GT TRBL W POL		3D05M	3D05M	3D05M	3D05M	3D05M	3D05M	3D05M	3D05M
9510	139	MJ CS NO PROBLEM			3D05M	3D05M	3D05M	3D05M	3D05M	3D05M	3D05M
9520	139	MJ NEVER USED DG			3D05M	3D05M	3D05M	3D05M	3D05M	3D05M	3D05M
9530	139	OT CS BEHV REGRT		3D05O	3D05O	3D05O	3D05O	3D05O	3D05O	3D05O	3D05O
9540	139	OT HURT REL PRNT		3D05O	3D05O	3D05O	3D05O	3D05O	3D05O	3D05O	3D05O
9550	139	OT HURT REL SPSE		3D05O	3D05O	3D05O	3D05O	3D05O	3D05O	3D05O	3D05O
9560	139	OT HURT REL FRND		3D05O	3D05O	3D05O	3D05O	3D05O	3D05O	3D05O	3D05O
9570	139	OT HURT REL TCHR		3D05O	3D05O	3D05O	3D05O	3D05O	3D05O	3D05O	3D05O
9580	139	OT INV PL BD INF		3D05O	3D05O	3D05O	3D05O	3D05O	3D05O	3D05O	3D05O
9590	139	OT HURT PERF JOB		3D05O	3D05O	3D05O	3D05O	3D05O	3D05O	3D05O	3D05O
9600	139	OT CAUS<INTERSTD		3D05O	3D05O	3D05O	3D05O	3D05O	3D05O	3D05O	3D05O
9610	139	OT CS<STABL EMTN		3D05O	3D05O	3D05O	3D05O	3D05O	3D05O	3D05O	3D05O
9620	139	OT CS HAV<ENERGY		3D05O	3D05O	3D05O	3D05O	3D05O	3D05O	3D05O	3D05O

(continued)

Item Reference Number	Page Loc. in this Volume	ITEM DESCRIPTION (ABBREVIATED)	QUESTIONNAIRE LOCATION BY YEAR (FORM, SECTION, AND QUESTION NUMBER)								
			1975	1976	1977	1978	1979	1980/81	1982/83	1984/85	1986

A07b: DRUGS. Other problems (continued)

Item Reference Number	Page Loc. in this Volume	ITEM DESCRIPTION (ABBREVIATED)	1975	1976	1977	1978	1979	1980/81	1982/83	1984/85	1986
9630	139	OT INTF THNK CLR		3D05O	3D05O	3D05O	3D05O	3D05O	3D05O	3D05O	3D05O
9640	139	OT BD PSYCH EFCT		3D05O	3D05O	3D05O	3D05O	3D05O	3D05O	3D05O	3D05O
9650	139	OT CS HEALTH BAD		3D05O	3D05O	3D05O	3D05O	3D05O	3D05O	3D05O	3D05O
9660	139	OT CS DRIV UNSAF		3D05O	3D05O	3D05O	3D05O	3D05O	3D05O	3D05O	3D05O
9670	139	OT GT TRBL W POL		3D05O	3D05O	3D05O	3D05O	3D05O	3D05O	3D05O	3D05O
9680	139	OT CS NO PROBLEM			3D05O	3D05O	3D05O	3D05O	3D05O	3D05O	3D05O
9690	139	OT NEVER USED DG			3D05O	3D05O	3D05O	3D05O	3D05O	3D05O	3D05O

A08a: DRUGS. Sources of help

Item Reference Number	Page Loc. in this Volume	ITEM DESCRIPTION (ABBREVIATED)	1975	1976	1977	1978	1979	1980/81	1982/83	1984/85	1986
7540		TRN FA/MO DRG HP			2E05A		2E07A				
7550		TRN SR/BR DRG HP			2E05B		2E07B				
7560		TRN RLTVS DRG HP			2E05C		2E07C				
7570		TRN FRND DRG HP			2E05D		2E07D				
7580		TRN DOCTR DRG HP			2E05E		2E07E				
7590		TRN CLINC DRG HP			2E05F		2E07F				
7600		TRN CNSLR DRG HP			2E05G		2E07G				
7610		TRN TCHR DRG HP			2E05H		2E07H				
7620		TRN MNSTR DRG HP			2E05I		2E07I				

A09a: DRUGS. Parental awareness of use

Item Reference Number	Page Loc. in this Volume	ITEM DESCRIPTION (ABBREVIATED)	1975	1976	1977	1978	1979	1980/81	1982/83	1984/85	1986
7510	116	PRNT THK U DRINK			2E02	2E01	2E04	2E05	2E05	2E05	2E05
7520	116	PRNT THK U SM MJ			2E03	2E02	2E05	2E06	2E06	2E06	2E06
7530		PRNT THK USE DRG			2E04	2E03	2E06	2E07			

A10a: DRUGS. Education and communication in school

Item Reference Number	Page Loc. in this Volume	ITEM DESCRIPTION (ABBREVIATED)	1975	1976	1977	1978	1979	1980/81	1982/83	1984/85	1986
7690	118	HAD DRUG EDUCATN		2E05	2E09	2E09	2E11	2E12	2E15	2E15	2E15
7840	119	DG ED,>DG INTRST		2E06	2E10	2E10	2E12	2E13	2E16	2E16	2E16
7850	119	DG ED,SPC COURSE		2E07A	2E11A	2E11A	2E13A	2E14A	2E17A	2E17A	2E17A
7860	119	DG ED,IN REG CRS		2E07B	2E11B	2E11B	2E13B	2E14B	2E17B	2E17B	2E17B
7870	119	DG ED,NT REG CRS		2E07C	2E11C	2E11C	2E13C	2E14C	2E17C	2E17C	2E17C
7880	119	DG ED,SPC DISCUS		2E07D	2E11D	2E11D	2E13D	2E14D	2E17D	2E17D	2E17D
7890	119	DG ED,GRT VALUE		2E08	2E12	2E12	2E14	2E15	2E18	2E18	2E18

A11a: DRUGS. Own attitudes about use by adults

Item Reference Number	Page Loc. in this Volume	ITEM DESCRIPTION (ABBREVIATED)	1975	1976	1977	1978	1979	1980/81	1982/83	1984/85	1986
8560	132	DAP SMK 1PCK CIG	(3A53A)	3A28A	3A28A	3A28A	3A28A	3A28A	3A28A	3A28A	3A28A
8570	132	DAP TRY MRJ 1-2T	(3A53B)	3A28B	3A28B	3A28B	3A28B	3A28B	3A28B	3A28B	3A28B
8580	132	DAP SMK MRJ OCCS	(3A53C)	3A28C	3A28C	3A28C	3A28C	3A28C	3A28C	3A28C	3A28C
8590	133	DAP SMK MRJ REGL	(3A53D)	3A28D	3A28D	3A28D	3A28D	3A28D	3A28D	3A28D	3A28D
8600	133	DAP TRY LSD 1-2T	(3A53E)	3A28E	3A28E	3A28E	3A28E	3A28E	3A28E	3A28E	3A28E
8610	133	DAP TKG LSD REGL	(3A53F)	3A28F	3A28F	3A28F	3A28F	3A28F	3A28F	3A28F	3A28F
8620	133	DAP TRY HRN 1-2T	(3A53G)	3A28G	3A28G	3A28G	3A28G	3A28G	3A28G	3A28G	3A28G
8630	133	DAP TKG HRN OCCS	(3A53H)	3A28H	3A28H	3A28H	3A28H	3A28H	3A28H	3A28H	3A28H
8640	133	DAP TKG HRN REGL	(3A53I)	3A28I	3A28I	3A28I	3A28I	3A28I	3A28I	3A28I	3A28I
8650	133	DAP TRY BRB 1-2T	(3A53J)	3A28J	3A28J	3A28J	3A28J	3A28J	3A28J	3A28J	3A28J
8660	133	DAP TKG BRB REGL	(3A53K)	3A28K	3A28K	3A28K	3A28K	3A28K	3A28K	3A28K	3A28K
8670	133	DAP TRY AMP 1-2T	(3A53L)	3A28L	3A28L	3A28L	3A28L	3A28L	3A28L	3A28L	3A28L
8680	134	DAP TKG AMP REGL	(3A53M)	3A28M	3A28M	3A28M	3A28M	3A28M	3A28M	3A28M	3A28M
8690	134	DAP TRY COC 1-2T	(3A53N)	3A28N	3A28N	3A28N	3A28N	3A28N	3A28N	3A28N	3A28N
8700	134	DAP TKG COC REGL	(3A53O)	3A28O	3A28O	3A28O	3A28O	3A28O	3A28O	3A28O	3A28O
8710	134	DAP TRY DRK ALCL	(3A53P)	3A28P	3A28P	3A28P	3A28P	3A28P	3A28P	3A28P	3A28P
8720	134	DAP 1-2 DRK/DAY	(3A53Q)	3A28Q	3A28Q	3A28Q	3A28Q	3A28Q	3A28Q	3A28Q	3A28Q
8730	134	DAP 4-5 DRK/DAY	(3A53R)	3A28R	3A28R	3A28R	3A28R	3A28R	3A28R	3A28R	3A28R
8740	134	DAP 5+ DRK WKNDS	(3A53S)	3A28S	3A28S	3A28S	3A28S	3A28S	3A28S	3A28S	3A28S

A11b: DRUGS. Own attitudes about use by own children

Item Reference Number	Page Loc. in this Volume	ITEM DESCRIPTION (ABBREVIATED)	1975	1976	1977	1978	1979	1980/81	1982/83	1984/85	1986
7210		FBD CHLD CIG RGL			2E01A						
7220		FBD CHLD MJ OCCS			2E01B						
7230		FBD CHLD MJ RGLY			2E01C						
		(continued)									

Item Reference Number	Page Loc. in this Volume	ITEM DESCRIPTION (ABBREVIATED)	QUESTIONNAIRE LOCATION BY YEAR (FORM, SECTION, AND QUESTION NUMBER)								
			1975	1976	1977	1978	1979	1980/81	1982/83	1984/85	1986

A11b: DRUGS. Own attitudes about use by own children (continued)

Item Reference Number	Page Loc.	ITEM DESCRIPTION	1975	1976	1977	1978	1979	1980/81	1982/83	1984/85	1986
7240		FBD CHLD LSD OCC			2E01D						
7250		FBD CHLD AMPH OC			2E01E						
7260		FBD CHLD BARB OC			2E01F						
7270		FBD CHLD COKE OC			2E01G						
7280		FBD CHLD HRN OCC			2E01H						
7290		FBD CHLD DRNK OC			2E01I						
7300		FBD CHLD DRNK RG			2E01J						
7310		FBD CHLD DRUNKOC			2E01K						

A11c: DRUGS. Own perceptions of users

Item Reference Number	Page Loc.	ITEM DESCRIPTION	1975	1976	1977	1978	1979	1980/81	1982/83	1984/85	1986
13060	196	I/MJ USR,>CREATV			5E01A	5E01A	5E01A	5E01A	5E01A	5E01A	5E01A
13070	196	I/MJ USR,<SENSBL			5E01B	5E01B	5E01B	5E01B	5E01B	5E01B	5E01B
13080	196	I/MJ USR,>INTRST			5E01C	5E01C	5E01C	5E01C	5E01C	5E01C	5E01C
13090	197	I/MJ USR,<HRDWKG			5E01D	5E01D	5E01D	5E01D	5E01D	5E01D	5E01D
13100	197	I/MJ USR,>INDPND			5E01E	5E01E	5E01E	5E01E	5E01E	5E01E	5E01E
13110	197	I/MJ USR,>UNSTBL			5E01F	5E01F	5E01F	5E01F	5E01F	5E01F	5E01F
13120	197	I/MJ USR,>CNCRND			5E01G	5E01G	5E01G	5E01G	5E01G	5E01G	5E01G
13130	197	I/MJ USR,>WKWLD			5E01H	5E01H	5E01H	5E01H	5E01H	5E01H	5E01H
13140	197	I/MJ USR,>CRMNL			5E01I	5E01I	5E01I	5E01I	5E01I	5E01I	5E01I
13330	197	I/DG USR,>CREATV			5E03A	5E03A		5E03A†	5E03A	5E02A	5E02A
13340	197	I/DG USR,<SENSBL			5E03B	5E03B		5E03B†	5E03B	5E02B	5E02B
13350	198	I/DG USR,>INTRST			5E03C	5E03C		5E03C†	5E03C	5E02C	5E02C
13360	198	I/DG USR,<HRDWKG			5E03D	5E03D		5E03D†	5E03D	5E02D	5E02D
13370	198	I/DG USR,>INDPND			5E03E	5E03E		5E03E†	5E03E	5E02E	5E02E
13380	198	I/DG USR,>UNSTBL			5E03F	5E03F		5E03F†	5E03F	5E02F	5E02F
13390	198	I/DG USR,>CNCRND			5E03G	5E03G		5E03G†	5E03G	5E02G	5E02G
13400	198	I/DG USR,>WKWLD			5E03H	5E03H		5E03H†	5E03H	5E02H	5E02H
13410	198	I/DG USR,>CRMNL			5E03I	5E03I		5E03I†	5E03I	5E02I	5E02I
13670	142	DRG USE+,MY FLGS			5E07C	5E07C	5E05C	5E07C†	3E07C	3E07C	3E07C
20880	198	GUY SMK COOL						5E03A‡	5E05A	5E03A	5E03A
20890	199	GUY SMK INSECURE						5E03B‡	5E05B	5E03B	5E03B
20900	199	GUY SMK INDPNDNT						5E03C‡	5E05C	5E03C	5E03C
20910	199	GUY SMK CONFORMG						5E03D‡	5E05D	5E03D	5E03D
20920	199	GUY SMK MATURE						5E03E‡	5E05E	5E03E	5E03E
20930	199	GUY SM TRY MATUR						5E03F‡	5E05F	5E03F	5E03F
20940	199	GIRL SMK COOL						5E04A‡	5E06A	5E04A	5E04A
20950	199	GRL SMK INSECURE						5E04B‡	5E06B	5E04B	5E04B
20960	200	GRL SMK INDPNDNT						5E04C‡	5E06C	5E04C	5E04C
20970	200	GRL SMK CONFORMG						5E04D‡	5E06D	5E04D	5E04D
20980	200	GRL SMK MATURE						5E04E‡	5E06E	5E04E	5E04E
20990	200	GRL SM TRY MATUR						5E04F‡	5E06F	5E04F	5E04F
21000	200	SMKRS ENJOY LIFE						5E05A‡	5E07A	5E05A	5E05A
21010	200	PRFR DATE N-SMKR						5E05B‡	5E07B	5E05B	5E05B
21020	200	HARMFUL CIG EXAG						5E05C‡	5E07C	5E05C	5E05C
21030	201	SMKR POOR JDGMNT						5E05D‡	5E07D	5E05D	5E05D
21040	201	DONT MIND SMOKNG						5E05E‡	5E07E	5E05E	5E05E
21050	201	SMKG DIRTY HABIT						5E05F‡	5E07F	5E05F	5E05F
21055	201	DTEST NEAR SMKRS									5E05G

A11d: DRUGS. Own attitudes about use by people of high school age

Item Reference Number	Page Loc.	ITEM DESCRIPTION	1975	1976	1977	1978	1979	1980/81	1982/83	1984/85	1986
22070	205	PR PTY-OTH HI AL								5E09C	5E09C
22090	205	PR PTY-OT USE MJ								5E09E	5E09E
22110	206	PR PTY-OT USE OT								5E09G	5E09G

A12a: DRUGS. Parents' attitudes about use

Item Reference Number	Page Loc.	ITEM DESCRIPTION	1975	1976	1977	1978	1979	1980/81	1982/83	1984/85	1986
11380		PRNT DAP CIGS	4A35A	4E09A	4E09A	4E08A	4E08A				
11390		PRNT DAP TRY MRJ	4A35B	4E09B	4E09B	4E08B	4E08B				
11400		PRNT DAP MJ OCC	4A35C	4E09C	4E09C	4E08C	4E08C				
11410		PRNT DAP MJ REG	4A35D	4E09D	4E09D	4E08D	4E08D				
11420		PRNT DAP TRY LSD	4A35E	4E09E	4E09E	4E08E	4E08E				
		(continued)									

† This question appears in 1980 but does not appear in 1981.   ‡ This question appears in 1981 but does not appear in 1980.

Item Reference Number	Page Loc. in this Volume	ITEM DESCRIPTION (ABBREVIATED)	QUESTIONNAIRE LOCATION BY YEAR (FORM, SECTION, AND QUESTION NUMBER)								
			1975	1976	1977	1978	1979	1980/81	1982/83	1984/85	1986

A12a: DRUGS. Parents' attitudes about use *(continued)*

11430		PRNT DAP TRY AMP	4A35F	4E09F	4E09F	4E08F	4E08F				
11440		PRNT DAP 1-2DR/D	4A35G	4E09G	4E09G	4E08G	4E08G				
11450		PRNT DAP 4-5DR/D	4A35H	4E09H	4E09H	4E08H	4E08H				
11460		PRNT DAP 5+DR/WE	4A35I	4E09I	4E09I	4E08I	4E08I				

A12b: DRUGS. Friends' and students' attitudes about use

11470	172	FRD DAP CIGS			4E10A		4E09A	4E08A	4E08A	4E08A	4E08A
11480	172	FRD DAP TRY MARJ			4E10B		4E09B	4E08B	4E08B	4E08B	4E08B
11490	173	FRD DAP MJ OCC			4E10C		4E09C	4E08C	4E08C	4E08C	4E08C
11500	173	FRD DAP MJ REG			4E10D		4E09D	4E08D	4E08D	4E08D	4E08D
11510	173	FRD DAP TRY LSD			4E10E		4E09E	4E08E	4E08E	4E08E	4E08E
11520	173	FRD DAP TRY AMP			4E10F		4E09F	4E08F	4E08F	4E08F	4E08F
11525	173	FRD DAP TRY COKE									4E08G
11526	173	FRD DAP COKE OCC									4E08H
11530	173	FRD DAP 1-2DR/DA			4E10G		4E09G	4E08G	4E08G	4E08G	4E08I
11540	173	FRD DAP 4-5DR/DA			4E10H		4E09H	4E08H	4E08H	4E08H	4E08J
11550	173	FRD DAP 5+DR/WKD			4E10I		4E09I	4E08I	4E08I	4E08I	4E08K
11551	174	FRD DAP DRIV+2DR								4E08J	4E08L
11552	174	FRD DAP DRIV+5DR								4E08K	4E08M
13650	142	DRG USE+,MAJ STD		5E06A	5E07A	5E07A	5E05A	5E07A†	3E07A	3E07A	3E07A
13660	142	DRG USE+,MY FRND		5E06B	5E07B	5E07B	5E05B	5E07B†	3E07B	3E07B	3E07B

A12c: DRUGS. Others' perceptions of users

12780		PSN TKG MJ/AMBTS		5D02A							
12790		PSN TKG MJ/-SOCL		5D02B							
12800		PSN TKG MJ/CNFMG		5D02C							
12810		PSN TKG MJ/CRMNL		5D02D							
12820		PSN TKG MJ/-STBL		5D02E							
12830		PSN TKG MJ/INTRS		5D02F							
12840		PSN TKG MJ/RBLS		5D02G							
12850		PSN TKG MJ/SNSBL		5D02H							
12860		PSN TKG MJ/SX PR		5D02I							
12870		PSN TKG MJ/WKWLD		5D02J							
12890		PSN TKG DG/AMBTS		5D03A							
12900		PSN TKG DG/-SOCL		5D03B							
12910		PSN TKG DG/CNFMG		5D03C							
12920		PSN TKG DG/CRMNL		5D03D							
12930		PSN TKG DG/-STBL		5D03E							
12940		PSN TKG DG/INTRS		5D03F							
12950		PSN TKG DG/RBLS		5D03G							
12960		PSN TKG DG/SNSBL		5D03H							
12970		PSN TKG DG/SX PR		5D03I							
12980		PSN TKG DG/WKWLD		5D03J							
13190		PPL/MJUSR>CREATV			5E02A	5E02A		5E02A	5E02A		
13200		PPL/MJUSR<SENSBL			5E02B	5E02B		5E02B	5E02B		
13210		PPL/MJUSR>INTRST			5E02C	5E02C		5E02C	5E02C		
13220		PPL/MJUSR<HRDWKG			5E02D	5E02D		5E02D	5E02D		
13230		PPL/MJUSR>INDPND			5E02E	5E02E		5E02E	5E02E		
13240		PPL/MJUSR>UNSTBL			5E02F	5E02F		5E02F	5E02F		
13250		PPL/MJUSR>CNCRND			5E02G	5E02G		5E02G	5E02G		
13260		PPL/MJUSR>WKWLD			5E02H	5E02H		5E02H	5E02H		
13270		PPL/MJUSR>CRMNL			5E02I	5E02I		5E02I	5E02I		
13490		PPL/DGUSR>CREATV			5E04A	5E04A		5E04A†	5E04A		
13500		PPL/DGUSR<SENSBL			5E04B	5E04B		5E04B†	5E04B		
13510		PPL/DGUSR>INTRST			5E04C	5E04C		5E04C†	5E04C		
13520		PPL/DGUSR<HRDWKG			5E04D	5E04D		5E04D†	5E04D		
13530		PPL/DGUSR>INDPND			5E04E	5E04E		5E04E†	5E04E		
13540		PPL/DGUSR>UNSTBL			5E04F	5E04F		5E04F†	5E04F		
13550		PPL/DGUSR>CNCRND			5E04G	5E04G		5E04G†	5E04G		
13560		PPL/DGUSR>WKWLD			5E04H	5E04H		5E04H†	5E04H		
13570		PPL/DGUSR>CRMNL			5E04I	5E04I		5E04I†	5E04I		

† This question appears in 1980 but does not appear in 1981.

Item Reference Number	Page Loc. in this Volume	ITEM DESCRIPTION (ABBREVIATED)	QUESTIONNAIRE LOCATION BY YEAR (FORM, SECTION, AND QUESTION NUMBER)								
			1975	1976	1977	1978	1979	1980/81	1982/83	1984/85	1986

A13a: DRUGS. Preferred legality for adults

10760	161	LAW 4 SMK TOBPUB			4A20K	4A20K	4A20K	4A20K	4A20K	4A20K	4A20K
10770		ILGL AD SMK CIG		4A20A							
10780	160	ILGL AD MRJ PRIV		4A20B	4A20A	4A20A	4A20A	4A20A	4A20A	4A20A	4A20A
10790	160	ILGL AD MRJ PUBL		4A20C	4A20B	4A20B	4A20B	4A20B	4A20B	4A20B	4A20B
10800	160	ILGL AD LSD PRIV		4A20D	4A20C	4A20C	4A20C	4A20C	4A20C	4A20C	4A20C
10810	160	ILGL AD LSD PUBL		4A20E	4A20D	4A20D	4A20D	4A20D	4A20D	4A20D	4A20D
10820	160	ILGL AD AMP PRIV		4A20F	4A20E	4A20E	4A20E	4A20E	4A20E	4A20E	4A20E
10830	161	ILGL AD AMP PUBL		4A20G	4A20F	4A20F	4A20F	4A20F	4A20F	4A20F	4A20F
10840	161	ILGL AD HRN PRIV		4A20H	4A20G	4A20G	4A20G	4A20G	4A20G	4A20G	4A20G
10850	161	ILGL AD HRN PUBL		4A20I	4A20H	4A20H	4A20H	4A20H	4A20H	4A20H	4A20H
10860	161	ILGL AD DRNK PRV		4A20J	4A20I	4A20I	4A20I	4A20I	4A20I	4A20I	4A20I
10870	161	ILGL AD DRNK PBL		4A20K	4A20J	4A20J	4A20J	4A20J	4A20J	4A20J	4A20J

A13b: DRUGS. Own response to legalization

10880	161	CRIME 2 USE MARJ	4A32	4A21	4A21	4A21	4A21	4A21	4A21	4A21	4A21
10890	161	LEGAL 2 SELL MRJ	4A33	4A22	4A22	4A22	4A22	4A22	4A22	4A22	4A22
10900	162	USE<MJ IF LEGAL	4A34	4A23	4A23	4A23	4A23	4A23	4A23	4A23	4A23

A13c: DRUGS. Knowledge of marijuana laws

13050		R'S STATE LAW/MJ		5D04	5D05	5D05	5D05	5D05†			

A14a: DRUGS. Risk of harm to self

12360	187	RSK OF CIG1+PK/D	5A41A	5A23A	5A23A	5A23A	5A23A	5A23A	5A23A	5A23A	5A23A
12365	190	RSK OF SMKLSS RG									5A23U
12370	187	RSK OF MJ 1-2 X	5A41B	5A23B	5A23B	5A23B	5A23B	5A23B	5A23B	5A23B	5A23B
12380	187	RSK OF MJ OCSNLY	5A41C	5A23C	5A23C	5A23C	5A23C	5A23C	5A23C	5A23C	5A23C
12390	188	RSK OF MJ REGLY	5A41D	5A23D	5A23D	5A23D	5A23D	5A23D	5A23D	5A23D	5A23D
12400	188	RSK OF LSD 1-2 X	5A41E	5A23E	5A23E	5A23E	5A23E	5A23E	5A23E	5A23E	5A23E
12410	188	RSK OF LSD REGLY	5A41F	5A23F	5A23F	5A23F	5A23F	5A23F	5A23F	5A23F	5A23F
12420	188	RSK OF 'H' 1-2 X	5A41G	5A23G	5A23G	5A23G	5A23G	5A23G	5A23G	5A23G	5A23G
12430	188	RSK OF 'H' OCSNL	5A41H	5A23H	5A23H	5A23H	5A23H	5A23H	5A23H	5A23H	5A23H
12440	188	RSK OF 'H' REGLY	5A41I	5A23I	5A23I	5A23I	5A23I	5A23I	5A23I	5A23I	5A23I
12450	188	RSK OF BARB 1-2X	5A41J	5A23J	5A23J	5A23J	5A23J	5A23J	5A23J	5A23J	5A23J
12460	189	RSK OF BARB REGY	5A41K	5A23K	5A23K	5A23K	5A23K	5A23K	5A23K	5A23K	5A23K
12470	189	RSK OF AMPH 1-2X	5A41L	5A23L	5A23L	5A23L	5A23L	5A23L	5A23L	5A23L	5A23L
12480	189	RSK OF AMPH REG	5A41M	5A23M	5A23M	5A23M	5A23M	5A23M	5A23M	5A23M	5A23M
12490	189	RSK OF COKE 1-2X	5A41N	5A23N	5A23N	5A23N	5A23N	5A23N	5A23N	5A23N	5A23N
12495	190	RSK OF COKE OCSN									5A23T
12500	189	RSK OF COKE REG	5A41O	5A23O	5A23O	5A23O	5A23O	5A23O	5A23O	5A23O	5A23O
12510	189	RSK OF 1-2 DRINK	5A41P	5A23P	5A23P	5A23P	5A23P	5A23P	5A23P	5A23P	5A23P
12520	189	RSK OF 1-2 DR/DA	5A41Q	5A23Q	5A23Q	5A23Q	5A23Q	5A23Q	5A23Q	5A23Q	5A23Q
12530	190	RSK OF 4-5 DR/DA	5A41R	5A23R	5A23R	5A23R	5A23R	5A23R	5A23R	5A23R	5A23R
12540	190	RSK OF 5+DR/WKND	5A41S	5A23S	5A23S	5A23S	5A23S	5A23S	5A23S	5A23S	5A23S

A14b: DRUGS. Risk of harm to others

7320		RSK/OT CIG1+PK/D		2E01A							
7330		RSK/OT MJ 1-2 X		2E01B							
7340		RSK/OT MJ OCSNLY		2E01C							
7350		RSK/OT MJ REGLY		2E01D							
7360		RSK/OT LSD 1-2 X		2E01E							
7370		RSK/OT LSD REGLY		2E01F							
7380		RSK/OT 'H' 1-2 X		2E01G							
7390		RSK/OT 'H' OCSNL		2E01H							
7400		RSK/OT 'H' REGLY		2E01I							
7410		RSK/OT BARB 1-2X		2E01J							
7420		RSK/OT BARB REGY		2E01K							
7430		RSK/OT AMPH 1-2X		2E01L							
7440		RSK/OT AMPH REG		2E01M							
7450		RSK/OT COKE 1-2X		2E01N							
		(continued)									

† This question appears in 1980 but does not appear in 1981.

Item Reference Number	Page Loc. in this Volume	ITEM DESCRIPTION (ABBREVIATED)	QUESTIONNAIRE LOCATION BY YEAR (FORM, SECTION, AND QUESTION NUMBER)								
			1975	1976	1977	1978	1979	1980/81	1982/83	1984/85	1986

A14b: DRUGS. Risk of harm to others (continued)

Item Reference Number	Page Loc.	ITEM DESCRIPTION	1975	1976	1977	1978	1979	1980/81	1982/83	1984/85	1986
7460		RSK/OT COKE REG		2E01O							
7470		RSK/OT 1-2 DRINK		2E01P							
7480		RSK/OT 1-2 DR/DA		2E01Q							
7490		RSK/OT 4-5 DR/DA		2E01R							
7500		RSK/OT 5+DR/WKND		2E01S							

A15a: DRUGS. Admitting use in questionnaire

Item Reference Number	Page Loc.	ITEM DESCRIPTION	1975	1976	1977	1978	1979	1980/81	1982/83	1984/85	1986
20800	206	WLD ADMT USE MJ					5E09	5E09=	5E13	5E10	5E10
20810	206	WLD ADMT USE AMP					5E10	5E10=	5E14	5E11	5E11
20820	206	WLD ADMT USE HER					5E11	5E11=	5E15	5E12	5E12

A16a: DRUGS. Parent groups

Item Reference Number	Page Loc.	ITEM DESCRIPTION	1975	1976	1977	1978	1979	1980/81	1982/83	1984/85	1986
21730	174	IDEA PARENTS GRP							4E09§	4E09	4E09
21740	174	#FRNDS PRNTS GRP							4E10§	4E10	4E10
21750	174	OWN PRNTS IN GRP							4E11§	4E11	4E11
21760	174	GP IMPCT OWN FLG							4E12§	4E12	4E12
21770	175	GP CHG RELP PRNT							4E13§	4E13	4E13
21780	175	#FRNDS ANTIDG GP							4E14§	4E14	4E14
21790	175	EVR IN ANTIDG GP							4E15§	4E15	4E15

B01: EDUCATION. High school: scholastic status, objectives, experiences

Item Reference Number	Page Loc.	ITEM DESCRIPTION	1975	1976	1977	1978	1979	1980/81	1982/83	1984/85	1986
390	19	WHEN R XPCT GRAD		+C14	+C14	+C14	+C14	+C14	+C14	+C14	+C14
400	19	R'S HS PROGRAM		+C15	+C15	+C15	+C15	+C15	+C15	+C15	+C15
410	19	RT SF SCH AB>AVG		+C16	+C16	+C16	+C16	+C16	+C16	+C16	+C16
420	19	RT SF INTELL>AVG		+C17	+C17	+C17	+C17	+C17	+C17	+C17	+C17
470	20	R HS GRADE/D=1		+C20	+C20	+C20	+C20	+C20	+C20	+C20	+C20
1310	35	SAT EDUC EXPRNCS	1A009E	1A006E	1A006E	1A006E	1A006E	1A006E	1A006E	1A006E	1A006E
1660	40	GO SCH ENJY XPR	1A013I	1A011I	1A011I	1A011I	1A011I	1A011I	1A011I	1A011I	1A011I
1670	40	DO WL SC IMP/JB	1A013H	1A011J	1A011J	1A011J	1A011J	1A011J	1A011J	1A011J	1A011J
5700	83	*SC WRK NVR MNG		1D002	1D002	1D002	1D002	1D002	1D002	1D002	1D002
5710	84	*MST COUR V DUL		1D003	1D003	1D003	1D003	1D003	1D003	1D003	1D003
5720	84	*LRN SCH NT IMP		1D004	1D004	1D004	1D004	1D004	1D004	1D004	1D004
7630	83	R LIKES SCHOOL		1D001	1D001	1D001	1D001	1D001	1D001	1D001	1D001
	117			2E02	2E06	2E06	2E08	2E09	2E12	2E12	2E12
				3E08	3E07	3E07	3E07	3E07			
				4E10	5E05	5E05	5E03	5E05†			
				5E04							
7640	118	HRS/WK SPND HMWK		2E03	2E07	2E07	2E09	2E10	2E13	2E13	2E13
9860	140	HAD SEX ED IN HS		3E09	3E08	3E08	3E08	3E08	3E04	3E04	3E04
9870	141	STUDY BC IN HS		3E10	3E09	3E09	3E09	3E09	3E05	3E05	3E05
22170	116	SCH ACTV-PBLCTNS									2E07A
22180	116	SCH ACTV-PRF ART									2E07B
22190	116	SCH ACTV-ATHLTCS									2E07C
22200	117	SCH ACTV-OTH ACT									2E07D

B02: EDUCATION. Combining work and school: attitudes, experiences

Item Reference Number	Page Loc.	ITEM DESCRIPTION	1975	1976	1977	1978	1979	1980/81	1982/83	1984/85	1986
5770	85	R IN WK-STDY PG		1D009	1D009	1D009	1D009	1D009	1D009	1D009	1D009
10260	153	JOB IMPC LRNING	4A08R	4A08R	4A08R	4A08R	4A08R	4A08R	4A08R	4A08R	4A08R

B03: EDUCATION. Interracial contact at school

Item Reference Number	Page Loc.	ITEM DESCRIPTION	1975	1976	1977	1978	1979	1980/81	1982/83	1984/85	1986
8220	127	DES AL CHL SM RC	3A19L	3A10A	3A10A	3A10A	3A10A	3A10A	3A10A	3A10A	3A10A
8230	127	DES SM CHL OT RC	3A19M	3A10B	3A10B	3A10B	3A10B	3A10B	3A10B	3A10B	3A10B
8240	127	DES MS CHL OT RC	3A19N	3A10C	3A10C	3A10C	3A10C	3A10C	3A10C	3A10C	3A10C
8270	127	ELEMSCH AL OT RC	3A21	3A13	3A13	3A13	3A13	3A13	3A13	3A13	3A13
8280	127	HISCH AL OT RC	3A20	3A14	3A14	3A14	3A14	3A14	3A14	3A14	3A14
11890	179	RCL CNTCT SCHOOL		5A07A	5A07A	5A07A	5A07A	5A07A	5A07A	5A07A	5A07A

= Questions 5E9–5E11 were numbered 5E14–5E16 in 1981.   § This question appears in 1983 but does not appear in 1982.

† This question appears in 1980 but does not appear in 1981.

Item Reference Number	Page Loc. in this Volume	ITEM DESCRIPTION (ABBREVIATED)	QUESTIONNAIRE LOCATION BY YEAR (FORM, SECTION, AND QUESTION NUMBER)								
			1975	1976	1977	1978	1979	1980/81	1982/83	1984/85	1986

B04: EDUCATION. Student norms

5730	84	LOT CMPTN GRADE		1D005	1D005	1D005	1D005	1D005	1D005	1D005	1D005
5740	84	STDTS DSLK CHTG		1D006	1D006	1D006	1D006	1D006	1D006	1D006	1D006
5750	84	ST -LK PROV TCH		1D007	1D007	1D007	1D007	1D007	1D007	1D007	1D007
5760	84	FRD NCG/TCH -LK		1D008	1D008	1D008	1D008	1D008	1D008	1D008	1D008
13580	141	STS SCH RT FAMLY		5E05A	5E06A	5E06A	5E04A	5E06A†	3E06A	3E06A	3E06A
13590	141	STS SCH LDS STU		5E05B	5E06B	5E06B	5E04B	5E06B†	3E06B	3E06B	3E06B
13600	141	STS SCH NIC CAR		5E05C	5E06C	5E06C	5E04C	5E06C†	3E06C	3E06C	3E06C
13610	141	STS SCH HI GRDE		5E05D	5E06D	5E06D	5E04D	5E06D†	3E06D	3E06D	3E06D
13620	141	STS SCH GD ATHLT		5E05E	5E06E	5E06E	5E04E	5E06E†	3E06E	3E06E	3E06E
13630	141	STS SCH INTLCTL		5E05F	5E06F	5E06F	5E04F	5E06F†	3E06F	3E06F	3E06F
13640	142	STS SCH PLN CLG		5E05G	5E06G	5E06G	5E04G	5E06G†	3E06G	3E06G	3E06G

B05: EDUCATION. Counseling

5780	85	#X/YR COUNS IND		1D010	1D010	1D010	1D010	1D010	1D010	1D010	1D010
5790	85	#X/YR COUNS GRP		1D011	1D011	1D011	1D011	1D011	1D011	1D011	1D011
5800	85	R LK C COUNS MR		1D012	1D012	1D012	1D012	1D012	1D012	1D012	1D012
5810	85	CSLNG VRY HLPFL		(1D013)	1D013	1D013	1D013	1D013	1D013	1D013	1D013
5811	85	CNSL COURSES					1D014A	1D014A	1D014A	1D014A	1D014A
5812	86	CNSL CL PROB					1D014B	1D014B	1D014B	1D014B	1D014B
5813	86	CNSL TRBL R IN					1D014C	1D014C	1D014C	1D014C	1D014C
5814	86	CNSL MILTRY PLN					1D014D	1D014D	1D014D	1D014D	1D014D
5815	86	CNSL EDUC PLANS					1D014E	1D014E	1D014E	1D014E	1D014E
5816	86	CNSL CAREER PLN					1D014F	1D014F	1D014F	1D014F	1D014F
5817	86	CNSL PRNL PROB					1D014G	1D014G	1D014G	1D014G	1D014G

B06: EDUCATION. Absenteeism and truancy

430	19	#DA/4W SC MS ILL		+C18A	+C18A	+C18A	+C18A	+C18A	+C18A	+C18A	+C18A
440	20	#DA/4W SC MS CUT		+C18B	+C18B	+C18B	+C18B	+C18B	+C18B	+C18B	+C18B
450	20	#DA/4W SC MS OTH		+C18C	+C18C	+C18C	+C18C	+C18C	+C18C	+C18C	+C18C
460	20	#DA/4W SKP CLASS		+C19	+C19	+C19	+C19	+C19	+C19	+C19	+C19

B07: EDUCATION. Delinquency and victimization at school

6540	103	FRQ FGT WRK/SCHL	2A39C	2A19C	2A19C	2A19C	2A19C	2A19C	2A19C	2A19C	2A19C
6650	104	FRQ DMG SCH PPTY	2A39N	2A19N	2A19N	2A19N	2A19N	2A19N	2A19N	2A19N	2A19N
9871	142	SM1 SCL ROB <$50		4E11A	3E10A	3E10A	5E06A	5E08A=	3E08A	3E08A	3E08A
9872	142	SM1 SCL ROB >$50		4E11B	3E10B	3E10B	5E06B	5E08B=	3E08B	3E08B	3E08B
9873	143	SM1 SCL DMG PRTY		4E11C	3E10C	3E10C	5E06C	5E08C=	3E08C	3E08C	3E08C
9874	143	SM1 SCL IN U W/W		4E11D	3E10D	3E10D	5E06D	5E08D=	3E08D	3E08D	3E08D
9875	143	SM1 SCL TH U W/W		4E11E	3E10E	3E10E	5E06E	5E08E=	3E08E	3E08E	3E08E
9876	143	SM1 SCL IN U -WP		4E11F	3E10F	3E10F	5E06F	5E08F=	3E08F	3E08F	3E08F
9877	143	SM1 SCL TH U W/I		4E11G	3E10G	3E10G	5E06G	5EO8G=	3E08G	3E08G	3E08G

B08: EDUCATION. Opinions regarding competency testing

7900		16YR+,TEST->DIPL				2E13A	(2E13A)	5E07A	2E16A	2E19A	
7910		14YR+,TEST->DIPL				2E13B	(2E13B)	5E07B	2E16B	2E19B	
7920		ALL STD H.S.TEST				2E13C	(2E13C)	5E07C	2E16C	2E19C	

B09: EDUCATION. Post high school: status, plans, characteristics

480	20	R WL DO VOC/TEC		+C21A	+C21A	+C21A	+C21A	+C21A	+C21A	+C21A	+C21A
490	20	R WL DO ARMD FC		+C21B	+C21B	+C21B	+C21B	+C21B	+C21B	+C21B	+C21B
500	21	R WL DO 2YR CLG		+C21C	+C21C	+C21C	+C21C	+C21C	+C21C	+C21C	+C21C
510	21	R WL DO 4YR CLG		+C21D	+C21D	+C21D	+C21D	+C21D	+C21D	+C21D	+C21D
520	21	R WL DO GRD/PRF		+C21E	+C21E	+C21E	+C21E	+C21E	+C21E	+C21E	+C21E
530	21	R WNTDO VOC/TEC		+C22A	+C22A	+C22A	+C22A	+C22A	+C22A	+C22A	+C22A
540	21	R WNTDO ARMD FC		+C22B	+C22B	+C22B	+C22B	+C22B	+C22B	+C22B	+C22B
550	21	R WNTDO 2YR CLG		+C22C	+C22C	+C22C	+C22C	+C22C	+C22C	+C22C	+C22C
560	21	R WNTDO 4YR CLG		+C22D	+C22D	+C22D	+C22D	+C22D	+C22D	+C22D	+C22D
570	21	R WNTDO GRD/PRF		+C22E	+C22E	+C22E	+C22E	+C22E	+C22E	+C22E	+C22E
		(continued)									

† This question appears in 1980 but does not appear in 1981.   = Questions 5E8a–g were numbered 5E13a–g in 1981.

Item Reference Number	Page Loc. in this Volume	ITEM DESCRIPTION (ABBREVIATED)	1975	1976	1977	1978	1979	1980/81	1982/83	1984/85	1986
						QUESTIONNAIRE LOCATION BY YEAR (FORM, SECTION, AND QUESTION NUMBER)					

B09: EDUCATION. Post high school: status, plans, characteristics *(continued)*

Item Reference Number	Page Loc. in this Volume	ITEM DESCRIPTION (ABBREVIATED)	1975	1976	1977	1978	1979	1980/81	1982/83	1984/85	1986
580	21	R WNTDO NONE		+C22F	+C22F	+C22F	+C22F	+C22F	+C22F	+C22F	+C22F
10410	155	JOB OBSTC EDUCTN		4A13F	4A13F	4A13F	4A13F	4A13F	4A13F	4A13F	4A13F
11320	171	P'IDEA OF EDUC	4A27J	4E08J	4E08J	4E07J	4E07J	4E07J	4E07J	4E07J	4E07J

B10: EDUCATION. Attitudes regarding educational institutions

Item Reference Number	Page Loc. in this Volume	ITEM DESCRIPTION (ABBREVIATED)	1975	1976	1977	1978	1979	1980/81	1982/83	1984/85	1986
6910	108	DHNSTY COLL&UNIV	2A20C	2D04C	2D04C	2D04C	2D04C	2D04C	2D04C	2D04C	2D04C
6920	108	DHNSTY PBLC SCHL	2A20D	2D04D	2D04D	2D04D	2D04D	2D04D	2D04D	2D04D	2D04D
7650	118	PRCL INFL SCL RN		2E04A	2E08A	2E08A	2E10A	2E11A	2E14A	2E14A	2E14A
7660	118	TCHR INFL SCL RN		2E04B	2E08B	2E08B	2E10B	2E11B	2E14B	2E14B	2E14B
7670	118	STDS INFL SCL RN		2E04C	2E08C	2E08C	2E10C	2E11C	2E14C	2E14C	2E14C
7680	118	PRTS INFL SCL RN		2E04D	2E08D	2E08D	2E10D	2E11D	2E14D	2E14D	2E14D
8400	129	GD JB COLLG&UNIV	3A27C	3A24C	3A24C	3A24C	3A24C	3A24C	3A24C	3A24C	3A24C
8410	130	GD JB PBLC SCHOL	3A27D	3A24D	3A24D	3A24D	3A24D	3A24D	3A24D	3A24D	3A24D
11130	169	MLTRY MORE ED		4E01B	4E01B	4E01B	4E01B	4E01B	4E01B	4E01B	4E01B
11840	178	PLC WRK SCH/UNIV	5A09E	5A05E	5A05E	5A05E	5A05E	5A05E	5A05E	5A05E	5A05E

C01: WORK and LEISURE. Present or recent work experience

Item Reference Number	Page Loc. in this Volume	ITEM DESCRIPTION (ABBREVIATED)	1975	1976	1977	1978	1979	1980/81	1982/83	1984/85	1986
590	21	HRS/W WRK SCHYR		+C23	+C23	+C23	+C23	+C23	+C23	+C23	+C23
1270	34	SAT PRESENT JOB	1A009A	1A006A	1A006A	1A006A	1A006A	1A006A	1D009	1D009	1D009
5770	85	R IN WK-STDY PG		1D009	1D009	1D009	1D009	1D009	1D009	1D009	1D009
6540	103	FRQ FGT WRK/SCHL	2A39C	2A19C	2A19C	2A19C	2A19C	2A19C	2A19C	2A19C	2A19C
6660	104	FRQ DMG WK PRPTY	2A39O	2A19O	2A19O	2A19O	2A19O	2A19O	2A19O	2A19O	2A19O
10910	162	CMP SATFD W/JOB		4D02	4D02	4D02	4D02	4D02	4D02	4D02	4D02
11790	178	XPRC MK R GD WKR		5A04C	5A04C	5A04C	5A04C	5A04C	5A04C	5A04C	5A04C
11940	180	RCL CNTCT JOB		5A07F	5A07F	5A07F	5A07F	5A07F	5A07F	5A07F	5A07F
21530	162	RCNT EMPLYMT EXP							4D03A	4D03A	4D03A
21540	162	JOB-#HRS/WEEK							4D03B	4D03B	4D03B
21550	163	JOB-SUPERVSR AGE							4D04	4D04	4D04
21560	163	JOB-#WKRS OWN AG							4D05	4D05	4D05
21570	163	JOB-USE BEST SKL							4D06A	4D06A	4D06A
21580	163	JOB-TEACH SKILLS							4D06B	4D06B	4D06B
21590	163	JOB-USE LRND SKL							4D06C	4D06C	4D06C
21600	163	JOB-DIF SOC BKGD							4D06D	4D06D	4D06D
21610	163	JOB-OVER AGE 30							4D06E	4D06E	4D06E
21620	164	JOB->STRESS							4D06F	4D06F	4D06F
21630	164	JOB-INTRFR W ED							4D06G	4D06G	4D06G
21640	164	JOB-INTRFR W SOC							4D06H	4D06H	4D06H
21650	164	JOB-INTRFR W FAM							4D06I	4D06I	4D06I
21660	164	JOB-INTERESTING							4D07A	4D07A	4D07A
21670	164	JOB-HAPPY FR LIF							4D07B	4D07B	4D07B
21680	164	JOB-EXPCT FR LIF							4D07C	4D07C	4D07C
21690	165	JOB-STEP STONE							4D07D	4D07D	4D07D
21700	165	JOB-DO JST FOR $							4D07E	4D07E	4D07E
21710	165	JOB-TCHR HELP GT							4D08	4D08	4D08
21720	165	JOB-WORK STUDY							4D09	4D09	4D09

C02: WORK and LEISURE. Income sources; financial security

Item Reference Number	Page Loc. in this Volume	ITEM DESCRIPTION (ABBREVIATED)	1975	1976	1977	1978	1979	1980/81	1982/83	1984/85	1986
600	21	R$/AVG WEEK JOB		+C24A	+C24A	+C24A	+C24A	(+C24A)	+C24A	+C24A	+C24A
610	22	R$/AVG WEEK OTH		+C24B	+C24B	+C24B	+C24B	(+C24B)	+C24B	+C24B	+C24B
12990	194	I HAVE ENOUGH $			5D04A	5D04A	5D04A	5D04A=	5D04A	5D04A	5D04A
13000	194	I LACK $FR BILL			5D04B	5D04B	5D04B	5D04B=	5D04B	5D04B	5D04B
13010	195	I WRY@-FINDG JOB			5D04C	5D04C	5D04C	5D04C=	5D04C	5D04C	5D04C
13020	195	I CAN FIND JOB			5D04D	5D04D	5D04D	5D04D=	5D04D	5D04D	5D04D
13030	195	I CAN KEEP MYJOB			5D04E	5D04E	5D04E	5D04E=	5D04E	5D04E	5D04E
13040	195	I WRY@LOSS MYJOB			5D04F	5D04F	5D04F	5D04F=	5D04F	5D04F	5D04F
20830	195	%$SAVE FUTR EDUC						5D03A‡	5D05A	5D05A	5D05A
20840	195	%$SAVE/SPEND CAR						5D03B‡	5D05B	5D05B	5D05B
20850	196	%$SAVE OTHER						5D03C‡	5D05C	5D05C	5D05C
20860	196	%$SPEND ON SELF						5D03D‡	5D05D	5D05D	5D05D
20870	196	%$SPEND HELP FAM						5D03E‡	5D05E	5D05E	5D05E

‡ This question appears in 1981 but does not appear in 1980.   = Questions 5D4a–f were numbered 5D2a–f in 1981.

Item Reference Number	Page Loc. in this Volume	ITEM DESCRIPTION (ABBREVIATED)	QUESTIONNAIRE LOCATION BY YEAR (FORM, SECTION, AND QUESTION NUMBER)								
			1975	1976	1977	1978	1979	1980/81	1982/83	1984/85	1986

C03: WORK and LEISURE. Vocational plans, aspirations, expectations

Item Reference Number	Page Loc. in this Volume	ITEM DESCRIPTION (ABBREVIATED)	1975	1976	1977	1978	1979	1980/81	1982/83	1984/85	1986
480	20	R WL DO VOC/TEC		+C21A	+C21A	+C21A	+C21A	+C21A	+C21A	+C21A	+C21A
530	21	R WNTDO VOC/TEC		+C22A	+C22A	+C22A	+C22A	+C22A	+C22A	+C22A	+C22A
6870	108	HOW GD AS WORKER	2A19C	2D02C	2D02C	2D02C	2D02C	2D02C	2D02C	2D02C	2D02C
8090	125	SAME JOB MST LIF	3A08I	3A05E	3A05E	3A05E	3A05E	3A05E	3A05E	3A05E	3A05E
10320	154	KIND OF WORK @30	4A09	4A09	4A09	4A09	4A09	4A09	4A09	4A09	4A09
10330	154	R SURE GT THS WK		4A10	4A10	4A10	4A10	4A10	4A10	4A10	4A10
10340	154	R SURE WK GD CHC		4A11	4A11	4A11	4A11	4A11	4A11	4A11	4A11
10350	155	R THNK WK BE SAT		4A12	4A12	4A12	4A12	4A12	4A12	4A12	4A12
10360	155	JOB OBSTC RELGN		4A13A	4A13A	4A13A	4A13A	4A13A	4A13A	4A13A	4A13A
10370	155	JOB OBSTC SEX		4A13B	4A13B	4A13B	4A13B	4A13B	4A13B	4A13B	4A13B
10380	155	JOB OBSTC RACE		4A13C	4A13C	4A13C	4A13C	4A13C	4A13C	4A13C	4A13C
10390	155	JOB OBSTC BKGRND		4A13D	4A13D	4A13D	4A13D	4A13D	4A13D	4A13D	4A13D
10400	155	JOB OBSTC POL VW		4A13E	4A13E	4A13E	4A13E	4A13E	4A13E	4A13E	4A13E
10410	155	JOB OBSTC EDUCTN		4A13F	4A13F	4A13F	4A13F	4A13F	4A13F	4A13F	4A13F
10420	155	JOB OBSTC -VOC T		4A13G	4A13G	4A13G	4A13G	4A13G	4A13G	4A13G	4A13G
10430	156	JOB OBSTC -ABLTY		4A13H	4A13H	4A13H	4A13H	4A13H	4A13H	4A13H	4A13H
10440	156	JOB OBSTC - PULL		4A13I	4A13I	4A13I	4A13I	4A13I	4A13I	4A13I	4A13I
10450	156	JOB OBSTC -WK HD		4A13J	4A13J	4A13J	4A13J	4A13J	4A13J	4A13J	4A13J
10460	156	JOB OBSTC -CONFM		4A13K	4A13K	4A13K	4A13K	4A13K	4A13K	4A13K	4A13K

C04: WORK and LEISURE. Preferences regarding job characteristics

Item Reference Number	Page Loc. in this Volume	ITEM DESCRIPTION (ABBREVIATED)	1975	1976	1977	1978	1979	1980/81	1982/83	1984/85	1986
1460	37	IMP STEADY WORK		1A007F	1A007F	1A007F	1A007F	1A007F	1A007F	1A007F	1A007F
8050	124	LIK WRK CAN FRGT	3A08D	3A05A	3A05A	3A05A	3A05A	3A05A	3A05A	3A05A	3A05A
10090	150	JOB IMPC SE RSLT	4A08A	4A08A	4A08A	4A08A	4A08A	4A08A	4A08A	4A08A	4A08A
10100	151	JOB IMPC STATUS	4A08B	4A08B	4A08B	4A08B	4A08B	4A08B	4A08B	4A08B	4A08B
10110	151	JOB IMPC INTRSTG	4A08C	4A08C	4A08C	4A08C	4A08C	4A08C	4A08C	4A08C	4A08C
10120	151	JOB IMPC ADVNCMT	4A08D	4A08D	4A08D	4A08D	4A08D	4A08D	4A08D	4A08D	4A08D
10130	151	JOB IMPC HLP OTH	4A08E	4A08E	4A08E	4A08E	4A08E	4A08E	4A08E	4A08E	4A08E
10140	151	JOB IMPC EARN $	4A08F	4A08F	4A08F	4A08F	4A08F	4A08F	4A08F	4A08F	4A08F
10150	151	JOB IMPC CREATVY	4A08G	4A08G	4A08G	4A08G	4A08G	4A08G	4A08G	4A08G	4A08G
10160	151	JOB IMPC UTILITY	4A08H	4A08H	4A08H	4A08H	4A08H	4A08H	4A08H	4A08H	4A08H
10170	151	JOB IMPC MK FRND	4A08I	4A08I	4A08I	4A08I	4A08I	4A08I	4A08I	4A08I	4A08I
10180	152	JOB IMPC USE SKL	4A08J	4A08J	4A08J	4A08J	4A08J	4A08J	4A08J	4A08J	4A08J
10190	152	JOB IMPC WRTHWLE	4A08K	4A08K	4A08K	4A08K	4A08K	4A08K	4A08K	4A08K	4A08K
10200	152	JOB IMPC VACATN	4A08L	4A08L	4A08L	4A08L	4A08L	4A08L	4A08L	4A08L	4A08L
10210	152	JOB IMPC MK DCSN	4A08M	4A08M	4A08M	4A08M	4A08M	4A08M	4A08M	4A08M	4A08M
10220	152	JOB IMPC FRE TIM		4A08N	4A08N	4A08N	4A08N	4A08N	4A08N	4A08N	4A08N
10230	152	JOB IMPC NO MVNG	4A08O	4A08O	4A08O	4A08O	4A08O	4A08O	4A08O	4A08O	4A08O
10240	152	JOB IMPC NO SPRV	4A08P	4A08P	4A08P	4A08P	4A08P	4A08P	4A08P	4A08P	4A08P
10250	153	JOB IMPC SECURTY	4A08Q	4A08Q	4A08Q	4A08Q	4A08Q	4A08Q	4A08Q	4A08Q	4A08Q
10260	153	JOB IMPC LRNING	4A08R	4A08R	4A08R	4A08R	4A08R	4A08R	4A08R	4A08R	4A08R
10270	153	JOB IMPC BE SELF	4A08S	4A08S	4A08S	4A08S	4A08S	4A08S	4A08S	4A08S	4A08S
10280	153	JOB IMPC RESPECT	4A08T	4A08T	4A08T	4A08T	4A08T	4A08T	4A08T	4A08T	4A08T
10290	153	JOB IMPC CNTC PL	4A08U	4A08U	4A08U	4A08U	4A08U	4A08U	4A08U	4A08U	4A08U
10300	153	JOB IMPC EZ PACE		4A08V	4A08V	4A08V	4A08V	4A08V	4A08V	4A08V	4A08V
10310	153	JOB IMPC HRD PRB		4A08W	4A08W	4A08W	4A08W	4A08W	4A08W	4A08W	4A08W

C05: WORK and LEISURE. Desirability of different working arrangements and settings

Item Reference Number	Page Loc. in this Volume	ITEM DESCRIPTION (ABBREVIATED)	1975	1976	1977	1978	1979	1980/81	1982/83	1984/85	1986
6160	97	-CHL,HB WK1.,W=0	2A15A	2A08A	2A08A	2A08A	2A08A	2A08A	2A08A	2A08A	2A08A
6170	97	-CHL,HB WK1.,W.5	2A15B	2A08B	2A08B	2A08B	2A08B	2A08B	2A08B	2A08B	2A08B
6180	97	-CHL,HB&WF WK 1.	2A15C	2A08C	2A08C	2A08C	2A08C	2A08C	2A08C	2A08C	2A08C
6190	97	-CHL,HB&WF WK .5	2A15D	2A08D	2A08D	2A08D	2A08D	2A08D	2A08D	2A08D	2A08D
6200	97	-CHL,W WK 1.,H.5	2A15E	2A08E	2A08E	2A08E	2A08E	2A08E	2A08E	2A08E	2A08E
6210	97	-CHL,W WK 1.,H=0	2A15F	2A08F	2A08F	2A08F	2A08F	2A08F	2A08F	2A08F	2A08F
6220	98	PSCH,HB WK1.,W=0	2A16A	2A09A	2A09A	2A09A	2A09A	2A09A	2A09A	2A09A	2A09A
6230	98	PSCH,HB WK1.,W.5	2A16B	2A09B	2A09B	2A09B	2A09B	2A09B	2A09B	2A09B	2A09B
6240	98	PSCH,HB&WF WK 1.	2A16C	2A09C	2A09C	2A09C	2A09C	2A09C	2A09C	2A09C	2A09C
6250	98	PSCH,HB&WF WK .5	2A16D	2A09D	2A09D	2A09D	2A09D	2A09D	2A09D	2A09D	2A09D
6260	98	PSCH,WF WK1.,H.5	2A16E	2A09E	2A09E	2A09E	2A09E	2A09E	2A09E	2A09E	2A09E
6270	98	PSCH,WF WK1.,H=0	2A16F	2A09F	2A09F	2A09F	2A09F	2A09F	2A09F	2A09F	2A09F
8120	125	DES SUPVR DIF RC	3A19B	3A07B	3A07B	3A07B	3A07B	3A07B	3A07B	3A07B	3A07B

(continued)

Item Reference Number	Page Loc. in this Volume	ITEM DESCRIPTION (ABBREVIATED)	QUESTIONNAIRE LOCATION BY YEAR (FORM, SECTION, AND QUESTION NUMBER)								
			1975	1976	1977	1978	1979	1980/81	1982/83	1984/85	1986

C05: WORK and LEISURE. Desirability of different working arrangements and settings (continued)

Item Reference Number	Page Loc. in this Volume	ITEM DESCRIPTION	1975	1976	1977	1978	1979	1980/81	1982/83	1984/85	1986
8160	126	DES AL WKS SM RC	3A19F	3A08A	3A08A	3A08A	3A08A	3A08A	3A08A	3A08A	3A08A
8170	126	DES SO WKS DF RC	3A19G	3A08B	3A08B	3A08B	3A08B	3A08B	3A08B	3A08B	3A08B
8180	126	DES MS WKS DF RC	3A19H	3A08C	3A08C	3A08C	3A08C	3A08C	3A08C	3A08C	3A08C
11150	169	MLTRY >FLFLLG JB		4E01D	4E01D	4E01D	4E01D	4E01D	4E01D	4E01D	4E01D
11800	178	PLC WRK LG CORPN	5A09A	5A05A	5A05A	5A05A	5A05A	5A05A	5A05A	5A05A	5A05A
11810	178	PLC WRK SM BSNSS	5A09B	5A05B	5A05B	5A05B	5A05B	5A05B	5A05B	5A05B	5A05B
11820	178	PLC WRK GVT AGCY	5A09C	5A05C	5A05C	5A05C	5A05C	5A05C	5A05C	5A05C	5A05C
11830	178	PLC WRK MLTY SVC	5A09D	5A05D	5A05D	5A05D	5A05D	5A05D	5A05D	5A05D	5A05D
11840	178	PLC WRK SCH/UNIV	5A09E	5A05E	5A05E	5A05E	5A05E	5A05E	5A05E	5A05E	5A05E
11850	178	PLC WRK PLC DEPT	5A09F	5A05F	5A05F	5A05F	5A05F	5A05F	5A05F	5A05F	5A05F
11860	178	PLC WRK SOC SVCS	5A09G	5A05G	5A05G	5A05G	5A05G	5A05G	5A05G	5A05G	5A05G
11870	179	PLC WRK SML GRP	5A09H	5A05H	5A05H	5A05H	5A05H	5A05H	5A05H	5A05H	5A05H
11880	179	PLC WRK SLF EMPL	5A09I	5A05I	5A05I	5A05I	5A05I	5A05I	5A05I	5A05I	5A05I

C06: WORK and LEISURE. Work ethic/success orientation

Item Reference Number	Page Loc. in this Volume	ITEM DESCRIPTION	1975	1976	1977	1978	1979	1980/81	1982/83	1984/85	1986
1410	36	IMP B SUCCSS WK		1A007A	1A007A	1A007A	1A007A	1A007A	1A007A	1A007A	1A007A
8060	124	WRK=ONLY MK LVNG	3A08E	3A05B	3A05B	3A05B	3A05B	3A05B	3A05B	3A05B	3A05B
8070	124	WRK CNTRL PRT LF	3A08G	3A05C	3A05C	3A05C	3A05C	3A05C	3A05C	3A05C	3A05C
8080	124	OVTM 2DO BST JOB	3A08H	3A05D	3A05D	3A05D	3A05D	3A05D	3A05D	3A05D	3A05D
8100	125	ENUF$,NT WNT WRK	3A10	3A06	3A06	3A06	3A06	3A06	3A06	3A06	3A06
	156		4A09A	4A14	4A14	4A14	4A14	4A14	4A14	4A14	4A14
	179		5A11	5A06	5A06	5A06	5A06	5A06	5A06	5A06	5A06

C07: WORK and LEISURE. Leisure time: extent, activities

Item Reference Number	Page Loc. in this Volume	ITEM DESCRIPTION	1975	1976	1977	1978	1979	1980/81	1982/83	1984/85	1986
620	22	#X/AV WK GO OUT		+C25	+C25	+C25	+C25	+C25	+C25	+C25	+C25
630	22	#X DATE 3+/WK		+C26	+C26	+C26	+C26	+C26	+C26	+C26	+C26
5820	92	DALY WATCH TV		2A02A	2A02A	2A02A	2A02A	2A02A	2A02A	2A02A	2A02A
5830	92	DALY GO TO MOVIE		2A02B	2A02B	2A02B	2A02B	2A02B	2A02B	2A02B	2A02B
5840		DALY ART,MSC,PLA		2A02C	2A02C	2A02C	2A02C	2A02C			
5845	92	DALY ROCK CONCRT								2A02C	2A02C
5850	92	DALY RIDE FORFUN			2A02D	2A02D	2A02D	2A02D	2A02D	2A02D	2A02D
5860	92	DALY CMNTY AFFRS		2A02E	2A02E	2A02E	2A02E	2A02E	2A02E	2A02E	2A02E
5870	92	DALY PLA MSC,SNG		2A02F	2A02F	2A02F	2A02F	2A02F	2A02F	2A02F	2A02F
5880	93	DALY CREAT WRTNG		2A02G	2A02G	2A02G	2A02G	2A02G	2A02G	2A02G	2A02G
5890	93	DALY ACTV SPORTS		2A02H	2A02H	2A02H	2A02H	2A02H	2A02H	2A02H	2A02H
5900	93	DALY ART/CRAFTS		2A02I	2A02I	2A02I	2A02I	2A02I	2A02I	2A02I	2A02I
5910	93	DALY WRK HSE,CAR		2A02J	2A02J	2A02J	2A02J	2A02J	2A02J	2A02J	2A02J
5920	93	DALY VIST W/FRDS		2A02K	2A02K	2A02K	2A02K	2A02K	2A02K	2A02K	2A02K
5930	93	DALY GO SHOPPING		2A02L	2A02L	2A02L	2A02L	2A02L	2A02L	2A02L	2A02L
5940	93	DALY ALONE LEISR		(2A02M)	2A02M	2A02M	2A02M	2A02M	2A02M	2A02M	2A02M
5950	94	DALY READ BK,MAG		2A02N	2A02N	2A02N	2A02N	2A02N	2A02N	2A02N	2A02N
5960	94	DALY GO TO BARS		2A02O	2A02O	2A02O	2A02O	2A02O	2A02O	2A02O	2A02O
5970	94	DALY GO TO PARTY		2A02P	2A02P	2A02P	2A02P	2A02P	2A02P	2A02P	2A02P
5980		DALY GO CHURCH		2A02D							
10550	158	#HRS TV/DAY/5+		4A16	4A16	4A16	4A16	4A16	4A16	4A16	4A16
10560	158	#BKS LAST YR/10+		4A17	4A17	4A17	4A17	4A17	4A17	4A17	4A17
21900	203	#X/LAST12M PARTY								5E07	5E07
21910	203	PARTY-PPL OVR 30								5E08A	5E08A
21920	203	PARTY-ONE HI ALC								5E08B	5E08B
21930	203	PARTY-OTH HI ALC								5E08C	5E08C
21940	203	PARTY-YOU HI ALC								5E08D	5E08D
21950	203	PARTY-PRESS ALCL								5E08E	5E08E
21960	204	PARTY-PRS HI ALC								5E08F	5E08F
21970	204	PARTY-ONE HI MJ								5E08G	5E08G
21980	204	PARTY-OTH HI MJ								5E08H	5E08H
21990	204	PARTY-YOU HI MJ								5E08I	5E08I
22000	204	PARTY-PRESS MJ								5E08J	5E08J
22010	204	PARTY-ONE HI OTD								5E08K	5E08K
22020	204	PARTY-OTH HI OTD								5E08L	5E08L
22030	205	PARTY-YOU HI OTD								5E08M	5E08M
22040	205	PARTY-PRESS OTDG								5E08N	5E08N
		(continued)									

Item Reference Number	Page Loc. in this Volume	ITEM DESCRIPTION (ABBREVIATED)	QUESTIONNAIRE LOCATION BY YEAR (FORM, SECTION, AND QUESTION NUMBER)								
			1975	1976	1977	1978	1979	1980/81	1982/83	1984/85	1986

C07: WORK and LEISURE. Leisure time: extent, activities (continued)

Item Reference Number	Page Loc. in this Volume	ITEM DESCRIPTION (ABBREVIATED)	1975	1976	1977	1978	1979	1980/81	1982/83	1984/85	1986
22170	116	SCH ACTV-PBLCTNS									2E07A
22180	116	SCH ACTV-PRF ART									2E07B
22190	116	SCH ACTV-ATHLTCS									2E07C
22200	117	SCH ACTV-OTH ACT									2E07D

C08: WORK and LEISURE. Attitudes toward leisure time

Item Reference Number	Page Loc. in this Volume	ITEM DESCRIPTION (ABBREVIATED)	1975	1976	1977	1978	1979	1980/81	1982/83	1984/85	1986
1370	36	SAT SPD LEISR	1A009K	1A006K	1A006K	1A006K	1A006K	1A006K	1A006K	1A006K	1A006K
1440	37	IMP TM RCRN&HBY		1A007D	1A007D	1A007D	1A007D	1A007D	1A007D	1A007D	1A007D
9880		DK DO W LEISR TM			3E11A		3E11A	3E11A			
9890		TM QUIK/LEIS HRS			3E11B		3E11B	3E11B			
9900		WASTE LEIS TIME			3E11C		3E11C	3E11C			
9910		ENUF TIME FR THG			3E11D		3E11D	3E11D			
11240	170	P'IDEA OF LSR TM	4A27B	4E08B	4E08B	4E07B	4E07B	4E07B	4E07B	4E07B	4E07B
22050	205	PRFR PTY-PPL >30								5E09A	5E09A
22060	205	PRF PTY-U HI ALC								5E09B	5E09B
22070	205	PR PTY-OTH HI AL								5E09C	5E09C
22080	205	PRF PTY-U USE MJ								5E09D	5E09D
22090	205	PR PTY-OT USE MJ								5E09E	5E09E
22100	206	PR PTY-U USE OTD								5E09F	5E09F
22110	206	PR PTY-OT USE OT								5E09G	5E09G

D01: SEX ROLES and FAMILY. Dating and marriage: status, attitudes, expectations

Item Reference Number	Page Loc. in this Volume	ITEM DESCRIPTION (ABBREVIATED)	1975	1976	1977	1978	1979	1980/81	1982/83	1984/85	1986
60	16	R NOT MARRIED		+C06	+C06	+C06	+C06	+C06	+C06	+C06	+C06
6120	96	DFNTLY PRFR MATE	2A10	2A05	2A05	2A05	2A05	2A05	2A05	2A05	2A05
6130	96	THINK WILL MARRY	2A11	2A06	2A06	2A06	2A06	2A06	2A06	2A06	2A06
6140	96	LIKLY STAY MARRD	2A12A	2A07A	2A07A	2A07A	2A07A	2A07A	2A07A	2A07A	2A07A
6850	107	HOW GD AS SPOUSE	2A19A	2D02A	2D02A	2D02A	2D02A	2D02A	2D02A	2D02A	2D02A
8320	128	MARRD OR ENGAGED	3A41	3A18	3A18	3A18	3A18	3A18	3A18	3A18	3A18
8330	128	WHN WANT GT MARR	3A42	3A19	3A19	3A19	3A19	3A19	3A19	3A19	3A19
11770	177	XPRC MK R GD SPS		5A04A	5A04A	5A04A	5A04A	5A04A	5A04A	5A04A	5A04A

D02: SEX ROLES and FAMILY. Parenthood: status, attitudes, expectations

Item Reference Number	Page Loc. in this Volume	ITEM DESCRIPTION (ABBREVIATED)	1975	1976	1977	1978	1979	1980/81	1982/83	1984/85	1986
6150	96	LIKLY HAVE KIDS	2A12B	2A07B	2A07B	2A07B	2A07B	2A07B	2A07B	2A07B	2A07B
6860	107	HOW GD AS PARENT	2A19B	2D02B	2D02B	2D02B	2D02B	2D02B	2D02B	2D02B	2D02B
8340	128	THGT LOT HAV CHL	3A43	3A20	3A20	3A20	3A20	3A20	3A20	3A20	3A20
8350	128	# CHLDN WANT(6+)	3A44	3A21	3A21	3A21	3A21	3A21	3A21	3A21	3A21
8360	129	IF -POP, MR CHLD	3A45	3A22	3A22	3A22	3A22	3A22	3A22	3A22	3A22
8370	129	WHN 1ST CHL(5+Y)	3A46	3A23	3A23	3A23	3A23	3A23	3A23	3A23	3A23
11780	177	XPRC MK R GD PRT		5A04B	5A04B	5A04B	5A04B	5A04B	5A04B	5A04B	5A04B

D03: SEX ROLES and FAMILY. Values surrounding marriage and family

Item Reference Number	Page Loc. in this Volume	ITEM DESCRIPTION (ABBREVIATED)	1975	1976	1977	1978	1979	1980/81	1982/83	1984/85	1986
1420	37	IMP GD MRRG&FAM		1A007B	1A007B	1A007B	1A007B	1A007B	1A007B	1A007B	1A007B
10470	156	FEW GD MAR, ? IT	4A11A	4A15A	4A15A	4A15A	4A15A	4A15A	4A15A	4A15A	4A15A
10480	156	GD LIV TG BF MRG	4A11B	4A15B	4A15B	4A15B	4A15B	4A15B	4A15B	4A15B	4A15B
10490	157	1 PRTNR=RSTRCTVE	4A11C	4A15C	4A15C	4A15C	4A15C	4A15C	4A15C	4A15C	4A15C
12150	183	FULLR LVS IF MRY	5A12A	5A18J	5A18J	5A18J	5A18J	5A18J	5A18J	5A18J	5A18J
12770	194	LV TGTH=BD MRLTY		5D05	5D02	5D02	5D02	5D02†	5D02	5D02	5D02
12775	194	FAM-MAR=BD MRLTY		5D06	5D03	5D03	5D03	5D03†	5D03	5D03	5D03

D04: SEX ROLES and FAMILY. Preferences regarding marital/familial arrangements

Item Reference Number	Page Loc. in this Volume	ITEM DESCRIPTION (ABBREVIATED)	1975	1976	1977	1978	1979	1980/81	1982/83	1984/85	1986
6160	97	-CHL,HB WK1.,W=0	2A15A	2A08A	2A08A	2A08A	2A08A	2A08A	2A08A	2A08A	2A08A
6170	97	-CHL,HB WK1.,W.5	2A15B	2A08B	2A08B	2A08B	2A08B	2A08B	2A08B	2A08B	2A08B
6180	97	-CHL,HB&WF WK 1.	2A15C	2A08C	2A08C	2A08C	2A08C	2A08C	2A08C	2A08C	2A08C
6190	97	-CHL,HB&WF WK .5	2A15D	2A08D	2A08D	2A08D	2A08D	2A08D	2A08D	2A08D	2A08D
6200	97	-CHL,W WK 1.,H.5	2A15E	2A08E	2A08E	2A08E	2A08E	2A08E	2A08E	2A08E	2A08E
6210	97	-CHL,W WK 1.,H=0	2A15F	2A08F	2A08F	2A08F	2A08F	2A08F	2A08F	2A08F	2A08F
6220	98	PSCH,HB WK1.,W=0	2A16A	2A09A	2A09A	2A09A	2A09A	2A09A	2A09A	2A09A	2A09A
6230	98	PSCH,HB WK1.,W.5	2A16B	2A09B	2A09B	2A09B	2A09B	2A09B	2A09B	2A09B	2A09B
		(continued)									

† This question appears in 1980 but does not appear in 1981.

Item Reference Number	Page Loc. in this Volume	ITEM DESCRIPTION (ABBREVIATED)	QUESTIONNAIRE LOCATION BY YEAR (FORM, SECTION, AND QUESTION NUMBER)								
			1975	1976	1977	1978	1979	1980/81	1982/83	1984/85	1986

D04: SEX ROLES and FAMILY. Preferences regarding marital/familial arrangements *(continued)*

6240	98	PSCH,HB&WF WK 1.	2A16C	2A09C	2A09C	2A09C	2A09C	2A09C	2A09C	2A09C	2A09C
6250	98	PSCH,HB&WF WK .5	2A16D	2A09D	2A09D	2A09D	2A09D	2A09D	2A09D	2A09D	2A09D
6260	98	PSCH,WF WK1.,H.5	2A16E	2A09E	2A09E	2A09E	2A09E	2A09E	2A09E	2A09E	2A09E
6270	98	PSCH,WF WK1.,H=0	2A16F	2A09F	2A09F	2A09F	2A09F	2A09F	2A09F	2A09F	2A09F
6280	98	H WK,W -WK,W CCR	2A17A	2A10A	2A10A	2A10A	2A10A	2A10A	2A10A	2A10A	2A10A
6290	99	H WK,W -WK,W>CCR	2A17B	2A10B	2A10B	2A10B	2A10B	2A10B	2A10B	2A10B	2A10B
6300	99	H WK,W -WK,=CHCR	2A17C	2A10C	2A10C	2A10C	2A10C	2A10C	2A10C	2A10C	2A10C
6310	99	H WK,W -WK,H>CCR	2A17D	2A10D	2A10D	2A10D	2A10D	2A10D	2A10D	2A10D	2A10D
6320	99	H WK,W -WK,H CCR	2A17E	2A10E	2A10E	2A10E	2A10E	2A10E	2A10E	2A10E	2A10E
11560		H&W WK,WF AL HWK			4E11A	4E10A	4E10A	4E10A			
11570		H&W WK,WF MS HWK			4E11B	4E10B	4E10B	4E10B			
11580		H&W WK,DO = HWRK			4E11C	4E10C	4E10C	4E10C			
11590		H&W WK,HB MS HWK			4E11D	4E10D	4E10D	4E10D			
11600		H&W WK,HB AL HWK			4E11E	4E10E	4E10E	4E10E			
11610		H&W WK+CH,W CHCR			4E12A	4E11A	4E11A	4E11A			
11620		H&W WK+CH,W>CHCR			4E12B	4E11B	4E11B	4E11B			
11630		H&W WK+CH,=CHCAR			4E12C	4E11C	4E11C	4E11C			
11640		H&W WK+CH,H>CHCR			4E12D	4E11D	4E11D	4E11D			
11650		H&W WK+CH,H CHCR			4E12E	4E11E	4E11E	4E11E			
13150		FAM+REL GD/CHILD		5E01A							
13160		FAM+REL GD/PARNT		5E01B							
13170		FAM+REL GD/GRPNT		5E01C							
13180		FAM+REL,R LIK/PT		5E01D							
13280		FAM+CPL GD/CHILD		5E02A							
13290		FAM+CPL GD/PARNT		5E02B							
13300		FAM+CPL GD/CPLS		5E02C							
13310		FAM+CPL,LIK/PRNT		5E02D							
13320		FAM+CPL,LIK/-CHD		5E02E							
13420		CPL+OTH +CHD MAR		5E03A							
13430		CPL+OTH +CHD DVC		5E03B							
13440		CPL+OTH +MAR CPL		5E03C							
13450		CPL+OTH +DIV PRT		5E03D							
13460		CPL+OTH +UNMARRD		5E03E							
13470		CPL+OTH,LK,MR PT		5E03F							
13480		CPL+OTH,LK,DVC P		5E03G							

D05: SEX ROLES and FAMILY. Sex role attitudes

7970	123	MN=ACHV/WMN=HOME	3A17H	3A03E	3A03E	3A03E	3A03E	3A03E	3A03E	3A03E	3A03E
7980	123	CHL SUFF W WK MO	3A17I	3A03F	3A03F	3A03F	3A03F	3A03F	3A03F	3A03F	3A03F
7990	123	WK MO AS WRM REL	3A17J	3A03G	3A03G	3A03G	3A03G	3A03G	3A03G	3A03G	3A03G
10500	157	JB INTFR REL HBD	4A11E	4A15D	4A15D	4A15D	4A15D	4A15D	4A15D	4A15D	4A15D
10510	157	JB DVLP WF PERSN	4A11G	4A15E	4A15E	4A15E	4A15E	4A15E	4A15E	4A15E	4A15E
10520	157	RS CHLD + FR MAN	4A11H	4A15F	4A15F	4A15F	4A15F	4A15F	4A15F	4A15F	4A15F
10530	157	MO SH B W CHL>TM	4A11I	4A15G	4A15G	4A15G	4A15G	4A15G	4A15G	4A15G	4A15G
10540	157	WF WK,HBD SHD>HW	4A11K	4A15H	4A15H	4A15H	4A15H	4A15H	4A15H	4A15H	4A15H
11330	172	P'IDEA OF SX RLS	4A27K	4E08K	4E08K	4E07K	4E07K	4E07K	4E07K	4E07K	4E07K
12160	183	ENCRG=INDP DT/SN	5A12B	5A18K	5A18K	5A18K	5A18K	5A18K	5A18K	5A18K	5A18K
12170	184	BNG MOTH V FULFL	5A12D	5A18L	5A18L	5A18L	5A18L	5A18L	5A18L	5A18L	5A18L
12180	184	FTHR>TIME W CHLD	5A12G	5A18M	5A18M	5A18M	5A18M	5A18M	5A18M	5A18M	5A18M
12190	184	HSB MAK IMP DCSN	5A12H	5A18N	5A18N	5A18N	5A18N	5A18N	5A18N	5A18N	5A18N

D06: SEX ROLES and FAMILY. Opinions regarding sex discrimination

7930	122	MEN&WOMN/=$,=WRK	3A17A	3A03A	3A03A	3A03A	3A03A	3A03A	3A03A	3A03A	3A03A
7940	122	CNSDR WMN/HI JOB	3A17B	3A03B	3A03B	3A03B	3A03B	3A03B	3A03B	3A03B	3A03B
7950	122	WMN SHD =JOB OPP	3A17C	3A03C	3A03C	3A03C	3A03C	3A03C	3A03C	3A03C	3A03C
7960	122	WMN SHD =ED OPP	3A17D	3A03D	3A03D	3A03D	3A03D	3A03D	3A03D	3A03D	3A03D
10370	155	JOB OBSTC SEX		4A13B	4A13B	4A13B	4A13B	4A13B	4A13B	4A13B	4A13B
11180	169	MLTRY DSCRM WOMN		4E03	4E03	4E03	4E03	4E03	4E03	4E03	4E03
12290	186	DSCM WN COLLG ED	5A21A	5A22A	5A22A	5A22A	5A22A	5A22A	5A22A	5A22A	5A22A
12300	186	DSCM WN LDRSHP	5A21B	5A22B	5A22B	5A22B	5A22B	5A22B	5A22B	5A22B	5A22B
12310	186	DSCM WN EXEC/BSN	5A21C	5A22C	5A22C	5A22C	5A22C	5A22C	5A22C	5A22C	5A22C
		(continued)									

Item Reference Number	Page Loc. in this Volume	ITEM DESCRIPTION (ABBREVIATED)	QUESTIONNAIRE LOCATION BY YEAR (FORM, SECTION, AND QUESTION NUMBER)								
			1975	1976	1977	1978	1979	1980/81	1982/83	1984/85	1986

D06: SEX ROLES and FAMILY. Opinions regarding sex discrimination *(continued)*

12320	186	DSCM WN TOP/PRFN	5A21D	5A22D	5A22D	5A22D	5A22D	5A22D	5A22D	5A22D	5A22D
12330	187	DSCM WN SKL LABR	5A21E	5A22E	5A22E	5A22E	5A22E	5A22E	5A22E	5A22E	5A22E
12340	187	DSCM WN PLTCL OF	5A21F	5A22F	5A22F	5A22F	5A22F	5A22F	5A22F	5A22F	5A22F
12350	187	DSCM WN =PAY =WK	5A21G	5A22G	5A22G	5A22G	5A22G	5A22G	5A22G	5A22G	5A22G

E01: POPULATION CONCERNS. Overpopulation

8360	129	IF -POP, MR CHLD	3A45	3A22	3A22	3A22	3A22	3A22	3A22	3A22	3A22
9760	139	GOV HP PRB POPL	3A32N	3E04A	3E04A	3E04A	3E04A	3E04A	3E03A	3E03A	3E03A
9770	140	GOV NO POP PLCY	3A32A	3E04B	3E04B	3E04B	3E04B	3E04B	3E03B	3E03B	3E03B
9780	140	STR OVPOP,LMT FM	3A32B	3E04C	3E04C	3E04C	3E04C	3E04C	3E03C	3E03C	3E03C
9790	140	PRV OVPOP,NO CHL	3A32C	3E04D	3E04D	3E04D	3E04D	3E04D	3E03D	3E03D	3E03D
9830		US POP SZ LRGER	3A34	3E06	3E05	3E05	3E05	3E05			
9840		GVNG FOOD O CNTY	3A33	3E05							
9850		WRLD POP SZ LRGR	3A35	3E07	3E06	3E06	3E06	3E06			
11670	176	WR/NT POP GROWTH	5A04B	5A03B	5A03B	5A03B	5A03B	5A03B	5A03B	5A03B	5A03B
12270	185	CTB TO POP PRBMS	5A20H	5A20H	5A20H	5A20H	5A20H	5A20H	5A20H	5A20H	5A20H

E02: POPULATION CONCERNS. Birth control

9800	140	HISCH INS BRTH C	3A32E	3E04E	3E04E	3E04E	3E04E	3E04E	3E03E	3E03E	3E03E
9810	140	BRTH CNT IMMORAL	3A32I	3E04F	3E04F	3E04F	3E04F	3E04F	3E03F	3E03F	3E03F
9820	140	GOV BRTHC NO CST	3A32M	3E04G	3E04G	3E04G	3E04G	3E04G	3E03G	3E03G	3E03G
9860	140	HAD SEX ED IN HS		3E09	3E08	3E08	3E08	3E08	3E04	3E04	3E04
9870	141	STUDY BC IN HS		3E10	3E09	3E09	3E09	3E09	3E05	3E05	3E05

F01: CONSERVATION, MATERIALISM, EQUITY, ETC. Personal materialism

1350	35	SAT STD OF LVG	1A009I	1A006I	1A006I	1A006I	1A006I	1A006I	1A006I	1A006I	1A006I
1430	37	IMP LOTS OF $		1A007C	1A007C	1A007C	1A007C	1A007C	1A007C	1A007C	1A007C
5930	93	DALY GO SHOPPING		2A02L	2A02L	2A02L	2A02L	2A02L	2A02L	2A02L	2A02L
7700		NOW OWN HAIR DRY		2E09A							
7710		NOW OWN WT/S SKI		2E09B							
7720		NOW OWN CAMERA		2E09C							
7730		NOW OWN WATCH		2E09D							
7740		NOW OWN HKG BKPK		2E09E							
7750		NOW OWN CK RADIO		2E09F							
7760		NOW OWN EL SHAVR		2E09G							
7770		NOW OWN TENIS RQ		2E09H							
7780		NOW OWN TV SET		2E09I							
7790		NOW OWN BICYCLE		2E09J							
7800		NOW OWN CAR		2E09K							
7810		NOW OWN TAPE REC		2E09L							
7820		NOW OWN ELT CALC		2E09M							
7830		NOW OWN BT/SNMBL		2E09N							
8020	123	MR$FR LASTG THG	3A31E	3A04C	3A04C	3A04C	3A04C	3A04C	3A04C	3A04C	3A04C
10060	150	FAM BUYS THG -ND	4A22L	4A06J	4A06J	4A06J	4A06J	4A06J	4A06J	4A06J	4A06J
	183				5A18I	5A18I	5A18I	5A18I	5A18I	5A18I	5A18I
10140	151	JOB IMPC EARN $	4A08F	4A08F	4A08F	4A08F	4A08F	4A08F	4A08F	4A08F	4A08F
12020	181	ENJOY SHOPPING	5A35A	5A15A	5A15A	5A15A	5A15A	5A15A	5A15A	5A15A	5A15A
12030	181	CARE LATST FASHN	5A35B	5A15B	5A15B	5A15B	5A15B	5A15B	5A15B	5A15B	5A15B
12040	181	CR FAM HV NBR HV	5A35C	5A15C	5A15C	5A15C	5A15C	5A15C	5A15C	5A15C	5A15C
12050	181	XPCT 2 OWN>PRNTS	5A36	5A16	5A16	5A16	5A16	5A16	5A16	5A16	5A16
12060	182	LST CNT OWN>PRNT	5A37	5A17	5A17	5A17	5A17	5A17	5A17	5A17	5A17
13600	141	STS SCH NIC CAR		5E05C	5E06C	5E06C	5E04C	5E06C†	3E06C	3E06C	3E06C
13700		BY SOON HAIR DRY		2E10A							
13710		BY SOON WT/S SKI		2E10B							
13720		BY SOON CAMERA		2E10C							
13730		BY SOON WATCH		2E10D							
13740		BY SOON HKG BKPK		2E10E							
13750		BY SOON CK RADIO		2E10F							
13760		BY SOON EL SHAVR		2E10G							
13770		BY SOON TENIS RQ		2E10H							
		(continued)									

† This question appears in 1980 but does not appear in 1981.

Item Reference Number	Page Loc. in this Volume	Item Description (Abbreviated)	QUESTIONNAIRE LOCATION BY YEAR (FORM, SECTION, AND QUESTION NUMBER)								
			1975	1976	1977	1978	1979	1980/81	1982/83	1984/85	1986

F01: CONSERVATION, MATERIALISM, EQUITY, ETC. Personal materialism *(continued)*

Item Reference Number	Page Loc. in this Volume	Item Description (Abbreviated)	1975	1976	1977	1978	1979	1980/81	1982/83	1984/85	1986
13780		BY SOON TV SET			2E10I						
13790		BY SOON BICYCLE			2E10J						
13800		BY SOON CAR			2E10K						
13810		BY SOON TAPE REC			2E10L						
13820		BY SOON ELT CALC			2E10M						
13830		BY SOON BT/SNMBL			2E10N						
13835	143	IMP HAV 1 CAR		3E12A		3E11A	3E10A	3E10A	3E09A	3E09A	3E09A
13840	143	IMP HAV 2 CARS		3E12B		3E11B	3E10B	3E10B	3E09B	3E09B	3E09B
13850	144	IMP HAV LARG CAR		3E12C		3E11C	3E10C	3E10C	3E09C	3E09C	3E09C
13860	144	IMP HAV NW CR OF		3E12D		3E11D	3E10D	3E10D	3E09D	3E09D	3E09D
13870	144	IMP HAV NW CLTHS		3E12E		3E11E	3E10E	3E10E	3E09E	3E09E	3E09E
13880	144	IMP HAV OWN HSE		3E12F		3E11F	3E10F	3E10F	3E09F	3E09F	3E09F
13890	144	IMP HAV BIG YARD		3E12G		3E11G	3E10G	3E10G	3E09G	3E09G	3E09G
13900	144	IMP HAV NEAT LWN		3E12H		3E11H	3E10H	3E10H	3E09H	3E09H	3E09H
13910	144	IMP HAV APPLINCS		3E12I		3E11I	3E10I	3E10I	3E09I	3E09I	3E09I
13920	144	IMP HAV G STEREO		3E12J		3E11J	3E10J	3E10J	3E09J	3E09J	3E09J
13930	145	IMP HAV VAC HSE		3E12K		3E11K	3E10K	3E10K	3E09K	3E09K	3E09K
13940	145	IMP HAV REC VEH		3E12L		3E11L	3E10L	3E10L	3E09L	3E09L	3E09L

F02: CONSERVATION, MATERIALISM, EQUITY, ETC. Societal materialism and advertising

Item Reference Number	Page Loc. in this Volume	Item Description (Abbreviated)	1975	1976	1977	1978	1979	1980/81	1982/83	1984/85	1986
6000	94	2MUCH CNCRN MTRL	2A23K	2A03B	2A03B	2A03B	2A03B	2A03B	2A03B	2A03B	2A03B
6010	94	ENCOURG PPL BUY>	2A23L	2A03C	2A03C	2A03C	2A03C	2A03C	2A03C	2A03C	2A03C
6020	95	-WRNG ADVERTISNG	2A23M	2A03D	2A03D	2A03D	2A03D	2A03D	2A03D	2A03D	2A03D
6030	95	MOR SHORTGS FUTR	2A23N	2A03E	2A03E	2A03E	2A03E	2A03E	2A03E	2A03E	2A03E
10040	150	TV COMM CRT NDS	4A22H	4A06H	4A06H	4A06H	4A06H	4A06H	4A06H	4A06H	4A06H
10050	150	TV COMMRCLS GOOD	4A22I	4A06I	4A06I	4A06I	4A06I	4A06I	4A06I	4A06I	4A06I

F03: CONSERVATION, MATERIALISM, EQUITY, ETC. Concern with world hunger and poverty

Item Reference Number	Page Loc. in this Volume	Item Description (Abbreviated)	1975	1976	1977	1978	1979	1980/81	1982/83	1984/85	1986
5990	94	US 2 MUCH PROFIT	2A23J	2A03A	2A03A	2A03A	2A03A	2A03A	2A03A	2A03A	2A03A
8040	124	EAT DIF->FD STRV	3A31G	3A04E	3A04E	3A04E	3A04E	3A04E	3A04E	3A04E	3A04E
11720	177	WR/NT HNGR&PVRTY	5A04G	5A03G	5A03G	5A03G	5A03G	5A03G	5A03G	5A03G	5A03G
12090	182	-SYMP TWD STARVG	5A19E	5A18C	5A18C	5A18C	5A18C	5A18C	5A18C	5A18C	5A18C
12140	183	RB CHNG ETG HABT		5A18H	5A18H	5A18H	5A18H	5A18H	5A18H	5A18H	5A18H
16440		SAT EAT<BEEF>GRN				2E05B					
19470		EAT<FD,>OWN CITY					5E08A				
19480		EAT<FD,>NRBY STT					5E08B				
19490		EAT<FD,>DIF REGN					5E08C				
19500		EAT<FD,>ASIAN CN					5E08D				

F04: CONSERVATION, MATERIALISM, EQUITY, ETC. Ecological concerns

Item Reference Number	Page Loc. in this Volume	Item Description (Abbreviated)	1975	1976	1977	1978	1979	1980/81	1982/83	1984/85	1986
1640	40	US NEEDS GROWTH	1A013E	1A011G	1A011G	1A011G	1A011G	1A011G	1A011G	1A011G	1A011G
8000	123	POLLUT INCREASED	3A31A	3A04A	3A04A	3A04A	3A04A	3A04A	3A04A	3A04A	3A04A
8010	123	GOVT DEAL ENV PR	3A31D	3A04B	3A04B	3A04B	3A04B	3A04B	3A04B	3A04B	3A04B
9700		PRVNT POL TOO >$		3E02A	3E02A	3E02A	3E02A	3E02A	3E01A	3E01A	
9710		PRVNT POL CST JB		3E02B	3E02B	3E02B	3E02B	3E02B	3E01B	3E01B	
9720		PRVNT POL PPL DK		3E02C	3E02C	3E02C	3E02C	3E02C	3E01C	3E01C	
9730		PRVNT POL -ENUF		3E02D	3E02D	3E02D	3E02D	3E02D	3E01D	3E01D	
9740		PRVNT POL USELSS		3E02E	3E02E	3E02E	3E02E	3E02E	3E01E	3E01E	
9970	148	PLLTN INCR IN US	4A22A	4A06A	4A06A	4A06A	4A06A	4A06A	4A06A	4A06A	4A06A
9980	149	PLLTN NT SO DANG	4A22B	4A06B	4A06B	4A06B	4A06B	4A06B	4A06B	4A06B	4A06B
9990	149	PLLTN NEC 4 GRTH	4A22C	4A06C	4A06C	4A06C	4A06C	4A06C	4A06C	4A06C	4A06C
10000	149	INDVL RESP 4 ENV	4A22D	4A06D	4A06D	4A06D	4A06D	4A06D	4A06D	4A06D	4A06D
10010	149	GOVT RESP 4 ENV	4A22E	4A06E	4A06E	4A06E	4A06E	4A06E	4A06E	4A06E	4A06E
10020	149	GOVT TAX PLLTRS	4A22F	4A06F	4A06F	4A06F	4A06F	4A06F	4A06F	4A06F	4A06F
10030	149	GOVT BAN DSPSBLE	4A22G	4A06G	4A06G	4A06G	4A06G	4A06G	4A06G	4A06G	4A06G
10070	150	POL SLVD BY 2000	4A22M	4A06K	4A06K	4A06K	4A06K	4A06K	4A06K	4A06K	4A06K
10080	150	R EFRT 2 HLP ENV	4A23	4A07	4A07	4A07	4A07	4A07	4A07	4A07	4A07
11340	172	P'IDEA OF ECLOGY	4A27L	4E08L	4E08L	4E07L	4E07L	4E07L	4E07L	4E07L	4E07L
11690	176	WR/NT POLLUTION	5A04D	5A03D	5A03D	5A03D	5A03D	5A03D	5A03D	5A03D	
12280	186	CTB TO ENVIR PBM	5A20I	5A20I	5A20I	5A20I	5A20I	5A20I	5A20I	5A20I	
16450		SAT TAX FR ECLGY				2E05C					

Item Reference Number	Page Loc. in this Volume	ITEM DESCRIPTION (ABBREVIATED)	QUESTIONNAIRE LOCATION BY YEAR (FORM, SECTION, AND QUESTION NUMBER)								
			1975	1976	1977	1978	1979	1980/81	1982/83	1984/85	1986

F05: CONSERVATION, MATERIALISM, EQUITY, ETC. Concern with conservation of resources

Item Reference Number	Page Loc.	ITEM DESCRIPTION	1975	1976	1977	1978	1979	1980/81	1982/83	1984/85	1986
9750	139	FUTR,HAV2 CNSUM<		3E03	3E03	3E03	3E03	3E03	3E02	3E02	3E02
10930	165	SOCTY WONT LAST	4A28B	4D03B	4D03B	4D03B	4D03B	4D03B	4D10B	4D10B	4D10B
11700	176	WR/NT ENRGY SHRT	5A04E	5A03E	5A03E	5A03E	5A03E	5A03E	5A03E	5A03E	5A03E
11730	177	WR/NT USE OPN LD	5A04H	5A03H	5A03H	5A03H	5A03H	5A03H	5A03H	5A03H	5A03H
12000	181	R CUT ELECTRICTY		5A13	5A13	5A13	5A13	5A13	5A13	5A13	5A13
12010	181	RDCE HEAT R'S HM		5A14	5A14	5A14	5A14	5A14	5A14	5A14	5A14

F06: CONSERVATION, MATERIALISM, EQUITY, ETC. Preferences regarding dwelling type and urbanicity

Item Reference Number	Page Loc.	ITEM DESCRIPTION	1975	1976	1977	1978	1979	1980/81	1982/83	1984/85	1986
17860		DESRD LVG RURAL				4E09A		4E09A	4E09A¶		
17870		DESRD LVG SM TWN				4E09B		4E09B	4E09B¶		
17880		DESRD LVG SM CTY				4E09C		4E09C	4E09C¶		
17890		DESRD LVG SUBURB				4E09D		4E09D	4E09D¶		
17900		DESRD LVG LG CTY				4E09E		4E09E	4E09E¶		
17910		DSRD HSG 1 FAMLY				4E09F		4E09F	4E09F¶		
17920		DSRD HSG 2 FAMLY				4E09G		4E09G	4E09G¶		
17930		DSRD HSG CNDMINM				4E09H		4E09H	4E09H¶		
17940		DSRD HSG APT BLD				4E09I		4E09I	4E09I¶		
17910		DSRD HSG 1 FAMLY				4E09F		4E09F	4E09F¶		

F07: CONSERVATION, MATERIALISM, EQUITY, ETC. Driving and use of mass transit

Item Reference Number	Page Loc.	ITEM DESCRIPTION	1975	1976	1977	1978	1979	1980/81	1982/83	1984/85	1986
640	22	DRIVE>200 MI/WK		+C27	+C27	+C27	+C27	+C27	+C27	+C27	+C27
8030	124	USE BYC/MAS TRAN	3A31F	3A04D	3A04D	3A04D	3A04D	3A04D	3A04D	3A04D	3A04D
11960	180	DNT HV DRVR LCNS	5A22	5A09	5A09	5A09	5A09	5A09	5A09	5A09	5A09
11970	180	DONT OWN CAR	5A23	5A10	5A10	5A10	5A10	5A10	5A10	5A10	5A10
11980	180	NEVR USE OTHS CR	5A24	5A11	5A11	5A11	5A11	5A11	5A11	5A11	5A11
11990	180	R CUT DRIVING		5A12	5A12	5A12	5A12	5A12	5A12	5A12	5A12
16430		SAT EVB CAR POOL				2E05A					
22210	121	USE SEATBLT-DRVR									2E22
22220	121	USE SEATBLT-RIDR									2E23

G: RELIGION. Religious preferences, activities, views

Item Reference Number	Page Loc.	ITEM DESCRIPTION	1975	1976	1977	1978	1979	1980/81	1982/83	1984/85	1986
360	18	R'S RELGS PRFNC		+C13A	+C13A	+C13A	+C13A	(+C13A)	+C13A	+C13A	+C13A
370	18	R'ATTND REL SVC		+C13B	+C13B	+C13B	+C13B	+C13B	+C13B	+C13B	+C13B
380	19	RLGN IMP R'S LF		+C13C	+C13C	+C13C	+C13C	+C13C	+C13C	+C13C	+C13C
5980		DALY GO CHURCH		2A02D							
6930	109	DHNSTY CHURCHES	2A20E	2D04E	2D04E	2D04E	2D04E	2D04E	2D04E	2D04E	2D04E
8420	130	GD JB CHURCHES	3A27E	3A24E	3A24E	3A24E	3A24E	3A24E	3A24E	3A24E	3A24E
10360	155	JOB OBSTC RELGN		4A13A	4A13A	4A13A	4A13A	4A13A	4A13A	4A13A	4A13A
10590	159	>INFLC CHURCHES	4A14C	4A19C	4A19C	4A19C	4A19C	4A19C	4A19C	4A19C	4A19C
11360	172	P'IDEA OF RLGION	4A27N	4E08N	4E08N	4E07N	4E07N	4E07N	4E07N	4E07N	4E07N
11910	179	RCL CNTCT CHURCH		5A07C	5A07C	5A07C	5A07C	5A07C	5A07C	5A07C	5A07C
12230	185	CTB TO RELGS ORG		5A20D	5A20D	5A20D	5A20D	5A20D	5A20D	5A20D	5A20D

H01: POLITICS. Political interest and preferences

Item Reference Number	Page Loc.	ITEM DESCRIPTION	1975	1976	1977	1978	1979	1980/81	1982/83	1984/85	1986
340	18	R'S POLTL PRFNC		+C11	+C11	+C11	+C11	+C11	+C11	+C11	+C11
350	18	R'POL BLF RADCL		+C12	+C12	+C12	+C12	+C12	+C12	+C12	+C12
6330	99	INTEREST IN GOVT	2A31	2A11	2A11	2A11	2A11	2A11	2A11	2A11	2A11
	158		4A29	3E01	3E01	3E01	3E01	3E01	4A18	4A18	4A18
	184		5A40	4A18	4A18	4A18	4A18	4A18	5A19	5A19	5A19
				5A19	5A19	5A19	5A19	5A19			
10400	155	JOB OBSTC POL VW		4A13E	4A13E	4A13E	4A13E	4A13E	4A13E	4A13E	4A13E
11370	172	P'IDEA OF PLTICS	4A27O	4E08O	4E08O	4E07O	4E07O	4E07O	4E07O	4E07O	4E07O

H02: POLITICS. Attitudes toward governmental policies and practices

Item Reference Number	Page Loc.	ITEM DESCRIPTION	1975	1976	1977	1978	1979	1980/81	1982/83	1984/85	1986
1390	36	SAT GOVT OPRTNG		1A006M	1A006M	1A006M	1A006M	1A006M	1A006M	1A006M	1A006M
5690	101	US GO WAR FR OTH	2A38B	2A18B	2A18B	2A18B	2A18B	2A18B	2A18B	2A18B	2A18B
6450	101	US SHD DISARM	2A38A	2A18A	2A18A	2A18A	2A18A	2A18A	2A18A	2A18A	2A18A
6460	101	US WAR PRTCT ECN	2A38C	2A18C	2A18C	2A18C	2A18C	2A18C	2A18C	2A18C	2A18C
		(continued)									

¶ This question appears in 1982 but does not appear in 1983.

Item Reference Number	Page Loc. in this Volume	ITEM DESCRIPTION (ABBREVIATED)	QUESTIONNAIRE LOCATION BY YEAR (FORM, SECTION, AND QUESTION NUMBER)								
			1975	1976	1977	1978	1979	1980/81	1982/83	1984/85	1986

H02: POLITICS. Attitudes toward governmental policies and practices *(continued)*

Item Reference Number	Page Loc.	Item Description	1975	1976	1977	1978	1979	1980/81	1982/83	1984/85	1986
6470	101	US ONLY WAR DFNS	2A38D	2A18D	2A18D	2A18D	2A18D	2A18D	2A18D	2A18D	2A18D
6480	102	-US MIL PWR>USSR	2A38E	2A18E	2A18E	2A18E	2A18E	2A18E	2A18E	2A18E	2A18E
6490	102	US NEED>PWR OTHS	2A38F	2A18F	2A18F	2A18F	2A18F	2A18F	2A18F	2A18F	2A18F
6500	102	US FRN PLCY NRRW	2A38G	2A18G	2A18G	2A18G	2A18G	2A18G	2A18G	2A18G	2A18G
7940	122	CNSDR WMN/HI JOB	3A17B	3A03B	3A03B	3A03B	3A03B	3A03B	3A03B	3A03B	3A03B
8010	123	GOVT DEAL ENV PR	3A31D	3A04B	3A04B	3A04B	3A04B	3A04B	3A04B	3A04B	3A04B
9760	139	GOV HP PRB POPL	3A32N	3E04A	3E04A	3E04A	3E04A	3E04A	3E03A	3E03A	3E03A
9770	140	GOV NO POP PLCY	3A32A	3E04B	3E04B	3E04B	3E04B	3E04B	3E03B	3E03B	3E03B
9820	140	GOV BRTHC NO CST	3A32M	3E04G	3E04G	3E04G	3E04G	3E04G	3E03G	3E03G	3E03G
10010	149	GOVT RESP 4 ENV	4A22E	4A06E	4A06E	4A06E	4A06E	4A06E	4A06E	4A06E	4A06E
10020	149	GOVT TAX PLLTRS	4A22F	4A06F	4A06F	4A06F	4A06F	4A06F	4A06F	4A06F	4A06F
10030	149	GOVT BAN DSPSBLE	4A22G	4A06G	4A06G	4A06G	4A06G	4A06G	4A06G	4A06G	4A06G
11210		-MLTRY COUP U.S.		4E06	4E06						
12340	187	DSCM WN PLTCL OF	5A21F	5A22F	5A22F	5A22F	5A22F	5A22F	5A22F	5A22F	5A22F

H03: POLITICS. Views about the role of citizens in government (See also I02: Attitudes regarding activism)

Item Reference Number	Page Loc.	Item Description	1975	1976	1977	1978	1979	1980/81	1982/83	1984/85	1986
1580	39	-OBY LW=-GD CTZN		1A011A	1A011A	1A011A	1A011A	1A011A	1A011A	1A011A	1A011A
1590	39	GD CTZN ALG GOVT		1A011B	1A011B	1A011B	1A011B	1A011B	1A011B	1A011B	1A011B
1600	39	GD CTZN CHG GOVT	1A013B	1A011C	1A011C	1A011C	1A011C	1A011C	1A011C	1A011C	1A011C
1620	39	CTZN GRP HV EFCT		1A011E	1A011E	1A011E	1A011E	1A011E	1A011E	1A011E	1A011E

H04: POLITICS. Confidence in government

Item Reference Number	Page Loc.	Item Description	1975	1976	1977	1978	1979	1980/81	1982/83	1984/85	1986
1630	39	OUR SYST ST BS	1A013C	1A011F	1A011F	1A011F	1A011F	1A011F	1A011F	1A011F	1A011F
6340	99	GOVT PPL -DSHNST	2A32	2A12	2A12	2A12	2A12	2A12	2A12	2A12	2A12
6350	99	GOVT DSNT WASTE$	2A33	2A13	2A13	2A13	2A13	2A13	2A13	2A13	2A13
6360	100	NEVER TRUST GOVT	2A34	2A14	2A14	2A14	2A14	2A14	2A14	2A14	2A14
6370	100	GVT PPL DK DOING	2A35	2A15	2A15	2A15	2A15	2A15	2A15	2A15	2A15
6380	100	GOVT RUN FOR PPL	2A36	2A16	2A16	2A16	2A16	2A16	2A16	2A16	2A16
6950	109	DHNSTY PRES&ADMN	2A20G	2D04G	2D04G	2D04G	2D04G	2D04G	2D04G	2D04G	2D04G
6960	109	DHNSTY CONGRESS	2A20H	2D04H	2D04H	2D04H	2D04H	2D04H	2D04H	2D04H	2D04H
6970	109	DHNSTY SUPRM CRT	2A20I	2D04I	2D04I	2D04I	2D04I	2D04I	2D04I	2D04I	2D04I
6980	109	DHNSTY JUSTC SYS	2A20J	2D04J	2D04J	2D04J	2D04J	2D04J	2D04J	2D04J	2D04J
8440	130	GD JB PRES&ADMN	3A27G	3A24G	3A24G	3A24G	3A24G	3A24G	3A24G	3A24G	3A24G
8450	130	GD JB CONGRESS	3A27H	3A24H	3A24H	3A24H	3A24H	3A24H	3A24H	3A24H	3A24H
8460	130	GD JB SUPRM CRT	3A27I	3A24I	3A24I	3A24I	3A24I	3A24I	3A24I	3A24I	3A24I
8470	130	GD JB JUSTC SYST	3A27J	3A24J	3A24J	3A24J	3A24J	3A24J	3A24J	3A24J	3A24J
10610	159	>INFLC PRES&ADMN	4A14E	4A19E	4A19E	4A19E	4A19E	4A19E	4A19E	4A19E	4A19E
10620	159	>INFLC CONGRESS	4A14F	4A19F	4A19F	4A19F	4A19F	4A19F	4A19F	4A19F	4A19F
10630	159	>INFLC SUPRM CRT	4A14G	4A19G	4A19G	4A19G	4A19G	4A19G	4A19G	4A19G	4A19G
10640	159	>INFLC JUSTC SYS	4A14H	4A19H	4A19H	4A19H	4A19H	4A19H	4A19H	4A19H	4A19H

H05: POLITICS. Voting, political activism

Item Reference Number	Page Loc.	Item Description	1975	1976	1977	1978	1979	1980/81	1982/83	1984/85	1986
1610	39	VOTE->MAJ IMPCT		1A011D	1A011D	1A011D	1A011D	1A011D	1A011D	1A011D	1A011D
6390	100	DO OR PLN VOTE	2A37A	2A17A	2A17A	2A17A	2A17A	2A17A	2A17A	2A17A	2A17A
6400	100	DO OR PLN WRITE	2A37B	2A17B	2A17B	2A17B	2A17B	2A17B	2A17B	2A17B	2A17B
6410	100	DO OR PLN GIVE $	2A37C	2A17C	2A17C	2A17C	2A17C	2A17C	2A17C	2A17C	2A17C
6420	101	DO OR PLN WK CPG	2A37D	2A17D	2A17D	2A17D	2A17D	2A17D	2A17D	2A17D	2A17D
6430	101	DO OR PLN DEMNST	2A37E	2A17E	2A17E	2A17E	2A17E	2A17E	2A17E	2A17E	2A17E
6440	101	DO OR PLN BOYCOT	2A37F	2A17F	2A17F	2A17F	2A17F	2A17F	2A17F	2A17F	2A17F
9920		R WL VOTE IN '76		3E11							
11820	178	PLC WRK GVT AGCY	5A09C	5A05C	5A05C	5A05C	5A05C	5A05C	5A05C	5A05C	5A05C
12240	185	CTB TO PLTCL PTY	5A20E	5A20E	5A20E	5A20E	5A20E	5A20E	5A20E	5A20E	5A20E
12250	185	CTB TO CTZN LBBY	5A20F	5A20F	5A20F	5A20F	5A20F	5A20F	5A20F	5A20F	5A20F
16340		EFCTV VOTING				2E04C					

I01: SOCIAL CHANGE. Expectations concerning societal change

Item Reference Number	Page Loc.	Item Description	1975	1976	1977	1978	1979	1980/81	1982/83	1984/85	1986
1200	33	US NEEDS PLANNG	1A004A	1A002A	1A002A	1A002A	1A002A	1A002A	1A002A	1A002A	1A002A
1230	33	X AHEAD TOUGHER	1A004G	1A002D	1A002D	1A002D	1A002D	1A002D	1A002D	1A002D	1A002D
9940	148	FUTR CNTRY WORSE	+A01	4A02	4A02	4A02	4A02	4A02	4A02	4A02	4A02

(continued)

Item Reference Number	Page Loc. in this Volume	ITEM DESCRIPTION (ABBREVIATED)	QUESTIONNAIRE LOCATION BY YEAR (FORM, SECTION, AND QUESTION NUMBER)								
			1975	1976	1977	1978	1979	1980/81	1982/83	1984/85	1986

I01: SOCIAL CHANGE. Expectations concerning societal change *(continued)*

9950	148	FUTR WORLD WORSE	+A02	4A03	4A03	4A03	4A03	4A03	4A03	4A03	4A03
9960	148	FUTR R LIFE WRSE	+A03	4A04	4A04	4A04	4A04	4A04	4A04	4A04	4A04
10940	165	THG TUF,TCHN SLV	4A28C	4D03C	4D03C	4D03C	4D03C	4D03C	4D10C	4D10C	4D10C

I02: SOCIAL CHANGE. Attitudes regarding activism

1610	39	VOTE->MAJ IMPCT		1A011D	1A011D	1A011D	1A011D	1A011D	1A011D	1A011D	1A011D
1620	39	CTZN GRP HV EFCT		1A011E	1A011E	1A011E	1A011E	1A011E	1A011E	1A011E	1A011E
1650	40	LV THNGS TO GOD	1A004C	1A011H	1A011H	1A011H	1A011H	1A011H	1A011H	1A011H	1A011H
6040	95	APRV PETITIONS	2A21A	2A04A	2A04A	2A04A	2A04A	2A04A	2A04A	2A04A	2A04A
6050	95	APRV BOYCOTT	2A21B	2A04B	2A04B	2A04B	2A04B	2A04B	2A04B	2A04B	2A04B
6060	95	APRV LWFL DMSTN	2A21C	2A04C	2A04C	2A04C	2A04C	2A04C	2A04C	2A04C	2A04C
6070	95	APRV OCCUPY BLDG	2A21D	2A04D	2A04D	2A04D	2A04D	2A04D	2A04D	2A04D	2A04D
6080	95	APRV WLDCAT STRK	2A21E	2A04E	2A04E	2A04E	2A04E	2A04E	2A04E	2A04E	2A04E
6090	96	APRV BLK TRAFFIC	2A21F	2A04F	2A04F	2A04F	2A04F	2A04F	2A04F	2A04F	2A04F
6100	96	APRV DAMAG THING	2A21G	2A04G	2A04G	2A04G	2A04G	2A04G	2A04G	2A04G	2A04G
6110	96	APRV PSNL VIOLNC	2A21H	2A04H	2A04H	2A04H	2A04H	2A04H	2A04H	2A04H	2A04H
6390	100	DO OR PLN VOTE	2A37A	2A17A	2A17A	2A17A	2A17A	2A17A	2A17A	2A17A	2A17A
6400	100	DO OR PLN WRITE	2A37B	2A17B	2A17B	2A17B	2A17B	2A17B	2A17B	2A17B	2A17B
6410	100	DO OR PLN GIVE $	2A37C	2A17C	2A17C	2A17C	2A17C	2A17C	2A17C	2A17C	2A17C
6420	101	DO OR PLN WK CPG	2A37D	2A17D	2A17D	2A17D	2A17D	2A17D	2A17D	2A17D	2A17D
6430	101	DO OR PLN DEMNST	2A37E	2A17E	2A17E	2A17E	2A17E	2A17E	2A17E	2A17E	2A17E
6440	101	DO OR PLN BOYCOT	2A37F	2A17F	2A17F	2A17F	2A17F	2A17F	2A17F	2A17F	2A17F
10920	165	I CNT CHNG WORLD	4A28A	4D03A	4D03A	4D03A	4D03A	4D03A	4D10A	4D10A	4D10A
12250	185	CTB TO CTZN LBBY	5A20F	5A20F	5A20F	5A20F	5A20F	5A20F	5A20F	5A20F	
16320		EFCTV WRIT OFCLS				2E04A					
16330		EFCTV WRK PL CPN				2E04B					
16340		EFCTV VOTING				2E04C					
16350		EFCTV PETITIONS				2E04D					
16360		EFCTV BOYCOTT				2E04E					
16370		EFCTV LWFL DMSTN				2E04F					
16380		EFCTV OCPY BLDGS				2E04G					
16390		EFCTV WLDCT STRK				2E04H					
16400		EFCTV BLK TRAFIC				2E04I					
16410		EFCTV DAMAG THNG				2E04J					
16420		EFCTV PSNL VLNC				2E04K					

I03: SOCIAL CHANGE. Reactions to personal and social change

1210	33	ENJOY FAST PACE	1A004B	1A002B	1A002B	1A002B	1A002B	1A002B	1A002B	1A002B	1A002B
1220	33	THG CHG 2 QUICK	1A004D	1A002C	1A002C	1A002C	1A002C	1A002C	1A002C	1A002C	1A002C
13950	193	EAGR TO LEAV HOM						5D01W	5D01W	5D01W	5D01W
13960	194	HEST PRT ADLT WL						5D01X	5D01X	5D01X	5D01X

J: SOCIAL PROBLEMS. Interest and concerns

1230	33	X AHEAD TOUGHER	1A004G	1A002D	1A002D	1A002D	1A002D	1A002D	1A002D	1A002D	1A002D
6880	108	THK ABT SOC ISSU	*A06	2D03	2D03	2D03	2D03	2D03	2D03	2D03	2D03
	122			3A02	3A02	3A02	3A02	3A02	3A02	3A02	3A02
	148				4A05	4A05	4A05	4A05	4A05	4A05	4A05
	176			5A02	5A02	5A02	5A02	5A02	5A02	5A02	5A02
10920	165	I CNT CHNG WORLD	4A28A	4D03A	4D03A	4D03A	4D03A	4D03A	4D10A	4D10A	4D10A
10930	165	SOCTY WONT LAST	4A28B	4D03B	4D03B	4D03B	4D03B	4D03B	4D10B	4D10B	4D10B
10940	165	THG TUF,TCHN SLV	4A28C	4D03C	4D03C	4D03C	4D03C	4D03C	4D10C	4D10C	4D10C
10950	166	NO HOPE 4 WORLD	4A28D	4D03D	4D03D	4D03D	4D03D	4D03D	4D10D	4D10D	4D10D
10960	166	WNDR PURPS 2 LIF	4A28E	4D03E	4D03E	4D03E	4D03E	4D03E	4D10E	4D10E	4D10E
10970	166	WRLD UPHVL 10 YR	4A28F	4D03F	4D03F	4D03F	4D03F	4D03F	4D10F	4D10F	4D10F
10980	166	ANNIHLTN IN LFTM	4A28G	4D03G	4D03G	4D03G	4D03G	4D03G	4D10G	4D10G	4D10G
10990	166	HMN RCE RSILIENT	4A28H	4D03H	4D03H	4D03H	4D03H	4D03H	4D10H	4D10H	4D10H
11660	176	WR/NT NUCLER WAR	5A04A	5A03A	5A03A	5A03A	5A03A	5A03A	5A03A	5A03A	5A03A
11670	176	WR/NT POP GROWTH	5A04B	5A03B	5A03B	5A03B	5A03B	5A03B	5A03B	5A03B	5A03B
11680	176	WR/NT CRIME&VLNC	5A04C	5A03C	5A03C	5A03C	5A03C	5A03C	5A03C	5A03C	5A03C
11690	176	WR/NT POLLUTION	5A04D	5A03D	5A03D	5A03D	5A03D	5A03D	5A03D	5A03D	5A03D
		(continued)									

Item Reference Number	Page Loc. in this Volume	ITEM DESCRIPTION (ABBREVIATED)	QUESTIONNAIRE LOCATION BY YEAR (FORM, SECTION, AND QUESTION NUMBER)								
			1975	1976	1977	1978	1979	1980/81	1982/83	1984/85	1986

J: SOCIAL PROBLEMS. Interest and concerns *(continued)*

11700	176	WR/NT ENRGY SHRT	5A04E	5A03E	5A03E	5A03E	5A03E	5A03E	5A03E	5A03E	5A03E
11710	177	WR/NT RACE RELTN	5A04F	5A03F	5A03F	5A03F	5A03F	5A03F	5A03F	5A03F	5A03F
11720	177	WR/NT HNGR&PVRTY	5A04G	5A03G	5A03G	5A03G	5A03G	5A03G	5A03G	5A03G	5A03G
11730	177	WR/NT USE OPN LD	5A04H	5A03H	5A03H	5A03H	5A03H	5A03H	5A03H	5A03H	5A03H
11740	177	WR/NT URBN DECAY	5A04I	5A03I	5A03I	5A03I	5A03I	5A03I	5A03I	5A03I	5A03I
11750	177	WR/NT ECON PRBLM	5A04J	5A03J	5A03J	5A03J	5A03J	5A03J	5A03J	5A03J	5A03J
11760	177	WR/NT DRUG ABUSE	5A04K	5A03K	5A03K	5A03K	5A03K	5A03K	5A03K	5A03K	5A03K

K01: MAJOR SOCIAL INSTITUTIONS. Trust (See also C05: Institutions as work settings)

6340	99	GOVT PPL -DSHNST	2A32	2A12	2A12	2A12	2A12	2A12	2A12	2A12	2A12
6350	99	GOVT DSNT WASTE$	2A33	2A13	2A13	2A13	2A13	2A13	2A13	2A13	2A13
6360	100	NEVER TRUST GOVT	2A34	2A14	2A14	2A14	2A14	2A14	2A14	2A14	2A14
6370	100	GVT PPL DK DOING	2A35	2A15	2A15	2A15	2A15	2A15	2A15	2A15	2A15
6380	100	GOVT RUN FOR PPL	2A36	2A16	2A16	2A16	2A16	2A16	2A16	2A16	2A16
6890	108	DHNSTY LARG CORP	2A20A	2D04A	2D04A	2D04A	2D04A	2D04A	2D04A	2D04A	2D04A
6900	108	DHNSTY LBR UNION	2A20B	2D04B	2D04B	2D04B	2D04B	2D04B	2D04B	2D04B	2D04B
6910	108	DHNSTY COLL&UNIV	2A20C	2D04C	2D04C	2D04C	2D04C	2D04C	2D04C	2D04C	2D04C
6920	108	DHNSTY PBLC SCHL	2A20D	2D04D	2D04D	2D04D	2D04D	2D04D	2D04D	2D04D	2D04D
6930	109	DHNSTY CHURCHES	2A20E	2D04E	2D04E	2D04E	2D04E	2D04E	2D04E	2D04E	2D04E
6940	109	DHNSTY NEWS MDIA	2A20F	2D04F	2D04F	2D04F	2D04F	2D04F	2D04F	2D04F	2D04F
6950	109	DHNSTY PRES&ADMN	2A20G	2D04G	2D04G	2D04G	2D04G	2D04G	2D04G	2D04G	2D04G
6960	109	DHNSTY CONGRESS	2A20H	2D04H	2D04H	2D04H	2D04H	2D04H	2D04H	2D04H	2D04H
6970	109	DHNSTY SUPRM CRT	2A20I	2D04I	2D04I	2D04I	2D04I	2D04I	2D04I	2D04I	2D04I
6980	109	DHNSTY JUSTC SYS	2A20J	2D04J	2D04J	2D04J	2D04J	2D04J	2D04J	2D04J	2D04J
6990	110	DHNSTY POLICE	2A20K	2D04K	2D04K	2D04K	2D04K	2D04K	2D04K	2D04K	2D04K
7000	110	DHNSTY MILITARY	2A20L	2D04L	2D04L	2D04L	2D04L	2D04L	2D04L	2D04L	2D04L

K02: MAJOR SOCIAL INSTITUTIONS. Satisfaction with performance

1390	36	SAT GOVT OPRTNG		1A006M	1A006M	1A006M	1A006M	1A006M	1A006M	1A006M	1A006M
8380	129	GD JB LARG CORPS	3A27A	3A24A	3A24A	3A24A	3A24A	3A24A	3A24A	3A24A	3A24A
8390	129	GD JB LBR UNIONS	3A27B	3A24B	3A24B	3A24B	3A24B	3A24B	3A24B	3A24B	3A24B
8400	129	GD JB COLLG&UNIV	3A27C	3A24C	3A24C	3A24C	3A24C	3A24C	3A24C	3A24C	3A24C
8410	130	GD JB PBLC SCHOL	3A27D	3A24D	3A24D	3A24D	3A24D	3A24D	3A24D	3A24D	3A24D
8420	130	GD JB CHURCHES	3A27E	3A24E	3A24E	3A24E	3A24E	3A24E	3A24E	3A24E	3A24E
8430	130	GD JB NEWS MEDIA	3A27F	3A24F	3A24F	3A24F	3A24F	3A24F	3A24F	3A24F	3A24F
8440	130	GD JB PRES&ADMIN ·	3A27G	3A24G	3A24G	3A24G	3A24G	3A24G	3A24G	3A24G	3A24G
8450	130	GD JB CONGRESS	3A27H	3A24H	3A24H	3A24H	3A24H	3A24H	3A24H	3A24H	3A24H
8460	130	GD JB SUPRM CRT	3A27I	3A24I	3A24I	3A24I	3A24I	3A24I	3A24I	3A24I	3A24I
8470	130	GD JB JUSTC SYST	3A27J	3A24J	3A24J	3A24J	3A24J	3A24J	3A24J	3A24J	3A24J
8480	131	GD JB POLICE	3A27K	3A24K	3A24K	3A24K	3A24K	3A24K	3A24K	3A24K	3A24K
8490	131	GD JB MILITARY	3A27L	3A24L	3A24L	3A24L	3A24L	3A24L	3A24L	3A24L	3A24L

K03: MAJOR SOCIAL INSTITUTIONS. Preferred influence

8500	131	MIL TOO MCH INFL	3A28	3A25	3A25	3A25	3A25	3A25	3A25	3A25	3A25
8510	131	US TOO MCH$MILT	3A29	3A26	3A26	3A26	3A26	3A26	3A26	3A26	3A26
10570	158	>INFLC LARG CORP	4A14A	4A19A	4A19A	4A19A	4A19A	4A19A	4A19A	4A19A	4A19A
10580	158	>INFLC LBR UNION	4A14B	4A19B	4A19B	4A19B	4A19B	4A19B	4A19B	4A19B	4A19B
10590	159	>INFLC CHURCHES	4A14C	4A19C	4A19C	4A19C	4A19C	4A19C	4A19C	4A19C	4A19C
10600	159	>INFLC NEWS MDIA	4A14D	4A19D	4A19D	4A19D	4A19D	4A19D	4A19D	4A19D	4A19D
10610	159	>INFLC PRES&ADMN	4A14E	4A19E	4A19E	4A19E	4A19E	4A19E	4A19E	4A19E	4A19E
10620	159	>INFLC CONGRESS	4A14F	4A19F	4A19F	4A19F	4A19F	4A19F	4A19F	4A19F	4A19F
10630	159	>INFLC SUPRM CRT	4A14G	4A19G	4A19G	4A19G	4A19G	4A19G	4A19G	4A19G	4A19G
10640	159	>INFLC JUSTC SYS	4A14H	4A19H	4A19H	4A19H	4A19H	4A19H	4A19H	4A19H	4A19H
10650	160	>INFLC POLICE	4A14I	4A19I	4A19I	4A19I	4A19I	4A19I	4A19I	4A19I	4A19I
10660	160	>INFLC MILITARY	4A14J	4A19J	4A19J	4A19J	4A19J	4A19J	4A19J	4A19J	4A19J

Item Reference Number	Page Loc. in this Volume	ITEM DESCRIPTION (ABBREVIATED)	QUESTIONNAIRE LOCATION BY YEAR (FORM, SECTION, AND QUESTION NUMBER)								
			1975	1976	1977	1978	1979	1980/81	1982/83	1984/85	1986

L01: MILITARY. Plans for military service

490	20	R WL DO ARMD FC		+C21B	+C21B	+C21B	+C21B	+C21B	+C21B	+C21B	+C21B
540	21	R WNTDO ARMD FC		+C22B	+C22B	+C22B	+C22B	+C22B	+C22B	+C22B	+C22B
730	24	R'S BRANCH SERV		+C32	+C32	+C32	+C32	+C32	+C32	+C32	+C32
740	24	R XPCTS B OFFCR		+C33	+C33	+C33	+C33	+C33	+C33	+C33	+C33
750	24	R XPCTS MLTR CR		+C34	+C34	+C34	+C34	+C34	+C34	+C34	+C34

L02: MILITARY. Attitudes toward a draft

21060	117	FAVOR MLTY DRAFT						5E06‡	2E08	2E08	2E08
21070	117	DRAFT INCL WOMEN						5E07‡	2E09	2E09	2E09

L03: MILITARY. Views about the use of military force

5690	101	US GO WAR FR OTH	2A38B	2A18B	2A18B	2A18B	2A18B	2A18B	2A18B	2A18B	2A18B
6450	101	US SHD DISARM	2A38A	2A18A	2A18A	2A18A	2A18A	2A18A	2A18A	2A18A	2A18A
6460	101	US WAR PRTCT ECN	2A38C	2A18C	2A18C	2A18C	2A18C	2A18C	2A18C	2A18C	2A18C
6470	101	US ONLY WAR DFNS	2A38D	2A18D	2A18D	2A18D	2A18D	2A18D	2A18D	2A18D	2A18D
6480	102	-US MIL PWR>USSR	2A38E	2A18E	2A18E	2A18E	2A18E	2A18E	2A18E	2A18E	2A18E
6490	102	US NEED>PWR OTHS	2A38F	2A18F	2A18F	2A18F	2A18F	2A18F	2A18F	2A18F	2A18F
6500	102	US FRN PLCY NRRW	2A38G	2A18G	2A18G	2A18G	2A18G	2A18G	2A18G	2A18G	2A18G
6510	102	SRVCMEN SHD OBEY	2A38H	2A18H	2A18H	2A18H	2A18H	2A18H	2A18H	2A18H	2A18H
11210		-MLTRY COUP U.S.		4E06	4E06						
11220	170	NT VOL 4 NEC WAR		4E07	4E07	4E06	4E06	4E06	4E06	4E06	4E06

L04: MILITARY. Attitudes toward the military as an institution and occupation

7000	110	DHNSTY MILITARY	2A20L	2D04L	2D04L	2D04L	2D04L	2D04L	2D04L	2D04L	2D04L
8490	131	GD JB MILITARY	3A27L	3A24L	3A24L	3A24L	3A24L	3A24L	3A24L	3A24L	3A24L
8500	131	MIL TOO MCH INFL	3A28	3A25	3A25	3A25	3A25	3A25	3A25	3A25	3A25
8510	131	US TOO MCH$MILT	3A29	3A26	3A26	3A26	3A26	3A26	3A26	3A26	3A26
10660	160	>INFLC MILITARY	4A14J	4A19J	4A19J	4A19J	4A19J	4A19J	4A19J	4A19J	4A19J
11120	169	MLTRY GET AHEAD		4E01A	4E01A	4E01A	4E01A	4E01A	4E01A	4E01A	4E01A
11130	169	MLTRY MORE ED		4E01B	4E01B	4E01B	4E01B	4E01B	4E01B	4E01B	4E01B
11140	169	MLTRY ADVNC RESP		4E01C	4E01C	4E01C	4E01C	4E01C	4E01C	4E01C	4E01C
11150	169	MLTRY >FLFLLG JB		4E01D	4E01D	4E01D	4E01D	4E01D	4E01D	4E01D	4E01D
11160	169	MLTRY IDEAS HERD		4E01E	4E01E	4E01E	4E01E	4E01E	4E01E	4E01E	4E01E
11170	169	EXTNT MLTRY JSTC		4E02	4E02	4E02	4E02	4E02	4E02	4E02	4E02
11180	169	MLTRY DSCRM WOMN		4E03	4E03	4E03	4E03	4E03	4E03	4E03	4E03
11190	170	MLTRY DSCRM BLKS		4E04	4E04	4E04	4E04	4E04	4E04	4E04	4E04
11200	170	>FAIR MLTRY CVLN		4E05	4E05	4E05	4E05	4E05	4E05	4E05	4E05
11830	178	PLC WRK MLTY SVC	5A09D	5A05D	5A05D	5A05D	5A05D	5A05D	5A05D	5A05D	5A05D
21080	117	MLTRY PAY CLG GD						5E08‡	2E10	2E10	2E10
21090	117	R WD DO MLTY/CLG						5E09‡	2E11	2E11	2E11

M01: INTERPERSONAL RELATIONSHIPS. Dating

620	22	#X/AV WK GO OUT		+C25	+C25	+C25	+C25	+C25	+C25	+C25	+C25
630	22	#X DATE 3+/WK		+C26	+C26	+C26	+C26	+C26	+C26	+C26	+C26

M02: INTERPERSONAL RELATIONSHIPS. Cross-age relationships with adults outside the family (See also B05)

1240	33	TM SPT ADLT MST	1A006	1A003	1A003	1A003	1A003	1A003	1A003	1A003	1A003
1250	34	LK MR TM ADLT	1A007	1A004	1A004	1A004	1A004	1A004	1A004	1A004	1A004
1260	34	LK MR TM YG CHD	1A008	1A005	1A005	1A005	1A005	1A005	1A005	1A005	1A005
6530	102	FRQ HIT SUPRVISR	2A39B	2A19B	2A19B	2A19B	2A19B	2A19B	2A19B	2A19B	2A19B
21550	163	JOB-SUPERVSR AGE							4D04	4D04	4D04
21610	163	JOB-OVER AGE 30							4D06E	4D06E	4D06E
21710	165	JOB-TCHR HELP GT							4D08	4D08	4D08
21910	203	PARTY-PPL OVR 30								5E08A	5E08A
22050	205	PRFR PTY-PPL >30								5E09A	5E09A

‡ This question appears in 1981 but does not appear in 1980.

Item Reference Number	Page Loc. in this Volume	ITEM DESCRIPTION (ABBREVIATED)	QUESTIONNAIRE LOCATION BY YEAR (FORM, SECTION, AND QUESTION NUMBER)								
			1975	1976	1977	1978	1979	1980/81	1982/83	1984/85	1986

M03: INTERPERSONAL RELATIONSHIPS. Agreement/disagreement with parents

Item Reference Number	Page Loc. in this Volume	ITEM DESCRIPTION (ABBREVIATED)	1975	1976	1977	1978	1979	1980/81	1982/83	1984/85	1986
1330	35	SAT GT ALNG PRNT	1A009G	1A006G	1A006G	1A006G	1A006G	1A006G	1A006G	1A006G	1A006G
1500	38	IMP LIV CLS PRNT		1A007J	1A007J	1A007J	1A007J	1A007J	1A007J	1A007J	1A007J
6520	102	FRQ FIGHT PARNTS	2A39A	2A19A	2A19A	2A19A	2A19A	2A19A	2A19A	2A19A	2A19A
11230	170	P'IDEA OF DO LIF	4A27A	4E08A	4E08A	4E07A	4E07A	4E07A	4E07A	4E07A	4E07A
11240	170	P'IDEA OF LSR TM	4A27B	4E08B	4E08B	4E07B	4E07B	4E07B	4E07B	4E07B	4E07B
11250	170	P'IDEA OF CLTHES	4A27C	4E08C	4E08C	4E07C	4E07C	4E07C	4E07C	4E07C	4E07C
11260	171	P'IDEA OF SPND $	4A27D	4E08D	4E08D	4E07D	4E07D	4E07D	4E07D	4E07D	4E07D
11270	171	P'IDEA OF DATE	4A27E	4E08E	4E08E	4E07E	4E07E	4E07E	4E07E	4E07E	4E07E
11280	171	P'IDEA OF OK DRK	4A27F	4E08F	4E08F	4E07F	4E07F	4E07F	4E07F	4E07F	4E07F
11290	171	P'IDEA OF OK MRJ	4A27G	4E08G	4E08G	4E07G	4E07G	4E07G	4E07G	4E07G	4E07G
11300	171	P'IDEA OF OK DRG	4A27H	4E08H	4E08H	4E07H	4E07H	4E07H	4E07H	4E07H	4E07H
11310	171	P'IDEA OF VALUES	4A27I	4E08I	4E08I	4E07I	4E07I	4E07I	4E07I	4E07I	4E07I
11320	171	P'IDEA OF EDUC	4A27J	4E08J	4E08J	4E07J	4E07J	4E07J	4E07J	4E07J	4E07J
11330	172	P'IDEA OF SX RLS	4A27K	4E08K	4E08K	4E07K	4E07K	4E07K	4E07K	4E07K	4E07K
11340	172	P'IDEA OF ECLOGY	4A27L	4E08L	4E08L	4E07L	4E07L	4E07L	4E07L	4E07L	4E07L
11350	172	P'IDEA OF RCL IS	4A27M	4E08M	4E08M	4E07M	4E07M	4E07M	4E07M	4E07M	4E07M
11360	172	P'IDEA OF RLGION	4A27N	4E08N	4E08N	4E07N	4E07N	4E07N	4E07N	4E07N	4E07N
11370	172	P'IDEA OF PLTICS	4A27O	4E08O	4E08O	4E07O	4E07O	4E07O	4E07O	4E07O	4E07O
13150		FAM+REL GD/CHILD		5E01A							
13160		FAM+REL GD/PARNT		5E01B							
13170		FAM+REL GD/GRPNT		5E01C							
13180		FAM+REL,R LIK/PT		5E01D							
19530		3MO/DLY ARG PRNT						2E08A	2E07A	2E07A	
21800	201	PRNT SUPRV PARTY								5E06A	5E06A
21810	201	PRNT SUPRV DATES								5E06B	5E06B
21820	202	PRNT SUPRV DRESS								5E06C	5E06C
21830	202	PRNT SUPRV MONEY								5E06D	5E06D
21840	202	PRNT SUPRV EVENG								5E06E	5E06E
21850	202	PRNT SUPRV HOMWK								5E06F	5E06F
21860	202	PRN SUPRV COURSE								5E06G	5E06G
21870	202	PRNT SUPRV WORK								5E06H	5E06H
21880	202	PRN SUPR TV QNTY								5E06I	5E06I
21890	203	PRN SUPR TV QLTY								5E06J	5E06J

M04: INTERPERSONAL RELATIONSHIPS. Friendships (See also Q03: Loneliness)

Item Reference Number	Page Loc. in this Volume	ITEM DESCRIPTION (ABBREVIATED)	1975	1976	1977	1978	1979	1980/81	1982/83	1984/85	1986
1320	35	SAT OWN FRIENDS	1A009F	1A006F	1A006F	1A006F	1A006F	1A006F	1A006F	1A006F	1A006F
1450	37	IMP STRG FRDSHP		1A007E	1A007E	1A007E	1A007E	1A007E	1A007E	1A007E	1A007E
5920	93	DALY VIST W/FRDS		2A02K	2A02K	2A02K	2A02K	2A02K	2A02K	2A02K	2A02K
10170	151	JOB IMPC MK FRND	4A08I	4A08I	4A08I	4A08I	4A08I	4A08I	4A08I	4A08I	4A08I

M05: INTERPERSONAL RELATIONSHIPS. Community at large

Item Reference Number	Page Loc. in this Volume	ITEM DESCRIPTION (ABBREVIATED)	1975	1976	1977	1978	1979	1980/81	1982/83	1984/85	1986
1480	37	IMP LDR COMUNTY		1A007H	1A007H	1A007H	1A007H	1A007H	1A007H	1A007H	1A007H
10290	153	JOB IMPC CNTC PL	4A08U	4A08U	4A08U	4A08U	4A08U	4A08U	4A08U	4A08U	4A08U
13590	141	STS SCH LDS STU		5E05B	5E06B	5E06B	5E04B	5E06B†	3E06B	3E06B	3E06B
21600	163	JOB-DIF SOC BKGD							4D06D	4D06D	4D06D
21730	174	IDEA PARENTS GRP							4E09§	4E09	4E09
21740	174	#FRNDS PRNTS GRP							4E10§	4E10	4E10
21750	174	OWN PRNTS IN GRP							4E11§	4E11	4E11
21760	174	GP IMPCT OWN FLG							4E12§	4E12	4E12
21770	175	GP CHG RELP PRNT							4E13§	4E13	4E13
21780	175	#FRNDS ANTIDG GP							4E14§	4E14	4E14
21790	175	EVR IN ANTIDG GP							4E15§	4E15	4E15

N01: RACE RELATIONS. Preferred interracial contact

Item Reference Number	Page Loc. in this Volume	ITEM DESCRIPTION (ABBREVIATED)	1975	1976	1977	1978	1979	1980/81	1982/83	1984/85	1986
8110	125	DES FRND OTH RC	3A19A	3A07A	3A07A	3A07A	3A07A	3A07A	3A07A	3A07A	3A07A
8120	125	DES SUPVR DIF RC	3A19B	3A07B	3A07B	3A07B	3A07B	3A07B	3A07B	3A07B	3A07B
8130	125	DES FAM NX DF RC	3A19C	3A07C	3A07C	3A07C	3A07C	3A07C	3A07C	3A07C	3A07C
8140	125	DES CHL FD SM RC	3A19D	3A07D	3A07D	3A07D	3A07D	3A07D	3A07D	3A07D	3A07D
8150	126	DES CHL FD OT RC	3A19E	3A07E	3A07E	3A07E	3A07E	3A07E	3A07E	3A07E	3A07E
8160	126	DES AL WKS SM RC	3A19F	3A08A	3A08A	3A08A	3A08A	3A08A	3A08A	3A08A	3A08A
		(continued)									

† This question appears in 1980 but does not appear in 1981.   § This question appears in 1983 but does not appear in 1982.

Item Reference Number	Page Loc. in this Volume	ITEM DESCRIPTION (ABBREVIATED)	QUESTIONNAIRE LOCATION BY YEAR (FORM, SECTION, AND QUESTION NUMBER)								
			1975	1976	1977	1978	1979	1980/81	1982/83	1984/85	1986
N01: RACE RELATIONS. Preferred interracial contact *(continued)*											
8170	126	DES SO WKS DF RC	3A19G	3A08B	3A08B	3A08B	3A08B	3A08B	3A08B	3A08B	3A08B
8180	126	DES MS WKS DF RC	3A19H	3A08C	3A08C	3A08C	3A08C	3A08C	3A08C	3A08C	3A08C
8190	126	DES AL NGB SM RC	3A19I	3A09A	3A09A	3A09A	3A09A	3A09A	3A09A	3A09A	3A09A
8200	126	DES SO NGB OT RC	3A19J	3A09B	3A09B	3A09B	3A09B	3A09B	3A09B	3A09B	3A09B
8210	126	DES MS NGB OT RC	3A19K	3A09C	3A09C	3A09C	3A09C	3A09C	3A09C	3A09C	3A09C
8220	127	DES AL CHL SM RC	3A19L	3A10A	3A10A	3A10A	3A10A	3A10A	3A10A	3A10A	3A10A
8230	127	DES SM CHL OT RC	3A19M	3A10B	3A10B	3A10B	3A10B	3A10B	3A10B	3A10B	3A10B
8240	127	DES MS CHL OT RC	3A19N	3A10C	3A10C	3A10C	3A10C	3A10C	3A10C	3A10C	3A10C
N02: RACE RELATIONS. Attitudes about discrimination											
1520	38	IMP CRRCT INEQL		1A007L	1A007L	1A007L	1A007L	1A007L	1A007L	1A007L	1A007L
10380	155	JOB OBSTC RACE		4A13C	4A13C	4A13C	4A13C	4A13C	4A13C	4A13C	4A13C
11190	170	MLTRY DSCRM BLKS		4E04	4E04	4E04	4E04	4E04	4E04	4E04	4E04
11350	172	P'IDEA OF RCL IS	4A27M	4E08M	4E08M	4E07M	4E07M	4E07M	4E07M	4E07M	4E07M
11710	177	WR/NT RACE RELTN	5A04F	5A03F	5A03F	5A03F	5A03F	5A03F	5A03F	5A03F	5A03F
11950	180	B/W RLTNS WRSE	5A15	5A08	5A08	5A08	5A08	5A08	5A08	5A08	5A08
12100	182	MNRTY NT MY BSNS	5A19F	5A18D	5A18D	5A18D	5A18D	5A18D	5A18D	5A18D	5A18D
12220	185	CTB TO MNRTY GRP	5A20C	5A20C	5A20C	5A20C	5A20C	5A20C	5A20C	5A20C	5A20C
N03: RACE RELATIONS. Actual interracial contacts											
8250	127	FRNDS AL OT RC	3A22	3A11	3A11	3A11	3A11	3A11	3A11	3A11	3A11
8260	127	NGBHD AL OT RC	3A23	3A12	3A12	3A12	3A12	3A12	3A12	3A12	3A12
8270	127	ELEMSCH AL OT RC	3A21	3A13	3A13	3A13	3A13	3A13	3A13	3A13	3A13
8280	127	HISCH AL OT RC	3A20	3A14	3A14	3A14	3A14	3A14	3A14	3A14	3A14
8290	128	WRKRS AL OT RC		3A15	3A15	3A15	3A15	3A15	3A15	3A15	3A15
8300	128	DO LOT THG OT RC	3A24	3A16	3A16	3A16	3A16	3A16	3A16	3A16	3A16
8310	128	VRY GD EXP OT RC	3A25	3A17	3A17	3A17	3A17	3A17	3A17	3A17	3A17
11890	179	RCL CNTCT SCHOOL		5A07A	5A07A	5A07A	5A07A	5A07A	5A07A	5A07A	5A07A
11900	179	RCL CNTCT NGHBHD		5A07B	5A07B	5A07B	5A07B	5A07B	5A07B	5A07B	5A07B
11910	179	RCL CNTCT CHURCH		5A07C	5A07C	5A07C	5A07C	5A07C	5A07C	5A07C	5A07C
11920	179	RCL CNTCT SPORTS		5A07D	5A07D	5A07D	5A07D	5A07D	5A07D	5A07D	5A07D
11930	180	RCL CNTCT CLUBS		5A07E	5A07E	5A07E	5A07E	5A07E	5A07E	5A07E	5A07E
11940	180	RCL CNTCT JOB		5A07F	5A07F	5A07F	5A07F	5A07F	5A07F	5A07F	5A07F
O01: CONCERN FOR OTHERS. Attitudes regarding social service, charitable activism											
1470	37	IMP CNTRBTN SOC		1A007G	1A007G	1A007G	1A007G	1A007G	1A007G	1A007G	1A007G
1520	38	IMP CRRCT INEQL		1A007L	1A007L	1A007L	1A007L	1A007L	1A007L	1A007L	1A007L
10130	151	JOB IMPC HLP OTH	4A08E	4A08E	4A08E	4A08E	4A08E	4A08E	4A08E	4A08E	4A08E
10190	152	JOB IMPC WRTHWLE	4A08K	4A08K	4A08K	4A08K	4A08K	4A08K	4A08K	4A08K	4A08K
11860	178	PLC WRK SOC SVCS	5A09G	5A05G	5A05G	5A05G	5A05G	5A05G	5A05G	5A05G	5A05G
O02: CONCERN FOR OTHERS. Involvement in community, altruistic activities											
5860	92	DALY CMNTY AFFRS		2A02E	2A02E	2A02E	2A02E	2A02E	2A02E	2A02E	2A02E
12200	184	CTB TO UNTD FUND	5A20A	5A20A	5A20A	5A20A	5A20A	5A20A	5A20A	5A20A	5A20A
12210	184	CTB TO INTL RELF	5A20B	5A20B	5A20B	5A20B	5A20B	5A20B	5A20B	5A20B	5A20B
12220	185	CTB TO MNRTY GRP	5A20C	5A20C	5A20C	5A20C	5A20C	5A20C	5A20C	5A20C	5A20C
12230	185	CTB TO RELGS ORG	5A20D	5A20D	5A20D	5A20D	5A20D	5A20D	5A20D	5A20D	5A20D
12240	185	CTB TO PLTCL PTY	5A20E	5A20E	5A20E	5A20E	5A20E	5A20E	5A20E	5A20E	5A20E
12250	185	CTB TO CTZN LBBY	5A20F	5A20F	5A20F	5A20F	5A20F	5A20F	5A20F	5A20F	5A20F
12260	185	CTB TO VS DISEAS	5A20G	5A20G	5A20G	5A20G	5A20G	5A20G	5A20G	5A20G	5A20G
12270	185	CTB TO POP PRBMS	5A20H	5A20H	5A20H	5A20H	5A20H	5A20H	5A20H	5A20H	5A20H
12280	186	CTB TO ENVIR PBM	5A20I	5A20I	5A20I	5A20I	5A20I	5A20I	5A20I	5A20I	5A20I
O03: CONCERN FOR OTHERS. Concern with the problems of others											
5990	94	US 2 MUCH PROFIT	2A23J	2A03A	2A03A	2A03A	2A03A	2A03A	2A03A	2A03A	2A03A
8040	124	EAT DIF->FD STRV	3A31G	3A04E	3A04E	3A04E	3A04E	3A04E	3A04E	3A04E	3A04E
9840		GVNG FOOD O CNTY	3A33	3E05							
12070	182	WRRY ABT OW CTRY	5A19A	5A18A	5A18A	5A18A	5A18A	5A18A	5A18A	5A18A	5A18A
		(continued)									

Item Reference Number	Page Loc. in this Volume	ITEM DESCRIPTION (ABBREVIATED)	QUESTIONNAIRE LOCATION BY YEAR (FORM, SECTION, AND QUESTION NUMBER)								
			1975	1976	1977	1978	1979	1980/81	1982/83	1984/85	1986

O03: CONCERN FOR OTHERS. Concern with the problems of others *(continued)*

Item Reference Number	Page Loc. in this Volume	ITEM DESCRIPTION (ABBREVIATED)	1975	1976	1977	1978	1979	1980/81	1982/83	1984/85	1986
12080	182	BTTR IF CTZ WRLD	5A19C	5A18B	5A18B	5A18B	5A18B	5A18B	5A18B	5A18B	5A18B
12090	182	-SYMP TWD STARVG	5A19E	5A18C	5A18C	5A18C	5A18C	5A18C	5A18C	5A18C	5A18C
12100	182	MNRTY NT MY BSNS	5A19F	5A18D	5A18D	5A18D	5A18D	5A18D	5A18D	5A18D	5A18D
12110	182	UPST PL TR -FAIR	5A19G	5A18E	5A18E	5A18E	5A18E	5A18E	5A18E	5A18E	5A18E
12120	183	HELP POOR W MY $	5A19I	5A18F	5A18F	5A18F	5A18F	5A18F	5A18F	5A18F	5A18F
12130	183	-MY PRB OT ND HP	5A19K	5A18G	5A18G	5A18G	5A18G	5A18G	5A18G	5A18G	5A18G
12140	183	RB CHNG ETG HABT		5A18H	5A18H	5A18H	5A18H	5A18H	5A18H	5A18H	5A18H
16430		SAT EVB CAR POOL				2E05A					
16440		SAT EAT <BEEF>GRN				2E05B					
19470		EAT <FD,>OWN CITY					5E08A				
19480		EAT <FD,>NRBY STT					5E08B				
19490		EAT <FD,>DIF REGN					5E08C				
19500		EAT <FD,>ASIAN CN					5E08D				

P01: HAPPINESS. Happiness; satisfaction with life and self

Item Reference Number	Page Loc. in this Volume	ITEM DESCRIPTION (ABBREVIATED)	1975	1976	1977	1978	1979	1980/81	1982/83	1984/85	1986
1190	33	VRY HPY THS DAYS		1A001	1A001	1A001	1A001	1A001	1A001	1A001	1A001
	92			2A01	2A01	2A01	2A01	2A01	2A01	2A01	2A01
	122			3A01	3A01	3A01	3A01	3A01	3A01	3A01	3A01
	148			4A01	4A01	4A01	4A01	4A01	4A01	4A01	4A01
	176			5A01	5A01	5A01	5A01	5A01	5A01	5A01	5A01
1340	35	SAT YOURSELF	1A009H	1A006H	1A006H	1A006H	1A006H	1A006H	1A006H	1A006H	1A006H
1380	36	SAT LIFE AS WHLE	1A009L	1A006L	1A006L	1A006L	1A006L	1A006L	1A006L	1A006L	1A006L
6840	107	CMP SATFD W/LIFE		2D01	2D01	2D01	2D01	2D01	2D01	2D01	2D01
	136			3D01	3D01	3D01	3D01	3D01	3D01	3D01	3D01
	162			4D01	4D01	4D01	4D01	4D01	4D01	4D01	4D01
	186			5A21	5A21	5A21	5A21	5A21	5A21	5A21	5A21
12620	111	SATISFD W MYSELF	5A39H	5D01H	5D01H	5D01H	5D01H	5D01H	5D01H	2D05J	2D05J
	191									5D01H	5D01H

P02: HAPPINESS. Satisfaction with specific life domains

Item Reference Number	Page Loc. in this Volume	ITEM DESCRIPTION (ABBREVIATED)	1975	1976	1977	1978	1979	1980/81	1982/83	1984/85	1986
1270	34	SAT PRESENT JOB	1A009A	1A006A	1A006A	1A006A	1A006A	1A006A	1A006A	1A006A	1A006A
1280	34	SAT NEIGHBORHOD	1A009B	1A006B	1A006B	1A006B	1A006B	1A006B	1A006B	1A006B	1A006B
1290	34	SAT PRSNL SAFTY	1A009C	1A006C	1A006C	1A006C	1A006C	1A006C	1A006C	1A006C	1A006C
1300	35	SAT OWN PROP SF	1A009D	1A006D	1A006D	1A006D	1A006D	1A006D	1A006D	1A006D	1A006D
1310	35	SAT EDUC EXPRNCS	1A009E	1A006E	1A006E	1A006E	1A006E	1A006E	1A006E	1A006E	1A006E
1320	35	SAT OWN FRIENDS	1A009F	1A006F	1A006F	1A006F	1A006F	1A006F	1A006F	1A006F	1A006F
1330	35	SAT GT ALNG PRNT	1A009G	1A006G	1A006G	1A006G	1A006G	1A006G	1A006G	1A006G	1A006G
1350	35	SAT STD OF LVG	1A009I	1A006I	1A006I	1A006I	1A006I	1A006I	1A006I	1A006I	1A006I
1360	36	SAT TIME FR THGS	1A009J	1A006J	1A006J	1A006J	1A006J	1A006J	1A006J	1A006J	1A006J
1370	36	SAT SPD LEISR	1A009K	1A006K	1A006K	1A006K	1A006K	1A006K	1A006K	1A006K	1A006K
1400	36	SAT AMT OF FUN		1A006N	1A006N	1A006N	1A006N	1A006N	1A006N	1A006N	1A006N
10350	155	R THNK WK BE SAT		4A12	4A12	4A12	4A12	4A12	4A12	4A12	4A12
10910	162	CMP SATFD W/JOB		4D02	4D02	4D02	4D02	4D02	4D02	4D02	4D02

Q01: OTHER PERSONALITY VARIABLES. Attitudes about self, self-esteem

Item Reference Number	Page Loc. in this Volume	ITEM DESCRIPTION (ABBREVIATED)	1975	1976	1977	1978	1979	1980/81	1982/83	1984/85	1986
1190	33	VRY HPY THS DAYS		1A001	1A001	1A001	1A001	1A001	1A001	1A001	1A001
	92			2A01	2A01	2A01	2A01	2A01	2A01	2A01	2A01
	122			3A01	3A01	3A01	3A01	3A01	3A01	3A01	3A01
	148			4A01	4A01	4A01	4A01	4A01	4A01	4A01	4A01
	176			5A01	5A01	5A01	5A01	5A01	5A01	5A01	5A01
1340	35	SAT YOURSELF	1A009H	1A006H	1A006H	1A006H	1A006H	1A006H	1A006H	1A006H	1A006H
1400	36	SAT AMT OF FUN		1A006N	1A006N	1A006N	1A006N	1A006N	1A006N	1A006N	1A006N
6840	107	CMP SATFD W/LIFE		2D01	2D01	2D01	2D01	2D01	2D01	2D01	2D01
	136			3D01	3D01	3D01	3D01	3D01	3D01	3D01	3D01
	162			4D01	4D01	4D01	4D01	4D01	4D01	4D01	4D01
	186			5A21	5A21	5A21	5A21	5A21	5A21	5A21	5A21
6850	107	HOW GD AS SPOUSE	2A19A	2D02A	2D02A	2D02A	2D02A	2D02A	2D02A	2D02A	2D02A
6860	107	HOW GD AS PARENT	2A19B	2D02B	2D02B	2D02B	2D02B	2D02B	2D02B	2D02B	2D02B
6870	108	HOW GD AS WORKER	2A19C	2D02C	2D02C	2D02C	2D02C	2D02C	2D02C	2D02C	2D02C
12550	111	POS ATT TWD SELF	5A39A	5D01A	5D01A	5D01A	5D01A	5D01A	5D01A	2D05G	2D05G
		(continued)									

Item Reference Number	Page Loc. in this Volume	ITEM DESCRIPTION (ABBREVIATED)	QUESTIONNAIRE LOCATION BY YEAR (FORM, SECTION, AND QUESTION NUMBER)								
			1975	1976	1977	1978	1979	1980/81	1982/83	1984/85	1986

Q01: OTHER PERSONALITY VARIABLES. Attitudes about self, self-esteem *(continued)*

Item Ref.	Page Loc.	Description	1975	1976	1977	1978	1979	1980/81	1982/83	1984/85	1986
12570	190, 111, 191	AM PRSN OF WORTH	5A39C	5D01C	5D01C	5D01C	5D01C	5D01C	5D01C	5D01A 2D05H 5D01C	5D01A 2D05H 5D01C
12580	111, 191	DO WELL AS OTHRS	5A39D	5D01D	5D01D	5D01D	5D01D	5D01D	5D01D	2D05I 5D01D	2D05I 5D01D
12620	111, 191	SATISFD W MYSELF	5A39H	5D01H	5D01H	5D01H	5D01H	5D01H	5D01H	2D05J 5D01H	2D05J 5D01H
12660	111, 192	-MUCH TO B PROUD			5D01L	5D01L	5D01L	5D01L	5D01L	2D05K 5D01L	2D05K 5D01L
12680	112, 192	I AM NO GOOD			5D01N	5D01N	5D01N	5D01N	5D01N	2D05L 5D01N	2D05L 5D01N
12720	112, 193	I DO WRONG THING			5D01R	5D01R	5D01R	5D01R	5D01R	2D05M 5D01R	2D05M 5D01R
12750	112, 193	MY LIFE NT USEFL			5D01U	5D01U	5D01U	5D01U	5D01U	2D05N 5D01U	2D05N 5D01U
13950	193	EAGR TO LEAV HOM						5D01W	5D01W	5D01W	5D01W
13960	194	HEST PRT ADLT WL						5D01X	5D01X	5D01X	5D01X

Q02: OTHER PERSONALITY VARIABLES. Locus of control

Item Ref.	Page Loc.	Description	1975	1976	1977	1978	1979	1980/81	1982/83	1984/85	1986
1210	33	ENJOY FAST PACE	1A004B	1A002B	1A002B	1A002B	1A002B	1A002B	1A002B	1A002B	1A002B
1220	33	THG CHG 2 QUICK	1A004D	1A002C	1A002C	1A002C	1A002C	1A002C	1A002C	1A002C	1A002C
12560	190	LUCK>IMP HRD WRK	5A39B	5D01B	5D01B	5D01B	5D01B	5D01B	5D01B	5D01B	5D01B
12590	191	TRY GT AHD,STOPD	5A39E	5D01E	5D01E	5D01E	5D01E	5D01E	5D01E	5D01E	5D01E
12600	191	PLNNG MKS UNHPPY	5A39F	5D01F	5D01F	5D01F	5D01F	5D01F	5D01F	5D01F	5D01F
12610	191	ACPT LIFE->HAPPR	5A39G	5D01G	5D01G	5D01G	5D01G	5D01G	5D01G	5D01G	5D01G
12630	191	PPL LK ME -CHANC	5A39I	5D01I	5D01I	5D01I	5D01I	5D01I	5D01I	5D01I	5D01I
12640	192	MY PLANS DO WORK			5D01J	5D01J	5D01J	5D01J	5D01J	5D01J	5D01J
12700	192	PPL MASTER FATE			5D01P	5D01P	5D01P	5D01P	5D01P	5D01P	5D01P
12740	193	PLANS->BTR RSLTS			5D01T	5D01T	5D01T	5D01T	5D01T	5D01T	5D01T

Q03: OTHER PERSONALITY VARIABLES. Loneliness

Item Ref.	Page Loc.	Description	1975	1976	1977	1978	1979	1980/81	1982/83	1984/85	1986
12650	192	OFTN FEEL LONELY			5D01K	5D01K	5D01K	5D01K	5D01K	5D01K	5D01K
12670	192	ALWYS SM1 HELP R			5D01M	5D01M	5D01M	5D01M	5D01M	5D01M	5D01M
12690	192	OFTN FL LEFT OUT			5D01O	5D01O	5D01O	5D01O	5D01O	5D01O	5D01O
12710	193	USLY SM1 TALK TO			5D01Q	5D01Q	5D01Q	5D01Q	5D01Q	5D01Q	5D01Q
12730	193	OFT WSH MOR FRND			5D01S	5D01S	5D01S	5D01S	5D01S	5D01S	5D01S
12760	193	USLY FRDS BE WTH			5D01V	5D01V	5D01V	5D01V	5D01V	5D01V	5D01V

Q04: OTHER PERSONALITY VARIABLES. Risk taking

Item Ref.	Page Loc.	Description	1975	1976	1977	1978	1979	1980/81	1982/83	1984/85	1986
7050	111	KICK DO DANGR TH		2D05E	2D05E	2D05E	2D05E	2D05E	2D05E	2D05E	2D05E
7060	111	LIKE RISK SOME X		2D05F	2D05F	2D05F	2D05F	2D05F	2D05F	2D05F	2D05F

Q05: OTHER PERSONALITY VARIABLES. Trust in others

Item Ref.	Page Loc.	Description	1975	1976	1977	1978	1979	1980/81	1982/83	1984/85	1986
1550	38	PPL CAN B TRSTD	1A010	1A008	1A008	1A008	1A008	1A008	1A008	1A008	1A008
1560	38	PPL TRY B HLPFL	1A011	1A009	1A009	1A009	1A009	1A009	1A009	1A009	1A009
1570	38	PPL TRY BE FAIR	1A012	1A010	1A010	1A010	1A010	1A010	1A010	1A010	1A010

Q06: OTHER PERSONALITY VARIABLES. See Subject Area T: HEALTH

Q07: OTHER PERSONALITY VARIABLES. Importance placed on various life goals

Item Ref.	Page Loc.	Description	1975	1976	1977	1978	1979	1980/81	1982/83	1984/85	1986
1410	36	IMP B SUCCSS WK		1A007A	1A007A	1A007A	1A007A	1A007A	1A007A	1A007A	1A007A
1420	37	IMP GD MRRG&FAM		1A007B	1A007B	1A007B	1A007B	1A007B	1A007B	1A007B	1A007B
1430	37	IMP LOTS OF $		1A007C	1A007C	1A007C	1A007C	1A007C	1A007C	1A007C	1A007C
1440	37	IMP TM RCRN&HBY		1A007D	1A007D	1A007D	1A007D	1A007D	1A007D	1A007D	1A007D
1450	37	IMP STRG FRDSHP		1A007E	1A007E	1A007E	1A007E	1A007E	1A007E	1A007E	1A007E
1460	37	IMP STEADY WORK		1A007F	1A007F	1A007F	1A007F	1A007F	1A007F	1A007F	1A007F
1470	37	IMP CNTRBTN SOC		1A007G	1A007G	1A007G	1A007G	1A007G	1A007G	1A007G	1A007G

(continued)

Item Reference Number	Page Loc. in this Volume	ITEM DESCRIPTION (ABBREVIATED)	QUESTIONNAIRE LOCATION BY YEAR (FORM, SECTION, AND QUESTION NUMBER)								
			1975	1976	1977	1978	1979	1980/81	1982/83	1984/85	1986

Q07: OTHER PERSONALITY VARIABLES. Importance placed on various life goals *(continued)*

Item Reference Number	Page Loc.	ITEM DESCRIPTION	1975	1976	1977	1978	1979	1980/81	1982/83	1984/85	1986
1480	37	IMP LDR COMUNTY		1A007H	1A007H	1A007H	1A007H	1A007H	1A007H	1A007H	1A007H
1490	37	IMP CHLD BTR OPP		1A007I	1A007I	1A007I	1A007I	1A007I	1A007I	1A007I	1A007I
1500	38	IMP LIV CLS PRNT		1A007J	1A007J	1A007J	1A007J	1A007J	1A007J	1A007J	1A007J
1510	38	IMP GT AWY AREA		1A007K	1A007K	1A007K	1A007K	1A007K	1A007K	1A007K	1A007K
1520	38	IMP CRRCT INEQL		1A007L	1A007L	1A007L	1A007L	1A007L	1A007L	1A007L	1A007L
1530	38	IMP NEW XPRNCE		1A007M	1A007M	1A007M	1A007M	1A007M	1A007M	1A007M	1A007M
1540	38	IMP FND PRPS LF		1A007N	1A007N	1A007N	1A007N	1A007N	1A007N	1A007N	1A007N

Q08: OTHER PERSONALITY VARIABLES. Social, political, cultural orientation

Item Reference Number	Page Loc.	ITEM DESCRIPTION	1975	1976	1977	1978	1979	1980/81	1982/83	1984/85	1986
6330	99	INTEREST IN GOVT	2A31	2A11	2A11	2A11	2A11	2A11	2A11	2A11	2A11
	158		4A29	3E01	3E01	3E01	3E01	3E01	4A18	4A18	4A18
	184		5A40	4A18	4A18	4A18	4A18	4A18	5A19	5A19	5A19
				5A19	5A19	5A19	5A19	5A19			
6880	108	THK ABT SOC ISSU	*A06	2D03	2D03	2D03	2D03	2D03	2D03	2D03	2D03
	122			3A02	3A02	3A02	3A02	3A02	3A02	3A02	3A02
	148			4A05	4A05	4A05	4A05	4A05	4A05	4A05	4A05
	176			5A02	5A02	5A02	5A02	5A02	5A02	5A02	5A02
7010	110	2MCH COMPTN SCTY	2A23C	2D05A	2D05A	2D05A	2D05A	2D05A	2D05A	2D05A	2D05A
7020	110	2MANY YNG SLOPPY	2A23H	2D05B	2D05B	2D05B	2D05B	2D05B	2D05B	2D05B	2D05B
7030	110	2MUCH HARD ROCK	2A23I	2D05C	2D05C	2D05C	2D05C	2D05C	2D05C	2D05C	2D05C
7040	110	SHD DO OWN THING	2A23A	2D05D	2D05D	2D05D	2D05D	2D05D	2D05D	2D05D	2D05D
7630	83	R LIKES SCHOOL		1D001	1D001	1D001	1D001	1D001	1D001	1D001	1D001
	117			2E02	2E06	2E06	2E08	2E09	2E12	2E12	2E12
				3E08	3E07	3E07	3E07	3E07			
				4E10	5E05	5E05	5E03	5E05†			
				5E04							
10460	156	JOB OBSTC -CONFM		4A13K	4A13K	4A13K	4A13K	4A13K	4A13K	4A13K	4A13K
17570		PPL SHD CONFORM					5E02A				
17580		PPL SHD LV HRMNY					5E02B				
17590		PPL SHD B FRANK					5E02C				
17600		PPL SHD THK FREE					5E02D				
17610		PPL SHD B INDPNT					5E02E				

Q09: OTHER PERSONALITY VARIABLES. Hostility

Item Reference Number	Page Loc.	ITEM DESCRIPTION	1975	1976	1977	1978	1979	1980/81	1982/83	1984/85	1986
19530		3MO/DLY ARG PRNT						2E08A	2E07A	2E07A	
19540		3MO/DLY ARG AUTH						2E08B	2E07B	2E07B	
19550		3MO/DLY MAD						2E08C	2E07C	2E07C	
19560		3MO/DLY MAD,SMSH						2E08D	2E07D	2E07D	
19570		3MO/DLY WANT FGT						2E08E	2E07E	2E07E	
19580		3MO/DLY DID FGHT						2E08F	2E07F	2E07F	

R01: BACKGROUND. Age, sex, race, and marital status

Item Reference Number	Page Loc.	ITEM DESCRIPTION	1975	1976	1977	1978	1979	1980/81	1982/83	1984/85	1986
10	16	R'S BIRTH YEAR		+C01	+C01	+C01	+C01	+C01	+C01	+C01	+C01
20	16	R'S BIRTH MONTH		+C02	+C02	+C02	+C02	+C02	+C02	+C02	+C02
30	16	R'S SEX		+C03	+C03	+C03	+C03	+C03	+C03	+C03	+C03
40	16	R'S RACE		+C04	+C04	+C04	+C04	+C04	+C04	+C04	+C04
60	16	R NOT MARRIED		+C06	+C06	+C06	+C06	+C06	+C06	+C06	+C06
8320	128	MARRD OR ENGAGED	3A41	3A18	3A18	3A18	3A18	3A18	3A18	3A18	3A18

R02: BACKGROUND. Family characteristics

Item Reference Number	Page Loc.	ITEM DESCRIPTION	1975	1976	1977	1978	1979	1980/81	1982/83	1984/85	1986
75	17	# OLDER BR/SIS								+C07A	+C07A
76	17	# YOUNGER BR/SR								+C07B	+C07B
310	17	FATHR EDUC LEVEL		+C08	+C08	+C08	+C08	+C08	+C08	+C08	+C08
320	17	MOTHR EDUC LEVEL		+C09	+C09	+C09	+C09	+C09	+C09	+C09	+C09
330	18	MOTH PD JB R YNG		+C10	+C10	+C10	+C10	+C10	+C10	+C10	+C10

† This question appears in 1980 but does not appear in 1981.

Item Reference Number	Page Loc. in this Volume	ITEM DESCRIPTION (ABBREVIATED)	QUESTIONNAIRE LOCATION BY YEAR (FORM, SECTION, AND QUESTION NUMBER)								
			1975	1976	1977	1978	1979	1980/81	1982/83	1984/85	1986

R03: BACKGROUND. Living arrangements and household characteristics

50	16	R SPD >TIM R-URB		+C05	+C05	+C05	+C05	+C05	+C05	+C05	+C05
80	17	R'S HSHLD ALONE		+C07A	+C07A	+C07A	+C07A	+C07A	+C07A	+C07Ca	+C07Ca
90	17	R'S HSHLD FATHER		+C07B	+C07B	+C07B	+C07B	+C07B	+C07B	+C07Cb	+C07Cb
100	17	R'S HSHLD MOTHER		+C07C	+C07C	+C07C	+C07C	+C07C	+C07C	+C07Cc	+C07Cc
110	17	R'S HSHLD BR/SR		+C07D	+C07D	+C07D	+C07D	+C07D	+C07D	+C07Cd	+C07Cd
120	17	R'S HSHLD GRPRNT		+C07E	+C07E	+C07E	+C07E	+C07E	+C07E	+C07Ce	+C07Ce
130	17	R'S HSHLD SPOUSE		+C07F	+C07F	+C07F	+C07F	+C07F	+C07F	+C07Cf	+C07Cf
140	17	R'S HSHLD CHLDRN		+C07G	+C07G	+C07G	+C07G	+C07G	+C07G	+C07Cg	+C07Cg
150	17	R'S HSHLD RELTVS		+C07H	+C07H	+C07H	+C07H	+C07H	+C07H	+C07Ch	+C07Ch
160	17	R'S HSHLD NONRLT		+C07I	+C07I	+C07I	+C07I	+C07I	+C07I	+C07Ci	+C07Ci

S01: DEVIANCE AND VICTIMIZATION. Delinquent behaviors

6520	102	FRQ FIGHT PARNTS	2A39A	2A19A	2A19A	2A19A	2A19A	2A19A	2A19A	2A19A	2A19A
6530	102	FRQ HIT SUPRVISR	2A39B	2A19B	2A19B	2A19B	2A19B	2A19B	2A19B	2A19B	2A19B
6540	103	FRQ FGT WRK/SCHL	2A39C	2A19C	2A19C	2A19C	2A19C	2A19C	2A19C	2A19C	2A19C
6550	103	FRQ GANG FIGHT	2A39D	2A19D	2A19D	2A19D	2A19D	2A19D	2A19D	2A19D	2A19D
6560	103	FRQ HURT SM1 BAD	2A39E	2A19E	2A19E	2A19E	2A19E	2A19E	2A19E	2A19E	2A19E
6570	103	FRQ THREAT WEAPN	2A39F	2A19F	2A19F	2A19F	2A19F	2A19F	2A19F	2A19F	2A19F
6580	103	FRQ STEAL <$50	2A39G	2A19G	2A19G	2A19G	2A19G	2A19G	2A19G	2A19G	2A19G
6590	103	FRQ STEAL >$50	2A39H	2A19H	2A19H	2A19H	2A19H	2A19H	2A19H	2A19H	2A19H
6600	103	FRQ SHOPLIFT	2A39I	2A19I	2A19I	2A19I	2A19I	2A19I	2A19I	2A19I	2A19I
6610	104	FRQ CAR THEFT	2A39J	2A19J	2A19J	2A19J	2A19J	2A19J	2A19J	2A19J	2A19J
6620	104	FRQ STEAL CAR PT	2A39K	2A19K	2A19K	2A19K	2A19K	2A19K	2A19K	2A19K	2A19K
6630	104	FRQ TRESPAS BLDG	2A39L	2A19L	2A19L	2A19L	2A19L	2A19L	2A19L	2A19L	2A19L
6640	104	FRQ ARSON	2A39M	2A19M	2A19M	2A19M	2A19M	2A19M	2A19M	2A19M	2A19M
6650	104	FRQ DMG SCH PPTY	2A39N	2A19N	2A19N	2A19N	2A19N	2A19N	2A19N	2A19N	2A19N
6660	104	FRQ DMG WK PRPTY	2A39O	2A19O	2A19O	2A19O	2A19O	2A19O	2A19O	2A19O	2A19O
6670	104	FRQ TRUBL POLICE	2A39P	2A19P	2A19P	2A19P	2A19P	2A19P	2A19P	2A19P	2A19P

S02: DEVIANCE AND VICTIMIZATION. Driving violations and accidents

650	22	#X/12MO R TCKTD		+C28	+C28	+C28	+C28	+C28	+C28	+C28	+C28
660	22	#TCKTS AFT DRNK		+C29A	+C29A	+C29A	+C29A	+C29A	+C29A	+C29A	+C29A
670	23	#TCKTS AFT MARJ		+C29B	+C29B	+C29B	+C29B	+C29B	+C29B	+C29B	+C29B
680	23	#TCKTS AFT OTDG		+C29C	+C29C	+C29C	+C29C	+C29C	+C29C	+C29C	+C29C
690	23	#ACCIDNTS/12 MO		+C30	+C30	+C30	+C30	+C30	+C30	+C30	+C30
700	23	#ACDTS AFT DRNK		+C31A	+C31A	+C31A	+C31A	+C31A	+C31A	+C31A	+C31A
710	23	#ACDTS AFT MARJ		+C31B	+C31B	+C31B	+C31B	+C31B	+C31B	+C31B	+C31B
720	23	#ACDTS AFT OTDG		+C31C	+C31C	+C31C	+C31C	+C31C	+C31C	+C31C	+C31C
22210	121	USE SEATBLT-DRVR									2E22
22220	121	USE SEATBLT-RIDR									2E23

S03: DEVIANCE AND VICTIMIZATION. Victimization experiences

6680	105	SM1 ROB YRS <$50		2A20A	2A20A	2A20A	2A20A	2A20A	2A20A	2A20A	2A20A
6690	105	SM1 ROB YRS >$50		2A20B	2A20B	2A20B	2A20B	2A20B	2A20B	2A20B	2A20B
6700	105	SM1 DMG YR PRPTY		2A20C	2A20C	2A20C	2A20C	2A20C	2A20C	2A20C	2A20C
6710	105	SM1 INJR U W/WPN		2A20D	2A20D	2A20D	2A20D	2A20D	2A20D	2A20D	2A20D
6720	105	SM1 THRTN U W/WP		2A20E	2A20E	2A20E	2A20E	2A20E	2A20E	2A20E	2A20E
6730	105	SM1 INJR YU -WPN		2A20F	2A20F	2A20F	2A20F	2A20F	2A20F	2A20F	2A20F
6740	106	SM1 THRT U W/INJ		2A20G	2A20G	2A20G	2A20G	2A20G	2A20G	2A20G	2A20G
9871	142	SM1 SCL ROB <$50		4E11A	3E10A	3E10A	5E06A	5E08A=	3E08A	3E08A	3E08A
9872	142	SM1 SCL ROB >$50		4E11B	3E10B	3E10B	5E06B	5E08B=	3E08B	3E08B	3E08B
9873	143	SM1 SCL DMG PRTY		4E11C	3E10C	3E10C	5E06C	5E08C=	3E08C	3E08C	3E08C
9874	143	SM1 SCL IN U W/W		4E11D	3E10D	3E10D	5E06D	5E08D=	3E08D	3E08D	3E08D
9875	143	SM1 SCL TH U W/W		4E11E	3E10E	3E10E	5E06E	5E08E=	3E08E	3E08E	3E08E
9876	143	SM1 SCL IN U -WP		4E11F	3E10F	3E10F	5E06F	5E08F=	3E08F	3E08F	3E08F
9877	143	SM1 SCL TH U W/I		4E11G	3E10G	3E10G	5E06G	5EO8G=	3E08G	3E08G	3E08G

= Questions 5E8a–g were numbered 5E13a–g in 1981.

Item Reference Number	Page Loc. in this Volume	ITEM DESCRIPTION (ABBREVIATED)	QUESTIONNAIRE LOCATION BY YEAR (FORM, SECTION, AND QUESTION NUMBER)								
			1975	1976	1977	1978	1979	1980/81	1982/83	1984/85	1986

T01: HEALTH. Symptoms

Item Reference Number	Page Loc.	ITEM DESCRIPTION	1975	1976	1977	1978	1979	1980/81	1982/83	1984/85	1986
8850	136	OFTN SHRTNS BRTH		(3D02A)	3D02A	3D02A	3D02A	3D02A	3D02A	3D02A	3D02A
8860	136	OFTN HEART BEATG		(3D02B)	3D02B	3D02B	3D02B	3D02B	3D02B	3D02B	3D02B
8870	136	OFTN SPLLS DZZNS		(3D02C)	3D02C	3D02C	3D02C	3D02C	3D02C	3D02C	3D02C
8880	136	OFTN HNDS TRMBLE		(3D02D)	3D02D	3D02D	3D02D	3D02D	3D02D	3D02D	3D02D
8890	136	OFTN HNDS SWEATG		(3D02E)	3D02E	3D02E	3D02E	3D02E	3D02E	3D02E	3D02E
8900	137	OFTN CDNT GT GNG		(3D02F)	3D02F	3D02F	3D02F	3D02F	3D02F	3D02F	3D02F
21310	86	#DA HEADACHE							1D015A	1D015A	1D015A
21320	87	#DA SORE THROAT							1D015B	1D015B	1D015B
21330	87	#DA SINUS CONG							1D015C	1D015C	1D015C
21340	87	#DA COUGHING							1D015D	1D015D	1D015D
21350	87	#DA CHEST COLD							1D015E	1D015E	1D015E
21360	87	#DA COUGH PHLM							1D015F	1D015F	1D015F
21370	87	#DA SHORT BRTH							1D015G	1D015G	1D015G
21380	88	#DA WHEEZING							1D015H	1D015H	1D015H
21390	88	#DA TRBL REMEM							1D015I	1D015I	1D015I
21400	88	#DA DFCT THINK							1D015J	1D015J	1D015J
21410	88	#DA TRBL LEARN							1D015K	1D015K	1D015K
21420	88	#DA TRBL SLEEP							1D015L	1D015L	1D015L
21430	88	#DA TRBL START							1D015M	1D015M	1D015M
21440	89	#DA STAY HOME							1D015N	1D015N	1D015N
21520	90	RLTV PHY HEALTH							1D018	1D018	1D018

T02: HEALTH. Habits

Item Reference Number	Page Loc.	ITEM DESCRIPTION	1975	1976	1977	1978	1979	1980/81	1982/83	1984/85	1986
20690		ATTN TO NUTRITON					2E15A				
20700		MIN CHOLESTEROL					2E15B				
20710		AVOID ADDITIVES					2E15C				
20720		TRY GET EXERCISE					2E15D				
20730		CNTRL OWN HEALTH					2E16				
20740	120	OFTN EAT BRKFST					2E17A	2E17A	2E20A	2E21A	2E21A
20750	120	OFTN EAT GN VEG					2E17B	2E17B	2E20B	2E21B	2E21B
20760	120	OFTN EAT FRUIT					2E17C	2E17C	2E20C	2E21C	2E21C
20770	120	OFTN EXERCISE					2E17D	2E17D	2E20D	2E21D	2E21D
20780	120	OFTN 7HRS SLEEP					2E17E	2E17E	2E20E	2E21E	2E21E
20790	121	OFTN SLEEP <SHLD					2E17F	2E17F	2E20F	2E21F	2E21F
22210	121	USE SEATBLT-DRVR									2E22
22220	121	USE SEATBLT-RIDR									2E23

T03: HEALTH. Height and weight

Item Reference Number	Page Loc.	ITEM DESCRIPTION	1975	1976	1977	1978	1979	1980/81	1982/83	1984/85	1986
22150	90	CURRENT HEIGHT									1D019
22160	91	CURRENT WEIGHT									1D020

T04: HEALTH. Medical treatment

Item Reference Number	Page Loc.	ITEM DESCRIPTION	1975	1976	1977	1978	1979	1980/81	1982/83	1984/85	1986
21450	89	#X/12M DOC-CHEK							1D016A	1D016A	1D016A
21460	89	#X/12M DOC-FGHT							1D016B	1D016B	1D016B
21470	89	#X/12M DOC-INJ							1D016C	1D016C	1D016C
21480	89	#X/12M DOC-ILL							1D016D	1D016D	1D016D
21490	89	#X/12M DOC-PSY							1D016E	1D016E	1D016E
21500	90	#X/12M HSP-INJ							1D017A	1D017A	1D017A
21510	90	#X/12M HSP-ILL							1D017B	1D017B	1D017B

Appendix A
Sampling Error Estimates and Tables

All of the percentages reported in this volume are really *estimates* of the response percentages that would have been obtained if, instead of using a sample survey, we had asked all high schools throughout the United States to participate, and in all schools that agreed to participate we had invited the whole senior class to fill out the questionnaires. The question naturally arises: How accurate are the present percentage estimates based on a limited number of schools and seniors? For any particular percentage resulting from a sample survey we cannot know exactly how much error has resulted from sampling, but we can make reasonably good estimates of "confidence intervals" — ranges within which the "true" population value is very likely to fall. The word "true" in this context is defined quite narrowly; it refers only to the value that would be found if we had set out to survey the total population — all high school seniors in the United States. Thus this concept of "true" population value does *not* take account of biases that might occur due to refusals, distortion of responses, faulty question wording, and other factors. Each of these sources of possible error is discussed in the "Representativeness and Validity" section of the Introduction to this volume. The reader is urged to review this material and take it into account along with the sampling error estimates included in this appendix.

The estimation of confidence intervals in surveys involving complex samples can be a highly complicated combination of statistical science plus informed judgment. It is an area in which there is no single "right answer" or "best approach." We suspect that many of those using this volume will not be especially interested in *how* we have chosen to solve the problems involved in estimating confidence intervals, so long as we provide guidelines that can be applied in a fairly simple and straightforward manner. This appendix is designed to accomplish that. Appendix B provides a more extensive discussion of how we obtained the confidence intervals shown here, and it also provides guidelines for computing specific confidence intervals for a wider range of possible applications than can be covered in the tables provided in this appendix.

A very rough example of a confidence interval can be stated in these terms: For percentages based on the total sample (all five questionnaire forms), the "true" values are rarely more than 1.5 percent higher or lower than the percentage estimates reported in this volume. How rarely? The chances are much lower than 1 in 20. Indeed, many of the percentages reported for the total sample are accurate to within one percent.

Of course, most of the data reported here are based on items included only in one or another of the five questionnaire forms. Since such percentages are based on only one-fifth of the total sample, they are somewhat less accurate. The loss in accuracy is less than might be imagined, however, for reasons spelled out in Appendix B. For present purposes, it is enough to say that percentages based on 3,000 or more seniors responding to one questionnaire form are rarely (less than 1 in 20) farther than 2.4 percent away from the "true" value.

We have thus far provided two very rough illustrations of confidence intervals — a range of ± 1.5 percent for percentages based on the total sample, and a range of ± 2.4 percent for percentages based on the number of seniors responding to one questionnaire form. While these two intervals provide some notion of the overall range of accuracy of the sample, they fall short of our needs in a number of respects. We need to be able to assign confidence intervals for subgroups such as males, females, those who plan to complete college, and so forth, all of which involve smaller numbers of cases and thus some reduction in accuracy. We also need to take account of the fact that, other things equal, confidence intervals grow smaller when one moves from the middle of the scale (percentages near 50 percent) to the extremes (e.g., 4 percent or 96 percent). Further, we need to provide guidelines for evaluating the *difference* between two percentages; for example, we may wish to know whether the difference between male and female percentages in response to a particular question is large enough so that it is not likely to be merely the result of sampling error. Another type of difference of considerable interest is that between percentages from two different years; for example, we may wish to know whether an increase in the percentage of daily marijuana users from one year to the next is large enough to be considered a statistically significant change.

Each of the requirements mentioned above is taken into account in the tables of confidence intervals which follow.

Confidence Intervals for Single Percentages

Table A-1 provides confidence intervals for single percentages that are reasonably good approximations for most *variables* and for most *subgroups* (as well as for the total sample). The table entries slightly underestimate the confidence intervals for regional subgroups and for blacks. These underestimates can be corrected reasonably well by multiplying the entries in Table A-1 by a factor of 1.1 for data based on a single form and by a factor of 1.33 for data based on all five forms. A more serious problem is that the table entries substantially underestimate the confidence intervals for certain variables which tend to be somewhat homogeneous within schools, as well as other factors likely to show clustering according to geographical area or socioeconomic level. A discussion of some of these variables is provided at the end of this appendix.

Table A-1 accommodates various numbers of cases (presented as different columns in the table), and various percentages (presented as different rows in the table). The table entries, when added to and subtracted from the observed percentage, establish the 95 percent confidence interval (calculated as 1.96 sampling errors). Thus, for example, to determine the accuracy of a result of 67.4 percent based on a sample of 1,632 cases, one should first look for the closest values in the table (in this case, about 70 percent and a number of cases approximately equal to 1,500); next determine the values to be added to and subtracted from the observed percentage (in this case the values

would be + 2.8 percent and − 2.9 percent); and then compute the confidence interval around the observed percentage of 67.4 percent (in this case an interval ranging from 64.5 percent to 70.2 percent). This procedure yields an interval such that, for most variables, the chances are 95 in 100 that if all high school seniors in the country had been asked to participate in the survey the resulting percentage would fall within the interval.

Confidence Intervals for Differences between Two Percentages

Table A-2 provides confidence intervals for differences between certain percentages. Specifically, the table can be used for *comparisons* between males and females, between those who do and do not plan to complete four years of college, and between those falling into different categories of the five-level index of drug usage. The above comparisons are appropriate for data from any single year (e.g., male seniors in 1976 compared with female seniors in 1976, or the "marijuana only" seniors in 1977 compared with the "no illicit drugs" seniors in 1977). Table A-2 is also useful in assessing *one-year* trends for any of the above subgroups as well as for the total sample. For example, one may be interested in a confidence interval (or significance level) for the difference between the percentage of female seniors in 1977 who used marijuana and the percentage of female seniors in 1978 who did so. The values in Table A-2 are appropriate for confidence intervals across adjacent years (e.g., 1976 compared with 1977), provided the same subgroup (e.g., females) is being considered both years. The confidence intervals for comparisons across non-adjacent years (e.g., 1976 compared with 1978), are slightly larger.

With appropriate corrections, the entries in Table A-2 can be used for trends covering more than one year and for trends or comparisons involving regional subgroups and blacks. Each of these applications requires some upward adjustment of the table entries; guidelines for such adjustments are provided in the notes accompanying Table A-2.

For information on the derivation of Table A-2 and for guidelines to be used in computing confidence intervals not covered in that table, the reader is referred to Appendix B.

In order to find the appropriate confidence interval in Table A-2, one must first locate that portion of the table which deals with percentage values closest to the two percentages being compared (for example, if one wished to compare a value of 28.1 percent with one of 35.4 percent, the "p = 30 percent or 70 percent" portion of the table would be closest). The next step is to locate the specific table entry which corresponds most closely to the numbers of cases involved in the two percentages being compared (e.g., if those numbers were 1,478 and 1,563 for 28.1 percent and 35.4 percent, the correct table entry would be 3.9 percent). That table entry, when added to and subtracted from the difference between the two percentages, yields the 95 percent confidence interval for the difference. (In the above illustration that would be 7.3 percent ± 3.9 percent or an interval from 3.4 percent to 11.2 percent.) The chances are only 1 in 20 that the "true" difference between two percentages lies outside of this interval.

Another use of Table A-2 is to test whether a difference between two percentages is "statistically significant." If the table entry is smaller than the difference between the two percentages (as is true in the above illustration), then the difference is statistically significant at the 95 percent level (sometimes indicated as p<.05).

Some Cautions

The tables provided here are based on averages of large numbers of sampling errors computed across a wide range of the variables which appear in this volume, as well as across all of the subgroups for which data are reported here. We are confident that the values in the tables are reasonably accurate for most purposes, but we must repeat the caution that the tables slightly underestimate confidence intervals for the following groups and comparisons:

> Blacks
> Regions (Northeast, North Central,
>   South, West)
> Comparisons among regions
> Comparisons across non-adjacent years
>   (e.g., 1976 vs. 1978)

A more important problem is that the tables substantially underestimate the confidence intervals for certain variables that, for various reasons, show greater than average homogeneity within schools. After an extensive, but by no means exhaustive, sampling of the kinds of variables which might show such clustering by school, we can provide the following examples of the kinds of variables for which Tables A-1 and A-2 substantially underestimate the confidence intervals.

Variables Related to Educational Background and Aspirations. The questionnaire items dealing with father's education, mother's education, high school curriculum (college preparatory versus all other), and plans for completing four years of college, all show an appreciable amount of clustering by school. Accordingly, for such variables the confidence intervals provided in the tables should be doubled.

Other items dealing with plans for technical/vocational schooling, a two-year college program, or graduate/professional study, also require adjustment. The confidence intervals in the tables should be multiplied by a factor of 1.5 in order to be applicable to these variables.

It seems clear that the common factor underlying these particular variables is the tendency for family socioeconomic level to be somewhat homogeneous within school districts — some schools serve wealthier populations than others. That makes the form of sampling we use somewhat less efficient for measuring those variables (like those listed above) which are closely associated with family socioeconomic level. Therefore, we urge the reader to treat with caution any variables which are likely to be strongly linked to socioeconomic factors. In the absence of more specific computations of sampling errors, a good rule of thumb for dealing with such variables would be to double the confidence intervals provided in Tables A-1 and A-2.

Variables Related to Geographic Location. Another category of variables which are somewhat homogeneous within schools and school districts consists of those things which reflect differences in region and/or urbanicity. An obvious example is a background question asking where the respondent grew up; the response category "on a farm" shows a very high degree of clustering within schools. One would have to more than double the confidence intervals in the tables to deal with such a measure. Similarly high clustering was found for some responses about religious preference; for example, those whose preference is Baptist are located primarily in the South (and probably heavily in rural areas), whereas those whose preference is Jewish are located primarily in the Northeast (especially in larger cities). The confidence intervals in Tables A-1 and A-2 should be multiplied by a factor as large as 3 in order to be applicable to such variables.

Other variables which show some greater than average homogeneity within schools include such ideologically related dimensions as frequency of attending religious services, importance of religion, and political preference. Still other variables showing high homogeneity, probably because of their association with urbanicity, include driving (percentage who usually do not drive at all), working (percentage with no job), and household composition (percentage with father not living in the home). For each of the variables mentioned in this paragraph, the confidence intervals shown in Tables A-1 and A-2 should be multiplied by a factor of about 1.5.

Variables Involving Use of Alcohol and Marijuana. Extensive work has been done to compute sampling errors and confidence intervals for the drug use measures included in this volume (see Johnston, Bachman, and O'Malley, 1977, 1979a, 1982; Johnston, O'Malley, and Bachman, 1984; especially Appendix B). Most drug use variables show sampling errors which lie within the range of those provided in Tables A-1 and A-2. Usage levels for alcohol and marijuana, however, show some degree of homogeneity within schools, thus requiring that the table levels be adjusted. For items dealing with alcohol use, the entries in Table

A-1 should be multiplied by a factor of 1.6; for items dealing with marijuana use, the correction factor is 1.35.

As noted earlier, this appendix has presented guidelines for using the tables of confidence intervals provided herein. Those readers interested in learning more about the rationale underlying such tables, the procedures used to derive the particular tables presented here, and guidelines for further computations of confidence intervals may consult Appendix B of this volume.

Notes to Table A-1

Caution: The entries in this table systematically underestimate confidence intervals for regional subgroups and for blacks. In order to correct these underestimates, the table entries should be multiplied by a factor of 1.10 for data from a single form and by a factor of 1.33 for data based on five forms. Further cautions and corrections are required for some specific variables which relate to educational background and aspirations, geographic location, and the use of alcohol and marijuana (see discussion in the final sections of Appendix A).

The values in this table, when added to and subtracted from an observed percentage, establish the 95 percent confidence interval around that percentage, incorporating a design effect. Table values were calculated using the following formula (adapted from Hays, 1973, p. 379):

$$\text{lower limit} = p - \frac{2N'p + (1.96)^2 - 1.96\sqrt{4N'p(1-p) + (1.96)^2}}{2[N' + (1.96)^2]}$$

$$\text{upper limit} = \frac{2N'p + (1.96)^2 + 1.96\sqrt{4N'p(1-p) + (1.96)^2}}{2[N' + (1.96)^2]} - p$$

where p = the proportion, and N' is the "effective N," $N' = N/(1.3 + .00015N)$. (See Appendix B for a discussion of the concept of "effective N.")

Table A-1

Confidence Intervals (95% Level) around Percentage Values

Number of Cases

	100	200	300	400	500	700	1000	1500	2000	2500	3000	3500	4000	5000	7000	10000	15000	20000
99%+	0.9	0.8	0.7	0.7	0.6	0.6	0.5	0.5	0.4	0.4	0.4	0.4	0.3	0.3	0.3	0.3	0.3	0.2
−	5.6	3.2	2.4	1.9	1.7	1.3	1.1	0.8	0.7	0.6	0.6	0.6	0.5	0.5	0.4	0.4	0.3	0.3
97%+	2.1	1.8	1.6	1.4	1.3	1.2	1.0	0.9	0.8	0.8	0.7	0.7	0.6	0.6	0.6	0.5	0.5	0.5
−	6.6	4.1	3.2	2.6	2.3	1.9	1.6	1.3	1.1	1.0	0.9	0.9	0.8	0.8	0.7	0.6	0.6	0.5
95%+	3.1	2.5	2.2	2.0	1.8	1.6	1.4	1.2	1.1	1.0	0.9	0.9	0.9	0.8	0.7	0.7	0.6	0.6
−	7.4	4.7	3.7	3.1	2.7	2.3	1.9	1.5	1.4	1.2	1.1	1.1	1.0	0.9	0.8	0.8	0.7	0.7
90%+	4.9	3.8	3.3	2.9	2.7	2.3	2.0	1.7	1.5	1.4	1.3	1.3	1.2	1.1	1.0	0.9	0.9	0.8
−	8.8	5.8	4.6	4.0	3.5	2.9	2.5	2.0	1.8	1.6	1.5	1.4	1.4	1.3	1.1	1.0	0.9	0.9
85%+	6.6	4.8	4.1	3.6	3.3	2.9	2.5	2.1	1.9	1.7	1.6	1.5	1.5	1.4	1.2	1.1	1.0	1.0
−	9.7	6.6	5.3	4.5	4.0	3.4	2.9	2.4	2.1	1.9	1.8	1.7	1.6	1.5	1.3	1.2	1.1	1.1
80%+	7.4	5.6	4.7	4.2	3.8	3.3	2.8	2.4	2.1	2.0	1.8	1.7	1.7	1.5	1.4	1.3	1.2	1.1
−	10.3	7.1	5.7	4.9	4.4	3.7	3.1	2.6	2.3	2.1	2.0	1.8	1.8	1.6	1.5	1.3	1.2	1.2
70%+	9.1	6.8	5.6	5.0	4.5	3.9	3.3	2.8	2.5	2.3	2.1	2.0	1.9	1.8	1.6	1.5	1.4	1.3
−	11.1	7.7	6.3	5.5	4.9	4.2	3.5	2.9	2.6	2.4	2.2	2.1	2.0	1.8	1.7	1.5	1.4	1.3
50%+	11.0	7.9	6.5	5.7	5.1	4.4	3.7	3.1	2.8	2.5	2.4	2.2	2.1	2.0	1.8	1.6	1.5	1.4
−	11.0	7.9	6.5	5.7	5.1	4.4	3.7	3.1	2.8	2.5	2.4	2.2	2.1	2.0	1.8	1.6	1.5	1.4
30%+	11.1	7.7	6.3	5.5	4.9	4.2	3.5	2.9	2.6	2.4	2.2	2.1	2.0	1.8	1.7	1.5	1.4	1.3
−	9.1	6.8	5.6	5.0	4.5	3.9	3.3	2.8	2.5	2.3	2.1	2.0	1.9	1.8	1.6	1.5	1.4	1.3
20%+	10.3	7.1	5.7	4.9	4.4	3.7	3.1	2.6	2.3	2.1	2.0	1.8	1.8	1.6	1.5	1.3	1.2	1.2
−	7.4	5.6	4.7	4.2	3.8	3.3	2.8	2.4	2.1	2.0	1.6	1.7	1.7	1.5	1.4	1.3	1.2	1.1
15%+	9.7	6.6	5.3	4.5	4.0	3.4	2.9	2.4	2.1	1.9	1.8	1.7	1.6	1.5	1.3	1.2	1.1	1.1
−	6.3	4.8	4.1	3.6	3.3	2.9	2.5	2.1	1.9	1.7	1.6	1.5	1.5	1.4	1.2	1.1	1.0	1.0
10%+	8.8	5.8	4.6	4.0	3.5	2.9	2.5	2.0	1.8	1.6	1.5	1.4	1.4	1.3	1.1	1.0	0.9	0.9
−	4.9	3.8	3.3	2.9	2.7	2.3	2.0	1.7	1.5	1.4	1.3	1.3	1.2	1.1	1.0	0.9	0.9	0.8
5%+	7.4	4.7	3.7	3.1	2.7	2.3	1.9	1.5	1.4	1.2	1.1	1.1	1.0	0.9	0.8	0.8	0.7	0.7
−	3.1	2.5	2.2	2.0	1.8	1.6	1.4	1.2	1.1	1.0	0.9	0.9	0.9	0.8	0.7	0.7	0.6	0.6
3%+	6.6	4.1	3.2	2.6	2.3	1.9	1.6	1.3	1.1	1.0	0.9	0.9	0.8	0.8	0.7	0.6	0.6	0.5
−	2.1	1.8	1.6	1.4	1.3	1.2	1.0	0.9	0.8	0.8	0.7	0.7	0.6	0.6	0.6	0.5	0.5	0.5
1%+	5.6	3.2	2.4	1.9	1.7	1.3	1.1	0.8	0.7	0.6	0.6	0.6	0.5	0.5	0.4	0.4	0.3	0.3
−	0.9	0.8	0.7	0.7	0.6	0.6	0.5	0.5	0.4	0.4	0.4	0.4	0.3	0.3	0.3	0.3	0.3	0.2

Notes to Table A-2

The entries in this table (which appear on the next two pages) are appropriate for *comparisons* between (a) males and females, (b) those who do and do not plan four years of college, and (c) those falling into different categories of the five-level index of drug usage. The table entries are also appropriate for *one-year trends* for the total sample and any of the subgroups except region. Most other trends and subgroup comparisons require that the table entries be multiplied by an adjustment factor, given below.

Outline of Steps to Follow (see text of appendix for illustrations)

1. Locate the portion of the table with "p" values closest to the two percentages being compared.

2. Locate the specific entry closest to the weighted Ns for the two percentages.

3. Multiply that entry by any necessary adjustment factor (see below).

4. That table value (or adjusted table value), when added to and subtracted from the difference between the two percentages, yields the 95 percent confidence interval for the difference.

5. Also, if the table value (or adjusted table value) is smaller than the difference between the two percentages, then the difference may be described as "statistically significant at the 95 percent level."

	Adjustment Factor (to be multiplied by table entry)
Adjustment Factors	
For comparisons between blacks and whites	
based on single form data	*
based on five form data	1.25
For comparisons between any two regions	
based on single form data	1.15
based on five form data	1.50
For one-year trends involving any region	
based on single form data	*
based on five form data	1.25
For trends over two or more years involving any region	
based on single form data	*
based on five form data	1.35
For trends over two or more years involving all other groups	
based on single form data	*
based on five form data	1.15

*indicates that no adjustment is necessary for category shown

NOTE: The table entries were calculated using the following formula: $1.96 \sqrt{p(1-p)\left[\frac{1}{N'_1} + \frac{1}{N'_2}\right]}$

where $N'_1 = N_1/DEFF$, and $N'_2 = N_2/DEFF$, $DEFF = 1.3 + .000075 \left[\frac{N_1 N_2}{N_1 + N_2}\right]$

Table A-2

Confidence Intervals (95% Confidence Level) for Differences Between Two Percentages

p = 1% or 99%

	N_1 = 100	200	300	400	500	700	1000	1500	2000	3000	4000	5000	7000	10000	15000	20000
N_2 = 100	3.2															
200	2.7	2.2														
300	2.6	2.0	1.8													
400	2.5	1.9	1.7	1.6												
500	2.4	1.9	1.6	1.5	1.4											
700	2.4	1.8	1.6	1.4	1.3	1.2										
1000	2.3	1.7	1.5	1.3	1.2	1.1	1.0									
1500	2.3	1.7	1.4	1.3	1.2	1.0	0.9	0.8								
2000	2.3	1.7	1.4	1.2	1.1	1.0	0.9	0.8	0.7							
3000	2.3	1.6	1.4	1.2	1.1	1.0	0.8	0.7	0.7	0.6						
4000	2.3	1.6	1.4	1.2	1.1	0.9	0.8	0.7	0.7	0.6	0.6					
5000	2.3	1.6	1.3	1.2	1.1	0.9	0.8	0.7	0.6	0.6	0.5	0.5				
7000	2.3	1.6	1.3	1.2	1.1	0.9	0.8	0.7	0.6	0.5	0.5	0.5	0.4			
10000	2.2	1.6	1.3	1.2	1.0	0.9	0.8	0.7	0.6	0.5	0.5	0.5	0.4	0.4		
15000	2.2	1.6	1.3	1.2	1.0	0.9	0.8	0.6	0.6	0.5	0.5	0.4	0.4	0.4	0.4	
20000	2.2	1.6	1.3	1.1	1.0	0.9	0.8	0.6	0.6	0.5	0.5	0.4	0.4	0.4	0.3	0.3

p = 3% or 97%

	N_1 = 100	200	300	400	500	700	1000	1500	2000	3000	4000	5000	7000	10000	15000	20000
N_2 = 100	5.4															
200	4.7	3.8														
300	4.4	3.5	3.1													
400	4.3	3.3	2.9	2.7												
500	4.2	3.2	2.8	2.6	2.4											
700	4.1	3.1	2.7	2.4	2.3	2.1										
1000	4.0	3.0	2.5	2.3	2.1	1.9	1.8									
1500	4.0	2.9	2.4	2.2	2.0	1.8	1.6	1.5								
2000	3.9	2.9	2.4	2.1	1.9	1.7	1.5	1.4	1.3							
3000	3.9	2.8	2.3	2.1	1.9	1.7	1.5	1.3	1.2	1.1						
4000	3.9	2.8	2.3	2.0	1.9	1.6	1.4	1.2	1.1	1.0	0.9					
5000	3.9	2.8	2.3	2.0	1.8	1.6	1.4	1.2	1.1	1.0	0.9	0.9				
7000	3.9	2.8	2.3	2.0	1.8	1.6	1.4	1.2	1.0	0.9	0.9	0.8	0.8			
10000	3.9	2.8	2.3	2.0	1.8	1.5	1.3	1.1	1.0	0.9	0.8	0.8	0.7	0.7		
15000	3.8	2.7	2.3	2.0	1.8	1.5	1.3	1.1	1.0	0.9	0.8	0.7	0.7	0.6	0.6	
20000	3.8	2.7	2.3	2.0	1.8	1.5	1.3	1.1	1.0	0.9	0.8	0.7	0.7	0.6	0.6	0.6

Table A-2 (continued)

	N_1 = 100	200	300	400	500	700	1000	1500	2000	3000	4000	5000	7000	10000	15000	20000
N_2 = 100	6.9															
200	6.0	4.9														
300	5.6	4.5	4.0													
400	5.5	4.3	3.8	3.5												
500	5.4	4.1	3.6	3.3	3.1											
700	5.2	3.9	3.4	3.1	2.9	2.7										
1000	5.1	3.8	3.2	2.9	2.7	2.5	2.2									
1500	5.1	3.7	3.1	2.8	2.6	2.3	2.1	1.9								
2000	5.0	3.6	3.1	2.7	2.5	2.2	2.0	1.7	1.6							
3000	5.0	3.6	3.0	2.6	2.4	2.1	1.9	1.6	1.5	1.4						
4000	5.0	3.6	3.0	2.6	2.4	2.1	1.8	1.6	1.4	1.3	1.2					
5000	4.9	3.6	2.9	2.6	2.3	2.0	1.8	1.5	1.4	1.2	1.2	1.1				
7000	4.9	3.5	2.9	2.6	2.3	2.0	1.7	1.5	1.3	1.2	1.1	1.0	1.0			
10000	4.9	3.5	2.9	2.5	2.3	2.0	1.7	1.4	1.3	1.1	1.1	1.0	0.9	0.9		
15000	4.9	3.5	2.9	2.5	2.3	2.0	1.7	1.4	1.3	1.1	1.0	1.0	0.9	0.8	0.8	
20000	4.9	3.5	2.9	2.5	2.3	1.9	1.7	1.4	1.3	1.1	1.0	0.9	0.9	0.8	0.7	0.7

p = 5% or 95%

	N_1 = 100	200	300	400	500	700	1000	1500	2000	3000	4000	5000	7000	10000	15000	20000
N_1 = 100	9.5															
200	8.2	6.7														
300	7.8	6.2	5.5													
400	7.5	5.9	5.2	4.8												
500	7.4	5.7	4.9	4.6	4.3											
700	7.2	5.4	4.7	4.3	4.0	3.7										
1000	7.1	5.2	4.5	4.0	3.7	3.4	3.1									
1500	7.0	5.1	4.3	3.8	3.5	3.2	2.8	2.6								
2000	6.9	5.0	4.2	3.7	3.4	3.0	2.7	2.4	2.2							
3000	6.9	4.9	4.1	3.6	3.3	2.9	2.6	2.2	2.1	1.9						
4000	6.8	4.9	4.1	3.6	3.3	2.8	2.5	2.2	2.0	1.8	1.7					
5000	6.8	4.9	4.0	3.6	3.2	2.8	2.4	2.1	1.9	1.7	1.6	1.5				
7000	6.8	4.9	4.0	3.5	3.2	2.8	2.4	2.0	1.8	1.6	1.5	1.4	1.3			
10000	6.8	4.8	4.0	3.5	3.2	2.7	2.3	2.0	1.8	1.6	1.4	1.4	1.3	1.2		
15000	6.8	4.8	4.0	3.5	3.1	2.7	2.3	2.0	1.8	1.5	1.4	1.3	1.2	1.1	1.1	
20000	6.8	4.8	4.0	3.5	3.1	2.7	2.3	1.9	1.7	1.5	1.4	1.3	1.2	1.1	1.0	1.0

p = 10% or 90%

Table A-2 (continued)

$p = 15\%$ or 85%

	$N_1=100$	200	300	400	500	700	1000	1500	2000	3000	4000	5000	7000	10000	15000	20000
$N_2=100$	11.3															
200	9.8	8.0														
300	9.3	7.3	6.6													
400	9.0	7.0	6.2	5.7												
500	8.8	6.7	5.9	5.4	5.1											
700	8.6	6.5	5.6	5.1	4.8	4.4										
1000	8.4	6.2	5.3	4.8	4.5	4.0	3.7									
1500	8.3	6.1	5.1	4.6	4.2	3.8	3.4	3.0								
2000	8.2	6.0	5.0	4.5	4.1	3.6	3.2	2.9	2.7							
3000	8.2	5.9	4.9	4.3	3.9	3.5	3.0	2.7	2.5	2.2						
4000	8.1	5.8	4.9	4.3	3.9	3.4	2.9	2.6	2.3	2.1	2.0					
5000	8.1	5.8	4.8	4.2	3.8	3.3	2.9	2.5	2.3	2.0	1.9	1.8				
7000	8.1	5.8	4.8	4.2	3.8	3.3	2.8	2.4	2.2	1.9	1.8	1.7	1.6			
10000	8.1	5.8	4.8	4.2	3.8	3.2	2.8	2.4	2.1	1.9	1.7	1.6	1.5	1.4		
15000	8.1	5.7	4.7	4.1	3.7	3.2	2.7	2.3	2.1	1.8	1.7	1.6	1.4	1.3	1.3	
20000	8.0	5.7	4.7	4.1	3.7	3.2	2.7	2.3	2.1	1.8	1.6	1.5	1.4	1.3	1.2	1.2

$p = 20\%$ or 80%

	$N_1=100$	200	300	400	500	700	1000	1500	2000	3000	4000	5000	7000	10000	15000	20000
$N_2=100$	12.7															
200	11.0	9.0														
300	10.4	8.2	7.4													
400	10.0	7.8	6.9	6.4												
500	9.8	7.5	6.6	6.1	5.7											
700	9.6	7.2	6.2	5.7	5.3	4.9										
1000	9.4	7.0	6.0	5.4	5.0	4.5	4.1									
1500	9.3	6.8	5.7	5.1	4.7	4.2	3.8	3.4								
2000	9.2	6.7	5.6	5.0	4.6		3.6	3.2	3.0							
3000	9.1	6.6	5.5	4.9	4.4	3.9	3.4	3.0	2.8	2.5						
4000	9.1	6.5	5.4	4.8	4.3	3.8	3.3	2.9	2.6	2.4	2.2					
5000	9.1	6.5	5.4	4.7	4.3	3.7	3.2	2.8	2.6	2.3	2.1	2.0				
7000	9.1	6.5	5.4	4.7	4.2	3.7	3.2	2.7	2.5	2.2	2.0	1.9	1.8			
10000	9.0	6.5	5.3	4.7	4.2	3.6	3.1	2.7	2.4	2.1	1.9	1.8	1.7	1.6		
15000	9.0	6.4	5.3	4.6	4.2	3.6	3.1	2.6	2.3	2.0	1.9	1.7	1.6	1.5	1.4	
20000	9.0	6.4	5.3	4.6	4.2	3.6	3.1	2.6	2.3	2.0	1.8	1.7	1.6	1.5	1.4	1.3

Table A-2 (continued)

N_2 \ N_1	100	200	300	400	500	700	1000	1500	2000	3000	4000	5000	7000	10000	15000	20000
100	14.5															
200	12.6	10.3														
300	11.9	9.4	8.4													
400	11.5	8.9	7.9	7.3												
500	11.3	8.6	7.6	7.0	6.6											
700	11.0	8.3	7.2	6.5	6.1	5.6										
1000	10.8	8.0	6.8	6.2	5.7	5.2	4.7									
1500	10.6	7.8	6.6	5.9	5.4	4.8	4.3	3.9								
2000	10.6	7.7	6.4	5.7	5.2	4.6	4.1	3.7	3.4							
3000	10.5	7.6	6.3	5.6	5.1	4.4	3.9	3.4	3.2	2.9						
4000	10.4	7.5	6.2	5.5	5.0	4.3	3.8	3.3	3.0	2.7	2.5					
5000	10.4	7.5	6.2	5.4	4.9	4.3	3.7	3.2	2.9	2.6	2.4	2.3				
7000	10.4	7.4	6.1	5.4	4.9	4.2	3.6	3.1	2.5	2.3	2.2	2.1				
10000	10.4	7.4	6.1	5.3	4.8	4.2	3.6	3.0	2.7	2.4	2.2	2.1	1.9	1.8		
15000	10.3	7.4	6.1	5.3	4.8	4.1	3.5	3.0	2.7	2.3	2.1	2.0	1.8	1.7	1.6	
20000	10.3	7.4	6.1	5.3	4.8	4.1	3.5	3.0	2.6	2.3	2.1	2.0	1.8	1.7	1.6	1.5

p = 30% or 70%

N_2 \ N_1	100	200	300	400	500	700	1000	1500	2000	3000	4000	5000	7000	10000	15000	20000
100	15.8															
200	13.7	11.2														
300	13.0	10.3	9.2													
400	12.6	9.8	8.6	8.0												
500	12.3	9.4	8.2	7.6	7.2											
700	12.0	9.0	7.8	7.1	6.7	6.1										
1000	11.8	8.7	7.5	6.7	6.2	5.6	5.1									
1500	11.6	8.5	7.2	6.4	5.9	5.3	4.7	4.3								
2000	11.5	8.4	7.0	6.2	5.7	5.1	4.5	4.0	3.7							
3000	11.4	8.2	6.9	6.1	5.5	4.8	4.3	3.7	3.4	3.1						
4000	11.4	8.2	6.8	6.0	5.4	4.7	4.1	3.6	3.3	3.0	2.8					
5000	11.3	8.1	6.7	5.9	5.4	4.7	4.1	3.5	3.2	2.8	2.7	2.5				
7000	11.3	8.1	6.7	5.9	5.3	4.6	4.0	3.4	3.1	2.7	2.5	2.4	2.2			
10000	11.3	8.1	6.7	5.8	5.3	4.5	3.9	3.3	3.0	2.6	2.4	2.3	2.1	2.0		
15000	11.3	8.0	6.6	5.8	5.2	4.5	3.8	3.3	2.9	2.5	2.3	2.2	2.0	1.9	1.8	
20000	11.3	8.0	6.6	5.8	5.2	4.5	3.8	3.2	2.9	2.5	2.3	2.1	2.0	1.8	1.7	1.6

p = 35% or 65%

Appendix B
Procedures Used to Derive Design Effects and Sampling Errors

Appendix A provided a very brief and relatively nontechnical explanation of sampling error estimates, accompanied by two tables of confidence intervals which can be used to ascertain the accuracy of most percentages reported in this volume. The present appendix is intended to provide some background concerning the strategy and rationale involved in computing these confidence intervals. It also offers guidance for those wishing to make sampling computations beyond those contained in Appendix A.

This appendix, like the first, is intended to be readable and usable by the nonstatistician. For that reason, we take the time to outline (albeit briefly) a number of relatively elementary factors involved in estimating confidence intervals.

Factors Influencing the Size of Confidence Intervals

The most straightforward types of samples, from a statistical standpoint at least, are simple random samples. In such samples the confidence limits for a proportion are influenced by the size of the sample or subgroups being considered and also by the size of the proportion. For example, the 95 percent confidence interval for a proportion p based on a simple random sample of N cases is approximated by:
$p \pm 1.96 \sqrt{p(1-p)/N}$. In a complex probability sample such as the present one, there are a number of other factors which influence the size of confidence limits. This section lists all of the factors which have been taken into account in calculating confidence intervals for use with the data in this volume, beginning with the most simple factors and then proceeding to the more complex.

Number of Cases (N). Other things equal, the larger a sample (or subgroup within a sample), the smaller or more precise will be the confidence interval for a percentage based on that sample. One of the factors determining the size of the confidence interval is $1/\sqrt{N}$. Thus, for example, if all other things were equal, a sample of 400 would have confidence intervals half as large (or twice as precise) as a sample of 100, because $1/\sqrt{400}$ is half as large as $1/\sqrt{100}$.

Size of Percentage. Other things equal, percentage values around 50 percent have larger confidence intervals than higher or lower percentage values. This is because another of the factors determining the size of the confidence interval is $\sqrt{p(1-p)}$ where p is a proportion ranging from 0 to 1.0 (or, to put it in percentage terms, the factor is $\sqrt{x\%(100-x\%)}$). Thus, for example, a proportion of either .1 or .9 (a percentage of either 10 percent or 90 percent) will have a confidence interval only three-fifths as large as the confidence interval around a proportion of .5 (or 50 percent), because $\sqrt{.1(1-.1)}$ is three-fifths as large as $\sqrt{.5(1-.5)}$.

Design Effects in Complex Samples. Under conditions of simple random sampling, a confidence interval can be determined solely on the basis of the number of cases and the percentage value involved. More complex samples such as the one used in the present study make use of stratification and clustering and often differential weighting of respondent scores, and these all influence sampling error. While stratification tends to heighten the precision of a sample, the effects of clustering and weighting reduce precision (compared with a simple random sample of the same size). Therefore, it is not appropriate to apply the

261

standard, simple random sampling formulas to such complex samples in order to obtain estimates of sampling errors, because they would almost always underestimate the actual sampling errors.

Methods exist for correcting for this underestimation, however. Kish (1965, p. 258) defines a correction term called the design effect (DEFF), where:

$$\text{DEFF} = \frac{\text{actual sampling variance}}{\begin{array}{l}\text{expected sampling variance} \\ \text{from a simple random sample} \\ \text{with same number of elements}\end{array}}$$

Thus, if the actual sampling variance in a complex sample is four times as large as the expected sampling variance from a simple random sample with the same number of cases, the DEFF is 4.0. Since confidence intervals are proportionate to the square root of variance, the confidence intervals for such a sample would be twice as large (because the square root of 4 is 2) as the confidence interval for a simple random sample with the same number of cases. A fairly simple and straightforward way of applying the concept of design effect may be to note that an increase in design effect has the same impact on precision as a reduction in the number of cases in a simple random sample. For example, a sample of 16,000 cases with a design effect of 4.0 would have the same degree of precision (the same size confidence intervals around various percentages) as a simple random sample of 4,000.

In principle, every different statistic resulting from a complex sample can have its own design effect, and different statistics in the same sample may have quite different design effects. However, it is not feasible to compute every design effect, nor would it be feasible to report every one. Thus, in practice, design effects are averaged across a number of statistics and these average values are used to estimate the design effects for other statistics based on the same sample. Sometimes a single design effect is applied to all statistics of a given type (e.g., percentages) for a given sample. In the present study, however, a rather extensive exploration of design effects revealed a number of systematic differences. These systematic differences have to do with the particular measures being examined, the subgroups involved, and the question of whether a trend over time is being considered. The most consistent difference involves the number of cases in the group or subgroup for which the design effect is computed.

The Relationship between Subgroup Size and Design Effects. Kish et al. (1976) have observed that design effects tend to be smaller for subgroups than for total samples; moreover, the smaller the subgroup the smaller the design effect is likely to be. The ex-

planation for this widespread phenomenon is that the average number of cases in each sampling cluster is an important factor in determining the size of the design effect, and as subgroup size decreases so does this average number of cases per cluster. This point is illustrated by several subgroups treated in the present volume — males, females, those planning four years of college, and those not planning four years of college. All (or virtually all) of the schools in the sample have both male and female students, as well as some students who plan four years of college and others who do not. Thus, each of these four subgroups is spread more or less evenly across the full number of clusters (schools). Since each of these subgroups includes roughly half of the total sample, the average number of cases per cluster is about half as large as for the total sample, and this leads to a smaller design effect than is found for the total sample. Other subgroups involving different patterns of drug use are also distributed more or less evenly across all clusters and thus are subject to the same phenomenon of smaller design effects because of the smaller number of cases per cluster.

One very important exception to the pattern of smaller design effects for subgroups involves the four geographic region subgroups presented in this volume. These subgroups do not cut across all clusters; instead, regions have been described as "segregated" subgroups, in contrast to the "cross-class" subgroups discussed above. For such segregated subgroups the average number of cases per cluster is about the same as is found in the total sample, and thus the design effects are not lower than those for the total sample (Kish et al., 1976). Another subgroup which is in some respects similar to regional subgroups is the category of blacks. Black respondents are not found equally across high schools throughout the United States. There are, of course, regional differences in proportions of blacks, and these contribute substantially to this lack of equal distribution. In addition, there are patterns of segregation in housing which continue to be reflected in the unequal distribution of blacks in high schools. The net effect of these several factors is that the black subgroup in our sample is "partially segregated" in a sampling sense as well as in the more usual usage of that word. For that reason, the design effects for blacks are somewhat larger than for other subgroups of approximately similar size.

Because the subgroups consisting of blacks and the four regional groups all have larger design effects than other subgroups of the same size, it is necessary to adjust the confidence intervals for these subgroups as indicated in Appendix A. (At a later point in the present appendix we will say more about these adjustment factors.)

One other kind of "subgroup" must be noted in this discussion of the relationship between subgroup size and design effects. One-fifth of the total sample filled out each of the five separate questionnaire forms, and thus the respondents to each of these forms may be viewed as a "cross-class" subgroup of the total sample. The average cluster size for a single form is exactly 20 percent of the average cluster size for the total sample. That means, of course, that the single form samples (which are the basis for the large majority of the data presented in this volume) are distinctly more "efficient" than the sample based on all five forms. Accordingly, single form data have much smaller design effects (as displayed later in this appendix).

Design Effects for Comparisons between Subgroups. We noted above that a number of subgroups treated in this volume can be described as "cross-class" subgroups, meaning that members of the subgroup are distributed more or less evenly across sampling clusters. For these kinds of subgroups, it turns out that *comparisons* are relatively efficient, from a sampling standpoint. The technical explanation for this phenomenon is that there is a higher degree of covariance between such subgroup pairs than would be the case in a comparison of independent subgroups. Now let us offer a fairly nontechnical illustration to indicate why this is so. Suppose that a researcher interested in use of marijuana during the senior year of high school obtained data from five high schools concerning female seniors' marijuana use and data from five other high schools concerning male seniors' marijuana use. Suppose that the percentage values for marijuana use during senior year were as follows:

Female seniors (five schools): 60%, 20%,
65%, 30%, 50%
Male seniors (five other schools): 40%,
80%, 25%, 70%, 60%

Even though there is a difference of ten percentage points between males and females (if the five schools in each case are averaged), there is still so much variability among schools that one would not conclude with very much confidence that females in general are less likely than males to use marijuana during the senior year of high school. Suppose, on the other hand, that the researcher had obtained data from a total of only five schools and had obtained data concerning both male and female seniors in each school as follows:

	Females	Males
School A	60%	70%
School B	20%	25%
School C	65%	80%
School D	30%	40%
School E	50%	60%

The same group of percentages, this time based on five pairings of males and females rather than independent observations, are much more strongly suggestive of systematic differences between the sexes.

A process analogous to that illustrated above is involved when "cross-class" subgroups are compared, and the increased accuracy or sampling efficiency is reflected in relatively small sampling errors and design effects.

Design Effects for Trends. Thus far this discussion of factors influencing design effects and confidence intervals has focused only on groups and subgroups within a single year. But one of the central purposes of the Monitoring the Future project is to monitor trends over time; indeed, the study procedures have been standardized across years insofar as possible in order to provide the opportunity for sensitive measurement of change. One of the factors designed to produce an added degree of consistency from one year to the next is the use of each school for two data collections, which means that for any two successive years half of the sample of schools is the same. This, plus the fact that the other half of the school sample in a given year is from the same primary sampling units as the half sample it replaced, means that there is a good deal of consistency in the sampling and clustering of the sample from one year to the next. As a result, when cross-year comparisons are made (say, between 1976 and 1977), the design effects are appreciably smaller (i.e., the efficiency is greater) than if completely independent samples of schools had been drawn each year. In other words, the 1976 and 1977 samples are not independent; on the contrary, there is a considerable degree of covariance between them. A similar level of covariance occurs between any pair of adjacent-year samples (e.g., 1977 and 1978), because about half of the schools in both samples were the same. This covariance, or partial "matching," reduces the design effect for differences observed between adjacent years, compared to what they would have been with totally independent samples.

It follows from the discussion above that a trend over an interval greater than one year (e.g., a comparison between 1976 and 1978 which involves totally non-overlapping school samples) is likely to have a design effect which is larger than that for a comparison between adjacent-year samples.

Variables with Unusually Large Design Effects. Kish et al. (1976) stress the importance of computing sampling errors for many kinds of variables, and they point out that they have found "very wide ranges in values of sampling errors (standard errors and design effects) between diverse variables within the same survey" (p. 21). Our own experience has been that, among most variables, the variation in sampling errors and design effects seems more random than consistent, and thus we are reasonably comfortable with the use of averaging procedures (described below) in order to derive a set of general purpose tables. There are some important exceptions to the above generalization, however. Variables which are likely to be grouped according to geographical area (region and/or urbanicity), as well as variables that may differ systematically from one school to another, show much higher than usual amounts of homogeneity within sample clusters. It follows necessarily that such variables also have much higher than usual design effects. The variables in the Monitoring the Future study which seem most likely to show such high design effects tend to be grouped into the questionnaire segment dealing with background factors and educational aspirations (Section C of all questionnaire forms). These variables were excluded from the process of computing overall design effects and the confidence intervals provided in Tables A-1 and A-2. Appendix A provides a further discussion of some of these variables and offers some suggestions for adjusting the confidence interval tables to deal with them.

Procedures Used in Deriving Design Effects and Tables of Confidence Intervals

Having taken some pains to review the several factors which can influence design effects and confidence intervals, it is now a fairly simple matter for us to summarize the steps followed to compute the tables of confidence intervals shown in Appendix A. We were heavily influenced in this effort by the work of Kish and his colleagues (Kish, 1965; Kish et al., 1976) in two ways. First, we followed their recommendation that sampling errors be computed and averaged across a goodly number of variables and subgroups. Second, we paid particular attention to their observation that design effects tend to be smaller for subgroups than for total samples (a point discussed earlier in this appendix).

Confidence Intervals for Single Percentages. Our procedure was to compute sampling errors and design effects for most of the variables which are common to all five forms (those in the C sections of all questionnaires, and those in the B sections of Forms 2 through 5), and for every twentieth variable in the A, D, and E sections of Forms 2 through 5. (Form 1 was omitted because most of this form is comprised of drug-related items, and such items involve high proportions of missing data because respondents are instructed to skip over many questions which are not applicable to them). Design effects were computed for each of the subgroups reported in this volume, as well as for the total sample. Design effects for each subgroup and for the total were averaged across variables for the C sec-

tion material (all five forms), the B section material (drug use measures, all five forms), and the sampling of variables from the A, D, and E sections (single form data). As noted earlier, the variables which showed unusually high levels of homogeneity within sample clusters were excluded from the C section variables when they were averaged. The 1977 data were used for this analysis. Later replication using 1976 data provided nearly identical values.

The averaging process consisted of taking a mean of the *square roots* of the design effects. Kish and his colleagues (1976) refer to the design effect as DEFF, and to the square root of the design effect as DEFT; thus, $\sqrt{DEFF} = DEFT$. We will find it useful to use this terminology in what follows. The rationale for computing means of DEFT rather than DEFF is that the former value is directly proportionate to the size of confidence intervals. A further reason for doing so is that the values of DEFT approximate a normal distribution much more closely than the values of DEFF, which are skewed upward. (A comparison of mean DEFTs and median DEFTs showed them to be quite similar, something which certainly is not true of mean and median DEFFs).

Bearing in mind that design effects tend to be smaller for subgroups than for total samples, and bearing in mind also that confidence intervals are directly proportionate to DEFT and to $\sqrt{N}$, we plotted the mean DEFT values for the total sample and for all subgroups, in each case relating DEFT to $\sqrt{N}$. The results are shown in Figure B-1. Note that distinctions are made between "cross-class" and "segregated" subgroups, and between mean DEFTs based on five forms and those based on single forms (the $\sqrt{N}$ values for the latter are, of course, much smaller).*

Setting aside the "segregated" subgroups (regions and blacks) for the moment, it is clear that the rest of the mean DEFTs in Figure B-1 show a very clear and consistent pattern: the higher the value $\sqrt{N}$ the higher the mean DEFT. It turns out that these mean DEFT values are very closely approximated by the function $DEFT = \sqrt{1.3 + .00015N}$, as shown by the solid line in the figure. (The function can also be stated as $DEFF = 1.3 + .00015N$.) The particular parameters in that function were derived empirically, but the basic function (i.e., $DEFT = \sqrt{a + bN}$) was adapted directly from the work of Kish et al. (1976).

Given the above function that fitted the mean DEFT values for the total sample and the "cross-class" subgroups, we returned to the problem of assigning DEFT values for the "segregated" subgroups. The simplest solution was to select two adjustment factors which could be multiplied by the confidence interval values in Table A-1. These adjustment factors are shown by the dashed lines in Figure B-1; they cor-

---

* The five form data consisted of C section material, excluding those variables related to region, urbanicity, and/or socioeconomic level.

Figure B-1
Design Effects for Single Percentages

respond to multiplying the "standard" DEFT (solid line) by a factor of 1.1 for single form data and by a factor of 1.33 for five form data. These adjustments, which were selected on empirical grounds, yield design effects for the "segregated" subgroups which are approximately equal to the design effects for the total sample (treating single form and five form data separately, of course). This is reassuring, since Kish et al. (1976) have reported that "segregated" subgroups can in general be expected to show design effects approximately equivalent to the design effects for the total sample.

After the data in Figure B-1 were plotted and the form of the main function (indicated by the solid line) was determined, DEFT values for drug use measures (material in Section B of all forms) were checked. It was found that the DEFTs for only two drug categories, alcohol and marijuana, exceeded the values indicated by the function; accordingly, adjustment factors were developed for these two drugs (1.6 and 1.35, respectively).

Confidence Intervals for Differences between Two Percentages. Our procedure here was directly parallel to that followed in determining confidence intervals for single percentages. DEFT values for the differences between 1977 and 1976 percentages were computed using virtually the same set of items as used earlier. Also computed were mean DEFT values for comparisons in the same year between subgroups such as males and females, those who did and did not plan to complete four years of college, blacks and whites, pairings of regions, and pairings of drug use groups. It was found that, for any given level of N, the mean DEFT values for subgroup comparisons were quite similar to the mean DEFT values for one-year trends; accordingly, all of these mean DEFTs were included in Figure B-2, which plots mean DEFTs for differences between percentages. In this figure, as in Figure B-1, the strong relationship was evident between mean DEFTs and the numbers of cases in the two groups being compared. This relationship can be very closely approximated by the function DEFT = $\sqrt{1.3 + .000075N}$ (which can also be stated DEFF = 1.3 + .000075N), where N = $2N_1N_2/N_1 + N_2$.

It was expected on grounds of sampling theory that as we found earlier, the function which fit most differences between percentages would not fit differences involving regions and differences involving blacks. In fact, the data indicated that some adjustment is necessary for black-white comparisons using data from all five forms, and also for comparisons as well as trends involving any region. We have not tried to show those adjustments in Figure B-2, but the several values involved are shown in the guidelines to Table A-2.

It was also expected on the grounds of sampling theory that trends across an interval of two or more years would show somewhat higher values of DEFT than one-year trends. It turned out that this was true only for data from all five forms; data based on one form only did not show significantly higher values. The adjustment factors for trends involving five forms over two or more years are shown in Table A-2.

Use of Weighted Numbers of Cases in Entering Confidence Interval Tables. We should mention in passing that the recommendations for using the tables in Appendix A indicate that *weighted* N values should be used. The computer program which generated our design effect statistics makes use of weights in calculating percentages and actual sampling variances. But in computing the DEFF ratio, defined as the actual sampling variance divided by the expected sampling variance from a simple random sample with the same number of elements, the program makes use of the *unweighted* numbers of cases to determine "the same number of elements." Since the mean weights used in the 1975, 1976, and 1977 data tables are slightly lower than 1.0, this means that when entering the tables in Appendix A with weighted data from those years, one is being very slightly "conservative" (slightly reduced risk of a Type 1 error, slightly increased risk of a Type 2 error). It is important to realize that if one took the trouble to make corrections for this "conservatism," the correction would rarely be as great as multiplying the Table A-1 and Table A-2 entries by a factor of .95; and in the large majority of cases the correction would involve multiplying by a factor of about .98. We find such discrepancies to be trivially small, particularly when compared with what Kish et al. (1976, p. 12) describe as the "heroic simplifications" required in some of the steps leading to general purpose tables of design effects and confidence intervals.

Before the 1978 data tables were produced we had come to realize the advantages in having weighted values which averaged 1.0; accordingly, beginning with the 1978 data, the weighted N values in the tables do approximate the actual numbers of cases quite closely. But it was impractical to redo the 1975 through 1977 data tables to incorporate this refinement. Another alternative would have been to employ slightly different versions of Tables A-1 and A-2, containing slightly different confidence intervals for each of those three years; however, we felt that such an approach could introduce confusion when cross-year comparisons were made. Thus, we opted for the solution which seems to us to be most simple and manageable, even though it involves the slight degree of "conservatism" noted above. For readers who find this solution undesirable, we have included Tables B-1 and B-2, which present weighted and unweighted Ns for the various subgroups for each year. Table B-1 contains Ns for all five forms (except for 1975 which shows Ns for Forms 2 through 5), and Table B-2 con-

Figure B-2
Design Effects for Differences Between Percentages

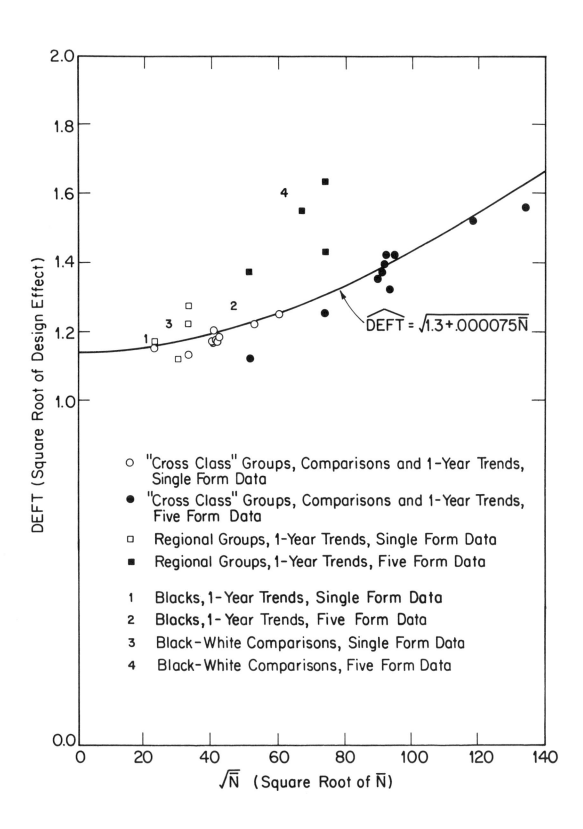

tains approximate Ns for a single form. Thus, readers who wish to avoid the slight "conservatism" (and also to be more precise for subgroups in 1978 and later whose average weight is not exactly 1.0) may determine the unweighted Ns. Some correction for missing data should be made in this case; this can be accomplished by calculating the percentage of missing data (using the weighted Ns from the data table and the weighted N from Table B-1 or B-2) and adjusting the unweighted N accordingly. These adjusted unweighted Ns can then be used in Appendix A.

TABLE B-1
Sample Sizes (Unweighted and Weighted) in Subgroups by Year

Number of Cases

	Class of 1975*		Class of 1976		Class of 1977		Class of 1978		Class of 1979		Class of 1980		Class of 1981		Class of 1982		Class of 1983		Class of 1984		Class of 1985		Class of 1986	
	Unwtd	Wtd	Unwtd	Wtd	Unwtd	Wtd	Unwtd	Wtd	Unwtd	Wtd	Unwtd	Wtd	Unwtd	Wtd	Unwtd	Wtd	Unwtd	Wtd	Unwtd	Wtd	Unwtd	Wtd	Unwtd	Wtd
Total Sample	12627	12108	16678	15138	18436	15830	18924	18916	16662	16662	16524	16524	18267	18267	18348	18348	16947	16947	16499	16499	16502	16502	15713	15713
Sex:																								
Male	5799	5571	7999	7241	8449	7358	8603	8779	7889	7778	7935	7744	8775	8725	8979	8828	8106	8074	7653	7800	7620	7776	7231	7261
Female	6371	6100	7924	7257	9188	7850	9416	9266	8139	8232	7874	8078	8752	8865	8610	8788	8160	8227	8144	8029	8287	8164	7843	7855
Race:																								
White	**	**	12933	11796	13818	12240	14663	14847	13432	13299	12894	12846	13625	13985	13753	13887	12697	12806	12223	12337	12162	12291	11311	11713
Black	**	**	1806	1716	2500	1938	2205	2096	1617	1742	1939	2098	2495	2265	2203	2080	2191	2067	2281	2244	2195	1995	1901	1649
Region:																								
Northeast	3014	2695	4034	3570	4760	3959	4841	4607	3926	4016	4281	3877	4269	4290	4719	4741	4130	4056	3658	3387	3615	3878	3433	3720
North Central	3951	3832	5098	4687	5697	4758	5576	5411	5385	4874	4340	4873	5069	5484	5223	5383	4245	4784	4018	4612	4612	4516	4392	4440
South	3366	3857	4177	4597	4908	4820	5566	6292	4713	5055	4667	5049	5513	5600	5191	5551	5522	5434	5726	5568	5263	5028	4910	4855
West	2296	1724	3369	2284	3071	2294	2941	2605	2638	2717	3236	2726	3416	2893	3215	2672	3050	2673	3097	2932	3012	3079	2978	2698
College Plans:																								
Complete 4 yrs	**	**	7963	6994	8933	7407	9264	8844	8571	8203	9191	8658	10256	9878	9851	9360	9342	9062	9114	9103	9592	9448	9655	9291
None or under 4 yrs	**	**	7179	6877	7764	7048	7857	8413	6715	7063	5995	6578	6486	7008	6971	7507	6214	6555	6002	6124	5588	5770	4855	5277
Illicit Drug Use:																								
None	4329	4400	6532	6091	6672	5878	6400	6595	5426	5654	5322	5591	5954	6148	6157	6328	6001	6082	6124	6199	6401	6412	6491	6535
Marijuana Only	2044	1894	3950	3457	4955	4050	5354	5214	4756	4610	4480	4357	4313	4179	4127	4040	3657	3599	3585	3529	3541	3449	3228	3125
Few Pills	1163	1113	1942	1736	2173	1813	2329	2304	2171	2168	2150	2104	2297	2306	2449	2439	2308	2315	2198	2196	2228	2264	2147	2223
More Pills	2157	1989	3427	2987	3857	3266	3906	3885	3622	3543	3873	3760	4972	4925	4896	4839	4333	4306	3946	3936	3737	3802	3261	3264
Any Heroin	231	216	319	268	321	280	289	302	193	186	186	180	183	189	210	210	210	206	206	207	196	193	160	161

*The number of cases shown for 1975 is based on Forms 2 through 5 only, because the data from Form 1 are intentionally not included in tabulations based on drug and demographic items which appeared in all forms.

**Missing data problems were severe for race and college plans in 1975; accordingly, these data have been excluded from all tables in the 1975 report.

TABLE B-2
Sample Sizes (Unweighted and Weighted) in Subgroups by Year
for Questions on a Single Form*

Number of Cases

	Class of 1975		Class of 1976		Class of 1977		Class of 1978		Class of 1979		Class of 1980		Class of 1981		Class of 1982		Class of 1983		Class of 1984		Class of 1985		Class of 1986	
	Unwtd	Wtd	Unwtd	Wtd	Unwtd	Wtd	Unwtd	Wtd	Unwtd	Wtd	Unwtd	Wtd	Unwtd	Wtd	Unwtd	Wtd	Unwtd	Wtd	Unwtd	Wtd	Unwtd	Wtd	Unwtd	Wtd
Total Sample	3157	3027	3336	3028	3687	3166	3785	3783	3332	3332	3305	3305	3653	3653	3670	3670	3389	3389	3300	3300	3300	3300	3143	3143
Sex:																								
Male	1450	1393	1600	1488	1690	1472	1721	1756	1578	1556	1587	1549	1755	1745	1796	1766	1621	1615	1531	1560	1524	1555	1446	1452
Female	1593	1525	1585	1451	1838	1570	1883	1853	1628	1646	1575	1616	1750	1773	1722	1758	1632	1645	1629	1606	1657	1633	1569	1571
Race:																								
White	**	**	2587	2359	2764	2448	2933	2969	2686	2660	2579	2569	2725	2797	2751	2777	2540	2561	2445	2467	2432	2458	2262	2343
Black	**	**	361	343	500	388	441	419	323	348	388	420	499	453	441	416	438	413	456	449	439	399	380	330
Region:																								
Northeast	754	674	807	714	952	792	968	921	785	803	856	775	854	858	944	948	826	811	732	677	723	776	687	744
North Central	988	958	1020	937	1139	952	1115	1082	1077	975	868	975	1014	1097	1045	1077	849	957	804	922	922	903	878	888
South	842	964	835	919	982	964	1113	1258	943	1011	933	1010	1103	1120	1038	1110	1104	1087	1145	1114	1053	1006	982	971
West	574	431	674	457	614	459	588	521	528	543	647	545	683	579	643	534	610	535	619	586	602	616	596	540
College Plans:																								
Complete 4 yrs	**	**	1593	1399	1787	1481	1853	1769	1714	1641	1838	1732	2051	1976	1970	1872	1868	1812	1823	1821	1918	1890	1931	1858
None or under 4 yrs	**	**	1436	1375	1553	1410	1571	1683	1343	1413	1199	1316	1297	1402	1394	1501	1243	1311	1200	1225	1118	1154	971	1055
Illicit Drug Use																								
None	1082	1100	1306	1218	1334	1176	1280	1319	1085	1131	1064	1118	1191	1230	1231	1266	1200	1216	1225	1240	1280	1282	1298	1307
Marijuana Only	511	474	790	691	991	810	1071	1043	951	922	896	871	863	836	825	808	731	720	717	706	708	690	646	625
Few Pills	291	278	388	347	435	363	466	461	434	434	430	421	459	461	490	488	462	463	440	439	446	453	429	445
More Pills	539	497	685	597	771	653	781	777	724	709	775	752	994	985	979	968	867	861	789	787	747	760	652	653
Any Heroin	58	54	64	54	64	56	58	60	39	37	37	36	37	38	42	42	42	41	41	41	39	39	32	32

*The Ns given here are very close approximations of the N in the given subgroup for any of the five different questionnaire forms used in the year.

**Missing data problems were severe for race and college plans in 1975; accordingly, these data have been excluded from all tables in the 1975 report.

Further Applications of these Design Effects and Sampling Errors

One of the reasons for providing the above review of the factors influencing design effects and confidence intervals, and the procedures used in computing our confidence interval tables, is to provide sufficient background and data to permit the interested reader to go beyond the material provided in Appendix A. In this section we consider two specific extensions, the calculation of levels of "statistical significance" higher than 95 percent and the computation of means and their confidence intervals.

Calculating Confidence Intervals for Higher Levels of Statistical Significance. The entries contained in Tables A-1 and A-2 provide the 95 percent confidence level (also referred to as the .05 level of significance). These entries were computed by multiplying the standard error (square root of sample variance) by a factor of 1.96. The 99 percent confidence interval (.01 level of significance) uses a factor of 2.58 standard errors, and the 99.9 percent confidence interval (.001 level of significance) uses a factor of 3.29 standard errors. To convert the entries in Tables A-1 and A-2 to these higher levels, it is necessary only to multiply the entries by the appropriate constant shown below (keeping in mind that any other adjustments required in the tables must also be applied):

Confidence Interval	Significance Level	Multiply entries in Tables A-1 and A-2 by the following:
99%	.01	2.58/1.96 = 1.32
99.9%	.001	3.29/1.96 = 1.68

Computing Means and Their Confidence Intervals. Many of the questionnaire items included in this volume have ordinal response scales (e.g., agree, agree mostly, neither, disagree mostly, disagree), and it is often the case that a survey analyst will be willing to treat such scales as if they involved equal intervals. In such cases, means and standard deviations are more "efficient" in their use of information than are dichotomies which yield a single percentage or a pair of percentages (e.g., those who respond "agree" or "agree mostly," versus all others). It is a relatively straightforward matter to compute means and standard deviations for the total sample or any of the subgroups treated in this volume. The problem, then, is to be able to specify confidence intervals for the means, or for the differences between pairs of means. In the case of simple random samples, one needs only the means, standard deviations (or variances), and numbers of cases in order to compute confidence intervals. But in complex samples such as the present one,

it is also necessary to take account of design effects. If an estimate of design effect is available, one of the simplest procedures to follow is to divide the actual numbers of cases by the design effect (thereby "depreciating" the actual number to its equivalent value in simple random sample terms) and then employ the standard statistical procedures which have been developed for application to simple random samples. Thus, for example, if the design effect (DEFF) for a sample of 18,000 were 4.0, then one could divide the 18,000 by 4.0 and the result, 4,500, could be entered as the value of "N" in statistical tables and formulas designed for use with simple random samples. To take another example, if one were comparing means based on two subgroups, each involving about 9,000 cases, and if DEFF (for both subgroups) was 2.0, then one could compute the significance of the difference between the two means as if the N for each group were 4,500 (i.e., 9,000 divided by 2.0).

In short, the strategy involves dividing the actual number of cases by the appropriate DEFF in order to get a "simple random sampling equivalent N" or, more simply, an "effective N" for use in statistical procedures designed for random samples.

Design Effects for Use in Computing "Effective Ns." In order to employ the strategy outlined above, one must have estimates of design effects which are judged to be appropriate for one's purposes. In the case of means based on the percentages reported in this volume, we are confident (based on personal communications with Kish) that it is appropriate to use the same DEFF values as were used in developing Tables A-1 and A-2. For other, more complex statistics, we cannot make the same assertion, although it is generally the case that design effects for such statistics are not larger than those for means and percentages (Kish and Frankel, 1970; Frankel, 1971).

In Table B-3 we provide guidelines for computing DEFF values for single percentages (or means) and for differences between two percentages (or means). For reasons discussed elsewhere in this appendix, we must provide for different (and somewhat higher) DEFFs for "segregated" subgroups (regional subgroups and sometimes also blacks), and for trends over two or more years (in contrast to one-year trends). And in all instances, of course, the DEFF values are very much influenced by the average size of sampling clusters, which is always dependent on the number of cases (N). Accordingly, all of the design effect formulas in Table B-3 require computations which take account of N. (It should also be noted that the formulas in Table B-3 correspond exactly to the values of design effects and adjustment factors used in Tables A-1 and A-2 in Appendix A.)

A Concluding Note. In their very useful paper dealing with sampling errors for fertility surveys, Kish

Table B-3
Guidelines for Computing Design Effects (DEFFs) for Percentages
and Means Derived from Monitoring the Future Samples

DEFINITIONS

$$\text{DEFF (design effect} = \frac{\text{(estimated sampling variance}}{\text{expected sampling variance from simple random sample with same number of elements}}$$

N = number of respondents on whom a single percentage or mean is based

$\overline{N} = 2N_1N_2/(N_1 + N_2)$, for use in comparisons of two percentages or means, based on two groups of sizes N_1 and N_2.

DESIGN EFFECT FORMULAS

1. For single percentages or means involving . . .
    a. regional subgroups or blacks
        DEFF for single form data ....$(1.3 + .00015N)\,(1.21)$
        DEFF for five form data ....$(1.3 + .00015N)\,(1.78)$

    b. all other subgroups or total sample
        DEFF for single form or five form data ....$1.3 + .00015N$

2. For comparisons between . . .
    a. any two regions
        DEFF for single form data ....$(1.3 + .000075\overline{N})\,(1.32)$
        DEFF for five form data ....$(1.3 + .000075\overline{N})\,(2.25)$

    b. blacks and whites
        DEFF for single form data..$1.3 + .000075\overline{N}$
        DEFF for five form data ....$(1.3 + .000075\overline{N})\,(1.56)$

    c. genders, college plans groups, or any two "drug use" subgroups
        DEFF for single form or five form data ....$1.3 + .000075\overline{N}$

3. For one-year trends involving . . .
    a. any region
        DEFF for single form data..$1.3 + .000075\overline{N}$
        DEFF for five form data ....$(1.3 + .000075\overline{N})\,(1.56)$
    b. all other subgroups or total sample
        DEFF for single form or five form data ....$1.3 + .000075\overline{N}$

4. For trends over two or more years involving . . .
    a. any region
        DEFF for single form data..$1.3 + .000075\overline{N}$
        DEFF for five form data ....$(1.3 + .000075\overline{N})\,(1.82)$
    b. all other subgroups or total sample
        DEFF for single form data..$1.3 + .000075\overline{N}$
        DEFF for five form data ....$(1.3 + .000075\overline{N})\,(1.32)$

et al. (1976) commented that some of the methods they used ". . . emerged after several false starts." They went on to say that the volume and diversity of the data they were dealing with ". . . presented new challenges and opportunities." And they added, "Our methods are subject to further developments and modifications, and we invite participation and suggestions" (p. 10). Our own attempts to apply the methods of Kish and his colleagues to the data reported in this volume have been challenged by the diversity of the data, have involved several false starts, and we hope are subject to further developments and modifications. We invite readers to offer their suggestions, and we also encourage readers to inquire about further work that we and/or others may carry out during the coming months and years.

Appendix C
Questionnaire Covers, Instructions, and Sample Page

monitoring the future

a continuing study of the lifestyles and values of youth

This questionnaire is part of a nationwide study of high school seniors, conducted each year by the University of Michigan's Institute for Social Research. The questions ask your opinions about a number of things — the way things are now and the way you think they ought to be in the future. In a sense, many of your answers on this questionnaire will count as "votes" on a wide range of important issues.

If this study is to be helpful, it is important that you answer each question as thoughtfully and frankly as possible. All your answers will be kept strictly confidential, and will never be seen by anyone who knows you.

This study is completely voluntary. If there is any question that you or your parents would find objectionable for any reason, just leave it blank.

In a few months, we would like to mail each of you a summary of the nationwide results from this study. Also, in about a year we would like to mail another questionnaire to some of you, asking about how your plans have worked out and what's happening in your lives.

In order to include you in these mailings, we ask for your name and address on a special form at the end of this questionnaire. This form is to be torn out and handed in separately. Once the address form and the questionnaire have been separated, there is no way they can be matched again, except by using a special computer tape at the University of Michigan. The only purpose for that tape is to match a follow-up questionnaire with this one.

Other seniors have said that these questionnaires are very interesting and that they enjoy filling them out. We hope you will too. Be sure to read the instructions on the other side of this cover page before you begin to answer. Thank you very much for being an important part of this project.

INSTITUTE FOR SOCIAL RESEARCH
THE UNIVERSITY OF MICHIGAN
ANN ARBOR, MICHIGAN

INSTRUCTIONS

1.   This is not a test, so there are no right or wrong answers; we would
     like you to work fairly quickly, so that you can finish.

2.   All of the questions should be answered by marking one of the answer spaces.
     If you don't always find an answer that fits exactly, use the one that comes
     closest. If any question does not apply to you, or you are not sure of what it
     means, just leave it blank.

3.   Your answers will be read automatically by a machine called an optical mark
     reader. Please follow these instructions carefully:

     •Use only the black lead pencil you have been given.
     •Make heavy black marks inside the circles.
     •Erase cleanly any answer you wish to change.
     •Make no other markings or comments on the
       answer pages, since they interfere with the
       automatic reading. (If you want to add a
       comment about any question, please use the
       space provided below.)

These kinds of markings
will work: ●   ●   ●

These kinds of markings
will NOT work: ⊙   ✸   ○

- -

(THIS SPACE FOR WRITTEN COMMENTS)

WHY YOUR NAME AND ADDRESS?

As we told you earlier, we'd like to send you a summary of the nationwide results of the present study, and in about a year we want to mail a shorter questionnaire to some of you. In order to include you in these follow-ups, we would like to have an address where information will be sure to reach you during the coming year.

HOW IS CONFIDENTIALITY PROTECTED?

- The information on this page will be used ONLY for mailing, and will always be kept separate from your answers. A special Grant of Confidentiality from the U.S. government protects all information gathered in this research project.

- The questionnaire and address pages will be collected separately, sealed immediately in separate envelopes, and sent to two different cities for processing.

- Once a questionnaire and address page have been separated, there is no way they can be matched, except by using a special computer tape at the University of Michigan. That tape contains the two DIFFERENT numbers that appear on the back of this address page and on the back of the questionnaire. These numbers will be used ONLY to match a follow-up questionnaire with this one.

> Before filling out this address page, please separate it from the rest of the questionnaire by FOLDING ALONG THE PERFORATED LINE AND TEARING CAREFULLY.

Please **PRINT** your name and the address where you can most likely be reached during the coming year.

```
Mr.
Miss _ _ _ _ _ _ _ _ _ _ _ _ _ _ _ _ _ _ _ _ _ _ _ _ _ _ _ _
Ms.   FIRST NAME        INITIAL        LAST NAME
Mrs.

STREET _ _ _ _ _ _ _ _ _ _ _ _ _ _ _ _ _ _ _ _ _ _ _ _ _

CITY _ _ _ _ _ _ _ _ _ _ _ _ _ _ _ _ _ _ _ _ _ _ _ _ _ _

STATE _ _ _ _ _ _ _ _ _ _ _ _ _ _ _ _ _ ZIP _ _ _ _ _ _ _ _

TELEPHONE NO.  (        ) _ _ _ _ _ _ _ _ _ _ _ _ _ _ _
                   AREA
```

In case we should have trouble getting mail to you, if you move, please **PRINT** the name and address of one other person (with a different address than your own) who will know where to reach you in the future. (Examples of such a person: aunt or uncle, older sister or brother, or close friend.)

```
Mr.
Miss _ _ _ _ _ _ _ _ _ _ _ _ _ _ _ _ _ _ _ _ _ _ _ _ _ _ _ _
Ms.   FIRST NAME        INITIAL        LAST NAME
Mrs.

STREET _ _ _ _ _ _ _ _ _ _ _ _ _ _ _ _ _ _ _ _ _ _ _ _ _

CITY _ _ _ _ _ _ _ _ _ _ _ _ _ _ _ _ _ _ _ _ _ _ _ _ _ _

STATE _ _ _ _ _ _ _ _ _ _ _ _ _ _ _ _ _ ZIP _ _ _ _ _ _ _ _

TELEPHONE NO.  (        ) _ _ _ _ _ _ _ _ _ _ _ _ _ _ _
                   AREA
```

THANK YOU AGAIN FOR YOUR HELP

PART A

* **BEFORE BEGINNING BE SURE YOU HAVE READ THE INSTRUCTIONS ON THE COVER.**

1. Taking all things together, how would you say things are these days—would you say you're very happy, pretty happy, or not too happy these days?

   ○ Very happy
   ○ Pretty happy
   ○ Not too happy

2. Some people think a lot about the social problems of the nation and the world, and about how they might be solved. Others spend little time thinking about these issues. How much do you think about such things?

   ① Never
   ② Seldom
   ③ Sometimes
   ④ Quite often
   ⑤ A great deal

3. Of all the problems facing the nation today, how often do you worry about each of the following? (Mark one circle for each line.)

   Never Seldom Sometimes Often

   a. Chance of nuclear war .... ①②③④
   b. Population growth .... ①②③④
   c. Crime and violence .... ①②③④
   d. Pollution .... ①②③④
   e. Energy shortages .... ①②③④
   f. Race relations .... ①②③④
   g. Hunger and poverty .... ①②③④
   h. Using open land for housing or industry .... ①②③④
   i. Urban decay .... ①②③④
   j. Economic problems .... ①②③④
   k. Drug abuse .... ①②③④

4. How well do you think your experiences and training (at home, school, work, etc.) have prepared you to be a good. . .

   Poorly Not So Well Fairly Well Well Very Well

   a. ...husband or wife? .... ①②③④⑤
   b. ...parent? .... ①②③④⑤
   c. ...worker on a job? .... ①②③④⑤

5. Apart from the particular kind of work you want to do, how would you rate each of the following settings as a place to work? (Mark one circle for each line.)

   Not At All Acceptable Somewhat Acceptable Acceptable Desirable

   a. Working in a large corporation .... ①②③④
   b. Working in a small business .... ①②③④
   c. Working in a government agency .... ①②③④
   d. Working in the military service .... ①②③④
   e. Working in a school or university ...... ①②③④
   f. Working in a police department or police agency .... ①②③④
   g. Working in a social service organization .. ①②③④
   h. Working with a small group of partners ... ①②③④
   i. Working on your own (self-employed) ..... ①②③④

6. If you were to get enough money to live as comfortably as you'd like for the rest of your life, would you want to work?

   ① I would want to work
   ② I would not want to work

—1—

(Base Year & Follow-up: Form 5—Part A)

References

Adelson, J. "What Generation Gap?" *New York Times Magazine*, January 18, 1970, pp. 1–11.

Adelson, J. "Adolescence and the Generation Gap." *Psychology Today*, February 1979, pp. 33–37.

Bachman, J.G., and Johnston, L.D. "The Monitoring the Future Project Design and Procedures," (Occasional Paper #1). Institute for Social Research, The University of Michigan, Ann Arbor, 1978.

Bachman, J.D., and Johnston, L.D. "The Freshmen, 1979." *Psychology Today*, September 1979, pp. 79–87.

Bachman, J.G.; Johnston, L.D.; and O'Malley, P.M. "Smoking, Drinking, and Drug Use Among American High School Students: Correlates and Trends, 1975–1979." *American Journal of Public Health* 71 (1981):59–69.

Bachman, J.G., and O'Malley, P.M. "When Four Months Equal a Year: Inconsistencies in Students' Reports of Drug Use." *Public Opinion Quarterly* 45 (1981):536–548.

Bachman, J.G., and O'Malley, P.M. "Yea-saying, Nay-saying, and Going to Extremes: Are Black-White Differences in Survey Results Due to Response Styles?" *Public Opinion Quarterly*, 48 (1984):409–427.

Bachman, J.G.; O'Malley, P.M.; and Johnston, J. Youth in Transition, Volume VI: *Adolescence to Adulthood — A Study of Change and Stability in the Lives of Young Men*. Ann Arbor: Institute for Social Research, The University of Michigan, 1978.

Dearman, N.B., and Plisko, V.W. *The Condition of Education*. (National Center for Education Statistics). Washington, D.C.: U.S. Government Printing Office, 1982.

Frankel, M.R. *Inference from Survey Samples: An Empirical Investigation*. Ann Arbor: Institute for Social Research, The University of Michigan, 1971.

Hays, W.L. *Statistics for the Social Sciences* (2nd ed.). New York: Holt, Rinehart, & Winston, 1973.

Johnston, L.D. *Drugs and American Youth*. Ann Arbor: Institute for Social Research, The University of Michigan, 1973.

Johnston, L.D.; Bachman, J.G.; and O'Malley, P.M. *Drug Use Among American High School Students, 1975–1977* (National Institute on Drug Abuse). Washington, D.C.: U.S. Government Printing Office, 1977.

Johnston, L.D.; Bachman, J.G.; and O'Malley, P.M. *Drugs and the Class of 1978: Behaviors, Attitudes, and Recent National Trends* (National Institute on Drug Abuse). Washington, D.C.: U.S. Government Printing Office, 1979(a).

Johnston, L.D.; Bachman, J.G.; and O'Malley, P.M. *1979 Highlights: Drugs and the Nation's High School Students, Five Year National Trends* (National Institute on Drug Abuse). Washington, D.C.: U.S. Government Printing Office, 1979(b).

Johnston, L.D.; Bachman, J.G.; and O'Malley, P.M. *Highlights from Student Drug Use in America: 1975–1980* (National Institute on Drug Abuse). Washington, D.C.: U.S. Government Printing Office, 1981.

Johnston, L.D.; Bachman, J.G.; and O'Malley, P.M. *Student Drug Use in America, 1975–1981*. (National Institute on Drug Abuse). Washington, D.C.: U.S. Government Printing Office, 1982.

Johnston, L.D.; O'Malley, P.M.; and Bachman, J.G. *Drugs and American High School Students, 1975–1983*. (National Institute on Drug Abuse). Washington, D.C.: U.S. Government Printing Office, 1984.

Johnston, L.D.; O'Malley, P.M.; and Bachman, J.G. *Drug Use Among American High School Students, College Students, and Other Young Adults, National Trends Through 1985*. (National Institute on Drug Abuse). Washington, D.C.: U.S. Government Printing Office, 1986.

Kish, L. *Survey Sampling*. New York: John Wiley & Sons, 1965.

Kish, L., and Frankel, M.R. "Balanced Repeated Replication for Standard Errors." *Journal of the American Statistical Association* 65 (1970):1071–1094.

Kish, L.; Groves, R.M.; and Krotki, K.P. *Sampling Errors for Fertility Surveys* (Occasional Papers Series No. 17). Voorburg, The Netherlands: International Statistical Institute, 1976.

U.S. Bureau of the Census, *Current Population Reports*. Series P-20, No. 319, School enrollment — social and economic characteristics of students, October 1976. Washington, D.C.: U.S. Government Printing Office, 1978.